Challenging
Perspectives

Challenging Perspectives

 Reading Critically about Ethics and Values

Deborah H. Holdstein
Governors State University

HOUGHTON MIFFLIN COMPANY

Boston   New York

"The highest form of wisdom is kindness."

I dedicate this book in loving memory of my father, Reinhard Holdstein (7 March 1915–14 March 2003), who by his life of struggle, honor, and commitment encouraged me to challenge perspectives.

Editor in Chief: Pat Coryell
Executive Editor: Suzanne Phelps Weir
Development Manager: Sarah Helyar Smith
Senior Project Editor: Florence Kilgo
Editorial Assistant: Eddie Fournier
Art and Design Coordinator: Jill Haber
Photo Editor: Jennifer Meyer-Dare
Composition Buyer: Sarah Ambrose
Senior Manufacturing Coordinator: Marie Barnes
Senior Marketing Manager: Cindy Graff Cohen
Marketing Associate: Wendy Thayer

Cover photo: Jeremy Woodhouse, Shadow on Balloon © Gettyimages.

Permissions and credits are found following the index at the end of this book. This Acknowledgments page constitutes an extension of the copyright page.

Printed in the U.S.A.

Library of Congress Catalog Card Number: 2003109850

ISBN: 0-618-21503-4

1 2 3 4 5 6 7 8 9 - QUF - 08 07 06 05 04

Contents

⊞

Chapter 1
Becoming Myself: What Kind of Person Do I Want to Be?   3
⊞

Chapter 2
Evaluating Ideas: How Do I Make Sense of My World?   105
⊞

Chapter 3
Defining Belief Systems: What Do I Believe? 197
⊞

*ing wheel by one immense power that had willed us into being and
intended our futures, wherever they led.*

Chapter 4
Broadening My View: How Do I Perceive Difference?   307
⌗

*There are always the women, who make pots and weave baskets,
who fashion clothes and cheer their children on at powwow,
who make fry bread and piki bread, and corn soup and chili stew,
who dance and sing and remember and hold within their hearts
the dream of their ancient peoples—that one day the woman
who thinks will speak to us again, and everywhere there will
be peace.*

*The fact of the separation of white and black was clear to me; it
was its effect upon the personalities of people that stumped and
dismayed me. I did not feel that I was a threat to anybody; yet, as
soon as I had grown old enough to think, I had learned that my
entire personality, my aspirations, had long ago been discounted;
that, in a measure, the very meaning of the words I spoke could
not be fully understood.*

*Hollywood producers must have an instant Ali Baba kit that con-
tains scimitars, veils, sunglasses and such Arab clothing as
chadors and kufiyahs.*

*Anger, channeled creatively and used to galvanize us into con-
structive action, is an important emotion not to be wasted. In the
spiritual place to which I was journeying, I wanted my anger to
count, to stay on the high road of resistance, where it could target
changes in the socioeconomic reality of my people rather than
changes in colors worn at wedding ceremonies.*

*"Whether I can write or can't write—I can't stop writing. I can't
rest. I can't breathe. There's no peace, no running away for me on
earth except in the struggle to give out what's in me. The beat from
my heart—the blood from my veins—must flow out into my
words."*

Chapter 5
Getting Educated: What Have Others Taught Me?   419
❖

Chapter 6
Conversing and Confiding: How Do I Respond ? 505
⊞

Chapter 7
Speaking My Mind: How Can I Persuade?   613
⊞

Chapter 8
Taking a Stand: What Are My Politics?   725
⊞

Rhetorical Contents

ARGUMENT

CLASSIFICATION

CAUSE AND EFFECT

COMPARISON/CONTRAST

PROCESS

DEFINITION

Preface

*Questioning the Questions and Assumptions
Behind This Book: It's Not About "I"*
⊞

Challenging Perspectives: Reading Critically About Ethics and Values is an anthology of readings organized around timeless questions. Although ethics and social philosophy each represents a significant scholarly enterprise within philosophy, this book does not teach the philosophical underpinnings of these specialized, complex disciplines. Rather, the organization and content of the book ask students, as thinkers, readers, and writers, to formulate a point of view and then hold themselves accountable for it by supporting their viewpoints with substance, fairness, and reason. Each of the readings in *Challenging Perspectives* allows you and your students to discuss issues of ethics and values and to develop well-considered, thoughtfully argued written responses to often-difficult questions. I have designed the book to be as flexible as possible to allow for a variety of approaches, not only to the ethical issues included but also to the teaching of rhetoric and writing.

Perhaps most importantly, *Challenging Perspectives* illustrates the value of careful analysis and questioning, not only in the classroom, but also as part of life experiences. For instance, as students question and challenge these readings and the issues they raise, and as they question and challenge their own assumptions and perspectives about the world, students learn to apply these skills not only to complex issues, but also, say, to specific daily decisions such as evaluating content on the Web. *Challenging Perspectives* affirms that there are few simple answers when we engage in a complex world, and it offers students the opportunity to question and challenge not only the perspectives of others, but also their own, whether to make those held perspectives stronger than before—or to change them.

Features
⊞

Opportunities for and Approaches to Argument

Many college composition textbooks specialize in traditional argumentation. *Challenging Perspectives* does not—at least not in the conventional sense. Traditional definitions of argument often are win-lose oriented. The language of argument is also often combative: consider *argue, defend, take a stand, refute.* Nonetheless, it's the language we have for conveying the need to analyze, to create the conversation to support a carefully considered stance on a complex subject. In this case, *Challenging Perspectives* asks students to examine their own thoughts in light of the various viewpoints included here. At its best, argument is invigorating conversation—a cooperative, even amiable attempt to arrive at an understanding by asking and answering questions. This book offers students the opportunity to better understand their own views and to explain those views to others, so that, in turn, they can appreciate the thinking of others. Above all, *Challenging Perspectives* holds students accountable, encouraging them to be clear, reasoned, and fair when explaining why they feel the way they do about certain issues, and why others might respond as they do.

It is all too easy to claim to be neutral on various subjects. In that very neutrality, however, some of us actually take a position—that is, by choosing not to take a stand, we actually take one in a passive, potentially damaging way. But a very basic concern for all of us is the way we believe we should lead our lives: how we treat others, our position on difficult, moral decisions, our choices regarding faith, and many others. *Challenging Perspectives* asks students to take positions on complex moral and ethical issues through essays that don't always demonstrate explicit treatment of those issues. The selections in the book are organized around questions beginning with "I" *not* to encourage wholly personal storytelling (although these stories can become the foundations for strong argument), but rather to *make each of us accountable* for the ways we see and respond to complex issues, cultures, belief systems, and persons.

Flexible Organization

Each chapter title contains a broad question and a variety of possible reflections upon and responses to that question. Many of the readings could appear in chapters other than those in which I've categorized them. This is deliberate. For instance, Bertrand Russell's work is included under the question, "How do I respond to others?" rather than in the more obvious category, "What do I believe?" The placement of each reading is meant to encourage questioning and to affirm the myriad ways of approaching each of these texts as your students read, discuss, and write. The questions your students raise and discuss will likely provide the opportunity for additional research on their part—perhaps other works by Russell, in this case, or writers who sought to refute Russell's stance. See the Instructor's Resource Manual for sample syllabi and suggestions for clustering readings across the chapters, either thematically or by rhetorical structure.

Diverse, Challenging Readings

The wide-ranging selections in this text include personal essays, writing from sources, poetry, op-ed pieces, cartoons, photography, and short fiction. The range demonstrates that the challenging questions that confront us can be voiced and examined through a variety of forms. The questions asked in each chapter's title have been raised across many centuries, cultures, and spiritual traditions, and the diverse array of perspectives that the readings offer reflect upon each broad question. Each chapter features selections ranging from the classic to the contemporary and writers working within (and sometimes against) specific rhetorical genres.

Thoughtful, Unobtrusive Apparatus

Each reading is prefaced by a brief headnote that provides context for students to think about issues of authority and *ethos*. Following each reading, "Questioning and Discussing" prompts students to consider both the rhetorical strategies and choices an author makes, as well as reflect upon and respond to larger issues of ethics and values. At the end of each chapter, "Questions for Reading and Responding" suggest connections among and between all of the readings and visuals in the chapter—with occasional connections to readings in other chapters. These questions may be used as prompts for journal writing, launching pads for discussion and additional, contextual research, or as the basis for in-class or extended essays. The apparatus within the book is deliberately spare, to allow students to develop their own understandings and interpretations of each reading and illustration. Additional ideas for teaching and writing about *Challenging Perspectives* are in the Instructors Resource Manual and on the website.

Visuals That Challenge Perspectives

Photographs at the end of each chapter provide opportunities for students to research and reflect critically upon the ways visual arts are created and read as texts. Each photograph potentially offers more than just one set of responses to or reflections upon the chapter's fundamental question, and can be used to enhance students' own readings or to discover contextual material about the images that enhance their own analyses.

Additional Resources

Instructor's Resource Manual
The Instructor's Resource Manual contains possible responses to the writing and discussion prompts that follow each reading and chapter; additional ideas for writing; suggestions for incorporating argument into the discussion of, and response to, the readings and images; strategies for creating a supportive classroom environment for the discussion of complex and substantive issues; strategies for evaluating and discussing visual texts; and several sample syllabi and suggestions for clustering readings across the chapters, either thematically or by rhetorical structure.

Web-site
The web-site for *Challenging Perspectives* offers additional assignments and exercises, links to further information about featured photographers and essayists, reliable web-based sources for research regarding ethics, and additional articles and sites that reflect the issues raised by the selections in the volume. Further, the site for *Challenging Perspectives* connects students to the wealth of online support for writing available through Houghton Mifflin.

Acknowledgments

While most of us who prepare textbooks with just one name on the cover would like to think that we are wholly responsible for the end result, we clearly are not. As a result, there are many people to thank. Barbara Collins Rosenberg, my agent, provides good advice and takes care of business. At Houghton Mifflin, Suzanne Phelps Weir, executive editor, has been important to this project from the beginning. Her intelligence, common sense, and willingness to step in and be available make her unique among present-day editors. Florence Kilgo, project editor, deserves high praise for her exacting work and her terrific sense of humor. I also thank Sarah Helyar Smith, development manager, and Anne Leung, editorial assistant, for their diligence and helpfulness.

Perhaps most profoundly worthy of thanks in my Houghton Mifflin family is my development editor *supreme*, Meg Botteon. Meg is not only well-read and intelligent, but she also *gets it* at a level of sophistication and humor that in my experience is rare in the publishing game. I sincerely hope to work with her again.

Close to home, there are more people to thank. My daughter, Emily Gilman, spent a good part of one summer as my research assistant, ably providing the background information for several of the head notes you see here. My son, David Gilman, always provides moments of intelligent humor and surprise. Roger Gilman advised about definitions of ethics for the IM. Cecilia Jackson, while working on her M.A. in English at Governors State University, toiled at the photocopier and in the library, making certain that I would have substantial background research for head notes and information about permissions.

I thank those friends in my life—you know who you are—without whom things seem impossible.

Part of the process of publishing a textbook involves the often-extensive feedback from a variety of colleagues at various institutions throughout the United States. For their good work, I thank the following persons:

Joseph J. Essid, University of Richmond
Carol S. Franks, Portland State University
Lisa Gerrard, University of California, Los Angeles
Phyllis R. Gooden, Northern Illinois University
Betty L. Hart, University of Southern Indiana
John W. Hodgson, Cameron University
Kate Kessler, James Madison University
Michael Lee, Columbia Basin College
Michael B. Mahon, Minnesota State University, Mankato
Sara McLaughlin, Texas Tech University
Sarah Mohler, Truman State University
John G. Parks, Miami University
Cyrus R. K. Patell, New York University
James Person, Grand Valley State University
Sylvia Rackow, Baruch College

Jayetta Slawson, Southeastern Louisiana University
Cynthia Spencer, Pennsylvania State University
Richard C. Taylor, East Carolina University
Deborah Coxwell Teague, Florida State University
Dan K. Thorpe, College of DuPage
Kate Waites, Nova Southeastern University
Rosemary Winslow, Catholic University of America

Deborah H. Holdstein

1

Becoming Myself

What Kind of Person Do I Want to Be?

"I went to a bookstore and asked the saleswoman, 'Where's the self-help section?' She said if she told me, it would defeat the purpose."

STEVEN WRIGHT, *comedian*

Linda Pastan

Linda Pastan (1932–) was graduated from Radcliffe College in 1954 and earned her master's degree from Brandeis University in 1957. Her poems have appeared in various, noted periodicals, including *The Atlantic Monthly*, *The New Yorker*, *The Georgia Review*, and *The New Republic*. She is also the recipient of several awards, and her work has been nominated for the National Book Award.

⌗

Ethics

In ethics class so many years ago   1
our teacher asked this question every fall:
if there were a fire in a museum
which would you save, a Rembrandt painting
or an old woman who hadn't many   5
years left anyhow? Restless on hard chairs
caring little for pictures or old age
we'd opt one year for life, the next for art
and always half-heartedly. Sometimes
the woman borrowed my grandmother's face   10
leaving her usual kitchen to wander
some drafty, half-imagined museum.
One year, feeling clever, I replied
why not let the woman decide herself?
Linda, the teacher would report, eschews   15
the burdens of responsibility.
This fall in a real museum I stand
before a real Rembrandt, old woman,
or nearly so, myself. The colors
within this frame are darker than autumn,   20
darker even than winter—the browns of earth,
though earth's most radiant elements burn
through the canvas. I know now that woman
and painting and season are almost one
and all beyond saving by children.   25

QUESTIONING AND DISCUSSING
Pastan, "Ethics"

1. How would you articulate the difficult ethical question that the speaker of this poem suggests? Analyze whether the choices here actually concern a choice between saving someone's life and saving a valuable artwork.

2. Several people responding to the poem after an initial reading have suggested that the simple solution to the "problem" would be to have the old woman carry the painting while the rescuer carried her. Comment on the ways in which this "solution" is either beside or part of the point, and use the text to help you support your analysis.

3. Explicit the following lines within the context of your reading of the poem. Look at "Restless on hard chairs / caring little for pictures or old age / we'd opt one year for life, the next for art / and always half-heartedly" and examine these lines' relationship to the final lines of the poem: "I know now that woman / and painting and season are almost one / and all beyond saving by children."

⊞

STEPHEN CRANE

Stephen Crane (1871–1900), often called the first modern American writer, was the fourteenth child of a Methodist minister. He is reputed to have led a wild life; in 1897, he married Cora Taylor, a woman who ran a brothel in Florida. Along with his marriage, slanderous rumors that he was a drug addict and a Satanist led to his spending his last years abroad. Crane died at twenty-nine in Germany. Called by critics a superb literary stylist, Crane was innovative in his use of imagery and symbolism. His works are particularly noted for their intense realism and treatment of social issues.

⊞

The Blue Hotel

I

The Palace Hotel at Fort Romper was painted a light blue, a shade that is on the legs of a kind of heron, causing the bird to declare its position against any background. The Palace Hotel, then, was always screaming and howling in a way that made the dazzling winter landscape of Nebraska seem only a gray swampish hush. It stood alone on the prairie, and when the snow was falling the town two hundred yards away was not visible. But when the traveler alighted at the railway station he was obliged to pass the Palace Hotel before he could come upon the company of low clap-board houses which composed Fort Romper, and it was not to be thought that any traveler could pass the Palace Hotel without looking at it. Pat Scully, the proprietor, had proved himself a master of strategy when he chose his paints. It is true that on clear days, when the great transconti-nental express, long lines of swaying Pullmans, swept through Fort Romper, passengers were overcome at the sight, and the cult that knows the brown-reds and the subdivisions of the dark greens of the East expressed shame, pity, horror, in a laugh. But to the citizens of this prairie town and to the people who would naturally stop there, Pat Scully had performed a feat. With this opulence and splendor, these creeds, classes, egotisms, that streamed through Romper on the rails day after day, they had no color in common.

2   As if the display delights of such a blue hotel were not sufficiently en-ticing, it was Scully's habit to go every morning and evening to meet the leisurely trains that stopped at Romper and work his seductions upon any man that he might see wavering, gripsack in hand.

3   One morning, when a snow-crusted engine dragged its long string of freight cars and its one passenger coach to the station, Scully performed the marvel of catching three men. One was a shaky and quick-eyed Swede, with a great shining cheap valise; one was a tall bronzed cowboy, who was on his way to a ranch near the Dakota line; one was a little silent man from the East, who didn't look it, and didn't announce it. Scully practi-cally made them prisoners. He was so nimble and merry and kindly that each probably felt it would be the height of brutality to try to escape. They trudged off over the creaking board sidewalks in the wake of the eager lit-tle Irishman. He wore a heavy fur cap squeezed tightly down on his head. It caused his two red ears to stick out stiffly, as if they were made of tin.

4   At last, Scully, elaborately, with boisterous hospitality, conducted them through the portals of the blue hotel. The room which they entered was small. It seemed to be merely a proper temple for an enormous stove, which, in the center, was humming with godlike violence. At various points on its surface the iron had become luminous and glowed yellow from the heat. Beside the stove Scully's son Johnnie was playing High-Five with an old farmer who had whiskers both gray and sandy. They were quarrelling. Frequently the old farmer turned his face toward a box of sawdust—colored brown from tobacco juice—that was behind the stove, and spat with an air of great impatience and irritation. With a loud flourish of

words Scully destroyed the game of cards, and bustled his son upstairs with part of the baggage of the new guests. He himself conducted them to three basins of the coldest water in the world. The cowboy and the Easterner burnished themselves fiery red with this water, until it seemed to be some kind of metal polish. The Swede, however, merely dipped his fingers gingerly and with trepidation. It was notable that throughout this series of small ceremonies the three travelers were made to feel that Scully was very benevolent. He was conferring great favors upon them. He handed the towel from one to another with an air of philanthropic impulse.

Afterward they went to the first room, and sitting about the stove, lis- 5
tened to Scully's officious clamor at his daughters, who were preparing the midday meal. They reflected in the silence of experienced men who tread carefully amid new people. Nevertheless, the old farmer, stationary, invincible in his chair near the warmest part of the stove, turned his face from the sawdust-box frequently and addressed a glowing commonplace to the strangers. Usually he was answered in short but adequate sentences by either the cowboy or the Easterner. The Swede said nothing. He seemed to be occupied in making furtive estimates of each man in the room. One might have thought that he had the sense of silly suspicion which comes to guilt. He resembled a badly frightened man.

Later, at dinner, he spoke a little, addressing his conversation entirely 6
to Scully. He volunteered that he had come from New York, where for ten years he had worked as a tailor. These facts seemed to strike Scully as fascinating, and afterward he volunteered that he had lived at Romper for fourteen years. The Swede asked about the crops and the price of labor. He seemed barely to listen to Scully's extended replies. His eyes continued to rove from man to man.

Finally, with a laugh and a wink, he said that some of these Western 7
communities were very dangerous; and after his statement he straightened his legs under the table, tilted his head, and laughed again, loudly. It was plain that the demonstration had no meaning to the others. They looked at him wondering and in silence.

II

As the men trooped heavily back into the front room, the two little win- 8
dows presented views of a turmoiling sea of snow. The huge arms of the wind were making attempts—mighty, circular, futile—to embrace the flakes as they sped. A gate-post like a still man with a blanched face stood aghast amid this profligate fury. In a hearty voice Scully announced the presence of a blizzard. The guests of the blue hotel, lighting their pipes,

assented with grunts of lazy masculine contentment. No island of the sea could be exempt in the degree of this little room with its humming stove. Johnnie, son of Scully, in a tone which defined his opinion of his ability as a card-player, challenged the old farmer of both gray and sandy whiskers to a game of High-Five. The farmer agreed with a contemptuous and bitter scoff. They sat close to the stove, and squared their knees under a wide board. The cowboy and the Easterner watched the game with interest. The Swede remained near the window, aloof, but with a countenance that showed signs of inexplicable excitement.

9   The play of Johnnie and the gray-beard was suddenly ended by another quarrel. The old man arose while casting a look of heated scorn at his adversary. He slowly buttoned his coat, and then stalked with fabulous dignity from the room. In the discreet silence of all the other men the Swede laughed. His laughter rang somehow childish. Men by this time had begun to look at him askance, as if they wished to inquire what ailed him.

10   A new game was formed jocosely. The cowboy volunteered to become the partner of Johnnie, and they all then turned to ask the Swede to throw in his lot with the little Easterner. He asked some questions about the game, and learning that it wore many names, and that he had played it when it was under an alias, he accepted the invitation. He strode toward the men nervously, as if he expected to be assaulted. Finally, seated, he gazed from face to face and laughed shrilly. This laugh was so strange that the Easterner looked up quickly, the cowboy sat intent and with his mouth open, and Johnnie paused, holding the cards with still fingers.

11   Afterward there was a short silence. Then Johnnie said, "Well, let's get at it. Come on now!" They pulled their chairs forward until their knees were bunched under the board. They began to play, and their interest in the game caused the others to forget the manner of the Swede.

12   The cowboy was a board-whacker. Each time that he held superior cards he whanged them, one by one, with exceeding force, down upon the improvised table, and took the tricks with a glowing air of prowess and pride that sent thrills of indignation into the hearts of his opponents. A game with a board-whacker in it is sure to become intense. The countenances of the Easterner and the Swede were miserable whenever the cowboy thundered down his aces and kings, while Johnnie, his eyes gleaming with joy, chuckled and chuckled.

13   Because of the absorbing play none considered the strange ways of the Swede. They paid strict heed to the game. Finally, during a lull caused by a new deal, the Swede suddenly addressed Johnnie: "I suppose there have been a good many men killed in this room." The jaws of the others dropped and they looked at him.

14   "What in hell are you talking about?" asked Johnnie.

The Swede laughed again his blatant laugh, full of a kind of false 15
courage and defiance. "Oh, you know what I mean all right," he answered.

"I'm a liar if I do!" Johnnie protested. The card was halted, and the men 16
stared at the Swede. Johnnie evidently felt that as the son of the proprietor he should make a direct inquiry. "Now, what might you be drivin' at,
mister?" he asked. The Swede winked at him. It was a wink full of cunning. His fingers shook on the edge of the board. "Oh, maybe you think I
have been to nowheres. Maybe you think I'm a tenderfoot?"

"I don't know nothin' about you," answered Johnnie, "and I don't give a 17
damn where you've been. All I got to say is that I don't know what you're
driving at. There hain't never been nobody killed in this room."

The cowboy, who had been steadily gazing at the Swede, then spoke: 18
"What's wrong with you, mister?"

Apparently it seemed to the Swede that he was formidably menaced. 19
He shivered and turned white near the corners of his mouth. He sent an
appealing glance in the direction of the little Easterner. During these moments he did not forget to wear his air of advanced pot-valor. "They say
they don't know what I mean," he remarked mockingly to the Easterner.

The latter answered after prolonged and cautious reflection. "I don't
understand you," he said, impassively.

The Swede made a movement then which announced that he thought 20
he had encountered treachery from the only quarter where he had expected sympathy, if not help. "Oh, I see you are all against me. I see—"

The cowboy was in a state of deep stupefaction. "Say," he cried, as he 21
tumbled the deck violently down upon the board, "say, what are you gittin'
at, hey?"

The Swede sprang up with the celerity of a man escaping from a snake 22
on the floor. "I don't want to fight!" he shouted. "I don't want to fight!"

The cowboy stretched his long legs indolently and deliberately. His 23
hands were in his pockets. He spat into the sawdust box. "Well, who the
hell thought you did?" he inquired.

The Swede backed rapidly toward a corner of the room. His hands were 24
out protectingly in front of his chest, but he was making an obvious struggle to control his fright. "Gentlemen," he quavered, "I suppose I am going
to be killed before I can leave this house! I suppose I am going to be killed
before I can leave this house!" In his eyes was the dying-swan look.
Through the windows could be seen the snow turning blue in the shadow
of dusk. The wind tore at the house, and some loose thing beat regularly
against the clapboards like a spirit tapping.

A door opened, and Scully himself entered. He paused in surprise as 25
he noted the tragic attitude of the Swede. Then he said, "What's the
matter here?"

26   The Swede answered him swiftly and eagerly: "These men are going to kill me."

27   "Kill you!" ejaculated Scully. "Kill you! What are you talkin'?"

28   The Swede made the gesture of a martyr.

29   Scully wheeled sternly upon his son. "What is this, Johnnie?"

30   The lad had grown sullen. "Damned if I know," he answered. "I can't make no sense to it." He began to shuffle the cards, fluttering them together with an angry snap. "He says a good many men have been killed in this room, or something like that. And he says he's goin' to be killed here too. I don't know what ails him. He's crazy, I shouldn't wonder."

31   Scully then looked for explanation to the cowboy, but the cowboy simply shrugged his shoulders.

32   "Kill you?" said Scully again to the Swede. "Kill you? Man, you're off your nut."

33   "Oh, I know," burst out the Swede. "I know what will happen. Yes, I'm crazy—yes. Yes, of course, I'm crazy—yes. But I know one thing—" There was a sort of sweat of misery and terror upon his face. "I know I won't get out of here alive."

34   The cowboy drew a deep breath, as if his mind was passing into the last stages of dissolution. "Well, I'm doggoned," he whispered to himself.

35   Scully wheeled suddenly and faced his son. "You've been troublin' this man!"

36   Johnnie's voice was loud with its burden of grievance. "Why, good Gawd. I ain't done nothin' to 'im."

37   The Swede broke in. "Gentlemen, do not disturb yourselves. I will leave this house. I will go away, because"—he accused them dramatically with his glance—"because I do not want to be killed."

38   Scully was furious with his son. "Will you tell me what is the matter, you young divil? What's the matter, anyhow? Speak out!"

39   "Blame it!" cried Johnnie in despair, "don't I tell you I don't know? He—he says we want to kill him, and that's all I know. I can't tell what ails him."

40   The Swede continued to repeat: "Never mind, Mr. Scully; never mind. I will leave this house. I will go away, because I do not wish to be killed. Yes, of course, I am crazy—yes. But I know one thing! I will go away. I will leave this house. Never mind, Mr. Scully; never mind. I will go away."

41   "You will not go 'way," said Scully. "You will not go 'way until I hear the reason of this business. If anybody has troubled you I will take care of him. This is my house. You are under my roof, and I will not allow any peaceable man to be troubled here." He cast a terrible eye upon Johnnie, the cowboy, and the Easterner.

"Never mind, Mr. Scully, never mind. I will go away. I do not wish to be   42
killed." The Swede moved toward the door which opened upon the stairs.
It was evidently his intention to go at once for his baggage.

"No, no," shouted Scully peremptorily; but the white-faced man slid by   43
him and disappeared. "Now," said Scully severely, "what does this mane?"

Johnnie and the cowboy cried together: "Why, we didn't do nothin'   44
to 'im!"

Scully's eyes were cold. "No," he said, "you didn't?"   45

Johnnie swore a deep oath. "Why, this is the wildest loon I ever see. We   46
didn't do nothin' at all. We were jest sittin' here playin' cards, and he—"

The father suddenly spoke to the Easterner. "Mr. Blanc," he asked,   47
"what has these boys been doin'?"

The Easterner reflected again. "I didn't see anything wrong at all," he   48
said at last, slowly.

Scully began to howl. "But what does it mane?" He stared ferociously at   49
his son. "I have a mind to lather you for this, my boy."

Johnnie was frantic. "Well, what have I done?" he bawled at his father.   50

III

"I think you are tongue-tied," said Scully finally to his son, the cowboy, and   51
the Easterner; and at the end of this scornful sentence he left the room.

Upstairs the Swede was swiftly fastening the straps of his great valise.   52
Once his back happened to be half turned toward the door, and, hearing a
noise there, he wheeled and sprang up, uttering a loud cry. Scully's wrinkled
visage showed grimly in the light of the small lamp he carried. This yellow
effulgence, streaming upward, colored his only prominent features, and left
his eyes, for instance, in mysterious shadow. He resembled a murderer.

"Man! man!" he exclaimed, "have you gone daffy?"   53

"Oh, no! Oh, no!" rejoined the other. "There are people in this world   54
who know pretty nearly as much as you do—understand?"

For a moment they stood gazing at each other. Upon the Swede's   55
deathly pale cheeks were two spots brightly crimson and sharply edged, as
if they had been carefully painted. Scully placed the light on the table and
sat himself on the edge of the bed. He spoke ruminatively. "By cracky, I
never heard of such a thing in my life. It's a complete muddle. I can't, for
the soul of me, think how you ever got this idea into your head." Presently
he lifted his eyes and asked: "And did you sure think they were going to
kill you?"

The Swede scanned the old man as if he wished to see into his mind. "I   56
did," he said at last. He obviously suspected that his answer might precipitate

an outbreak. As he pulled on a strap his whole arm shook, the elbow wavering like a bit of paper.

57   Scully banged his hand impressively on the footboard of the bed. "Why, man, we're goin' to have a line of ilictric street-cars in this town next spring."

58   "'A line of electric street-cars,'" repeated the Swede, stupidly.

59   "And," said Scully, "there's a new railroad goin' to be built down from Broken Arm to here. Not to mintion the four churches and the smashin' big brick schoolhouse. Then there's the big factory, too. Why, in two years Romper'll be a met-tro-*pol*-is."

60   Having finished the preparation of his baggage, the Swede straightened himself. "Mr. Scully," he said, with sudden hardihood, "how much do I owe you?"

61   "You don't owe me anythin'," said the old man, angrily.

62   "Yes, I do," retorted the Swede. He took seventy-five cents from his pocket and tendered it to Scully; but the latter snapped his fingers in disdainful refusal. However, it happened that they both stood gazing in a strange fashion at three silver pieces on the Swede's open palm.

63   "I'll not take your money," said Scully at last. "Not after what's been goin' on here." Then a plan seemed to strike him. "Here," he cried, picking up his lamp and moving toward the door. "Here! Come with me a minute."

64   "No," said the Swede, in overwhelming alarm.

65   "Yes," urged the old man. "Come on! I want you to come and see a picter—just across the hall—in my room."

66   The Swede must have concluded that his hour was come. His jaw dropped and his teeth showed like a dead man's. He ultimately followed Scully across the corridor, but he had the step of one hung in chains.

67   Scully flashed the light high on the wall of his own chamber. There was revealed a ridiculous photograph of a little girl. She was leaning against a balustrade of gorgeous decoration, and the formidable bang to her hair was prominent. The figure was as graceful as an upright sled-stake, and, withal, it was the hue of lead. "There," said Scully tenderly, "that's the picter of my little girl that died. Her name was Carrie. She had the purtiest hair you ever saw! I was that fond of her, she—"

68   Turning then, he saw that the Swede was not contemplating the picture at all, but, instead, was keeping keen watch on the gloom in the rear.

69   "Look, man!" cried Scully, heartily. "That's the picter of my little gal that died. Her name was Carrie. And then here's the picter of my oldest boy, Michael. He's a lawyer in Lincoln, an' doin' well. I gave that boy a grand eddication, and I'm glad for it now. He's a fine boy. Look at 'im now. Ain't he bold as blazes, him there in Lincoln, an honored an' respicted

gintleman! An honored and respected gintleman," concluded Scully with
a flourish. And, so saying, he smote the Swede jovially on the back.

The Swede faintly smiled.   70

"Now," said the old man, "there's only one more thing." He dropped   71
suddenly to the floor and thrust his head beneath the bed. The Swede
could hear his muffled voice. "I'd keep it under me piller if it wasn't for
that boy Johnnie. Then there's the old woman—Where is it now? I never
put it twice in the same place. Ah, now come out with you!"

Presently he backed clumsily from under the bed, dragging with him an   72
old coat rolled into a bundle. "I've fetched him," he muttered. Kneeling on
the floor, he unrolled the coat and extracted from its heart a large yellow-
brown whiskey-bottle.

His first manoeuver was to hold the bottle up to the light. Reassured,   73
apparently, that nobody had been tampering with it, he thrust it with a
generous movement toward the Swede.

The weak-kneed Swede was about to eagerly clutch this element of   74
strength, but he suddenly jerked his hand away and cast a look of horror
upon Scully.

"Drink," said the old man affectionately. He had risen to his feet, and   75
now stood facing the Swede.

There was a silence. Then again Scully said: "Drink!"   76

The Swede laughed wildly. He grabbed the bottle, put it to his mouth;   77
and as his lips curled absurdly around the opening and his throat worked,
he kept his glance, burning with hatred, upon the old man's face.

IV

After the departure of Scully the three men, with the cardboard still upon   78
their knees, preserved for a long time an astounded silence. Then Johnnie
said: "That's the doddangedest Swede I ever see."

"He ain't no Swede," said the cowboy, scornfully.   79

"Well, what is he then?" cried Johnnie. "What is he then?"   80

"It's my opinion," replied the cowboy deliberately, "he's some kind of a   81
Dutchman." It was a venerable custom of the country to entitle as Swedes
all light-haired men who spoke with a heavy tongue. In consequence the
idea of the cowboy was not without its daring. "Yes, sir," he repeated. "It's
my opinion this feller is some kind of a Dutchman."

"Well, he says he's a Swede, anyhow," muttered Johnnie, sulkily. He   82
turned to the Easterner: "What do you think, Mr. Blanc?"

"Oh, I don't know," replied the Easterner.   83

"Well, what do you think makes him act that way?" asked the cowboy.   84

85   "Why, he's frightened." The Easterner knocked his pipe against a rim of the stove. "He's clear frightened out of his boots."

86   "What at?" cried Johnnie and the cowboy together.

87   The Easterner reflected over his answer.

88   "What at?" cried the others again.

89   "Oh, I don't know, but it seems to me this man has been reading dime novels, and he thinks he's right out in the middle of it—the shootin' and stabbin' and all."

90   "But," said the cowboy, deeply scandalized, "this ain't Wyoming, ner none of them places. This is Nebrasker."

91   "Yes," added Johnnie, "an' why don't he wait till he gits *out West?*"

92   The travelled Easterner laughed. "It isn't different there even—not in these days. But he thinks he's right in the middle of hell."

93   Johnnie and the cowboy mused long.

94   "It's awful funny," remarked Johnnie at last.

95   "Yes," said the cowboy. "This is a queer game. I hope we don't git snowed in, because then we'd have to stand this here man bein' around with us all the time. That wouldn't be no good."

96   "I wish pop would throw him out," said Johnnie.

97   Presently they heard a loud stamping on the stairs, accompanied by ringing jokes in the voice of old Scully, and laughter, evidently from the Swede. The men around the stove stared vacantly at each other. "Gosh!" said the cowboy. The door flew open, and old Scully, flushed and anecdotal, came into the room. He was jabbering at the Swede, who followed him, laughing bravely. It was the entry of two roisterers from a banquet ball.

98   "Come now," said Scully sharply to the three seated men, "move up and give us a chance at the stove." The cowboy and the Easterner obediently sidled their chairs to make room for the newcomers. Johnnie, however, simply arranged himself in a more indolent attitude, and then remained motionless.

99   "Come! Git over, there," said Scully.

100   "Plenty of room on the other side of the stove," said Johnnie.

101   "Do you think we want to sit in the draught?" roared the father.

102   But the Swede here interposed with a grandeur of confidence. "No, no. Let the boy sit where he likes," he cried in a bullying voice to the father.

103   "All right! All right!" said Scully, deferentially. The cowboy and the Easterner exchanged glances of wonder.

104   The five chairs were formed in a crescent about one side of the stove. The Swede began to talk; he talked arrogantly, profanely, angrily. Johnnie, the cowboy, and the Easterner maintained a morose silence, while old

Scully appeared to be receptive and eager, breaking in constantly with sympathetic ejaculations.

Finally the Swede announced that he was thirsty. He moved in his chair, and said that he would go for a drink of water.   105

"I'll git it for you," cried Scully at once.   106

"No," said the Swede, contemptuously. "I'll get it for myself." He arose and stalked with the air of an owner off into the executive parts of the hotel.   107

As soon as the Swede was out of hearing Scully sprang to his feet and whispered intensely to the others: "Up-stairs he thought I was tryin' to poison 'im."   108

"Say," said Johnnie, "this makes me sick. Why don't you throw 'im out in the snow?"   109

"Why, he's all right now," declared Scully. "It was only that he was from the East, and he thought this was a tough place. That's all. He's all right now."   110

The cowboy looked with admiration upon the Easterner. "You were straight," he said. "You were on to that there Dutchman."   111

"Well," said Johnnie to his father, "he may be all right now, but I don't see it. Other time he was scared, but now he's too fresh."   112

Scully's speech was always a combination of Irish brogue and idiom, Western twang and idiom, and scraps of curiously formal diction taken from the story-books and newspapers. He now hurled a strange mass of language at the head of his son. "What do I keep? What do I keep? What do I keep?" he demanded, in a voice of thunder. He slapped his knee impressively, to indicate that he himself was going to make reply, and that all should heed. "I keep a hotel," he shouted. "A hotel, do you mind? A guest under my roof has sacred privileges. He is to be intimidated by none. Not one word shall he hear that would prijudice him in favor of goin' away. I'll not have it. There's no place in this here town where they can say they iver took in a guest of mine because he was afraid to stay here." He wheeled suddenly upon the cowboy and the Easterner. "Am I right?"   113

"Yes, Mr. Scully," said the cowboy, "I think you're right."   114

"Yes, Mr. Scully," said the Easterner, "I think you're right."   115

V

At six-o'clock supper, the Swede fizzed like a fire-wheel. He sometimes seemed on the point of bursting into riotous song, and in all his madness he was encouraged by old Scully. The Easterner was encased in reserve; the cowboy sat in wide-mouthed amazement, forgetting to eat, while Johnnie wrathily demolished great plates of food. The daughters of the   116 house, when they were obliged to replenish the biscuits, approached as warily as Indians, and, having succeeded in their purposes, fled with ill-concealed trepidation. The Swede domineered the whole feast, and he gave it the appearance of a cruel bacchanal. He seemed to have grown suddenly taller; he gazed, brutally disdainful, into every face. His voice rang through the room. Once when he jabbed out harpoon-fashion with his fork to pinion a biscuit, the weapon nearly impaled the hand of the Easterner, which had been stretched quietly out for the same biscuit.

117   After supper, as the men filed toward the other room, the Swede smote Scully ruthlessly on the shoulder. "Well, old boy, that was a good, square meal." Johnnie looked hopefully at his father; he knew that shoulder was tender from an old fall; and, indeed, it appeared for a moment as if Scully was going to flame out over the matter, but in the end he smiled a sickly smile and remained silent. The others understood from his manner that he was admitting his responsibility for the Swede's new view-point.

118   Johnnie, however, addressed his parent in an aside. "Why don't you license somebody to kick you downstairs?" Scully scowled darkly by way of reply.

119   When they were gathered about the stove, the Swede insisted on another game of High-Five. Scully gently deprecated the plan at first, but the Swede turned a wolfish glare upon him. The old man subsided, and the Swede canvassed the others. In his tone there was always a great threat. The cowboy and the Easterner both remarked indifferently that they would play. Scully said that he would presently have to go to meet the 6:58 train, and so the Swede turned menacingly upon Johnnie. For a moment their glances crossed like blades, and then Johnnie smiled and said, "Yes, I'll play."

120   They formed a square, with the little board on their knees. The Easterner and the Swede were again partners. As the play went on, it was noticeable that the cowboy was not board-whacking as usual. Meanwhile, Scully, near the lamp, had put on his spectacles and, with an appearance curiously like an old priest, was reading a newspaper. In time he went out to meet the 6:58 train, and, despite his precautions, a gust of polar wind whirled into the room as he opened the door. Besides scattering the cards, it chilled the players to the marrow. The Swede cursed frightfully. When Scully returned, his entrance disturbed a cozy and friendly scene. The Swede again cursed. But presently they were once more intent, their heads bent forward and their hands moving swiftly. The Swede had adopted the fashion of board-whacking.

121   Scully took up his paper and for a long time remained immersed in matters which were extraordinarily remote from him. The lamp burned badly, and once he stopped to adjust the wick. The newspaper, as he turned from

page to page, rustled with a slow and comfortable sound. Then suddenly he heard three terrible words: "You are cheatin'!"

Such scenes often prove that there can be little of dramatic import in environment. Any room can present a tragic front: any room can be comic. This little den was now hideous as a torture-chamber. The new faces of the men themselves had changed it upon the instant. The Swede held a huge fist in front of Johnnie's face, while the latter looked steadily over it into the blazing orbs of his accuser. The Easterner had grown pallid; the cowboy's jaw had dropped in that expression of bovine amazement which was one of his important mannerisms. After the three words, the first sound in the room was made by Scully's paper as it floated forgotten to his feet. His spectacles had also fallen from his nose, but by a clutch he had saved them in air. His hand, grasping the spectacles, now remained poised awkwardly and near his shoulder. He stared at the card-players. 122

Probably the silence was while a second elapsed. Then, if the floor had been suddenly twitched out from under the men they could not have moved quicker. The five had projected themselves headlong toward a common point. It happened that Johnnie, in rising to hurl himself upon the Swede, had stumbled slightly because of his curiously instinctive care for the cards and the board. The loss of the moment allowed time for the arrival of Scully, and also allowed the cowboy time to give the Swede a great push which sent him staggering back. The men found tongue together, and hoarse shouts of rage, appeal, or fear burst from every throat. The cowboy pushed and jostled feverishly at the Swede, and the Easterner and Scully clung wildly to Johnnie; but through the smoky air, above the swaying bodies of the peace-compellers, the eyes of the two warriors ever sought each other in glances of challenge that were at once hot and steely. 123

Of course the board had been overturned, and now the whole company of cards was scattered over the floor, where the boots of the men trampled the fat and painted kings and queens as they gazed with their silly eyes at the war that was waging above them. 124

Scully's voice was dominating the yells. "Stop now! Stop, I say! Stop, now—" 125

Johnnie, as he struggled to burst through the rank formed by Scully and the Easterner, was crying, "Well, he says I cheated! He says I cheated! I won't allow no man to say I cheated! If he says I cheated, he's a———!" 126

The cowboy was telling the Swede, "Quit, now! Quit, d'ye hear—" 127

The screams of the Swede never ceased: "He did cheat! I saw him! I saw him—" 128

As for the Easterner, he was importuning in a voice that was not heeded: "Wait a moment, can't you? Oh, wait a moment. What's the good of a fight over a game of cards? Wait a moment—" 129

130   In this tumult no complete sentences were clear. "Cheat"—"Quit"—"He says"—these fragments pierced the uproar and rang out sharply. It was remarkable that, whereas Scully undoubtedly made the most noise, he was the least heard of any of the riotous band.

131   Then suddenly there was a great cessation. It was as if each man had paused for breath; and although the room was still lighted with the anger of men, it could be seen that there was no danger of immediate conflict, and at once Johnnie, shouldering his way forward, almost succeeded in confronting the Swede. "What did you say I cheated for? What did you say I cheated for? I don't cheat, and I won't let no man say I do!"

132   The Swede said, "I saw you! I saw you!"

133   "Well," cried Johnnie, "I'll fight any man what says I cheat!"

134   "No, you won't," said the cowboy. "Not here."

135   "Ah, be still, can't you?" said Scully, coming between them.

136   The quiet was sufficient to allow the Easterner's voice to be heard. He was repeating, "Oh, wait a moment, can't you? What the good of a fight over a game of cards? Wait a moment!"

137   Johnnie, his red face appearing above his father's shoulder, hailed the Swede again. "Did you say I cheated?"

138   The Swede showed his teeth. "Yes."

139   "Then," said Johnnie, "we must fight."

140   "Yes, fight," roared the Swede. He was like a demoniac. "Yes, fight! I'll show you what kind of a man I am! I'll show you who you want to fight! Maybe you think I can't fight! Maybe you think I can't! I'll show you, you skin, you card-sharp! Yes, you cheated! You cheated! You cheated!"

141   "Well, let's go at it, then, mister," said Johnnie, coolly.

142   The cowboy's brow was beaded with sweat from his efforts in intercepting all sorts of raids. He turned in despair to Scully. "What are you goin' to do now?"

143   A change had come over the Celtic visage of the old man. He now seemed all eagerness; his eyes glowed.

144   "We'll let them fight," he answered stalwartly. "I can't put up with it any longer. I've stood this damned Swede till I'm sick. We'll let them fight."

VI

145   The men prepared to go out-of-doors. The Easterner was so nervous that he had great difficulty in getting his arms into the sleeves of his new leather coat. As the cowboy drew his fur cap down over his ears his hands trembled. In fact, Johnnie and old Scully were the only ones who displayed no agitation. These preliminaries were conducted without words.

Scully threw open the door. "Well, come on," he said. Instantly a ter-   146
rific wind caused the flame of the lamp to struggle at its wick, while a puff
of black smoke sprang from the chimney-top. The stove was in mid-current
of the blast, and its voice swelled to equal the roar of the storm. Some of
the scarred and bedabbled cards were caught up from the floor and dashed
helplessly against the further wall. The men lowered their heads and plunged
into the tempest as into a sea.

No snow was falling, but great whirls and clouds of flakes, swept up from   147
the ground by the frantic winds, were streaming southward with the speed
of bullets. The covered land was blue with the sheen of an unearthly satin,
and there was no other hue save where, at the low, black railway station—
which seemed incredibly distant—one light gleamed like a tiny jewel. As
the men floundered into a thigh-deep drift, it was known that the Swede
was bawling out something. Scully went to him, put a hand on his shoulder,
and projected an ear. "What's that you say?" he shouted.

"I say," bawled the Swede again, "I won't stand much show against this   148
gang. I know you'll all pitch on me."

Scully smote him reproachfully on the arm. "Tut, man!" he yelled. The   149
wind tore the words from Scully's lips and scattered them far a-lee.

"You are all a gang of—" boomed the Swede, but the storm also seized   150
the remainder of his sentence.

Immediately turning their backs upon the wind, the men had swung   151
around a corner to the sheltered side of the hotel. It was the function of
the little house to preserve here, amid this great devastation of snow, an
irregular V-shape of heavily encrusted grass, which crackled beneath their
feet. One could imagine the great drifts piled against the windward side.
When the party reached the comparative peace of this spot it was found
that the Swede was still bellowing.

"Oh, I know what kind of a thing this is! I know you'll all pitch on me.   152
I can't lick you all!"

Scully turned upon him panther-fashion. "You'll not have to whip all of   153
us. You'll have to whip my son Johnnie. An' the man what troubles you
durin' that time will have me to dale with."

The arrangements were swiftly made. The two men faced each other,   154
obedient to the harsh commands of Scully, whose face, in the subtly luminous gloom, could be seen set in the austere impersonal lines that are
pictured on the countenances of the Roman veterans. The Easterner's teeth
were chattering, and he was hopping up and down like a mechanical toy.
The cowboy stood rocklike.

The contestants had not stripped off any clothing. Each was in his ordi-   155
nary attire. Their fists were up, and they eyed each other in a calm that
had the elements of leonine cruelty in it.

156 During this pause, the Easterner's mind, like a film, took lasting impressions of three men—the iron-nerved master of the ceremony; the Swede, pale, motionless, terrible; and Johnnie, serene yet ferocious, brutish yet heroic. The entire prelude had in it a tragedy greater than the tragedy of action, and this aspect was accentuated by the long, mellow cry of the blizzard, as it sped the tumbling and wailing flakes into the black abyss of the south.

157 "Now!" said Scully.

158 The two combatants leaped forward and crashed together like bullocks. There was heard the cushioned sound of blows, and of a curse squeezing out from between the tight teeth of one.

159 As for the spectators, the Easterner's pent-up breath exploded from him with a pop of relief, absolute relief from the tension of the preliminaries. The cowboy bounded into the air with a yowl. Scully was immovable as from supreme amazement and fear at the fury of the fight which he himself had permitted and arranged.

160 For a time the encounter in the darkness was such a perplexity of flying arms that it presented no more detail than would a swiftly revolving wheel. Occasionally a face, as if illumined by a flash of light, would shine out, ghastly and marked with pink spots. A moment later, the men might have been known as shadows, if it were not for the involuntary utterance of oaths that came from them in whispers.

161 Suddenly a holocaust of warlike desire caught the cowboy, and he bolted forward with the speed of a broncho. "Go it, Johnnie! Go it! Kill him! Kill him!"

162 Scully confronted him. "Kape back," he said; and by his glance the cowboy could tell that this man was Johnnie's father.

163 To the Easterner there was a monotony of unchangeable fighting that was an abomination. This confused mingling was eternal to his sense, which was concentrated in a longing for the end, the priceless end. Once the fighters lurched near him, and as he scrambled hastily backward he heard them breathe like men on the rack.

164 "Kill him, Johnnie! Kill him! Kill him! Kill him!" The cowboy's face was contorted like one of those agony masks in museums.

165 "Keep still," said Scully, icily.

166 Then there was a sudden loud grunt, incomplete, cut short, and Johnnie's body swung away from the Swede and fell with sickening heaviness to the grass. The cowboy was barely in time to prevent the mad Swede from flinging himself upon his prone adversary. "No, you don't," said the cowboy, interposing an arm. "Wait a second."

Scully was at his son's side. "Johnnie! Johnnie, me boy!" His voice had 167
a quality of melancholy tenderness. "Johnnie! Can you go on with it?"
He looked anxiously down into the bloody, pulpy face of his son.

There was a moment of silence, and then Johnnie answered in his ordi- 168
nary voice, "Yes, I—it—yes."

Assisted by his father he struggled to his feet. "Wait a bit now till you 169
git your wind," said the old man.

A few paces away the cowboy was lecturing the Swede. "No, you don't! 170
Wait a second!"

The Easterner was plucking at Scully's sleeve. "Oh, this is enough," he 171
pleaded. "This is enough! Let it go as it stands. This is enough!"

"Bill," said Scully, "git out of the road." The cowboy stepped aside. 172
"Now." The combatants were actuated by a new caution as they advanced
toward collision. They glared at each other, and then the Swede aimed a
lightning blow that carried with it his entire weight. Johnnie was evidently half stupid from weakness, but he miraculously dodged, and his fist
sent the overbalanced Swede sprawling.

The cowboy, Scully, and the Easterner burst into a cheer that was like a 173
chorus of triumphant soldiery, but before its conclusion the Swede had
scuffled agilely to his feet and come in berserk abandon at his foe. There
was another perplexity of flying arms, and Johnnie's body again swung
away and fell, even as a bundle might fall from a roof. The Swede instantly
staggered to a little wind-waved tree and leaned upon it, breathing like an
engine, while his savage and flame-lit eyes roamed from face to face as the
men bent over Johnnie. There was a splendor of isolation in his situation
at this time which the Easterner felt once when, lifting his eyes from the
man on the ground, he beheld that mysterious and lonely figure, waiting.

"Are you any good yet, Johnnie?" asked Scully in a broken voice. 174

The son gasped and opened his eyes languidly. After a moment he an- 175
swered, "No—I ain't—any good—any—more." Then, from shame and
bodily ill, he began to weep, the tears furrowing down through the bloodstains on his face. "He was too—too—too heavy for me."

Scully straightened and addressed the waiting figure. "Stranger," he 176
said, evenly, "it's all up with our side." Then his voice changed into that
vibrant huskiness which is commonly the tone of the most simple and
deadly announcements. "Johnnie is whipped."

Without replying, the victor moved off on the route to the front door of 177
the hotel.

The cowboy was formulating new and unspellable blasphemies. The 178
Easterner was startled to find that they were out in a wind that seemed to
come direct from the shadowed arctic floes. He heard again the wail of the

snow as it was flung to its grave in the south. He knew now that all this time the cold had been sinking into him deeper and deeper, and he wondered that he had not perished. He felt indifferent to the condition of the vanquished man.

179   "Johnnie, can you walk?" asked Scully.

180   "Did I hurt—hurt him any?" asked the son.

181   "Can you walk, boy? Can you walk?"

182   Johnnie's voice was suddenly strong. There was a robust impatience in it. "I asked you whether I hurt him any!"

183   "Yes, yes, Johnnie," answered the cowboy, consolingly; "he's hurt a good deal."

184   The raised him from the ground, and as son as he was on his feet he went tottering off, rebuffing all attempts at assistance. When the party rounded the corner they were fairly blinded by the pelting of the snow. It burned their faces like fire. The cowboy carried Johnnie through the drift to the door. As they entered, some cards again rose from the floor and beat against the wall.

185   The Easterner rushed to the stove. He was so profoundly chilled that he almost dared to embrace the glowing iron. The Swede was not in the room. Johnnie sank into a chair and, folding his arms on his knees, buried his face in them. Scully, warming one foot and then the other at the rim of the stove, muttered to himself with Celtic mournfulness. The cowboy had removed his fur cap, and with a dazed and rueful air he was running one hand through his tousled locks. From overhead they could hear the creaking of boards, as the Swede tramped here and there in his room.

186   The sad quiet was broken by the sudden flinging open of a door that led toward the kitchen. It was instantly followed by an inrush of women. They precipitated themselves upon Johnnie amid a chorus of lamentations. Before they carried their prey off to the kitchen, there to be bathed and harangued with that mixture of sympathy and abuse which is a feat of their sex, the mother straightened herself and fixed old Scully with an eye of stern reproach. "Shame be upon you, Patrick Scully!" she cried. "Your own son, too. Shame be upon you!"

187   "There, now! Be quiet, now!" said the old man, weakly.

188   "Shame be upon you, Patrick Scully!" The girls, rallying to this slogan, sniffed disdainfully in the direction of those trembling accomplices, the cowboy and the Easterner. Presently they bore Johnnie away, and left the three men to dismal reflection.

VII

"I'd like to fight this here Dutchman myself," said the cowboy, breaking a   189
long silence.

Scully wagged his head sadly. "No, that wouldn't do. It wouldn't be   190
right. It wouldn't be right."

"Well, why wouldn't it?" argued the cowboy. "I don't see no harm in it."   191

"No," answered Scully, with mournful heroism. "It wouldn't be right. It   192
was Johnnie's fight, and now we mustn't whip the man just because he
whipped Johnnie."

"Yes, that's true enough," said the cowboy; "but—he better not get fresh   193
with me, because I couldn't stand no more of it."

"You'll not say a word to him," commanded Scully, and even then they   194
heard the tread of the Swede on the stairs. His entrance was made the-
atric. He swept the door back with a bang and swaggered to the middle of
the room. No one looked at him. "Well," he cried, insolently, at Scully. "I
s'pose you'll tell me now how much I owe you?"

The old man remained stolid. "You don't owe me nothin'."   195

"Huh!" said the Swede, "huh! Don't own 'im nothin'."   196

The cowboy addressed the Swede. "Stranger, I don't see how you come   197
to be so gay around here."

Old Scully was instantly alert. "Stop!" he shouted, holding his hand   198
forth, fingers upward. "Bill, you shut up!"

The cowboy spat carelessly into the sawdust-box. "I didn't say a word,   199
did I?" he asked.

"Mr. Scully," called the Swede, "how much do I owe you?" It was seen   200
that he was attired for departure, and that he had his valise in his hand.

"You don't owe me nothin'," repeated Scully in his same imper-   201
turbable way.

"Huh!" said the Swede. "I guess you're right. I guess if it was any way at   202
all, you'd owe me somethin'. That's what I guess." He turned to the cowboy.

"'Kill him! Kill him! Kill him!'" he mimicked, and then guffawed   203
victoriously. "'Kill him!'" He was convulsed with ironical humor.

But he might have been jeering at the dead. The three men were im-   204
movable and silent, staring with glassy eyes at the stove.

The Swede opened the door and passed into the storm, one derisive   205
glance backward at the still group.

As soon as the door was closed, Scully and the cowboy leaped to their   206
feet and began to curse. They trampled to and fro, waving their arms and
smashing into the air with their fists. "Oh, but that was a hard minute!"
wailed Scully. "That was a hard minute! Him there leerin' and scoffin'!

One bang at his nose was worth forty dollars to me that minute! How did you stand it, Bill?"

207 "How did I stand it?" cried the cowboy in a quivering voice. "How did I stand it? Oh!"

208 The old man burst into sudden brogue. "I'd loike to take that Swade," he wailed, "and hould 'im down on a shtone flure and bate 'im to a jelly wid a shtick!"

209 The cowboy groaned in sympathy. "I'd like to git him by the neck and hammer him"—he brought his hand down on a chair with a noise like a pistol-shot—"hammer that there Dutchman until he couldn't tell himself from a dead coyote!"

210 "I'd bate 'im until he—"

211 "I'd show *him* some things—"

212 And then together they raised a yearning, fanatic cry— "Oh-o-oh! if we only could—"

213 "Yes!"

214 "Yes!"

215 "And then I'd—"

216 "O-o-oh!"

VIII

217 The Swede, tightly gripping his valise, tacked across the face of the storm as if he carried sails. He was following a line of little naked, gasping trees which he knew, must mark the way of the road. His face, fresh from the pounding of Johnnie's fists, felt more pleasure than pain in the wind and the driving snow. A number of square shapes loomed upon him finally, and he knew them as the houses of the main body of the town. He found a street and made travel along it, leaning heavily upon the wind whenever, at a corner, a terrific blast caught him.

218 He might have been in a deserted village. We picture the world as thick with conquering and elate humanity, but here, with the bugles of the tempest pealing, it was hard to imagine a peopled earth. One viewed the existence of man then as a marvel, and conceded a glamor of wonder to these lice which were caused to cling to a whirling, fire-smitten, ice-locked, disease-stricken, space-lost bulb. The conceit of man was explained by this storm to be the very engine of life. One was a coxcomb not to die in it. However, the Swede found a saloon.

219 In front of it an indomitable red light was burning, and the snowflakes were made blood-color as they flew through the circumscribed territory of the lamp's shining. The Swede pushed open the door of the saloon and entered. A sanded expanse was before him, and at the end of it four men sat

about a table drinking. Down one side of the room extended a radiant bar, and its guardian was leaning upon his elbows listening to the talk of the men at the table. The Swede dropped his valise upon the floor and, smiling fraternally upon the barkeeper, said, "Gimme some whiskey, will you?" The man placed a bottle, a whiskey-glass, and a glass of ice-thick water upon the bar. The Swede poured himself an abnormal portion of whiskey and drank it in three gulps. "Pretty bad night," remarked the bartender, indifferently. He was making the pretension of blindness which is usually a distinction of his class; but it could have been seen that he was furtively studying the half-erased bloodstains on the face of the Swede. "Bad night," he said again.

"Oh, it's good enough for me," replied the Swede, hardily, as he poured 220 himself more whiskey. The barkeeper took his coin and maneuvered it through its reception by the highly nickelled cash-machine. A bell rang; a card labeled "20 cts." had appeared.

"No," continued the Swede, "this isn't too bad weather. It's good 221 enough for me."

"So?" murmured the barkeeper, languidly. 222

The copious drams made the Swede's eyes swim, and he breathed a tri- 223 fle heavier. "Yes, I like this weather. I like it. It suits me." It was apparently his design to impart a deep significance to these words.

"So?" murmured the bartender again. He turned to gaze dreamily at the 224 scroll-like birds and bird-like scrolls which had been drawn with soap upon the mirrors in the back of the bar.

"Well, I guess I'll take another drink," said the Swede, presently. "Have 225 something?"

"No, thanks; I'm not drinkin'," answered the bartender. Afterward he 226 asked, "How did you hurt your face?"

The Swede immediately began to boast loudly. "Why, in a fight. I 227 thumped the soul of a man down here at Scully's hotel."

The interest of the four men at the table was at last aroused. 228

"Who was it?" said one. 229

"Johnnie Scully," blustered the Swede. "Son of the man what runs it. 230 He will be pretty near dead for some weeks, I can tell you. I made a nice thing of him, I did. He couldn't get up. They carried him in the house. Have a drink?"

Instantly the men in some subtle way encased themselves in reserve. 231 "No, thanks," said one. The group was of curious formation. Two were prominent local business men; one was the district attorney; and one was a professional gambler of the kind known as "square."[1] But a scrutiny of

1 Honest

the group would not have enabled an observer to pick the gambler from the men of more reputable pursuits. He was, in fact, a man so delicate in manner, when among people of fair class, and so judicious in his choice of victims, that in the strictly masculine part of the town's life he had come to be explicitly trusted and admired. People called him a thoroughbred. The fear and contempt with which his craft was regarded were undoubtedly the reason why his quiet dignity shone conspicuous above the quiet dignity of men who might be merely hatters, billiard-markers, or grocery clerks. Beyond an occasional unwary traveller who came by rail, this gambler was supposed to prey solely upon reckless and senile farmers, who, when flush with good crops, drove into town in all the pride and confidence of an absolutely invulnerable stupidity. Hearing at times in circuitous fashion of the despoilment of such a farmer, the important men of Romper invariably laughed in contempt of the victim, and if they thought of the wolf at all, it was a kind of pride at the knowledge that he would never dare think of attacking their wisdom and courage. Besides, it was popular that this gambler had a real wife and two real children in a neat cottage in a suburb, where he led an exemplary home life; and when any one even suggested a discrepancy in his character, the crowd immediately vociferated descriptions of this virtuous family circle. Then men who led exemplary home lives, and men who did not lead exemplary home lives, all subsided in a bunch, remarking that there was nothing more to be said.

232   However, when a restriction was placed upon him—as, for instance, when a strong clique of members of the new Pollywog Club refused to permit him, even as a spectator, to appear in the rooms of the organization— the candor and gentleness with which he accepted the judgment disarmed many of his foes and made his friends more desperately partisan. He invariably distinguished between himself and a respectable Romper man so quickly and frankly that his manner actually appeared to be a continual broadcast compliment.

233   And one must not forget to declare the fundamental fact of his entire position in Romper. It is irrefutable that in all affairs outside his business, in all matters that occur eternally and commonly between man and man, this thieving card-player was so generous, so just, so moral, that, in a contest, he could have put to flight the consciences of nine tenths of the citizens of Romper.

234   And so it happened that he was seated in this saloon with the two prominent local merchants and the district attorney.

235   The Swede continued to drink raw whiskey, meanwhile babbling at the barkeeper and trying to induce him to indulge in potations. "Come on. Have a drink. Come on. What—no? Well, have a little one, then. By gawd,

I've whipped a man tonight, and I want to celebrate. I whipped him good, too. Gentlemen," the Swede cried to the men at the table, "have a drink?"

"Ssh!" said the barkeeper.   236

The group at the table, although furtively attentive, had been pretend-   237
ing to be deep in talk, but now a man lifted his eyes toward the Swede and said, shortly, "Thanks. We don't want any more."

At this reply the Swede ruffled out his chest like a rooster. "Well," he   238
exploded, "it seems I can't get anybody to drink with me in this town. Seems so, don't it? Well!"

"Ssh!" said the barkeeper.   239

"Say," snarled the Swede, "don't you try to shut me up. I won't have it.   240
I'm a gentleman, and I want people to drink with me. And I want 'em to drink with me now. *Now*—do you understand?" He rapped the bar with his knuckles.

Years of experience had calloused the bartender. He merely grew sulky.   241
"I hear you," he answered.

"Well," cried the Swede, "listen hard then. See those men over there?   242
Well, they're going to drink with me, and don't you forget it. Now you watch."

"Hi!" yelled the barkeeper, "this won't do!"   243

"Why won't it?" demanded the Swede. He stalked over to the table, and   244
by chance laid his hand upon the shoulder of the gambler. "How about this?" he asked wrathfully. "I asked you to drink with me."

The gambler simply twisted his head and spoke over his shoulder. "My   245
friend, I don't know you."

"Oh, hell!" answered the Swede, "come and have a drink."   246

"Now, my boy," advised the gambler, kindly, "take your hand off my   247
shoulder and go 'way and mind your own business." He was a little, slim man, and it seemed strange to hear him use this tone of heroic patronage to the burly Swede. The other men at the table said nothing.

"What! You won't drink with me, you little dude? I'll make you, then!   248
I'll make you!" The Swede had grasped the gambler frenziedly at the throat, and was dragging him from his chair. The other men sprang up. The barkeeper dashed around the corner of his bar. There was a great tu-mult, and then was seen a long blade in the hand of the gambler. It shot forward, and a human body, this citadel of virtue, wisdom, power, was pierced as easily as if it had been a melon. The Swede fell with a cry of supreme astonishment.

The prominent merchants and the district attorney must have at once   249
tumbled out of the place backward. The bartender found himself hanging limply to the arm of a chair and gazing into the eyes of a murderer.

250　　"Henry," said the latter, as he wiped his knife on one of the towels that hung beneath the bar rail, "you tell 'em where to find me. I'll be home, waiting for 'em." Then he vanished. A moment afterward the barkeeper was in the street dinning through the storm for help and, moreover, companionship.

251　　The corpse of the Swede, alone in the saloon, had its eye fixed upon a dreadful legend that dwelt atop of the cash-machine: "This registers the amount of your purchase."

IX

252　Months later, the cowboy was frying pork over the stove of a little ranch near the Dakota line, where there was a quick thud of hoofs outside, and presently the Easterner entered with the letters and the papers.

253　　"Well," said the Easterner at once, "the chap that killed the Swede has got three years? Wasn't much, was it?"

254　　"He has? Three years?" The cowboy poised his pan of pork, while he ruminated upon the news. "Three years. That ain't much."

255　　"No. It was a light sentence," replied the Easterner as he unbuckled his spurs. "Seems there was a good deal of sympathy for him in Romper."

256　　"If the bartender had been any good," observed the cowboy, thoughtfully, "he would have gone in and cracked that there Dutchman on the head with a bottle in the beginnin' of it and stopped all this here murderin'."

257　　"Yes, a thousand things might have happened," said the Easterner, tartly.

258　　The cowboy returned his pan of pork to the fire, but his philosophy continued. "It's funny, ain't it? If he hadn't said Johnnie was cheatin' he'd be alive this minute. He was an awful fool. Game played for fun, too. Not for money. I believe he was crazy."

259　　"I feel sorry for that gambler," said the Easterner.

260　　"Oh, so do I," said the cowboy. "He don't deserve none of it for killin' who he did."

261　　"The Swede might not have been killed if everything had been square."

262　　"Might not have been killed?" exclaimed the cowboy. "Everythin' square? Why, when he said that Johnnie was cheatin' and acted like such a jackass? And then in the saloon he fairly walked up to git hurt?" With these arguments the cowboy browbeat the Easterner and reduced him to rage.

263　　"You're a fool!" cried the Easterner, viciously. "You're a bigger jackass than the Swede by a million majority. Now let me tell you one thing. Let me tell you something. Listen! Johnnie *was* cheating!"

264　　"'Johnnie,'" said the cowboy, blankly. There was a minute of silence, and then he said, robustly, "Why, no. The game was only for fun."

"Fun or not," said the Easterner, "Johnnie was cheating. I saw him. I   265
know it. I saw him. And I refused to stand up and be a man. I let the
Swede fight it out alone. And you—you were simply puffing around the
place and wanting to fight. And then old Scully himself! We are all in it!
This poor gambler isn't even a noun. He is a kind of an adverb. Every sin
is the result of a collaboration. We, five of us, have collaborated in the
murder of this Swede. Usually there are from a dozen to forty women really
involved in every murder, but in this case it seems to be only five men—
you, I, Johnnie, old Scully; and that fool of an unfortunate gambler came
merely as a culmination, the apex of a human movement, and gets all the
punishment."

The cowboy, injured and rebellious, cried out blindly into this fog of   266
mysterious theory: "Well, I didn't do anythin', did I?"

Questioning and Discussing

Crane, "The Blue Hotel"

1. Analyze and comment on the ways in which this story reveals the alternating power struggles among the characters. What might be Crane's purpose in
   presenting these varying shifts of power? Analyze the various forms of personal power—the circumstances in which characters are hurt or punished,
   for instance—and the implications of the ways in which they are or are not
   put to use.

2. Literary critic Robert Gleckner concludes about the characters in "The
   Blue Hotel" that "they were all collaborators . . . yet no one of them really
   actually had complete control at any moment." What does Gleckner seem
   to imply is the most powerful factor controlling the fates of these characters? What might this say about the human ability to make choices that
   are ethical?

3. Discuss the implications of the narrator's and the cowboy's language in the
   final sentences of the story, using other examples from the text to support
   your point of view: "The cowboy, injured and rebellious, cried out blindly
   into this fog of mysterious theory: 'Well, I didn't do anythin', did I?'" What,
   then, might you argue are the major themes of this narrative?

⊞

ADRIENNE RICH

Adrienne Rich's most recent books of poetry are *Midnight Salvage: Poems 1995–1998*, and *Fox: Poems 1998–2000*. A new selection of her essays, *Arts of the Possible: Essays and Conversations*, was published in 2001. She has recently been the recipient of the Dorothea Tanning Prize of the Academy of American Poets "for mastery in the art of poetry," and the Lannan Foundation Lifetime Achievement Award. She lives in California.

⊞

When We Dead Awaken:
Writing as Re-Vision

1   The challenge flung by feminists at the accepted literary canon, at the methods of teaching it, and at the biased and astigmatic view of male "literary scholarship," has not diminished in the decade since the first Women's Forum; it has become broadened and intensified more recently by the challenges of black and lesbian feminists pointing out that feminist literary criticism itself has overlooked or held back from examining the work of black women and lesbians. The dynamic between a political vision and the demand for a fresh vision of literature is clear: without a growing feminist movement, the first inroads of feminist scholarship could not have been made; without the sharpening of a black feminist consciousness, black women's writing would have been left in limbo between misogynist black male critics and white feminists still struggling to unearth a white women's tradition; without an articulate lesbian/feminist movement, lesbian writing would still be lying in that closet where many of us used to sit reading forbidden books "in a bad light."

2   Much, much more is yet to be done; and university curricula have of course changed very little as a result of all this. What *is* changing is the availability of knowledge, of vital texts, the visible effects on women's lives of seeing, hearing our wordless or negated experience affirmed and pursued further in language.

3   Ibsen's *When We Dead Awaken* is a play about the use that the male artist and thinker—in the process of creating culture as we know it—has made of women, in his life and in his work; and about a woman's slow

struggling awakening to the use to which her life has been put. Bernard Shaw wrote in 1900 of this play:

> [Ibsen] shows us that no degradation ever devized or permitted is as disastrous as this degradation; that through it women can die into luxuries for men and yet can kill them; that men and women are becoming conscious of this; and that what remains to be seen as perhaps the most interesting of all imminent social developments is what will happen "when we dead awaken."[1]

It's exhilarating to be alive in a time of awakening consciousness; it can   4
also be confusing, disorienting, and painful. This awakening of dead or sleeping consciousness has already affected the lives of millions of women, even those who don't know it yet. It is also affecting the lives of men, even those who deny its claims upon them. The argument will go on whether an oppressive economic class system is responsible for the oppressive nature of male/female relations, or whether, in fact, patriarchy— the domination of males—is the original model of oppression on which all others are based. But in the last few years the women's movement has drawn inescapable and illuminating connections between our sexual lives and our political institutions. The sleepwalkers are coming awake, and for the first time this awakening has a collective reality; it is no longer such a lonely thing to open one's eyes.

Re-vision—the act of looking back, of seeing with fresh eyes, of enter-   5
ing an old text from a new critical direction—is for women more than a chapter in cultural history: it is an act of survival. Until we can understand the assumptions in which we are drenched we cannot know ourselves. And this drive to self-knowledge, for women, is more than a search for identity: it is part of our refusal of the self-destructiveness of male-dominated society. A radical critique of literature, feminist in its impulse, would take the work first of all as a clue to how we live, how we have been living, how we have been led to imagine ourselves, how our language has trapped as well as liberated us, how the very act of naming has been till now a male prerogative, and how we can begin to see and name—and therefore live—afresh. A change in the concept of sexual identity is essential if we are not going to see the old political order reassert itself in every new revolution. We need to know the writing of the past, and know it differently than we have ever known it; not to pass on a tradition but to break its hold over us.

For writers, and at this moment for women writers in particular, there   6
is the challenge and promise of a whole new psychic geography to be

1 G. B. Shaw, *The Quintessence of Ibsenism* (New York: Hill & Wang, 1922), p. 139.

explored. But there is also a difficult and dangerous walking on the ice, as we try to find language and images for a consciousness we are just coming into, and with little in the past to support us. I want to talk about some aspect of this difficulty and this danger.

7   Jane Harrison, the great classical anthropologist, wrote in 1914 in a letter to her friend Gilbert Murray:

> By the by, about "Women," it has bothered me often—why do women never want to write poetry about Man as a sex—why is Woman a dream and a terror to man and not the other way around? . . . Is it mere convention and propriety, or something deeper?[2]

I think Jane Harrison's question cuts deep into the myth-making tradition, the romantic tradition; deep into what women and men have been to each other; and deep into the psyche of the woman writer. Thinking about that question, I began thinking of the work of two twentieth-century women poets, Sylvia Plath and Diane Wakoski. It strikes me that in the work of both Man appears as, if not a dream, a fascination and a terror; and that the source of the fascination and the terror is, simply, Man's power—to dominate, tyrannize, choose, or reject the woman. The charisma of Man seems to come purely from his power over her and his control of the world by force, not from anything fertile or life-giving in him. And, in the work of both these poets, it is finally the woman's sense of *herself*— embattled, possessed—that gives the poetry its dynamic charge, its rhythms of struggle, need, will, and female energy. Until recently this female anger and this furious awareness of the Man's power over her were not available materials to the female poet, who tended to write of Love as the source of her suffering, and to view that victimization by Love as an almost inevitable fate. Or, like Marianne Moore and Elizabeth Bishop, she kept sexuality at a measured and chiseled distance in her poems.

8   One answer to Jane Harrison's question has to be that historically men and women have played very different parts in each others' lives. Where woman has been a luxury for man, and has served as the painter's model and the poet's muse, but also as comforter, nurse, cook, bearer of his seed, secretarial assistant, and copyist of manuscripts, man has played a quite different role for the female artist. Henry James repeats an incident which the writer Prosper Mérimée described, of how, while he was living with George Sand,

---

2 J. G. Stewart, *Jane Ellen Harrison: A Portrait from Letters* (London: Merlin, 1959), p. 140.

he once opened his eyes, in the raw winter dawn, to see his companion, in a dressing-gown, on her knees before the domestic hearth, a candle-stick beside her and a red *madras* round her head, making bravely, with her own hands the fire that was to enable her to sit down betimes to urgent pen and paper. The story represents him as having felt that the spectacle chilled his ardor and tried his taste; her appearance was unfortunate, her occupation an inconsequence, and her industry a reproof—the result of all which was a lively irritation and an early rupture.[3]

The specter of this kind of male judgment, along with the misnaming and thwarting of her needs by a culture controlled by males, has created problems for the woman writer: problems of contact with herself, problems of language and style, problems of energy and survival.

In reading Virginia Woolf's *A Room of One's Own* (1929) for the first   9
time in some years, I was astonished at the sense of effort, of pains taken, of dogged tentativeness, in the tone of that essay. And I recognized that tone. I had heard it often enough, in myself and in other women. It is the tone of a woman almost in touch with her anger, who is determined not to appear angry, who is *willing* herself to be calm, detached, and even charming in a roomful of men where things have been said which are attacks on her very integrity. Virginia Woolf is addressing an audience of women, but she is acutely conscious—as she always was—of being overheard by men: by Morgan and Lytton and Maynard Keynes and for that matter by her father, Leslie Stephen.[4] She drew the language out into an exacerbated thread in her determination to have her own sensibility yet protect it from those masculine presences. Only at rare moments in that essay do you hear the passion in her voice; she was trying to sound as cool as Jane Austen, as Olympian as Shakespeare, because that is the way the men of the culture thought a writer should sound.

No male writer has written primarily or even largely for women, or with   10
the sense of women's criticism as a consideration when he chooses his materials, his theme, his language. But to a lesser or greater extent, every woman writer has written for men even when, like Virginia Woolf, she was supposed to be addressing women. If we have come to the point when

---

3 Henry James, "Notes on Novelists," in *Selected Literary Criticism of Henry James*, Morris Shapira, ed. (London: Heinemann, 1965), pp. 157–58.

4 "A. R., 1978: This intuition of mine was corroborated when, early in 1978, I read the correspondence between Woolf and Dame Ethel Smyth (Henry W. and Albert A. Berg Collection, The New York Public Library, Astor, Lenox and Tilden Foundations); in a letter dated June 8, 1933, Woolf speaks of having kept her own personality out of *A Room of One's Own* lest she not be taken seriously: '. . . how personal, so will they say, rubbing their hands with glee, women always are; *I even hear them as I write.*' (Italics mine.)"

this balance might begin to change, when women can stop being haunted, not only by "convention and propriety" but by internalized fears of being and saying themselves, then it is an extraordinary moment for the woman writer—and reader.

11 I have hesitated to do what I am going to do now, which is to use myself as an illustration. For one thing, it's a lot easier and less dangerous to talk about other women writers. But there is something else. Like Virginia Woolf, I am aware of the women who are not with us here because they are washing the dishes and looking after the children. Nearly fifty years after she spoke, that fact remains largely unchanged. And I am thinking also of women whom she left out of the picture altogether—women who are washing other people's dishes and caring for other people's children, not to mention women who went on the streets last night in order to feed their children. We seem to be special women here, we have liked to think of ourselves as special, and we have known that men would tolerate, even romanticize us as special, as long as our words and actions didn't threaten their privilege of tolerating or rejecting us and our work according to *their* ideas of what a special woman ought to be. An important insight of the radical women's movement has been how divisive and how ultimately destructive is this myth of the special woman, who is also the token woman. Every one of us here in this room has had great luck—we are teachers, writers, academicians; our own gifts could not have been enough, for we all know women whose gifts are buried or aborted. Our struggles can have meaning and our privileges—however precarious under patriarchy—can be justified only if they can help to change the lives of women whose gifts—and whose very being—continue to be thwarted and silenced.

12 My own luck was being born white and middle-class into a house full of books, with a father who encouraged me to read and write. So for about twenty years I wrote for a particular man, who criticized and praised me and made me feel I was indeed "special." The obverse side of this, of course, was that I tried for a long time to please him, or rather, not to displease him. And then of course there were other men—writers, teachers— the Man, who was not a terror or a dream but a literary master and a master in other ways less easy to acknowledge. And there were all those poems about women, written by men: it seemed to be a given that men wrote poems and women frequently inhabited them. These women were almost always beautiful, but threatened with the loss of beauty, the loss of youth—the fate worse than death. Or, they were beautiful and died young, like Lucy and Lenore. Or, the woman was like Maud Gonne, cruel and disastrously mistaken, and the poem reproached her because she had refused to become a luxury for the poet.

A lot is being said today about the influence that the myths and images   13
of women have on all of us who are products of culture. I think it has been
a peculiar confusion to the girl or woman who tries to write because she is
peculiarly susceptible to language. She goes to poetry or fiction looking for
her way of being in the world, since she too has been putting words and
images together; she is looking eagerly for guides, maps, possibilities; and
over and over in the "words' masculine persuasive force" of literature she
comes up against something that negates everything she is about: she
meets the image of Woman in books written by men. She finds a terror
and a dream, she finds a beautiful pale face, she finds La Belle Dame Sans
Merci, she finds Juliet or Tess or Salomé, but precisely what she does not
find is that absorbed, drudging, puzzled, sometimes inspired creature, herself, who sits at a desk trying to put words together.

So what does she do? What did I do? I read the older women poets with   14
their peculiar keenness and ambivalence: Sappho, Christina Rossetti,
Emily Dickinson, Elinor Wylie, Edna Millay, H. D. I discovered that the
woman poet most admired at the time (by men) was Marianne Moore,
who was maidenly, elegant, intellectual, discreet. But even in reading
these women I was looking in them for the same things I had found in the
poetry of men, because I wanted women poets to be the equals of men,
and to be equal was still confused with sounding the same.

I know that my style was formed first by male poets: by the men I was   15
reading as an undergraduate—Frost, Dylan Thomas, Donne, Auden,
MacNeice, Stevens, Yeats. What I chiefly learned from them was craft.[5]
But poems are like dreams: in them you put what you don't know you
know. Looking back at poems I wrote before I was twenty-one, I'm startled
because beneath the conscious craft are glimpses of the split I even then
experienced between the girl who wrote poems, who defined herself in
writing poems, and the girl who was to define herself by her relationships
with men. "Aunt Jennifer's Tigers" (1951), written while I was a student,
looks with deliberate detachment at this split. In writing this poem, composed and apparently cool as it is, I thought I was creating a portrait of an
imaginary woman. But this woman suffers from the opposition of her
imagination, worked out in tapestry, and her life-style, "ringed with or-
deals she was mastered by." It was important to me that Aunt Jennifer was
a person as distinct from myself as possible—distanced by the formalism of

---

5 A. R., 1978: Yet I spent months, at sixteen, memorizing and writing imitations of Millay's son-
nets; and in notebooks of that period I find what are obviously attempts to imitate Dickinson's
metrics and verbal compression. I knew H. D. only through anthologized lyrics; her epic poetry was
not then available to me.

the poem, by its objective, observant tone—even by putting the woman in a different generation.

16   In those years formalism was part of the strategy—like asbestos gloves, it allowed me to handle materials I couldn't pick up bare-handed. A later strategy was to use the persona of a man, as I did in "The Loser" (1958):

A man thinks of the woman he once loved: first, after her
wedding, and then nearly a decade later.

I
I kissed you, bride and lost, and went
home from that bourgeois sacrament,
your cheek still tasting cold upon
my lips that gave you benison
with all the swagger that they knew—   5
as losers somehow learn to do.

Your wedding made my eyes ache; soon
the world would be worse off for one
more golden apple dropped to ground
without the least protesting sound,   10
and you would windfall lie, and we
forget your shimmer on the tree.

Beauty is always wasted: if
not Mignon's song sung to the deaf,
at all events to the unmoved.   15
A face like yours cannot be loved
long or seriously enough.
Almost, we seem to hold it off.

II
Well, you are tougher than I thought.
Now when the wash with ice hangs taut   20
this morning of St. Valentine,
I see you strip the squeaking line,
you body weighed against the load,
and all my groans can do no good.

Because you are still beautiful,   25
though squared and stiffened by the pull
of what nine windy years have done.
You have three daughters, lost a son.
I see all your intelligence
flung into that unwearied stance.   30

My envy is of no avail.
I turn my head and wish him well
who chafed your beauty into use
and lives forever in a house
lit by the friction of your mind.   35
You stagger in against the wind.

I finished college, published my first book by a fluke, as it seemed to me,   17
and broke off a love affair. I took a job, lived alone, went on writing, fell
in love. I was young, full of energy, and the book seemed to mean that others agreed I was a poet. Because I was also determined to prove that as a
woman poet I could also have what was then defined as a "full" woman's
life, I plunged in my early twenties into marriage and had three children
before I was thirty. There was nothing overt in the environment to warn
me: these were the fifties, and in reaction to the earlier wave of feminism,
middle-class women were making careers of domestic perfection, working
to send their husbands through professional schools, then retiring to raise
large families. People were moving out to the suburbs, technology was going to be the answer to everything, even sex; the family was in its glory.
Life was extremely private; women were isolated from each other by the
loyalties of marriage. I have a sense that women didn't talk to each other
much in the fifties—not about their secret emptiness, their frustrations. I
went on trying to write; my second book and first child appeared in the
same month. But by the time that book came out I was already dissatisfied
with those poems, which seemed to me mere exercises for poems I hadn't
written. The book was praised, however, for its "gracefulness"; I had a
marriage and a child. If there were doubts, if there were periods of null depression or active despairing, these could only mean that I was ungrateful,
insatiable, perhaps a monster.

About the time my third child was born, I felt that I had either to con-   18
sider myself a failed woman and a failed poet, or to try to find some synthesis by which to understand what was happening to me. What frightened
me most was the sense of drift, of being pulled along on a current which
called itself my destiny, but in which I seemed to be losing touch with
whoever I had been, with the girl who had experienced her own will and
energy almost ecstatically at times, walking around a city or riding a train
at night or typing in a student room. In a poem about my grandmother I
wrote (of myself): "A young girl, thought sleeping, is certified dead"
("Halfway"). I was writing very little, partly from fatigue, that female fatigue of suppressed anger and loss of contact with my own being; partly
from the discontinuity of female life with its attention to small chores, errands, work that others constantly undo, small children's constant needs.

What I did write was unconvincing to me; my anger and frustration were hard to acknowledge in or out of poems because in fact I cared a great deal about my husband and my children. Trying to look back and understand that time I have tried to analyze the real nature of the conflict. Most, if not all, human lives are full of fantasy—passive day-dreaming which need not be acted on. But to write poetry or fiction, or even to think well, is not to fantasize, or to put fantasies on paper. For a poem to coalesce, for a character or an action to take shape, there has to be an imaginative transformation of reality which is no way passive. And a certain freedom of the mind is needed—freedom to press on, to enter the currents of your thought like a glider pilot, knowing that your motion can be sustained, that the buoyancy of your attention will not be suddenly snatched away. Moreover, if the imagination is to transcend and transform experience it has to question, to challenge, to conceive of alternatives, perhaps to the very life you are living at that moment. You have to be free to play around with the notion that day might be night, love might be hate; nothing can be too sacred for the imagination to turn into its opposite or to call experimentally by another name. For writing is re-naming. Now, to be maternally with small children all day in the old way, to be with a man in the old way of marriage, requires a holding-back, a putting-aside of that imaginative activity, and demands instead a kind of conservatism. I want to make it clear that I am *not* saying that in order to write well, or think well, it is necessary to become unavailable to others, or to become a devouring ego. This has been the myth of the masculine artist and thinker; and I do not accept it. But to be a female human being trying to fulfill traditional female functions in a traditional way *is* in direct conflict with the subversive function of the imagination. The word traditional is important here. There must be ways, and we will be finding out more and more about them, in which the energy of creation and the energy of relation can be united. But in those years I always felt the conflict as a failure of love in myself. I had thought I was choosing a full life: the life available to most men, in which sexuality, work, and parenthood could coexist. But I felt, at twenty-nine, guilt toward the people closest to me, and guilty toward my own being.

19   I wanted, then, more than anything, the one thing of which there was never enough: time to think, time to write. The fifties and early sixties were years of rapid revelations: the sit-ins and marches in the South, the Bay of Pigs, the early antiwar movement, raised large questions—questions for which the masculine world of the academy around me seemed to have expert and fluent answers. But I needed to think for myself—about pacifism and dissent and violence, about poetry and society, and about my own relationship to all these things. For about ten years I was reading in

fierce snatches, scribbling in notebooks, writing poetry in fragments; I was looking desperately for clues, because if there were no clues then I thought I might be insane. I wrote in a notebook about this time:

> Paralyzed by the sense that there exists a mesh of relationships—e.g., between my anger at the children, my sensual life, pacifism, sex (I mean sex in its broadest significance, not merely sexual desire)—an interconnectedness which, if I could see it, make it valid, would give me back myself, make it possible to function lucidly and passionately. Yet I grope in and out among these dark webs.

I think I began at this point to feel that politics was not something "out there" but something "in here" and of the essence of my condition.

In the late fifties I was able to write, for the first time, directly about experiencing myself as a woman. The poem was jotted in fragments during children's naps, brief hours in a library, or at 3:00 A.M. after rising with a wakeful child. I despaired of doing any continuous work at this time. Yet I began to feel that my fragments and scraps had a common consciousness and a common theme, one which I would have been very unwilling to put on paper at an earlier time because I had been taught that poetry should be "universal," which meant, of course, nonfemale. Until then I had tried very much *not* to identify myself as a female poet. Over two years I wrote a ten-part poem called "Snapshots of a Daughter-in-Law" (1958–1960), in a longer looser mode than I'd ever trusted myself with before. It was an extraordinary relief to write that poem. It strikes me now as too literary, too dependent on allusion; I hadn't found the courage yet to do without authorities, or even to use the pronoun "I"—the woman in the poem is always "she." One section of it, No. 2, concerns a woman who thinks she is going mad; she is haunted by voices telling her to resist and rebel, voices which she can hear but not obey.

2.
Banging the coffee-pot into the sink
she hears the angels chiding, and looks out
past the raked gardens to the sloppy sky.
Only a week since They said: *Have no patience.*

The next time it was: *Be insatiable.*
Then: *Save yourself; others you cannot save.*
Sometimes she's let the tapstream scald her arm,
a match burn to her thumbnail,

or held her hand above the kettle's snout
right in the woolly stream. They are probably angels,

since nothing hurts her anymore, except
each morning's grit blowing into her eyes.

21   The poem "Orion," written five years later, is a poem of reconnection
with a part of myself I had felt I was losing—the active principle, the energetic imagination, the "half-brother" whom I projected, as I had for many
years, into the constellation Orion. It's no accident that the words "cold
and egotistical" appear in this poem, and are applied to myself.

Far back when I went zig-zagging
through tamarack pastures
you were my genius, you
my cast-iron Viking, my helmed
lion-heart king in prison.   5
Years later now you're young

my fierce half-brother, staring
down from that simplified west
your breast open, your belt dragged down
by an oldfashioned thing, a sword   10
the last bravado you won't give over
though it weighs you down as you stride

and the stars in it are dim
and maybe have stopped burning.
But you burn, and I know it;   15
as I throw back my head to take you in
an old transfusion happens again:
divine astronomy is nothing to it.

Indoors I bruise and blunder,
break faith, leave ill enough   20
alone, a dead child born in the dark.
Night cracks up over the chimney,
pieces of time, frozen geodes
come showering down in the grate.

A man reaches behind my eyes   25
and finds them empty
a woman's head turns away
from my head in the mirror
children are dying my death
and eating crumbs of my life.   30

Pity is not your forte.
Calmly you ache up there

pinned aloft in your crow's nest,
my speechless pirate!
You take it all for granted   35
and when I look you back

it's with a starlike eye
shooting its cold and egotistical spear
where it can do least damage.
Breathe deep! No hurt, no pardon   40
out here in the cold with you
you with your back to the wall.

The choice still seemed to be between "love"—womanly, maternal love,
altruistic love—a love defined and ruled by the weight of an entire culture; and egotism—a force directed by men into creation, achievement,
ambition, often at the expense of others, but justifiably so. For weren't
they men, and wasn't that their destiny as womanly, selfless love was ours?
We know now that the alternatives are false ones—that the word "love"
is itself in need of revision.

There is a companion poem to "Orion," written three years later, in   22
which at last the woman in the poem and the woman writing the poem
become the same person. It is called "Planetarium," and it was written after a visit to a real planetarium, where I read an account of the work of
Caroline Herschel, the astronomer, who worked with her brother William,
but whose name remained obscure, as his did not.

A woman in the shape of a monster
a monster in the shape of a woman
the skies are full of them

a woman   'in the snow
among the Clocks and instruments   5
or measuring the ground with poles'
in her 98 years to discover
8 comets

she whom the moon ruled
likes us   10
levitating into the night sky
riding the polished lenses

Galaxies of women, there
doing penance for impetuousness
ribs chilled   15
in those spaces   of the mind

An eye,

> 'virile, precise and absolutely certain'
> from the mad webs of Uranusborg

> encountering the NOVA   20

every impulse of light exploding
from the core
as life flies out of us

> Tycho whispering at last
> 'Let me not seem to have lived in vain'   25

What we see, we see
and seeing is changing

the light that shrivels a mountain
and leaves a man alive

Heartbeat of the pulsar   30
heart sweating through my body

The radio impulse
pouring in from Taurus

> I am bombarded yet   I stand

I have been standing all my life in the   35
direct path of a battery of signals
the most accurately transmitted most
untranslatable language in the universe
I am a galactic cloud so deep   so invo-
luted that a light wave could take 15   40
years to travel through me   And has
taken   I am an instrument in the shape
of a woman trying to translate pulsations
into images   for the relief of the body
and the reconstruction of the mind.   45

23   In closing I want to tell you about a dream I had last summer. I dreamed
I was asked to read my poetry at a mass women's meeting, but when I
began to read, what came out were the lyrics of a blues song. I share
this dream with you because it seemed to me to say something about the
problems and the future of the woman writer, and probably of women
in general. The awakening of consciousness is not like the crossing of a

frontier—one step and you are in another country. Much of woman's poetry has been of the nature of the blues song: a cry of pain, of victimization, or a lyric of seduction.[6] And today, much poetry by women—and
prose for that matter—is charged with anger. I think we need to go
through that anger, and we will betray our own reality if we try, as Virginia
Woolf was trying, for an objectivity, a detachment, that would make us
sound more like Jane Austen or Shakespeare. We know more than Jane
Austen or Shakespeare knew: more than Jane Austen because our lives
are more complex, more than Shakespeare because we know more about
the lives of women—Jane Austen and Virginia Woolf included.

Both the victimization and the anger experienced by women are real,   24
and have real sources, everywhere in the environment, built into society,
language, the structures of thought. They will go on being tapped and explored by poets, among others. We can neither deny them, nor will we rest
there. A new generation of women poets is already working out the psychic energy released when women begin to move out towards what the
feminist philosopher Mary Daly has described as the "new space" on the
boundaries of patriarchy. Women are speaking to and of women in these
poems, out of a newly released courage to name, to love each other, to
share risk and grief and celebration.

To the eye of a feminist, the work of Western male poets now writing   25
reveals a deep, fatalistic pessimism as to the possibilities of change,
whether societal or personal, along with a familiar and threadbare use of
women (and nature) as redemptive on the one hand, threatening on the
other; and a new tide of phallocentric sadism and overt woman-hating
which matches the sexual brutality of recent films. "Political" poetry by
men remains stranded amid the struggles for power among male groups; in
condemning U.S. imperialism or the Chilean junta the poet can claim to
speak for the oppressed while remaining, as male, part of a system of sexual oppression. The enemy is always outside the self, the struggle somewhere else. The mood of isolation, self-pity, and self-imitation that
pervades "nonpolitical" poetry suggests that a profound change in masculine consciousness will have to precede any new male poetic—or other—
inspiration. The creative energy of patriarchy is fast running out; what
remains is its self-generating energy for destruction. As women, we have
our work cut out for us.

---

6 A. R., 1978: When I dreamed that dream, was I wholly ignorant of the tradition of Bessie Smith and
other women's blues lyrics which transcended victimization to sing of resistance and independence?

Questioning and Discussing
Rich, "When We Dead Awaken"

1. As Adrienne Rich explains, this essay was originally given as a talk to the Modern Language Association, the organization of professors of literature and language. To what use does Rich put her literary references? How might the meaning of her references transcend her (mostly) literary audience?

2. Consider the words that Rich defines. Why, for instance, is *revision* spelled as "re-vision"? What might be Rich's purpose here?

3. Analyze Rich's assertions regarding anger, using examples from the text. What are her conclusions about anger? How is the use of anger justified?

4. What does Rich imply about the ethical responsibilities of the reader? What is your response to this? On what basis?

5. Analyze and discuss Rich's notion of "imaginative transformation." When is it appropriate to know tradition and yet resist it? Why might doing this be valuable?

⊞

Garrett Hardin

Garrett Hardin (1915–), trained as a biologist, has written extensively on the social, political, and moral implications of his field. Feisty, direct, and particularly concerned about ecology and the scarcity of resources, Hardin received his Ph.D. in biology from Stanford University in 1941. It has been said that Hardin is "especially skilled at telling people things that they do not necessarily want to hear." His books include *Stalking the Wild Taboo* (1973), *Mandatory Motherhood* (1974), and *How to Survive Despite Economists, Ecologists, and the Merely Eloquent* (1985). The following essay appeared in *Psychology Today* in 1974.

⊞

Lifeboat Ethics: The Case Against Helping the Poor*

1 Environmentalists use the metaphor of the earth as a "spaceship" in trying to persuade countries, industries and people to stop wasting and polluting

*Reprinted with permission from *Psychology Today* magazine, copyright © 1974, Sussex Publishers, Inc.

our natural resources. Since we all share life on this planet, they argue, no single person or institution has the right to destroy, waste, or use more than a fair share of its resources.   2

But does everyone on earth have an equal right to an equal share of its resources? The spaceship metaphor can be dangerous when used by misguided idealists to justify suicidal policies for sharing our resources through uncontrolled immigration and foreign aid. In their enthusiastic but unrealistic generosity, they confuse the ethics of a spaceship with those of a lifeboat.   3

A true spaceship would have to be under the control of a captain, since no ship could possibly survive if its course were determined by committee. Spaceship Earth certainly has no captain; the United Nations is merely a toothless tiger, with little power to enforce any policy upon its bickering members.   4

If we divide the world crudely into rich nations and poor nations, two thirds of them are desperately poor, and only one third comparatively rich, with the United States the wealthiest of all. Metaphorically each rich nation can be seen as a lifeboat full of comparatively rich people. In the ocean outside each lifeboat swim the poor of the world, who would like to get in, or at least to share some of the wealth. What should the lifeboat passenger do?   5

First, we must recognize the limited capacity of any lifeboat. For example, a nation's land has a limited capacity to support a population and as the current energy crisis has shown us, in some ways we have already exceeded the carrying capacity of our land.   6

So here we sit, say 50 people in our lifeboat. To be generous let us assume it has room for 10 more, making a total capacity of 60. Suppose the 50 of us in the lifeboat see 100 others swimming in the water outside, begging for admission to our boat or for handouts. We have several options: we may be tempted to try to live by the Christian ideal of being "our brother's keeper," or by the Marxist ideal of "to each according to his needs." Since the needs of all in the water are the same, and since they can all be seen as "our brothers," we could take them all into our boat, making a total of 150 in a boat designed for 60. The boat swamps, everyone drowns. Complete justice, complete catastrophe.   7

Since the boat has an unused excess capacity of 10 more passengers, we could admit just 10 more to it. But which 10 do we let in? How do we choose? Do we pick the best 10, the neediest 10, "first come, first served"? And what do we say to the 90 we exclude? If we do let an extra 10 into our lifeboat, we will have lost our "safety factor," an engineering principle of critical importance. For example, if we don't leave room for excess capacity as a safety factor in our country's agriculture, a new plant disease or a bad change in the weather could have disastrous consequences.

8   Suppose we decide to preserve our small safety factor and admit no more to the lifeboat. Our survival is then possible although we shall have to be constantly on guard against boarding parties.

9   While this last solution clearly offers the only means of our survival, it is morally abhorrent to many people. Some say they feel guilty about their good luck. My reply is simple: "Get out and yield your place to others." This may solve the problem of the guilt-ridden person's conscience, but it does not change the ethics of the lifeboat. The needy person to whom the guilt-ridden person yields his place will not himself feel guilty about his good luck. If he did, he would not climb aboard. The net result of conscience-stricken people giving up their unjustly held seats is the elimination of that sort of conscience from the lifeboat.

10   This is the basic metaphor within which we must work out our solutions. Let us now enrich the image, step by step, with substantive additions from the real world, a world that must solve real and pressing problems of overpopulation and hunger.

11   The harsh ethics of the lifeboat become even harsher when we consider the reproductive differences between the rich nations and the poor nations. The people inside the lifeboats are doubling in numbers every 87 years; those swimming around outside are doubling on the average, every 35 years, more than twice as fast as the rich. And since the world's resources are dwindling, the difference in prosperity between the rich and the poor can only increase.

12   As of 1973, the U.S. had a population of 210 million people, who were increasing by 0.8 percent per year. Outside our lifeboat, let us imagine another 210 million people (say the combined populations of Colombia, Ecuador, Venezuela, Morocco, Pakistan, Thailand and the Philippines), who are increasing at a rate of 3.3 percent per year. Put differently, the doubling time for this aggregate population is 21 years, compared to 87 years for the U.S.

13   Now suppose the U.S. agreed to pool its resources with those seven countries, with everyone receiving an equal share. Initially the ratio of Americans to non-Americans in this model would be one-to-one but consider what the ratio would be after 87 years, by which time the Americans would have doubled to a population of 420 million. By then, doubling every 21 years, the other group would have swollen to 354 billion. Each American would have to share the available resources with more than eight people.

14   But, one could argue, this discussion assumes that current population trends will continue, and they may not. Quite so. Most likely the rate of

population increase will decline much faster in the U.S. than it will in the other countries, and there does not seem to be much we can do about it. In sharing with "each according to his needs," we must recognize that needs are determined by population size, which is determined by the rate of reproduction, which at present is regarded as a sovereign right of every nation, poor or not. This being so, the philanthropic load created by the sharing ethic of the spaceship can only increase.

The fundamental error of spaceship ethics, and the sharing it requires, 15 is that it leads to what I call "the tragedy of the commons." Under a system of private property, the men who own property recognize their responsibility to care for it, for if they don't they will eventually suffer. A farmer, for instance, will allow no more cattle in a pasture than its carrying capacity justifies. If he overloads it, erosion sets in, weeds take over, and he loses the use of the pasture.

If a pasture becomes a commons open to all, the right of each to use it 16 may not be matched by a corresponding responsibility to protect it. Asking everyone to use it with discretion will hardly do, for the considerate herdsman who refrains from overloading the commons suffers more than a selfish one who says his needs are greater. If everyone would restrain himself all would be well; but it takes only one less than everyone to ruin a system of voluntary restraint. In a crowded world of less than perfect human beings, mutual ruin is inevitable if there are no controls. This is the tragedy of the commons.

One of the major tasks of education today should be the creation of such 17 an acute awareness of the dangers of the commons that people will recognize its many varieties. For example, the air and water have become polluted because they are treated as commons. Further growth in the population or per-capita conversion of natural resources into pollutants will only make the problem worse. The same holds true for the fish of the oceans. Fishing fleets have nearly disappeared in many parts of the world, technological improvements in the art of fishing are hastening the day of complete ruin. Only the replacement of the system of the commons with a responsible system of control will save the land, air, water and oceanic fisheries.

In recent years there has been a push to create a new commons called a 18 World Food Bank, an international depository of food reserves to which nations would contribute according to their abilities and from which they would draw according to their needs. This humanitarian proposal has received support from many liberal international groups, and from such prominent citizens as Margaret Mead, U.N. Secretary General Kurt Waldheim, and Senators Edward Kennedy and George McGovern.

A world food bank appeals powerfully to our humanitarian impulses. 19 But before we rush ahead with such a plan, let us recognize where the greatest political push comes from, lest we be disillusioned later. Our experience with the "Food for Peace program," or Public Law 480, gives us the answer. This program moved billions of dollars' worth of U.S. surplus grain to food-short, population-long countries during the past two decades. But when P.L. 480 first became law, a headline in the business magazine *Forbes* revealed the real power behind it: "Feeding the World's Hungry Millions: How It Will Mean Billions for U.S. Business."

20   And indeed it did. In the years 1960 to 1970, U.S. taxpayers spent a total of $7.9 billion on the Food for Peace program. Between 1948 and 1970, they also paid an additional $50 billion for other economic-aid programs, some of which went for food for food-producing machinery and technology. Though all U.S. taxpayers were forced to contribute to the cost of P.L. 480, certain special interest groups gained handsomely under the program. Farmers did not have to contribute the grain; the Government, or rather the taxpayers, bought it from them at full market prices. The increased demand raised prices of farm products generally. The manufacturers of farm machinery, fertilizers and pesticides benefited by the farmers' extra efforts to grow more food. Grain elevators profited from storing the surplus until it could be shipped. Railroads made money hauling it to ports, and shipping lines profited from carrying it overseas. The implementation of P.L. 480 required the creation of a vast Government bureaucracy, which then acquired its own vested interest in continuing the program regardless of its merits.

21   Those who proposed and defended the Food for Peace program in public rarely mentioned its importance to any of these special interests. The public emphasis was always on its humanitarian effects. The combination of silent selfish interests and highly vocal humanitarian apologists made a powerful and successful lobby for extracting money from taxpayers. We can expect the same lobby to push now for the creation of a World Food Bank.

22   However great the potential benefit to selfish interests, it should not be a decisive argument against a truly humanitarian program. We must ask if such a program would actually do more good than harm, not only momentarily but also in the long run. Those who propose the food bank usually refer to a current "emergency" or "crisis" in terms of world food supply. But what is an emergency? Although they may be infrequent and sudden, everyone knows that emergencies will occur from time to time. A well-run family, company, organization or country prepares for the likelihood of accidents and emergencies. It expects them, it budgets for them, it saves for them.

23   What happens if some organizations or countries budget for accidents and others do not? If each country is solely responsible for its own well-

being, poorly managed ones will suffer. But they can learn from experience. They may mend their ways, and learn to budget for infrequent but certain emergencies. For example, the weather varies from year to year, and periodic crop failures are certain. A wise and competent government saves out of the production of the good years in anticipation of bad years to come. Joseph taught this policy to Pharoah in Egypt more than 2,000 years ago. Yet the great majority of the governments in the world today do not follow such a policy. They lack either the wisdom or the competence, or both. Should those nations that do manage to put something aside be forced to come to the rescue each time an emergency occurs among the poor nations?

"But it isn't their fault!" Some kind-hearted liberals argue, "How can we   24
blame the poor people who are caught in an emergency? Why must they suffer for the sins of their governments?" The concept of blame is simply not relevant here. The real question is, what are the operational consequences of establishing a world food bank? If it is open to every country every time a need develops, slovenly rulers will not be motivated to take Joseph's advice. Someone will always come to their aid. Some countries will deposit food in the world food bank, and others will withdraw it. There will be almost no overlap. As a result of such solutions to food shortage emergencies, the poor countries will not learn to mend their ways, and will suffer progressively greater emergencies as their populations grow.

On the average, poor countries undergo a 2.5 percent increase in popu-   25
lation each year; rich countries, about 0.8 percent. Only rich countries have anything in the way of food reserves set aside, and even they do not have as much as they should. Poor countries have none. If poor countries received no food from the outside, the rate of their population growth would be periodically checked by crop failures and famines. But if they can always draw on a world food bank in time of need, their population can continue to grow unchecked, and so will their "need" for aid. In the short run, a world food bank may diminish that need, but in the long run it actually increases the need without limit.

Without some system of worldwide food sharing, the proportion of people   26
in the rich and poor nations might eventually stabilize. The overpopulated poor countries would decrease in numbers, while the rich countries that had room for more people would increase. But with a well-meaning system of sharing, such as a world food bank, the growth differential between the rich and poor countries will not only persist, it will increase. Because of the higher rate of population growth in the poor countries of the world, 88 percent of today's children are born poor, and only 12 percent

rich. Year by year the ratio becomes worse, as the fast-reproducing poor outnumber the slow-reproducing rich.

27   A world food bank is thus a commons in disguise. People will have more motivation to draw from it than to add to any common store. The less provident and less able will multiply at the expense of the abler and more provident, bringing eventual ruin upon all who share in the commons. Besides, any system of "sharing" that amounts to foreign aid from the rich nations to the poor nations will carry the taint of charity, which will contribute little to the world peace so devoutly desired by those who support the idea of a world food bank.

28   As past U.S. foreign-aid programs have amply and depressingly demonstrated, international charity frequently inspires mistrust and antagonism rather than gratitude on the part of the recipient nation [see "What Other Nations Hear When the Eagle Screams," by Kenneth J. and Mary M. Gergen, *Psychology Today*, June 1974].

29   The modern approach to foreign aid stresses the export of technology and advice, rather than money and food. As ancient Chinese proverb goes: "Give a man a fish and he will eat for a day; teach him how to fish and he will eat for the rest of his days." Acting on this advice, the Rockefeller and Ford Foundations have financed a number of programs for improving agriculture in the hungry nations. Known as the "Green Revolution," these programs have led to the development of "miracle rice" and "miracle wheat," new strains that offer bigger harvests and greater resistance to crop damage. Norman Borlaug, the Nobel Prize winning agronomist who, supported by the Rockefeller Foundation, developed "miracle wheat," is one of the most prominent advocates of a world food bank.

30   Whether or not the Green Revolution can increase food production as much as its champions claim is a debatable but possible irrelevant point. Those who support this well-intended humanitarian effort should first consider some of the fundamentals of human ecology. Ironically, one man who did was the late Alan Gregg, a vice president of the Rockefeller Foundation. Two decades ago he expressed strong doubts about the wisdom of such attempts to increase food production. He likened the growth and spread of humanity over the surface of the earth to the spread of cancer in the human body, remarking that "cancerous growths demand food, but, as far as I know, they have never been cured by getting it."

31   Every human born constitutes a draft on all aspects of the environment: food, air, water, forests, beaches, wildlife, scenery and solitude. Food can, perhaps, be significantly increased to meet a growing demand. But what about clean beaches, unspoiled forests, and solitude? If we satisfy a growing

population's need for food, we necessarily decrease its per capita supply of the other resources needed by men.

India, for example, now has a population of 600 million, which in- 32
creases by 15 million each year. This population already puts a huge load on a relatively impoverished environment. The country's forests are now only a small fraction of what they were three centuries ago, and floods and erosion continually destroy the insufficient farmland that remains. Every one of the 15 million new lives added to India's population puts an additional burden on the environment, and increases the economic and social costs of crowding. However humanitarian our intent, every Indian life saved through medical or nutritional assistance from abroad diminishes the quality of life for those who remain, and for subsequent generations. If rich countries make it possible, through foreign aid, for 600 million Indians to swell to 1.2 billion in a mere 28 years, as their current growth rate threatens, will future generations of Indians thank us for hastening the destruction of their environment? Will our good intentions be sufficient excuse for the consequences of our actions?

My final example of a commons in action is one for which the public 33
has the least desire for rational discussion—immigration. Anyone who publicly questions the wisdom of current U.S. immigration policy is promptly charged with bigotry, prejudice, ethnocentrism, chauvinism, isolationism or selfishness. Rather than encounter such accusations, one would rather talk about other matters, leaving immigration policy to wallow in the crosscurrents of special interests that take no account of the good of the whole, or the interests of posterity.

Perhaps we still feel guilty about things we said in the past. Two gener- 34
ations ago the popular press frequently referred to Dagos, Wops, Polacks, Chinks and Krauts, in articles about how America was being "overrun" by foreigners of supposedly inferior genetic stock [see "The Politics of Genetic Engineering: Who Decides Who's Defective?" *Psychology Today*, June 1974]. But because the implied inferiority of foreigners was used then as justification for keeping them out, people now assume that restrictive policies could only be based on such misguided notions. There are other grounds.

Just consider the numbers involved. Our Government acknowledges a 35
net inflow of 400,000 immigrants a year. While we have no hard data on the extent of illegal entries, educated guesses put the figure at about 600,000 a year. Since the natural increase (excess of births over deaths) of the resident population now runs about 1.7 million per year, the yearly gain from immigration amounts to at least 19 percent of the total annual increase, and may be as much as 37 percent if we include the estimate for

illegal immigrants. Considering the growing use of birth-control devices, the potential effect of educational campaigns by such organizations as Planned Parenthood Federation of America and Zero Population Growth, and the influence of inflation and the housing shortage, the fertility rate of American women may decline so much that immigration could account for all the yearly increase in population. Should we not at least ask if that is what we want?

36   For the sake of those who worry about whether the "quality" of the average immigrant compares favorably with the quality of the average resident, let us assume that immigrants and nativeborn citizens are of exactly equal quality, however one defines that term. We will focus here only on quality; and since our conclusions will depend on nothing else, all charges of bigotry and chauvinism become irrelevant.

37   World food banks *move food to the people*, hastening the exhaustion of the environment of the poor countries. Unrestricted immigration, on the other hand, *moves people to the food*, thus speeding up the destruction of the environment of the rich countries. We can easily understand why poor people should want to make this latter transfer, but why should rich hosts encourage it?

38   As in the case of foreign-air programs, immigration receives support from selfish interests and humanitarian impulses. The primary selfish interest in unimpeded immigration is the desire of employers for cheap labor, particularly in industries and trades that offer degrading work. In the past, one wave of foreigners after another was brought into the U.S. to work at wretched jobs for wretched wages. In recent years the Cubans, Puerto Ricans and Mexicans have had this dubious honor. The interests of the employers of cheap labor mesh well with the guilty silence of the country's liberal intelligentsia. White Anglo-Saxon Protestants are particularly reluctant to call for a closing of the doors to immigration for fear of being called bigots.

39   But not all countries have such reluctant leadership. Most educated Hawaiians, for example, are keenly aware of the limits of their environment, particularly in terms of population growth. There is only so much room on the islands, and the islanders know it. To Hawaiians, immigrants from the other 49 states present as great a threat as those from other nations. At a recent meeting of Hawaiian government officials in Honolulu, I had the ironic delight of hearing a speaker, who like most of his audience was of Japanese ancestry, ask how the country might practically and constitutionally close its doors to further immigration. One member of the audience countered: "How can we shut the doors now? We have many friends and relatives in Japan that we'd like to bring here some day so that

they can enjoy Hawaii too." The Japanese-American speaker smiled sympathetically and answered: "Yes, but we have children now, and someday we'll have grandchildren too. We can bring more people here from Japan only by giving away some of the land that we hope to pass on to our grandchildren some day. What right do we have to do that?"

At this point, I can hear U.S. liberals asking: "How can you justify slamming the door once you're inside? You say that immigrants should be kept out. But aren't we all immigrants, or the descendants of immigrants? If we insist on staying, must we not admit all others?" Our craving for intellectual order leads us to seek and prefer symmetrical rules and morals: a single rule for me and everybody else; the same rule yesterday, today and tomorrow. Justice, we feel, should not change with time and place. 40

We Americans of non-Indian ancestry can look upon ourselves as the descendants of thieves who are guilty morally, if not legally, of stealing this land from its Indian owners. Should we then give back the land to the now living American descendants of those Indians? However morally or logically sound this proposal may be, I, for one, am unwilling to live by it and I know no one else who is. Besides, the logical consequence would be absurd. Suppose that, intoxicated with a sense of pure justice, we should decide to turn our land over to the Indians. Since all our other wealth has also been derived from the land, wouldn't we be morally obliged to give that back to the Indians too? 41

Clearly, the concept of pure justice produces an infinite regression to absurdity. Centuries ago, wise men invented statutes of limitations to justify the rejection of such pure justice, in the interest of preventing continual disorder. The law zealously defends property rights. Drawing a line after an arbitrary time has elapsed may be unjust, but the alternatives are worse. 42

We are all the descendants of thieves, and the world's resources are inequitably distributed. But we must begin the journey to tomorrow from the point where we are today. We cannot remake the past. We cannot safely divide the wealth equitably among all peoples so long as people reproduce at different rates. To do so would guarantee that our grandchildren, and everyone else's grandchildren, would have only a ruined world to inhabit. 43

To be generous with one's own possessions is quite different from being generous with those of posterity. We should call this point to the attention of those who, from a commendable love of justice and equality, would institute a system of the commons, either in the form of a world food bank, or of restricted immigration. We must convince them if we wish to save at least some parts of the world from environmental ruin. 44

45   Without a true world government to control reproduction and the use of available resources, the sharing ethic of the spaceship is impossible. For the foreseeable future, our survival demands that we govern our actions by the ethics of a lifeboat, harsh though they may be. Posterity will be satisfied with nothing less.

QUESTIONING AND DISCUSSING

Hardin, "Lifeboat Ethics"

1. Analyze and comment on Hardin's use of his central metaphor, discussing his assumptions that underlie his use of "the harsh ethics of the lifeboat." Discuss whether these assumptions are faulty, solid—or a bit of both. On what basis can you judge here?

2. Looking at current articles regarding world hunger and ethical approaches to solving that problem, determine if, in your opinion, Hardin's views are supported or refuted. Support your viewpoint with examples from your reading. Does the fact that Hardin's essay is thirty years old undermine its point of view, or do you find that it is still relevant—for positive and negative reasons?

3. Carefully consider Hardin's views regarding the "fundamental error of spaceship ethics" and the "tragedy of the commons" and the examples that he uses to explore his view of this "tragedy." Research what has happened in the many years since this article was published—the fate of a world food bank, for instance. What light does newer information shed on Hardin's stance?

4. Hardin engages in some fairly blatant name-calling—"U.S. liberals," for instance—that make his political stance clear. What effect does this have on his credibility? In your view, is this an ethical form of argument? Why or why not?

⊞

M ARY E. W ILKINS F REEMAN

Mary E. Wilkins Freeman (1852–1930) is considered a regionalist and realist, having spent her life in Randolph, Massachusetts, a town of industry workers, house carpenters, and farmers. She had two years of formal education. After she had experienced isolation and poverty, her career began when she earned fifty dollars in a literary contest. Freeman's writing often explores the lives of defiant, impoverished heroines struggling to overcome their isolation. After winning the Howell Medal for Fiction in 1926 and having published thirty-nine volumes of stories, novels, and drama, Freeman (along with Edith Wharton) became one of the first women to be elected to membership in the National Institute of Arts and Letters.

⊞

A Mistaken Charity

There were in a green field a little, low, weather-stained cottage, with a foot-path leading to it from the highway several rods distant, and two old women—one with a tin pan and old knife searching for dandelion greens among the short young grass, and the other sitting on the door-step watching her, or, rather, having the appearance of watching her.

"Air there enough for a mess, Harriét?" asked the old woman on the door-step. She accented oddly the last syllable of the Harriet, and there was a curious quality in her feeble, cracked old voice. Besides the question denoted by the arrangement of her words and the rising inflection, there was another, broader and subtler, the very essence of all questioning, in the tone of her voice itself; the cracked, quavering notes that she used reached out of themselves, and asked, and groped like fingers in the dark. One would have known by the voice that the old woman was blind.

The old woman on her knees in the grass searching for dandelions did not reply; she evidently had not heard the question. So the old woman on the door-step, after waiting a few minutes with her head turned expectantly, asked again, varying her question slightly, and speaking louder:

"Air there enough for a mess, do ye s'pose, Harriét?"

The old woman in the grass heard this time. She rose slowly and laboriously; the effort of straightening out the rheumatic old muscles was evidently a painful one; then she eyed the greens heaped up in the tin pan, and pressed them down with her hand.

"Wa'al, I don't know, Charlotte," she replied, hoarsely. "There's plenty on 'em here, but I 'ain't got near enough for a mess; they do bile down so when you get 'em in the pot; an' it's all I can do to bend my j'ints enough to dig 'em."

7   "I'd give consider'ble to help ye, Harriét," said the old woman on the door-step.

8   But the other did not hear her; she was down on her knees in the grass again, anxiously spying out the dandelions.

9   So the old woman on the door-step crossed her little shrivelled hands over her calico knees, and sat quite still, with the soft spring wind blowing over her.

10   The old wooden door-step was sunk low down among the grasses, and the whole house to which it belonged had an air of settling down and mouldering into the grass as into its own grave.

11   When Harriet Shattuck grew deaf and rheumatic, and had to give up her work as tailoress, and Charlotte Shattuck lost her eyesight, and was unable to do any more sewing for her livelihood, it was a small and trifling charity for the rich man who held a mortgage on the little house in which they had been born and lived all their lives to give them the use of it, rent and interest free. He might as well have taken credit to himself for not charging a squirrel for his tenement in some old decaying tree in his woods.

12   So ancient was the little habitation, so wavering and mouldering, the hands that had fashioned it had lain still so long in their graves, that it almost seemed to have fallen below its distinctive rank as a house. Rain and snow had filtered through its roof, mosses had grown over it, worms had eaten it, and birds built their nests under its eaves; nature had almost completely overrun and obliterated the work of man, and taken her own to herself again, till the house seemed as much a natural ruin as an old tree-stump.

13   The Shattucks had always been poor people and common people; no especial grace and refinement or fine ambition had ever characterized any of them; they had always been poor and coarse and common. The father and his father before him had simply lived in the poor little house, grubbed for their living, and then unquestioningly died. The mother had been of no rarer stamp, and the two daughters were cast in the same mould.

14   After their parents' death Harriet and Charlotte had lived alone in the old place from youth to old age, with the one hope of ability to keep a roof over their heads, covering on their backs, and victuals in their mouths— an all-sufficient one with them.

15   Neither of them had ever had a lover; they had always seemed to repel rather than attract the opposite sex. It was not merely because they were poor, ordinary, and homely; there were plenty of men in the place who would have matched them well in that respect; the fault lay deeper—in their characters. Harriet, even in her girlhood, had a blunt, defiant man-

ner that almost amounted to surliness, and was well calculated to alarm timid adorers, and Charlotte had always had the reputation of not being any too strong in her mind.

Harriet had gone about from house to house doing tailor-work after the   16 primitive country fashion, and Charlotte had done plain sewing and mending for the neighbors. They had been, in the main, except when pressed by some temporary anxiety about their work or the payment thereof, happy and contented, with that negative kind of happiness and contentment which comes not from gratified ambition, but a lack of ambition itself. All that they cared for they had had in tolerable abundance, for Harriet at least had been swift and capable about her work. The patched, mossy old roof had been kept over their heads, the coarse, hearty food that they loved had been set on their table, and their cheap clothes had been warm and strong.

After Charlotte's eyes failed her, and Harriet had the rheumatic fever,   17 and the little hoard of earnings went to the doctors, times were harder with them, though still it could not be said that they actually suffered.

When they could not pay the interest on the mortgage they were al-   18 lowed to keep the place interest free; there was as much fitness in a mort-gage on the little house, anyway, as there would have been on a rotten old apple-tree; and the people about, who were mostly farmers, and good friendly folk, helped them out with their living. One would donate a bar-rel of apples from his abundant harvest to the two poor old women, one a barrel of potatoes, another a load of wood for the winter fuel, and many a farmer's wife had bustled up the narrow foot-path with a pound of butter, or a dozen fresh eggs, or a nice bit of pork. Besides all this, there was a tiny garden patch behind the house, with a straggling row of currant bushes in it, and one of gooseberries, where Harriet contrived every year to raise a few pumpkins, which were the pride of her life. On the right of the garden were two old apple-trees, a Baldwin and a Porter, both yet in a tolerably good fruit-bearing state.

The delight which the two poor old souls took in their own pumpkins,   19 their apples and currants, was indescribable. It was not merely that they contributed largely towards their living; they were their own, their private share of the great wealth of nature, the little taste set apart for them alone out of her bounty, and worth more to them on that account, though they were not conscious of it, than all the richer fruits which they received from their neighbors' gardens.

This morning the two apple-trees were brave with flowers, the currant   20 bushes looked alive, and the pumpkin seeds were in the ground. Harriet cast complacent glances in their direction from time to time, as she painfully dug her dandelion greens. She was a short, stoutly built old woman, with a large face coarsely wrinkled, with a suspicion of a stubble of beard on the square chin.

21 When her tin pan was filled to her satisfaction with the sprawling, spidery greens, and she was hobbling stiffly towards her sister on the door-step, she saw another woman standing before her with a basket in her hand.

22 "Good-morning, Harriet," she said, in a loud, strident voice, as she drew near. "I've been frying some doughnuts, and I brought you over some warm."

23 "I've been tellin' her it was real good in her," piped Charlotte from the door-step, with an anxious turn of her sightless face towards the sound of her sister's footstep.

24 Harriet said nothing but a hoarse "Good-mornin', Mis' Simonds." Then she took the basket in her hand, lifted the towel off the top, selected a doughnut, and deliberately tasted it.

25 "Tough," said she. "I s'posed so. If there is anything I 'spise on this airth it's a tough doughnut."

26 "Oh, Harriét!" said Charlotte, with a frightened look.

27 "They air tough," said Harriet, with hoarse defiance, "and if there is anything I 'spise on this airth it's a tough doughnut."

28 The woman whose benevolence and cookery were being thus ungratefully received only laughed. She was quite fleshy, and had a round, rosy, determined face.

29 "Well, Harriet," said she, "I am sorry they are tough, but perhaps you had better take them out on a plate, and give my basket. You may be able to eat two or three of them if they are tough."

30 "They air tough—turrible tough," said Harriet, stubbornly; but she took the basket into the house and emptied it of its contents nevertheless.

31 "I suppose your roof leaked as bad as ever in that heavy rain day before yesterday?" said the visitor to Harriet, with an inquiring squint towards the mossy shingles, as she was about to leave with her empty basket.

32 "It was turrible," replied Harriet, with crusty acquiescence—"turrible. We had to set pails an' pans everywheres, an' move the bed out."

33 "Mr. Upton ought to fix it."

34 "There ain't any fix to it; the old ruff ain't fit to nail new shingles on to; the hammerin' would bring the whole thing down on our heads," said Harriet, grimly.

35 "Well, I don't know as it can be fixed, it's so old. I suppose the wind comes in bad around the windows and doors too?"

36 "It's like livin' with a piece of paper, or mebbe a sieve, 'twixt you an' the wind an' the rain," quoth Harriet, with a jerk of her head.

"You ought to have a more comfortable home in your old age," said the   37
visitor, thoughtfully.

"Oh, it's well enough," cried Harriet, in quick alarm, and with a com-   38
plete change of tones; the woman's remark had brought an old dread over
her. "The old house'll last as long as Charlotte an' me do. The rain ain't so
bad, nuther is the wind; there's room enough for us in the dry places, an'
out of the way of the doors an' windows. It's enough sight better than goin'
on the town." Her square, defiant old face actually looked pale as she uttered the last words and stared apprehensively at the woman.

"Oh, I did not think of your doing that," she said, hastily and kindly.   39
"We all know how you feel about that, Harriet, and not one of us neighbors will see you and Charlotte go to the poorhouse while we've got a
crust of bread to share with you."

Harriet's face brightened. "Thank ye Mis' Simonds," she said, with re-   40
luctant courtesy. "I'm much obleeged to you an' the neighbors. I think
mebbe we'll be able to eat some of them doughnuts if they air tough," she
added, mollifyingly, as her caller turned down the foot-path.

"My, Harriét," said Charlotte, lifting up a weakly, wondering, peaked   41
old face, "what did you tell her them doughnuts was tough fur?"

"Charlotte, do you want everybody to look down on us, an' think we   42
ain't no account at all, just like any beggars, 'cause they bring us in vittles?" said Harriet, with a grim glance at her sister's meek, unconscious
face.

"No, Harriét." The poor little old woman on the doorstep fairly cow-   43
ered before her aggressive old sister.

"Then don't hender me agin when I tell folks their doughnuts is tough   44
an' their pertaters is poor. If I don't kinder keep up an' show some sperrit,
I sha'n't think nothing of myself, an' other folks won't nuther, and fust
thing we know they'll kerry us to the poorhouse. You'd 'a been there before now if it hadn't been for me, Charlotte."

Charlotte looked meekly convinced, and her sister sat down on a chair   45
in the doorway to scrape her dandelions.

"Did you git a good mess, Harriét?" asked Charlotte, in a humble tone.   46
"Toler'ble."   47

"They'll be proper relishin' with that piece of pork Mis' Mann brought   48
in yesterday. O Lord, Harriét, it's a chink!"

Harriet sniffed.   49

Her sister caught with her sensitive ear the little contemptuous sound.   50
"I guess," she said, querulously, and with more pertinacity than she had
shown in the matter of the doughnuts, "that if you was in the dark, as I
am, Harriét, you wouldn't make fun an' turn up your nose at chinks. If you
had seen the light streamin' in all of a sudden through some little hole

that you hadn't known of before when you set down on the door-step this mornin', and the wind with the smell of the apple blows in it came in your face, an' when Mis' Simonds brought them hot doughnuts, an' when I thought of the pork an' greens jest now—O Lord, how it did shine in! An' it does now. If you was me, Harriét, you would know there was chinks."

51 Tears began starting from the sightless eyes, and streaming pitifully down the pale old cheeks.

52 Harriet looked at her sister, and her grim face softened.

53 "Why, Charlotte, hev it that thar *is* chinks if you want to. Who cares?"

54 "Thar *is* chinks, Harriét."

55 "Wa'al, thar *is* chinks, then. If I don't hurry, I sha'n't get these greens in in time for dinner."

56 When the two old women sat down complacently to their meal of pork and dandelion greens in their little kitchen they did not dream how destiny slowly and surely was introducing some new colors into their web of life, even when it was almost completed, and that this was one of the last meals they would eat in their old home for many a day. In about a week from that day they were established in the "Old Ladies' Home" in a neighboring city. It came about in this wise: Mrs. Simonds, the woman who had brought the gift of hot doughnuts, was a smart, energetic person, bent on doing good, and she did a great deal. To be sure, she always did it in her own way. If she chose to give hot doughnuts, she gave hot doughnuts; it made not the slightest difference to her if the recipients of her charity would infinitely have preferred ginger cookies. Still, a great many would like hot doughnuts, and she did unquestionably a great deal of good.

57 She had a worthy coadjutor in the person of a rich and childless elderly widow in the place. They had fairly entered into a partnership in good works, with about an equal capital on both sides, the widow furnishing the money, and Mrs. Simonds, who had much the better head of the two, furnishing the active schemes of benevolence.

58 The afternoon after the doughnut episode she had gone to the widow with a new project, and the result was that entrance fees had been paid, and old Harriet and Charlotte made sure of a comfortable home for the rest of their lives. The widow was hand in glove with officers of missionary boards and trustees of charitable institutions. There had been an unusual mortality among the inmates of the "Home" this spring, there were several vacancies, and the matter of the admission of Harriet and Charlotte was very quickly and easily arranged. But the matter which would have seemed the least difficult—inducing the two old women to accept the bounty which Providence, the widow, and Mrs. Simonds were ready to bestow on them—proved the most so. The struggle to persuade them to abandon their tottering old home for a better was a terrible one. The

widow had pleaded with mild surprise, and Mrs. Simonds with benevolent determination; the counsel and reverend eloquence of the minister had been called in; and when they yielded at last it was with a sad grace for the recipients of a worth charity.

It had been hard to convince them that the "home" was not an almshouse under another name, and their yielding at length to anything short of actual force was only due probably to the plea, which was advanced most eloquently to Harriet, that Charlotte would be so much more comfortable.

The morning they came away, Charlotte cried pitifully, and trembled all over her little shrivelled body. Harriet did not cry. But when her sister had passed out the low, sagging door she turned the key in the lock, then took it out and thrust it slyly into her pocket, shaking her head to herself with an air of fierce determination.

Mrs. Simonds's husband, who was to take them to the depot, said to himself, with disloyal defiance of his wife's active charity, that it was a shame, as he helped the two distressed old souls into his light wagon, and put the poor little box, with their homely clothes in it, in behind.

Mrs. Simonds, the widow, the minister, and the gentleman from the "Home" who was to take charge of them, were all at the depot, and their faces beaming with the delight of successful benevolence. But the two poor old women looked like two forlorn prisoners in their midst. It was an impressive illustration of the truth of the saying "that it is more blessed to give than to receive."

Well, Harriet and Charlotte Shattuck went to the "Old Ladies' Home" with reluctance and distress. They stayed two months, and then—they ran away.

The "Home" was comfortable, and in some respects even luxurious; but nothing suited those two unhappy, unreasonable old women.

The fare was of a finer, more delicately served variety than they had been accustomed to; those finely flavored nourishing soups for which the "Home" took great credit to itself failed to please palates used to common, coarser food.

"O Lord, Harriét, when I set down to the table here there ain't no chinks," Charlotte used to say. "If we could hev some cabbage, or some pork an' greens, how the light would stream in!"

Then they had to be more particular about their dress. They had always been tidy enough, but now it had to be something more; the widow, in the kindness of her heart, had made it possible, and the good folks in charge of the "Home," in the kindness of their hearts, tried to carry out the widow's designs.

68 But nothing could transform these two unpolished old women into two nice old ladies. They did not take kindly to white lace caps and delicate neckerchiefs. They liked their new black cashmere dresses well enough, but they felt as if they broke a commandment when they put them on every afternoon. They had always worn calico with long aprons at home, and they wanted to now; and they wanted to twist up their scanty gray locks into little knots at the back of their heads, and go without caps, just as they always had done.

69 Charlotte in a dainty white cap was pitiful, but Harriet was both pitiful and comical. They were totally at variance with their surroundings, and they felt it keenly, as people of their stamp always do. No amount of kindness and attention—and they had enough of both—sufficed to reconcile them to their new abode. Charlotte pleaded continually with her sister to go back to their old home.

70 "O Lord, Harriét," she would exclaim (by the way, Charlotte's "O Lord," which, as she used it, was innocent enough, had been heard with much disfavor in the "Home," and she, not knowing at all why, had been remonstrated with concerning it), "let us go home. I can't stay here no ways in this world. I don't like their vittles, an' I don't like to wear a cap; I want to go home and do different. The currants will be ripe, Harriét. O Lord, thar was almost a chink, thinking about 'em. I want some of 'em; an' the Porter apples will be gittin' ripe, an' we could have some apple-pie. This here ain't good; I want merlasses fur sweeting. Can't we get back no ways, Harriét? It ain't far, an' we could walk, an' they don't lock us in, nor nothing'. I don't want to die her; it ain't so straight up to heaven from here. O Lord, I've felt as if I was slantendicular from heaven ever since I've been here, an' it's been so awful dark. I ain't had any chinks. I want to go home, Harriét."

71 "We'll go to-morrow mornin'," said Harriet, finally; "we'll pack up our things an' go; we'll put on our old dresses, an' we'll do up the new ones in bundles, an' we'll jest shy out the back way to-morrow mornin'; an' we'll go. I kin find the way, an' I reckon we kin git thar, if it is fourteen mile. Mebbe somebody will give us a lift."

72 And they went. With a grim humor Harriet hung the new white lace caps with which she and Charlotte had been so pestered, one on each post at the head of the bedstead, so they would meet the eyes of the first person who opened the door. Then they took their bundles, stole slyly out, and were soon on the high-road, hobbling along, holding each other's hands, as jubilant as two children, and chuckling to themselves over their escape, and the probable astonishment there would be in the "Home" over it."

"O Lord, Harriét, what do you s'pose they will say to them caps?" cried 73
Charlotte, with a gleeful cackle.

"I guess they'll see as folks ain't goin' to be made to wear caps agin their 74
will in a free kentry," returned Harriet, with an echoing cackle, as they
sped feebly and bravely along.

The "Home" stood on the very outskirts of the city, luckily for them. 75
They would have found it a difficult undertaking to traverse the crowded
streets. As it was, a short walk brought them into the free country road—
free comparatively, for even here at ten o'clock in the morning there was
considerable travelling to and from the city on business or pleasure.

People whom they met on the road did not stare at them as curiously as 76
might have been expected. Harriet held her bristling chin high in air, and
hobbled along with an appearance of being well aware of what she was
about, that led folks to doubt their own first opinion that there was something unusual about the two old women.

Still their evident feebleness now and then occasioned from one and 77
another more particular scrutiny. When they had been on the road a half-
hour or so, a man in a covered wagon drove up behind them. After he had
passed them, he poked his head around the front of the vehicle and
looked back. Finally he stopped, and waited for them to come up to him.

"Like a ride, ma'am?" said he, looking at once bewildered and compas- 78
sionate.

"Thankee," said Harriet, "we'd be much obleeged." 79

After the man had lifted the old women into the wagon, and estab- 80
lished them on the back seat, he turned around, as he drove slowly along,
and gazed at them curiously.

"Seems to me you look pretty feeble to be walking far," said he. "Where 81
were you going?"

Harriet told him with an air of defiance. 82

"Why," he exclaimed, "it is fourteen miles out. You could never walk it 83
in the world. Well, I am going within three miles of there, and I can go on
a little farther as well as not. But I don't see—Have you been in the city?"

"I have been visitin' my married darter in the city," said Harriet, calmly. 84

Charlotte started, and swallowed convulsively. 85

Harriet had never told a deliberate falsehood before in her life, but this 86
seemed to her one of the tremendous exigencies of life which justify a lie.
She felt desperate. If she could not contrive to deceive him in some way,
the man might turn directly around and carry Charlotte and her back to
the "Home" and the white caps.

"I should not have thought your daughter would have let you start for 87
such a walk as that," said the man. "Is this lady your sister? She is blind,
isn't she? She does not look fit to walk a mile."

88 "Yes, she's my sister," replied Harriet, stubbornly: "an' she's blind; an' my darter didn't want us to walk. She felt reel bad about it. But she couldn't help it. She's poor, and her husband's dead, an' she's got four leetle children."

89 Harriet recounted the hardships of her imaginary daughter with a glibness that was astonishing. Charlotte swallowed again.

90 "Well," said the man, "I am glad I overtook you, for I don't think you would ever have reached home alive."

91 About six miles from the city an open buggy passed them swiftly. In it were seated the matron and one of the gentlemen in charge of the "Home." They never thought of looking into the covered wagon—and indeed one can travel in one of those vehicles, so popular in some parts of New England, with as much privacy as he could in his tomb. The two in the buggy were seriously alarmed, and anxious for the safety of the old women, who were chuckling maliciously in the wagon they soon left far behind. Harriet had watched them breathlessly until they disappeared on a curve of the road; then she whispered to Charlotte.

92 A little after noon the two old women crept slowly up the foot-path across the field to their old home.

93 "The clover is up to our knees," said Harriet; "an' the sorrel and the white-weed; an' there's lots of yaller butterflies."

94 O Lord, Harriét, thar's a chink, an' I do believe I saw one of them yaller butterflies go past it," cried Charlotte, trembling all over, and nodding her gray head violently.

95 Harriet stood on the old sunken door-step and fitted the key, which she drew triumphantly from her pocket, in the lock, while Charlotte stood waiting and shaking behind her.

96 Then they went in. Everything was there just as they had left it. Charlotte sank down on a chair and began to cry. Harriet hurried across to the window that looked out on the garden.

97 "The currants air ripe," said she; "an' them pumpkins hev run all over everything."

98 "O Lord, Harriét," sobbed Charlotte, "thar is so many chinks that they air all runnin' together!"

QUESTIONING AND DISCUSSING
Freeman, "A Mistaken Charity"

1. What are the ironies of this story regarding charity? In the use of the old saying "It is more blessed to give than to receive"? What are the ethical implications of the title of the story?

2. What ethical issues raised by this story—written in 1888—are relevant and useful for today's readers? How does it shed light on current examples from the media or your own life? Be sure to use the story itself to back up your ideas.

3. Comment on the following lines, both as they relate to the story (using the text to support your points) and as a general commentary about life and behavior: "Harriet had never told a deliberate falsehood before in her life, but this seemed to her one of the tremendous exigencies of life which justify a lie." Are there other times at which "tremendous exigencies" might justify a lie? What might those be? How or why are they justified—or not justified?

⊞

GEORGE ORWELL

The pseudonym of Eric Arthur Blair, George Orwell (1903–1950) is known for his numerous novels, biographical works, and essays, particularly his frightening and satirical political novels, *Animal Farm* (1946) and *1984* (1949). After attending private school, he served with the Indian imperial police in what was then called Burma. Orwell fought in the Spanish Civil War after spending a number of years living in poverty as a writer in London and Paris. Most significantly, Orwell's works are concerned with the sociopolitical conditions of his time and the issue of human freedom. Critics call Orwell's prose style "lucid and superb," and many consider his literary essays—of which this is one—to be superior to his novels.

⊞

Shooting an Elephant

In Moulmein, in Lower Burma, I was hated by large numbers of people— the only time in my life that I have been important enough for this to happen to me. I was sub-divisional police officer of the town, and in an aimless, petty kind of way anti-European feeling was very bitter. No one had the guts to raise a riot, but if a European woman went through the bazaars alone somebody would probably spit betel juice over her dress. As a police officer I was an obvious target and was baited whenever it seemed safe to do so. When a nimble Burman tripped me up on the football field and the referee (another Burman) looked the other way, the crowd yelled with hideous laughter. This happened more than once. In the end the sneering yellow faces of young men that met me everywhere, the insults hooted after me when I was at a safe distance, got badly on my nerves. The young Buddhist priests were the worst of all. There were several thousands of them in the town and none of them seemed to have anything to do except stand on street corners and jeer at Europeans.

2   All this was perplexing and upsetting. For at that time I had already made up my mind that imperialism was an evil thing and the sooner I chucked up my job and got out of it the better. Theoretically—and secretly, of course—I was all for the Burmese and all against their oppressors, the British. As for the job I was doing, I hated it more bitterly than I can perhaps make clear. In a job like that you see the dirty work of Empire at close quarters. The wretched prisoners huddling in the stinking cages of the lock-ups, the grey, cowed faces of the long-term convicts, the scarred buttocks of the men who had been flogged with bamboos—all these oppressed me with an intolerable sense of guilt. But I could get nothing into perspective. I was young and ill-educated and I had had to think out my problems in the utter silence that is imposed on every Englishman in the East. I did not even know that the British Empire is dying, still less did I know that it is a great deal better than the younger empires that are going to supplant it. All I knew was that I was stuck between my hatred of the empire I served and my rage against the evil-spirited little beasts who tried to make my job impossible. With one part of my mind I thought of the British Raj as an unbreakable tyranny, as something clamped down, in *saecula saeculorum*,* upon the will of prostrate peoples; with another part I thought that the greatest joy in the world would be to drive a bayonet into a Buddhist priest's guts. Feelings like these are the normal by-products of imperialism; ask any Anglo-Indian official, if you can catch him off duty.

3   One day something happened which in a roundabout way was enlightening. It was a tiny incident in itself, but it gave me a better glimpse than I had had before of the real nature of imperialism—the real motives for which despotic governments act. Early one morning the sub-inspector at a police station [on] the other end of town rang me up on the 'phone and said that an elephant was ravaging the bazaar. Would I please come and do something about it? I did not know what I could do, but I wanted to see

---

* in *saecula saeculorum*—for ever and ever (Latin)

what was happening and I got on to a pony and started out. I took my rifle, an old .44 Winchester and much too small to kill an elephant, but I thought the noise might be useful *in terrorem*. Various Burmans stopped me on the way and told me about the elephant's doings. It was not, of course, a wild elephant, but a tame one which had gone "must." It had been chained up, as tame elephants always are when their attack of "must" is due, but on the previous night it had broken its chain and escaped. Its mahout, the only person who could manage it when it was in that state, had set out in pursuit, but had taken the wrong direction and was now twelve hours' journey away, and in the morning the elephant had suddenly reappeared in the town. The Burmese population had no weapons and were quite helpless against it. It had already destroyed somebody's bamboo hut, killed a cow and raided some fruit-stalls and devoured the stock; also it had met the municipal rubbish van and, when the driver jumped out and took to his heels, had turned the van over and inflicted violences upon it.

The Burmese sub-inspector and some Indian constables were waiting   4
for me in the quarter where the elephant had been seen. It was a very poor quarter, a labyrinth of squalid bamboo huts, thatched with palm-leaf, winding all over a steep hillside. I remember that it was a cloudy, stuffy morning at the beginning of the rains. We began questioning the people as to where the elephant had gone and, as usual, failed to get any definite information. That is invariably the case in the East; a story always sounds clear enough at a distance, but the nearer you get to the scene of events the vaguer it becomes. Some of the people said that the elephant had gone in one direction, some said that he had gone in another, some professed not even to have heard of any elephant. I had almost made up my mind that the whole story was a pack of lies, when we heard yells a little distance away. There was a loud, scandalized cry of "Go away, child! Go away this instant!" and an old woman with a switch in her hand came around the corner of a hut, violently shooing away a crowd of naked children. Some more women followed, clicking their tongues and exclaiming; evidently there was something that the children ought not to have seen. I rounded the hut and saw a man's dead body sprawling in the mud. He was an Indian, a black Dravidian coolie, almost naked, and he could not have been dead many minutes. The people said that the elephant had come suddenly upon him round the corner of the hut, caught him with its trunk, put its foot on his back and ground him into the earth. This was the rainy season and the ground was soft, and his face had scored a trench a foot deep and a couple of yards long. He was lying on his belly with arms crucified and head sharply twisted to one side. His face was coated with

mud, the eyes wide open, the teeth bared and grinning with an expression of unendurable agony. (Never tell me, by the way, that the dead look peaceful. Most of the corpses I have seen looked devilish.) The friction of the great beast's foot had stripped the skin from his back as neatly as one skins a rabbit. As soon as I saw the dead man I sent an orderly to a friend's house nearby to borrow an elephant rifle. I had already sent back the pony, not wanting it to go mad with fright and throw me if it smelt the elephant.

5   The orderly came back in a few minutes with a rifle and five cartridges, and meanwhile some Burmans had arrived and told us that the elephant was in the paddy fields below, only a few hundred yards away. As I started forward practically the whole population of the quarter flocked out of the houses and followed me. They had seen the rifle and were all shouting excitedly that I was going to shoot the elephant. They had not shown much interest in the elephant when he was merely ravaging their homes, but it was different now that he was going to be shot. It was a bit of fun to them, as it would be to an Eanglish crowd; besides they wanted the meat. It made me vaguely uneasy. I had no intention of shooting the elephant—I had merely sent for the rifle to defend myself if necessary—and it is always unnerving to have a crowd following you. I marched down the hill, looking and feeling a fool, with the rifle over my shoulder and an ever-growing army of people jostling at my heels. At the bottom, when you got away from the huts, there was a metalled road and beyond that a miry waste of paddy fields a thousand yards across, not yet ploughed but soggy from the first rains and dotted with coarse grass. The elephant was standing eight yards from the road, his left side towards us. He took not the slightest notice of the crowd's approach. He was tearing up bunches of grass, beating them against his knees to clean them and stuffing them into his mouth.

6   I had halted on the road. As soon as I saw the elephant I knew with perfect certainty that I ought not to shoot him. It is a serious matter to shoot a working elephant—it is comparable to destroying a huge and costly piece of machinery—and obviously one ought not to do it if it can possibly be avoided. And at that distance, peacefully eating, the elephant looked no more dangerous than a cow. I thought then and I think now that his attack of "must" was already passing off; in which case he would merely wander harmlessly about until the mahout came back and caught him. Moreover, I did not in the least want to shoot him. I decided that I would watch him for a little while to make sure that he did not turn savage again, and then go home.

7   But at that moment I glanced round at the crowd that had followed me. It was an immense crowd, two thousand at the least and growing every

minute. It blocked the road for a long distance on either side. I looked at
the sea of yellow faces above the garish clothes—faces all happy and excited over this bit of fun, all certain that the elephant was going to be
shot. They were watching me as they would watch a conjurer about to
perform a trick. They did not like me, but with the magical rifle in my
hands I was momentarily worth watching. And suddenly I realized that I
should have to shoot the elephant after all. The people expected it of me
and I had to do it; I could feel their two thousand wills pressing me forward, irresistibly. And it was at this moment, as I stood there with the rifle in my hands, that I first grasped the hollowness, the futility of the white
man's dominion in the East. Here was I, the white man with his gun,
standing in front of the unarmed native crowd—seemingly the leading actor of the piece; but in reality I was only an absurd puppet pushed to and
fro by the will of those yellow faces behind. I perceived in this moment
that when the white man turns tyrant it is his own freedom that he destroys. He becomes a sort of hollow, posing dummy, the conventionalized
figure of a sahib. For it is the condition of his rule that he shall spend his
life in trying to impress the "natives," and so in every crisis he has got to
do what the "natives" expect of him. He wears a mask, and his face grows
to fit it. I had got to shoot the elephant. I had committed myself to doing
it when I sent for the rifle. A sahib has got to act like a sahib; he has got
to appear resolute, to know his own mind and do definite things. To come
all that way, rifle in hand, with two thousand people marching at my
heels, and then to trail feebly away, having done nothing—no, that was
impossible. The crowd would laugh at me. And my whole life, every white
man's life in the East, was one long struggle not to be laughed at.

But I did not want to shoot the elephant. I watched him beating his   8
bunch of grass against his knees, with that preoccupied grandmotherly air
that elephants have. It seemed to me that it would be murder to shoot him.
At that age I was not squeamish about killing animals, but I had never shot
an elephant and never wanted to. (Somehow it always seems worse to kill
a *large* animal.) Besides, there was the beast's owner to be considered.
Alive, the elephant was worth at least a hundred pounds; dead, he would
only be worth the value of his tusks, five pounds, possibly. But I had got to
act quickly. I turned to some experienced-looking Burmans who had been
there when we arrived, and asked them how the elephant had been behaving. They all said the same thing: he took no notice of you if you left
him alone, but he might charge if you went too close to him.

It was perfectly clear to me what I ought to do. I ought to walk up to   9
within, say, twenty-five yards of the elephant and test his behavior. If he
charged, I could shoot; if he took no notice of me, it would be safe to leave

him until the mahout came back. But also I knew that I was going to do no such thing. I was a poor shot with a rifle and the ground was soft mud into which one would sink at every step. If the elephant charged and I missed him, I should have about as much chance as a toad under a steamroller. But even then I was not thinking particularly of my own skin, only of the watchful yellow faces behind. For at that moment, with the crowd watching me, I was not afraid in the ordinary sense, as I would have been if I had been alone. A white man mustn't be frightened in front of "natives"; and so, in general, he isn't frightened. The sole thought in my mind was that if anything went wrong those thousand Burmans would see me pursued, caught, trampled on and reduced to a grinning corpse like that Indian up the hill. And if that happened it was quite probable that some of them would laugh. That would never do. There was only one alternative. I shoved the cartridges into the magazine and lay down on the road to get a better aim.

10   The crowd grew very still, and a deep, low, happy sigh, as of people who see the theatre curtain go up at last, breathed from innumerable throats. They were going to have their bit of fun after all. The rifle was a beautiful German thing with cross-hair sights. I did not then know that in shooting an elephant one would shoot to cut an imaginary bar running from ear-hole to ear-hole. I ought, therefore, as the elephant was sideways on, to have aimed straight at his ear-hole; actually I aimed several inches in front of this, thinking the brain would be further forward.

11   When I pulled the trigger I did not hear the bang or feel the kick—one never does when a shot goes home—but I heard the devilish roar of glee that went up from the crowd. In that instant, in too short a time, one would have thought, even for the bullet to get there, a mysterious, terrible change had come over the elephant. He neither stirred nor fell, but every line of his body had altered. He looked suddenly stricken, shrunken, immensely old, as though the frightful impact of the bullet had paralysed him without knocking him down. At last, after what seemed a long time—it might have been five seconds, I dare say—he sagged flabbily to his knees. His mouth slobbered. An enormous senility seemed to have settled upon him. One could have imagined him thousands of years old. I fired again into the same spot. At the second shot he did not collapse but climbed with desperate slowness to his feet and stood weakly upright, with legs sagging and head drooping. I fired a third time. That was the shot that did for him. You could see the agony of it jolt his whole body and knock the last remnant of strength from his legs. But in falling he seemed for a moment to rise, for as his hind legs collapsed beneath him he seemed to tower upward like a huge rock toppling, his trunk reaching skywards like a tree. He trumpeted, for the first and only time. And then down he came, his belly towards me, with a crash that seemed to shake the ground even where I lay.

I got up. The Burmans were already racing past me across the mud. It 12
was obvious that the elephant would never rise again, but he was not
dead. He was breathing very rhythmically with long rattling gasps, his
great mound of a side painfully rising and falling. His mouth was wide
open—I could see far down into caverns of pale pink throat. I waited a
long time for him to die, but his breathing did not weaken. Finally I fired
my two remaining shots into the spot where I thought his heart must be.
The thick blood welled out of him like red velvet, but still he did not die.
His body did not even jerk when the shots hit him, the tortured breathing
continued without a pause. He was dying, very slowly and in great agony,
but in some world remote from me where not even a bullet could damage
him further. I felt that I had got to put an end to that dreadful noise. It
seemed dreadful to see the great beast lying there, powerless to move and
yet powerless to die, and not even to be able to finish him. I sent back for
my small rifle and poured shot after shot into his heart and down his
throat. They seemed to make no impression. The tortured gasps continued as steadily as the ticking of a clock.

In the end I could not stand it any longer and went away. I heard later 13
that it took him half an hour to die. Burmans were bringing dahs and baskets even before I left, and I was told they had stripped his body almost to
the bones by the afternoon.

Afterwards, of course, there were endless discussions about the shooting 14
of the elephant. The owner was furious, but he was only an Indian and
could do nothing. Besides, legally I had done the right thing, for a mad
elephant has to be killed, like a mad dog, if its owner fails to control it.
Among the Europeans opinion was divided. The older men said I was
right, the younger men said it was a damn shame to shoot an elephant for
killing a coolie, because an elephant was worth more than any damn
Coringhee coolie. And afterwards I was very glad that the coolie had been
killed; it put me legally in the right and it gave me a sufficient pretext for
shooting the elephant. I often wondered whether any of the others
grasped that I had done it solely to avoid looking a fool.

QUESTIONING AND DISCUSSING

Orwell, "Shooting an Elephant"

1. "Shooting an Elephant" reveals through specific, personal events—and one
   in particular—"the real nature of imperialism," in Orwell's words. How does
   it also reveal the pressures of personal decision-making? Using the text for
   examples, discuss how, in your view, Orwell fares in this regard.

2. Research the concept of *imperialism*, looking specifically at British imperialism in Burma. On what assumptions is imperialism based? How does this
context shape your view of Orwell's narrative? Given that Orwell was writing in 1936, to what might he be alluding when he writes, "I did not even
know that the British Empire is dying, still less did I know that it is a great
deal better than the younger empires that are going to supplant it."

3. Orwell writes, "All I knew was that I was stuck between my hatred of the
empire I served and my rage against the evil-spirited little beasts . . ." What
other passages in this essay reinforce Orwell's divided sense of self? (Consider, for instance, "Among the Europeans opinion was divided. The older
men said I was right, the younger men said it was a damn shame to shoot an
elephant . . . ," and other similar statements.)

4. Comment on the final sentence of the essay: "I often wondered whether any
of the others grasped that I had done it solely to avoid looking a fool." How
does Orwell's personal decision transcend the larger contexts of imperialism
that drive this essay?

⊞

ALICE WALKER

Alice Walker (1944–) was educated at Sarah Lawrence College, after which she
worked as a caseworker for the New York City welfare department and participated in
the civil rights movement. She has taught creative writing and African American literature at Jackson State College, Tougaloo College, Wellesley College, and Yale University.
Walker's stories, novels, and political essays are many and include *In Love and Trouble: Stories of Black Women* (1973); *The Color Purple* (1982), for which she won the
Pulitzer Prize; and *Possessing the Secret of Joy* (1992). Her volume of social and political essays, entitled *Anything We Love Can Be Saved*, was published in 1997. She has
also published a memoir, *The Same River Twice: Honoring the Defficult* (1996), and *By
the Light of My Father's Smile* (1998).

⊞

Everyday Use

For your grandmamma

1   I will wait for her in the yard that Maggie and I made so clean and wavy
yesterday afternoon. A yard like this is more comfortable than most
people know. It is not just a yard. It is like an extended living room. When

the hard clay is swept clean as a floor and the fine sand around the edges lined with tiny, irregular grooves, anyone can come and sit and look up into the elm tree and wait for the breezes that never come inside the house.

Maggie will be nervous until after her sister goes: she will stand hope- lessly in corners, homely and ashamed of the burn scars down her arms and legs, eying her sister with a mixture of envy and awe. She thinks her sister has held life always in the palm of one hand, that "no" is a word the world never learned to say to her. 2

You've no doubt seen those TV shows where the child who has "made it" is confronted, as a surprise, by her own mother and father, tottering in weakly from backstage. (A pleasant surprise, of course: What would they do if parent and child came on the show only to curse out and insult each other?) On TV mother and child embrace and smile into each other's faces. Sometimes the mother and father weep, the child wraps them in her arms and leans across the table to tell how she would not have made it without their help. I have seen these programs. 3

Sometimes I dream a dream in which Dee and I are suddenly brought to- gether on a TV program of this sort. Out of a dark and soft-seated limou- sine I am ushered into a bright room filled with many people. There I meet a smiling, gray, sporty man like Johnny Carson who shakes my hand and tells me what a fine girl I have. Then we are on the stage and Dee is em- bracing me with tears in her eyes. She pins on my dress a large orchid, even though she has told me once that she thinks orchids are tacky flowers. 4

In real life I am a large, big-boned woman with rough, man-working hands. In the winter I wear flannel nightgowns to bed and overalls during the day. I can kill and clean a hog as mercilessly as a man. My fat keeps me hot in zero weather. I can work outside all day, breaking ice to get water for washing; I can eat pork liver cooked over the open fire minutes after it comes steaming from the hog. One winter I knocked a bull calf straight in the brain between the eyes with a sledge hammer and had the meat hung up to chill before nightfall. But of course all this does not show on televi- sion. I am the way my daughter would want me to be: a hundred pounds lighter, my skin like an uncooked barley pancake. My hair glistens in the hot bright lights. Johnny Carson has much to do to keep up with my quick and witty tongue. 5

But that is a mistake. I know even before I wake up. Who ever knew a Johnson with a quick tongue? Who can even imagine me looking a strange white man in the eye? It seems to me I have talked to them always with one foot raised in flight, with my head turned in whichever way is 6 farthest from them. Dee, though. She would always look anyone in the eye. Hesitation was no part of her nature.

7   "How do I look, Mama?" Maggie says, showing just enough of her thin body enveloped in pink skirt and red blouse for me to know she's there, almost hidden by the door.

8   "Come out into the yard," I say.

9   Have you ever seen a lame animal, perhaps a dog run over by some careless person rich enough to own a car, sidle up to someone who is ignorant enough to be kind to them? That is the way my Maggie walks. She has been like this, chin on chest, eyes on ground, feet in shuffle, ever since the fire that burned the other house to the ground.

10   Dee is lighter than Maggie, with nicer hair and a fuller figure. She's a woman now, though sometimes I forget. How long ago was it that the other house burned? Ten, twelve years? Sometimes I can still hear the flames and feel Maggie's arms sticking to me, her hair smoking and her dress falling off her in little black papery flakes. Her eyes seemed stretched open, blazed open by the flames reflected in them. And Dee. I see her standing off under the sweet gum tree she used to dig gum out of; a look of concentration on her face as she watched the last dingy gray board of the house fall in toward the red-hot brick chimney. Why don't you do a dance around the ashes? I'd wanted to ask her. She had hated the house that much.

11   I used to think she hated Maggie, too. But that was before we raised the money, the church and me, to send her to Augusta to school. She used to read to us without pity; forcing words, lies, other folks' habits, whole lives upon us two, sitting trapped and ignorant underneath her voice. She washed us in a river of make-believe, burned us with a lot of knowledge we didn't necessarily need to know. Pressed us to her with the serious way she read, to shove us away at just the moment, like dimwits, we seemed about to understand.

12   Dee wanted nice things. A yellow organdy dress to wear to her graduation from high school; black pumps to match a green suit she'd made from an old suit somebody gave me. She was determined to stare down any disaster in her efforts. Her eyelids would not flicker for minutes at a time. Often I fought off the temptation to shake her. At sixteen she had a style of her own: and knew what style was.

13   I never had an education myself. After second grade the school was closed down. Don't ask me why: in 1927 colored asked fewer questions than they do now. Sometimes Maggie reads to me. She stumbles along

good naturedly but can't see well. She knows she is not bright. Like good looks and money, quickness passed her by. She will marry John Thomas (who has mossy teeth in an earnest face) and then I'll be free to sit here and I guess just sing church songs to myself. Although I never was a good singer. Never could carry a tune. I was always better at a man's job. I used to love to milk till I was hooked in the side in '49. Cows are soothing and slow and don't bother you, unless you try to milk them the wrong way.

I have deliberately turned my back on the house. It is three rooms, just   14
like the one that burned, except the roof is tin; they don't make shingle roofs any more. There are no real windows, just some holes cut in the sides, like the portholes in a ship, but not round and not square, with rawhide holding the shutters up on the outside. This house is in a pasture, too, like the other one. No doubt when Dee sees it she will want to tear it down. She wrote me once that no matter where we "choose" to live, she will manage to come see us. But she will never bring her friends. Maggie and I thought about this and Maggie asked me, "Mama, when did Dee ever *have* any friends?"

She had a few. Furtive boys in pink shirts hanging about on washday af-   15
ter school. Nervous girls who never laughed. Impressed with her they wor-shiped the well-turned phrase, the cute shape, the scalding humor that erupted like bubbles in lye. She read to them.

When she was courting Jimmy T she didn't have much time to pay to   16
us, but turned all her faultfinding power on him. He *flew* to marry a cheap city girl from a family of ignorant flashy people. She hardly had time to re-compose herself.

When she comes I will meet—but there they are!   17

Maggie attempts to make a dash for the house, in her shuffling way, but   18
I stay her with my hand. "Come back here," I say. And she stops and tries to dig a well in the sand with her toe.

It is hard to see them clearly through the strong sun. But even the first   19
glimpse of leg out of the car tells me it is Dee. Her feet were always neat-looking, as if God himself had shaped them with a certain style. From the other side of the car comes a short, stocky man. Hair is all over his head a foot long and hanging from his chin like a kinky mule tail. I hear Maggie suck in her breath. "Uhnnnh," is what it sounds like. Like when you see the wriggling end of a snake just in front of your foot on the road. "Uhnnnh."

Dee next. A dress down to the ground, in this hot weather. A dress so   20
loud it hurts my eyes. There are yellows and oranges enough to throw back the light of the sun. I feel my whole face warming from the heat waves it

throws out. Earrings gold, too, and hanging down to her shoulders. Bracelets dangling and making noises when she moves her arm up to shake the folds of the dress out of her armpits. The dress is loose and flows, and as she walks closer, I like it. I hear Maggie go "Uhnnnh" again. It is her sister's hair. It stands straight up like the wool on a sheep. It is black as night and around the edges are two long pigtails that rope about like small lizards disappearing behind her ears.

21 "Wa-su-zo-Tean-o!" she says, coming on in that gliding way the dress makes her move. The short stocky fellow with the hair to his navel is all grinning and he follows up with "Asalamalakim, my mother and sister!" He moves to hug Maggie but she falls back, right up against the back of my chair. I feel her trembling there and when I look up I see the perspiration falling off her chin.

22 "Don't get up," says Dee. Since I am stout it takes something of a push. You can see me trying to move a second or two before I make it. She turns, showing white heels through her sandals, and goes back to the car. Out she peeks next with a Polaroid. She stoops down quickly and lines up picture after picture of me sitting there in front of the house with Maggie cowering behind me. She never takes a shot without making sure the house is included. When a cow comes nibbling around the edge of the yard she snaps it and me and Maggie *and* the house. Then she puts the Polaroid in the back seat of the car, and comes up and kisses me on the forehead.

23 Meanwhile Asalamalakim is going through motions with Maggie's hand. Maggie's hand is as limp as a fish, and probably as cold, despite the sweat, and she keeps trying to pull it back. It looks like Asalamalakim wants to shake hands but wants to do it fancy. Or maybe he don't know how people shake hands. Anyhow, he soon gives up on Maggie.

24 "Well," I say. "Dee."

25 "No, Mama," she says. "Not 'Dee,' Wangero Leewanika Kemanjo!"

26 "What happened to 'Dee'?" I wanted to know.

27 "She's dead," Wangero said. "I couldn't bear it any longer, being named after the people who oppress me."

28 "You know as well as me you was named after your aunt Dicie," I said. Dicie is my sister. She named Dee. We called her "Big Dee" after Dee was born.

29 "But who was *she* named after?" asked Wangero.

30 "I guess after Grandma Dee," I said.

31 "And who was she named after?" asked Wangero.

32 "Her mother," I said, and saw Wangero was getting tired. "That's about as far back as I can trace it." I said. Though, in fact, I probably could have carried it back beyond the Civil War through the branches.

"Well," said Asalamalakim, "there you are." 33

"Uhnnnh," I heard Maggie say. 34

"There I was not," I said, "before 'Dicie' cropped up in our family, so 35
why should I try to trace it that far back?"

He just stood there grinning, looking down on me like somebody in- 36
specting a Model A car. Every once in a while he and Wangero sent eye
signals over my head.

"How do you pronounce this name?" I asked. 37

"You don't have to call me by it if you don't want to," said Wangero. 38

"Why shouldn't I?" I asked. "If that's what you want us to call you, we'll 39
call you."

"I know it might sound awkward at first," said Wangero. 40

"I'll get used to it," I said. "Ream it out again." 41

Well, soon we got the name out of the way. Asalamalakim had a name 42
twice as long and three times as hard. After I tripped over it two or three
times he told me to just call him Hakim-a-barber. I wanted to ask him was
he a barber, but I didn't really think he was, so I didn't ask.

"You must belong to those beef-cattle peoples down the road," I said. 43
They said "Asalamalakim" when they met you, too, but they didn't shake
hands. Always too busy: feeding the cattle, fixing the fences, putting up
salt-lick shelters, throwing down hay. When the white folks poisoned
some of the herd the men stayed up all night with rifles in their hands. I
walked a mile and a half just to see the sight.

Hakim-a-barber said, "I accept some of their doctrines, but farming and 44
raising cattle is not my style." (They didn't tell me, and I didn't ask,
whether Wangero (Dee) had really gone and married him.)

We sat down to eat and right away he said he didn't eat collards and 45
pork was unclean. Wangero, though, went on through the chitlins and
corn bread, the greens and everything else. She talked a blue streak over
the sweet potatoes. Everything delighted her. Even the fact that we still
used the benches her daddy made for the table when we couldn't afford to
buy chairs.

"Oh, Mama!" she cried. Then turned to Hakim-a-barber. "I never knew 46
how lovely these benches are. You can feel the rump prints," she said, running her hands underneath her and along the bench. Then she gave a sigh
and her hand closed over Grandma Dee's butter dish. "That's it!" she said.
"I knew there was something I wanted to ask you if I could have." She
jumped up from the table and went over in the corner where the churn
stood, the milk in it clabber by now. She looked at the churn and looked
at it.

47   "This churn top is what I need," she said. "Didn't Uncle Buddy whittle it out of a tree you all used to have?"

48   "Yes," I said.

49   "Uh huh," she said happily. "And I want the dasher, too."

50   "Uncle Buddy whittle that, too?" asked the barber.

51   Dee (Wangero) looked up at me.

52   "Aunt Dee's first husband whittled the dash," said Maggie so low you almost couldn't hear her. "His name was Henry, but they called him Stash."

53   "Maggie's brain is like an elephant's," Wangero said, laughing. "I can use the churn top as a centerpiece for the alcove table," she said, sliding a plate over the churn, "and I'll think of something artistic to do with the dasher."

54   When she finished wrapping the dasher the handle stuck out. I took it for a moment in my hands. You didn't even have to look close to see where hands pushing the dasher up and down to make butter had left a kind of sink in the wood. In fact, there were a lot of small sinks; you could see where thumbs and fingers had sunk into the wood. It was beautiful light yellow wood, from a tree that grew in the yard where Big Dee and Stash had lived.

55   After dinner Dee (Wangero) went to the trunk at the foot of my bed and started rifling through it. Maggie hung back in the kitchen over the dishpan. Out came Wangero with two quilts. They had been pieced by Grandma Dee and then Big Dee and me had hung them on the quilt frames on the front porch and quilted them. One was in the Lone Star pattern. The other was Walk Around the Mountain. In both of them were scraps of dresses Grandma Dee had worn fifty and more years ago. Bits and pieces of Grandpa Jarrell's Paisley shirts. And one teeny faded blue piece, about the size of a penny matchbox, that was from Great Grandpa Ezra's uniform that he wore in the Civil War.

56   "Mama," Wangero said sweet as a bird. "Can I have these old quilts?"

57   I heard something fall in the kitchen, and a minute later the kitchen door slammed.

58   "Why don't you take one or two of the others?" I asked. "These old things was just done by me and Big Dee from some tops your grandma pieced before she died."

59   "No," said Wangero. "I don't want those. They are stitched around the borders by machine."

60   "That'll make them last better," I said.

61   "That's not the point," said Wangero. "These are all pieces of dresses Grandma used to wear. She did all this stitching by hand. Imagine!" She held the quilts securely in her arms, stroking them.

"Some of the pieces, like those lavender ones, come from old clothes   62
her mother handed down to her," I said, moving up to touch the quilts.
Dee (Wangero) moved back just enough so that I couldn't reach the
quilts. They already belonged to her.

"Imagine!" she breathed again, clutching them closely to her bosom.   63

"The truth is," I said, "I promised to give them quilts to Maggie, for   64
when she marries John Thomas."

She gasped like a bee had stung her.   65

"Maggie can't appreciate these quilts!" she said. "She'd probably be   66
backward enough to put them to everyday use."

"I reckon she would," I said. "God knows I been saving 'em for long   67
enough with nobody using 'em. I hope she will!" I didn't want to bring up
how I had offered Dee (Wangero) a quilt when she went away to college.
Then she had told me they were old-fashioned, out of style.

"But they're *priceless*!" she was saying now, furiously; for she has a tem-   68
per. "Maggie would put them on the bed and in five years they'd be in rags.
Less than that!"

"She can always make some more," I said. "Maggie knows how to quilt."   69

Dee (Wangero) looked at me with hatred. "You just will not under-   70
stand. The point is these quilts, *these* quilts!"

"Well," I said, stumped. "What would *you* do with them?"   71

"Hang them," she said. As if that was the only thing you *could* do with   72
quilts.

Maggie by now was standing in the door. I could almost hear the sound   73
her feet made as they scraped over each other.

"She can have them, Mama," she said, like somebody used to never   74
winning anything, or having anything reserved for her. "I can 'member
Grandma Dee without the quilts."

I looked at her hard. She had filled her bottom lip with checkerberry   75
snuff and it gave her face a kind of dopey, hangdog look. It was Grandma
Dee and Big Dee who taught her how to quilt herself. She stood there
with her scarred hands hidden in the folds of her skirt. She looked at her
sister with something like fear but she wasn't mad at her. This was Maggie's portion. This was the way she knew God to work.

When I looked at her like that something hit me in the top of my head   76
and ran down to the soles of my feet. Just like when I'm in church and the
spirit of God touches me and I get happy and shout. I did something I
never had done before: hugged Maggie to me, then dragged her on into
the room, snatched the quilts out of Miss Wangero's hands and dumped
them into Maggie's lap. Maggie just sat there on my bed with her mouth
open.

77   "Take one or two of the others," I said to Dee.

78   But she turned without a word and went out to Hakim-a-barber.

79   "You just don't understand," she said, as Maggie and I came out to the car.

80   "What don't I understand?" I wanted to know.

81   "Your heritage," she said. And then she turned to Maggie, kissed her, and said, "You ought to try to make something of yourself, too, Maggie. It's really a new day for us. But from the way you and Mama still live you'd never know it."

82   She put on some sunglasses that hid everything above the tip of her nose and her chin.

83   Maggie smiled; maybe at the sunglasses. But a real smile, not scared. After we watched the car dust settle I asked Maggie to bring me a dip of snuff. And then the two of us sat there just enjoying, until it was time to go in the house and go to bed.

QUESTIONING AND DISCUSSING

Walker, "Everyday Use"

1. "Everyday Use" concerns not only the clashes and differences among family members but also, and perhaps more significantly, the ways in which these clashes represent differences in values. What are these differences in values? How does each character represent or reinforce these values? Which seem the most sincere? Why?

2. Analyze the various possible meanings of the title of the story and its relationship to the theme(s) of the story.

3. A number of people reading the story for the first time find it to be clear-cut in terms of indicating whose values are better. In your view, is this so? What issues might make the notion of "values" more complex, and why?

4. Comment on the symbolic value of the quilts and their function in this story.

⊞

DANIEL CALLAHAN

Daniel Callahan (1930–) cofounded and from 1989 to 1996 directed the Hastings Center for Biomedical Ethics. Trained as a philosopher and having received his Ph.D. from Harvard University, Callahan writes extensively on abortion and medical ethics. The author or editor of thirty-five books. Callahan has also served as visiting professor at numerous institutions.
⊞

What Do Children Owe Elderly Parents?

In the spring of 1983 the Reagan administration announced that states may under Medcaid legally require children to contribute to the support of their elderly parents. At the time a number of states were considering or enacting just such laws. The administration, one spokesman said, was not proposing anything inherently new. It was simply responding to a state request for clarification of the existing Medicaid law, and wanted only to say that state statutes enforcing family responsibility laws were not in conflict with federal policy. [1]

As it turned out, the administration's initiative was a policy shift whose time had not come. While a number of states flirted for a time with new family responsibility policies, only a few (Virginia, Idaho, and Mississippi, for example) actually adopted them, and even fewer seem to be enforcing them. As pressing as the state Medicaid nursing home burden is, it rapidly became clear that there is little general sentiment to force children to provide financially for their elderly parents. [2]

Nonetheless, Reagan's initiative was an important social and policy event and raises significant moral issues. In one form or another, the idea is likely to arise again. Anything that can be done to raise revenue to reduce the Medicaid burden probably will be done. Three questions are thus worth considering. What kind of a moral obligation do children have toward the welfare of their elderly parents? Can it be said that the changed health, longevity, and social circumstances of the elderly justify a shift in traditional moral obligations? Even if children do have some significant duties to parents, is it still legitimate to ask the state to take over much of the direct burden of care? [3]

The first question is of course an old one. Each generation has had to make its own sense of the biblical injunction that we should honor our fathers [4] and mothers. It neither tells us in what "honor" consists nor how far filial obligation should be carried. As a piece of practical advice, however, it once made considerable sense. In most traditional and agricultural societies, parents had considerable power over the lives of their offspring. Children who did not honor their parents risked not only immediate privation, but also the loss of the one inheritance that would enable them to raise and support their own families—land they could call their own.

5   The advent of industrialization brought about a radical change. It reduced the direct coercive power of parents over their children, setting into motion a trend toward the independence of both parents and children that has been a mark of contemporary society. Though the affective bond between parents and children has so far endured in the face of industrialization and modernity, the combination of actual attachment and potential independence frames the question of the obligation of children toward their elderly parents.

6   The moral ideal of the parent-child relationship is that of love, nurture, and the mutual seeking for the good of the other. While the weight of the relationship will ordinarily shift according to the age of children and their parents, mutual respect and reciprocity have been a central part of the moral standard. Yet the reality of human lives can stand in the way of the realization of moral ideals. Just as not all children are lovable, neither do all parents give the welfare of their children their serious attention and highest priority. Many children do not find their parents lovable and feel no special sense of duty toward them. Many parents are not happy with the way their children turn out, or with the kind of lives they live, and do not seek to remain intertwined with them.

7   To what extent, and under what circumstances, flaws and faults of that kind can be said to alter the mutual obligations is obviously an important question. Yet even when the affectional bonds between parent and child are strong, it is still by no means clear what each morally owes to the other. If parents ought to help their children to grow up and flourish, should they go so far as to seriously jeopardize their own future welfare in doing so? If children should honor their elderly parents, how great a sacrifice ought that to entail?

The Changing Status of the Elderly

8   The present relationship between children and their elderly parents is shaped in part by the changing status of the elderly in society. A rising number and increasing proportion of our population are elderly. The "young old" (65–75) appear to be in better health than ever, but as people

live longer, there is also an increasing number of the "old old" (75+) who are frail and dependent. Despite a variety of public programs and considerable improvement in recent decades, a significant proportion of the elderly (about 25 percent in 1980) still live in poverty or near-poverty. A large proportion do not have immediate family or relatives to whom they can turn for either financial or emotional assistance, and many—particularly women—live alone or in institutions. Even so, as Victor Fuchs notes in summarizing available data, rising income has "made it possible for an ever higher percentage [of the elderly] to maintain their own households, health permitting."

Independence, however, need not mean an absence of family ties. Gerontologists take great pleasure in demolishing what they tell us are two prevalent myths, that the caring family has disappeared, and that the elderly are isolated from their children. There has indeed been a decline in the number of elderly who live with their children or other relatives, from three-fifths in 1960 to one-third in 1980, and an equally sharp drop— down to 1 percent—in the number of elderly who depend upon their children for financial support. Yet it still seems to be true, as Ethel Shanas has noted, that "most old people live close to at least one of their children and see at least one child often. Most old people see their siblings and relatives often, and old people, whether bedfast or housebound because of ill health, are twice as likely to be living at home as to be residents in an institution. . . ." In addition, it is estimated that 60–80 percent of all disabled or impaired persons receive significant family help.

One important change involves the proportion of young and old who believe that children should be financially responsible for their elderly parents. This has shifted downward (from about 50 percent in the midfifties to 10 percent in the mid-seventies), and a simultaneous reduction in financial assistance has occurred. However, this need not be taken as an indication of a diminished sense of filial responsibility. The advent of Social Security, and the increasing financial strength of the elderly for other reasons, all indicate important social variables that have reduced financial pressure on children to support parents.

Other social changes could eventually alter that situation. The increasing number of divorced families, of small families, and of families where both spouses work, [has] created the possibility of a reduced sense of obligation in the future, though that has yet clearly to materialize. In his 1981 book *New Rules*, the pollster Daniel Yankelovich wrote that "one of the most far-reaching changes in [moral] norms relates to what parents believe they owe their children and what their children owe them. Nowhere are the changes in the unwritten social contract more significant or agonizing. The overall pattern is clear: today's parents expect to make fewer sacrifices for their children than in the past, but they also demand less from their offspring in the form of future obligations than their parents demanded of them. . . . Sixty-seven percent [of Americans surveyed] believe that 'children do not have an obligation to their parents regardless of what their parents have done for them.'" . . .

What the Law Says

12 Some twenty-six states at present have statutes that can require children to provide financial support for needy parents. Though erratically administered, difficult to implement, and of doubtful financial value, they remain as testimony to an effort dating back to the early seventeenth century to shift from the public to the private sphere the care of poverty-stricken elderly. While such laws had no precedent in either common law or medieval law, they came into being in England with the Elizabethan Poor Law of 1601, representing a culmination of at least three centuries of efforts to cope with the problem of the poor in general. The Poor Law did not concentrate on the children of the elderly, but extended the network of potential support to include the fathers and mothers, and the grandfathers and grandmothers, of the poor. The family, as a unit, was to be responsible for poverty-stricken kinfolk.

13 When these laws passed over into the American scene, during the seventeenth and eighteenth centuries, the focus was on the responsibility of children toward their elderly parents, though a few states have retained the wider scope. Blackstone's famous *Commentaries* succinctly state the moral basis of such a responsbility: "The duties of children to their parents arise from a principle of natural justice and retribution. For to those who gave us existence we naturally owe subjection and obedience during our minority, and honor and reverence ever after; they who protected the weakness of our infancy are entitled to our protection in the infirmity of their age; they who by sustenance and education have enabled their offspring to prosper ought in return to be supported by that offspring in case they stand in need of assistance."

14 The American state laws were little invoked during the eighteenth and nineteenth centuries, but they were increasingly turned to during the twentieth century, particularly in the aftermath of the depression and World War II. While there is broad historical agreement that the primary purpose of the laws was to protect the public from the burden of caring for the poor, including the elderly, the laws were buttressed by a variety of moral assumptions.

Martin R. Levy and Sara W. Gross have identified three moral premises   15
that underlie the American laws and developed some cogent criticisms of
them. First, "the duty of a child to support his parents is a mirror-image of
the parents' responsbility to support a child." They point out the doubtful
logic of that position. In procreation parents not only bring a child into
the world, but by the same action undertake the moral obligation of sustaining that child, whose existence is entirely dependent upon the parents. As Levy and Gross put it, "In the converse situation of the duty of a
child to support a parent, there is no proximate cause, no volitional act,
and no rational basis for the demand of support. The child has not acted
to bring about the life of the parent. While the father assumes the voluntary status of fatherhood, the child assumes no duty by having been born.
His birth is the result of the act of the father and mother, and such a result cannot logically or physically be turned into a proximate cause."
While they do not deny that there can be a moral bond of love and affection, "moral duty and gratitude, or lofty ideals, cannot be used as a justification for the taking of property." By focusing on "the taking of property,"
the authors focus on a relatively narrow point.

The second general moral premise turns on what they call "the rela-   16
tional interest of family status." They mean that the simple fact of a family relationship—creating a special tie between parent and child, both
biological and social—may itself engender the basis for a demand made
upon children to support their elderly parents. Yet they point out that the
relational interests are both too broad and too narrow to serve as a reasonable criterion for determining the duty to provide support. "It is too
broad in . . . that not all children love and revere their parents. The status
of a child confers no special emotional tie in and of itself." It is too narrow
in that, if emotional commitment is the standard, then a child would logically be bound to support everyone to whom he or she is tied by emotional commitment, whether family member or not.

The analogy of a contract provides the third moral premise. Since the   17
child was at one time supported by the parent, does not that create an implicit contract requiring that the child in turn support the parent when
that becomes necessary? Levy and Gross point out that no direct contract
is negotiated between parent and child when the child is procreated, and
that any analogy of an implied contract does not work: the two parties
necessary to the making of a contract did not exist simultaneously. A
common standard in the law, moreover, is that neither the carrying out of
a duty, nor the promise of rendering a performance already required by
duty, is a sufficient condition of a return promise—an obligation to do
likewise.

Parents as "Friends"

18   Although Levy and Gross effectively dispatch the argument that the benefits bestowed by parents upon children automatically entail a duty of the children in return to aid parents, there is considerably more that needs to be said. Are we to hold that the obligation flows in one direction only, that because children were given no choice about being born, they owe nothing whatever to their parents? That seems too extreme. At the least, it fails to explain why in fact many children feel an obligation toward their parents, nor does it sufficiently plumb the moral depths of the family relationship.

19   The late Jane English also argued that the language of "owing" is mistakenly applied in the circumstances. Children "owe" parents nothing at all—which is not to say that there are not many things that children ought to do for their parents. Instead, she held that "the duties of grown children are those of friends and result from love between them and their parents, rather than being things owed in repayment for the parents' earlier sacrifices." In situations where one person does a favor for another, there may be an obligation to reciprocate, but parents do not do favors for their children in the same sense that strangers or acquaintances may do them for each other. The bond that should unite parents and children is that of friendship, and "friendship ought to be characterized by *mutuality* rather than reciprocity: friends offer what they can give and accept what they need without regard for the total amount of benefits exchanged. And friends are motivated by love rather than by the prospect of repayment. Hence, talk of 'owing' is singularly out of place in friendship." Thus children ought to do things for their parents but the "ought" is that which follows from friendship; it resists both quantitative measurement and the stricter language of owing something in return for earlier benefits.

20   While English's argument has some plausibility, it is ultimately unsatisfying. Friendship can certainly exist between parent and child, but it often does not. Quite apart from those circumstances where parents have neglected their children or otherwise alienated their affection, they may have little in common other than their biological origins. Moreover, the nature of the friendship that exists between parent and child can and usually will be different from the kind that exists between and among those who are unrelated. A child might plausibly say that, while he is not a friend of his parents, he nonetheless feels toward them respect and love. To push the same point further, many children actively dislike their parents, find no pleasure in their company, and yet feel they ought to do things for them despite those feelings. In distinguishing between favors and friendship, English says that "another difference between favors and

friendships is that after a friendship ends, the duties of friendship end." That may be true enough in the case of nonfamily relationships, but it then raises all the more forcefully the question of whether friendship, however much it may mark a relationship between parent and child, can catch the fullness of the moral bond.

The origin and nature of the parent-child bond—or whatever other re- 21 lationship may exist—is unique. By the procreation of children parents create a social unit that otherwise would not and could not exist. If children do not select their parents, neither do parents select their individual children (they choose to have *a* child, not *this* child). Even so, the family relationship is not something one can simply take or leave. It is a fundamental and unavoidable part of our social nature as human beings. That psychotherapists can spend a good deal of time untangling problems between parents and children provides at least a clue to the emotional depth of the biological relationship, whether marked by unhappiness or happiness. We can and do drift away from ordinary friendships, but parents stay in our memory and exert their influence even in the face of distance or active hostility. Whether we like it or not, we are in some sense always one with our parents, both because of the unique circumstances by which we came to know them and because of the long period of nurture when we were utterly dependent upon them. The mutual interaction of parents and children, even when friendships exist, cannot then entirely be reduced to the category of friendship. The emotional and biological bond between parent and child gives the relationship a permanent and central place in our lives, quite apart from whether that relationship turns out well or poorly. That cannot be said of friendship in the usual sense of the term.

Capturing Intimacy in Moral Language

Ferdinand Schoeman catches some of this flavor when he argues that the 22 traditional language of morality, that of rights and obligations, does not seem to fit well in describing the bond among family members: "We *share ourselves* with those with whom we are intimate and are aware that they do the same with us. Traditional moral boundaries, which give rigid shape to the self, are transparent to this kind of sharing. This makes for nonabstract moral relationships in which talk about rights of others, respect for others, and even welfare of others is to a certain extent irrelevant." Perhaps Schoeman takes things a bit far, but he tries to make clear that the intimacy of family relationships forces us into revealing and sharing a self that may not be revealed to others on the public stage. While it is often the case that parents do not really know their own child, just as often they do, even when their perceptions differ from those of the child. Whether they understand their child or not, the fact that they shared considerable intimacy when the child was young gives them access to a self that others may never see. For their part, children have unique access to parents, seeing a side of them that may never be revealed to others.

23   Another powerful candidate for the source of obligation is that of gratitude on the part of children toward their parents. Gratitude would be due, not simply because parents discharged their obligations toward the children, but because in their manner of doing so they went beyond the demands of mere duty, giving voluntarily of themselves in a way neither required nor ordinarily expected of them. As Jeffrey Blustein notes, "Duties of gratitude are owed only to those who have helped or benefited us freely, without thought of personal gain, simply out of a desire to protect or promote our well-being. The givers may hope for some return, but they do not give in expectation of it." A consequence of this line of reasoning, however, is that only those parents who did more than was morally required could be said to have a right to the gratitude of their children. And it is by no means obvious that a "debt of gratitude" carries with it a strict obligation to provide like goods or services, that is, to be beyond what is otherwise required.

24   I am searching here with some difficulty for a way to characterize the ethical nature of the parent-child relationship, a relationship that appears almost but not quite self-evident in its reciprocal moral claims and yet oddly elusive also. We seem to say too much if we try to reduce the relationship to mutual moral duties, rights, and obligations. That implies a rigor and formalism which distorts the moral bond. We say too little if we try to make it a matter of voluntary affection only. Yet we cannot, I suspect, totally dismiss the language of oblgiation nor would we want to give up the ideal of mutual affection either. If the procreation and physical rearing of a child does not automatically entail reciprocal duties toward the parents when they are needy and dependent, it is certainly possible to imagine a sense of obligation arising when parents have done far more for children than would morally be required of them. My own parents, for example, did not throw me out on my own when I reached eighteen. They sacrificed a good deal to provide me with a higher education, and in fact provided financial support for my graduate education until I was thirty, topping that off by giving my wife and me a down-payment on our first house. They did it out of affection, rather than duty, but I certainly felt I owed them something in return in their old age. There need not be, then, any necessary incompatibility between feeling both affection and a sense of duty. But we lack a moral phrase that catches both notions in one concept; and neither taken separately is quite right.

The Power of Dependence

Another aspect of the relationship between children and their elderly 25
parents bears reflection. Much as young children will have a special dependence upon parents, as those human beings above all others who have
a fateful power over their destinies, so many elderly parents can come in
dire circumstances similarly to depend upon their children. In a world of
strangers or fleeting casual acquaintances, of distant government agencies
and a society beyond their control, elderly parents can see in their children their only hope for someone who ought to care for them. Neither
parent nor child may want this kind of emotional dependence, and each
might wish that there were an alternative. Nonetheless, parents may be
forced to throw themselves upon their children simply because there is no
other alternative. Who else is likely to care?

Can that sense of utter need, if not for money then only for affection and 26
caring, in and of itself create a moral obligation? It is surely a difficult question whether, as a general matter, a moral obligation is incurred when one
human being is rendered by circumstance wholly dependent upon another—whether, that is, the dependency itself creates the obligation, quite
apart from any other features of the relationship. A moral claim of that
kind will inevitably be controversial, if only because it is (regretfully) common to rest claims of obligation upon implicit or explicit contracts of one
kind or another; or upon features of the relationship that can be subjected
to a utilitarian calculation. It is difficult in this case plausibly to invoke
such norms. Still, the power of sheer dependence—whether of newborn
child upon parent or elderly, dependent parent upon child—can be potent
in its experienced moral demands. The fate of one or more persons rests in
the hands of another. The issue, as it presents itself, may be less one of trying to discover the grounds of obligation that would require a response
than one of trying to find grounds for ignoring a demand that so patently
assaults the sensibilities. It is not so much "must I?" as it is "how can I not?"

Joel Feinberg, commenting on the moral place of gratitude, moves in a 27
similar direction when he writes, "My benefactor once freely offered me
his services when I needed them. . . . But now circumstances have arisen
in which he needs help, and I am in a position to help him. Surely, I owe
him my services now, and he would be entitled to resent my failure to
come through." A qualification is in order here: gratitude is ordinarily
thought due only when, as noted above, a benefactor has gone beyond ordinary duties. In some cases, parents may have only done their duty, and
in such a minimal way that no gratitude seems due them. We are then
brought back to the starkest moral situation—in which the dependency
only seeks to establish a claim on us.

28   In trying to unravel the nature of the possible moral obligations, it may be helpful to speak of some specific claims or demands that might be made. Money is by no means the only, or necessarily the most important, benefit that parents can ask of their children. Children can also contribute their time and physical energy, and provide affection and psychological support. On a scale of moral priorities, it would be difficult to persuasively argue that parents have an obligation to deprive their own dependent children of necessary financial support in order to support their elderly parents. By virtue of procreating those children, the latter have been taken care of, the financial support of needy parents might become obligatory, particularly if there were no other available sources of support. Ordinarily, however, their principal economic duties will be toward their own children.

29   The same cannot necessarily be said of providing either physical help or affection to their parents. While the giving of physical help or affection could readily be merged, I think it is useful to distinguish between them. Physical help—such as assistance in moving, cleaning, shopping, and trips to visit friends or doctors—is a somewhat different contribution to the welfare of the elderly than simply talking with them. Parents of young children may not readily be able to adapt their schedules to such demands upon their time or energy. Yet they may be able to provide affection, either by visits at times they find convenient, or through letters and telephone calls. An inability to provide some kinds of care does not exempt children from providing other forms. In fact, the available evidence suggests that affection is most wanted, and it is not difficult to understand why. The uncertainties of old age, the recognition of growing weakness and helplessness, can above all generate the desire to believe that at least some people in the world care about one's fate, and are willing to empathetically share that burden which few of us would care to bear alone—a recognition that life is gradually coming to an end and that nature is depriving us of our body, our individuality, and our future.

30   In terms of financial obligations, there is considerable evidence from human experience in general, and from state efforts to impose financial burdens upon children in particular, that enforced legal obligations of children toward parents are mutually destructive. If only from the viewpoint of promoting family unity and affection, the provision of economic and medical care for the elderly by the government makes considerable sense. Ben Wattenberg quotes someone who nicely catches an important point: "We [older folks] don't like to take money from our kids. We don't want to be a burden. They don't like giving us money, either. We all get angry at each other if we do it that way. So we all sign a political contract to deal with what anthropologists would call the 'intergenerational transfer of wealth.' The young people *give* money to the government. I *get*

money from the government. That way we can both get mad at the government and keep on loving each other."

If the burden of economic care of the elderly can be difficult even for   31
the affluent, it can be impossible for the poor. Moreover, adults with elderly parents ought not to be put in the position of trying to balance the moral claims of their own children against those of their parents, or jeopardizing their own old age in order to sustain their parents in their old age. Though such conflicts may at times be inescapable, society ought to be structured in a way that minimizes them. The great increase in life expectancy provides a solid reason, if one was ever needed, for arguing that all of us collectively through the state—rather than the children of the elderly—should supply their basic economic support. Both parents and children legitimately want an appropriate independence, not the kind that sunders their relationship altogether or makes it merely contingent upon active affection. A balance is sought between that independence which enables people to have a sense of controlling their own destinies, and those ties of obligation and affection that render each an indispensable source of solace in the face of a world that has no special reason to care for them.

A minimal duty of any government should be to do nothing to hinder,   32
and if possible do something to protect, the natural moral and filial ties that give families their power to nurture and sustain. To exploit that bond by coercively taxing families is, I believe, to threaten them with great harm. It is an action that presupposes a narrower form of moral obligation of children to parents than can rationally be defended. At the same time it promises to rupture those more delicate moral bonds, as powerful as they are conceptually elusive, that sustain parents and children in their lives together. Such bonds do not necessarily rule out financial incentives for children to care for their aged parents, as some recent legislative proposals suggest. But if such incentives are to receive support, in that case considerable care would be needed to guard against an exploitation of parents by avaricious children. There are, I ruefully note, as many ways to corrupt the parent-child relationship as ways to sustain it.

QUESTIONING AND DISCUSSING

Callahan, "What Do Children Owe Elderly Parents?"

1. What are the "significant moral issues" raised by the Reagan administration's attempt to make adult children more responsible for their elderly parents? Why, in Callahan's view, is it "still by no means clear what each morally owes to the other"?

2. The abstract of this article, originally published in *The Hastings Center Report*, is as follows: "On a scale of moral priorities, children owe affection and some kinds of care to elderly parents, but their principle economic duties are to their own offspring." How does Callahan delineate this "scale of moral priorities"? What is your response to it?

3. Research economic and medical issues of concern to older people in such popular magazines as *AARP* and in news reports regarding Medicare and initiatives promoted (or thwarted) by the federal government. What additional perspective do these contexts bring to your reading of Callahan's article? With what result? How do the issues articulated in the 1980s seem relevant and controversial today?

4. Carefully consider (and, if it would be helpful, research) Callahan's view that "A minimal duty of any government should be to do nothing to hinder, and if possible do something to protect, the natural moral and filial ties that give families their power to nurture and sustain." Is this a defensible position in moral and political terms? Why or why not?

⊞

LOUIS MENAND

Louis Menand is Distinguished Professor of English at the City University of New York Graduate Center. A regular contributor to *The New Yorker*, in which this article appeared, Menand earned his Ph.D. at Columbia University. Among his many books are *American Studies* (2003), *The Metaphysical Club* (2001), *The Future of Academic Freedom* (1998), and *Discovering Modernism: T. S. Eliot and His Context* (1987). Menand's essay about college admissions gave authoritative voice to the suspicions of many a nervous parent and college-bound high school senior.

The Thin Envelope
Why College Admissions Has Become Unpredictable

1   In the spring semester of my senior year of high school, my father got a call from the headmaster of the school I was about to graduate from. The headmaster said that he was expecting to speak soon with the admissions office at the single Ivy League college to which, on the headmaster's advice, I had applied. He was wondering whether my father planned to attend a local cocktail-party fund-raiser for my school that Sunday. My

father (rightly, in my opinion) hung up on him, and a few weeks later I received a rejection letter from the Ivy League college. This was my introduction to the meritocracy.

Apart from the tactlessness (made grotesque by the circumstance that I was a scholarship student), this little episode was not entirely anomalous. My headmaster was not gaming the system; the system was already a game. He ran what is known as a feeder school: for many years, its most favored students had been admitted to the Ivy League college to which I had applied. More qualified students applied than the college could accept, of course, which is why it continued to seek my headmaster's recommendations at the end of the admissions process. If the college could accommodate, say, six graduates (it was a small school), he could name them, and the college would not be disappointed. I expect that, as part of a tacit understanding, the best students were not encouraged to apply to the other Ivy League colleges, since most of them seemed, every year, to end up going to that one.

My headmaster assumed, therefore, that his school's reputation for getting students into this particular college was one reason parents paid to send their children there. Why he thought that he could squeeze a few more dollars from my family, which did not have the money to give, is something I've never understood; but, in the calculation of which high-school bodies get directed where, dollars are part of the equation. Headmasters of expensive prep schools are no longer given the degree of carte blanche they once enjoyed at college admissions offices (their powers were fading even in my time), but college admissions offices do have long-term "informal" relations with guidance counsellors at feeder schools. Colleges are sometimes told by counsellors which of two equally attractive applicants has wealthier parents, since that might increase the chances for a donation; or which applicant is less likely to qualify for financial aid; or which is more likely, if accepted, to enroll. These considerations may or may not figure in the final decision. It is a mistake, though, to imagine that they are never on the table.

In the ongoing debate about affirmative action, with the Supreme Court expecting to decide a case involving admissions procedures at the University of Michigan, the term "meritocracy" is a canard. American education is not meritocratic, and it never has been. Merit, defined as quantifiable aptitude and achievement, is just one of the variables that decide educational outcomes. Success in college admissions, as in almost every sphere of life, is a function of some combination of ability, connections, persistence, wealth, and special markers—that is, attributes valued for the difference they make to "the mix." Since 1978, the year of the Supreme

Court decision in Regents of the University of California v. Bakke, race has been a judicially approved special marker in higher education. As Justice Lewis Powell pointed out in the majority opinion, quoting from the amici curiae brief filed jointly for Columbia, Harvard, Stanford, and Penn, college admissions offices have always given preference to various types of candidates whose grades and standardized-test scores may be below average. They have done so because they have other institutional needs besides putting scholars in the classrooms. They have football teams to field, orchestras and marching bands to staff, student organizations to be led, alumni to be kept in a giving mood, and feeder schools to be kept in a feeding mood. They have a gender balance to preserve. They can't have ten times as many poets as physicists, or thirty students from Exeter and none from the local high school. Racial diversity, Powell concluded, is just another institutional need. What the Bakke decision basically said to universities was: Stop talking about redressing the effects of past discrimination and start talking about the educational benefits of mixed-race student bodies, and you'll be on the safe side of the law. It preserved the practice by changing the rationale.

5   How admissions offices contrive to meet all these institutional needs— how they manage to enroll pre-meds, painters, children of alumni ("legacies"), soccer players, Exeter grads, and African-Americans in roughly the same proportions, year after year—while maintaining (or improving) the college's median S.A.T. score is a good story, and it's made better by the understandable reluctance of most colleges to speak frankly about the process. In 1999, Jacques Steinberg, a reporter at the Times, was permitted to observe the selection of the class of 2004 at Wesleyan. "The Gatekeepers: Inside the Admissions Process of a Premier College" (Viking; $25.95) is his account. In 2001, James Fallows published an influential article in The Atlantic Monthly on the use of early admissions (the system that allows students who apply early to receive a quick decision), which drew on work done by Christopher Avery, Andrew Fairbanks, and Richard Zeckhauser; their book, "The Early Admissions Game: Joining the Elite" (Harvard; $29.95), has just been published. "The Gatekeepers" is mostly case studies of a small number of Wesleyan applicants; "The Early Admissions Game" is mostly statistical analyses of admissions rates at élite colleges. Together, they will pretty much scare the daylights out of people with children approaching college age (not to mention the children themselves). They do not show the admissions process to be unfair or corrupt; it is not—although Avery and his co-writers think that it is less transparent than it should be. They do show it to be, as psychiatrists say, highly overdetermined, affected by so many variables that it has become, for most intents and purposes, unpredictable. Avery and his colleagues describe college admissions as a

casino on Mars: you have to guess the rules of the game you are playing, and the rules can change while you are playing it.

There are many reasons that college admission has become so complex, but the main one is demand. In 1932, 1,330 people applied for admission to Yale. Seventy-two per cent—nine hundred and fifty-nine—were accepted. Eight hundred and eighty-four students enrolled; twenty-seven per cent of them were the sons of Yale graduates. Last year, Yale had 15,466 applicants and accepted 2,009, or thirteen per cent. Thirteen hundred enrolled; sixteen per cent were legacies. In 1999–2000, the eight Ivy League colleges together received 121,948 applications and rejected more than eighty per cent. This means that colleges like Harvard and Yale can cherry-pick their classes. If Harvard needs an outside linebacker, it can probably choose between an All-Division player with 1450 combined S.A.T. scores and an All-State with 1350. Yale can choose between a legacy, a Latina, and a national-science-competition finalist, depending on which hole needs another pigeon, each applicant with two 800s on the S.A.T.s (a credential known as "dialling toll-free"). Ivy League colleges can reach very deep into their pools before they start coming up with underqualified applicants.

Most colleges cannot go so deep. There are more than two thousand four-year colleges in the United States. Only about two hundred reject more students than they accept. The vast majority of American colleges accept eighty per cent or more of those who apply. But among the top fifty there is a constant Darwinian struggle to improve selectivity. These colleges want two things from their admissions offices: a low acceptance rate and a high matriculation rate (that is, a high percentage of admits who actually enroll—the "yield"). Both these numbers—the acceptance rate and the yield—figure in *U.S. News and World Report's* annual rankings of American colleges.

The *U.S. News* rankings began in 1983, and they drive colleges nuts, because they are based on notoriously unstable and sometimes incomparable categories, but they have a demonstrated effect on both applications and donations. They can make a college "hot" overnight. The factors that, this year, make Pomona fifth among liberal-arts colleges (tied with Carleton) and Middlebury seventh (tied with Bowdoin)—things like class size, alumni donations, and faculty salaries—are so prone to change that the rankings can flip during the summer, so that next year Middlebury might be able to begin its fundraising letter with the good news that it has leapfrogged from seventh to fifth in the national rankings, while Pomona's letter must boast of other things.

9   One of the colleges aggrieved by the *U.S. News* rankings is Cornell, which has several peculiarities that throw its numbers out of alignment with those of other Ivy League universities; it is cheaper to live in Ithaca than in Boston or New York, for example, so the average faculty salary is lower at Cornell, and this counts against it in the rankings. Ronald Ehrenberg, a Cornell economist frustrated with the rankings obsession, points out, in "Tuition Rising: Why College Costs So Much" (Harvard; $18.95), that the figures colleges send to *U.S. News* can, hypothetically, be massaged in any number of ways to yield a better ranking. If, for example, one alumna gives a million dollars and the rest of her class gives nothing, what *U.S. News* calls the "alumni giving rank" (total dollars) will be high, but the "alumni giving rate" (total participation) will be low. If you divide up the million dollars and send some to every member of the class, with the request that it be donated right back to Cornell, the rank will stay the same and the rate will shoot up to a hundred per cent. Similarly, the category "percentage of classes with fifty or more students" (the lower the percentage the better) leaves no room for a distinction between classes with sixty students and classes with six hundred. One class with six hundred will count much less against a college than ten classes with sixty.

10   The effect of the ranking system on admissions has been that colleges encourage as many applications as possible, even from students who are unlikely to be accepted, since this increases selectivity, and they place a premium on accepting students who are very likely to enroll, since this increases the yield. This is one of the reasons, according to the authors of "The Early Admissions Game," that so many selective colleges have instituted early-admissions programs. There are two types. Early Action programs allow students to submit applications before the regular deadline with the promise of a quick decision—accept, reject, or defer. Accepted students are still free to apply elsewhere. Early Decision programs, though, are binding on the applicants. If they are accepted, they are honor-bound (there is no legal penalty) to withdraw their applications to other colleges. Around twenty-five per cent of American colleges offer one or the other program, and a few have both. Among the Ivies, Harvard offers Early Action; the rest offer Early Decision.

11   The chief finding reached by the authors of "The Early Admissions Game" is that applying early significantly increases the chances of acceptance. Their conclusions are based on data from the admissions offices at fourteen élite colleges and on a survey of three thousand high-school seniors. The average student in their sample who applied Early Action increased his or her chances of admission by 18.9 percentage points; an Early Decision application increased the chances of the average applicant in the sample by 34.8 points. The authors calculate that the advantage is the

equivalent of a hundred additional points on the combined S.A.T. scores. An Early Decision application doubled the average applicant's chances at Brown and nearly tripled them at Princeton. An Early Action application nearly tripled the chances at Harvard. Half of all current Harvard students were early applicants; only ten per cent of the regular applicants to Harvard were accepted. This suggests that unless an applicant is what admissions officers call "hooked"—unless he or she is a legacy, a recruited athlete, or a "clear priority" (Wesleyan's label for nonwhite applicants)—the chances for acceptance in the regular pool are very reduced. As the college counsellor at the Collegiate School, in New York, told Avery and his co-authors, "If you're an 'unhooked' white male applying regular to Harvard or Princeton, might as well just stick a fork in you, because you're done."

Colleges argue that the early-admissions pool is stronger than the regular   12 pool, and that this accounts for the higher acceptance rate, but the authors of "The Early Admissions Game" dispute that claim. They find that Early Decision applicants at Princeton are admitted at close to three times the rate of regular applicants (fifty-five per cent versus nineteen per cent), but have lower average S.A.T. scores. In general, they conclude that Early Action applicants are slightly stronger on average than regular applicants, but that Early Decision applicants are weaker. "The Early Admissions Game" is intended as an exposé, for high-school students and their parents, of the realities of college admissions, but it is also a protest against the practice of early admissions. The authors believe that these programs benefit privileged students, who are more likely to get informed guidance about how the "game" is played; that they cheat disadvantaged students who do use them, because with Early Decision the students have to accept whatever aid package they are awarded under the standard formula; and that they entice students to choose a college before they have intelligently explored their options.

So why do colleges do it? There are several theories, not all compatible   13 but probably all relevant in one way or another. Early Decision programs obviously enhance the yield, since the ratio of admits to matricks in those programs is close to one. For some colleges, early admissions is a way of plucking a candidate from the pools of higher-ranked colleges. The comfort of knowing in January that you have been accepted by Wesleyan may outweigh the attractions of Yale, where the slope is somewhat steeper. But there are other considerations at work. For one thing, colleges do not always accept their strongest applicants. A shoo-in at Yale—an applicant who, in admissions talk, can "walk on water"—may be rejected at Wesleyan, on the theory that she will just be lowering the yield when she turns Wesleyan down to go to Yale. Admissions officers are wary of what they call "scalp-hunters," hot shots out to rack up acceptances. When they spot them, they mail them the thin envelope. Early Decision pro-grams guarantee the commitment of the stellar applicant—which is one reason their admission rate is so high. At the same time, a college can de-fer an Early Action applicant, if it thinks it is being used as a backup, and still have a chance to get him or her in the regular pool. Early admissions gives colleges more control over the process.

14   As Avery and his co-authors point out, though, early-admissions appli-cants are not necessarily stronger than regular applicants, and this points to another theory, which is that colleges use early admissions, particularly Early Decision, to select not the best students in the class but the weakest. There will be a bottom tier in every class, and early admissions is a way of handpicking it, making sure of getting students who really want to attend, and who satisfy one or another institutional need as well. It is also a way of taking care of the athletes and the legacies and the "clear priorities" right at the start. Knowing in January the makeup of a third of the in-coming class gives admissions committees greater flexibility down the road. A lot of poets in the early round makes it easier to pick the physicist later on (and is bad news for the poet who applies late). A high median S.A.T. in the group accepted by January—something that is more likely in the case of a college with Early Action Admissions—opens the door for the president's godson, whose hitherto undiagnosed allergy to No. 2 pen-cils probably explains his unusual test scores.

15   Finally, Avery and his colleagues think that there is a dollars issue. All the Ivies now have needs-blind admissions. Because candidates for early admission are more likely to be from affluent schools with well-informed guidance counsellors, they are also more likely to be "full pay" students. The odds are, therefore, that the more students a college takes in the early round, the less financial aid it is going to have to shell out in the end. And, as "The Early Admissions Game" points out, Early Decision pre-vents students who do need aid from using another offer to negotiate a better deal. They are not allowed to get another offer.

16   Is early admissions unfair, though? One of the effects of the increase in demand from the days when headmasters could chauffeur their preferred students into élite colleges is a shift in emphasis from what some admis-sions officers refer to as B.W.R.K.s—bright well-rounded kids—to what are known as "well-lopsided" students. It's no longer the students who are well-rounded, in other words; it's the class. This is why an applicant's spe-cial markers matter so much: differentiation is what colleges are looking for. Harvard rejects twenty-five percent of its "toll free" candidates. It is not looking for the perfect student; it is looking for the perfect class. In ef-fect, the admissions office has a dozen mini-quotas to fill. If it waits until

March, it is leaving a lot to chance. But increasing the predictability for the college is precisely what reduces the predictability for the applicant. Applicants have no idea which niche they are competing for, and at each college it's likely to be a different niche, anyway.

Most people feel that a heterogeneous class is better than a homogeneous one, and the fact that this makes it harder to get in does not mean that the process is unjust. It's just a supply-side system: excess demand gives the colleges the advantage in deciding what they want their student demographics to look like. And the truth is that anything that reduces the power of the S.A.T. is a good thing. It is absurd to believe that a test taken when a person is sixteen can predict how well that person will be performing when she is twenty-two. In fact, S.A.T. scores claim to predict academic performance only for the first year of college, and, even then, they explain less of the variation in grades than does high-school class rank or parents' education. They have little correlation with performance in the last two years, which is when students start to specialize. There seems to be a developmental jump that people make when they are nineteen or twenty which can render past measures of merit irrelevant. When you're suddenly publishing your stuff in *Poetry*, that 500 on the math S.A.T. seems pretty insignificant. 17

Still, the process can go haywire in interesting ways. Steinberg's book, on admissions at Wesleyan, makes it clear that a personal relationship with the school college counsellor and, either through the counsellor or directly, with an officer on the college's admissions committee can make a big difference for what might be called the average exceptional student, the applicant who is fully qualified, and even well-lopsided, but who happens not to walk on water. There are moments when the counsellor or the admissions officer can administer a crucial nudge to the application of a student he or she has a personal interest in. But then comes the one moment when the applicant has control: the moment he or she gets to decide whether to accept the acceptance. 18

At this point, a variable that is generally masked, or cosmetically altered, during the courtship ritual of admissions suddenly comes into play. This is the nature of college life itself. As Steinberg shows, admissions officers are not usually academics themselves. Their backgrounds tend to be in service work: they are people who have devoted their lives to helping people. Cornell is one of the few colleges where faculty play a regular role in admissions. At Wesleyan, the previous occupations of members of the admissions committee included (in 1999–2000) food-stamp interviewer, resident administrator in a psychiatric halfway house, high-school English teacher, and 19 management trainee at Sears. Admissions officers therefore tend to be highly interested in, and experienced judges of, character. At the same time, they may be a step removed from the realities of campus life. Their ideas about college can be a little purer than the situation merits.

20   One of the applicants Steinberg chose to track through the admissions process was Becca, a student at Harvard-Westlake, which is an élite private school near Los Angeles. Becca had been involved in a small scandal at Harvard-Westlake. On the way to class one day, she took a bite of a pot brownie another student was handing around. The student was caught (she had become ill), and Becca turned herself in. She was the only one of the several students who had eaten a piece of the brownie who did so, and though she was disciplined, she was also praised by the school administration for her integrity and maturity. The following year, she was elected president of the student government, and she became the chair of the honor board.

21   Becca and her college counsellor debated about what to do with this incident when she applied to college; they decided to make it a selling point, as a story about accepting responsibility and rising above past mistakes. Becca used the pot-brownie story as the subject of her application essay, and was turned down by all the top colleges to which she applied. At Wesleyan, the committee could not see the wisdom of admitting a student who had confessed to using drugs. The Wesleyan admissions officer whose district included Harvard-Westlake, though, believed the accept-responsibility-and-rise-above-past-mistakes line, and he contrived to get Becca onto the waiting list and then, surreptitiously, to the top of that list. A visit to Wesleyan was arranged for her. When she arrived, a student escort took her to the dorm where she would be staying. As soon as she entered the building, Becca could smell marijuana everywhere. Her visit turned out to coincide with what what is known at Wesleyan as Zonker Harris Day, a day devoted to the celebration of pot smoking. Becca was later accepted at Wesleyan, but she was also accepted off the waiting list at Cornell. She went to Cornell.

22   One of Becca's classmates at Harvard-Westlake was among the most heavily recruited high-school students in the country in 1999–2000. Her name was Julianna. She had missed only one question on her P.S.A.T.s, she was an accomplished dancer, and her father was black and Brazilian. She was wooed by dozens of colleges, and was accepted everywhere she applied, including Stanford, Texas, Chicago, Michigan, Swarthmore, Harvard, Wesleyan, and Yale. Wesleyan had been courting Julianna for several years, and believed that it had a chance to get her. A visit was arranged. Again, a student escort showed up to take her around. The escort asked

whether she would like to attend a meeting of a student club. Julianna said she would, and soon found herself sitting in a conference room with a dozen other students. One of them opened a bag and took out a collection of vibrators and other sex toys. It was a meeting of the Wesleyan University Cunt Club. Julianna went to Yale. It was a good thing for Yale, probably, that she did not visit the campus during the seven days of lectures, films, panels, concerts, and parties known as Campus-Wide Sex Week.

QUESTIONING AND DISCUSSING

Menand, "The Thin Envelope"

1. The caption under an illustration accompanying this article in *The New Yorker* reads, "The best colleges have so many well-qualified applicants to choose from that they can effectively cherry-pick their classes. How they contrive to enroll geniuses, legacies, athletes, and nonwhites in the same proportions every year is a good story." How does the word choice in this caption suggest the author's view of his subject? How does this wording affect the way you might approach this article?

2. What does this caption say about the relative influence of values on the part of college admissions committees? What are these values?

3. Why would an article like this appear in *The New Yorker*? That is, who reads this magazine? To whom is this article targeted? Why?

4. It could be argued that only students and families who benefit from elitist forms of education are the subject of this article. How might the implications of this article seem relevant to anyone who applies to college? Does what happens at selective colleges affect circumstances at less selective colleges? How and why?

⊞

RUTH ORKIN

Ruth Orkin (1921–1985) was given a Univex camera when she was ten, and she started developing her own photographs when she was twelve. She began by photographing celebrities in her native Hollywood but moved to New York in 1943. By day, she photographed babies; at night, she was a nightclub photographer. As her reputation grew, she began photographing renowned musicians (including Isaac Stern and Leonard Bernstein) and later was named one of the "Ten Top Women Photographers" in 1959. She took a noted series of photographs from the window of her Central Park West apartment to document the seasons and various day-to-day occurrences in New York. "An American Girl in Italy" is considered her signature photo.
⊞

QUESTIONING AND DISCUSSING

Orkin, "An American Girl in Italy"

1. Is there an implicit argument to "An American Girl in Italy"? What about the arrangement of people within the image supports your point of view: stance, expression, and the like?

2. Does the photograph evoke different responses if the reader of this image is female? Male? Should it make a difference? Why or why not?

3. Ruth Orkin captured this image as she worked in Italy on a project entitled "Don't Be Afraid to Travel Alone." The woman at the center of this photograph is an American art student Orkin met in Florence; Orkin took both staged and spontaneous photographs of her in various situations. This particular image happened spontaneously, as the art student walked through a group of men. At once cinematic and enigmatic, this photograph has been reproduced worldwide since its original publication in *Cosmopolitan* magazine in 1952. What kind of narrative do you tell yourself to explain what is happening in this photograph? Are you responding to gesture, expression, or something else? How is it that a silent, still photo can convey so much dramatic tension and a sense of story?

⊞

QUESTIONS FOR READING AND RESPONDING

Chapter 1 Becoming Myself:
What Kind of Person Do I Want to Be?

1. Analyze the content of Linda Pastan's "Ethics," looking at the questions that follow the poem. How might your conclusions about the poem's theme and conflict speak to the concerns voiced by other authors in this chapter? Consider, for instance, Stephan Crane's "The Blue Hotel," Mary E. Wilkins Freeman's "A Mistaken Charity," and Alice Walker's "Everyday Use" as ripe subjects for comparing and contrasting, using Pastan's poem as your lens.

2. Garrett Hardin's "Lifeboat Ethics" and Daniel Callahan's "What Do Children Owe Elderly Parents?" both deal controversially with ethical choices. Analyzing each piece carefully, consider the ways in which Callahan might respond to Hardin's position—and vice versa—or if such an exchange might even seem feasible. Conduct research, as appropriate and necessary, to give yourself other, substantive contexts for a response in addition to what you are able to infer from specific passages in each text.

3. What are the ways in which Ruth Orkin's "An American Girl in Italy" and Adrienne Rich's "When We Dead Awaken" raise issues that fall under the heading of "feminist ethics" as well as raising what might be generally accepted issues of values and ethics? You might consider and then argue how each piece sheds light on the other, conducting some research for additional contexts, as appropriate.

4. How do the selections in this chapter imply connections between privilege and decision making? Consider disparate works that include George Orwell's "Shooting an Elephant" and Louis Menand's "The Thin Envelope." What issues that reflect values might be found in these two very different essays?

⊞

2

Evaluating Ideas

How Do I Make Sense of My World?

"Justice is conscience, not a
personal conscience but the
conscience of the whole of
humanity. Those who clearly
recognize the voice of their
own conscience usually recognize also the voice of justice."

ALEXANDER SOLZHENITSYN (B. 1918),

Russian writer and winner of Nobel Prize in Literature (1970)

THE ONION

According to its website, *The Onion* is "a satirical weekly publication published 47 times a year on Thursdays" and refers to itself (humorously and seriously, it appears) as "America's Finest News Source." Known for its biting wit, humor, and intelligence, *The Onion*'s articles critique everything and everyone from celebrities to politicians and current events. This article appeared on *The Onion*'s website on September 24, 2003.

⊞

U.S. Government to Discontinue Long-Term, Low-Yield Investment in Nation's Youth

WASHINGTON, D.C.—In an effort to streamline federal financial holdings and spur growth, Treasury Secretary John Snow announced Monday that the federal government will discontinue its long-term, low-yield investment in the nation's youth.

President Bush explains the nation's new investment strategy at an inner-city school in Baltimore.

"For generations, we've viewed spending on our nation's young people   2
as an investment in the future," Snow said. "Unfortunately, investments
of this type take a minimum of 18 years to mature, and even then, there's
no guarantee of a profit. It's just not good business."

Snow compared funneling money into public schools, youth programs,   3
and child health-care clinics to letting the nation's money languish in a
low-interest savings account.

"This is taxpayer money we're talking about," Snow said. "We can't   4
keep pouring it into slow-growth ventures, speculating on a minuscule
payout some time in the future."

"Federal expenditures are recouped when a child grows up and becomes   5
a productive, taxpaying member of society," Snow said. "But we don't see
a sizable return on our investment unless a child invents something profitable, or cures a costly disease, like cancer. The wisdom of making such
long-range, long-shot investments is questionable at best, especially when
you consider inflation. America would do better to invest in profitable
business ventures. It's just that simple."

In the first quarter of 2004, the U.S. will scale back such youth-market   6
investments as Head Start, a federal preschool program for the poor, and
D.A.R.E., a drug-use prevention program for minors. Snow said such programs focus on preparing tomorrow's leaders at the expense of turning a
profit today. The extensive federal public-education system will also experience major cutbacks.

"With the economy showing signs of recovery, now is the time to cut   7
away the dead wood," Snow said. "As the stock market turns around, we
have a real opportunity to make some money. But that's only if we shift
the nation's funds into high-yield, short-term investments."

Snow said he plans to support the private sector with corporate subsi-   8
dies, and to invest overseas.

"This nation needs something really big to turn it around, something   9
like the '90s tech bubble," Snow said. "We need a winning business
model, something that after-school art workshops and inner-city basketball programs simply do not offer."

Federal Reserve Chairman Alan Greenspan expressed cautious support   10
for the divestments.

"Investments in our nation's young people have never yielded very im-   11
pressive gains," Greenspan said. "On the other hand, as the market im-
proves, disinflation is a major concern for future quarters. The education
system is a huge employer in this country, and consumer spending could
be affected."

12   Jack Carpenter, a financial consultant for Deloitte Touche Tohmatsu, said he is excited by the prospects for the nation's financial future.

13   "In such tough markets, the federal government should be putting its money in fliers, but instead, it's wasting it all on crawlers," Carpenter said. "Right now, we should focus on high-growth industries. Professional and technical services, finance and insurance, and information management are hot right now. Inner-city community youth programs—not so much."

14   Carpenter noted that not all investments in America's youth are low-yield, pointing to several youth-targeted efforts in the private sector that have generated immense returns.

15   "Coca-Cola and Microsoft," Carpenter said. "Both organizations have done very well in the youth market. Coke markets their beverages largely to children and young adults, showing steady gains. And Microsoft, maker of the X-Box, has increased profits and beat earnings expectations in each of the past eight quarters. The federal government has a lot to learn from these businesses."

16   In spite of an outcry from teachers and union leaders, Snow insisted that the divestment will be a boon for all Americans.

17   "Taking a student through high school costs the federal government nearly $100,000 in taxpayer money," Snow said. "If that figure upsets you,

An advertisement that supports divestment of our stake in the nation's youth.

then think about the times that we invest in a child and then he pulls out of the program before he matures."

Secretary of Education Rod Paige, whose post has historically been   18
strongly committed to investment in youth and the bridges from one century to the next, surprised many when he came out in favor of the controversial plan. Paige said data collected over the past five years shows
that there is reason to divest our stake in the nation's youth.

"Look at our recent graduates," Paige said. "So many recipients of years   19
of federal investments are laying around in a state of unemployment. It's
just not reasonable to continue to invest billions of dollars in such risky
ventures."

Paige was quick to add that the new investment strategy doesn't in-   20
volve dismantling the public school system, just restructuring it.

"The proposed plan actually includes *increased* investments in vouchers   21
for private schools," Paige said. "Through the years, we've seen consistent
returns from blue-chip schools."

In addition, Paige said Republican leaders are investing record levels of   22
federal money in support of President Bush's No Child Left Behind program, which calls for expanded testing, higher-quality teachers, and
greater achievement among students, particularly those in poor districts.

"Testing is exactly the sort of research the government should do before   23
making spending decisions," Paige said. "How else will we know which individuals are sound investments and which are likely to waste our time
and money?"

Questioning and Discussing

The Onion, "U.S. Government to Discontinue Long-Term, Low-Yield Investment in Nation's Youth"

1. Comment on the ways in which this satire takes the word *investment* and
   deliberately uses it in a context other than the one expected by the reader.
   What is the effect?

2. Given that this is, indeed, satire, what might be the more serious point of
   this article?

3. As noted elsewhere—particularly regarding Jonathan Swift's "A Modest
   Proposal" and Seth Stevenson's piece about term paper sites—satire works
   when conditions are such that it might suggest the truth. What do you infer,
   then, about the opinions behind the tone and content of this article regarding the political climate during which it was written? What in the article
   indicates this response?

4. What does the article seem to imply, then, about what the United States, as a whole, values? What are the ethical implications of this?

⊞

MARGARET ATWOOD

One of Canada's premier writers of poetry, fiction, and essays, Margaret Atwood (1939–) was educated at the University of Toronto, Radcliffe College, and Harvard University. She has taught at numerous colleges and universities, both in Canada and in the United States. Among her many books, essays, and volumes of poetry (with the first, entitled *Double Persephone*, published in 1961), Atwood's novel *The Handmaid's Tale* (1986) is among her most well known and is often compared with Aldous Huxley's *Brave New World*. *The Handmaid's Tale* won the *Los Angeles Times* Book Award, the Commonwealth Literature Prize, and the Arthur C. Clarke Award for Best Science Fiction (despite Atwood's protests that the book is not science fiction). "Pornography," first published in 1983, reflects Atwood's conviction that writing—especially the novel—exists for "social examination."

⊞

Pornography

1   When I was in Finland a few years ago for an international writers' conference, I had occasion to say a few paragraphs in public on the subject of pornography. The context was a discussion of political repression, and I was suggesting the possibility of a link between the two. The immediate result was that a male journalist took several large bites out of me. Prudery and pornography are two halves of the same coin, said he, and I was clearly a prude. What could you expect from an Anglo-Canadian? Afterward, a couple of pleasant Scandinavian men asked me what I had been so worked up about. All "pornography" means, they said, is graphic depictions of whores, and what was the harm in that?

2   Not until then did it strike me that the male journalist and I had two entirely different things in mind. By "pornography," he meant naked bodies and sex. I, on the other hand, had recently been doing the research for my novel *Bodily Harm,* and was still in a state of shock from some of the material I had seen, including the Ontario Board of Film Censors' "outtakes." By "pornography," I meant women getting their nipples snipped off with garden shears, having meat hooks stuck into their vaginas, being

disemboweled; little girls being raped; men (yes, there are some men) being smashed to a pulp and forcibly sodomized. The cutting edge of pornography, as far as I could see, was no longer simple old copulation, hanging from the chandelier or otherwise: it was death, messy, explicit and highly sadistic. I explained this to the nice Scandinavian men. "Oh, but that's just the United States," they said. "Everyone knows they're sick." In their country, they said, violent "pornography" of that kind was not permitted on television or in movies; indeed, excessive violence of any kind was not permitted. They had drawn a clear line between erotica, which earlier studies had shown did not incite men to more aggressive and brutal behavior toward women, and violence, which later studies indicated did.

Some time after that I was in Saskatchewan, where, because of the scenes in *Bodily Harm*, I found myself on an open-line radio show answering questions about "pornography." Almost no one who phoned in was in favor of it, but again they weren't talking about the same stuff I was, because they hadn't seen it. Some of them were all set to stamp out bathing suits and negligees, and, if possible, any depictions of the female body whatsoever. God, it was implied, did not approve of female bodies, and sex of any kind, including that practiced by bumblebees, should be shoved back into the dark, where it belonged. I had more than a suspicion that *Lady Chatterley's Lover*, Margaret Laurance's *The Diviners*, and indeed most books by most serious modern authors would have ended up as confetti if left in the hands of these callers.

For me, these two experiences illustrate the two poles of the emotionally heated debate that is now thundering around this issue. They also underline the desirability and even the necessity of defining the terms. "Pornography" is now one of those catchalls, like "Marxism" and "feminism," that have become so broad they can mean almost anything, ranging from certain verses in the Bible, ads for skin lotion and sex texts for children to the contents of *Penthouse*, Naughty '90s postcards and films with titles containing the word *Nazi* that show vicious scenes of torture and killing. It's easy to say that sensible people can tell the difference. Unfortunately, opinions on what constitutes a sensible person vary.

But even sensible people tend to lose their cool when they start talking about this subject. They soon stop talking and start yelling, and the name-calling begins. Those in favor of censorship (which may include groups not noticeably in agreement on other issues, such as some feminists and religious fundamentalists) accuse the others of exploiting women through the use of degrading images, contributing to the corruption of children, and adding to the general climate of violence and threat in which both women and children live in this society; or, though they may not give much of a hoot about actual women and children, they invoke moral standards and God's supposed aversion to "filth," "smut" and deviated *per-version*, which may mean ankles.

6   The camp in favor of total "freedom of expression" often comes out howling as loud as the Romans would have if told they could no longer have innocent fun watching the lions eat up Christians. It too may include segments of the population who are not natural bedfellows: those who proclaim their God-given right to freedom, including the freedom to tote guns, drive when drunk, drool over chicken porn and get off on videotapes of women being raped and beaten, may be waving the same anticensorship banner as responsible liberals who fear the return of Mrs. Grundy, or gay groups for whom sexual emancipation involves the concept of "sexual theater." *Whatever turns you on* is a handy motto, as is *A man's home is his castle* (and if it includes a dungeon with beautiful maidens strung up in chains and bleeding from every pore, that's his business).

7   Meanwhile, theoreticians theorize and speculators speculate. Is today's pornography yet another indication of the hatred of the body, the deep mind–body split, which is supposed to pervade Western Christian society? Is it a backlash against the women's movement by men who are threatened by uppity female behavior in real life, so like to fantasize about women done up like outsize parcels, being turned into hamburger, kneeling at their feet in slavelike adoration or sucking off guns? Is it a sign of collective impotence, of a generation of men who can't relate to real women at all but have to make do with bits of celluloid and paper? Is the current flood just a result of smart marketing and aggressive promotion by the money men in what has now become a multibillion-dollar industry? If they were selling movies about men getting their testicles stuck full of knitting needles by women with swastikas on their sleeves, would they do as well, or is this penchant somehow peculiarly male? If so, why? Is pornography a power trip rather than a sex one? Some say that those ropes, chains, muzzles and other restraining devices are an argument for the immense power female sexuality still wields in the male imagination: you don't put these things on dogs unless you're afraid of them. Others, more literary, wonder about the shift from the 19th-century Magic Woman or Femme Fatale image to the lollipoplicker, airhead or turkey-carcass treatment of women in porn today. The proporners don't care much about theory: they merely demand product. The antiporners don't care about it in the final analysis either: there's dirt on the street, and they want it cleaned up, now.

8   It seems to me that this conversation, with its *You're-a-prude/You're-a-pervert* dialectic, will never get anywhere as long as we continue to think of this material as just "entertainment." Possibly we're deluded by the

packaging, the format: magazine, book, movie, theatrical presentation. We're used to thinking of these things as part of the "entertainment industry," and we're used to thinking of ourselves as free adult people who ought to be able to see any kind of "entertainment" we want to. That was what the First Choice pay-TV debate was all about. After all, it's only entertainment, right? Entertainment means fun, and only a killjoy would be antifun. What's the harm?

This is obviously the central question: *What's the harm?* If there isn't any 9 real harm to any real people, then the antiporners can tsk-tsk and/or throw up as much as they like, but they can't rightfully expect more legal controls or sanctions. However, the no-harm position is far from being proven.

(For instance, there's a clear-cut case for banning—as the federal gov- 10 ernment has proposed—movies, photos and videos that depict children engaging in sex with adults: real children are used to make the movies, and hardly anybody thinks this is ethical. The possibilities for coercion are too great.)

To shift the viewpoint, I'd like to suggest three other models for looking 11 at "pornography"—and here I mean the violent kind.

Those who find the idea of regulating pornographic materials repugnant 12 because they think it's Fascist or Communist or otherwise not in accordance with the principles of an open democratic society should consider that Canada has made it illegal to disseminate material that may lead to hatred toward any group because of race or religion. I suggest that if pornography of the violent kind depicted these acts being done predominantly to Chinese, to blacks, to Catholics, it would be off the market immediately, under the present laws. Why is hate literature illegal? Because whoever made the law thought that such material might incite real people to do real awful things to other real people. The human brain is to a certain extent a computer: garbage in, garbage out. We only hear about the extreme cases (like that of American multimurderer Ted Bundy) in which pornography has contributed to the death and/or mutilation of women and/or men. Although pornography is not the only factor involved in the creation of such deviance, it certainly has upped the ante by suggesting both a variety of techniques and the social acceptability of such actions. Nobody knows yet what effect this stuff is having on the less psychotic.

Studies have shown that a large part of the market for all kinds of porn, 13 soft and hard, is drawn from the 16-to-21-year-old population of young men. Boys used to learn about sex on the street, or (in Italy, according to Fellini movies) from friendly whores, or, in more genteel surroundings, from girls, their parents, or, once upon a time, in school, more or less. Now porn has been added, and sex education in the schools is rapidly being phased out. The buck has been passed, and boys are being taught that all women secretly like to be raped and that real men get high on scooping out women's digestive tracts.

14　　Boys learn their concept of masculinity from other men: is this what most men want them to be learning? If word gets around that rapists are "normal" and even admirable men, will boys feel that in order to be normal, admirable and masculine they will have to be rapists? Human beings are enormously flexible, and how they turn out depends a lot on how they're educated, by the society in which they're immersed as well as by their teachers. In a society that advertises and glorifies rape or even implicitly condones it, more women get raped. It becomes socially acceptable. And at a time when men and the traditional male role have taken a lot of flak and men are confused and casting around for an acceptable way of being male (and, in some cases, not getting much comfort from women on that score), this must be at times a pleasing thought.

15　　It would be naïve to think of violent pornography as just harmless entertainment. It's also an educational tool and a powerful propaganda device. What happens when boy educated on porn meets girl brought up on Harlequin romances? The clash of expectations can be heard around the block. She wants him to get down on his knees with a ring, he wants her to get down on all fours with a ring in her nose. Can this marriage be saved?

16　　Pornography has certain things in common with such addictive substances as alcohol and drugs: for some, though by no means for all, it induces chemical changes in the body, which the user finds exciting and pleasurable. It also appears to attract a "hard core" of habitual users and a penumbra of those who use it occasionally but aren't dependent on it in any way. There are also significant numbers of men who aren't much interested in it, not because they're undersexed but because real life is satisfying their needs, which may not require as many appliances as those of users.

17　　For the "hard core," pornography may function as alcohol does for the alcoholic: tolerance develops, and a little is no longer enough. This may account for the short viewing time and fast turnover in porn theatres. Mary Brown, chairwoman of the Ontario Board of Film Censors, estimates that for every one mainstream movie requesting entrance to Ontario, there is one porno flick. Not only the quantity consumed but the quality of explicitness must escalate, which may account for the growing violence: once the big deal was breasts, then it was genitals, then copulation, then that was no longer enough and the hard users had to have more. The ultimate kick is death, and after that, as the Marquis de Sade[1] so boringly demonstrated, multiple death.

The existence of alcoholism has not led us to ban social drinking. On the other hand, we do have laws about drinking and driving, excessive drunkenness and other abuses of alcohol that may result in injury or death to others. 18

This leads us back to the key question: what's the harm? Nobody knows, but this society should find out fast, before the saturation point is reached. The Scandinavian studies that showed a connection between depictions of sexual violence and increased impulse toward it on the part of male viewers would be a starting point, but many more questions remain to be raised as well as answered. What, for instance, is the crucial difference between men who are users and men who are not? Does using affect a man's relationship with actual women, and, if so, adversely? Is there a clear line between erotica and violent pornography, or are they on an escalating continuum? Is this a "men versus women" issue, with all men secretly siding with the proporners and all women secretly siding against? (I think not; there *are* lots of men who don't think that running their true love through the Cuisinart is the best way they can think of to spend a Saturday night, and they're just as nauseated by films of someone else doing it as women are.) Is pornography merely an expression of the sexual confusion of this age or an active contributor to it? 19

Nobody wants to go back to the age of official repression, when even piano legs were referred to as "limbs" and had to wear pantaloons to be decent. Neither do we want to end up in George Orwell's *1984*, in which pornography is turned out by the State to keep the proles in a state of torpor, sex itself is considered dirty and the approved practice it only for reproduction. But Rome under the emperors isn't such a good model either. 20

If all men and women respected each other, if sex were considered joyful and life-enhancing instead of a wallow in germ-filled glop, if everyone were in love all the time, if, in other words, many people's lives were more satisfactory for them than they appear to be now, pornography might just go away on its own. But since this is obviously not happening, we as a society are going to have to make some informed and responsible decisions about how to deal with it. 21

---

1 *Marquis de Sade* Donatien Alphonse François (1740–1814), a French writer and soldier who was imprisoned for his cruelty and sexual perversions. When he died, he was insane. The word *sadism* comes from his name.

QUESTIONING AND DISCUSSING

Atwood, "Pornography"

1. What are the various definitions of *pornography* revealed in this essay? What was your definition before you read the essay? After? How do these views compare with one another?

2. How is the "sensible person" defined here? What is Atwood's "central question"? How effective is her argument?

3. Reread the final paragraph of the essay. Why does Atwood end the essay as follows: "But since this is obviously not happening, we as a society are going to have to make some informed and responsible decisions about how to deal with it." Why is there no clear answer here?

4. Does the advent of the Internet add to or detract from Atwood's argument? Support your point of view. How else have things changed—or not changed—in the two decades since this essay was written?

⊞

GERALD EARLY

Professor of English and African American Studies at Washington University in St. Louis, Gerald Early (1952–) received his PhD from Cornell and writes extensively about cultural studies and African American issues. He has also written a memoir and a volume of poetry. Among his many books are *One Nation Under a Groove: Motown and American Culture* (1995) and *Tuxedo Junction: Essays on American Culture* (1990). This essay was written in 1996; it is important to remember as you read it that Early is not an Afrocentrist.

Understanding Afrocentrism: Why Blacks Dream of a World Without Whites

The White man will never admit his real references. He will steal everything you have and still call you those names.

　　　　　　　　—Ishmael Reed, Mumbo Jumbo (1972)

Furthermore, no one can be thoroughly educated until he learns as much about the Negro as he knows about other people.

　　　　　　　　—Carter G. Woodson, The Mis-Education of the Negro (1933)

*[Alexander] Crummell's black nationalism was marked by certain inconsistencies,
but they derived from the inconsistencies and hypocrisy of American racism,
rather than from any intellectual shortcomings on his part. It was impossible to
create an ideology that responded rationally to an irrational system.*
                    —Wilson Jeremiah Moses, *Alexander Crummell:
                    A Study of Civilization and Discontent* (1989)

In a span of three weeks during the early spring semester of 1995, Angela   1
Davis and bell hooks, two notable black leftist, feminist thinkers, visited
the campus of Washington University in St. Louis, invited by different
student groups. They were generally well received, indeed, enthusiastically so. But there was, for each of them during these visits, something of
a jarring note, both involving black students.

Professor Davis, entertaining questions during a panel session after hav-   2
ing spoken earlier on the subject of prison reform, was asked by a black
woman student what she had to offer black people as a solution to their
problems. The student went on to explain that she did not consider herself an African American. She was simply an African, wishing to have
nothing to do with being an American or with America itself. She wanted
black people to separate themselves entirely from "Europeans," as she
called white Americans, and wanted to know what Davis could suggest to
further that aim.

Davis answered that she was not inclined to such stringent race separa-   3
tion. She was proud of being of African descent but wished to be around
a variety of people, not just people like herself. Davis felt further that
blacks should not isolate themselves but accept in partnership anyone
who was sincerely interested in the cause of overthrowing capitalism, a
standard and reasonable Marxist response to the "essentializing" of race in
a way that would divert true political engagement "against the system."
The student was visibly annoyed with the answer, which presumably
smacked of "white" intellectualism.

Professor bell hooks, after her address on ending racism and sexism in   4
America—love, I think, was the answer—was asked by a black woman
student how feminism was relevant to black women. Hooks explained
that feminism was not only for white women, that black women needed
to read more feminist texts, even if some of them were racist. After all,
Karl Marx was racist, but he did give the world a brilliant analysis of capitalism. She had said in her speech how disappointed she was that her
black women students at City College of New York were not inclined to
embrace feminism, rejecting it as something white. She felt that these
black women were unduly influenced by black male rappers who bashed
feminism. The answer did not persuade or please the student.

5   Later that day, I heard many black undergraduates dismiss hooks's talk as not addressing the needs of black people, as being too geared to the white feminists in the audience. Some were disturbed that hooks would feel that they formed their opinions on the basis of listening to rap records. None of this was said, necessarily, with hostility, but rather with regret and a shade of condescension that only the young can so keenly and innocently express when speaking about the foolishness of their elders.

6   I recall a fairly recent incident where a black student, a very bright young woman, asked if, when doing research, one had to acknowledge racist books. I told her that a certain amount of objectivity was part of the discipline of being a scholar. Anger at unjust or inaccurate statements and assessments was understandable, but personalizing everything often caused a kind of tunnel vision where crude self-affirmation seemed to be the only fit end of scholarship. She responded that she would refuse to acknowledge racist sources, that if the book was racist, then everything it said was tainted and should be disregarded.

7   The attitudes of these students have been shaped by Afrocentrism, an insistence by a growing number of black Americans on seeing the world from an "African-centered" perspective in response to the dominant "European-centered" perspective, to which they feel they have been subjected throughout their lives. Afrocentrism is many things and has many degrees of advocacy. It can range from the commercialism and pretense of the shallow holiday called Kwanza (no shallower, it should be said, than the commercialized celebration of Christmas) to the kente-cloth ads and nationalist talk that one finds in most black publications these days; from talk about racist European scholarship to a view that world culture is essentially African in origin and that Europeans are usurpers, thieves, and generally inferior. On the one hand, we have the recent cover story "Is Jesus Black?" in *Emerge*, an Afrocentric-tinged news magazine for the black middle class. The answer in this instance, of course, is clearly yes. (Obviously, this is grounds for competing claims between blacks and Jews; whatever can be said about Jesus' skin color or the religious movement that bears his name, there is no question that he was a Jew.) On the other hand, we have the first explicitly Afrocentric Hollywood western in Mario Van Peebles's 1993 film *Posse*, a jumbled multicultural critique of white fin-de-siècle imperialism and the myth of how the West was won.

8   No doubt, Afrocentrists specifically and black folk generally found it to be a signal victory that in the recent television dramatization of the love affair between Solomon and Sheba, Sheba was played by a black actress and Solomon by a swarthy Hispanic. In the 1959 Hollywood film version

of *Solomon and Sheba*, directed by King Vidor—who, incidentally, made the first all-black Hollywood film—Solomon was played by Yul Brynner and Sheba by Gina Lollobrigida. It is safe to say that the real Solomon and the real Sheba, if they ever existed, did not look remotely like any of the actors who ever played them. But whom we want them to look like is very important. The Afrocentrists will feel their triumph to be complete when black actors portray Beethoven, Joseph Haydn, Warren G. Harding, Alexander Hamilton, Hannibal, Abraham Lincoln, Dwight Eisenhower, Cleopatra, Moses, Jesus Christ, and Saint Augustine. Many African Americans are inclined to believe that any noted white with ambiguous ancestry must be black. They are also inclined to believe that any white with dark skin tones, one who hangs around blacks or who "acts black" in some way is truly black. At various times in my life, I have heard blacks argue vehemently that Madonna, Phoebe Snow, Keith Jarrett, Mae West, Ava Gardner, and Dorothy Parker were black, even though they did not have a shred of evidence to support the claims. Blacks have always been fascinated by "passing," by the possibility that some whites are really black—"fooling old massa," so to speak.

Afrocentrism is an intellectual movement, a political view, a historically   9
traceable evolution, a religious orthodoxy. It derives in part from Negritude and Pan-Africanism, which stressed the culture and achievements of Africans. Both movements were started by Africans, West Indians, and African Americans in response to European colonialism and the worldwide oppression of African-descended people. But Afrocentrism is also a direct offshoot of earlier forms of black nationalism, in which blacks around the world believed they had a special destiny to fulfill and a special consciousness to redeem. More important, Afrocentrism is a mood that has largely erupted in the past ten to fifteen years in response to integration, or, perhaps more precisely, to the failure of integration. Many blacks who have succeeded in the white world tend to feel most Afrocentric, although I think it would be a mistake to see Afrocentrism purely as middle class, since significant numbers of working-class blacks are attracted to some elements of it. The bourgeois, "midcult" element of Afrocentrism, nonetheless, is very strong. "Integrated" middle-class blacks see it as a demonstration of their race loyalty and solidarity with their brothers and sisters throughout the world, whether in American cities or on African farms. (It is worth noting the economic clout of the black middle class, which can be seen in the growing number of black Hollywood films and filmmakers, in new black magazines ranging from *Body and Soul* to

The Source to *Upscale,* and in the larger audience for black books. It is the market power of this class that has given Afrocentrism its force as a consumer ideology.)

10   So the middle-class black, having had more contact with whites and their institutions, is expected to speak for and to other blacks. Afrocentrism, like Negritude and Pan-Africanism, is meant to be an ideological glue to bring black people together, not just on the basis of color but as the expression of a cultural and spiritual will that crosses class and geographical lines. As W. E. B. Du Bois wrote in 1940: "Since the fifteenth century these ancestors of mine and their other descendants have had a common history; have suffered a common disaster and have one long memory. . . . The real essence of this kinship is its social heritage of slavery; the discrimination and insults; and this heritage binds together not simply the children of Africa, but extends through yellow Asia and into the South Seas. It is this unity that draws me to Africa."

11   Louis H. Farrakhan, the head of the Nation of Islam, is probably the most familiar figure associated with Afrocentrism. (Muhammad Ali introduced Islamic conversion to an even bigger public, suffering greatly for his religious and political beliefs and becoming the most noted and charismatic dissident of his era. Ali's prodigious athletic abilities and his genial temperament succeeded in endearing him to the American public despite his religion. He never became a member of Farrakhan's sect.) Farrakhan is a fiery preacher, prone to making extreme statements, with a militant flair and a racist edge, that have the conviction of truth among some blacks. He especially exploits the idea that he is a heroic black man at grave risk for daring to tell the truth about the white man. (Malcolm X used this device effectively, too.) He is also a master demagogue who exploits the paranoia of his audience. But then, as a friend once said to me, "What black person isn't justified in being at least half paranoid?"

12   Farrakhan has found three effective lines of entry among blacks, particularly voting blacks, that draw on the Afrocentric impulse: First, that Islam is the true religion of black people. (This has led to a move among black Christian leaders to point out with great vehemence the African origins of Christianity, to make it, in effect, a black religion.) Second, that black people need business enterprise in their community in order to liberate themselves (an old belief among blacks, going back to at least the early part of the nineteenth century). And third, that Jews of European descent (whom he calls "false Jews") are not to be trusted, a charge that exploits the current tension between blacks and Jews—and that Farrakhan has used to move into the black civil rights establishment. All three positions enjoy remarkable support within the black middle class, a situation that

has helped Farrakhan tap people's insecurities for his own purposes. The Nation of Islam may be famous for converting addicts and criminals, but above all, it wants, as all religions do, to win over the middle class, with its money, its respectability, and its organizational know-how.

Whatever might be said of Farrakhan's importance as a political figure in the black community or in the United States, he is a minor figure in the development of Afrocentrism. His position in the history of Afrocentrism is similar to that of, say, Rush Limbaugh in the development of American conservatism. He is, like Limbaugh, a figure the media can use to give a sellable face and voice to a unique temper among a group of people. For both Limbaugh and Farrakhan represent an intense sentimentality in American life, a yearning for a fantasized, idealized past of racial grandeur and simplicity. This sentimentality appeals powerfully to the black middle class, which yearns for a usable, untainted past. This partly explains why Farrakhan and the Muslims can often be found speaking to black college students. 13

In thinking about the connection between class and nationalistic feelings, it should be recalled that in Harriet Beecher Stowe's 1852 novel *Uncle Tom's Cabin*, the most light-complexioned blacks, the ones with the greatest skills, George, Eliza, and Cassy, return to Africa at the novel's end to retrieve their degraded patrimony. It might be said that this is purely Stowe's own perverse vision, since some of the fiercest advocates for returning to Africa have been Martin Delany, Alexander Crummell, and Marcus Garvey, all very dark men. Yet there is more than a little truth to the idea that class, caste, and race consciousness are closely interwoven. Nationalism of whatever sort has almost always been an affair of a disaffected middle class. And until the 1920s, the black middle class in America was disproportionately made up of light-skinned people. 14

The paradox of the bourgeois aspect of Afrocentrism is that it rejects cosmopolitanism as being "white" or "Eurocentric." Yet Afrocentrism has no other way of seeing cosmopolitanism except on the "Eurocentric" model, so it tries to make Africa for black Americans the equivalent of what Europe is for white Americans: the source of civilization. Indeed, by trying to argue that Africa is the source of Western civilization, the Afrocentric sees the African, symbolically, as the mother of white Europe (just as the black mother, the mammy, is the mythic progenitor of the white South, or so Langston Hughes seemed to believe, in his famous short story "Father and Son," which became his even more famous play *Mulatto*). The African becomes, in this view, the most deeply cultured person on the planet, which matches his status as the oldest person on the planet, with the longest and deepest genetic history. In short, Afrocentrism becomes another form of the American apologizing for being American to people he imagines are 15 his cultural superiors. Afrocentrism tries to mask a quest for American filiopiety behind a facade of African ancestor and culture worship.

16 It would be easy, on one level, to dismiss Afrocentrism as an expression, in white workplaces and white colleges, of intimidated black folk who are desperately trying to find a space for themselves in what they feel to be alien, unsympathetic environments. Seen this way, Afrocentrism becomes an expression of the low self-esteem and inferiority that blacks feel most intensely when they are around whites; their response is to become more "black," estranged from the environment that they find so unaccepting of them. The greatest psychic burden of the African American is that he must not only think constantly about being different but about what his difference means. And it might be suggested that Afrocentrism does not solve this problem but merely reflects it in a different mirror. There is a certain amount of truth to this, especially at a time when affirmative action, which promotes group identification and group difference, tends to intensify black self-consciousness. And black people, through no fault of their own, are afflicted with a debilitating sense of self-consciousness when around whites. When whites are in the rare situation of being a minority in a sea of blacks, they often exhibit an abject self-consciousness as well, but the source of that self-consciousness is quite different. The white is used to traveling anywhere in the world and having his cultural inclinations accommodated. The black is neither used to this nor does he realistically expect it. The European exults in his culture, while the African is utterly degraded by his. That blacks should want to free themselves from the white gaze seems not merely normal but essential to the project of reconstructing themselves as a people on their own terms. And the history of blacks in the United States has been an ongoing project—tragic, pathetic, noble, heroic, misguided, sublime—of self-reconstruction.

> When it comes to black folk in America, the white man wants to say that if you have a ⅟32 portion of black blood, a mere drop of black blood, then you are black, no matter what your skin color. But when it comes to the ancient Egyptians, it doesn't matter if they have a drop of black blood—and we know that they had at least a ⅟32 portion of African blood. It doesn't matter how much African blood they have, they are still white. The white man wants to have his cake and eat it too. When it's convenient he wants you to be black, and when it's convenient he wants you to be white. Either you're a nigger, because he thinks you're nothing. Or you're white, if you have done anything he's bound to respect. The white man wants to control all the definitions of blackness.
>
> —A conversation with an Afrocentric friend

. . . There are several texts that might be considered the literary and in- 17
tellectual cornerstones of the Afrocentrism movement. Molefi K. Asante,
professor and chair of African American studies at Temple University in
Philadelphia, is credited with inventing the name "Afrocentrism" or
"Afrocentricity" (although currently the term "Africentrism" is on the
rise in certain quarters, probably because there is a group of black folk
who, for some reason, despise the prefix "Afro," as if the word "Africa" itself
were created by the people of the continent rather than by Europeans).
Asante's very short books, including *The Afrocentric Idea*, published in
1987, and *Afrocentrcity: The Theory of Social Change*, published in 1980,
are frequently the starting points for people seeking a basic explanation of
this ideology. As defined by Asante, Afrocentrism seems to take the terms
and values of Eurocentrism—intense individualism, crass greed, lack of
spirituality, warlike inclinations, dominance and racism, dishonesty and
hypocrisy—and color their opposites black, giving us a view of black
people not terribly different from the romantic racism of Harriet Beecher
Stowe and other whites like her in the nineteenth and twentieth centuries. I cannot recount the number of "race sensitivity" meetings I have
attended where blacks begin to describe themselves (or those they perceive
to be Africans) as more spiritual, more family-oriented, more community-
oriented, more rhythmic, more natural, and less combative than whites.
All of which is, of course, a crock of nonsense, largely the expression of
wishes for qualities that blacks see as absent from their community life
now. But, thanks to Asante, this has become the profile of the African in
the Afrocentric vision.

Martin Bernal's massively researched two-volume *Black Athena* (pub- 18
lished in 1987 and 1991) is a popular title in Afrocentric circles, in large
measure because Bernal, a Professor at Cornell, is one of the few white
scholars to take Afrocentrism seriously—William Piersen, Robert Farris
Thompson, and Andrew Hacker, in decidedly different ways, are others—
and one of the few to write an academic treatise in its defense that forces
whites to take it seriously too. (The irony that blacks still need whites, in
some measure, to sell their ideas and themselves to other whites is not entirely lost on those who have thought about this.)

Black Athena supports three major contentions of the Afrocentrists: 19
1) ancient Egypt was a black civilization; 2) the Greeks derived a good
deal, if not all, of their philosophy and religion from the Egyptians; 3)
European historiography has tried strenuously and with clear political
objectives to deny both. Bernal's book provoked a scathing attack by
Mary R. Lefkowitz, a professor at Wellesley, who characterizes Afrocentrism as a perversion of the historiography of antiquity and a degradation
of academic standards for political ends. Lefkowitz has also battled with

Tony Martin, a cultural historian, barrister, and Marcus Garvey specialist, who began using and endorsing the Nation of Islam's anti-Semitic *The Secret Relationship Between Blacks and Jews* (Volume 1) in his classes on slavery at Wellesley. Martin responded in 1993 with his own account of the dispute, *The Jewish Onslaught: Despatches from the Wellesley Battlefront,* which elaborates his claims of Jewish racism and the hypocrisy of academic freedom. . . .

20   Perhaps the most popular Afrocentric text is Chancellor Williams's *The Destruction of Black Civilization: Great Issues of a Race from 4500 BC to 2000 AD* (published in 1987), an account of his exhaustive research trips to Africa. Although not directly trained in the study of African history, Williams studied under William Leo Hansberry, a history professor at Howard University and probably the leading black American authority on Africa during the 1930s, 1940s, and 1950s. Hansberry did path-breaking work in an utterly neglected field, eventually becoming known as "the father of African studies" in the United States. (Scholars, until recently, did not think Africa had a "history." The continent, especially its sub-Saharan regions, had an "anthropology" and an "archaeology," folkways to be discovered and remains to be unearthed, but never a record of institutions, traditions, political ideologies, and complex societies.) Williams also did reasearch on African history at Oxford and at the University of London, where, because of colonialism, interest in the nature of African societies was far keener than in the United States. His book *The Re-Birth of African Civilization,* an account of his 1953–1957 research project investigating the nature of education in Europe and Africa, calls for Pan-African education of blacks in Africa and around the world. Williams concluded that "European" and "Eurocentric" education was antithetical, both politically and intellectually, to African interests, a common refrain in Afrocentrist thought. . . .

21   In some ways, the rise of Afrocentrism is related to the rise of "black psychology" as a discipline. The Association of Black Psychologists was organized in 1968, a time when a number of black professional offshoots were formed in political and ideological protest against the mainstream, white-dominated versions of their organizations. Somewhat later came the *Journal of Black Psychology,* given impetus by the initial assaults against black intelligence or pointed suggestions of black genetic inferiority by Richard Herrnstein, Arthur Jensen, and others in the early 1970s; this was also the time of the first wave of court challenges against affirmative action. The black psychology movement argued for new modes of treatment for black mental illness, the medical efficacy of using black history to repair a collectively damaged black psyche, and the destruction of "Eurocentrism" and the values it spawned—from the idealization of white standards of beauty to the scientific measurement of intelligence—as to-

tally inimical to the political and psychological interests of black people. Rationality, order, individualism, dominance, sexual repression as well as sexual license, aggression, warmaking, moneymaking, capitalism itself— all soon became "white values."

That all of this happened during the era of Vietnam War protests, when white Western civilization was coming under withering intellectual attack from the radical left, is not without significance. Radical white intellectuals, who otherwise had no more use for a black epic history than a white one, found the black version useful as a weapon against "Eurocentrism," which, as a result of the Vietnam War, they held in utter contempt. In short, Jean-Paul Sartre and Susan Sontag were as instrumental, albeit indirectly, in the formation of Afrocentrism as, say, the Black Power movement of the late 1960s or the writings of African psychiatrist Frantz Fanon, whose *The Wretched of the Earth* became the revolutionary psychological profile of the oppressed black diaspora. Also occurring at this time was the movement on white college campuses to establish black studies programs, which provided a black intellectual wedge into the white academy. These programs, largely multidisciplinary, required an ideological purpose and mission to bind together the various disciplines, which is why many began to articulate some kind of Afrocentrism or, as it was called in the 1970s, "black aesthetic"—in other words, an ideological framework to give black studies a reason for being. When used to challenge the dominance of Western thought, Afrocentrism becomes part of a multicultural wave of complaint and resentment against the white man by a number of groups that feel they have been oppressed.

In an age of dysfunction and psychotherapy, no one can have greater claim to having been made dysfunctional by political oppression than the African American, who was literally a slave; and no one can have a greater need for recourse to psychotherapy in the form of Afrocentrism. But what made the black psychology movement possible was the rise of the Nation of Islam, particularly the rise of Malcolm X.

The charismatic Muslim minister did two things. First, he forced the white mainstream press to take notice of black nationalism, Pan-Africanism, and the concept of African unity. Previously these ideas had been marginalized as ridiculous or even comic expressions of black nationalism, to be read by blacks in block barbershops and beauty salons as they thumbed through the Ripley's-Believe-It-or-Not-type work of the self-taught black historian J. A. Rogers (*One Hundred Amazing Facts about the Negro, Five Negro Presidents*, and the like). Malcolm X revitalized the ideas of Marcus Garvey, the great black nationalist leader of the 1910s and 1920s, whose Universal Negro Improvement Association became, for a time, one of the most popular black political groups in America. Malcolm,

22

23

24

like Garvey, felt that the Negro still needed to be "improved," but unlike Garveyites, the Muslims did not offer costumes and parades but sober suits, puritanical religion, dietary discipline, and no-nonsense business practices. Malcolm himself was also, by his physical appearance alone, a figure who would not be dismissed as a buffoon, as Garvey often was by both blacks and whites. According to Malcolm's *Autobiography*, his father had been a Garveyite as well as a wife beater who favored his lighter-skinned children. Malcolm's Islamic-based black nationalism, his sexual abstinence, which lasted from his religious conversion until his marriage a decade later, and his triumph over his own preference for lighter-skinned blacks and whites were all meant to demonstrate vividly how he superseded his father as a nationalist and how the Nation of Islam had superseded Garveyism.

25   Malcolm enlisted a body of enforcers, the feared Fruit of Islam, grim-faced men who, one imagines, were supposed to personify the essence of an unbowed yet disciplined black manhood. In this way, he dramatically associated black nationalism with a new type of regenerated black male. It was said in the black community, and may still be, that no one bothers a Muslim for fear of retribution from the Fruit of Islam. Certainly, there was a point in the development of the Fruit of Islam and the Nation itself in the 1960s and early 1970s (Malcolm was assassinated in 1965) when both were closely associated with racketeering and gangster activity. During this period, many East Coast mosques were among the most terrifying organizations in the black community.

26   Second, Malcolm, in his *Autogiography,* also managed to link the psychological redemption of the Negro with his reacquaintance with his history. The prison chapters of the *Autobiography* have become nearly mythic as a paradigm of black reawakening. Malcolm's religious conversion became, in a sense, the redemption of the black male and the rehabilitation of black masculinity itself. Lately, we have seen two major black male public figures who were incarcerated for serious crimes, Marion Barry and Mike Tyson, use the Malcolm paradigm to resuscitate their standing with the black public. The martyrdom of Malcolm gave this paradigm a blood-endorsed political heroism that has virtually foreclosed any serious criticism of either its origins or its meaning.

27   It is extraordinary to contemplate how highly regarded Malcolm X is in the black community today, especially in comparison with Martin Luther King. (When I wrote an article for *Harper's Magazine* that was critical of Malcolm X, I received three death threats.) Despite the fact that King's achievements were enormous—and that Malcolm left really nothing behind other than a book—King's association with integration, with nonviolence, even with Christianity has reduced him in the eyes of many blacks. When blacks in major cities, inspired by figures like Malcolm X

and the romanticization of Africa that Malcolm's nationalism wrought, began to organize African-oriented celebrations, such as my aunts did in Philadelphia with the creation of the Yoruba-inspired Odunde festival in 1975, then Afrocentrism has succeeded not only in intellectual spheres but on the grassroots level as well. Its triumph as the legitimation of the black mind and the black aesthetic vision was complete.

Afrocentrism may eventually wane in the black community, but proba- 28 bly not very soon. Moreover, a certain type of nationalistic mood, a kind of racial preoccupation, will always exist among blacks. It always has, in varying degrees. Homesickness is strong among black Americans, although it is difficult to point to a homeland. What Afrocentrism reflects is the inability of a large number of black people to deal with the reality of being American and with the meaning of their American experience.

Stanley Crouch is right in pointing out that the Afrocentrist is similar 29 to the white Southerner after the Civil War. To black nationalists, the lost war was the "war of liberation" led by black "revolutionaries" in the late 1960s, which in their imagination was modeled on the struggles against colonialism then taking place around the world. (The enslavement of the Africans, of course, was an earlier lost war, and it also weighs heavily on the Afrocentrist. He, like the white Southerner, hates the idea of belonging to a defeated people.) This imaginative vision of a restored and indomitable ethnicity is not to be taken lightly. In a culture as driven by the idea of redemption and as corrupted by racism as this one, race war is our Armageddon. It can be seen in works as various as Thomas Jefferson's *Notes on the State of Virginia,* David Walker's *Appeal to the Colored Citizens of the World,* Joseph Smith's *Book of Mormon,* D. W. Griffith's *Birth of a Nation,* and Mario Van Peebles's *Posse.*

Today, Afrocentrism is not a mature political movement but rather a cul- 30 tural style and a moral stance. There is a deep, almost lyrical poignancy in the fantasy of the Afrocentrist, as there is in the white Southerner's. What would I have been had I not lost the war? The Afrocentrist is devoted to his ancestry and his blood, fixated on the set of traditions that define his nobility, preoccupied with an imagined lost way of life. What drives the Afrocentrist and the white Southerner is not the expression of a group self-interest but concern with pride and honor. One group's myth is built on the surface of honor and pride, the other on the total absence of them.

Like the white Southerner, the Afrocentrist is in revolt against liberal- 31 ism itself, against the idea of individual liberty. In a way, the Afrocentrist is right to rage against it, because liberalism set free the individual but did not encourage the development of a community within which the individual could flower. This is what the Afrocentrist wishes to retrieve, a place for himself in his own community. Wilson Jeremiah Moses, a black historian, is right: Afrocentrism is a historiography of decline, like the mythic epic of the South. The tragedy is that black people fail to see their "Americaniza-tion" as one of the great human triumphs of the past five hundred years. The United States is virtually the only country where the ex-masters and the ex-slaves try to live together as equals, not only by consent of the ex-masters but by the demand of the ex-slaves. Ironically, what the Afrocen-trist can best hope for is precisely what multiculturalism offers: the idea that American culture is a blend of many white and nonwhite cultures. In the end, although many Afrocentrists claim they want this blending, mul-ticulturalism will not satisfy. For if the Euro-American is reminded through this that he is not European or wholly white, the African American will surely be reminded that he is not African or wholly black. The Afrocentrist does not wish to be a mongrel. He wants, like the Southerner, to be pure.

32   Afrocentrism is intense now because blacks are in a special period of so-cial development in a nation going through a period of fearsome transi-tion. Social development, by its nature, is ambivalent, characterized by a sense of exchange, of gaining and losing. Afrocentrism, in its conservatism, is opposed to this ambivalence and to this sense of exchange. What blacks desire during these turbulent times is exactly what whites want: the secu-rity of a golden past that never existed. A significant number of both blacks and whites want, strangely, to go back to an era of segregation, a fantasy time between 1920 and 1955, when whites felt secure in a stable culture and when blacks felt unified and strong because black people were forced to live together. Afrocentrism wants social change without having to pay the psychic price for it. Perhaps many black folk feel that they have paid too much already, and who is to say they are not right.

33   The issue raised by Afrocentrism is the meaning and formation of iden-tity, which is the major fixation of the American, especially the black American. In a country that relentlessly promotes the myth of self-reliance because it is unable to provide any sense of security in a cauldron of capi-talistic change, identity struggle is so acute because so much is at stake. Afrocentrism may be wrong in many respects, and it certainly can be sti-fling and restrictive, but some of its impulses are right. In a culture where information and resources of knowledge are the main levers for social and economic advancement, psychological well-being has become increasingly important as, in the words of one scholar, "a social resource," just as "social networks of care and community support [have become] central features of a dynamic economy." Black folk know, and rightly so, that their individual identities are tied to the strength of their community. The struggle over black identity in the United States has been the struggle over the creation of a true black community here. What integration has done to the indi-

vidual black mind in the United States is directly related to what it has done to the black community. This is the first lesson we must learn. The second is that perhaps many black folk cling to Afrocentrism because the black *American* experience still costs more, requires more courage, than white Americans—and black Americans—are willing to admit.

QUESTIONING AND DISCUSSING

Early, "Understanding Afrocentrism"

1. Why is it somehow befitting the subject of this article that as I write these questions using Microsoft *Word*, the automatic dictionary didn't recognize the word *Afrocentrism* and underlined it in red? What does this say about the values of those who create the preferences and parameters for Word?
2. Why does Early say that "[t]he issue raised by Afrocentrism is the meaning and formation of identity, which is the major fixation of the American, especially the black American"? How is this point revealed elsewhere in the essay?
3. What are the various permutations of Afrocentrism, and how does Early use these to explain the appeal of this ideology?
4. How are Afrocentrism and Eurocentrism similar? Different? How does Early discuss each of these ideologies, and for what purpose?

⊞

NATHANIEL HAWTHORNE

Nathaniel Hawthorne (1804–1864) was born in Salem, Massachusetts, the descendant of a venerable Puritan family. He attended Bowdoin College in Maine and upon graduation determined to make his living as a writer. While living with his mother for the next twelve years, he produced a number of short stories (including "Young Goodman Brown," first published in 1835). Alternative culture in the United States at that time was profoundly idealistic, and Hawthorne joined an experimental utopian community in Massachusetts called Brook Farm. Although he left Brook Farm after a few months, he maintained friendships with the leading figures of transcendentalism, New England's literary and philosophical movement, including writer-philosophers Ralph Waldo Emerson and Henry David Thoreau. Hawthorne's best-known writings explore the darker recesses of the American character and express ambivalence toward women and sexuality. His best-known novel, *The Scarlet Letter*, was published in 1850.

⊞

Young Goodman Brown

1   Young Goodman Brown came forth at sunset into the street at Salem village; but put his head back, after crossing the threshold, to exchange a parting kiss with his young wife. And Faith, as the wife was aptly named, thrust her own pretty head into the street, letting the wind play with the pink ribbons of her cap while she called to Goodman Brown.

2   "Dearest heart," whispered she, softly and rather sadly, when her lips were close to his ear, "prithee put off your journey until sunrise and sleep in your own bed to-night. A lone woman is troubled with such dreams and such thoughts that she's afeard of herself sometimes. Pray tarry with me this night, dear husband, of all nights in the year."

3   "My love and my Faith," replied young Goodman Brown, "of all nights in the year, this one night must I tarry away from thee. My journey, as thou callest it, forth and back again, must needs be done 'twixt now and sunrise. What, my sweet, pretty wife, dost thou doubt me already, and we but three months married?"

4   "Then God bless youe!" said Faith, with the pink ribbons; "and may you find all well when you come back."

5   "Amen!" cried Goodman Brown. "Say thy prayers, dear Faith, and go to bed at dusk, and no harm will come to thee."

6   So they parted; and the young man pursued his way until, being about to turn the corner by the meeting-house, he looked back and saw the head of Faith still peeping after him with a melancholy air, in spite of her pink ribbons.

7   "Poor little Faith!" thought he, for his heart smote him. "What a wretch am I to leave her on such an errand! She talks of dreams, too. Methought as she spoke there was trouble in her face, as if a dream had warned her what work is to be done tonight. But no, no; 't would kill her to think it. Well, she's a blessed angel on earth; and after this one night I'll cling to her skirts and follow her to heaven."

8   With this excellent resolve for the future, Goodman Brown felt himself justified in making more haste on his present evil purpose. He had taken a dreary road, darkened by all the gloomiest trees of the forest, which barely stood aside to let the narrow path creep through, and closed immediately behind. It was all as lonely as could be; and there is this peculiarity in such a solitude, that the traveller knows not who may be concealed by the innumerable trunks and the thick boughs overhead; so that with lonely footsteps he may yet be passing through an unseen multitude.

9   "There may be a devilish Indian behind every tree," said Goodman Brown to himself; and he glanced fearfully behind him as he added, "What if the devil himself should be at my very elbow!"

His head being turned back, he passed a crook of the road, and, looking   10
forward again, beheld the figure of a man, in grave and decent attire,
seated at the foot of an old tree. He arose at Goodman Brown's approach
and walked onward side by side with him.

"You are late, Goodman Brown," said he. "The clock of the Old South   11
was striking as I came through Boston, and that is full fifteen minutes
agone."

"Faith kept me back a while," replied the young man, with a tremor in   12
his voice, caused by the sudden appearance of his companion, though not
wholly unexpected.

It was now deep dusk in the forest, and deepest in that part of it where   13
these two were journeying. As nearly as could be discerned, the second
traveller was about fifty years old, apparently in the same rank of life as
Goodman Brown, and bearing a considerable resemblance to him, though
perhaps more in expression than features. Still they might have been
taken for father and son. And yet, though the elder person was as simply
clad as the younger, and as simple in manner too, he had an indescribable
air of one who knew the world, and who would not have felt abashed at
the governor's dinner table or in King William's court, were it possible
that his affairs should call him thither. But the only thing about him that
could be fixed upon as remarkable was his staff, which bore the likeness of
a great black snake, so curiously wrought that it might almost be seen to
twist and wriggle itself like a living serpent. This, of course, must have
been an ocular deception, assisted by the uncertain light.

"Come, Goodman Brown," cried his fellow-traveller, "this is a dull pace   14
for the beginning of a journey. Take my staff, if you are so soon weary."

"Friend," said the other, exchanging his slow pace for a full stop, "hav-   15
ing kept covenant by meeting thee here, it is my purpose now to return
whence I came. I have scruples touching the matter thou wot'st of."

"Sayest thou so?" replied he of the serpent, smiling apart. "Let us walk   16
on, nevertheless, reasoning as we go; and if I convince thee not thou shalt
turn back. We are but a little way in the forest yet."

"Too far! too far!" exclaimed the goodman, unconsciously resuming his   17
walk. "My father never went into the woods on such an errand, nor his father before him. We have been a race of honest men and good Christians
since the days of the martyrs; and shall I be the first of the name of Brown
that ever took this path and kept ——"

"Such company, thou wouldst say," observed the elder person, interpret-   18
ing his pause. "Well said, Goodman Brown! I have been as well acquainted
with your family as with ever a one among the Puritans; and that's no trifle
to say. I helped your grandfather, the constable, when he lashed the
Quaker woman so smartly through the streets of Salem; and it was I that

brought your father a pitch-pine knot, kindled at my own hearth, to set fire to an Indian village, in King Philip's war. They were my good friends, both; and many a pleasant walk have we had along this path, and returned merrily after midnight. I would fain be friends with you for their sake."

19 "If it be as thou sayest," replied Goodman Brown, "I marvel they never spoke of these matters; or, verily, I marvel not, seeing that the least rumor of the sort would have driven them from New England. We are a people of prayer, and good works to boot, and abide no such wickedness."

20 "Wickedness or not," said the traveller with the twisted staff, "I have a very general acquaintance here in New England. The deacons of many a church have drunk the communion wine with me; the selectmen of divers towns make me their chairman; and a majority of the Great and General Court are firm supporters of my interest. The governor and I, too—But these are state secrets."

21 "Can this be so?" cried Goodman Brown, with a stare of amazement at his undisturbed companion. "Howbeit, I have nothing to do with the governor and council; they have their own ways, and are no rule for a simple husbandman like me. But, were I to go on with thee, how should I meet the eye of that good old man, our minister, at Salem village? Oh, his voice would make me tremble both Sabbath day and lecture day."

22 Thus far the elder traveller had listened with due gravity; but now burst into a fit of irrepressible mirth, shaking himself so violently that his snake-like staff actually seemed to wriggle in sympathy.

23 "Ha! ha! ha!" shouted he again and again; then composing himself, "Well, go on, Goodman Brown, go on; but, prithee, don't kill me with laughing."

24 "Well, then, to end the matter at once," said Goodman Brown, considerably nettled, "there is my wife, Faith. It would break her dear little heart; and I'd rather break my own."

25 "Nay, if that be the case," answered the other, "e'en go thy ways, Goodman Brown. I would not for twenty old women like the one hobbling before us that Faith should come to any harm."

26 As he spoke he pointed his staff at a female figure on the path, in whom Goodman Brown recognized a very pious and exemplary dame, who had taught him his catechism in youth, and was still his moral and spiritual adviser, jointly with the minister and Deacon Gookin.

27 "A marvel, truly, that Goody Cloyse should be so far in the wilderness at nightfall," said he. "But with your leave, friend, I shall take a cut through the woods until we have left this Christian woman behind. Being a stranger to you, she might ask whom I was consorting with and whither I was going."

"Be it so," said his fellow-traveller. "Betake you to the woods, and let me   28
keep the path."

Accordingly the young man turned aside, but took care to watch his   29
companion, who advanced softly along the road until he had come within
a staff's length of the old dame. She, meanwhile, was making the best of
her way, with singular speed for so aged a woman, and mumbling some
indistinct words—a prayer, doubtless—as she went. The traveller put
forth his staff and touched her withered neck with what seemed the
serpent's tail.

"The devil!" screamed the pious old lady.   30

"Then Goody Cloyse knows her old friend?" observed the traveller,   31
confronting her and leaning on his writhing stick.

"Ah, forsooth, and is it your worship indeed?" cried the good dame.   32
"Yea, truly is it, and in the very image of my old gossip, Goodman Brown,
the grandfather of the silly fellow that now is. But—would your worship
believe it?—my broomstick hath strangely disappeared, stolen, as I suspect, by that unhanged witch, Goody Cory, and that, too, when I was all
anointed with the juice of smallage, and cinquefoil, and wolf's bane."

"Mingled with fine wheat and the fat of a new-born babe," said the   33
shape of old Goodman Brown.

"Ah, your worship knows the recipe," cried the old lady, cackling aloud.   34
"So, as I was saying, being all ready for the meeting, and no horse to ride
on, I made up my mind to foot it; for they tell me there is a nice young
man to be taken into communion to-night. But now your good worship
will lend me your arm, and we shall be there in a twinkling."

"That can hardly be," answered her friend. "I may not spare you my arm,   35
Goody Cloyse; but here is my staff, if you will."

So saying, he threw it down at her feet, where, perhaps, it assumed life,   36
being one of the rods which its owner had formerly lent to the Egyptian
magi. Of this fact, however, Goodman Brown could not take cognizance.
He had cast up his eyes in astonishment, and, looking down again, beheld
neither Goody Cloyse nor the serpentine staff, but his fellow-traveller
alone, who waited for him as calmly as if nothing had happened.

"That old woman taught me my catechism," said the young man; and   37
there was a world of meaning in this simple comment.

They continued to walk onward, while the elder traveller exhorted his   38
companion to make good speed and persevere in the path, discoursing so
aptly that his arguments seemed rather to spring up in the bosom of his auditor than to be suggested by himself. As they went, he plucked a branch
of maple to serve for a walking stick, and began to strip it of the twigs and
little boughs, which were wet with evening dew. The moment his fingers

touched them they became strangely withered and dried up as with a week's sunshine. Thus the pair proceeded, at a good free pace, until suddenly, in a gloomy hollow of the road, Goodman Brown sat himself down on the stump of a tree and refused to go any farther.

39   "Friend," said he, stubbornly, "my mind is made up. Not another step will I budge on this errand. What if a wretched old woman do choose to go to the devil when I thought she was going to heaven: is that any reason why I should quit my dear Faith and go after her?"

40   "You will think better of this by and by," said his acquaintance, composedly. "Sit here and rest yourself a while; and when you feel like moving again, there is my staff to help you along."

41   Without more words, he threw his companion the maple stick, and was as speedily out of sight as if he had vanished into the deepening gloom. The young man sat a few moments by the roadside, applauding himself greatly, and thinking with how clear a conscience he should meet the minister in his morning walk, nor shrink from the eye of good old Deacon Gookin. And what calm sleep would be his that very night, which was to have been spent so wickedly, but so purely and sweetly now, in the arms of Faith! Amidst these pleasant and praiseworthy meditations, Goodman Brown heard the tramp of horses along the road, and deemed it advisable to conceal himself within the verge of the forest, conscious of the guilty purpose that had brought him thither, though now so happily turned from it.

42   On came the hoof tramps and the voices of the riders, two grave old voices, conversing soberly as they drew near. These mingled sounds appeared to pass along the road, within a few yards of the young man's hiding-place; but, owing doubtless to the depth of the gloom at that particular spot, neither the travellers nor their steeds were visible. Though their figures brushed the small boughs by the wayside, it could not be seen that they intercepted, even for a moment, the faint gleam from the strip of bright sky athwart which they must have passed. Goodman Brown alternately crouched and stood on tiptoe, pulling aside the branches and thrusting forth his head as far as he durst without discerning so much as a shadow. It vexed him the more, because he could have sworn, were such a thing possible, that he recognized the voices of the minister and Deacon Gookin, jogging along quietly, as they were wont to do, when bound to some ordination or ecclesiastical council. While yet within hearing, one of the riders stopped to pluck a switch.

43   "Of the two, reverend sir," said the voice like the deacon's, "I had rather miss an ordination dinner than to-night's meeting. They tell me that some of our community are to be here from Falmouth and beyond, and

others from Connecticut and Rhode Island, besides several of the Indian powwows, who, after their fashion, know almost as much deviltry as the best of us. Moreover, there is a goodly young woman to be taken into communion."

"Mighty well, Deacon Gookin!" replied the solemn old tones of the   44
minister. "Spur up, or we shall be late. Nothing can be done, you know, until I get on the ground."

The hoofs clattered again; and the voices, talking so strangely in the   45
empty air, passed on through the forest, where no church had ever been gathered or solitary Christian prayed. Whither, then, could these holy men be journeying so deep into the heathen wilderness? Young Goodman Brown caught hold of a tree for support, being ready to sink down on the ground, faint and overburdened with the heavy sickness of his heart. He looked up to the sky, doubting whether there really was a heaven above him. Yet there was the blue arch, and the stars brightening in it.

"With heaven above and Faith below, I will yet stand firm against the   46
devil!" cried Goodman Brown.

While he still gazed upward into the deep arch of the firmament and   47
had lifted his hands to pray, a cloud, though no wind was stirring, hurried across the zenith and hid the brightening stars. The blue sky was still visible, except directly overhead, where this black mass of cloud was sweeping swiftly northward. Aloft in the air, as if from the depths of the cloud, came a confused and doubtful sound of voices. Once the listener fancied that he could distinguish the accents of towns-people of his own, men and women, both pious and ungodly, many of whom he had met at the communion table, and had seen others rioting at the tavern. The next moment, so indistinct were the sounds, he doubted whether he had heard aught but the murmur of the old forest, whispering without a wind. Then came a stronger swell of those familiar tones, heard daily in the sunshine at Salem village, but never until now from a cloud of night. There was one voice of a young woman, uttering lamentations, yet with an uncertain sorrow, and entreating for some favor, which, perhaps, it would grieve her to obtain; and all the unseen multitude, both saints and sinners, seemed to encourage her onward.

"Faith!" shouted Goodman Brown, in a voice of agony and desperation;   48
and the echoes of the forest mocked him, crying, "Faith! Faith!" as if bewildered wretches were seeking her all through the wilderness.

The cry of grief, rage, and terror was yet piercing the night, when the   49
unhappy husband held his breath for a response. There was a scream, drowned immediately in a louder murmur of voices, fading into far-off laughter, as the dark cloud swept away, leaving the clear and silent sky

above Goodman Brown. But something fluttered lightly down through the air and caught on the branch of a tree. The young man seized it, and beheld a pink ribbon.

50   "My Faith is gone!" cried he, after one stupefied moment. "There is no good on earth; and sin is but a name. Come, devil; for to thee is this world given."

51   And, maddened with despair, so that he laughed loud and long, did Goodman Brown grasp his staff and set forth again, at such a rate that he seemed to fly along the forest path rather than to walk or run. The road grew wilder and drearier and more faintly traced, and vanished at length, leaving him in the heart of the dark wilderness, still rushing onward with the instinct that guides mortal man to evil. The whole forest was peopled with frightful sounds—the creaking of the trees, the howling of wild beasts, and the yell of Indians; while sometimes the wind tolled like a distant church bell, and sometimes gave a broad roar around the traveller, as if all Nature were laughing him to scorn. But he was himself the chief horror of the scene, and shrank not from its other horrors.

52   "Ha! ha! ha!" roared Goodman Brown when the wind laughed at him.

53   "Let us hear which will laugh loudest. Think not to frighten me with your deviltry. Come witch, come wizard, come Indian powwow, come devil himself, and here comes Goodman Brown. You may as well fear him as he fear you."

54   In truth, all through the haunted forest there could be nothing more frightful than the figure of Goodman Brown. On he flew among the black pines, brandishing his staff with frenzied gestures, now giving vent to an inspiration of horrid blasphemy, and now shouting forth such laughter as set all the echoes of the forest laughing like demons around him. The fiend in his own shape is less hideous than when he rages in the breast of man. Thus sped the demoniac on his course, until, quivering among the trees, he saw a red light before him, as when the felled trunks and branches of a clearing have been set on fire, and throw up their lurid blaze against the sky, at the hour of midnight. He paused, in a lull of the tempest that had driven him onward, and heard the swell of what seemed a hymn, rolling solemnly from a distance with the weight of many voices. He knew the tune; it was a familiar one in the choir of the village meeting-house. The verse died heavily away, and was lengthened by a chorus, not of human voices, but of all the sounds of the benighted wilderness pealing in awful harmony together. Goodman Brown cried out, and his cry was lost to his own ear by its unison with the cry of the desert.

55   In the interval of silence he stole forward until the light glared full upon his eyes. At one extremity of an open space, hemmed in by the dark wall

of the forest, arose a rock, bearing some rude, natural resemblance either to an alter or a pulpit, and surrounded by four blazing pines, their tops aflame, their stems untouched, like candles at an evening meeting. The mass of foliage that had overgrown the summit of the rock was all on fire, blazing high into the night and fitfully illuminating the whole field. Each pendent twig and leafy festoon was in a blaze. As the red light arose and fell, a numerous congregation alternately shone forth, then disappeared in shadow, and again grew, as it were, out of the darkness, peopling the heart of the solitary woods at once.

"A grave and dark-clad company," quoth Goodman Brown. 56

In truth they were such. Among them, quivering to and fro between gloom and splendor, appeared faces that would be seen next day at the council board of the province, and others which, Sabbath after Sabbath, looked devoutly heavenward, and benignantly over the crowded pews, from the holiest pulpits in the land. Some affirm that the lady of the governor was there. At least there were high dames well known to her, and wives of honored husbands, and widows, a great multitude, and ancient maidens, all of excellent repute, and fair young girls, who trembled lest their mothers should espy them. Either the sudden gleams of light flashing over the obscure field bedazzled Goodman Brown, or he recognized a score of the church members of Salem village famous for their especial sanctity. Good old Deacon Gookin had arrived, and waited at the skirts of that venerable saint, his revered pastor. But, irreverently consorting with these grave, reputable, and pious people, these elders of the church, these chaste dames and dewy virgins, there were men of dissolute lives and women of spotted fame, wretches given over to all mean and filthy vice, and suspected even of horrid crimes. It was strange to see that the good shrank not from the wicked, nor were the sinners abashed by the saints. Scattered also among their pale-faced enemies were the Indian priests, or powwows, who had often scared their native forest with more hideous incantations than any known to English witchcraft. 57

"But where is Faith?" thought Goodman Brown; and, as hope came into his heart, he trembled. 58

Another verse of the hymn arose, a slow and mournful strain, such as the pious love, but joined to words which expressed all that our nature can conceive of sin, and darkly hinted at far more. Unfathomable to mere mortals is the lore of fiends. Verse after verse was sung; and still the chorus of the desert swelled between like the deepest tone of a mighty organ; and with the final peal of that dreadful anthem there came a sound, as if the roaring wind, the rushing streams, the howling beasts, and every other voice of the unconcerted wilderness were mingling and according with 59 the voice of guilty man in homage to the prince of all. The four blazing pines threw up a loftier flame, and obscurely discovered shapes and visages of horror on the smoke wreaths above the impious assembly. At the same moment the fire on the rock shot redly forth and formed a glowing arch above its base, where now appeared a figure. With reverence be it spoken, the figure bore no slight similitude, both in garb and manner, to some grave divine of the New England churches.

60   "Bring forth the converts!" cried a voice that echoed through the field and rolled into the forest.

61   At the word, Goodman Brown stepped forth from the shadow of the trees and approached the congregation, with whom he felt a loathful brotherhood by the sympathy of all that was wicked in his heart. He could have well-nigh sworn that the shape of his own dead father beckoned him to advance, looking downward from a smoke wreath, while a woman, with dim features of despair, threw out her hand to warn him back. Was it his mother? But he had no power to retreat one step, nor to resist, even in thought, when the minister and good old Deacon Gookin seized his arms and led him to the blazing rock. Thither came also the slender form of a veiled female, led between Goody Cloyse, that pious teacher of the cate-chism, and Martha Carrier, who had received the devil's promise to be queen of hell. A rampant hag was she. And there stood the proselytes be-neath the canopy of fire.

62   "Welcome, my children," said the dark figure, "to the communion of your race. Ye have found thus young your nature and your destiny. My children, look behind you!"

63   They turned; and flashing forth, as it were, in a sheet of flame, the fiend worshippers were seen; the smile of welcome gleamed darkly on every visage.

64   "There," resumed the sable form, "are all whom ye have reverenced from youth. Ye deemed them holier than yourselves, and shrank from your own sin, contrasting it with their lives of righteousness and prayerful aspi-rations heavenward. Yet here are they all in my worshipping assembly. This night it shall be granted you to know their secret deeds: how hoary-bearded elders of the church have whispered wanton words to the young maids of their households; how many a woman, eager for widows' weeds, has given her husband a drink at bedtime and let him sleep his last sleep in her bosom; how beardless youths have made haste to inherit their fa-thers' wealth; and how fair damsels—blush not, sweet ones—have dug lit-tle graves in the garden, and bidden me, the sole guest to an infant's funeral. By the sympathy of your human hearts for sin ye shall scent out all the places—whether in church, bedchamber, street, field, or forest—

where crime has been committed, and shall exult to behold the whole earth one stain of guilt, one mighty blood spot. Far more than this. It shall be yours to penetrate, in every bosom, the deep mystery of sin, the fountain of all wicked arts, and which inexhaustibly supplies more evil impulses than human power—than my power at its utmost—can make manifest in deeds. And now, my children, look upon each other."

They did so; and, by the blaze of the hell-kindled torches, the wretched man beheld his Faith, and the wife her husband, trembling before that unhallowed altar. 65

"Lo, there ye stand, my children," said the figure, in a deep and solemn tone, almost sad with its despairing awfulness, as if his once angelic nature could yet mourn for our miserable race. "Depending upon one another's hearts, ye had still hoped that virtue were not all a dream. Now are ye undeceived. Evil is the nature of mankind. Evil must be your only happiness. Welcome again, my children, to the communion of your race." 66

"Welcome," repeated the fiend worshippers, in one cry of despair and triumph. 67

And there they stood, the only pair, as it seemed, who were yet hesitating on the verge of wickedness in this dark world. A basin was hollowed, naturally, in the rock. Did it contain water, reddened by the lurid light? or was it blood? or, perchance, a liquid flame? Herein did the shape of evil dip his hand and prepare to lay the mark of baptism upon their foreheads, that they might be partakers of the mystery of sin, more conscious of the secret guilt of others, both in deed and thought, than they could now be of their own. The husband cast one look at his pale wife, and Faith at him. What polluted wretches would the next glance show them to each other, shuddering alike at what they disclosed and what they saw! 68

"Faith! Faith!" cried the husband, "look up to heaven, and resist the wicked one." 69

Whether Faith obeyed he knew not. Hardly had he spoken when he found himself amid calm night and solitude, listening to a roar of the wind which died heavily away through the forest. He staggered against the rock, and felt it chill and damp; while a hanging twig, that had been all on fire, besprinkled his cheek with the coldest dew. 70

The next morning young Goodman Brown came slowly into the street of Salem village, staring around him like a bewildered man. The good old minister was taking a walk along the graveyard to get an appetite for breakfast and meditate his sermon, and bestowed a blessing, as he passed, on Goodman Brown. He shrank from the venerable saint as if to avoid an anathema. Old Deacon Gookin was at domestic worship, and the holy words of his prayer were heard through the open window. "What God 71 doth the wizard pray to?" quoth Goodman Brown. Goody Cloyse, that excellent old Christian, stood in the early sunshine at her own lattice, catechizing a little girl who had brought her a pint of morning's milk. Goodman Brown snatched away the child as from the grasp of the fiend himself. Turning the corner by the meeting-house, he spied the head of Faith, with the pink ribbons, gazing anxiously forth, and bursting into such joy at sight of him that she skipped along the street and almost kissed her husband before the whole village. But Goodman Brown looked sternly and sadly into her face, and passed on without a greeting.

72   Had Goodman Brown fallen asleep in the forest and only dreamed a wild dream of a witch-meeting?

73   Be it so if you will; but, alas! it was a dream of evil omen for young Goodman Brown. A stern, a sad, a darkly meditative, a distrustful, if not a desperate man did he become from the night of that fearful dream. On the Sabbath day, when the congregation were singing a holy psalm, he could not listen because an anthem of sin rushed loudly upon his ear and drowned all the blessed strain. When the minister spoke from the pulpit with power and fervid eloquence, and, with his hand on the open Bible, of the sacred truths of our religion, and of saint-like lives and triumphant deaths, and of future bliss or misery unutterable, then did Goodman Brown turn pale, dreading lest the roof should thunder down upon the gray blasphemer and his hearers. Often, waking suddenly at midnight, he shrank from the bosom of Faith; and at morning or eventide, when the family knelt down at prayer, he scowled and muttered to himself, and gazed sternly at his wife, and turned away. And when he had lived long, and was borne to his grave a hoary corpse, followed by Faith, an aged woman, and children and grandchildren, a goodly procession, besides neighbors not a few, they carved no hopeful verse upon his tombstone, for his dying hour was gloom.

Questioning and Discussing

Hawthorne, "Young Goodman Brown"

1. How do the first paragraphs of "Young Goodman Brown" foreshadow later events? Pay particular attention to Faith's references to dreams. How do these opening paragraphs foreshadow the moral conflicts of the story?

2. In many ways "Young Goodman Brown" is an example of *allegory*, beginning with the names of its key characters. Research the term *allegory* as a literary device and explore the many different levels at which this story functions as

allegory. Pay particular attention to the way in which the allegory suggests the values articulated in the story—and perhaps the author's own values as well. How might a story set in the time of "Young Goodman Brown" speak to contemporary issues?

3. What exactly is the nature of Young Goodman Brown's' "errand" in the forest? Although you certainly know the most common definition of this word, look up *errand* in a reference source such as the *Oxford English Dictionary*. How does a deeper knowledge of this word's connotations enhance your understanding of this story as an allegory?

4. Nathaniel Hawthorne had conflicted feelings about his Puritan ancestors and their legacy of intolerance and persecution. What aspects of Puritan society (and, perhaps, American society in his own time) does Hawthorne critique in "Young Goodman Brown"?

⊞

Henry Louis Gates, Jr.

Noted American scholar and critic Henry Louis Gates, Jr. (1950–) is credited with rediscovering and reinterpreting African American literature, a project that began when he located, authenticated, and published the first known novel by an African American, Harriet E. Wilson's *Our Nig* (1859). He has brought other lost works to light but is also well known for his numerous books of criticism, including *The Signifying Monkey: A Theory of African-American Literary Criticism* (1988), and a number of popular works, including *Thirteen Ways of Looking at a Black Man* (1997). In 1999, Gates wrote and hosted a public television series on Africa and prepared its text, *Wonders of the African World.* He heads the Afro-American Studies Program at Harvard University.

⊞

The Charmer

The drive to Louis Farrakhan's house, on South Woodlawn Avenue, took me through the heart of black Chicago—past campaign billboards for a hot city-council race, past signs for Harold the Fried Chicken King and Tony's Vienna Beef Hotdogs. Much of the area is flecked with housing projects and abandoned lots, but when you turn the corner at Woodlawn and Forty-ninth Street things abruptly look different. You can see why the late Elijah Muhammad, who led the Nation of Islam—the Black Muslims—for almost four decades, built his house in this little pocket of opulence. It's a street of large brick houses, enshrining the vision of black-bourgeois respectability, and even grandeur, that has always been at the nostalgic heart of the Nation of Islam's creed. The neighborhood, known as South Kenwood, is integrated and professional. In 1985, Farrakhan bought Elijah Muhammad's house—a yellow-brick neo-Mediterranean structure—and he has lived there ever since; the creed and the neighborhood remain intact.

2   It was a warm spring morning the week after Easter, 1996, and everything was peaceful, quiet, orderly, which somehow made matters all the more unsettling. I wasn't expecting the Death Star, exactly, but I wouldn't have been surprised to see a formidable security detail: the Fruit of Islam patrolling the roof and gates with automatic weapons; perhaps a few attack dogs roaming the grounds. In fact, the only security measure in evidence was a rather elegant wrought-iron fence. After I spent a minute or so fumbling around, trying to find a hinge, a baby-faced young man with close-cropped hair and gleaming black combat boots came over and flicked the gate open. Together, we walked up a short, curved driveway, past two marble lions flanking the front door, and into the house that Elijah Muhammad built.

3   People in the Nation of Islam refer to the house as the Palace, and it does have an undeniable, vaguely Orientalist splendor. There is a large center hall, two stories high, filled with well-tended tropical plants, some reaching up between ten and twenty feet. Sunlight floods in from a huge dome of leaded glass; at its center, Arabic characters spell out "Allahu Akbar," or "God Is Great." To the right is a large and vibrant triptych: the Nation's founder, Wallace D. Fard; his prophet, Elijah Muhammad (with a set of gold keys in his hands); and Elijah's successor as the head of the Nation, a very youthful-looking Louis Farrakhan. The walls are spanking white, the floors are tiled in white and gray marble. A C-shaped sofa is upholstered in white fabric and covered with clear vinyl—the same stuff my mother put on to protect *her* good furniture, back in Piedmont, West Virginia.

4   Farrakhan's wife, Khadijah, came down to check on me, and to make sure everything was tidy now that company had arrived. Khadijah Farrakhan has a soft brown face and a warm smile. I had a bad cold that day, and she offered me some advice on how to unblock my ears, which still hadn't recovered from the flight to Chicago. "Open your mouth wide, and shift your jaw from side to side," she said, helpfully demonstrating the motion. We stood facing each other, our mouths contorted like those of a pair of groupers.

5   That is about when America's great black Satan himself came gliding into the room. Farrakhan was resplendent in a three-button suit of chocolate-brown silk, a brown-and-beige bow tie, and a matching pocket square. Only then did I notice that my own trousers did not match my suit jacket. Moments later, I referred to his wife as "Mrs. Muhammad," and there was a glint

of amusement in his eyes. The truth is, I was having a bad case of nerves that morning. For good reason. After I criticized Farrakhan in print three years ago, a few of his more impetuous followers had shared with me their fervent hope for my death. Now that I was face to face with Farrakhan, I did feel, in fact, pretty deathly. "I'm a wounded warrior," I admitted.

Farrakhan, relaxed and gracious, made sure I was supplied with hot tea   6
and honey. "Get the battlefield ready," he said, laughing. For the rest of a long day, we sat together at his big dining-room table, and it became clear that Farrakhan is a man of enormous intelligence, curiosity, and charm. He can also be deeply strange. It all depends on the moment and the subject. When he talks about the need for personal responsibility or of his fondness for Johnny Mathis and Frank Sinatra, he sounds as jovial and bourgeois as Bill Cosby; when he is warning of the wicked machinations of Jewish financiers, he seems as odd and obsessed as Pat Robertson.

Not long after we began talking, Farrakhan told me about an epiphany   7
he had recently about the waning of white cultural supremacy. Farrakhan takes moments of revelation very seriously; one of his most profound occurred, he has said, while he was aboard a giant spacecraft. This particular revelation, less marvelously, took place at a Lionel Ritchie concert. There Farrakhan saw a beautiful young blond woman and her little daughter, who both clearly idolized this black performer. And when Ritchie told the mostly white crowd to raise their hands in the air almost everyone joined in. Farrakhan saw this as something not only amazing but telling.

"I see something happening in America," he said. "You go into white folks'   8
homes, you see Michael Jackson on the wall, you see Michael Jordan on the wall, you see Hank Aaron on the wall. Their children are being influenced by black faces. And I say to myself, 'Where is this leading?' And what I see is that white supremacy is being challenged in so many subtle and overt ways, and gradually children are losing that thing about being superior."

The myths of black superiority are also going by the wayside. Someone   9
might believe that a white cannot play the horn, he said, "then Kenny G. blows that all away." (Joe Lovano, maybe, but Kenny G.?) It used to be that white people listened to the blues but could never sing it. Now, though, "white people are experiencing that out of which the blues came," he said. "White people are suffering. Now you drive your streets and you see a white person with stringy hair sitting by the side of the road plucking his guitar, like we used to do in the South. Now *they're* into that." What people must do is "outgrow the narrowness of their own nationalistic feelings," Farrakhan declared. "When we outgrow the color thing, outgrow the race and the ethnic thing, outgrow the religious thing to see the oneness of God and the oneness of humanity, then we can begin to approach our divinity."

10   I scratched my head: we'd gone from Kenny G. to God in a matter of seconds; "the blue-eyed devils"—Elijah Muhammad's favorite designation for white folk—are learning the blues, and we're mightily impressed.

11   It turns out that there is in Farrakhan's discourse a strain that sounds awfully like liberal universalism; there is also, of course, its brutal opposite. The two tendencies, in all their forms, are constantly in tension. Pundits like to imagine that Farrakhan is a kind of radio program: the incendiary Louis Farrakhan Show. In fact, Farrakhan is more like a radio station: what you hear depends on when you tune in. His talk ranges from far-fetched conspiracy theories to Dan Quayle-like calls for family values. Farrakhan really does believe that a cabal of Jews secretly controls the world; he also suspects, I learned later in our conversation, that one of his own grandparents was a Portuguese Jew. Apologists and detractors alike feel free to decide which represents the "real" Farrakhan. The result may score debating points, but it has little to do with the man who lives at South Woodlawn and Forty-ninth Street.

12   Much is made of Farrakhan's capacity to strike fear into the hearts of white liberals. And it does seem that for many of them Farrakhan represents their worst nightmare: the Nat Turner figure, crying out for racial vengeance. As Adolph Reed, Jr., writes of Farrakhan, "he has become uniquely notorious because his inflammatory nationalist persona has helped to center public discussion of Afro-American politics on the only issue (except affirmative action, of course) about which most whites ever show much concern: What do blacks think of whites?"

13   A subject that receives far less attention is the fear that Farrakhan inspires in blacks. The truth is that blacks—across the economic and ideological spectrum—often feel astonishingly vulnerable to charges of inauthenticity, of disloyalty to the race. I know that I do, despite my vigorous efforts to deconstruct that vocabulary of reproach. Farrakhan's sway over blacks—the answering chord his rhetoric finds—attests to the enduring strength of our own feelings of guilt, our own anxieties of having been false to our people, of having sinned against our innermost identity. He denounces the fallen in our midst, invokes the wrath of heaven against us: and his outlandish vitriol occasions both terror and a curious exhilaration. . . .

14   The truly paranoid heart of Farrakhan's world view has been revealed in recent speeches in which he has talked about a centuries-old conspiracy of international bankers—with names like Rothschild and Warburg— who have captured control over the central banks in many countries, and who incite wars to increase the indebtedness of others and maximize their own wealth. The Federal Reserve, the I.R.S., the F.B.I., and the Anti-Defamation League

were all founded in 1913, Farrakhan says (actually, the I.R.S. was founded in 1862 and the F.B.I. in 1908, but never mind), and then he poses the favorite rhetorical question of all paranoid historians: "Is that a coincidence?"

What do you do with a religious demagogue who promulgates the the-   15
ory that Jewish financiers have manipulated world events for centuries? Well, if you're a Republican contender for the presidency, and the dema-gogue's name is Pat Robertson, you genuflect. It turns out that Farrakhan's conspiracy theory of Jewish cabals is essentially identical to Robertson's. "Rest assured, there is a behind-the-scenes Establishment in this nation, as in every other," Robertson writes in *The New World Order,* his recent best-selling book. "It has enormous power. It has controlled the economic and foreign policy objectives of the United States for the past seventy years, whether the man sitting in the White House is a Democrat or a Re-publican, a liberal or a conservative, a moderate or an extremist." Robert-son goes on to inveigh against the tentacular Rothschilds and Warburgs. Michael Lind, who has analyzed Robertson's conspiracy theories at length, suggests that not since the days of Father Coughlin[1] has the grass-roots right been as overtly anti-Semitic as it is now.

And Farrakhan? He, too, believes all this conspiracy stuff, and thinks he's   16
just telling it like it is. He must realize that such talk goes down well with in-ner-city audiences hungry for secret histories that explain how things went wrong. He turns mainstream criticism to his advantage, winning ovations by representing himself as the persecuted truth-teller. But turnabout isn't al-ways fair play: and the fact that Farrakhan is a black American only makes his deafness to historical context all the more dismaying. Within his own lifetime, one of every three Jews on the face of the earth died at the hands of a regime suffused by the same language about nefarious Jewish influence. Ultimately, Farrakhan's anti-Semitism has the characteristics of a psycho-logical obsession, and once in a while he shows signs of recognizing this. "I would prefer that this whole conflict would go away, in truth," he said to me. His voice sounded husky, and a little tired. "But it's like I'm locked now in a struggle. It's like both of us got a hold on each other, and each of us is filled with electricity. I can't let them go, and they can't let me go."

Farrakhan's peculiar mixture of insight and delusion would be a matter   17
of mainly academic interest if it weren't for his enormous populist appeal among black Americans—an appeal that was clearly demonstrated in the 1995 Million Man March. That occasion has been widely seen as an

1 Charles Edward Coughlin (1891–1979), a Catholic priest famous for his vitriolic radio addresses in the 1930s.

illustration both of Farrakhan's strengths and of his weaknesses. "If only somebody else had convened it," the liberal-minded are prone to say. But nobody else—not Colin Powell, not Jesse Jackson—could have.

18   Some of the most heartfelt tributes to the event's success are also the most grudging. There's little doubt, after all, that the Farrakhan phenomenon owes much to a vacuum of radical black leadership. (Jesse Jackson has emerged over the past decade as the leading spokesman of the American left, one could argue, rather than of black America.) "We have the worst leadership in the black community since slavery," Eldridge Cleaver maintains. "Farrakhan saw that vacuum, saw nothing motivating the people, no vision being projected to the people, and he came up with the defining event for a generation of people, this Million Man March."

19   Timing had a lot to do with the event's success, of course. As Roger Wilkins likes to say, Newt Gingrich was one of the main organizers of the march. "If the white middle class feels it's losing ground, the black working class and unskilled working class are being slaughtered—hit by a blitzkrieg that no one notices," Wilkins points out. "And their plight is not on anyone's agenda anymore. Farrakhan supplies an answer, and an emotional discharge."

20   Farrakhan's people have won some real credibility in the black community. "It's as if Malcolm was having a march on Washington," Robert Moses, the civil-rights activist and education reformer, says. And Wilkins says, "Nobody else can go into the prisons and save souls to the degree that they have. Nobody else is able to put as many neat and clean young people on the streets of the inner city as they are. You think about the fellows who are selling their papers as opposed to those fellows you see standing around the liquor stores. Their men have this enviable sense of discipline, orderliness, and human purpose." (The Nation of Islam continues to have very conservative sexual politics, and Farrakhan is vehemently anti-abortion, but he has also inveighed against domestic violence, and—in a sharp break from tradition—even named a woman to be a Nation of Islam minister.) Hugh Price, the president of the National Urban League, calls the march "the largest family-values rally in the history of the United States." Indeed, another sign of its success was the number of mainstream civil-rights leaders who were present. Whatever their discomfort with Farrakhan's extremist rhetoric, they calculated that their absence might well imperil their legitimacy with the black public.

21   Attendance or nonattendance was a delicate decision. General Colin Powell was prominent among those blacks who decided that they could not afford to appear. When I asked Farrakhan if he would consider sup-

porting a future Powell presidential bid, he said, "I don't want to support anybody because he's black—I think I have outgrown the need to support somebody because of the color of his skin. What is in the best interest of our people is really in the best interest of the country. So if General Powell had an agenda that is good for the totality of our people—the American people first—and in that package is something that can lift our people, he's got our support."

Farrakhan's level of support among black Americans is vigorously debated. If you gauge his followers by the number who regularly attend mosques affiliated with the Nation of Islam and eschew lima beans and corn bread, they are not very numerous. Estimates range from twenty thousand to ten times that. On the other hand, if you go by the number of people who consider him a legitimate voice of black protest, the ranks are much larger. (In a recent poll, more than half the blacks surveyed reported a favorable impression of him.) The march was inspired by the Muslims but not populated by them. Farrakhan knows that the men who came to the march were not his religious followers. They tended to be middle class and college-educated and Christian. Farrakhan is convinced that those men came "to a march called by a man who is considered radical, extremist, anti-Semitic, anti-white" because of a yearning "to connect with the masses." 22

Not everyone, to be sure, was quite so deeply impressed. "This was an opportunity for the black middle class to feel this symbolic connection, but what were the solutions that were proposed, except atonement?" Angela Davis asks. Julian Bond says bluntly, "You know, that Negro didn't even vote until 1984. He's the leader in the sense that he can gather people to him, but they don't go anyplace when they leave him." And Jesse Jackson, who addressed the marchers, now views the march as fatally flawed by its failure to reach out to Capitol Hill. "The 1963 March on Washington was connected to public policy—public accommodations," he says, and notes that the result was the signing into law of the Civil Rights Act the following year. By contrast, he argues, the Million Man March had "essentially a religious theme—atonement—disconnected from public policy," so it brought no political dividends in its aftermath. "On the very next day—the very next day, *the very next day*—there was the welfare bill," he said, referring to the House and Senate conferences to work out a final draft of a bill excusing the federal government from a degree of responsibility toward the poor. "The next day was the vote on the unfair sentence guidelines. The next day was the Medicare bill," another hostile measure. "The big debates in Congress took place between that Wednesday and Thursday. And so those who were taking away our 23 rights and attacking us did not see any connection between the gathering and public policy." The lesson he draws is straightforward: "The march was essentially disconnected from our political leadership. Any mass action must be connected to the public-policy leaders."

24　　Some critics express a sense that the mass mobilization may itself be a relic of a bygone era. It was an arena where Farrakhan was able to stake a claim for mass black leadership, in part because of the near-sacralization of the 1963 precursor; but its continued political viability has not been demonstrated. Indeed, the growing fragmentation of black leadership— the irrelevance of the old-fashioned notion of a "head nigger in charge"— is one sign that an elite now exists in black America that does enjoy an unmediated relation to power. Privately, many black leaders say that Farrakhan's moment has passed. Such remarks inevitably carry an air of wishful thinking. White liberal allies sometimes worry that pressure is required to keep black leaders from being "soft on Farrakhan": in reality, no love is lost among those who would compete for the hearts and souls of black America. At the helm of the mainstream black-advocacy groups are men and women who may say conciliatory things about the Nation of Islam, but their jaws are tense and their smiles are tight. They reassure themselves that Farrakhan is bound to remain a marginal phenomenon because of his extremism. Yet the organic leaders of the disenfranchised are seldom moderate in tone; and since, from all indications, the underclass is continuing to expand, Farrakhan's natural power base will only increase.

25　　In the months following the march, Farrakhan dropped out of public view, and he spoke of having suffered from depression, in part because he was still being misrepresented by the press. This response highlights Farrakhan's paradoxical relation to the wider public—that of a pariah who wants to be embraced. "Both Malcolm and Farrakhan had a very tough ideology but at the same time wanted a degree of public acceptance in the white community," Ron Walters, a political scientist and an adviser to Jackson, says. "To me, that's a tremendous contradiction. I don't know whether it's a personality thing or just what happens to you when you reach a certain level of prominence—that you do want a sort of universal acceptance."

26　　Such acceptance has been elusive so far. A few weeks before the Million Man March, Farrakhan gave an interview to make it clear that when he referred to Jewish "bloodsuckers" he didn't mean Jews in particular—he meant all non-black shopkeepers in the inner city, some of them Jewish but these days more often Koreans or Arabs. He must have found it galling when many newspapers wrested his remarks out of context, leaving the

impression that he had merely repeated the original accusation: Farrakhan calls Jews bloodsuckers. Farrakhan's image also suffered when,
early last year, the *Chicago Tribune* published an investigative series, by
David Jackson and William Gaines, revealing financial disarray among
Nation-owned businesses. Farrakhan's calls for economic self-sufficiency,
it appeared, were not matched by his organization's performance.

Farrakhan hurt himself yet again, with his so-called World Friendship   27
Tour, in January and February. He claims that his decision to make this
trip to Third World capitals was a matter of divine inspiration, but it isn't
hard to imagine human motivations as well. Public figures who feel that
they have been badly used by the local papers often find that solace awaits
them in admiring throngs overseas: call it the Jerry Lewis syndrome. Besides, how better to shore up your position as the leader of black America
than by being received as such by foreign potentates?

The domestic fallout, however, has lingered. Even many of those who   28
supported Farrakhan were chagrined to find him holding friendly meetings with some of the world's worst dictators: Nigeria's Sam Abacha,
Libya's Muammar Qaddafi, Zaire's Mobutu, and Sudan's Omar al-Bashir.
Ron Walters observes, "He gave all those people who wanted an opportunity not to have to deal with him the golden reason. The tremendous political capital of the march had been dissipated." Black nationalists were
among those who were the most horrified. Molefi Kete Asante, the Afrocentric scholar, says, "What Farrakhan did, in my judgment, was to take
the legitimacy of the march and put it in his back pocket, and march
around to these terrible governments, as if somehow he were the leader of
a million black people. That upset me."

It is a sore subject with Farrakhan. Sure, he met with dictators, he said   29
to me, but when you are dealing with atonement, sin, and reconciliation
you don't travel to the blameless. "It's all right for Jesse to sit down with
George Wallace in Alabama and for them to pray together—and there's
applause," he went on. "But I can't go sit down with my brother who is a
sinner? Nixon died a hero, but I cannot forgive a black man?" There was
a surge of anger in his voice. "That's the damnable thing that I hate about
this whole damned thing," he said. "If I go to a black man to retrieve him,
all of a sudden I'm cavorting with a damned dictator, but Jesus could sit
down with the sinners and you give him honor and credit. And Reagan
can sit down with Gorbachev, and he gets honor and credit. He sits with
the evil empire, but I can't sit with my own brother. To hell with you for
that. That's why I am not a politician."

"Has the tour compromised the achievement of the march?" I asked him.   30

31   He sounded subdued when he said, "If I lost momentum, I believe it's only temporary."

32   Farrakhan lays much stress on the imagery of dialogue and conciliation these days. Certainly the Farrakhan I met was a model of civility and courtesy. I was reminded of Eric Lincoln's account of the last couple of visits he had paid to Farrakhan at his home: "Louis insisted on getting down on his hands and knees on the floor to take my shoes off. You know, I'm overweight and it's a difficult task to get shoes and socks off. And so Louis said, 'I will do that.' And I said, 'No, no.' And Louis said, 'No, I want to do it.' He took my shoes off and rubbed my feet to get the blood circulating."

33   If the Farrakhan phenomenon remains disquieting, the man himself seems oddly, jarringly vulnerable. I met someone who was eager, even hungry, for conversation; someone of great intelligence who seemed intellectually lonely. In fiery speeches before packed auditoriums, Farrakhan speaks of plots against his life, and does so in alarmingly messianic tones. ("I don't care nothing about my life," he told his audience on Saviour's Day in 1995, his voice breaking. "It's your life that I want to save!") To me he spoke of his mortality in a quieter mode. He spoke movingly of watching the funeral of Yitzhak Rabin—about the tragedy of a wise and tempered elder statesman assassinated by a callow extremist. He spoke about having a growing appreciation for compromise, about coming to see the value in the positions of his ideological antagonists within the civil-rights tradition. And he told me about a fight of his own, against prostate cancer, over the past several years.

34   "At first, it was frightening to me—how could I have cancer? I've eaten well, I've tried to live clean. Then I fasted and I prayed and I went into the desert, and after a month I went and had an M.R.I. and one of those rectal ultrasounds, and all they could find was a little scar." He paused, and added quietly, "But then it came back." He looks in splendid health: he is sixty-three, and his skin remains soft and almost unlined. He recently made a health-and-exercise video, which shows him going through an arduous regimen of weight-training. And he *is* remarkably fit. He has undergone seed-implantation radiation-therapy for his cancer, and remains optimistic about the results. "I've never had to take a pain pill, and I hope and pray that God will bless me ultimately to overcome it. At least, all accounts up to date, the P.S.A."—the blood-screening test for prostate cancer—"has been normal. And so I'm going on with my life, but warning all of us that this is such a hell of a killer of our people. And when you reach your early forties, many of us won't like somebody poking around in our

rectum, but we have to encourage our young men and our middle-aged brothers, and the population as a whole, to do that for themselves, because all we have is our health."

We all know that the world isn't divided between saints and sinners. And yet the private Farrakhan's very humanness—those traits of kindness, concern, humor—makes his paranoia all the more disconcerting. He rails against the way the mainstream has demonized him, and yet he refuses to renounce the anti-Semitic conspiracy theories that have made him anathema: to him, it would be like denying the law of gravity. And so he is trapped, immobilized by his contradictory desires. His ongoing calls for dialogue are seemingly heartfelt; he genuinely wants a seat at the table, craves the legitimation of power. Yet he will not engage in the compromises and concessions that true dialogue requires. He cannot afford to. This is a man whose political identity is constituted by antagonism to the self-image of America. To moderate his stance of unyielding opposition would be to destroy the edifice he has spent his life constructing. Moreover, Farrakhan knows that there are people around him whose militancy puts his to shame. Some of them are former lieutenants of his in the Nation of Islam, such as Khalid Muhammad, whom Farrakhan suspended after judging him to have been *too* intemperate in his public pronouncements. Others have established an independent base of support, such as Silas Muhammad, another Elijah loyalist who split with the organization, and whose sect is now based in Atlanta. For leaders whose appeal is based on intransigence, outrage, and wrath, there is always the danger of being outflanked by those even more intransigent, more outrageous, more wrathful. This, in part, is why Farrakhan could not truly atone even at his own day of atonement.

In the end, however, it isn't Farrakhan but Farrakhan's following that demands explanation. We might start by admitting the moral authority that black nationalism commands even among those blacks who ostensibly disapprove of it. In the village where I grew up, there was a Holiness Church, where people spoke in tongues and fell down in religious ecstasy. It was not my church; my family and I shunned the Pentecostal fervor. And yet, on some level, we believed it to be the real thing, realer than our own, more temperate Episcopal services. It was the place to go if you really needed something—if you got desperately sick, say—because the Holy Ghost lived there. (There are Reform Jews who admit to a similar attitude toward their Hasidic brethren.) In this same vein, the assimilated black American, who lives in Scarsdale and drives a Lexus, responds to Farrakhan and Farrakhanism as a presence at once threatening and exhilarating, dismaying and cathartic. Though blackness isn't exactly a religion, it has become invested with a quasi-religious structure. Black nationalism is a tradition extending at least back to Martin R. Delany, in the nineteenth century. Cross it with the black messianic tradition—which spawned the legendary likes of Father Divine, Daddy Grace, and Prophet Jones— and you have the Nation of Islam.

37   Hard as it is to take stock of the organization's membership, it's harder to take stock of Farrakhan's place in the mind of black America. For his dominion is, in a sense, a dominion of metaphor, which is to say that it is at once factitious and factual. The political theorist Benedict Anderson has defined nations as "imagined communities," and the black nation is even more imaginary than most. We know that thirty-six million sepia Americans do not a collective make, but in our minds we sometimes insist upon it.

38   The Million Man March had all the hallmarks of a watershed event, yet a march is not a movement. I asked Farrakhan at one point what the country would look like if, by magic, he could turn his hopes into reality. The answer he gave me was long and meandering, but it centered on things like "revamping the educational system" to make it less Eurocentric—proposals of the sort debated by the New York State Board of Regents, rather than something that was radically transformative in any obvious way.

39   That was, in a sense, the most dismaying response I'd heard all day. Farrakhan is a man of visions. Just weeks before the march, he told congregants in a Washington, D.C., church about the "Mother Wheel"—a heavily armed spaceship the size of a city, which will rain destruction upon white America but save those who embrace the Nation of Islam. ("Ezekiel saw the wheel, way up in the middle of the air," in the words of the old spiritual.) What gave me pause was the realization that such visions coexist in Farrakhan's mind with a real poverty of—well, vision, which is to say a broader conception of the human future.

40   Farrakhan is a man of unhealthy fixations, but the reciprocal fixation on Farrakhan that you find in the so-called mainstream is a sign of our own impoverished political culture. Thirteen decades have passed since Emancipation, and half of our black men between twenty-four and thirty-five are without full-time employment. One black man graduates from college for every hundred who go to jail. Almost half of black children live in poverty. People say that Farrakhan is now the leading voice of black rage in America. One day, America will realize it got off easy.

QUESTIONING AND DISCUSSING
Gates, "The Charmer"

1. Reading the text carefully, determine the ways in which Gates reveals the complex, paradoxical, and often disturbing values of Louis Farrakhan. What seems to be Gates's attitude toward Farrakhan's values in this essay? What in the text supports your response?

2. Comment on Gates's choice of a title for this essay. How is it possible for Farrakhan to be persuasive to one group and so offensive to most others? What are possible historical contexts and lessons regarding leaders—demagogues, to some—who are charismatic but whose charisma involves hatred for particular groups?

3. Analyze Gates's statements that the black community is an "imagined community," that "Farrakhan's anti-Semitism has the characteristics of a psychological obsession," and that Farrakhan comprises a "peculiar mixture of insight and delusion."

⊞

ANONYMOUS

Old Horse, which was published anonymously, appeared in a 1959 edition of the religiously oriented magazine *Lutheran Life.*

⊞

Old Horse

Old Horse was the algebra instructor at the school where I teach. I don't remember his real name anymore. But he had a long face with big, square teeth, and so the students called him "Old Horse."

Perhaps they would have liked him more if he hadn't been so sarcastic. With his cutting remarks, Old Horse could force the most brazen student to stare at the floor in silence. Even the faculty had a healthy respect for his sharp tongue.

One day a boy named Jenkins flared back at Old Horse, "But I don't understand this," pointing to a part of a problem on the board.

"I'm doing the best I can considering the material I have to work with," said Old Horse.

5   "You're trying to make a jackass out of me," said Jenkins, his face turning red.

6   "But, Jenkins, you make it so easy for me," said Old Horse—and Jenkins's eyes retreated to the floor.

7   Old Horse retired shortly after I came. Something went wrong with his liver or stomach and so he left. No one heard from him again.

8   One day, however, not too long before Old Horse left, a new boy came to school. Because he had buck teeth and a hare lip, everybody called him Rabbit. No one seemed to like Rabbit much either. Most of the time he stood by himself chewing his fingernails.

9   Since Rabbit came to school in the middle of October, he had make-up work to do in algebra every day after school. Old Horse was surprisingly patient during these sessions. He would explain anything Rabbit asked. Rabbit in turn always did his homework. In fact, he came early to class, if he could manage it. Then, after the lesson, he would walk with Old Horse to the parking lot.

10 One Friday, because of a faculty meeting, Old Horse didn't meet with Rabbit. This afternoon I walked with Old Horse. We were passing the athletic field when suddenly he stopped and pointed. "What's the matter with that one?" he asked. He was referring to Rabbit, standing alone, chewing his fingernails, while watching some boys pass a football.

11 "What do you mean?" I asked.

12 "Why doesn't he play ball, too?" Old Horse demanded.

13 "Oh, you know how it is. He came in later than the others, and besides—."

14 "Besides what?"

15 "Well, he's different, you know? He'll fit in sooner or later."

16 "No, no, no. That won't do. They mustn't leave him out like that."

17 Then we had to break off our conversation because Rabbit had hurried over to join with us. With a smile, he walked beside his teacher, asking him questions.

18 Suddenly, one of the boys from the athletic field called out, "Yea, Old Horse! Yea, Old Horse!" and then he threw back his head and went, "Wheeeeeeeee!" like a horse's whinny. Rabbit's face reddened with embarrassment. Old Horse tossed his head, but said nothing.

19 The next day the students from my fifth hour class came to my room awfully excited. Old Horse had gone too far, they said. He ought to be fired. When I asked what had happened, they said he had picked on Rabbit. He had called on Rabbit first thing and deliberately made him look ridiculous.

Apparently Rabbit had gone to the board with confidence. But when   20
he began to put down some numbers, Old Horse said they looked like animal tracks in the snow. Everyone snickered, and Rabbit got nervous.

Then Old Horse taunted him for a mistake in arithmetic. "No, no, no.   21
Can't you multiply now? Even a rabbit can do that."

Everyone laughed, although they were surprised. They thought Rabbit   22
was Old Horse's pet. By now, Rabbit was so mixed up he just stood there,
chewing his fingernails.

"Don't nibble!" Old Horse shouted. "Those are your fingers, boy, not   23
carrots!"

At that, Rabbit took his seat without being told and put his red face in   24
his hands. But the class wasn't laughing anymore. They were silent with
anger at Old Horse.

I went in to see Old Horse after my last class. I found him looking out   25
the window.

"Now listen here—," I began, but he waved me into silence.   26

"Now, now, now, look at that. See?" He pointed to Rabbit walking to   27
the athletic field with one of the boys who had complained about how
mean Old Horse had been.

"Doesn't he have special class with you now?" I asked after a moment.   28

"He doesn't need that class anymore," said Old Horse.   29

That afternoon I walked with Old Horse to the parking lot. He was in   30
one of his impatient moods, so I didn't try to say much. Suddenly, from
the players on the athletic field, a wild chorus broke out. "Yea, Old Horse!
Yea, Old Horse!" And then Rabbit, who was with them, stretched his
long neck and screamed, "Wheeeeeeeee!"

Old Horse tossed his head as if a large fly were bothering him. But he   31
said nothing.

QUESTIONING AND DISCUSSING

"Old Horse"

1. "Old Horse" originally appeared in the magazine *Lutheran Life* in 1959,
   which might suggest that the story is supposed to have a moral from which
   the reader will learn an important lesson. What might that lesson be?

2. Comment on the story itself. What do you think of the way in which the
   story makes its points? What about the text reveals qualities about the main
   characters and the narrator? What are these qualities? What effect do these
   details have, and what do they reveal about the narrator's and the characters'
   values?

3. As the editor of this volume, I'll readily admit that this story is a bit odd, but it's useful for articulating one's moral compass at a variety of levels. One of the reviewers for this book was concerned that students would misread this story and see it as endorsing and fostering cruelty. What do you think of that concern?

4. Consider this story in the light of the next selection, an excerpt from *Words that Hurt, Words that Heal*. Does it provide additional context for "Old Horse"? Explain why and how—or doesn't it?

⌗

JOSEPH TELUSHKIN

Joseph Telushkin (1948–), ordained a rabbi by Yeshiva University in New York, lectures throughout the United States and is the author of many books, including *Jewish Literacy* (1991), *Biblical Literacy* (1997), *Jewish Humor* (1992), and *Words that Hurt, Words that Heal* (1998), from which this excerpt is taken. Focusing on historical and ethical concerns in his nonfiction books, Telushkin has written novels, several of which have been adapted (also by Telushkin) for popular shows on television. He is credited with making Jewish philosophy, theology, and history accessible to the general public.

⌗

The Cost of Public Humiliation

1 Some eighteen hundred years ago in Israel, Rabbi Judah the Prince, the leading scholar of his age, was delivering an important lecture when suddenly he found himself in a very aggravating circumstance: A member of the audience who had eaten a large amount of garlic was emitting such an unpleasant odor that the rabbi found it difficult to concentrate. Rabbi Judah abruptly stopped speaking and called out: "Whoever ate the garlic, leave!"

2 Almost immediately Rabbi Hiyya, a scholar only slightly less prominent than the speaker, rose from his seat and started toward the back. Many other listeners, mortified by Rabbi Hiyya's public embarrassment, followed him out, and the lecture was canceled.

3 The next morning, Rabbi Judah's son confronted Rabbi Hiyya, and criticized him for spoiling his father's lecture.

4 "God forbid that I would ever trouble your father," Rabbi Hiyya responded.

"How can you deny what you did?" the son answered. "Wasn't it you 5
who stood up when my father demanded that the one who had eaten the
garlic leave?"

"I stood up only to avoid the public humiliation of the person whose 6
breath was bothering your father. Since I already have a certain status
among the rabbis, I was willing to accept the embarrassment of being publicly singled out like that. Imagine, though, if the person who had eaten
the garlic was a rabbi of lesser stature than me, or worse, a student. *That*
person would have been deeply humiliated, and likely would have become an object of mockery."*

So far we have been examining the cost of harsh words spoken in anger 7
or criticism. But what of the occasional cruelties to which we are all
prone? In the preceding example, Rabbi Hiyya was concerned with more
than just guarding the unfortunate garlic eater's dignity. He also wished to
prevent Rabbi Judah from violating one of Judaism's most serious ethical
offenses: humiliating a fellow human being.

"Whoever shames his neighbor in public," the Talmud teaches, "it is as 8
if he shed his blood." The analogy is deemed apt, because a shamed person's skin blanches as the blood drains from his face.

Abhorrence at the thought of publicly shaming others, however, does 9
not seem to preoccupy a large number of contemporary journalists, prominent figures, and opinion makers, or, for that matter, ordinary citizens.

In 1959 a prominent businessman donated half a million dollars to a 10
university in Saint Louis, Missouri. The *St. Louis Post-Dispatch* assigned
reporters to write a feature about him. The reporters soon discovered that
the man had served three prison terms, totaling almost ten years, for for-
gery, larceny, and issuing fraudulent checks. In the thirty-five years since
he had left prison, his record had been spotless; in fact, the FBI had
cleared him for defense-related work. More significantly, there was no reason to believe that any of his current money, including the half-million
dollars he had donated to the university, had been earned illegally.

Nonetheless, the reporters headlined the article, which initially was 11
supposed to be complimentary: [SO-AND-SO] . . . MAIN UNIVERSAL MATCH
OWNER, IS EX-CONVICT. The man's wife and son, both of whom did not
know of his earlier criminal record, denounced the piece as "vicious," to
which Raymond L. Crowley, the paper's managing editor, responded: "I
think the stories simply speak for themselves."

---

* The Babylonian Talmud, *Sanhedrin* 11a, recounts this incident. I have greatly expanded on Rabbi
Hiyya's terse explanation for his behavior, putting into his mouth statements that are only suggested
in the text and commentaries.

12   The Talmud's moral standard differs markedly from Crowley's. "If a person is a penitent," it teaches, "it is forbidden to say to him, 'Remember your early deeds.'" Needless to say, it's even more cruel to spread embarrassing reports about the person *to others* when his or her subsequent behavior has been exemplary.

13   The *St. Louis Post-Dispatch* article was harmful to far more people than just this man and his family; it sent a very demoralizing message to everyone who has tried to undo past misdeeds. It told them that no matter how hard they try, through hard work, charitable contributions, or anything that constitutes "doing good," they will forever be linked to the worst acts of their lives; they can never win back their good name. Wouldn't this alone make a person feel that there is little point in changing his ways?

14   The irony of the message communicated by the *St. Louis Post-Dispatch* "exposé" is profound. Years earlier, criminal courts had justifiably punished the man for doing evil. Now, the newspaper was punishing him for doing good.

15   This case is unusual. As a rule, reporters and newspapers rarely go out of their way to humiliate someone against whom they have no grudge. More commonly, journalists, like many of us, are apt to shame only those at whom they already are angry.

16   The desire to humiliate adversaries is particularly common in politics. When South Carolinian Tom Turnipseed ran for Congress in 1980, his Republican rival unearthed and publicized evidence that Turnipseed once had suffered an episode of depression for which he had received electric shock treatment. When Turnipseed responded with an anguished attack on his opponent's campaign ethics, Lee Atwater (who later became famous as the director of George Bush's 1988 presidential campaign, but was then directing the Republican campaign in South Carolina) responded that he had no intention of answering charges made by a person "hooked up to jumper cables."

17   What a grotesque violation of privacy and the dictum against publicly humiliating another! Atwater put into the voters' heads a vicious, graphic image that potentially poisoned not only their perceptions of Turnipseed, but of everyone who has had electric shock therapy.

18   Is it any wonder that some ten years later, when Atwater himself was stricken with an inoperable brain tumor, and found himself attached to unpleasant hospital machinery, that he was moved to write Turnipseed a letter asking forgiveness?

19   In contemporary America, one of the most prestigious and highly paid professions, the law, commonly encourages its practitioners to humiliate those who oppose them in court. Particularly among criminal defense

lawyers, *humiliating* an opposing witness is sometimes regarded as a singularly effective way to discredit testimony. Seymour Wishman, a successful and well-known criminal defense attorney, recalls a difficult defense he had to mount for a client accused of raping and sodomizing a nurse.

Although Wishman had no reason to assume the nurse had fabricated   20
the allegation, he was ecstatic upon learning that the examining police physician had neglected to mention in his medical report whether there was any physical evidence that force had been used against the nurse. This omission freed him to pursue a particularly aggressive cross-examination of the woman, one filled with reputation-damaging and humiliating questions:

Wishman: Isn't it a fact that after you met the defendant at a bar, you
   asked him if he wanted to have a good time?
Witness: No! That's a lie!
Wishman: Isn't it true that you took him and his three friends back to
   your apartment and had that good time?
Witness: No!
Wishman: And, after you had that good time, didn't you ask for money?
Witness: No such way!
Wishman: Isn't it a fact that the only reason you made a complaint was
   because you were furious for not getting paid?
Witness: No! No! That's a lie!
Wishman: You claim to have been raped and sodomized. As a nurse, you
   surely have an idea of the effect of such an assault on a woman's body.
   Are you aware, Mrs. Lewis, that the police doctors found no evidence
   of force or trauma?
Witness: I don't know what the doctors found.

After the trial ended, Wishman was proud when the presiding judge   21
congratulated him for dealing with the woman "brilliantly." He felt considerably less proud half a year later when he accidentally encountered the nurse at her workplace. As soon as she recognized Wishman, she started screaming: "That's the son-of-a-bitch that did it to me!"

Of course, she was referring not to the alleged rape and sodomy, but to   22
the verbal "rape" to which the lawyer had subjected her. According to Wishman, this encounter left him shaken and feeling somewhat guilty.

What *is* amazing is the lawyer's surprise at his own reaction. Why   23
shouldn't he have felt guilty? It's difficult to imagine a greater cruelty toward, and humiliation of, a woman than to suggest that she was a prostitute who had made a false allegation of rape because she hadn't been paid.

24   Atwater's and Wishman's very sincere regrets bring to mind a striking image in the epilogue to George Bernard Shaw's play *Saint Joan*. The scene is set some twenty-five years after Joan of Arc has been convicted of heresy and burned at the stake. When a group of people gather to discuss her impact on their lives, one man says that he feels fortunate to have been present at her execution, because having seen how dreadful it was to burn a person, he subsequently became much kinder. "Must then a Christ perish in torment in every age," another character asks, "for the sake of those who have no imagination?"

25   Is it just some journalists, politicians, and lawyers who lack the empathy to understand how wrong it is to humiliate others? Apparently many of us share in this failing, because the shaming of individuals occurs thousands of times each day. The settings in which this emotional pain is inflicted may be less public, but the damage done can be just as devastating:

26   Take the case of Joanne, a woman I know in her mid-thirties, who is a middle manager at a large corporation. Her job ideally requires her to make public addresses and briefings, but for years her professional advancement has been stunted because of her inordinate fear of public speaking.

27   To Joanne and her many friends, her extreme nervousness has never made sense. Since she has considerable professional expertise, and is very articulate about her work in one-on-one settings, there exists no *logical* reason for her to freeze up every time she is called to make an address in public.

28   In desperation Joanne consulted a psychologist, who hypnotized her. After inducing a deep state of relaxation, the psychologist instructed her to focus on any recollections or associations involving discomfort around public speaking. Joanne began to regress, and was soon vividly reliving a series of episodes that had occurred when she was seven years old. At that time, her parents had recently moved from Chile to Brazil. Although Joanne quickly acquired an adequate grasp of Portuguese, she still made many grammatical mistakes. Unfortunately, her second-grade teacher delighted in summoning Joanne to the blackboard at the front of the classroom and questioning her on material the class had been studying. On several occasions when she answered correctly but made grammatical mistakes, the teacher would ridicule her. After a few such episodes, Joanne chose not to answer at all. "Why do you stand there like a dummy?" the teacher would ask her. "Do you expect the answer to drop down to you from God in heaven?"

29   Twenty-five years later, this highly accomplished adult still finds herself paralyzed when called upon to speak in front of an audience. The schoolteacher's gratification of a sadistic impulse has left Joanne with a lifelong emotional scar. To this day, she continues to go to great (and, from a career standpoint, self-destructive) lengths to avoid situations where she again might be humiliated.

Roberta, another woman I know, recalls a recurring and humiliating   30
trauma from her teenage years. As a young child, she had been her mother's
favorite. But when she became an adolescent and gained twenty pounds,
her mother's expressions of love turned to withering verbal attacks.

Once, when her aunt was visiting, Roberta brought some food to the   31
kitchen table. As she walked away, her mother said to her aunt in a loud
voice: "Do you see how big her ass is, how fat she's become? Doesn't it
look disgusting?" The mother repeated this sentiment many times, always
in the presence of others.

During her high school years, Roberta would wait until every other stu-   32
dent had left the room when a class ended; she did not want people to see
her from the rear. Although she's now over fifty, and her mother has long
been dead, her miserable physical self-image remains perhaps the largest
part of the legacy her mother bequeathed her.

When You've Humiliated Another Person

The great Jewish writer Rabbi Milton Steinberg once said, "When I was   33
young, I admired clever people. Now that I am older, I admire kind
people." Steinberg understood that it's a greater accomplishment to be
kind than to be brilliant.

Harry Truman might not have been the greatest intellectual ever to oc-   34
cupy the office of president. But in addition to his penetrating common
sense, Truman possessed kind instincts, epitomized by the extraordinary
care he took not to humiliate others.

In 1962, some ten years after he left the White House, Truman lectured   35
before a group of university students in Los Angeles. During the question-
and-answer period, a student asked him: "What do you think of our local
yokel?" referring to California Governor Pat Brown.

Mr. Truman bristled and told the boy he should be ashamed of himself   36
for speaking of the governor in so disrespectful a manner. He continued
scolding the boy a while longer; by the time he finished, the student was
close to tears.

What marks this story off as different from every other account until   37
now is what happened next: "When the question period was over," writes
Merle Miller, author of an oral biography of the president, "Mr. Truman
went to the boy and said that he hoped he would understand that what he
had said had to do with the principle involved and that he meant nothing
personal. The boy said that he did understand, and the two shook hands.
Afterward Mr. Truman went to see the dean to ask him to send reports
from time to time on the boy's progress in school. The dean said he
would. . . . I asked Mr. Truman if he had ever heard from the boy himself,

and he said, 'He's written me two or three times, and I've written him back. He's doing very well.'"*

38   Compare Truman's behavior with that of Winston Churchill, arguably the greatest statesman of this century and a man of penetrating mind and wit. In an adulatory compilation of Churchill's greatest quotes and quips, James Hume writes of an incident during the 1930s in which a teenager annoyed and heckled Churchill during a speech. The second time the young man spoke up, Churchill replied: "I admire a manly man, and I rejoice in a womanly woman—but I cannot abide a boily boy. Come back in a few years when your cause is as free from spots as your complexion [will then be]." The boy's arguments might well have deserved to be attacked, but if this story is true, why did Churchill have to mock the fact that he had pimples?†

39   While there is little question that the British leader was a greater statesman and intellectual than Truman, it was Truman who had the awareness and sensitivity to realize—not ten years later or even one year later but immediately—that the public scolding he had given the boy, *even if justified*, could subject him to ridicule and contempt. Imagine how different Joanne's life would have been if the teacher who had mocked her had realized right away the unfairness and evil of what she was doing, and desisted and apologized.

40   Other observers of Truman have noted that being attentive to others' feelings was very important to him. In 1964, when newsman Eric Sevareid interviewed him about his presidential experiences, Truman commented: "What you don't understand is the power of a President to hurt."

41   Sevareid was struck by this remark. "An American President has the power to build, to set fateful events in motion, to destroy an enemy civilization. . . . But the power of a President to hurt the feelings of another human being—this, I think, had scarcely occurred to me, and still less had it occurred to me that a President in office would have the time and need to be aware of this particular power among so many others. Mr. Truman went on to observe that a word, a harsh glance, a peremptory motion by a President of the United States, could so injure another man's pride that it would remain a scar on his emotional system all his life."

---

* President Truman's concern about not inflicting gratuitous hurt is confirmed in an anecdote related by Tip O'Neill, the late speaker of the House: "I met [President Truman] with a group of us freshmen when I came to Congress in 1953, and the conversation turned to Mamie Eisenhower [wife of the newly elected Republican president]. Truman said that he had no use for Ike. 'But leave his family alone,' the President continued, his voice rising. 'If I ever hear that one of you attacked the wife or a family member of the President of the United States, I'll personally go into your district and campaign against you'" (Tip O'Neill with Gary Hymel, *All Politics Is Local* [New York: Times Books, 19941, p. 35).
† There is reason to suspect that as Churchill grew older, he became far more sensitive to the power of cruel words to hurt.

If an American president, constantly besieged with personal, administrative, and political demands, can find the time to reflect on whether his words unintentionally shame another, doesn't it behoove all of us to do the same?

Guidelines for Ensuring That We Don't Humiliate Others

What was it about Harry Truman that caused him to be so conscious of the damage words can cause? It wasn't an exceedingly mild disposition, for the many Truman biographies indicate that he was an impassioned man who frequently lost his temper. But even when he expressed anger, what stopped him from humiliating others, or caused him immediately to set out to repair the damage if he feared he had done so, was his conscious internalization of the observation he made to Sevareid: "What you don't understand is the power of a President to hurt."

Change "the power of a President" to "the power of words," and you realize that we all have the ability to shame others.

If you reflect for a few moments, you'll realize how many people you can wound verbally (and perhaps already have): your spouse, parents, other relatives, friends, and/or people who work for you.

The first step in ensuring that we don't abuse this power is to be aware that we have it; otherwise, we'll feel no need to guard our tongues.

While it is important to recognize the power of words to hurt, such recognition alone is certainly not sufficient to stop us from using words destructively. No doubt many readers have nodded as they have read each episode in this chapter, mentally acknowledging the great evil of shaming others. However, unless you make such an acknowledgment *again and again*, you will probably forget it, particularly during moments of anger.

A popular British story tells of a very prominent politician who one night had imbibed too much liquor, and stumbled into a heavy-set female member of Parliament from the opposition party. Annoyed, the woman said to him, "You are drunk, and what's more, you are disgustingly drunk." To which the British parliamentarian responded: "And might I say, you are ugly, and what's more, disgustingly ugly. But tomorrow, I shall be sober."

If you, like the politician in question, have a quick temper and pride yourself on having a sharp wit, it is important that you *reflect again and again on the moral evil of shaming another person.*

For Lee Atwater it was only when he was lying on his deathbed that it became obvious to him how cruel it was to have mocked one of the most painful episodes in another man's life. I am sure that had Atwater been taught throughout his life *again and again*, as I believe all of us must be taught *again and again*, that humiliating another person is as evil as going up to someone in the street and punching him in the face, he wouldn't have done so in the first place.

51　　Similarly, if my friend Roberta's mother, who jeered at her for being overweight, had reminded herself repeatedly how hurtful her words could be—so much so that, *forty years later,* her daughter still looks contemptuously at herself in the mirror—would she not have learned to curb her tongue? I suspect she would have, for Roberta is certain that her mother loved her, since she expressed many warm feelings toward her daughter on other occasions. Yet because Roberta's mother never learned to reflect on her potentially destructive power of words, she didn't feel the need to restrain her tongue when angry. She went through life like a reckless child playing with a loaded gun, and never understood that words are like bullets, and the damage they wreak often cannot be undone.

52　　An ancient Jewish teaching observes: "It would be better for a person not to have been born at all than to experience these seven things: the death of his children in his lifetime, economic dependence upon others, an unnatural death, forgetting his learning, suffering, slavery, and publicly shaming his fellow man."

53　　The first six items on this list represent some of the most horrific fates imaginable. Anyone who knows someone who has buried a child realizes that no parent ever fully recovers from such pain. Similarly, the prospect of becoming totally dependent on others, or even worse becoming another's slave, is horrifying. As for "forgetting his learning," we have all heard of people committing suicide after being diagnosed with Alzheimer's disease. Although most people won't take so drastic a step, I suspect most of us would prefer to die than to go through life with severe brain damage.

54　　It's striking that the Rabbis included "and publicly shaming his fellow man" on the listing of terrible occurrences. Note that they did not say "being *publicly shamed,*" but "*publicly shaming* his fellow man." To the Rabbis, becoming the kind of malevolent human being who humiliates others is as appalling a fate as losing a child—or one's mind.

55　　Why? Every monotheistic faith believes that our mental capacities are God-given and that human beings were brought into this world to do good. If it's wrong to squander the gifts bestowed by God, how much worse it is to turn them to such an evil purpose as deliberately hurting another!

56　　Finally, remember that *it is when you are most upset that you need to consider your words most carefully.* Admittedly, thinking about the consequences of what you say before you say it is particularly difficult at such a time. Rabbi Judah the Prince was so bothered by the smell of garlic that he didn't reflect on the shame his words might inflict on the person who had eaten it. Winston Churchill was so annoyed by the young man's irritating behavior that he only wished to find a "put-down" that would make others laugh at the boy's unappealing physical traits. But while Rabbi Judah and Churchill were justified in being annoyed at the provocative behavior directed toward them, the "punishment" inflicted by their sharp words far outweighed the victims' "crimes."

Jewish law asks us to take care not to humiliate others even in far-fetched 57 cases: "If someone was hanged in a person's family, don't say to him, 'Hang up this fish for me,'" lest you trigger that distressful memory or remind others who are present of the shameful event. If we are supposed to be morally vigilant even in such a remote case, how much more careful should we be not to publicly mock someone's bad breath, acne, or ugliness.

If you have humiliated another person, of course you should apologize 58 to him or her. But the far more moral thing to do is to exercise restraint *before* you inflict shame, for the greatest remorse and the best will in the world never can erase your words. You can do everything possible to try to minimize their impact, but unfortunately, that is all you can do.

QUESTIONING AND DISCUSSING

Telushkin, "The Cost of Public Humiliation"

1. Telushkin takes a strong moral stand in "The Cost of Public Humiliation." How does Telushkin reveal his point of view?
2. Comment on Telushkin's use of a range of examples to back up his overall argument. What purpose might this serve?
3. How does Telushkin's notion of moral vigilance provide additional context for your readings of "Old Horse" and Gates's essay on Louis Farrakhan?

⊞

ALBERT CAMUS

Considered one of the most significant writers and thinkers of the twentieth century, Albert Camus (1913–1960) was born in Algiers. In his youth, he was active in social reform and was for a short time a member of the Communist Party. During the Second World War, Camus joined the French Resistance to the Nazis and was the editor of an underground newspaper entitled *Combat*. Camus's belief that the human condition is absurd aligned him with the existentialists. However, he refused to be aligned with that group, and many critics affirm that his works express a "courageous humanism" against oppressive forces. The author of many political essays, novels—including *La Peste* (*The Plague*, 1948)—journalistic essays, and stories, Camus won the Nobel Prize for Literature in 1957. An early draft of an autobiographical novel was found in his briefcase after his death in a car crash; it was later published as *Le Premier Homme* (*The First Man*, 1995).

⊞

The Guest

1   The schoolmaster was watching the two men climb toward him. One was on horseback, the other on foot. They had not yet tackled the abrupt rise leading to the schoolhouse built on the hillside. They were toiling onward, making slow progress in the snow, among the stones, on the vast expanse of the high, deserted plateau. From time to time the horse stumbled. Without hearing anything yet, he could see the breath issuing from the horse's nostrils. One of the men, at least, knew the region. They were following the trail although it had disappeared days ago under a layer of dirty white snow. The schoolmaster calculated that it would take them half an hour to get onto the hill. It was cold; he went back into the school to get a sweater.

2   He crossed the empty, frigid classroom. On the blackboard the four rivers of France, drawn with four different colored chalks, had been flowing toward their estuaries for the past three days. Snow had suddenly fallen in mid-October after eight months of drought without the transition of rain, and the twenty pupils, more or less, who lived in the villages scattered over the plateau had stopped coming. With fair weather they would return. Daru now heated only the single room that was his lodging, adjoining the classroom and giving also onto the plateau to the east. Like the class windows, his window looked to the south too. On that side the school was a few kilometers from the point where the plateau began to slope toward the south. In clear weather could be seen the purple mass of the mountain range where the gap opened onto the desert.

Somewhat warmed, Daru returned to the window from which he had

first seen the two men. They were no longer visible. Hence they must
have tackled the rise. The sky was not so dark, for the snow had stopped
falling during the night. The morning had opened with a dirty light which
had scarcely become brighter as the ceiling of clouds lifted. At two in the
afternoon it seemed as if the day were merely beginning. But still this was
better than those three days when the thick snow was falling amidst un-
broken darkness with little gusts of wind that rattled the double door of
the classroom. Then Daru had spent long hours in his room, leaving it
only to go to the shed and feed the chickens or get some coal. Fortunately
the delivery truck from Tadjid, the nearest village to the north, had
brought his supplies two days before the blizzard. It would return in forty-
eight hours.

Besides, he had enough to resist a siege, for the little room was cluttered
with bags of wheat that the administration left as a stock to distribute to
those of his pupils whose families had suffered from the drought. Actually
they had all been victims because they were all poor. Every day Daru
would distribute a ration to the children. They had missed it, he knew,
during these bad days. Possibly one of the fathers or big brothers would
come this afternoon and he could supply them with grain. It was just a
matter of carrying them over to the next harvest. Now shiploads of wheat
were arriving from France and the worst was over. But it would be hard to
forget that poverty, that army of ragged ghosts wandering in the sunlight,
the plateaus burned to a cinder month after month, the earth shriveled up
little by little, literally scorched, every stone bursting into dust under
one's foot. The sheep had died then by thousands and even a few men,
here and there, sometimes without anyone's knowing.

In contrast with such poverty, he who lived almost like a monk in his
remote schoolhouse, nonetheless satisfied with the little he had and with
the rough life, had felt like a lord with his whitewashed walls, his narrow
couch, his unpainted shelves, his well, and his weekly provision of water
and food. And suddenly this snow, without warning, without the foretaste
of rain. This is the way the region was, cruel to live in, even without
men—who didn't help matters either. But Daru had been born here.
Everywhere else, he felt exiled.

He stepped out onto the terrace in front of the schoolhouse. The two
men were now halfway up the slope. He recognized the horseman as Balducci, the old gendarme he had known for a long time. Balducci was holding on the end of a rope an Arab who was walking behind him with hands
bound and head lowered. The gendarme waved a greeting to which Daru
did not reply, lost as he was in contemplation of the Arab dressed in a
faded blue jellaba, his feet in sandals but covered with socks of heavy raw
wool, his head surmounted by a narrow, short *chèche*. They were ap-

proaching. Balducci was holding back his horse in order not to hurt the Arab, and the group was advancing slowly.

7 　Within earshot, Balducci shouted: "One hour to do the three kilometers from El Ameur!" Daru did not answer. Short and square in his thick sweater, he watched them climb. Not once had the Arab raised his head, "Hello," said Daru when they got up onto the terrace. "Come in and warm up," Balducci painfully got down from his horse without letting go the rope. From under his bristling mustache he smiled at the schoolmaster. His little dark eyes, deep-set under a tanned forehead, and his mouth surrounded with wrinkles made him look attentive and studious. Daru took the bridle, led the horse to the shed, and came back to the two men, who were now waiting for him in the school. He led them into his room. "I am going to heat up the classroom," he said. "We'll be more comfortable there." When he entered the room again, Balducci was on the couch. He had undone the rope tying him to the Arab, who had squatted near the stove. His hands still bound, the *chèche* pushed back on his head, he was looking toward the window. At first Daru noticed only his huge lips, fat, smooth, almost Negroid; yet his nose was straight, his eyes were dark and full of fever. The *chèche* revealed an obstinate forehead and, under the weathered skin now rather discolored by the cold, the whole face had a restless and rebellious look that struck Daru when the Arab, turning his face toward him, looked him straight in the eyes. "Go into the other room," said the schoolmaster, "and I'll make you some mint tea." "Thanks," Balducci said. "What a chore! How I long for retirement." And addressing his prisoner in Arabic: "Come on, you." The Arab got up and, slowly, holding his bound wrists in front of him, went into the classroom.

8 　With the tea, Daru brought a chair. But Balducci was already enthroned on the nearest pupil's desk and the Arab had squatted against the teacher's platform facing the stove, which stood between the desk and the window. When he held out the glass of tea to the prisoner, Daru hesitated at the sight of his bound hands. "He might perhaps be untied." "Sure," said Balducci. "That was for the trip." He started to get to his feet. But Daru, setting the glass on the floor, had knelt beside the Arab. Without saying anything, the Arab watched him with his feverish eyes. Once his hands were free, he rubbed his swollen wrists against each other, took the glass of tea, and sucked up the burning liquid in swift little sips.

9 　"Good," said Daru. "And where are you headed?"

10 　Balducci withdrew his mustache from the tea. "Here, son."

　　"Odd pupils! And you're spending the night?"

12 　"No. I'm going back to El Ameur. And you will deliver this fellow to Tinguit. He is expected at police headquarters."

13 　Balducci was looking at Daru with a friendly little smile.

"What's this story?" asked the schoolmaster. "Are you pulling my leg?"   14

"No, son. Those are the orders."   15

"The orders? I'm not . . ." Daru hesitated, not wanting to hurt the old   16
Corsican. "I mean, that's not my job."

"What! What's the meaning of that? In wartime people do all kinds   17
of jobs."

"Then I'll wait for the declaration of war!"   18

Balducci nodded.   19

"O.K. But the orders exist and they concern you too. Things are brew-   20
ing, it appears. There is talk of a forthcoming revolt. We are mobilized, in
a way."

Daru still had his obstinate look.   21

"Listen, son," Balducci said. "I like you and you must understand.   22
There's only a dozen of us at El Ameur to patrol throughout the whole territory of a small department and I must get back in a hurry. I was told to
hand this guy over to you and return without delay. He couldn't be kept
there. His village was beginning to stir; they wanted to take him back. You
must take him to Tinguit tomorrow before the day is over. Twenty kilometers shouldn't faze a husky fellow like you. After that, all will be over.
You'll come back to your pupils and your comfortable life."

Behind the wall the horse could be heard snorting and pawing the   23
earth. Daru was looking out the window. Decidedly, the weather was
clearing and the light was increasing over the snowy plateau. When all
the snow was melted, the sun would take over again and once more would
burn the fields of stone. For days, still, the unchanging sky would shed its
dry light on the solitary expanse where nothing had any connection
with man.

"After all," he said, turning around toward Balducci, "what did he do?"   24
And, before the gendarme had opened his mouth, he asked: "Does he
speak French?"

"No, not a word. We had been looking for him for a month, but they   25
were hiding him. He killed his cousin."

"Is he against us?"   26

"I don't think so. But you can never be sure."   27

"Why did he kill?"   28

"A family squabble, I think. One owed the other grain, it seems. It's not   29
at all clear. In short, he killed his cousin with a billhook. You know, like a
sheep, *kreezk!*"

Balducci made the gesture of drawing a blade across his throat and the   30
Arab, his attention attracted, watched him with a sort of anxiety. Daru
felt a sudden wrath against the man, against all men with their rotten
spite, their tireless hates, their blood lust.

31 But the kettle was singing on the stove. He served Balducci more tea, hesitated, then served the Arab again, who, a second time, drank avidly. His raised arms made the jellaba fall open and the schoolmaster saw his thin, muscular chest.

32 "Thanks, kid," Balducci said. "And now, I'm off."

33 He got up and went toward the Arab, taking a small rope from his pocket.

34 "What are you doing?" Daru asked dryly.

35 Balducci, disconcerted, showed him the rope.

36 "Don't bother."

37 The old gendarme hesitated. "It's up to you. Of course, you are armed?"

38 "I have my shotgun."

39 "Where?"

40 "In the trunk."

41 "You ought to have it near your bed."

42 "Why? I have nothing to fear."

43 "You're crazy, son. If there's an uprising, no one is safe, we're all in the same boat."

44 "I'll defend myself. I'll have time to see them coming."

45 Balducci began to laugh, then suddenly the mustache covered the white teeth.

46 "You'll have time? O.K. That's just what I was saying. You have always been a little cracked. That's why I like you, my son was like that."

47 At the same time he took out his revolver and put it on the desk.

48 "Keep it; I don't need two weapons from here to El Ameur."

49 The revolver shone against the black paint of the table. When the gendarme turned toward him, the schoolmaster caught the smell of leather and horseflesh.

50 "Listen, Balducci," Daru said suddenly, "every bit of this disgusts me, and first of all your fellow here. But I won't hand him over. Fight, yes, if I have to. But not that."

51 The old gendarme stood in front of him and looked at him severely.

52 "You're being a fool," he said slowly. "I don't like it either. You don't get used to putting a rope on a man even after years of it, and you're even ashamed—yes, ashamed. But you can't let them have their way."

53 "I won't hand him over," Daru said again.

54 "It's an order, son, and I repeat it."

55 "That's right. Repeat to them what I've said to you: I won't hand him over."

56 Balducci made a visible effort to reflect. He looked at the Arab and at Daru. At last he decided.

57 "No, I won't tell them anything. If you want to drop us, go ahead; I'll

not denounce you. I have an order to deliver the prisoner and I'm doing so. And now you'll just sign this paper for me."

"There's no need. I'll not deny that you left him with me." 58

"Don't be mean with me. I know you'll tell the truth. You're from here- 59
abouts and you are a man. But you must sign, that's the rule."

Daru opened his drawer, took out a little square bottle of purple ink, the 60
red wooden penholder with the "sergeant-major" pen he used for making models of penmanship, and signed. The gendarme carefully folded the paper and put it into his wallet. Then he moved toward the door.

"I'll see you off," Daru said. 61

"No," said Balducci. "There's no use being polite. You insulted me." 62

He looked at the Arab, motionless in the same spot, sniffed peevishly, 63
and turned away toward the door. "Good-by, son," he said. The door shut behind him. Balducci appeared suddenly outside the window and then disappeared. His footsteps were muffled by the snow. The horse stirred on the other side of the wall and several chickens fluttered in fright. A moment later Balducci reappeared outside the window leading the horse by the bridle. He walked toward the little rise without turning around and disappeared from sight with the horse following him. A big stone could be heard bouncing down. Daru walked back toward the prisoner, who, without stirring, never took his eyes off him. "Wait," the schoolmaster said in Arabic and went toward the bedroom. As he was going through the door, he had a second thought, went to the desk, took the revolver, and stuck it in his pocket. Then, without looking back, he went into his room.

For some time he lay on his couch watching the sky gradually close 64
over, listening to the silence. It was this silence that had seemed painful to him during the first days here, after the war. He had requested a post in the little town at the base of the foothills separating the upper plateaus from the desert. There, rocky walls, green and black to the north, pink and lavender to the south, marked the frontier of eternal summer. He had been named to a post farther north, on the plateau itself. In the beginning, the solitude and the silence had been hard for him on these wastelands peopled only by stones. Occasionally, furrows suggested cultivation, but they had been dug to uncover a certain kind of stone good for building. The only plowing here was to harvest rocks. Elsewhere a thin layer of soil accumulated in the hollows would be scraped out to enrich paltry village gardens. This is the way it was: bare rock covered three quarters of the region. Towns sprang up, flourished, then disappeared; men came by, loved one another or fought bitterly, then died. No one in this desert, neither he nor his guest, mattered. And yet, outside this desert neither of them, Daru knew, could have really lived.

When he got up, no noise came from the classroom. He was amazed at 65 the unmixed joy he derived from the mere thought that the Arab might have fled and that he would be alone with no decision to make. But the prisoner was there. He had merely stretched out between the stove and the desk. With eyes open, he was staring at the ceiling. In that position, his thick lips were particularly noticeable, giving him a pouting look. "Come," said Daru. The Arab got up and followed him. In the bedroom, the schoolmaster pointed to a chair near the table under the window. The Arab sat down without taking his eyes of Daru.

66   "Are you hungry?"

67   "Yes," the prisoner said.

68   Daru set the table for two. He took flour and oil, shaped a cake in a frying-pan, and lighted the little stove that functioned on bottled gas. While the cake was cooking, he went out to the shed to get cheese, eggs, dates, and condensed milk. When the cake was done he set it on the window sill to cool, heated some condensed milk diluted with water, and beat up the eggs into an omelette. In one of his motions he knocked against the revolver stuck in his right pocket. He set the bowl down, went into the classroom, and put the revolver in his desk drawer. When he came back to the room, night was falling. He put on the light and served the Arab. "Eat," he said. The Arab took a piece of the cake, lifted it eagerly to his mouth, and stopped short.

69   "And you?" he asked.

70   "After you. I'll eat too."

71   The thick lips opened slightly. The Arab hesitated, then bit into the cake determinedly.

72   The meal over, the Arab looked at the schoolmaster. "Are you the judge?"

73   "No, I'm simply keeping you until tomorrow."

74   "Why do you eat with me?"

75   "I'm hungry."

76   The Arab fell silent. Daru got up and went out. He brought back a folding bed from the shed, set it up between the table and the stove, perpendicular to his own bed. From a large suitcase which, upright in a corner, served as a shelf for papers, he took two blankets and arranged them on the camp bed. Then he stopped, felt useless, and sat down on his bed. There was nothing more to do or to get ready. He had to look at this man. He looked at him, therefore, trying to imagine his face bursting with rage. He couldn't do so. He could see nothing but the dark yet shining eyes and the animal mouth.

77   "Why did you kill him?" he asked in a voice whose hostile tone surprised him.

78   The Arab looked away.

79   "He ran away. I ran after him."

He raised his eyes to Daru again and they were full of a sort of woeful in- 80
terrogation. "Now what will they do to me?"

"Are you afraid?" 81

He stiffened, turning his eyes away. 82

"Are you sorry?" 83

The Arab stared at him openmouthed. Obviously he did not under- 84
stand. Daru's annoyance was growing. At the same time he felt awkward
and self-conscious with his big body wedged between the two beds.

"Lie down there," he said impatiently. "That's your bed." 85

The Arab didn't move. He called to Daru: 86

"Tell me!" 87

The schoolmaster looked at him. 88

"Is the gendarme coming back tomorrow?" 89

"I don't know." 90

"Are you coming with us?" 91

"I don't know. Why?" 92

The prisoner got up and stretched out on top of the blankets, his feet 93
toward the window. The light from the electric bulb shone straight into
his eyes and he closed them at once.

"Why?" Daru repeated, standing beside the bed. 94

The Arab opened his eyes under the blinding light and looked at him, 95
trying not to blink.

"Come with us," he said. 96

In the middle of the night, Daru was still not asleep. He had gone to bed 97
after undressing completely; he generally slept naked. But when he suddenly realized that he had nothing on, he hesitated. He felt vulnerable
and the temptation came to him to put his clothes back on. Then he
shrugged his shoulders; after all, he wasn't a child and, if need be, he could
break his adversary in two. From his bed he could observe him, lying on
his back, still motionless with his eyes closed under the harsh light. When
Daru turned out the light, the darkness seemed to coagulate all of a sudden. Little by little, the night came back to life in the window where the
starless sky was stirring gently. The schoolmaster soon made out the body
lying at his feet. The Arab still did not move, but his eyes seemed open. A
faint wind was prowling around the schoolhouse. Perhaps it would drive
away the clouds and the sun would reappear.

During the night the wind increased. The hens fluttered a little and 98
then were silent. The Arab turned over on his side with his back to Daru,
who thought he heard him moan. Then he listened for his guest's breathing, become heavier and more regular. He listened to that breath so close
to him and mused without being able to go to sleep. In this room where

he had been sleeping alone for a year, this presence bothered him. But it bothered him also by imposing on him a sort of brotherhood he knew well but refused to accept in the present circumstances. Men who share the same rooms, soldiers or prisoners, develop a strange alliance as if, having cast off their armor with their clothing, they fraternized every evening, over and above their differences, in the ancient community of dream and fatigue. But Daru shook himself; he didn't like such musings, and it was essential to sleep.

99   A little later, however, when the Arab stirred slightly, the schoolmaster was still not asleep. When the prisoner made a second move, he stiffened, on the alert. The Arab was lifting himself slowly on his arms with almost the motion of a sleepwalker. Seated upright in bed, he waited motionless without turning his head toward Daru, as if he were listening attentively. Daru did not stir; it had just occurred to him that the revolver was still in the drawer of his desk. It was better to act at once. Yet he continued to observe the prisoner, who, with the same slithery motion, put his feet on the ground, waited again, then began to stand up slowly. Daru was about to call out to him when the Arab began to walk, in a quite natural but extraordinarily silent way. He was heading toward the door at the end of the room that opened into the shed. He lifted the latch with precaution and went out, pushing the door behind him but without shutting it. Daru had not stirred. "He is running away," he merely thought. "Good riddance!" Yet he listened attentively. The hens were not fluttering; the guest must be on the plateau. A faint sound of water reached him, and he didn't know what it was until the Arab again stood framed in the doorway, closed the door carefully, and came back to bed without a sound. Then Daru turned his back on him and fell asleep. Still later he seemed, from the depths of his sleep, to hear furtive steps around the schoolhouse. "I'm dreaming! I'm dreaming!" he repeated to himself. And he went on sleeping.

100   When he awoke, the sky was clear; the loose window let in a cold, pure air. The Arab was asleep, hunched up under the blankets now, his mouth open, utterly relaxed. But when Daru shook him, he started dreadfully, staring at Daru with wild eyes as if he had never seen him and such a frightened expression that the schoolmaster stepped back. "Don't be afraid. It's me. You must eat." The Arab nodded his head and said yes. Calm had returned to his face, but his expression was vacant and listless.

101   The coffee was ready. They drank it seated together on the folding bed as they munched their pieces of the cake. Then Daru led the Arab under the shed and showed him the faucet where he washed. He went back into the room, folded the blankets and the bed, made his own bed and put the room in order. Then he went through the classroom and out onto the terrace. The sun was already rising in the blue sky; a soft, bright light was

bathing the deserted plateau. On the ridge the snow was melting in spots. The stones were about to reappear. Crouched on the edge of the plateau, the schoolmaster looked at the deserted expanse. He thought of Balducci. He had hurt him, for he had sent him off in a way as if he didn't want to be associated with him. He could still hear the gendarme's farewell and, without knowing why, he felt strangely empty and vulnerable. At that moment, from the other side of the schoolhouse, the prisoner coughed. Daru listened to him almost despite himself and then, furious, threw a pebble that whistled through the air before sinking into the snow. That man's stupid crime revolted him, but to hand him over was contrary to honor. Merely thinking of it made him smart with humiliation. And he cursed at one and the same time his own people who had sent him this Arab and the Arab too who had dared to kill and not managed to get away. Daru got up, walked in a circle on the terrace, waited motionless, and then went back into the schoolhouse.

The Arab, leaning over the cement floor of the shed, was washing his 102 teeth with two fingers. Daru looked at him and said: "Come." He went back into the room ahead of the prisoner. He slipped a hunting-jacket on over his sweater and put on walking-shoes. Standing, he waited until the Arab had put on his *chèche* and sandals. They went into the classroom and the schoolmaster pointed to the exit, saying: "Go ahead." The fellow didn't budge. "I'm coming," said Daru. The Arab went out. Daru went back into the room and made a package of pieces of rusk, dates, and sugar. In the classroom, before going out, he hesitated a second in front of his desk, then crossed the threshold and locked the door. "That's the way," he said. He started toward the east, followed by the prisoner. But, a short distance from the schoolhouse, he thought he heard a slight sound behind them. He retraced his steps and examined the surroundings of the house; there was no one there. The Arab watched him without seeming to understand. "Come on," said Daru.

They walked for an hour and rested beside a sharp peak of limestone. 103 The snow was melting faster and faster and the sun was drinking up the puddles at once, rapidly cleaning the plateau, which gradually dried and vibrated like the air itself. When they resumed walking, the ground rang under their feet. From time to time a bird rent the space in front of them with a joyful cry. Daru breathed in deeply the fresh morning light. He felt a sort of rapture before the vast familiar expanse, now almost entirely yellow under its dome of blue sky. They walked an hour more, descending toward the south. They reached a level height made up of crumbly rocks. From there on, the plateau sloped down, eastward, toward a low plain where there were a few spindly trees and, to the south, toward outcroppings of rock that gave the landscape a chaotic look.

104   Daru surveyed the two directions. There was nothing but the sky on the horizon. Not a man could be seen. He turned toward the Arab, who was looking at him blankly. Daru held out the package to him. "Take it," he said. "There are dates, bread, and sugar. You can hold out for two days. Here are a thousand francs too." The Arab took the package and the money but kept his full hands at chest level as if he didn't know what to do with what was being given him. "Now look," the schoolmaster said as he pointed in the direction of the east, "there's the way to Tinguit. You have a two-hour walk. At Tinguit you'll find the administration and the police. They are expecting you." The Arab looked toward the east, still holding the package and the money against his chest. Daru took his elbow and turned him rather roughly toward the south. At the foot of the height on which they stood could be seen a faint path. "That's the trail across the plateau. In a day's walk from here you'll find pasturelands and the first no-mads. They'll take you in and shelter you according to their law." The Arab had now turned toward Daru and a sort of panic was visible in his expression. "Listen," he said. Daru shook his head: "No, be quiet. Now I'm leaving you." He turned his back on him, took two long steps in the di-rection of the school, looked hesitantly at the motionless Arab, and started off again. For a few minutes he heard nothing but his own step re-sounding on the cold ground and did not turn his head. A moment later, however, he turned around. The Arab was still there on the edge of the hill, his arms hanging now, and he was looking at the schoolmaster. Daru felt something rise in his throat. But he swore with impatience, waved vaguely, and started off again. He had already gone some distance when he again stopped and looked. There was no longer anyone on the hill.

105   Daru hesitated. The sun was now rather high in the sky and was begin-ning to beat down on his head. The schoolmaster retraced his steps, at first somewhat uncertainly, then with decision. When he reached the lit-tle hill, he was bathed in sweat. He climbed it as fast as he could and stopped, out of breath, at the top. The rock-fields to the south stood out sharply against the blue sky, but on the plain to the east a steamy heat was already rising. And in that slight haze, Daru, with heavy heart, made out the Arab walking slowly on the road to prison.

106   A little later, standing before the window of the classroom, the school-master was watching the clear light bathing the whole surface of the plateau, but he hardly saw it. Behind him on the blackboard, among the winding French rivers, sprawled the clumsily chalked-up words he had just read: "You handed over our brother. You will pay for this." Daru looked at the sky, the plateau, and, beyond, the invisible lands stretching all the way to the sea. In this vast landscape he had loved so much he was alone.

QUESTIONING AND DISCUSSING
Camus, "The Guest"

1. In awarding Albert Camus the Nobel Prize for Literature in 1957, the Committee commented that Camus's work "illuminates the problem of the human conscience of our time." How is this demonstrated in "The Guest"?

2. What is the significance of the title, particularly at the end of the story? Consider the last sentence, concerning the schoolmaster: "In this vast landscape he had loved so much he was alone."

3. What are the values demonstrated by the characters' choices? What are the ironies of those choices? How are these choices and ironies complicated by the gendarme's assertion about responsibilities in times of war? (In addition, you might want to do a bit of research about French colonialism.)

⊞

CYNTHIA OZICK

Cynthia Ozick (1928–) often centers her work on the plight of the immigrant. A short-story writer, translator, critic, essayist, novelist, and poet, Ozick uses language that is marked, in the words of one critic, by "eloquence and intricacy." "The Shawl," written in 1980, is among her most famous stories, and it moved famed writer and Holocaust survivor Elie Wiesel to comment, "Non-survivor [of the Holocaust] novelists who treat the Holocaust ought to learn from Ozick the art of economy and what the French call *pudeur* (modesty)." Another critic commented on Ozick's "impressive intellect" and the way in which it "pervades the words she chooses" and the "stories she elects to tell."

⊞

The Shawl

Stella, cold, cold, the coldness of hell. How they walked on the roads together, Rosa with Magda curled up between sore breasts, Magda wound up in the shawl. Sometimes Stella carried Magda. But she was jealous of Magda. A thin girl of fourteen, too small, with thin breasts of her own, Stella wanted to be wrapped in a shawl, hidden away, asleep, rocked by the march, a baby, a round infant in arms. Magda took Rosa's nipple, and Rosa never stopped walking, a walking cradle. There was not enough milk; sometimes Magda sucked air; then she screamed. Stella was ravenous. Her knees were tumors on sticks, her elbows chicken bones.

2   Rosa did not feel hunger; she felt light, not like someone walking but like someone in a faint, in trance, arrested in a fit, someone who is already a floating angel, alert and seeing everything, but in the air, not there, not touching the road. As if teetering on the tips of her fingernails. She looked into Magda's face through a gap in the shawl: a squirrel in a nest, safe, no one could reach her inside the little house of the shawl's windings. The face, very round, a pocket mirror of a face: but it was not Rosa's bleak complexion, dark like cholera, it was another kind of face altogether, eyes blue as air, smooth feathers of hair nearly as yellow as the Star sewn into Rosa's coat. You could think she was one of *their* babies.

3   Rosa, floating, dreamed of giving Magda away in one of the villages. She could leave the line for a minute and push Magda into the hands of any woman on the side of the road. But if she moved out of line they might shoot. And even if she fled the line for half a second and pushed the shawl-bundle at a stranger, would the woman take it? She might be surprised, or afraid; she might drop the shawl, and Magda would fall out and strike her head and die. The little round head. Such a good child, she gave up screaming, and sucked now only for the taste of the drying nipple itself. The neat grip of the tiny gums. One mite of a tooth tip sticking up in the bottom gum, how shining, an elfin tombstone of white marble gleaming there. Without complaining, Magda relinquished Rosa's teats, first the left, then the right; both were cracked, not a sniff of milk. The duct-crevice extinct, a dead volcano, blind eye, chill hole, so Magda took the corner of the shawl and milked it instead. She sucked and sucked, flooding the threads with wetness. The shawl's good flavor, milk of linen.

4   It was a magic shawl, it could nourish an infant for three days and three nights. Magda did not die, she stayed alive, although very quiet. A peculiar smell, of cinnamon and almonds, lifted out of her mouth. She held her eyes open every moment, forgetting how to blink or nap, and Rosa and sometimes Stella studied their blueness. On the road they raised one burden of a leg after another and studied Magda's face. "Aryan," Stella said, in a voice grown as thin as a string; and Rosa thought how Stella gazed at Magda like a young cannibal. And the time that Stella said "Aryan," it sounded to Rosa as if Stella had really said "Let us devour her."

5   But Magda lived to walk. She lived that long, but she did not walk very well, partly because she was only fifteen months old, and partly because the spindles of her legs could not hold up her fat belly. It was fat with air, full and round. Rosa gave almost all her food to Magda, Stella gave nothing; Stella was ravenous, a growing child herself, but not growing much. Stella did not menstruate. Rosa did not menstruate. Rosa was ravenous, but also not; she learned from Magda how to drink the taste of a

finger in one's mouth. They were in a place without pity, all pity was an-nihilated in Rosa, she looked at Stella's bones without pity. She was sure that Stella was waiting for Magda to die so she could put her teeth into the little thighs.

Rosa knew Magda was going to die very soon; she should have been 6 dead already, but she had been buried away deep inside the magic shawl, mistaken there for the shivering mound of Rosa's breasts; Rosa clung to the shawl as if it covered only herself. No one took it away from her. Magda was mute. She never cried. Rosa hid her in the barracks, under the shawl, but she knew that one day someone would inform; or one day someone, not even Stella, would steal Magda to eat her. When Magda be-gan to walk Rosa knew that Magda was going to die very soon, something would happen. She was afraid to fall asleep; she slept with the weight of her thigh on Magda's body; she was afraid she would smother Magda un-der her thigh. The weight of Rosa was becoming less and less; Rosa and Stella were slowly turning into air.

Magda was quiet, but her eyes were horribly alive, like blue tigers. She 7 watched. Sometimes she laughed—it seemed a laugh, but how could it be? Magda had never seen anyone laugh. Still, Magda laughed at her shawl when the wind blew its corners, the bad wind with pieces of black in it, that made Stella's and Rosa's eyes tear. Magda's eyes were always clear and tearless. She watched like a tiger. She guarded her shawl. No one could touch it; only Rosa could touch it. Stella was not allowed. The shawl was Magda's own baby, her pet, her little sister. She tangled herself up in it and sucked on one of the corners when she wanted to be very still.

Then Stella took the shawl away and made Magda die. 8

Afterward Stella said: "I was cold." 9

And afterward she was always cold, always. The cold went into her 10 heart: Rosa saw that Stella's heart was cold. Magda flopped onward with her little pencil legs scribbling this way and that, in search of the shawl; the pencils faltered at the barracks opening, where the light began. Rosa saw and pursued. But already Magda was in the square outside the bar-racks, in the jolly light. It was the roll-call arena. Every morning Rosa had to conceal Magda under the shawl against a wall of the barracks and go out and stand in the arena with Stella and hundreds of others, sometimes for hours, and Magda, deserted, was quiet under the shawl, sucking on her corner. Every day Magda was silent, and so she did not die. Rosa saw that today Magda was going to die, and at the same time a fearful joy ran in Rosa's two palms, her fingers were on fire, she was astonished, febrile: Magda, in the sunlight, swaying on her pencil legs, was howling. Ever since the drying up of Rosa's nipples, ever since Magda's last scream on the road, Magda had been devoid of any syllable; Magda was a mute. Rosa believed that something had gone wrong with her vocal cords, with her windpipe, with the cave of her larynx; Magda was defective, without a voice; perhaps she was deaf; there might be something amiss with her intelligence; Magda was dumb. Even the laugh that came when the ash-stippled wind made a clown out of Magda's shawl was only the air-blown showing of her teeth. Even when the lice, head lice and body lice, crazed her so that she became as wild as one of the big rats that plundered the barracks at daybreak looking for carrion, she rubbed and scratched and kicked and bit and rolled without a whimper. But now Magda's mouth was spilling a long viscous rope of clamor.

11   "Maaaa—"

12   It was the first noise Magda had ever sent out from her throat since the drying up of Rosa's nipples.

13   "Maaaa . . . aaa!"

14   Again! Magda was wavering in the perilous sunlight of the arena, scribbling on such pitiful little bent shins. Rosa saw. She saw that Magda was grieving for the loss of her shawl, she saw that Magda was going to die. A tide of commands hammered in Rosa's nipples: Fetch, get, bring! But she did not know which to go after first, Magda or the shawl. If she jumped out into the arena to snatch Magda up, the howling would not stop, because Magda would still not have the shawl; but if she ran back into the barracks to find the shawl, and if she found it, and if she came after Magda holding it and shaking it, then she would get Magda back, Magda would put the shawl in her mouth and turn dumb again.

15   Rosa entered the dark. It was easy to discover the shawl. Stella was heaped under it, asleep in her thin bones. Rosa tore the shawl free and flew—she could fly, she was only air—into the arena. The sunheat murmured of another life, of butterflies in summer. The light was placid, mellow. On the other side of the steel fence, far away, there were green meadows speckled with dandelions and deep-colored violets; beyond them, even farther, innocent tiger lilies, tall, lifting their orange bonnets. In the barracks they spoke of "flowers," of "rain": excrement, thick turd-braids, and the slow stinking maroon waterfall that slunk down from the upper bunks, the stink mixed with a bitter fatty floating smoke that greased Rosa's skin. She stood for an instant at the margin of the arena. Sometimes the electricity inside the fence would seem to hum; even Stella said it was only an imagining, but Rosa heard real sounds in the wire: grainy sad voices. The farther she was from the fence, the more clearly the voices crowded at her. The lamenting voices strummed so convincingly, so passionately, it was impossible to suspect them of being phantoms. The voices

told her to hold up the shawl, high; the voices told her to shake it, to whip with it, to unfurl it like a flag. Rosa lifted, shook, whipped, unfurled. Far off, very far, Magda leaned across her air-fed belly, reaching out with the rods of her arms. She was high up, elevated, riding someone's shoulder. But the shoulder that carried Magda was not coming toward Rosa and the shawl, it was drifting away, the speck of Magda was moving more and more into the smoky distance. Above the shoulder a helmet glinted. The light tapped the helmet and sparkled in into a goblet. Below the helmet a black body like a domino and a pair of black boots hurled themselves in the direction of the electrified fence. The electric voices began to chatter wildly. "Maamaa, maaa-maaa," they all hummed together. How far Magda was from Rosa now, across the whole square, past a dozen barracks, all the way on the other side! She was no bigger than a moth.

All at once Magda was swimming through the air. The whole of Magda traveled through loftiness. She looked like a butterfly touching a silver vine. And the moment Magda's feathered round head and her pencil legs and balloonish belly and zigzag arms splashed against the fence, the steel voices went mad in their growling, urging Rosa to run and run to the spot where Magda had fallen from her flight against the electrified fence; but of course Rosa did not obey them. She only stood, because if she ran they would shoot, and if she tried to pick up the sticks of Magda's body they would shoot, and if she let the wolf's screech ascending now through the ladder of her skeleton break out, they would shoot; so she took Magda's shawl and filled her own mouth with it, stuffed it in and stuffed it in, until she was swallowing up the wolf's screech and tasting the cinnamon and al-mond depth of Magda's saliva; and Rosa drank Magda's shawl until it dried. 16

QUESTIONING AND DISCUSSING

Ozick "The Shawl"

1. Critic Francesca Battinieri writes, "Progress has not changed man's tendency to oppress his fellow men, and the so-called 'civilization' of which we are so proud has not prevented [. . .] the appalling atrocities of the Holocaust and its innocent victims. Six million Jews were subjugated, deprived of their houses and their rights, deprived of their dignity, tortured, and murdered without pity." What indications are there that this is a story of the Holo-caust? What are the events of this story?

2. What is the struggle within Rosa? What are the ethical implications of situa-tions in which people are forced to struggle with ethical decisions within completely unethical contexts not of their own making?

3. Look carefully at Ozick's use of language. How does the imagery play counterpoint to the brutality of the situation? Consider, for instance, that Rosa is
a "walking cradle" in a situation that is, essentially, a death march. What
other use of language is equally notable and ironic?

4. Comment on the tragedy of the story and its ending. Why does Rosa cram
the shawl down her throat? What is the additional irony here?

⊞

HOWARD RHEINGOLD

Howard Rheingold has written science fiction and books on science and technology.
Often praised for his ability to translate the complex into simple language, he is
among the few writers who early on tackled the implications of newer technologies.
For instance, in 1985, he published *Tools for Thought: The People and Ideas Behind
the Next Computer Revolution*. Before that, in 1982, he and coauthor Howard Levine
defined seventy scientific terms in language for lay readers in *Talking Tech: A Conver-
sational Guide to Science and Technology*. His other books include *Virtual Community:
Homesteading on the Electronic Frontier* (1993) and *Virtual Reality* (1991). This essay
is taken from *Virtual Community*.

⊞

Disinformocracy

1 Virtual communities could help citizens revitalize democracy, or they
could be luring us into an attractively packaged substitute for democratic
discourse. A few true believers in electronic democracy have had their say.
It's time to hear from the other side. We owe it to ourselves and future
generations to look closely at what the enthusiasts fail to tell us, and to listen attentively to what the skeptics fear. . . .

2 Three different kinds of social criticisms of technology are relevant to
claims of CMC as a means of enhancing democracy. One school of criticism emerges from the longer-term history of communications media, and
focuses on the way electronic communications media already have pre-
empted public discussions by turning more and more of the content of the
media into advertisements for various commodities—a process these critics call commodification. Even the political process, according to this
school of critics, has been turned into a commodity. The formal name for
this criticism is "the commodification of the public sphere." The public

sphere is what these social critics claim we used to have as citizens of a democracy, but have lost to the tide of commodization. The public sphere is also the focus of the hopes of online activists, who see CMC as a way of revitalizing the open and wide-spread discussions among citizens that feed the roots of democratic societies.

The second school of criticism focuses on the fact that high-bandwidth interactive networks could be used in conjunction with other technologies as a means of surveillance, control, and disinformation as well as a conduit for useful information. This direct assault on personal liberty is compounded by a more diffuse erosion of old social values due to the capabilities of new technologies; the most problematic example is the way traditional notions of privacy are challenged on several fronts by the ease of collecting and disseminating detailed information about individuals via cyberspace technologies. When people use the convenience of electronic communication or transaction, we leave invisible digital trails; now that technologies for tracking those trails are maturing, there is cause to worry. The spreading use of computer matching to piece together the digital trails we all leave in cyberspace is one indication of privacy problems to come.

Along with all the person-to-person communications exchanged on the world's telecommunications networks are vast flows of other kinds of personal information—credit information, transaction processing, health information. Most people take it for granted that no one can search through all the electronic transactions that move through the world's networks in order to pin down an individual for marketing—or political—motives. Remember the "knowbots" that would act as personal servants, swimming in the info-tides, fishing for information to suit your interests? What if people could turn loose knowbots to collect all the information digitally linked to *you?* What if the Net and cheap, powerful computers give that power not only to governments and large corporations but to everyone?

Every time we travel or shop or communicate, citizens of the credit-card society contribute to streams of information that travel between point of purchase, remote credit bureaus, municipal and federal information systems, crime information databases, central transaction databases. And all these other forms of cyberspace infraction take place via the same packet-switched, high-bandwidth network technology—those packets can contain transactions as well as video clips and text files. When these streams of information begin to connect together, the unscrupulous or would-be tyrants can use the Net to catch citizens in a more ominous kind of net.

The same channels of communication that enable citizens around the world to communicate with one another also allow government and private interests to gather information about them. This school of criticism is known as Panoptic in reference to the perfect prison proposed in the eighteenth century by Jeremy Bentham—a theoretical model that happens to fit the real capabilities of today's technologies.

7   Another category of critical claim deserves mention, despite the rather bizarre and incredible imagery used by its most well known spokesmen—the hyper-realist school. These critics believe that information technologies have already changed what used to pass for reality into a slicked-up electronic simulation. Twenty years before the United States elected a Hollywood actor as president, the first hyper-realists pointed out how politics had become a movie, a spectacle that raised the old Roman tactic of bread and circuses to the level of mass hypnotism. We live in a hyper-reality that was carefully constructed to mimic the real world and extract money from the pockets of consumers: the forests around the Matterhorn might be dying, but the Disneyland version continues to rake in the dollars. The television programs, movie stars, and theme parks work together to create global industry devoted to maintaining a web of illusion that grows more lifelike as more people buy into it and as technologies grow more powerful.

8   Many other social scientists have intellectual suspicions of the hyper-realist critiques, because so many are abstract and theoretical, based on little or no direct knowledge of technology itself. Nevertheless, this perspective does capture something about the way the effects of communications technologies have changed our modes of thought. One good reason for paying attention to the claims of the hyper-realists is that the society they predicted decades ago bears a disturbingly closer resemblance to real life than do the forecasts of the rosier-visioned technological utopians. While McLuhan's image of the global village has taken on a certain irony in light of what has happened since his predictions of the 1960s, "the society of the spectacle"—another prediction from the 1960s, based on the advent of electronic media—offered a far less rosy and, as events have proved, more realistic portrayal of the way information technologies have changed social customs.

The Selling of Democracy: Commodification and the Public Sphere

9   There is an intimate connection between informal conversations, the kind that take place in communities and virtual communities, in the coffee shops and computer conferences, and the ability of large social groups to govern themselves without monarchs or dictators. This social-political connection shares a metaphor with the idea of cyberspace, for it takes place in a kind of virtual space that has come to be known by specialists as the public sphere.

Here is what the preeminent contemporary writer about the public   10
sphere, social critic and philosopher Jurgen Habermas, had to say about
the meaning of this abstraction:

> By "public sphere," we mean first of all a domain of our social life in which
> such a thing as public opinion can be formed. Access to the public sphere is
> open in principle to all citizens. A portion of the public sphere is constituted
> in every conversation in which private persons come together to form a
> public. They are then acting neither as business or professional people con-
> ducting their private affairs, nor as legal consociates subject to the legal reg-
> ulations of a state bureaucracy and obligated to obedience. Citizens act as a
> public when they deal with matters of general interest without being subject
> to coercion; thus with the guarantee that they may assemble and unite
> freely, and express and publicize their opinions freely.

In this definition, Habermas formalized what people in free societies   11
mean when we say "The public wouldn't stand for that" or "It depends on
public opinion." And he drew attention to the intimate connection between this web of free, informal, personal communications and the foundations of democratic society. People can govern themselves only if they
communicate widely, freely, and in groups—publicly. The First Amendment of the U.S. Constitution's Bill of Rights protects citizens from government interference in their communications—the rights of speech,
press, and assembly are communication rights. Without those rights, there
is no public sphere. Ask any citizen of Prague, Budapest, or Moscow.

Because the public sphere depends on free communication and discus-   12
sion of ideas, as soon as your political entity grows larger than the number
of citizens you can fit into a modest town hall, this vital marketplace for
political ideas can be powerfully influenced by changes in communications technology. According to Habermas,

> When the public is large, this kind of communication requires certain
> means of dissemination and influence; today, newspapers and periodicals, ra-
> dio and television are the media of the public sphere. . . . The term "public
> opinion" refers to the functions of criticism and control or organized state
> authority that the public exercises informally, as well as formally during pe-
> riodic elections. Regulations concerning the publicness (or publicity [Pub-
> lizitat] in its original meaning) of state-related activities, as, for instance, the
> public accessibility required of legal proceedings, are also connected with
> this function of public opinion. To the public sphere as a sphere mediat-
> ing between state and society, a sphere in which the public is the vehicle
> of publicness—the publicness that once had to win out against the secret

politics of monarchs and that since then has permitted democratic control of state activity.

13   Ask anybody in China about the right to talk freely among friends and neighbors, to own a printing press, to call a meeting to protest government policy, or to run a BBS. But brute totalitarian seizure of communications technology is not the only way that political powers can neutralize the ability of citizens to talk freely. It is also possible to alter the nature of discourse by inventing a kind of paid fake discourse. If a few people have control of what goes into the daily reporting of the news, and those people are in the business of selling advertising, all kinds of things become possible for those who can afford to pay.

14   Habermas had this to say about the corrupting influence of ersatz public opinion:

> Whereas at one time publicness was intended to subject persons or things to the public use of reason and to make political decisions subject to revision before the tribunal of public opinion, today it has often enough already been enlisted in the aid of the secret policies of interest groups; in the form of "publicity" it now acquires public prestige for persons or things and renders them capable of acclamation in a climate of nonpublic opinion. The term "public relations" itself indicates how a public sphere that formerly emerged from the structure of society must now be produced circumstantially on a case-by-case basis.

15   The idea that public opinion can be manufactured and the fact that electronic spectacles can capture the attention of a majority of the citizenry damaged the foundations of democracy. According to Habermas,

> It is no accident that these concepts of the public sphere and public opinion were not formed until the eighteenth century. They derive their specific meaning from a concrete historical situation. It was then that one learned to distinguish between opinion and public opinion. . . . Public opinion, in terms of its very idea, can be formed only if a public that engages in rational discussion exists. Public discussions that are institutionally protected and that take, with critical intent, the exercise of political authority as their theme have not existed since time immemorial.

The public sphere and democracy were born at the same time, from the same sources. Now that the public sphere, cut off from its roots, seems to be dying, democracy is in danger, too.

16   The concept of the public sphere as discussed by Habermas and others includes several requirements for authenticity that people who live in democratic societies would recognize: open access, voluntary participa-

tion, participation outside institutional roles, the generation of public opinion through assemblies of citizens who engage in rational argument, the freedom to express opinions, and the freedom to discuss matters of the state and criticize the way state power is organized. Acts of speech and publication that specifically discuss the state are perhaps the most important kind protected by the First Amendment of the U.S. Constitution and similar civil guarantees elsewhere in the world. Former Soviets and Eastern Europeans who regained it after decades of censorship offer testimony that the most important freedom of speech is the freedom to speak about freedoms.

In eighteenth-century America, the Committees of Correspondence 17 were one of the most important loci of the public sphere in the years of revolution and constitution-building. If you look closely at the roots of the American Revolution, it becomes evident that a text-based, horseback-transported version of networking was an old American tradition. In their book *Networking*, Jessica Lipnack and Jeffrey Stamps describe these committees as

> a communications forum where homespun political and economic thinkers hammered out their ideological differences, sculpting the form of a separate and independent country in North America. Writing to one another and sharing letters with neighbors, this revolutionary generation nurtured its adolescent ideas into a mature politics. Both men and women participated in the debate over independence from England and the desirable shape of the American future. . . .
>
> During the years in which the American Revolution was percolating, letters, news-sheets, and pamphlets carried from one village to another were the means by which ideas about democracy were refined. Eventually, the correspondents agreed that the next step in their idea exchange was to hold a face-to-face meeting. The ideas of independence and government had been debated, discussed, discarded, and reformulated literally hundreds of times by the time people in the revolutionary network met in Philadelphia.
>
> Thus, a network of correspondence and printed broadsides led to the formation of an organization after the writers met in a series of conferences and worked out a statement of purpose—which they called a "Declaration of Independence." Little did our early networking grandparents realize that the result of their youthful idealism, less than two centuries later, would be a global superpower with an unparalleled ability to influence the survival of life on the planet.

As the United States grew and technology changed, the ways in which 18 these public discussions of "matters of general interest," as Habermas called them—slavery and the rights of the states versus the power of the federal government were two such matters that loomed large—began to change as well. The text-based media that served as the channel for discourse gained more and more power to reshape the nature of that discourse. The communications media of the nineteenth century were the newspapers, the penny press, the first generation of what has come to be known as the mass media. At the same time, the birth of advertising and the beginnings of the public-relations industry began to undermine the public sphere by inventing a kind of buyable and sellable phony discourse that displaced the genuine kind.

19   The simulation (and therefore destruction) of authentic discourse, first in the United States, and then spreading to the rest of the world, is what Guy Debord would call the first quantum leap into the "society of the spectacle" and what Jean Baudrillard would recognize as a milestone in the world's slide into hyper-reality. Mass media's colonization of civil society turned into a quasi-political campaign promoting technology itself when the image-making technology of television came along. ("Progress is our most important product," said General Electric spokesman Ronald Reagan, in the early years of television.) And in the twentieth century, as the telephone, radio, and television became vehicles for public discourse, the nature of political discussion has mutated into something quite different from anything the framers of the Constitution could have foreseen.

20   A politician is now a commodity, citizens are consumers, and issues are decided via sound-bites and staged events. The television camera is the only spectator that counts at a political demonstration or convention. According to Habermas and others, the way the new media have been commoditized through this evolutionary process from hand-printed broadside to telegraph to penny press to mass media has led to the radical deterioration of the public sphere. The consumer society has become the accepted model both for individual behavior and political decision making. Discourse degenerated into publicity, and publicity used the increasing power of electronic media to alter perceptions and shape beliefs.

21   The consumer society, the most powerful vehicle for generating short-term wealth ever invented, ensures economic growth by first promoting the idea that the way to be is to buy. The engines of wealth depend on a fresh stream of tabloids sold at convenience markets and television programs to tell us what we have to buy next in order to justify our existence. What used to be a channel for authentic communication has become a channel for the updating of commercial desire.

22   Money plus politics plus network television equals an effective system. It works. When the same packaging skills that were honed on automobile tail fins and fast foods are applied to political ideas, the highest bidder can

influence public policy to great effect. What dies in the process is the rational discourse at the base of civil society. That death manifests itself in
longings that aren't fulfilled by the right kind of shoes in this month's
color or the hot new prime-time candidate everybody is talking about.
Some media scholars are claiming a direct causal connection between the
success of commercial television and the loss of citizen interest in the political process.

Another media critic, Neal Postman, in his book *Amusing Ourselves to* 23
Death, pointed out that Tom Paine's *Common Sense* sold three hundred
thousand copies in five months in 1776. The most successful democratic
revolution in history was made possible by a citizenry that read and debated widely among themselves. Postman pointed out that the mass media, and television in particular, had changed the mode of discourse itself,
by substituting fast cuts, special effects, and sound-bites for reasoned discussion or even genuine argument.

The various hypotheses about commodification and mode of discourse 24
focus on an area of apparent agreement among social observers who have
a long history of heated disagreements.

When people who have become fascinated by BBSs or networks start 25
spreading the idea that such networks are inherently democratic in some
magical way, without specifying the hard work that must be done in real
life to harvest the fruits of that democratizing power, they run the danger
of becoming unwitting agents of commodification. First, it pays to understand how old the idea really is. Next, it is important to realize that the
hopes of technophiles have often been used to sell technology for commercial gain. In this sense, CMC enthusiasts run the risk of becoming un-
paid, unwitting advertisers for those who stand to gain financially from
adoption of new technology.

The critics of the idea of electronic democracy have unearthed exam- 26
ples from a long tradition of utopian rhetoric that James Carey has called
"the rhetoric of the 'technological sublime.'" He put it this way:

> Despite the manifest failure of technology to resolve pressing social issues
> over the last century, contemporary intellectuals continue to see revolu-
> tionary potential in the latest technological gadgets that are pictured as a
> force outside history and politics. . . . In modern futurism, it is the machines
> that possess teleological insight. Despite the shortcomings of town meetings,
> newspaper, telegraph, wireless, and television to create the conditions of
> a new Athens, contemporary advocates of technological liberation regu-
> larly describe a new postmortem age of instantaneous daily plebiscitory
> democracy through a computerized system of electronic voting and opin-
> ion polling.

27   Carey was prophetic in at least one regard—he wrote this years before Ross Perot and William Clinton both started talking about their versions of electronic democracy during the 1992 U.S. presidential campaign. If the United States is on the road to a version of electronic democracy in which the president will have electronic town hall meetings, including instant voting-by-telephone to "go directly to the people" (and perhaps bypass Congress?) on key issues, it is important for American citizens to understand the potential pitfalls of decision making by plebiscite. Media-manipulated plebiscites as political tools go back to Joseph Goebbels, who used radio so effectively in the Third Reich. Previous experiments in instant home polling and voting had been carried out by Warners, with their Qube service, in the early 1980s. One critic, political scientist Jean Betheke Elshtain, called the television-voting model an

> interactive shell game [that] cons us into believing that we are participating when we are really simply performing as the responding "end" of a prefabricated system of external stimuli. . . . In a plebiscitary system, the views of the majority . . . swamp minority or unpopular views. Plebiscitism is compatible with authoritarian politics carried out under the guise of, or with the connivance of, majority views. That opinion can be registered by easily manipulated, ritualistic plebiscites, so there is no need for debate on substantive questions.

28   What does it mean that the same hopes, described in the same words, for a decentralization of power, a deeper and more widespread citizen involvement in matters of state, a great equalizer for ordinary citizens to counter the forces of central control, have been voiced in the popular press for two centuries in reference to steam, electricity, and television? We've had enough time to live with steam, electricity, and television to recognize that they did indeed change the world, and to recognize that the utopia of technological millenarians has not yet materialized.

29   An entire worldview and sales job are packed into the word *progress*, which links the notion of improvement with the notion of innovation, highlights the benefits of innovation while hiding the toxic side-effects of extractive and lucrative technologies, and then sells more of it to people via television as a cure for the stress of living in a technology-dominated world. The hope that the next technology will solve the problems created by the way the last technology was used is a kind of millennial, even messianic, hope, apparently ever-latent in the breasts of the citizenry. The myth of technological progress emerged out of the same Age of Reason that gave us the myth of representative democracy, a new organizing vi-

sion that still works pretty well, despite the decline in vigor of the old democratic institutions. It's hard to give up on one Enlightenment ideal while clinging to another.

I believe it is too early to judge which set of claims will prove to be ac- 30
curate. I also believe that those who would prefer the more democratic vision of the future have an opportunity to influence the outcome, which is precisely why online activists should delve into the criticisms that have been leveled against them. If electronic democracy advocates can address these critiques successfully, their claims might have a chance. If they cannot, perhaps it would be better not to raise people's hopes. Those who are not aware of the history of dead ends are doomed to replay them, hopes high, again and again.

The idea that putting powerful computers in the hands of citizens will 31
shield the citizenry against totalitarian authorities echoes similar, older beliefs about citizen-empowering technology. As Langdon Winner (an author every computer revolutionary ought to read) put it in his essay "Mythinformation,"

> Of all the computer enthusiasts' political ideas, there is none more poignant than the faith that the computer is destined to become a potent equalizer in modern society. . . . Presumably, ordinary citizens equipped with microcomputers will be able to counter the influence of large, computer-based organizations.
>
> Notions of this kind echo beliefs of eighteenth-century revolutionaries that placing fire arms in the hands of the people was crucial to overthrowing entrenched authority. In the American Revolution, French Revolution, Paris Commune, and Russian Revolution the role of "the people armed" was central to the revolutionary program. As the military defeat of the Paris Commune made clear, however, the fact that the popular forces have guns may not be decisive. In a contest of force against force, the larger, more sophisticated, more ruthless, better equipped competitor often has the upper hand. Hence, the availability of low-cost computing power may move the baseline that defines electronic dimensions of social influence, but it does not necessarily alter the relative balance of power. Using a personal computer makes one no more powerful vis-à-vis, say, the National Security Agency than flying a hang glider establishes a person as a match for the U.S. Air Force.

The great power of the idea of electronic democracy is that technical 32
trends in communications technologies can help citizens break the monopoly on their attention that has been enjoyed by the powers behind the broadcast paradigm—the owners of television networks, newspaper

syndicates, and publishing conglomerates. The great weakness of the idea of electronic democracy is that it can be more easily commodified than explained. . . .

33   What should those of us who believe in the democratizing potential of virtual communities do about the technological critics? I believe we should invite them to the table and help them see the flaws in our dreams, the bugs in our designs. I believe we should study what the historians and social scientists have to say about the illusions and power shifts that accompanied the diffusion of previous technologies. CMC and technology in general [have] real limits; it's best to continue to listen to those who understand the limits, even as we continue to explore the technologies' positive capabilities. Failing to fall under the spell of the "rhetoric of the logical sublime," actively questioning and examining social assumptions about the effects of new technologies, [and] reminding ourselves that electronic communication has powerful illusory capabilities are all good steps to take to prevent disasters.

34   If electronic democracy is to succeed, however, in the face of all the obstacles, activists must do more than avoid mistakes. Those who would use computer networks as political tools must go forward and actively apply their theories to more and different kinds of communities. If there is a last good hope, a bulwark against the hyper-reality of Baudrillard or Forster, it will come from a new way of looking at technology. Instead of falling under the spell of a sales pitch, or rejecting new technologies as instruments of illusion, we need to look closely at new technologies and ask how they can help build stronger, more humane communities—and ask how they might be obstacles to that goal. The late 1990s may eventually be seen in retrospect as a narrow window of historical opportunity, when people either acted or failed to act effectively to regain control over communications technologies. Armed with knowledge, guided by a clear, human-centered vision, governed by a commitment to civil discourse, we the citizens hold the key levers at a pivotal time. What happens next is largely up to us.

QUESTIONING AND DISCUSSING

Rheingold, "Disinformocracy"

1. Rheingold believes in "the democratizing potential of virtual communities." Given this text and your own observations, is the Internet a valuable forum for democracy? How has technology evolved since this essay was published? How is the Internet democratic? How not? How does virtual reality often replicate "reality" itself?

2. Consider the other technologies that have evolved since 1993: text messaging and picture phones, for instance. Do these support or refute Rheingold's contention that there is the risk of a "direct assault on personal liberty" and the "erosion of old social values"? (And what are these "old social values"? Are they worth keeping, in many ways? Defend your point of view here.)

3. How would you critique Rheingold's use of the views of the philosopher Habermas to make his points about "authenticity" and "open access"?

4. Discuss Rheingold's citing of the term *technological sublime* and its implications. Do images foster participatory democracy? What else do they foster? Why?

🔲

BANNED PHOTOGRAPH:
"THE UNIVERSITY OF ARIZONA CLASS OF 1898–1899"

Part of the photographic archive of the University of Arizona, this photograph was banned after it was taken because of the two couples who (it was felt) dared to hold hands not only in public but also as the image was being taken.

🔲

QUESTIONING AND DISCUSSING
"Banned Photograph"

1. Some will look at this photograph, learn about its context, and decide that it symbolizes the sexual repression that still exists in the United States despite greater openness in the media. Others will look at and yearn for the "good old days," when a code of acceptable behavior existed and dominated—a code that has been steadily eroded into the twenty-first century. What do you think? Why? Be sure to back up your point of view with specific examples from newspapers, other media, or your general reading.

2. Research the on-again off-again controversy surrounding the banning of photographs (or books, if you prefer) and the ethical and legal issues that come into play with such censorship. Argue the pitfalls of (or, if you wish to try it, the valid reasons) restricting or barring controversial images or books from public view.

⊞

QUESTIONS FOR READING AND RESPONDING

Chapter 2 Evaluating Ideas: How Do I Make Sense of My World?

1. Several of the authors in this chapter deal with the conflicts of freedom versus oppression. Examples might include Howard Rheingold's essay on technology, Cynthia Ozick's story about the Holocaust, and Gerald Early's essay on Afrocentrism. Consider these or any three selections of your choosing. What does each say about oppression and freedom? Use the texts carefully to support your argument.

2. Research definitions of the complex term *ideology*. Looking at the ideological assumptions that underlie arguments, consider the University of Arizona graduation photograph, Margaret Atwood's essay on pornography, or the satire from *The Onion*. What are the ideological assumptions behind these different works? What assumptions do you bring to them as you analyze them?

3. Choose several of the selections in this chapter, noting the ways in which values you believe to be universally held are challenged or subject to change. Consider analyzing Nathaniel Hawthorne's "Young Goodman Brown" and Henry Louis Gates, Jr.'s "The Charmer." How would you describe these values? Do some values seem to change over time, and is such change inevitable? In your view, is this change a positive or negative phenomenon? Why? (It might also be useful to research the philosophical term *moral relativism* and its implications for ethical judgments and behaviors.)

4. How do "Old Horse" and Joseph Telushkin's' "The Cost of Public Humiliation" shed light on one another? What might Telushkin say about the ethics of the situation described in "Old Horse"? What specifically in the Telushkin essay might imply support for your argument or support it directly?

5. The main characters in Albert Camus's "The Guest" and Cynthia Ozick's "The Shawl" are forced to make important ethical choices in contexts that are anything but typical, contexts in which they are, in making their choices, essentially alone. You might wish to research the various definitions of the philosophical movement called *existentialism* as you analyze these similarities and differences in each character's situation and consider them, if you wish, through that lens. Be sure to refer to the text to support your point of view.

⊞

3

Defining Belief Systems

What Do I Believe?

MAD MAGAZINE

The first edition of *Mad Magazine* was published in 1956 by Bill Gaines and Harvey Kurtzman, and, according to *Publisher's Weekly*, "American satirical humor has never been the same since." Known for its idiosyncratic management, *Mad* has never accepted advertising or run reader surveys. Moreover, any attempt to find a cartoonist's or author's name in the magazine will be frustrated by the masthead's own way of acknowledging credit: a notation that the writers and artists are "the usual bunch of idiots."

⊞

The Blasphemous American Satan Family

QUESTIONING AND DISCUSSING

Mad Magazine, "The Blasphemous American Satan Family"

1. This is part of *Mad Magazine's* "Pillage Idiots Department," the subtitle of which notes, "Unfortunately, the subtleties and nuances of American humor often escape [Europeans, Asians, and Middle Easterners], as you'll see in these [. . . .].

    Considering the context, are there other ways to read this cartoon other than the way in which it was intended? What might those readings be? (For instance, there might be people for whom this strip rings all too true.)

2. Discuss the ways in which *Mad Magazine's* choice of the characters from *The Simpsons* for this particular cartoon strip is appropriate (even if it's annoyingly appropriate). What are some of the manifestations of religious beliefs on that television show, and the show's attitude toward those beliefs, that

make this cartoon effective? In what ways are the Simpsons themselves—
and the show itself—often controversial for similar reasons?

3. Note that the foreign country to which this joke assessment of American
culture is attributed is Iraq. Is it only that culture that might find aspects of
American humor offensive? Explain.

FLANNERY O'CONNOR

Born in Savannah, Georgia, Flannery O'Connor (1925–1964) was the only child of
Roman Catholic parents in a Protestant environment. O'Connor attended Georgia
State College for Women and earned a fellowship to the Writers' Workshop at the
University of Iowa, based on the stories she had written for the literary magazine
at Georgia State. In 1950, she was diagnosed with the disease that had killed her
father—lupus—and underwent a series of medical treatments that temporarily put the
disease into remission. Writer Joyce Carol Oates calls O'Connor a devout Catholic,
"one of the great religious writers of modern times." O'Connor's first book, *Wise
Blood* (1952), indicted a popular tendency to secularize religion. In 1955, she published a collection of stories, *A Good Man Is Hard to Find*, followed by a second novel
and stories for a second collection, *Everything That Rises Must Converge* (1965),
which was published posthumously. O'Connor has written that she meant for her
stories to be read as parables, not as examples of realism.

Good Country People

Besides the neutral expression that she wore when she was alone, Mrs.   1
Freeman had two others, forward and reverse, that she used for all her human dealings. Her forward expression was steady and driving like the advance of a heavy truck. Her eyes never swerved to left or right but turned
as the story turned as if they followed a yellow line down the center of it.
She seldom used the other expression because it was not often necessary
for her to retract a statement, but when she did, her face came to a complete stop, there was an almost imperceptible movement of her black eyes,
during which they seemed to be receding, and then the observer would
see that Mrs. Freeman, though she might stand there as real as several
grain sacks thrown on top of each other, was no longer there in spirit. As

for getting anything across to her when this was the case, Mrs. Hopewell had given it up. She might talk her head off. Mrs. Freeman could never be brought to admit herself wrong on any point. She would stand there and if she could be brought to say anything, it was something like, "Well, I wouldn't of said it was and I wouldn't of said it wasn't" or letting her gaze range over the top kitchen shelf where there was an assortment of dusty bottles, she might remark, "I see you ain't ate many of them figs you put up last summer."

2   They carried on their most important business in the kitchen at breakfast. Every morning Mrs. Hopewell got up at seven o'clock and lit her gas heater and Joy's. Joy was her daughter, a large blonde girl who had an artificial leg. Mrs. Hopewell thought of her as a child though she was thirty-two years old and highly educated. Joy would get up while her mother was eating and lumber into the bathroom and slam the door, and before long, Mrs. Freeman would arrive at the back door. Joy would hear her mother call, "Come on in," and then they would talk for a while in low voices that were indistinguishable in the bathroom. By the time Joy came in, they had usually finished the weather report and were on one or the other of Mrs. Freeman's daughters, Glynese or Carramae. Joy called them Glycerin and Caramel. Glynese, a redhead, was eighteen and had many admirers; Carramae, a blonde, was only fifteen but already married and pregnant. She could not keep anything on her stomach. Every morning Mrs. Freeman told Mrs. Hopewell how many times she had vomited since the last report.

3   Mrs. Hopewell liked to tell people that Glynese and Carramae were two of the finest girls she knew and that Mrs. Freeman was a *lady* and that she was never ashamed to take her anywhere or introduce her to anybody they might meet. Then she would tell how she had happened to hire the Freemans in the first place and how they were a godsend to her and how she had had them four years. The reason for her keeping them so long was that they were not trash. They were good country people. She had telephoned the man whose name they had given as reference and he had told her that Mr. Freeman was a good farmer but that his wife was the nosiest woman ever to walk the earth. "She's got to be into everything," the man said. "If she don't get there before the dust settles, you can bet she's dead, that's all. She'll want to know all your business. I can stand him real good," he had said, "but me nor my wife neither could have stood that woman one more minute on this place." That had put Mrs. Hopewell off for a few days.

4   She had hired them in the end because there were no other applicants but she had made up her mind beforehand exactly how she would handle the woman. Since she was the type who had to be into everything, then,

Mrs. Hopewell had decided, she would not only let her be into every-thing, she would *see to it* that she was into everything—she would give her the responsibility of everything, she would put her in charge. Mrs. Hopewell had no bad qualities of her own but she was able to use other people's in such a constructive way that she had kept them four years.

Nothing is perfect. This is one of Mrs. Hopewell's favorite sayings. An- 5
other was: that is life! And still another, the most important, was: well, other people have their opinions too. She would make these statements, usually at the table, in a tone of gentle insistence as if no one held them but her, and the large hulking Joy, whose constant outrage had obliterated every expression from her face, would stare just a little to the side of her, her eyes icy blue, with the look of someone who has achieved blindness by an act of will and means to keep it.

When Mrs. Hopewell said to Mrs. Freeman that life was like that, Mrs. 6
Freeman would say, "I always said so myself." Nothing had been arrived at by anyone that had not first been arrived at by her. She was quicker than Mr. Freeman. When Mrs. Hopewell said to her after they had been on the place a while, "You know, you're the wheel behind the wheel," and winked, Mrs. Freeman had said, "I know it. I've always been quick. It's some that are quicker than others."

"Everybody is different," Mrs. Hopewell said. 7

"Yes, most people is," Mrs. Freeman said. 8

"It takes all kinds to make the world." 9

"I always said it did myself." 10

The girl was used to this kind of dialogue for breakfast and more of it for 11
dinner; sometimes they had it for supper too. When they had no guest they ate in the kitchen because that was easier. Mrs. Freeman always managed to arrive at some point during the meal and to watch them fin-ish it. She would stand in the doorway if it were summer but in the winter she would stand with one elbow on top of the refrigerator and look down on them, or she would stand by the gas heater, lifting the back of her skirt slightly. Occasionally she would stand against the wall and roll her head from side to side. At no time was she in any hurry to leave. All this was very trying on Mrs. Hopewell but she was a woman of great patience. She realized that nothing is perfect and that in the Freemans she had good country people and that if, in this day and age, you get good country people, you had better hang onto them.

She had had plenty of experience with trash. Before the Freemans she 12
had averaged one tenant family a year. The wives of these farmers were not the kind you would want to be around you for very long. Mrs. Hopewell, who had divorced her husband long ago, needed someone to walk over the fields with her; and when Joy had to be impressed for these

services, her remarks were usually so ugly and her face so glum that Mrs. Hopewell would say, "If you can't come pleasantly, I don't want you at all," to which the girl, standing square and rigid-shouldered with her neck thrust slightly forward, would reply, "If you want me, here I am— LIKE I AM."

13   Mrs. Hopewell excused this attitude because of the leg (which had been shot off in a hunting accident when Joy was ten). It was hard for Mrs. Hopewell to realize that her child was thirty-two now and that for more than twenty years she had had only one leg. She thought of her still as a child because it tore her heart to think instead of the poor stout girl in her thirties who had never danced a step or had any *normal* good times. Her name was really Joy but as soon as she was twenty-one and away from home, she had had it legally changed. Mrs. Hopewell was certain that she had thought and thought until she had hit upon the ugliest name in the language. Then she had gone and had the beautiful name, Joy, changed without telling her mother until after she had done it. Her legal name was Hulga.

14   When Mrs. Hopewell thought the name, Hulga, she thought of the broad blank hull of a battleship. She would not use it. She continued to call her Joy to which the girl responded but in a purely mechanical way.

15   Hulga had learned to tolerate Mrs. Freeman who saved her from taking walks with her mother. Even Glynese and Carramae were useful when they occupied attention that might otherwise have been directed at her. At first she had thought she could not stand Mrs. Freeman for she had found that it was not possible to be rude to her. Mrs. Freeman would take on strange resentments and for days together she would be sullen but the source of her displeasure was always obscure; a direct attack, a positive leer, blatant ugliness to her face—these never touched her. And without warning one day, she began calling her Hulga.

16   She did not call her that in front of Mrs. Hopewell who would have been incensed but when she and the girl happened to be out of the house together, she would say something and add the name Hulga to the end of it, and the big spectacled Joy-Hulga would scowl and redden as if her privacy had been intruded upon. She considered the name her personal affair. She had arrived at it first purely on the basis of its ugly sound and then the full genius of its fitness had struck her. She had a vision of the name working like the ugly sweating Vulcan who stayed in the furnace and to whom, presumably, the goddess had to come when called. She saw it as the name of her highest creative act. One of her major triumphs was that her mother had not been able to turn her dust into Joy, but the greater one was that she had been able to turn it herself into Hulga. However, Mrs. Freeman's relish for using the name only irritated her. It was as if Mrs. Freeman's beady steel-pointed eyes had penetrated far enough behind her face to reach some se-

cret fact. Something about her seemed to fascinate Mrs. Freeman and then one day Hulga realized that it was the artificial leg. Mrs. Freeman had a special fondness for the details of secret infections, hidden deformities, assaults upon children. Of diseases, she perferred the lingering or incurable. Hulga had heard Mrs. Hopewell give her the details of the hunting accident, how the leg had been literally blasted off, how she had never lost consciousness. Mrs. Freeman could listen to it any time as if it had happened an hour ago.

When Hulga stumped into the kitchen in the morning (she could walk   17
without making the awful noise but she made it—Mrs. Hopewell was certain—because it was ugly-sounding), she glanced at them and did not speak. Mrs. Hopewell would be in her red kimono with her hair tied around her head in rags. She would be sitting at the table, finishing her breakfast and Mrs. Freeman would be hanging by her elbow outward from the refrigerator, looking down at the table. Hulga always put her eggs on the stove to boil and then stood over them with her arms folded, and Mrs. Hopewell would look at her—a kind of indirect gaze divided between her and Mrs. Freeman—and would think that if she would only keep herself up a little, she wouldn't be so bad looking. There was nothing wrong with her face that a pleasant expression wouldn't help. Mrs. Hopewell said that people who looked on the bright side of things would be beautiful even if they were not.

Whenever she looked at Joy this way, she could not help but feel that it   18
would have been better if the child had not taken the PhD. It had certainly not brought her out any and now that she had it, there was no more excuse for her to got to school again. Mrs. Hopewell thought it was nice for girls to go to school to have a good time but Joy had "gone through." Anyhow, she would not have been strong enough to go again. The doctors had told Mrs. Hopewell that with the best of care, Joy might see forty-five. She had a weak heart. Joy had made it plain that if it had not been for this condition, she would be far from these red hills and good country people. She would be in a university lecturing to people who knew what she was talking about. And Mrs. Hopewell could very well picture her there, looking like a scarecrow and lecturing to more of the same. Here she went about all day in a six-year-old skirt and a yellow sweat shirt with a faded cowboy on a horse embossed on it. She thought this was funny; Mrs. Hopewell thought it was idiotic and showed simply that she was still a child. She was brilliant but she didn't have a grain of sense. It seemed to Mrs. Hopewell that every year she grew less like other people and more like herself—bloated, rude, and squint-eyed. And she said such strange things! To her own mother she had said—without warning, without excuse, standing up in the middle of a meal with her face purple and her mouth half full—"Woman! do you ever look inside? Do you ever look inside and see

what you are *not?* God!" she had cried sinking down again and staring at her plate, "Malebranche was right: we are not our own light. We are not our own light!" Mrs. Hopewell had no idea to this day what brought that on. She had only made the remark, hoping Joy would take it in, that a smile never hurt anyone.

19   The girl had taken the PhD in philosophy and this left Mrs. Hopewell at a complete loss. You could say, "My daughter is a nurse," or "My daughter is a school teacher," or even, "My daughter is a chemical engineer." You could not say, "My daughter is a philosopher." That was something that had ended with the Greeks and Romans. All day Joy sat on her neck in a deep chair, reading. Sometimes she went for walks but she didn't like dogs or cats or birds or flowers or nature or nice young men. She looked at nice young men as if she could smell their stupidity.

20   One day Mrs. Hopewell had picked up one of the books the girl had just put down and opening it at random, she read, "Science, on the other hand, has to assert its soberness and seriousness afresh and declare that it is concerned solely with what-is. Nothing—how can it be for science anything but a horror and a phantasm? If science is right, then one thing stands firm: science wishes to know nothing of nothing. Such is after all the strictly scientific approach to Nothing. We know it by wishing to know nothing of Nothing." These words had been underlined with a blue pencil and they worked on Mrs. Hopewell like some evil incantation in gibberish. She shut the book quickly and went out of the room as if she were having a chill.

21   This morning when the girl came in, Mrs. Freeman was on Carramae. "She thrown up four times after supper," she said, "and was up twict in the night after three o'clock. Yesterday she didn't do nothing but ramble in the bureau drawer. All she did. Stand up there and see what she could run up on."

22   "She's got to eat," Mrs. Hopewell muttered, sipping her coffee, while she watched Joy's back at the stove. She was wondering what the child had said to the Bible salesman. She could not imagine what kind of conversation she could possibly have had with him.

23   He was a tall gaunt hatless youth who had called yesterday to sell them a Bible. He had appeared at the door, carrying a large black suitcase that weighted him so heavily on one side that he had to brace himself against the door facing. He seemed on the point of collapse but he said in a cheerful voice, "Good morning, Mrs. Cedars!" and set the suitcase down on the mat. He was not a bad-looking young man though he had on a bright blue suit and yellow socks that were not pulled up far enough. He had prominent face bones and a streak of sticky-looking brown hair falling across his forehead.

24   "I'm Mrs. Hopewell," she said.

"Oh!" he said, pretending to look puzzled but with his eyes sparkling. "I   25
saw it said 'The Cedars,' on the mailbox so I thought you was Mrs.
Cedars!" and he burst out in a pleasant laugh. He picked up the satchel
and under cover of a pant, he fell forward into her hall. It was rather as if
the suitcase had moved first, jerking him after it. "Mrs. Hopewell!" he said
and grabbed her hand. "I hope you are well!" and he laughed again and
then all at once his face sobered completely. He paused and gave her a
straight earnest look and said, "Lady, I've come to speak of serious things."

"Well, come in," she muttered, none too pleased because her dinner   26
was almost ready. He came into the parlor and sat down on the edge of a
straight chair and put the suitcase between his feet and glanced around
the room as if her were sizing her up by it. Her silver gleamed on the two
sideboards; she decided he had never been in a room as elegant as this.

"Mrs. Hopewell," he began, using her name in a way that sounded al-   27
most intimate, "I know you believe in Chrustian service."

"Well yes," she murmured.   28

"I know," he said and paused, looking very wise with his head cocked on   29
one side, "that you're a good woman. Friends have told me."

Mrs. Hopewell never liked to be taken for a fool. "What are you sell-   30
ing?" she asked.

"Bibles," the young man said and his eyes raced around the room before   31
he added, "I see you have no family Bible in your parlor, I see that is the
one lack you got!"

Mrs. Hopewell could not say, "My daughter is an atheist and won't let me   32
keep the Bible in the parlor." She said, stiffening slightly, "I keep my Bible
by my bedside." This was not the truth. It was in the attic somewhere.

"Lady," he said, "the word of God ought to be in the parlor."   33

"Well, I think that's a matter of taste," she began. "I think . . ."   34

"Lady," he said, "for a Chrustian, the word of God ought to be in every   35
room in the house besides in his heart. I know you're a Chrustian because
I can see it in every line of your face."

She stood up and said, "Well, young man, I don't want to buy a Bible   36
and I smell my dinner burning."

He didn't get up. He began to twist his hands and looking down at   37
them, he said softly, "Well lady, I'll tell you the truth—not many people
want to buy one nowadays and besides, I know I'm real simple. I don't
know how to say a thing but to say it. I'm just a country boy." He glanced
up into her unfriendly face. "People like you don't like to fool with country people like me!"

"Why!" she cried, "good country people are the salt of the earth! Be-   38
sides, we all have different ways of doing, it takes all kinds to make the
world go 'round. That's life!"

39   "You said a mouthful," he said.

40   "Why, I think there aren't enough good country people in the world!" she said, stirred. "I think that's what's wrong with it!"

41   His face brightened. "I didn't inraduce myself," he said. "I'm Manley Pointer from out in the country around Willohobie, not even from a place, just from near a place."

42   "You wait a minute," she said. "I have to see about my dinner." She went out to the kitchen and found Joy standing near the door where she had been listening.

43   "Get rid of the salt of the earth," she said, "and let's eat."

44   Mrs. Hopewell gave her a pained look and turned the heat down under the vegetables. "*I can't be rude to anybody,*" she murmured and went back into the parlor.

45   He had opened the suitcase and was sitting with a Bible on each knee.

46   "You might as well put those up," she told him. "I don't want one."

47   "I appreciate your honesty," he said. "You don't see any more real honest people unless you go way out in the country."

48   "I know," she said, "real genuine folks!" Through the crack in the door she heard a groan.

49   "I guess a lot of boys come telling you they're working their way through college," he said, "but I'm not going to tell you that. Somehow," he said, "I don't want to go to college. I want to devote my life to Chrustian service. See," he said, lowering his voice. "I got this heart condition. I may not live long. When you know it's something wrong with you and you may not live long, well then, lady . . ." He paused, with his mouth open, and stared at her.

50   He and Joy had the same condition! She knew that her eyes were filling with tears but she collected herself quickly and murmured, "Won't you stay for dinner? We'd love to have you!" and was sorry the instant she heard herself say it.

51   "Yes mam," he said in an abashed voice, "I would sher love to do that!"

52   Joy had given him one look on being introduced to him and then throughout the meal had not glanced at him again. He had addressed several remarks to her, which she had pretended not to hear. Mrs. Hopewell could not understand deliberate rudeness, although she lived with it, and she felt she had always to overflow with hospitality to make up for Joy's lack of courtesy. She urged him to talk about himself and he did. He said he was the seventh child of twelve and that his father had been crushed under a tree when he himself was eight years old. He had been crushed very badly, in fact, almost cut in two and was practically not recognizable. His mother had got along best she could by hard working and she had al-

ways seen that her children went to Sunday School and that they read the Bible every evening. He was now nineteen years old and he had been selling Bibles for four months. In that time he had sold seventy-seven Bibles and had the promise of two more sales. He wanted to become a missionary because he thought that was the way you could do most for people. "He who losest his life shall find it," he said simply and he was so sincere, so genuine and earnest that Mrs. Hopewell would not for the world have smiled. He prevented his peas from sliding onto the table by blocking them with a piece of bread which he later cleaned his plate with. She could see Joy observing sidewise how he handled his knife and fork and she saw too that every few minutes, the boy would dart a keen appraising glance at the girl as if he were trying to attract her attention.

After dinner Joy cleared the dishes off the table and disappeared and 53 Mrs. Hopewell was left to talk with him. He told her again about his childhood and his father's accident and about various things that had happened to him. Every five minutes or so she would stifle a yawn. He sat for two hours until finally she told him she must go because she had an appointment in town. He packed his Bibles and thanked her and prepared to leave, but in the doorway he stopped and wrung her hand and said that not on any of his trips had he met a lady as nice as her and he asked if he could come again. She had said she would always be happy to see him.

Joy had been standing in the road, apparently looking at something in 54 the distance, when he came down the steps toward her, bent to the side with his heavy valise. He stopped where she was standing and confronted her directly. Mrs. Hopewell could not hear what he said but she trembled to think what Joy would say to him. She could see that after a minute Joy said something and that then the boy began to speak again, making an excited gesture with his free hand. After a minute Joy said something else at which the boy began to speak once more. Then to her amazement, Mrs. Hopewell saw the two of them walk off together, toward the gate. Joy had walked all the way to the gate with him and Mrs. Hopewell could not imagine what they had said to each other, and she had not yet dared to ask.

Mrs. Freeman was insisting upon her attention. She had moved from 55 the refrigerator to the heater so that Mrs. Hopewell had to turn and face her in order to seem to be listening. "Glynese gone out with Harvey Hill again last night," she said. "She had this sty."

"Hill," Mrs. Hopewell said absently, "is that the one who works in 56 the garage?"

"Nome, he's the one that goes to chiropractor school," Mrs. Freeman 57 said. "She had this sty. Been had it two days. So she says when he brought her in the other night he says, 'Lemme get rid of that sty for you,' and she says, 'How?' and he says, 'You just lay yourself down acrost the seat of that car and I'll show you.' So she done it and he popped her neck. Kept on a-popping it several times until she made him quit. This morning," Mrs. Freeman said, "she ain't got no sty. She ain't got no traces of a sty."

58   "I never heard of that before," Mrs. Hopewell said.

59   "He ast her to marry him before the Ordinary," Mrs. Freeman went on, "and she told him she wasn't going to be married in no *office*."

60   "Well, Glynese is a fine girl," Mrs. Hopewell said. "Glynese and Carramae are both fine girls."

61   "Carramae said when her and Lyman was married Lyman said it sure felt sacred to him. She said he said he wouldn't take five hundred dollars for being married to a preacher."

62   "How much would he take?" the girl asked from the stove.

63   "He said he wouldn't take five hundred dollars," Mrs. Freeman repeated.

64   "Well we all have work to do," Mrs. Hopewell said.

65   "Lyman said it just felt more sacred to him," Mrs. Freeman said. "The doctor wants Carramae to eat prunes. Says instead of medicine. Says them cramps is coming from pressure. You know where I think it is?"

66   "She'll be better in a few weeks," Mrs. Hopewell said.

67   "In the tube," Mrs. Freeman said. "Else she wouldn't be as sick as she is."

68   Hulga had cracked her two eggs into a saucer and was bringing them to the table along with a cup of coffee that she had filled too full. She sat down carefully and began to eat, meaning to keep Mrs. Freeman there by questions if for any reason she showed an inclination to leave. She could perceive her mother's eye on her. The first round-about question would be about the Bible salesman and she did not wish to bring it on. "How did he pop her neck?" she asked.

69   Mrs. Freeman went into a description of how he had popped her neck. She said he owned a '55 Mercury but that Glynese said she would rather marry a man with only a '36 Plymouth who would be married by a preacher. The girl asked what if he had a '32 Plymouth and Mrs. Freeman said what Glynese had said was a '36 Plymouth.

70   Mrs. Hopewell said there were not many girls with Glynese's common sense. She said what she admired in those girls was their common sense. She said that reminded her that they had had a nice visitor yesterday, a young man selling Bibles. "Lord," she said, "he bored me to death but he was so sincere and genuine I couldn't be rude to him. He was just good country people, you know," she said, "—just the salt of the earth."

71   "I seen him walk up," Mrs. Freeman said, "and then later—I seen him walk off," and Hulga could feel the slight shift in her voice, the slight insinuation, that he had not walked off alone, had he? Her face remained

expressionless but the color rose into her neck and she seemed to swallow it down with the next spoonful of egg. Mrs. Freeman was looking at her as if they had a secret together.

"Well, it takes all kinds of people to make the world go 'round," Mrs. Hopewell said. "It's very good we aren't all alike." 72

"Some people are more alike than others," Mrs. Freeman said. 73

Hulga got up and stumped, with about twice the noise that was necessary, into her room and locked the door. She was to meet the Bible salesman at ten o'clock at the gate. She had thought about it half the night. She had started thinking of it as a great joke and then she had begun to see profound implications in it. She had lain in bed imagining dialogues for them that were insane on the surface but that reached below to depths that no Bible salesman would be aware of. Their conversation yesterday had been of this kind. 74

He had stopped in front of her and had simply stood there. His face was bony and sweaty and bright, with a little pointed nose in the center of it, and his look was different from what it had been at the dinner table. He was gazing at her with open curiosity, with fascination, like a child watching a new fantastic animal at the zoo, and he was breathing as if he had run a great distance to reach her. His gaze seemed somehow familiar but she could not think where she had been regarded with it before. For almost a minute he didn't say anything. Then on what seemed an insuck of breath, he whispered, "You ever ate a chicken that was two days old?" 75

The girl looked at him stonily. He might have just put his question up for consideration at the meeting of a philosophical association. "Yes," she presently replied as if she had considered it from all angles. 76

"It must have been might small!" he said triumphantly and shook all over with little nervous giggles, getting very red in the face, and subsiding finally into his gaze of complete admiration, while the girl's expression remained exactly the same. 77

"How old are you?" he asked softly. 78

She waited some time before she answered. Then in a flat voice she said, "Seventeen." 79

His smiles came in succession like waves breaking on the surface of a little lake. "I see you got a wooden leg," he said. "I think you're real brave. I think you're real sweet." 80

The girl stood blank and solid and silent. 81

"Walk to the gate with me," he said. "You're a brave sweet little thing and I liked you the minute I seen you walk in the door." 82

Hulga began to move forward. 83

"What's your name?" he asked, smiling down on the top of her head. 84

85   "Hulga," she said.

86   "Hulga," he murmured, "Hulga. Hulga. I never heard of anybody named Hulga before. You're shy, aren't you, Hulga?" he asked.

87   She nodded, watching his large red hand on the handle of the giant valise.

88   "I like girls that wear glasses," he said. "I think a lot. I'm not like these people that a serious thought don't ever enter their heads. It's because I may die."

89   "I may die too," she said suddenly and looked up at him. His eyes were very small and brown, glittering feverishly.

90   "Listen," he said, "don't you think some people was meant to meet on account of what all they got in common and all? Like they both think serious thoughts and all?" He shifted the valise to his other hand so that the hand nearest her was free. He caught hold of her elbow and shook it a little. "I don't work on Saturday," he said. "I like to walk in the woods and see what Mother Nature is wearing. O'er the hills and far away. Picnics and things. Couldn't we go on a picnic tomorrow? Say yes, Hulga," he said and gave her a dying look as if he felt his insides about to drop out of him. He had even seemed to sway slightly toward her.

91   During the night she had imagined that she seduced him. She imagined that the two of them walked on the place until they came to the storage barn beyond the two back fields and there, she imagined, that things came to such a pass that she very easily seduced him and that then, of course, she had to reckon with his remorse. True genius can get an idea across even to an inferior mind. She imagined that she took his remorse in hand and changed it into a deeper understanding of life. She took all his shame away and turned it into something useful.

92   She set off for the gate at exactly ten o'clock, escaping without drawing Mrs. Hopewell's attention. She didn't take anything to eat, forgetting that food is usually taken on a picnic. She wore a pair of slacks and a dirty white shirt, and as an afterthought, she had put some Vapex on the collar of it since she did not own any perfume. When she reached the gate no one was there.

93   She looked up and down the empty highway and had the furious feeling that she had been tricked, that he had only meant to make her walk to the gate after the idea of him. Then suddenly he stood up, very tall, from behind a bush on the opposite embankment. Smiling, he lifted his hat which was new and wide-brimmed. He had not worn it yesterday and she wondered if he had bought it for the occasion. It was toast-colored with a red and white band around it and was slightly too large for him. He stepped from behind the bush carrying the black valise. He had on the same suit and the same yellow socks sucked down in his shoes from walking. He crossed the highway and said, "I knew you'd come!"

The girl wondered acidly how he had known this. She pointed to the   94
valise and asked, "Why did you bring your Bibles?"

He took her elbow, smiling down on her as if he could not stop. "You   95
can never tell when you'll need the word of God, Hulga," he said. She had
a moment in which she doubted that this was actually happening and
then they began to climb the embankment. They went down into the pasture toward the woods. The boy walked lightly by her side, bouncing on
his toes. The valise did not seem to be heavy today: he even swung it.
They crossed half the pasture without saying anything and then, putting
his hand easily on the small of her back, he asked softly, "Where does your
wooden leg join on?"

She turned an ugly red and glared at him and for an instant the boy   96
looked abashed. "I didn't mean you no harm," he said. "I only meant
you're so brave and all. I guess God takes care of you."

"No," she said, looking forward and walking fast, "I don't even believe   97
in God."

At this he stopped and whistled. "No!" he exclaimed as if he were too   98
astonished to say anything else.

She walked on and in a second he was bouncing at her side, fanning   99
with his hat. "That's very unusual for a girl," he remarked, watching her
out of the corner of his eye. When they reached the edge of the wood, he
put his hand on her back again and drew her against him without a word
and kissed her heavily.

The kiss, which had more pressure than feeling behind it, produced that   100
extra surge of adrenalin in the girl that enables one to carry a packed
trunk out of a burning house, but in her, the power went at once to the
brain. Even before he released her, her mind, clear and detached and
ironic anyway, was regarding him from a great distance, with amusement
but with pity. She had never been kissed before and she was pleased to discover that it was an unexceptional experience and all a matter of the mind's
control. Some people might enjoy drain water if they were told it was
vodka. When the boy, looking expectant but uncertain, pushed her gently
away, she turned and walked on, saying nothing as if such business, for
her, were common enough.

He came along panting at her side, trying to help her when he saw a   101
root that she might trip over. He caught and held back the long swaying
blades of thorn vine until she had passed beyond them. She led the way
and he came breathing heavily behind her. Then they came out on a sun-
lit hillside, sloping softly into another one a little smaller. Beyond, they
could see the rusted top of the old barn where the extra hay was stored.

The hill was sprinkled with small pink weeds. "Then you ain't saved?"   102
he asked suddenly, stopping.

103   The girl smiled. It was the first time she had smiled at him at all. "In my economy," she said, "I'm saved and you are damned but I told you I didn't believe in God."

104   Nothing seemed to destroy the boy's look of admiration. He gazed at her now as if the fantastic animal at the zoo had put its paw through the bars and given him a loving poke. She thought he looked as if he wanted to kiss her again and she walked on before he had the chance.

105   "Ain't there somewheres we can sit down sometime?" he murmured, his voice softening toward the end of the sentence.

106   "In that barn," she said.

107   They made for it rapidly as if it might slide away like a train. It was a large two-story barn, cool and dark inside. The boy pointed up the ladder that led into the loft and said, "It's too bad we can't go up there."

108   "Why can't we?" she asked.

109   "Yer leg," he said reverently.

110   The girl gave him a contemptuous look and putting both hands on the ladder, she climbed it while he stood below, apparently awestruck. She pulled herself expertly through the opening and then looked down at him and said, "Well, come on if you're coming," and he began to climb the ladder, awkwardly bringing the suitcase with him.

111   "We won't need the Bible," she observed.

112   "You never can tell," he said, panting. After he had got into the loft, he was a few seconds catching his breath. She had sat down in a pile of straw. A wide sheath of sunlight, filled with dust particles, slanted over her. She lay back against a bale, her face turned away, looking out the front opening of the barn where hay was thrown from a wagon into the loft. The two pink-speckled hillsides lay back against a dark ridge of woods. The sky was cloudless and cold blue. The boy dropped down by her side and put one arm under her and the other over her and began methodically kissing her face, making little noises like a fish. He did not remove his hat but it was pushed far enough back not to interfere. When her glasses got in his way, he took them off of her and slipped them into his pocket.

113   The girl at first did not return any of his kisses but presently she began to and after she had put several on his cheek, she reached his lips and remained there, kissing him again and again as if she were trying to draw all the breath out of him. His breath was clear and sweet like a child's and the kisses were sticky like a child's. He mumbled about loving her and about knowing when he first seen her that he loved her, but the mumbling was like the sleepy fretting of a child being put to sleep by his mother. Her mind, throughout this, never stopped or lost itself for a second to her feelings. "You ain't said you loved me none," he whispered finally, pulling back from her. "You got to say that."

She looked away from him off into the hollow sky and then down at a 114
black ridge and then down farther into what appeared to be two green
swelling lakes. She didn't realize he had taken her glasses but this landscape could not seem exceptional to her for she seldom paid any close attention to her surroundings.

"You got to say it," he repeated. "You got to say you love me." 115

She was always careful how she committed herself. "In a sense," she began, 116
"if you use the word loosely, you might say that. But it's not a word I use. I
don't have illusions. I'm one of those people who see *through* to nothing."

The boy was frowning. "You got to say it. I said it and you got to say it," 117
he said.

The girl looked at him almost tenderly. "You poor baby," she murmured. 118
"It's just as well you don't understand," and she pulled him by the neck,
face-down, against her. "We are all damned," she said, "but some of us
have taken off our blindfolds and see that there's nothing to see. It's a kind
of salvation."

The boy's astonished eyes looked blankly through the ends of her hair. 119
"Okay," he almost whined, "but do you love me or don'tcher?"

"Yes," she said and added, "in a sense. But I must tell you something. 120
There mustn't be anything dishonest between us." She lifted his head and
looked him in the eye. "I am thirty years old," she said. "I have a number
of degrees."

The boy's look was irritated but dogged. "I don't care," he said. "I don't 121
care a thing about what all you done. I just want to know if you love me
or don'tcher?" and he caught her to him and wildly planted her face with
kisses until she said, "Yes, yes."

"Okay then," he said, letting her go. "Prove it." 122

She smiled, looking dreamily out on the shifty landscape. She had se- 123
duced him without even making up her mind to try. "How?" she asked,
feeling that he should be delayed a little.

He leaned over and put his lips to her ear. "Show me where your 124
wooden leg joins on," he whispered.

The girl uttered a sharp little cry and her face instantly drained of color. 125
The obscenity of the suggestion was not what shocked her. As a child she
had sometimes been subject to feelings of shame but education had removed the last traces of that as a good surgeon scrapes for cancer; she
would no more have felt it over what he was asking than she would have
believed in his Bible. But she was as sensitive about the artificial leg as a
peacock about his tail. No one ever touched it but her. She took care of it
as someone else would his soul, in private and almost with her own eyes
turned away. "No," she said.

"I known it," he muttered, sitting up. "You're just playing me for a sucker." 126

127 "Oh no no!" she cried. "It joins at the knee. Only at the knee. Why do you want to see it?"

128 The boy gave her a long penetrating look. "Because," he said, "it's what makes you different. You ain't like anybody else."

129 She sat staring at him. There was nothing about her face or her round freezing-blue eyes to indicate that this had moved her; but she felt as if her heart had stopped and left her mind to pump her blood. She decided that for the first time in her life she was face to face with real innocence. This boy, with an instinct that came from beyond wisdom, had touched the truth about her. When after a minute, she said in a hoarse high voice, "All right," it was like surrendering to him completely. It was like losing her own life and finding it again, miraculously, in his.

130 Very gently he began to roll the slack leg up. The artificial limb, in a white sock and brown flat shoe, was bound in a heavy material like canvas and ended in an ugly jointure where it was attached to the stump. The boy's face and his voice were entirely reverent as he uncovered it and said, "Now show me how to take it off and on."

131 She took it off for him and put it back on again and then he took it off himself, handling it as tenderly as if it were a real one. "See!" he said with a delighted child's face. "Now I can do it myself!"

132 "Put it back on," she said. She was thinking that she would run away with him and that every night he would take the leg off and every morning put it back on again. "Put it back on," she said.

133 "Not yet," he murmured, setting it on its foot out of her reach. "Leave it off for awhile. You got me instead."

134 She gave a little cry of alarm but he pushed her down and began to kiss her again. Without the leg she felt entirely dependent on him. Her brain seemed to have stopped thinking altogether and to be about some other function that it was not very good at. Different expressions raced back and forth over her face. Every now and then the boy, his eyes like two steel spikes, would glance behind him, where the leg stood. Finally she pushed him off and said, "Put it back on me now."

135 "Wait," he said. He leaned the other way and pulled the valise toward him and opened it. It had a pale blue spotted lining and there were only two Bibles in it. He took one of these out and opened the cover of it. It was hollow and contained a pocket flask of whiskey, a pack of cards, and a small blue box with printing on it. He laid these out in front of her one at a time in an evenly-spaced row, like one presenting offerings at the shrine of a goddess. He put the blue box in her hand. THIS PRODUCT TO BE USED ONLY FOR THE PREVENTION OF DISEASE, she read, and dropped it. The boy was unscrewing the top of the flask. He stopped and pointed, with a smile, to the

deck of cards. It was not an ordinary deck but one with an obscene picture on the back of each card. "Take a swig," he said, offering her the bottle first. He held it in front of her, but like one mesmerized, she did not move.

Her voice when she spoke had an almost pleading sound. "Aren't you," she murmured, "aren't you just good country people?" 136

The boy cocked his head. He looked as if he were just beginning to understand that she might be trying to insult him. "Yeah," he said, curling his lip slightly, "but it ain't held me back none. I'm as good as you any day in the week." 137

"Give me my leg," she said. 138

He pushed it farther away with his foot. "Come on now, let's begin to have us a good time," he said coaxingly. "We ain't got to know one another good yet." 139

"Give me my leg!" she screamed and tried to lunge for it but he pushed her down easily. 140

"What's the matter with you all of a sudden?" he asked, frowning as he screwed the top on the flask and put it quickly back inside the Bible. "You just a while ago said you didn't believe in nothing. I thought you was some girl!" 141

Her face was almost purple. "You're a Christian!" she hissed. "You're a fine Christian! You're just like them all—say one thing and do another. You're a perfect Christian, you're . . ." 142

The boy's mouth was set angrily. "I hope you don't think," he said in a lofty indignant tone, "that I believe in that crap! I may sell Bibles but I know which end is up and I wasn't born yesterday and I know where I'm going!" 143

"Give me my leg!" she screeched. He jumped up so quickly that she barely saw him sweep the cards and the blue box back into the Bible and throw the Bible into the valise. She saw him grab the leg and then she saw it for an instant slanted forlornly across the inside of the suitcase with a Bible at either side of its opposite ends. He slammed the lid shut and snatched up the valise and swung it down the hole and then stepped through himself. 144

When all of him had passed but his head, he turned and regarded her with a look that no longer had any admiration in it. "I've gotten a lot of interesting things," he said. "One time I got a woman's glass eye this way. And you needn't think you'll catch me because Pointer ain't my real name. I use a different name at every house I call at and don't stay nowhere long. And I'll tell you another thing, Hulga," he said, using the name as if he didn't think much of it, "you ain't so smart. I been believing in nothing ever since I was born!" and then the toast-colored hat disappeared down the hole and the girl was left, sitting on the straw in the dusty sunlight. 145

When she turned her churning face toward the opening, she saw his blue figure struggling successfully over the green speckled lake.

146   Mrs. Hopewell and Mrs. Freeman, who were in the back pasture, digging up onions, saw him emerge a little later from the woods and head across the meadow toward the highway. "Why, that looks like that nice dull young man that tried to see me a Bible yesterday," Mrs. Hopewell said, squinting. "He must have been selling them to the Negroes back in there. He was so simple," she said, "but I guess the world would be better off if we were all that simple."

147   Mrs. Freeman's gaze drove forward and just touched him before he disappeared under the hill. Then she returned her attention to the evil-smelling onion shoot she was lifting from the ground. "Some can't be that simple," she said. "I know I never could."

Questioning and Discussing

O' Connor, "Good Country People"

1. Analyze the implications of the story's title, "Good Country People." What are the assumptions behind the serious use of that phrase? How are these undercut? What are the ironies in the title? In the Bible quotations? How are these developed through the story—and at the end?

2. What are the various belief systems that are challenged throughout the story?

3. Comment on the possible meaning of the characters' names and how these contribute to the tone of the story.

4. What is the purpose of the rather macabre series of events at the end of the story? How do "believing," having a "soul," and belief in "nothing" contribute to an overall point to the story? What might that point be? (Refer to the text to support your point of view.)

⊞

REYNOLDS PRICE

Reynolds Price (1933–) has taught at Duke University for more than forty years. A novelist and professor of English, Price also attended Duke and was a Rhodes Scholar. In 1962, Price received the William Faulkner Award for his first novel, *A Long and Happy Life,* and he has since published more than thirty books and works of fiction. Price's work frequently concerns the presence of Christianity in everyday life: *A Palpable God* "contains translations from the Old and New Testaments with an essay on the origins and aims of narrative"; *Three Gospels* features his "translations of the Gospels of Mark and John with introductory essays." Price and his work have also been featured on National Public Radio and the Public Broadcasting System (PBS).

⊞

Dear Harper: A Letter to a Godchild About God

It'll be some years before you read this, if ever. But given the uncertainties of all our futures, I'll set it down here at the time of your baptism and will hope that—should you ever need it—it will be legible still. Since you're under the age of two, chances are slim that you'll feel the need for well more than a decade. By then the twenty-first century will be thoroughly under way. Since it's likely to move as unforeseeably as the twentieth, I'll make no effort to predict how the world will feel then about religious faith.

And I certainly won't guess at what your own relation to faith may be, though your parents and godparents have vowed to guide you toward it. Those adults have old ties to churches, though those ties vary. Above all, none of us know you in the bright wonder of your laughing, open-armed childhood can begin to imagine who you'll be and where you'll want—or need—to go in your youth or your maturity. So here, by way of a gift, are some thoughts that may interest you in time.

As I write, in the spring of 2000, a large majority of the world's people say that they're religious. This year, for instance, 84 percent of the residents of the United States identified themselves as Christian, associates in the world's largest religion. What did they mean by their claim? The *Oxford English Dictionary* says that religion is:

Belief in, reverence for, and desire to please, a divine ruling power; the exercise or practice of rites or observances implying this.

Most Americans today would agree, and I'd suggest only one change. Instead of "divine ruling power," I'd substitute "supreme creative power." And I'd wonder if it mightn't be desirable to strip the definition to its bones—"religion is the belief in a supreme creative power." But perhaps those bones define the word *faith* more adequately than the word *religion*.

6   I hope you'll be interested to know that I—near the start of a new millennium and at the age of sixty-seven—am still able to believe, with no serious effort, that the entire universe was willed into being by an unsurpassed power whom most human beings call God. I believe that God remains conscious of his creation and interested in it. I believe that his interest may be described, intermittently at least, as love (and I say "his" with no strong suspicion that he shares qualities with the earthly male gender).

7   Whether he's attentive to every moment of every human's life, as some religions claim, I'm by no means sure. But I do believe that he has standards of action that he means us to observe. I believe that he has communicated those standards—and most of whatever else we know about his transcendent nature—through a few human messengers and through the mute spectacles of nature in all its manifestations, around and inside us (the human kidney is as impressive a masterwork as the Grand Canyon).

8   God created those spectacles many billion years ago and began to send those messengers, to this planet at least, as long ago as four thousand years, maybe earlier. Those messengers are parents and teachers, prophets and poets (sacred and secular), painters and musicians, healers and lovers; the generous saints of Hinduism, Judaism, Buddhism, Christianity, Islam, and a few other faiths—all the deep feeders of our minds and bodies. One of the matchless gifts of our present life lies in the fact that those messengers continue to come, though the task of distinguishing valid messages from the false or merely confused is hard and often dangerous. At least one of those messengers, I believe, was in some mysterious sense an embodiment of God; and it's to him—Jesus of Nazareth—that you were recently dedicated.

9   Finally, I believe that some essential part of our nature is immortal. The core of each of us is immune to death and will survive forever. Whether we'll experience the eternity as good or bad may depend upon the total record of our obedience to God's standards of action. Most of the long-enduring faith say that we accumulate the weight of our wrongs—our sins, our karma—and will ultimately be confronted with that weight.

10   A wide lobe of my brain finds it difficult to believe that the maker of anything so immense as our universe—and of who knows what beyond it—is permanently concerned with how I behave in relation to my diet (so long as I'm not a cannibal), or my genitals (as long as they don't do willful damage to another creature), or my hair (so long as it doesn't propagate disease-bearing vermin), or a good deal else that concerns many religious people.

11   God likely cares how I treat the planet Earth, its atmosphere, and its nonhuman inhabitants (I think it's possible that he wants us not to kill or

eat other conscious creatures, though I'm a restrained carnivore who feels no real guilt). Above all, the Creator intends that I honor my fellow human beings—whoever and from wherever—and that I do everything in my power never to harm them and to alleviate, as unintrusively as possible, any harm they suffer. God likely expects me to extend that honor to other forms of life, though how far down the scale that honor is to run, I don't know—surely I'm not meant to avoid killing, say, an anthrax bacillus.

12 Though I've mentioned that a preponderance of Americans presently share some version of my beliefs, it's fair to tell you that a possible majority of the social class I've occupied since my mid-twenties—those who've experienced extensive years of academic training—don't share my beliefs nor hold any beliefs that might be called religious. That characteristic of the intellectual classes of the Western world and China (at a minimum) is more than a century old and is the result largely of a few discoveries of the physical sciences and of the worldwide calamities of war and suffering that have convinced many witnesses that no just God exists.

13 My own educational credentials include nineteen years of formal schooling. I've likewise read extensively in the literatures of many cultures that are not my own. How then can I explain my defection, in the matter of faith, from the doubts or flat rejection of so many in my social class? And am I suggesting that the reasons for my defection should have any weight with you, if you should face a crossroads of belief and rejection, at whatever point in your life?

14 In fact, I haven't defected. Put plainly, I have never held all the central dogmas of my caste. I received the rudiments of my faith long before I began to read or attend school. And while that faith has undergone assaults—from myself and others—it's never buckled. To be honest, I've sometimes been suspicious of that apparent strength. Shouldn't anyone who's lived as long as I, on two continents, and who's sustained more than one maiming catastrophe, have felt occasional very dark nights? Well, of course I have; but they've been dark nights of the sort described by the Spanish monk and poet Saint John of the Cross—certain souls may feel God's absence as a form of near desperation, but that pain (which may last a very long while) never tumbles finally into disbelief.

15 Note that I said just above that I received the rudiments of faith. They came from the usual sources—my parents and other kin, the natural world around me (which tended to be rural or wooded suburban), and from God and his various messengers. To say that much, here and now, runs the severe risk of pomposity, an absurd degree of self-love, and a ludicrous elitism. Yet I know of no more accurate way to describe a situation that's far from uncommon.

16   My preparation for faith likely began with the gift of two Bible storybooks—one from my Grandmother Price when I was two or three, the second a year or so later from my parents. They proved to be long-range endowments for the only child I then was (my brother was born just as I turned eight). Each of the books contained strikingly realistic illustrations; and with a small amount of guidance from my parents, I launched myself on an early fascination with the prime characters and stories from Hebrew and Christian sacred texts—Abraham, Isaac, and Sarah; Ruth and Naomi; David, Jonathan, and Saul; Samson and Delilah; Joseph, Mary, and Jesus; Jesus and the girl he raises from the dead; Jesus himself rising from the dead.

17   At about the same time I began occasionally to go to Sunday school with my father; and there I glimpsed the fact that those stories meant something important to other men, women, and children. I must likewise have begun to sense how vital this thing—whatever it was—was to my father. It would be years before I understood that he was, at just that time, withdrawing from years of alcoholism. And in the absence of Alcoholics Anonymous in our part of the world, help for him could only have come from my mother, his minister, and his own tenacious will to quit (he'd reached the age of thirty-three before beginning his battle).

18   When I was six years old, we lived on the edge of a small town. Within roaming distance for me were thickets of pine with plentiful birds, rabbits, foxes, possums, and raccoons; and there was a small stream filled with crawfish, toads, turtles, minnows, and snakes. I spent countless solitary and silent hours exploring that teeming world. And there I began to store up an invaluable sense of the endless inventiveness of life and the savage conditions of so much animal existence. In those same woods, I even found and saved my first flint arrowheads from long-vanished Indians. The simple endurance of those shaped stones helped me further onward with their intimations of the doggedness, and yet the frailty, of human life.

19   Then late one afternoon, still alone but blissful in that world, I was given my first visionary experience. I'm still convinced it came from some inhuman force outside my own mind and body. And though it would be years before I knew it, it was a vision of a kind experienced by more than a few lucky children. In brief, in a single full moment, I was allowed to see how intricately the vast contraption of nature all around me—and nature included me, my parents a few yards away in the house, and every other creature alive on Earth—was bound into a single huge ongoing wheel by one immense power that had willed us into being and intended our futures, wherever they led.

20   We were all, somehow, one vibrant thing; and even the rattlesnakes, the lethal microbes, and the plans of men like Adolf Hitler (whom I'd heard of from my father; it was 1939) were bound with the rest of us

toward a final harmony. At the age of six, of course, I couldn't have described it in such words, but memory tells me that the description is honest. And there that day, in the core of a much loved by often unaccompanied childhood, it seemed a benign revelation.

While it didn't result in an immediate certainty that God exists and   21
knows me and tends me, it left me watchful for further intimations. And in some way that I've only just realized six decades later, it became the first private knowledge of my life. I never mentioned what I'd suddenly learned, not to my parents nor to any child I knew and trusted. My life as a largely solitary mystic had begun.

I don't recall other such climactic moments in my childhood. But my   22
interest in Bible stories continued; and because at the age of nine I won a free New Testament for bringing a new member to Sunday school, I eventually began to read the Christian scriptures directly, not in someone else's version. Above all, the four Gospels interested me with their varying but complementary pictures of a man as mysterious and potent, yet credible, as Jesus. For reasons I can't explain, Jesus became one of the figures I often thought about and drew pictures of, along with Tarzan and King Arthur.

Since I was then hoping to become a painter in my adult life, I was also   23
increasingly aware of the towering presence in Western art of Jesus at every stage of his short, and brilliantly depictable, life. In a way that it may be difficult for you to imagine years from now, the world around me—which was most of America from the 1930s onward—was as permeated with reverberations of the life of Jesus as the sea is with salt. For good or ill—and he's still outrageously invoked as the guarantor of hatred, violence, and endless fantasy—he was a constant component (even for those who entirely rejected him) of the air we breathed.

The fact that Jesus was also plainly a man who'd suffered and died for   24
his acts made him more and more interesting to me as I entered adolescence and encountered the usual daunting amount of unhappiness. Mine, like that of so many others, came at the hands of a pair of school bullies. Like many boys who grew up in Christian cultures then, and perhaps even now, I spent a fair amount of secret time in prayer to Jesus. I'd ask for the meanness to stop and for kinder friends to materialize (my demons had once been my friends). It was my first acquaintance with unanswered, or partially answered, prayer. Other friends appeared but the bullies never relented till we moved from the town.

Somehow that partial success with prayer didn't stop me. I thought I'd   25
heard the beginning of a dialogue. And life improved rapidly. Relations with my schoolmates in the new town were free of hostility, and I made a handful of friends who've lasted. But almost anyone's adolescence, as you may know by the time you read this, is subject to frequent attacks of self-

doubt and melancholy, even bouts of hopelessness. Life sometimes seems too bleak to continue. Why should young people believe that things change—and often for the better? They've frequently had little experience of such improvements.

26   I don't recall ever plunging so low; but still I went on investing a fair amount of time in prayers to Jesus and his mother (a beautiful Catholic girl had taught me the rosary, and it became a part of my attempts at reaching and persuading the Creator and—what?—his household). And in the absence of the old tormentors who'd even made churchgoing difficult, I began attending church—my mother's Methodist and my father's Baptist. The Methodist minister took an interest in my developing curiosities about the historical Jesus and the origins of Christianity; and he readily agreed to what must have seemed peculiar requests from a boy—requests for private communion at times when I needed special help, like college scholarship competitions.

27   By age seventeen I clearly had some sort of vocation for a life with regular attempts at persuading God's attention and cooperation. I don't think my daily behavior looked unusually "holy," and I don't recall that my parents or my minister ever mentioned the possibility. But toward the end of high school, one of my teachers suggested that I think of preparing for life as a pastor. Though by then I'd joined the Methodist church, I felt at once that the idea was wrong. My sexual energies and their direction seemed far too powerful and heretical for such a career. In any case I'd already decided on the parallel careers I've ultimately followed—life as a writer and a teacher—and as I moved on to college, I headed for those choices.

28   As I worked even more steadily at my undergraduate studies and my writing (especially poetry)—and as I began to express my sexual needs—I slowly began to feel less compelled toward the public worship I'd enjoyed for the past few years. I'd begun to suspect that a yen for display played a part in public worship, especially my own. Yet despite my involvement in a number of academic courses that questioned, and occasionally mocked, the foundations of religious thought, my withdrawal from church represented no loss of the faith that had grown as I grew.

29   My withdrawal was likewise a response to my increasing awareness of the hostility or indifference of all major American churches to the coming crises in radical justice and sexual tolerance. Most honestly, though, I was returning to a means of worship that was more natural for me: private prayer, reading, and meditation, and the beginnings of a comprehension that the chief aim of any mature religious life is union with the will of God, as opposed to one's own, and the finding of ways to assist other creatures.

30   My first year of graduate study in England, where study is largely self-monitored, marked also my launching on a near full-time dedication to

my writing and on my first real delight in reciprocated love. In the chilly atmosphere of one of the oldest colleges at Oxford and the beautiful thirteenth-century chapel whose emptiness echoed the rapid expiration of Protestant Anglicanism, it was easy enough not to seek out a congenial church, and my sense of the Creator—of the duties I might owe him and the means of communicating with him—continued on the solitary track to which they'd reverted. Yet in normal human fashion, I was now praying mainly when I needed quick help.

I felt mind guilt at my separation from a religious community, especially   31
when my mother or my old minister inquired about my British church-going. But I told myself I'd made a necessary choice. I imagined I'd learned to locate—through my teaching and writing—communities where my own questions and whatever useful findings I might make could be best conveyed to others, potentially a wider community than I might have found in a dedicated building and a congregation.

In retrospect, I estimate that my subsequent years of work may have   32
communicated to a few thousand readers and a few thousand students how one relatively lucid and respectably educated man, in the final two-thirds of the twentieth century and somewhat thereafter, has managed to live at least six decades of a life that (while it's committed a heavy share of self-intoxicated incursions on others and has broken at least five of the Ten Commandments) has so far hurled no dead bodies to the roadside, abandoned no sworn partners or children, and has managed to turn up— shaved and sober—in a writing office, a teaching classroom, a kinsman's or lover's or friend's place in time of need on most promised occasions.

I've been especially chary of broaching discussions of my relations with   33
God in the arenas of either of my careers, in books or in classrooms. That's partly because, by nature, I'm among the world's least evangelical souls but also because my own beliefs were acquired so gradually, and in response to such personal tides, as to be almost incommunicable if not incomprehensible. In recent years, however, I've relaxed a little in that reluctance.

I've spoken of my faith in two volumes of memoirs, a number of poems,   34
and a published letter to a dying young man who asked for my views; and I'm writing this new letter to you. After more than thirty years of teaching Milton's *Paradise Lost*, I've begun, very lightly, to confess to my students that I'm a renegade Christian and that they might be at a certain advantage in studying a Christian poet with me. Wouldn't they like to study Homer with, say, an actual Zeusian?

So my life has gone through youth and middle age. It was normally sub-   35
ject, as I've said, to serious wrongdoing. And it was frequently challenged by disappointment and at least one bitter remorse. Throughout—despite several deep dives into self-blame and the sporadic lack of any clear view

ahead—my faith has been the prime stabilizer. Like many other navigational aids, it's done most of its work when I had only the dimmest awareness of its service.

36   Then, when I was fifty-one, I found myself having difficulties walking. After a few weeks of denial, I was discovered to have a large and intricately entangled cancer of the spinal cord. Despite surgery, with the best technology of the early 1980s, the tumor couldn't be removed; and no chemotherapy was available. The only medical hope was five weeks of searing radiation, directly to the fragile cord. I was warned that such a brutal therapy might leave me paraplegic or worse. The alternative, however, was to wait while the tumor paralyzed my legs, then my arms and hands, and finally my lungs. With no other imaginable choice, I agreed to the radiation.

37   A few mornings before the daily treatments were to start, I was propped wide awake in bed at home, when I experienced the second visionary moment of my life, some forty-six years after my childhood glimpse of the unity of nature. I've written about this second moment in other places. Enough to say here that I was, suddenly and without apparent transport, in a different place—by the Sea of Galilee—and a man whom I knew to be Jesus was washing and healing the long wound from my failed surgery, the site of my coming radiation.

38   My conviction, since the second vision, is that the experience was in some crucial sense real. In that moment I was healed, and the fact that my legs were subsequently paralyzed by radiation two years before a new ultrasonic device made the removal of the tumor possible, the tumor was merely a complexity in the narrative that God intended. There does seem a possibility that, had I avoided the withering radiation, I might have been healed in any case. My doctors felt that, along with its damage, the radiation had stalled the tumor for a lucky while.

39   I'm aware that many of my contemporaries will read such a statement as groundless, if not howling crazy, and I can all but share their laughter. Yet sixteen years after my initial diagnosis, I'm an energetic man working when virtually none of my therapists thought I had a serious chance (one of them told my brother that I had eighteen months at best). And since I've mentioned my healing in print, I've had dozens of letters from patently sane strangers who confide similar transcendent experiences in a time of crisis.

40   They mostly describe an experience in which some entirely real figure, whether Jesus or some matter-of-fact plainclothes angel, comes and consoles or heals them. Such confidences almost always end with their telling me that they'd mentioned their experience to no one else for fear of ridicule. My correspondents also generally say that their experience, like mine, was

singular—that is, never repeated, thereby eliminating the possibility that we'd all been merely cheering ourselves with pleasant dreams in the face of calamity.

My moment by the Sea of Galilee occurred sixteen years ago and has not recurred in any form. Those years have brought me an unprecedented amount of work—twenty-one books since the cancer—and an outpouring of affection and meticulous care of a sort I wouldn't have allowed myself to expect from kin, friends, and strangers. In addition to the books, I've continued my regular schedule of teaching. I've traveled for business and for pleasure more than in my able-bodied life. And those changes have only deepened my certainty that my illness—its devastations and its legacies of paralysis and chronic pain—was intended for me at that point in my life and perhaps ever after. 41

What the ultimate intention of such a blow may be, I barely guess at. Time, or beyond, will presumably uncover as much of that mystery as I'll ever need to know. I can say, however, that the drastic reversal led me to abandon certain choices that I'd always explored with both pleasure and uncertainty of purpose. I've made that simplification because I've slowly come to suspect that a curbing of past choices was intended. And while this new course has left me deprived of a few physical rewards, I've all but ceased to miss them. If nothing else, paraplegia either leads to a rapid refining of human focus and one's expectations from other creatures or it plunges its cripple into querulous, or wailing, neurosis or worse. 42

Yet now I've outlived both my parents; and though I'm nearly seventy, I'm hopeful of as much more time as I have work to do, the resources with which to do it, and the help I need in my straitened circumstances. My relations with God run a fairly normal course. They intensify when I'm in trouble; and when things go smoothly, they tend to resemble the domestic relations of family members—a good deal of taking-for-granted on my part, with a dozen or so snatches of prayer per day (mostly requests to understand God's intent, if any; to learn patience, to bear what I can't change and then to incorporate it). I'm aware of no substantial fears of age or death, though I won't say I welcome either prospect. And I have no doubt that the usual calm I live in—and here I tap on the nearest wood—comes as a form of mercy from whatever force created the world and knows of me in it. 43

Can I expect that spotty run through sixty-some years of faith to be of any weight for you, years from now, or for anyone else to whom religious belief is either a baffling phenomenon, an inviting curiosity, or an intellectually impossible position? From a friend, I might hope for the patience required to read these pages—something less than an hour. But I can 44 hardly expect it to be convincing or even comprehensible for unbelieving strangers. One of the characteristics of faith that can seem so repellent is the apparent necessity that faith be given help from God. The most sophisticated theologies of the Western past—millennia of rabbinical debate, the treatises of Augustine, Aquinas, Calvin, and Barth—deduce a

45   similar necessity.

The leap of faith that believers so often recommend is preceded by a serious hitch. It almost invariably requires God's presence, on the far side of the abyss, saying, "Jump!" In Christianity, anyhow, Calvinists agree. God calls certain creatures to believe in him and thus win salvation; others he simply permits to live and die in preordained damnation. It's another idea that looks absurd to anyone who has not been inclined to faith by a propitious early atmosphere and training. For me, as for more than a few writers of the early Christian documents comprised in the New Testament, that terrible prior choosing by God seems at times the baldest deduction

46   from attentive witness of the world.

How can anyone reared in the desert air of contemporary science—physics seems the most relevant science—even begin to move in the murky direction of faith, especially when so many manifestations of religious faith lead to violence, disdain, if not outright hatred, and dithering or murderous nonsense? In any day's news, half the world's human wrongs are done in God's name. That one obstacle to faith, if no other, is all but impassably high. (Yet, again, the majority of human beings claim some form of faith.)

47   It's my seasoned instinct, then, that any slow scrutiny of contemporary science will demonstrate at many points its intellectual inadequacy as an ample chain of theories to explain the face and the actions of the world. Thus Isaac Newton, who in many ways invented modern science, was a fervently convinced believer; and physics, here at the beginning of the third millennium, is uncovering at a breathtaking rate subatomic phenomena that surpass the imaginings of the wildest hierophant scraping his sores with a cast-off potsherd.

48   That's not to claim that anyone should fling posthaste into the arms of an invisible God or any religious cult simply because science has proven so prissily bankrupt as a guide to what's here and what's there (here and there seem increasingly to be the same thing). Helium-filled New Age unfortunates are steadily chattering away on television to warn us about that. Yet if nothing else, an honest, well-informed creature must now acknowledge that the world—the universe of physical objects, forces, and actions above, within, or below the range of human or instrumental vision—far surpasses in extent and wonder what we can see and absorb.

49   But if anyone with a persistent curiosity about faith, anyone who has lacked a sane early grounding in one of the central faiths of his on her cul-

ture, were to ask me where to go to begin to understand the inevitability of belief and its mixed rewards (faith is more difficult than unbelief), I'd suggest two initial courses, each to be pursued with quiet steadiness. First, begin to read the sacred texts of your native culture. For the majority of Americans, those texts would include the Christian Bible (which includes the Hebrew scriptures).

Simultaneously, begin to read the thoughts of the great believing 50
minds. For you, friend, those would include a concentration on the actual words of Jesus as preserved in the four Gospels of Matthew, Mark, Luke, and John and then an awareness of the lives and works of figures (among hundreds) such as Francis of Assisi, Søren Kierkegaard, Albert Schweitzer, Simone Weil, W. H. Auden, Dorothy Day, and Flannery O'Connor.

Second, considering that your family will have reared you in a world 51
deep in the knowledge and the resonance of the arts, I'd urge you (and others) to immerse yourself in the lives and works of the great believing musicians and painters—such witnesses as the preservers of Gregorian chant, Giotto and Michelangelo, Palestrina, Rembrandt, Bach and Handel, Mozart and Beethoven, Van Gogh and Rouault, Messiaen and Pärt. None of those believers was a fool nor a mere hired hand of the pope nor some prince with an idle and unadorned chapel.

On the contrary, the inspiration of their work, the craft it employs, the 52
makers' surviving personal statements, show them to be intellectually and emotionally tough-minded and trustworthy—and I've omitted the whole world of poetry, which is, if anything, even more bountiful than music and painting. The same advice can be given for virtually all the world's religions, freighted as they are with glorifications of the mystery and presence and the dreaded absence of God, though the artists of Judaism and Islam (because of their prohibitions against the portrayal of living things) have brilliantly concentrated their findings in such nonvisual forms as prophecy, poetry, and music.

While you're reading and listening, you might want to try—if you never 53
have—speaking short sentences to the air around you (be sure no one is watching; people have been carted off for less). Call the air God if you can, though it's not a god; and state as honestly as possible some immediate need, some hope for guidance. With luck and further effort, your sentences will grow less self-obsessed. They may even begin to express occasional thanks. For long months you may get no trace of notice or reply. In time, however, you may hear answers on the same scale as that on which we measure the masters I've just named. And if an answer comes, you can be almost sure it wasn't simply the air that answered.

There are numerous possible next steps. You might want to begin fre- 54
quenting spaces that have a natural benignity for you—whether it's the

lobby of Grand Central Station or a quiet corner church or a one-man fire-watch tower high above some primal forest. You might begin to talk about your findings with some friend whom you suspect of having similar curiosities. You might commit some part of your time to working with the wretched of your neighborhood or town—the homeless, hungry, abused, the unloved whom most religions insist that we comfort. You might want to try attending some regular religious ceremonies. If they fail you, go back to yourself and the ambient air.

55   Soon or late, you'll likely get some response from that space to which you first spoke. It may say what it's said to many good people: "There's nothing here but atoms of air. Get a life." It may also say what it's said persuasively to even more of the earth's human beings: "Keep talking. Learn how. You're listened to. One day you may hear me, should I need or want you."

56   You may, in short—and finally, my valued young friend—have begun to speak with and to hear from the truth, some form of the truth that wears many masks for its likely sole face.

Yours in hope,
Reynolds

Questioning and Discussing

Price, "Dear Harper"

1. Why would Price write a "letter" to his godchild regarding "thoughts that may interest" the person "in time"? What function does this letter serve? What might be Price's strategy in writing it?

2. Despite the letter format and personal language of this selection, Price appears to have a central argument. Analyze and comment on Price's argument. Are his points convincing? Might they pertain to religions other than Christianity? Why? Why not? (You might need to research the tenets of other faiths to answer this question more fully and specifically.)

3. Price attributes to God "standards of action that he means us to observe." What might those standards be? Is it possible to attain those standards without a conventional system of religious belief? Explain your response.

4. Comment on the personal stories about faith that Price uses to convince his audience—his godchild—of the importance of faith. How does Price seem to anticipate the possible arguments advanced against faith that might be encountered by his godchild? (Consider his discussion of science, for instance.) How might Price's intended audience extend beyond his godchild? What aspects of the essay might indicate this?

⊞

ADAM GOPNIK

Since 1986, Adam Gopnik has written for *The New Yorker*, and that work has earned him the National Magazine Award for Essay and Criticism and the George Polk Award for Magazine Reporting. In addition to writing regular broadcasts for the Canadian Broadcasting Corporation, he has written the entry on culture for the last two editions of the *Encyclopedia Britannica*. From 1995 to 2000, Gopnik and his wife lived in Paris; his observations are recounted in his book *Paris to the Moon*. The French newspaper *Le Monde* praises his "witty and Voltairean picture of French life" while the magazine *Le Point* notes, "It is impossible to resist delighting in the nuances of his articles, for the details concerning French culture that one discovers even when one is French oneself."

⊞

American Electric
Did Franklin Fly That Kite?

We are said to be living in an icon-smashing age, but the odd thing is how few shards can be found on the floor. Joe DiMaggio may now be chilly and Bing Crosby charmless, but the essential pantheon of heroes remains in place. Lincoln, John Adams, Lewis and Clark, Seabiscuit—those who matter most to us are intact, and the common activity is not to smash their images but to trace on them, as though with a diamond pen, the signature of our own favored flaws, allowing their heroism to shine through more brightly. The thrust of popular history has been to remake old heroes as more like us than we knew, and better than us than we could imagine. (Even John Kennedy, if sicker than we recognized, was braver, too.) The Founding Fathers have been remade as Founding Brothers, our superior siblings.

Of them all, Benjamin Franklin seems the most secure, since he has always been the most "human," the one Founding Father who has no trace of asceticism, neither Massachusetts Puritan nor Virginia Neo-Roman. He is all godless materialist Pennsylvania merchant (although he borrowed some simplicity from the Quakers from time to time, as the need suited him). You could swing a baseball bat of propriety at him, and he would bounce back, beaming. This gives him, and his legend, endless vitality. If you were a child growing up in Philadelphia in the nineteen-sixties, Franklin was still alive, everywhere you looked. At night, his electric profile, wattles outlined in neon, hovered above the city in the sign for the Benjamin Franklin Hotel. He was known in Philadelphia the way St. Francis was known in Assisi, as both presiding deity and local boy.

3   Central to his myth was the story of the Kite and Key. (An honors society at the University of Pennsylvania still has that name.) He went out to a field in a thunderstorm, flew his kite, saw it struck by lightning, and then watched the lightning sparkle around a key held in a jar at the end of the kite twine. If he put his knuckle on the twine, he could feel the spark. What this accomplished, exactly, was something that schoolboys were vague about: "He discovered electricity" was the usual formula. In fact, he had shown that lightning was a form of electricity, and that ingenuity could hold its own against book learning. In one of the two greatest editorial emendations in American letters (the other is Maxwell Perkins keeping Fitzgerald from calling "Gatsby" "Trimalchio in West Egg"), Franklin changed Jefferson's "We hold these truths to be sacred and undeniable" to the modest, conclusive "We hold these truths to be self-evident"—and Franklin could make that change because he was known as the master of self-evidence, with all the authority of a man willing to face down lightning with a kite while everyone else was safe inside arguing about ideas. "He Took Lightning from the Sky and the Scepter from the Tyrant's Hand" was the (originally Latin) inscription that a French poet would later offer, conclusively.

4   Now, however, a new book argues that the legend on which Franklin's reputation rests is dubious. There was no kite, no key, no bolt, no knuckle, no charge. He let people believe that he had been places he never went, done things he never did, and seen things that never happened. No wonder he's been called the father of American journalism.

5   The new book, "Bolt of Fate," by Tom Tucker (Pubic Affairs; $25), is part of an apparently unstoppable wave of Franklin biography. In the past three years, we have had Edmund S. Morgan's short, loving "Benjamin Franklin" (Yale; $24.95) and H. W. Brands's "The First American" (Doubleday; $35), and this month Walter Isaacson's energetic, entertaining, and worldly "Benjamin Franklin: An American Life" (Simon & Schuster; $30) joins them. Two more Franklin biographies are supposedly on the way. Tucker's book, it should be said, is not so much a wet blanket cast over the party as an "Aw, nuts" uttered at it; his evidence is far from conclusive, but neither does his book have any of the usual telltale signs of overreaching, special pleading, paranoia, or conspiracy-mongering. This is Franklin unmasked, but not, so to speak, Franklin dressed up in women's clothing. True or false, Tucker's argument touches on the heart of who Franklin was, who we want him to be, and who he might have been. *"Eripuit coelo fulmen"*—he snatched the lightning from the sky. What if, just conceivably, he didn't?

6   There are no bad biographies of Franklin for the same reason that there are no bad Three Stooges movies, or, for that matter, demolition derbies:

something always happens. Just when Franklin is getting becalmed in diplomatic squabbles, say, or running a tedious printing business in a provincial city, he writes about farts or invents bifocals. Yet there is, even in Isaacson's genial book and Morgan's almost hagiographic one, a sense that this figure is seen at a distance, and remains hard to know. Where John Adams comes before us in all his bad-tempered intelligence, and Washington in his thin-lipped realism, Franklin is elusive: he can at times be Santa Claus or William James, bubbly and intelligent, and at times he is Franklin Roosevelt, with a carefully composed affability overlaying a character essentially calculating and remote.

In part, this is because he had to adapt to two different times, one of   7
which, at least, he helped to make. His career, as Isaacson suggests, bridges two centuries of sensibility: in the first half of his life, up until the seventeen-fifties, we are in a largely seventeenth-century world of nascent capitalism and virtuous upward mobility. Franklin is an ambitious early capitalist operator at the edge of the empire, a provincial Pepys. He starts a business from scratch and chases women, and both the culture and the science around him feel skin-thin. By the end of the Franklin biographies, we are in a late-Enlightment world of fully fledged science and sensibility—where the reign of violence and feeling is beginning. This is partly a question of place, Philadelphia traded for Paris, but it is also an effect of growing knowledge and an expanded universe, and science is the crossing point. The electrical experiments are the link between the early Franklin and the later Franklin—between the young striver and the Papa Savant.

Franklin was born in Boston in 1706, to a family of freethinking arti-   8
sans, and was apprenticed as a boy to his half brother James, a printer. A printer in those Colonial days often had his own newspaper, and James's was the *New England Courant*, America's first independent paper. Benjamin picked up the newspapering habit—for a brief period, still an adolescent, he ran the paper while his bother was in jail over a censorship dispute. But he disliked his brother ("I fancy his harsh and tyrannical treatment of me might be a means of impressing me with that aversion to arbitrary power that has stuck to me through my whole life," he wrote years later) and, at seventeen, ran away to Philadelphia, a village of two thousand people that nonetheless dreamed of itself as a metropolis of tolerance. Compared with Mathered Boston, it was.

Franklin, tall and physically formidable—he was a terrific swimmer and   9
runner—almost immediately brought himself to the center of Philadelphia life. He earned a reputation as the publisher and editor of the *Pennsylvania Gazette*, a newspaper begun by a printer whom he helped drive out of business. Like Dr. Johnson, his almost exact contemporary, he made

his way by sheer force of talent as a miscellaneous journalist; unlike the bulldoggish Dr. Johnson, he understood, and pioneered, the American principle that it pays to be liked. "The consummate networker," as Isaacson calls him, he turned a little circle of fellow-apprentices and small tradesmen, the Junto, into a kind of freewheeling all-purpose civic association. He was a funny writer, with a dry, pawky prose style, modelled on Addison's, and a taste for pseudonymous pranks; he hid his most acerbic opinions behind the masks of made-up characters. But he had world-class ambitions, and he understood that those ambitions were probably best served by achievement in natural philosophy—the sciences. No one in London gave a damn about Philadelphia politics, but they cared about Philadelphia lightning. Distance lends authority to experiments: if it can be done out there, it can be done anywhere.

10   Franklin had just given up his career as a printer when he began his work as an "electrician," fascinated by the small shocks you could make out of amber rods and glass jars. Electricity was not yet a serious science. Though everyone agreed that it was a phenomenon, no one was sure at first if it was a phenomenon like the hula hoop or a phenomenon like gravity. People played with it for fun. Then, in the seventeen-forties, the Leyden jar, and early capacitor, showed that an electrical charge could be held in place and made to pass through glass. Essentially, you could collect and store electricity; and in 1749 Franklin reported to the Royal Academy in London that he had created the first electric battery.

11   In his correspondence with the academy, he understood that he would inevitably be viewed as a provincial, and that it paid to play the clown a little. In the midst of his serious submissions, he also wrote to the academy, apropos the state of "American electricity," that "a turkey is to be killed for our dinners by the electrical shock, and roasted by the electrical jack, before a fire kindled by the electrified bottle, when the healths of all the famous electricians in England, France and Germany, are to be drank in electrified bumpers, under the discharge of guns from the electrical battery." The metropolis, while it mistrusts an upstart, forgives a lovable provincial eccentric. (Though he was being funny about the American enthusiasm for electricity, he wasn't entirely joking. He electrocuted at least one turkey, and boasted of how tender it was, a thing typical of the way he could turn a joke into a fact.)

12   Previously, it had been proposed that there were two different kinds of electricity, both fluid: one generated by glass and one generated by resin. Franklin, experimenting with varieties of electric shock, swiftly arrived at a fundamental insight: that electricity was a single fluid, and that what he was the first to call "positive" and "negative" charges came from having too

much or too little of it. The importance of Franklin's theory, as the great historian of science I. Bernard Cohen has shown, was not only that it insisted on the conservation of charge but that it accepted "action at a distance": there didn't have to be holes for the charge to pass through, or invisible levers in the sky to send it along; electricity was just there, like gravity.

Many people, whatever theory they held, had noticed that lightning in 13
the sky looked a lot like electricity in a jar, only there was more of it. In 1749, it seems, Franklin himself made a list of the resemblances, a list that reveals the tenor of his scientific mind, at once disarmingly particular and searching for unity: "Electrical fluid agrees with lightning in these particulars. 1. Giving light. 2. Color of the light. 3. Crooked direction. 4. Swift motion. 5. Being conducted by metals. 6. Crack or noise in exploding. 7. Subsisting in water or ice. . . . Since they agree in all particulars wherein we can already compare them, is it not probable they agree likewise in this? Let the experiment be made." The lightning experiment would be suggestive about the centrality of electricity in an essentially Newtonian world picture. The simpler the world picture, the less intricate the celestial mechanics, and the greater the play of universal forces, however bizarre their action. *E pluribus unum* applied—a motto that Franklin, once again running from the absurd to the solemn, took from a classical recipe for salad dressing.

Did he really do it? There were actually two experiments. In 1750, 14
Franklin proposed that if you could get up high enough to be above trees and other natural obstacles, on a steeple or a spire, safely insulated in a sentry box (about the size of a telephone booth), you might be able to draw electricity from a thundercloud through a long iron rod, and "determine whether the clouds that contain lightning are electrified or not." A group of French scientists who read the proposal—for all that it took six weeks for mail to cross the Atlantic, there was a constant and meaningful exchange of ideas and data—tried it, in a town called Marly, outside Paris, and found that it worked. (Significantly, the apparatus didn't function right away—no experiment ever really works the first time you try it, for the same reason that no child's toy ever works on Christmas morning, the first time you assemble it—and it was a fairly lowly assistant who eventually made the discovery.)

Well, if you didn't have a steeple or a spire, you could use a kite to make 15
the same experiment, with a key attached at a silk ribbon to the twine on the kite; the key and the twine would conduct the electricity. Franklin published an account of this experiment—which took place, if it did, sometime in 1752—in the *Pennsylvania Gazette*, and it is worth quoting,

for its clarity and for its odd future tenses. After some details about the construction of the kite, which is to be made of a "large thin silk handkerchief," Franklin explains:

> The kite is to be raised, when a thunder-gust appears to be coming on, (which is very frequent in this country) and the person, who holds the string, must stand within a door, or window, or under some cover, so that the silk riband may not be wet. . . . As soon as any of the thunder-clouds come over the kite, the pointed wire will draw the electric fire from them; and the kite, with all the twine, will be electrified; and the loose filaments of the twine will stand out every way, and be attracted by the approaching finger. When the rain has wet the kite and twine, so that it can conduct the electric fire freely, you will find it stream out plentifully from the key on the approach of your knuckle. . . . All the other electrical experiments [can] be performed, which are usually done by the help of a rubbed glass globe or tube, and thereby the sameness of the electric matter with that of lightning completely demonstrated.

16   The first thing to note is that there is no bolt of lightning. Lightning, as Tucker points out, is a weird phenomenon. You won't find it by waiting in a field, and, if you did, it might fry you like a turkey; it would certainly vaporize the twine. What Franklin was trying to get was the electrostatic energy in clouds, which is usually there.

17   The next thing to note is the conditional spirit in which Franklin tells the story: he doesn't say he did it; he says that it can be done. This, Tucker notes, is not the era's usual scientific style, and in other cases Franklin is very careful, to the fetishistic degree beloved of eighteenth-century science, to say exactly what, when, and how. Tucker writes, "In his letter to George Whatley, on old London friend, describing the invention of bifocal glasses and in his 'Description of an Instrument for Taking Down Books from High Shelves' Franklin is unambiguous: he invented both items, he writes at length, he gives specifics, he uses active voice, he offers diagrams, *he says he did it*." In this first account, anyway, he doesn't.

18   The third thing to note is how hard it is to do. Tucker argues that a kite made of the kind of handkerchief that would have been available (a thirty-inch square of lingerie-thin silk), dragging a standard chunky key of the time (a quarter-pound brass latchkey), would have been nearly impossible to fly in the first place, especially if you were trying to keep it aloft from inside a shed—you can't get the key out and up. (Tucker notes that the job of keeping the key from falling to the ground while you're still flying the kite—and doing both from inside some kind of box—is one that has defeated the imagination of every illustrator, including Currier & Ives, who put Franklin's hand above the key, on the electrified twine, to

support the weight.) He says that he himself tried the experiment and couldn't get the kite off the ground: "My wife held a large picture frame as a stand-in for a window frame. When I tried to keep the key safely on my side of the picture frame and 'dry' and not let the line brush against the frame, especially with the reduced handling caused by the dangling key, there came the sudden realization: *He—really—didn't—do—this*." Which may have been a good thing. Tucker says that the experiment was also fantastically dangerous, and Franklin was lucky not to get killed trying to do it, if he did it.

Isaacson, for this part, rejects Tucker, and sensibly directs us toward Cohen's books on Franklin's science. Cohen notes that other people claimed to have reproduced the experiment not long afterward, but for Cohen perhaps the most important consideration in its favor is the simple fact that Franklin said that he did it. The idea that Franklin might have made up his account is simply alien to his conception of Franklin.

Who is to decide when doctors disagree? It is, finally, as conservatives like to say, all about character. And here one approaches an area of subtle gradations, easy to misinterpret. Tucker points to evidence of Franklin's series of hoaxes as conclusive, or anyway highly suggestive. He offers a long list and shows how they often advanced Franklin's career; for instance, when he was just starting out as a printer he wrote a pseudonymous essay in favor of paper currency and then, after the legislature had been persuaded, got the government contract to print money. As Tucker recognizes, the majority of these impostures are closer to deadpan satiric jokes than they are to self-seeking lies. Franklin like to write letters claiming to be from other people—a "famous Jesuit," or a Scottish Presbyterian—in order to dramatize some political point through obvious overload. The last thing he wrote was a letter purportedly from a Muslim slaver, "Sidi Mehemet Ibrahim," whose lust for slavery was intended to hold a mirror up to the American slaveholder's own, and shame him.

This is the reason for Franklin's opacity and, perhaps, for the doubts about the kite, which do not begin with Tucker. Franklin was an instinctive ironist. That is not to make him contemporary; it was Enlightenment irony, not Duchampian irony—begun as a way of getting past censorship. But it was his natural mode, as in the joke about the electrocuted turkeys: which *was* a joke, and had a serious point, and was something he actually did, and the whole thing depended on being reported with an absolutely straight face. It was not that he did not value honesty. He did. It is that he did not value sincerity, a different thing. He would have been reluctant to say something that he believed to be a lie. But, as a businessman and a writer and a diplomat, he might very well have been willing to dramatize, or even overdramatize, something he believed to be essentially the truth.

*   *   *

22   Everyone, doubters and believers, meets in Paris, for what all can agree on
is that the image of Franklin, the American electrician, was more essential to his success as a diplomat in France than any other element of his
legend. By 1776, Franklin was, of course, a very senior American, and his
tastes and allegiances, which throughout his life had been almost passionately English and imperial, seemed fully formed. He came home from a
long posting to London as a representative of the Pennsylvania legislature, and was immediately asked to join the first Congress. He was, at the
start, suspected by the more radical patriots of being a "wet," if not actually a spy. (His son William, with whom he was said to have done the kite-
flying, was then the loyal Tory governor of New Jersey.) But he soon
proved to be as ardently in favor of unilateral independence as Adams or
Jefferson. ("He does not hesitate at our boldest Measures, but rather seems
to think us too irresolute," John wrote to Abigail, perpetually annoyed at
Franklin's gift for arriving late at a party and then lighting all the candles
on the cake.) And, when it became plain that the war for independence
would live or die on French aid, he was the obvious candidate to go to
France and ask for it. "There can be no question that when Franklin arrived in France on that grave mission he was already a public figure," Cohen writes. "And this was so because of his stature as a scientist and
because of the spectacular nature of his work on lightning." We may have
thought we were sending over Will Rogers; they thought they were getting Richard Feynman.

23   Franklin's essentially ironic, distancing turn of mind, which was often
so baffling to his literal-minded American colleagues—Isaacson's funniest
pages are supplied by John Adams's stunned and alarmed accounts of
Franklin's nonchalant diplomacy on the Paris mission—gave him a kind
of second sight into the minds of his hosts. There is little sham in French
life, but a lot of show, a lot of rhetorical gesturing. Franklin understood
the style instantly. He was pretending to be a naïf (he left his wig and
powder, which he normally wore, back home in Philadelphia), which the
French knew to be faux, and they were pretending to be worldly, which he
knew to be an illusion.

24   Franklin was not just shrewder than he seemed, having the measure of
his host very well down. He was also politically far more skillful. As Morgan points out, there was no necessity for the French to side with the
Americans, whose cause looked like the longest of long shots and involved
making league with a frankly king-hating new republic. Adams and the
ornery Arthur Lee, another member of the French mission, were exasperated by Franklin's attention to social trivia. Why didn't he just bluntly insist on the power political formula that stared them in the face? America is

the enemy of England, England is the enemy of France. Franklin understood that the "realistic" formula was essentially empty, and that there was, and is, no more maddeningly fatuous cliché than that nations have interests rather then affections. It was in France's interest to supplant the British, against its interest to support a republic, in its interest to form an alliance with the Spanish and leave the Americans alone, and on and on. But the logic of power depends largely on the perceptions, and feelings, of the people who have it. Franklin understood that, above all, the good opinion of the French mattered. It paid to be liked and admired, and he made sure that he was. He knew that he could not make his country, and its needs, inescapable if he did not make himself, and his cause, irresistible.

Was Franklin, because he was calculating and clear-eyed, a fraud? Nothing seems more false. Might he have, in the American, or, for that matter, the electrical, cause, massaged the data in what he thought was the pursuit of truth, or told a half-truth and then been enclosed within it? Nothing seems more human. 25

One need not have a pragmatic or skeptical vision of truth to have a charitable view of the frailty of those who pursue it. The electrical kite could never have really been a hoax, because it was never really a claim. Even if the experiment did take place, it would not, on its own, have counted as scientific data by any standard, Enlightenment or modern. There was no specification, no replication by the experimenter, no protocol. It was, really, a thought experiment: if you did this, then what might happen? Despite all the rhetoric, much of it self-created, of Franklin as natural man, pragmatic man, empirical man, man with a kite, the plain truth is that his genius was, in every realm, for airy abstraction brought to earth, the single-fluid theory of life. 26

Franklin the political theorist was not drawing on his own experience, either, which consisted entirely of more or less slavish negotiations with colonial powers and absolute monarchs. He was, in the end, proposing a system of governance that no one had experienced at all. It was a pure thought experiment, a kite that might fly. 27

The moral of the kite is not that truth is relative. It is that nothing is really self-evident. Scientific truths, like political beliefs, are guesses and arguments, not certainties. Dr. Johnson's great, comforting gloss on the Christian funeral service comes to mind: "In the sure and certain hope of a resurrection" did not mean that the resurrection was certain, only that the hope was certain. "We hold these truths to be self-evident," similarly, means that we hold them to be so. We hold these truths as we hold the twine, believing, without being sure, that the tugs and shocks are what we think they are. We hold the string, and hope for the best. Often, there is no lightning. Sometimes, there is no kite. 28

QUESTIONING AND DISCUSSING

Gopnik, "American Electric"

---

1. Gopnik's article from *The New Yorker* is presented as a review of a recent book, "part of an apparently unstoppable wave of Franklin biography." However, Gopnik seems to be arguing larger points as he begins his review: "We are said to be living in an icon-smashing age, but the odd thing is how few shards can be found on the floor." First, analyze and discuss Gopnik's metaphor in this sentence. Second, determine whether or not you agree. Does the rest of Gopnik's review support or refute his own initial statement? How?

2. What is the overall tone of Gopnik's article? For instance, consider the transitional paragraph that begins, "Now, however, a new book argues that the legend on which Franklin's reputation rests in dubious," and such contentions as "There are no bad biographies of Franklin for the same reason that there are no bad Three Stooges movies, or for that matter, demolition derbies. Something always happens." How does Gopnik's choice of language—and allusions—enhance his writing? With what purpose and to what effect?

3. Using aspects of Gopnik's article as the basis of your argument, discuss the ways in which human beings tend to create and hold on to their belief in heroes—often public figures, particularly people in sports and entertainment. Referring not only to Franklin but perhaps also to our general belief in heroes, Gopnik concludes, "We hold these truths as we hold the twine, believing, without being sure, that the tugs and shocks are what we think they are. We hold the string, and hope for the best." How does Gopnik's metaphor potentially address larger systems of belief?

⊞

GABRIEL GARCÍA MÁRQUEZ

Gabriel García Márquez (1928–) was born in Colombia, the oldest of twelve children. Raised by his maternal grandparents, García Márquez was sent to school near Bogotá when he was eight. He studied law after graduating in 1946. Dedicated to writing since childhood, García Márquez published his first book, *Leaf Storm and Other Stories* (which includes the story that follows), in 1955. He is also a screenwriter and journalist, and in 1982, he received the Nobel Prize for Literature. His masterpiece, *One Hundred Years of Solitude* (1967), was followed by novels that include *The Autumn of the Patriarch* (1957) and the stirring *Love in the Time of Cholera* (1988) and volumes of short fiction. García Márquez has said that his stories begin with an image: "The image grows in my head until the whole story takes shape as it might in real life."

⊞

A Very Old Man with Enormous Wings

Translated by Gregory Rabassa

On the third day of rain they had killed so many crabs inside the house   1
that Pelayo had to cross his drenched courtyard and throw them into the sea, because the newborn child had a temperature all night and they thought it was due to the stench. The world had been sad since Tuesday. Sea and sky were a single ash-gray thing and the sands of the beach, which on March nights glimmered like powdered light, had become a stew of mud and rotten shellfish. The light was so weak at noon that when Pelayo was coming back to the house after throwing away the crabs, it was hard for him to see what it was that was moving and groaning in the rear of the courtyard. He had to go very close to see that it was an old man, a very old man, lying face down in the mud, who, in spite of his tremendous efforts, couldn't get up, impeded by his enormous wings.

Frightened by that nightmare, Pelayo ran to get Elisenda, his wife, who   2
was putting compresses on the sick child, and he took her to the rear of the courtyard. They both looked at the fallen body with mute stupor. He was dressed like a ragpicker. There were only a few faded hairs left on his bald skull and very few teeth in his mouth, and his pitiful condition of a drenched great-grandfather had taken away any sense of grandeur he might have had. His huge buzzard wings, dirty and half-plucked, were forever entangled in the mud. They looked at him so long and so closely that Pelayo and Elisenda very soon overcame their surprise and in the end

found him familiar. Then they dared to speak to him, and he answered in an incomprehensible dialect with a strong sailor's voice. That was how they skipped over the inconvenience of the wings and quite intelligently concluded that he was a lonely castaway from some foreign ship wrecked by the storm. And yet, they called in a neighbor woman who knew everything about life and death to see him, and all she needed was one look to show them their mistake.

3   "He's an angel," she told them. "He must have been coming for the child, but the poor fellow is so old that the rain knocked him down."

4   On the following day everyone knew that a flesh-and-blood angel was held captive in Pelayo's house. Against the judgment of the wise neighbor woman, for whom angels in those times were the fugitive survivors of a celestial conspiracy, they did not have the heart to club him to death. Pelayo watched over him all afternoon from the kitchen, armed with his baliff's club, and before going to bed he dragged him out of the mud and locked him up with the hens in the wire chicken coop. In the middle of the night, when the rain stopped, Pelayo and Elisenda were still killing crabs. A short time afterward the child woke up without a fever and with a desire to eat. Then they felt magnanimous and decided to put the angel on a raft with fresh water and provisions for three days and leave him to his fate on the high seas. But when they went out into the courtyard with the first light of dawn, they found the whole neighborhood in front of the chicken coop having fun with the angel, without the slightest reverence, tossing him things to eat through the openings in the wire as if he weren't a supernatural creature but a circus animal.

5   Father Gonzaga arrived before seven o'clock, alarmed at the strange news. By that time onlookers less frivolous than those at dawn had already arrived and they were making all kinds of conjectures concerning the captive's future. The simplest among them thought that he should be named mayor of the world. Others of sterner mind felt that he should be promoted to the rank of five-star general in order to win all wars. Some visionaries hoped that he could be put to stud in order to implant on earth a race of winged wise men who could take charge of the universe. But Father Gonzaga, before becoming a priest, had been a robust woodcutter. Standing by the wire, he reviewed his catechism in an instant and asked them to open the door so that he could take a close look at that pitiful man who looked more like a huge decrepit hen among the fascinated chickens. He was lying in a corner drying his open wings in the sunlight among the fruit peels and breakfast leftovers that the early risers had thrown him. Alien to the impertinences of the world, he only lifted his antiquarian eyes and murmured something in his dialect when Father Gonzaga went into the chicken coop and said good morning to him in Latin. The parish priest had his first

suspicion of an impostor when he saw that he did not understand the language of God or know how to greet His ministers. Then he noticed that seen close up he was much too human: he had an unbearable smell of the outdoors, the back side of his wings was strewn with parasites and his main feathers had been mistreated by terrestrial winds, and nothing about him measured up to the proud dignity of angels. Then he came out of the chicken coop and in a brief sermon warned the curious against the risks of being ingenuous. He reminded them that the devil had the bad habit of making use of carnival tricks in order to confuse the unwary. He argued that if wings were not the essential element in determining the difference between a hawk and an airplane, they were even less so in the recognition of angels. Nevertheless, he promised to write a letter to his bishop so that the latter would write to his primate so that the latter would write to the Supreme Pontiff in order to get the final verdict from the highest courts.

His prudence fell on sterile hearts. The news of the captive angel spread with such rapidity that after a few hours the courtyard had the bustle of a marketplace and they had to call in troops with fixed bayonets to disperse the mob that was about to knock the house down. Elisenda, her spine all twisted from sweeping up so much marketplace trash, then got the idea of fencing in the yard and charging five cents admission to see the angel. 6

The curious came from far away. A traveling carnival arrived with a flying acrobat who buzzed over the crowd several times, but no one paid any attention to him because his wings were not those of an angel but, rather, those of a sidereal bat. The most unfortunate invalids on earth came in search of health: a poor woman who since childhood had been counting her heartbeats and had run out of numbers; a Portuguese man who couldn't sleep because the noise of the stars disturbed him; a sleep-walker who got up at night to undo the things he had done while awake; and many others with less serious ailments. In the midst of that shipwreck disorder that made the earth tremble, Pelayo and Elisenda were happy with fatigue, for in less than a week they had crammed their room with money and the line of pilgrims waiting their turn to enter still reached beyond the horizon. 7

The angel was the only one who took no part in his own act. He spent his time trying to get comfortable in his borrowed nest, befuddled by the hellish heat of the oil lamps and sacramental candles that had been placed along the wire. At first they tried to make him eat some mothballs, which, according to the wisdom of the wise neighbor woman, were the food prescribed for angels. But he turned them down, just as he turned down the papal lunches that the penitents brought him, and they never found out whether it was because he was an angel or because he was an old man that in the end he ate nothing but eggplant mush. His only supernatural virtue 8 seemed to be patience. Especially during the first days, when the hens pecked at him, searching for the stellar parasites that proliferated in his wings, and the cripples pulled out feathers to touch their defective parts with, and even the most merciful threw stones at him, trying to get him to rise so they could see him standing. The only time they succeeded in arousing him was when they burned his side with an iron for branding steers, for he had been motionless for so many hours that they thought he was dead. He awoke with a start, ranting in his hermetic language and with tears in his eyes, and he flapped his wings a couple of times, which brought on a whirlwind of chicken dung and lunar dust and a gale of panic that did not seem to be of this world. Although many thought that his reaction had been one not of rage but of pain, from then on they were careful not to annoy him, because the majority understood that his passivity was not that of a hero taking his ease but that of a cataclysm in repose.

9   Father Gonzaga held back the crowd's frivolity with formulas of maid-servant inspiration while awaiting the arrival of a final judgment on the nature of the captive. But the mail from Rome showed no sense of urgency. They spent their time finding out if the prisoner had a navel, if his dialect had any connection with Aramaic, how many times he could fit on the head of a pin, or whether he wasn't just a Norwegian with wings. Those meager letters might have come and gone until the end of time if a providential event had not put an end to the priest's tribulations.

10   It so happened that during those days, among so many other carnival attractions, there arrived in town the traveling show of the woman who had been changed into a spider for having disobeyed her parents. The admission to see her was not only less than the admissions to see the angel, but people were permitted to ask her all manner of questions about her absurd state and to examine her up and down so that no one would ever doubt the truth of her horror. She was a frightful tarantula the size of a ram and with the head of a sad maiden. What was most heart-rending, however, was not her outlandish shape but the sincere affliction with which she recounted the details of her misfortune. While still practically a child she had sneaked out of her parents' house to go to a dance, and while she was coming back through the woods after having danced all night without permission, a fearful thunderclap rent the sky in two and through the crack came the lightning bolt of brimstone that changed her into a spider. Her only nourishment came from the meatballs that chari-table souls chose to toss into her mouth. A spectacle like that, full of so much human truth and with such a fearful lesson, was bound to defeat without even trying that of a haughty angel who scarcely deigned to look at mortals. Besides, the few miracles attributed to the angel showed a certain mental disorder, like the blind man who didn't recover his sight but

grew three new teeth, or the paralytic who didn't get to walk but almost won the lottery, and the leper whose sores sprouted sunflowers. Those consolation miracles, which were more like mocking fun, had already ruined the angel's reputation when the woman who had been changed into a spider finally crushed him completely. That was how Father Gonzaga was cured forever of his insomnia and Pelayo's courtyard went back to being as empty as during the time it had rained for three days and crabs walked through the bedrooms.

The owners of the house had no reason to lament. With the money they saved they built a two-story mansion with balconies and gardens and high netting so that crabs wouldn't get in during the winter, and with iron bars on the windows so that angels wouldn't get in. Pelayo also set up a rabbit warren close to town and gave up his job as baliff for good, and Elisenda bought some satin pumps with high heels and many dresses of iridescent silk, the kind worn on Sunday by the most desirable women in those times. The chicken coop was the only thing that didn't receive any attention. If they washed it down with creolin and burned tears of myrrh inside it every so often, it was not in homage to the angel but to drive away the dungheap stench that still hung everywhere like a ghost and was turning the new house into an old one. At first, when the child learned to walk, they were careful that he not get too close to the chicken coop. But then they began to lose their fears and got used to the smell, and before the child got his second teeth he'd gone inside the chicken coop to play, where the wires were falling apart. The angel was no less standoffish with him than with other mortals, but he tolerated the most ingenious infamies with the patience of a dog who had no illusions. They both came down with chicken pox at the same time. The doctor who took care of the child couldn't resist the temptation to listen to the angel's heart, and he found so much whistling in the heart and so many sounds in his kidneys that it seemed impossible for him to be alive. What surprised him most, however, was the logic of his wings. They seemed so natural on that completely human organism that he couldn't understand why the other men didn't have them too.

When the child began school it had been some time since the sun and rain had caused the collapse of the chicken coop. The angel went dragging himself about here and there like a stray dying man. They would drive him out of the bedroom with a broom and a moment later find him in the kitchen. He seemed to be in so many places at the same time that they grew to think that he'd been duplicated, that he was reproducing himself all through the house, and the exasperated and unhinged Elisenda shouted that it was awful living in that hell full of angels. He could scarcely eat and his antiquarian eyes had also become so foggy that he went about

11

12

bumping into posts. All he had left were the bare cannulae of his last feathers. Pelayo threw a blanket over him and extended him the charity of letting him sleep in the shed, and only then did they notice that he had a temperature at night, and was delirious with the tongue twisters of an old Norwegian. That was one of the few times they became alarmed, for they thought he was going to die and not even the wise neighbor woman had been able to tell them what to do with dead angels.

13   And yet he not only survived his worst winter, but seemed improved with the first sunny days. He remained motionless for several days in the farthest corner of the courtyard, where no one would see him, and at the beginning of December some large, stiff feathers began to grow on his wings, the feathers of a scarecrow, which looked more like another misfortune of decrepitude. But he must have known the reason for those changes, for he was quite careful that no one should notice them, that no one should hear the sea chanteys that he sometimes sang under the stars. One morning Elisenda was cutting some bunches of onions for lunch when a wind that seemed to come from the high seas blew into the kitchen. Then she went to the window and caught the angel in his first attempts at flight. They were so clumsy that his fingernails opened a furrow in the vegetable patch and he was on the point of knocking the shed down with the ungainly flapping that slipped on the light and couldn't get a grip on the air. But he did manage to gain altitude. Elisenda let out a sigh of relief, for herself and for him, when she saw him pass over the last houses, holding himself up in some way with the risky flapping of a senile vulture. She kept watching him even when she was through cutting the onions and she kept on watching until it was no longer possible for her to see him, because then he was no longer an annoyance in her life but an imaginary dot on the horizon of the sea.

QUESTIONING AND DISCUSSING

García Márquez, "A Very Old Man with Enormous Wings"

1. The words *nightmare* and *imaginary* appear in the story at the beginning and the end. Are we to take this story as mere imagination and fancy? Why or why not?

2. What comment is being made on the notion of angels and belief in them—their appearance, their function, their origins?

3. Analyze and comment on Elisenda's idea: "fencing in the yard and charging five cents admission to see the angel." What are the implications of this decision in practical and spiritual terms?

4. Consider carefully the passages concerning Father Gonzaga and his communications with Rome and the circumstances under which the angel loses his attraction. What might García Márquez be suggesting here about belief— or faith?

⊞

WRAY HERBERT, JEFFERY L. SHELER, AND TRACI WATSON

Wray Herbert, Jeffery L. Sheler, and Traci Watson are freelance writers and staff writers for *U.S. News and World Report,* from which this piece is excerpted. The coauthors describe the chief ethical issues raised by human cloning and consider the possible repercussions of cloning on society as a whole.

⊞

Ethical Issues Concerning Human Cloning

At first it was just plain startling. Word from Scotland in late February   1
1997 that a scientist named Ian Wilmut had succeeded in cloning an adult mammal—a feat long thought impossible—caught the imagination of even the most jaded technophobe. The laboratory process that produced Dolly, an unremarkable-looking sheep, theoretically would work for humans as well. A world of clones and drones, of *The Boys From Brazil* and *Multiplicity* [two science fiction movies about cloning], was suddenly within reach. It was science fiction come to life. And scary science fiction at that.

In the wake of Wilmut's shocker, governments scurried to formulate   2
guidelines for the unknown, a future filled with mind-boggling possibilities. The Vatican called for a worldwide ban on human cloning. President Bill Clinton ordered a national commission to study the legal and ethical implications. Leaders in Europe, where most nations already prohibit human cloning, began examining the moral ramifications of cloning other species.

Like the splitting of the atom, the first space flight, and the discovery of   3
"life" on Mars, Dolly's debut has generated a long list of difficult puzzles for scientists and politicians, philosophers and theologians. And at dinner tables and office coolers, in bars and on street corners, the development of wild scenarios spun from the birth of a simple sheep has only just begun. *U.S. News* sought answers from experts to the most intriguing and frequently asked questions.

The Possibilities of Human Cloning

4   Why would anyone want to clone a human being in the first place? The human cloning scenarios that ethicists ponder most frequently fall into two broad categories: 1) parents who want to clone a child, either to provide transplants for a dying child or to replace that child, and 2) adults who for a variety of reasons might want to clone themselves.

5   Many ethicists, however, believe that after the initial period of uproar, there won't be much interest in cloning humans. Making copies, they say, pales next to the wonder of creating a unique human being the old-fashioned way.

6   Could a human being be cloned today? What about other animals? It would take years of trial and error before cloning could be applied successfully to other mammals. For example, scientists will need to find out if the donor egg is best used when it is resting quietly or when it is growing.

7   Will it be possible to clone the dead? Perhaps, if the body is fresh, says Randall Prather, a cloning expert at the University of Missouri–Columbia. The cloning method used by Wilmut's lab requires fusing an egg cell with the cell containing the donor's DNA. And that means the donor cell must have an intact membrane around its DNA. The membrane starts to fall apart after death, as does DNA. But, yes, in theory at least it might be possible.

8   Can I set up my own cloning lab? Yes, but maybe you'd better think twice. All the necessary chemicals and equipment are easily available and relatively low-tech. But out-of-pocket costs would run $100,000 or more, and that doesn't cover the pay for a skilled developmental biologist. The lowest-priced of these scientists, straight out of graduate school, makes about $40,000 a year. If you tried to grow the cloned embryos to maturity, you'd encounter other difficulties. The Scottish team implanted 29 very young clones in 13 ewes, but only one grew into a live lamb. So if you plan to clone Fluffy, buy enough cat food for a host of surrogate mothers.

A Twin, Not a Copy

9   Would a cloned human be identical to the original? Identical genes don't produce identical people, as anyone acquainted with identical twins can tell you. In fact, twins are more alike than clones would be, since they have at least shared the uterine environment, are usually raised in the same family, and so forth. Parents could clone a second child who eerily resembled their first in appearance, but all the evidence suggests the two would have very different personalities. Twins separated at birth do sometimes share quirks of personality, but such quirks in a cloned son or daughter would be haunting reminders of the child who was lost—and the failure to re-create that child.

Even biologically, a clone would not be identical to the "master copy."   10
The clone's cells, for example, would have energy-processing machinery
(mitochondria) that came from the egg donor, not from the nucleus
donor. But most of the physical differences between originals and copies
wouldn't be detectable without a molecular-biology lab. The one possible
exception is fertility. Wilmut and his coworkers are not sure that Dolly
will be able to have lambs. They will try to find out once she's old enough
to breed.

Will a cloned animal die sooner or have other problems because its   11
DNA is older? Scientists don't know. For complex biological reasons, creating a clone from an older animal differs from breeding an older animal
in the usual way. So clones of adults probably wouldn't risk the same birth
defects as the offspring of older women, for example. But the age of the
DNA used for the clone still might affect life span. The Scottish scientists
will monitor how gracefully Dolly ages.

What if parents decided to clone a child in order to harvest organs?   12
Most experts agree that it would be psychologically harmful if a child
sensed he had been brought into the world simply as a commodity. But
some parents already conceive second children with nonfatal bone marrow transplants in mind, and many ethicists do not oppose this. Cloning
would increase the chances for a biological match from 25 percent to
nearly 100 percent.

If cloned animals could be used as organ donors, we wouldn't have to   13
worry about cloning twins for transplants. Pigs, for example, have organs
similar in size to humans'. But the human immune system attacks and
destroys tissue from other species. To get around that, the Connecticut
biotech company Alexion Pharmaceuticals Inc. is trying to alter the pig's
genetic codes to prevent rejection. If Alexion succeeds, it may be more efficient to mass-produce porcine organ donors by cloning then by current
methods, in which researchers inject pig embryos with human genes and
hope the genes get incorporated into the embryo's DNA.

Wouldn't it be strange for a cloned twin to be several years younger   14
than his or her sibling? When the National Advisory Board on Ethics in
Reproduction studied a different kind of cloning a few years ago, its members split on the issue of cloned twins separated in time. Some thought the
children's individuality might be threatened, while others argued that
identical twins manage to keep their individuality intact.

Redefining Family Relationships

John Robertson of the University of Texas raises several other issues   15
worth pondering: What about the cloned child's sense of free will and

parental expectations? Since the parents chose to duplicate their first child, will the clone feel obliged to follow in the older sibling's footsteps? Will the older child feel he has been duplicated because he was inadequate or because he is special? Will the two have a unique form of sibling rivalry, or a special bond? These are, of course, just special versions of questions that come up whenever a new child is introduced into a family.

16   Could a megalomaniac decide to achieve immortality by cloning an "heir"? Sure, and there are other situations where adults might be tempted to clone themselves. For example, a couple in which the man is infertile might opt to clone one of them rather than introduce an outsider's sperm. Or a single woman might choose to clone herself rather than involve a man in any way. In both cases, however, you would have adults raising children who are also their twins—a situation ethically indistinguishable from the megalomaniac cloning himself. On adult cloning, ethicists are more united in their discomfort. In fact, the same commission that was divided on the issues of twins was unanimous in its conclusion that cloning an adult's twin is "bizarre . . . narcissistic and ethically impoverished." What's more, the commission argued that the phenomenon would jeopardize our very sense of who's who in the world, especially in the family.

17   How would a human clone refer to the donor of its DNA? "Mom" is not right, because the woman or women who supplied the egg and the womb would more appropriately be called Mother. "Dad" isn't right, either. A traditional father supplies only half the DNA in an offspring. Judith Martin, etiquette's "Miss Manners," suggests, "Most honored sir or madame." Why? "One should always respect one's ancestors," she says, "regardless of what they did to bring one into the world."

18   That still leaves some linguistic confusion. Michael Agnes, editorial director of *Webster's New World Dictionary*, says that "clonee" may sound like a good term, but it's too ambiguous. Instead, he prefers "original" and "copy." And above all else, advises Agnes, "Don't use 'Xerox.'"

19   A scientist joked that cloning could make men superfluous. Is it true? Yes, theoretically. A woman who wanted to clone herself would not need a man. Besides her DNA, all she would require are an egg and a womb—her own or another woman's. A man who wanted to clone himself, on the other hand, would need to buy the egg and rent the womb—or find a very generous woman.

Implications for Society

20   What are the other implications of cloning for society? The gravest concern about the misuse of genetics isn't related to cloning directly, but to genetic engineering—the deliberate manipulation of genes to enhance human tal-

ents and create human beings according to certain specifications. But some ethicists also are concerned about the creation of a new (and stigmatized) social class: "the clones." Albert Jonsen of the University of Washington believes the confrontation could be comparable to what occurred in the 16th century, when Europeans were perplexed by the unfamiliar inhabitants of the New World and endlessly debated their status as humans.

Whose pockets will cloning enrich in the near future? Not Ian Wilmut's. He's a government employee and owns no stock in PPL Therapeutics, the British company that holds the rights to the cloning technology. On the other hand, PPL stands to make a lot of money. Also likely to cash in are pharmaceutical and agricultural companies and maybe even farmers. The biotech company Genzyme has already bred goats that are genetically engineered to give milk laced with valuable drugs. Wilmut and other scientists say it would be much easier to produce such animals with cloning than with today's methods. Stock breeders could clone champion dairy cows or the meatiest pigs.   21

Could cloning be criminally misused? If the technology to clone humans existed today, it would be almost impossible to prevent someone from cloning you without your knowledge or permission, says Philip Bereano, professor of technology and public policy at the University of Washington. Everyone gives off cells all the time—whenever we give a blood sample, for example, or visit the dentist—and those cells all contain one's full complement of DNA. What would be the goal of such "drive-by" cloning? Well, what if a woman were obsessed with having the child of an apathetic man? Or think of the commercial value of a dynasty-building athletic pedigree or a heavenly singing voice. Even though experience almost certainly shapes these talents as much as genetic gifts, the unscrupulous would be unlikely to be deterred.   22

Religious Attitudes

Is organized religion opposed to cloning? Many of the ethical issues being raised about cloning are based in theology. Concern for preserving human dignity and individual freedom, for example, is deeply rooted in religious and biblical principles. But until Wilmut's announcement, there had been surprisingly little theological discourse on the implications of cloning per se. The response so far from the religious community, while overwhelmingly negative, has been far from monolithic.   23

Roman Catholic, Protestant, and Jewish theologians all caution against applying the new technology to humans, but for varying reasons. Catholic opposition stems largely from the church's belief that "natural moral law" prohibits most kinds of tampering with human reproduction. A 1987   24

Vatican document, *Donum Vitae*, condemned cloning because it violates "the dignity both of human procreation and of the conjugal union."

25   Protestant theology, on the other hand, emphasizes the view that nature is "fallen" and subject to improvement. "Just because something occurs naturally doesn't mean it's automatically good," explains Max Stackhouse of Princeton Theological Seminary. But while they tend to support using technology to fix flaws in nature, Protestant theologians say cloning of humans crosses the line. It places too much power in the hands of sinful humans, who, says philosophy Prof. David Flectcher of Wheaton College in Wheaton, Ill., are subject to committing "horrific abuses."

26   Judaism also tends to favor using technology to improve on nature's shortcomings, says Rabbi Richard Address of the Union of American Hebrew Congregations. But cloning humans, he says, "is an area where we cannot go. It violates the mystery of what it means to be human."

27   Doesn't cloning encroach on the Judeo-Christian view of God as the creator of life? Would a clone be considered a creature of God or of science? Many theologians worry about this. Cloning, at first glance, seems to be a usurpation of God's role as creator of humans "in his own image." The scientist, rather than God or chance, determines the outcome. "Like Adam and Eve, we want to be like God, to be in control," says philosophy Prof. Kevin Wildes of Georgetown University. "The question is, what are the limits?"

28   But some theologians argue that cloning is not the same as creating life from scratch. The ingredients used are alive or contain the elements of life, says Fletcher of Wheaton College. It is still only God, he says, who creates life.

29   Would a clone person have its own soul? Most theologians agree with scientists that a human clone and its DNA donor would be separate and distinct persons. That means each would have his or her own body, mind, and soul.

30   Would cloning upset religious views about death, immortality, and even resurrection? Not really. Cloned or not, we all die. The clone that outlives its "parent"—or that is generated from the DNA of a dead person, if that were possible—would be a different person. It would not be a reincarnation or a resurrected version of the deceased. Cloning could be said to provide immortality, theologians say, only in the sense that, as in normal reproduction, one might be said to "live on" in the genetic traits passed to one's progeny.

QUESTIONING AND DISCUSSING
Herbert, Sheler, and Watson, "Ethical Issues Concerning Human Cloning"

1. The initial viewpoint suggested by this article features words such as *startling, shocker,* and *scary science fiction.* Does the rest of this brief overview of issues surrounding cloning bear out this tone? How so? How not?

2. This article was published in 1997. Research recent scientific information related to cloning—the use of stem cells to ease chronic diseases such as Parkinson's, for instance. Does any of this information correct or modify the authors' concerns? Support your view by using specific examples from the texts you consult.

3. Select one of the areas considered by the authors—religion, general implications, redefining family—and research the views of other philosopher/ ethicists and scientists on the subject. What do you conclude? Why?

⊞

HENRY DAVID THOREAU

Social rebel, intellectual, journalist, and philosophical essayist, Henry David Thoreau (1817–1862) influenced important leaders who themselves would influence others, including Mahatma Gandhi and Dr. Martin Luther King, Jr. Thoreau celebrated solitude and nature, which suited his adherence to transcendentalism, a philosophical perspective emphasizing mysticism and individualism. He contributed to *The Dial,* a magazine of transcendentalism, and for three years lived near Walden Pond in solitude, a sojourn that resulted in his most famous book, *Walden* (1854). Thoreau said he finally left Walden because he had "several more lives to live and could not spare any more for that one." "Civil Disobedience" is Thoreau's most famous essay, prompted by the night he spent in a Concord, Massachusetts, jail. Thoreau hadn't paid his taxes, opposing the use of taxes to support slavery and the United States' war with Mexico.

⊞

Civil Disobedience

I heartily accept the motto,—"That government is best which governs least"; and I should like to see it acted up to more rapidly and systematically. Carried out, it finally amounts to this, which also I believe,—"That government is best which governs not at all"; and when men are prepared for it, that will be the kind of government which they will have. Government is at best but an expedient; but most governments are usually, and all governments are sometimes, inexpedient. The objections which have been brought against a standing army, and they are many and weighty, and deserve to prevail, may also at last be brought against a standing government. The standing army is only an arm of the standing government. The government itself, which is only the mode which the people have chosen to execute their will, is equally liable to be abused and perverted before the people can act through it. Witness the present Mexican war, the work of comparatively a few individuals using the standing government as their tool; for, in the outset, the people would not have consented to this measure.

2   This American Government,—what is it but a tradition, though a recent one, endeavoring to transmit itself unimpaired to posterity, but each instant losing some of its integrity? It has not the vitality and force of a single living man; for a single man can bend it to his will. It is a sort of wooden gun to the people themselves. But it is not the less necessary for this; for the people must have some complicated machinery or other, and hear its din, to satisfy that idea of government which they have. Governments show thus how successfully men can be imposed on, even impose on themselves, for their own advantage. It is excellent, we must all allow. Yet this government never of itself furthered any enterprise, but by the alacrity with which it got out of its way. *It* does not keep the country free. *It* does not settle the West. *It* does not educate. The character inherent in the American people has done all that has been accomplished; and it would have done somewhat more, if the government had not sometimes got in its way. For government is an expedient by which men would fain succeed in letting one another alone; and, as has been said, when it is most expedient, the governed are most let alone by it. Trade and commerce, if they were not made of India-rubber, would never manage to bounce over the obstacles which legislators are continually putting in their way; and, if one were to judge these men wholly by the effects of their actions and not partly by their intentions, they would deserve to be classed and punished with those mischievous persons who put obstructions on the railroads.

3   But, to speak practically and as a citizen, unlike those who call themselves no-government men, I ask for, not at once no government, but *at once* a better government. Let every man make known what kind of government would command his respect, and that will be one step toward obtaining it.

After all, the practical reason why, when the power is once in the hands   4
of the people, a majority are permitted, and for a long period continue, to
rule is not because they are most likely to be in the right, nor because this
seems fairest to the minority, but because they are physically the strongest.
But a government in which the majority rule in all cases cannot be based
on justice, even as far as men understand it. Can there not be a government in which majorities do not virtually decide right and wrong, but
conscience?—in which majorities decide only those questions to which
the rule of expediency is applicable? Must the citizen ever for a moment,
or in the least degree, resign his conscience to the legislator? Why has
every man a conscience, then? I think that we should be men first, and
subjects afterward. It is not desirable to cultivate a respect for the law, so
much as for the right. The only obligation which I have a right to assume
is to do at any time what I think right. It is truly enough said, that a corporation has no conscience; but a corporation of conscientious men is a
corporation *with* a conscience. Law never made men a whit more just;
and, by all means of their respect for it, even the well-disposed are daily
made the agents of injustice. A common and natural result of any undue
respect for law is, that you may see a file of soldiers, colonel, captain, corporal, privates, powder-monkeys, and all, marching in admirable order
over hill and dale to the wars, against their wills, ay, against their common
sense and consciences, which makes it very steep marching indeed, and
produces a palpitation of the heart. They have no doubt that it is a damnable
business in which they are concerned; they are all peaceably inclined.
Now, what are they? Men at all? or small movable forts and magazines, at
the service of some unscrupulous man in power? Visit the Navy-Yard, and
behold a marine, such a man as an American government can make, or
such as it can make a man with its black arts,—a mere shadow and remi-
niscence of humanity, a man laid out alive and standing, and already, as
one may say, buried under arms with funeral accompaniments, though it
may be,—

> "Not a drum was heard, not a funeral note,
>   As his corse to the rampart we hurried;
> Not a soldier discharged his farewell shot
>   O'er the grave where our hero we buried."

The mass of men serve the state thus, not as men mainly, but as ma-   5
chines, with their bodies. They are the standing army, and the militia, jail-
ers, constables, posse comitatus, etc. In most cases there is no free exercise
whatever of the judgment or of the moral sense; but they put themselves

on a level with wood and earth and stones; and wooden men can perhaps be manufactured that will serve the purpose as well. Such command no more respect than men of straw or a lump of dirt. They have the same sort of worth only as horses and dogs. Yet such as these even are commonly esteemed good citizens. Others—as most legislators, politicians, lawyers, ministers, and office-holders—serve the state chiefly with their heads; and, as they rarely make any moral distinctions, they are as likely to serve the Devil, without *intending* it, as God. A very few, as heroes, patriots, martyrs, reformers in the great sense, and *men*, serve the state with their consciences also, and so necessarily resist it for the most part; and they are commonly treated as enemies by it. A wise man will only be useful as a man, and will not submit to be "clay," and "stop a hole to keep the wind away," but leave that office to his dust at least:—

"I am too high-born to be propertied,
To be a secondary at control,
Or useful serving-man and instrument
To any sovereign state throughout the world."

6   He who gives himself entirely to his fellow-men appears to them useless and selfish; but he who gives himself partially to them is pronounced a benefactor and philanthropist.

7   How does it become a man to behave toward this American government to-day? I answer, that he cannot without disgrace be associated with it. I cannot for an instant recognize that political organization as *my* government which is the *slave's* government also.

8   All men recognize the right of revolution; that is, the right to refuse allegiance to, and to resist, the government, when its tyranny or its inefficiency are great and unendurable. But almost all say that such is not the case now. But such was the case, they think, in the Revolution of '75. If one were to tell me that this was a bad government because it taxed certain foreign commodities brought to its ports, it is most probable that I should not make an ado about it, for I can do without them. All machines have their friction; and possibly this does enough good to counterbalance the evil. At any rate, it is a great evil to make a stir about it. But when the friction comes to have its machine, and oppression and robbery are organized, I say, let us not have such a machine any longer. In other words, when a sixth of the population of a nation which has undertaken to be the refuge of liberty are slaves, and a whole country is unjustly overrun and conquered by a foreign army, and subjected to military law, I think that it is not too soon for honest men to rebel and revolutionize. What makes

this duty the more urgent is the fact that the country so overrun is not our own, but ours is the invading army.

Paley, a common authority with many on moral questions, in his chapter on the "Duty of Submission to Civil Government," resolves all civil obligation into expediency; and he proceeds to say, "that so long as the interest of the whole society requires it, that is, so long as the established government cannot be resisted or changed without public inconveniency, it is the will of God that the established government be obeyed, and no longer. . . . This principle being admitted, the justice of every particular case of resistance is reduced to a computation of the quantity of the danger and grievance on the one side, and of the probability and expense of redressing it on the other." Of this, he says, every man shall judge for himself. But Paley appears never to have contemplated those cases to which the rule of expediency does not apply, in which a people, as well as an individual, must do justice, cost what it may. If I have unjustly wrested a plank from a drowning man, I must restore it to him though I drown myself. This, according to Paley, would be inconvenient. But he that would save his life, in such a case, shall lose it. This people must cease to hold slaves, and to make war on Mexico, though it cost them their existence as a people.

In their practice, nations agree with Paley; but does any one think that Massachusetts does exactly what is right at the present crisis?

> "A drab of state, a cloth-o'-silver slut,
> To have her train borne up, and her soul trail in the dirt."

Practically speaking, the opponents to a reform in Massachusetts are not a hundred thousand politicians at the South, but a hundred thousand merchants and farmers here, who are more interested in commerce and agriculture than they are in humanity, and are not prepared to do justice to the slave and to Mexico, *cost what it may*. I quarrel not with far-off foes, but with those who, near at home, coöperate with, and do the bidding of, those far away, and without whom the latter would be harmless. We are accustomed to say, that the mass of men are unprepared; but improvement is slow, because the few are not materially wiser or better than the many. It is not so important that many should be as good as you, as that there be some absolute goodness somewhere; for that will leaven the whole lump. There are thousands who are *in opinion* opposed to slavery and to the war, who yet in effect do nothing to put an end to them; who, esteeming themselves children of Washington and Franklin, sit down with their hands in their pockets, and say that they know not what to do, and do nothing; who even postpone the question of freedom to the question of free-trade, and quietly read the prices-current along with the latest advices from Mexico, after dinner, and, it may be, fall asleep over them both. What is the price-current of an honest man and patriot to-day? They hesitate, and they regret, and sometimes they petition; but they do nothing in earnest and with effect. They will wait, well disposed, for others to remedy the evil, that they may no longer have it to regret. At most, they give only a cheap vote, and a feeble countenance and Godspeed, to the right, as it goes by them. There are nine hundred and ninety-nine patrons of virtue to one virtuous man. But it is easier to deal with the real possessor of a thing than with the temporary guardian of it.

11   All voting is a sort of gaming, like checkers or backgammon, with a slight moral tinge to it, a playing with right and wrong, with moral questions; and betting naturally accompanies it. The character of the voters is not staked. I cast my vote, perchance, as I think right; but I am not vitally concerned that that right should prevail. I am willing to leave it to the majority. Its obligation, therefore, never exceeds that of expediency. Even voting *for the right* is *doing* nothing for it. It is only expressing to men feebly your desire that it should prevail. A wise man will not leave the right to the mercy of chance, nor wish it to prevail through the power of the majority. There is but little virtue in the action of masses of men. When the majority shall at length vote for the abolition of slavery, it will be because they are indifferent to slavery, or because there is but little slavery left to be abolished by their vote. *They* will then be the only slaves. Only *his* vote can hasten the abolition of slavery who asserts his own freedom by his vote.

12   I hear of a convention to be held at Baltimore, or elsewhere, for the selection of a candidate for the Presidency, made up chiefly of editors, and men who are politicians by profession; but I think, what is it to any independent, intelligent, and respectable man what decision they may come to? Shall we not have the advantage of his wisdom and honesty, nevertheless? Can we not count upon some independent votes? Are there not many individuals in the country who do not attend conventions? But no: I find that the respectable man, so called, has immediately drifted from his position, and despairs of his country, when his country has more reason to despair of him. He forthwith adopts one of the candidates thus selected as the only *available* one, thus proving that he is himself *available* for any purposes of the demagogue. His vote is of no more worth than that of any unprincipled foreigner or hireling native, who may have been bought. O for a man who is a *man*, and, as my neighbor says, has a bone in his back which you cannot pass your hand through! Our statistics are at fault: the population has been returned too large. How many *men* are there to a square thousand miles in this country? Hardly one. Does not America of-

fer any inducement for men to settle here? The American has dwindled into an Odd Fellow,—one who may be known by the development of his organ of gregariousness, and a manifest lack of intellect and cheerful self-reliance; whose first and chief concern, on coming into the world, is to see that Almhouses are in good repair; and, before yet he has lawfully donned the virile garb, to collect a fund for the support of the widows and orphans that may be; who, in short, ventures to live only by the aid of the Mutual Insurance company, which has promised to bury him decently.

It is not a man's duty, as a matter of course, to devote himself to the   13 eradication of any, even the most enormous wrong; he may still properly have other concerns to engage him; but it is his duty, at least, to wash his hands of it, and, if he gives it no thought longer, not to give it practically his support. If I devote myself to other pursuits and contemplations, I must first see, at least, that I do not pursue them sitting upon another man's shoulders. I must get off him first, that he may pursue his contemplations too. See what gross inconsistency is tolerated. I have heard some of my townsmen say, "I should like to have them order me out to help put down an insurrection of the slaves, or to march to Mexico;—see if I would go"; and yet these very men have each, directly by their allegiance, and so indirectly, at least, by their money, furnished a substitute. The soldier is applauded who refuses to serve in an unjust war by those who do not refuse to sustain the unjust government which makes the war; is applauded by those whose own act and authority he disregards and sets at naught; as if the state were penitent to that degree that it hired one to scourge it while it sinned, but not to that degree that it left off sinning for a moment. Thus, under the name of Order and Civil Government, we are all made at last to pay homage to and support our own meanness. After the first blush of sin comes its indifference; and from immoral it becomes, as it were, *un*-moral, and not quite unnecessary to that life which we have made.

The broadest and most prevalent error requires the most disinterested   14 virtue to sustain it. The slight reproach to which the virtue of patriotism is commonly liable, the noble are most likely to incur. Those who, while they disapprove of the character and measures of a government, yield to it their allegiance and support are undoubtedly its most conscientious supporters, and so frequently the most serious obstacles to reform. Some are petitioning the state to dissolve the Union, to disregard the requisitions of the President. Why do they not dissolve it themselves,—the union between themselves and the state,—and refuse to pay their quota into its treasury? Do not they stand in the same relation to the state that the state does to the Union? And have not the same reasons prevented the state from resisting the Union which have prevented them from resisting the state?

15   How can a man be satisfied to entertain an opinion merely, and enjoy *it*? Is there any enjoyment in it, if his opinion is that he is aggrieved? If you are cheated out of a single dollar by your neighbor, you do not rest satisfied with knowing that you are cheated, or with saying that you are cheated, or even with petitioning him to pay you your due; but you take effectual steps at once to obtain the full amount, and see that you are never cheated again. Action from principle, the perception and the performance of right, changes things and relations; it is essentially revolutionary, and does not consist wholly with anything which was. It not only divides states and churches, it divides families; ay, it divides the *individual*, separating the diabolical in him from the divine.

16   Unjust laws exist: shall we be content to obey them, or shall we endeavor to amend them, and obey them until we have succeeded, or shall we transgress them at once? Men generally, under such a government as this, think that they ought to wait until they have persuaded the majority to alter them. They think that, if they should resist, the remedy would be worse than the evil. But it is the fault of the government itself that the remedy *is* worse than the evil. *It* makes it worse. Why is it not more apt to anticipate and provide for reform? Why does it not cherish its wise minority? Why does it cry and resist before it is hurt? Why does it not encourage its citizens to be on the alert to point out its faults, and *do* better than it would have them? Why does it always crucify Christ, and excommunicate Copernicus and Luther, and pronounce Washington and Franklin rebels?

17   One would think, that a deliberate and practical denial of its authority was the only offense never contemplated by government; else, why has it not assigned its definite, its suitable and proportionate penalty? If a man who has no property refuses but once to earn nine shillings for the state, he is put in prison for a period unlimited by any law that I know, and determined only by the discretion of those who placed him there; but if he should steal ninety times nine shillings from the state, he is soon permitted to go at large again.

18   If the injustice is part of the necessary friction of the machine of government, let it go, let it go: perchance it will wear smooth,—certainly the machine will wear out. If the injustice has a spring, or a pulley, or a rope, or a crank, exclusively for itself, then perhaps you may consider whether the remedy will not be worse than the evil; but if it is of such a nature that it requires you to be the agent of injustice to another, then, I say, break the law. Let your life be a counter friction to stop the machine. What I have to do is to see, at any rate, that I do not lend myself to the wrong which I condemn.

19   As for adopting the ways which the state has provided for remedying the evil, I know not of such ways. They take too much time, and a man's

life will be gone. I have other affairs to attend to. I came into this world, not chiefly to make this a good place to live in, but to live in it, be it good or bad. A man has not everything to do, but something; and because he cannot do *everything*, it is not necessary that he should do *something* wrong. It is not my business to be petitioning the Governor or the Legislature any more than it is theirs to petition me; and if they should not hear my petition, what should I do then? But in this case the state has provided no way: its very Constitution is the evil. This may seem to be harsh and stubborn and unconciliatory; but it is to treat with the utmost kindness and consideration the only spirit that can appreciate or deserve it. So is all change for the better, like birth and death, which convulse the body.

I do not hesitate to say, that those who call themselves Abolitionists   20 should at once effectually withdraw their support, both in person and property, from the government of Massachusetts, and not wait till they constitute a majority of one, before they suffer the right to prevail through them. I think that it is enough if they have God on their side, without waiting for the other one. Moreover, any man more right than his neighbors constitutes a majority of one already.

I meet this American government, or its representative, the state gov-   21 ernment, directly, and face to face, once a year—no more—in the person of its tax-gatherer; this is the only mode in which a man situated as I am necessarily meets it; and then says distinctly, Recognize me; and the simplest, the most effectual, and, in the present posture of affairs, the indispensablest mode of treating with it on this head, of expressing your little satisfaction with and love for it, is to deny it then. My civil neighbor, the tax-gatherer, is the very man I have to deal with,—for it is, after all, with men and not with parchment that I quarrel,—and he has voluntarily chosen to be an agent of the government. How shall he ever know well what he is and does as an officer of the government, or as a man, until he is obliged to consider whether he shall treat me, his neighbor, for whom he has respect, as a neighbor and well-disposed man, or as a maniac and disturber of the peace, and see if he can get over this obstruction to his neighborliness without a ruder and more impetuous thought or speech corresponding with his action. I know this well, that if one thousand, if one hundred, if ten men whom I could name,—if ten *honest* men only,— say if *one* HONEST man, in this State of Massachusetts, *ceasing to hold slaves*, were actually to withdraw from this copartnership, and be locked up in the county jail therefor, it would be the abolition of slavery in America. For it matters not how small the beginning may seem to be: what is once well done is done forever. But we love better to talk about it: that we say is our mission. Reform keeps many scores of newspapers in its service, but not one man. If my esteemed neighbor, the State's ambassador, who will devote his days to the settlement of the question of human rights in the Council Chamber, instead of being threatened with the prisons of Carolina, were to sit down the prisoner of Massachusetts, that State which is so anxious to foist the sin of slavery upon her sister,—though at present she can discover only an act of inhospitality to be the ground of a quarrel with her,—the Legislature would not wholly waive the subject the following winter.

22   Under a government which imprisons any unjustly, the true place for a just man is also a prison. The proper place to-day, the only place which Massachusetts has provided for her freer and less desponding spirits, is in her prisons, to be put out and locked out of the State by her own act, as they have already put themselves out by their principles. It is there that the fugitive slave, and the Mexican prisoner on parole, and the Indian come to plead the wrongs of his race should find them; on that separate, but more free and honorable gound, where the State places those who are not *with* her, but *against* her,—the only house in a slave State in which a free man can abide with honor. If any think that their influence would be lost there, and their voices no longer afflict the ear of the State, that they would not be as an enemy within its walls, they do not know by how much truth is stronger than error, nor how much more eloquently and effectively he can combat injustice who has experienced a little in his own person. Cast your whole vote, not a strip of paper merely, but your whole influence. A minority is powerless while it conforms to the majority; it is not even a minority then; but it is irresistible when it clogs by its whole weight. If the alternative is to keep all just men in prison, or give up war and slavery, the State will not hesitate which to choose. If a thousand men were not to pay their tax-bills this year, that would not be a violent and bloody measure, as it would be to pay them, and enable the State to commit violence and shed innocent blood. This is, in fact, the definition of a peaceable revolution, if any such is possible. If the tax-gatherer, or any other public officer, asks me, as one has done, "But what shall I do?" my answer is, "If you really wish to do anything, resign your office." When the subject has refused allegiance, and the officer has resigned his office, then the revolution is accomplished. But even suppose blood should flow. Is there not a sort of blood shed when the conscience is wounded? Through this wound a man's real manhood and immortality flow out, and he bleeds to an everlasting death. I see this blood flowing now.

23   I have contemplated the imprisonment of the offender, rather than the seizure of his goods,—though both will serve the same purpose,—because they who assert the purest right, and consequently are most dangerous to

a corrupt State, commonly have not spent much time in accumulating property. To such the State renders comparatively small service, and a slight tax is wont to appear exorbitant, particularly if they are obliged to earn it by special labor with their hands. If there were one who lived wholly without the use of money, the State itself would hesitate to demand it of him. But the rich man—not to make any invidious comparison—is always sold to the institution which makes him rich. Absolutely speaking, the more money, the less virtue; for money comes between a man and his objects, and obtains them for him; and it was certainly no great virtue to obtain it. It puts to rest many questions which he would otherwise be taxed to answer; while the only new question which it puts is the hard but superfluous one, how to spend it. Thus his moral ground is taken from under his feet. The opportunities of living are diminished in proportion as what are called the "means" are increased. The best thing a man can do for his culture when he is rich to endeavor to carry out those schemes which he entertained when he was poor. Christ answered the Herodians according to their condition. "Show me the tribute-money," said he;—and one took a penny out of his pocket;—if you use money which has the image of Caesar on it, which he has made current and valuable, that is, *if you are men of the State*, and gladly enjoy the advantages of Caesar's government, then pay him back some of his own when he demands it. "Render therefore to Caesar that which is Caesar's, and to God those things which are God's,"—leaving them no wiser than before as to which was which; for they did not wish to know.

When I converse with the freest of my neighbors, I perceive that, whatever they may say about the magnitude and seriousness of the question, and their regard for the public tranquility, the long and the short of the matter is, that they cannot spare the protection of the existing government, and they dread the consequences to their property and families of disobedience to it. For my own part, I should not like to think that I ever rely on the protection of the State. But, if I deny the authority of the State when it presents its tax-bill, it will soon take and waste all my property, and so harass me and my children without end. This is hard. This makes it impossible for a man to live honestly, and at the same time comfortably, in outward respects. It will not be worth the while to accumulate property; that would be sure to go again. You must hire or squat somewhere, and raise but a small crop, and eat that soon. You must live within yourself, and depend upon yourself always tucked up and ready for a start, and not have many affairs. A man may grow rich in Turkey even, if he will be in all respects a good subject of the Turkish government. Confucius said: "If a state is governed by the principles of reason, poverty and misery are subjects of shame; if a state is not governed by the principles of reason, riches and honors are the subjects of shame." No: until I want the protection of Massachusetts to be extended to me in some distant Southern port, where my liberty is endangered, or until I am bent solely on building up an estate at home by peaceful enterprise, I can afford to refuse allegiance to Massachusetts, and her right to my property and life. It costs me less in every sense to incur the penalty of disobedience to the State than it would to obey. I should feel as if I were worth less in that case.

25   Some years ago, the State met me in behalf of the Church, and commanded me to pay a certain sum toward the support of a clergyman whose preaching my father attended, but never I myself. "Pay," it said, "or be locked up in jail." I declined to pay. But, unfortunately, another man saw fit to pay it. I did not see why the schoolmaster should be taxed to support the priest, and not the priest the schoolmaster; for I was not the State's schoolmaster, but I supported myself by voluntary subscription. I did not see why the lyceum should not present its tax-bill, and have the State to back its demand, as well as the Church. However, at the request of the selectmen, I condescended to make some such statement as this in writing:— "Know all men by these presents, that I, Henry Thoreau, do not wish to be regarded as a member of any incorporated society which I have not joined." This I gave to the town clerk; and he has it. The State, having thus learned that I did not wish to be regarded as a member of that church, has never made a like demand on me since; though it said that it must adhere to its original presumption that time. If I had known how to name them, I should have then signed off in detail from all the societies which I never signed on to; but I did not know where to find a complete list.

26   I have paid no poll-tax for six years. I was put into a jail once on this account, for one night; and, as I stood considering the walls of solid stone, two or three feet thick, the door of wood and iron, a foot thick, and the iron grating which strained the light, I could not help being struck with the foolishness of that institution which treated me as if I were mere flesh and blood and bones, to be locked up. I wondered that it should have concluded at length that this was the best use it could put me to, and had never thought to avail itself of my services in some way. I say that, if there was a wall of stone between me and my townsmen, there was a still more difficult one to climb or break through before they could get to be as free as I was. I did not for a moment feel confined, and the walls seemed a great waste of stone and mortar. I felt as if I alone of all my townsmen had paid my tax. They plainly did not know how to treat me, but behaved like persons who are underbred. In every threat and in every compliment there was a blunder; for they thought that my chief desire was to stand the other

side of that stone wall. I could not but smile to see how industriously they locked the door on my meditations, which followed them out again without let or hindrance, and *they* were really all that was dangerous. As they could not reach me, they had resolved to punish my body; just as boys, if they cannot come at some person against whom they have a spite, will abuse his dog. I saw that the State was half-witted, that it was timid as a lone woman with her silver spoons, and that it did not know its friends from its foes, and I lost all my remaining respect for it, and pitied it.

Thus the State never intentionally confronts a man's sense, intellectual or moral, but only his body, his senses. It is not armed with superior wit or honesty, but with superior physical strength. I was not born to be forced. I will breathe after my own fashion. Let us see who is the strongest. What force has a multitude? They only can force me who obey a higher law than I. They force me to become like themselves. I do not hear of *men* being *forced* to live this way or that by masses of men. What sort of life were that to live? When I meet a government which says to me, "Your money or your life," why should I be in haste to give it my money? It may be in a great strait, and not know what to do: I cannot help that. It must help itself; do as I do. It is not worth the while to snivel about it. I am not responsible for the successful working of the machinery of society. I am not the son of the engineer. I perceive that, when an acorn and a chestnut fall side by side, the one does not remain inert to make way for the other, but both obey their own laws, and spring and grow and flourish as best they can, till one, perchance, overshadows and destroys the other. If a plant cannot live according to its nature, it dies; and so a man. 27

That night in prison was novel and interesting enough. The prisoners in their shirt-sleeves were enjoying a chat and the evening air in the doorway, when I entered. But the jailer said, "Come, boys, it is time to lock up"; and so they dispersed, and I heard the sound of their steps returning into the hollow apartments. My room-mate was introduced to me by the jailer as "a first-rate fellow and a clever man." When the door was locked, he showed me where to hang my hat, and how he managed matters there. The rooms were whitewashed once a month; and this one, at least, was the whitest, most simply furnished, and probably the neatest apartment in the town. He naturally wanted to know where I came from, and what brought me there; and, when I had told him, I asked him in my turn how he came there, presuming him to be an honest man, of course; and, as the world goes, I believe he was. "Why," said he, "they accuse me of burning a barn; but I never did it." As near as I could discover, he had probably gone to bed in a barn when drunk, and smoked his pipe there; and so a barn was burnt. He had the reputation of being a clever man, had been there some 28 three months waiting for his trial to come on, and would have to wait as much longer; but he was quite domesticated and contented, since he got his board for nothing, and thought that he was well treated.

29   He occupied one window, and I the other; and I saw that if one stayed there long, his principal business would be to look out the window. I had soon read all tracts that were left there, and examined where former prisoners had broken out, and where a grate had been sawed off, and heard the history of the various occupants of that room; for I found that even here there was a history and a gossip which never circulated beyond the walls of the jail. Probably this is the only house in the town where verses are composed, which are afterward printed in a circular form, but not published. I was shown quite a long list of verses which were composed by some young men who had been detected in an attempt to escape, who avenged themselves by signing them.

30   I pumped up my fellow-prisoner as dry as I could, for fear I should never see him again; but at length he showed me which was my bed, and left me to blow out the lamp.

31   It was like traveling into a far country, such as I had never expected to behold, to lie there for one night. It seemed to me that I never had heard the town-clock strike before, nor the evening sounds of the village; for we slept with the windows open, which were inside the grating. It was to see my native village in the light of the Middle Ages, and our Concord was turned into a Rhine stream, and visions of knights and castles passed before me. They were the voices of old burghers that I heard in the streets. I was an involuntary spectator and auditor of whatever was done and said in the kitchen of the adjacent village-inn,—a wholly new and rare experience to me. It was a closer view of my native town. I was fairly inside of it. I never had seen its institutions before. This is one of its peculiar institutions; for it is a shire town. I began to comprehend what its inhabitants were about.

32   In the morning, our breakfasts were put through the hole in the door, in small oblong-square tin pans, made to fit, and holding a pint of chocolate, with brown bread, and an iron spoon. When they called for the vessels again, I was green enough to return what bread I had left; but my comrade seized it, and said that I should lay that up for lunch or dinner. Soon after he was let out to work at haying in a neighboring field, whither he went every day, and would not be back till noon; so he bade me good-day, saying that he doubted if he should see me again.

33   When I came out of prison,—for some one interfered, and paid that tax,—I did not perceive that great changes had taken place on the com-

mon, such as he observed who went in a youth and emerged a tottering and gray-headed man; and yet a change had to my eyes come over the scene,—the town, and State, and country,—greater than any that mere time could effect. I saw yet more distinctly the State in which I lived. I saw to what extent the people among whom I lived could be trusted as good neighbors and friends; that their friendship was for summer weather only; that they did not greatly propose to do right; that they were a distinct race from me by their prejudices and superstitions, as the Chinamen and Malays are; that in their sacrifices to humanity they ran no risks, not even to their property; that after all they were not so noble but they treated the thief as he had treated them, and hoped, by a certain outward observance and a few prayers, and by walking in a particular straight though useless path from time to time, to save their souls. This may be to judge my neighbors harshly; for I believe that many of them are not aware that they have such an institution as the jail in their village.

It was formerly the custom in our village; when a poor debtor came out   34
of jail, for his acquaintances to salute him, looking through their fingers, which were crossed to represent the grating of a jail window, "How do ye do?" My neighbors did not thus salute me, but first looked at me, and then at one another, as if I had returned from a long journey. I was put into jail as I was going to the shoemaker's to get a shoe which was mended. When I was let out the next morning, I proceeded to finish my errand, and, having put on my mended shoe, joined a huckleberry party, who were impatient to put themselves under my conduct; and in half an hour,—for the horse was soon tackled,—was in the midst of a huckleberry field, on one of our highest hills, two miles off, and then the State was nowhere to be seen.

This is the whole history of "My Prisons."   35

I have never declined paying the highway tax, because I am as desirous   36
of being a good neighbor as I am of being a bad subject; and as for supporting schools, I am doing my part to educate my fellow-countrymen now. It is for no particular item in the tax-bill that I refuse to pay it. I simply wish to refuse allegiance to the State, to withdraw and stand aloof from it effectually. I do not care to trace the course of my dollar, if I could, till it buys a man or a musket to shoot one with,—the dollar is innocent,—but I am concerned to trace the effects of my allegiance. In fact, I quietly declare war with the State, after my fashion, though I will still make what use and get what advantage of her I can, as is usual in such cases.

If others pay the tax which is demanded of me, from a sympathy with   37
the State, they do but what they have already done in their own case, or

rather they abet injustice to a greater extent than the State requires. If they pay the tax from a mistaken interest in the individual taxed, to save his property, or prevent his going to jail, it is because they have not considered wisely how far they let their private feelings interfere with the public good.

38   This, then, is my position at present. But one cannot be too much on his guard in such a case, lest his action be biased by obstinacy or an undue regard for the opinions of men. Let him see that he does only what belongs to himself and to the hour.

39   I think sometimes, Why, this people mean well, they are only ignorant; they would do better if they knew how: why give your neighbors this pain to treat you as they are not inclined to? But I think again, This is no reason why I should do as they do, or permit others to suffer much greater pain of a different kind. Again, I sometimes say to myself, When many millions of men, without heat, without ill will, without personal feeling of any kind, demand of you a few shillings only, without the possibility, such is their constitution, of retracting or altering their present demand, and without the possibility, on your side, of appeal to any other millions, why expose yourself to this overwhelming brute force? You do not resist cold and hunger, the winds and the waves, thus obstinately; you quietly submit to a thousand similar necessities. You do not put your head into the fire. But just in proportion as I regard this as not wholly a brute force, but partly a human force, and consider that I have relations to those millions as to so many millions of men, and not of mere brute or inanimate things, I see that appeal is possible, first and instantaneously, from them to the Maker of them, and secondly, from them to themselves. But if I put my head deliberately into the fire, there is no appeal to fire or to the maker of fire, and I have only myself to blame. If I could convince myself that I have any right to be satisfied with men as they are, and to treat them accordingly, and not accordingly, in some respects, to my requisitions and expectations of what they and I ought to be, then, like a good Mussulman and fatalist, I should endeavor to be satisfied with things as they are, and say it is the will of God. And, above all, there is this difference between resisting this and a purely brute or natural force that I can resist this with some effect; but I cannot expect, like Orpheus, to change the nature of rocks and trees and beasts.

40   I do not wish to quarrel with any man or nation. I do not wish to split hairs, to make the fine distinctions, or set myself up as better than my neighbors. I seek rather, I may say, even an excuse for conforming to the laws of the land. I am but too ready to conform to them. Indeed, I have reason to suspect myself on this head; and each year, as the tax-gatherer

comes round, I find myself disposed to review the acts and position of the general and State governments, and the spirit of the people, to discover a pretext for conformity.

> "We must affect our country as our parents,
> And if at any time we alienate
> Our love or industry from doing it honor,
> We must respect effects and teach the soul
> Matter of conscience and religion,
> And not desire of rule or benefit."

I believe that the State will soon be able to take all my work of this sort out of my hands, and then I shall be no better a patriot than my fellow-countrymen. Seen from a lower point of view, the Constitution, with all its faults, is very good; the law and the courts are very respectable; even this State and this American government are, in many respects, very admirable, and rare things, to be thankful for, such as a great many have described them; but seen from a point of view a little higher, they are what I have described them; seen from a higher still, and the highest, who shall say what they are, or that they are worth looking at or thinking of at all?

However, the government does not concern me much, and I shall bestow the fewest possible thoughts on it. It is not many moments that I live under a government, even in this world. If a man is thought-free, fancy-free, imagination-free, that which *is not* never for a long time appearing *to be* him, unwise rulers or reformers cannot fatally interrupt him.   41

I know that most men think differently from myself; but those whose lives are by profession devoted to the study of these or kindred subjects content me as little as any. Statesmen and legislators, standing so completely within the institution, never distinctly and nakedly behold it. They speak of moving society, but have no resting-place without it. They may be men of a certain experience and discrimination, and have no doubt invented ingenious and even useful systems, for which we sincerely thank them; but all their wit and usefulness lie within certain not very wide limits. They are wont to forget that the world is not governed by policy and expediency. Webster never goes behind government, and so cannot speak with authority about it. His words are wisdom to those legislators who contemplate no essential reform in the existing government; but for thinkers, and those who legislate for all time, he never once glances at the subject. I know of those whose serene and wise speculations on this theme would soon reveal the limits of his mind's range and hospitality. Yet, compared with the cheap professions of most reformers, and the still cheaper wisdom and eloquence of politicians in general, his are almost the only   42 sensible and valuable words, and we thank Heaven for him. Comparatively, he is always strong, original, and, above all, practical. Still, his quality is not wisdom, but prudence. The lawyer's truth is not Truth, but consistency or a consistent expediency. Truth is always in harmony with herself, and is not concerned chiefly to reveal the justice that may consist with wrong-doing. He well deserves to be called, as he has been called, the Defender of the Constitution. There are really no blows to be given to him but defensive ones. He is not a leader, but a follower. His leaders are the men of '87. "I have never made an effort," he says, "and never propose to make an effort; I have never countenanced an effort, and never mean to countenance an effort, to disturb the arrangement as originally made, by which the various States came into the Union." Still thinking of the sanction which the Constitution gives to slavery, he says, "Because it was a part of the original compact,—let it stand." Notwithstanding his special acuteness and ability, he is unable to take a fact out of its merely political relations, and behold it as it lies absolutely to be disposed of by the intellect,—what, for instance, it behooves a man to do here in America to-day with regard to slavery,—but ventures, or is driven, to make some such desperate answer as the following, while professing to speak absolutely, and as a private man,—from which what new and singular code of social duties might be inferred? "The manner," says he, "in which the governments of those States where slavery exists are to regulate it is for their own consideration, under their responsibility to their constituents, to the general laws of propriety, humanity, and justice, and to God. Associations formed elsewhere, springing from a feeling of humanity, or any other cause, have nothing whatever to do with it. They have never received any encouragement from me, and they never will."

43   They who know of no purer sources of truth, who have traced up its stream no higher, stand, and wisely stand, by the Bible and the Constitution, and drink at it there with reverence and humility; but they who behold where it comes trickling into this lake or that pool, gird up their loins once more, and continue their pilgrimage toward its fountain-head.

44   No man with a genius for legislation has appeared in America. They are rare in the history of the world. There are orators, politicians, and eloquent men, by the thousand; but the speaker has not yet opened his mouth to speak who is capable of settling the much-vexed questions of the day. We love eloquence for its own sake, and not for any truth which it may utter, or any heroism it may inspire. Our legislators have not yet learned the comparative value of free-trade and of freedom, of union, and of rectitude, to a nation. They have no genius or talent for comparatively humble questions of taxation and finance, commerce and manufacturers and agri-

culture. If we were left solely to the worldly wit of legislators in Congress for our guidance, uncorrected by the seasonable experience and the effectual complaints of the people, America would not long retain her rank among the nations. For eighteen hundred years, though perchance I have no right to say it, the New Testament has been written; yet where is the legislator who has wisdom and practical talent enough to avail himself of the light which it sheds on the science of legislation?

The authority of government, even such as I am willing to submit to,— for I will cheerfully obey those who know and can do better than I, and in many things even those who neither know nor can do so well,—is still an impure one: to be strictly just, it must have the sanction and consent of the governed. It can have no pure right over my person and property but what I concede to it. The progress from an absolute to a limited monarchy, from a limited monarchy to a democracy, is a progress toward a true respect for the individual. Even the Chinese philosopher was wise enough to regard the individual as the basis of the empire. Is a democracy, such as we know it, the last improvement possible in government? Is it not possible to take a further step towards recognizing and organizing the rights of man? There will never be a really free and enlightened State until the State comes to recognize the individual as a higher and independent power, from which all its own power and authority are derived, and treats him accordingly. I please myself with imagining a State at last which can afford to be just to all men, and to treat the individual with respect as a neighbor; which even would not think it inconsistent with its own repose if a few were to live aloof from it, not meddling with it, nor embraced by it, who fulfilled all the duties of neighbors and fellow-men. A State which bore this kind of fruit, and suffered it to drop off as fast as it ripened, would prepare the way for a still more perfect and glorious State, which also I have imagined, but not yet anywhere seen.

45

QUESTIONING AND DISCUSSING

Thoreau, "Civil Disobedience"

1. Thoreau believes that he must "do what I think is right." If, in fact, democracies also depend on a belief in what is best for the greater good, how can we reconcile Thoreau's view with a traditional definition of *democracy*? Discuss the notion of majority rule and its relationship to an individual's desire and conscience. If necessary, consult other sources, and cite them carefully.

2. Select and analyze some of Thoreau's key statements. For instance, consider "That government is best which governs least," "All voting is a sort of gaming,

like checkers or backgammon," and "Under a government which imprisons any unjustly, the true place for a just man is also a prison." Find other equally challenging statements. What are the moral consequences of each? Consider recent events in the United States and the world. What are the moral implications of Thoreau's positions given current events?

3. What is good citizenship, according to Thoreau? (What about those Americans of Thoreau's time who were opposed to slavery, for instance?) Using your assessment of Thoreau's definition, what is *good citizenship* today? Be specific.

4. When, if ever, is civil disobedience appropriate or morally necessary?

⊞

Svi Shapiro

Professor of Education at the University of North Carolina at Greensboro, Svi Shapiro (1948–) also chairs the Department of Educational Leadership and Cultural Foundations. His areas of research include issues of political change and educational policy. Shapiro's numerous books on educational reform include *Between Capitalism and Democracy* (1990), in which he argues that educational policy in the United States is the result of competing and unresolved ideological points of view. Published in 1999, Shapiro's most recent book, *Strangers in a Strange Land: Modernity, Pedagogy, and Jewish Identity,* articulates Jews' oppression and marginalization in the United States, providing a context that might explain the following article. In it, Shapiro struggles with the idea of sending his daughter to a private school despite his personal and professional support for public education.

⊞

A Parent's Dilemma: Public vs. Jewish Education

The time for decision always seemed to be far off. It would be six years from the beginning of kindergarten before my daughter would complete her elementary schooling—a seemingly endless period of time during which I would surely find the clarity of thinking to decide on the future course of her education. Yet fifth grade at B'nai Shalom Day School had arrived far more rapidly than I wanted. I would now have to seriously confront my own commitments to public education, and to Jewish education—to say nothing of my ambivalence about private schooling and the privileges of class, the rootlessness of a postmodern America, and the comforts of parochial communities.

For leftist academics, there is always the danger of allowing the particularities of one person's life to become lost in the much grander narratives of moral, ideological, and political considerations. This is, after all, a decision about where my eleven-year-old daughter Sarah is to spend her sixth grade. Nor, as I have reminded myself many times, can I hold her needs hostage to my own heavily worked concerns about the course of social justice and identity in this country.

We live in Greensboro, North Carolina. This is not New York or Philadelphia. The Jewish community (well established and comfortable as it is) exists as a very small island in an overwhelmingly dominant Christian milieu. This is what is sometimes referred to as the New South—middle class, moderately conservative. Greensboro is a city of several colleges and universities; we recycle garbage; our mayor is a woman and an environmentalist. Despite a notorious 1979 shoot-out involving the Ku Klux Klan, this is not Klan country.

To grow up Jewish here is certainly a minority experience. But it is far from the culturally marginalizing and politely silent experience I had growing up Jewish in England in the 1950s. Here, Jewish holidays are visibly and positively commented on in the local media, the television stations wish their viewers a happy Chanukah, and the downtown Christmas decorations are referred to as the "Festival of Lights." Even our supermarkets consult with our Conservative rabbi on Jewish dietary laws and culinary tastes.

The Jewish day school my daughter attends is a quite beautiful institution. Its enrollment is about 190 students—fairly remarkable in a city of about 1,200 Jewish families. Recently celebrating its twenty-fifth anniversary, the school provides a warm, very *haimish* Jewish environment, where holidays and Shabbat are richly celebrated, and the Hebrew language ubiquitous. Its religiosity is traditional though nondogmatic, and it affirms the notions of *tikkun olam*. While I find the pedagogy too conventional, my daughter has found the place to be nurturant and loving. She has, for the most part, found delight in being there—a place where schooling has sustained her, not opposed her life.

What was at stake in my choice of Sarah's schooling was no abstract pedagogic exercise. I want my daughter's heart and soul to be shaped and nurtured by a *Yiddishkeyt* that would ensure her allegiance to a Jewish identity. As spiritually or historically compelling as this might be, I make no claim that this is not, at root, a selfish act. Such an education would ensure my continuing ability to recognize my own self in my daughter's being— the natural, if not entirely laudable, desire of most parents. Until now, my decision has been richly repaid; she had indeed absorbed not only some of the knowledge and culture of Jewish life, but more significantly its texture and feel. She senses its importance and its uniqueness. The joys and significance of this belong not only to the private sphere of family life, but also for her to the sphere of communal participation. Jewish life exists not merely in home or synagogue, but richly and vibrantly in the everyday, Monday-through-Friday world from which, for most of us, it is abstracted.

7   The mobilization of support for a politics that eviscerates public institutions is bound up with the widely felt hostility in modern societies toward the state, with all of its impersonality, inefficiency, and waste. It is precisely this perception that has fueled the relentless drive of the Right to gut almost everything that has the word "public" in it.

8   At the heart of this assault is an ideology that lionizes the marketplace and scorns society's attempts to ameliorate social injustice. In this view, the marketplace and market forces are regarded as the only legitimate means to allocate resources and to assign economic or cultural values. The reultant push for smaller government and a balanced budget has the effect of drastically reducing the scope and scale of the social safety net. It means ever more drastic cutbacks in society's supports to the elderly, children, the unemployed, the poor, and the sick.

9   So our culture continues to foster self-interest and a lack of concern for the common good. Where the marketplace alone is to be arbiter of economic investment and social values, attempts are made to eliminate or reduce publicly financed education and culture. Prisons become one of the few areas of public investment. And where public policy collides with the imperatives of the market, as in environmental and consumer regulation, then the latter need be scaled back if not eradicated.

10   The political discourse that has sought to achieve these ends is not without its own conflicts and contradictions. It is clear, for example, that many people subscribe to the notion of smaller, less wasteful government, but also support a state that lessens the hazards and dangers of the free market. In this sense the state is, paradoxically, both the focus of much popular anger and repository of much of our needs and aspirations as a community. It irks us with its demands and intrusiveness, but it also instantiates our collective responsibilities and obligations. For all of its flaws, the state embodies some notion of a shared purpose; its ultimate client purports to be the public good, not simply the desirous ego.

11   The irony is that those conservatives who have often been the loudest in their condemnation of the decline of community and an ethic of responsibility have pursued a politics that has sought to allow the standards and ethics of the market to exert ever more freedom and dominance in

our social, economic, and cultural lives. In working to ensure a world in which private interests and profits are less and less hindered by broad public responsibilities, and where the public arena is endlessly demeaned and savagely attacked, these free-marketeers have helped create a society that more and more resembles a predatory jungle. The violence of the Oklahoma bombing and the shut-down of the federal government, with its callous layoffs of workers and undelivered unemployment checks, are the most recent visible evidence of a discourse which has effectively trashed the public domain.

Sadly, it is often only when cuts in services and benefits are directly felt that individuals become more critical of what is happening on a broader level. Until then, the politics of racism and division succeed in legitimating the Right's social policies. A bunker mentality spreads, which calls for a social ethic of each for him or herself; individualism, separateness, and isolation frame our disposition toward the rest of the world. All of this has been given added impetus by corporate behavior in the 1980s and '90s, replete with layoffs, downsizing, closings, and relocations. It is a world that mocks any notions of obligation or commitment to workers, consumers, or community. Nothing really counts except the hunt for immediate profitability. Public accountability is a barrier to be subverted by whatever means necessary. 12

Yet in spite of all of this, there is still a deep hunger for communal life and the public good in America. Despite the shift to the Right, large majorities continue to affirm the importance of protecting our environment, maintaining investments in public libraries and cultural resources, and ensuring the availability of health care. Sometimes it becomes crystallized in ways that seem narrow or even repressive (protecting "our" flag). Yet behind these can be heard a cry for a society in which our collective concerns, not just our private interests, are honored, and where there is a strong sense of the public good instantiated in our civic world and in our social institutions. 13

Perhaps nowhere has this struggle been more focused than around the institutions of public education. Indeed, all of our societal schizophrenia around questions of public and private, marketplace and equity, democracy and capitalism, are in evidence there. In its most ideal rendering, public schooling represents a space where all of our children may be educated, a place where the rights of citizenship take precedence over the privileges or disadvantages of social and economic life. Understood in this way, public education becomes a crucial element in the making of a democratic civil society. It is an indispensable site for the nurturing of a new generation in those attitudes and values that ensure the possibility of meaningful democratic life. 14

15   Public school brings together in one setting children who, regardless of their class, race, gender or ethnicity, may acquire the capacity for critical intelligence, the sense of community, and the cultural literacy that are requisites for democracy. As many political commentators have pointed out, the current crisis of democracy in the United States is closely related to the decline of meaningful public spaces where citizens can engage in a thoughtful and critical consideration of our society's pressing issues and concerns. In a world where commercial malls and presidential debates simulate real public interaction and involvement, there is a growing urgency to preserve those places where notions of equity, community, citizenship, and the public good still have validity.

16   Sadly, the reality of public schools has always been a long way from its democratic promise. The fundamental ideal of a place where the offspring of all citizens might meet and come together as a community has always been upset by the harsh realities of privilege, inequity, and racism. The historic struggles to eradicate the effects of a racially segregated system of public education are well known. Less obvious have been the continuing pernicious effects of class and race in maintaining schools vastly different in their resources, funding, expectations of students, and educational climate. Jonathan Kozol, among others, vividly documented the horrendous conditions that beset schools in poor and underfunded districts, producing debilitating and demoralizing third-world environments for kids in many of this nation's cities.

17   This public sphere mirrors the increasing polarization of wealth and opportunity found in the wider society. Urban schools with their violence, high drop-out rates, low achievement, and poor morale exist as altogether different institutions from those in suburban areas that function as conduits to good colleges and economic well-being.

18   Far from equalizing opportunities for diverse groups of students, education typically reinforces the already existing advantages and disadvantages found in the larger culture. The bitter irony of the process is that it occurs under the apparently well-meaning rhetoric of educational theories that promise to teach to the intellectual and emotional differences among students. Yet, in practice, the effect is usually to rationalize racism and classism. The ubiquitous grouping and tracking of students become little more than a way of affirming the "cultural capital" of some individuals and invalidating that of others. It takes only a cursory look at many schools to see how education dignifies the knowledge and experiences of some people and silences and marginalizes that of others.

19   Typically, schooling represents a process of mindless absorption of knowledge separated from any notion of existential or social meaning. Successful learning comes to be seen as a regurgitation of bits and pieces

of knowledge abstracted from a context that might provide them with relevance to the lives, hopes, interests, and dreams of kids' lives. And the "hidden curriculum" of schooling is such that the emphasis on achievement, individual success, and competition undermines efforts to build communities of respect and care. Indeed, where the latter are taken seriously, they must confront the contradictions not only of school culture but that of the large social milieu. The daily grind of public school life with its boredom, alienation, and bureaucratic regimentation are the resonant features of contemporary, adolescent popular culture.

In my struggle to decide the fate of my fifth-grade daughter, I am mindful 20 of the desperate need to sustain the promise of public life in this country. The withdrawal of the middle class from public institutions is the certain vehicle for their demoralization and decline. Not only in this country but in other places such as the United Kingdom, the turn toward more individualistic lifestyles and privatized institutions, promoted by conservative governments, has turned the public space into one of neglect and decay. Whether in health care, housing, or in education, the story is one of double-standards—where publicly provided institutions or systems are synonymous with the poor, and where standards are increasingly inferior as compared to those found in the private domain.

In wrestling with whether to send my daughter to a public school, I feel 21 compelled to weigh my own moral responsibility as to whether I am to be part of the flight from our public world into the safety and privileges of a private institution. A commitment to progressive politics would seem to demand commitment to those public institutions where we may share, to some degree, our lives with those who inhabit economic, cultural, or racial worlds quite different from our own.

Among all these concerns, one is of particular significance to me. How 22 do we reconcile a commitment to public education with the need to recognize and affirm cultural, religious, or other differences? For many on the Left, this validation of differences has been central to the contemporary struggle to deepen the meaning of democratic life. It has been seen as a critical feature of democracy in a "postmodern" world. The struggle to recognize the multiplicity of voices and the diversity of histories and experiences of those who inhabit our nation and world has been a key focus of progressive educators.

And there has been increasing recognition of the ways that education has 23 for so long denied the contributions and presence of many kinds of people. Whether because of class or race or ethnicity or gender or religion or nationality, it has become clear just how much we have ignored or invalidated the knowledge and traditions of others—those who fall outside the constructed norms of the culture. As educators, we have come to see how this process demeans and silences our students as the classroom becomes a place that is quite foreign to their homes, neighborhood, or communities.

24   In this regard, the emergence of a "multicultural" awareness in our schools is an important and liberating phenomenon. It is certainly a mark of progress that children are being taught to question the notion that "Columbus discovered America" with all its ethnocentric and racist assumptions about civilization; or that history, social studies, and English are beginning to be taught in more expansive and inclusive ways. Even where there are good-faith efforts, multiculturalism too often becomes trivialized—a matter of food, fiestas, and dressing up. It offers a very superficial appreciation indeed of what difference has meant to communities often denigrated or despised by those in the mainstream of society. Whatever its limitations, these efforts represent real cracks in the wall of cultural assumptions that have confronted generations of young people, shutting out or silencing those whose language, history, beliefs, and culture have been made to seem peripheral to the society.

25   Yet even where difference is valued and the plural nature of cultures in America is celebrated, the texture of the particular cultures recognized by our public schools is likely to be "thin." For my daughter, no multicultural environment can offer the judaically rich, evocative, and full experience that would be available to her in a Jewish day school. Only in that environment does Jewishness become a form of life that colors moral expression, joyful celebration, the moments of soulful reflection and sadness, and the days and seasons of the calendar. Jewishness becomes more than an abstract focus of intellectual discussion: the living vehicle through which my daughter can construct her identity and articulate her ethical and spiritual commitments.

26   Such a voice is a matter of both the heart and the mind, and only a pedagogic environment that is flooded with the resonance of Jewish memory and experience can nurture it. Nor is a deep sense of value about Jewish life easily available outside of a context which integrates it into a community's daily practice—one that draws in some way from the moral and spiritual meanings of our people's historical wisdom. The "thick" texture of Jewish life—the pervasive sounds of Hebrew, the smell of challah, the *niggunim* and Israeli songs, the benching after meals—are the resources upon which are built an identity that contains an enduring commitment to Jewish life and continuity.

27   The intensity of this experience, however, holds the potential danger of nurturing parochial or arrogant attitudes. Such schooling may produce a *shtetl* consciousness that shuns or disparages anything foreign—one that

later fuels the intolerance of "*goyim*-bashing," or the self-righteousness that underlays so much of the American-Jewish support for chauvinistic, right-wing Israeli politics.

While at B'nai Shalom, much hard work goes toward developing a 28 sense of social responsibility and celebrating the values of human community and global connectedness, the school my daughter attends is nevertheless a sheltered, limited community that is separated from much that other children must confront and deal with in their lives. Certainly its ambiance is too competitive, oriented to the goals of individual success and achievements. In selectivity as a Jewish and predominantly middle- and upper-middle-class institution ensures that it is the kind of secure and cohesive community so appealing to parents. Yet in this sense it also provides a powerful, if disturbing, answer to some of the dilemmas of a post-modern world.

In their observations of postmodern society, there is a surprising con- 29 vergence among both left- and right-wing critics. At the center is the belief that the world we have entered is one in which barriers—spatial, moral, political, intellectual, and aesthetic—have collapsed. Even the boundaries of gender appear permeable in an age in which sexual borders are easily crossed and labile. Our age is one of unfixity, uncertainty, and flux.

There is much to celebrate in all of this. The unfixing of boundaries, 30 verities, and distinctions has given us the promise of a world that is more fluid, open, and free. Yet there is a price to pay—one, I believe, that has traumatic consequences for the young. And in this the conservative critique finds a powerful resonance in the anguish of many parents, by no means all of whom can be dismissed as simply and predictably right wing.

It is quite clear that the desire for discipline and structure in the raising of 31 the young now hits a powerful chord across a wide range of parents. This desire emanates from the increasing recognition of a world in which a moral and spiritual homelessness is the prevailing sensibility. More and more there is the sense of being uprooted from the stabilities of place, family, and normative communities. The postmodern world is one in which individuals increasingly feel as if they are in exile—existentially and morally adrift in a world that constantly disrupts and dissolves any sense of situatedness in an enduring web of meaning and community. Indeed, far from acknowledging the pain of so much alienation, we are urged by Madison Avenue as well as the hipper cultural critics to enjoy the tumultuous ride.

In ways that distort the broad concern for the disintegration of ethical 32 life and the erosion of the sense of social responsibility, talk of tradition, values, and discipline is mistakenly understood as only a discourse of the Right. Yet a world in which all that is solid melts—moral commitment, identity, community, social connection—is a matter that confronts all of us. And nowhere is this more painfully so than in regard to the upbringing of our own children. Daily, all of us, especially parents, are forced to confront the fallout from the postmodern condition—the self-destructiveness of adolescent suicide, drugs, alcoholism and compulsive dieting, widespread depression and generalized rage, and a cynical detachment from social institutions. However manipulative or distorting, conservative discourse succeeds because it speaks to the widespread anguish of an older generation.

33   In this context of disintegration, rootlessness, and the culture of images, Jewish schooling offers a sense of possibility not easily found elsewhere. Here there is the hope of nurturing an identity grounded in the Jewish people's long history—a history rich with the struggles for a world of justice and freedom. Here, too, is the real possibility of transmitting what it means to be a "stranger in the land"—developing personalities, empathic to the pain of exclusion and human indignity.

34   Jewish "memory" roots us in a temporal community of unbelievable human tragedies, celebrations, suffering, courage, and the will for physical and spiritual survival. And such history makes powerful claims on the living—an insistence on the vision of *tikkun olam*; to act as if we ourselves had experienced the bondage of Egypt. Far from the Disney World theme park of historical images, Jewish pedagogy can offer a deep sense of historic and communal identification. Such identification is one of connectedness to an enduring moral and spiritual vision.

35   The religious sensibility forged in this history is one that continually demands that we create and recognize boundaries—distinctions within our world between ways of living that express the sacred and those that are profane. Judaism is a religion of everyday life that constantly seeks to make sacred the so-called ordinary, taken-for-granted acts of daily existence. Those of us who grew up in Orthodox homes know the rigidity and frequently stultifying nature of halakhic Judaism. Yet, at the same time, one can find here a powerful rejoinder to the dehumanization and degradation of our common world—one that insists that we seek to make holy human life and behavior, as well as the whole environment that makes life possible.

36   Certainly Judaism, like all religions, can become dogmatic and reified; a series of mindless rituals and practices. Yet I have reason to believe that B'nai Shalom offers my daughter the beginning of a deeper set of meanings that points to the limits and boundaries that structure our relationship to the world as one of respect, consciousness of the needs of others, and responsibility toward them. In this school's Judaism there is, too, a sense of celebration and festivity—one that seeks to teach the young something about experiencing lives of joy, wonder, and appreciation. It is, I be-

lieve, in this synthesis of social responsibility and joyful mindfulness that we can find the beginnings of a meaningful response to the rampant cynicism and nihilism of our culture.

It is true that the school offers an environment that is only very cautiously questioning or critical of the injustices of our world. And I am concerned lest it limit the importance of developing the critical mind and spirit—the lifeblood of a democratic culture. But beyond the need for our young to be educated to enable them to challenge their world, there is a need for the sense of hope and possibility that the world can be changed and transformed. And this, I believe, happens best in an environment where we feel a deeply shared, and inspiring, sense of connected fate. For Jews, there is our long history of struggle in a harsh world of brutality and oppression, and the will to maintain our hope for a better world.

Without this communal rootedness and affirmation of a way of life there is, I think, little emotional capacity to act in the world—at least not where acting means trying to transform the moral character of our lives and the political shape of our society. There is only disconnected apathy and cynicism—the world of the young so well reflected in the recent popular movies, *Slacker* and *Clueless*.

The Right is correct to argue that without an internalized discipline the self becomes passive, unable to act in the world. Yet the discipline that empowers is not that of the obedient drone but the structure that comes from participation and responsibility in the life of a meaningful and enduring community.

These are not easy times. Such communities are not easy to find. All of us must somehow find the capacity for commitment in a world where all beliefs seem uncertain, visions uncertain, and social relations fragile or broken. Yet the need to find a place in which our commitments are shared and our identities confirmed is the necessary ground of our being as moral agents in the world.

Let me be clear that my real interest is not in what is referred to today as "Jewish continuity." The continuation of a set of practices and rituals is of no particular significance to me. The ultimate value of Jewish education is not found in my daughter's capacity to read or speak Hebrew, or her knowledge of Judaica, but in whether she will become a human being deeply concerned for the worth and dignity of all the lives that share our world. My hope is that her Jewish education will be a powerful vehicle for developing such a way of being. The particular here, I hope, will provide a gateway to the universal.

Yet I worry that my desire for this education will also boost the arguments of those who favor "school choice." These are often no more than thinly veiled attempts to promote educational policies that are elitist,

37

38

39

40

41

42

racially separatist, or religiously fundamentalist, and have little to do with creating a more compassionate or respectful civic culture. As I wrestle with my daughter's future, I feel the strong and inescapable claims of the particular in a world that more and more demands a recognition of our universal connectedness and responsibilities.

QUESTIONING AND DISCUSSING

Shapiro, "A Parent's Dilemma"

1. What does the "dilemma" of the title seem to promise about the discussion? What are the bases for this dilemma? In what ways is it a dilemma that is, to the author, a moral one?

2. This article originally appeared in a magazine called *Tikkun*, which is a Hebrew word for "to mend, repair, and transform the world." How might this definition, the stated purpose of this magazine, somehow reflect the conflict that Shapiro delineates?

3. Shapiro writes, "It is precisely this perception that has fueled the relentless drive of the Right to gut almost everything that has the word 'public' in it." What is that perception? Why is there a "hostility in modern societies toward the state"?

4. What are the various ways in which Shapiro makes his argument? How effective are they? Explain.

5. Comment on Shapiro's contentions that "our culture continues to foster self-interest and a lack of concern for the common good" and that in our society, "[t]here is only disconnected apathy and cynicism [. . .] reflected in the recent popular movies, *Slacker* and *Clueless*."

6. Analyze Shapiro's arguments about multiculturalism in the public schools. What has been your experience? Back up your point of view with specific examples, referring also to Shapiro's article.

⊞

RAYMOND S. DUFF AND A. G. M. CAMPBELL

Renowned in the fields of pediatric care and medical sociology, Raymond S. Duff
(1923–1995) has been particularly cited for his 1968 book (coauthored with C. Hol-
lingshead), *Sickness and Society*, in which he examines hospital care and its impact on
patients and their families. Duff extends this examination of doctors and patients to
the New Haven, Connecticut, area in his 1990 book, *Assessing Pediatric Practice—
A Critical Study*. Duff, who was also a professor of pediatrics at Yale, was known for
speaking out on controversial issues. The 1973 article from the *New England Journal
of Medicine* that follows (coauthored with A. G. M. Campbell) has proven to be influential in examining "emotionally and intellectually challenging" topics related to
health care.

⊞

Moral and Ethical Dilemmas
in the Special-Care Nursery

Abstract   *Of 299 consecutive deaths occurring in a special-care nursery, 43 (14 per
cent) were related to withholding treatment. In this group were 15 with cardiopulmonary disease, seven with meningomyelocele, three with other central-nervous-
system disorders, and two with short-bowel syndrome. After careful consideration of
each of these 43 infants, parents and physicians in a group decision concluded that
prognosis for meaningful life was extremely poor or hopeless, and therefore rejected
further treatment. The awesome finality of these decisions, combined with a potential
for error in prognosis, made the choice agonizing for families and health professionals.
Nevertheless, the issue has to be faced, for not to decide is an arbitrary and potentially
devastating decision of default. (N Engl J Med 289:890–894, 1973)*

From the Department of Pediatrics, Yale University School of Medicine, 333 Cedar St.,
New Haven, Conn. 06510, where reprint requests should be addressed to Dr. Duff.

Between 1940 and 1970 there was a 58 per cent decrease in the infant
death rate in the United States.[1] This reduction was related in part to the
application of new knowledge to the care of infants. Neonatal mortality
rates in hospitals having infant intensive-care units have been about ½
those reported in hospitals without such units.[2] There is now evidence
that in many conditions of early infancy the long-term morbidity may also
be reduced.[3] Survivors of these units may be healthy, and their parents
grateful, but some infants continue to suffer from such conditions as
chronic cardiopulmonary disease, short-bowel syndrome or various manifestations of brain damage; others are severely handicapped by a myriad of

congenital malformations that in previous times would have resulted in early death. Recently, both lay and professional persons have expressed increasing concern about the quality of life for these severely impaired survivors and their families.[4,5] Many pediatricians and others are distressed with the long-term results of pressing on and on to save life at all costs and in all circumstances. Eliot Slater stated, "If this is one of the consequences of the sanctity-of-life ethic, perhaps our formulation of the principle should be revised."

2   The experiences described in this communication document some of the grave moral and ethical dilemmas now faced by physicians and families. They indicate some of the problems in a large special-care nursery where medical technology has prolonged life and where "informed" parents influence the management decisions concerning their infants.

Background and Methods

3   The special-care nursery of the Yale–New Haven Hospital not only serves an obstetric service for over 4,000 live births annually but also acts as the principal referral center in Connecticut for infants with major problems of the newborn period. From January 1, 1970, through June 30, 1972, 1,615 infants born at the Hospital were admitted, and 556 others were transferred for specialized care from community hospitals. During this interval, the average daily census was 26, with a range of 14 to 37.

4   For some years the unit has had a liberal policy for parental visiting, with the staff placing particular emphasis on helping parents adjust to and participate in the care of their infants with special problems. By encouraging visiting, attempting to create a relaxed atmosphere within the unit, exploring carefully the special needs of the infants, and familiarizing parents with various aspects of care, it was hoped to remove much of the apprehension—indeed, fear—with which parents at first view an intensive-care nursery.[7] At any time, parents may see and handle their babies. They commonly observe or participate in most routine aspects of care and are often present when some infant is critically ill or moribund. They may attend, as they choose, the death of their own infant. Since an average of two to three deaths occur each week and many infants are critically ill for long periods, it is obvious that the concentrated, intimate social interactions between personnel, infants and parents in an emotionally charged atmosphere often make the work of the staff very difficult and demanding. However, such participation and recognition of parents' rights to information about their infant appear to be the chief foundations of "informed consent" for treatment.

5   Each staff member must know how to cope with many questions and problems brought up by parents, and if he or she cannot help, they must

have access to those who can. These requirements can be met only when staff members work closely with each other in all the varied circumstances from simple to complex, from triumph to tragedy. Formal and informal meetings take place regularly to discuss the technical and family aspects of care. As a given problem may require, some or all of several persons (including families, nurses, social workers, physicians, chaplains and others) may convene to exchange information and reach decisions. Thus, staff and parents function more or less as a small community in which a concerted attempt is made to ensure that each member may participate in and know about the major decisions that concern him or her. However, the physician takes appropriate initiative in final decision making, so that the family will not have to bear that heavy burden alone.

For several years, the responsibilities of attending pediatrician have been assumed chiefly by ourselves, who, as a result, have become acquainted intimately with the problems of the infants, the staff, and the parents. Our almost constant availability to staff, private pediatricians and parents has resulted in the raising of more and more ethical questions about various aspects of intensive care for critically ill and congenitally deformed infants. The penetrating questions and challenges, particularly of knowledgeable parents (such as physicians, nurses, or lawyers), brought increasing doubts about the wisdom of many of the decisions that seemed to parents to be predicated chiefly on technical considerations. Some thought their child had a right to die since he could not live well or effectively. Others thought that society should pay the costs of care that may be so destructive to the family economy. Often, too, the parents' or siblings' rights to relief from the seemingly pointless, crushing burdens were important considerations. It seemed right to yield to parent wishes in several cases as physicians have done for generations. As a result, some treatments were withheld or stopped with the knowledge that earlier death and relief from suffering would result. Such options were explored with the less knowledgeable parents to ensure that their consent for treatment of their defective children was truly informed. As Eisenberg[8] pointed out regarding the application of technology, "At long last, we are beginning to ask, not *can* it be done, but *should* it be done?" In lengthy, frank discussions, the anguish of the parents was shared, and attempts were made to support fully the reasoned choices, whether for active treatment and rehabilitation or for an early death.

To determine the extent to which death resulted from withdrawing or withholding treatment, we examined the hospital records of all children who died from January 1, 1970, through June 30, 1972.

Results

8   In total, there were 299 deaths; each was classified in one of two categories; deaths in Category 1 resulted from pathologic conditions in spite of treatment given; 256 (86 per cent) were in this category. Of these, 66 per cent were the result of respiratory problems or complications associated with extreme prematurity (birth weight under 1,000 g). Congenital heart disease and other anomalies accounted for an additional 22 per cent (Table 1).

Table 1. Problems Causing Death in Category 1.

Problem	No. of Deaths	Percentage
Respiratory	108	42.2
Extreme prematurity	60	23.4
Heart disease	42	16.4
Multiple anomalies	14	5.5
Other	32	12.5
Totals	256	100.0

9   Deaths in Category 2 were associated with severe impairment, usually from congenital disorders (Table 2): 43 (14 per cent) were in this group. These deaths or their timing was associated with discontinuance or withdrawal of treatment. The mean duration of life in Category 2 (Table 3) was greater than that in Category 1. This was the result of a mean life of 55 days for eight infants who became chronic cardiopulmonary cripples but for whom prolonged and intensive efforts were made in the hope of eventual recovery. They were infants who were dependent on oxygen, digoxin and diuretics, and most of them had been treated for the idiopathic respiratory-distress syndrome with high oxygen concentrations and positive-pressure ventilation.

Table 2. Problems Associated with Death in Category 2.

Problem	No. of Deaths	Percentage
Multiple anomalies	15	34.9
Trisomy	8	18.6
Cardiopulmonary	8	18.6
Meningomyelocele	7	16.3
Other central-nervous-system defects	3	7.0
Short-bowel syndrome	2	4.6
Totals	43	100.0

Table 3. Selected Comparisons of 256 Cases in Category 1 and 43 in Category 2.

Attribute	Category 1	Category 2
Mean length of life	4.8 days	7.5 days
Standard deviation	8.8	34.3
Range	1–69	1–150
Portion living for < 2 days	50.0%	12.0%

Some examples of management choices in Category 2 illustrate the problems. An infant with Down's syndrome and intestinal atresia, like the much-publicized one at John Hopkins Hospital,[9] was not treated because his parents thought that surgery was wrong for their baby and themselves. He died seven days after birth. Another child had chronic pulmonary disease after positive-pressure ventilation with high oxygen concentrations for treatment of severe idiopathic respiratory-distress syndrome. By five months of age, he still required 40 per cent oxygen to survive, and even then, he was chronically dyspneic and cyanotic. He also suffered from cor pulmonale, which was difficult to control with digoxin and diuretics. The nurses, parents and physicians considered it cruel to continue, and yet difficult to stop. All were attached to this child, whose life they had tried so hard to make worthwhile. The family had endured high expenses (the hospital bill exceeding $15,000), and the strains of the illness were believed to be threatening the marriage bonds and to be causing sibling behavioral disturbances. Oxygen supplementation was stopped, and the child died in about three hours. The family settled down and 18 months later had another baby, who was healthy.

A third child had meningomyelocele, hydrocephalus and major anomalies of every organ in the pelvis. When the parents understood the limits of medical care and rehabilitation, they believed no treatment should be given. She died at five days of age.

We have maintained contact with most families of children in Category 2. Thus far, these families appear to have experienced a normal mourning for their losses. Although some have exhibited doubts that the choices were correct, all appear to be as effective in their lives as they were before this experience. Some claim that their profoundly moving experience has provided a deeper meaning in life, and from this they believe they have become more effective people.

Members of all religious faiths and atheists were participants as parents and as staff in these experiences. There appeared to be no relation between participation and a person's religion. Repeated participation in these troubling events did not appear to reduce the worry of the staff about the awesome nature of the decisions.

Discussion

14   That decisions are made not to treat severely defective infants may be no surprise to those familiar with special-care facilities. All laymen and professionals familiar with our nursery appeared to set some limits upon their application of treatment to extend life or to investigate a pathologic process. For example, an experienced nurse said about one child, "We lost him several weeks ago. Isn't it time to quit?" In another case, a house officer said to a physician investigating an aspect of a child's disease, "For this child, don't you think it's time to turn off your curiosity so you can turn on your kindness?" Like many others, these children eventually acquired the "right to die."

15   Arguments among staff members and families for and against such decisions were based on varied notions of the rights and interests of defective infants, their families, professionals and society. They were also related to varying ideas about prognosis. Regarding the infants, some contended that individuals should have a right to die in some circumstances such as anencephaly, hydranencephaly, and some severely deforming and incapacitating conditions. Such very defective individuals were considered to have little or no hope of achieving meaningful "humanhood."[10] For example, they have little or no capacity to love or be loved. They are often cared for in facilities that have been characterized as "hardly more than dying bins,"[11] an assessment with which, in our experience, knowledgeable parents (those who visited chronic-care facilities for placement of their children) agreed. With institutionalized well children, social participation may be essentially nonexistent, and maternal deprivation severe; this is known to have an adverse, usually disastrous, effect upon the child.[12] The situation for the defective child is probably worse, for he is restricted socially both by his need for care and by his defects. To escape "wrongful life,"[13] a fate rated as worse than death, seemed right. In this regard, Lasagna[14] notes, "We may, as a society, scorn the civilizations that slaughtered their infants, but our present treatment of the retarded is in some ways more cruel."

16   Others considered allowing a child to die wrong for several reasons. The person most involved, the infant, had no voice in the decision. Prognosis was not always exact, and a few children with extensive care might live for months, and occasionally years. Some might survive and function satisfactorily. To a few persons, withholding treatment and accepting death was condemned as criminal.

17   Families had strong but mixed feelings about management decisions. Living with the handicapped is clearly a family affair, and families of deformed infants thought there were limits to what they could bear or

should be expected to bear. Most of them wanted maximal efforts to sustain life and to rehabilitate the handicapped; in such cases, they were supported fully. However, some families, especially those having children with severe defects, feared that they and their other children would become socially enslaved, economically deprived, and permanently stigmatized, all perhaps for a lost cause. Such a state of "chronic sorrow" until death has been described by Olshansky.[15] In some cases, families considered the death of the child right both for the child and for the family. They asked if that choice could be theirs or their doctors.

As Feifel has reported,[16] physicians on the whole are reluctant to deal with the issues. Some, particularly specialists based in the medical center, gave specific reasons for this disinclination. There was a feeling that to "give up" was disloyal to the cause of the profession. Since major research, teaching and patient-care efforts were being made, professionals expected to discover, transmit and apply knowledge and skills; patients and families were supposed to co-operate fully even if they were not always grateful. Some physicians recognized that the wishes of families went against their own, but they were resolute. They commonly agreed that if they were the parents of very defective children, withholding treatment would be most desirable for them. However, they argued that aggressive management was indicated for others. Some believed that allowing death as a management option was euthanasia and must be stopped for fear of setting a "poor ethical example" or for fear of personal prosecution or damage to their clinical departments or to the medical center as a whole. Alexander's report on Nazi Germany[17] was cited in some cases as providing justification for pressing the effort to combat disease. Some persons were concerned about the loss through death of "teaching material." They feared the training of professionals for the care of defective children in the future and the advancing of the state of the art would be compromised. Some parents who became aware of this concern thought their children should not become experimental subjects.

Practicing pediatricians, general practitioners and obstetricians were often familiar with these families and were usually sympathetic with their views. However, since they were more distant from the special-care nursery than the specialists of the medical center, their influence was often minimal. As a result, families received little support from them, and tension in community-medical relations was a recurring problem.

Infants with severe types of meningomyelocele precipitated the most controversial decisions. Several decades ago, those who survived this condition beyond a few weeks usually became hydrocephalic and retarded, in addition to being crippled and deformed. Without modern treatment, they died earlier.[18] Some may have been killed or at least not resuscitated at

18

19

20

birth.[19] From the early 1960's, the tendency has been to treat vigorously all infants with meningomyelocele. As advocated by Zachary[20] and Shurt-leff,[21] aggressive management of these children became the rule in our unit as in many others. Infants were usually referred quickly. Parents routinely signed permits for operation though rarely had they seen their children's defects or had the nature of various management plans and their respec-tive prognoses clearly explained to them. Some physicians believed that parents were too upset to understand the nature of the problems and the options for care. Since they believed informed consent had no meaning in these circumstances, they either ignored the parents or simply told them that the child needed an operation on the back as the first step in cor-recting several defects. As a result, parents often felt completely left out while the activities of care proceeded at a brisk pace.

Some physicians experienced in the care of these children and famil-iar with the impact of such conditions upon families had early reserva-tions about this plan of care.[22] More recently, they were influenced by the pessimistic appraisal of vigorous management schemes in some cases.[5] Meningomyelocele, when treated vigorously, is associated with higher survival rates,[21] but the achievement of satisfactory rehabilitation is at best difficult and usually impossible for almost all who are severely affected. Knowing this, some physicians and some families[23] decide against treat-ment of the most severely affected. If treatment is not carried out, the child's condition will usually deteriorate from further brain damage, urinary-tract infections and orthopedic difficulties, and death can be expected much earlier. Two thirds may be dead by three months, and over 90 per cent by one year of age. However, the quality of life during that time is poor, and the strains on families are great, but not necessarily greater than with treatment.[24] Thus, both treatment and nontreatment constitute unsatis-factory dilemmas for everyone, especially for the child and his family. When maximum treatment was viewed as unacceptable by families and physicians in our unit, there was a growing tendency to seek early death as a management option, to avoid that cruel choice of gradual, often slow, but progressive deterioration of the child who was required under these circumstances in effect to kill himself. Parents and the staff then asked if his dying needed to be prolonged. If not, what were the most appropriate medical responses?

Is it possible that some physicians and some families may join in a con-spiracy to deny the right of a defective child to live or to die? Either could occur. Prolongation of the dying process by resident physicians having a vested interest in their careers has been described by Sudnow.[25] On the other hand, from the fatigue of working long and hard some physicians may give up too soon, assuming that their cause is lost. Families, similarly, may have mixed motives. They may demand death to obtain relief from the high costs and the tensions inherent in suffering, but their sense of guilt in this thought may produce the opposite demand, perhaps in violation of the sick person's rights. Thus, the challenge of deciding what course to take can be most tormenting for the family and the physician. Unquestionably, not facing the issue would appear to be the easier course, at least temporarily; no doubt many patients, families, and physicians decline to join in an effort to solve the problems. They can readily assume that what is being done is right and sufficient and ask no questions. But pretending there is no decision to be made is an arbitrary and potentially devastating decision of default. Since families and patients must live with the problems one way or another in any case, the physician's failure to face the issues may constitute a victimizing abandonment of patients and their families in times of greatest need. As Lasagna[14] pointed out, "There is no place for the physician to hide."

Can families in the shock resulting from the birth of a defective child   23 understand what faces them? Can they give truly "informed consent" for treatment or withholding treatment? Some of our colleagues answer no to both questions. In our opinion, if families regardless of background are heard sympathetically and at length and are given information and answers to their questions in words they understand, the problems of their children as well as the expected benefits and limits of any proposed care can be understood clearly in practically all instances. Parents *are* able to understand the implications of such things as chronic dyspnea, oxygen dependency, incontinence, paralysis, contractures, sexual handicaps and mental retardation.

Another problem concerns who decides for a child. It may be accept-   24 able for a person to reject treatment and bring about his own death. But it is quite a different situation when others are doing this for him. We do not know how often families and their physicians will make just decisions for severely handicapped children. Clearly, this issue is central in evaluation of the process of decision making that we have described. But we also ask, if these parties cannot make such decisions justly, who can?

We recognize great variability and often much uncertainty in prognoses   25 and in family capacities to deal with defective newborn infants. We also acknowledge that there are limits of support that society can or will give to assist handicapped persons and their families. Severely deforming conditions that are associated with little or no hope of a functional existence pose painful dilemmas for the laymen and professionals who must decide how to cope with severe handicaps. We believe the burdens of decision making must be borne by families and their professional advisers because they are most familiar with the receptive situations. Since families primarily must live with and are most affected by the decisions, it therefore appears that society and the health professions should provide only general guidelines for decision making. Moreover, since variations between situations are so great, and the situations themselves are so complex, it follows that much latitude in decision making should be expected and tolerated. Otherwise, the rules of society or the policies most convenient for medical technologists may become cruel masters of human beings instead of their servants. Regarding any "allocation of death"[26] policy we readily acknowledge that the extreme excesses of Hegelian "rational utility" under dictatorships must be avoided.[17] Perhaps it is less recognized that the uncontrolled application of medical technology may be detrimental to individuals and families. In this regard, our views are similar to those of Waitzkin and Stoekle.[27] Physicians may hold excessive power over decision making by limiting or controlling the information made available to patients or families. It seems appropriate that the profession be held accountable for presenting fully all management options and their expected consequences. Also, the public should be aware that professionals often face conflicts of interest that may result in decisions against individual preferences.

What are the legal implications of actions like those described in this paper? Some persons may argue that the law has been broken, and others would contend otherwise. Perhaps more than anything else, the public and professional silence on a major social taboo and some common practices has been broken further. That seems appropriate, for out of the ensuing dialogue perhaps better choices for patients and families can be made. If working out these dilemmas in ways such as those we suggest is in violation of the law, we believe the law should be changed.

References

1. Wegman ME: Annual summary of vital statistics—1970. Pediatrics 48:979-983, 1971
2. Swyer PR: The regional organization of special care for the neonate. Pediatr Clin North Am 17:761-776, 1970
3. Rawlings G, Reynold EOR, Stewart A, et al.: Changing prognosis for infants of very low birth weight. Lancet 1:516-519, 1971
4. Freeman E: The god committee. New York Times Magazine. May 21, 1972, pp 84-90
5. Lorber J: Results of treatment of myelomeningocele. Dev Med Child Neurol 13:279-303, 1971
6. Slater E: Health service or sickness service. Br Med J 4:734-736, 1971
7. Klaus MH, Kennell JH: Mothers separated from their newborn infants. Pediatr Clin North Am 17:1015-1037, 1970
8. Eisenberg L: The human nature of human nature. Science 176:123-128, 1972
9. Report of the Joseph P. Kennedy Foundation International Symposium on Human Rights, Retardation and Research. Washington, DC, The John F. Kennedy Center for the Performing Arts, October 16, 1971
10. Fletcher J: Indicators of humanhood: a tentative profile of man. The Hastings Center Report Vol 2, No 5. Hastings-on-Hudson, New York, Institute of Society, Ethics and the Life Sciences, November, 1972, pp 1-4

11. Freeman HE, Brim OG Jr, Williams G: New dimensions of dying. The Dying Patient. Edited by OG Brim Jr. New York, Russell Sage Foundation, 1970, pp xiii-xxvi

12. Spitz RA: Hospitalism: an inquiry into the genesis of psychiatric conditions in early childhood. Psychoanal Study Child 1:53-74, 1945

13. Engelhardt HT Jr.: Euthanasia and children: the injury of continued existence. J Pediatr 83:170-171, 1973

14. Lasagna L: Life, Death and the Doctor. New York, Alfred A Knopf, 1968

15. Olshansky S: Chronic sorrow: a response to having a mentally defective child. Soc Casework 43:190-193, 1962

16. Feifel H: Perception of death. Ann NY Acad Sci 164:669-677, 1969

17. Alexander L: Medical science under dictatorship. N Engl J Med 241:39-47, 1949

18. Laurence KM and Tew BJ: Natural history of spina bifida cystica and cranium bifidum cysticum: major central nervous system malfunctions in South Wales. Part IV. Arch Dis Child 46:127-138, 1971

19. Forrest DM: Modern trends in the treatment of spina bifida: early closure in spina bifida: results and problems. Proc R Soc Med 60:763-767, 1967

20. Zachary RB: Ethical and social aspects of treatment of spina bifida. Lancet 2:274-276, 1968

21. Shurtleff DB: Care of the myelodysplastic patient, Ambulatory Pediatrics. Edited by M Green, R Haggerty. Philadelphia, WB Saunders Company, 1968, pp 726-741

22. Matson DD: Surgical treatment of myelomeningocele. Pediatrics 42:225-227, 1968

23. Mac Keith RC: A new look at spina bifida aperta. Dev Med Child Neurol 13:277-278, 1971

24. Hide DW, Williams HP, Ellis HL: The outlook for the child with a myelomeningocele for whom early surgery was considered inadvisable. Dev Med Child Neurol 14:304-307,1972

25. Sudnow D: Passing On. Englewood Cliffs, New Jersey, Prentice Hall, 1967

26. Manning B: Legal and policy issues in the allocation of death, The Dying Patient. Edited by OG Brim Jr. New York, Russell Sage Foundation, 1970, pp 253-274

27. Waitzkin H. Stoeckle JD: The communication of information about illness. Adv Psychosom Med 8:180-215, 1972

QUESTIONING AND DISCUSSING

Duff and Campbell, "Moral and Ethical Dilemmas in the Special-Care Nursery"

1. How do the authors frame their notion of the "right to die" in paragraph 14? What is your initial response to the remarks of the nurse and the hospital official (house officer)? Why?

2. What is the authors' central argument?

3. What is the potential "conspiracy" of which the authors write? What are these mixed motives? Why are these difficult to resolve?

4. In what ways is this article controversial? Consider the authors' conclusion: "If working out these dilemmas in ways such as those we suggest is in violation of the law, we believe the law should be changed."

5. This article was published in 1973. Conduct a bit of your own research to discover what other thinking by philosopher-ethicists and others regarding premature and other infants has been published since then. Has Duff and

Campbell's perspective been adopted or changed? How? With what result? Judging by what you have read, what is your position on these dilemmas?

⊞

MICHAEL DORRIS

A celebrated writer of Native American heritage, Michael Dorris (1945–1997) founded the Native American Studies Department at Dartmouth College. His interest in his ancestry led to his conducting ethnographic work in an Athapaskan village in Alaska. Dorris writes movingly in *The Broken Cord* (1989) about being the adoptive father of a child affected with fetal alcohol syndrome; it is his most celebrated book. In addition, Dorris wrote a number of novels, including *A Yellow Raft in Blue Water* (1987), *The Crown of Columbus* (1991, written with noted author Louise Erdrich, to whom he was married), and *Paper Trail* (1994), a volume of essays. He published the following essay and the book *Cloud Chamber* (1997) shortly before his death.

⊞

The Myth of Justice

1   Where did we ever get the idea that life is ultimately fair? Who promised that there was a balance to things, a yin and yang that perfectly cancels each other out, a divine score sheet that makes sure that all the totals eventually ring even? Who exactly reaps what they sow? Does everything that goes around come around?

2   If that's some people's experience, I haven't met them, and my guess is, if they still believe it, they simply haven't lived long enough to know better.

3   Justice is one of those palliative myths—like afterlife with acquired personality and memory intact—that makes existence bearable. As long as we can think that our experience of being periodically screwed by fate is the exception to the rule we can hope for, as they used to say in commercials, a brighter tomorrow. As long as we can trust in an ultimate squaring of accounts, we can suffer what we assume to be temporary setbacks, transitory stumbles on our path toward redemption through good works and sacrifice.

4   When I was a child we were told of a Golden Ledger in which God (or one of his executive assistants) kept tabs on our every plus and minus, and as long

as we wound up in the black we were "in"—as *in* heaven for all eternity. Our journey through the years was a test that was passable, if only we stretched hard enough. We were in control of our destinies. We were, at worst, Job: Hang in there, and you will be paid back with compound interest.

Uh huh. In your dreams, sucker. 5

Religion isn't the opiate of the people, the conception of justice is. It's 6 our last bastion of rationality, our logical lighthouse on a stormy sea, our anchor. We extend its parameters beyond death—if we haven't found equity in this life, all the great belief systems assure us, just wait until the next. Or the next, or the next. Someday our prince will come.

That may be true, but the paradigm is based on faith, not fact. We *can* 7 believe in the tooth fairy until the alarm goes off, but unless there's a benevolent parent to value our loss as worth a quarter, we wake up with used calcium, not negotiable currency, under our pillows.

Anthropologists and other social scientists make a distinction between 8 contextual and blind justice. In the former archetype, the goddess has her eyes wide open. It matters—boy, does it matter—who does what to whom, when, how much, and why. In contextual-justice-crazy societies like ours, or like the Yurok of precontact California, rich folks get to pay off their victims, either through a dream team of attorneys or via a prearranged valuation in woodpecker scalps—the murder of an aristocrat worth ever so much more than the slaying of a commoner. If you can afford it, you can do it, and that's the way the game is played. You can't even complain, have begrudging thoughts, or retry the case if the price is right and coughed up in full.

In the theoretical latter case—and is there any manifest and irrefutable 9 instance, really?—it matters not what your station is or what you intended: The act's the thing. All equal before the law. Don't ask, don't tell. A level field, a blank slate. The verdict is impartial and therefore fair. Gripe and you're a sore loser, short-sighted, an excuser of your own incapacities. Strike out and it's because you wanted to in your heart, you didn't wait through the rain, you didn't expend maximum effort. Because if you had, well, you'd wind up—justified. It's a utopian notion, blind justice, an Eden where expectations are perfectly in tune with possibility. But for each of us there comes an undeniable catch, a flaw in the argument. What any human being not convicted of a capital crime has to one day wonder is: What did I do to deserve the death penalty? Be born?

Yet despite the evidence of our private and cultural histories, de- 10 spite the inevitability of the maximum sentence, when things *don't* work out, we are perpetually surprised. Is this a naiveté carried to an absurd extreme? Wouldn't it be wiser, safer to be shocked at a fleeting *happy* outcome? Wouldn't a pleasant astonishment, however brief, beat bitter disappointment?

11 But that's too dour. It's downright discouraging. We watch our gritty TV dramas with assurance of retribution, of confirmation. Right prevails, if not this week, then next. Good wins out against all odds. When the innocent victim is convicted on *NYPD Blue* or *Law and Order,* we are outraged; and when the perp goes free, we're appalled. It's not supposed to be that way. We recognize injustice when we see it. We're positively Old Testament in our condemnation. We know how things *should* be.

12 Our truth. As if it were happening to us.

13 As it is. All the time.

14 I've talked to underpaid public defenders, idealistic law school top-ten percenters who chose working within this system over six-figure starting salaries. First year, they're motivated, blessed. Second year, they're cynically busting their chops to spring drug dealers. Third year, they're burnt out, ready for corporate, a health plan, into locking up the very bad guys they've been so busy turning loose. Sellouts, but just ask them and they'll tell you why not. They sleep at night now, go to bed with clear conscience, know what's what, and act on it.

15 Are their serial analyses accurate? Unless you're an avower of the innate goodness of human nature at twenty-one you'll never be, so use or lose it. Because at thirty you'll know better, you'll have your own kids to protect, you'll be wise to the ways of the world, clear-eyed, maybe even a Republican. Was Kunstler just an old kid, a guy who wouldn't admit harsh facts when they stared him square in the face? Is a $300 suit a give-up buy-in or the minimum salary for upholding civilization as we know it?

16 Questions, questions, questions. If we knew the answers or were sure of them we wouldn't have to ask. We yearn to be proven wrong, returned to the innocence of righteous hope. We don't want to be our parents. We want to be as we were: true believers. Please.

17 We're every generation with a minimal sense of integrity who came before us and reluctantly, partially conceded the fight. We're us. We're our children in twenty years. We're wish. We're further disillusionment waiting to happen.

18 Do I need examples from "real life" to prove my point? Read the newspaper. Look at world history. Examine your own family. People got what they deserve, right? Oh, really? They didn't?

19 Okay, call me a downer. There's divine justice, we're assured, a future payday in which everybody knows everything about everybody and rewards and punishments are meted out in precisely the correct quotients.

We all stand there on judgment day, quivering, humiliated by our secret transgressions, dreading exposure. There's this apocalyptic division point, like at the Nazi camps: go right, go left. Life, death.

But all that is beside the point, finally. If there's punishment for trans-   20
gression, that means that order does actually prevail—and the alternative is arguably scarier than hell itself. What if all is chaos and it is simply our own fear, our own cosmological terror, our own instinct as a species to impose structure on whatever we behold? There are scientists who specialize in precisely this kind of bubble-popping on a minor scale: Dr. Amos Tversky, a Stanford University psychologist, working with Dr. Donald Redelmeier, an internist at the University of Toronto, has neatly disproven the long-held truism that people with arthritis can anticipate rainy weather and that a chill brings on a cold; Dr. Albert Kligman, a dermatology professor at the University of Pennsylvania, roundly disproved the widely held notion that eating chocolate exacerbates acne in teenagers. According to these and other researchers, human beings innately desire predictability and so search out patterns even when there are none. We disregard contrary indications in order to stick firm to our collective wishful thought that events conform to knowable design.

This is the basis, after all, of ritual act. If I do X and Y, then Z will nec-   21
essarily follow. If once upon a time when I wanted it to rain I sang a certain song at a certain time of day, decked out in a particular outfit, having either eaten or not eaten, had sex or abstained, vocalized or remained silent—and it rained!—then next drought I'd better replicate all the details as precisely as possible. Who knows what caused the moisture to arrive: Was it the sequence? All the ingredients? And if not all, which ones dare I omit? So to be sure, replay, and if the heavens don't open it must have been *my* fault, *I* must have messed up on some aspect. We wear ourselves out in pursuit of the right key to understanding the nature of things, whether we call it physics or witch-doctoring or philosophy. What other sane option is there? If we are ineffectual, if there isn't any grand scheme to discover and plug into, then we're simply spinning wheels. When the sun goes down, it might not rise again. When we go to sleep, we might not wake up. When we die, regardless of whether we've been a sinner or a saint—yikes!

The good news about this impulse of ours is that it begets common as-   22
sumptions, which are the next best thing to reality. When we give group credence to the same hypotheses we function as if they're absolute, we allow them to define us. When a culture is healthy, cohesive, intellectually homogenous and in sync, we agree that our explanations work—and they

seem to. But when we're clustered in a society that's atomized, discordant, at odds, psychological clarity explodes like confetti from a firecracker. If truth is relative, if law is haphazard, if what we term justice is nothing more than occasional and statistical circumstance that we utilize bogusly to reenforce our hope for righteousness, then we dwell not just on a shaky foundation but mired in quicksand.

23   Not all cultures have grounded their sense of reality in cause-effect relationships. While Genesis postulates a planned, intentionally ordered universe and later books of the Bible stipulate the myriad of rules and regulations we must follow in order to placate, if not please, the divinity, the Nootka Tribe of the Pacific Northwest takes a different approach. In their scheme the culture hero is a unisex trickster personified as Raven. Their human creation story goes something like this:

24   Once, Raven was flying around when it spied a bush loaded with luscious, purple, irresistible berries. Down swoops Raven and gobbles up every one. Finally its breast feathers are stained with juice and its belly is so bloated that it has to get a running start and jump off a cliff to again become airborne. In no time at all, Raven experiences the worst stomach cramps it has ever known, and shortly thereafter a horrible case of diarrhea. It seems to last forever, but when the attack is over, Raven breathes a sigh of relief and looks down to the earth to see the mess it has made. And there we are!

25   In the Nootka cosmology, justice, like much else, is chance not ordained. Things simply happen without structure or divine plan. The proper response to the tale—and to the organization of the world that it implies—is laughter rather than smugness or indignation. Don't expect from me, the universe seems to suggest, but don't blame me either. You're on your own.

26   An interesting notion, but we in the West are programmed to content ourselves with being appalled, insisting that we're stunned when injustice seems to triumph. The *human*-created system has broken down, we persuade ourselves. This is but a temporary aberration. Just hold out for the eventual guaranteed happy ending. Cling to the Beatitudes and the meek *will* inherit the earth. Be like Pascal and choose to behave as if we're sure in our convictions, betting that if, God forbid, we're wrong, we'll never have to find out. Like the ground beneath the circling trickster, we'll never know what hit us.

QUESTIONING AND DISCUSSING

Dorris, "The Myth of Justice"

1. Dorris makes his viewpoint clear from the beginning of his essay: "Where did we get the idea that life is ultimately fair?" How does he back up his overall point? Is there any way to answer Dorris's initial question differently than the way that he ultimately does in the essay? Discuss and explain your response.

2. Comment on the particularly evocative language and tone that Dorris chooses to make his argument. (Consider, for instance, "Uh-uh. In your dreams, sucker.") How do these rhetorical strategies affect you as a reader? Are they persuasive? What do these suggest about Dorris's attitude toward his subject?

3. Analyze Dorris's rejection of the Bible and his discussion of the Nootka myth, in which "[t]hings simply happen without structure or divine plan." If we accept aspects of Dorris's reasoning, how might his view of justice seem more "fair," "just," and "ethical" than the traditional conceptions against which he rails?

4. Why does Dorris argue that in the West, we are "programmed to content ourselves with being appalled, insisting that we're stunned when injustice seems to triumph"? Why might it be important for people to believe in that "eventual happy ending"?

JOY HARJO

A member of the Muskogee tribe, Joy Harjo (1951–) was born in Tulsa, Oklahoma. Known as a poet and writer of fiction, Harjo has taught at a number of colleges and universities, including Arizona State, the University of Arizona, and the University of New Mexico. She has published in a variety of journals and magazines, and she is also a screenwriter and musician, performing with her band, Poetic Justice. Harjo has received numerous awards and fellowships. She emphasizes in her work "a responsibility to all the sources that I am: to all the past and future ancestors, to my home country, to all voices, all women, all of my tribe, all people [. . .]." Joy Harjo has also served on national advisory committees, including the PEN Advisory Board and the Native American Public Broadcasting Consortium Board of Directors.

Three Generations of Native American Women's Birth Experience

1   It was still dark when I awakened in the stuffed back room of my mother-in-law's small rented house with what felt like hard cramps. At 17 years of age I had read everything I could from the Tahlequah Public Library about pregnancy and giving birth. But nothing prepared me for what was coming. I awakened my child's father and then ironed him a shirt before we walked the four blocks to the Indian hospital because we had no car and no money for a taxi. He had been working with another Cherokee artist silk-screening signs for specials at the supermarket and making $5 a day, and had to leave me alone at the hospital because he had to go to work. We didn't awaken his mother. She had to get up soon enough to fix breakfast for her daughter and granddaughter before leaving for her job at the nursing home. I knew my life was balanced at the edge of a great, precarious change and I felt alone and cheated. Where was the circle of women to acknowledge and honor this birth?

2   It was still dark as we walked through the cold morning, under oaks that symbolized the stubbornness and endurance of the Cherokee people who had made Tahlequah their capital in the new lands. I looked for hand-holds in the misty gray sky, for a voice announcing this impending miracle. I wanted to change everything: I wanted to go back to a place before childhood, before our tribe's removal to Oklahoma. What kind of life was I bringing this child into? I was a poor, mixed-blood woman heavy with a child who would suffer the struggle of poverty, the legacy of loss. For the second time in my life I felt the sharp tug of my own birth cord, still connected to my mother. I believe it never pulls away, until death, and even then it becomes a streak in the sky symbolizing that most important warrior road. In my teens I had fought my mother's weaknesses with all my might, and here I was at 17, becoming as my mother, who was in Tulsa, cooking breakfasts and preparing for the lunch shift at a factory cafeteria as I walked to the hospital to give birth. I should be with her; instead, I was far from her house, in the house of a mother-in-law who later would try to use witchcraft to destroy me.

3   After my son's father left me I was prepped for birth. This meant my pubic area was shaved completely and then I endured the humiliation of an enema, all at the hands of strangers. I was left alone in a room painted government green. An overwhelming antiseptic smell emphasized the sterility of the hospital, a hospital built because of the U.S. government's treaty and responsibility to provide health care to Indian people.

I intellectually understood the stages of labor, the place of transition, of   4
birth—but it was difficult to bear the actuality of it, and to bear it alone.
Yet in some ways I wasn't alone, for history surrounded me. It is with the
birth of children that history is given form and voice. Birth is one of the
most sacred acts we take part in and witness in our lives. But sacredness
seemed to be far from my lonely labor room in the Indian hospital. I heard
a woman screaming in the next room with her pain, and I wanted to comfort her. The nurse used her as a bad example to the rest of us who were
struggling to keep our suffering silent.

The doctor was a military man who had signed on this watch not for   5
the love of healing or out of awe at the miracle of birth, but to fulfill a
contract for medical school payments. I was another statistic to him; he
touched me as if he were moving equipment from one place to another.
During my last visit I was given the option of being sterilized. He explained to me that the moment of birth was the best time to do it. I was
handed the form but chose not to sign it, and am amazed now that I didn't
think too much of it at the time. Later I would learn that many Indian
women who weren't fluent in English signed, thinking it was a form giving consent for the doctor to deliver their babies. Others were sterilized
without even the formality of signing. My light skin had probably saved
me from such a fate. It wouldn't be the first time in my life.

When my son was finally born I had been deadened with a needle in   6
my spine. He was shown to me—the incredible miracle nothing prepared me for—then taken from me in the name of medical progress. I fell
asleep with the weight of chemicals and awoke yearning for the child
I had suffered for, had anticipated in the months proceeding from his
unexpected genesis when I was still 16 and a student at Indian school. I
was not allowed to sit up or walk because of the possibility of paralysis
(one of the drug's side effects), and when I finally got to hold him, the
nurse stood guard as if I would hurt him. I felt enmeshed in a system in
which the wisdom that had carried my people from generation to generation was ignored. In that place I felt ashamed I was an Indian woman. But
I was also proud of what my body had accomplished despite the rape by
the bureaucracy's machinery, and I got us out of there as soon as possible.
My son would flourish on beans and fry bread, and on the dreams and
stories we fed him.

My daughter was born four years later, while I was an art student at the   7
University of New Mexico. Since my son's birth I had waitressed, cleaned
hospital rooms, filled cars with gas (while wearing a miniskirt), worked as
a nursing assistant, and led dance classes at a health spa. I knew I didn't
want to cook and waitress all my life, as my mother had done. I watched

the varicose veins grow branches on her legs, and as they grew, her zest for dancing and sports dissolved into utter tiredness. She had been born with a caul over her face, the sign of a gifted visionary.

8   My earliest memories are of my mother writing songs on an ancient Underwood typewriter after she had washed and waxed the kitchen floor on her hands and knees. She too had wanted something different for her life. She had left an impoverished existence at age 17, bound for the big city of Tulsa. She was shamed in a time in which to be even part Indian was to be an outcast in the great U.S. system. Half her relatives were Cherokee full-bloods from near Jay, Oklahoma, who for the most part had nothing to do with white people. The other half were musically inclined "white trash" addicted to country-western music and Holy Roller fervor. She thought she could disappear in the city; no one would know her family, where she came from. She had dreams of singing and had once been offered a job singing on the radio but turned it down because she was shy. Later one of her songs would be stolen before she could copyright it and would make someone else rich. She would quit writing songs. She and my father would divorce and she would be forced to work for money to feed and clothe four children, all born within two years of each other.

9   As a child growing up in Oklahoma, I liked to be told the story of my birth. I would beg for it while my mother cleaned and ironed. "You almost killed me," she would say. "We almost died." That I could kill my mother filled me with remorse and shame. And I imagined the push-pull of my life, which is a legacy I deal with even now when I am twice as old as my mother was at my birth. I loved to hear the story of my warrior fight for my breath. The way it was told, it had been my decision to live. When I got older, I realized we were both nearly casualties of the system, the same system flourishing in the Indian hospital where later my son Phil would be born.

10   My parents felt lucky to have insurance, to be able to have their children in the hospital. My father came from a fairly prominent Muscogee Creek family. *His* mother was a full-blood who in the early 1920s got her degree in art. She was a painter. She gave birth to him in a private hospital in Oklahoma City; at least that's what I think he told me before he died at age 53. It was something of which they were proud.

11   This experience was much different from my mother's own birth. She and five of her six brothers were born at home, with no medical assistance. The only time a doctor was called was when someone was dying. When she was born her mother named her Wynema, a Cherokee name my

mother says means beautiful woman, and Jewell, for a can of shortening stored in the room where she was born.

I wanted something different for my life, for my son, and for my daughter, who later was born in a university hospital in Albuquerque. It was a bright summer morning when she was ready to begin her journey. I still had no car, but I had enough money saved for a taxi for a ride to the hospital. She was born "naturally," without drugs. I could look out of the hospital window while I was in labor at the bluest sky in the world. I had support. Her father was present in the delivery room—though after her birth he disappeared on a drinking binge. I understood his despair, but did not agree with the painful means to describe it. A few days later Rainy Dawn was presented to the sun at her father's pueblo and given a name so that she will always be recognized as a part of the people, as a child of the sun.

That's not to say that my experience in the hospital reached perfection. The clang of metal against metal in the delivery room had the effect of a tuning fork reverberating fear in my pelvis. After giving birth I held my daughter, but they took her from me for "processing." I refused to lie down to be wheeled to my room after giving birth; I wanted to walk out of there to find my daughter. We reached a compromise and I rode in a wheelchair. When we reached the room I stood up and walked to the nursery and demanded my daughter. I knew she needed me. That began my war with the nursery staff, who deemed me unknowledgeable because I was Indian and poor. Once again I felt the brushfire of shame, but I'd learned to put it out much more quickly, and I demanded early release so I could take care of my baby without the judgment of strangers.

I wanted something different for Rainy, and as she grew up I worked hard to prove that I could make "something" of my life. I obtained two degrees as a single mother. I wrote poetry, screenplays, became a professor, and tried to live a life that would be a positive influence for both of my children. My work in this life has to do with reclaiming the memory stolen from our peoples when we were dispossessed from our lands east of the Mississippi; it has to do with restoring us. I am proud of our history, a history so powerful that it both destroyed my father and guarded him. It's a history that claims my mother as she lives not far from the place her mother was born, names her as she cooks in the cafeteria of a small college in Oklahoma.

When my daughter told me she was pregnant, I wasn't surprised. I had known it before she did, or at least before she would admit it to me. I felt despair, as if nothing had changed or ever would. She had run away from Indian school with her boyfriend and they had been living in the streets of Gallup, a border town notorious for the suicides and deaths of Indian peoples. I brought her and her boyfriend with me because it was the only way I could bring her home. At age 16, she was fighting me just as I had so fiercely fought my mother. She was making the same mistakes. I felt as if everything I had accomplished had been in vain. Yet I felt strangely empowered, too, at this repetition of history, this continuance, by a new possibility of life and love, and I steadfastly stood by my daughter.

16   I had a university job, so I had insurance that covered my daughter. She saw an obstetrician in town who was reputed to be one of the best. She had the choice of a birthing room. She had the finest care. Despite this, I once again battled with a system in which physicians are taught the art of healing by dissecting cadavers. My daughter went into labor a month early. We both knew intuitively the baby was ready, but how to explain that to a system in which numbers and statistics provide the base of understanding? My daughter would have her labor interrupted; her blood pressure would rise because of the drug given to her to stop the labor. She would be given an unneeded amniocentesis and would have her labor induced—after having it artificially stopped! I was warned that if I took her out of the hospital so her labor could occur naturally my insurance would cover nothing.

17   My daughter's induced labor was unnatural and difficult, monitored by machines, not by touch. I was shocked. I felt as if I'd come full circle, as if I were watching my mother's labor and the struggle of my own birth. But I was there in the hospital room with her, as neither my mother had been for me, nor her mother for her. My daughter and I went through the labor and birth together.

18   And when Krista Rae was born she was born to her family. Her father was there for her, as were both her grandmothers and my friend who had flown in to be with us. Her paternal great-grandparents and aunts and uncles had also arrived from the Navajo Reservation to honor her. Something *had* changed.

19   Four days later, I took my granddaughter to the Saguaro forest before dawn and gave her the name I had dreamed for her just before her birth. Her name looks like clouds of mist settling around a sacred mountain as it begins to speak. A female ancestor approaches on a horse. We are all together.

QUESTIONING AND DISCUSSING

Harjo, "Three Generations of Native American Women's Birth Experience"

1. How does Harjo construct her argument? Examine and comment on her use of narrative and the language she chooses to prepare the reader for her point of view.

2. Harjo suggests particular values through this essay—for instance, when she writes, "I once again battled with a system in which physicians are taught the art of healing by dissecting cadavers." What are other aspects of this essay that demonstrate her values regarding birth? In short, what are these values?

3. Are there ways in which the desire for a spiritual, whole birth experience that Harjo describes can be reconciled with modern medicine? Are there times when one might have to take precedence over the other? Explain.

⌗

"CHURCH DIRECTORY"

The image here called "Church Directory" is one of seven million digitalized prints that are part of the Library of Congress' expansive website. Located in the historical collection entitled "American Memory," the print is one among many "primary source materials that pertain to the history and culture of the United States."

⌗

QUESTIONING AND DISCUSSING

"Church Directory"

1. This photograph might be one of those examples that illustrate the maxim "A picture is worth a thousand words." Why, in this case, would that statement seem appropriate?

2. What are the ironies presented in this particular image? How do they convey larger meanings? What might those meanings be? However unintentionally, how does the sign seem to minimize the importance of houses of worship and belief while attempting to draw attention to them?

⊞

QUESTIONS FOR READING AND RESPONDING

Chapter 3 Defining Belief Systems: What Do I Believe?

1. Flannery O'Connor, Reynolds Price, and Gabriel García Márquez all deal, in part, with systems of religious belief. Using the texts from this chapter for your examples (and also looking at other works by these authors, if you choose), discuss the various ways in which each writer critiques or advances certain types of religious thought or belief. Consider the ways in which the photograph called "Church Directory" and the cartoon strip from *Mad Magazine* advance your point of view or contrast with the writing of a particular author.

2. This chapter also deals with the notion of *belief* in a very broad sense. For instance, Svi Shapiro and Henry David Thoreau advance differing systems of belief regarding a person's responsibility to himself or herself and to the world—that is, to the greater good. Michael Dorris questions belief in justice. Determine the ways in which each author argues for or against forms of belief. How are these belief systems alike? How are they different?

3. We in the United States often make heroes of celebrities or athletes. Adam Gopnik and Joy Harjo, while not doing so explicitly, seem to discuss other types of heroes—for good or ill. Discuss this notion, arguing a point of view with specific examples from these texts.

4. Both of the philosophical articles dealing explicitly with ethics—the special-care nursery and human cloning—have been followed by the publication of more recent work concerning the same issues. How does more current information reinforce or reshape the points of view advanced in these articles—or make their arguments seem more complex than ever? Fashion your argument carefully, using specific examples to prove your points.

⊞

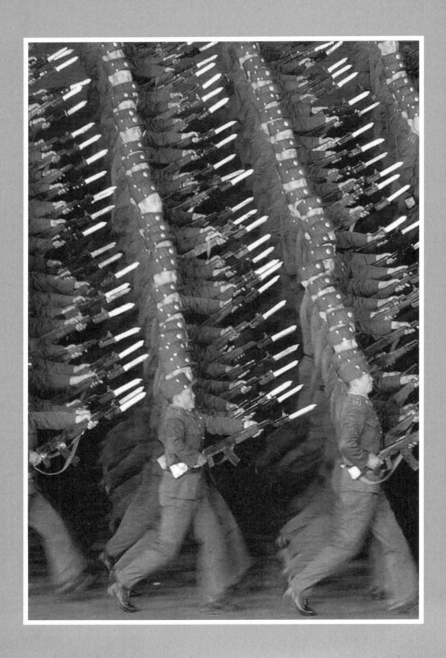

4

Broadening My View

How Do I Perceive Difference?

"To be a tourist is to escape
accountability. Errors and
failings don't cling to you the
way they do back home. . . .
Together with thousands, you
are granted immunities and
broad freedoms. You are an
army of fools, wearing bright
polyesters, riding camels,
taking pictures of each other,
haggard, dysenteric, thirsty.
There is nothing to think about
but the next shapeless event."
DON DELILLO (B. 1926),
American writer.

GAIL SHISTER

Gail Shister is a columnist for the *Philadelphia Inquirer,* specializing in issues related to popular culture. Although the series that is the subject of her article—*Queer Eye for the Straight Guy*—became popular, Shister's piece raises other issues within the context of its time: political and cultural movements supporting benefits for same-sex couples, for instance, and Supreme Court decisions regarding affirmative action that speak to other issues about diversity and inclusion.

⊞

NBC Has Its Eye on Reality Series Coming to Bravo

1 Call it *Trading Spaces With Will & Grace*. Literally.

2 Should the new reality makeover series, *The Queer Eye for the Straight Guy,* become a hit on NBC-owned Bravo, it could move to the Peacock, says Jeff Gaspin, executive vice president, programming, NBC/Bravo.

3 "We'd love for Bravo to be a breeding ground for potential network series," says Gaspin. "The makeover genre is very popular on cable. It would be great to see it transfer to broadcast TV."

4 Bravo, acquired by NBC in November [2002], has ordered 12 episodes of *Queer,* to launch in July. In each hourlong segment, a hopelessly square straight guy will be molded into a hip straight guy.

5 Providing the hip will be five gay experts in personal grooming, fashion, interior design, etiquette, and food and wine. David Collins (gay) and his creative partner, David Metzler (straight) are co-exec producers.

6 "The title is stranger than the show," says NBC's Gaspin. "The pilot was really charming. . . . It made me laugh. It's not as over-the-top as it could be."

7 Collins, 36, a former movie producer who lives in Boston with his boyfriend of 13 years, came up with the idea for *Queer* at an art opening.

8 He and his buddies cracked up as they observed a woman in her 30s drag her schlumpy husband over to three impossibly stylish gay men and ask for pointers on how to improve his look.

9 "It hit me like a brick," Collins recalls. "Those guys had the queer eyes for the straight guys. I said, 'There's something here.'"

10 *Queer's* "Fab 5" will class up each subject's act, including redecorating a room or two in his home. The first season will focus on New York, then hit other big burgs, Collins says.

Production will begin March 3. The experts, still being cast, will be un-   11
knowns. The tone of *Queer* will be, in Collins' words, tongue in cheek.

"We're not trying to turn the guy gay. We want him to go back to his   12
wife or girlfriend cooler and feeling better about himself. We want him to
know it's OK to think about his shoes or get a manicure."

While Collins maintains that *Queer* will break down gay stereotypes,   13
Ron Cowen, co-exec producer of Showtime's hit *Queer as Folk,* worries it
will reinforce them.

"Not all gay guys have perfect bodies and great hair. It's a superficial way   14
to judge somebody's worth, and it perpetuates the notion that gay men are
silly queens only interested in the latest fashion or fabulous restaurant."

Queer as Folk co-e.p. Daniel Lipman, Cowen's partner of 30 years, dis-   15
agrees. "People in the gay community have always been a step ahead."

Suzanna Walters, director of the women's studies program at George-   16
town and author of *All the Rage: The Story of Gay Visibility in America,*
compares Bravo's *Queer* to a *Saturday Night Live* bit.

"It could be so camp that it actually undoes the stereotype," says Wal-   17
ters, 40, a lesbian. "I'm not sure that stereotype is so pernicious. Straight
people have been feeding off gay culture for years."

As for a lesbian *Queer,* Collins and Gaspin says it's possible, but Walters   18
"can't imagine it."

"The stereotyped lesbian is a man-hating feminist from hell. A stereo-   19
typed gay man is the witty best girlfriend. Clearly, the lesbian image is far
more threatening."

QUESTIONING AND DISCUSSING

Shister, "NBC Has Its Eye on Reality Series Coming to Bravo"

1. This article seems to operate on several assumptions about what's popular
   and what's acceptable—from reality shows to stereotypes. What are these?
   Are the assumptions, in your view, correct? Why or why not?

2. Considering your own views and analyses you have read about the phenomenon of reality television, what accounts for its popularity? What does it
   seem to say about values—both positively and negatively?

3. Shister writes that one successful television producer worries that shows like
   this will perpetuate "the notion that gay men are silly queens only interested
   in the latest fashion or fabulous restaurant," that "it's a superficial way to
   judge someone's worth." Given Shister's description of this particular program—whether you have seen it or not—what do you think?

4. While some maintain that this program breaks down gay stereotypes, some of the same people suggest that it would be impossible for a program to do the same for lesbian stereotypes: "Clearly, the lesbian image is far more threatening." Is there a contradiction here? Why? Is it dangerous? Explain.

⊞

DR. MARTIN LUTHER KING, JR.

The preeminent civil rights leader of this or any other time, Dr. Martin Luther King, Jr., (1929–1968) was born in Atlanta, Georgia. He attended Morehouse College, Crozer Theological Seminar, and Boston University. While serving as a Baptist minister in Montgomery, Alabama, King led a successful boycott against segregated bus lines and consequently gained national prominence. King organized and led the Southern Christian Leadership Conference, a group dedicated to civil rights, and in 1964, he won the Nobel Peace Price. In 1968, King was assassinated while in Memphis, Tennessee; at the time, he was supporting a strike by garbage workers. When he wrote the "Letter" (in response to "A Call for Unity," which had been written by local clergymen and published in the local newspaper), King had been jailed for organizing and participating in a march for which there had been no parade permit.

⊞

Letter from Birmingham Jail

A Call for Unity

April 12, 1963

1   We the undersigned clergymen are among those who, in January, issued "An Appeal for Law and Order and Common Sense," in dealing with racial problems in Alabama. We expressed understanding that honest convictions in racial matters could properly be pursued in the courts, but urged that decisions of those courts should in the meantime be peacefully obeyed.

2   Since that time there had been some evidence of increased forbearance and a willingness to face facts. Responsible citizens have undertaken to work on various problems which cause racial friction and unrest. In Birmingham, recent public events have given indication that we all

have opportunity for a new constructive and realistic approach to racial problems.

However, we are now confronted by a series of demonstrations by some 3 of our Negro citizens, directed and led in part by outsiders. We recognize the natural impatience of people who feel that their hopes are slow in being realized. But we are convinced that these demonstrations are unwise and untimely.

We agree rather with certain local Negro leadership which has called 4 for honest and open negotiation of racial issues in our area. And we believe this kind of facing of issues can best be accomplished by citizens of our own metropolitan area, white and Negro, meeting with their knowledge and experience of the local situation. All of us need to face that responsibility and find proper channels for its accomplishment.

Just as we formerly pointed out that "hatred and violence have no 5 sanction in our religious and political traditions," we also point out that such actions as incite to hatred and violence, however technically peaceful those actions may be, have not contributed to the resolution of our local problems. We do not believe that these days of new hope are days when extreme measures are justified in Birmingham.

We commend the community as a whole, and the local news media and 6 law enforcement officials in particular, on the calm manner in which these demonstrations have been handled. We urge the public to continue to show restraint should the demonstrations continue, and the law enforcement officials to remain calm and continue to protect our city from violence.

We further strongly urge our own Negro community to withdraw support from these demonstrations, and to unite locally in working peacefully 7 for a better Birmingham. When rights are consistently denied, a cause should be pressed in the courts and in negotiations among local leaders, and not in the streets. We appeal to both our white and Negro citizenry to observe the principles of law and order and common sense.

C. C. J. Carpenter, DD, LLD, Bishop of Alabama; Joseph A. Durick, 8 DD, Auxiliary Bishop, Diocese of Mobile–Birmingham; Rabbi Milton L. Grafman, Temple Emanu-El, Birmingham, Alabama; Bishop Paul Hardin, Bishop of the Alabama–West Florida Conference of the Methodist Church; Bishop Nolan B. Harmon, Bishop of the North Alabama Conference of the Methodist Church; George M. Murray, DD, LLD, Bishop Coadjutor, Episcopal Diocese of Alabama; Edward V. Ramage, Moderator, Synod of the Alabama Presbyterian Church in the United States; Earl Stallings, Pastor, First Baptist Church, Birmingham, Alabama.

Letter from Birmingham Jail

April 16, 1963

9 My Dear Fellow Clergymen:

10   While confined here in the Birmingham city jail, I cam across your recent statement calling my present activities "unwise and untimely."[1] Seldom do I pause to answer criticism of my work and ideas. If I sought to answer all criticisms that cross my desk, my secretaries would have little time for anything other than such correspondence in the course of the day, and I would have no time for constructive work. But since I feel that you are men of genuine good will and that your criticisms are sincerely set forth, I want to try to answer your statement in what I hope will be patient and reasonable terms.

11   I think I should indicate why I am here in Birmingham, since you have been influenced by the view which argues against "outsiders coming in." I have the honor of serving as president of the Southern Christian Leadership Conference, an organization operating in every southern state, with headquarters in Atlanta, Georgia. We have some eighty-five affiliated organizations across the South, and one of them is the Alabama Christian Movement for Human Rights. Frequently we share staff, educational, and financial resources with our affiliates. Several months ago the affiliate here in Birmingham asked us to be on call to engage in a nonviolent direct-action program if such were deemed necessary. We readily consented, and when the hour came we lived up to our promise. So I, along with several members of my staff, am here because I was invited here. I am here because I have organizational ties here.

12   But more basically, I am in Birmingham because injustice is here. Just as the prophets of the eighth century BC left their villages and carried their "thus saith the Lord" far beyond the boundaries of their home towns, and just as the Apostle Paul left his village of Tarsus and carried the gospel of Jesus Christ to the far corners of the Greco-Roman world, so am I compelled to carry the gospel of freedom beyond my own home town. Like Paul, I must constantly respond to the Macedonian call for aid.

13   Moreover, I am cognizant of the interrelatedness of all communities and states. I cannot sit idly by in Atlanta and not be concerned about

---

1 This response to a published statement by eight fellow clergymen from Alabama (Bishop C. C. J. Carpenter, Bishop Joseph A. Durick, Rabbi Milton L. Grafman, Bishop Paul Hardin, Bishop Nolan B. Harmon, the Reverend George M. Murray, the Reverend Edward V. Ramage, and the Reverend Earl Stallings) was composed under somewhat constricting circumstances. Begun on the margins of the newspaper in which the statement appeared while I was in jail, the letter was continued on scraps of writing paper supplied by a friendly Negro trusty, and concluded on a pad my attorneys were eventually permitted to leave me. Although the text remains in substance unaltered, I have indulged in the author's prerogative of polishing it for publication. [King's note.]

what happens in Birmingham. Injustice anywhere is a threat to justice everywhere. We are caught in an inescapable network of mutuality; tied in a single garment of destiny. Whatever affects one directly, affects all indirectly. Never again can we afford to live with the narrow, provincial "outside agitator" idea. Anyone who lives inside the United States can never be considered an outsider anywhere within its bounds.

You deplore the demonstrations taking place in Birmingham. But your statement, I am sorry to say, fails to express a similar concern for the conditions that brought about the demonstrations. I am sure that none of you would want to rest content with the superficial kind of social analysis that deals merely with effects and does not grapple with underlying causes. It is unfortunate that demonstrations are taking place in Birmingham, but it is even more unfortunate that the city's white power structure left the Negro community with no alternative.   14

In any nonviolent campaign there are four basic steps: collection of the facts to determine whether injustices exist; negotiation; self-purification; and direct action. We have gone through all these steps in Birmingham. There can be no gainsaying the fact that racial injustice engulfs this community. Birmingham is probably the most thoroughly segregated city in the United States. Its ugly record of brutality is widely known. Negroes have experienced grossly unjust treatment in the courts. There have been more unsolved bombings of Negro homes and churches in Birmingham than in any other city in the nation. These are the hard, brutal facts of the case. On the basis of these conditions, Negro leaders sought to negotiate with the city fathers. But the latter consistently refused to engage in good-faith negotiation.   15

Then, last September, came the opportunity to talk with leaders of Birmingham's economic community. In the course of the negotiations, certain promises were made by the merchants—for example, to remove the stores' humiliating racial signs. On the basis of these promises, the Reverend Fred Shuttleworth and the leaders of the Alabama Christian Movement for Human Rights agreed to a moratorium on all demonstrations. As the weeks and months went by, we realized that we were the victims of a broken promise. A few signs, briefly removed, returned; the others remained.   16

As in so many past experiences, our hopes had been blasted, and the shadow of deep disappointment settled upon us. We had no alternative except to prepare for direct action, whereby we would present our very bodies as a means of laying our case before the conscience of the local and the national community. Mindful of the difficulties involved, we decided to undertake a process of self-purification. We began a series of workshops on nonviolence, and we repeatedly asked ourselves: "Are you able to accept   17 blows without retaliating?" "Are you able to endure the ordeal of jail?" We decided to schedule our direct-action program for the Easter season, realizing that except for Christmas, this is the main shopping period of the year. Knowing that a strong economic-withdrawal program would be the by-product of direct action, we felt that this would be the best time to bring pressure to bear on the merchants for the needed change.

18   Then it occurred to us that Birmingham's mayoralty election was coming up in March, and we speedily decided to postpone action until after election day. When we discovered that the Commissioner of Public Safety, Eugene "Bull" Connor, had piled up enough votes to be in the run-off, we decided again to postpone action until the day after the run-off so that the demonstrations could not be used to cloud the issues. Like many others, we waited to see Mr. Connor defeated, and to this end we endured postponement after postponement. Having aided in this community need, we felt that our direct-action program could be delayed no longer.

19   You may well ask: "Why direct action? Why sit-ins, marches, and so forth? Isn't negotiation a better path?" You are quite right in calling for negotiation. Indeed, this is the very purpose of direct action. Nonviolent direct action seeks to create such a crisis and foster such a tension that a community which has constantly refused to negotiate is forced to confront the issue. It seeks so to dramatize the issue that it can no longer be ignored. My citing the creation of tension as part of the work of the nonviolent-resister may sound rather shocking. But I must confess that I am not afraid of the word "tension." I have earnestly opposed violent tension, but there is a type of constructive, nonviolent tension which is necessary for growth. Just as Socrates felt that it was necessary to create a tension in the mind so that individuals could rise from the bondage of myths and half-truths to the unfettered realm of creative analysis and objective appraisal, so must we see the need for nonviolent gadflies to create the kind of tension in society that will help men rise from the dark depths of prejudice and racism to the majestic heights of understanding and brotherhood.

20   The purpose of our direct-action program is to create a situation so crisis-packed that it will inevitably open the door to negotiation. I therefore concur with you in your call for negotiation. Too long has our beloved Southland been bogged down in a tragic effort to live in monologue rather than dialogue.

21   One of the basic points in your statement is that the action that I and my associates have taken in Birmingham is untimely. Some have asked: "Why didn't you give the new city administration time to act?" The only answer that I can give to this query is that the new Birmingham administration must be prodded about as much as the outgoing one, before it will

act. We are sadly mistaken if we feel that the election of Albert Boutwell as mayor will bring the millennium to Birmingham. While Mr. Boutwell is a much more gentle person than Mr. Connor, they are both segrega-tionists, dedicated to maintenance of the status quo. I have hope that Mr. Boutwell will be reasonable enough to see the futility of massive resis-tance to desegregation. But he will not see this without pressure from devotees of civil rights. My friends, I must say to you that we have not made a single gain in civil rights without determined legal and nonviolent pressure. Lamentably, it is an historical fact that privileged groups seldom give up their privileges voluntarily. Individuals may see the moral light and voluntarily give up their unjust posture; but as Reinhold Niebuhr[2] has reminded us, groups tend to be more immoral than individuals.

We know through painful experience that freedom is never voluntarily   22
given by the oppressor; it must be demanded by the oppressed. Frankly, I have yet to engage in a direct-action campaign that was "well timed" in the view of those who have not suffered unduly from the disease of segre-gation. For years now I have heard the word "Wait!" It rings in the ear of every Negro with piercing familiarity. This "Wait" has almost always meant "Never." We must come to see, with one of our distinguished jurists, that "justice too long delayed is justice denied."[3]

We have waited for more than 340 years for our constitutional and God-   23
given rights. The nations of Asia and Africa are moving with jetlike speed toward gaining political independence, but we still creep at horse-and-buggy pace toward gaining a cup of coffee at a lunch counter. Perhaps it is easy for those who have never felt the stinging darts of segregation to say, "Wait." But when you have seen vicious mobs lynch your mothers and fathers at will and drown your sisters and brothers at whim; when you have seen hate-filled policemen curse, kick, and even kill your black brothers and sisters; when you see the vast majority of your twenty million Negro brothers smothering in an airtight cage of poverty in the midst of an afflu-ent society; when you suddenly find your tongue twisted and your speech stammering as you seek to explain to your six-year-old daughter why she can't go to the public amusement park that has just been advertised on tel-evision, and see tears welling up in her eyes when she is told that Funtown is closed to colored children, and see ominous clouds of inferiority begin-ning to form in her little mental sky, and see her beginning to distort her

---

2 **Reinhold Niebuhr** Niebuhr (1892–1971) was a minister, political activist, author, and professor of applied Christianity at Union Theological Seminary. [All notes are the editors' unless otherwise specified.]
3 **Justice . . . denied** A quotation attributed to William E. Gladstone (1809–1898), British states-man and prime minister.

personality by developing an unconscious bitterness toward white people; when you have to concoct an answer for a five-year-old son who is asking: "Daddy, why do white people treat colored people so mean?"; when you take a cross-country drive and find it necessary to sleep night after night in the uncomfortable corners of your automobile because no motel will accept you; when you are humiliated day in and day out by nagging signs reading "white" and "colored"; when your first name becomes "nigger," your middle name becomes "boy" (however old you are) and your last name becomes "John," and your wife and mother are never given the respected title "Mrs."; when you are harried by day and haunted by night by the fact that you are a Negro, living constantly at tiptoe stance, never quite knowing what to expect next, and are plagued with inner fears and outer resentments; when you are forever fighting a degenerating sense of "nobodiness"—then you will understand why we find it difficult to wait. There comes a time when the cup of endurance runs over, and men are no longer willing to be plunged into the abyss of despair. I hope, sirs, you can understand our legitimate and unavoidable impatience.

24   You express a great deal of anxiety over our willingness to break laws. This is certainly a legitimate concern. Since we so diligently urge people to obey the Supreme Court's decision of 1954 outlawing segregation in the public schools, at first glance it may seem rather paradoxical for us consciously to break laws. One may well ask: "How can you advocate breaking some laws and obeying others?" The answer lies in the fact that there are two types of laws: just and unjust. I would be the first to advocate obeying just laws. One has not only a legal but a moral responsibility to obey just laws. Conversely, one has a moral responsibility to disobey unjust laws. I would agree with St. Augustine that "an unjust law is no law at all."

25   Now, what is the difference between the two? How does one determine whether a law is just or unjust? A just law in a man-made code that squares with the moral law or the law of God. An unjust law is a code that is out of harmony with the moral law. To put it in the terms of St. Thomas Aquinas: An unjust law is a human law that is not rooted in eternal law and natural law. Any law that uplifts human personality is just. Any law that degrades human personality is unjust. All segregation statutes are unjust because segregation distorts the soul and damages the personality. It gives the segregator a false sense of superiority and the segregated a false sense of inferiority. Segregation, to use the terminology of the Jewish philosopher Martin Buber, substitutes an "I-it" relationship for an "I-thou" relationship and ends up relegating persons to the status of things. Hence segregation is not only politically, economically, and sociologically

unsound, it is morally wrong and sinful. Paul Tillich[4] has said that sin is separation. Is not segregation an existential expression of man's tragic separation, his awful estrangement, his terrible sinfulness? Thus it is that I can urge men to obey the 1954 decision of the Supreme Court, for it is morally right; and I can urge them to disobey segregation ordinances, for they are morally wrong.

Let us consider a more concrete example of just and unjust laws. An unjust law is a code that a numerical or power majority group compels a minority group to obey but does not make binding on itself. This is *difference* made legal. By the same token, a just law is a code that a majority compels a minority to follow and that it is willing to follow itself. This is *sameness* made legal.   26

Let me give another explanation. A law is unjust if it is inflicted on a minority that, as a result of being denied the right to vote, had no part in enacting or devising the law. Who can say that the legislature of Alabama which set up that state's segregation laws was democratically elected? Throughout Alabama all sorts of devious methods are used to prevent Negroes from becoming registered voters, and there are some counties in which, even though Negroes constitute a majority of the population, not a single Negro is registered. Can any law enacted under such circumstances be considered democratically structured?   27

Sometimes a law is just on its face and unjust in its application. For instance, I have been arrested on a charge of parading without a permit. Now, there is nothing wrong in having an ordinance which requires a permit for a parade. But such an ordinance becomes unjust when it is used to maintain segregation and to deny citizens the First Amendment privilege of peaceful assembly and protest.   28

I hope you are able to see the distinction I am trying to point out. In no sense do I advocate evading or defying the law, as would the rabid segregationist. That would lead to anarchy. One who breaks an unjust law must do so openly, lovingly, and with a willingness to accept the penalty. I submit that an individual who breaks a law that conscience tells him is unjust, and who willingly accepts the penalty of imprisonment in order to arouse the conscience of the community over its injustice, is in reality expressing the highest respect for law.   29

---

4 **Paul Tillich** Tillich (1886–1965), born in Germany, taught theology at several German universities, but in 1933 he was dismissed from his post at the University of Frankfurt because of his opposition to the Nazi regime. At the invitation of Reinhold Niebuhr, he came to the United States and taught at Union Theological Seminary.

30   Of course, there is nothing new about this kind of civil disobedience. It was evidenced sublimely in the refusal of Shadrach, Meshach, and Abednego to obey the laws of Nebuchadnezzar, on the ground that a higher moral law was at stake. It was practiced superbly by the early Christians, who were willing to face hungry lions and the excruciating pain of chopping blocks rather than submit to certain unjust laws of the Roman Empire. To a degree, academic freedom is a reality today because Socrates practiced civil disobedience. In our own nation, the Boston Tea Party represented a massive act of civil disobedience.

31   We should never forget that everything Adolf Hitler did in Germany was "legal" and everything the Hungarian freedom fighters did in Hungary was "illegal." It was "illegal" to aid and comfort a Jew in Hitler's Germany. Even so, I am sure that, had I lived in Germany at the time, I would have aided and comforted my Jewish brothers. If today I lived in a Communist country where certain principles dear to the Christian faith are suppressed, I would openly advocate disobeying that country's anti-religious laws.

32   I must make two honest confessions to you, my Christian and Jewish brothers. First, I must confess that over the past few years I have been gravely disappointed with the white moderate. I have almost reached the regrettable conclusion that the Negro's great stumbling block in his stride toward freedom is not the White Citizen's Councilor or the Ku Klux Klanner, but the white moderate, who is more devoted to "order" than to justice; who prefers a negative peace which is the absence of tension to a positive peace which is the presence of justice; who constantly says: "I agree with you in the goal you seek, but I cannot agree with your methods or direct action"; who paternalistically believes he can set the timetable for another man's freedom; who lives by a mythical concept of time and who constantly advises the Negro to wait for a "more convenient season." Shallow understanding from people of good will is more frustrating than absolute misunderstanding from people of ill will. Lukewarm acceptance is much more bewildering than outright rejection.

33   I had hoped that the white moderate would understand that law and order exist for the purpose of establishing justice and that when they fail in this purpose they become the dangerously structured dams that block the flow of social progress. I had hoped that the white moderate would understand that the present tension in the south is a necessary phase of the transition from an obnoxious negative peace, in which the Negro passively accepted his unjust plight, to a substantive and positive peace, in which all men will respect the dignity and worth of human personality. Actually, we who engage in nonviolent direct action are not the creators of tension. We merely bring to the surface the hidden tension that is already alive. We

bring it out in the open, where it can be seen and dealt with. Like a boil that can never be cured so long as it is covered up but must be opened with all its ugliness to the natural medicines of air and light, injustice must be exposed, with all the tension its exposure creates, to the light of human conscience and the air of national opinion before it can be cured.

In your statement you assert that our actions, even though peaceful,   34
must be condemned because they precipitate violence. But is this a logical assertion? Isn't this like condemning a robbed man because his possession of money precipitated the evil act of robbery? Isn't this like condemning Socrates because his unswerving commitment to truth and his philosophical inquiries precipitated the act by the misguided populace in which they made him drink hemlock? Isn't this like condemning Jesus because his unique God-consciousness and never-ceasing devotion to God's will precipitated the evil act of crucifixion? We must come to see that, as the federal courts have consistently affirmed, it is wrong to urge an individual to cease his efforts to gain his basic constitutional rights because the quest may precipitate violence. Society must protect the robbed and punish the robber.

I had also hoped that the white moderate would reject the myth con-   35
cerning time in relation to the struggle for freedom. I have just received a letter from a white brother in Texas. He writes: "All Christians know that the colored people will receive equal rights eventually, but it is possible that you are in too great a religious hurry. It has taken Christianity almost two thousand years to accomplish what it has. The teachings of Christ take time to come to earth." Such an attitude stems from a tragic misconception of time, from the strangely irrational notion that there is something in the very flow of time that will inevitably cure all ills. Actually, time itself is neutral; it can be used either destructively or constructively. More and more I feel that the people of ill will have used time much more effectively than have the people of good will. We will have to repent in this generation not merely for the hateful words and actions of the bad people but for the appalling silence of the good people. Human progress never rolls in on wheels of inevitability; it comes through the tireless efforts of men willing to be co-workers with God, and without this hard work, time itself becomes an ally of the forces of social stagnation. We must use time creatively, in the knowledge that the time is always ripe to do right. Now is the time to make real the promise of democracy and transform our pending national elegy into a creative psalm of brotherhood. Now is the time to lift our national policy from the quicksand of racial injustice to the solid rock of human dignity.

You speak of our activity in Birmingham as extreme. At first I was rather   36 disappointed that fellow clergymen would see my nonviolent efforts as those of an extremist. I began thinking about the fact that I stand in the middle of two opposing forces in the Negro community. One is a force of complacency, made up in part of Negroes who, as a result of long years of oppression, are so drained of self-respect and a sense of "somebodiness" that they have adjusted to segregation; and in part of a few middle-class Negroes who, because of a degree of academic and economic security and because in some ways they profit by segregation, have become insensitive to the problems of the masses. The other force is one of bitterness and ha-tred, and it comes perilously close to advocating violence. It is expressed in the various black nationalist groups that are springing up across the na-tion, the largest and best-known being Elijah Muhammad's Muslim movement. Nourished by the Negro's frustration over the continued exis-tence of racial discrimination, this movement is made up of people who have lost faith in America, who have absolutely repudiated Christianity, and who have concluded that the white man is an incorrigible "devil."

37   I have tried to stand between these two forces, saying that we need em-ulate neither the "do-nothingism" of the complacent nor the hatred and despair of the black nationalists. For there is the more excellent way of love and nonviolent protest. I am grateful to God that, through the influ-ence of the Negro church, the way of nonviolence became an integral part of our struggle.

38   If this philosophy had not emerged, by now many streets of the South should, I am convinced, be flowing with blood. And I am further con-vinced that if our white brothers dismiss as "rabble-rousers" and "outside agitators" those of us who employ nonviolent direct action, and if they refuse to support our nonviolent efforts, millions of Negroes will, out of frustration and despair, seek solace and security in black-nationalist ideologies—a development that would inevitably lead to a frightening racial nightmare.

39   Oppressed people cannot remain oppressed forever. The yearning for freedom eventually manifests itself, and that is what has happened to the American Negro. Something within has reminded him of his birthright of freedom, and something without has reminded him that it can be gained. Consciously or unconsciously, he has been caught up by the *Zeitgeist*,[5] and with his black brothers of Africa and his brown and yellow brothers of Asia, South America, and the Caribbean, the United States Negro is moving with a sense of great urgency toward the promised land of racial justice. If one recognizes this vital urge that has engulfed the Negro com-

5 **Zeitgeist** German for "spirit of the age."

munity, one should readily understand why public demonstrations are taking place. The Negro has many pent-up resentments and latent frustrations, and he must release them. So let him march; let him make prayer pilgrimages to the city hall; let him go on freedom rides—and try to understand why he must do so. If his repressed emotions are not released in nonviolent ways, they will seek expression through violence; this is not a threat but a fact of history. So I have not said to my people: "Get rid of your discontent." Rather, I have tried to say that this normal and healthy discontent can be channeled into the creative outlet of nonviolent direct action. And now this approach is being termed extremist.

But though I was initially disappointed at being categorized as an extremist, as I continued to think about the matter I gradually gained a measure of satisfaction from the label. Was not Jesus an extremist for love: "Love your enemies, bless them that curse you, do good to them that hate you, and pray for them which despitefully use you, and persecute you." Was not Amos an extremist for justice: "Let justice roll down like waters and righteousness like an ever-flowing stream." Was not Paul an extremist for the Christian gospel: "I bear in my body the marks of the Lord Jesus." Was not Martin Luther an extremist: "Here I stand; I cannot do otherwise, so help me God." And John Bunyan: "I will stay in jail to the end of my days before I make a butchery of my conscience." And Abraham Lincoln: "This nation cannot survive half slave and half free." And Thomas Jefferson: "We hold these truths to be self-evident, that all men are created equal. . . ." So the question is not whether we will be extremists, but what kind of extremists we will be. Will we be extremists for hate or for love? Will we be extremists for the preservation of injustice or for the extension of justice? In that dramatic scene on Calvary's hill three men were crucified. We must never forget that all three were crucified for the same crime—the crime of extremism. Two were extremists for immorality, and thus fell below their environment. The other, Jesus Christ, was an extremist for love, truth, and goodness, and thereby rose above his environment. Perhaps the South, the nation, and the world are in dire need of creative extremists.

I had hoped that the white moderate would see this need. Perhaps I was too optimistic; perhaps I expected too much. I suppose I should have realized that few members of the oppressor race can understand the deep groans and passionate yearnings of the oppressed race, and still fewer have the vision to see that injustice must be rooted out by strong, persistent, and determined action. I am thankful, however, that some of our white brothers in the South have grasped the meaning of this social revolution and committed themselves to it. They are still all too few in quantity, but they are big in quality. Some—such as Ralph McGill, Lillian Smith,

Harry Golden, James McBride Dabbs, Ann Braden, and Sarah Patton Boyle—have written about our struggle in eloquent and prophetic terms. Others have marched with us down nameless streets of the South. They have languished in filthy, roach-infested jails, suffering the abuse and brutality of policemen who view them as "dirty nigger-lovers." Unlike so many of their moderate brothers and sisters, they have recognized the urgency of the moment and sensed the need for powerful "action" antidotes to combat the disease of segregation.

42   Let me take note of my other major disappointment. I have been so greatly disappointed with the white church and its leadership. Of course, there are some notable exceptions. I am not unmindful of the fact that each of you has taken some significant stands on this issue. I commend you, Reverend Stallings, for your Christian stand on this past Sunday, in welcoming Negroes to your worship service on a nonsegregated basis. I commend the Catholic leaders of this state for integrating Spring Hill College several years ago.

43   But despite these notable exceptions, I must honestly reiterate that I have been disappointed with the church. I do not say this as one of those negative critics who can always find something wrong with the church. I say this as a minister of the gospel, who loves the church; who was nurtured in its bosom; who has been sustained by its spiritual blessings and who will remain true to it as long as the cord of life shall lengthen.

44   When I was suddenly catapulted into the leadership of the bus protest in Montgomery, Alabama, a few years ago, I felt we would be supported by the white church. I felt that the white ministers, priests, and rabbis of the South would be among our strongest allies. Instead, some have been outright opponents, refusing to understand the freedom movement and misrepresenting its leaders; all too many others have been more cautious than courageous and have remained silent behind the anesthetizing security of stained-glass windows.

45   In spite of my shattered dreams, I came to Birmingham with the hope that the white religious leadership of this community would see the justice of our cause and, with deep moral concern, would serve as the channel through which our just grievances could reach the power structure. I had hoped that each of you would understand. But again I have been disappointed.

46   I have heard numerous southern religious leaders admonish their worshipers to comply with a desegregation decision because it is the law, but I have longed to hear white ministers declare: "Follow this decree because integration is morally right and because the Negro is your brother." In the midst of blatant injustices inflicted upon the Negro, I have watched white churchmen stand on the sideline and mouth pious irrelevancies and sanc-

timonious trivialities. In the midst of a mighty struggle to rid our nation of racial and economic injustice, I have heard many ministers say: "Those are social issues, with which the gospel has no real concern." And I have watched many churches commit themselves to a completely otherworldly religion which makes a strange, unbiblical distinction between body and soul, between the sacred and the secular.

I have traveled the length and breadth of Alabama, Mississippi, and all the other southern states. On sweltering summer days and crisp autumn mornings I have looked at the South's beautiful churches with their lofty spires pointing heavenward. I have beheld the impressive outlines of her massive religious-education buildings. Over and over I have found myself saying: "What kind of people worship here? Who is their God? Where were their voices when the lips of Governor Barnett dripped with words of interposition and nullification? Where were they when Governor Wallace gave a clarion call for defiance and hatred? Where were their voices of support when bruised and weary Negro men and women decided to rise from the dark dungeons of complacency to the bright hills of creative protest?" 47

Yes, these questions are still in my mind. In deep disappointment I have wept over the laxity of the church. But be assured that my tears have been tears of love. There can be no deep disappointment where there is not deep love. Yes, I love the church. How could I do otherwise? I am in the rather unique position of being the son, the grandson, and the great-grandson of preachers. Yes, I see the church as the body of Christ. But, Oh! How we have blemished and scarred that body through social neglect and through fear of being nonconformists. 48

There was a time when the church was very powerful—in the time when the early Christians rejoiced at being deemed worthy to suffer for what they believed. In those days the church was not merely a thermometer that recorded the ideas and principles of popular opinion; it was a thermostat that transformed the mores of society. Whenever the early Christians entered a town, the people in power became disturbed and immediately sought to convict the Christians for being "disturbers of the peace" and "outside agitators." But the Christians pressed on, in the conviction that they were "a colony of heaven," called to obey God rather than man. Small in number, they were big in commitment. They were too God-intoxicated to be "astronomically intimidated." By their effort and example they brought an end to such ancient evils as infanticide and gladiatorial contests. 49

Things are different now. So often the contemporary church is a weak, ineffectual voice with an uncertain sound. So often it is an archdefender of the status quo. Far from being disturbed by the presence of the church, 50 the power structure of the average community is consoled by the church's silent—and often even vocal—sanction of things as they are.

51   But the judgment of God is upon the church as never before. If today's church does not recapture the sacrificial spirit of the early church, it will lose its authenticity, forfeit the loyalty of millions, and be dismissed as an irrelevant social club with no meaning for the twentieth century. Every day I meet young people whose disappointment with the church has turned into outright disgust.

52   Perhaps I have once again been too optimistic. Is organized religion too inextricably bound to the status quo to save our nation and the world? Perhaps I must turn my faith to the inner spiritual church, the church within the church, as the true *ekklesia*[6] and the hope of the world. But again I am thankful to God that some noble souls from the ranks of organized religion have broken loose from the paralyzing chains of conformity and joined us as active partners in the struggle for freedom. They have left their secure congregations and walked the streets of Albany, Georgia, with us. They have gone down the highways of the South on tortuous rides for freedom. Yes, they have gone to jail with us. Some have been dismissed from their churches, have lost the support of their bishops and fellow ministers. But they have acted in the faith that right defeated is stronger than evil triumphant. Their witness has been the spiritual salt that has preserved the true meaning of the gospel in these troubled times. They have carved a tunnel of hope through the dark mountain of disappointment.

53   I hope the church as a whole will meet the challenge of this decisive hour. But even if the church does not come to the aid of justice, I have no despair about the future. I have no fear about the outcome of our struggle in Birmingham, even if our motives are at present misunderstood. We will reach the goal of freedom in Birmingham and all over the nation, because the goal of America is freedom. Abused and scorned though we may be, our destiny is tied up with America's destiny. Before the pilgrims landed at Plymouth, we were here. Before the pen of Jefferson etched the majestic words of the Declaration of Independence across the pages of history, we were here. For more than two centuries our forebears labored in this country without wages; they made cotton king; they built the homes of their masters while suffering gross injustice and shameful humiliation—and yet out of a bottomless vitality they continue to thrive and develop. If the inexpressible cruelties of slavery could not stop us, the opposition we now face will surely

---

6 *ekklesia:* Greek for "a gathering or assembly of citizens."

fail. We will win our freedom because the sacred heritage of our nation and the eternal will of God are embodied in our echoing demands.

Before closing I feel impelled to mention one other point in your state-   54
ment that has troubled me profoundly. You warmly commended the Birmingham police force for keeping "order" and "preventing violence." I doubt that you would have so warmly commended the police force if you had seen its dogs sinking their teeth into unarmed, nonviolent Negroes. I doubt that you would so quickly commend the policemen if you were to observe their ugly and inhumane treatment of Negroes here in the city jail; if you were to watch them push and curse old Negro women and young Negro girls; if you were to see them slap and kick old Negro men and young boys; if you were to observe them, as they did on two occasions, refuse to give us food because we wanted to sing our grace together. I cannot join you in your praise of the Birmingham police department.

It is true that the police have exercised a degree of discipline in han-   55
dling the demonstrators. In this sense they have conducted themselves rather "nonviolently" in public. But for what purpose? To preserve the evil system of segregation. Over the past few years I have consistently preached that nonviolence demands that the means we use must be as pure as the end we seek. I have tried to make clear that it is wrong to use immoral means to attain moral ends. But now I must affirm that it is just as wrong, or perhaps even more so, to use moral means to preserve immoral ends. Perhaps Mr. Connor and his policemen have been rather nonviolent in public, as was Chief Pritchett in Albany, Georgia, but they used the moral means of nonviolence to maintain the immoral end of racial injustice. As T. S. Eliot has said: "The last temptation is the greatest treason: To do the right deed for the wrong reason."

I wish you had commended the Negro sit-inners and demonstrators of   56
Birmingham for their sublime courage, their willingness to suffer, and their amazing discipline in the midst of great provocation. One day the South will recognize its real heroes. They will be the James Merediths, with the noble sense of purpose that enables them to face jeering and hostile mobs, and with the agonizing loneliness that characterizes the life of the pioneer. They will be old, oppressed, battered Negro women, symbolized in a seventy-two-year-old woman in Montgomery, Alabama, who rose up with a sense of dignity and with her people decided not to ride segregated buses, and who responded with ungrammatical profundity to one who inquired about her weariness: "My feets is tired, but my soul is at rest." They will be the young high school and college students, the young ministers of the gospel and a host of their elders, courageously and nonviolently sitting in at lunch counters and willingly going to jail for conscience's sake. One day

the South will know that when these disinherited children of God sat down at lunch counters, they were in reality standing up for what is best in the American dream and for the most sacred values in our Judaeo-Christian heritage, thereby bringing our nation back to those great wells of democracy which were dug deep by the founding fathers in their formulation of the Constitution and the Declaration of Independence.

57   Never before have I written so long a letter. I'm afraid it is much too long to take your precious time. I can assure you that it would have been much shorter if I had been writing from a comfortable desk, but what else can one do when he is alone in a narrow jail cell, other than write long letters, think long thoughts, and pray long prayers?

58   If I have said anything in this letter that overstates the truth and indicates an unreasonable impatience, I beg you to forgive me. If I have said anything that understates the truth and indicates my having a patience that allows me to settle for anything less than brotherhood, I beg God to forgive me.

59   I hope this letter finds you strong in the faith. I also hope that circumstances will soon make it possible for me to meet each of you, not as an integrationist or a civil-rights leader but as a fellow clergyman and a Christian brother. Let us all hope that the dark clouds of racial prejudice will soon pass away and the deep fog of misunderstanding will be lifted from our fear-drenched communities, and in some not too distant tomorrow the radiant stars of love and brotherhood will shine over our great nation with all their scintillating beauty.

Yours for the cause of Peace and Brotherhood,
Martin Luther King Jr.

QUESTIONING AND DISCUSSING

King, "Letter from Birmingham Jail"

1. How would you describe King's strategies for developing his argument? For instance, look carefully at the first five paragraphs. Why does King select the references that he does? For what purpose?

2. Consider the following statements: "One who breaks an unjust law must do so openly, lovingly, and with a willingness to accept the penalty," and "I had hoped that the white moderate would understand that law and order exist for the purpose of establishing justice and that when they fail in this purpose they become the dangerously structured dams that block the flow of social progress." How does King defend his defiance of unjust laws? What types of evidence does he use for his support?

3. How does King mix arguments that are personal and historical? How effective are these arguments?

4. Compare Dr. King's arguments with those Thoreau presents in "Civil Disobedience." What similarities and differences do you find?

⊞

BERTRAND RUSSELL

Bertrand Russell (1872–1970) was a trained mathematician and logician, but he became well known to the public as a social philosopher. His most popular books included *History of Western Philosophy* (1945) and *Why I Am Not a Christian* (1957). A consistently provocative and controversial figure, Russell lost his teaching position at Cambridge University because of his pacifist beliefs during World War I. In 1938, he was prevented from taking a position at the City University of New York when a judge refused him a visa for what were Russell's allegedly dangerous views on sex. The following selection is Russell's most famous essay on religion.

⊞

Why I Am Not a Christian

As your Chairman has told you, the subject about which I am going to speak to you tonight is "Why I Am Not a Christian." Perhaps it would be as well, first of all, to try to make out what one means by the word *Christian*. It is used these days in a very loose sense by a great many people. Some people mean no more by it than a person who attempts to live a good life. In that sense I suppose there would be Christians in all sects and creeds; but I do not think that that is the proper sense of the word, if only because it would simply imply that all the people who are not Christians— all the Buddhists, Confucians, Mohammedans, and so on—are not trying to live a good life. I do not mean by a Christian any person who tries to live decently according to his lights. I think that you must have a certain amount of definite belief before you have a right to call yourself a Christian. The word does not have quite such a full-blooded meaning now as it had in the times of St. Augustine and St. Thomas Aquinas. In those days, if a man said that he was a Christian it was known what he meant. You accepted a whole collection of creeds which were set out with great precision, and every single syllable of those creeds you believed with the whole strength of your convictions.

What Is a Christian?

2 Nowadays it is not quite that. We have to be a little more vague in our meaning of Christianity. I think, however, that there are two different items which are quite essential to anybody calling himself a Christian. The first is one of a dogmatic nature—namely, that you must believe in God and immortality. If you do not believe in those two things, I do not think that you can properly call yourself a Christian. Then, further than that, as the name implies, you must have some kind of belief about Christ. The Mohammedans, for instance, also believe in God and in immortality, and yet they would not call themselves Christians. I think you must have at the very lowest the belief that Christ was, if not divine, at least the best and wisest of men. If you are not going to believe that much about Christ, I do not think you have any right to call yourself a Christian. Of course, there is another sense, which you find in *Whitaker's Almanack* and in geography books, where the population of the world is said to be divided into Christians, Mohammedans, Buddhists, fetish worshipers, and so on; and in that sense we are all Christians. The geography books count us all in, but that is a purely geographical sense, which I suppose we can ignore. Therefore I take it that when I tell you why I am not a Christian I have to tell you two different things: first, why I do not believe in God and in immortality; and, secondly, why I do not think Christ was the best and wisest of men, although I grant him a very high degree of moral goodness.

3 But for the successful efforts of unbelievers in the past, I could not take so elastic a definition of Christianity as that. As I said before, in olden days it had a much more full-blooded sense. For instance, it included the belief in hell. Belief in eternal hell-fire was an essential item of Christian belief until pretty recent times. In this country, as you know, it ceased to be an essential item because of a decision of the Privy Council, and from that decision the Archbishop of Canterbury and the Archbishop of York dissented; but in this country our religion is settled by Act of Parliament, and therefore the Privy Council was able to override their Graces and hell was no longer necessary to a Christian. Consequently I shall not insist that a Christian must believe in hell.

The Existence of God

4 To come to this question of the existence of God: It is a large and serious question, and if I were to attempt to deal with it in any adequate manner I should have to keep you here until Kingdom Come, so that you will have to excuse me if I deal with it in a somewhat summary fashion. You know, of course, that the Catholic Church has laid it down as a dogma that the exis-

tence of God can be proved by the unaided reason. That is a somewhat curious dogma, but it is one of their dogmas. They had to introduce it because at one time the freethinkers adopted the habit of saying that there were such and such arguments which mere reason might urge against the existence of God, but of course they knew as a matter of faith that God did exist. The arguments and the reasons were set out at great length, and the Catholic Church felt that they must stop it. Therefore they laid it down that the existence of God can be proved by the unaided reason and they had to set up what they considered were arguments to prove it. There are, of course, a number of them, but I shall take only a few.

The First Cause Argument

Perhaps the simplest and easiest to understand is the argument of the First   5
Cause. (It is maintained that everything we see in this world has a cause, and as you go back in the chain of causes further and further you must come to a First Cause, and to that First Cause you give the name of God.) That argument, I suppose, does not carry very much weight nowadays, because, in the first place, cause is not quite what it used to be. The philosophers and the men of science have got going on cause and it has not anything like the vitality it used to have; but, apart from that, you can see that the argument that there must be a First Cause is one that cannot have any validity. I may say that when I was a young man and was debating these questions very seriously in my mind, I for a long time accepted the argument of the First Cause, until one day, at the age of eighteen, I read John Stuart Mill's *Autobiography*, and I there found this sentence: "My father taught me that the question 'Who made me?' cannot be answered, since it immediately suggests the further question 'Who made God?'" That very simple sentence showed me, as I still think, the fallacy in the argument of the First Cause. If everything must have a cause, then God must have a cause. If there can be everything without a cause, it may just as well be the world as God, so that there cannot be any validity in that argument. It is exactly of the same nature as the Hindu's view that the world rested upon an elephant and the elephant rested upon a tortoise; and when they said, "How about the tortoise?" the Indian said, "Suppose we change the subject." The argument is really no better than that. There is no reason why the world could not have come into being without a cause; nor, on the other hand, is there any reason why it should not always have existed. There is no reason to suppose that the world had a beginning at all. The idea that things must have a beginning is really due to the poverty of our imagination. Therefore, perhaps I need not waste any more time upon the argument about the First Cause.

The Natural Law Argument

6 Then there is a very common argument from natural law. That was a favorite argument all through the eighteenth century, especially under the influence of Sir Isaac Newton and his cosmogony. People observed the planets going around the sun according to the law of gravitation, and they thought that God had given a behest to these planets to move in that particular fashion, and that was why they did so. That was, of course, a convenient and simple explanation that saved them the trouble of looking any further for explanations of the law of gravitation. Nowadays we explain the law of gravitation in a somewhat complicated fashion that Einstein has introduced. I do not propose to give you a lecture on the law of gravitation, as interpreted by Einstein, because that again would take some time; at any rate, you no longer have the sort of natural law that you had in the Newtonian system, where, for some reason that nobody could understand, nature behaved in a uniform fashion. We now find that a great many things we thought were natural laws are really human conventions. You know that even in the remotest depths of stellar space there are still three feet to a yard. That is, no doubt, a very remarkable fact, but you would hardly call it a law of nature. And a great many things that have been regarded as laws of nature are of that kind. On the other hand, where you can get down to any knowledge of what atoms actually do, you will find they are much less subject to law than people thought, and that the laws at which you arrive are statistical averages of just the sort that would emerge from chance. There is, as we all know, a law that if you throw dice you will get double sixes only about once in thirty-six times, and we do not regard that as evidence that the fall of the dice is regulated by design; on the contrary, if the double sixes came every time we should think that there was design. The laws of nature are of that sort as regards a great many of them. They are statistical averages such as would emerge from the laws of chance; and that makes this whole business of natural law much less impressive than it formerly was. Quite apart from that, which represents the momentary state of science that may change tomorrow, the whole idea that natural laws imply a lawgiver is due to a confusion between natural and human laws. Human laws are behests commanding you to behave a certain way, in which way you may choose to behave, or you may choose not to behave; but natural laws are a description of how things do in fact behave, and being a mere description of what they in fact do, you cannot argue that there must be somebody who told them to do that, because even supposing that there were, you are then faced with the question "Why did God issue just those natural laws and no others?" If you say that he did it simply from his own good pleasure, and without any rea-

son, you then find that there is something which is not subject to law, and so your train of natural law is interrupted. If you say, as more orthodox theologians do, that in all the laws which God issues he had a reason for giving those laws rather than others—the reason, of course, being to create the best universe, although you would never think it to look at it—if there were a reason for the laws which God gave, then God himself was subject to law, and therefore you do not get any advantage by introducing God as an intermediary. You have really a law outside and anterior to the divine edicts, and God does not serve your purpose, because he is not the ultimate lawgiver. In short, this whole argument about natural law no longer has anything like the strength that it used to have. I am traveling on in time in my review of the arguments. The arguments that are used for the existence of God change their character as time goes on. They were at first hard intellectual arguments embodying certain quite definite fallacies. As we come to modern times they become less respectable intellectually and more and more affected by a kind of moralizing vagueness.

The Argument from Design

The next step in this process brings us to the argument from design. You   7
all know the argument from design: Everything in the world is made just so that we can manage to live in the world, and if the world was ever so little different, we could not manage to live in it. That is the argument from design. It sometimes takes a rather curious form; for instance, it is argued that rabbits have white tails in order to be easy to shoot. I do not know how rabbits would view that application. It is an easy argument to parody. You all know Voltaire's remark, that obviously the nose was designed to be such as to fit spectacles. That sort of parody has turned out to be not nearly so wide of the mark as it might have seemed in the eighteenth century, because since the time of Darwin we understand much better why living creatures are adapted to their environment. It is not that their environment was made to be suitable to them but that they grew to be suitable to it, and that is the basis of adaptation. There is no evidence of design about it.

When you come to look into this argument from design, it is a most as-   8
tonishing thing that people can believe that this world, with all the things that are in it, with all its defects, should be the best that omnipotence and omniscience have been able to produce in millions of years. I really cannot believe it. Do you think that, if you were granted omnipotence and omniscience and millions of years in which to perfect your world, you could produce nothing better than the Ku Klux Klan or the Fascists? Moreover, if you accept the ordinary laws of science, you have to suppose

that human life and life in general on this planet will die out in due course: It is a stage in the decay of the solar system; at a certain stage of decay you get the sort of conditions of temperature and so forth which are suitable to protoplasm, and there is life for a short time in the life of the whole solar system. You see in the moon the sort of thing to which the earth is tending—something dead, cold, and lifeless.

9   I am told that that sort of view is depressing, and people will sometimes tell you that if they believed that, they would not be able to go on living. Do not believe it; it is all nonsense. Nobody really worries much about what is going to happen millions of years hence. Even if they think they are worrying much about that, they are really deceiving themselves. They are worried about something much more mundane, or it may merely be a bad digestion; but nobody is really seriously rendered unhappy by the thought of something that is going to happen to this world millions and millions of years hence. Therefore, although it is of course a gloomy view to suppose that life will die out—at least I suppose we may say so, although sometimes when I contemplate the things that people do with their lives I think it is almost a consolation—it is not such as to render life miserable. It merely makes you turn your attention to other things.

The Moral Arguments for Deity

10   Now we reach one stage further in what I shall call the intellectual descent that the Theists have made in their argumentations, and we come to what are called the moral arguments for the existence of God. You all know, of course, that there used to be in the old days three intellectual arguments for the existence of God, all of which were disposed of by Immanuel Kant in the *Critique of Pure Reason;* but no sooner had he disposed of those arguments than he invented a new one, a moral argument, and that quite convinced him. He was like many people: In intellectual matters he was skeptical, but in moral matters he believed implicitly in the maxims that he had imbibed at his mother's knee. That illustrates what the psychoanalysts so much emphasize—the immensely stronger hold upon us that our very early associations have than those of later times.

11   Kant, as I say, invented a new moral argument for the existence of God, and that in varying forms was extremely popular during the nineteenth century. It has all sorts of forms. One form is to say that there would be no right or wrong unless God existed. I am not for the moment concerned with whether there is a difference between right and wrong, or whether there is not: That is another question. The point I am concerned with is that, if you are quite sure there is a difference between right and wrong,

you are then in this situation: Is that difference due to God's fiat or is it not? If it is due to God's fiat, then for God himself there is no difference between right and wrong, and it is no longer a significant statement to say that God is good. If you are going to say, as theologians do, that God is good, you must then say that right and wrong have some meaning which is independent of God's fiat, because God's fiats are good and not bad independently of the mere fact that he made them. If you are going to say that, you will then have to say that it is not only through God that right and wrong came into being, but that they are in their essence logically anterior to God. You could, of course, if you liked, say that there was a superior deity who gave orders to God who made this world, or could take up the line that some of the gnostics took up—a line which I often thought was a very plausible one—that as a matter of fact this world that we know was made by the devil at a moment when God was not looking. There is a good deal to be said for that, and I am not concerned to refute it.

The Argument for the Remedying of Injustice

Then there is another very curious form of moral argument, which is this: They say that the existence of God is required in order to bring justice into the world. In the part of this universe that we know there is great injustice, and often the good suffer, and often the wicked prosper, and one hardly knows which of those is the more annoying; but if you are going to have justice in the universe as a whole you have to suppose a future life to redress the balance of life here on earth. So they say that there must be a God, and there must be a heaven and hell in order that in the long run there may be justice. That is a very curious argument. If you looked at the matter from a scientific point of view, you would say, "After all I know only this world. I do not know about the rest of the universe, but so far as one can argue at all on probabilities one would say that probably this world is a fair sample, and if there is injustice here the odds are that there is injustice elsewhere also." Supposing you got a crate of oranges that you opened, and you found all the top layer of oranges bad, you would not argue, "The underneath ones must be good, so as to redress the balance." You would say, "Probably the whole lot is a bad consignment"; and that is really what a scientific person would argue about the universe. He would say, "Here we find in this world a great deal of injustice, and so far as that goes that is a reason for supposing that justice does not rule in the world; and therefore so far as it goes it affords a moral argument against deity and not in favor of one." Of course I know that the sort of intellectual arguments that I have been talking to you about are not what really moves people. What really moves people to believe in God is not any intellectual

12

argument at all. Most people believe in God because they have been taught from early infancy to do it, and that is the main reason.

13 Then I think that the next most powerful reason is the wish for safety, a sort of feeling that there is a big brother who will look after you. That plays a very profound part in influencing people's desire for a belief in God.

The Character of Christ

14 I now want to say a few words upon a topic which I often think is not quite sufficiently dealt with by Rationalists, and that is the question whether Christ was the best and the wisest of men. It is generally taken for granted that we should all agree that that was so. I do not myself. I think that there are a good many points upon which I agree with Christ a great deal more than the professing Christians do. I do not know that I could go with Him all the way, but I could go with Him much further than most professing Christians can. You will remember that He said, "Resist not evil: But whosoever shall smite thee on thy right cheek, turn to him the other also." That is not a new precept or a new principle. It was used by Lao-tse and Buddha some 500 or 600 years before Christ, but it is not a principle which as a matter of fact Christians accept. I have no doubt that the present Prime Minister,[1] for instance, is a most sincere Christian, but I should not advise any of you to go and smite him on one cheek. I think you might find that he thought this text was intended in a figurative sense.

15 Then there is another point which I consider excellent. You will remember that Christ said, "Judge not lest ye be judged." That principle I do not think you would find as popular in the law courts of Christian countries. I have known in my time quite a number of judges who were very earnest Christians, and none of them felt that they were acting contrary to Christian principles in what they did. Then Christ says, "Give to him that asketh of thee, and from him that would borrow of thee turn not thou away." That is a very good principle. Your Chairman has reminded you that we are not here to talk politics, but I cannot help observing that the last general election was fought on the question of how desirable it was to turn away from him that would borrow of thee, so that one must assume that the Liberals and Conservatives of this country are composed of people who do not agree with the teaching of Christ, because they certainly did very emphatically turn away on that occasion.

---

1 Stanley Baldwin (1867–1947).

Then there is one other maxim of Christ which I think has a great deal 16
in it, but I do not find that it is very popular among some of our Christian
friends. He says, "If thou wilt be perfect, go and sell that which thou hast,
and give to the poor." That is a very excellent maxim, but, as I say, it is not
much practiced. All these, I think, are good maxims, although they are a
little difficult to live up to. I do not profess to live up to them myself; but
then, after all, it is not quite the same thing as for a Christian.

Defects in Christ's Teaching

Having granted the excellence of these maxims, I come to certain points 17
in which I do not believe that one can grant either the superlative wisdom or the superlative goodness of Christ as depicted in the Gospels; and
here I may say that one is not concerned with the historical question.
Historically it is quite doubtful whether Christ ever existed at all, and if
He did we do not know anything about Him, so that I am not concerned
with the historical question, which is a very difficult one. I am concerned
with Christ as He appears in the Gospels, taking the Gospel narrative
as it stands, and there one does find some things that do not seem to be
very wise. For one thing, He certainly thought that His second coming
would occur in clouds of glory before the death of all the people who
were living at that time. There are a great many texts that prove that. He
says, for instance, "Ye shall not have gone over the cities of Israel till the
Son of Man be come." Then He says, "There are some standing here
which shall not taste death till the Son of Man comes into His kingdom"; and there are a lot of places where it is quite clear that He believed
that His second coming would happen during the lifetime of many then
living. That was the belief of His earlier followers, and it was the basis
of a good deal of His moral teaching. When He said, "Take no thought for
the morrow," and things of that sort, it was very largely because He
thought that the second coming was going to be very soon, and that all ordinary mundane affairs did not count. I have, as a matter of fact, known
some Christians who did believe that the second coming was imminent. I
knew a parson who frightened his congregation terribly by telling them
that the second coming was very imminent indeed, but they were much
consoled when they found that he was planting trees in his garden. The
early Christians did really believe it, and they did abstain from such things
as planting trees in their gardens, because they did accept from Christ the
belief that the second coming was imminent. In that respect, clearly He
was not so wise as some other people have been, and He was certainly not
superlatively wise.

The Moral Problem

18   Then you come to moral questions. There is one very serious defect to my mind in Christ's moral character, and that is that He believed in hell. I do not myself feel that any person who is really profoundly humane can believe in everlasting punishment. Christ certainly as depicted in the Gospels did believe in everlasting punishment, and one does find repeatedly a vindictive fury against those people who would not listen to His preaching—an attitude which is not uncommon with preachers, but which does somewhat detract from superlative excellence. You do not, for instance, find that attitude in Socrates. You find him quite bland and urbane toward the people who would not listen to him; and it is, to my mind, far more worthy of a sage to take that line than to take the line of indignation. You probably all remember the sort of things that Socrates was saying when he was dying, and the sort of things that he generally did say to people who did not agree with him.

19   You will find that in the Gospels Christ said, "Ye serpents, ye generation of vipers, how can ye escape the damnation of hell." That was said to people who did not like His preaching. It is not really to my mind quite the best tone, and there are a great many of these things about hell. There is, of course, the familiar text about the sin against the Holy Ghost: "Whosoever speaketh against the Holy Ghost it shall not be forgiven him neither in this World nor in the world to come." That text has caused an unspeakable amount of misery in the world, for all sorts of people have imagined that they have committed the sin against the Holy Ghost, and thought that it would not be forgiven them either in this world or in the world to come. I really do not think that a person with a proper degree of kindliness in his nature would have put fears and terrors of that sort into the world.

20   Then Christ says, "The Son of Man shall send forth His angels, and they shall gather out of His kingdom all things that offend, and them which do iniquity, and shall cast them into a furnace of fire; there shall be wailing and gnashing of teeth"; and He goes on about the wailing and gnashing of teeth. It comes in one verse after another, and it is quite manifest to the reader that there is a certain pleasure in contemplating wailing and gnashing of teeth, or else it would not occur so often. Then you all, of course, remember about the sheep and the goats; how at the second coming He is going to divide the sheep from the goats, and He is going to say to the goats, "Depart from me, ye cursed, into everlasting fire." He continues, "And these shall go away into everlasting fire." Then He says again, "If thy hand offend thee, cut it off; it is better for thee to enter into life maimed, than having two hands to go into hell, into the fire that

never shall be quenched; where the worm dieth not and the fire is not quenched." He repeats that again and again also. I must say that I think all this doctrine, that hell-fire is a punishment for sin, is a doctrine of cruelty. It is a doctrine that put cruelty into the world and gave the world generations of cruel torture; and the Christ of the Gospels, if you could take Him as His chroniclers represent Him, would certainly have to be considered partly responsible for that.

There are other things of less importance. There is the instance of the 21
Gadarene swine, where it certainly was not very kind to the pigs to put the devils into them and make them rush down the hill to the sea. You must remember that He was omnipotent, and He could have made the devils simply go away; but He chose to send them into the pigs. Then there is the curious story of the fig tree, which always rather puzzled me. You remember what happened about the fig tree. "He was hungry; and seeing a fig tree afar off having leaves, He came if haply He might find anything thereon; and when He came to it He found nothing but leaves, for the time of figs was not yet. And Jesus answered and said unto it: 'No man eat fruit of thee hereafter for ever' . . . and Peter . . . saith unto Him: 'Master, behold the fig tree which thou cursedst is withered away.'" This is a very curious story, because it was not the right time of year for figs, and you really could not blame the tree. I cannot myself feel that either in the matter of wisdom or in the matter of virtue Christ stands quite as high as some other people known to history. I think I should put Buddha and Socrates above Him in those respects.

The Emotional Factor

As I said before, I do not think that the real reason why people accept re- 22
ligion has anything to do with argumentation. They accept religion on emotional grounds. One is often told that it is a very wrong thing to attack religion, because religion makes men virtuous. So I am told; I have not noticed it. You know, of course, the parody of that argument in Samuel Butler's book, *Erewhon Revisited*. You will remember that in *Erewhon* there is a certain Higgs who arrives in a remote country, and after spending some time there he escapes from that country in a balloon. Twenty years later he comes back to that country and finds a new religion in which he is worshipped under the name of the "Sun Child," and it is said that he ascended into heaven. He finds that the Feast of the Ascension is about to be celebrated, and he hears Professors Hanky and Panky say to each other that they never set eyes on the man Higgs, and they hope they never will; but they are the high priests of the religion of the Sun Child. He is very indignant, and he comes up to them, and he says, "I am going to expose

all this humbug and tell the people of Erewhon that it was only I, the man Higgs, and I went up in a balloon." He was told, "You must not do that, because all the morals of this country are bound round this myth, and if they once know that you did not ascend into heaven they will all become wicked"; and so he is persuaded of that and he goes quietly away.

23   That is the idea—that we should all be wicked if we did not hold to the Christian religion. It seems to me that the people who have held to it have been for the most part extremely wicked. You find this curious fact, that the more intense has been the religion of any period and the more profound has been the dogmatic belief, the greater has been the cruelty and the worse has been the state of affairs. In the so-called ages of faith, when men really did believe the Christian religion in all its completeness, there was the Inquisition, with its tortures; there were millions of unfortunate women burned as witches; and there was every kind of cruelty practiced upon all sorts of people in the name of religion.

24   You find as you look around the world that every single bit of progress in humane feeling, every improvement in the criminal law, every step toward the diminution of war, every step toward better treatment of the colored races, or every mitigation of slavery, every moral progress that there has been in the world, has been consistently opposed by the organized churches of the world. I say quite deliberately that the Christian religion, as organized in its churches, has been and still is the principal enemy of moral progress in the world.

How the Churches Have Retarded Progress

25   You may think that I am going too far when I say that that is still so. I do not think that I am. Take one fact. You will bear with me if I mention it. It is not a pleasant fact, but the churches compel one to mention facts that are not pleasant. Supposing that in this world that we live in today an inexperienced girl is married to a syphilitic man; in that case the Catholic Church says, "This is an indissoluble sacrament. You must endure celibacy or stay together. And if you stay together, you must not use birth control to prevent the birth of syphilitic children." Nobody whose natural sympathies have not been warped by dogma, or whose moral nature was not absolutely dead to all sense of suffering, could maintain that it is right and proper that that state of things should continue.

26   That is only an example. There are a great many ways in which, at the present moment, the church, by its insistence upon what it chooses to call morality, inflicts upon all sorts of people undeserved and unnecessary suffering. And of course, as we know, it is in its major part an opponent still of progress and of improvement in all the ways that diminish suffering in

the world, because it has chosen to label as morality a certain narrow set of rules of conduct which have nothing to do with human happiness; and when you say that this or that ought to be done because it would make for human happiness, they think that has nothing to do with the matter at all. "What has human happiness to do with morals? The object of morals is not to make people happy."

Fear, the Foundation of Religion

Religion is based, I think, primarily and mainly upon fear. It is partly the 27 terror of the unknown and partly, as I have said, the wish to feel that you have a kind of elder brother who will stand by you in all your troubles and disputes. Fear is the basis of the whole thing—fear of the mysterious, fear of defeat, fear of death. Fear is the parent of cruelty, and therefore it is no wonder if cruelty and religion have gone hand in hand. It is because fear is at the basis of those two things. In this world we can now begin a little to understand things, and a little to master them by help of science, which has forced its way step by step against the Christian religion, against the churches, and against the opposition of all the old precepts. Science can help us to get over this craven fear in which mankind has lived for so many generations. Science can teach us, and I think our own hearts can teach us, no longer to look around for imaginary supports, no longer to invent allies in the sky, but rather to look to our own efforts here below to make this world a fit place to live in, instead of the sort of place that the churches in all these centuries have made it.

What We Must Do

We want to stand upon our own feet and look fair and square at the 28 world—its good facts, its bad facts, its beauties, and its ugliness; see the world as it is and be not afraid of it. Conquer the world by intelligence and not merely by being slavishly subdued by the terror that comes from it. The whole conception of God is a conception derived from ancient Oriental despotisms. It is a conception quite unworthy of free men. When you hear people in church debasing themselves and saying that they are miserable sinners, and all the rest of it, it seems contemptible and not worthy of self-respecting human beings. We ought to stand up and look the world frankly in the face. We ought to make the best we can of the world, and if it is not so good as we wish, after all it will still be better than what these others have made of it in all these ages. A good world needs knowledge, kindliness, and courage; it does not need a regretful hankering after the past or a fettering of the free intelligence by the words uttered long ago by ignorant men. It needs a fearless outlook and a free intelligence.

It needs hope for the future, not looking back all the time toward a past that is dead, which we trust will be far surpassed by the future that our intelligence can create.

QUESTIONING AND DISCUSSING

Russell, "Why I Am Not a Christian"

1. Consider the ways in which Russell frames his argument—by presenting various arguments as the basis for Christian belief. What are they? Which arguments, to you, seem most effective? Less effective? Why?

2. Look up various definitions of *Christianity* in what might appear to be secular rather than religious sources, and compare them. Then, look up definitions in sources that are by definition religious. How do these definitions of the word differ? Based on this essay, what might be Russell's response to them?

3. Why does Russell concentrate only on Christianity? How might what he has written be said about any set of religious beliefs?

4. Russell argues to refute the "moral arguments for Deity." How is his argument moral—or not moral? Use examples from the text to make your points.

5. Comment on and analyze Russell's discussion of fear and emotions as contributing to religious belief. Whether you are religious or not, discuss ways in which you have witnessed this phenomenon in your own experience. How do these reactions contribute to organized religion? To what effect?

⊞

MICHAEL HARRINGTON

Once, during an appearance with conservative thinker and writer William Buckley, Michael Harrington (1928–1989) was introduced as a "foremost representative of socialist thought in the United States." Buckley wryly retorted, "That's like being called the tallest building in Topeka, Kansas." But Harrington is generally credited with being the person who awakened the United States to the searing issue of poverty. *The Other America* (1962) pointed out the contradictions of assumed prosperity in this country in the middle of the twentieth century. That is, more Americans were more prosperous than ever; however, one out of every four was locked in poverty. Born into a prosperous Irish Catholic Democratic family, Harrington said that he "only discovered the great Depression when he read about it in the serious Catholic schools" he attended. An outstanding student, Harrington graduated from Holy Cross College at nineteen and went to Yale Law School, doing so to please his parents. He left Yale to follow his desire to be a poet and went to the University of Chicago. According to the website of the Democratic Socialists of America, Harrington "eventually ended up at Dorothy Day's *Catholic Worker,* until he left not only the *Worker,* but the Catholic Church, eventually becoming the acknowledged socialist successor to Eugene V. Debs and Norman Thomas."

⊞

From *The Other America*

Introduction:
Poverty in the Seventies

In the Seventies the poor may become invisible again. And even if that 1
tragedy does not occur, there will still be tens of millions living in the other America when the country celebrates its two hundredth anniversary in 1976.

This prediction should be improbable. Lyndon B. Johnson declared an 2
"unconditional war" on poverty in 1964, Congress agreed, and for the next four years the White House recited awesome statistics on the billions that were being spent on social purposes. And the Sixties were a time of marches and militancy, of students and churches committing themselves to abolish want, and of documentary presentations of the nation's domestic shame by all the mass media. Indeed the impression of frenetic Government activity was so widespread that Richard Nixon campaigned in 1968 with a promise to slow down the pace of innovation. So how, then,

argue that poverty will persist in the Seventies and perhaps once again drop out of the society's conscience and consciousness?

3   As usual, the Government has carefully assembled the figures to debunk the former President's optimism and the current President's quietism. In every crucial area—food, housing, education and other social responsibilities—the United States provides its worst-off citizens only a percentage of what they desperately need. And since half of the poor are young people destined to enter a sophisticated economy at enormous disadvantage, unless countermeasures are taken the children of this generation's impoverished will become the parents of an even larger generation of the other America.

4   This is not to say there has been no progress. The boom generated by public policy in the Sixties did finally reduce the unemployment rates and there were people who made real, but precarious, gains as a result. And Medicare for the aged was the one program where there was something like a quantum jump in social investment, even though inflation vitiated part of its effect.

5   Still the very same groups which were poor when this book was written in 1961 and published in 1962 are poor today: the blacks, the Spanish-speaking, the unemployed and the underemployed, the citizens of depressed regions, the aging. And I should add one minority that I quite wrongly omitted from my original analysis: the American Indian, probably the poorest of all.

6   Yet even though the society has failed to redeem the pledges of the Sixties it has taken to celebrating paper triumphs over poverty. Thus in August of 1969 the Department of Commerce announced the happy news that the number of poverty-stricken had dropped from 39,000,000 to 25,000,000 in a matter of nine years. The only problem, as will be seen, is that the numbers prettied up the reality. This was a sign that, in the Seventies, America might be going back to the established procedures of the Eisenhower years, deluding itself with happy reports on the state of the nation. It was another ominous portent that one of Richard Nixon's top domestic advisers, Arthur Burns, said in the summer of 1969 that poverty is only an "intellectual concept" defined by "artificial statistics." That is precisely the kind of callous thinking that made the poor invisible in the first place. And it can happen again.

7   So in order to understand the cruel prospects for poverty in the Seventies, it is necessary to go behind the current optimism with its juggling of the social books. That is much more easily done now than in the early Sixties since this society, in one of its typical ironies, has spared no expense in recording its injustices. The problem is to examine the official figures critically and to glimpse the human faces and the tragic tendencies

that are hidden in them. Only then can we know how much still needs to be done.

In an economy drowning in data, many people think that statistics are 8 a neutral, scientific reflection of the objective world. Actually, the numbers depend on debatable and very political assumptions, which is how poverty can persist while some agencies of Government are preparing to celebrate its abolition.

When Lyndon Johnson declared his social war in the State of the 9 Union message of 1964, there was very little research to draw on. Much of it had been done by Robert Lampman, a dedicated scholar who had seen through the myth of universal prosperity in the Fifties. Using his work, the Council of Economic Advisers said in 1964 that poverty was a family income of less than $3,000 a year. That was a rough measure since it didn't take into account family size or geographic location, yet it was extremely useful in identifying the particular groups that were particularly afflicted.

In the next few years the criteria were made much more sophisticated. 10 In a brilliant attempt to define poverty objectively, the Social Security Administration took the Department of Agriculture's Economy Food Plan as a base figure. This was about 80 percent of the Low Cost Plan that many welfare agencies had used to figure budgets; it was a temporary, emergency diet. In January 1964 the Economy Plan provided $4.60 per person a week, or 22 cents a meal, and the "line" was $3,100. In 1967 it was $4.90 a week, and a four-person family was said to be poor if its income was below $3,335 a year. And in 1969, when the Department of Commerce was announcing its cheerful news, the poverty line was increased all the way up to $3,553 a year.

These definitions were drawn up by concerned public servants, some of 11 them with a deep personal commitment to abolish the outrage they were defining. But even when, in 1968, the poverty line was adjusted for increases in the cost of living on the Consumer Price Index, it was still much too low. For one thing, organized groups in the society, like the unions, and the professionals and technicians of the middle class, always strive to increase their annual income by more than the price of inflation. For it is assumed that one's absolute standard of living should increase every year. But the statisticians, by only correcting the poverty definition for rise of prices, are essentially saying that the poor should never progress as a group. And secondly, the inflationary increases of the late Sixties were most dramatic in the area of medical services and effectively canceled out all the increase in Medicare and forced some people out of Medicaid.

And before there is too much jubilation about the paper triumphs in 12 the war on poverty, it would be well to look at the report of the President's Commission on Income Maintenance Programs in 1969. It told the country that a Department of Labor study argued that the official definition should be increased by more than half (from $2.43 per person a day to $4.05). But even more revealing was the Commission's statement that, between 1965 and 1966, while 36% of the families were escaping poverty, 34% were falling into it. That emphasized how risky life was for those who had managed to scramble above the line; it meant that even in the middle of a boom and a "war" on poverty millions were being forced into the other America.

13   There was also another optimistic assumption in the official definition. The Economy Food Plan was taken as the base figure and it was assumed that all other needs would cost two times the grocery bill. As Herman Miller of the Bureau of the Census has pointed out, this relationship between diet and income was identified in 1955. So to keep up with changes in the economy and society since then, one should compute the other items at three times the price of food, not two. By using the assumptions of the Eisenhower Fifties, Miller concluded, the Government abolished the poverty of twelve million Americans who were still poor.

14   If it seems extreme to suggest that honest, and even concerned, experts could thus overlook the anguish of twelve million of their fellow citizens, consider the famous Census undercount in 1960. Almost six million Americans, mainly black adults living in Northern cities, were not even enumerated. Their lives were so marginal—no permanent address, no mail, no phone number, no regular job—that they did not even achieve the dignity of being a statistic. Here again the extent of misery was underestimated in drastic fashion but in this case the error has been publicly proclaimed.

15   When officialdom thus becomes too sanguine it is not simply the poor who suffer. To be sure they inhabit a subculture of special indignities in which institutions such as the police, the family and the schools behave differently than in the rest of the society. But they are also a part of the larger society and, when they are ignored, so are many, many millions who are not poor. Paradoxically, the white worker who was tempted to support George Wallace in 1968 because he was tired of the Government doing "too much" for the blacks and the poor will himself be hurt if the programs are cut back.

16   For there were in 1967 some twelve million citizens whom the Council of Economic Advisers called the "near poor" (with incomes between $3,335 and $4,345 for families of four). If these numbers were underestimated in the same way as the definition of poverty itself, then there are sixteen million Americans who are one illness, one accident, one recession away from being poor again. If, as now seems so possible, America in

the Seventies reduces its social efforts, this group will lose almost as much as the poor.

But there is another, and even larger, segment of the population whose destiny is, without their knowing it, related to that of the other Americans. In late 1966, which is light-years distant from the Seventies in terms of inflation, the Bureau of Labor Statistics figured that it would take $9,191 for a "moderate standard of living" for an urban family of four—you could buy a two-year-old used car and a new suit every four years. And a majority of the American people had less than that. They had to scrape for housing, food and education. And just as raising the minimum wage for the lowest paid workers tends to help raise the take of those who are organized and much better off, so turning our backs on the poor creates a political and social atmosphere in which the needs of the majority can be overlooked.   17

So the poor in the Seventies will be more numerous than the official figures admit. But perhaps the simplest way to get a summary view of the dangerous trends is to examine one generation of broken promises in the area of housing and to see that the Seventies will most likely be one more decade of failure.   18

The Government promised every citizen a decent dwelling in 1949. Under the leadership of a conservative Republican, Senator Robert A. Taft, the Congress agreed that the private housing market was not serving the needs of the poor. They therefore pledged to build 810,000 units of low-cost housing by 1955. In 1970, one generation later, that target has not yet been achieved. But then the problem was not just what the Government did not do but what it did instead. For while Washington was providing cheap money and princely tax deductions for more than ten million affluent home builders in suburbia, it was actually taking housing away from the poor. As the President's Commission on Urban Problems, chaired by Senator Paul Douglas, reported in January 1969, "Government action through urban renewal, highway programs, demolition on public housing sites, code enforcement and other programs has destroyed more housing for the poor than Government at all levels has built for them."   19

Thus it was that in 1968 a law was passed solemnly pledging the United States to do in the Seventies what it had solemnly pledged to do in the Fifties. But within a year it became clear that it was unlikely that the nation would redeem this second, shamefaced promise. To build twenty-six million new housing units in ten years, six million of them low-cost, would require speeding up the production of dwellings for the poor to twenty times the present rate. And as George Romney, the Secretary of Housing and Urban Development, admitted in 1969, it is quite possible that we will fall ten million units behind the official goal.   20

21   What this means for the Seventies is the further decay of the central cities of America, an increase in the already massive level of housing poverty which afflicts a third of the people—and the emergence of ghost towns in the middle of metropolis.

22   For the plight of the cities is becoming so grievous that even slums are not as profitable as they used to be. As a result, the Real Estate Research Corporation told the *Wall Street Journal* in 1969 that between ten and fifteen thousand buildings are being abandoned in the course of the year. In St. Louis, Missouri, for instance, there is a neighborhood I knew well as a child, for my grandfather lived there. It had big three-story homes and spacious lawns and backyards, and it was peopled by the white middle class. Returning to that familiar street twenty-five years later was like visiting a war zone. The houses were falling apart and some of them were boarded up and abandoned. That street was literally dying.

23   Many Americans would ride down that block and think that it proves that poor people don't care about property and will ruin a decent home if one is foolish enough to give them one. That is the exact opposite of the truth. That street, and the thousands like it in the big cities of America, is the result of one generation of broken promises, of massive economic trends like job relocation and inflation, which worked to isolate and imprison the poor, both black and white, in the ramshackle hand-me-down houses of the white middle class which had taken advantage of Federal subsidies and gone to suburbia.

24   On July 4, 1976, when the nation celebrates its two hundredth birthday, there will probably be more ghost towns in the cities.

25   But the statistics do not communicate the emotional quality of the Sixties when hopes were raised up so high and then dashed down. Perhaps a few personal experiences will.

26   In January 1964 Lyndon Johnson announced a war on poverty which John Kennedy had initiated within the Government but did not have the opportunity to proclaim publicly. In February, Sargent Shriver was named to head the effort. I went to Washington to have lunch with Shriver and stayed for two weeks as part of a task force which worked feverishly for sixteen or eighteen hours a day trying to define the basic concepts of the project.

27   The important thing was not just that the President was going to commit money to the war on poverty. More than that, the enormous moral and political power which the White House can summon was channeled into this undertaking. There was a sense of excitement, of social passion, in the capital. Friends of mine in the Government phoned to say that they would work at reduced pay and rank if only they could become a part of

this crusade. At the end of those hectic fourteen days, Frank Mankiewicz, Paul Jacobs and I drafted a memorandum for Shriver saying that bold innovations going beyond the New Deal were demanded if the job was going to be done. Shriver incorporated part of our analysis in his first presentation at the White House and, he told us, Mr. Johnson was not phased by the radical definition of the issue.

A few weeks later there was a rally at the Berkeley campus of the University of California. A large audience of students was enthusiastic when I talked of the Johnson program. These were the same young men and women who, within a matter of two or three years, were to become bitterly opposed to the President and who, in 1968, would help to drive him out of politics. And one of the reasons for their militant disenchantment would be, precisely, that they had trusted in the promises made in 1964.   28

In 1964 during the Presidential campaign the Teamsters Union in Los Angeles held a strike meeting. The leadership, knowing that strike and contract ratification votes always pull out a very large crowd, took the unusual step of scheduling an educational session before the business session. I told a jammed hall of white workers that it was in their economic interest to make common cause with the blacks and the poor in order to create a real full-employment economy. And there was loud, vocal support for that position.   29

Then the Community Action provisions of the Economic Opportunity Act had a positive effect. There was, as Daniel Patrick Moynihan has argued, a great deal of confusion over the meaning of "maximum feasible participation" of the poor in the war on poverty; mayors looked for more patronage and wanted the poor to be "deserving"; sociologists and psychologists saw an opportunity to test theories. But even though the Government began to retreat from the notion of democratic participation almost as soon as it was announced, the activists of the other America seized the moment.   30

In March of 1965 there was a demonstration in Oxnard, California. There was a mariachi band in the lead and a man on a horse and the procession wound its way through the Mexican-American section of town. This was an early manifestation of the movement which Cesar Chavez organized among the migrant farm workers—Philippine and Anglo as well as Mexican-American. With solid support from the established unions and help from students and religious people, Chavez for the first time in a generation had raised up the hopes of the men and women who harvest the grapes of wrath.   31

The farm workers in Oxnard were a new insurgency. That same month there was another demonstration in Montgomery, Alabama, which marked the culmination of a much older struggle. As the marchers from   32

Selma came to Montgomery with Martin Luther King, Jr., at their head, they were joined by tens of thousands who had come from every section of the country. As we moved toward the capital, we passed through black slums. The people sitting on the rickety porches were dazed by the massive show of solidarity. Some fell into the line of march; others stared in disbelief; some wept. The Negroes, with the trade unionists, priests, ministers, rabbis, nuns, liberal and radical politicals who were their allies, were in effect winning the Voting Rights Act of 1965.

33   We stood in front of the capitol and everywhere Confederate flags were flying. And so the crowd defiantly sang "The Star-Spangled Banner," and the national anthem suddenly became a hymn of militant hope that the nation could become one. And had the forces represented there in Montgomery remained united, they would have represented a majority of the electorate. But they did not. For at this very moment of triumph, President Johnson was preparing the escalation of the war in Vietnam. The anti-poverty programs continued and the rhetoric remained bold. But the moral and political energy of Washington, as well as tens of billions of dollars, were not channeled into the right war at home but into the wrong war in Southeast Asia.

34   The black poor became bitter and disillusioned, and the most militant among them turned against the whole system. A minority of the idealistic students were driven into an impotent, but shrill, intransigence; the majority joined the Robert Kennedy and Eugene McCarthy movements in 1968 and helped to force the President out of the race. The unionists maintained their commitment to fight poverty—they contribute more political strength to the legislative effort than any other group—but they also supported Johnson's war policy. So as Vietnam came increasingly to dominate all of American lives, the allies who had stood together that March afternoon in Montgomery turned upon one another.

35   And finally, there were the funerals of 1968.

36   Martin Luther King, Jr., died in the midst of a Poor People's Campaign which sought an economic bill of rights for all Americans. The day before he was buried, the groups that had assembled in Montgomery—the blacks, the unionists, the liberals and radicals from the middle class, the churches—came together in Memphis. For when King was murdered he was working with striking sanitation men who were fighting for union recognition. Now in the name of the dead leader, we marched through an almost completely deserted downtown. The people of Memphis had stayed home that day and the only sound in the center of the city was the eerie tread of feet. At the side streets there were contingents of Federalized guardsmen who were there to protect our constitutional rights.

For ironically, the death of the greatest American spokesman of nonvi- 37
olence had occasioned riots and tension throughout the land. That was
how bitter the struggle had become.

And then in June of 1968 Robert Kennedy was killed. To the people of 38
the other America, it seemed that fate was depriving them of the leaders
who understood them and fought for them. I had supported Kennedy because I believed that he was uniquely able to talk to both white trade
unionists and the poor, both black and white. One meeting in California
during the primary was symbolic of that hope to me: I spoke along with
Cesar Chavez and John Lewis, the chairman of the Student Nonviolent
Coordinating Committee in its early, nonviolent days. But in June an as-
sassin put an end to that dream of a movement which would reach out to
the blacks, the Spanish-speaking, the unionists, the middle-class idealists.

That funeral train seemed to me to carry the finest hopes of the decade 39
along with the body of the dead Senator. It passed through the other
America because the affluent never live in sight of the tracks but the poor
do. And those tens of thousands standing there—sometimes singing,
sometimes saluting, sometimes simply present, silent—were mourning their
own aspirations along with the man who had spoken for them. For in the
1960s, the greatest opportunity for social change since the New Deal was
sacrificed to the tragedy in Vietnam. And the Seventies will inherit a
legacy of disillusionment and the memory of these tragic deaths.

So after all the broken promises and false starts Richard Nixon was 40
elected President and told the people that the Federal Government had
tried to do too much and that he would therefore decentralize social programs and set more modest goals. There was a half-truth and a dangerous
falsehood in his analysis, and that bodes ill for the poor in the Seventies.

Under Lyndon Johnson the Administration had indeed talked as if it 41
were undertaking, and accomplishing, prodigies. One of the reasons why
a disturbing number of white workers turned toward George Wallace in
1968 (even though, outside the South, they eventually voted for Hubert
Humphrey) was that they were under the impression that Washington
had done so much for the poor, and particularly the Negroes among them.
They confused the bold rhetoric with action and did not understand that
life in the ghettos had changed very little. Insofar as Nixon taxes Johnson
for having talked too loudly, he is right. But the rest of his thesis—that the
Government was too activist, efforts must be cut back and turned over to
the states—is very much wrong.

In order to destroy this myth of the favored, pampered poor one need 42
only consider a few of the official figures. In 1968 the National Commission

on Civil Disorders—the "Riot" Commission—reported that in Detroit, New Haven and Newark, the cities where the violence was the most destructive in 1967, the median percentage of those eligible who were actually covered by any one of the major social programs was 33 percent. In other words, in the United States a majority of the poor are not on welfare at all. And, the Commission showed, the national average for welfare payments is "a little more than one half of need"—and in some cases one fourth of need. In January 1969 a special Cabinet committee reported to Lyndon Johnson that the existing domestic programs were already underfunded by $6 billion and that a moderate expansion of civilian efforts along lines already suggested by various commissions and study groups would cost another $40 billion by 1972.

43   So the statistics are clear enough: the Government by its own standards is falling billions of dollars behind modest estimates of what should be done. Among the minority of the poor lucky enough to get any money there are millions who must exist on a half or a fourth of their urgent needs. Moreover these people are often victimized by what the nonpoor think of them. To many citizens, people who receive welfare are thought of as a burden upon the hard-working common man. But, as Richard Titmus has pointed out, what is really happening is that many of the poor are being undercompensated for humiliations which the Government and the economy, or both, have visited upon them.

44   The most dramatic case in point is the rural poor who were driven into the cities in recent years. Billions of dollars in Federal subsidies were paid to rich individuals and corporate farmers—including hundreds of thousands to Senator James O. Eastland, the impartial plantation owner who sits on the Senate Agricultural Committee and helps determine his own rewards. These princely welfare payments to the wealthy allowed them to make a profit by reducing the land under cultivation and also provided them with funds for mechanization. So it was that productivity in the fields increased twice as fast as in the factories, and millions of the rural poor became economically superfluous.

45   Between 1950 and 1966 Federal monies thus helped to force 5.5 million black farm workers into the cities. They came from areas where education for Negroes was substandard and they were required to relate to a bewildering, complex urban environment and compete in a sophisticated labor market. They brought with them, as Harold Fleming has said, "the largest accumulation of social deficits ever visited upon an identifiable group. Now these people often seem to the average taxpayer to be a burden, yet the real source of the problem was the Federal policy to pay billions to the agricultural rich in such a way as to exile the poor from the land. In other words, most of the people on welfare rolls are victims of government ac-

tion and technological progress. They receive only a fraction of the compensation they deserve, not in charity but in justice.

In short, it is not that Washington has done too much but that it has so often done too much of the wrong thing. And the central thesis of Mr. Nixon's 1969 welfare message—"A third of a century of centralizing power in Washington has produced a bureaucratic monstrosity, cumbersome, unresponsive, ineffective"—is just not an accurate description of what happened. Moreover, Mr. Nixon's major welfare proposal to establish a minimum income for families contradicts his own analysis, for it proposes to *Federalize* welfare benefits at a certain level. Mr. Nixon was quite rightly disturbed that Mississippi pays an average of $39.35 a month to support an entire family while New York has much higher standards. He therefore wants to use the Federal power to force Mississippi from abusing its states' rights in such an inhumane way, which is hardly decentralization.

So the President who will set the policy guidelines for at least the first period of the Seventies has a superficial, contradictory theory of poverty. And some of the problems he will confront will be even more serious than those faced by Lyndon Johnson.

One of the most disturbing facts about the poor is that roughly half of them are young. They will be flooding into the labor market so fast in 1975 that the Department of Labor expects that there will be 25 percent more 16–19-year-olds looking for a job than in 1965—and 50 percent more black youths. This will happen at a time when the blue-collar positions for which they will be competing will be opening up at a rate of about 15 percent a year. In other words, there is a very real possibility that many, even most, of the children of the poor will become the fathers and mothers of the poor. If that were to take place, then America would, for the first time in history, have a hereditary underclass.

These dangerous trends did not explode in the Sixties, but two of the reasons were Vietnam and inflation. The nation's tragic commitment to the horror in Southeast Asia created 700,000 new "jobs" in the armed forces and a million new openings in defense industry. Since 80 percent of the draftees had high-school diplomas, the army did not actually take the poor in but removed some of their competition from the labor market. Then with inflation after 1965—which was triggered by a $10 billion "mistake" in Federal spending based upon optimistic assumptions about a victory in the war in 1966—the labor market tightened up even more.

But with peace in Vietnam, what are the acceptable substitutes for the employment generated by war and inflation? The policy answer to that question will not be found in a quietist Presidency but in radical new programs.

And yet every once in a while the President does recognize some of his difficulties rhetorically. In his Population Message to Congress in the summer of 1969, Nixon attacked a sweeping proposal of the National Committee on Urban Growth Policy for not being sufficiently daring. The Commission—which included Democratic regulars such as Hale Boggs and John Sparkman and even a Goldwater Republican, John Tower—had said that the nation must build ten new cities for one million citizens each and ten new towns for 100,000 inhabitants. After noting that there will be 100 million additional Americans by the year 2000, three quarters of them living in urbanized areas, the President said of the Commission's suggestion, "But the total number of people who would be accommodated if even those bold plans were implemented is *only* twenty million—a *mere* one fifth of the expected thirty-year increase." (Italics added.)

52   So Mr. Nixon is rightly saying that, unless there are radical innovations, the housing problem will become worse. Since his own Administration cut back on Model Cities spending and is doing even less than Mr. Johnson did, when Nixon insists upon how enormous the problem is, that is a way of saying that the failure of the 1949 Housing Act will endure half a century to the year 2000. In the 1968 campaign, the President would have dealt with the issue by suggesting that private enterprise would do the job for a profit. But the Committee he criticized for not going far enough found that private development of new towns and cities occurs only in "rare circumstances." For these ventures demand a tremendous investment in social capital, which free enterprise simply will not make.

53   In short, as the Seventies open there is every indication that housing poverty will become even more acute and that the children of the last decade's poor will, as parents in an economy without enough decent jobs, increase the size of the other America. Such tragedies are not, of course, fated; they will be the result of political choices. And even though the Nixon Administration has given every indication of not understanding the problem, it is still important to summarize briefly what must be done.

54   First of all there must be planning. There should be an Office of the Future attached to the Presidency and a Joint Congressional Committee on the Future which would receive, debate and adopt or modify annual reports from the White House (I spelled out this suggestion in *Toward a Democratic Left.*)

55   This proposition might sound strange to American ears, yet there are signs that moderates, and even conservatives, are beginning to appreciate its logic. In his Population Message, President Nixon considered the prospect of 100 million additional citizens in a third of a century and asked, "Are our cities prepared for such an influx? The chaotic history of urban growth suggests they are not and that many problems will be severely aggravated by a dramatic increase in numbers." And a little later he

got to the heart of the matter: "Perhaps the most dangerous element in the present situation is that so few people are examining these questions from the viewpoint of the whole society."

Precisely. Suburban home builders, automobile manufacturers and trucking companies all pick up their huge Federal subsidies without a thought of pollution, isolating the central-city slum or ravaging the countryside. And now—not simply if poverty is to be abolished, but if the quality of life in America is to be kept from deteriorating—we must adopt long-range priorities and consider the "side effects" of new technologies even more scrupulously than we do with new drugs. A year before his death, Dwight Eisenhower urged the building of new cities, racially and socially integrated and with new jobs. Mr. Nixon apparently agrees. But the enormously complex planning needed to accomplish such a task is not going to be done by the invisible hand of Adam Smith.   56

Secondly, there must be billions of dollars in social investments.   57

President Nixon, like President Johnson before him, hopes that all of these crises can be met by hiring private enterprise to do the job. Mr. Nixon's first version of this philosophy was called "black capitalism," and he ordered the concept extended to all the impoverished minorities when he took office. But the blunt economic facts of life are that costs in the slums are twice as high as in the suburbs, congestion much more serious, the labor market relatively untrained—i.e., all of the miseries which the nation has imposed upon the poor make their neighborhoods unprofitable for big business. Minority enterprises can, of course, make a contribution to their areas and should be helped generously, but for the vast majority they offer no real hope.   58

But then as the Sixties were ending there did seem to be one area when the cooperation of the public and the private sector worked: employment. The National Association of Businessmen, with strong Federal help, is trying to put poverty-stricken and minority workers into good jobs and there has been a lot of publicity about the gains that have been made. However, a 1969 analysis by the *Wall Street Journal* was not so sanguine. The main reason for these hirings, Alan Otten wrote, was the tight labor market, and any increase in unemployment—which is inevitable given the Nixon strategy against inflation—would turn these people back out on the streets. Yet when the Automobile Workers Union proposed to the Ford Corporation that its older members be permitted to take a voluntary layoff so that the new men could stay on, the company refused. The reason was simple enough: the supplementary unemployment compensation for a veteran is costlier than for a new worker. And in the winter of 1970 the layoffs in the auto industry began and hit precisely those men who had   59 been recruited with such fanfare. The calculus of profit was stronger than social conscience.

60   Therefore new cities for 100 million new Americans and decent jobs for all will come only if there are large social investments. Early in the Seventies the Gross National Product of the United States will pass the $1 trillion mark. As an article in *Fortune* calculated this trend, there would be a fiscal "dividend"—the automatic increase in Government income without any rise in taxes which takes place when the GNP becomes larger—of $38 billion in 1974 and around $80 billion by 1980. The problem under these circumstances is not finding the resources but being intelligent enough to use them democratically and creatively. To do that the nation should adopt the Economic Bill of Rights advocated by Martin Luther King, Jr., in the last days of his life: every citizen has a right either to a decent job or to an adequate income.

61   In his 1969 welfare message, President Nixon made that sharp attack on the unevenness of the present, states'-rights welfare system. But in his positive proposals he urged Congress to delegate even more power to the very local administrations which had previously abused it, and he came out for a Federal minimum which would leave people well below the poverty line. In the Nixon program, Washington would provide the funds to bring family payments up to $1600 a year (and food stamps would add another $900), and the twenty states which now pay less than that would be required to contribute only half of their present welfare spending to the total.

62   Instead of thus institutionalizing a Federal minimum which is well below the poverty line, the United States should adopt the principle that all of its citizens are legally entitled to a decent income. Lyndon Johnson's outgoing Cabinet computed that one version of such a social investment—a negative income tax—would cost between $15 and $20 billion a year. Given the *Fortune* prediction of an $80 billion dividend by 1980, that amount is clearly within the country's means.

63   Such a program should have, of course, a work incentive. Instead of the typical American practice of taxing the earnings of the welfare recipient 100 percent (by reducing his benefits by the amount of his wages), the individual should be allowed to keep a decreasing portion of his income supplement as his pay goes up. But this also means that there must be a vast increase in the number of decent jobs. In New York City, where Aid for Dependent Children payments are around the level of menial jobs in the economy, there is no motive for mothers to look for work and they haven't. So a guaranteed income with a work incentive means a commitment to genuine full employment.

And that is where the notion of a guaranteed income ties in with the 64 right to work. It was Franklin Roosevelt who first urged, in the campaign of 1944, that if the private economy does not provide jobs for the people, then the public economy must. If, after a generation of inexcusable hesitation, we finally adopt this proposal it would mean that the society could channel the enormous unused resource of the unemployed and the underemployed into constructing a new, livable environment. If the promises of the Housing Acts of 1949 and 1968 were carried out, there would be a labor shortage and the country would discover that it really needs the poor and the near poor. And the effect of such a program would not be inflationary because these workers would be producing valuable goods and services for their wages.

So the Seventies need planned, long-range social investments to pro- 65 vide a decent home for every citizen and to guarantee either a living income or a good job for all. But as the decade begins, the nation, including its Chief Executive, believes in myths which keep us from even defining the problem as it is. They think we tried too much when actually we did so little. And the official thinkers and statisticians are even winning paper victories over poverty and making the poor invisible.

Therefore there is reason for pessimism. But if these menacing trends 66 are to be reversed, then America must understand one crucial proposition: that it is in the interest of the entire society to end the outrage of the other America.

The poor are the most sorely tried and dramatic victims of economic 67 and social tendencies which threaten the entire nation. They suffer most grievously from unplanned, chaotic urbanization, but millions of the affluent are affected too. They are the first to experience technological progress as a curse which destroys the old muscle-power jobs that previous generations used as a means to fight their way out of poverty. Yet, as the current student radicalism makes clear, the nature of work is also becoming problematic for the most advantaged in the society. If, in other words, the cities sprawl and technology revolutionizes the land in a casual, thoughtless way, polluting the very fundamentals of human existence, like air and water, it is the poor who will be most cruelly used but the entire nation will experience a kind of decadence.

In morality and in justice every citizen should be committed to abolish- 68 ing the other America, for it is intolerable that the richest nation in human history should allow such needless suffering. But more than that, if we solve the problem of the other America we will have learned how to solve the problems of all of America.

Harrington, From *The Other America*

1. This is a revised introduction written in 1969 by Harrington for his ground-breaking 1962 exposé of poverty, *The Other America*. How does Harrington's revised introduction, looking back on the years before 1969 and forecasting the 1970s, illuminate his position on poverty in the United States? Research names and events that seem unfamiliar to you to expand the historical and political context of Harrington's positions.

2. Among Harrington's many quotable statements is this: "People who are much too sensitive to demand of cripples that they run races ask of the poor that they get up and act just like everybody else in society." How does this introduction also evidence Harrington's accusation of people's insensitivity toward the poor?

3. In 1969, Harrington predicted the following for the 1970s regarding poverty in America: "the further decay of the central cities of America, an increase in the already massive level of housing poverty which afflicts a third of the people—and the emergence of ghost towns in the middle of metropolis." How has history proven Harrington correct? Has there been any improvement? Conduct research to prove your points, and cite your sources carefully.

4. What does Harrington mean when he says that "every once in a while the President [referring to Nixon] does recognize some of his difficulties rhetorically." In what ways is Harrington making a moral as well as a rhetorical argument?

⊞

PAULA GUNN ALLEN

A critic, novelist, and poet concerned with issues related to American Indians (her background is Lebanese, Laguna, and Sioux), Paula Gunn Allen (1943–) was born and spent her childhood in New Mexico, the middle child of five. She earned her BA and MFA at the University of Oregon, and while completing her doctoral degree, she taught at DeAnza Community College and at the University of New Mexico. Allen earned her PhD in 1976 from the University of New Mexico and has since taught at UCLA, the University of California at Berkeley, San Diego State, and other institutions. Her publications include *Spider Woman's Granddaughters: Traditional Tales and Contemporary Writing* (1990), for which she received the American Book Award, and *Life Is a Fatal Disease: Collected Poems 1962–1995.* Paula Gunn Allen is currently Professor of English at the University of California at Los Angeles.

⌗

Where I Come from Is Like This

I

Modern American Indian women, like their non-Indian sisters, are deeply engaged in the struggle to redefine themselves. In their struggle they must reconcile traditional tribal definitions of women with industrial and postindustrial non-Indian definitions. Yet while these definitions seem to be more or less mutually exclusive, Indian women must somehow harmonize and integrate both in their own lives. 1

An American Indian woman is primarily defined by her tribal identity. In her eyes, her destiny is necessarily that of her people, and her sense of herself as a woman is first and foremost prescribed by her tribe. The definitions of woman's roles are as diverse as tribal cultures in the Americas. In some she is devalued, in others she wields considerable power. In some she is a familial/clan adjunct, in some she is as close to autonomous as her economic circumstances and psychological traits permit. But in no tribal definitions is she perceived in the same way as are women in Western industrial and postindustrial cultures. 2

In the West, few images of women form part of the cultural mythos, and these are largely sexually charged. Among Christians, the Madonna is the female prototype, and she is portrayed as essentially passive: her contribution is simply that of birthing. Little else is attributed to her and she certainly possesses few of the characteristics that are attributed to mythic 3 figures among Indian tribes. This image is countered (rather than balanced) by the witch-goddess/whore characteristics designed to reinforce cultural beliefs about women, as well as Western adversarial and dualistic perceptions of reality.

4   The tribes see women variously, but they do not question the power of femininity. Sometimes they see women as fearful, sometimes peaceful, sometimes omnipotent and omniscient, but they never portray women as mindless, helpless, simple, or oppressed. And while the women in a given tribe, clan, or band may be all these things, the individual woman is provided with a variety of images of women from the interconnected supernatural, natural, and social worlds she lives in.

5   As a half-breed American Indian woman, I cast about in my mind for negative images of Indian women, and I find none that are directed to Indian women alone. The negative images I do have are of Indians in general and in fact are more often of males than of females. All these images come to me from non-Indian sources, and they are always balanced by a positive image. My ideas of womanhood, passed on largely by my mother and grandmothers, Laguna Pueblo women, are about practicality, strength, reasonableness, intelligence, wit, and competence. I also remember vividly the women who came to my father's store, the women who held me and sang to me, the women at Feast Day, at Grab Days, the women in the kitchen of my Cubero home, the women I grew up with; none of them appeared weak or helpless, none of them presented herself tentatively. I remember a certain reserve on those lovely brown faces; I remember the direct gaze of eyes framed by bright-colored shawls draped over their heads and cascading down their backs. I remember the clean cotton dresses and carefully pressed hand-embroidered aprons they always wore; I remember laughter and good food, especially the sweet bread and the oven bread they gave us. Nowhere in my mind is there a foolish woman, a dumb woman, a vain woman, or a plastic woman, though the Indian women I have known have shown a wide range of personal style and demeanor.

6   My memory includes the Navajo woman who was badly beaten by her Sioux husband; but I also remember that my grandmother abandoned her Sioux husband long ago. I recall the stories about the Laguna woman beaten regularly by her husband in the presence of her children so that the children would not believe in the strength and power of femininity. And I remember the women who drank, who got into fights with other women and with the men, and who often won those battles. I have memories of tired women, partying women, stubborn women, sullen women, amicable women, selfish women, shy women, and aggressive women. Most of all I remember the women who laugh and scold and sit uncom-

plaining in the long sun on feast days and who cook wonderful food on wood stoves, in beehive mud ovens, and over open fires outdoors.

Among the images of women that come to me from various tribes as 7 well as my own are White Buffalo Woman, who came to the Lakota long ago and brought them the religion of the Sacred Pipe which they still practice; Tinotzin the goddess who came to Juan Diego to remind him that she still walked the hills of her people and sent him with her message, her demand, and her proof to the Catholic bishop in the city nearby. And from Laguna I take the images of Yellow Woman, Coyote Woman, Grandmother Spider (Spider Old Woman), who brought the light, who gave us weaving and medicine, who gave us life. Among the Keres she is known as Thought Woman who created us all and who keeps us in creation even now. I remember Iyatiku, Earth Woman, Corn Woman, who guides and counsels the people to peace and who welcomes us home when we cast off this coil of flesh as huskers cast off the leaves that wrap the corn. I remember Iyatiku's sister, Sun Woman, who held metals and cattle, pigs and sheep, highways and engines and so many things in her bundle, who went away to the east saying that one day she would return.

II

Since the coming of the Anglo-Europeans beginning in the fifteenth cen- 8 tury, the fragile web of identity that long held tribal people secure has gradually been weakened and torn. But the oral tradition has prevented the complete destruction of the web, the ultimate disruption of tribal ways. The oral tradition is vital; it heals itself and the tribal web by adapting to the flow of the present while never relinquishing its connection to the past. Its adaptability has always been required, as many generations have experienced. Certainly the modern American Indian woman bears slight resemblance to her forebears—at least on superficial examination—but she is still a tribal woman in her deepest being. Her tribal sense of relationship to all that is continues to flourish. And though she is at times beset by her knowledge of the enormous gap between the life she lives and the life she was raised to live, and while she adapts her mind and being to the circumstances of her present life, she does so in tribal ways, mending the tears in the web of being from which she takes her existence as she goes.

My mother told me stories all the time, though I often did not recognize 9 them as that. My mother told me stories about cooking and childbearing; she told me stories about menstruation and pregnancy; she told me stories about gods and heroes, about fairies and elves, about goddesses and spirits; she told me stories about the land and the sky, about cats and dogs, about snakes and spiders; she told me stories about climbing trees and exploring the mesas; she told me stories about going to dances and getting married; she told me stories about dressing and undressing, about sleeping and waking; she told me stories about herself, about her mother, about her grandmother. She told me stories about grieving and laughing, about thinking and doing; she told me stories about school and about people; about darning and mending; she told me stories about turquoise and about gold; she told me European stories and Laguna stories; she told me Catholic stories and Presbyterian stories; she told me city stories and country stories; she told me political stories and religious stories. She told me stories about living and stories about dying. And in all of those stories she told me who I was, who I was supposed to be, whom I came from, and who would follow me. In this way she taught me the meaning of the words she said, that all life is a circle and everything has a place within it. That's what she said and what she showed me in the things she did and the way she lives.

10   Of course, through my formal, white, Christian education, I discovered that other people had stories of their own—about women, about Indians, about fact, about reality—and I was amazed by a number of startling suppositions that others made about tribal customs and beliefs. According to the un-Indian, non-Indian view, for instance, Indians barred menstruating women from ceremonies and indeed segregated them from the rest of the people, consigning them to some space specially designed for them. This showed that Indians considered menstruating women unclean and not fit to enjoy the company of decent (nonmenstruating) people, that is, men. I was surprised and confused to hear this because my mother had taught me that white people had strange attitudes toward menstruation: they thought something was bad about it, that it meant you were sick, cursed, sinful, and weak and that you had to be careful during that time. She taught me that menstruation was a normal occurrence, that I could go swimming or hiking or whatever else I wanted to do during my period. She actively scorned women who took to their beds, who were incapacitated by cramps, who "got the blues."

11   As I struggled to reconcile these very contradictory interpretations of American Indians' traditional beliefs concerning menstruation, I realized that the menstrual taboos were about power, not about sin or filth. My conclusion was later borne out by some tribes' own explanations, which, as you may well imagine, came as quite a relief to me.

12   The truth of the matter as many Indians see it is that women who are at the peak of their fecundity are believed to possess power that throws male power totally out of kilter. They emit such force that, in their presence, any male-owned or -dominated ritual or sacred object cannot do its usual task. For instance, the Lakota say that a menstruating woman anywhere near a yuwipi man, who is a special sort of psychic, spirit-empowered

healer, for a day or so before he is to do his ceremony will effectively dis-empower him. Conversely, among many if not most tribes, important cer-emonies cannot be held without the presence of women. Sometimes the ritual woman who empowers the ceremony must be unmarried and vir-ginal so that the power she channels is unalloyed, unweakened by sexual arousal and penetration by a male. Other ceremonies require tumescent women, others the presence of mature women who have borne children, and still others depend for empowerment on postmenopausal women. Women may be segregated from the company of the whole band or village on certain occasions, but on certain occasions men are also segregated. In short, each ritual depends on a certain balance of power, and the positions of women within the phases of womanhood are used by tribal people to empower certain rites. This does not derive from a male-dominant view; it is not a ritual observance imposed on women by men. It derives from a tribal view of reality that distinguishes tribal people from feudal and in-dustrial people.

Among the tribes, the occult power of women, inextricably bound to our hormonal life, is thought to be very great; many hold that we possess innately the blood-given power to kill—with a glance, with a step, or with a judicious mixing of menstrual blood into somebody's soup. Medi-cine women among the Pomo of California cannot practice until they are sufficiently mature; when they are immature, their power is diffuse and is likely to interfere with their practice until time and experience have it under control. So women of the tribes are not especially inclined to see themselves as poor helpless victims of male domination. Even in those tribes where something akin to male domination was present, women are perceived as powerful, socially, physically, and metaphysically. In times past, as in times present, women carried enormous burdens with aplomb. We were far indeed from the "weaker sex," the designation that white aristocratic sisters unhappily earned for us all. 13

I remember my mother moving furniture all over the house when she wanted it changed. She didn't wait for my father to come home and help—she just went ahead and moved the piano, a huge upright from the old days, the couch, the refrigerator. Nobody had told her she was too weak to do such things. In imitation of her, I would delight in loading trucks at my father's store with cases of pop or fifty-pound sacks of flour. Even when I was quite small I could do it, and it gave me a belief in my own physical strength that advancing middle age can't quite erase. My mother used to tell me about the Acoma Pueblo women she had seen as a child carrying huge ollas (water pots) on their heads as they wound their way up the tortuous stairwell carved into the face of the "Sky City" mesa, a feat I tried to imitate with books and tin buckets. ("Sky City" is the term 14 used by the chamber of commerce for the mother village of Acoma, which is situated atop a high sandstone table mountain.) I was never very successful, but even the attempt reminded me that I was supposed to be strong and balanced to be a proper girl.

15　　Of course, my mother's Laguna people are Keres Indian, reputed to be the last extreme mother-right people on earth. So it is no wonder that I got notably nonwhite notions about the natural strength and prowess of women. Indeed, it is only when I am trying to get non-Indian approval, recognition, or acknowledgment that my "weak sister" emotional and intellectual ploys get the better of my tribal woman's good sense. At such times I forget that I just moved the piano or just wrote a competent paper or just completed a financial transaction satisfactorily or have supported myself and my children for most of my adult life.

16　　Nor is my contradictory behavior atypical. Most Indian women I know are in the same bicultural bind: we vacillate between being dependent and strong, self-reliant and powerless, strongly motivated and hopelessly insecure. We resolve the dilemma in various ways: some of us party all the time; some of us drink to excess; some of us travel and move around a lot; some of us land good jobs and then quit them; some of us engage in violent exchanges; some of us blow our brains out. We act in these destructive ways because we suffer from the societal conflicts caused by having to identify with two hopelessly opposed cultural definitions of women. Through this destructive dissonance we are unhappy prey to the self-disparagement common to, indeed demanded of, Indians living in the United States today. Our situation is caused by the exigencies of a history of invasion, conquest, and colonization whose searing marks are probably ineradicable. A popular bumper sticker on many Indian cars proclaims: "If You're Indian You're In," to which I always find myself adding under my breath, "Trouble."

17　　No Indian can grow to any age without being informed that her people were "savages" who interfered with the march of progress pursued by respectable, loving, civilized white people. We are the villains of the scenario when we are mentioned at all. We are absent from much of white history except when we are calmly, rationally, succinctly, and systematically dehumanized. On the few occasions we are noticed in any way other than as howling, bloodthirsty beings, we are acclaimed for our noble quaintness. In this definition, we are exotic curios. Our ancient arts and customs are used to draw tourist money to state coffers, into the pocketbooks and bank accounts of scholars, and into support of the American-in-Disneyland promoters' dream.

18　　As a Roman Catholic child I was treated to bloody tales of how the savage Indians martyred the hapless priests and missionaries who went among them in an attempt to lead them to the one true path. By the time I was through high school I had the idea that Indians were people who had benefited mightily from the advanced knowledge and superior morality of the Anglo-Europeans. At least I had, perforce, that idea to lay beside the other one that derived from my daily experience of Indian life, an idea less dehumanizing and more accurate because it came from my mother and the other Indian people who raised me. That idea was that Indians are a people who don't tell lies, who care for their children and their old people. You never see an Indian orphan, they said. You always know when you're old that someone will take care of you—one of your children will. Then they'd list the old folks who were being taken care of by this child or that. No child is ever considered illegitimate among the Indians, they said. If a girl gets pregnant, the baby is still part of the family, and the mother is too. That's what they said, and they showed me real people who lived according to those principles.

Of course the ravages of colonization have taken their toll; there are orphans in Indian country now, and abandoned, brutalized old folks; there are even illegitimate children, though the very concept still strikes me as absurd. There are battered children and neglected children, and there are battered wives and women who have been raped by Indian men. Proximity to the "civilizing" effects of white Christians has not improved the moral quality of life in Indian country, though each group, Indian and white, explains the situation differently. Nor is there much yet in the oral tradition that can enable us to adapt to these inhuman changes. But a force is growing in that direction, and it is helping Indian women reclaim their lives. Their power, their sense of direction and of self will soon be visible. It is the force of the women who speak and work and write, and it is formidable. 19

Through all the centuries of war and death and cultural and psychic destruction have endured the women who raise the children and tend the fires, who pass along the tales and the traditions, who weep and bury the dead, who are the dead, and who never forget. There are always the women, who make pots and weave baskets, who fashion clothes and cheer their children on at powwow, who make fry bread and piki bread, and corn soup and chili stew, who dance and sing and remember and hold within their hearts the dream of their ancient peoples—that one day the woman who thinks will speak to us again, and everywhere there will be peace. Meanwhile we tell the stories of fun and scandal and laugh over all manner of things that happen every day. We watch and we wait. 20

My great-grandmother told my mother: Never forget you are Indian. And my mother told me the same thing. This, then, is how I have gone about remembering, so that my children will remember too. 21

QUESTIONING AND DISCUSSING

Gunn Allen, *"Where I Come From Is Like This"*

1. What are the stereotypes of American Indians? How are these stereotypes fashioned by the larger society? How does Gunn Allen attempt to reframe those stereotypes?

2. Analyze and discuss the "dualities" presented in this essay—for instance, being defined by one's tribal identity and also by one's "other" identity—and the additional conflicts Gunn Allen articulates. What are the effects of these dualities and conflicts?

3. How are issues of power important factors to Gunn Allen in explaining issues of identity? Consider, for instance, the statement that "the menstrual taboos were about power, not about sin or filth." How might this—and other examples from the text—be true in other cultures?

4. In what ways are Gunn Allen's arguments also about ethics and values? Consider the closing paragraph: "My great-grandmother told my mother: Never forget you are Indian. And my mother told me the same thing. This, then, is how I have gone about remembering, so that my children will remember too." What are the importance and the significance of remembering? What are the components of this remembering, and why is one obligated to do it? (Is it as important, say, for those from more "mainstream" cultures within the United States, or is it of equal importance for everyone? Why?)

⊞

RICHARD WRIGHT

A powerful, influential American writer, Richard Wright (1908–1960) was born to sharecroppers in Natchez, Mississippi. Wright attended high school in Jackson, and he began his writing career when he moved to Memphis, Tennessee. In 1927, he moved to Chicago, worked a variety of jobs, and in the 1930s became part of the Federal Writing Project, joining the Communist Party for several years. Wright moved to Paris after the Second World War. Particularly noted for his novel *Native Son* (1940) and his autobiography, *Black Boy* (1945), Wright also published story collections that include *Uncle Tom's Children* (1938) and *Eight Men* (1961).

⊞

The Man Who Went to Chicago

When I rose in the morning the temperature had dropped below zero. The house was as cold to me as the Southern streets had been in winter. I dressed, doubling my clothing. I ate in a restaurant, caught a streetcar, and rode south, rode until I could see no more black faces on the sidewalks. I had now crossed the boundary line of the Black Belt and had entered the territory where jobs were perhaps to be had from white folks. I walked the streets and looked into shop windows until I saw a sign in a delicatessen: PORTER WANTED.

I went in and a stout white woman came to me. 2

"Vat do you vant?" she asked. 3

The voice jarred me. She's Jewish, I thought, remembering with shame 4 the obscenities I used to shout at Jewish storekeepers in Arkansas.

"I thought maybe you needed a porter," I said. 5

"Meester 'Offman, he eesn't here yet," she said. "Vill you vait?" 6

"Yes, ma'am." 7

"Seet down." 8

"No, ma'am, I'll wait outside." 9

"But eet's cold out zhere," she said. 10

"That's all right," I said. 11

She shrugged. I went to the sidewalk. I waited for half an hour in the 12 bitter cold, regretting that I had not remained in the warm store, but unable to go back inside. A bald, stoutish white man went into the store and pulled off his coat. Yes, he was the boss man . . .

"Zo you vant a job?" he asked. 13

"Yes, sir," I answered, guessing at the meaning of his words. 14

15   "Vhere you vork before?"

16   "In Memphis, Tennessee."

17   "My brudder-in-law vorked in Tennessee vonce," he said.

18   I was hired. The work was easy, but I found to my dismay that I could not understand a third of what was said to me. My slow Southern ears were baffled by their clouded, thick accents. One morning Mrs. Hoffman asked me to go to a neighboring store—it was owned by a cousin of hers—and get a can of chicken *à la king*. I had never heard the phrase before and I asked her to repeat it.

19   "Don't you know nosing?" she demanded of me.

20   "If you would write it down for me, I'd know what to get," I ventured timidly.

21   "I can't vite!" she shouted in a sudden fury. "Vat kinda boy iss you?"

22   I memorized the separate sounds that she had uttered and went to the neighboring store.

23   "Mrs. Hoffman wants a can of Cheek Keeng Awr Lar Keeng," I said slowly, hoping he would not think I was being offensive.

24   "All vite," he said, after staring at me a moment.

25   He put a can into a paper bag and gave it to me; outside in the street I opened the bag and read the label: Chicken *à la* King. I cursed, disgusted with myself. I knew those words. It had been her thick accent that had thrown me off. Yet I was not angry with her for speaking broken English; my English, too, was broken. But why could she not have taken more patience? Only one answer came to my mind. I was black and she did not care. Or so I thought . . . I was persisting in reading my present environment in the light of my old one. I reasoned thus: though English was my native tongue and America my native land, she, an alien, could operate a store and earn a living in a neighborhood where I could not even live. I reasoned further that she was aware of this and was trying to protect her position against me.

26   It was not until I had left the delicatessen job that I saw how grossly I had misread the motives and attitudes of Mr. Hoffman and his wife. I had not yet learned anything that would have helped me to thread my way through these perplexing racial relations. Accepting my environment at its face value, trapped by my own emotions, I kept asking myself what had black people done to bring this crazy world upon them?

27   The fact of the separation of white and black was clear to me; it was its effect upon the personalities of people that stumped and dismayed me. I did not feel that I was a threat to anybody; yet, as soon as I had grown old enough to think, I had learned that my entire personality, my aspirations,

had long ago been discounted; that, in a measure, the very meaning of the words I spoke could not be fully understood.

And when I contemplated the area of No Man's Land into which the   28
Negro mind in America had been shunted I wondered if there had ever been in all human history a more corroding and devastating attack upon the personalities of men than the idea of racial discrimination. In order to escape the racial attack that went to the roots of my life, I would have gladly accepted any way of life but the one in which I found myself. I would have agreed to live under a system of feudal oppression, not because I preferred feudalism but because I felt that feudalism made use of a limited part of a man, defined man, his rank, his function in society. I would have consented to live under the most rigid type of dictatorship, for I felt that dictatorships, too, defined the use of men, however degrading that use might be.

While working as a porter in Memphis I had often stood aghast as a   29
friend of mine had offered himself to be kicked by the white men; but now, while working in Chicago, I was learning that perhaps even a kick was better than uncertainty . . . I had elected, in my fevered search for honorable adjustment to the American scene, not to submit and in doing so I had embraced the daily horror of anxiety, of tension, of eternal disquiet. I could now sympathize with—though I could never bring myself to approve—those tortured blacks who had given up and had gone to their white tormentors and had said: "Kick me, if that's all there is for me; kick me and let me feel at home, let me have peace!"

Color-hate defined the place of black life as below that of white life; and   30
the black man, responding to the same dreams as the white man, strove to bury within his heart his awareness of this difference because it made him lonely and afraid. Hated by whites and being an organic part of the culture that hated him, the black man grew in turn to hate in himself that which others hated in him. But pride would make him hate his self-hate, for he would not want whites to know that he was so thoroughly conquered by them that his total life was conditioned by their attitude; but in the act of hiding his self-hate, he could not help but hate those who evoked his self-hate in him. So each part of his energy would be consumed in a war with himself, a good part of his energy would be spent in keeping control of his unruly emotions, emotions which he had not wished to have, but could not help having. Held at bay by the hate of others, preoccupied with his own feelings, he was continuously at war with reality. He became inefficient, less able to see and judge the objective world. And when he reached that state, the white people looked at him and laughed and said:

"Look, didn't I tell you niggers were that way?"   31

32   To solve this tangle of balked emotion, I loaded the empty part of the ship of my personality with fantasies of ambition to keep it from toppling over into the sea of senselessness. Like any other American, I dreamed of going into business and making money; I dreamed of working for a firm that would allow me to advance until I reached an important position; I even dreamed of organizing secret groups of blacks to fight all whites . . . And if the blacks would not agree to organize, then they would have to be fought. I would end up again with self-hate, but it was now a self-hate that was projected outward upon other blacks. Yet I knew—with that part of my mind that the whites had given me—that none of my dreams were possible. Then I would hate myself for allowing my mind to dwell upon the unattainable. Thus the circle would complete itself.

33   Slowly I began to forge in the depths of my mind a mechanism that repressed all the dreams and desires that the Chicago streets, the newspapers, the movies were evoking in me. I was going through a second childhood; a new sense of the limit of the possible was being born in me. What could I dream of that had the barest possibility of coming true? I could think of nothing. And, slowly, it was upon exactly that nothingness that my mind began to dwell, that constant sense of wanting without having, of being hated without reason. A dim notion of what life meant to a Negro in America was coming to consciousness in me, not in terms of external events, lynchings, Jim Crowism, and the endless brutalities, but in terms of crossed-up feeling, of emotional tension. I sensed that Negro life was a sprawling land of unconscious suffering, and there were but few Negroes who knew the meaning of their lives, who could tell their story.

34   Word reached me that an examination for postal clerk was impending and at once I filed an application and waited. As the date for the examination drew near, I was faced with another problem. How could I get a free day without losing my job? In the South it would have been an unwise policy for a Negro to have gone to his white boss and asked for time to take an examination for another job. It would have implied that the Negro did not like to work for the white boss, that he felt he was not receiving just consideration and, inasmuch as most jobs that Negroes held in the South involved a personal, paternalistic relationship, he would have been risking an argument that might have led to violence.

35   I now began to speculate about what kind of man Mr. Hoffman was, and I found that I did not know him; that is, I did not know his basic attitude toward Negroes. If I asked him, would he be sympathetic enough to allow me time off with pay? I needed the money. Perhaps he would say: "Go home and stay home if you don't like this job!" I was not sure of him. I de-

cided, therefore, that I had better not risk it. I would forfeit the money and stay away without telling him.

The examination was scheduled to take place on a Monday; I had been working steadily and I would be too tired to do my best if I took the examination without benefit of rest. I decided to stay away from the shop Saturday, Sunday, and Monday. But what could I tell Mr. Hoffman? Yes, I would tell him that I had been ill. No, that was too thin. I would tell him that my mother had died in Memphis and that I had gone down to bury her. That lie might work. 36

I took the examination and when I came to the store on Tuesday, Mr. Hoffman was astonished, of course. 37

"I didn't sink you vould ever come back," he said. 38

"I'm awfully sorry, Mr. Hoffman." 39

"Vat happened?" 40

"My mother died in Memphis and I had to go down and bury her," I lied. 41

He looked at me, then shook his head. 42

"Rich, you lie," he said. 43

"I'm not lying," I lied stoutly. 44

"You vanted to do somesink, zo you zayed ervay," he said shrugging. 45

"No, sir. I'm telling the truth," I piled another lie upon the first one. 46

"No. You lie. You disappoint me," he said. 47

"Well, all I can do is tell you the truth," I lied indignantly. 48

"Vy didn't you use the phone?" 49

"I didn't think of it," I told a fresh lie. 50

"Rich, if your mudder die, you vould tell me," he said. 51

"I didn't have time. Had to catch the train," I lied yet again. 52

"Vhere did you get the money?" 53

"My aunt gave it to me," I said, disgusted that I had to lie and lie again. 54

"I don't vant a boy vat tells lies," he said. 55

"I don't lie," I lied passionately to protect my lies. 56

Mrs. Hoffman joined in and both of them hammered at me. 57

"Ve know. You come from ze Zouth. You feel you can't tell us ze truth. But ve don't bother you. Ve don't feel like people in ze Zouth. Ve treat you nice, don't ve?" they asked. 58

"Yes, ma'am," I mumbled. 59

"Zen vy lie?" 60

"I'm not lying," I lied with all my strength. 61

I became angry because I knew that they knew that I was lying. I had lied to protect myself, and then I had to lie to protect my lie. I had met so many white faces that would have violently disapproved of my taking the examination that I could not have risked telling Mr. Hoffman the truth. 62

But how could I tell him that I had lied because I was so unsure of myself? Lying was bad, but revealing my own sense of insecurity would have been worse. It would have been shameful, and I did not like to feel ashamed.

63 Their attitudes had proved utterly amazing. They were taking time out from their duties in the store to talk to me, and I had never encountered anything like that from whites before. A Southern white man would have said: "Get to hell out of here!" or "All right, nigger. Get to work." But no white people had ever stood their ground and probed at me, questioned me at such length. It dawned upon me that they were trying to treat me as an equal, which made it even more impossible for me ever to tell them that I had lied, why I had lied. I felt that if I confessed I would be giving them a moral advantage over me that would have been unbearable.

64 "All vight, zay and vork," Mr. Hoffman said. "I know you're lying, but I don't care, Rich."

65 I wanted to quit. He had insulted me. But I liked him in spite of myself. Yes, I had done wrong; but how on earth could I have known the kind of people I was working for? Perhaps Mr. Hoffman would have gladly consented for me to take the examination; but my hopes had been far weaker than my powerful fears.

66 Working with them from day to day and knowing that they knew I had lied from fear crushed me. I knew that they pitied me and pitied the fear in me. I resolved to quit and risk hunger rather than stay with them. I left the job that following Saturday, not telling them that I would not be back, not possessing the heart to say good-by. I just wanted to go quickly and have them forget that I had ever worked for them.

67 After an idle week, I got a job as a dishwasher in a North Side café that had just opened. My boss, a white woman, directed me in unpacking barrels of dishes, setting up new tables, painting, and so on. I had charge of serving breakfast; in the late afternoon I carted trays of food to patrons in the hotel who did not want to come down to eat. My wages were fifteen dollars a week; the hours were long, but I ate my meals on the job.

68 The cook was an elderly Finnish woman with a sharp, bony face. There were several white waitresses. I was the only Negro in the café. The waitresses were a hard, brisk lot, and I was keenly aware of how their attitudes contrasted with those of Southern white girls. They had not been taught to keep a gulf between me and themselves; they were relatively free of the heritage of racial hate.

69 One morning as I was making coffee, Cora came forward with a tray loaded with food and squeezed against me to draw a cup of coffee.

70 "Pardon me, Richard," she said.

"Oh, that's all right," I said in an even tone.   71

But I was aware that she was a white girl and that her body was pressed   72
closely against mine, an incident that had never happened to me before in
my life, an incident charged with the memory of dread. But she was not
conscious of my blackness or of what her actions would have meant in the
South. And had I not been born in the South, her trivial act would have
been as unnoticed by me as it was by her. As she stood close to me, I could
not help thinking that if a Southern white girl had wanted to draw a cup
of coffee, she would have commanded me to step aside so that she might
not come in contact with me. The work of the hot and busy kitchen
would have had to cease for the moment so that I could have taken my
tainted body far enough away to allow the Southern white girl a chance
to get a cup of coffee. There lay a deep, emotional safety in knowing that
the white girl who was now leaning carelessly against me was not thinking of me, had not deep, vague, irrational fright that made her feel that I
was a creature to be avoided at all costs.

One summer morning a white girl came late to work and rushed into   73
the pantry where I was busy. She went into the women's room and
changed her clothes; I heard the door open and a second later I was surprised to hear her voice:

"Richard, quick! Tie my apron!"   74

She was standing with her back to me and the strings of her apron dan-   75
gled loose. There was a moment of indecision on my part, then I took the
two loose strings and carried them around her body and brought them
again to her back and tied them in a clumsy knot.

"Thanks a million," she said, grasping my hand for a split second, and   76
was gone.

I continued my work, filled with all the possible meanings that the tiny   77
simple, human event could have meant to any Negro in the South where
I had spent most of my hungry days.

I did not feel any admiration or any hate for the girls. My attitude was   78
one of abiding and friendly wonder. For the most part I was silent with
them, though I knew that I had a firmer grasp of life than most of them.
As I worked I listened to their talk and perceived its puzzled, wandering,
superficial fumbling with the problems and facts of life. There were many
things they wondered about that I could have explained to them, but I
never dared.

During my lunch hour, which I spent on a bench in a near-by park, the   79
waitresses would come and sit beside me, talking at random, laughing,
joking, smoking cigarettes. I learned about their tawdry dreams, their simple hopes, their home lives, their fear of feeling anything deeply, their sex

problems, their husbands. They were an eager, restless, talkative, ignorant bunch, but casually kind and impersonal for all that. They knew nothing of hate and fear, and strove instinctively to avoid all passion.

80   I often wondered what they were trying to get out of life, but I never stumbled upon a clue, and I doubt if they themselves had any notion. They lived on the surface of their days; their smiles were surface smiles, and their tears were surface tears. Negroes lived a truer and deeper life than they, but I wished that Negroes, too, could live as thoughtlessly, serenely, as they. The girls never talked of their feelings; none of them possessed the insight or the emotional equipment to understand themselves or others. How far apart in culture we stood! All my life I had done nothing but strive for petty goals, the trivial material prizes of American life. We shared a common tongue, but my language was a different language from theirs.

81   It was in the psychological distance that separated the races that the deepest meaning of the problem of the Negro lay for me. For these poor, ignorant white girls to have understood my life would have meant nothing short of a vast revolution in theirs. And I was convinced that what they needed to make them complete and grown-up in their living was the inclusion in their personalities of a knowledge of lives such as I lived and suffered containedly.

82   As I, in memory, think back now upon those girls and their lives I feel that for white America to understand the significance of the problem of the Negro will take a bigger and tougher America than any we have yet known. I feel that America's past is too shallow, her national character too superficially optimistic, her very morality too suffused with color hate for her to accomplish so vast and complex a task. Culturally the Negro represents a paradox: Though he is an organic part of the nation, he is excluded by the entire tide and direction of American culture. Frankly, it is felt to be right to exclude him, and it is felt to be wrong to admit him freely. Therefore if, within the confines of its present culture, the nation ever seeks to purge itself of its color hate, it will find itself at war with itself, convulsed by a spasm of emotional and moral confusion. If the nation ever finds itself examining its real relation to the Negro, it will find itself doing infinitely more than that; for the anti-Negro attitude of whites represents but a tiny part—though a symbolically significant one—of the moral attitude of the nation. Our too-young and too-new America, lusty because it is lonely, aggressive because it is afraid, insists upon seeing the world in terms of good and bad, the holy and the evil, the high and the low, the white and the black; our America is frightened by fact, by history, by processes, by necessity. It hugs the easy way of damning those whom it

cannot understand, of excluding those who look different; and it salves its conscience with a self-draped cloak of righteousness. Am I damning my native land? No; for I, too, share these faults of character! And I really do not think that America, adolescent and cocksure, a stranger to suffering and travail, an enemy of passion and sacrifice, is ready to probe into its most fundamental beliefs.

I knew that not race alone, not color alone, but daily values that gave   83
meaning to life stood between me and those white girls with whom I worked. Their constant outwardlooking, their mania for radios, cars, and a thousand other trinkets, made them dream and fix their eyes upon the trash of life, made it impossible for them to learn a language that could have taught them to speak of what was in theirs or others' hearts. The words of their souls were the syllables of popular songs.

The essence of the irony of the plight of the Negro in America, to me,   84
is that he is doomed to live in isolation, while those who condemn him seek the basest goals of any people on the face of the earth. Perhaps it would be possible for the Negro to become reconciled to his plight if he could be made to believe that his sufferings were for some remote, high, sacrificial end; but sharing the culture that condemns him, and seeing that a lust for trash is what blinds the nation to his claims, is what sets storms to rolling in his soul.

Though I had fled the pressure of the South, my outward conduct had   85
not changed. I had been schooled to present an unalteringly smiling face and I continued to do so despite the fact that my environment allowed more open expression. I hid my feelings and avoided all relationships with whites that might cause me to reveal them.

Tillie, the Finnish cook, was a tall, ageless, red-faced, raw-boned woman   86
with long snow-white hair, which she balled in a knot at the nape of her neck. She cooked expertly and was superbly efficient. One morning as I passed the sizzling stove, I thought I heard Tillie cough and spit, but I saw nothing; her face, obscured by steam, was bent over a big pot. My senses told me that Tillie had coughed and spat into that pot, but my heart told me that no human being could possibly be so filthy. I decided to watch her. An hour or so later I heard Tillie clear her throat with a grunt, saw her cough and spit into the boiling soup. I held my breath; I did not want to believe what I had seen.

Should I tell the boss lady? Would she believe me? I watched Tillie for   87
another day to make sure that she was spitting into the food. She was; there was no doubt of it. But who would believe me if I told them what was happening? I was the only black person in the café. Perhaps they

would think that I hated the cook. I stopped eating my meals there and bided my time.

88   The business of the café was growing rapidly and a Negro girl was hired to make salads. I went to her at once.

89   "Look, can I trust you?" I asked.

90   "What are you talking about?" she asked.

91   "I want you to say nothing, but watch that cook."

92   "For what?"

93   "Now, don't get scared. Just watch the cook."

94   She looked at me as though she thought I was crazy; and frankly, I felt that perhaps I ought not say anything to anybody.

95   "What do you mean?" she demanded.

96   "All right," I said. "I'll tell you. That cook spits in the food."

97   "What are you saying?" she asked aloud.

98   "Keep quiet," I said.

99   "Spitting?" she asked me in a whisper. "Why would she do that?"

100   "I don't know. But watch her."

101   She walked away from me with a funny look in her eyes. But half an hour later she came rushing to me, looking ill, sinking into a chair.

102   "Oh, God, I feel awful!"

103   "Did you see it?"

104   "She *is* spitting in the food!"

105   "What ought we do?" I asked.

106   "Tell the lady," she said.

107   "She wouldn't believe me," I said.

108   She widened her eyes as she understood. We were black and the cook was white.

109   "But I can't work here if she's going to do that," she said.

110   "Then you tell her," I said.

111   "She wouldn't believe me either," she said.

112   She rose and ran to the women's room. When she returned she stared at me. We were two Negroes and we were silently asking ourselves if the white boss lady would believe us if we told her that her expert white cook was spitting in the food all day long as it cooked on the stove.

113   "I don't know," she wailed, in a whisper, and walked away.

114   I thought of telling the waitresses about the cook, but I could not get up enough nerve. Many of the girls were friendly with Tillie. Yet I could not let the cook spit in the food all day. That was wrong by any human standard of conduct. I washed dishes, thinking, wondering; I served breakfast, thinking, wondering; I served meals in the apartments of patrons upstairs, think-

ing, wondering. Each time I picked up a tray of food I felt like retching. Finally the Negro salad girl came to me and handed me her purse and hat.

"I'm going to tell her and quit, goddamn," she said.   115

"I'll quit too, if she doesn't fire her," I said.   116

"Oh, she won't believe me," she wailed, in agony.   117

"You tell her. You're a woman. She might believe you."   118

Her eyes welled with tears and she sat for a long time; then she rose and   119
went abruptly into the dining room. I went to the door and peered. Yes,
she was at the desk, talking to the boss lady. She returned to the kitchen
and went into the pantry. I followed her.

"Did you tell her?" I asked.   120

"Yes."   121

"What did she say?"   122

"She said I was crazy."   123

"Oh, God!" I said.   124

"She just looked at me with those gray eyes of hers," the girl said. "Why   125
would Tillie do that?"

"I don't know," I said.   126

The boss lady came to the door and called the girl; both of them went into   127
the dining room. Tillie came over to me; a hard cold look was in her eyes.

"What's happening here?" she asked.   128

"I don't know," I said, wanting to slap her across the mouth.   129

She muttered something and went back to the stove, coughed, and spat   130
into a bubbling pot. I left the kitchen and went into the back areaway to
breathe. The boss lady came out.

"Richard," she said.   131

Her face was pale. I was smoking a cigarette and I did not look at her.   132

"Is this true?"   133

"Yes, ma'am."   134

"It couldn't be. Do you know what you're saying?"   135

"Just watch her," I said.   136

"I don't know," she moaned.   137

She looked crushed. She went back into the dining room, but I saw her   138
watching the cook through the doors. I watched both of them, the boss
lady and the cook, praying that the cook would spit again. She did. The
boss lady came into the kitchen and stared at Tillie, but she did not utter
a word. She burst into tears and ran back into the dining room.

"What's happening here?" Tillie demanded.   139

No one answered. The boss lady came out and tossed Tillie her hat,   140
coat, and money.

141   "Now, get out of here, you dirty dog!" she said.

142   Tillie stared, then slowly picked up her hat, coat, and the money; she stood a moment, wiped sweat from her forehead with her hand, then spat—this time on the floor. She left.

143   Nobody was ever able to fathom why Tillie liked to spit into the food.

144   Brooding over Tillie, I recalled the time when the boss man in Mississippi had come to me and had tossed my wages to me and said:

145   "Get out, nigger! I don't like your looks."

146   And I wondered if a Negro who did not smile and grin was as morally loathsome to whites as a cook who spat into the food.

147   The following summer I was called for temporary duty in the post office, and the work lasted into the winter. Aunt Cleo succumbed to a severe cardiac condition and, hard on the heels of her illness, my brother developed stomach ulcers. To rush my worries to a climax, my mother also became ill. I felt that I was maintaining a private hospital. Finally, the post office work ceased altogether and I haunted the city for jobs. But when I went into the streets in the morning I saw sights that killed my hope for the rest of the day. Unemployed men loitered in doorways with blank looks in their eyes, sat dejectedly on front steps in shabby clothing, congregated in sullen groups on street corners, and filled all the empty benches in the parks of Chicago's South Side.

148   Luck of a sort came when a distant cousin of mine, who was a superintendent for a Negro burial society, offered me a position on his staff as an agent. The thought of selling insurance policies to ignorant Negroes disgusted me.

149   "Well, if you don't sell them, somebody else will," my cousin told me. "You've got to eat, haven't you?"

150   During that year I worked for several burial and insurance societies that operated among Negroes, and I received a new kind of education. I found that the burial societies, with some exceptions, were mostly "rackets." Some of them conducted their business legitimately, but there were many that exploited the ignorance of their black customers.

151   I was paid under a system that netted me fifteen dollars for every dollar's worth of new premiums that I placed upon the company's books, and for every dollar's worth of old premiums that lapsed I was penalized fifteen dollars. In addition, I was paid a commission of ten per cent on total premiums collected, but during the Depression it was extremely difficult to persuade a black family to buy a policy carrying even a dime premium. I considered myself lucky if, after subtracting the lapses from new business, there remained fifteen dollars that I could call my own.

This "gambling" method of remuneration was practiced by some of the   152
burial companies because of the tremendous "turnover" in policyholders,
and the companies had to have a constant stream of new business to keep
afloat. Whenever a black family moved or suffered a slight reverse in fortune, it usually let its policy lapse and later bought another policy from
some other company.

Each day now I saw how the Negro in Chicago lived, for I visited hun-   153
dreds of dingy flats filled with rickety furniture and ill-clad children. Most
of the policyholders were illiterate and did not know that their policies
carried clauses severely restricting their benefit payments, and, as an insurance agent, it was not my duty to tell them.

After tramping the streets and pounding on doors to collect premiums, I   154
was dry, strained, too tired to read or write. I hungered for relief and, as a
salesman of insurance to many young black girls, I found it. There were
many comely black housewives who, trying desperately to keep up their insurance payments, were willing to make bargains to escape paying a ten-cent
premium. I had a long, tortured affair with one girl by paying her ten-cent
premium each week. She was an illiterate black child with a baby whose father she did not know. During the entire period of my relationship with her,
she had but one demand to make of me: she wanted me to take her to a circus. Just what significance circuses had for her, I was never able to learn.

After I had been with her one morning—in exchange for the dime pre-   155
mium—I sat on the sofa in the front room and began to read a book I had
with me. She came over shyly.

"Lemme see that," she said.   156
"What?" I asked.   157
"That book," she said.   158
I gave her the book; she looked at it intently. I saw that she was holding   159
it upside down.

"What's in here you keep reading?" she asked.   160
"Can't you really read?" I asked.   161
"Naw," she giggled. "You know I can't read."   162
"You can read *some*," I said.   163
"Naw," she said.   164
I stared at her and wondered just what a life like hers meant in the   165
scheme of things, and I came to the conclusion that it meant absolutely
nothing. And neither did my life mean anything.

"How come you looking at me that way for?"   166
"Nothing."   167
"You don't talk much."   168
"There isn't much to say."   169

170   "I wished Jim was here," she sighed.

171   "Who's Jim?" I asked, jealous. I knew that she had other men, but I resented her mentioning them in my presence.

172   "Just a friend," she said.

173   I hated her then, then hated myself for coming to her.

174   "Do you like Jim better than you like me?" I asked.

175   "Naw. Jim just likes to talk."

176   "Then why do you be with me, if you like Jim better?" I asked, trying to make an issue and feeling a wave of disgust because I wanted to.

177   "You all right," she said, giggling. "I like you."

178   "I could kill you," I said.

179   "What?" she exclaimed.

180   "Nothing," I said, ashamed.

181   "Kill me, you said? You crazy, man," she said.

182   "Maybe I am," I muttered, angry that I was sitting beside a human being to whom I could not talk, angry with myself for coming to her, hating my wild and restless loneliness.

183   "You oughta go home and sleep," she said. "You tired."

184   "What do you ever think about?" I demanded harshly.

185   "Lotta things."

186   "What, for example?"

187   "You," she said, smiling.

188   "You know I mean just one dime to you each week," I said.

189   "Naw, I thinka lotta you."

190   "Then what do you think?"

191   "'Bout how you talk when you talk. I wished I could talk like you," she said seriously.

192   "Why?" I taunted her.

193   "When you gonna take me to a circus?" she demanded suddenly.

194   "You ought to be in a circus," I said.

195   "I'd like it," she said, her eyes shining.

196   I wanted to laugh, but her words sounded so sincere that I could not.

197   "There's no circus in town," I said.

198   "I bet there is and you won't tell me 'cause you don't wanna take me," she said, pouting.

199   "But there's no circus in town, I tell you!"

200   "When will one come?"

201   "I don't know."

202   "Can't you read it in the papers?" she asked.

203   "There's nothing in the papers about a circus."

204   "There is," she said. "If I could read, I'd find it."

I laughed, and she was hurt. 205

"There *is* a circus in town," she said stoutly. 206

"There's no circus in town," I said. "But if you want to learn to read, 207
then I'll teach you."

She nestled at my side, giggling. 208

"See that word?" I said, pointing. 209

"Yeah." 210

"That's an 'and,'" I said. 211

She doubled, giggling. 212

"What's the matter?" I asked. 213

She rolled on the floor, giggling. 214

"What's so funny?" I demanded. 215

"You," she giggled. "You so funny." 216

I rose. 217

"The hell with you," I said. 218

"Don't you go and cuss me now," she said. "I don't cuss you." 219

"I'm sorry," I said. 220

I got my hat and went to the door. 221

"I'll see you next week?" she asked. 222

"Maybe," I said. 223

When I was on the sidewalk, she called to me from a window. 224

"You promised to take me to a circus, remember?" 225

"Yes." I walked close to the window. "What is it you like about a circus?" 226

"The animals," she said simply. 227

I felt that there was a hidden meaning, perhaps, in what she had said, 228
but I could not find it. She laughed and slammed the window shut.

Each time I left her I resolved not to visit her again. I could not talk to 229
her; I merely listened to her passionate desire to see a circus. She was not
calculating; if she liked a man, she just liked him. Sex relations were the
only relations she had ever had; no others were possible with her, so limited was her intelligence.

Most of the other agents also had their bought girls and they were ex- 230
tremely anxious to keep other agents from tampering with them. One day
a new section of the South Side was given to me as a part of my collection
area, and the agent from whom the territory had been taken suddenly became very friendly with me.

"Say, Wright," he asked, "did you collect from Ewing on Champlain 231
Avenue yet?"

"Yes," I answered, after consulting my book. 232

"How did you like her?" he asked, staring at me. 233

"She's a good-looking number," I said. 234

235   "You had anything to do with her yet?" he asked.

236   "No, but I'd like to," I said laughing.

237   "Look," he said. "I'm a friend of yours."

238   "Since when?" I countered.

239   "No, I'm really a friend," he said.

240   "What's on your mind?"

241   "Listen, that gal's sick," he said seriously.

242   "What do you mean?"

243   "She's got the clap," he said. "Keep away from her. She'll lay with anybody."

244   "Gee, I'm glad you told me," I said.

245   "You had your eye on her, didn't you?" he asked.

246   "Yes, I did," I said.

247   "Leave her alone," he said. "She'll get you down."

248   That night I told my cousin what the agent had said about Miss Ewing. My cousin laughed.

249   "That gal's all right," he said. "That agent's been fooling around with her. He told you she had a disease so that you'd be scared to bother her. He was protecting her from you."

250   That was the way the black women were regarded by the black agents. Some of the agents were vicious; if they had claims to pay to a sick black woman and if the woman was able to have sex relations with them, they would insist upon it, using the claims money as a bribe. If the woman refused, they would report to the office that the woman was a malingerer. The average black woman would submit because she needed the money badly.

251   As an insurance agent it was necessary for me to take part in one swindle. It appears that the burial society had originally issued a policy that was—from their point of view—too liberal in its provisions, and the officials decided to exchange the policies then in the hands of their clients for other policies carrying stricter clauses. Of course, this had to be done in a manner that would not allow the policyholder to know that his policy was being switched—that he was being swindled. I did not like it, but there was only one thing I could do to keep from being a party to it: I could quit and starve. But I did not feel that being honest was worth the price of starvation.

252   The swindle worked in this way. In my visits to the homes of the policyholders to collect premiums, I was accompanied by the superintendent who claimed to the policyholder that he was making a routine inspection. The policyholder, usually an illiterate black woman, would dig up her policy from the bottom of a trunk or chest and hand it to the superintendent. Meanwhile I would be marking the woman's premium book, an act which

would distract her from what the superintendent was doing. The superintendent would exchange the old policy for a new one which was identical in color, serial number, and beneficiary, but which carried smaller payments. It was dirty work and I wondered how I could stop it. And when I could think of no safe way I would curse myself and the victims and forget about it. (The black owners of the burial societies were leaders in the Negro communities and were respected by whites.)

When I reached the relief station, I felt that I was making a public confession of my hunger. I sat waiting for hours, resentful of the mass of hungry people about me. My turn finally came and I was questioned by a middle-class Negro woman who asked me for a short history of my life. As I waited, I became aware of something happening in the room. The black men and women were mumbling quietly among themselves; they had not known one another before they had come here, but now their timidity and shame were wearing off and they were exchanging experiences. Before this they had lived as individuals, each somewhat afraid of the other, each seeking his own pleasure, each stanch in that degree of Americanism that had been allowed him. But now life had tossed them together, and they were learning to know the sentiments of their neighbors for the first time; their talking was enabling them to sense the collectivity of their lives, and some of their fear was passing. 253

Did the relief officials realize what was happening? No. If they had, they would have stopped it. But they saw their "clients" through the eyes of their profession, saw only what their "science" allowed them to see. As I listened to the talk, I could see black minds shedding many illusions. These people now knew that the past had betrayed them, had cast them out; but they did not know what the future would be like, did not know what they wanted. Yes, some of the things that the Communists said were true; they maintained that there came times in history when a ruling class could no longer rule. And now I sat looking at the beginnings of anarchy. To permit the birth of this new consciousness in these people was proof that those who ruled did not quite know what they were doing, assuming that they were trying to save themselves and their class. Had they understood what was happening, they would never have allowed millions of perplexed and defeated people to sit together for long hours and talk, for out of their talk was rising a new realization of life. And once this new conception of themselves had formed, no power on earth could alter it. 254

I left the relief station with the promise that food would be sent to me, but I also left with a knowledge that the relief officials had not wanted to give to me. I had felt the possibility of creating a new understanding of 255 life in the minds of people rejected by the society in which they lived, people to whom the Chicago *Tribune* referred contemptuously as the "idle" ones, as though these people had deliberately sought their present state of helplessness.

256 Who would give these people a meaningful way of life? Communist theory defined these people as the molders of the future of mankind, but the Communist speeches I had heard in the park had mocked that definition. These people, of course, were not ready for a revolution; they had not abandoned their past lives by choice, but because they simply could not live the old way any longer. Now, what new faith would they embrace? The day I begged bread from the city officials was the day that showed me I was not alone in my loneliness; society had cast millions of others with me. But how could I be with them? How many understood what was happening? My mind swam with questions that I could not answer.

257 I was slowly beginning to comprehend the meaning of my environment; a sense of direction was beginning to emerge from the conditions of my life. I began to feel something more powerful than I could express. My speech and manner changed. My cynicism slid from me. I grew open and questioning. I wanted to know.

258 If I were a member of the class that rules, I would post men in all the neighborhoods of the nation, not to spy upon or club rebellious workers, not to break strikes or disrupt nations, but to ferret out those who no longer respond to the system under which they live. I would make it known that the real danger does not stem from those who seek to grab their share of wealth through force, or from those who try to defend their property through violence, for both of these groups, by their affirmative acts, support the values of the system under which they live. The millions that I would fear are those who do not dream of the prizes that the nation holds forth, for it is in them, though they may not know it, that a revolution has taken place and is biding its time to translate itself into a new and strange way of life.

259 I feel that the Negroes' relation to America is symbolically peculiar, and from the Negroes' ultimate reactions to their trapped state a lesson can be learned about America's future. Negroes are told in a language they cannot possibly misunderstand that their native land is not their own; and when, acting upon impulses which they share with whites, they try to assert a claim to their birthright, whites retaliate with terror, never pausing to consider the consequences should the Negroes give up completely. The whites never dream that they would face a situation far more terrifying if they were confronted by Negroes who made no claims at all than by those who are buoyed up by social aggressiveness. My knowledge of how Negroes react to their plight makes me declare that no man can possibly be individu-

ally guilty of treason, that an insurgent act is but a man's desperate answer
to those who twist his environment so that he cannot fully share the spirit
of his native land. Treason is a crime of the State.

Christmas came and I was once more called to the post office for tem-   260
porary work. This time I met many young white men and we discussed
world happenings, the vast armies of unemployed, the rising tide of radical action. I now detected a change in the attitudes of the whites I met;
their privations were making them regard Negroes with new eyes, and, for
the first time, I was invited to their homes.

When the work in the post office ended, I was assigned by the relief sys-   261
tem as an orderly to a medical research institute in one of the largest and
wealthiest hospitals in Chicago. I cleaned operating rooms, dog, rat, mice,
cat, and rabbit pans, and fed guinea pigs. Four of us Negroes worked there
and we occupied an underworld position, remembering that we must restrict ourselves—when not engaged upon some task—to the basement corridors, so that we would not mingle with white nurses, doctors, or visitors.

The sharp line of racial division drawn by the hospital authorities came   262
to me the first morning when I walked along an underground corridor and
saw two long lines of women coming toward me. A line of white girls
marched past, clad in starched uniforms that gleamed white; their faces
were alert, their step quick, their bodies lean and shapely, their shoulders
erect, their faces lit with the light of purpose. And after them came a line of
black girls, old, fat, dressed in ragged gingham, walking loosely, carrying tin
cans of soap powder, rags, mops, brooms . . . I wondered what law of the universe kept them from being mixed? The sun would not have stopped shining had there been a few black girls in the first line, and the earth would not
have stopped whirling on its axis had there been a few white girls in the second line. But the two lines I saw graded social status in purely racial terms.

Of the three Negroes who worked with me, one was a boy about my own   263
age, Bill, who was either sleepy or drunk most of the time. Bill straightened
his hair and I suspected that he kept a bottle hidden somewhere in the piles
of hay which we fed to the guinea pigs. He did not like me and I did not like
him, though I tried harder than he to conceal my dislike. We had nothing
in common except that we were both black and lost. While I contained my
frustration, he drank to drown his. Often I tried to talk to him, tried in simple words to convey to him some of my ideas, and he would listen in sullen
silence. Then one day he came to me with an angry look on his face.

"I got it," he said.   264

"You've got what?" I asked.   265

"This old race problem you keep talking about," he said.   266

267   "What about it?"

268   "Well, it's this way," he explained seriously. "Let the government give every man a gun and five bullets, then let us all start over again. Make it just like it was in the beginning. The ones who come out on top, white or black, let them rule."

269   His simplicity terrified me. I had never met a Negro who was so irredeemably brutalized. I stopped pumping my ideas into Bill's brain for fear that the fumes of alcohol might send him reeling toward some fantastic fate.

270   The two other Negroes were elderly and had been employed in the institute for fifteen years or more. One was Brand, a short, black, morose bachelor; the other was Cooke, a tall, yellow, spectacled fellow who spent his spare time keeping track of world events through the Chicago *Tribune*. Brand and Cooke hated each other for a reason that I was never able to determine, and they spent a good part of each day quarreling.

271   When I began working at the institute, I recalled my adolescent dream of wanting to be a medical research worker. Daily I saw young Jewish boys and girls receiving instruction in chemistry and medicine that the average black boy or girl could never receive. When I was alone, I wandered and poked my fingers into strange chemicals, watched intricate machines trace red and black lines on ruled paper. At times I paused and stared at the walls of the rooms, at the floors, at the wide desks at which the white doctors sat; and I realized—with a feeling that I could never quite get used to—that I was looking at the world of another race.

272   My interest in what was happening in the institute amused the three other Negroes with whom I worked. They had no curiosity about "white folks' things," while I wanted to know if the dogs being treated for diabetes were getting well; if the rats and mice in which cancer had been induced showed any signs of responding to treatment. I wanted to know the principle that lay behind the Aschheim-Zondek tests that were made with rabbits, the Wassermann tests that were made with guinea pigs. But when I asked a timid question I found that even Jewish doctors had learned to imitate the sadistic method of humbling a Negro that the others had cultivated.

273   "If you know too much, boy, your brains might explode," a doctor said one day.

274   Each Saturday morning I assisted a young Jewish doctor in slitting the vocal cords of a fresh batch of dogs from the city pound. The object was to devocalize the dogs so that their howls would not disturb the patients in the other parts of the hospital. I held each dog as the doctor injected Nembutal into its veins to make it unconscious; then I held the dog's jaws open as the doctor inserted the scalpel and severed the vocal cords. Later, when the dogs came to, they would lift their heads to the ceiling and gape

in a soundless wail. The sight became lodged in my imagination as a symbol of silent suffering.

To me Nembutal was a powerful and mysterious liquid, but when I   275
asked questions about its properties I could not obtain a single intelligent
answer. The doctor simply ignored me with:

"Come on. Bring me the next dog. I haven't got all day."   276

One Saturday morning, after I had held the dogs for their vocal cords to   277
be slit, the doctor left the Nembutal on a bench. I picked it up, uncorked
it, and smelled it. It was odorless. Suddenly Brand ran to me with a
stricken face.

"What're you doing?" he asked.   278

"I was smelling this stuff to see if it had any odor," I said.   279

"Did you really smell it?" he asked me.   280

"Yes."   281

"Oh, God!" he exclaimed.   282

"What's the matter?" I asked.   283

"You shouldn't've done that!" he shouted.   284

"Why?"   285

He grabbed my arm and jerked me across the room.   286

"Come on!" he yelled, snatching open the door.   287

"What's the matter?" I asked.   288

"I gotta get you to a doctor 'fore it's too late," he gasped.   289

Had my foolish curiosity made me inhale something dangerous?   290

"But—Is it poisonous?"   291

"Run, boy!" he said, pulling me. "You'll fall dead."   292

Filled with fear, with Brand pulling my arm, I rushed out of the room,   293
raced across a rear areaway, into another room, then down a long corridor. I
wanted to ask Brand what symptoms I must expect, but we were running
too fast. Brand finally stopped, gasping for breath. My heart beat wildly and
my blood pounded in my head. Brand then dropped to the concrete floor,
stretched out on his back, and yelled with laughter, shaking all over. He
beat his fists against the concrete; he moaned, giggled, he kicked.

I tried to master my outrage, wondering if some of the white doctors had   294
told him to play the joke. He rose and wiped tears from his eyes, still laughing. I walked away from him. He knew that I was angry and he followed me.

"Don't get mad," he gasped through his laughter.   295

"Go to hell," I said.   296

"I couldn't help it," he giggled. "You looked at me like you'd believe   297
anything I said. Man, you was scared."

He leaned against the wall, laughing again, stomping his feet. I was an-   298
gry, for I felt that he would spread the story. I knew that Bill and Cooke
never ventured beyond the safe bounds of Negro living, and they would

never blunder into anything like this. And if they heard about this, they would laugh for months.

299   "Brand, if you mention this, I'll kill you," I swore.

300   "You ain't mad?" he asked, laughing, staring at me through tears.

301   Sniffing, Brand walked ahead of me. I followed him back into the room that housed the dogs. All day, while at some task, he would pause and giggle, then smother the giggling with his hand, looking at me out of the corner of his eyes, shaking his head. He laughed at me for a week. I kept my temper and let him amuse himself. I finally found out the properties of Nembutal by consulting medical books; but I never told Brand.

302   One summer morning, just as I began work, a young Jewish boy came to me with a stop watch in his hand.

303   "Dr. _____ wants me to time you when you clean a room," he said. "We're trying to make the institute more efficient."

304   "I'm doing my work, and getting through on time," I said.

305   "This is the boss's order," he said.

306   "Why don't you work for a change?" I blurted, angry.

307   "Now, look," he said. *"This* is my work. Now *you* work."

308   I got a mop and pail, sprayed the room with disinfectant, and scrubbed at coagulated blood and hardened dog, rat, and rabbit feces. The normal temperature of a room was ninety, but, as the sun beat down upon the skylights, the temperature rose above a hundred. Stripped to my waist, I slung the mop, moving steadily like a machine, hearing the boy press the button on the stop watch when I finished cleaning a room.

309   "Well, how is it?" I asked.

310   "It took you seventeen minutes to clean that last room," he said. "That ought to be the time for each room."

311   "But that room was not very dirty," I said.

312   "You have seventeen rooms to clean," he went on as though I had not spoken. "Seventeen times seventeen makes four hours and forty-nine minutes." He wrote upon a little pad. "After lunch, clean the five flights of stone stairs. I timed a boy who scrubbed one step and multiplied that time by the number of those steps. You ought to be through by six."

313   "Suppose I want relief?" I asked.

314   "You'll manage," he said and left.

315   Never had I felt so much the slave as when I scoured those stone steps each afternoon. Working against time, I would wet five steps, sprinkle soap powder, and then a white doctor or a nurse would come along and, instead of avoiding the soapy steps, would walk on them and track the dirty water onto the steps that I had already cleaned. To obviate this, I cleaned but two steps at a time, a distance over which a ten-year-old child could step. But

it did no good. The white people still plopped their feet down into the dirty water and muddied the other clean steps. If I ever really hotly hated unthinking whites, it was then. Not once during my entire stay at the institute did a single white person show enough courtesy to avoid a wet step. I would be on my knees, scrubbing, sweating, pouring out what limited energy my body could wring from my meager diet, and I would hear feet approaching. I would pause and curse with tense lips:

"These sonofabitches are going to dirty these steps again, goddamn   316
their souls to hell!"

Sometimes a sadistically observant white man would notice that he had   317
tracked dirty water up the steps, and he would look back down at me and smile and say:

"Boy, we sure keep you busy, don't we?"   318

And I would not be able to answer.   319

The feud that went on between Brand and Cooke continued. Although   320
they were working daily in a building where scientific history was being made, the light of curiosity was never in their eyes. They were conditioned to their racial "place," had learned to see only a part of the whites and the white world; and the whites, too, had learned to see only a part of the lives of the blacks and their world.

Perhaps Brand and Cooke, lacking interests that could absorb them,   321
fuming like children over trifles, simply invented their hate of each other in order to have something to feel deeply about. Or perhaps there was in them a vague tension stemming from their chronically frustrating way of life, a pain whose cause they did not know; and, like those devocalized dogs, they would whirl and snap at the air when their old pain struck them. Anyway, they argued about the weather, sports, sex, war, race, politics, and religion; neither of them knew much about the subjects they debated, but it seemed that the less they knew the better they could argue.

The tug of war between the two elderly men reached a climax one win-   322
ter day at noon. It was incredibly cold and an icy gale swept up and down the Chicago streets with blizzard force. The door of the animal-filled room was locked, for we always insisted that we be allowed one hour in which to eat and rest. Bill and I were sitting on wooden boxes, eating our lunches out of paper bags. Brand was washing his hands at the sink. Cooke was sitting on a rickety stool, munching an apple and reading the Chicago *Tribune*.

Now and then a devocalized dog lifted his nose to the ceiling and howled   323
soundlessly. The room was filled with many rows of high steel tiers. Perched upon each of these tiers were layers of steel cages containing the dogs, rats, mice, rabbits, and guinea pigs. Each cage was labeled in some indecipherable scientific jargon. Along the walls of the room were long charts with zigzagging red and black lines that traced the success or failure of some

experiment. The lonely piping of guinea pigs floated unheeded about us. Hay rustled as a rabbit leaped restlessly about in its pen. A rat scampered around in its steel prison. Cooke tapped the newspaper for attention.

324 "It says here," Cooke mumbled through a mouthful of apple, "that this is the coldest day since 1888."

325 Bill and I sat unconcerned. Brand chuckled softly.

326 "What in hell you laughing about?" Cooke demanded of Brand.

327 "You can't believe what that damn *Tribune* says," Brand said.

328 "How come I can't?" Cooke demanded. "It's the world's greatest newspaper."

329 Brand did not reply; he shook his head pityingly and chuckled again.

330 "Stop that damn laughing at me!" Cooke said angrily.

331 "I laugh as much as I wanna," Brand said. "You don't know what you talking about. The *Herald-Examiner* says it's the coldest day since 1873."

332 "But the *Trib* oughta know," Cooke countered. "It's older'n that *Examiner.*"

333 "That damn *Trib* don't know nothing!" Brand drowned out Cooke's voice.

334 "How in hell you know?" Cooke asked with rising anger.

335 The argument waxed until Cooke shouted that if Brand did not shut up he was going to "cut his black throat."

336 Brand whirled from the sink, his hands dripping soapy water, his eyes blazing.

337 "Take that back," Brand said.

338 "I take nothing back! What you wanna do about it?" Cooke taunted.

339 The two elderly Negroes glared at each other. I wondered if the quarrel was really serious, or if it would turn out harmlessly as so many others had done.

340 Suddenly Cooke dropped the Chicago *Tribune* and pulled a long knife from his pocket; his thumb pressed a button and a gleaming steel blade leaped out. Brand stepped back quickly and seized an ice pick that was stuck in a wooden board above the sink.

341 "Put that knife down," Brand said.

342 "Stay 'way from me, or I'll cut your throat," Cooke warned.

343 Brand lunged with the ice pick. Cooke dodged out of range. They circled each other like fighters in a prize ring. The cancerous and tubercular rats and mice leaped about in their cages. The guinea pigs whistled in fright. The diabetic dogs bared their teeth and barked soundlessly in our direction. The Aschheim-Zondek rabbits flopped their ears and tried to hide in the corners of their pens. Cooke now crouched and sprang forward with the knife. Bill and I jumped to our feet, speechless with surprise. Brand retreated. The eyes of both men were hard and unblinking; they were breathing deeply.

344 "Say, cut it out!" I called in alarm.

"Them damn fools is really fighting," Bill said in amazement.   345

Slashing at each other, brand and Cooke surged up and down the aisles   346
of steel tiers. Suddenly Brand uttered a bellow and charged into Cooke
and swept him violently backward. Cooke grasped Brand's hand to keep
the ice pick from sinking into his chest. Brand broke free and charged
Cooke again, sweeping him into an animal-filled steel tier. The tier balanced itself on its edge for an indecisive moment, then toppled.

Like kingpins, one steel tier lammed into another, then they all crashed   347
to the floor with a sound as of the roof falling. The whole aspect of the
room altered quicker than the eye could follow. Brand and Cooke stood
stock-still, their eyes fastened upon each other, their pointed weapons
raised; but they were dimly aware of the havoc that churned about them.

The steel tiers lay jumbled; the doors of the cages swung open. Rats and   348
mice and dogs ad rabbits moved over the floor in wild panic. The Wassermann guinea pigs were squealing as though judgment day had come. Here
and there an animal had been crushed beneath a cage.

All four of us looked at one another. We knew what this meant. We   349
might lose our jobs. We were already regarded as black dunces; and if the
doctors saw this mess they would take it as final proof. Bill rushed to the
door to make sure that it was locked. I glanced at the clock and saw that
it was 12:30. We had one half-hour of grace.

"Come on," Bill said uneasily. "We got to get this place cleaned."   350

Brand and Cooke stared at each other, both doubting.   351

"Give me your knife, Cooke," I said.   352

"Naw! Take Brand's ice pick *first*," Cooke said.   353

"The hell you say!" Brand said. "Take his knife *first*!"   354

A knock sounded at the door.   355

"Sssssh," Bill said.   356

We waited. We heard footsteps going away. We'll all lose our jobs, I   357
thought.

Persuading the fighters to surrender their weapons was a difficult task,   358
but at last it was done and we could begin to set things right. Slowly Brand
stooped and tugged at one end of a steel tier. Cooke stooped to help him.
Both men seemed to be acting in a dream. Soon, however, all four of us
were working frantically, watching the clock.

As we labored we conspired to keep the fight a secret; we agreed to tell   359
the doctors—if any should ask—that we had not been in the room during
our lunch hour; we felt that that lie would explain why no one had unlocked the door when the knock had come.

We righted the tiers and replaced the cages; then we were faced with   360
the impossible task of sorting the cancerous rats and mice, the diabetic
dogs, the Aschheim-Zondek rabbits, and the Wassermann guinea pigs.

Whether we kept our jobs or not depended upon how shrewdly we could cover up all evidence of the fight. It was pure guesswork, but we had to try to put the animals back into the correct cages. We knew that certain rats or mice went into certain cages, but we did not know *what* rat or mouse went into *what* cage. We did not know a tubercular mouse from a cancerous mouse—the white doctors had made sure that we would not know. They had never taken time to answer a single question; though we worked in the institute, we were as remote from the meaning of the experiments as if we lived in the moon. The doctors had laughed at what they felt was our childlike interest in the fate of the animals.

361   First we sorted the dogs; that was fairly easy, for we could remember the size and color of most of them. But the rats and mice and guinea pigs baffled us completely.

362   We put our heads together and pondered, down in the underworld of the great scientific institute. It was a strange scientific conference; the fate of the entire medical research institute rested in our ignorant, black hands.

363   We remembered the number of rats, mice, or guinea pigs—we had to handle them several times a day—that went into a given cage, and we supplied the number helter-skelter from those animals that we could catch running loose on the floor. We discovered that many rats, mice, and guinea pigs were missing—they had been killed in the scuffle. We solved that problem by taking healthy stock from other cages and putting them into cages with sick animals. We repeated this process until we were certain that, numerically at least, all the animals with which the doctors were experimenting were accounted for.

364   The rabbits came last. We broke the rabbits down into two general groups: those that had fur on their bellies and those that did not. We knew that all those rabbits that had shaven bellies—our scientific knowledge adequately covered this point because it was our job to shave the rabbits— were undergoing the Aschheim-Zondek tests. But in what pen did a given rabbit belong? We did not know. I solved the problem very simply. I counted the shaven rabbits; they numbered seventeen. I counted the pens labeled "Aschheim-Zondek," then proceeded to drop a shaven rabbit into each pen at random. And again we were numerically successful. At least white America had taught us how to count. . . .

365   Lastly we carefully wrapped all the dead animals in newspapers and hid their bodies in a garbage can.

366   At a few minutes to one the room was in order; that is, the kind of order that we four Negroes could figure out. I unlocked the door and we sat waiting, whispering, vowing secrecy, wondering what the reaction of the doctors would be.

Finally a doctor came, gray-haired, white-coated, spectacled, efficient, serious, taciturn, bearing a tray upon which sat a bottle of mysterious fluid and a hypodermic needle.   367

"My rats, please."   368

Cooke shuffled forward to serve him. We held our breath. Cooke got the cage which he knew the doctor always called for at that hour and brought it forward. One by one, Cooke took out the rats and held them as the doctor solemnly injected the mysterious fluid under their skins.   369

"Thank you, Cooke," the doctor murmured.   370

"Not at all, sir," Cooke mumbled with a suppressed gasp.   371

When the doctor had gone we looked at one another, hardly daring to believe that our secret would be kept. We were so anxious that we did not know whether to curse or laugh. Another doctor came.   372

"Give me A-Z rabbit number 14."   373

"Yes, sir," I said.   374

I brought him the rabbit and he took it upstairs to the operating room. We waited for repercussions. None came.   375

All that afternoon the doctors came and went. I would run into the room—stealing a few seconds from my step-scrubbing—and ask what progress was being made and would learn that the doctors had detected nothing. At quitting time we felt triumphant.   376

"They won't ever know," Cooke boasted in a whisper.   377

I saw Brand stiffen. I knew that he was aching to dispute Cooke's optimism, but the memory of the fight he had just had was so fresh in his mind that he could not speak.   378

Another day went by and nothing happened. Then another day. The doctors examined the animals and wrote in their little black books, in their big black books, and continued to trace red and black lines upon the charts.   379

A week passed and we felt out of danger. Not one question had been asked.   380

Of course, we four black men were much too modest to make our contribution known, but we often wondered what went on in the laboratories after that secret disaster. Was some scientific hypothesis, well on its way to validation and ultimate public use, discarded because of unexpected findings on that cold winter day? Was some tested principle given a new and strange refinement because of fresh, remarkable evidence? Did some brooding research worker—those who held stop watches and slopped their feet carelessly in the water of the steps I tried so hard to keep clean—get a wild, if brief, glimpse of a new scientific truth? Well, we never heard. . . .   381

I brooded upon whether I should have gone to the director's office and told him what had happened, but each time I thought of it I remembered that the director had been the man who had ordered the boy to stand   382 over me while I was working and time my movements with a stop watch. He did not regard me as a human being. I did not share his world. I earned thirteen dollars a week and I had to support four people with it, and should I risk that thirteen dollars by acting idealistically? Brand and Cooke would have hated me and would have eventually driven me from the job had I "told" on them. The hospital kept us four Negroes as though we were close kin to the animals we tended, huddled together down in the underworld corridors of the hospital, separated by a vast psychological distance from the significant processes of the rest of the hospital—just as America had kept us locked in the dark underworld of American life for three hundred years—and we had made our own code of ethics, values, loyalty.

QUESTIONING AND DISCUSSING

Wright, "The Man Who Went to Chicago"

1. Richard Wright's story is a compelling illustration of the ways in which literature reflects both the overt and the subtle concerns of humankind. Note, especially, the ways in which what seem to be off-handed, seemingly insignificant comments reveal much larger truths. Consider, for instance, "Of course, we four black men were much too modest to make our contribution known, but we often wondered what went on in the laboratories after that secret disaster," and "Cooke shuffled forward to serve him." How do deliberately subtle—yet not-so-subtle—examples such as these reflect the results of oppression and the ways in which it affects self-regard and behavior? How do these views become ingrained—even in the language of the narrator? What are the ways in which Wright reveals that he is not prejudice-free?

2. How do the narrator and his friends change their values and codes of behavior ("and we had made our own code of ethics, values, loyalty")? Why was doing this necessary—and what were the motivations? Discuss the experiences and insights gained by the narrator throughout the story.

3. What symbol does Wright use to add significance to the story? Analyze their effectiveness and determine the ways in which they enhance the story.

⊞

JACK G. SHAHEEN

Professor Emeritus of Mass Communications at Southern Illinois University at Carbondale, Jack G. Shaheen (1935–) is also a former CBS News consultant on Middle East affairs. He is the author of *Reel Bad Arabs: How Hollywood Villifies a People, The TV Arab,* and *Nuclear War Films 1978.* Shaheen, who has received two Fulbright-Hays Lectureships, is frequently invited to college campuses and other venues to lecture on subjects that include "Hollywood's Arabs: Problems and Prospects."

⌗

The Media's Image of Arabs

America's bogyman is the Arab. Until the nightly news brought us TV pictures of Palestinian boys being punched and beaten, almost all portraits of Arabs seen in America were dangerously threatening. Arabs were either billionaires or bombers—rarely victims. They were hardly ever seen as ordinary people practicing law, driving taxis, singing lullabies or healing the sick. Though TV news may portray them more sympathetically now, the absence of positive media images nurtures suspicion and stereotype. As an Arab-American, I have found that ugly caricatures have had an enduring impact on my family.

I was sheltered from prejudicial portraits at first. My parents came from Lebanon in the 1920s; they met and married in America. Our home in the steel city of Clairton, Pa., was a center for ethnic sharing—black, white, Jew and gentile. There was only one major source of media images then, at the State movie theater where I was lucky enough to get a part-time job as an usher. But in the late 1940s, Westerns and war movies were popular, not Middle Eastern dramas. Memories of World War II were fresh, and the screen heavies were the Japanese and the Germans. True to the cliché of the times, the only good Indian was a dead Indian. But when I mimicked or mocked the bad guys, my mother cautioned me. She explained that stereotypes blur our vision and corrupt the imagination. "Have compassion for all people, Jackie," she said. "This way, you'll learn to experience the joy of accepting people as they are, and not as they appear in films. Stereotypes hurt."

Mother was right. I can remember the Saturday afternoon when my son, Michael, who was seven, and my daughter, Michele, six, suddenly called out: "Daddy, Daddy, they've got some bad Arabs on TV." They were watching that great American morality play, TV wrestling. Akbar the Great, who liked to hear the cracking of bones, and Abdullah the Butcher, a dirty fighter who liked to inflict pain, were pinning their foes with "camel locks." From that day on, I knew I had to try to neutralize the media caricatures.

4   It hasn't been easy. With my children, I have watched animated heroes Heckle and Jeckle pull the rug from under "Ali Boo-Boo, the Desert Rat," and Laverne and Shirley stop "Sheik Ha-Mean-Ie" from conquering "the U.S. and the world." I have read comic books like the "Fantastic Four" and "G.I. Combat" whose characters have sketched Arabs as "lowlifes" and "human hyenas." Negative stereotypes were everywhere. A dictionary informed my youngsters that an Arab is a "vagabond, drifter, hobo and vagrant." Whatever happened, my wife wondered, to Aladdin's good genie?

5   To a child, the world is simple: good versus evil. But my children and others with Arab roots grew up without ever having seen a humane Arab on the silver screen, someone to pattern their lives after. Is it easier for a camel to go through the eye of a needle than for a screen Arab to appear as a genuine human being?

6   Hollywood producers must have an instant Ali Baba kit that contains scimitars, veils, sunglasses and such Arab clothing as *chadors* and *kufiyahs*. In the mythical "Ay-rabland," oil wells, tents, mosques, goats and shepherds prevail. Between the sand dunes, the camera focuses on a mock-up of a palace from "Arabian Nights"—or a military air base. Recent movies suggest that Americans are at war with Arabs, forgetting the fact that out of 21 Arab nations, America is friendly with 19 of them. And in "Wanted Dead or Alive," a movie that starred Gene Simmons, the leader of the rock group Kiss, the war comes home when an Arab terrorist comes to the United States dressed as a rabbi and, among other things, conspires with Arab-Americans to poison the people of Los Angeles. The movie was released last year.

7   The Arab remains American culture's favorite whipping boy. In his memoirs, Terrel Bell, Ronald Reagan's first secretary of education, writes about an "apparent bias among mid-level, right-wing staffers at the White House" who dismissed Arabs as "sand niggers." Sadly, the racial slurs continue. At a recent teacher's conference, I met a woman from Sioux Falls, S.D., who told me about the persistence of discrimination. She was in the process of adopting a baby when an agency staffer warned her that the infant had a problem. When she asked whether the child was mentally ill, or physically handicapped, there was silence. Finally, the worker said: "The baby is Jordanian."

8   To me, the Arab demon of today is much like the Jewish demon of yesterday. We deplore the false portrait of Jews as a swarthy menace. Yet a similar portrait has been accepted and transferred to another group of Semites—the Arabs. Print and broadcast journalists have started to challenge this stereotype. They are now revealing more humane images of Palestinian Arabs, a people who traditionally suffered from the myth that

Palestinian equals terrorist. Others could follow that lead and retire the stereotypical Arab to a media Valhalla.

It would be a step in the right direction if movie and TV producers developed characters modeled after real-life Arab-Americans. We could then see a White House correspondent like Helen Thomas, whose father came from Lebanon, in "The Golden Girls," a heart surgeon patterned after Dr. Michael DeBakey on "St. Elsewhere," or a Syrian-American playing tournament chess like Yasser Seirawan, the Seattle grandmaster.   9

Politicians, too, should speak out against the cardboard caricatures. They should refer to Arabs as friends, not just as moderates. And religious leaders could state that Islam like Christianity and Judaism maintains that all mankind is one family in the care of God. When all imagemakers rightfully begin to treat Arabs and all other minorities with respect and dignity, we may begin to unlearn our prejudices.   10

QUESTIONING AND DISCUSSING

Shaheen, "The Media's Image of Arabs"

1. This article was written in the late 1980s. Analyze Shaheen's examples and arguments. How might Shaheen have to extend his article since the events of September 11, 2001? Have the stereotypes become worse? How so? What attempts have there been to change them?

2. It might be argued that the media often stereotype a variety of groups. Consider beer commercials and the ways in which they portray men, for instance. Why do these stereotypes "work"? Are they harmful? Explain.

3. Again look closely at Shaheen's examples and overall argument—and then at other examples of stereotyping in the media or in your daily life—and determine whether stereotypes are ever appropriate. Explain your argument.

⊞

GLORIA WADE-GAYLES

Professor of English at Spelman College in Atlanta, Georgia, Gloria Wade-Gayles (1938–) writes that her mother's love for knowledge and education encouraged her own career: "She saw the freedom to trust your own power to think, a validation of yourself as something other than just a sponge that receives. We were so bound in time and circumstances that the books were liberating, empowering, motivating." Wade-Gayles received a full scholarship to LeMoyne College in Memphis, Tennessee, in 1955. Initially a math major and English minor, she was persuaded to write during a visit by a scholar of literature. Former Spelman president Johnetta B. Cole has written that "Gayles is a tough and tender teacher who sets impossible standards for her students to reach and then works with them until they get there." With a PhD from Emory University, Wade-Gayles has written a number of books on interdisciplinary, literary, and popular subjects, including *Pushed Back to Strength* (1993), a memoir; *No Crystal Stair: Race and Sex in Black Women's Novels, 1946–76* (1984), an interdisciplinary study; and *Rooted Against the Wind* (1996), from which this excerpt is taken.

⊞

Interracial Relationships Can Be Difficult to Accept

Black women face considerable difficulty overcoming their hostile feelings toward black men who marry white women. These relationships inspire feelings of abandonment and shame in African American women. Many feel that by marrying white women, black men send the message that white is better, a message that causes many black women to question their self-worth. Black women must learn to let go of their anger toward interracial relationships. There are more important things that deserve their anger, such as poverty and racial injustice.

1   I remember in my high school and college years being proud of the black man in *Mod Squad*. He was so very hip, so very visible, so very much an equal in the trio that fought crime. "Day-O. Day-O. Daylight come and me wanna' go home." I would Calypso dance in front of the mirror to [Harry] Belafonte's scratchy voice singing melodiously. And like other black women, I was proud of Sidney Poitier, that ebony brother of tight smoothness, who was the first of the big stars. There was something in the way he walked, leaning down in his hips, in the way he read a script through his eyes, in the way his deep blackness spoke of a power that was

mine to claim. I remember wanting the mellifluous voice that made James Earl Jones brilliant in any role—from "street" to Shakespearean. All married white women.

The pain we experience as black teenagers follows many of us into adulthood, and, if we are professional black women, it follows with a vengeance. As a colleague in an eastern school explained our situation, "Black men don't want us as mates because we are independent; white men, because we are black." We have to organize our own venting sessions. The only difference between us and black teenagers is the language we use, our attempt at some kind of analysis, and our refusal to mourn. Teenagers see an individual heartthrob; we see an entire championship basketball team: "Can you believe that every single black starter on the team has a white wife?" Teenagers know about athletes and entertainers; we know about politicians and scholars. Teenagers see faces; we see symbols that, in our opinion, spin the image of white women to the rhythm of symphonic chords. In our critique of *Jungle Fever,* for example, we see the carnival walk, the music, the cotton candy, the playful wrestling, which all precede sex between the black man and his white lover; and therefore we cannot miss seeing the very different symbols for the man and his black wife. The movie begins with them making such hard love—passion is what it is supposed to be—that the daughter asks, "Daddy, why were you hurting Mama?" Teenagers are so preoccupied with heartthrobs who marry "wrong" that they forget the men who marry "right." We don't. Adult black women all but cheer when we hear that a black male luminary is married to a black woman. Sadly, we do not discuss how the right-thinking brother treats his wife. What matters is that he *chose* one of us.

Choice

Choice is the key word in our reading of marriages between black women and white men and good treatment is our focus. The sister didn't do the choosing. She was *chosen.* Isn't that how it works in patriarchy? The man, not the woman, asks, "Will you marry me?" And didn't many of us in the Civil Rights movement, myself included, support the notion that marriages between black women and white men (unlike those between black men and white women) said more about the gains we thought we had achieved than the new laws which were never meant to be aggressively enforced? The men shook the very foundation of the system by legally marrying women the system saw as anybody's sexual property. We tended, therefore, to see white men and black women through a more accepting lens. Our logic might have been flawed, but the issue was never about logic in the first place.

4　　What's more, our argument continued, black women are immune to the charge of disloyalty, having demonstrated down through the ages and in all circumstances unswerving, unshakable—and perhaps insane—devotion to black men. For us, there was no credence to the idea that black women who marry interracially suffer the affliction of their counterparts among black men, that is, a preference for white. Since women love so easily, and so well, often foolishly, for us, the choice is more than likely a matter of the heart. Case closed for black women married to white men because the number is comparatively minuscule. Trial in session for black men married to white women because they were, in our opinion, too many of them who went that way immediately after their success in white America.

A Preference for White

5　　The trial is still in session, and because of the nature of race relations in our nation, we are pounding an iron-heavy gavel. We think we can read these men without ever seeing lines in the palms of their hands. We believe we know them by the signs they wear, flashing neon and without apology. They are the men who date only white; who attend only predominantly, or so-called integrated, gatherings; who can't remember expressions, songs, places, or people from home; who make as few trips home as possible; who refer to black people as "they"; and who have a long list of what "black people/they" shouldn't say and how "black people/they" shouldn't act.

6　　But not always. Sometimes black men in interracial relationships are like the character Truman in Alice Walker's *Meridian:* "blacker than thou" and equipped with the rhetoric, the walk, and the haircut to prove as much. For them, everything good is black, or, more precisely, African. And what better good for the nation than black babies, and who other than black women can give the people, or them, those new soldiers/warriors?

7　　But we believe we know them most certainly by a contempt they cannot conceal. It is in their body movements, their words, their eyes, and the odor of their perspiration when they are forced to be in close proximity with us.

8　　Those we do not know personally who shape a steep mountain on the graph of interracial marriages—the entertainers, athletes, politicians, etcetera—we nevertheless judge. Regardless of the signs they wear, our verdict is the same: they marry white because they prefer white. It is a matter of the mind, not the heart. Isn't that what Frantz Fanon told us in *Black Skin, White Masks?* Never mind that Fanon was *not* an African-American and was *not* writing about our unique racial reality in these United States. We dig into a dung heap of Freudian analysis until we locate the phrase that says what we want to hear:

> By loving me [the white woman] proves that I am worthy
> of white love. I am loved like a white man.
> I am a white man.

We know about exceptions to this rule, but give them little time in our 9
venting sessions. We say, "It's not like that with _____," or "They are in
love, period," and we promise to fight any Ku-Kluxer or rabid black nationalist who attempts to disturb their hearth. But the second in which we acknowledge they exist is followed by an hour of venting. This seems to make
good sense, for exceptions in any situation never represent the problem.
They are precisely that: *exceptions*. They do not change the rule.

The Pain of Self-Hatred

Nor do they change our history of pain as black women, or save us from 10
the self-hatred that turns us into erupting volcanoes at the sight of a black
man with a white woman. We see them, and we feel abandoned. We feel
abandoned because we have been abandoned in so many ways, by so many
people, and for so many centuries. We are the group of women furthest removed from the concept of beauty and femininity which invades almost
every spot on the planet, and, as a result, we are taught not to like ourselves, or, as my student said, not to believe that we can never do enough
or be enough to be loved and desired. The truth is we experience a pain
unique to us as a group when black men marry white women and even
when they don't.

It is a pain our mothers knew and their mothers before them. A pain 11
passed on from generation to generation because the circumstances that
create the pain have remained unchanged generation after generation. It
has become a part of us, this pain, finding its way to the placenta and to
the amniotic waters in which we swim before birth. "From the moment
we are born black and female," Audre Lorde writes, we are

> Steeped in hatred—for our color, for our sex, for our effrontery in daring to pre-
> sume we had a right to live. As children we absorbed that hatred, passed it through
> ourselves, and for the most part, we still live our lives outside of the recognition of
> what that hatred is and how it functions.

We struggle to be whole in a society of "entrenched loathing and contempt 12
for whatever is Black and female." I have been writing specifically about the
pain heterosexual women feel when black men choose white women, but
heterosexuals do not own this pain. Black lesbians experience it also, for in
their world race choices or race rejections are evident in love relationships.

I look at my past participation in venting sessions with gratitude for the 13
liberation I now experience, a liberation that was slow and gradual, and yet

that seems to have happened overnight, as if while I slept someone or something cut the straps of the straightjacket that was stealing my breath and, miraculously, I awoke able to breathe with arms freed for embracing. It must have been a good spirit who knew the weight of anger had become too much for me, too much, and that I wanted to be done with it. Relieved of it. Freed from it. The truth is, I was carrying too much anger—anger over what integration did not mean for the masses of black people; anger over the deterioration of black schools; anger over battering and homicide of black women; anger over violence against our children, our elderly, and our young men; anger over the writing of books (by blacks no less) that lie about our character and misread the cause of our suffering; anger over misogynist lyrics; anger over . . . ANGER. It was a long list; it was a heavy weight which I had to lighten or lose my mind. The question was, What could I/should I remove? What was important and what was not important? What could I change and what couldn't I change? What should a former activist take on as a mission and not take on? What was my business and not my business? What could make a difference in the world?

Out of Focus

14   The answer to those questions came with the clarity of a mockingbird singing from a rooftop in a North Carolina dawn, identifying herself and the place she has claimed as her own. I could see myself flying to a spiritually high place, identifying myself as a woman who loves herself, and claiming as my own a different place for struggle. Perched there, singing, I knew I would never again give my mind and my emotions over to something I could not change, did not have the right to change, and something that was not the cause of suffering in the world. I decided to remain focused in my anger, the better to be useful in a struggle for change, for the new justice we so desperately need. Anger over black men with white women, I sang, took me out of focus.

15   The percentage of black men marrying out of the race might be greater than the percentage of white men, but what are we talking about in terms of numbers? I began to ask myself. "Minuscule," I answered. There are twenty-plus million African-Americans (actually more, given tricks census plays) and I was sucking in all of that negativity because of a personal decision that a small group makes! The numbers don't add up to a million; at last count they constituted less than five percent of all black marriages. I talked to myself:

"Nonsense."
"No, it's not nonsense at all."
"Less than five percent. That's small."

"Not really. Actually, small is big for us."
"What do you mean?"
"The small number includes the big men. Men of influence."

Even so, I was quite simply weary of the weight of "the problem." I sang   16
about going elsewhere with my anger. Anger, channeled creatively and
used to galvanize us into constructive action, is an important emotion not
to be wasted. In the spiritual place to which I was journeying, I wanted my
anger to count, to stay on the high road of resistance, where it could target changes in the socioeconomic reality of my people rather than
changes in colors worn at wedding ceremonies. I decided that interracial
marriages did not deserve so precious an emotion.

Imprisoned by Race

Weariness was one factor in my liberation; my love for children, another.   17
How strange (and yet not so strange if I believe Spirit works in our lives)
that when I was struggling with my liberation, interracial children became
more visible than ever in grocery stores, shopping centers, and other public places. In almost all cases, their mothers were white. In the past, I would
see them and think about the same old pattern: white mother, black father.
Now I see the children and forget their parents, having decided that I cannot truly accept them if I question the union in which they were conceived. And the children I will never *not* accept. As if they are making a
point, babies drop their pacifiers at my feet, toddlers bump into me, and at
checkout counters, infants, propped in padded seats, face me rather than
their white mothers. How innocent they are! How unaware they are of the
insanity in the world we have created. How necessary it is for us to stop
talking about who married whom and receive the children without qualification into the circle of our embrace. Our failure to do so pushes them as
teenagers into the quicksand of peer acceptance, forcing them to choose to
be either black or white. Given this pressure, it is not surprising that they
are sometimes the most strident voices of anger in the venting session and
that their journal entries are often the most pained. That was the case with
a student in the seminar on autobiography. She didn't "look" biracial (but,
then, how do *they* always look?), but in a poignant autobiographical narrative, entitled "Trapped by Silence," she wrote about the pain of being the
daughter of a white mother and a black father. Trapped in a nation imprisoned by race, she was uncomfortable with the "cotton-white" skin of her
mother and obsessed with becoming black.

> *Everything my mother loved, I hated. Everything she did, I avoided. With every-*
> *thing she said, I disagreed. . . . How great a darkness that was! My only hope*

seemed to appear in places which glittered like pyrite. "The blacker, the better"
seemed to be my theme. . . . I began worshipping black boys, the same boys I had
avoided like liver and onions only a year before because they reminded me that I,
too, was a part of their culture. "But now I am BLACK," I thought.

18   What pain can be more consummate, I thought as I read her narrative, than rejection, no matter how brief, of the mother who births us.

19   The student wanted me to share her experiences in hopes that they would open the lens of our understanding to other dimensions of "the problem" and thereby make possible for other biracial children the acceptance of self she finally celebrates.

I had tried so hard for so long to be white, and then to be black, that I intentionally
or foolishly forgot that I am both. After being accepted to Spelman College, I real-
ized that I would have the opportunity to experience the world I had never known,
and my mother would be the provider of that opportunity. . . . I anticipated my
chance to be my white and black self. I began to close the chapter of my life replete
with cultural confusion and open a chapter filled with acceptance of my complete
self. I no longer felt I had to choose one or the other, so I embraced both as I gath-
ered my stuff.

A New List of Concerns

20   A maternal woman (who is ready for grandchildren), I have always delighted in waving bye-bye or playing peek-a-boo with children I see in grocery stores and shopping malls, but recently it seems that biracial children are seeking me out for a hug; and ever since I read "Trapped by Silence," they seem to be in all the public places I find myself. They reach toward me, perhaps to test me. I give them what I give all children: my love. I am reminded, as I was not before my enlightenment, that the only difference between these children and my grandmother and probably my great-great-grandmother is that, unlike them, these children exist because of a union entered into willingly, for whatever the reason, and lived in the full light of day. That is what the student who wrote the poignant narrative came to understand: in the full light of day, her parents celebrated their coming together and her birth.

21   At a different spiritual place, I made a new list of concerns that, working in coalition with others, I should address, have a moral obligation to address. Black men with white wives didn't make it on the list. I would be false to truth and, therefore, to my soul if I said I no longer believe that most black men with white wives have problems with themselves, with the race, and with black women. I will not lie. I believe many of them wear the aroma

of disdain we can smell miles away. I believe that for most of them the choice is not a matter of the heart; but not knowing who in the group followed his heart (How *can* I know?), I have decided not to judge. Like a recovering alcoholic who is hooked all over again with one sip, I have written my own recovery program. It is composed of one step: remember how much lighter you feel without the weight of anger and the weight of judging.

QUESTIONING AND DISCUSSING

Wade-Gayles, "Interracial Relationships Can Be Difficult to Accept"

1. This excerpt is from Wade-Gayles's 1996 book, *Rooted Against the Wind*. How does the title of that book suggest and enhance the arguments of this excerpt? How would you express Wade-Gayles's central argument?

2. Comment on Wade-Gayles's quoting of a colleague's controversial statement, "Black men don't want us because we are independent; white men, because we are black." What are the assumptions, and possible contradictions, behind this statement?

3. What are the ways in which Wade-Gayles achieves credibility in what is arguably an emotionally rooted stance? Consider, for instance, "Adult black women all but cheer when we hear that a black male luminary is married to a black woman. Sadly, we do not discuss how the right-thinking brother treats his wife."

4. How does Wade-Gayles liberate herself "from the self-hatred that turns us into erupting volcanoes at the sight of a black man with a white woman"? What are the roots and further manifestations of this self-hatred? How is it resolved? What types of values does her argument reveal?

5. Explain the list of concerns that Wade-Gayles feels that she has "a moral obligation to address." That said, however, explain what you might see as the difficulties of separating a moral, political stand from an emotionally valid, and perhaps equally political, one.

⊞

Born to poverty in a mud hut in Plinsk, near the border between Russia and Poland, Anzia Yezierska (1880–1970) came to New York City with her parents when she was fifteen and worked in a sweatshop while she went to night school to learn English. She won a scholarship to Columbia University to become a domestic-science teacher, an unusual event given the existing prejudice against women and immigrants, particularly Jewish immigrants. Unlike writers born to privilege, Yezierska documents immigrants' struggles for acceptance in the so-called "New World," a place where hopeful immigrants encounter hostility and xenophobia. After publishing several collections of stories and a novel recording the difficulties of Jewish immigrants and seeing her royalties all but evaporate during the Depression, Yezierska worked for the Works Progress Administration's Writers' Project, cataloguing trees in Central Park. In her later years, she continued to document and work to relieve the struggles of more recent immigrants—this time, Puerto Rican arrivals who found obstacles similar to those encountered by their predecessors.

⊞

My Own People

1   With the suitcase containing all her worldly possessions under her arm, Sophie Sapinsky elbowed her way through the noisy ghetto crowds. Push-cart peddlers and pullers-in shouted and gesticulated. Women with market-baskets pushed and shoved one another, eyes straining with the one thought—how to get the food a penny cheaper. With the same strained intentness, Sophie scanned each tenement, searching for a room cheap enough for her dwindling means.

2   In a dingy basement window a crooked sign, in straggling, penciled letters, caught Sophie's eye: "Room to let, a bargain, cheap."

3   The exuberant phrasing was quite in keeping with the extravagant dilapidation of the surroundings. "This is the very place," thought Sophie. "There couldn't be nothing cheaper in all New York."

4   At the foot of the basement steps she knocked.

5   "Come in!" a voice answered.

6   As she opened the door she saw an old man bending over a pot of potatoes on a shoemaker's bench. A group of children in all degrees of rags surrounded him, greedily snatching at the potatoes he handed out.

7   Sophie paused for an instant, but her absorption in her own problem was too great to halt the question: "Is there a room to let?"

8   "Hanneh Breineh, in the back, has a room." The old man was so preoccupied filling the hungry hands that he did not even look up.

Sophie groped her way to the rear hall. A gaunt-faced woman answered 9
her inquiry with loquacious enthusiasm. "A grand room for the money. I'll
let it down to you only for three dollars a month. In the whole block is no
bigger bargain. I should live so."

As she talked, the woman led her through the dark hall into an airshaft 10
room. A narrow window looked out into the bottom of a chimney-like pit,
where lay the accumulated refuse from a score of crowded kitchens.

"Oi Weh!" gasped Sophie, throwing open the sash. "No air and no 11
light. Outside shines the sun and here it's so dark."

"It ain't so dark. It's only a little shady. Let me only turn up the gas for 12
you and you'll quick see everything like with sunshine."

The claw-fingered flame revealed a rusty, iron cot, an inverted potato 13
barrel that served for a table, and two soap-boxes for chairs.

Sophie felt of the cot. It sagged and flopped under her touch. "The bed 14
has only three feet!" she exclaimed in dismay.

"You can't have Rockefeller's palace for three dollars a month," de- 15
fended Hanneh Breineh, as she shoved one of the boxes under the legless
corner of the cot. "If the bed ain't so steady, so you got good neighbors.
Upstairs lives Shprintzeh Gittle, the herring-woman. You can buy by her
the biggest bargains in fish, a few days older. . . . What she got left over
from the Sabbath, she sells to the neighbors cheap. . . . In the front lives
Shmendrik, the shoemaker. I'll tell you the truth, he ain't no real shoemaker. He never yet made a pair of whole shoes in his life. He's a learner
from the old country—a tzadik, a saint; but every time he sees in the street
a child with torn feet, he calls them in and patches them up. His own eating, the last bite from his mouth, he divides up with them."

"Three dollars," deliberated Sophie, scarcely hearing Hanneh Breineh's 16
chatter. "I will never find anything cheaper. It has a door to lock and I can
shut this woman out. . . . I'll take it," she said, handing her the money.

Hanneh Breineh kissed the greasy bills gloatingly. "I'll treat you like a 17
mother! You'll have it good by me like in your own home."

"Thanks—but I got no time to shmoos. I got to be alone to get my 18
work done."

The rebuff could not penetrate Hanneh Breineh's joy over the sudden 19
possession of three dollars.

"Long years on you! May we be to good luck to one another!" was Han- 20
neh Breineh's blessing as she closed the door.

Alone in her room—*her* room, securely hers—yet with the flash of tri- 21
umph, a stab of bitterness. All that was hers—so wretched and so ugly!
Had her eager spirit, eager to give and give, no claim to a bit of beauty—
a shred of comfort?

22   Perhaps her family was right in condemning her rashness. Was it worth while to give up the peace of home, the security of a regular job—suffer hunger, loneliness, and want—for what? For something she knew in her heart was beyond her reach. Would her writing ever amount to enough to vindicate the uprooting of her past? Would she ever become articulate enough to express beautifully what she saw and felt? What had she, after all, but a stifling, sweat shop experience, a meager, night-school education, and this wild, blind hunger to release the dumbness that choked her?

23   Sophie spread her papers on the cot beside her. Resting her elbows on the potato barrel, she clutched her pencil with tense fingers. In the notebook before her were a hundred beginnings, essays, abstractions, outbursts of chaotic moods. She glanced through the titles: "Believe in Yourself," "The Quest of the Ideal."

24   Meaningless tracings on the paper, her words seemed to her now—a restless spirit pawing at the air. The intensity of experience, the surge of emotion that had been hers when she wrote—where were they? The words had failed to catch the life-beat—had failed to register the passion she had poured into them.

25   Perhaps she was not a writer, after all. Had the years and years of night-study been in vain? Choked with discouragement, the cry broke from her, "O—God—God help me! I feel—I see, but it all dies in me—dumb!"

26   Tedious days passed into weeks. Again Sophie sat staring into her notebook. "There's nothing here that's alive. Not a word yet says what's in me . . .

27   "But it *is* in me!" with clenched fist she smote her bosom. "It must be in me! I believe in it! I got to get it out—even if it tears my flesh in pieces—even if it kills me! . . .

28   "But these words—these flat, dead words . . .

29   "Whether I can write or can't write—I can't stop writing. I can't rest. I can't breathe. There's no peace, no running away for me on earth except in the struggle to give out what's in me. The beat from my heart—the blood from my veins—must flow out into my words."

30   She returned to her unfinished essay, "Believe in Yourself." Her mind groping—clutching at the misty incoherence that clouded her thoughts—she wrote on.

31   "These sentences are yet only wood—lead; but I can't help it—I'll push on—on—I'll not eat—I'll not sleep—I'll not move from this spot till I get it to say on the paper what I got in my heart!"

32   Slowly the dead words seemed to begin to breathe. Her eyes brightened. Her cheeks flushed. Her very pencil trembled with the eager onrush of words.

Then a sharp rap sounded on her door. With a gesture of irritation So- 33
phie put down her pencil and looked into the burning, sunken eyes of her
neighbor, Hanneh Breineh.

"I got yourself a glass of tea, good friend. It ain't much I got to give away, 34
but it's warm even if it's nothing."

Sophie scowled. "You must n't bother yourself with me. I'm so busy— 35
thanks."

"Don't thank me yet so quick. I got no sugar." Hanneh Breineh edged 36
herself into the room confidingly. "At home, in Poland, I not only had
sugar for tea—but even jelly—a jelly that would lift you up to heaven. I
thought in America everything would be so plenty, I could drink the tea
out from my sugar-bowl. But ach! Not in Poland did my children starve
like in America!"

Hanneh Breineh, in a friendly manner, settled herself on the sound end 37
of the bed, and began her jeremaid.

"Yosef, my man, ain't no bread-giver. Already he got consumption the 38
second year. One week he works and nine weeks he lays sick."

In despair Sophie gathered her papers, wondering how to get the 39
woman out of her room. She glanced through the page she had written,
but Hanneh Breineh, unconscious of her indifference, went right on.

"How many times it is tearing the heart out from my body—should I take 40
Yosef's milk to give to the baby, or the baby's milk to give to Yosef? If he was
dead the pensions they give to widows would help feed my children. Now
I got only the charities to help me. A black year on them! They should only
have to feed their own children on what they give me."

Resolved not to listen to the intruder, Sophie debated within herself. 41
"Should I call my essay 'Believe in Yourself,' or wouldn't it be stronger to
say, 'Trust Yourself'? But if I say, 'Trust Yourself,' would n't they think that
I got the words from Emerson?"

Hanneh Breineh's voice went on, but it sounded to Sophie like a faint 42
buzzing from afar. "Gotteniu! How much did it cost me my life to go and
swear myself that my little Fannie—only skin and bones—that she is already fourteen! How it chokes me the tears every morning when I got to
wake her and push her out to the shop when her eyes are yet shutting
themselves with sleep!"

Sophie glanced at her wrist-watch as it ticked away the precious min- 43
utes. She must get rid of the woman! Had she not left her own sister, sacrificed all the comfort, all association, for solitude and its golden
possibilities? For the first time in her life she had the chance to be by herself and think. And now, the thoughts which a moment ago had seemed

like a flock of fluttering birds had come so close—and this woman with her sordid wailing had scattered them.

44 "I'm a savage, a beast, but I got to ask her to get out—this very minute," resolved Sophie. But before she could summon the courage to do what she wanted to do, there was a timid knock at the door, and the wizened little Fannie, her face streaked with tears, stumbled in.

45 "The inspector said it's a lie. I ain't yet fourteen," she whimpered.

46 Hanneh Breineh paled. "Woe is me! Sent back from the shop? God from the world—is there no end to my troubles? Why did n't you hide yourself when you saw the inspector come?"

47 "I was running to hide myself under the table, but she caught me and she said she'll take me to the Children's Society and arrest me and my mother for sending me to work too soon."

48 "Arrest me?" shrieked Hanneh Breineh, beating her breast. "Let them only come and arrest me! I'll show America who I am! Let them only begin themselves with me! . . . Black is for my eyes . . . the groceryman will not give us another bread till we pay him the bill!"

49 "The inspector said . . ." The child's brow puckered in an effort to recall the words.

50 "What did the inspector said? Gotteniu!" Hanneh Breineh wrung her hands in passionate entreaty. "Listen only once to my prayer! Send on the inspector only a quick death! I only wish her to have her own house with twenty-four rooms and each of the twenty-four rooms should be twenty-four beds and the chills and the fever should throw her from one bed to another!"

51 "Hanneh Breineh, still yourself a little," entreated Sophie.

52 "How can I still myself without Fannie's wages? Bitter is me! Why do I have to live so long?"

53 "The inspector said . . ."

54 "What did the inspector said? A thunder should strike the inspector! Ain't I as good a mother as other mothers? Would n't I better send my children to school? But who'll give us to eat? And who'll pay us the rent?"

55 Hanneh Breineh wiped her red-lidded eyes with the corner of her apron.

56 "The president from America should only come to my bitter heart. Let him go fighting himself with the pushcarts how to get the eating a penny cheaper. Let him try to feed his children on the money the charities give me and we'd see if he would n't better send his littlest ones to the shop better than to let them starve before his eyes. Woe is me! What for did I come to America? What's my life—nothing but one terrible, never-stopping fight with the grocer and the butcher and the landlord . . ."

57 Suddenly Sophie's resentment for her lost morning was forgotten. The crying waste of Hanneh Breineh's life lay open before her eyes like pic-

tures in a book. She saw her own life in Hanneh Breineh's life. Her efforts to write were like Hanneh Breineh's efforts to feed her children. Behind her life and Hanneh Breineh's life she saw the massed ghosts of thousands upon thousands beating—beating out their hearts against rock barriers.

"The inspector said . . ." Fannie timidly attempted again to explain. 58

"The inspector!" shrieked Hanneh Breineh, as she seized hold of Fannie 59 in a rage. "Hell-fire should burn the inspector! Tell me again about the inspector and I'll choke the life out from you—"

Sophie sprang forward to protect the child from the mother. "She's only 60 trying to tell you something."

"Why should she yet throw salt on my wounds? If there was enough 61 bread in the house would I need an inspector to tell me to send her to school? If America is so interested in poor people's children, then why don't they give them to eat till they should go to work? What learning can come into a child's head when the stomach is empty?"

A clutter of feet down the creaking cellar steps, a scuffle of broken shoes, 62 and a chorus of shrill voices, as the younger children rushed in from school.

"Mamma—what's to eat?" 63

"It smells potatoes!" 64

"Pfui! The pot is empty! It smells over from Cohen's." 65

"Jake grabbed all the bread!" 66

"Mamma—he kicked the piece out from my hands!" 67

"Mamma—it's so empty in my stomach! Ain't there nothing?" 68

"Gluttons—wolves—thieves!" Hanneh Breineh shrieked. "I should 69 only live to bury you all in one day!"

The children, regardless of Hanneh Breineh's invectives, swarmed 70 around her like hungry bees, tearing at her apron, her skirt. Their voices rose in increased clamor, topped only by their mother's imprecations. "Gotteniu! Tear me away from these leeches on my neck! Send on them only a quick death! . . . Only a minute's peace before I die!"

"Hanneh Breineh—children! What's the matter?" Shmendrik stood at 71 the door. The sweet quiet of the old man stilled the raucous voices as the coming of evening stills the noises of the day.

"There's no end to my troubles! Hear them hollering for bread, and the 72 grocer stopped to give till the bill is paid. Woe is me! Fannie sent home by the inspector and not a crumb in the house!"

"I got something." The old man put his hands over the heads of the chil- 73 dren in silent benediction. "All come in by me. I got sent me a box of cake."

"Cake!" The children cried, catching at the kind hands and snuggling 74 about the shabby coat.

"Yes. Cake and nuts and raisins and even a bottle of wine." 75

76   The children leaped and danced around him in their wild burst of joy.

77   "Cake and wine—a box—to you? Have the charities gone crazy?" Hanneh Breineh's eyes sparkled with light and laughter.

78   "No—no," Shmendrik explained hastily. "Not from the charities—from a friend—for the holidays."

79   Shmendrik nodded invitingly to Sophie, who was standing in the door of her room. "The roomerkeh will also give a taste with us our party?"

80   "Sure will she!" Hanneh Breineh took Sophie by the arm. "Who'll say no in this black life to cake and wine?"

81   Young throats burst into shrill cries. "Cake and wine—wine and cake—raisins and nuts—nuts and raisins!" The words rose in a triumphant chorus. The children leaped and danced in time to their chant, almost carrying the old man bodily into his room in the wildness of their joy.

82   The contagion of this sudden hilarity erased from Sophie's mind the last thought of work and she found herself seated with the others on the cobbler's bench.

83   From under his cot the old man drew forth a wooden box. Lifting the cover he held up before wondering eyes a large frosted cake embedded in raisins and nuts.

84   Amid the shouts of glee Shmendrik now waved aloft a large bottle of grape-juice.

85   The children could contain themselves no longer and dashed forward.

86   "Shah—shah! Wait only!" He gently halted their onrush and waved them back to their seats.

87   "The glasses for the wine!" Hanneh Breineh rushed about hither and thither in happy confusion. From the sink, the shelf, the windowsill, she gathered cracked glasses, cups without handles—anything that would hold even a few drops of the yellow wine.

88   Sacrificial solemnity filled the basement as the children breathlessly watched Shmendrik cut the precious cake. Mouths—even eyes—watered with the intensity of their emotion.

89   With almost religious fervor Hanneh Breineh poured the grape-juice into the glasses held in the trembling hands of the children. So overwhelming was the occasion that none dared to taste till the ritual was completed. The suspense was agonizing as one and all waited for Shmendrik's signal.

90   "Hanneh Breineh—you drink from my Sabbath wine-glass!"

91   Hanneh Breineh clinked glassed with Shmendrik. "Long years on you—long years on us all!" Then she turned to Sophie, clinked glasses once more. "May you yet marry yourself from our basement to a millionaire!" Then she lifted the glass to her lips.

92   The spell was broken. With a yell of triumph the children gobbled the cake in huge mouthfuls and sucked the golden liquid. All the traditions of

wealth and joy that ever sparkled from the bubbles of champagne smiled at Hanneh Breineh from her glass of California grape-juice.

"Ach!" she sighed. "How good it is to forget your troubles, and only those that's got troubles have the chance to forget them!" 93

She sipped the grape-juice leisurely, thrilled into ecstasy with each lingering drop. "How it laughs yet in me, the life, the minute I turn my head from my worries!" 94

With growing wonder in her eyes, Sophie watched Hanneh Breineh. This ragged wreck of a woman—how passionately she clung to every atom of life! Hungrily, she burned through the depths of every experience. How she flared against wrongs—and how every tiny spark of pleasure blazed into joy! 95

Within a half-hour this woman had touched the whole range of human emotions, from bitterest agony to dancing joy. The terrible despair at the onrush of her starving children when she cried out, "O that I should only bury you all in one day!" And now the leaping light of the words: "How it laughs yet in me, the life, the minute I turn my head from my worries." 96

"Ach, if I could only write like Hanneh Breineh talks!" thought Sophie. "Her words dance with a thousand colors. Like a rainbow it flows from her lips." Sentences from her own essays marched before her, stiff and wooden. How clumsy, how unreal, were her most labored phrases compared to Hanneh Breineh's spontaneity. Fascinated, she listed to Hanneh Breineh, drinking her words as a thirst-perishing man drinks water. Every bubbling phrase filled her with a drunken rapture to create. 97

"Up till now I was only trying to write from my head. It was n't real—it was n't life. Hanneh Breineh is real. Hanneh Breineh is life." 98

"Ach! What do the rich people got but dried-up dollars? Pfui on them and their money!" Hanneh Breineh held up her glass to be refilled. "Let me only win a fortune on the lotteree and move myself in my own bought house. Let me only have my first hundred dollars in the bank and I'll lift up my head like a person and tell the charities to eat their own cornmeal. I'll get myself an automobile like the kind rich ladies and ride up to their houses on Fifth Avenue and feed them only once on the eating they like so good for me and my children." 99

With a smile of benediction Shmendrik refilled the glasses and cut for each of his guests another slice of cake. Then came the handful of nuts and raisins. 100

As the children were scurrying about for hammers and iron lasts with which to crack their nuts, the basement door creaked. Unannounced, a woman entered—the "friendly visitor" of the charities. Her look of awful amazement swept the group of merry-makers. 101

"Mr. Shmendrik!—Hanneh Breineh!" Indignation seethed in her voice. "What's this? A feast—a birthday?" 102

Gasps—bewildered glances—a struggle for utterance! 103

104   "I came to make my monthly visit—evidently I'm not needed."

105   Shmendrik faced the accusing eyes of the "friendly visitor." "Holiday eating . . ."

106   "Oh—I'm glad you're so prosperous."

107   Before any one had gained presence of mind enough to explain things, the door had clanked. The "friendly visitor" had vanished.

108   "Pfui!" Hanneh Breineh snatched up her glass and drained its contents. "What will she do now? Will we get no more dry bread from the charities because once we ate cake?"

109   "What for did she come?" asked Sophie.

110   "To see that we don't over-eat ourselves!" returned Hanneh Breineh. "She's a 'friendly visitor'! She learns us how to cook cornmeal. By pictures and lectures she shows us how the poor people should live without meat, without milk, without butter, and without eggs. Always it's on the end of my tongue to ask her, 'You learned us to do without so much, why can't you yet learn us how to eat without eating?'"

111   The children seized the last crumbs of the cake that Shmendrik handed them and rushed for the street.

112   "What a killing look was on her face," said Sophie. "Could n't she be a little glad for your gladness?"

113   "Charity ladies—gladness?" The joy of the grape-wine still rippled in Hanneh Breineh's laughter. "For poor people is only cornmeal. Ten cents a day—to feed my children!"

114   Still in her rollicking mood Hanneh Breineh picked up the baby and tossed it like a Bacchante. "Could you be happy a lot with ten cents in your stomach? Ten cents—half a can of condensed milk—then fill yourself the rest with water! . . . Maybe yet feed you with all water and save the ten-cent pieces to buy you a carriage like the Fifth Avenue babies! . . ."

115   The soft sound of a limousine purred through the area grating and two well-fed figures in seal-skin coats, led by the "friendly visitor," appeared at the door.

116   "Mr. Bernstein, you can see for yourself." The "friendly visitor" pointed to the table.

117   The merry group shrank back. It was as if a gust of icy wind had swept all the joy and laughter from the basement.

118   "You are charged with intent to deceive and obtain assistance by dishonest means," said Mr. Bernstein.

119   "Dishonest?" Shmendrik paled.

120   Sophie's throat strained with passionate protest, but no words came to her release.

121   "A friend—a friend"—stammered Shmendrik—"sent me the holiday eating."

The superintendent of the Social Betterment Society faced him accus- | 122
ingly. "You told us that you had no friends when you applied to us for
assistance."

"My friend—he knew me in my better time." Shmendrik flushed | 123
painfully. "I was once a scholar—respected. I wanted by this one friend to
hold myself like I was."

Mr. Bernstein had taken from the bookshelf a number of letters, | 124
glanced through them rapidly and handed them one by one to the defer-
ential superintendent.

Shmendrik clutched at his hart in an agony of humiliation. Suddenly his | 125
bent body straightened. His eyes dilated. "My letters—my life—you dare?"

"Of course we dare!" The superintendent returned Shmendrik's livid | 126
gaze, made bold by the confidence that what he was doing was the only
scientific method of administering philanthropy. "These dollars so generously given, must go to those most worthy. . . . I find in these letters references to gifts of fruit and other luxuries you did not report at our office."

"He never kept nothing for himself!" Hanneh Breineh broke in defen- | 127
sively. "He gave it all for the children."

Ignoring the interruption Mr. Bernstein turned to the "friendly visitor." | 128
"I'm glad you brought my attention to this case. It's but one of the many
impositions on our charity . . . Come . . ."

"Kossacks! Pogromschiks!" Sophie's rage broke at last. "You call your- | 129
selves Americans? You dare call yourselves Jews? You bosses of the poor!
This man Shmendrik, whose house you broke into, whom you made to
shame like a beggar—he is the one Jew from whom the Jews can be proud!
He gives all he is—all he has—as God gives. He *is* charity.

"But you—you are the greed—the shame of the Jews! *All-right-niks*—fat | 130
bellies in fur coats! What do you give from yourselves? You may eat and
bust eating! Nothing you give till you've stuffed yourselves so full that
your hearts are dead!"

The door closed in her face. Her wrath fell on indifferent backs as the | 131
visitors mounted the steps to the street.

Shmendrik groped blindly for the Bible. In a low, quavering voice, he | 132
began the chant of the oppressed—the wail of the downtrodden. "I am
afraid, and a trembling taketh hold of my flesh. Wherefore do the wicked
live, become old, yea, mighty in power?"

Hanneh Breineh and the children drew close around the old man. They | 133
were weeping—unconscious of their weeping—deep-buried memories
roused by the music, the age-old music of the Hebrew race.

Through the grating Sophie saw the limousine pass. The chant flowed | 134
on: "Their houses are safe from fear; neither is the rod of God upon them."

Silently Sophie stole back to her room. She flung herself on the cot, | 135 pressed her fingers to her burning eyeballs. For a long time she lay rigid, clenched—listening to the drumming of her heart like the sea against rock barriers. Presently the barriers burst. Something in her began pouring itself out. She felt for her pencil—paper—and began to write. Whether she reached out to God or man she knew not, but she wrote on and on all through that night.

136   The gray light entering her grated window told her that beyond was dawn. Sophie looked up: "Ach! At last it writes itself in me!" she whispered triumphantly. "It's not me—it's their cries—my own people—crying in me! Hanneh Breineh, Shmendrik, they will not be stilled in me, till all America stops to listen."

Questioning and Discussing

Yezierska, "My Own People"

1. Carefully analyze the characters in this story. What can you infer about their situation? How so? Refer specifically to examples you discern in the text.

2. Who is the "friendly visitor," and why does the visit provoke such outrage?

3. What are the various sets of values—questionable and otherwise—suggested by the story? What is the irony of the title, and how does it shed light on these various "values"?

4. What is the irony of this tale, and how might it be a call to political action? For what purpose? How might Yezierska's story of early-twentieth-century immigration shed light on our own times?

5. Research information about and personal accounts of immigrants to the United States in the early twentieth century. Consider not only Jewish immigrants (Yezierska's primary focus) but also Italians, Irish, and other nationalities. How does Yezierska's story reflect the experiences of these groups as well?

⊞

"UNIDENTIFIED CONCENTRATION CAMP, GERMANY, AT TIME OF LIBERATION BY U.S. ARMY," 1945 (U.S. ARMY PHOTOGRAPHIC PRINT)

This is one among many horrors photographed by the U.S. Army Signal Corps and available through the Library of Congress Prints and Photographs Division in Washington, D.C. These images were taken in 1945 (noted on the image as April 8–24, 1945) as the Allied Forces liberated German concentration camps and found the tragic evidence of the Nazis' plan to exterminate the Jewish people and other "undesirable" minorities. ⊞

"Unidentified Concentration Camp, Germany, at Time of Liberation by U.S. Army, 1945"

1. The title of this horrifying photograph likely came about naturally as the image was being made by an unidentified U.S. Army photographer documenting what the Allies found as they liberated Nazi concentration camps at the end of World War II in 1945. How does the title, however, take on unintentional irony, given what is depicted in the image itself?

2. It is difficult to discern the justification for hatred so extreme that it could lead to outcomes such as this. Research information not only on the liberation of concentration camps by Allied soldiers and what they found but also about the events leading up to the Nazi justification for the imprisonment, torture, and murder of millions of Jews and others. What is the importance of memory concerning events that occurred more than fifty years ago? What can we learn from our study of these atrocities that will inform the present?

Chapter 4 Broadening My View: How Do I Perceive Difference?

1. Several of the selections in this chapter take on the status quo—assumptions about "the way things should be" in society as a whole. Select three examples from this chapter that resist conventional thinking (or that resisted conventional thinking in their time) and argue the ways in which these selections do so in similar and/or different ways, using examples from each selection to support your point of view.

2. Selecting from among Gail Shister's "NBC Has Its Eye on Reality Series Coming to Bravo," Gloria Wade-Gayles's "Interracial Relationships Can Be Difficult to Accept," Jack G. Shaheen's "The Media's Image of Arabs," Richard Wright's "The Man Who Went to Chicago," and Michael Harrington's excerpt from *The Other America*, consider the various manifestations of stereotyping as discussed by each writer, even if she or he does not use that word specifically. To what conclusion can you come regarding the various subtle and not-so-subtle ways in which discrimination and stereotyping exist?

3. Examine Dr. Martin Luther King, Jr.'s "Letter from a Birmingham Jail" and Bertrand Russell's "Why I Am Not a Christian" and comment on the values

and moral attitudes demonstrated by each, contrasting it with the U.S. Army 1945 image from a concentration camp in Germany. When contrasted with the reality depicted in the photo, what are the ironies of the essays' assumptions about belief and morality?

⊞

5

Getting Educated

What Have Others Taught Me?

"That is the great advantage
of inner life: it grants everyone
the privilege of preferring
himself to all others."
SIMONE DE BEAUVOIR

One of many sites providing term papers (usually for a fee), CheatHouse.com is among those unabashedly direct, similar purveyors that include Cheat.com. The easy availability of "pre-fab" papers of often questionable quality raises a variety of serious issues, not only about the marketplace but also about the value of education, accountability—and honesty. That instructors suspecting students of plagiarism can now go to powerful search engines to reveal that dishonesty raises further questions about the purposes of education and the ways in which teachers must often spend their time.

⊞

CheatHouse.com

See facing page.

QUESTIONING AND DISCUSSING

"CheatHouse.com homepage"

1. The ethical concerns raised by sites of this type are, one might argue, obvious. But are they? How do sites like this potentially change the nature of education?

2. What is the extent to which students have become immune to the ethical issues surrounding the use of sites such as this one? What is the remedy? What are the educational implications for students who become dependent on sites such as this?

3. In addition to the concerns of accountability and honesty, are there other, practical concerns that one should consider regarding these sites? What are they? How do these concerns relate to the use of technology in general— and to the dependence on the Internet in particular? How does the design of this site suggest some of these concerns?

⊞

Select a TERM PAPER topic:

Essays & Papers On Literature ▼   View Papers!

50,000+ Essays & Papers

SEARCH

Search for Essays:

[   ]

○ Essays in all languages
○ Only English essays

Search!

STATS

Essays:	26091
Essays pending:	147
Today's essays:	116
Comments:	9512
Ratings:	96788
Members:	103970
Members online:	6
Guests online:	155

CHAT

[a67sm]
anyone alive
[a_beautifulmistake]
im alive and well :P
[a67sm]
damn I was hoping for no
response for no reason
[mortalixe]
neh

[   ]

Talk

(chat history)

Welcome to CheatHouse.com!

THOUSANDS OF *FREE ESSAYS* IN OVER 130 CATEGORIES. LEADING THE INDUSTRY SINCE 1995

CheatHouse is the perfect site for research, late assignments and general reference. Have a look at a complete list of all the essays we have, or try out our search engine.

There are over 10,000 **free essays** waiting for you if you contribute to the database.

To use any of our services, you need to register which is free and only takes 42 seconds. If this is your first visit, then check out our essays right now. If you want a general overview of CheatHouse and how it works, see "What is CheatHouse?"

If you want full, totally unlimited access NOW, then:

CLICK HERE TO GET THE SYSTEM PASSWORD

SUBJECT LIST

Subject name:	Description:	Total:
AREA & COUNTRY STUDIES Travel Descriptions.	Specific countries and regions.	513
ARTS Film & TV Studies, Music History & Studies, Drama.	Various paintings and works of art, artist, periods and styles, movies, TV shows and film analysis.	1931
BUSINESS Management, Case Studies, Marketing.	Business in general, accounting, marketing and cases.	1654
HISTORY North American History, European History, World History.	World and regional history.	3423
HUMANITIES Health & Medicine, Philosophy, Religion & Faith, ...	History, literature, book, authors, philosophy and classical studies.	3012
LAW & GOVERNMENT Law, Civil Rights, Government ...	Human rights, laws, government and organisations.	1876
LITERATURE European Literature, North American, Creative Writing, ...	Book reports, reviews, analysis of classic and modern literature.	7100
SCIENCES Biology, Computer Science, Environmental Science, ...	Biology, chemistry, computers science, mathematics, physics and more.	2655
SOCIAL SCIENCES Controversial Issues, Society and community, Political Science, ...	Economics, current issues, politics, sociology and psychology.	3877

ARTICLES

Administrator, 25.08.2003, 08:28:34

Using sources without plagiarizing

In conjunction with last weeks article about how to properly cite your sources, this week we focus on how to use that information when dealing with essays.

LOGIN

username:

[   ]

password:

[   ]   login

☐ Remember login

I forgot my login info

I want full access now

I want to register

NEWS

14 Jan 2004
Change password feature
30 Nov 2003
Our best wishes for the holiday season
18 Nov 2003
20,000 Essays and server power
06 Oct 2003
19,000 Essays and growing!

Older News ...

NEW ESSAYS

A concept paper ...
This is an edit ...
Holi - the fest ...
Conflict manage ...
Treasury Human ...
Ban Smoking
Tundra Biom cli ...
The French Revo ...
This is an outl ...
Personal effect ...

RANKING

Highest Ranking Users
• couclove7(53885)
• ccriustangs2001(46355)
• Eqqy(45320)
• masterpuppet(42335)
• yankee842(28895)
• Robert Kestenbaum (20520)
• c0lriski(17070)
• glengem(16705)
• hoba(16090)
• mrjafinchopra(15945)

SETH STEVENSON

Seth Stevenson "shops for *Slate*," as noted in the online magazine, and also writes reports from faraway places that include India during the Monsoon season. He is noted for witty, insightfully irreverent articles that purport to give consumer-related guidance to *Slate* readers. At a time when plagiarism is more rampant than ever—thanks to the Internet—Stevenson's online article appears to offer a shopper's guide but in fact offers a bit more.

Adventures in Cheating
*A Guide to Buying Term Papers Online**

1   Students, your semester is almost over. This fall, did you find yourself pulling many bong hits but few all-nighters? Absorbing much Schlitz but little Nietzsche? Attending Arizona State University? If the answer is yes to any or (especially) all these questions, you will no doubt be plagiarizing your term papers.

2   Good for you—we're all short on time these days. Yes, it's ethically blah blah blah to cheat on a term paper blah. The question is: How do you do it right? For example, the chump move is to find some library book and copy big hunks out of it. No good: You still have to walk to the library, find a decent book, and link the hunks together with your own awful prose. Instead, why not just click on a term paper Web site and buy the whole damn paper already written by some smart dude? *Que bella!* Ah, but which site?

3   I shopped at several online term paper stores to determine where best to spend your cheating dollar. After selecting papers on topics in history, psychology, and biology, I had each paper graded by one of my judges. These were: *Slate* writer David Greenberg, who teaches history at Columbia; my dad, who teaches psychology at the University of Rhode Island (sometimes smeared as the ASU of the East); and my girlfriend, who was a teaching assistant in biology at Duke (where she says cheating was quite common). So, which site wins for the best combination of price and paper quality? I compared free sites, sites that sell "pre-witten papers," and a site that writes custom papers to your specifications.

*© *Slate*/Distributed by United Feature Syndicate, Inc.

Free Sites

A quick Web search turns up dozens of sites filled with free term papers. 4
Some ask you to donate one of your own papers in exchange, but most
don't. I chose one from each of our fields for comparison and soon found
that when it comes to free papers, you get just about what you pay for.

EssaysFree.com: From this site I chose a history paper titled "The Infa- 5
mous Watergate Scandal." Bad choice. This paper had no thesis, no argument, random capitalization, and bizarre spell-checking errors—including
"taking the whiteness stand" (witness) and "the registration of Nixon"
(resignation). My judge said if they gave F's at Columbia, well . . . Instead,
it got a good old "Please come see me."

BigNerds.com: Of the free bio paper I chose from this site, my judge said, 6
"Disturbing. I am still disturbed." It indeed read less like a term paper than
a deranged manifesto. Rambling for 11 single-spaced pages and ostensibly
on evolutionary theory, it somehow made reference to Lamarck, Sol In-
victus, and "the blanket of a superficial American Dream." Meanwhile, it
garbled its basic explanation of population genetics. Grade: "I would not
give this a grade so much as suggest tutoring, a change in majors, some sort
of counseling . . ."

OPPapers.com: This site fared much better. A paper titled "Critically 7
Evaluate Erikson's Psychosocial Theory" spelled Erikson's name wrong in
the first sentence, yet still won a C+/B- from my dad. It hit most of the important points—the problem was no analysis. And the citations all came
from textbooks, not real sources. Oddly, this paper also used British
spellings ("behaviour") for no apparent reason. But all in all not terrible,
considering it was free. OPPapers.com, purely on style points, was my favorite site. The name comes from an old hip-hop song ("You down with
O-P-P?" meaning other people's . . . genitalia), the site has pictures of
coed babes, and one paper in the psych section was simply the phrase "I
wanna bang Angelina Jolie" typed over and over again for several pages.
Hey, whaddaya want for free?

Sites Selling Pre-Written Papers

There are dozens of these—I narrowed it down to three sites that seemed 8
fairly reputable and were stocked with a wide selection. (In general, the
selection offered on pay sites was 10 times bigger than at the free ones.)

Each pay site posted clear disclaimers that you're not to pass off these papers as your own work. Sure you're not.

9 **AcademicTermPapers.com:** This site charged $7 per page, and I ordered "The Paranoia Behind Watergate" for $35. Well worth it. My history judge gave it the highest grade of all the papers he saw—a B or maybe even a B+. Why? It boasted an actual argument. A few passages, however, might set off his plagiarism radar (or "pladar"). They show almost too thorough a command of the literature.

10 My other purchase here was a $49 bio paper titled "The Species Concept." Despite appearing in the bio section of the site, this paper seemed to be for a philosophy class. Of course, no way to know that until after you've bought it (the pay sites give you just the title and a very brief synopsis of each paper). My judge would grade this a C- in an intro bio class, as its conclusion was "utterly meaningless," and it tossed around "airy" philosophies without actually understanding the species concept at all.

11 **PaperStore.net:** For about $10 per page, I ordered two papers from the Paper Store, which is also BuyPapers.com and AllPapers.com. For $50.23, I bought "Personality Theory: Freud and Erikson," by one Dr. P. McCabe (the only credited author on any of these papers. As best I can tell, the global stock of papers for sale is mostly actual undergrad stuff with a few items by hired guns thrown in). The writing style here was oddly mixed, with bad paraphrasing of textbooks—which is normal for a freshman— side by side with surprisingly clever and polished observations. Grade: a solid B.

12 My other Paper Store paper was "Typical Assumptions of Kin Selection," bought for $40.38. Again, a pretty good buy. It was well written, accurate, and occasionally even thoughtful. My bio judge would give it a B in a freshman class. Possible pladar ping: The writer seemed to imply that some of his ideas stemmed from a personal chat with a noted biologist. But overall, the Paper Store earned its pay.

13 **A1Termpaper.com (aka 1-800-Termpaper.com):** In some ways this is the strangest site, as most of the papers for sale were written between 1978 and '83. I would guess this is an old term paper source, which has recently made the jump to the Web. From its history section, I bought a book report on Garry Wills' *Nixon Agonistes* for $44.75, plus a $7.45 fee for scanning all the pages—the paper was written in 1981, no doubt on a typewriter. Quality? It understood the book but made no critique—a high-school paper. My judge would give it a D.

I next bought "Personality as Seen by Erikson, Mead, and Freud" from A1 Termpaper for $62.65 plus a $10.43 scanning fee. Also written in 1981, this one had the most stylish prose of any psych paper and the most sophisticated thesis, but it was riddled with factual errors. For instance, it got Freud's psychosexual stages completely mixed up and even added some that don't exist (the correct progression is oral-anal-phallic-latency-genital, as if you didn't know). Showing its age, it cited a textbook from 1968 and nothing from after '69 (and no, that's not another Freudian stage, gutter-mind). Grade: Dad gave it a C+. In the end, A1 Termpaper.com was pricey, outdated, and not a good buy. 14

With all these pre-written papers, though, it occurred to me that a smart but horribly lazy student could choose to put his effort into editing instead of researching and writing: Buy a mediocre paper that's done the legwork, then whip it into shape by improving the writing and adding some carefully chosen details. Not a bad strategy. 15

Papers Made to Order

PaperMasters.com: My final buy was a custom-made paper written to my specifications. Lots of sites do this, for between $17 and $20 per page. PaperMasters.com claims all its writers have "at least one Master's Degree" and charges $17.95 per page. I typed this request (posing as a professor's assignment, copied verbatim) into its Web order form: "A 4-page term paper on David Foster Wallace's *Infinite Jest*. Investigate the semiotics of the 'addicted gaze' as represented by the mysterious film of the book's title. Possible topics to address include nihilism, figurative transgendering, the culture of entertainment, and the concept of 'infinite gestation.'" 16

This assignment was total hooey. It made no sense whatsoever. Yet it differed little from papers I was assigned as an undergrad English major at Brown. 17

After a few tries (one woman at the 800 number told me they were extremely busy), my assignment was accepted by Paper Masters, with a deadline for one week later. Keep in mind, *Infinite Jest* is an 1,100-page novel (including byzantine footnotes), and it took me almost a month to read even though I was completely engrossed by it. In short, there's no way anyone could 1) finish the book in time; and 2) write anything coherent that addressed the assignment. 18

I began to feel guilty. Some poor writer somewhere was plowing through this tome, then concocting a meaningless mishmash of words simply to fill four pages and satisfy the bizarre whims of a solitary, heartless taskmaster (me). But then I realized this is exactly what I did for all four years of college—and I paid them for the privilege! 19

20   When the custom paper came back, it was all I'd dreamed. Representative sentence: "The novel's diverse characters demonstrate both individually and collectively the fixations and obsessions that bind humanity to
the pitfalls of reality and provide a fertile groundwork for the semiotic explanation of addictive behavior." Tripe. The paper had no thesis and in
fact had no body—not one sentence actually advanced a cogent idea. I'm
guessing it would have gotten a C+ at Brown—maybe even a B-. If I were
a just slightly lesser person, I might be tempted by this service. One custom paper off the Web: $71.80. Not having to dredge up pointless poppy-
cock for some po-mo obsessed, overrated lit-crit professor: priceless.

Bulletin Board Responses

NOTES FROM THE FRAY EDITOR:
Magellan had a pertinent question: "Do you want the guy at the nuclear
power plant to have gotten his degree through a barrage of online papers
without knowing his/her stuff?" And Charles had another: "Good job,
Seth. So, tell us, really, how much did you pay Paper Masters for this article?" A university English instructor was horrified by the article, and received good advice from mfbenson and others ("in-class essays"). Many
other professors wrote in, too, some shocked, some very knowledgeable
about catching plagiarists: watch out, cheaters, particularly at the University of Iowa (see Silvano Wueschner's post, below). Nick Carbone has a
great post here with advice for teachers: "Better assignments . . . collect
drafts . . . talk about honesty: . . . [this] beats relying on search engines
after that fact . . . If students know you take this stuff seriously and you
care, and that you're as interested in teaching as catching them, most will
play fair. Not all will, but then not all ever did." And Mr. Carbone also
introduces the idea of nakedwriters.com "papers written while you wait and
watch": an interactive web moneymaker if ever we heard of one. [. . .]
Meanwhile, Kit suggests Fray posts could be bought and sold, and Mangar
is ready to organize a system to turn Fray posts into college papers.

COMMENTS:
Pure lander. As an ASU grad, I strongly resemble your characterization
of my alma mater in your article. Yet no self-respecting Sun Devil would
ever enroll in a major that demanded of all things . . . work.
                                                                    —Tim Gauthier

Yes one can indeed obtain a wide variety and quality of term papers via
the world wide web. I had suspected this for the past few years and began

to run the "Google" test on all papers submitted during a semester. I will not divulge how this is accomplished, suffice it to say that at the last institution I taught I managed to nab 12 bought papers in just one of my classes. (At the University of Virginia over 100 students were discovered to be cheating on their term papers.) When word leaked out that I was putting the papers to the "Google test" a number of my eager to please scholars called my office to beg for extensions—it seems the computer system was running out of ink and paper or floppy disks were being destroyed by vicious PCs. Needless to say I was not sympathetic. Those who cheated were promptly brought to the Academic Dean's attention. To my delight I can acknowledge that the Internet is indeed user friendly.

—Silvano Wueschner

Gee, I hate to sound like a jerk, but isn't buying a term paper cheating? Should you be trying to provide consumer advice so that students can cheat more effectively? I hope that you plan to follow this up with a story that provides consumer advice to the various journalists who want to invent news stories or to plagiarize.

—DJG

It's not about ethics, or money, or not wanting to "shovel the b.s." yourself. It's about being willing to pay for an A or a B on a paper and not learning a damn thing about how to do research yourself nor about the topic. If you aspire to graduate and still be a mindless dolt, then you're not only doing yourself a disservice, but you're also making the reputations of America's universities go downhill. (Not that I care, but it's still a fact.)

I made good money writing papers for idiots in law school and in their 4th year who were for all intents and purposes, functionally illiterate. The bottom line is that in the end, if you want to cut corners with your education, you'll be the one playing the fool, while those who did the work to learn how to research and write their own work will be mopping up in your place. . . .

—Aristos

Sorry to say that I was expecting more! Not quality, you understand, but really prime dreck, suitable for wrapping fish and lining birdcages. Instead, Seth Stevenson turns up papers that probably would *not* be distinguishable from many students' own work. How to separate out the cheaters when your initial expectations are so low? I did like Seth's request to PaperMasters.com; opaquely fiendish, piquantly vapid.

—Diane

Stevenson, "Adventures in Cheating"

1. Analyze and comment on the tone of Seth Stevenson's article. How are aspects of his attitude toward his subject evident in the first paragraph—and throughout the article?

2. Stevenson ostensibly seems to argue the following: "Yes, it's ethically blah blah blah to cheat on a term paper blah. The question is: How do you do it right?" Do his examples and the rest of his article support the thesis he purports to argue? How so? How not?

3. In what ways does Stevenson point out the pitfalls of this type of consumerism? How does this consumerism also become a critique of undergraduate education?

4. How do the bulletin board comments—slamming Stevenson, for instance, about his lack of ethics—indicate that Stevenson's readers either didn't understand his overall points or perhaps understood them too well? Which? Why?

⌗

JONATHAN SWIFT

Jonathan Swift (1667–1745) is considered among the greatest writers of prose in the English language, his work being marked by clarity and directness. Swift was born in Dublin to English parents. He devoted a good deal of his life to politics and religion, and he was known in his time as a man of charm and integrity. He was dean of St. Patrick's Cathedral in Dublin, but he is remembered less for his religious interests and more for his writing—particularly his satirical writings. In a letter to poet Alexander Pope, Swift declared that although he could love people as individuals, he "hated that animal called man," believing that men are "merely *capable* of reason." Interestingly, although his classic tale, *Gulliver's Travels* (1726), was written as satire, it is celebrated now as a children's book. Swift's writing of satire knew few bounds: Ireland, already weakened by England's economic policies, was further strained by severe famine. Affected by the conditions in that country, Swift used "A Modest Proposal" (1729) to demonstrate his searing use of irony and satire to comment on the situation.

⌗

A Modest Proposal

*For Preventing the Children of Poor People in Ireland
from Being a Burden to Their Parents or Country, and for
Making Them Beneficial to the Public*

It is a melancholy object to those who walk through this great town or   1
travel in the country, when they see the streets, the roads, and cabin
doors, crowded with beggars of the female sex, followed by three, four, or
six children, all in rags and importuning every passenger for an alms.
These mothers, instead of being able to work for their honest livelihood,
are forced to employ all their time in strolling to beg sustenance for their
helpless infants: who as they grow up either turn thieves for want of work,
or leave their dear native country to fight for the Pretender in Spain, or
sell themselves to the Barbadoes.

I think it is agreed by all parties that this prodigious number of children   2
in the arms, or on the backs, or at the heels of their mothers, and frequently of their fathers, is in the present deplorable state of the kingdom
a very great additional grievance; and, therefore, whoever could find out a
fair, cheap, and easy method of making these children sound, useful members of the commonwealth, would deserve so well of the public as to have
his statue set up for a preserver of the nation.

But my intention is very far from being confined to provide only for the   3
children of professed beggars; it is of a much greater extent, and shall take
in the whole number of infants at a certain age who are born of parents in
effect as little able to support them as those who demand our charity in
the streets.

As to my own part, having turned my thoughts for many years upon this   4
important subject, and maturely weighed the several schemes of our pro-
jectors, I have always found them grossly mistaken in their computation.
It is true, a child just dropped from its dam may be supported by her milk
for a solar year, with little other nourishment; at most not above the value
of 2s., which the mother may certainly get, or the value in scraps, by her
lawful occupation of begging; and it is exactly at one year old that I propose to provide for them in such a manner as instead of being a charge
upon their parents or the parish, or wanting food and raiment for the rest
of their lives, they shall on the contrary contribute to the feeding, and
partly to the clothing, of many thousands.

There is likewise another great advantage in my scheme, that it will pre-   5
vent those voluntary abortions, and that horrid practice of women murdering their bastard children, alas! too frequent among us! sacrificing the

poor innocent babes I doubt more to avoid the expense than the shame, which would move tears and pity in the most savage and inhuman breast.

6 The number of souls in this kingdom being usually reckoned one million and a half, of these I calculate there may be about 200,000 couple whose wives are breeders; from which number I subtract 30,000 couple who are able to maintain their own children (although I apprehend there cannot be so many, under the present distress of the kingdom); but this being granted, there will remain 170,000 breeders. I again subtract 50,000 for those women who miscarry, or whose children die by accident or disease within the year. There only remain 120,000 children of poor parents annually born. The question therefore is, how this number shall be reared and provided for? which, as I have already said, under the present situation of affairs, is utterly impossible by all the methods hitherto proposed. For we can neither employ them in handicraft or agriculture; we neither build houses (I mean in the country) nor cultivate land; they can very seldom pick up a livelihood by stealing, till they arrive at six years old, except where they are of towardly parts; although I confess they learn the rudiments much earlier; during which time they can, however, be properly looked upon only as probationers; as I have been informed by a principal gentleman in the county of Cavan, who protested to me that he never knew above one or two instances under the age of six, even in a part of the kingdom so renowned for the quickest proficiency in that art.

7 I am assured by our merchants, that a boy or a girl before twelve years old is no salable commodity; and even when they come to this age they will not yield above 3£. or 3£. 2s. 6d. at most on the exchange; which cannot turn to account either to the parents or kingdom, the charge of nutriment and rags having been at least four times that value.

8 I shall now therefore humbly propose my own thoughts, which I hope will not be liable to the least objection.

9 I have been assured by a very knowing American of my acquaintance in London, that a young healthy child well nursed is at a year old a most delicious, nourishing, and wholesome food, whether stewed, roasted, baked, or broiled; and I make no doubt that it will equally serve in a fricassee or a ragout.

10 I do therefore humbly offer it to public consideration that of the 120,000 children already computed, 20,000 may be reserved for breed, whereof only one-fourth part to be males; which is more than we allow to sheep, black cattle, or swine; and my reason is, that these children are seldom the fruits of marriage, a circumstance not much regarded by our savages; therefore one male will be sufficient to serve four females. That the remaining 100,000 may, at a year old, be offered in sale to the persons of quality and fortune through the kingdom; always advising the mother to

let them suck plentifully in the last month, so as to render them plump and fat for a good table. A child will make two dishes at an entertainment for friends; and when the family dines alone, the fore or hind quarter will make a reasonable dish, and seasoned with a little pepper or salt will be very good boiled on the fourth day, especially in winter.

I have reckoned upon a medium that a child just born will weigh twelve pounds, and in a solar year, if tolerably nursed, will increase to twenty-eight pounds.   11

I grant this food will be somewhat dear, and therefore very proper for landlords, who, as they have already devoured most of the parents, seem to have the best title to the children.   12

Infant's flesh will be in season throughout the year, but more plentiful in March, and a little before and after: for we are told by a grave author, an eminent French physician, that fish being a prolific diet, there are more children born in Roman Catholic countries about nine months after Lent than at any other season; therefore, reckoning a year after Lent, the markets will be more glutted than usual, because the number of popish infants is at least three to one in this kingdom: and therefore it will have one other collateral advantage, by lessening the number of papists among us.   13

I have already computed the charge of nursing a beggar's child (in which list I reckon all cottagers, laborers, and four-fifths of the farmers) to be about 2s. per annum, rags included; and I believe no gentleman would repine to give 10s. for the carcass of a good fat child, which, as I have said, will make four dishes of excellent nutritive meat, when he has only some particular friend or his own family to dine with him. Thus the squire will learn to be a good landlord, and grow popular among the tenants; the mother will have 8s. net profit, and be fit for work till she produces another child.   14

Those who are more thrifty (as I must confess the times require) may flay the carcass; the skin of which artificially dressed will make admirable gloves for ladies, and summer boots for fine gentlemen.   15

As to our city of Dublin, shambles may be appointed for this purpose in the most convenient parts of it, and butchers we may be assured will not be wanting: although I rather recommend buying the children alive, and dressing them hot from the knife as we do roasting pigs.   16

A very worthy person, a true lover of his country, and whose virtues I highly esteem, was lately pleased in discoursing on this matter to offer a refinement upon my scheme. He said that many gentlemen of this kingdom, having of late destroyed their deer, he conceived that the want of venison might be well supplied by the bodies of young lads and maidens, not exceeding fourteen years of age nor under twelve; so great a number of both sexes in every country being now ready to starve for want of work   17 and service; and these to be disposed of by their parents, if alive, or otherwise by their nearest relations. But with due deference to so excellent a friend and so deserving a patriot, I cannot be altogether in his sentiments; for as to the males, my American acquaintance assured me from frequent experience that their flesh was generally tough and lean, like that of our schoolboys by continual exercise, and their taste disagreeable; and to fatten them would not answer the charge. Then as to the females, it would, I think, with humble submission be a loss to the public, because they soon would become breeders themselves: and besides, it is not improbable that some scrupulous people might be apt to censure such a practice (although indeed very unjustly), as a little bordering upon cruelty; which, I confess, has always been with me the strongest objection against any project, how well soever intended.

18   But in order to justify my friend, he confessed that this expedient was put into his head by the famous Psalmanazar[,] a native of the island Formosa, who came from thence to London about twenty years ago: and in conversation told my friend, that in his country when any young person happened to be put to death, the executioner sold the carcass to persons of quality as a prime dainty; and that in his time the body of a plump girl of fifteen, who was crucified for an attempt to poison the emperor, was sold to his imperial majesty's prime minister of state, and other great mandarins of the court, in joints from the gibbet, at 400 crowns. Neither indeed can I deny, that if the same use were made of several plump young girls in this town, who without one single groat to their fortunes cannot stir abroad without a chair, and appear at the playhouse and assemblies in foreign fineries which they never will pay for, the kingdom would not be the worse.

19   Some persons of a depending spirit are in great concern about the vast number of poor people, who are aged, diseased, or maimed, and I have been desired to employ my thoughts what course may be taken to ease the nation of so grievous an encumbrance. But I am not in the least pain upon that matter, because it is very well known that they are every day dying and rotting by cold and famine, and filth and vermin, as fast as can be reasonably expected. And as to the young laborers, they are now in as hopeful a condition: They cannot get work, and consequently pine away for want of nourishment, to a degree that if at any time they are accidentally hired to common labor, they have not strength to perform it; and thus the country and themselves are happily delivered from the evils to come.

20   I have too long digressed, and therefore shall return to my subject. I think the advantages by the proposal which I have made are obvious and many, as well as of the highest importance.

For first, as I have already observed, it would greatly lessen the number   21
of papists, with whom we are yearly overrun, being the principal breeders
of the nation as well as our most dangerous enemies; and who stay at
home on purpose to deliver the kingdom to the Pretender, hoping to take
their advantage by the absence of so many good Protestants, who have
chosen rather to leave their country than stay at home and pay tithes
against their conscience to an Episcopal curate.

Secondly, The poor tenants will have something valuable of their   22
own, which by law may be made liable to distress and help to pay their
landlord's rent, their corn and cattle being already seized, and money a
thing unknown.

Thirdly, Whereas the maintenance of 100,000 children from two years   23
old and upward, cannot be computed at less than 10s. apiece per annum,
the nation's stock will be thereby increased £50,000 per annum, beside
the profit of a new dish introduced to the tables of all gentlemen of fortune in the kingdom who have any refinement in taste. And the money
will circulate among ourselves, the goods being entirely of our own growth
and manufacture.

Fourthly, The constant breeders beside the gain of 8s. sterling per an-   24
num by the sale of their children, will be rid of the charge of maintaining
them after the first year.

Fifthly, This food would likewise bring great custom to taverns, where   25
the vintners will certainly be so prudent as to procure the best receipts for
dressing it to perfection, and consequently have their houses frequented
by all the fine gentlemen, who justly value themselves upon their knowledge in good eating; and a skillful cook who understands how to oblige his
guests, will contrive to make it as expensive as they please.

Sixthly, This would be a great inducement to marriage, which all wise   26
nations have either encouraged by rewards or enforced by laws and penal-
ties. It would increase the care and tenderness of mothers toward their
children, when they were sure of a settlement for life to the poor babes,
provided in some sort by the public, to their annual profit instead of expense. We should see an honest emulation among the married women,
which of them would bring the fattest child to the market. Men would become as fond of their wives during the time of their pregnancy as they are
now of their mares in foal, their cows in calf, their sows when they are
ready to farrow; nor offer to beat or kick them (as is too frequent a practice) for fear of a miscarriage.

Many other advantages might be enumerated. For instance, the addi-   27
tion of some thousand carcasses in our exportation of barreled beef, the
propagation of swine's flesh, and improvement in the art of making good

bacon, so much wanted among us by the great destruction of pigs, too frequent at our table; which are no way comparable in taste or magnificence to a well-grown, fat, yearling child, which roasted whole will make a considerable figure at a lord mayor's feast or any other public entertainment. But this and many others I omit, being studious of brevity.

28   Supposing that 1,000 families in this city would be constant customers for infants' flesh, besides others who might have it at merrymeetings, particularly at weddings and christenings, I compute that Dublin would take off annually about 20,000 carcasses; and the rest of the kingdom (where probably they will be sold somewhat cheaper) the remaining 80,000.

29   I can think of no one objection that will possibly be raised against this proposal, unless it should be urged that the number of people will be thereby much lessened in the kingdom. This I freely own, and it was indeed one principal design in offering it to the world. I desire the reader will observe, that I calculate my remedy for this one individual kingdom of Ireland and for no other that ever was, is, or I think ever can be upon earth. Therefore let no man talk to me of other expedients: of taxing our absentees at 5s. a pound; of using neither clothes nor household furniture except what is of our own growth and manufacture; of utterly rejecting the materials and instruments that promote foreign luxury; of curing the expensiveness of pride, vanity, idleness, and gaming in our women; of introducing a vein of parsimony, prudence, and temperance; of learning to love our country, in the want of which we differ even from Laplanders and the inhabitants of Topinamboo; of quitting our animosities and factions, nor acting any longer like the Jews, who were murdering one another at the very moment their city was taken; of being a little cautious not to sell our country and conscience for nothing; of teaching landlords to have at least one degree of mercy toward their tentants; lastly, of putting a spirit of honesty, industry, and skill into our shopkeepers; who, if a resolution could now be taken to buy only our native goods, would immediately unite to cheat and exact upon us in the price the measure, and the goodness, nor could ever yet be brought to make one fair proposal of just dealing, though often and earnestly invited to it.

30   Therefore I repeat, let no man talk to me of these and the like expedients, till he has at least some glimpse of hope that there will be ever some hearty and sincere attempt to put them in practice.

31   But as to myself, having been wearied out for many years with offering vain, idle, visionary thoughts, and at length utterly despairing of success, I fortunately fell upon this proposal; which, as it is wholly new, so it has something solid and real, of no expense and little trouble, full in our own power, and whereby we can incur no danger in disobliging England. For

this kind of commodity will not bear exportation, the flesh being of too tender a consistence to admit a long continuance in salt, although perhaps I could name a country which would be glad to eat up our whole nation without it.

After all, I am not so violently bent upon my own opinion as to reject 32 any offer proposed by wise men, which shall be found equally innocent, cheap, easy, and effectual. But before something of that kind shall be advanced in contradiction to my scheme, and offering a better, I desire the author or authors will be pleased maturely to consider two points. First, as things now stand, how they will be able to find food and raiment for 100,000 useless mouths and backs. And secondly, there being a round million of creatures in human figure throughout this kingdom, whose subsistence put into a common stock would leave them in debt 2,000,000£. sterling, adding those who are beggars by profession to the bulk of farmers, cottagers, and laborers, with the wives and children who are beggars in effect; I desire those politicians who dislike my overture, and may perhaps be so bold as to attempt an answer, that they will first ask the parents of these mortals, whether they would not at this day think it a great happiness to have been sold for food at a year old in the manner I prescribe, and thereby have avoided such a perpetual scene of misfortunes as they have since gone through by the oppression of landlords, the impossibility of paying rent without money or trade, the want of common sustenance, with neither house nor clothes to cover them from the inclemencies of the weather, and the most inevitable prospect of entailing the like or greater miseries upon their breed for ever.

I profess, in the sincerity of my heart, that I have not the least personal 33 interest in endeavoring to promote this necessary work, having no other motive than the public good of my country, by advancing our trade, providing for infants, relieving the poor, and giving some pleasure to the rich. I have no children by which I can propose to get a single penny; the youngest being nine years old, and my wife past childbearing.

QUESTIONING AND DISCUSSING

Swift, "A Modest Proposal"

1. How are irony and satire at play in this essay? For instance, is there a distinction between the way that the speaker sees himself and the way that the reader sees him? (How would you characterize the speaker? Consider language and tone, for example.) Explain your point of view, using examples from the text.

2. Analyze and comment on the speaker's various solutions for the Irish poor. Research the historical contexts of this essay. Are there other facts that Swift might have included to explain the reasons for the plight of the poor in Ireland?

3. It is said that satire works only when it suggests the truth. What are the truths that are revealed in Swift's essay despite its satire? Consider current contexts of poverty in the United States, conducting research to provide substantive information for your discussion. How might satire work for discussing such issues as the homeless and the health care crisis—and not for others?

⊞

Steve Lopez

A columnist known for his eclectic topics and pull-no-punches style, Steve Lopez joined the *Los Angeles Times* in May 2001 after spending four years at Time, Inc. While there, he wrote for *Time Magazine* as well as for *Life, Entertainment Weekly* (as editor-at-large), and *Sports Illustrated*. Lopez won a Society of Professional Journalists Award for his story about Philadelphia murderer Ira Einhorn, a former hippie guru captured by the French and extradited to the United States for trial. Lopez also wrote columns for the *Philadelphia Inquirer* (often filing stories from abroad), for which he won the H. L. Mencken Writing Award, the Ernie Pyle Award for human interest writing, and a National Headliner Award. A number of his columns have been anthologized in *Land of Giants: Where No Good Deed Goes Unpunished*. Also a novelist, Lopez has published *Third and Indiana, The Sunday Macaroni Club*, and *In the Clear*.

Lopez's essay is followed by a transcript from the television newsmagazine *60 Minutes* that more fully describes the situation to which Lopez is responding. Read both texts together, and then reflect upon the "Questioning and Discussing" prompts found after the *60 Minutes* reading.

⊞

Doin' Time with a New Ticker

1 When my parents got dumped by their medical insurance company and found that a new plan was going to cost at least twice as much, they asked my two cents' worth. My dad has a heart condition, so I told him they ought to lay out some cash and get the best plan available.

2 Now I realize it was bad advice. I should have told them to get a couple of Saturday night specials and start knocking off convenience stores.

A California convict, serving time for a 1996 robbery in Los Angeles, 3
got a heart transplant on Jan. 3 at Stanford Medical Center. A story by the
Times' Mitchell Landsberg reported that the bill will come to as much as
$1 million. But the patient didn't have Blue Cross, so you and I will be
covering the tab.

Now I'm not someone who will argue that prisoners surrender all rights 4
the moment the door slams shut. People often tell me they're appalled
that inmates have televisions or ball fields, and I can't get worked up
about it. I've been on the inside of enough prisons to know there are no
holidays there. What appalls me is that a huge percentage of the prison
population is doing time for simple drug addiction, essentially, while
deep-pocketed execs from the likes of Enron and Arthur Andersen pillage
and plunger and still walk the streets.

But getting back to the crooks who are actually behind bars, the ques- 5
tion is whether they should get taken care of when they're sick, even if
treatment is complicated and expensive. And the answer is yes. They're
still citizens, and more important, they're human beings. The law doesn't
offer a choice in the matter, anyway.

But should it be the best care available when you and I are the ones pay- 6
ing? Do we really want to make that kind of top-shelf investment in the
future of somebody who lives on a cell block?

My dad worked his entire life, has not been in jail that I know of, and 7
pays a growing chunk of his fixed income on health care. The only time
he's been to Stanford is to see a football game. He's been having a rough
time lately because his doctors, forced by insurance company bean counters to practice cut-rate, assembly-line medicine, failed to treat him for a
condition that was diagnosed two years ago. A convict, meanwhile, is being fussed over at one of the finest hospitals in the world, and my dad is
paying for it.

According to Landsberg's story, the average heart transplant costs 8
$209,000, plus $15,000 a year for follow-up treatment. That being the case,
it's not clear to me why this guy got the Cadillac of heart transplants. Did
state prison officials shop around at all? Have they heard of priceline.com?
Did it have to be Stanford?

When I first heard about it, I wondered how this con managed to get to 9
the top of the waiting list. You don't just show up at the hospital, have
them zip you open, and go home with a new heart. You've got to get your
name on a list and wait your turn, and for some people, that turn doesn't
come in time. A lot of factors are taken into account, such as the location
of the donor heart, the location of the recipient, the degree of illness, and
other compatibility factors.

10   On the day this 31-year-old, two-time felon hit the jackpot, there were 4,119 people in this country waiting for a new heart that might save their lives. You have to wonder if a law-abiding, tax-paying citizen drew one last breath while Jailhouse Joe was getting a second wind.

11   A person's moral standing ought to be irrelevant, a bioethicist argued in Landsberg's story. "Should merit be considered a criteria?" she asked skeptically. "Should organs go to people who are 'good,' who have lived good lives?"

12   Let me put it this way:

13   Yes.

14   When it comes to organ transplants, we're already playing God to a certain degree, extending life beyond its natural course. I'm not saying a prison inmate should never receive a life-saving medical procedure. But when a fresh donor heart is on ice and the choice is between a two-time loser or someone who doesn't wear a jumpsuit every day, I don't have a problem giving extra points to the latter.

15   Before his transplant, the inmate had applied for a so-called compassionate release because of his condition. He might still get one, because even though he's got a new pump, he may be classified as terminally ill. Taking up a life of crime could be the smartest thing this guy ever did.

16   I've got to talk to my parents.

60 MINUTES

---

60 Minutes was the first newsmagazine television show, having first been broadcast in 1968. What follows is a transcript of a 2002 feature by correspondent Steve Kroft concerning the ethics of providing a heart transplant for a convicted felon.

⊞

Change of Heart

If you or someone in your family is in need of a heart transplant, then you know they're not easy to get. Donor hearts are scarce and the procedure is expensive.

So, as 60 Minutes first reported last December, when an elite transplant team at one of the finest hospitals in the country performed one on a prison inmate at a cost to taxpayers of roughly $1 million, it raised lots of eyebrows and lots of questions.

Why did a prison get the heart? Prison officials in California say they had no choice in the matter. In fact, they believe the Supreme Court has, in effect, granted prisoners a constitutional right it has never granted to law-abiding citizens—the right to health care. Correspondent Steve Kroft reports.

The California prisoner got his heart transplant at Stanford University 1
Medical Center, which has one of the finest transplant programs in the
country. It was the first time ever a prisoner had gotten a new heart.

The California Department of Corrections won't release the name of 2
the prisoner who received the heart transplant, citing regulations on medical confidentiality. It did say, however, that he is a 31-year-old inmate—
a twice-convicted felon—serving a 14-year-sentence for armed robbery.

His heart was irreparably damaged by a viral infection, and over the 3
years his condition deteriorated to the point where his physicians decided
he would die without a transplant.

He was put on a waiting list at the United Networks for Organ Sharing 4
in Richmond, Va., where donor organs are matched to appropriate patients. The computer found a heart in January 2002, and doctors notified
the prison system.

Steve Green, a California corrections official, says the state said, "Go 5
ahead." He also says they didn't have a choice in the matter: "The administration at that time refused to give it to him. He sued. The U.S. District Court ruled that he was entitled to the transplant, and that he was
also entitled to $35,000 from the state because of the state's deliberate in-
difference. So we have direct court rulings saying that we will meet medical needs of our inmates. And we do."

By denying him a heart transplant, Green says it would have been de- 6
liberate indifference: "We think that's what the court would decide. The
inmate would probably die, and his estate would sue us, and we'd lose."

And he's probably right. In 1976, the Supreme Court ruled that "delib- 7
erate indifference" to an inmate's medical needs is "cruel and unusual
punishment," something specifically prohibited by the Eighth Amendment to the Constitution. It's an amendment that applies solely to people
in custody.

"Inmates have a constitutional right that you and I don't have, Steve," 8
says Green. "To health care."

This has surprised and angered a lot of people in California, and one 9
of them was *Los Angeles Times* columnist Steve Lopez, who wrote about
the situation.

"What is this telling people? What's the message here to the public," 10
asks Lopez. "You know, you had two robbery convictions, you're in jail,
you get sick, you're going to the top of the line, buddy. I mean, that's the
problem here."

11   Lopez says it doesn't seem fair to people like his father, who has heart trouble, lives on a fixed income and at one point had his health insurance cancelled. The only way his father will ever get to Stanford, he says, is for a football game.

12   "When I wrote a column about my Dad, who I assumed was sitting there reading the paper going nuts, I suggested that he and my Mom get a couple of berets and do a Bonnie and Clyde act," says Lopez. "I mean, it might be the best way to get the best health care available. You know, knock off a few banks."

13   And maybe some other people are thinking about it too. There are seven million Californians who don't have health insurance and probably would not qualify for a transplant. They are, by definition, working poor who don't have health insurance with their jobs and can't afford to buy it on their own.

14   It's not unusual for hospitals to require hundreds of thousands of dollars up front before an uninsured qualifies for the list.

15   "I had this conversation with a woman who calls me and says my brother needs a heart transplant and he could not get on the list. And they said, 'Well, you're going to have to raise $150,000.' And he says, 'Well, I don't have $150,000.' They're practically having bake sales," says Lopez.

16   "Now here's a guy who works for a living and has three children. Why should he have to give up everything that he's worked for while somebody in prison is getting the best treatment available. It's not equitable."

17   Dr. Lawrence Schneiderman, a medical ethicist at the University of California at San Diego, says even getting onto the transplant list can be difficult. Hospitals set all kinds of medical criteria, including the ability to pay for expensive follow-up care.

18   "I think there are very few centers who would do that, unless you were special, they had a kind of endowment for teaching. But in general, don't count on it, no," he says.

19   But in this case, the prisoner's heart transplant was being paid for by the taxpayers. However, prison officials say if they hadn't given the inmate his million-dollar heart transplant, they would have been giving the armed robber a death sentence. But every day, 12 Americans die waiting for a transplant. And by giving the prisoner the heart, a death sentence was being passed to someone else—most likely someone who had never threatened anyone else's life with a gun.

20   Schneiderman says doctors can't take that into consideration. Medical ethics require physicians to give the organs to the patient who will benefit the most, regardless of their status in society. But he believes that soci-

ety, as a whole, can make its own decisions about social worth and could pass laws to do it.

"Now society may say, 'Look, in the case of a heart transplant, we don't have enough to go around. We have to make choices.' Then we, as a society, try to express our values through our choices," says Schneiderman. 21

So, basically doctors have to decide based on medical need, but society can decide who it thinks deserves a heart? 22

"Yeah. And that's, that's because we have such a hodgepodge of health care coverage, and not universal health care coverage, society has decided," says Schneiderman. "And so prisoners are, in fact, given what the rest of us in society deserve. But nobody has written that law. Nobody has made that Supreme Court determination." 23

Does Schneiderman think it's fine for society to say "No heart transplants for murderers?" 24

"I, personally, yes," he says. 25

What about heart transplants for robbers? 26

"Now we're starting on the slippery slope, you know. 'Well, then what about people who get a parking ticket,'" says Schneiderman. 27

But when doctors make the decision to not give the heart to the murderer but give it to the armed robber, are they playing God? 28

"When people say, 'You're playing God, you're rationing.' We're doing it right now. We're doing it often without thinking about it. And we're doing it in a way that when you step back and look at it, it really is hard to justify," says Schneiderman. 29

Corrections official Steve Green readily acknowledges that when it comes to transplants the uninsured may have to beg and borrow. But people who steal, or worse, already qualify. 30

He says that he would have approved this heart transplant if the person had been a murderer. They haven't faced the question of what would be decided if it were an inmate on death row. However, he says they have 600 people on death row right now. 31

If you walk around the exercise yard at the California Medical Facility in Vacaville, it's clear that prisoners are getting older and medically more needy. 32

Denton Johns is a diabetic with colon cancer: "I'm waiting for surgery right now. I'm supposed to be going out any time within the next two weeks to have a bowel resection done." 33

Does it surprise him that somebody received a heart transplant? "When I was at Salinas Valley, they did a $160,000 quadruple bypass on me. And that kind of surprised me," he says. "But when they said it was $1 million, 34 that heart transplant, I said, 'They, they can definitely afford to do my cancer surgery then.'"

35 He admits that there's a bit of a controversy on the outside about the heart transplant: "They're saying, 'Oh, our tax dollars are going to pay for it.' We're in the care of the state. And the state has to take care of us and do what they can to keep us alive."

36 California will spend over $900 million this year on medical care for its prisoners. And the cost is going up at a rate of 10 percent a year. And while no one pretends that prison medicine is the best, with procedures like transplants, it's becoming some of the most expensive.

37 And Green expects this is going to happen again: "Probably quite a bit in the future, because we have a very serious Hepatitis C problem in prisons nationwide. And the demand for liver transplants will be going up."

38 It's ethical dilemmas like that that Schneiderman deals with every day. What do you do if someone who's a hard-working, tax-paying American needs a heart transplant, and can't get it. But someone who takes a gun [and] robs a bank or a store can?

39 "Doesn't seem fair, does it?" says Schneiderman. "What I would say to that hard-working person is don't blame the criminal. Don't blame the docs who are doing the heart transplant. Blame ourselves and our politicians who have made such a hodgepodge and patchwork of health care insurance in this country."

40 "When we look for the next name that the computer is going to spit out, and it comes up an inmate, I don't think it's a sin to say, to pause and to say, 'Okay, wait a minute. What is this guy's story and who is No. 2 on the list and what is his story[?]'" says Lopez.

41 "Yes, the ethics of it are complicated, but I personally don't think it's a sin to take a look at two lives, and to give a few points to the guy on the outside who is paying for his health insurance—who is caring for a family, who can be a productive tax-paying citizen . . . just on the grounds of common sense."

42 In spite of the State of California's expenditures and the Stanford University Medical Center's expertise, the inmate transplant patient died last December 18. California corrections officials say he was "not a model transplant patient" and did not follow the strict medical rules laid out for transplant recipients.

QUESTIONING AND DISCUSSING

Lopez, "Doin' Time with a New Ticker" and 60 Minutes, "Change of Heart"

1. Lopez quotes a bioethicist as asking "Should merit be considered a criteria [sic]? [. . .] Should organs go to people who are 'good,' who have lived good lives?" The ethicist mentioned in the 60 Minutes transcript believes it is fine to "play God" and decide not to give heart transplants to murderers. Research others' positions on this matter. What is your response? Use examples from the Lopez article and the 60 Minutes transcript to help support your point of view.

2. Research issues regarding health care and health insurance in light of these articles. What are some of the major issues that confront us in these areas? How do these issues reflect not only ethical concerns but also our values as a society?

3. Consider the Supreme Court's 1976 ruling that "deliberate indifference" to an inmate's medical needs is "cruel and unusual punishment." How has this clear, apparently uncomplicated decision, which is based on the Eighth Amendment, taken on additional considerations as time has passed?

⌗

HERMAN MELVILLE

Although his literary genius was not recognized and appreciated until the 1920s, Herman Melville (1819–1891) broke new ground in nineteenth-century American prose fiction. Born into genteel poverty, Melville had little formal schooling. To support his family after the death of his father, he became a sailor. For almost ten years he worked on whalers and merchant ships around the world, drawing upon his adventures for his first novel, *Typee: A Peep at Polynesian Life* (1846). The success of that exotic novel encouraged Melville to read more widely and to move with his new wife and young family to a farm in the Berkshires. In subsequent novels he began exploring more metaphysical themes, culminating in his 1851 masterpiece *Moby-Dick, or The Whale*. The sprawling book, with its mythic quest and unresolved philosophical and psychological drama, was unlike any fiction published in the English language; unfortunately, it was virtually ignored by the reading public. Discouraged, Melville turned again to more realistic settings and conflicts, including the short story *Bartleby, the Scrivener*. With a growing family to support, he moved to New York in 1857 and took a job as a customs inspector, which he worked at for the next twenty years. In his later years he wrote poetry, which was also largely ignored.

⌗

Bartleby, the Scrivener

A Story of Wall Street

1   I am a rather elderly man. The nature of my avocations, for the last thirty years, has brought me into more than ordinary contact with what would seem an interesting and somewhat singular set of men, of whom, as yet, nothing, that I know of, has ever been written—I mean, the law-copyists, or scriveners. I have known very many of them, professionally and privately, and, if I pleased, could relate divers histories, at which good-natured gentlemen might smile, and sentimental souls might weep. But I waive the biographies of all other scriveners, for a few passages in the life of Bartleby, who was a scrivener, the strangest I ever saw, or heard of. While, of other law-copyists, I might write the complete life, of Bartleby nothing of that sort can be done. I believe that no materials exist, for a full and satisfactory biography of this man. It is an irreparable loss to literature. Bartleby was one of those beings of whom nothing is ascertainable, except from the original sources, and, in his case, those are very small. What my own astonished eyes saw of Bartleby, *that* is all I know of him, except, indeed, one vague report, which will appear in the sequel.

2   Ere introducing the scrivener, as he first appeared to me, it is fit I make some mention of myself, my *employés*, my business, my chambers, and general surroundings, because some such description is indispensable to an adequate understanding of the chief character about to be presented. Imprimis: I am a man who, from his youth upwards, has been filled with a profound conviction that the easiest way of life is the best. Hence, though I belong to a profession proverbially energetic and nervous, even to turbulence, at times, yet nothing of that sort have I ever suffered to invade my peace. I am one of those unambitious lawyers who never address a jury, or in any way draw down public applause; but, in the cool tranquillity of a snug retreat, do a snug business among rich men's bonds, and mortgages, and title-deeds. All who know me, consider me an eminently *safe* man. The late John Jacob Astor, a personage little given to poetic enthusiasm, had no hesitation in pronouncing my first grand point to be prudence; my next, method. I do not speak it in vanity, but simply record the fact, that I was not unemployed in my profession by the late John Jacob Astor; a name which, I admit, I love to repeat; for it hath a rounded and orbicular sound to it, and rings like unto bullion. I will freely add, that I was not insensible to the late John Jacob Astor's good opinion.

3   Some time prior to the period at which this little history begins, my avocations had been largely increased. The good old office, now extinct in

the State of New York, of a Master in Chancery, had been conferred upon me. It was not a very arduous office, but very pleasantly remunerative. I seldom lose my temper; much more seldom indulge in dangerous indignation at wrongs and outrages; but I must be permitted to be rash here and declare, that I consider the sudden and violent abrogation of the office of Master in Chancery, by the new Constitution, as a ——— premature act; inasmuch as I had counted upon a life-lease of the profits, whereas I only received those of a few short years. But this is by the way.

My chambers were up stairs, at No.— Wall Street. At one end, they looked upon the white wall of the interior of a spacious skylight shaft, penetrating the building from top to bottom.   4

This view might have been considered rather tame than otherwise, deficient in what landscape painters call "life." But, if so, the view from the other end of my chambers offered, at least, a contrast, if nothing more. In that direction, my windows commanded an unobstructed view of a lofty brick wall, black by age and everlasting shade; which wall required no spy-glass to bring out its lurking beauties, but, for the benefit of all near-sighted spectators, was pushed up to within ten feet of my window-panes. Owing to the great height of the surrounding buildings, and my chambers being on the second floor, the interval between this wall and mine not a little resembled a huge square cistern.   5

At the period just preceding the advent of Bartleby, I had two persons as copyists in my employment, and a promising lad as an office-boy. First, Turkey; second, Nippers; third, Ginger Nut. These may seem names, the like of which are not usually found in the Directory. In truth, they were nicknames, mutually conferred upon each other by my three clerks, and were deemed expressive of their respective persons or characters. Turkey was a short, pursy Englishman, of about my own age—that is, somewhere not far from sixty. In the morning, one might say, his face was of a fine florid hue, but after twelve o'clock, meridian—his dinner hour—it blazed like a grate full of Christmas coals; and continued blazing—but, as it were, with a gradual wane—till six o'clock, P.M., or thereabouts; after which, I saw no more of the proprietor of the face, which, gaining its meridian with the sun, seemed to set with it, to rise, culminate, and decline the following day, with the like regularity and undiminished glory. There are many singular coincidences I have known in the course of my life, not the least among which was the fact, that, exactly when Turkey displayed his fullest beams from his red and radiant countenance, just then, too, at that critical moment, began the daily period when I considered his business capacities as seriously disturbed for the remainder of the twenty-four hours. Not that he was absolutely idle, or averse to business then; far from it. The   6 difficulty was, he was apt to be altogether too energetic. There was a strange, inflamed, flurried, flighty recklessness of activity about him. He would be incautious in dipping his pen into his inkstand. All his blots upon my documents were dropped there after twelve o'clock, meridian. Indeed, not only would he be reckless, and sadly given to making blots in the afternoon, but, some days, he went further, and was rather noisy. At such times, too, his face flamed with augmented blazonry, as if cannel coal had been heaped on anthracite. He made an unpleasant racket with his chair; spilled his sand-box; in mending his pens, impatiently split them all to pieces, and threw them on the floor in a sudden passion; stood up, and leaned over his table, boxing his papers about in a most indecorous manner, very sad to behold in an elderly man like him. Nevertheless, as he was in many ways a most valuable person to me, and all the time before twelve o'clock, meridian, was the quickest, steadiest creature, too, accomplishing a great deal of work in a style not easily to be matched—for these reasons, I was willing to overlook his eccentricities, though, indeed, occasionally, I remonstrated with him. I did this very gently, however, because, though the civilest, nay, the blandest and most reverential of men in the morning, yet, in the afternoon, he was disposed, upon provocation, to be slightly rash with his tongue—in fact, insolent. Now, valuing his morning services as I did, and resolved not to lose them—yet, at the same time, made uncomfortable by his inflamed ways after twelve o'clock—and being a man of peace, unwilling by my admonitions to call forth unseemly retorts from him, I took upon me, one Saturday noon (he was always worse on Saturdays) to hint to him, very kindly, that, perhaps, now that he was growing old, it might be well to abridge his labors; in short, he need not come to my chambers after twelve o'clock, but, dinner over, had best go home to his lodgings, and rest himself till tea-time. But no; he insisted upon his afternoon devotions. His countenance became intolerably fervid, as he oratorically assured me—gesticulating with a long ruler at the other end of the room—that if his services in the morning were useful, how indispensable, then, in the afternoon?

7   "With submission, sir," said Turkey, on this occasion, "I consider myself your right-hand man. In the morning I but marshal and deploy my columns; but in the afternoon I put myself at their head, and gallantly charge the foe, thus"—and he made a violent thrust with the ruler.

8   "But the blots, Turkey," intimated I.

9   "True; but, with submission, sir, behold these hairs! I am getting old. Surely, sir, a blot or two of a warm afternoon is not to be severely urged against gray hairs. Old age—even if it blot the page—is honorable. With submission, sir, we *both* are getting old."

This appeal to my fellow-feeling was hardly to be resisted. At all events,   10
I saw that go he would not. So, I made up my mind to let him stay, resolving, nevertheless, to see to it that, during the afternoon, he had to do
with my less important papers.

Nippers, the second on my list, was a whiskered, sallow, and, upon the   11
whole, rather piratical-looking young man, of about five-and-twenty. I always deemed him the victim of two evil powers—ambition and indigestion. The amibition was evinced by a certain impatience of the duties of
a mere copyist, an unwarrantable usurpation of strictly professional affairs
such as the original drawing up of legal documents. The indigestion
seemed betokened in an occasional nervous testiness and grinning irritability, causing the teeth to audibly grind together over mistakes committed in copying; unnecessary maledictions, hissed, rather than spoken,
in the heat of business; and especially by a continual discontent with the
height of the table where he worked. Though of a very ingenious mechanical turn, Nippers could never get this table to suit him. He put chips
under it, blocks of various sorts, bits of pasteboard, and at last went so far
as to attempt an exquisite adjustment, by final pieces of folded blotting
paper. But no invention would answer. If, for the sake of easing his back,
he brought the table-lid at a sharp angle well up towards his chin, and
wrote there like a man using the steep roof of a Dutch house for his desk,
then he declared that it stopped the circulation in his arms. If now he lowered the table to his waistbands, and stooped over it in writing, then there
was a sore aching in his back. In short, the truth of the matter was, Nippers knew not what he wanted. Or, if he wanted anything, it was to be rid
of a scrivener's table altogether. Among the manifestations of his diseased
ambition was a fondness he had for receiving visits from certain ambiguous-
looking fellows in seedy coats, whom he called his clients. Indeed, I was
aware that not only was he, at times, considerable of a ward-politician,
but he occasionally did a little business at the justices' courts, and was not
unknown on the steps of the Tombs. I have good reason to believe, however, that one individual who called upon him at my chambers, and who,
with a grand air, he insisted was his client, was no other than a dun, and
the alleged title-deed, a bill. But, with all his failings, and the annoyances
he caused me, Nippers, like his compatriot Turkey, was a very useful man
to me; wrote a neat, swift hand; and, when he chose, was not deficient in
a gentlemanly sort of deportment. Added to this, he always dressed in a
gentlemanly sort of way; and so, incidentally, reflected credit upon my
chambers. Whereas, with respect to Turkey, I had much ado to keep him
from being a reproach to me. His clothes were apt to look oily, and smell
of eating-houses. He wore his pantaloons very loose and baggy in summer.

His coats were execrable, his hat not to be handled. But while the hat was a thing of indifference to me, inasmuch as his natural civility and deference, as a dependent Englishman, always led him to doff it the moment he entered the room, yet his coat was another matter. Concerning his coats, I reasoned with him; but with no effect. The truth was, I suppose, that a man with so small an income could not afford to sport such a lustrous face and a lustrous coat at one and the same time. As Nippers once observed, Turkey's money went chiefly for red ink. One winter day, I presented Turkey with a highly respectable-looking coat of my own—a padded gray coat, of a most comfortable warmth, and which buttoned straight up from the knee to the neck. I thought Turkey would appreciate the favor, and abate his rashness and obstreperousness of afternoons. But no; I verily believe that buttoning himself up in so downy and blanket-like a coat had a pernicious effect upon him the same principle that too much oats are bad for horses. In fact, precisely as a rash, restive horse is said to feel his oats, so Turkey felt his coat. It made him insolent. He was a man whom prosperity harmed.

12 Though, concerning the self-indulgent habits of Turkey, I had my own private surmises, yet, touching Nippers, I was well persuaded that, whatever might be his faults in other respects, he was, at least, a temperate young man. But, indeed, nature herself seemed to have been his vintner, and, at his birth, charged him so thoroughly with an irritable, brandy-like disposition, that all subsequent potations were needless. When I consider how, amid the stillness of my chambers, Nippers would sometimes impatiently rise from his seat, and stooping over his table, spread his arms wide apart, seize the whole desk, and move it, and jerk it, with a grim, grinding motion on the floor, as if the table were a perverse voluntary agent, intent on thwarting and vexing him, I plainly perceive that, for Nippers, brandy-and-water were altogether superfluous.

13 It was fortunate for me that, owing to its peculiar cause—indigestion—the irritability and consequent nervousness of Nippers were mainly observable in the morning, while in the afternoon he was comparatively mild. So that, Turkey's paroxysms only coming on about twelve o'clock, I never had to do with their eccentricities at one time. Their fits relieved each other, like guards. When Nippers' was on, Turkey's was off; and *vice versa*. This was a good natural arrangement, under the circumstances.

14 Ginger Nut, the third on my list, was a lad, some twelve years old. His father was a carman, ambitious of seeing his son on the bench instead of a cart, before he died. So he sent him to my office, as student at law, errand-boy, cleaner, and sweeper, at the rate of one dollar a week. He had a little desk to himself, but he did not use it much. Upon inspection, the drawer

exhibited a great array of the shells of various sorts of nuts. Indeed, to this quick-witted youth, the whole noble science of the law was contained in a nutshell. Not the least among the employments of Ginger Nut, as well as one which he discharged with the most alacrity, was his duty as cake and apple purveyor for Turkey and Nippers. Copying lawpapers being proverbially a dry, husky sort of business, my two scriveners were fain to moisten their mouths very often with Spitzenbergs, to be had at the numerous stalls nigh the Custom House and Post Office. Also, they sent Ginger Nut very frequently for that peculiar cake—small, flat, round, and very spicy—after which he had been named by them. Of a cold morning, when business was but dull, Turkey would gobble up scores of these cakes, as if they were mere wafers—indeed, they sell them at the rate of six or eight for a penny—the scrape of his pen blending with the crunching of the crisp particles in his mouth. Of all the fiery afternoon blunders and flurried rashness of Turkey, was his once moistening a ginger-cake between his lips, and clapping it on to a mortgage, for a seal. I came within an ace of dismissing him then. But he mollified me by making an oriental bow, and saying—

"With submission, sir, it was generous of me to find you in stationery on   15
my own account."

Now my original business—that of a conveyancer and title hunter, and   16
drawer-up of recondite documents of all sorts—was considerably increased by receiving the Master's office. There was now great work for scriveners. Not only must I push the clerks already with me, but I must have additional help.

In answer to my advertisement, a motionless young man one morning   17
stood upon my office threshold, the door being open, for it was summer. I can see that figure now—pallidly neat, pitiably respectable, incurably forlorn! It was Bartleby.

After a few words touching his qualifications, I engaged him, glad to   18
have among my corps of copyists a man of so singularly sedate an aspect, which I thought might operate beneficially upon the flighty temper of Turkey, and the fiery one of Nippers.

I should have stated before that ground-glass folding-doors divided my   19
premises into two parts, one of which was occupied by my scriveners, the other by myself. According to my humor, I threw open these doors, or closed them. I resolved to assign Bartleby a corner by the folding-doors, but on my side of them, so as to have this quiet man within easy call, in case any trifling thing was to be done. I placed his desk close up to a small side-window in that part of the room, a window which originally had afforded a lateral view of certain grimy brickyards and bricks, but which,

owing to subsequent erections, commanded at present no view at all, though it gave some light. Within three feet of the panes was a wall, and the light came down from far above, between two lofty buildings, as from a very small opening in a dome. Still further to a satisfactory arrangement, I procured a high green folding screen, which might entirely isolate Bartleby from my sight, though not remove him from my voice. And thus, in a manner, privacy and society were conjoined.

20　　At first, Bartleby did an extraordinary quantity of writing. As if long famishing for something to copy, he seemed to gorge himself on my documents. There was no pause for digestion. He ran a day and night line, copying by sunlight and by candle-light. I should have been quite delighted with his application, had he been cheerfully industrious. But he wrote on silently, palely, mechanically.

21　　It is, of course, an indispensable part of a scrivener's business to verify the accuracy of his copy, word by word. Where there are two or more scriveners in an office, they assist each other in this examination, one reading from the copy, the other holding the original. It is a very dull, wearisome, and lethargic affair. I can readily imagine that, to some sanguine temperaments, it would be altogether intolerable. For example, I cannot credit that the mettlesome poet, Byron, would have contentedly sat down with Bartleby to examine a law document of, say five hundred pages, closely written in a crimpy hand.

22　　Now and then, in the haste of business, it had been my habit to assist in comparing some brief document myself, calling Turkey or Nippers for this purpose. One object I had, in placing Bartleby so handy to me behind the screen, was, to avail myself of his services on such trivial occasions. It was on the third day, I think, of his being with me, and before any necessity had arisen for having his own writing examined, that, being much hurried to complete a small affair I had in hand, I abruptly called to Bartleby. In my haste and natural expectancy of instant compliance, I sat with my head bent over the original on my desk, and my right hand sideways, and somewhat nervously extended with the copy, so that, immediately upon emerging from his retreat, Bartleby might snatch it and proceed to business without the least delay.

23　　In this very attitude did I sit when I called to him, rapidly stating what it was I wanted him to do—namely, to examine a small paper with me. Imagine my surprise, nay, my consternation, when, without moving from his privacy, Bartleby, in a singularly mild, firm voice, replied, "I would prefer not to."

24　　I sat awhile in perfect silence, rallying my stunned faculties. Immediately it occurred to me that my ears had deceived me, or Bartleby had entirely misunderstood my meaning. I repeated my request in the clearest tone I could assume; but in quite as clear a one came the previous reply, "I would prefer not to."

"Prefer not to," echoed I, rising in high excitement, and crossing the room with a stride. "What do you mean? Are you moonstruck? I want you to help me compare this sheet here—take it," and I thrust it towards him.   25

"I would prefer not to," said he.   26

I looked at him steadfastly. His face was leanly composed; his gray eye dimly calm. Not a wrinkle of agitation rippled him. Had there been the least uneasiness, anger, impatience, or impertinence in his manner; in other words, had there been anything ordinarily human about him, doubtless I should have violently dismissed him from the premises. But as it was, I should have as soon thought of turning my pale plaster-of-paris bust of Cicero out of doors. I stood gazing at him awhile, as he went on with his own writing, and then reseated myself at my desk. This is very strange, thought I. What had one best do? But my business hurried me. I concluded to forget the matter for the present, reserving it for my future leisure. So, calling Nippers from the other room, the paper was speedily examined.   27

A few days after this, Bartleby concluded four lengthy documents, being quadruplicates of a week's testimony taken before me in my High Court of Chancery. It became necessary to examine them. It was an important suit, and great accuracy was imperative. Having all things arranged, I called Turkey, Nippers, and Ginger Nut, from the next room, meaning to place the four copies in the hands of my four clerks, while I should read from the original. Accordingly, Turkey, Nippers, and Ginger Nut had taken their seats in a row, each with his document in his hand, when I called to Bartleby to join this interesting group.   28

"Bartleby! quick, I am waiting."   29

I heard a slow scrape of his chair legs on the uncarpeted floor, and soon he appeared standing at the entrance of his hermitage.   30

"What is wanted?" said he, mildly.   31

"The copies, the copies," said I, hurriedly. "We are going to examine them. There"—and I held towards him the fourth quadruplicate.   32

"I would prefer not to," he said, and gently disappeared behind the screen.   33

For a few moments I was turned into a pillar of salt, standing at the head of my seated column of clerks. Recovering myself, I advanced towards the screen, and demanded the reason for such extraordinary conduct.   34

"*Why* do you refuse?"   35

"I would prefer not to."   36

With any other man I should have flown outright into a dreadful passion, scorned all further words, and thrust him ignominiously from my   37 presence. But there was something about Bartleby that not only strangely disarmed me, but, in a wonderful manner, touched and disconcerted me. I began to reason with him.

38 "These are your own copies we are about to examine. It is labor saving to you, because one examination will answer for your four papers. It is common usage. Every copyist is bound to help examine his copy. Is it not so? Will you not speak? Answer!"

39 "I prefer not to," he replied in a flute-like tone. It seemed to me that, while I had been addressing him, he carefully revolved every statement that I made; fully comprehended the meaning; could not gainsay the irresistible conclusion; but, at the same time, some paramount consideration prevailed with him to reply as he did.

40 "You are decided, then, not to comply with my request, a request made according to common usage and common sense?"

41 He briefly gave me to understand, that on that point my judgment was sound. Yes: his decision was irreversible.

42 It is not seldom the case that, when a man is browbeaten in some unprecedented and violently unreasonable way, he begins to stagger in his own plainest faith. He begins, as it were, vaguely to surmise that, wonderful as it may be, all the justice and all the reason is on the other side. Accordingly, if any disinterested persons are present, he turns to them for some reinforcement for his own faltering mind.

43 "Turkey," said I, "what do you think of this? Am I not right?"

44 "With submission, sir," said Turkey, in his blandest tone, "I think that you are."

45 "Nippers," said I, "what do *you* think of it?"

46 "I think I should kick him out of the office."

47 (The reader of nice perceptions will have perceived that, it being morning, Turkey's answer is couched in polite and tranquil terms, but Nippers replies in ill-tempered ones. Or, to repeat a previous sentence, Nippers' ugly mood was on duty, and Turkey's off.)

48 "Ginger Nut," said I, willing to enlist the smallest suffrage in my behalf, "what do *you* think of it?"

49 "I think, sir, he's a little *luny*," replied Ginger Nut, with a grin.

50 "You hear what they say," said I, turning towards the screen, "come forth and do your duty."

51 But he vouchsafed no reply. I pondered a moment in sore perplexity. But once more business hurried me. I determined again to postpone the consideration of this dilemma to my future leisure. With a little trouble we made out to examine the papers without Bartleby, though at every

page or two Turkey deferentially dropped his opinion, that this proceeding was quite out of the common; while Nippers, twitching in his chair with a dyspeptic nervousness, ground out, between his set teeth, occasional hissing maledictions against the stubborn oaf behind the screen. And for his (Nippers') part, this was the first and the last time he would do another man's business without pay.

Meanwhile Bartleby sat in his hermitage, oblivious to everything but his own peculiar business there. 52

Some days passed, the scrivener being employed upon another lengthy work. His late remarkable conduct led me to regard his ways narrowly. I observed that he never went to dinner; indeed, that he never went anywhere. As yet I had never, of my personal knowledge, known him to be outside of my office. He was a perpetual sentry in the corner. At about eleven o'clock though, in the morning, I noticed that Ginger Nut would advance towards the opening in Bartleby's screen, as if silently beckoned thither by a gesture invisible to me where I sat. The boy would then leave the office, jingling a few pence, and reappear with a handful of ginger-nuts, which he delivered in the hermitage, receiving two of the cakes for his trouble. 53

He lives, then, on ginger-nuts, thought I; never eats a dinner, properly speaking; he must be a vegetarian, then, but no; he never eats even vegetables, he eats nothing but ginger-nuts. My mind then ran on in reveries concerning the probable effects upon the human constitution of living entirely on ginger-nuts. Ginger-nuts are so called, because they contain ginger as one of their peculiar constituents, and the final flavoring one. Now, what was ginger? A hot, spicy thing. Was Bartleby hot and spicy? Not at all. Ginger, then, had no effect upon Bartleby. Probably he preferred it should have none. 54

Nothing so aggravates an earnest person as a passive resistance. If the individual so resisted be of a not inhumane temper, and the resisting one perfectly harmless in his passivity, then, in the better moods of the former, he will endeavor charitably to construe to his imagination what proves impossible to be solved by his judgment. Even so, for the most part, I regarded Bartleby and his ways. Poor fellow! thought I, he means no mischief; it is plain he intends no insolence; his aspect sufficiently evinces that his eccentricities are involuntary. He is useful to me. I can get along with him. If I turn him away, the chances are he will fall in with some less indulgent employer, and then he will be rudely treated, and perhaps driven forth miserably to starve. Yes. Here I can cheaply purchase a delicious self-approval. To befriend Bartleby; to humor him in his strange 55 wilfulness, will cost me little or nothing, while I lay up in my soul what will eventually prove a sweet morsel for my conscience. But this mood was not invariable with me. The passiveness of Bartleby sometimes irritated me. I felt strangely goaded on to encounter him in new opposition—to elicit some angry spark from him answerable to my own. But, indeed, I might as well have essayed to strike fire with my knuckles against a bit of Windsor soap. But one afternoon the evil impulse in me mastered me, and the following little scene ensued:

56   "Bartleby," said I, "when those papers are all copied, I will compare them with you."

57   "I would prefer not to."

58   "How? Surely you do not mean to persist in that mulish vagary?"

59   No answer.

60   I threw open the folding-doors nearby, and turning upon Turkey and Nippers, exclaimed:

61   "Bartleby a second time says, he won't examine his papers. What do you think of it, Turkey?"

62   It was afternoon, be it remembered. Turkey sat glowing like a brass boiler; his bald head steaming; his hands reeling among his blotted papers.

63   "Think of it?" roared Turkey. "I think I'll just step behind his screen, and black his eyes for him!"

64   So saying, Turkey rose to his feet and threw his arms into a pugilistic position. He was hurrying away to make good his promise, when I detained him, alarmed at the effect of incautiously rousing Turkey's combativeness after dinner.

65   "Sit down, Turkey," said I, "and hear what Nippers has to say. What do you think of it, Nippers? Would I not be justified in immediately dismissing Bartleby?"

66   "Excuse me, that is for you to decide, sir. I think his conduct quite unusual, and, indeed, unjust, as regards Turkey and myself. But it may only be a passing whim."

67   "Ah," exclaimed I, "you have strangely changed your mind, then—you speak very gently of him now."

68   "All beer," cried Turkey; "gentleness is effects of beer—Nippers and I dined together to-day. You see how gentle I am, sir. Shall I go and black his eyes?"

69   "You refer to Bartleby, I suppose. No, not to-day, Turkey," I replied; "pray, put up your fists."

70   I closed the doors, and again advanced towards Bartleby. I felt additional incentives tempting me to my fate. I burned to be rebelled against again. I remembered that Bartleby never left the office.

"Bartleby," said I, "Ginger Nut is away; just step around to the Post Of- 71
fice, won't you?" (it was but a three minutes' walk) "and see if there is anything for me."

"I would prefer not to." 72

"You *will* not?" 73

"I *prefer* not." 74

I staggered to my desk, and sat there in a deep study. My blind inveter- 75
acy returned. Was there any other thing in which I could procure myself
to be ignominiously repulsed by this lean, penniless wight? my hired clerk?
What added thing is there, perfectly reasonable, that he will be sure to refuse to do?

"Bartleby!" 76

No answer. 77

"Bartleby," in a louder tone. 78

No answer. 79

"Bartleby," I roared. 80

Like a very ghost, agreeably to the laws of magical invocation, at the 81
third summons, he appeared at the entrance of his hermitage.

"Go to the next room, and tell Nippers to come to me." 82

"I would prefer not to," he respectfully and slowly said, and mildly 83
disappeared.

"Very good, Bartleby," said I, in a quiet sort of serenely-severe self- 84
possessed tone, intimating the unalterable purpose of some terrible retribution very close at hand. At the moment I half intended something of
the kind. But upon the whole, as it was drawing towards my dinner-hour,
I thought it best to put on my hat and walk home for the day, suffering
much from perplexity and distress of mind.

Shall I acknowledge it? The conclusion of this whole business was, that 85
it soon became a fixed fact of my chambers, that a pale young scrivener, by
the name of Bartleby, had a desk there; that he copied for me at the usual
rate of four cents a folio (one hundred words); but he was permanently exempt from examining the work done by him, that duty being transferred
to Turkey and Nippers, out of compliment, doubtless, to their superior
acuteness; moreover, said Bartleby was never, on any account, to be dis-
patched on the most trivial errand of any sort; and that even if entreated
to take upon him such a matter, it was generally understood that he would
"prefer not to"—in other words, that he would refuse point blank.

As days passed on, I became considerably reconciled to Bartleby. His 86
steadiness, his freedom from all dissipation, his incessant industry (except
when he chose to throw himself into a standing revery behind his screen),
his great stillness, his unalterableness of demeanor under all circumstances,

made him a valuable acquisition. One prime thing was this—*he was always there*—first in the morning, continually through the day, and the last at night. I had a singular confidence in his honesty. I felt my most precious papers perfectly safe in his hands. Sometimes, to be sure, I could not, for the very soul of me, avoid falling into sudden spasmodic passions with him. For it was exceeding difficult to bear in mind all the time those strange peculiarities, privileges, and unheard-of exemptions, forming the tacit stipulations on Bartleby's part under which he remained in my office. Now and then, in the eagerness of dispatching pressing business, I would inadvertently summon Bartleby, in a short, rapid tone, to put his finger, say, in the incipient tie of a bit of red tape with which I was about compressing some papers. Of course, from behind the screen the usual answer, "I prefer not to," was sure to come; and then, how could a human creature, with the common infirmities of our nature, refrain from bitterly exclaiming upon such perverseness—such unreasonableness? However, every added repulse of this sort which I received only tended to lessen the probability of my repeating the inadvertence.

87   Here it must be said, that, according to the custom of most legal gentlemen occupying chambers in densely populated law buildings, there were several keys to my door. One was kept by a woman residing in the attic, which person weekly scrubbed and daily swept and dusted my apartments. Another was kept by Turkey for convenience sake. The third I sometimes carried in my own pocket. The fourth I knew not who had.

88   Now, one Sunday morning I happened to go to Trinity Church, to hear a celebrated preacher, and finding myself rather early on the ground I thought I would walk round to my chambers for a while. Luckily I had my key with me; but upon applying it to the lock, I found it resisted by something inserted from the inside. Quite surprised, I called out; when to my consternation a key was turned from within; and thrusting his lean visage at me, and holding the door ajar, the apparition of Bartleby appeared, in his shirt-sleeves, and otherwise in a strangely tattered *deshabille,* saying quietly that he was sorry, but he was deeply engaged just then, and preferred not admitting me at present. In a brief word or two, he moreover added, that perhaps I had better walk round the block two or three times, and by that time he would probably have concluded his affairs.

89   Now, the utterly unsurmised appearance of Bartleby, tenanting my lawchambers of a Sunday morning, with his cadaverously gentlemanly *nonchalance,* yet withal firm and self-possessed, had such a strange effect upon me, that incontinently I slunk away from my own door, and did as desired. But not without sundry twinges of impotent rebellion against the mild effrontery of this unaccountable scrivener. Indeed, it was his wonderful

mildness chiefly, which not only disarmed me, but unmanned me, as it were. For I consider that one, for the time, is sort of unmanned when he tranquilly permits his hired clerk to dictate to him, and order him away from his own premises. Furthermore, I was full of uneasiness as to what Bartleby could possibly be doing in my office in his shirt-sleeves, and in an otherwise dismantled condition on a Sunday morning. Was anything amiss going on? Nay, that was out of the question. It was not to be thought of for a moment that Bartleby was an immoral person. But what could he be doing there?—copying? Nay again, whatever might be his eccentricities, Bartleby was an eminently decorous person. He would be the last man to sit down to his desk in any state approaching to nudity. Besides, it was Sunday; and there was something about Bartleby that forbade the supposition that he would by any secular occupation violate the proprieties of the day.

Nevertheless, my mind was not pacified; and full of a restless curiosity, at last I returned to the door. Without hindrance I inserted my key, opened it, and entered. Bartleby was not to be seen. I looked round anxiously, peeped behind his screen; but it was very plain that he was gone. Upon more closely examining the place, I surmised that for an indefinite period Bartleby must have ate, dressed, and slept in my office, and that too without plate, mirror, or bed. The cushioned seat of a rickety old sofa in one corner bore the faint impress of a lean, reclining form. Rolled away under his desk, I found a blanket; under the empty grate, a blacking box and brush; on a chair, a tin basin, with soap and a ragged towel; in a newspaper a few crumbs of ginger-nuts and a morsel of cheese. Yes, thought I, it is evident enough that Bartleby has been making his home here, keeping bachelor's hall all by himself. Immediately then the thought came sweeping across me, what miserable friendlessness and loneliness are here revealed! His poverty is great; but his solitude, how horrible! Think of it. Of a Sunday, Wall Street is deserted as Petra; and every night of every day it is an emptiness. This building, too, which of week-days hums with industry and life, at nightfall echoes with sheer vacancy, and all through Sunday is forlorn. And here Bartleby makes his home; sole spectator of a solitude which he has seen all populous—a sort of innocent and transformed Marius brooding among the ruins of Carthage!

For the first time in my life a feeling of overpowering stinging melancholy seized me. Before, I had never experienced aught but a not unpleasing sadness. The bond of a common humanity now drew me irresistibly to gloom. A fraternal melancholy! For both I and Bartleby were sons of Adam. I remembered the bright silks and sparkling faces I had seen that day, in gala trim, swan-like sailing down the Mississippi of Broadway; and

I contrasted them with the pallid copyist, and thought to myself, Ah, happiness courts the light, so we deem the world is gay; but misery hides aloof, so we deem that misery there is none. These sad fancyings—chimeras, doubtless, of a sick and silly brain—led on to other and more special thoughts, concerning the eccentricities of Bartleby. Presentiments of strange discoveries hovered round me. The scrivener's pale form appeared to me laid out, among uncaring strangers, in its shivering winding-sheet.

92   Suddenly I was attracted by Bartleby's closed desk, the key in open sight left in the lock.

93   I mean no mischief, seek the gratification of no heartless curiosity, thought I; besides, the desk is mine, and its contents, too, so I will make bold to look within. Everything was methodically arranged, the papers smoothly placed. The pigeon-holes were deep, and removing the files of documents, I groped into their recesses. Presently I felt something there, and dragged it out. It was an old bandanna handkerchief, heavy and knotted. I opened it, and saw it was a saving's bank.

94   I now recalled all the quiet mysteries which I had noted in the man. I remembered that he never spoke but to answer; that, though at intervals he had considerable time to himself, yet I had never seen him reading— no, not even a newspaper; that for long periods he would stand looking out, at his pale window behind the screen, upon the dead brick wall; I was quite sure he never visited any refectory or eating-house; while his pale face clearly indicated that he never drank beer like Turkey; or tea and coffee even, like other men; that he never went anywhere in particular that I could learn; never went out for a walk, unless, indeed, that was the case at present; that he had declined telling who he was, or whence he came, or whether he had any relatives in the world; that though so thin and pale, he never complained of ill-health. And more than all, I remembered a certain unconscious air of pallid—how shall I call it?—of pallid haughtiness, say, or rather an austere reserve about him, which has positively awed me into my tame compliance with his eccentricities, when I had feared to ask him to do the slightest incidental thing for me, even though I might know, from his long-continued motionlessness, that behind his screen he must be standing in one of those dead-wall reveries of his.

95   Revolving all these things, and coupling them with the recently discovered fact, that he made my office his constant abiding place and home, and not forgetful of his morbid moodiness; revovling all these things, a prudential feeling began to steal over me. My first emotions had been those of pure melancholy and sincerest pity; but just in proportion as the forlornness of Bartleby grew and grew to my imagination, did that same

melancholy merge into fear, that pity into repulsion. So true it is, and so terrible, too, that up to a certain point the thought or sight of misery enlists our best affections; but, in certain special cases, beyond that point it does not. They err who would assert that invariably this is owing to the inherent selfishness of the human heart. It rather proceeds from a certain hopelessness of remedying excessive and organic ill. To a sensitive being, pity is not seldom pain. And when at last it is perceived that such pity cannot lead to effectual succor, common sense bids the soul be rid of it. What I saw that morning persuaded me that the scrivener was the victim of innate and incurable disorder. I might give alms to his body; but his body did not pain him; it was his soul that suffered, and his soul I could not reach.

I did not accomplish the purpose of going to Trinity Church that morning. Somehow, the things I had seen disqualified me for the time from church-going. I walked homeward, thinking what I would do with Bartleby. Finally, I resolved upon this—I would put certain calm questions to him the next morning, touching his history, etc., and if he declined to answer them openly and unreservedly (and I supposed he would prefer not), then to give him a twenty dollar bill over and above whatever I might owe him, and tell him his services were no longer required; but that if in any other way I could assist him, I would be happy to do so, especially if he desired to return to his native place, wherever that might be, I would willingly help to defray his expenses. Moreover, if, after reaching home, he found himself at any time in want of aid, a letter from him would be sure of a reply. 96

The next morning came. 97

"Bartleby," said I, gently calling to him behind his screen. 98

No reply. 99

"Bartleby," said I, in a still gentler tone, "come here; I am not going to ask you to do anything you would prefer not to do—I simply wish to speak to you." 100

Upon this he noiselessly slid into view. 101

"Will you tell me, Bartleby, where you were born?" 102

"I would prefer not to." 103

"Will you tell me *anything* about yourself?" 104

"I would prefer not to." 105

"But what reasonable objection can you have to speak to me? I feel friendly towards you." 106

He did not look at me while I spoke, but kept his glance fixed upon my bust of Cicero, which, as I then sat, was directly behind me, some six inches above my head. 107

108   "What is your answer, Bartleby?" said I, after waiting a considerable time for a reply, during which his countenance remained immovable, only there was the faintest conceivable tremor of the white attenuated mouth.

109   "At present I prefer to give no answer," he said, and retired into his hermitage.

110   It was rather weak in me I confess, but his manner, on this occasion, nettled me. Not only did there seem to lurk in it a certain calm disdain, but his perverseness seemed ungrateful, considering the undeniable good usage and indulgence he had received from me.

111   Again I sat ruminating what I should do. Mortified as I was at his behavior, and resolved as I had been to dismiss him when I entered my office, nevertheless I strangely felt something superstitious knocking at my heart, and forbidding me to carry out my purpose, and denouncing me for a villain if I dared to breathe one bitter word against his forlornest of mankind. At last, familiarly drawing my chair behind his screen, I sat down and said: "Bartleby, never mind, then, about revealing your history; but let me entreat you, as a friend, to comply as far as may be with the usages of this office. Say now, you will help to examine papers tomorrow or next day: in short, say now, that in a day or two you will begin to be a little reasonable:—say so, Bartleby."

112   "At present I would prefer not to be a little reasonable," was his mildly cadaverous reply.

113   Just then the folding-doors opened, and Nippers approached. He seemed suffering from an unusually bad night's rest, induced by severer indigestion than common. He overheard those final words of Bartleby.

114   "*Prefer not*, eh?" gritted Nippers—"I'd *prefer* him, if I were you, sir," addressing me—"I'd *prefer* him; I'd give him preferences, the stubborn mule! What is it, sir, pray, that he *prefers* not to do now?"

115   Bartleby moved not a limb.

116   "Mr. Nippers," said I, "I'd prefer that you would withdraw for the present."

117   Somehow, of late, I had got into the way of involuntarily using this word "prefer" upon all sorts of not exactly suitable occasions. And I trembled to think that my contact with the scrivener had already and seriously affected me in a mental way. And what further and deeper aberration might it not yet produce? This apprehension had not been without efficacy in determining me to summary measures.

118   As Nippers, looking very sour and sulky, was departing, Turkey blandly and deferentially approached.

119   "With submission, sir," said he, "yesterday I was thinking about Bartleby here, and I think that if he would but prefer to take a quart of good ale

every day, it would do much towards mending him, and enabling him to assist in examining his papers."

"So you have got the word, too," said I, slightly excited. 120

"With submission, what word, sir?" asked Turkey, respectfully crowding 121 himself into the contracted space behind the screen, and by so doing, making me jostle the scrivener. "What word, sir?"

"I would prefer to be left alone here," said Bartleby, as if offended at be- 122 ing mobbed in his privacy.

"*That's* the word, Turkey," said I—"*that's* it." 123

"Oh, *prefer?* oh yes—queer word. I never use it myself. But, sir, as I was 124 saying, if he would but prefer—"

"Turkey," interrupted I, "you will please withdraw." 125

"Oh certainly, sir, if you prefer that I should." 126

As he opened the folding-door to retire, Nippers at his desk caught a 127 glimpse of me, and asked whether I would prefer to have a certain paper copied on blue paper or white. He did not in the least roguishly accent the word "prefer." It was plain that it involuntarily rolled from his tongue. I thought to myself, surely I must get rid of a demented man, who already has in some degree turned the tongues, if not the heads of myself and clerks. But I thought it prudent not to break the dismission at once.

The next day I noticed that Bartleby did nothing but stand at his win- 128 dow in his dead-wall revery. Upon asking him why he did not write, he said that he had decided upon doing no more writing.

"Why, how now? what next?" exclaimed I, "do no more writing?" 129

"No more." 130

"And what is the reason?" 131

"Do you not see the reason for yourself?" he indifferently replied. 132

I looked steadfastly at him, and perceived that his eyes looked dull and 133 glazed. Instantly it occurred to me, that his unexampled diligence in copy- ing by his dim window for the first few weeks of his stay with me might have temporarily impaired his vision.

I was touched. I said something in condolence with him. I hinted that 134 of course he did wisely in abstaining from writing for a while; and urged him to embrace that opportunity of taking wholesome exercise in the open air. This, however, he did not do. A few days after this, my other clerks being absent, and being in a great hurry to dispatch certain letters by the mail, I thought that, having nothing else earthly to do, Bartleby would surely be less inflexible than usual, and carry these letters to the Post Office. But he blankly declined. So, much to my inconvenience, I went myself.

135   Still added days went by. Whether Bartleby's eyes improved or not, I could not say. To all appearance, I thought they did. But when I asked him if they did he vouchsafed no answer. At all events, he would do no copying. At last, in replying to my urgings, he informed me that he had permanently given up copying.

136   "What!" exclaimed I; "suppose your eyes should get entirely well—better than ever before—would you not copy then?"

137   "I have given up copying," he answered, and slid aside.

138   He remained as ever, a fixture in my chamber. Nay—if that were possible—he became still more of a fixture than before. What was to be done? He would do nothing in the office; why should he stay there? In plain fact, he had now become a millstone to me, not only useless as a necklace, but afflictive to bear. Yet I was sorry for him. I speak less than truth when I say that, on his own account, he occasioned me uneasiness. If he would but have named a single relative or friend, I would instantly have written, and urged their taking the poor fellow away to some convenient retreat. But he seemed alone, absolutely alone in the universe. A bit of wreck in the mid-Atlantic. At length, necessities connected with my business tyrannized over all other considerations. Decently as I could, I told Bartleby that in six days' time he must unconditionally leave the office. I warned him to take measures, in the interval, for procuring some other abode. I offered to assist him in this endeavor, if he himself would but take the first step towards a removal. "And when you finally quit me, Bartleby," added I, "I shall see that you go not away entirely unprovided. Six days from this hour, remember."

139   At the expiration of that period, I peeped behind the screen, and lo! Bartleby was there.

140   I buttoned up my coat, balanced myself; advanced slowly towards him, touched his shoulder, and said, "The time has come; you must quit this place; I am sorry for you; here is money; but you must go."

141   "I would prefer not," he replied, with his back still towards me.

142   "You *must*."

143   He remained silent.

144   Now I had an unbounded confidence in this man's common honesty. He had frequently restored to me sixpences and shillings carelessly dropped upon the floor, for I am apt to be very reckless in such shirt-button affairs. The proceeding, then, which followed will not be deemed extraordinary.

145   "Bartleby," said I, "I owe you twelve dollars on account; here are thirty-two; the odd twenty are yours—Will you take it?" and I handed the bills towards him.

But he made no motion. 146

"I will leave them here, then," putting them under a weight on the 147
table. Then taking my hat and cane and going to the door, I tranquilly
turned and added—"After you have removed your things from these offices, Bartleby, you will of course lock the door—since every one is now
gone for the day but you—and if you please, slip your key underneath the
mat, so that I may have it in the morning. I shall not see you again; so
good-bye to you. If, hereafter, in your new place of abode, I can be of any
service to you, do not fail to advise me by letter. Good-bye, Bartleby, and
fare you well."

But he answered not a word; like the last column of some ruined tem- 148
ple, he remained standing mute and solitary in the middle of the otherwise deserted room.

As I walked home in a pensive mood, my vanity got the better of my 149
pity. I could not but highly plume myself on my masterly management in
getting rid of Bartleby. Masterly I call it, and such it must appear to any
dispassionate thinker. The beauty of my procedure seemed to consist in its
perfect quietness. There was no vulgar bullying, no bravado of any sort, no
choleric hectoring, and striding to and fro across the apartment, jerking
out vehement commands for Bartleby to bundle himself off with his beg-
garly traps. Nothing of the kind. Without loudly bidding Bartleby depart—
as an inferior genius might have done—I *assumed* the ground that depart
he must; and upon that assumption built all I had to say. The more I
thought over my procedure, the more I was charmed with it. Nevertheless, next morning, upon awakening, I had my doubts—I had somehow
slept off the fumes of vanity. One of the coolest and wisest hours a man
has, is just after he awakes in the morning. My procedure seemed as saga-
cious as ever—but only in theory. How it would prove in practice—there
was the rub. It was truly a beautiful thought to have assumed Bartleby's departure; but, after all, that assumption was simply my own, and none of
Bartleby's. The great point was, not whether I had assumed that he would
quit me, but whether he would prefer to do so. He was more a man of preferences than assumptions.

After breakfast, I walked down town, arguing the probabilities *pro* and 150
con. One moment I thought it would prove a miserable failure, and
Bartleby would be found all alive at my office as usual; the next moment
it seemed certain that I should find his chair empty. And so I kept veering
about. At the corner of Broadway and Canal Street, I saw quite an excited
group of people standing in earnest conversation.

"I'll take odds he doesn't," said a voice as I passed. 151

152 "Doesn't go?—done!" said I, "put up your money."

153 I was instinctively putting my hand in my pocket to produce my own, when I remembered that this was an election day. The words I had overheard bore no reference to Bartleby, but to the success or non-success of some candidate for the mayoralty. In my intent frame of mind, I had, as it were, imagined that all Broadway shared in my excitement, and were debating the same question with me. I passed on, very thankful that the uproar of the street screened my momentary absent-mindedness.

154 As I had intended, I was earlier than usual at my office door. I stood listening for a moment. All was still. He must be gone. I tried the knob. The door was locked. Yes, my procedure had worked to a charm; he indeed must be vanished. Yet a certain melancholy mixed with this: I was almost sorry for my brilliant success. I was fumbling under the door mat for the key, which Bartleby was to have left there for me, when accidentally my knee knocked against a panel, producing a summoning sound, and in response a voice came to me from within—"Not yet; I am occupied."

155 It was Bartleby.

156 I was thunderstruck. For an instant I stood like the man who, pipe in mouth, was killed one cloudless afternoon long ago in Virginia, by summer lightning; at his own warm open window he was killed, and remained leaning out there upon the dreamy afternoon, till someone touched him, when he fell.

157 "Not gone!" I murmured at last. But again obeying that wondrous ascendancy which the inscrutable scrivener had over me, and from which ascendancy, for all my chafing, I could not completely escape, I slowly went down stairs and out into the street, and while walking round the block, considered what I should next do in this unheard-of perplexity. Turn the man out by an actual thrusting I could not; to drive him away by calling him hard names would not do; calling in the police was an unpleasant idea; and yet, permit him to enjoy his cadaverous triumph over me—this, too, I could not think of. What was to be done? or, if nothing could be done, was there anything further that I could *assume* in the matter? Yes, as before I had prospectively assumed that Bartleby would depart, so now I might retrospectively assume that departed he was. In the legitimate carrying out of this assumption, I might enter my office in a great hurry, and pretending not to see Bartleby at all, walk straight against him as if he were air. Such a proceeding would in a singular degree have the appearance of a home-thrust. It was hardly possible that Bartleby could withstand such an application of the doctrine of assumption. But upon second thoughts the success of the plan seemed rather dubious. I resolved to argue the matter over with him again.

"Bartleby," said I, entering the office, with a quietly severe expression, 158
"I am seriously displeased. I am pained, Bartleby. I had thought better of
you. I had imagined you of such a gentlemanly organization, that in any
delicate dilemma a slight hint would suffice—in short, an assumption. But
it appears I am deceived. Why," I added, unaffectedly starting, "You have
not even touched that money yet," pointing to it, just where I had left it
the evening previous.

He answered nothing. 159

"Will you, or will you not, quit me?" I now demanded in a sudden pas- 160
sion, advancing close to him.

"I would prefer *not* to quit you," he replied, gently emphasizing the *not*. 161

"What earthly right have you to stay here? Do you pay any rent? Do you 162
pay my taxes? Or is this property yours?"

He answered nothing. 163

"Are you ready to go on and write now? Are your eyes recovered? Could 164
you copy a small paper for me this morning? or help examine a few lines?
or step round to the Post Office? In a word, will you do anything at all, to
give a coloring to your refusal to depart the premises?"

He silently retired into his hermitage. 165

I was now in such a state of nervous resentment that I thought it but 166
prudent to check myself at present from further demonstrations. Bartleby
and I were alone. I remembered the tragedy of the unfortunate Adams and
the still more unfortunate Colt in the solitary office of the latter; and how
poor Colt, being dreadfully incensed by Adams, and imprudently permitting himself to get wildly excited, was at unawares hurried into his fatal
act an act which certainly no man could possibly deplore more than the
actor himself.[1] Often it had occurred to me in my ponderings upon the
subject that had that altercation taken place in the public street, or at a
private residence, it would not have terminated as it did. It was the circumstance of being alone in a solitary office, up stairs, of a building entirely unhallowed by humanizing domestic associations—an uncarpeted
office, doubtless, of a dusty, haggard sort of appearance—this it must have
been, which greatly helped to enhance the irritable desperation of the
hapless Colt.

But when this old Adam of resentment rose in me and tempted me con- 167
cerning Bartleby, I grappled him and threw him. How? Why, simply by re-
calling the divine injunction: "A new commandment give I unto you,

---

1 John C. Colt murdered Samuel Adams in January 1842. Later that year, after his conviction, Colt
committed suicide a half-hour before he was to be hanged. The case received wide and sensational-
istic press coverage at the time.

that ye love one another." Yes, this it was that saved me. Aside from higher considerations, charity often operates as a vastly wise and prudent principle—a great safeguard to its possessor. Men have committed murder for jealousy's sake, and anger's sake, and hatred's sake, and selfishness' sake, and spiritual pride's sake; but no man, that ever I heard of, ever committed a diabolical murder for sweet charity's sake. Mere self-interest, then, if no better motive can be enlisted, should, especially with high-tempered men, prompt all beings to charity and philanthropy. At any rate, upon the occasion in question, I strove to drown my exasperated feelings towards the scrivener by benevolently construing his conduct. Poor fellow, poor fellow! thought I, he don't mean anything; and besides, he has seen hard times, and ought to be indulged.

168   I endeavored, also, immediately to occupy myself, and at the same time to comfort my despondency. I tried to fancy, that in the course of the morning, at such time as might prove agreeable to him, Bartleby, of his own free accord, would emerge from his hermitage and take up some decided line of march in the direction of the door. But no. Half-past twelve o'clock came; Turkey began to glow in the face, overturn his inkstand, and become generally obstreperous; Nippers abated down into quietude and courtesy; Ginger Nut munched his noon apple; and Bartleby remained standing at his window in one of his profoundest dead-wall reveries. Will it be credited? Ought I to acknowledge it? That afternoon I left the office without saying one further word to him.

169   Some days now passed, during which, at leisure intervals I looked a little into "Edwards on the Will," and "Priestley on Necessity." Under the circumstances, those books induced a salutary feeling. Gradually I slid into the persuasion that these troubles of mine, touching the scrivener, had been all predestined from eternity, and Bartleby was billeted upon me for some mysterious purpose of an all-wise Providence, which it was not for a mere mortal like me to fathom. Yes, Bartleby, stay there behind your screen, thought I; I shall persecute you no more; you are harmless and noiseless as any of these old chairs; in short, I never feel so private as when I know you are here. At last I see it, I feel it; I penetrate to the predestined purpose of my life. I am content. Others may have loftier parts to enact; but my mission in this world, Bartleby, is to furnish you with office-room for such period as you may see fit to remain.

170   I believe that this wise and blessed frame of mind would have continued with me, had it not been for the unsolicited and uncharitable remarks obtruded upon me by my professional friends who visited the rooms. But thus it often is, that the constant friction of illiberal minds wears out at last the best resolves of the more generous. Though to be sure, when I re-

flected upon it, it was not strange that people entering my office should be struck by the peculiar aspect of the unaccountable Bartleby, and so be tempted to throw out some sinister observations concerning him. Sometimes an attorney, having business with me, and calling at my office, and finding no one but the scrivener there, would undertake to obtain some sort of precise information from him touching my whereabouts; but without heeding his idle talk, Bartleby would remain standing immovable in the middle of the room. So after contemplating him in that position for a time, the attorney would depart, no wiser than he came.

Also, when a reference was going on, and the room full of lawyers and 171 witnesses, and business driving fast, some deeply-occupied legal gentleman present, seeing Bartleby wholly unemployed, would request him to run round to his (the legal gentleman's) office and fetch some papers for him. Thereupon, Bartleby would tranquilly decline, and yet remain idle as before. Then the lawyer would give a great stare, and turn to me. And what could I say? At last I was made aware that all through the circle of my professional acquaintance, a whisper of wonder was running round, having reference to the strange creature I kept at my office. This worried me very much. And as the idea came upon me of his possibly turning out a long-lived man, and keeping occupying my chambers, and denying my authority; and perplexing my visitors; and scandalizing my professional reputation; and casting a general gloom over the premises; keeping soul and body together to the last upon his savings (for doubtless he spent but half a dime a day), and in the end perhaps outlive me, and claim possession of my office by right of his perpetual occupancy: as all these dark anticipations crowded upon me more and more, and my friends continually intruded their relentless remarks upon the apparition in my room; a great change was wrought in me. I resolved to gather all my faculties together, and forever rid me of this intolerable incubus.

Ere revolving any complicated project, however, adapted to this end, I 172 first simply suggested to Bartleby the propriety of his permanent departure. In a calm and serious tone, I commended the idea to his careful and mature consideration. But, having taken three days to meditate upon it, he apprised me, that his original determination remained the same; in short, that he still preferred to abide with me.

What shall I do? I now said to myself, buttoning up my coat to the last 173 button. What shall I do? what ought I to do? what does conscience say I *should* do with this man, or, rather, ghost. Rid myself of him, I must; go, he shall. But how? You will not thrust him, the poor, pale, passive mortal you will not thrust such a helpless creature out of your door? you will not dishonor yourself by such cruelty? No, I will not, I cannot do that. Rather would I let him live and die here, and then mason up his remains in the wall. What, then, will you do? For all your coaxing, he will not budge. Bribes he leaves under your own paper-weight on your table; in short, it is quite plain that he prefers to cling to you.

174 Then something severe, something unusual must be done. What! surely you will not have him collared by a constable, and commit his innocent pallor to the common jail? And upon what ground could you procure such a thing to be done?—a vagrant, is he? What! he a vagrant, a wanderer, who refuses to budge? It is because he will not be a vagrant, then, that you seek to count him *as* a vagrant. That is too absurd. No visible means of support: there I have him. Wrong again: for indubitably he *does* support himself, and that is the only unanswerable proof that any man can show of his possessing the means so to do. No more, then. Since he will not quit me, I must quit him. I will change my offices; I will move elsewhere, and give him fair notice, that if I find him on my new premises I will then proceed against him as a common trespasser.

175 Acting accordingly, next day I thus addressed him: "I find these chambers too far from the City Hall; the air is unwholesome. In a word, I propose to remove my offices next week, and shall no longer require your services. I tell you this now, in order that you may seek another place."

176 He made no reply, and nothing more was said.

177 On the appointed day I engaged carts and men, proceeded to my chambers, and, having but little furniture, everything was removed in a few hours. Throughout, the scrivener remained standing behind the screen, which I directed to be removed the last thing. It was withdrawn; and, being folded up like a huge folio, left him the motionless occupant of a naked room. I stood in the entry watching him a moment, while something from within me upbraided me.

178 I re-entered, with my hand in my pocket—and—and my heart in my mouth.

179 "Good-bye, Bartleby; I am going—good-bye, and God some way bless you; and take that," slipping something in his hand. But it dropped upon the floor, and then—strange to say—I tore myself from him whom I had so longed to be rid of.

180 Established in my new quarters, for a day or two I kept the door locked, started at every footfall in the passages. When I returned to my rooms, after any little absence, I would pause at the threshold for an instant, and attentively listen, ere applying my key. But these fears were needless. Bartleby never came nigh me.

181 I thought all was going well, when a perturbed-looking stranger visited me, inquiring whether I was the person who had recently occupied rooms at No. — Wall Street.

Full of forebodings, I replied that I was.   182

"Then, sir," said the stranger, who proved a lawyer, "you are responsible   183
for the man you left there. He refuses to do any copying; he refuses to do
anything; he says he prefers not to; and he refuses to quit the premises."

"I am very sorry, sir," said I, with assumed tranquillity, but an inward   184
tremor, "but, really, the man you allude to is nothing to me—he is no relation or apprentice of mine, that you should hold me responsible for him."

"In mercy's name, who is he?"   185

"I certainly cannot inform you. I know nothing about him. Formerly I   186
employed him as a copyist; but he has done nothing for me now for some
time past."

"I shall settle him, then—good morning, sir."   187

Several days passed, and I heard nothing more; and, though I often felt   188
a charitable prompting to call at the place and see poor Bartleby, yet a certain squeamishness, of I know not what, withheld me.

All is over with him, by this time, thought I, at last, when, through an-   189
other week, no further intelligence reached me. But, coming to my room
the day after, I found several persons waiting at my door in a high state of
nervous excitement.

"That's the man here—he comes," cried the foremost one, whom I rec-   190
ognized as the lawyer who had previously called upon me alone.

"You must take him away, sir, at once," cried a portly person among   191
them, advancing upon me, and whom I knew to be the landlord of No. —
Wall Street. "These gentlemen, my tenants, cannot stand it any longer;
Mr. B ——" pointing to the lawyer, "has turned him out of his room, and
he now persists in haunting the building generally, sitting upon the banis-
ters of the stairs by day, and sleeping in the entry by night. Everybody is
concerned; clients are leaving the offices; some fears are entertained of a
mob; something you must do, and that without delay."

Aghast at this torrent, I fell back before it, and would fain have locked   192
myself in my new quarters. In vain I persisted that Bartleby was nothing
to me—no more than to any one else. In vain—I was the last person
known to have anything to do with him, and they held me to the terrible
account. Fearful, then, of being exposed in the papers (as one person present obscurely threatened), I considered the matter, and, at length, said, that
if the lawyer would give me a confidential interview with the scrivener, in
his (the lawyer's) own room, I would, that afternoon, strive my best to rid
them of the nuisance they complained of.

Going up stairs to my old haunt, there was Bartleby silently sitting upon   193
the banister at the landing.

"What are you doing here, Bartleby?" said I.   194

"Sitting upon the banister," he mildly replied.   195

196   I motioned him into the lawyer's room, who then left us.

197   "Bartleby," said I, "are you aware that you are the cause of great tribulation to me, by persisting in occupying the entry after being dismissed from the office?"

198   No answer.

199   "Now one of two things must take place. Either you must do something, or something must be done to you. Now what sort of business would you like to engage in? Would you like to re-engage in copying for some one?"

200   "No; I would prefer not to make any change."

201   "Would you like a clerkship in a dry-goods store?"

202   "There is too much confinement about that. No, I would not like a clerkship; but I am not particular."

203   "Too much confinement," I cried, "why, you keep yourself confined all the time!"

204   "I would prefer not to take a clerkship," he rejoined, as if to settle that little item at once.

205   "How would a bar-tender's business suit you? There is no trying of the eye-sight in that."

206   "I would not like it at all; though, as I said before, I am not particular."

207   His unwonted wordiness inspirited me. I returned to the charge.

208   "Well, then, would you like to travel through the country collecting bills for the merchants? That would improve your health."

209   "No, I would prefer to be doing something else."

210   "How, then, would going as a companion to Europe, to entertain some young gentleman with your conversation—how would that suit you?"

211   "Not at all. It does not strike me that there is anything definite about that. I like to be stationary. But I am not particular."

212   "Stationary you shall be, then," I cried, now losing all patience, and, for the first time in all my exasperating connections with him, fairly flying into a passion. "If you do not go away from these premises before night, I shall feel bound—indeed, I *am* bound—to—to—to quit the premises myself!" I rather absurdly concluded, knowing not with what possible threat to try to frighten his immobility into compliance. Despairing of all further efforts, I was precipitately leaving him, when a final thought occurred to me—one which had not been wholly indulged before.

213   "Bartleby," said I, in the kindest tone I could assume under such exciting circumstances, "will you go home with me now not to my office, but my dwelling—and remain there till we can conclude upon some convenient arrangement for you at our leisure? Come, let us start now, right away."

214   "No: at present I would prefer not to make any change at all."

215   I answered nothing; but, effectually dodging every one by the suddenness and rapidity of my flight, rushed from the building, ran up Wall Street

towards Broadway, and, jumping into the first omnibus, was soon removed from pursuit. As soon as tranquillity returned, I distinctly perceived that I had now done all that I possibly could, both in respect to the demands of the landlord and his tenants, and with regard to my own desire and sense of duty, to benefit Bartleby, and shield him from rude persecution. I now strove to be entirely care-free and quiescent; and my conscience justified me in the attempt; though, indeed, it was not so successful as I could have wished. So fearful was I of being again hunted out by the incensed land-lord and his exasperated tenants, that, surrendering my business to Nip-pers, for a few days, I drove about the upper part of the town and through the surburbs, in my rockaway; crossed over to Jersey City and Hoboken, and paid fugitive visits to Manhattanville and Astoria. In fact, I almost lived in my rockaway for the time.

When again I entered my office, lo, a note from the landlord lay upon the desk. I opened it with trembling hands. It informed me that the writer had sent to the police, and had Bartleby removed to the Tombs as a va-grant. Moreover, since I knew more about him than any one else, he wished me to appear at that place, and make a suitable statement of the facts. These tidings had a conflicting effect upon me. At first I was indig-nant; but, at last, almost approved. The landlord's energetic, summary dis-position, had led him to adopt a procedure which I do not think I would have decided upon myself; and yet, as a last resosrt, under such peculiar circumstances, it seemed the only plan.   216

As I afterwards learned, the poor scrivener, when told that he must be conducted to the Tombs, offered not the slightest obstacle, but, in his pale, unmoving way, silently acquiesced.   217

Some of the compassionate and curious by-standers joined the party; and headed by one of the constables arm-in-arm with Bartleby, the silent procession filed its way through all the noise, and heat, and joy of the roar-ing thoroughfares at noon.   218

The same I received the note, I went to the Tombs, or, to speak more properly, the Halls of Justice. Seeking the right officer, I stated the purpose of my call, and was informed that the individual I described was, indeed, within. I then assured the functionary that Bartleby was a perfectly hon-est man, and greatly to be compassionated, however unaccountably ec-centric. I narrated all I knew, and closed by suggesting the idea of letting him remain in as indulgent confinement as possible, till something less harsh might be done—though, indeed, I hardly knew what. At all events, if nothing else could be decided upon, the alms-house must receive him. I then begged to have an interview.   219

Being under no disgraceful charge, and quite serene and harmless in all his ways, they had permitted him freely to wander about the prison, and,   220 especially, in the inclosed grass-platted yards thereof. And so I found him there, standing all alone in the quietest of the yards, his face towards a high wall, while all around, from the narrow slits of the jail windows, I thought I saw peering out upon him the eyes of murderers and thieves.

221   "Bartleby!"

222   "I know you," he said, without looking around—"and I want nothing to say to you."

223   "It was not I that brought you here, Bartleby," said I, keenly pained at his implied suspicion. "And to you, this should not be so vile a place. Nothing reproachful attaches to you by being here. And see, it is not so sad a place as one might think. Look, there is the sky, and here is the grass."

224   "I know where I am," he replied, but would say nothing more, and so I left him.

225   As I entered the corridor again, a broad meat-like man, in an apron, accosted me, and, jerking his thumb over my shoulder, said "Is that your friend?"

226   "Yes."

227   "Does he want to starve? If he does, let him live on the prison fare, that's all."

228   "Who are you?" asked I, not knowing what to make of such an unofficially speaking person in such a place.

229   "I am the grub-man. Such gentlemen as have friends here, hire me to provide them with something good to eat."

230   "Is this so?" said I, turning to the turnkey.

231   He said it was.

232   "Well, then," said I, slipping some silver into the grub-man's hands (for so they called him), "I want you to give particular attention to my friend there; let him have the best dinner you can get. And you must be as polite to him as possible."

233   "Introduce me, will you?" said the grub-man, looking at me with an expression which seemed to say he was all impatience for an opportunity to give a specimen of his breeding.

234   Thinking it would prove of benefit to the scrivener, I acquiesced; and, asking the grub-man his name, went up with him to Bartleby.

235   "Bartleby, this is a friend; you will find him very useful to you."

236   "Your sarvant, sir, your sarvant," said the grub-man, making a low salutation behind his apron. "Hope you find it pleasant here, sir; nice grounds—cool apartments—hope you'll stay with us some time—try to make it agreeable. What will you have for dinner to-day?"

237   "I prefer not to dine to-day," said Bartleby, turning away. "It would disagree with me; I am unused to dinners." So saying, he slowly moved to the other side of the inclosure, and took up a position fronting the dead-wall.

"How's this?" said the grub-man, addressing me with a stare of astonishment. "He's odd, ain't he?" 238

"I think he is a little deranged," said I, sadly. 239

"Deranged? deranged is it? Well, now, upon my word, I thought that friend of yourn was a gentleman forger; they are always pale and genteel-like, them forgers. I can't help pity 'em—can't help it, sir. Did you know Monroe Edwards?" he added, touchingly, and paused. Then, laying his hand piteously on my shoulder, sighed, "he died of consumption at Sing-Sing. So you weren't acquainted with Monroe?" 240

"No, I was never socially acquainted with any forgers. But I cannot stop longer. Look to my friend younder. You will not lose by it. I will see you again." 241

Some few days after this, I again obtained admission to the Tombs, and went through the corridors in quest of Bartleby; but without finding him. 242

"I saw him coming from his cell not long ago," said a turnkey, "may be he's gone to loiter in the yards." 243

So I went in that direction. 244

"Are you looking for the silent man?" said another turnkey, passing me. "Yonder he lies—sleeping in the yard there. 'Tis not twenty minutes since I saw him lie down." 245

The yard was entirely quiet. It was not accessible to the common prisoners. The surrounding walls, of amazing thickness, kept off all sounds behind them. The Egyptian character of the masonry weighed upon me with its gloom. But a soft imprisoned turf grew under foot. The heart of the eternal pyramids, it seemed, wherein, by some strange magic, through the clefts, grass-seed, dropped by birds, had sprung. 246

Strangely huddled at the base of the wall, his knees drawn up, and lying on his side, his head touching the cold stones, I saw the wasted Bartleby. But nothing stirred. I paused; then went close up to him; stooped over, and saw that his dim eyes were open; otherwise he seemed profoundly sleeping. Something prompted me to touch him. I felt his hand, when a tingling shiver ran up my arm and down my spine to my feet. 247

The round face of the grub-man peered upon me now. "His dinner is ready. Won't he dine to-day, either? Or does he live without dining?" 248

"Lives without dining," said I, and closed the eyes. 249

"Eh!—He's asleep, ain't he?" 250

"With kings and counselors," murmured I. 251

There would seem little need for proceeding further in this history. Imagination will readily supply the meagre recital of poor Bartleby's interment. But, ere parting with the reader, let me say, that if this little narrative has sufficiently interested him, to awaken curiosity as to who Bartleby 252 was, and what manner of life he led prior to the present narrator's making his acquaintance, I can only reply, that in such curiosity I fully share, but am wholly unable to gratify it. Yet here I hardly know whether I should divulge one little item of rumor, which came to my ear a few months after the scrivener's decease. Upon what basis it rested, I could never ascertain; and hence, how true it is I cannot now tell. But, inasmuch as this vague report has not been without a certain suggestive interest to me, however sad, it may prove the same with some others; and so I will briefly mention it. The report was this: that Bartleby had been a subordinate clerk in the Dead Letter Office at Washington, from which he had been suddenly removed by a change in the administration. When I think over this rumor, hardly can I express the emotions which seize me. Dead letters! does it not sound like dead men? Conceive a man by nature and misfortune prone to a pallid hopelessness, can any business seem more fitted to heighten it than that of continually handling these dead letters, and assorting them for the flames? For by the cart-load they are annually burned. Sometimes from out the folded paper the pale clerk takes a ring the finger it was meant for, perhaps, moulders in the grave; a bank-note sent in swiftest charity he whom it would relieve, nor eats nor hungers any more; pardon for those who died despairing; hope for those who died unhoping; good tidings for those who died stifled by unrelieved calamities. On errands of life, these letters speed to death.

253   Ah, Bartleby! Ah, humanity!

QUESTIONING AND DISCUSSING

Melville, "Bartleby, the Scrivener"

1. Describe the narrator. What might be his motives for his treatment of Bartleby, in addition to those that he himself gives?

2. Describe Bartleby. What might be the source of his behavior? What would explain the motives of a person who says little besides "I would prefer not to"?

3. Analyze the close of the story and the narrator's assumptions about Bartleby's decline and demise. Explain why Melville ends the story with "Ah, Bartleby! Ah, humanity!"

RICHARD RODRIGUEZ

Richard Rodriguez (1944–), born in San Francisco, received his BA from Stanford University, MA from Columbia, and PhD in English from the University of California at Berkeley. A prolific writer often concerned with issues of race and color, Rodriguez authored essays for the PBS series *NewHour with Jim Lehrer* that earned him the prestigious George Foster Peabody Award in 1997. His articles and essays have also been published in newspapers and journals, including *Change, The American Scholar,* and *Harper's.* Rodriguez is also a contributing editor of the *Los Angeles Times* and *U.S. News and World Report.* His numerous books include *Hunger of Memory* (1982, the source of the following essay), *Mexico's Children* (1992), *Days of Obligation: An Argument with My Mexican Father* (1992), and *Brown: The Last Discovery of America* (2003).

⌗

Aria: A Memoir of a Bilingual Childhood

I remember, to start with, that day in Sacramento, in a California now nearly thirty years past, when I first entered a classroom—able to understand about fifty stray English words. The third of four children, I had been preceded by my older brother and sister to a neighborhood Roman Catholic school. But neither of them had revealed very much about their classroom experiences. They left each morning and returned each afternoon, always together, speaking Spanish as they climbed the five steps to the porch. And their mysterious books, wrapped in brown shopping-bag paper, remained on the table next to the door, closed firmly behind them.

An accident of geography sent me to a school where all my classmates were white and many were the children of doctors and lawyers and business executives. On that first day of school, my classmates must certainly have been uneasy to find themselves apart from their families, in the first institution of their lives. But I was astonished. I was fated to be the "problem student" in class.

The nun said, in a friendly but oddly impersonal voice: "Boys and girls, this is Richard Rodriguez." (I heard her sound it out: *Rich-heard Road-ree-guess.*) It was the first time I had heard anyone say my name in English. "Richard," the nun repeated more slowly, writing my name down in her book. Quickly I turned to see my mother's face dissolve in a watery blur behind the pebbled-glass door.

Now, many years later, I hear of something called "bilingual education"— a scheme proposed in the late 1960s by Hispanic-American social activists, later endorsed by a congressional vote. It is a program that seeks to permit non–English-speaking children (many from lower class homes) to use their "family language" as the language of school. Such, at least, is the aim its supporters announce. I hear them, and am forced to say no: It is not possible for a child, any child, ever to use his family's language in school. Not to understand this is to misunderstand the public uses of schooling and to trivialize the nature of intimate life.

5   Memory teaches me what I know of these matters. The boy reminds the adult. I was a bilingual child, but of a certain kind: "socially disadvantaged," the son of working-class parents, both Mexican immigrants.

6   In the early years of my boyhood, my parents coped very well in America. My father had steady work. My mother managed at home. They were nobody's victims. When we moved to a house many blocks from the Mexican-American section of town, they were not intimidated by those two or three neighbors who initially tried to make us unwelcome. ("Keep your brats away from my sidewalk!") But despite all they achieved, or perhaps because they had so much to achieve, they lacked any deep feeling of ease, of belonging in public. They regarded the people at work or in crowds as being very distant from us. Those were the others, *los gringos*. That term was interchangeable in their speech with another, even more telling: *los americanos*.

7   I grew up in a house where the only regular guests were my relations. On a certain day, enormous families of relatives would visit us, and there would be so many people that the noise and the bodies would spill out to the backyard and onto the front porch. Then for weeks no one would come. (If the doorbell rang, it was usually a salesman.) Our house stood apart—gaudy yellow in a row of white bungalows. We were the people with the noisy dog, the people who raised chickens. We were the foreigners on the block. A few neighbors would smile and wave at us. We waved back. But until I was seven years old, I did not know the name of the old couple living next door or the names of the kids living across the street.

8   In public, my father and mother spoke a hesitant, accented, and not always grammatical English. And then they would have to strain, their bodies tense, to catch the sense of what was rapidly said by *los gringos*. At home, they returned to Spanish. The language of their Mexican past sounded in counterpoint to the English spoken in public. The words would come quickly, with ease. Conveyed through those sounds was the pleasing, soothing, consoling reminder that one was at home.

9   During those years when I was first learning to speak, my mother and father addressed me only in Spanish; in Spanish I learned to reply. By contrast, English (*inglés*) was the language I came to associate with gringos,

rarely heard in the house. I learned my first words of English overhearing my parents speaking to strangers. At six years of age, I knew just enough words for my mother to trust me on errands to stores one block away—but no more.

I was then a listening child, careful to hear the very different sounds of Spanish and English. Wide-eyed with hearing, I'd listen to sounds more than to words. First, there were English (gringo) sounds. So many words still were unknown to me that when the butcher or the lady at the drug-store said something, exotic polysyllabic sounds would bloom in the midst of their sentences. Often the speech of people in public seemed to me very loud, booming with confidence. The man behind the counter would liter-ally ask, "What can I do for you?" But by being so firm and clear, the sound of his voice said that he was a gringo; he belonged in public society. There were also the high, nasal notes of middle-class American speech—which I rarely am conscious of hearing today because I hear them so often, but could not stop hearing when I was a boy. Crowds at Safeway or at bus stops were noisy with the birdlike sounds of *los gringos*. I'd move away from them all—all the chirping chatter above me.

My own sounds I was unable to hear, but I knew that I spoke English poorly. My words could not extend to form complete thoughts. And the words I did speak I didn't know well enough to make distinct sounds. (Lis-teners would usually lower their heads to hear better what I was trying to say.) But it was one thing for *me* to speak English with difficulty; it was more troubling to hear my parents speaking in public: their high-whining vowels and guttural consonants; their sentences that got stuck with "eh" and "ah" sounds; the confused syntax; the hesitant rhythm of sounds so different from the way gringos spoke. I'd notice, moreover, that my par-ents' voices were softer than those of gringos we would meet.

I am tempted to say now that none of this mattered. (In adulthood I am embarrassed by childhood fears.) And, in a way, it didn't matter very much that my parents could not speak English with ease. Their linguistic difficulties had no serious consequences. My mother and father made themselves understood at the county hospital clinic and at government offices. And yet, in another way, it mattered very much. It was unsettling to hear my parents struggle with English. Hearing them, I'd grow nervous, and my clutching trust in their protection and power would be weakened.

There were many times like the night at a brightly lit gasoline station (a blaring white memory) when I stood uneasily hearing my father talk to a teenage attendant. I do not recall what they were saying, but I cannot forget the sounds my father made as he spoke. At one point his words slid together to form one long word—sounds as confused as the threads of blue

10

11

12

13

and green oil in the puddle next to my shoes. His voice rushed through what he had left to say. Toward the end, he reached falsetto notes, appealing to his listener's understanding. I looked away at the lights of passing automobiles. I tried not to hear any more. But I heard only too well the attendant's reply, his calm, easy tones. Shortly afterward, headed for home, I shivered when my father put his hand on my shoulder. The very first chance that I got, I evaded his grasp and ran on ahead into the dark, skipping with feigned boyish exuberance.

14   But then there was Spanish: *español,* the language rarely heard away from the house; *español,* the language which seemed to me therefore a private language, my family's language. To hear its sounds was to feel myself specially recognized as one of the family, apart from *los otros.* A simple remark, an inconsequential comment could convey that assurance. My parents would say something to me and I would feel embraced by the sounds of their words. Those sounds said: *I am speaking with ease in Spanish. I am addressing you in words I never use with los gringos. I recognize you as someone special, close, like no one outside. You belong with us. In the family. Ricardo.*

15   At the age of six, well past the time when most middle-class children no longer notice the difference between sounds uttered at home and words spoken in public, I had a different experience. I lived in a world compounded of sounds. I was a child longer than most. I lived in a magical world, surrounded by sounds both pleasing and fearful. I shared with my family a language enchantingly private—different from that used in the city around us.

16   Just opening or closing the screen door behind me was an important experience. I'd rarely leave home all alone or without feeling reluctance. Walking down the sidewalk, under the canopy of tall trees, I'd warily notice the (suddenly) silent neighborhood kids who stood warily watching me. Nervously, I'd arrive at the grocery store to hear there the sounds of the gringo, reminding me that in this so-big world I was a foreigner. But if leaving home was never routine, neither was coming back. Walking toward our house, climbing the steps from the sidewalk, in summer when the front door was open, I'd hear voices beyond the screen door talking in Spanish. For a second or two I'd stay, linger there listening. Smiling, I'd hear my mother call out, saying in Spanish, "Is that you, Richard?" Those were her words, but all the while her sounds would assure me: *You are home now. Come close inside. With us.* "Sí," I'd reply.

17   Once more inside the house, I would resume my place in the family. The sounds would grow harder to hear. Once more at home, I would grow less conscious of them. It required, however, no more than the blurt of the doorbell to alert me all over again to listen to sounds. The house would

turn instantly quiet while my mother went to the door. I'd hear her hard English sounds. I'd wait to hear her voice turn to soft-sounding Spanish, which assured me, as surely as did the clicking tongue of the lock on the door, that the stranger was gone.

Plainly it is not healthy to hear such sounds so often. It is not healthy   18
to distinguish public from private sounds so easily. I remained cloistered by sounds, timid and shy in public, too dependent on the voices at home. I remember many nights when my father would come back from work, and I'd hear him call out to my mother in Spanish, sounding relieved. In Spanish, his voice would sound the light and free notes that he never could manage in English. Some nights I'd jump up just hearing his voice. My brother and I would come running into the room where he was with our mother. Our laughing (so deep was the pleasure!) became screaming. Like others who feel the pain of public alienation, we transformed the knowledge of our public separateness into a consoling reminder of our in-timacy. Excited, our voices joined in a celebration of sounds. *We are speak-ing now the way we never speak out in public—we are together,* the sounds told me. Some nights no one seemed willing to loosen the hold that sounds had on us. At dinner we invented new words that sounded Span-ish, but made sense only to us. We pieced together new words by taking, say, an English verb and giving it Spanish endings. My mother's instruc-tions at bedtime would be lacquered with mock-urgent tones. Or a word like *sí*, sounded in several notes, would convey added measures of feeling. Tongues lingered around the edges of words, especially fat vowels, and we happily sounded that military drum roll, the twirling roar of the Spanish *r*. Family language, my family's sounds: the voices of my parents and sisters and brother. Their voices insisting: *You belong here. We are family members. Related. Special to one another. Listen!* Voices singing and sighing, rising and straining, then surging, teeming with pleasure which burst syllables into fragments of laughter. At times it seemed there was steady quiet only when, from another room, the rustling whispers of my parents faded and I edged closer to sleep.

Supporters of bilingual education imply today that students like me   19
miss a great deal by not being taught in their family's language. What they seem not to recognize is that, as a socially disadvantaged child, I regarded Spanish as a private language. It was a ghetto language that deepened and strengthened my feeling of separateness. What I needed to learn in school was that I had the right, and the obligation, to speak the public language. The odd truth is that my first-grade classmates could have become bilin-gual, in the conventional sense of the word, more easily than I. Had they

been taught early (as upper-middle-class children often are taught) a "second language" like Spanish or French, they could have regarded it simply as another public language. In my case, such bilingualism could not have been so quickly achieved. What I did not believe was that I could speak a single public language.

20   Without question, it would have pleased me to have heard my teachers address me in Spanish when I entered the classroom. I would have felt much less afraid. I would have imagined that my instructors were somehow "related" to me; I would indeed have heard their Spanish as my family's language. I would have trusted them and responded with ease. But I would have delayed—postponed for how long?—having to learn the language of public society. I would have evaded—and for how long?—learning the great lesson of school: that I had a public identity.

21   Fortunately, my teachers were unsentimental about their responsibility. What they understood was that I needed to speak public English. So their voices would search me out, asking me questions. Each time I heard them I'd look up in surprise to see a nun's face frowning at me. I'd mumble, not really meaning to answer. The nun would persist. "Richard, stand up. Don't look at the floor. Speak up. Speak to the entire class, not just to me!" But I couldn't believe English could be my language to use. (In part, I did not want to believe it.) I continued to mumble. I resisted the teacher's demands. (Did I somehow suspect that once I learned this public language my family life would be changed?) Silent, waiting for the bell to sound, I remained dazed, diffident, afraid.

22   Because I wrongly imagined that English was intrinsically a public language and Spanish was intrinsically private, I easily noted the difference between classroom language and the language at home. At school, words were directed to a general audience of listeners. ("Boys and girls . . .") Words were meaningfully ordered. And the point was not self-expression alone, but to make oneself understood by many others. The teacher quizzed: "Boys and girls, why do we use that word in this sentence? Could we think of a better word to use there? Would the sentence change its meaning if the words were differently arranged? Isn't there a better way of saying much the same thing?" (I couldn't say. I wouldn't try to say.)

23   Three months passed. Five. A half year. Unsmiling, ever watchful, my teachers noted my silence. They began to connect my behavior with the slow progress my brother and sisters were making. Until, one Saturday morning, three nuns arrived at the house to talk to our parents. Stiffly they sat on the blue living-room sofa. From the doorway of another room, spying on the visitors, I noted the incongruity, the clash of two worlds, the

faces and voices of school intruding upon the familiar setting of home. I overheard one voice gently wondering, "Do your children speak only Spanish at home, Mrs. Rodriguez?" While another voice added, "That Richard especially seems so timid and shy."

That Rich-heard!   24

With great tact, the visitors continued, "Is it possible for you and your   25
husband to encourage your children to practice their English when they are home?" Of course my parents complied. What would they not do for their children's well-being? And how could they question the Church's authority which those women represented? In an instant they agreed to give up the language (the sounds) which had revealed and accentuated our family's closeness. The moment after the visitors left, the change was observed. "*Ahora,* speak to us only *en inglés,*" my father and mother told us.

At first, it seemed a kind of game. After dinner each night, the family   26
gathered together to practice "our" English. It was still then *inglés,* a language foreign to us, so we felt drawn to it as strangers. Laughing, we would try to define words we could not pronounce. We played with strange English sounds, often overanglicizing our pronunciations. And we filled the smiling gaps of our sentences with familiar Spanish sounds. But that was cheating, somebody shouted, and everyone laughed.

In school, meanwhile, like my brothers and sisters, I was required to at-   27
tend a daily tutoring session. I needed a full year of this special work. I also needed my teachers to keep my attention from straying in class by calling out, "*Rich-heard*"—their English voices slowly loosening the ties to my other name, with its three notes, *Ri-car-do.* Most of all, I needed to hear my mother and father speak to me in a moment of seriousness in "broken"— suddenly heartbreaking—English. This scene was inevitable. One Saturday morning I entered the kitchen where my parents were talking, but I did not realize that they were talking in Spanish until, the moment they saw me, their voices changed and they began speaking English. The gringo sounds they uttered startled me. Pushed me away. In that moment of trivial misunderstanding and profound insight, I felt my throat twisted by unsounded grief. I simply turned and left the room. But I had no place to escape to where I could grieve in Spanish. My brother and sisters were speaking English in another part of the house.

Again and again in the days following, as I grew increasingly angry, I   28
was obliged to hear my mother and father encouraging me: "Speak to us *en inglés.*" Only then did I determine to learn classroom English. Thus, sometime afterward it happened: One day in school, I raised my hand to

volunteer an answer to a question. I spoke out in a loud voice and I did not think it remarkable when the entire class understood. That day I moved very far from being the disadvantaged child I had been only days earlier. Taken hold at last was the belief, the calming assurance, that I *belonged* in public.

29   Shortly after, I stopped hearing the high, troubling sounds of *los gringos*. A more and more confident speaker of English, I didn't listen to how strangers sounded when they talked to me. With so many English-speaking people around me, I no longer heard American accents. Conversations quickened. Listening to persons whose voices sounded eccentrically pitched, I might note their sounds for a few seconds, but then I'd concentrate on what they were saying. Now when I heard someone's tone of voice—angry or questioning or sarcastic or happy or sad—I didn't distinguish it from the words it expressed. Sound and word were thus tightly wedded. At the end of each day I was often bemused, and always relieved, to realize how "soundless," though crowded with words, my day in public had been. An eight-year-old boy, I finally came to accept what had been technically true since my birth: I was an American citizen.

30   But diminished by then was the special feeling of closeness at home. Gone was the desperate, urgent, intense feeling of being at home among those with whom I felt intimate. Our family remained a loving family, but one greatly changed. We were no longer so close, no longer bound tightly together by the knowledge of our separateness from *los gringos*. Neither my older brother nor my sisters rushed home after school anymore. Nor did I. When I arrived home, often there would be neighborhood kids in the house. Or the house would be empty of sounds.

31   Following the dramatic Americanization of their children, even my parents grew more publicly confident—especially my mother. First she learned the names of all the people on the block. Then she decided we needed to have a telephone in our house. My father, for his part, continued to use the word gringo, but it was no longer charged with bitterness or distrust. Stripped of any emotional content, the word simply became a name for those Americans not of Hispanic descent. Hearing him, sometimes, I wasn't sure if he was pronouncing the Spanish word *gringo*, or saying gringo in English.

32   There was a new silence at home. As we children learned more and more English, we shared fewer and fewer words with our parents. Sentences needed to be spoken slowly when one of us addressed our mother or father. Often the parent wouldn't understand. The child would need to repeat himself. Still the parent misunderstood. The young voice, frus-

trated, would end up saying, "Never mind"—the subject was closed. Dinners would be noisy with the clinking of knives and forks against dishes. My mother would smile softly between her remarks; my father, at the other end of the table, would chew and chew his food while he stared over the heads of his children.

My mother! My father! After English became my primary language, I 33 no longer knew what words to use in addressing my parents. The old Spanish words (those tender accents of sound) I had earlier used—*mamá* and *papá*—I couldn't use anymore. They would have been all-too-painful reminders of how much had changed in my life. On the other hand, the words I heard neighborhood kids call their parents seemed equally unsatisfactory. "Mother" and "father," "ma," "pa," "dad," "pop" (how I hated the all-American sound of that last word)—all these I felt were unsuitable terms of address for *my* parents. As a result, I never used them at home. Whenever I'd speak to my parents, I would try to get their attention by looking at them. In public conversations, I'd refer to them as my "parents" or my "mother" and "father."

My mother and father, for their part, responded differently, as their chil- 34 dren spoke to them less. My mother grew restless, seemed troubled and anxious at the scarceness of words exchanged in the house. She would question me about my day when I came home from school. She smiled at my small talk. She pried at the edges of my sentences to get me to say something more. ("What . . . ?") She'd join conversations she overheard, but her intrusions often stopped her children's talking. By contrast, my father seemed to grow reconciled to the new quiet. Though his English somewhat improved, he tended more and more to retire into silence. At dinner he spoke very little. One night his children and even his wife helplessly giggled at his garbled English pronunciation of the Catholic "Grace Before Meals." Thereafter he made his wife recite the prayer at the start of each meal, even on formal occasions when there were guests in the house.

Hers became the public voice of the family. On official business it was 35 she, not my father, who would usually talk to strangers on the phone or in stores. We children grew so accustomed to his silence that years later we would routinely refer to his "shyness." (My mother often tried to explain: Both of his parents died when he was eight. He was raised by an uncle who treated him as little more than a menial servant. He was never encouraged to speak. He grew up alone—a man of few words.) But I realized my father was not shy whenever I'd watch him speaking Spanish with relatives. Using Spanish, he was quickly effusive. Especially when talking with other men, his voice would spark, flicker, flare alive with varied sounds. In Spanish he expressed ideas and feelings he rarely revealed when speaking English. With firm Spanish sounds he conveyed a confidence and authority that English would never allow him.

36 The silence at home, however, was not simply the result of fewer words passing between parents and children. More profound for me was the silence created by my inattention to sounds. At about the time I no longer bothered to listen with care to the sounds of English in public, I grew careless about listening to the sounds made by the family when they spoke. Most of the time I would hear someone speaking at home and didn't distinguish his sounds from the words people uttered in public. I didn't even pay much attention to my parents' accented and ungrammatical speech—at least not at home. Only when I was with them in public would I become alert to their accents. But even then their sounds caused me less and less concern. For I was growing increasingly confident of my own public identity.

37 I would have been happier about my public success had I not recalled, sometimes, what it had been like earlier, when my family conveyed its intimacy through a set of conveniently private sounds. Sometimes in public, hearing a stranger, I'd hark back to my lost past. A Mexican farm worker approached me one day downtown. He wanted directions to some place. "*Hijito,* . . ." he said. And his voice stirred old longings. Another time I was standing beside my mother in the visiting room of a Carmelite convent, before the dense screen which rendered the nuns shadowy figures. I heard several of them speaking Spanish in their busy, singsong, overlapping voices, assuring my mother that, yes, yes, we were remembered, all our family was remembered, in their prayers. Those voices echoed faraway family sounds. Another day a dark-faced old woman touched my shoulder lightly to steady herself as she boarded a bus. She murmured something to me I couldn't quite comprehend. Her Spanish voice came near, like the face of a never-before-seen relative in the instant before I was kissed. That voice, like so many of the Spanish voices I'd hear in public, recalled the golden age of my childhood.

38 Bilingual educators say today that children lose a degree of "individuality" by becoming assimilated into public society. (Bilingual schooling is a program popularized in the seventies, that decade when middle-class "ethnics" began to resist the process of assimilation—the "American melting pot.") But the bilingualists oversimplify when they scorn the value and necessity of assimilation. They do not seem to realize that a person is individualized in two ways. So they do not realize that, while one suffers a diminished sense of *private* individuality by being assimilated into public society, such assimilation makes possible the achievement of *public* individuality.

Simplistically again, the bilingualists insist that a student should be re- 39
minded of his difference from others in mass society, of his "heritage." But
they equate mere separateness with individuality. The fact is that only in
private—with intimates—is separateness from the crowd a prerequisite
for individuality; an intimate "tells" me that I am unique, unlike all others, apart from the crowd. In public, by contrast, full individuality is
achieved, paradoxically, by those who are able to consider themselves
members of the crowd. Thus it happened for me. Only when I was able to
think of myself as an American, no longer an alien in gringo society, could
I seek the rights and opportunities necessary for full public individuality.
The social and political advantages I enjoy as a man began on the day I
came to believe that my name is indeed *Rich-heard Road-ree-guess*. It is true
that my public society today is often impersonal; in fact, my public society
is usually mass society. But despite the anonymity of the crowd, and despite the fact that the individuality I achieve in public is often tenuous—
because it depends on my being one in a crowd—I celebrate the day I
acquired my new name. Those middle-class ethnics who scorn assimilation seem to me filled with decadent self-pity, obsessed by the burden of
public life. Dangerously, they romanticize public separateness and trivialize
the dilemma of those who are truly socially disadvantaged.

If I rehearse here the changes in my private life after my Americaniza- 40
tion, it is finally to emphasize a public gain. The loss implies the gain. The
house I returned to each afternoon was quiet. Intimate sounds no longer
greeted me at the door. Inside there were other noises. The telephone
rang. Neighborhood kids ran past the door of the bedroom where I was
reading my schoolbooks—covered with brown shopping-bag paper. Once
I learned the public language, it would never again be easy for me to hear
intimate family voices. More and more of my day was spent hearing words,
not sounds. But that may only be a way of saying that on the day I raised
my hand in class and spoke loudly to an entire roomful of faces, my childhood started to end.

QUESTIONING AND DISCUSSING

Rodriguez, "Aria"

---

1. Richard Rodriguez's essay is a strong example of "mixed modes"—that is, it
   is a story, a memoir, but it also argues a point of view. What is that central
   argument? How does Rodriguez's use of various modes—description, narration, and argument, for instance—enhance the essay? For example, what is
   the effect of beginning the essay with narration? What is his argument?

2. How does Rodriguez evoke the treatment given immigrants—and any people in a neighborhood other than their own? What is it like to be "nobody's victim" and yet to feel very distant from others—from *"los americanos"*?

3. Discuss Rodriguez's contention that "It is not possible for a child, any child, ever to use his family's language in school. Not to understand this is to misunderstand the public uses of schooling and to trivialize the nature of intimate life." You might want to do some research on the controversial movement in bilingual-bicultural education.

⊞

HENRY DEMAREST LLOYD

It is fitting that this excerpt from *Wealth Against Commonwealth* comes from a chapter entitled "The Old Self-Interest" since Henry Demarest Lloyd (1847–1903) was a political reformer as well as a journalist. In 1872, Lloyd became a financial writer for the *Chicago Tribune*, and he began to write about the connections and often conflicting interests among various businesses and corporations. As a result, he wrote an article published in *The Atlantic Monthly* about corporate collusion that was read and discussed widely. In *Wealth against Commonwealth*, published in 1894, Lloyd follows up the *Atlantic* piece, detailing the reticence or failure of the government to break up collusive activities between the railroad industry and Standard Oil. Unfortunately, Lloyd's popular work did not ultimately lead to reform.

⊞

The Old Self-Interest

1   The corn of the coming harvest is growing so fast that, like the farmer standing at night in his fields, we can hear it snap and crackle. We have been fighting fire on the well-worn lines of old-fashioned politics and political economy, regulating corporations, and leaving competition to regulate itself. But the flames of a new economic evolution run around us, and we turn to find that competition has killed competition, that corporations are grown greater than the State and have bred individuals greater than themselves, and that the naked issue of our time is with property becoming master instead of servant, property in many necessaries of life becoming monopoly of the necessaries of life.

2   We are still, in part, as Emerson says, in the quadruped state. Our industry is a fight of every man for himself. The prize we give the fittest is

monopoly of the necessaries of life, and we leave these winners of the powers of life and death to wield them over us by the same "self-interest" with which they took them from us. In all this we see at work a "principle" which will go into the records as one of the historic mistakes of humanity. Institutions stand or fall by their philosophy, and the main doctrine of industry since Adam Smith has been the fallacy that the self-interest of the individual was a sufficient guide to the welfare of the individual and society. . . .

"It is a law of business for each proprietor to pursue his own interest," 3
said the committee of Congress which in 1893 investigated the coal combinations. "There is no hope for any of us, but the weakest must go first," is the golden rule of business. There is no other field of human associations in which any such rule of action is allowed. The man who should apply in his family or his citizenship this "survival of the fittest" theory as it is practically professed and operated in business would be a monster, and would be speedily made extinct, as we do with monsters. To divide the supply of food between himself and his children according to their relative powers of calculation, to follow his conception of his own self-interest in any matter which the self-interest of all has taken charge of, to deal as he thinks best for himself with foreigners with whom his country is at war, would be a short road to the penitentiary or the gallows. In trade men have not yet risen to the level of the family life of the animals. The true law of business is that all must pursue the interest of all. In the law, the highest product of civilization, this has long been a commonplace. The safety of the people is the supreme law. We are in travail to bring industry up to this. Our century of the caprice of the individual as the lawgiver of the common toil, to employ or disemploy, to start or stop, to open or close, to compete or combine, has been the disorder of the school while the master slept. The happiness, self-interest, or individuality of the whole is not more sacred than that of each, but it is greater. They are equal in quality, but in quantity they are greater. In the ultimate which the mathematician, the poet, the reformer projects the two will coincide.

Meanwhile, we who are the creators of society have got the times out of 4
joint, because, less experienced than the Creator of the balanced matter of earth, we have given the precedence to the powers on one side. As gods we are but half-grown. For a hundred years or so our economic theory has been one of industrial government by the self-interest of the individual. Political government by the self-interest of the individual we call anarchy. It is one of the paradoxes of public opinion that the people of America, least tolerant of this theory of anarchy in political government, lead in practicing it in industry. Politically, we are civilized; industrially, not yet. Our century, given to this *laissez-faire*—"leave the individual alone; he

will do what is best for himself, and what is best for him is best for all"—
has done one good: It has put society at the mercy of its own ideals, and
has produced an actual anarchy in industry which is horrifying us into a
change of doctrines.

5   The true *laissez-faire* is, let the individual do what the individual can
do best, and let the community do what the community can do best. The
laissez-faire of social self-interest, if true, cannot conflict with the individual self-interest, if true, but it must outrank it always. What we have called
"free competition" has not been free, only freer than what went before.
The free is still to come. . . .

6   Where the self-interest of the individual is allowed to be the rule both
of social and personal action, the level of all is forced down to that of the
lowest. Business excuses itself for the things it does—cuts in wages, exac-
tions in hours, tricks of competition—on the plea that the merciful are
compelled to follow the cruel. . . . When the self-interest of society is
made the standard the lowest must rise to the average. The one pulls
down, the other up. That men's hearts are bad and that bad men will do
bad things has a truth in it. But whatever the general average of morals,
the anarchy which gives such individuals their head and leaves them to
set the pace for all will produce infinitely worse results than a policy
which applies mutual checks and inspirations. Bad kings make bad reigns,
but monarchy is bad because it is arbitrary power, and that, whether it be
political or industrial, makes even good men bad.

7   A partial truth universally applied as this of self-interest has been is
a universal error. Everything goes to defeat. Highways are used to prevent travel and traffic. Ownership of the means of production is sought in
order to "shut down" production, and the means of plenty make famine.
All follow self-interest to find that though they have created marvelous
wealth it is not theirs. We pledge "our lives, our fortunes, and our sacred
honor" to establish the rule of the majority, and end by finding that
the minority—a minority in morals, money, and men—are our masters
whichever way we turn. We agonize over "economy," but sell all our grain
and pork and oil and cotton at exchanges where we pay brokerage on a
hundred or a thousand barrels or bushels or bales of wind to get one real
one sold. These intolerabilities—sweatshops where model merchants buy
and sell the cast-off scarlet-fever skins of the poor, factory and mine where
childhood is forbidden to become manhood and manhood is forbidden
to die a natural death, mausoleums in which we bury the dead rich, slums
in which we bury the living poor, coal pools with their manufacture of
artificial winter—all these are the rule of private self-interest arrived at
its destination. . . .

We are very poor. The striking feature of our economic condition is our 8
poverty, not our wealth. We make ourselves "rich" by appropriating the
property of others by methods which lessen the total property of all. Spain
took such riches from American and grew poor. Modern wealth more and
more resembles the winnings of speculators in bread during famine—worse,
for to make the money it makes the famine. What we call cheapness shows
itself to be unnatural fortunes for a very few, monstrous luxury for them and
proportionate deprivation for the people, judges debauched, trustees dis-
honored, Congress and State legislatures insulted and defied, when not seduced, multitudes of honest men ruined and driven to despair. . . .

Syndicates, by one stroke, get the power of selling dear on one side, and 9
producing cheap on the other. Thus they keep themselves happy, prices
high, and the people hungry. What model merchant could ask more? The
dream of the king who wished that all his people had but one neck that he
might decapitate them at one blow is realized today in this industrial gar-
rote. The syndicate has but to turn its screw, and every neck begins to
break. Prices paid to such intercepters are not an exchange of service; they
are ransom paid by the people for their lives. The ability of the citizen to
pay may fluctuate; what he must pay remains fixed, or advances like the
rent of the Irish tenant to the absentee landlord until the community interfered. Those who have this power to draw the money from the people—
from every railroad station, every streetcar, every fireplace, every saltcellar,
every breadpan, washboard, and coal scuttle—to their own safes have the
further incentive to make this money worth the most possible. By contracting the issue of currency and contracting it again by hoarding it in
their banks, safe-deposit vaults, and the government treasury, they can de-
press the prices of all that belongs to the people. Their own prices are
fixed. These are "regular prices," established by price lists. Given, as a ruling motive, the principles of business—to get the most and give the least;
given the legal and economic, physical and mechanical control, possible
under our present social arrangements, to the few over the many, and the
certain end of all this, if unarrested, unreversed, can be nothing less than
a return to chattel slavery. There may be some finer name, but the fact will
not be finer. Between our present tolerance and our completed subjection
the distance is not so far as that from the equality and simplicity of our Pil-
grim Fathers to ourselves.

Everything withers—even charity. Aristocratic benevolence spends a 10
shrunken stream in comparison with democratic benevolence. In an address
to the public, soliciting subscriptions, the Committee of the United Hospitals Association of New York said, in December, 1893: "The committee
have found that, through the obliteration of old methods of individual

competition by the establishment of large corporations and trusts in modern times, the income of such charitable institutions as are supported by the individual gifts of the benevolent has been seriously affected."

11   In the worst governments and societies that have existed one good can be seen—so good that the horrors of them fall back into secondary places as extrinsic, accidental. That good is the ability of men to lead the life together. The more perfect monopoly makes itself the more does it bring into strong lights the greatest fact of our industry, of far more permanent value than the greed which has for the moment made itself the cynosure of all eyes. It makes this fair world more fair to consider the loyalties, intelligences, docilities of the multitudes who are guarding, developing, operating with the faithfulness of brothers and the keen interest of owners' properties and industries in which brotherhood is not known and their title is not more than a tenancy at will. One of the largest stones in the arch of "consolidation," perhaps the keystone, is that men have become so intelligent, so responsive and responsible, so cooperative that they can be entrusted in great masses with the care of vast properties owned entirely by others and with the operation of complicated processes, although but a slender cost of subsistence is awarded them out of fabulous profits. The spectacle of the million and more employees of the railroads of this country despatching trains, maintaining tracks, collecting fares and freights, and turning over hundreds of millions of net profits to the owners, not one in a thousand of whom would know how to do the simplest of these things for himself, is possible only where civilization has reached a high average of morals and culture. More and more the mills and mines and stores, and even the farms and forests, are being administered by others than the owners. The virtue of the people is taking the place Poor Richard thought only the eye of the owner could fill. If mankind, driven by their fears and the greed of others, can do so well, what will be their productivity and cheer when the "interest of all" sings them to their work?

12   This new morality and new spring of wealth have been seized first by the appropriating ones among us. But, as has been in government, their intervention of greed is but a passing phase. Mankind belongs to itself, not to kings or monopolists, and will supersede the one as surely as the other with the institutions of democracy. Yes, Callicles, said Socrates, the greatest are usually the bad, for they have the power. If power could continue paternal and benign, mankind would not be rising through one emancipation after another into a progressive communion of equalities. The individual society will always be wrestling with each other in a composition of forces. But to just the extent to which civilization prevails, society will be held as inviolable as the individual; not subordinate—indeed inaudible—as now in the counting room and corporation office. We have overworked the

self-interest of the individual. The line of conflict between individual and social is a progressive one of the discovery of point after point in which the two are identical. Society thus passes from conflict to harmony, and on to another conflict. Civilization is the unceasing accretion of these social solutions. We fight out to an equilibrium, as in the abolition of human slavery; then upon this new level thus built up we enter upon the struggle for a new equilibrium, as now in the labor movement. The man for himself destroys himself and all men; only society can foster him and them.

Children yet, we run everything we do—love or war, work or leisure, religion or liberty—to excess. Every possibility of body and mind must be played upon till it is torn to pieces, as toys by children. Priests, voluptuaries, tyrants, knights, ascetics—in the long procession of fanatics a newcomer takes his place; he is called "the model merchant"—the cruelest fanatic in history. He is the product of ages given to progressive devotion to "trading." He is the high priest of the latest idolatry, the self-worship of self-interest. Whirling dervish of the market, self, friends, and family, body and soul, loves, hopes, and faith, all are sacrificed to seeing how many "turns" he can make before he drops dead. Trade began, Sir Henry Sumner Maine tells us, not within the family or community, but without. Its first appearances are on the neutral borderland between hostile tribes. There, in times of peace, they meet to trade, and think it no sin that "the buyer must beware" since the buyer is an enemy. Trade has spread thence, carrying with itself into family and State the poison of enmity. From the fatherhood of the old patriarchal life, where father and brother sold each other nothing, the world has chaffered along to the anarchy of a "free" trade which sells everything. One thing after another has passed out from under the regime of brotherhood and passed in under that of bargainhood. . . . 13

Conceptions of duty take on a correspondingly unnatural complexion. The main exhortations the world gives beginners are how to "get on"— the getting on so ardently inculcated being to get, like the old-man-of-the-sea, on somebody's back. "If war fails you in the country where you are, you must go where there is war," said one of the successful men of the fourteenth century to a young knight who asked him for the Laws of Life. "I shall be perfectly satisfied with you," I heard one of the great business geniuses of America say to his son, "if you will only always go to bed at night worth more than when you got up in the morning." The system grows, as all systems do, more complicated, and gets further away from its first purposes of barter of real things and services. It goes more under the hands of men of apt selfishness, who push it further away from general comprehension and the general good. Tariffs, currencies, finances, freight-rate sheets, the laws, become instruments of privilege, and just in proportion become puzzles no people can decipher. "I have a right to buy my labor where I can 14 buy it cheapest"—beginning as a protest against the selfish exclusions of antiquated trade guilds outgrown by the new times—has at last come to mean, "I have a right to do anything to cheapen the labor I want to buy, even to destroying the family life of the people."

15   When steaming kettles grew into beasts of burden and public highways dwindled into private property administered by private motives for private ends, all previous tendencies were intensified into a sudden whirl redistributing wealth and labors. It appears to have been the destiny of the railroad to begin and of oil to lubricate to its finish the last stage of this crazy commercialism. Business colors the modern world as war reddened the ancient world. Out of such delirium monsters are bred, and their excesses destroy the system that brought them forth. There is a strong suggestion of moral insanity in the unrelieved sameness of mood and unvarying repetition of one act in the life in the model merchant. Sane minds by an irresistible law alternate one tension with another. Only a lunatic is always smiling or always weeping or always clamoring for dividends. Eras show their last stages by producing men who sum up individually the morbid characteristics of the mass. When the crisis comes in which the gathering tendencies of generations shoot forward in the avalanche, there is born some group of men perfect for their function—good be it or bad. They need to take time for no second thought, and will not delay the unhalting reparations of nature by so much as the time given to one tear over the battlefield or the bargain. With their birth their mission is given them, whether it be the mission of Lucifer or Gabriel. This mission becomes their conscience. The righteous indignation that other men feel against sin these men feel against that which withstands them. Sincere as rattlesnakes, they are selfish with the unconsciousness possible to only the entirely commonplace, without the curiosity to question their times or the imagination to conceive the pain they inflict, and their every ideal is satisfied by the conventionalities of church, parlor, and counting room. These men are the touchstones to wither the cant of an age.

16   We preach "Do as you would be done by" in our churches, and "A fair exchange no robbery" in our counting rooms, and "All citizens are equal as citizens" in courts and Congress. Just as we are in danger of believing that to say these things is to do them and be them, there come unto us these men, practical as granite and gravitation. Taking their cue not from our lips, but from our lives, they better the instruction, and, passing easily to the high seats at every table, prove that we are liars and hypocrites. Their only secret is that they do, better than we, the things we are all trying to do, but of which in our morning and evening prayers, seen of all men, we are continually making believe to pray: Good Lord, deliver us! When the hour strikes for such leaders, they come and pass as by a law of nature to the

front. All follow them. It is their fate and ours that they must work out to the end the destiny interwoven of their own insatiate ambition and the false ideals of us who have created them and their opportunity.

If our civilization is destroyed, as Macaulay predicted, it will not be by   17
his barbarians from below. Our barbarians come from above. Our great moneymakers have sprung in one generation into seats of power kings do not know. The forces and the wealth are new, and have been the opportunity of new men. Without restraints of culture, experience, the pride, or even the inherited caution of class or rank, these men, intoxicated, think they are the wave instead of the float, and that they have created the business which has created them. To them science is but a never-ending repertoire of investments stored up by nature for the syndicates, government but a fountain of franchises, the nations but customers in squads, and a million the unit of a new arithmetic of wealth written for them. They claim a power without control, exercised through forms which make it secret, anonymous, and perpetual. The possibilities of its gratification have been widening before them without interruption since they began, and even at a thousand millions they will feel no satiation and will see no place to stop. They are gluttons of luxury and power, rough, unsocialized, believing that mankind must be kept terrorized. Power of pity die out of them, because they work through agents and die in their agents, because what they do is not for themselves.

Of gods, friends, learnings, of the uncomprehended civilization they   18
overrun, they ask but one question: How much? What is a good time to sell? What is a good time to buy? The Church and the Capitol, incarnating the sacrifices and triumphs of a procession of martyrs and patriots since the dawn of freedom, are good enough for a money changer's shop for them, and a market and shambles. Their heathen eyes see in the law and its consecrated officers nothing but an intelligence office and hired men to help them burglarize the treasures accumulated for thousands of years at the altars of liberty and justice, that they may burn their marbles for the lime of commerce.

Business motivated by the self-interest of the individual runs into mo-   19
nopoly at every point it touches the social life—land monopoly, transportation monopoly, trade monopoly, political monopoly in all its forms, from contraction of the currency to corruption in office. The society in which in half a lifetime a man without a penny can become a hundred times a millionaire is as overripe, industrially, as was, politically, the Rome in which the most popular bully could lift himself from the ranks of the legion on to the throne of the Caesars. Our rising issue is with business. Monopoly is business at the end of its journey. It has got there. The irrepressible conflict is now as distinctly with business as the issue so lately

met was with slavery. Slavery went first only because it was the cruder form of business.

20   Our tyrants are our ideals incarnating themselves in men born to command. What these men are we have made them. All governments are representative governments; none of them more so than our government of industry. We go hopelessly astray if we seek the solution of our problems in the belief that our business rulers are worse men in kind than ourselves. Worse in degree; yes. It is a race to the bad, and the winners are the worst. A system in which the prizes go to meanness invariably marches with the meanest men at the head. But if any could be meaner than the meanest it would be they who run and fail and rail.

21   Every idea finds its especially susceptible souls. These men are our most susceptible souls to the idea of individual self-interest. They have believed implicitly what we have taught, and have been the most faithful in trying to make the talent given them grow into ten talents. They rise superior to our halfhearted social corrections: publicity, private competition, all devices of market opposition, private litigation, public investigation, legislation, and criminal prosecution—all. Their power is greater today than it was yesterday, and will be greater tomorrow. The public does not withhold its favor, but deals with them, protects them, refuses to treat their crimes as it treats those of the poor, and admits them to the highest places. The predominant mood is the more or less concealed regret of the citizens that they have not been able to conceive and execute the same lucky stroke or some other as profitable. The conclusion is irresistible that men so given the lead are the representatives of the real "spirit of the age," and that the protestants against them are not representative of our times— are at best but intimators of times which may be.

22   Two social energies have been in conflict, and the energy of reform has so far proved the weaker. We have chartered the self-interest of the individual as the rightful sovereign of conduct; we have taught that the scramble for profit is the best method of administering the riches of earth and the exchange of services. Only those can attack this system who attack its central principle, that strength gives the strong in the market the right to destroy his neighbor. Only as we have denied that right to the strong elsewhere have we made ourselves as civilized as we are. And we cannot make a change as long as our songs, customs, catchwords, and public opinion tell all to do the same thing if they can. Society, in each person of its multitudes, must recognize that the same principles of the interest of all being the rule of all, of the strong serving the weak, of the first being the last—"I am among you as one that serves"—which have given us the home where the weakest is the one surest of his rights and of the fullest service of the strongest, and have given us the republic in

which all join their labor that the poorest may be fed, the weakest defended, and all educated and prospered, must be applied where men associate in common toil as wherever they associate. Not until then can the forces be reversed which generate those obnoxious persons—our fittest.

Our system, so fair in its theory and so fertile in its happiness and prosperity in its first century, is now, following the fate of systems, becoming artifical, technical, corrupt; and, as always happens in human institutions, after noon, power is stealing from the many to the few. Believing wealth to be good, the people believed the wealthy to be good. But, again in history, power has intoxicated and hardened its possessors, and Pharoahs are bred in counting rooms as they were in palaces. Their furniture must be banished to the world garret, where lie the outworn trappings of the guilds and slavery and other old lumber of human institutions.

23

QUESTIONING AND DISCUSSING
Lloyd, "The Old Self-Interest"

1. What is Henry Demarest Lloyd's central argument, and how does it touch on ethical issues? Consider the ways in which Lloyd chooses to refute basic tenets of business: "[. . .] in trade men have not yet risen to the level of the family life of animals." How does Lloyd support his point of view?

2. Comment on Lloyd's concluding statement: "Our system, so fair in its theory and so fertile in its happiness and prosperity in its first century, is now, following the fate of systems, becoming artificial, technical, corrupt; and, as always happens in human institutions, after noon, power is stealing from the many to the few." Looking at the text and researching at least one business or government-related story from current events, compare Lloyd's late-nineteenth-century views with contemporary concerns.

3. Do our "barbarians" indeed "come from above"? Support your reply.

4. Why does Lloyd use biblical references in this essay, and for what purpose? Analyze these references and their effectiveness.

5. Analyze Lloyd's discussion of economic and political principles—and their ethical implications—that are practiced in the United States. What relevance does this analysis have in the twenty-first century?

⊞

CHRISTINA HOFF SOMMERS

Christina Hoff Sommers (1956–) graduated from New York University and earned her PhD in philosophy from Brandeis University. She is a fellow at a conservative think tank, the American Enterprise Institute. In addition to *The War Against Boys*, Hoff Sommers has published *Right and Wrong: Basic Readings in Ethics* (1985) and *Who Stole Feminism? How Women Have Betrayed Women* (1994). "The War Against Boys" is part of a larger essay that appeared in *The Atlantic Monthly*, coinciding with the publication of Hoff Sommers's most recent book, *The War Against Boys: How Misguided Feminism Is Harming Our Young Men* (2000).

⊞

The War Against Boys

1   It's a bad time to be a boy in America. The triumphant victory of the U.S. women's soccer team at the World Cup last summer has come to symbolize the spirit of American girls. The shooting at Columbine High last spring might be said to symbolize the spirit of American boys.

2   That boys are in disrepute is not accidental. For many years women's groups have complained that boys benefit from a school system that favors them and is biased against girls. "Schools shortchange girls," declares the *American Association of University Women*. Girls are "undergoing a kind of psychological foot-binding," two prominent educational psychologists say. A stream of books and pamphlets cite research showing not only that boys are classroom favorites but also that they are given to schoolyard violence and sexual harassment.

3   In the view that has prevailed in American education over the past decade, boys are resented, both as unfairly privileged sex and as obstacles on the path to gender justice for girls. This perspective is promoted in schools of education, and many a teacher now feels that girls need and deserve special indemnifying consideration. "It is really clear that boys are Number One in this society and in most of the world," says Patricia O'Reilly, a professor of education and the director of the Gender Equity Center, at the University of Cincinnati.

4   The idea that schools and society grind girls down has given rise to an array of laws and policies intended to curtail the advantage boys have and to redress the harm done to girls. That girls are treated as the second sex in school and consequently suffer, that boys are accorded privileges and consequently benefit—these are things everyone is presumed to know. But they are not true.

The research commonly cited to support claims of male privilege and   5
male sinfulness is riddled with errors. Almost none of it has been published in peer-reviewed professional journals. Some of the data turn out to
be mysteriously missing. A review of the facts shows boys, not girls, on the
weak side of an education gender gap. The typical boy is a year and a half
behind the typical girl in reading and writing; he is less committed to
school and less likely to go to college. In 1997 college full-time enroll-
ments were 45 percent male and 55 percent female. The Department of
Education predicts that the proportion of boys in college classes will continue to shrink.

Data from the U.S. Department of Education and from several recent   6
university studies show that far from being shy and demoralized, today's
girls outshine boys. They get better grades. They have higher educational
aspirations. They follow more rigorous academic programs and participate
in advanced-placement classes at higher rates. According to the National
Center for Education Statistics, slightly more girls than boys enroll in
high-level math and science courses. Girls, allegedly timorous and lacking
in confidence, now outnumber boys in student government, in honor societies, on school newspapers, and in debating clubs. Only in sports are
boys ahead, and women's groups are targeting the sports gap with a
vengeance. Girls read more books. They outperform boys on tests for
artistic and musical ability. More girls than boys study abroad. More join
the Peace Corps. At the same time, more boys than girls are suspended
from school. More are held back and more drop out. Boys are three times
as likely to receive a diagnosis of attention-deficit hyperactivity disorder.
More boys than girls are involved in crime, alcohol, and drugs. Girls attempt suicide more often than boys, but it is boys who more often succeed.
In 1997, a typical year, 4,483 young people aged five to twenty-four committed suicide: 701 females and 3,782 males.

In the technical language of education experts, girls are academically   7
more "engaged." Last year an article in *The CQ Researcher* about male and
female academic achievement described a common parental observation:
"Daughters want to please their teachers by spending extra time on projects, doing extra credit, making homework as neat as possible. Sons rush
through homework assignments and run outside to play, unconcerned
about how the teacher will regard the sloppy work."

School engagement is a critical measure of student success. The U.S.   8
Department of Education gauges student commitment by the following
criteria: "How much time do students devote to homework each night?"
and "Do students come to class prepared and ready to learn? (Do they
bring books and pencils? Have they completed their homework?)."

According to surveys of fourth, eighth, and twelfth graders, girls consistently do more homework than boys. By the twelfth grade boys are four times as likely as girls not to do homework. Similarly, more boys than girls report that they "usually" or "often" come to school without supplies or without having done their homework.

9   The performance gap between boys and girls in high school leads directly to the growing gap between male and female admissions to college. The Department of Education reports that in 1996 there were 8.4 million women but only 6.7 million men enrolled in college. It predicts that women will hold on to and increase their lead well into the next decade, and that by 2007 the numbers will be 9.2 million women and 6.9 million men.

Deconstructing the Test-Score Gap

10   Feminists cannot deny that girls get better grades, are more engaged academically, and are now the majority sex in higher education. They argue, however, that these advantages are hardly decisive. Boys, they point out, get higher scores than girls on almost every significant standardized test—especially the Scholastic Assessment Test and law school, medical school, and graduate school admissions tests.

11   In 1996 I wrote an article for *Education Week* about the many ways in which girl students were moving ahead of boys. Seizing on the test-score data that suggest boys are doing better than girls, David Sadker, a professor of education at American University and a co-author with his wife, Myra, of *Failing at Fairness: How America's Schools Cheat Girls* (1994), wrote, "If females are soaring in school, as Christina Hoff Sommers writes, then these tests are blind to their flight." On the 1998 SAT boys were thirty-five points (out of 800) ahead of girls in math and seven points ahead in English. These results seem to run counter to all other measurements of achievement in school. In almost all other areas boys lag behind girls. Why do they test better? Is Sadker right in suggesting that this is a manifestation of boys' privileged status?

12   The answer is no. A careful look at the pool of students who take the SAT and similar tests shows that the girls' lower scores have little or nothing to do with bias or unfairness. Indeed, the scores do not even signify lower achievement by girls. First of all, according to *College Bound Seniors*, an annual report on standardized-test takers published by the College Board, many more "at risk" girls than "at risk" boys take the SAT—girls from lower-income homes or with parents who never graduated from high school or never attended college. "These characteristics," the report says, "are associated with lower than average SAT scores." Instead of wrongly using SAT scores as evidence of bias against girls, scholars should be con-

cerned about the boys who never show up for the tests they need if they are to move on to higher education.

Another factor skews test results so that they appear to favor boys. 13 Nancy Cole, the president of the Educational Testing Service, calls it the "spread" phenomenon. Scores on almost any intelligence or achievement test are more spread out for boys than for girls—boys include more prodigies and more students of marginal ability. Or, as the political scientist James Q. Wilson once put it, "There are more male geniuses and more male idiots."

Boys also dominate dropout lists, failure lists, and learning-disability 14 lists. Students in these groups rarely take college-admissions tests. On the other hand, exceptional boys who take school seriously show up in disproportionately high numbers for standardized tests. Gender-equity activists like Sadker ought to apply their logic consistently: if the shortage of girls at the high end of the ability distribution is evidence of unfairness to girls, then the excess of boys at the low end should be deemed evidence of unfairness to boys.

Suppose we were to turn our attention away from the highly motivated, 15 self-selected two fifths of high school students who take the SAT and consider instead a truly representative sample of American schoolchildren. How would girls and boys then compare? Well, we have the answer. The National Assessment of Educational Progress started in 1969 and mandated by Congress, offers the best and most comprehensive measure of achievement among students at all levels of ability. Under the NAEP program 70,000 to 100,000 students, drawn from forty-four states, are tested in reading, writing, math, and science at ages nine, thirteen, and seventeen. In 1996, seventeen-year-old boys outperformed seventeen-year-old girls by five points in math and eight points in science, whereas the girls outperformed the boys by fourteen points in reading and seventeen points in writing. In the past few years girls have been catching up in math and science while boys have continued to lag far behind in reading and writing.

In the July, 1995, issue of *Science*, Larry V. Hedges and Amy Nowell, re- 16 searchers at the University of Chicago, observed that girls' deficits in math were small but not insignificant. These deficits, they noted, could adversely affect the number of women who "excel in scientific and technical occupations." Of the deficits in boys' writing skills they wrote, "The large sex differences in writing . . . are alarming. . . . The data imply that males are, on average, at a rather profound disadvantage in the performance of this basic skill." They went on to warn,

> The generally larger numbers of males who perform near the bottom of
> the distribution on reading comprehension and writing also have policy

implications. It seems likely that individuals with such poor literacy skills will have difficulty finding employment in an increasingly information-driven economy. Thus, some intervention may be required to enable them to participate constructively.

Hedges and Nowell were describing a serious problem of national scope, but because the focus elsewhere has been on girls' deficits, few Americans know much about the problem or even suspect that it exists.

17   Indeed, so accepted has the myth of girls in crisis become that even teachers who work daily with male and female students tend to reflexively dismiss any challenge to the myth, or any evidence pointing to the very real crisis among boys. Three years ago Scarsdale High School, in New York, held a gender-equity workshop for faculty members. It was the standard girls-are-being-shortchanged fare, with one notable difference. A male student gave a presentation in which he pointed to evidence suggesting that girls at Scarsdale High were well ahead of boys. David Greene, a social-studies teacher, thought the student must be mistaken, but when he and some colleagues analyzed department grading patterns, they discovered that the student was right. They found little or no difference in the grades of boys and girls in advanced-placement social-studies classes. But in standard classes the girls were doing a lot better.

18   And Greene discovered one other thing: few wanted to hear about his startling findings. Like schools everywhere, Scarsdale High has been strongly influenced by the belief that girls are systematically deprived. That belief prevails among the school's gender-equity committee and has led the school to offer a special senior elective on gender equity. Greene has tried to broach the subject of male underperformance with his colleagues. Many of them concede that in the classes they teach, the girls seem to be doing better than the boys, but they do not see this as part of a larger pattern. After so many years of hearing about silenced, diminished girls, teachers do not take seriously the suggestion that boys are not doing as well as girls even if they see it with their own eyes in their own classrooms.

QUESTIONING AND DISCUSSING

Hoff Sommers, "The War Against Boys"

1. Is it truly a "bad time to be a boy in America"? Is it "presumed" that boys are privileged while girls "are treated as the second sex in school"? Support your response with specific examples after researching federal and other mandates made over the past thirty or more years so that your findings can help you analyze Hoff Sommers's view.

2. What might be the solution to the crisis that Hoff Sommers describes?

3. There are those who accuse Hoff Sommers of being anti-feminist, especially because of her association with a conservative think thank. Why would this be the case? Does such an association diminish Hoff Sommers's argument? Should it be assumed that anything written in support of boys is then "anti-girl"? Why or why not?

4. Find a copy of the complete article from which this excerpt comes. How does it further explain Hoff Sommers's argument?

"Books Are Weapons" (WPA Poster)

The following poster was created during the WPA era of federal support for the arts. Regarding the Works Progress Administration (WPA) and other federal programs that were part of President Roosevelt's New Deal, Don Adams and Arlene Goldbard write, "Franklin Delano Roosevelt's New Deal cultural programs marked the U.S. government's first big, direct investment in cultural development." In the author's words, these federal cultural programs present a "mirror image of today's federal policy," in the following respects:

> [T]heir goals were clearly stated and democratic; they supported activities not already subsidized by private sector patrons, rather than following private patrons' leads; and they emphasized an interrelatedness of culture with all aspects of life, not the separatedness of a rarefied art world.

The WPA was the largest of these cultural programs, employing artists (often people who were out of work because of the Depression) selected through competition and the awarding commissions.

QUESTIONING AND DISCUSSING

"Books Are Weapons"

1. Several aspects of the poster might seem surprising to those of us living in the twenty-first century: first, its emphasis on reading and education as important weapons in a time of war. What are others? Is it surprising that this poster came about under a program funded by the federal government? Why or why not?

2. What does this poster—and others in the collection, which are available on the Web—say about the values fostered by the United States during World War II? Have things changed? How? How can books—or education rather than ignorance—be "weapons"?

3. Analyze and comment on the ways in which our perspectives on literacy and the promotion of literacy have changed since the time of this poster.

QUESTIONS FOR READING AND RESPONDING

Chapter 5 Getting Educated: What Have Others Taught Me?

1. Contrast the assumed values behind the WPA poster "Books Are Weapons" and the homepage for CheatHouse.com. Consider the tone and content of the Seth Stevenson article, "Adventures in Cheating," as you devise your point of view. Do these works represent a dramatic shift in the overt values of our culture at large? Explain your response.

2. Compare Jonathan Swift's "A Modest Proposal" with Seth Stevenson's "Adventures in Cheating" in terms of tone and purpose. How do humor and irony belie the possible ethical purposes behind these selections?

3. How might Henry Demarest Lloyd, Steve Lopez (and the 60 Minutes transcript), and Herman Melville provide similar points of view regarding business (or government)?

4. Richard Rodriguez and Christina Hoff Sommers each argue what might be considered "conservative" positions regarding education. Consider each of these arguments in light of the other. Research articles that attempt to refute Rodriguez's and Hoff Sommers's positions, supporting your own viewpoint with examples from your reading.

6

Conversing and Confiding

How Do I Respond?

"I like to think of my behavior
in the sixties as a 'learning
experience.' Then again, I
like to think of anything
stupid I've done as a 'learning
experience.' It makes me feel
less stupid."

P. J. O'ROURKE.

RANDY COHEN

An Emmy award–winning writer for David Letterman's *Late Show*, Randy Cohen (1946–) writes the weekly column entitled "The Ethicist" for the *New York Times Sunday Magazine*. In this column (recently syndicated around the United States as "Everyday Ethics"), he responds to letters from readers concerning their everyday— and often significant—ethical dilemmas. Cohen has written several books, among them *Diary of a Flying Man* and his most recent, *The Good, the Bad, and the Difference*. Cohen holds a master's degree in music composition from the California Institute of the Arts in Los Angeles and a BA from SUNY–Albany. He prefers receiving letters that do not begin "Dear Jerk" and admits that for the toughest ethical help, "For me or for anybody in an ethical quandary, your mom is always there in your head."

⊞

Get a Leash

My 80-pound unneutered (male) dog and I frequent a park where we often see a 90-pound unspayed female. The two basically ignore each other except when the female is in heat. At those times, I do my utmost to keep my dog away from the female, but her owner gives her total freedom, off-leash and running around. It drives my dog crazy! Who is acting irresponsibly? Can you suggest a solution?

A. L. H., New York City

1   You are both acting irresponsibly, and I thank you for it: when everyone in a situation behaves badly, my job is so much easier. (If only there had been some kind of gunplay here, I could take the rest of the day off.)

2   As most vets, the A.S.P.C.A. or nearly any other group concerned with animals will tell you, get your dog neutered. That could make him less responsive to females in heat and less susceptible to various health problems. Similarly, your nemesis should have her dog spayed. Unless either of you is planning to breed her dog—and imminently, not in some vague, puppy-laden future—you should do so promptly.

3   In the meantime, while you must strive to control your own dog, the burden of responsibility is on the owner of the female in heat: it is her dog that is unsettling many others. Every subculture has its particular ethos, and it is generally asserted among dog owners that a female in heat should be isolated from other dogs. For the duration, her owner should keep her on the leash and walk her outside the park.

4   It is a fact of city life that with millions of us living cheek by jowl, one boorish creature—canine or human—can disturb the tranquillity of many,

and so we must all act considerately. Thus, no unneutered dogs cavorting in the park until all hours, sniffing and barking and blasting their stereos. Think of the neighbors.

While my ex-wife was away, I went to her condo (which we own jointly, but I pay for) to retrieve some things our son needed for school. She knew this might happen. Snooping in her night stand, I found a prized coin from my childhood collection, one I thought long lost. Obviously, she had taken it, so I took it back. My brother, the Buddhist, says, "Two wrongs don't make a right." I, the pragmatist, say, "Hey, an eye for an eye, baby."
    What do you say?

                                                                    R. S., Los Angeles

Tallying the wrongs, I get a different total from your brother's. I count your snooping as wrong No. 3. Your ex-wife may have allowed you to enter her condo—and it is her condo, the salient fact being who lives there, not who pays the bills—but she didn't O.K. your rummaging through her night stand. In law, evidence turned up in an illegal search would generally be inadmissible in court.

In ethics, it is not so different. When you rummaged, you ceded the moral high ground.   5

The thing to do now is come clean. Tell your ex you snooped, and tell   6
her what you found. If, as you assert, you both agree the coin is yours, then you can accept her apology for taking it, and she can accept yours for the prying and the swiping. If, however, the ownership of the coin is in dispute, the way to resolve the conflict does not involve anyone's slipping anything into a pocket. You really must work it out openly and honestly.

Incidentally, are you sure that Buddha was the source of that "two wrongs"   7
remark? And the pragmatist who coined "an eye for an eye, baby"—Sinatra?

QUESTIONING AND DISCUSSING
Cohen, "Get a Leash"

---

1. What understanding of ethics do you bring to this *New York Times* column? In what ways would you concur with Cohen's responses? In what ways would you differ? Why?

2. As Randy Cohen states in a recent interview, "More and more I've come to feel that people will be about as virtuous as the society in which they live." What are the implications of Cohen's statement for the column you have just read? What are the implications for the other essays in this section or this volume?

3. How would you describe Cohen's rhetorical strategies? What seem to be Cohen's assumptions about the people who write to him, and how are these assumptions reflected in his tone? Consider, for instance, Cohen's initial salvo in his response to the first letter: "You are both acting irresponsibly, and I thank you for it."

⊞

MONROE H. FREEDMAN

Monroe H. Freedman (1928–) was in 1998 awarded the American Bar Association's Michael Franck Award in recognition of "a lifetime of original and influential scholarship in the field of lawyers' ethics." The *New York Times* has named Freedman a "pioneer in the field of legal ethics," and he is described by the *Harvard Law Bulletin* as "a lawyer's lawyer." He is currently dean of the Hofstra University School of Law in Hempstead, New York.

⊞

Professional Responsibility of the Criminal Defense Lawyer:
The Three Hardest Questions

In almost any area of legal counseling and advocacy, the lawyer may be faced with the dilemma of either betraying the confidential communications of his client or participating to some extent in the purposeful deception of the court. This problem is nowhere more acute than in the practice of criminal law, particularly in the representation of the indigent accused. The purpose of this article is to analyze and attempt to resolve three of the most difficult issues in this general area:

1. Is it proper to cross-examine for the purpose of discrediting the reliability or credibility of an adverse witness whom you know to be telling the truth?
2. Is it proper to put a witness on the stand when you know he will commit perjury?
3. Is it proper to give your client legal advice when you have reason to

believe that the knowledge you give him will tempt him to commit perjury?

These questions present serious difficulties with respect to a lawyer's ethical responsibilities. Moreover, if one admits the possibility of an affirmative answer, it is difficult even to discuss them without appearing to some to be unethical.[1] It is not surprising, therefore, that reasonable, rational discussion of these has been uncommon and that the problems have for so long remained unresolved. In this regard it should be recognized that the Canons of Ethics, which were promulgated in 1908 "as a general guide," are both inadequate and self-contradictory.

I. The Adversary System and the Necessity for Confidentiality

At the outset, we should dispose of some common question-begging responses. The attorney is indeed an officer of the court, and he does participate in a search for truth. These two propositions, however, merely serve to state the problem in different words: As an officer of the court, participating in a search for truth, what is the attorney's special responsibility, and how does that responsibility affect his resolution of the question posed above?

The attorney functions in an adversary system based upon the presupposition that the most effective means of determining truth is to present to a judge and jury a clash between proponents of conflicting views. It is essential to the effective functioning of this system that each adversary have, in the words of Canon 15, "entire devotion to the interest of the client, warm zeal in the maintenance and defense of his rights and the exertion of his utmost learning and ability." It is also essential to maintain the fullest uninhibited communication between the client and his attorney, so that the attorney can most effectively counsel his client and advocate the latter's cause. This policy is safeguarded by the requirement that the lawyer must, in the words of Canon 37, "preserve his client's confidences." Canon 15 does, of course, qualify these obligations by stating that "the office of attorney does not permit, much less does it demand of

---

1 The substance of this paper was recently presented to a Criminal Trial Institute attended by forty-five members of the District of Columbia Bar. As a consequence, several judges (none of whom had either heard the lecture or read it) complained to the Committee on Admissions and Grievances of the District Court for the District of Columbia, urging the author's disbarment or suspension. Only after four months of proceedings, including a hearing, two meetings, and a *de novo* review by eleven federal district court judges, did the Committee announce its decision to "proceed no further in the matter." Professor Freedman has expanded and updated his analysis in his latest book, *Understanding Lawyers' Ethics* (Matthew Bender / Irwin, 1990).

him for any client, violations of law or any manner of fraud or chicane."
In addition, Canon 22 requires candor toward the court.

5   The problem presented by these salutary generalities of the Canons in
the context of particular litigation is illustrated by the personal experience of Samuel Williston, which was related in his autobiography. Because of his examination of a client's correspondence file, Williston
learned of a fact extremely damaging to his client's case. When the judge
announced his decision, it was apparent that a critical factor in the favorable judgment for Williston's client was the judge's ignorance of this fact.
Williston remained silent and did not thereafter inform the judge of what
he knew. He was convinced . . . that it was his duty to remain silent.

6   In an opinion by the American Bar Association Committee on Professional Ethics and Grievances, an eminent panel headed by Henry Drinker
held that a lawyer should remain silent when his client lies to the judge by
saying that he has no prior record, despite the attorney's knowledge to the
contrary. The majority of the panel distinguished the situation in which
the attorney has learned of the client's prior record from a source other
than the client himself. William B. Jones, a distinguished trial lawyer and
now a judge in the United States District Court for the District of Columbia, wrote a separate opinion in which he asserted that in neither
event should the lawyer expose his client's lie. If these two cases do not
constitute "fraud or chicane" or lack of candor within the meaning of the
Canons (and I agree with the authorities cited that they do not), it is clear
that the meaning of the Canons is ambiguous.

7   The adversary system has further ramifications in a criminal case. The
defendant is presumed to be innocent. The burden is on the prosecution
to prove beyond a reasonable doubt that the defendant is guilty. The plea
of not guilty does not necessarily mean "not guilty in fact," for the defendant may mean "not legally guilty." Even the accused who knows that he
committed the crime is entitled to put the government to its proof. Indeed,
the accused who knows that he is guilty has an absolute constitutional
right to remain silent. The moralist might quite reasonably understand
this to mean that, under these circumstances, the defendant and his lawyer
are privileged to "lie" to the court in pleading not guilty. In my judgment,
the moralist is right. However, our adversary system and related notions of
the proper administration of criminal justice sanction the lie.

8   Some derive solace from the sophistry of calling the lie a "legal fiction,"
but this is hardly an adequate answer to the moralist. Moreover, this answer has no particular appeal for the practicing attorney, who knows that
the plea of not guilty commits him to the most effective advocacy of
which he is capable. Criminal defense lawyers do not win their cases by
arguing reasonable doubt. Effective trial advocacy requires that the attor-

ney's every word, action, and attitude be consistent with the conclusion that his client is innocent. As every trial lawyer knows, the jury is certain that the defense attorney knows whether his client is guilty. The jury is therefore alert to, and will be enormously affected by, any indication by the attorney that he believes the defendant to be guilty. Thus, the plea of not guilty commits the advocate to a trial, including a closing argument, in which he must argue that "not guilty" means "not guilty in fact."[2]

There is, of course, a simple way to evade the dilemma raised by the not guilty plea. Some attorneys rationalize the problem by insisting that a lawyer never knows for sure whether his client is guilty. The client who insists upon his guilt may in fact be protecting his wife, or may know that he pulled the trigger and that the victim was killed, but not that his gun was loaded with blanks and that the fatal shot was fired from across the street. For anyone who finds this reasoning satisfactory, there is, of course, no need to think further about the issue.   9

It is also argued that a defense attorney can remain selectively ignorant. He can insist in his first interview with his client that, if his client is guilty, he simply does not want to know. It is inconceivable, however, that an attorney could give adequate counsel under such circumstances. How is the client to know, for example, precisely which relevant circumstances his lawyer does not want to be told? The lawyer might ask whether his client has a prior record. The client, assuming that this is the kind of knowledge that might present ethical problems for his lawyer, might respond that he has no record. The lawyer would then put the defendant on the stand and, on cross-examination, be appalled to learn that his client has two prior convictions for offenses identical to that for which he is being tried.   10

Of course, an attorney can guard against this specific problem by telling his client that he must know about the client's past record. However, a lawyer can never anticipate all of the innumerable and potentially critical factors that his client, once cautioned, may decide not to reveal. In one instance, for example, the defendant assumed that his lawyer would prefer to be ignorant of the fact that the client had been having sexual relations with the chief defense witness. The client was innocent of the robbery with which he was charged, but was found guilty by the jury—probably   11

---

2 "The failure to argue the case before the jury, while ordinarily only a trial tactic not subject to review, manifestly enters the field of incompetency when the reason assigned is the attorney's conscience. It is as improper as though the attorney had told the jury that his client had uttered a falsehood in making the statement. The right to an attorney embraces effective representation throughout all stages of the trial, and where the representation is of such low caliber as to amount to no representation, the guarantee of due process has been violated," Johns v. Smyth, 176 E. Supp. 949, 953 E.D. Va. 1959); Schwartz, *Cases on Professional Responsibility and the Administration of Criminal Justice* 79 (1962).

because he was guilty of fornication, a far less serious offense for which he had not even been charged.

12 The problem is compounded by the practice of plea bargaining. It is considered improper for a defendant to plead guilty to a lesser offense unless he is in fact guilty. Nevertheless, it is common knowledge that plea bargaining frequently results in improper guilty pleas by innocent people. For example, a defendant falsely accused of robbery may plead guilty to simple assault, rather than risk a robbery conviction and a substantial prison term. If an attorney is to be scrupulous in bargaining pleas, however, he must know in advance that his client is guilty, since the guilty plea is improper if the defendant is innocent. Of course, if the attempt to bargain for a lesser offense should fail, the lawyer would know the truth and thereafter be unable to rationalize that he was uncertain of his client's guilt.

13 If one recognizes that professional responsibility requires that an advocate have full knowledge of every pertinent fact, it follows that he must seek the truth from his client, not shun it.[3] This means that he will have to dig and pry and cajole, and, even then, he will not be successful unless he can convince the client that full and confidential disclosure to his lawyer will never result in prejudice to the client by any word or action of the lawyer. This is, perhaps, particularly true in the case of the indigent defendant, who meets his lawyer for the first time in the cell block or the rotunda. He did not choose the lawyer, nor does he know him. The lawyer has been sent by the judge and is part of the system that is attempting to punish the defendant. It is no easy task to persuade this client that he can talk freely without fear of prejudice. However, the inclination to mislead one's lawyer is not restricted to the indigent or even to the criminal defendant. Randolph Paul has observed a similar phenomenon among the wealthier class in a far more congenial atmosphere:

> The tax advisor will sometimes have to dynamite the facts of his case out of the unwilling witnesses on his own side—witnesses who are nervous, witnesses who are confused about their own interest, witnesses who try to be too smart for their own good, and witnesses who subconsciously do not want to understand what has happened despite the fact that they must if they are to testify coherently.

14 Paul goes on to explain that the truth can be obtained only by persuading the client that it would be a violation of a sacred obligation for the lawyer ever to reveal a client's confidence. Beyond any question, once a lawyer

---

3 "Counsel cannot properly perform their duties without knowing the truth." Opinion 23, Committee on Professional Ethics and Grievances of the American Bar Association (1930).

has persuaded his client of the obligation of confidentiality, he must respect that obligation scrupulously.

II. The Specific Questions

The first of the difficult problems posed above will now be considered: Is it proper to cross-examine for the purpose of discrediting the reliability or the credibility of a witness whom you know to be telling the truth? Assume the following situation. Your client has been falsely accused of a robbery committed at 16th and P Streets at 11:00 p.m. He tells you at first that at no time on the evening of the crime was he within six blocks of that location. However, you are able to persuade him that he must tell you the truth and that doing so will in no way prejudice him. He then reveals to you that he was at 15th and P Streets at 10:55 that evening, but that he was walking east, away from the scene of the crime, and that, by 11:00 p.m., he was six blocks away. At the trial, there are two prosecution witnesses. The first mistakenly, but with some degree of persuasion identifies your client as the criminal. At that point, the prosecution's case depends on this single witness, who might or might not be believed. Since your client has a prior record, you do not want to put him on the stand, but you feel that there is at least a chance for acquittal. The second prosecution witness is an elderly woman who is somewhat nervous and who wears glasses. She testifies truthfully and accurately that she saw your client at 15th and P Streets at 10:55 p.m. She has corroborated the erroneous testimony of the first witness and made conviction virtually certain. However, if you destroy her reliability through cross-examination designed to show that she is easily confused and has poor eyesight, you may not only eliminate the corroboration, but also cast doubt in the jury's mind on the prosecution's entire case. On the other hand, if you should refuse to cross-examine her because she is telling the truth, your client may well feel betrayed, since you knew of the witnesses' veracity only because your client confided in you, under your assurance that his truthfulness would not prejudice him.

The client would be right. Viewed strictly, the attorney's failure to cross-examine would not be violative of the client's confidence because it would not constitute a disclosure. However, the same policy that supports the obligation of confidentiality precludes the attorney from prejudicing his client's interest in any other way because of knowledge gained in his professional capacity. When a lawyer fails to cross-examine only because his client, placing confidence in the lawyer, has been candid with him, the basis of such confidence and candor collapses. Our legal system cannot tolerate such a result.

The purposes and necessities of the relation between a client and his attorney require, in many cases, on the part of the client, the fullest and freest disclosures to the attorney of the client's objects, motives and acts. . . . To permit the attorney to reveal to others what is so disclosed, would be not only a gross violation of a sacred trust upon his part, but it would utterly destroy and prevent the usefulness and benefits to be derived from professional assistance.

17   The client's confidences must "upon all occasions be inviolable," to avoid the "greater mischiefs" that would probably result if a client could not feel free "to repose [confidence] in the attorney to whom he resorts for legal advice and assistance." Destroy that confidence, and "a man would not venture to consult any skillful person, or would only dare to tell his counsellor half his case."

18   Therefore, one must conclude that the attorney is obligated to attack, if he can, the reliability or credibility of an opposing witness whom he knows to be truthful. The contrary result would inevitably impair the "perfect freedom of consultation by client with attorney," which is "essential to the administration of justice."

19   The second question is generally considered to be the hardest of all: Is it proper to put a witness on the stand when you know he will commit perjury? Assume, for example, that the witness in question is the accused himself, and that he has admitted to you, in response to your assurances of confidentiality, that he is guilty. However, he insists upon taking the stand to protect his innocence. There is a clear consensus among prosecutors and defense attorneys that the likelihood of conviction is increased enormously when the defendant does not take the stand. Consequently the attorney who prevents his client from testifying only because the client has confided his guilt to him is violating that confidence by acting upon the information in a way that will seriously prejudice his client's interests.

20   Perhaps the most common method for avoiding the ethical problem just posed is for the lawyer to withdraw from the case, at least if there is sufficient time before trial for the client to retain another attorney.[4] The client will then go to the nearest law office, realizing that the obligation of confidentiality is not what it has been represented to be, and withhold incriminating information or the fact of his guilt from his new attorney. On ethical grounds, the practice of withdrawing from a case under such circumstances is indefensible, since the identical perjured testimony will ultimately be presented. More important, perhaps, is the practical consid-

---

4 Unless the lawyer has told the client at the outset that he will withdraw if he learns that the client is guilty, "it is plain enough as a matter of good morals and professional ethics" that the lawyer should not withdraw on this ground.

eration that the new attorney will be ignorant of the perjury and therefore will be in no position to attempt to discourage the client from presenting it. Only the original attorney, who knows the truth, has that opportunity, but he loses it in the very act of evading the ethical problem.

The problem is all the more difficult when the client is indigent. He 21 cannot retain other counsel, and in many jurisdictions, including the District of Columbia, it is impossible for appointed counsel to withdraw from a case except for extraordinary reasons. Thus, appointed counsel, unless he lies to the judge, can successfully withdraw only by revealing to the judge that the attorney has received knowledge of his client's guilt. Such a revelation in itself would seem to be a sufficiently serious violation of the obligation of confidentiality to merit severe condemnation. In fact, however, the situation is far worse, since it is entirely possible that the same judge who permits the attorney to withdraw will subsequently hear the case and sentence the defendant. When he does so, of course, he will have had personal knowledge of the defendant's guilt before the trial began.[5] Moreover, this will be knowledge of which the newly appointed counsel for the defendant will probably be ignorant.

The difficulty is further aggravated when the client informs the lawyer 22 for the first time during trial that he intends to take the stand and commit perjury. The perjury in question may not necessarily be a protestation of innocence by a guilty man. Referring to the earlier hypothetical of the defendant wrongly accused of a robbery at 16th and P, the only perjury may be his denial of the truthful, but highly damaging, testimony of the corroborating witness who placed him one block away from the intersection five minutes prior to the crime. Of course, if he tells the truth and thus verifies the corroborating witness, the jury will be far more inclined to accept the inaccurate testimony of the principal witness, who specifically identified him as the criminal.[6]

If a lawyer has discovered his client's intent to perjure himself, one possi- 23 ble solution to this problem is for the lawyer to approach the bench, explain

5 The judge may infer that the situation is worse than it is in fact. In the case related in note 8, the attorney's actual difficulty was that he did not want to permit a plea of guilty by a client who was maintaining his innocence. However, as is commonly done, he told the judge only that he had to withdraw because of "an ethical problem." The judge reasonably inferred that the defendant had admitted his guilt and wanted to offer a perjured alibi.

6 One lawyer, who considers it clearly unethical for the attorney to present the alibi in this hypothetical case, found no ethical difficulty himself in the following case. His client was prosecuted for robbery. The prosecution witness testified that the robbery had taken place at 10:15, and identified the defendant as the criminal. However, the defendant had a convincing alibi for 10:00 to 10:30. The attorney presented the alibi, and the client was acquitted. The alibi was truthful, but the attorney knew that the prosecution witness had been confused about the time, and that his client had in fact committed the crime at 10:45.

his ethical difficulty to the judge, and ask to be relieved, thereby causing a mistrial. This request is certain to be denied, if only because it would empower the defendant to cause a series of mistrials in the same fashion. At this point, some feel that the lawyer has avoided the ethical problem and can put the defendant on the stand. However, one objection to this solution, apart from the violation of confidentiality, is that the lawyer's ethical problem has not been solved, but has only been transferred to the judge. Moreover, the client in such a case might well have grounds for appeal on the basis of deprivation of due process and denial of the right to counsel, since he will have been tried before, and sentenced by, a judge who has been informed of the client's guilt by his own attorney.

24   A solution even less satisfactory than informing the judge of the defendant's guilt would be to let the client take the stand without the attorney's participation and to omit reference to the client's testimony in closing argument. The latter solution, of course, would be as damaging as to fail entirely to argue the case to the jury, and failing to argue the case is "as improper as though the attorney had told the jury that his client had uttered a falsehood in making the statement."

25   Therefore, the obligation of confidentiality, in the context of our adversary system, apparently allows the attorney no alternative to putting a perjurious witness on the stand without explicit or implicit disclosure of the attorney's knowledge to either the judge or the jury. Canon 37 does not proscribe this conclusion; the canon recognizes only two exceptions to the obligation of confidentiality. The first relates to the lawyer who is accused by his client and may disclose the truth to defend himself. The other exemption relates to the "announced intention of a client to commit a crime." On the basis of the ethical and practical considerations discussed above, the Canon's exception to the obligation of confidentiality cannot logically be understood to include the crime of perjury committed during the specific case in which the lawyer is serving. Moreover, even when the intention is to commit a crime in the future, Canon 37 does not require disclosure, but only permits it. Furthermore, Canon 15, which does proscribe "violation of law" by the attorney for his client, does not apply to the lawyer who unwillingly puts a perjurious client on the stand after having made every effort to dissuade him from committing perjury. Such an act by the attorney cannot properly be found to be subornation— corrupt inducement—of perjury. Canon 29 requires counsel to inform the prosecuting authorities of perjury committed in a case in which he has been involved, but this can only refer to perjury by opposing witnesses. For an attorney to disclose his client's perjury "would involve a direct violation of Canon 37." Despite Canon 29, therefore, the attorney should not reveal his client's perjury "to the court or to the authorities."

Of course, before the client testifies perjuriously, the lawyer has a duty   26
to attempt to dissuade him on grounds of both law and morality. In addition, the client should be impressed with the fact that his untruthful alibi
is tactically dangerous. There is always a strong possibility that the prosecutor will expose the perjury on cross-examination. However, for the reasons already given, the final decision must necessarily be the client's. The
lawyer's best course thereafter would be to avoid any further professional
relationship with a client whom he knew to have perjured himself.

The third question is whether it is proper to give your client legal ad-   27
vice when you have reason to believe that the knowledge you give him
will tempt him to commit perjury. This may indeed be the most difficult
problem of all, because giving such advice creates the appearance that the
attorney is encouraging and condoning perjury.

If the lawyer is not certain what the facts are when he gives the advice,   28
the problem is substantially minimized, if not eliminated. It is not the
lawyer's function to prejudge his client as a perjurer. He cannot presume
that the client will make unlawful use of his advice. Apart from this, there
is a natural predisposition in most people to recollect facts, entirely honestly, in a way most favorable to their own interest. As Randolph Paul has
observed, some witnesses are nervous, some are confused about their own
interests, some try to be too smart for their own good, and some subcon-
sciously do not want to understand what has happened to them. Before he
begins to remember essential facts, the client is entitled to know what his
own interests are.

The above argument does not apply merely to factual questions such as   29
whether a particular event occurred at 10:15 or at 10:45.[7] One of the most
critical problems in a criminal case, as in many others, is intention. A
German writer, considering the question of intention as a test of legal
consequences, suggests the following situations. A young man and a
young woman decide to get married. Each has a thousand dollars. They
decide to begin a business with these funds, and the young lady gives her
money to the young man for this purpose. Was the intention to form a
joint venture or a partnership? Did they intend that the young man be an
agent or a trustee? Was the transaction a gift or a loan? If the couple
should subsequently visit a tax attorney and discover that it is in their interest that the transaction be viewed as a gift, it is submitted that they
could, with complete honesty, so remember it. On the other hand, should
their engagement be broken and the young woman consult an attorney

---

[7] Even this kind of "objective fact" is subject to honest error. See note 6.

for the purpose of recovering her money, she could with equal honesty remember that her intention was to make a loan.

30   Assume that your client, on trial for his life in a first-degree murder case, has killed another man with a penknife but insists that the killing was in self-defense. You ask him, "Do you customarily carry this penknife in your pocket, do you carry it frequently or infrequently, or did you take it with you only on this occasion?" He replies, "Why do you ask me a question like that?" It is entirely appropriate to inform him that his carrying the knife only on this occasion, or infrequently, supports an inference of premeditation, while if he carried the knife constantly, or frequently, the inference of premeditation would be negated. Thus, your client's life may depend upon his recollection as to whether he carried the knife frequently or infrequently. Despite the possibility that the client or a third party might infer that the lawyer was prompting the client to lie, the lawyer must apprise the defendant of the significance of his answer. There is no conceivable ethical requirement that the lawyer trap his client into a hasty and ill-considered answer before telling him the significance of the question.

31   A similar problem is created if the client has given the lawyer incriminating information before being fully aware of its significance. For example, assume that a man consults a tax lawyer and says, "I am fifty years old. Nobody in my immediate family has lived past fifty. Therefore, I would like to put my affairs in order. Specifically, I understand that I can avoid substantial estate taxes by setting up a trust. Can I do it?" The lawyer informs the client that he can successfully avoid the estate taxes only if he lives at least three years after establishing the trust or, should he die within three years, if the trust is found not to have been created in contemplation of death. The client then might ask who decides whether the trust is in contemplation of death. After learning that the determination is made by the court, the client might inquire about the factors on which such a decision would be based.

32   At this point, the lawyer can do one of two things. He can refuse to answer the question, or he can inform the client that the court will consider the wording of the trust instrument and will hear evidence about any conversations which he may have or any letters he may write expressing motives other than avoidance of estate taxes. It is likely that virtually every tax attorney in the country would answer the client's question, and that no one would consider the answer unethical. However, the lawyer might well appear to have prompted his client to deceive the Internal Revenue Service and the courts, and this appearance would remain regardless of the lawyer's explicit disclaimer to the client of any intent so to prompt him. Nevertheless, it should not be unethical for the lawyer to give the advice.

In a criminal case, a lawyer may be representing a client who protests   33
his innocence, and whom the lawyer believes to be innocent. Assume, for
example, that the charge is assault with intent to kill, that the prosecution
has erroneous but credible eyewitness testimony against the defendant,
and that the defendant's truthful alibi witness is impeachable on the basis
of several felony convictions. The prosecutor, perhaps having doubts
about the case, offers to permit the defendant to plead guilty to simple assault. If the defendant should go to trial and be convicted, he might well
be sent to jail for fifteen years; on a plea of simple assault, the maximum
penalty would be one year, and sentence might well be suspended.

The common practice of conveying the prosecutor's offer to the defen-   34
dant should not be considered unethical, even if the defense lawyer is
convinced of his client's innocence. Yet the lawyer is clearly in the position of prompting his client to lie, since the defendant cannot make the
plea without saying to the judge that he is pleading guilty because he is
guilty. Furthermore, if the client does decide to plead guilty, it would be
improper for the lawyer to inform the court that his client is innocent,
thereby compelling the defendant to stand trial and take the substantial
risk of fifteen years' imprisonment.[8]

Essentially no different from the problem discussed above, but appar-   35
ently more difficult, is the so-called *Anatomy of a Murder* situation. The
lawyer, who has received from his client an incriminating story of murder
in the first degree, says, "If the facts are as you have stated them so far, you
have no defense, and you will probably be electrocuted. On the other
hand, if you acted in a blind rage, there is a possibility of saving your life.
Think it over, and we will talk about it tomorrow." As in the tax case, and
as in the case of the plea of guilty to a lesser offense, the lawyer has given
his client a legal opinion that might induce the client to lie. This is information which the lawyer himself would have, without advice, were he in

---

8 In a recent case, the defendant was accused of unauthorized use of an automobile, for which the
maximum penalty is five years. He told his court-appointed attorney that he had borrowed the car
from a man known to him only as "Junior," that he had not known the car was stolen, and that he
had an alibi for the time of the theft. The defendant had three prior convictions for larceny, and the
alibi was weak. The prosecutor offered to accept a guilty plea to two misdemeanors (taking property
without right and petty larceny) carrying a combined maximum sentence of eighteen months. The
defendant was willing to plead guilty to the lesser offenses, but the attorney felt that, because of his
client's alibi, he could not permit him to do so. The lawyer therefore informed the judge that he had
an ethical problem, and asked to be relieved. The attorney who was appointed in his place permitted the client to plead guilty to the two lesser offenses, and the defendant was sentenced to nine
months. The alternative would have been five or six months in jail while the defendant waited for
his jury trial, and a very substantial risk of conviction and a much heavier sentence. Neither the
client nor justice would have been well served by compelling the defendant to go to trial against his
will under these circumstances.

the client's position. It is submitted that the client is entitled to have this information about the law and to make his own decision as to whether to act upon it. To decide otherwise would not only penalize the less well-educated defendant, but would also prejudice the client because of his initial truthfulness in telling his story in confidence to the attorney.

III. Conclusion

36   The lawyer is an officer of the court, participating in a search for truth. Yet no lawyer would consider that he had acted unethically in pleading the statute of frauds or the statute of limitations as a bar to a just claim. Similarly, no lawyer would consider it unethical to prevent the introduction of evidence such as a murder weapon seized in violation of the fourth amendment or a truthful but involuntary confession, or to defend a guilty man on grounds of denial of a speedy trial. Such actions are permissible because there are policy considerations that at times justify frustrating the search for truth and the prosecution of a just claim. Similarly, there are policies that justify an affirmative answer to the three questions that have been posed in this article. These policies include the maintenance of an adversary system, the presumption of innocence, the prosecution's burden to prove guilt beyond a reasonable doubt, the right to counsel, and the obligation of confidentiality between lawyer and client.

QUESTIONING AND DISCUSSING

Freedman, "Professional Responsibility of the Criminal Defense Lawyer"

1. What is your understanding of what it is that criminal defense attorneys do? On what are your assumptions based? Discuss popular culture and its depictions of the criminal justice system—television shows, for instance, and other influences that have shaped your assumptions. How do these compare with the actual justice system and responsibilities of attorneys as delineated by Freedman?

2. What do you infer as being the "*Anatomy of a Murder* situation" as it is described by Freedman? Consider viewing the film to which Freedman alludes and discussing its implication in light of Freedman's article.

3. This article was published in 1996, and it is still considered a standard by which ethical conduct in these situations should be based. Research recent publicized cases involving criminal defense attorneys to present in class. What are the results when you compare what you have learned about the

cases with Freedman's three questions and the other issues that he raises in the article?

4. If, as Freedman declares, the Canons of Ethics for attorneys, published in 1908, are inadequate, what might that say about the assumptions of that segment of society at the time during which they were written? What does it say about society in the United States in 1966? About society now? Attempt to define what might be meant by *society* and give examples to support your points.

⊞

George Steiner

George Steiner (1929–) was born in Paris and has lived there, in Vienna, and in New York City. Steiner's father had moved his family from Vienna to Paris in 1924, before Steiner's birth, for what he had hoped would be a more welcoming, less anti-Semitic environment than that in Vienna. He is a distinguished literary critic who was schooled in three languages—French, German, and English. A fellow of Churchill College of Cambridge University in England, Steiner has written extensively and has published in such journals and magazines as *The New Yorker* and the *Times Literary Supplement*. His many books include *Language and Silence: Essays on Language, Literature,* and *the Inhuman* (1982), *No Passion Spent: Essays: 1976–1996* (1996), and *Errata: An Examined Life* (1998). "Heraldry" was part of a special issue of the prestigious journal *Granta* (1997) in which authors, both well known and lesser known, write about the ambition to become a writer. Steiner's concern centers on the complacency of a world that has still refused to come to terms with the Holocaust.

⊞

Heraldry

Rain, particularly to a child, carries distinct smells and colours. Summer rains in the Tyrol are relentless. They have a morose, flogging insistence and come in deepening shades of dark green. At night, the drumming is one of mice on or just under the roof. Even daylight can be sodden. But it is the smell which, after sixty years, stays with me. Of drenched leather and hung game. Or, at moments, of tubers steaming under drowned mud. A world made boiled cabbage.

That summer was already ominous. A family holiday in the dark yet magical landscape of a country condemned. In those mid-1930s, Jew-hatred and a lust for reunification with Germany hung in the Austrian air. My father, convinced that catastrophe was imminent, the gentile husband of my aunt still blandly optimistic, found conversation awkward. My mother and her fitfully hysterical sister sought to achieve an effect of normality. But the planned pastimes, swimming and boating on the lake, walks in the woods and hills, dissolved in the perpetual downpours. My impatience, my demands for entertainment in a cavernous chalet increasingly chill and, I imagine, mildewed, must have been pestilential. One morning Uncle Rudi drove into Salzburg. He brought back with him a small book in blue waxen covers.

3   It was a pictorial guide to coats of arms in the princely city and surrounding fiefs. Each blazon as reproduced in colour, together with a brief historical notice as to the castle, family domain, bishopric, or abbey which it identified. The little manual closed with a map marking the relevant sites, including ruins, and with a glossary of heraldic terms.

4   Even today I can feel the pressure of wonder, the inward shock which this chance "pacifier" triggered. What is difficult to render in adult language is the combination, almost the fusion of delight and menace, of fascination and unease I experienced as I retreated to my room, the drains spitting under the rain-lashed eaves, and sat, hour after entranced hour, turning the pages, committing to memory the florid names of those towers, keeps, and high personages.

5   Though I could not, obviously, have defined or phrased it in any such way, that armorial primer overwhelmed me with a sense of the numberless specificity, of the minutiae, of the manifold singularity of the substance and forms of the world. Each coat of arms differed from every other. Each had its symbolic organization, motto, history, locale, and date wholly proper, wholly integral to itself. It "heralded" a unique, ultimately intractable fact of being. Within its quarterings, each graphic component, colour, and pattern entailed its own prodigal signification. Heraldry often inserts coats of arms within coats of arms. The suggestive French designation of this device is a *mise en abyme*. My treasures included a magnifying glass. I pored over the details of geometric and "bestiary" shapes, the lozenges, diamonds, diagonal slashes of each emblem, over the helmeted crests and "supporters" crowning, flanking the diverse arms. Over the precise number of tassels which graced a bishop's, an archbishop's, or a cardinal's armorials.

6   The notion which, in some visceral impact, tided over me and held me mesmerized was this: if there are in this obscure province of one small country (diminished Austria) so many coats of arms, each unique, how

many must there be in Europe, across the globe? I do not recall what grasp I had, if any, of large numbers. But I do remember that the word "millions" came to me and left me unnerved. How was any human being to see, to master this plurality? Suddenly it came to me, in some sort of exultant but also appalled revelation, that no inventory, no heraldic encyclopedia, no *summa* of fabled beasts, inscriptions, chivalric hallmarks, however compendious, could ever be complete. The opaque thrill and desolation which came over me in that ill-lit and end-of-summer room on the Wolfgangsee—was it, distantly, sexual?—has, in good part, oriented my life.

I grew possessed by an intuition of the particular, of diversities so numerous that no labour of classification and enumeration could exhaust them. Each leaf differed from any other on each differing tree (I rushed out in the deluge to assure myself of this elementary and miraculous truth). Each blade of grass, each pebble on the lake shore was eternally "just so." No repetition of measurement, however closely calibrated, in whatever controlled vacuum it was carried out, could ever be perfectly the same. It would deviate by some trillionth of an inch, by a nanosecond, by the breadth of a hair—itself a teeming immensity—from any preceding measurement. I sat on my bed striving to hold my breath, knowing that the next breath would signal a new beginning, that the past was already unrecapturable in its differential sequence. Did I guess that there could be no perfect *facsimile* of anything, that the identical work spoken twice, even in lightning-quick reiteration, was not and could not be the same (much later, I was to learn that this unrepeatability had preoccupied both Heraclitus and Kierkegaard).

At that hour, in the days following, the totalities of personal experience, of human contacts, of landscape around me became a mosaic, each fragment at once luminous and resistant in its "quiddity"—the scholastic term for integral presence revived by Gerard Manley Hopkins. There could be, I knew, no finality to the raindrops, to the number and variousness of the stars, to the books to be read, to the languages to be learned. The mosaic of the possible could, at any instant, be splintered and reassembled into new images and motions of meaning. The idiom of heraldry, those "gules" and "bars sinister," even if I could not yet make it out, must, I sensed, be only one among countless systems of discourse specifically tailored to the teeming diversity of human purposes, artefacts, representations, or concealments (I still recall the strange excitement I felt at the thought that a coat of arms could hide as well as reveal).

I set out, as many children do, to compile lists. Of monarchs and mythological heroes, of popes, of castles, of numinous dates, of operas—I had been taken to see *Figaro* at the neighbouring Salzburg Festival. The wearied assurance of my parents that such lists already existed, that they could be looked up in any almanac or work of standard reference—my queries about antipopes and how to include them visibly irritated my somewhat ceremonious and Catholic uncle—brought no solace. The available indices of reality, be they a thousand pages thick, the atlases, the children's encyclopedias, could never be exhaustively comprehensive. This or that item, perhaps the hidden key to the edifice, would be left out. There was simply too much to everything. Existence thronged and hummed with obstinate difference like the midges around the light bulb. "Who can number the clouds in wisdom? Or who can stay the bottles of heaven . . . ?" (How did Job 38:37, already know about rains in the Salzhammergut?) I may not have cited the verse to myself in that drowned August, though the Old Testament was already a tutelary voice, but I did know of those bottles.

10   If the revelation of incommensurable "singleness" held me spellbound, it also generated fear. I come back to the *mise en abyme* of one blazon within another, to that "setting in the abyss." Consider a fathomless depth of differentiation, of nonidentity, always incipient with the eventuality of chaos. How could the senses, how could the brain impose order and coherence on the kaleidoscope, on the perpetuum mobile of swarming existence? I harboured vague nightmares at the fact, revealed in the nature column of some newspaper, that a small corner of the Amazon forest was habitat to thirty thousand rigorously distinct species of beetles. Gazing at, recopying with watercolours, the baronial or episcopal or civic arms, pondering the unlimited variations possible on formal and iconic motifs, I felt a peculiar dread. Detail could know no end.

11   How can a human voice cast a huge sickening shadow? On short waves, the wireless chirped and often dissolved in bursts of static. But Hitler's speeches, when broadcast, punctuated my childhood (whence, so many years later, *The Portage to San Cristobal of A.H.*). My father would be close to the wireless, straining to hear. We were in Paris, where I was born in 1929. One of the doctors assisting at my awkward birth then returned to Louisiana to assassinate Huey Long. History was always in attendance.

12   My parents had left Vienna in 1924. From meagre circumstances, from a Czech-Austrian milieu still in reach of the ghetto, my father had risen to meteoric eminence. Anti-Semitic Vienna, the cradle of Nazism, was, in certain respects, a liberal meritocracy. He had secured a senior legal position in the Austrian Central Bank, with fiacre (the use of a carriage and

horses). A brilliant career lay before the youthful Herr Doktor. With grim clairvoyance, my father perceived the nearing disaster. A systematic, doctrinal Jew-hatred seethed and stank below the glittering liberalities of Viennese culture. The world of Freud, of Mahler, of Wittgenstein was also that of Mayor Lueger, Hitler's exemplar. At their lunatic source, Nazism and the final solution are Austrian rather than German reflexes. Like his friend out of Galacia, one Lewis Namier, my father dreamed of England. For the East- and Central-European Jewish intelligentsia, the career of Disraeli had assumed a mythical, talismanic aura. But he suffered from rheumatic fevers, and medical sagacity of the day held France to be the milder climate. So Paris it was, and a new start under strained circumstances (my mother, Viennese to her fingertips, lamented this seemingly irrational move). And to the end of his days, my father never felt at home among what he judged to be the arrogant chauvinism, the frivolities, the myopia of French politics, finance, and society. He would mutter under his breath and unjustly that all nationals will sell you their mothers, but that the French delivered.

Of fragile physique, my father was compounded of formidable will and intellect. He found a surprisingly large portion of mankind unacceptable. Sloppiness, lies, be they "white," evasions of reality, infuriated him. He lacked the art of forgiveness. His contributions to the skills of international investment banking, to the techniques of corporate finance in the period between the wars are on record. His Zionism had the ardour of one who knew, even at the outset, that he would not emigrate to Palestine. His bookplate shows a barque, a seven-branched candelabrum at its bow, approaching Jerusalem. But the holy city remains on the far horizon. Papa embodied, as did every corner of our Paris home, the tenor, the prodigality and glow of Jewish-European and Central-European emancipation. The horrors which reduced this liberal humaneness and vision to ashes have distorted remembrance. Evocations of the Shoah have, tragically, privileged the remembrance of prior suffering, particularly throughout Eastern Europe. The proud Judaism of my father was, like that of an Einstein or a Freud, one of messianic agnosticism. It breathed rationality, the promise of the Enlightenment and tolerance. It owed as much to Voltaire as it did to Spinoza. High holidays, notably the Day of Atonement, were observed not for prescriptive or theological motives, but as a yearly summons to identity, to a homeland in millennial time.

By virtue of what was to become an unbearable paradox, this Judaism of secular hope looked to German philosophy, literature, scholarship, and music for its talismanic guarantees. German metaphysics and cultural criticism, from Kant to Schopenhauer and Nietzsche, the classics of German-language poetry and drama, the master historians, such as Ranke, Mommsen, Gregorovius, crowded the shelves of my father's library. As did first editions of Heine, in whose mordant wit, in whose torn and ambiguous destiny, in whose unhoused virtuosity in both German and French, my father saw the prophetic mirror of modern European Judaism. Like so many German, Austrian, and Central-European Jews, my father was immersed in Wagner. During his very brief spell under arms in Vienna in 1914, he had ridden a horse named Lohengrin; he had then married a woman called Elsa. It was, however, the whole legacy of German-Austrian music: it was Mozart, Beethoven, Schubert, Hugo Wolfe, Mahler who filled the house. As a very young child, at the edge of bedtime and through a crack in the living-room door, I was sometimes allowed to hear chamber music, a lieder recital, being performed by musicians invited into our home. They were, increasingly, refugees in desolate plight. Yet even in the thickening political twilight, a Schubert song, a Schumann study could light up my father's haunted mien. When concessions had to be made to encroaching reality, my father gave them an ironic touch: recordings of Wagner were not played in French.

15   Only in the posthumously published letters of Gershom Scholem have I come across the same note of helpless clearsightedness and warning. Over and over, even prior to 1933, my father laboured to warn, to alert, to awaken to refuge not only those whom he and my mother had left behind in Prague or in Vienna, but the French political-military establishment with which his international dealings had brought him into contact. His "pessimism," his "alarmist prognostications" elicited only officious dismissal or hostility. Family and friends refused to move. One could come to reasonable terms with Herr Hitler. The unpleasantness would soon pass. The age of pogroms was over. In diplomatic and ministerial circles, my father was regarded as a tedious Cassandra, prone to well-known traits of Jewish hysteria. Papa lived those rancid 1930s like a man trapped in cobwebs, lashing out and sick at heart. There was also, however, a more private and constant regret.

16   His own studies in law and economic theory had been of exceptional strength. He had published monographs on the utopian economics of Saint-Simon and on the Austrian banking crises of the later nineteenth century. The absolute need to support various less qualified members of his family, the collapse of the dual monarchy, and the aftermath of world war had thrust him into finance. He respected the importance, the technical ingenuities of his craft, but cultivated scant regard for most of those

who practiced it (one of the few contemporaries he acknowledged as preeminent, also in integrity and whom he came, in certain outward gestures
and tone, to resemble, was Siegmund Warburg). My father's innermost
passions lay elsewhere. His uncertain health had barred him from medical
studies. He turned to intellectual history, to the history and philosophic
aspects of biology. His learning was extensive and exact. His appetite for
languages remained unquenched to the very end (he was systematically
acquiring Russian at the time of his death). Investment banking occupied
the main of his outward existence. At the core, it left him almost indifferent. From this tension came his uncompromising resolve that his son
should know next to nothing of his father's profession. This partition
could reach absurd lengths: "I would rather that you did not know the difference between a bond and a share." I was to be a teacher and a thorough
scholar. On this last point, I have failed him.

Why this elevation of the teacher-scholar rather than, say, the artist,   17
the writer, the performer in a sensibility so responsive to music, literature,
and the arts? There was scarcely a museum in Paris and later, in New York,
to which he did not take me of a Saturday. It is in this instinctive preference for teaching and learning, for the discovery and transmission of the
truth, that my father, in his aching stoicism, was most profoundly Jewish.
Like Islam, Judaism is iconoclastic. It fears the image; it distrusts the
metaphor. Emancipated Judaism delights in the performing artist, especially the musician. It has produced masters of stage and film. Yet even to
this day, when it informs so much of American literature, when it can
look to a Kafka, a Proust, a Mandelstam or a Paul Celan, Judaism is not altogether at ease with the poetics of invention (*fabulation*), with the mus-
tard seed of "falsehood" or fiction, with the rivalry to God the creator
inherent in the arts. Given the limitless wonders of the created universe,
when there is such wealth of actual being to be recorded and grasped by
reason, when there is history to be untangled, law to be clarified, science
to be furthered, is the devising of fictions, of *mimesis* a truly responsible, a
genuinely adult pursuit? Freud, for one, did not think so. Fictions were to
be outgrown as man ripened into the "reality principle." Somewhere in
my father's restless spirit a comparable doubt may have nagged. Even the
most Voltairean, perhaps atheist—I do not know—of Jews knows that the
word *rabbi* simply means "teacher."

Only later did I come to realize the investment of hope against hope, of   18
watchful inventiveness, which my father made in educating me. This,
during years of private and public torment, when the bitter need to find
some future for us as Nazism drew near, left him emotionally and physically

worn out. I marvel still at the loving astuteness of his devices. No new book was allowed me till I had written down for his inspection a précis of the one I had just read. If I had not understood this or that passage—my father's choices and suggestions aimed carefully above my head—I was to read it to him out loud. Often the voice clears up a text. If misunderstanding persisted, I was to copy the relevant bit in my own writing. At which move, it would usually surrender its lode.

19   Though I was hardly aware of the design, my reading was held in balance between French, English, and German. My upbringing was totally trilingual, and the background always polyglot. My radiant mama would habitually begin a sentence in one tongue and end it in another. Once a week a diminutive Scottish lady appeared to read Shakespeare to and with me. I entered that world, I am not certain why, via *Richard II*. Adroitly, the first speech I was made to learn by heart was not that of Gaunt, but Mowbray's farewell, with its mordant music of exile. A refugee scholar coached me in Greek and Latin. He exhaled an odour of reduced soap and sorrow.

QUESTIONING AND DISCUSSING

Steiner, "Heraldry"

1. Research and discuss what you can about the history of Germany and Austria during the 1930s. Discuss what you know about the rise of Nazism and the situation of Jews in Europe. How does this knowledge provide valuable context for Steiner's memoir?

2. How does Steiner's use of language and tone convey the mood of these times? What does he assume about his audience with other language choices and specific references to writers and musicians who influenced him—people such as Kafka, Proust, Freud, and Celan? Research these writers and, additionally, define and analyze the phrases—such as *mise en abyme* and "liberal meritocracy"—that shape the essay.

3. What influence does "heraldry" have on this essay? In addition to contributing to the richness and implications of the essay itself, what larger purpose might it serve?

⊞

GAIL COLLINS

Having served as editorial page editor for the *New York Times* since 2001, Gail Collins (1946–) has also been a columnist for that newspaper and before that a columnist for *Newsday* and the *New York Daily News*. Before holding these positions, Collins was a financial reporter for United Press International in New York. She has received numerous awards and honors, among them the Associated Press Award for Commentary (1994), a Meyer Berger Award from Columbia University (1987), and a Women in Communications Matrix Award (1989). Collins holds a BA from Marquette University and an MA from the University of Massachusetts–Amherst. She is also the author of *Scorpion Tongues: Gossip, Celebrity, and American Politics* (1998), from which this excerpt is taken.

⊞

From *Scorpion Tongues*: Gossip, Celebrity, and American Politics

Introduction

1. Hillary's Lamp

"Suspicions have already been, um, aroused . . ."

Inaugural week, 1993: Barbra Streisand led the Celebrity Salute to the new president. Barney the purple dinosaur was the star of the parade. The crowds were so dense that people tried to hoist their kids on the Portosans to get a better view. Bill Clinton, contrary to his supporters' worst fears, did not talk too long after he took the oath of office. The insiders exchanged rumors about who was getting what job and everyone else talked about who was going to what party. The gossip du jour, however, was the story of Hillary Clinton and the lamp. The First Lady, it was whispered, had thrown a lamp at her husband during a fight in the White House. Sometimes the argument was said to have started because the president-elect ogled one of the celebrities at the pre-inaugural show. Sometimes it was about whether or not Hillary Clinton's offices would be located in the critical White House West Wing. Frequently, the story included a subplot about the antagonism between Mrs. Clinton and her Secret Service guards. It remained confined to the nation's capital for about as long as it took to say "e-mail." Up in New York City, Hillary and the lamp were soon a big topic at a party for a retiring city detective. Investigators from the Treasury Department's Bureau of Alcohol, Tobacco and Firearms who had dropped by to wish the detective good-bye entertained the guests with the story, which they said they'd heard from friends in the Secret Service. "Those guys must really hate the Clintons," said a lawyer who had been at the affair, and then called his own circle of acquaintances to spread the tale along.

2   The lamp story was not, of course, the only gossip of a personal nature about the Clintons during the administration's first days in office. *The Washington Monthly*'s "Who's Who" column tried to float a rumor that there was something more than economic indicators passing between the president and his new appointee to the Council of Economic Advisers. ("Suspicions have already been, um, aroused about one of Bill Clinton's better known weaknesses. Certain insiders say that . . . Laura Tyson has the ear and the eye of the president-elect, giving Hillary a new and compelling reason to sit in on all those top-level late night meetings.") There was some perfunctory talk about a woman on the transition team who was supposed to be having a liaison with the chief executive, but it faded away quickly, as would dozens of similar stories that sprang up over the next few years but failed to flower into serious gossip. And *The Washington Monthly* stampeded into retreat on its Laura Tyson rumor. ("The item was not intended to convey that anything more had happened or that Tyson had sought to use her physical charm to attract the president's attention. Indeed, from all we hear she is one of the more original intellects in his administration and deserves Clinton's attention strictly on the basis of merit.") But the lamp story endured. By March, major publications had begun printing it. By the summer it had achieved such legendary status that people were joking about it on network television. But long before the national media had decided the rumor was worth mentioning, people all across the country had picked it up through more informal communications networks. I went to Ohio for a family party in February, and when I was asked for inside Washington gossip, I offered up Hillary's lamp. But it was old news—my mother had already heard it on Rush Limbaugh's radio show.

3   Even before the birth of tabloid TV and talk radio, it was possible to pick up quite a bit of gossip about the personal lives of important political figures, no matter where you lived or how communicative the newspapers were feeling. When Boston schoolteacher Barbara Wilson was a child and Dwight Eisenhower was president, she knew there were rumors his wife, Mamie, was a heavy drinker. "I must have heard it from my mother," she recalled. "She loved politics. Not in an active way, but she was a very big reader." How Wilson's mother picked up the information is a mystery. In

the 1950s that sort of gossip had to be transmitted word of mouth—the *Boston Globe* didn't print it, and back then radio shows didn't encourage callers to phone in the latest rumors about the president's home life. Yet the Mamie-drinks rumor, like Hillary's lamp, had a remarkable ability to travel. One of the differences between that discreet age and today was that in the fifties and early sixties, people tended to hear only the gossip that appealed to their political prejudices, or their special interests. Steve Weisman, an editorial writer for the *New York Times*, grew up in Beverly Hills, where most of his junior high school class had heard that President Kennedy was having an affair with actress Angie Dickinson: "The hotel was right across from my old grade school." But back in Boston, the people in Wilson's neighborhood believed the nation's first Catholic president was a model husband. "He and Jackie had no faults. I couldn't imagine them fighting. I couldn't even imagine them brushing their teeth," she said. The entire Boston parochial school system, Wilson theorized, was out of the gossip loop on that one.

"Those pesky and unproved rumors"

The lamp story, of course, would turn out to be the least of the Clintons' problems when it came to public discussion of the president's private life. But it was gossip that spread without the help of legal inquiry or political spin—less sensational, but more spontaneous, than the talk that was to come. Like other stories that would follow, it spread through an incredibly dense network of gossip routes. Talk radio and the Internet had created a new kind of word of mouth that could spread a rumor across the country in minutes. By the time it reached television via tabloid news shows or a Jay Leno joke, people might have heard the same story from a half-dozen sources, and the mere repetition would make it seem true. The old-line media—newspapers, network news shows, newsmagazines—became less important as transmitters of gossip than as judges of credibility. By paying attention to a rumor, they could raise it to a new level of seriousness—a sort of official gossip.

In March of 1993, the conservative *Washington Times* became the first paper to print a variant of the lamp rumor, which had the First Lady throwing a book (perhaps a Bible) at a Secret Service guard. Although "trustworthy sources" had discounted the tales, the *Times* added, the story had spread to papers in "Middle America and Europe." Most reports of gossip about political figures are accompanied by these two elements— an excuse for printing the story (the rumor has gotten so out of control it's being repeated in Berlin and Boise) and a denial. The most powerful denials are the ones from some variation on "trustworthy sources." (The inference is that the reporter has consulted people so reliable they're worth quoting even if their names can't be used.) The weakest come from the subject's spokesperson. (After all, what else would you expect a spokesperson to say?)

6   The critical point, however, was that the *Times* story freed other publications from the onus of being the first to print the gossip, and everyone felt freer to leap in. *Newsweek* ran a story about the rumor in which an angry First Lady threw "a lamp, a briefing book or a Bible" at the president, and added a new fillip—that Mrs. Clinton was rumored to have lit a cigarette to torture her smoke-allergic husband. (The writers personally deemed the cigarette story "outrageous" but simply quoted White House spokesman George Stephanopoulos as denying the thrown-lamp rumor.) White House correspondents asked Press Secretary Dee Dee Myers whether the lamp gossip had created a rift between the president and the Secret Service. Myers called the story "ridiculous" and urged the press to focus on the president's programs, not "the gutter." Her comments were part of a tradition that began with George Washington's wistful suggestion that newspapers should forget about scandal and concentrate on "the debates in Congress on all great national questions."

7   Myers's comments opened the way for the *Washington Post* to report, briefly and somewhat impatiently, that "the White House finally felt compelled to deny those pesky and unproved rumors involving all manner of domestic disputes between Bill and Hillary Clinton." (In a one-paragraph story, the *Post* also managed to move the rumor ahead a step by adding "punches" to the things that might have been thrown.) *The Washingtonian* weighed in with a conclusion that the throws-lamp-at-Bill part of the story began on Inauguration Day, when the Senate Republicans were penned up in a holding room next to one where the Clintons were fighting. "One prominent senator says he overheard Hillary shouting at Bill and threatening to throw something at him," the magazine reported. The Secret Service had been leaking stories of its own, *The Washingtonian* said, "including separate bedrooms and lots of loud talk and bad language including lots of the twelve letter 'm' word. One agent claims that Hillary threw her Bible at an agent who was driving too slow."

8   The Hillary-lamp saga became one of those stories that is so well known it can be referred to in shorthand, without explanation, in a David Letterman Top Ten list or *Saturday Night Live* skit. By June, when Mrs. Clinton was taking NBC's Katie Couric on a televised White House tour, Couric cheerfully asked her to "point out just where you were when you threw the lamp at your husband."

9   "Well, you know that's—I'm looking for that spot, too," the First Lady responded.

2. Deconstructing Political Gossip

"Such a filthy old man he had become!"

Gossip covers such a sweeping variety of human behavior that we have to   10
define our terms narrowly. Many people think, for instance, of political
gossip as shoptalk—rumors about who's going to be running for Congress
next year. But for our purposes, it will only refer to unverified information
about a person's private life that he or she might prefer to keep hidden.
This is the classic form of gossip, and passing it around has been one of our
most popular social activities since privacy was invented. Politicians have
been a favorite target throughout history—or at least since the time of the
ancient Greeks, when Athenians speculated that Pericles always kept his
helmet on because he was embarrassed about his pear-shaped head. The
Romans were enthusiastic gossips in political matters—Mark Antony
spread the rumor that Augustus got to be emperor by sleeping with Julius
Caesar. Parts of Suetonius's *Lives of the Caesars*, one of Western civilization's most venerable histories, are pure gossip. Tiberius Caesar, Suetonius
wrote, trained small boys to "chase him while he went swimming and get
between his legs to lick and nibble them . . . such a filthy old man he had
become!" Americans have never been blessed with quite such colorful an-
ecdotes about their leaders. (Except, perhaps, for one nineteenth-century
presidential candidate who was rumored to be a cannibal.) But the public
has always passed around stories about politicians' private lives, even
though the respectable newspapers have not always printed them.

Gossip answers a wide range of human needs. It makes the teller feel   11
important. It bonds both teller and listener together with a sense of sharing something slightly forbidden. By revealing behavior that's normally
hidden, it helps people to understand how things really work in the mysterious world behind closed doors. (A young wife may figure out how to
judge and deal with her husband's infidelity by listening to the stories
about other straying spouses.) People express their hidden fears through
gossip, imposing on others the anxieties they haven't resolved in their
own lives. They sometimes also use gossip to reaffirm their commitment
to the social order. (Whispering about an acquaintance who wears golf
clothes at Sunday services shows you still hold to the tradition of dressing
up for church.)

But gossip has sometimes had a subversive role, too. For much of human   12
history, it was one of the few weapons available to the powerless: servants
who spread stories about their masters, peasants who irreverently speculated about the most private aspects of life in the manor. (The French
peasants had a song about Louis the XVI's penis that was popular as long
as the king failed to produce an heir.) Gossip has always been identified as

a woman's vice because from the time of the ancient Greeks, men realized that their homebound, anonymous wives had access to the secrets of the master of the house. Aristotle warned gloomily that democracy might lead to a society where women could seize the reins of domestic control, and begin carrying gossip about their husbands to the outside world. In the Middle Ages, "gossip" was connected with childbearing, because the birthing room was one of the few places women gathered without super-vision, free to make fun of the men in their lives, and tell their most em-barrassing secrets.

13   In American history, gossip has sometimes been a reaction against heavily marketed politicians who voters might suspect were being thrust upon them against their will. Nineteenth-century presidential candidates promoted as war heroes were often gossiped about as cowards, paragons of virtue as "illegitimate" by birth. Even today, voters who pass around sto-ries about a nominee's drinking habits or womanizing may be attempting to show that they aren't fooled by the barrage of commercials broadcast-ing his virtues.

14   Political gossip is, of course, very frequently a tactical weapon that one party or candidate uses to try to weaken an opponent. But while anybody can start a story, it isn't possible to force people to pick up on it and pass it around. The gossip that reverberates and endures isn't always true, but it usually reflects something real about the target, or the national anxi-eties at a given point in time. When the recently widowed Woodrow Wil-son suddenly married Edith Galt, people began to whisper that the two of them had murdered the president's first wife. That wasn't true, of course. But the gossip did express people's discomfort with such stark evidence of a husband's ability to recover from his spouse's death, as well as the gen-eral impression that Wilson was something of a cold fish. More balanced citizens relieved their emotions by telling catty jokes about the second Mrs. W. The late columnist Murray Kempton remembered as a boy in the 1920s hearing that when President Wilson asked Mrs. Galt to be his wife, she was so excited she fell out of bed. "I think my sainted mother told me that one," Kempton said.

15   Gossip that gets floated unsuccessfully tells us things as well. During the weeks before the New Hampshire Republican primary in 1996, Lars-Erik Nelson of the *New York Daily News* noticed that right-wing radio talk shows were circulating a rumor that Bob Dole had not really been wounded in World War II. His crippled hand, the story went, was just the result of an accident during basic training. That wasn't true. However, if it had caught on, and been repeated by people without any political ax to grind, it might have told us something about the country's mood: that Dole was

hanging too much of his campaign on his status as a wounded veteran, perhaps. Or that younger men who have not experienced a war were tired of hearing the older generation talk about theirs. But the story turned out to be more than false—it was unevocative. It tried to tug at emotions that didn't exist, failed gossip that was tossed aside like yesterday's fish.

The lamp story grew and grew because Hillary Clinton stirred up anxiety in many Americans, and the story about her smashed lighting fixture helped them express it without directly confronting the things that were bothering them. Mrs. Clinton was a new kind of First Lady who made it clear she planned to have a policy-making role in the administration. She was carving out that job at a time when the nation hadn't resolved its own feelings about how women should mix the duties of career and marriage. The gossip stirred up many voters' own unresolved concerns about working wives, powerful women, and the proper role of the First Lady. By passing along the rumor that Mrs. Clinton had physically attacked the president, people were expressing their secret fears that she (and maybe by implication all women) would try to push her husband aside and run things herself.

3. The Three Great Eras of Political Gossip

The Kaleidoscope Theory of History

The freedom with which people pass around rumors about their political leaders' private lives has changed dramatically over the last two hundred–odd years, but not necessarily in the way we imagine. We tend to think of history as a continuum, trending ever up or downward. We now know that John Kennedy invited his lovers to swim in the White House pool without fear of exposure, while the details of Bill Clinton's sex life get rehashed every day on talk radio and tabloid TV shows. So we assume that the nation was discreet, concentrating on the political issues rather than scandalous secrets, until some very recent period when we lost our bearings and began obsessively speculating about the private vices of our leaders.

The real progression has been much more erratic. Rather than a continuum, the interaction of gossip and politics is a sort of kaleidoscope, in which new patterns are created with every turn of the wheel. The national morality relaxes or stiffens. An irresistibly likable president is replaced by one with a downright irritating personality. A politician with a closet full of skeletons and an urge to party is followed by a string of men whose idea of a good time is taking a nap after dinner. Each year brings a new mix. The public is doomed to be shocked, hardened, and then reborn into hopeful innocence, over and over.

19   Still, we can divide the nation's history into three rough eras, depending on how freely people talked (and newspapers wrote) about their leading politicians' private lives. The era of the Founding Fathers was a sort of prologue. Our story really begins with the 1820s, when states began opening the elections up to all (white male) citizens. That was also the beginning of a long period, running through most of the nineteenth century, in which average people were very interested in politics. They were wildly patriotic, but not particularly reverent about their elected officials. People thought nothing of spreading stories that a candidate had an illegitimate child, was concealing his Negro ancestry or Catholic faith. They jeered at Andrew Jackson as a bully and adulterer, passed around stories that Martin Van Buren wore women's corsets, distributed leaflets listing how Henry Clay had broken each one of the Ten Commandments ("spends his days at a gaming table and his nights in a brothel"), and accused Daniel Webster of being a drunken boor who couldn't keep his hands off innocent female clerical workers. Abraham Lincoln was rumored in the South to be a secret Negro ("Abraham Africanus the First") and in the North to be a war profiteer. The press compared Andrew Johnson unfavorably to Caligula's horse and speculated that Grover Cleveland would turn the White House into a bordello.

20   Then, around the turn of the century, things slowly began to quiet down. The nation no longer found politics fascinating—it had discovered movies and radio band singers and professional baseball. There was much less idle talk about politicians once people had the opportunity to speculate about the private lives of Mary Pickford and Babe Ruth and discuss the shocking rumors about what comedian Fatty Arbuckle did to the starlet Virginia Rappe in his hotel room. Political figures weren't entirely exempt, of course, particularly during election years. People whispered that Woodrow Wilson had an affair with a mystery woman named Mrs. Peck, that Warren Harding was part Negro, that William McKinley beat his wife, and that Franklin Roosevelt and his entire family were alcoholics, as well as Theodore Roosevelt, and of course Mamie Eisenhower. But the media ignored this sort of talk. When one of Franklin Roosevelt's top officials got caught drunkenly propositioning the railroad porters on a train trip, the president confidently and accurately announced no newspaper would ever print the story.

21   This quiet and sometimes self-satisfied era ran from around World War I until the American involvement in Vietnam. Voters, if they chose, could easily convince themselves that the people running their government were faithful spouses and temperate drinkers, paragons whose public images were in perfect accord with their private behavior. "The fifties

were a curious age," said Russell Baker, who covered Washington during the apex of that discreet period. "You'd go on vacation with Eisenhower, and the local people would come up and say: 'What sort of man is he?' And you'd say 'Well, he's rather cold.' They didn't want to hear that. They were convinced he was a great guy and they didn't want to be disillusioned or have fun made of him."

In the 1970s, things changed again. The public moved from disinterest   22
in politics to something that bordered on contempt. There may actually have been less political gossip than ever, given the declining number of people interested in doing the talking. But what there was got printed, repeated, and, eventually, e-mailed, posted on the Internet, and masticated in talk radio and tabloid TV. The cynicism that began with scandals like Watergate and the disillusionment over the war in Vietnam prepared the public to hear almost anything—that the mayor of Seattle's wife had shot him when she caught him with another man, that the First Lady had murdered her lover, or that the Republican and Democratic candidates for president were both covering up an affair with a woman named J(G)ennifer. The politicians helped the process along by promoting themselves on television and radio in a manner guaranteed to remove any barriers the public felt to freely discussing their most personal secrets.

These shifts were created by all sorts of changes in the society and econ-   23
omy, particularly the development of communications technology, the decline of the power of political parties, and the growth of the entertainment industry. Of course, the deportment of the politicians mattered, too. If congressmen get shot by their mistresses, or a president is hit with a sexual harassment suit, people will talk, whatever the socioeconomic conditions. But when all the forces come together, like some sinister alignment of the planets, they can pull even the most discreet figures into the rumor mill. The public's hunger for gossip about President Cleveland's wife, Frances, was so intense that reporters felt compelled to invent it, and her admirers caused near riots whenever she appeared in public. But Mrs. Cleveland never encouraged the phenomenon with even a single interview. She behaved with as much circumspection as Mrs. Zachary Taylor, whose public profile was so low she had to be depicted in the president's deadbed portrait with her head in her hands. None of the painters had any idea what she looked like.

The Media: "Important If True"

In the early years of American democracy, the salient fact about the   24
newspaper business was that almost nobody made a profit at it. Most editors ran one-man shops, sold few ads, and usually boasted a readership of

only a few hundred souls, almost all of whom were slow in paying for their subscriptions. "Subsisting by a country newspaper is generally little better than starving," said a New Jersey editor. Their brightest hopes lay in pleasing a successful politician and snagging a government printing contract or—better yet—a government job. Some of the best spots went to people who had printed the most outrageous stories. The editor who claimed that John Quincy Adams slept with his wife before they were married was made governor of Florida by the triumphant Andrew Jackson. Another who spread the story that Adams had been a pimp for the czar of Russia was made a senator and a member of Jackson's "Kitchen Cabinet." It's hardly surprising that most editors were ready, willing, and able to print any scandal about an opposition candidate that they could find or manufacture. Accuracy was not regarded as an important quality, anyhow. Editors of the era had no shame in admitting they were simply recycling rumors. ("Important If True" was a common headline.)

25   As technology improved and the population began to congregate in large cities, papers were able to make money from circulation and advertising. As long as production costs were still relatively low, even a small city could support a couple of profitable publications, along with a handful of fly-by-night competitors who might still be in the game of jockeying for political patronage. These smaller papers were the ones most likely to print shocking stories about government officials and election candidates. In 1881, for instance, a rumor went roaring through New York's state capitol in Albany concerning U.S. senator Thomas Platt. Platt's political enemies had discovered he was having an assignation with a woman in a local hotel, and arranged to watch the proceedings over the transom from an adjoining room. The *Albany Argus* promptly reported every detail: the conspirators' long vigil armed with "a stepladder, some whiskey, some crackers and cheese and cigars"; their three hours of amusement "taking turns mounting the stepladder and playing Peeping Tom"; the names of everyone involved except the woman. (It did report that she was "of engaging form but unpleasing features.") The other papers' more staid response must have sent readers racing out to look for a copy of the *Argus*. "A scandalous story affecting the private character of a prominent politician of this state was reported on the streets here and in Albany yesterday," announced the *New York Tribune*, with maddening discretion. "And full particulars were telegraphed to this paper, which we declined to print."

26   As newspaper chains grew and competition began to shrink in the twentieth century, the small, scurrilous papers died out and the surviving media tended to prefer less controversial family fare. That was the quiet era, bracketed by the Harding administration (extremely popular presi-

dent makes love to his mistress in the Oval Office closet) and that of John Kennedy (extremely popular president makes love to rapidly revolving series of girlfriends just about everywhere but the White House press room). Newspaper editors, who were almost all men, found it distasteful to publicize the private misbehavior of politicians, who were almost always men, too. The periods in which newspapers did publish such personal revelations were generally marked by a strong female influence on the nation's social agenda. Women tended to focus on the problems of the family, and to regard male misbehavior in private life as a serious matter. Men tended to disagree.

Like all the sweeping generalizations, the one that said newspaper read-   27
ers could not pick up much about politicians' private misdeeds during this period didn't always hold true, especially if an arrest or court proceedings provided an excuse to pass on a truly juicy piece of scandal. In 1951, the *Birmingham News* published virtually every word of Police Commissioner "Bull" Connor's trial on morals charges, including the detective's claim that he found a towel "reeking with semen" in the bedroom of the hotel room where Connor was found with his secretary. (The defense brought in a gynecologist to testify that semen didn't reek, but to no avail.)

But the arrival of television news forced the newspapers and magazines   28
to stretch harder to give readers something they couldn't get from Walter Cronkite. By the 1980s, cable television, talk radio, twenty-four-hour news, and the Internet were creating an unprecedented competition for news consumers' attention. Because the old "scoops" of hard-news information could be transmitted so fast, the emphasis shifted to personality-driven stories that were harder for the competition to copy. With every public word recorded by TV and computerized services, reporters felt more pressure to learn the things that were hidden. When Gary Hart challenged them to follow him around if they thought he was cheating on his wife, the dare was hard to resist.

The Parties: "If so, mention it modestly"

People used to like to belong to a political party. It was one of the ways   29
they kept track of their own identities in a shifting, mobile society. It also greatly simplified the process of being a good citizen. If you knew you were a Democrat, you voted the party line and you did not need to study the League of Women Voters candidate summaries just to choose between two state senate hopefuls.

Even back in 1828, there were party image-makers who tried to maxi-   30
mize their candidates' good points. ("Does the old gentleman have prayers in his own house?" asked one of Andrew Jackson's handlers, Martin Van

Buren. ("If so, mention it modestly.") Their followers read newspapers that favored their party's side of things, and talked politics with people who shared their views. It was like belonging to a fraternal lodge or drinking club. That was one of the reasons that nineteenth-century voters went to the polls like crazy. They also happily spread rumors about the opposition candidates. It was part of the civic duty of preaching to the political heathen and helping the forces of justice to triumph.

31   The parties started losing their moral underpinnings around the turn of the century, when muckrakers published exposés about the corruption of the big-city bosses. Middle-class voters bolted from their traditional Republican affiliations in the name of reform. Politicians were praised for putting principle above party, and the word got around that a really well[-]informed citizen voted the man, not the party. Newspapers started to brag about being independent. Political gossip stopped being printed, and people stopped spreading it with quite as much avidity. Voter participation, unfortunately, plummeted.

32   A much bigger change occurred in the 1960s and 1970s, when Vietnam and Watergate left Republicans and Democrats—particularly Democrats—so alienated from their party bosses that they took away the power to nominate candidates. Instead of the smoke-filled room, there was the clean, well-lighted polling place. Nominating a president became a strange ritual that began years before the election, as hopeful politicians trotted out their wares before an indifferent nation. The real selection process telescoped into a few hectic months early in the election year, when candidates the public had hardly begun to focus on raced through a packed schedule of primary elections, most of which were conducted almost completely through TV ads.

33   The old system, under which political insiders picked the nominees, presumed that the decision-makers knew all the gossip about the candidates' personal lives and took it into consideration when they made their choices. It wasn't always true. (In 1920, when the party bosses asked Warren Harding if he had any secrets that might cause political problems, nobody seemed to think it was ominous that Harding thought for ten minutes before saying no.) But it was a sensible rationale for keeping rumors about candidates' private failings from the public. Once the voters took control of the nominations, however, it was inevitable that they would wind up being let in on the gossip, too.

Celebrity: Richard Gere and the Gerbil

34   Politicians are obviously not the only people whose personal lives get dissected by total strangers. For every story like that of Hillary's lamp there are a dozen popular legends about movie stars or rock singers or athletes, from

the 1960s rumor that Paul McCartney was dead to the more current one about Richard Gere and the gerbil. The gerbil story is a good example of the way gossip about entertainers has paralleled gossip about politicians. It also demonstrates the willingness of even family newspapers in the 1990s to print outrageous and unverified stories about famous people's personal lives. "Rumor: Richard Gere had a gerbil, the result of a bizarre sexual practice, removed from his rear end at a Los Angeles hospital in the mid-1980s" reported the *Indianapolis Star* in a sixteen-hundred-word rumor-roundup in 1997. "Fact: There has never been a verified medical case of a gerbil (or any other rodent) having been extracted from a patient's rectum."

The gerbil story's staying power was related to an anxiety as powerful as   35
the one about overreaching women—fear of AIDS. It was basically a cautionary tale about unsafe sex, like the famous anti-hairspray legend from the 1960s about the girl with a lacquered beehive hairdo who died when poisonous spiders built a nest inside it. *Playboy* claimed the original gerbil story was a homophobic fable dating back to 1990 that was linked to Gere after "the actor had joked to a magazine writer about having performed some youthful indiscretion with a chicken." A *Los Angeles Daily News* columnist got it into print through the time-honored method of decrying the people who were spreading the gossip. A prankster then sent people in the Hollywood community a phony fax from the Association for the Prevention of Cruelty to Animals, attacking Gere for abusing a gerbil. Like the Hillary lamp story, the gerbil rumor reached a status where it could be referred to in shorthand. In a 1995 *Vanity Fair* profile of actor Keanu Reeves, author Michael Shnayerson claimed a rumor that Reeves was having an affair with producer David Geffen "was everywhere. Like Richard Gere and gerbils."

The roots of American gossip about entertainment celebrities run back   36
deep into the nineteenth century, when romantic schoolgirls used to fantasize about the brooding poet Lord Byron. After Byron's death, the writer Harriet Beecher Stowe started an incredible uproar by announcing that she knew for a fact Byron had slept with his own half sister. Stowe was trying to defend her friend, Byron's much-abused wife. But she soon discovered a lesson from the history of political gossip: There are some stories that the public won't believe because they simply don't want to think prominent people do that kind of thing.

The class of entertainment celebrities that we know today was created   37
around the 1880s, then people started moving to the cities making money, acquiring leisure, and reading newspapers that celebrated the new heroes of sport and society and theater. In the early 1900s, movie stars were added to the mix. The public couldn't get enough information about these fabulous new creatures—even in the early years when the producers

stubbornly refused to reveal their names. But the identities emerged, followed by movie magazines bearing information about their backgrounds, their romances, their hobbies and favorite foods and clothes.

38   This was a very important development for politics, which until then had been just about the only source of entertainment for most Americans, as well as the main provider of celebrities to talk about. For average people in the nineteenth century, being politically involved meant going to picnics, marching in parades, and drinking toasts to the party nominees, many of whom were depicted as cartoonlike embodiments of utter heroism or (to the opposition) utter depravity. Once times changed and the candidates were no longer connected to entertainment, they became more remote, more dignified, more boring.

39   In the 1920s, movie stars went through a sort of shakedown in which one scandal after another prompted newspapers to dump all the accumulated gossip about people like (accused killer) Fatty Arbuckle and (admitted drug addict) Wallace Reid onto the shocked readers. But once things quieted down, entertainers and politicians both sailed into that long period in which they were gossiped about in public only in the most harmless terms. Alcoholic senators would be described for public consumption as "colorful," even as the most dysfunctional of Hollywood marriages was referred to in euphemisms like "those battling Bogarts." While the plethora of movie magazines made it appear as if actors and actresses were perpetual gossip victims, the information that was actually printed was "totally sanitized," said gossip columnist Liz Smith, who started her own career writing for the magazines. "Louella Parsons might predict that if Clark Gable married Carole Lombard he'd be ruined, but there was enormous restraint," she said. "They'd never put in anything that reflected on the stars' morals."

40   The most important difference between the gossip about the two professions was that the public really wasn't much interested in the politicians anyway. That was an advantage in the 1950s, when entertainers were being tortured by scandal magazine exposés but politicians were deemed too uninteresting to humiliate. But with the advent of television, political candidates slowly tried to win the voters' attention and affection by sneaking into the world of entertainment. Each generation pressed the envelope a little further. The Richard Nixon who made the traditional, if somewhat bizarre, "Checkers" speech on television in 1952 became the Richard Nixon who tried to promote his presidential candidacy in 1968 with an appearance on *Laugh-In*.

41   When the studio system and the political parties broke down, both entertainers and politicians had to market themselves directly to the public—a

process that involved embarrassment and ruined careers on both sides. But the same public indifference that protected politicians in the era of the scandal magazines forced them to expose themselves further and further in the eighties and nineties, as they desperately attempted to gain recognition. The deference bred by a combination of apathy and distance fell apart when presidential candidates began to appear on TV variety shows, when senators and governors vied to be interviewed by "shock-jock" radio hosts, and the president himself discussed his underwear preferences on MTV.

QUESTIONING AND DISCUSSING

Collins, from *Scorpion Tongues*

1. What is Gail Collins's central argument, and how do you respond to it in terms of its ethics? What are the ethical implications of the suggestion that "Gossip answers a wide range of human needs"? How is its "subversiveness" used to justify gossip?

2. Analyze and comment on the structure of Collins's argument. Why does she choose to begin the Introduction as she does? What purpose might that style serve? How would you describe Collins's tone—and why?

3. Compare these excerpts with the next article—"Oops! I Shouldn't Say This . . . or Should I?"—which, in fact, quotes Collins. How does each selection affect your reading of the other? Why?

⊞

MARGARET MOERS WENIG

Margaret Moers Wenig has served for more than a decade as spiritual leader of the People's Temple in New York City; she is currently rabbi emerita. An instructor in Homiletics at the Hebrew Union College, Wenig has published widely on popular, spiritual, and religious issues and is a frequent guest preacher and lecturer throughout the United States. She is also the author of "Sacred Speech—Sacred Communities," from *The Reconstructionist,* Vol. 67, No. 1, Fall 2002.

⊞

Oops! I Shouldn't Say This . . . or Should I?

"I've heard first-, second-, and third-hand gossip circulating at my synagogue—mostly untrue or, at best, only partially true," says a past president of a Reform congregation. "The most damaging gossip was about our rabbi. People assumed the worst about his conduct or motives, discredited him in ways that ranged from petty to slanderous. As a result, we lost members, teachers, staff . . . and the gossip hurt important temple relationships, both with local Jewish organizations and the non-Jewish community." Another past president concurs. "While sometimes congregants raised legitimate concerns with me in sensitive ways, at other times people were cruel. The net effect was, the synagogue felt less like a sanctuary, less holy, than it might have."

1 In Judaism, damaging a person's reputation through gossip is akin to taking his life. The Talmud teaches: "A person's tongue is more powerful than his sword. A sword can only kill someone who is nearby; a tongue can cause the death of someone who is far away" (Babylonian Talmud Shabbat 15b).

2 Rabbinic laws governing gossip, or *lashon hara,* are as extensive as they are strict. We are forbidden to relate *anything* derogatory about others. Even if a negative statement is true, it is still considered *lashon hara.* If it is false, even partially so, the offense is the more severe *motzi shem ra* (defamation of character). Also prohibited is *rechilut* (talebearing, or reporting to someone what others have said about him). *Lashon hara* violates no fewer than thirty-one biblical commandments, among them: "do not utter (or accept) a false report (Ex. 23:1), "do not go about as a talebearer among your people" (Lev. 19:16), and "cursed be one who smites his neighbor secretly" (Deut. 27:24).

3 In 1873, Rabbi Israel Meir Kagan, a commentator on the *Shulchan Aruch* and a teacher of *musar* (ethics), collected the laws of *lashon hara* and *rechilut* into one volume entitled *Sefer Chofetz Chayim.* So widely

studied is this work that its author became known as the Chofetz Chayim, a reference to Psalm 34:13–14: "Who is the person who desires life (*chofetz chayim*). . . . Guard your tongue from evil and your lips from speaking deceit." According to the Chofetz Chayim, we are forbidden:

- to discuss a person's negative character traits or to mention his/her misdeeds, even to a person who witnessed them
- to make derogatory remarks about someone, even when the information is common knowledge, and even if it causes no harm
- to convey a negative response about a person through hints, hand motions, facial expressions, coughs, winks, or tone of voice
- to make any statement, even if not explicitly derogatory, which might cause financial loss, physical pain, mental anguish, or any damage to reputation
- to reveal any personal or professional information about someone which he/she admitted to us, even if he/she did not request confidentiality
- to speak ill of a *talmid chacham* (scholar) or to ridicule his teaching—a particularly egregious sin if he is the practicing rabbi of a community

We are even forbidden: 4

- to listen to or sit next to someone who speaks *lashon hara*
- to praise another person excessively, for doing so might provoke a listener to disagree
- to make a seemingly neutral comment (such as, "Have you seen Sam lately?"), for it may prompt others to speak ill of him

The Chofetz Chayim adds that the greater the number of people who 5 hear one's *lashon hara*, the greater the sin. One who gossips habitually commits sins greater than idolatry, adultery, and murder.

Dangers of *Lashon Hara*

If some of the rabbinic injunctions against *lashon hara* appear exceptionally strict, consider what is at stake: 6

- Lashon hara *can destroy a human being's livelihood.* The "blacklisting" which was characteristic of the McCarthy era left many people jobless, and worse.
- Lashon hara *can inflict psychic pain and damage self-esteem.* "For all the misery that's crossed my path, no pain is more searingly etched in my

memory than the relatively slight deprecations I've endured or inflicted," writes UAHC Board member and social activist Evely Laser Shlensky. "Relatively minor personal humiliations can elicit a powerful enduring sense of degradation. I think of these intimate acts which crush the human soul as 'little murders.'"

- Lashon hara *can compromise truth*. Since standards of proof are rarely invoked in gossip, *lashon hara* violates the legal principle: innocent until proven guilty.
- Lashon hara *can violate our privacy*. "When other people intervene by telling someone information about us," Rabbi Margaret Holub observes, "they are violating our control of our personal information. This can feel like theft or even rape."
- Lashon hara *about an entire group of people can lead to racial/ethnic/religious hatred and violence*. Jews as a people have often been victimized by slanders emanating from pulpits, the media, and now the Internet.
- Lashon hara *can undermine a sacred community*. Congregants may flee from or avoid assuming leadership roles in synagogues in which backbiting is rampant, privacy is violated, and people are constantly being judged.

7 What makes *lashon hara* even more insidious is the near impossibility of undoing its damage. The Chofetz Chayim tells the story of a penitent who asks him for a way to repair the harm done by his gossip. The Chofetz Chayim hands the man a feather pillow and instructs him to take it outside, slit it open, and shake its contents into the wind. When the penitent returns with the empty pillow, the Chofetz Chayim says, "Now, go collect the feathers."

Benefits of *Lashon Hara*

8 Gossip can cause irreparable damage to a person's reputation and well-being, but it can also play a *constructive* social role. "Gossip provides an individual with a map of his social environment, including details which are inaccessible to him in his own everyday life," writes anthropologist John Beard Haviland in *Gossip, Reputation and Knowledge in Zincantan*. Quoting F. G. Bailey, he explains, "An event or an action is public not only to those who see it, but also to those who hear about it. . . . The map which a man has of the community around him, of what is going on and of how he should respond to others, is a map created by the spoken word, by the information circulating around his community." In *Scorpion Tongues: Gossip, Celebrity, and American Politics*, columnist Gail Collins says, "By revealing behavior that's normally hidden, [gossip] helps people understand

how things really work in the mysterious world behind closed doors." Philosopher Sisela Bok adds: "If we knew about people only what they wished to reveal, we would be subjected to ceaseless manipulation; and we would be deprived of the pleasure and suspense that comes from trying to understand them. . . . In order to live in both the inner and the shared worlds, the exchange of views about each other—in spite of all the difficulties of perception and communication—gossip is indispensable."

Gossip also helps to create and define the boundaries of a community of 9 shared values. It may even be instrumental in forming what F. G. Bailey calls "a moral community"—that is, "a group of people prepared to make moral judgments about one another." In fact, the first definition of a gossip in the *Oxford English Dictionary* is: "One who has contracted spiritual affinity with another by acting as a sponsor at a baptism (from god sib)." Consider the positive value of former classmates or camp buddies sharing information about members of their group: who is ill, who is getting divorced, whose child is having trouble, who is changing careers, who could use a friendly call. In other words, there is an appropriate connection between the intimacy of family or the closest of friends and the intimate information they share with one another.

In the realm of politics, *lashon hara* may be necessary in order to exer- 10 cise our responsible roles as citizens in a democratic society. To vote, to speak out for justice, to respond intelligently to the dilemmas of our era, we need access to information about the actions of our public officials, good and bad. "Considering the implications of Daniel Ellsberg's leaking the Pentagon Papers to *The New York Times*," writes Rabbi Margaret Holub. "One could make the case that gossip ended the Vietnam War."

For the oppressed, *lashon hara* may serve as a means of resistance. "For 11 much of human history," Gail Collins writes, "[gossip] was one of the few weapons available to the powerless: servants who spread stories about their masters, peasants who irreverently speculated about the most private aspects of life in the manor. . . ." Today, if an employee suspects she has been discriminated against, speaking *lashon hara* may lead to confirmation of her belief and may become the first step in mobilizing resources, her own and others', to fight the discrimination.

Lashon hara can lead to self-understanding and connection with those 12 closest to us. For example, discussing with a spouse, partner, or trusted friend a negative encounter with one's boss, though considered *lashon hara*, may help our loved one better understand why we are angry, uncommunicative, or depressed. Unburdening in this way may also result in our gaining a more balanced perspective on our situation and brainstorming strategies for resolving the conflict.

13　　*Lashon hara* also plays a role in fostering creativity and self-expression. In commenting on society and the human condition, literature and the performing arts often describe people with satire, irony, and humor. "If we are honest," adds Rabbi Margaret Holub, "there is probably some percentage of that awful gossip we all do which is just fun. It really doesn't fan the flames of our negativity. It doesn't keep us from more serious and intimate conversation. It doesn't harm the person at whose expense we laugh. I think we each need a little free zone—a few minutes a week, a single trusted companion, something like that—to keep ourselves from being insufferably self-conscious or, worse, sanctimonious. The very same energy which allows us to laugh and mock also keeps us curious and alive."

14　　In Jewish law, *lashon hara* is permitted when it is the only means available to alert someone of possible danger, and it is *required* when the intent is to warn others not to follow in the footsteps of one who has transgressed *mitzvot*. For example, *lashon hara* may be necessary if in private premarital counseling a rabbi learns that the groom-to-be has engaged in unsafe sex and refuses to be tested for HIV. In this case, telling the bride-to-be that her fiancé's behavior and attitude might pose some risk to her and to their future is a *mitzvah*.

15　　In business dealings as well, under certain limited circumstances, the rabbis permitted the exchange of negative assessments of a person's character and behavior. When asked for an employee reference, Rabbi Zelig Pliskin explains that you are "obliged to give a truthful answer, even if [your] reply . . . contain[s] derogatory facts . . . in order to prevent an unqualified person from being mistakenly hired." In such cases, a person is permitted to listen to *lashon hara* for cautionary purposes, but the listener is forbidden to take any negative information as the absolute truth.

16　　A consumer is also "permitted to speak of the poor quality of a [vendor's] merchandise in order to prevent [a potential customer] from being cheated." And "it is permitted to speak *lashon hara* if you believe your words will help an injured person receive compensation."

Finding the Right Balance

17　　How, then, do we determine when engaging in *lashon hara* is destructive and when it is desirable? The first step is to become more aware of the ramifications of our own speech. Try these guidelines for a week:

- Take note of everything you say about another person or about a group of people.
- Refrain from repeating anything you do not know firsthand to be true.

- Each time you are tempted to speak about another person, ask yourself: "Is there a better way to accomplish my goal [e.g., to become closer to the listener, to help a friend, to correct a problem]?"

Preventative Strategies

We can learn to avoid committing *lashon hara* in the first place by implementing "preventative" strategies, such as giving another the benefit of the doubt, rebuking with compassion, and nurturing appreciation for the good in others.

    Give others the benefit of the doubt. When we witness infuriating behavior, instead of automatically ascribing to the offender the worst of motives and then sharing our judgment with others, we might instead assume the best of intentions—or that the offender was simply misguided. "As we judge others favorably, so will God judge us favorably" (The Babylonian Talmud, Shabbat 127b).

    Rebuking wisely. If a situation arises which cannot be simply "explained away," our tradition enjoins us to rebuke the presumed offender directly and privately (publicly embarrassing someone is prohibited). Leviticus 19 states: "You shall surely rebuke your neighbor (*hocheyach tochiach et amitecha*), but incur no guilt [because of him]." Notably, this *mitzvah* appears immediately after the prohibition, "Do not go about as a talebearer" and immediately before, "You shall not take vengeance or bear a grudge against your kinsfolk. Love your neighbor as yourself. I am the Eternal God."

    Although we may hesitate to offer rebuke (*tochecha*) for fear of "hurting another human being, ruining a relationship, engaging in an unhealthy power struggle, or opening up our own sense of vulnerability and insecurity," says Rabbi Matthew Gewirtz of Rodeph Sholom Congregation in New York City, "we are nevertheless commanded to rebuke." To minimize the risk of causing hurt feelings, Rabbi Gewirtz offers these guidelines from Jewish tradition: Be aware of your motives before proceeding. Do not rebuke someone out of anger or jealousy arising out of your own sense of failure. Maimonides advises us to "speak to the offender gently and tenderly, so that he can hear the critique" (Mishneh Torah Hilchot Deot 6:7).

    Nurturing Appreciation. While rebuke, or direct criticism, can be a *mitzvah*, we must be mindful not to nurture negativity in human relations. As Rabbi Gewirtz says, "Let us not allow our responsibility to offer *tochecha* to prevent us from also seeing the good in each other. We all need to be appreciated. We all need to be loved. We all want to live with each other in peace. . . . [But] love unaccompanied by criticism is not love. . . . Peace unaccompanied by reproof is not peace" (Genesis Rabbah 54:3).

Sacred Speech, Sacred Communities

23 Just as *lashon hara* can diminish the sanctity of synagogue life, rebuke can enhance it. Even in a sacred community, a community in which each person
is regarded and treated as a creature of God, members still err. Sacred communities cannot grow stronger by ignoring the genuine weaknesses or faults
of their members, leaders, or collective culture. A truly sacred community
acknowledges that people transgress and that *tochecha* (rebuke), *teshuvah*
(repentance), reconciliation, and forgiveness are, in most situations, not
only possible but advisable. As Zelig Pliskin writes in *Guard Your Tongue: A
Practical Guide to the Laws of Loshon Hora Based on Chofetz Chaim:* "If a person diligently applies himself to studying the laws of *lashon hara*, God will
remove his *yetzer hora* (his urge) for forbidden speech. But if an entire group
will resolve together to guard their speech, the merit is [much] greater."

⊞

How to Avoid Listening to Lashon Hara

If someone begins speaking *lashon hara* which you do not wish
to hear:

- Change the subject
- Encourage the speaker to address his concerns directly to the
  person about whom he is speaking, and offer to help him do so
- Walk away (if in a group)
- If you have no choice but to listen to the *lashon hara*, do not
  believe it, act on it, or repeat it

24 Should the Reform Movement establish standards of acceptable and
undesirable *lashon hara?* Just as libel laws vary from state to state and have
changed over time, guidelines for *lashon hara* should be developed at the
local level to address each community's unique circumstance. Congregations notorious for stoking the destructive fire of *lashon hara* may have to
emphasize prohibitions and sanctions; on the other hand, congregations
in which all negative comments are suppressed may need to concentrate
on opening channels for permissible *lashon hara*.

25 Every synagogue can benefit from implementing steps to address the underlying causes of *lashon hara*. Congregants whose insightful questions or
concerns are ignored may gossip out of frustration. Those who persist in
raising thorny questions may be pegged as "chronic complainers" and dis-

missed. Others who may have legitimate complaints may simply leave the congregation without a sound. "A leader who is uncomfortable with dissension, who is unable to encourage others to express their differences, [and] who negatively judges those who do surface disagreements is going to cause even more organizational difficulty," says Stephen B. Leas, director of consulting for the Alban Institute, in *Leadership & Conflict*. The key to stemming the tide of *lashon hara* is to open avenues for direct criticism and honest feedback—practices which require good leadership.

When I arrived at Beth Am, The People's Temple in New York City in 26 1984, a bitter conflict between two warring factions had not yet been resolved. Though the focus of that conflict was no longer an issue, the war continued. To "create an atmosphere where gossip would not breed—in other words, to drain the swamp"—the temple president, Judah Rosenfeld, mandated a monthly "Liaison Committee" meeting, with representation from both sides as well as those with their ears closest to the grapevine and those in positions of power. Every month, committee members brought complaints from the congregation to my attention. One Liaison Committee member who had opposed my hiring carried a little notebook and, after each service, solicited criticism from those he knew might be dissatisfied; at each Liaison Committee meeting he drew the notebook from his pocket and went down that month's list.

For the first few years, the constant criticism was painful for me to hear. 27 But I preferred knowing the substance of congregants' complaints to the anxiety of not knowing what people were saying about me behind my back. In time, when it became clear that the criticism would not scare me away, the Liaison Committee meetings became the place where the synagogue leaders (who eventually came to see themselves not as adversaries but as allies) helped me figure out how to respond to the criticism and how to avoid provoking it in the first place. The committee also allowed me to air my own concerns and enlist help in addressing them.

Rosenfeld's strategy had succeeded. The creation of an appropriate av- 28 enue to discuss issues curtailed gossip which arose from congregants' legitimate concerns and grievances.

While the Chofetz Chayim prohibits "disgracing, belittling, or ridicule" 29 of a rabbi as *lashon hara*, legitimate disagreement with a rabbi's teaching is permitted. And so, at Beth Am, following a tradition established decades earlier by Rabbi Israel Raphael Margolies, *z'l*, after each Shabbat evening service, the congregation sat down for cake and coffee and an hour-long discussion of that night's sermon. I was granted absolute freedom of the pulpit; the congregation was granted equal freedom to disagree. I never worried that congregants might whisper about my sermons behind my back; they shared their reactions to my face—blunt, trenchant, no holds barred. On occasions when there was no sit-down discussion, congregants who objected to a sermon would tell me so on the receiving line, in a letter, or by phone. In recent years, on-line discussion of my High Holiday sermons sometimes lasted months and involved an ever-widening group of congregants. As a result of the objections voiced directly to me, valuable dialogue replaced *lashon hara,* turning the temple into a community energized by the exchange of viewpoints.

Excommunicating "Clergy Killers"

30 Sometimes, even in congregations with open channels of communication, a few members will intentionally introduce dissension by spreading nasty rumors. In *Pastoral Stress: Sources of Tension, Resources for Transformation,* Anthony G. Pappas of the Alban Institute refers to such members as "clergy killers"—people "with power needs and other pathologies" . . . who find congregations—composed mostly of "warm, loving, and tolerant" people— "a viable environment to act out their internal illness. Ideally, the congregation will react in responsible ways to transform or at least contain the harmful behavior. . . ." If all other strategies have failed, Pappas advises that "key congregational leaders [educate themselves] about the reasons and procedures for censure, removal, and/or excommunication of members."

31 Jewish law considers *lashon hara* against rabbis and other Jewish communal leaders a particularly egregious offense. If we witness a communal leader's transgression, we are instructed to assume that our eyes deceived us, or that the behavior was in error, or an aberration. And if we tell someone else what we saw, our punishment is the more severe because we committed *lashon hara* against a sage. In *Gossip: The Power of the Word,* Rabbi Stephen M. Wylen of Temple Beth Tikvah in Wayne, New Jersey rejects the Chafetz Chayim's hierarchy giving sages the greatest benefit of the doubt. Rabbi Wylen's wisdom has been borne out by revelations of sexual abuse of congregants and children by clergy who had been given the benefit of the doubt by their superiors.

32 With the exception of complaints from "clergy killers," grievances about synagogue leaders merit serious attention. In most cases, it is preferable that a synagogue president not censor a member's *lashon hara* by saying, "*Lashon hara* is a sin; I cannot listen to you," or cut off the objection midstream by refuting its contents. In many complaints there lies valuable information about the subject of the *lashon hara,* its speaker, and/or the circumstances which gave rise to its utterance. Rabbi Wylen advises: "Even a tongue-lashing from a spiteful person may contain some surprising insight into our character that we can use to our own advantage if we will only listen . . . 'Rebuke a wise man and he will love you' (Proverbs 9:8)."

As synagogue leaders will inevitably receive direct or indirect criticism, they are well advised to ask themselves: "What support do I need to listen to *lashon hara* (or rebuke) without feeling so vulnerable that I am compelled to respond defensively?" How well a leader meets this challenge will affect the synagogue's well-being. "The quality of interpersonal transactions between members of a congregation," writes Rabbi Lawrence Kushner, "is the single most important factor in determining its health. Do they bear witness to the piety the congregation claims to perpetuate? Where the human relationships are self-righteous, deceitful, and toxic, congregational life is wretched. Where they are tolerant, honest, and nurturing, congregational life can be a transforming joy."

In Mendocino, California, Rabbi Margaret Holub and members of her community have been discussing passages from the Chofetz Chayim and experimenting with standards of "right speech." "More than once of late, I've heard someone stop a sentence and say, 'Oops! I shouldn't say this,'" Rabbi Holub writes. "The very process of being aware of how we speak about others and how we hear others will itself guide us in the direction we want to go. This process . . . is exactly the opposite of the kind of frozen silence that I fear when speech is thoughtlessly curtailed. I have every confidence that we will find our answers as we keep talking."

As we keep talking, may we remember the wisdom of Proverbs 18:21: "Death and life are in the power of the tongue."

QUESTIONING AND DISCUSSING

Moers Wenig, "Oops! I Shouldn't Say This . . . or Should I?"

1. What is Margaret Moers Wenig's central argument? What types of examples and sources does Wenig use to back up her points? What are the distinctions among the types of gossip that might be acceptable and the types that are not?

2. Wenig's article appears in a journal aimed at a primarily Jewish and educated audience. However, she also quotes Protestant clergy and a variety of non-biblical sources. What might be her purpose in doing so?

3. Wenig quotes Gail Collins's book (excerpted in this chapter) *Scorpion Tongues*, noting that gossip "helps people understand how things really work in the mysterious world behind closed doors." In your view, and having read Wenig's article, do you agree that gossip is "indispensable," or is this pronouncement merely an excuse for "fun"?

⊞

GLORIA NAYLOR

Formally educated at Brooklyn College and at Yale University, Gloria Naylor (1950–)
began writing *The Women of Brewster Place,* from which this story is taken, while she
was still an undergraduate. Critics note that her fiction "avoids stereotypes [. . .] and
manages to make the reader understand how the economic and social situation of
black lives becomes one with personal lives." Naylor has received a number of important honors, among them the Guggenheim Fellowship.

⊞

Etta Mae Johnson

1   The unpainted walls of the long rectangular room were soaked with the
smell of greasy chicken and warm, headless beer. The brown and pink
faces floated above the trails of used cigarette smoke like bodiless carnival
balloons. The plump yellow woman with white gardenias pinned to the
side of her head stood with her back pressed against the peeling sides of
the baby grand and tried to pierce the bloated hum in the room with her
thin scratchy voice. Undisturbed that she remained for the most part ignored, she motioned for the piano player to begin.

2   It wasn't the music or the words or the woman that took that room by
its throat until it gasped for air—it was the pain. There was a young southern girl, Etta Johnson, pushed up in a corner table, and she never forgot.
The music, the woman, the words.

> I love my man
> I'm a lie if I say I don't
> I love my man
> I'm a lie if I say I don't
> But I'll quit my man
> I'm a lie if I say I won't
>
> My man wouldn't give me no breakfast
> Wouldn't give me no dinner
> Squawked about my supper
> Then he put me out of doors
> Had the nerve to lay
> A matchbox to my clothes
> I didn't have so many
> But I had a long, long, way to go

Children bloomed on Brewster Place during July and August with their colorful shorts and tops plastered against gold, ebony, and nut-brown legs and arms; they decorated the street, rivaling the geraniums and ivy found on the manicured boulevard downtown. The summer heat seemed to draw the people from their cramped apartments onto the stoops, as it drew the tiny drops of perspiration from their foreheads and backs.

The apple-green Cadillac with the white vinyl roof and Florida plates 3 turned into Brewster like a greased cobra. Since Etta had stopped at a Mobil station three blocks away to wash off the evidence of a hot, dusty 1200-mile odyssey home, the chrome caught the rays of the high afternoon sun and flung them back into its face. She had chosen her time well.

The children, free from the conditioned restraints of their older counter- 4 parts, ran along the sidewalks flanking this curious, slow-moving addition to their world. Every eye on the block, either openly or covertly, was on the door of the car when it opened. They were rewarded by the appearance of a pair of white leather sandals attached to narrow ankles and slightly bowed, shapely legs. The willow-green sundress, only ten minutes old on the short chestnut woman, clung to a body that had finished a close second in its race with time. Large two-toned sunglasses hid the weariness that had defied the freshly applied mascara and burnt-ivory shadow. After taking twice the time needed to stretch herself, she reached into the back seat of the car and pulled out her plastic clothes bag and Billie Holiday albums.

The children's curiosity reached the end of its short life span, and they 5 drifted back to their various games. The adults sucked their teeth in disappointment, and the more envious felt self-righteousness twist the corners of their mouths. It was only Etta. Looked like she'd done all right by herself—this time around.

Slowly she carried herself across the street—head high and eyes fixed 6 unwaveringly on her destination. The half-dozen albums were clutched in front of her chest like a cardboard armor.

There ain't nothing I ever do
Or nothing I ever saw
That folks don't criticize me
But I'm doing to do
Just what I want to, anyway
And don't care just what people say
If I should take a notion
To jump into the ocean
Ain't nobody's business if I do . . .

Any who bothered to greet her never used her first name. No one called 7 Etta Mae "Etta," except in their minds; and when they spoke to each other about her, it was Etta Johnson; but when they addressed her directly, it was always Miss Johnson. This baffled her because she knew what they thought about her, and she'd always call them by their first names and invited them to do the same with her. But after a few awkward attempts, they'd fall back into the pattern they were somehow comfortable with. Etta didn't know if this was to keep the distance on her side or theirs, but it was there. And she had learned to tread through these alien undercurrents so well that to a casual observer she had mastered the ancient secret of walking on water.

8   Mattie sat in her frayed brocade armchair, pushed up to the front window, and watched her friend's brave approach through the dusty screen. Still toting around them oversized records, she thought. That woman is a puzzlement.

9   Mattie rose to open the door so Etta wouldn't have to struggle to knock with her arms full. "Lord, child, thank you," she gushed, out of breath. "The younger I get, the higher those steps seem to stretch."

10   She dumped her load on the sofa and swept off her sunglasses. She breathed deeply of the freedom she found in Mattie's presence. Here she had no choice but to be herself. The carefully erected decoys she was constantly shuffling and changing to fit the situation were of no use here. Etta and Mattie went way back, a singular term that claimed coknowledge of all the important events in their lives and almost all of the unimportant ones. And by rights of this possession, it tolerated no secrets.

11   "Sit on down and take a breather. Must have been a hard trip. When you first said you were coming, I didn't expect you to be driving."

12   "To tell the truth, I didn't expect it myself, Mattie. But Simeon got very ornery when I said I was heading home, and he refused to give me the money he'd promised for my plane fare. So I said, just give me half and I'll take the train. Well, he wasn't gonna even do that. And Mattie, you know I'll be damned if I was coming into this city on a raggedy old Greyhound. So one night he was by my place all drunk up and snoring, and as kindly as you please, I took the car keys and registration and so here I am."

13   "My God, woman! You stole the man's car?"

14   "Stole—nothing. He owes me that and then some."

15   "Yeah, but the police don't wanna hear that. It's a wonder the highway patrol ain't stopped you before now."

16   "They ain't stopped me because Simeon didn't report it."

17   "How you know that?"

18   "His wife's daddy is the sheriff of that county." Laughter hung dangerously on the edge of the two women's eyes and lips.

19   "Yeah, but he could say you picked his pockets."

Etta went to her clothes bag and pulled out a pair of pink and red mono-   20
grammed shorts. "I'd have to be a damned good pickpocket to get away
with all this." The laughter lost its weak hold on their mouths and went
bouncing crazily against the walls of the living room.

> Them that's got, shall get
> Them that's not, shall lose
> So the Bible says
> And it still is news

Each time the laughter would try to lie still, the two women would look   21
at each other and send it hurling between them, once again.

> Mamma may have
> Papa may have
> But God bless the child
> That's got his own
> That's got his own

"Lord, Tut, you're a caution." Mattie wiped the tears off her cheeks with   22
the back of a huge dark hand.

Etta was unable to count the years that had passed since she had heard   23
someone call her that. Look a' that baby gal strutting around here like a
bantam. You think she'd be the wife of King Tut. The name had stayed because she never lost the walk. The washed-out grime and red mud of back-
woods Rock Vale, Tennessee, might wrap itself around her bare feet and
coat the back of her strong fleshy legs, but Etta always had her shoulders
flung behind her collarbone and her chin thrust toward the horizon that
came to mean everything Rock Vale did not.

Etta spent her teenage years in constant trouble. Rock Vale had no   24
place for a black woman who was not only unwilling to play by the rules,
but whose spirit challenged the very right of the game to exist. The whites
in Rock Vale were painfully reminded of this rebellion when she looked
them straight in the face while putting in her father's order at the dry
goods store, when she reserved her sirs and mams for those she thought
deserving, and when she smiled only if pleased, regardless of whose presence she was in. That Johnson gal wasn't being an uppity nigger, as talk
had it; she was just being herself.

> Southern trees bear strange fruit
> Blood on the leaves and blood at the root
> Black bodies swinging
> In the southern breeze

Strange fruit hanging
From the poplar trees

25   But Rutherford County wasn't ready for Etta's blooming independence, and so she left one rainy summer night about three hours ahead of dawn and Johnny Brick's furious pursuing relatives. Mattie wrote and told her they had waited in ambush for two days on the county line, and then had returned and burned down her father's barn. The sheriff told Mr. Johnson that he had gotten off mighty light—considering. Mr. Johnson thought so, too. After reading Mattie's letter, Etta was sorry she hadn't killed the horny white bastard when she had the chance.

26   Rock Vale had followed her to Memphis, Detroit, Chicago, and even to New York. Etta soon found out that America wasn't ready for her yet— not in 1937. And so along with the countless other disillusioned, restless children of Ham with so much to give and nowhere to give it, she took her talents to the street. And she learned to get over, to hook herself to any promising rising black star, and when he burnt out, she found another.

27   Her youth had ebbed away quickly under the steady pressure of the changing times, but she was existing as she always had. Even if someone had bothered to stop and tell her that the universe had expanded for her, just an inch, she wouldn't have known how to shine alone.

28   Etta and Mattie had taken totally different roads that with all of their deceptive winding had both ended up on Brewster Place. Their laughter now drew them into a conspiratorial circle against all the Simeons outside of that dead-end street, and it didn't stop until they were both weak from the tears that flowed down their faces.

29   "So," Mattie said, blowing her nose on a large cotton handkerchief, "trusting you say out of jail, what you plan on doing now?"

30   "Child, I couldn't tell you." Etta dropped back down on the couch. "I should be able to get a coupla thousand for the car to tide me over till another business opportunity comes along."

31   Mattie raised one eyebrow just a whisper of an inch. "Ain't it time you got yourself a regular job? These last few years them *business opportunities* been fewer and farther between."

32   Etta sucked her small white teeth. "A job doing what? Come on, Mattie, what kind of experience I got? Six months here, three there. I oughta find me a good man and settle down to live quiet in my old age." She combed her fingers confidently through the thick sandy hair that only needed slight tinting at the roots and mentally gave herself another fifteen years before she had to worry about this ultimate fate.

33   Mattie, watching the creeping tiredness in her eyes, gave her five. "You done met a few promising ones along the way, Etta."

"No, honey, it just seemed so. Let's face it, Mattie. All the good men are 34
either dead or waiting to be born."

"Why don't you come to meeting with me tonight. There's a few settle- 35
minded men in our church, some widowers and such. And a little prayer
wouldn't hurt your soul one bit."

"I'll thank you to leave my soul well alone, Mattie Michael. And if your 36
church is so full of upright Christian men, why you ain't snagged one yet?"

"Etta, I done banked them fires a long time ago, but seeing that you still 37
keeping up steam . . ." Her eyes were full of playful kindness.

"Just barely, Mattie, just barely." 38

And laughter rolled inside of 2E, once again. 39

"Etta, Etta Mae!" Mattie banged on the bathroom door. "Come on out 40
now. You making me late for the meeting."

"Just another second, Mattie. The church ain't gonna walk away." 41

"Lord," Mattie grumbled, "she ain't bigger than a minute, so it shouldn't 42
take more than that to get ready."

Etta came out of the bathroom in an exaggerated rush. "My, my, you the 43
most impatient Christian I know."

"Probably, the only Christian you know." Mattie refused to be humored 44
as she bent to gather up her sweater and purse. She turned and was
stunned with a barrage of colors. A huge white straw hat reigned over layers of gold and pearl beads draped over too much bosom and too little
dress. "You plan on dazzling the Lord, Etta?"

"Well, honey," Etta said, looking down the back of her stocking leg to 45
double-check for runs, "last I heard, He wasn't available. You got more recent news?"

"Um, um, um." Mattie pressed her lips together and shook her head 46
slowly to swallow down the laughter she felt crawling up her throat. Realizing she wasn't going to succeed, she quickly turned her face from Etta
and headed toward the door. "Just bring your blasphemin' self on downstairs. I done already missed morning services waiting on you today."

Canaan Baptist Church, a brooding, ashen giant, sat in the middle of a 47
block of rundown private homes. Its multi-colored, dome-shaped eyes
glowered into the darkness. Fierce clapping and thunderous organ chords
came barreling out of its mouth. Evening services had begun.

Canaan's congregation, the poor who lived in a thirty-block area 48
around Brewster Place, still worshiped God loudly. They could not afford
the refined, muted benediction of the more prosperous blacks who went to
Sinai Baptist on the northern end of the city, and because each of their requests for comfort was so pressing, they took no chances that He did not
hear them.

> When Israel was in Egypt's land
> Let my people go
> Oppressed so hard, they could not stand
> Let my people go

49   The words were as ancient as the origin of their misery, but the tempo had picked up threefold in its evolution from the cotton fields. They were now sung with the frantic determination of a people who realized that the world was swiftly changing but for some mystic, complex reason their burden had not.

> God said to go down
> Go down
> Brother Moses
> Brother Moses
> To the shore of the great Nile River

50   The choir clapped and stomped each syllable into a devastating reality, and just as it did, the congregation reached up, grabbed the phrase, and tried to clap and stomp it back into oblivion.

> Go to Egypt
> Go to Egypt
> Tell Pharaoh
> Tell Pharaoh
> Let my people go

51   Etta entered the back of the church like a reluctant prodigal, prepared at best to be amused. The alien pounding and the heat and the dark glistening bodies dragged her back, back past the cold ashes of her innocence to a time when pain could be castrated on the sharp edges of iron-studded faith. The blood rushed to her temples and began to throb in union with the musical pleas around her.

> Yes, my God is a mighty God
> Lord, deliver
> And he set old Israel free
> Swallowed that Egyptian army
> Lord, deliver
> With the waves of the great Red Sea

52   Etta glanced at Mattie, who was swaying and humming, and she saw that the lines in her face had almost totally vanished. She had left Etta in just that moment for a place where she was free. Sadly, Etta looked at her, at them all, and was very envious. Unaccustomed to the irritating texture

of doubt, she felt tears as its abrasiveness grated over the fragile skin of her life. Could there have been another way?

The song ended with a huge expulsion of air, and the congregation sat   53
down as one body.

"Come on, let's get us a seat." Mattie tugged her by the arm.   54

The grizzled church deacon with his suit hanging loosely off his stooped   55
shoulders went up to the pulpit to read the church business.

"That's one of the widowers I was telling you about," Mattie whispered,   56
and poked Etta.

"Unmm." The pressure on her arm brought Etta back onto the uncom-   57
fortable wooden pew. But she didn't want to stay there, so she climbed
back out the window, through the glass eyes of the seven-foot Good Shepherd, and started again the futile weaving of invisible ifs and slippery
mights into an equally unattainable past.

The scenes of her life reeled out before her with the same aging script;   58
but now hindsight sat as the omniscient director and had the young star
of her epic recite different brilliant lines and make the sort of stunning decisions that propelled her into the cushioned front pews on the right of
the minister's podium. There she sat with the deacons' wives, officers of
the Ladies' Auxiliary, and head usherettes. And like them, she would wear
on her back a hundred pairs of respectful eyes earned the hard way, and not
the way she had earned the red sundress, which she now self-consciously
tugged up in the front. Was it too late?

The official business completed, the treasurer pulled at his frayed lapels,   59
cleared his throat, and announced the guest speaker for the night.

The man was magnificent.   60

He glided to the podium with the effortlessness of a well-oiled machine   61
and stood still for an interminable long moment. He eyed the congregation confidently. He only needed their attention for that split second because once he got it, he was going to wrap his voice around their souls and
squeeze until they screamed to be relieved. The knew it was coming and
waited expectantly, breathing in unison as one body. First he played with
them and threw out fine silken threads that stroked their heart muscles
ever so gently. They trembled ecstatically at the touch and invited more.
The threads multiplied and entwined themselves solidly around the one
pulsating organ they had become and tightened slightly, testing them for
a reaction.

The "Amen, brothers" and "Yes, Jesus" were his permission to take that   62
short hop from the heart to the soul and lay all pretense of gentleness
aside. Now he would have to push and pound with clenched fists in order
to be felt, and he dared not stop the fierce rhythm of his voice until their
replies had reached that fevered pitch of satisfaction. Yes, Lord—grind

out the unheated tenements! Merciful Jesus—shove aside the low-paying boss man. Perfect Father—fill me, fill me till there's no room, no room for nothing else, not even that great big world out there that exacts such a strange penalty for my being born black.

63   It was hard work. There was so much in them that had to be replaced. The minister's chest was heaving in long spasms, and the sweat was pouring down his gray temples and rolling under his chin. His rich voice was now hoarse, and his legs and raised arms trembled on the edge of collapse. And as always they were satisfied a half-breath before he reached the end of his endurance. They sat back, limp and spent, but momentarily at peace. There was no price too high for this service. At that instant they would have followed him to do battle with the emperor of the world, and all he was going to ask of them was money for the "Lord's work." And they would willingly give over half of their little to keep this man in comfort.

64   Etta had not been listening to the message; she was watching the man. His body moved with the air of one who had not known recent deprivation. The tone of his skin and the fullness around his jawline told her that he was well-off, even before she got close enough to see the manicured hands and diamond pinkie ring.

65   The techniques he had used to brand himself on the minds of the congregation were not new to her. She'd encountered talent like that in poolrooms, nightclubs, grimy second-floor insurance offices, numbers dens, and on a dozen street corners. But here was a different sort of power. The jungle-sharpened instincts of a man like that could move her up to the front of the church, ahead of the deacons' wives and Ladies' Auxiliary, off of Brewster Place for good. She would find not only luxury but a place that complemented the type of woman she had fought all these years to become.

66   "Mattie, is that your regular minister?" she whispered.

67   "Who, Reverend Woods? No, he just visits on occasion, but he sure can preach, can't he?"

68   "What you know about him, he married?"

69   Mattie cut her eyes at Etta. "I should have figured it wasn't the sermon that moved you. At least wait till after the prayer before you jump all into the man's business."

70   During the closing song and prayer Etta was planning how she was going to maneuver Mattie to the front of the church and into introducing her to Reverend Woods. It wasn't going to be as difficult as she thought. Moreland T. Woods had noticed Etta from the moment she'd entered the church. She stood out like a bright red bird among the drab morality that dried up the breasts and formed rolls round the stomachs of the other church sisters. This woman was still dripping with the juices of a full-

fleshed life—the kind of life he was soon to get up and damn into hell for the rest of the congregation—but how it fitted her well. He had to swallow to remove the excess fluid from his mouth before he got up to preach.

Now the problem was to make his way to the back of the church before   71
she left without seeming to be in a particular hurry. A half-dozen back slaps, handshakes, and thank-you sisters only found him about ten feet up the aisle, and he was growing impatient. However, he didn't dare to turn his neck and look in the direction where he'd last seen her. He felt a hand on his upper arm and turned to see a grim-faced Mattie flanked by the woman in the scarlet dress.

"Reverend Woods, I really enjoyed your sermon," Mattie said.   72

"Why, thank you, sister—sister?"   73

"Sister Michael, Mattie Michael." While he was addressing his words to   74
her, the smile he sent over her shoulder to Etta was undeniable.

"Especially the part," Mattie raised her voice a little, "about throwing   75
away temptation to preserve the soul. That was a mighty fine point."

"The Lord moves me and I speak, Sister Michael. I'm just a humble in-   76
strument for his voice."

The direction and intent of his smile was not lost to Etta. She inched   77
her way in front of Mattie. "I enjoyed it, too, Reverend Woods. It's been a long time since I heard preaching like that." She increased the pressure of her fingers on Mattie's arm.

"Oh, excuse my manners. Reverend Woods, this is an old friend of   78
mine, Etta Mae Johnson. Etta Mae, Reverend Woods." She intoned the words as if she were reciting a eulogy.

"Pleased to meet you, Sister Johnson." He beamed down on the small   79
woman and purposely held her hand a fraction longer than usual. "You must be a new member—I don't recall seeing you the times I've been here before."

"Well, no, Reverend, I'm not a member of the congregation, but I was   80
raised up in the church. You know how it is, as you get older sometimes you stray away. But after your sermon, I'm truly thinking of coming back."

Mattie tensed, hoping that the lightning that God was surely going to   81
strike Etta with wouldn't hit her by mistake.

"Well, you know what the Bible says, sister. The angels rejoice more   82
over one sinner who turns around than over ninety-nine righteous ones."

"Yes, indeed, and I'm sure a shepherd like you has helped to turn many   83
back to the fold." She looked up and gave him the full benefit of her round dark eyes, grateful she hadn't put on that third coat of mascara.

"I try, Sister Johnson, I try."   84

"It's a shame Mrs. Woods wasn't here tonight to hear you. I'm sure she   85
must be mighty proud of your work."

86   "My wife has gone to her glory, Sister Johnson. I think of myself now as a man alone—rest her soul."

87   "Yes, rest her soul," Etta sighed.

88   "Please, Lord, yes," Mattie muttered, giving out the only sincere request among the three. The intensity of her appeal startled them, and they turned to look at her. "Only knows how hard this life is, she's better in the arms of Jesus."

89   "Yes"—Etta narrowed her eyes at Mattie and then turned back to the minister—"I can testify to that. Being a woman alone, it seems all the more hard. Sometimes you don't know where to turn."

90   Moreland Woods knew Etta was the type of woman who not only knew which way to turn, but, more often than not, had built her own roads when nothing else was accessible. But he was enjoying this game immensely—almost as much as the growing heat creeping into his groin.

91   "Well, if I can be of any assistance, Sister Johnson, don't hesitate to ask. I couldn't sleep knowing one of the Lord's sheep is troubled. As a matter of fact, if you have anything you would like to discuss with me this evening, I'd be glad to escort you home."

92   "I don't have my own place. You see, I'm just up from out of state and staying with my friend Mattie here."

93   "Well, perhaps we could all go out for coffee."

94   "Thank you, but I'll have to decline, Reverend," Mattie volunteered before Etta did it for her. "The services have me all tired out, but if Etta wants to, she's welcome."

95   "That'll be just fine," Etta said.

96   "Good, good." And now it was his turn to give her the benefit of a mouth full of strong gold-capped teeth. "Just let me say good-bye to a few folks here, and I'll meet you outside."

97   "Girl, you oughta patent that speed and sell it to the airplane companies," Mattie said outside. "'After that sermon, Reverend, I'm thinking of coming back'—indeed!"

98   "Aw, hush your fussing."

99   "I declare if you had batted them lashes just a little faster, we'd of had a dust storm in there."

100   "You said you wanted me to meet some nice men. Well, I met one."

101   "Etta, I meant a man who'd be serious about settling down with you." Mattie was exasperated. "Why, you're going on like a schoolgirl. Can't you see what he's got in mind?"

102   Etta turned an indignant face toward Mattie. "The only thing I see is that you're telling me I'm not good enough for a man like that. Oh, no, not Etta Johnson. No upstanding decent man could ever see anything in

her but a quick good time. Well, I'll tell you something, Mattie Michael. I've always traveled first class, maybe not in the way you'd approve with all your fine Christian principles, but it's done all right by me. And I'm gonna keep going top drawer till I leave this earth. Don't you think I got a mirror? Each year there's a new line to cover. I lay down with this body and get up with it every morning, and each morning it cries for just a little more rest than it did the day before. Well, I'm finally gonna get that rest, and it's going to be with a man like Reverend Woods. And you and the rest of those slack-mouthed gossips on Brewster be damned!" Tears frosted the edges of her last words. "They'll be humming a different tune when I show up there the wife of a big preacher. I've always known what they say about me behind my back, but I never thought you were right in there with them."

Mattie was stunned by Etta's tirade. How could Etta have so totally   103
misunderstood her words? What had happened back there to stuff up her senses to the point that she had missed the obvious? Surely she could not believe that the vibrations coming from that unholy game of charades in the church aisle would lead to something as permanent as marriage? Why, it had been nothing but the opening gestures to a mating dance. Mattie had gone through the same motions at least once in her life, and Etta must have known a dozen variations to it that were a mystery to her. And yet, somehow, back there it had been played to a music that had totally distorted the steps for her friend. Mattie suddenly felt the helplessness of a person who is forced to explain that for which there are no words.

She quietly turned her back and started down the steps. There was no   104
need to defend herself against Etta's accusations. They shared at least a hundred memories that could belie those cruel words. Let them speak for her.

Sometimes being a friend means mastering that art of timing. There is   105
a time for silence. A time to let go and allow people to hurl themselves into their own destiny. And a time to prepare to pick up the pieces when it's all over. Mattie realized that this moment called for all three.

"I'll see ya when you get home, Etta," she threw gently over her shoulder.   106

Etta watched the bulky figure become slowly enveloped by the shadows.   107
Her angry words had formed a thick mucus in her throat, and she couldn't swallow them down. She started to run into the darkness where she'd seen Mattie disappear, but at that instant Moreland Woods came out of the lighted church, beaming.

He took her arm and helped her into the front seat of his car. Her back   108
sank into the deep upholstered leather, and the smell of the freshly vacuumed carpet was mellow in her nostrils. All of the natural night sounds of the city were blocked by the thick tinted windows and the hum of the air

conditioner, but they trailed persistently behind the polished back of the vehicle as it turned and headed down the long gray boulevard.

> Smooth road
> Clear day
> But why am I the only one
> Traveling this way
> How strange the road to love
> Can be so easy
> Can there be a detour ahead?

109   Moreland Woods was captivated by the beautiful woman at his side. Her firm brown flesh and bright eyes carried the essence of nectar from some untamed exotic flower, and the fragrance was causing a pleasant disturbance at the pit of his stomach. He marveled at how excellently she played the game. A less alert observer might have been taken in, but his survival depended upon knowing people, knowing exactly how much to give and how little to take. It was this razor-thin instinct that had catapulted him to the head of his profession and that would keep him there.

110   And although she cut her cards with a reckless confidence, pushed her chips into the middle of the table as though the supply was unlimited, and could sit out the game until dawn, he knew. Oh, yes. Let her win a few, and then he would win just a few more, and she would be bankrupt long before the sun was up. And then there would be only one thing left to place on the table—and she would, because the stakes they were playing for were very high. But she was going to lose that last deal. She would lose because when she first sat down in that car she had everything riding on the fact that he didn't know the game existed.

111   And so it went. All evening Etta had been in another world, weaving his tailored suit and the smell of his expensive cologne into a custom-made future for herself. It took his last floundering thrusts into her body to bring her back to reality. She arrived in enough time to feel him beating against her like a dying walrus, until he shuddered and was still.

112   She kept her eyes closed because she knew when she opened them there would be the old familiar sights around her. To her right would be the plastic-coated nightstand that matched the cheaply carved headboard of the bed she lay in. She felt the bleached coarseness of the sheet under her sweaty back and predicted the roughness of the worn carpet path that led from the bed to the white-tiled bathroom with bright fluorescent light, sterilized towels, and tissue-wrapped water glasses. There would be two or three small thin rectangles of soap wrapped in bright waxy covers that bore the name of the hotel.

She didn't try to visualize what the name would be. It didn't matter. 113
They were all the same, all meshed together into one lump that rested like
an iron ball on her chest. And the expression on the face of this breathing
mass to her left would be the same as all the others. She could turn now
and go through the rituals that would tie up the evening for them both, but
she wanted just one more second of this smoothing darkness before she had
to face the echoes of the locking doors she knew would be in his eyes.

Etta got out of the car unassisted and didn't bother to turn and watch the 114
taillights as it pulled off down the deserted avenue adjacent to Brewster
Place. She had asked him to leave her at the corner because there was no
point in his having to make a U-turn in the dead-end street, and it was
less than a hundred yards to her door. Moreland was relieved that she had
made it easy for him, because it had been a long day and he was anxious
to get home and go to sleep. But then, the whole business had gone pretty
smoothly after they left the hotel. He hadn't even been called upon to use
any of the excuses he had prepared for why it would be a while before he'd
see her again. A slight frown crossed his forehead as he realized that she
had seemed as eager to get away from him as he had been to leave. Well,
he shrugged his shoulders and placated his dented ego, that's the nice part
about these worldly women. They understand the temporary weakness of
the flesh and don't make it out to be something bigger than it is. They can
have a good time without pawing and hanging all onto a man. Maybe I
should drop around sometime. He glanced into his rearview mirror and
saw that Etta was still standing on the corner, looking straight ahead into
Brewster. There was something about the slumped profile of her body, sil-
houetted against the dim street light, that caused him to press down on
the accelerator.

Etta stood looking at the wall that closed off Brewster from the avenues 115
farther north and found it hard to believe that it had been just this afternoon when she had seen it. It had looked so different then, with the August sun highlighting the browns and reds of the bricks and the young
children bouncing their rubber balls against its side. Now it crouched
there in the thin predawn light, like a pulsating mouth awaiting her arrival. She shook her head sharply to rid herself of the illusion, but an un-
canny fear gripped her, and her legs felt like lead. If I walk into the street,
she thought, I'll never come back. I'll never get out. Oh, dear God, I am
so tired—so very tired.

Etta removed her hat and massaged her tight forehead. Then, giving a 116
resigned sigh, she started slowly down the street. Had her neighbors been
out on their front stoops, she could have passed through their milling

clusters as anonymously as the night wind. They had seen her come down that street once in a broken Chevy that had about five hundred dollars' worth of contraband liquor in its trunk, and there was even the time she'd come home with a broken nose she'd gotten in some hair-raising escapade in St. Louis, but never had she walked among them with a broken spirit. This middle-aged woman in the wrinkled dress and wilted straw hat would have been a stranger to them.

117   When Etta got to the stoop, she noticed there was a light under the shade at Mattie's window, and she strained to hear what actually sounded like music coming from behind the screen. Mattie was playing her records! Etta stood very still, trying to decipher the broken air waves into intelligible sound, but she couldn't make out the words. She stopped straining when it suddenly came to her that it wasn't important what song it was—someone was waiting up for her. Someone who would deny fiercely that there had been any concern—just a little indigestion from them fried onions that kept me from sleeping. Thought I'd pass the time by figuring out what you seen in all this loose-life music.

118   Etta laughed softly to herself as she climbed the steps toward the light and the love and the comfort that awaited her.

QUESTIONING AND DISCUSSING

Naylor, "Etta Mae Johnson"

1. What are the central conflicts in this story? How can these be described as moral or ethical conflicts?

2. Analyze Gloria Naylor's use of language in describing Mattie and Etta. How do the two women differ? How would you characterize their relationship? How is it pivotal to the story?

3. Examine and analyze the paragraphs introducing Reverend Woods—and note when Naylor stops using *Reverend* before his name. What impression do you have of him? What might Naylor want the reader to feel when she describes Woods's thinking toward the end of the story: "Well [. . .] that's the nice part about these worldly women. They understand the temporary weakness of the flesh and don't make it out to be something bigger than it is"?

4. How does Naylor suggest that notions of morality depend on whether the person is male or female? Why would Naylor use the extended metaphor of a poker game—in itself not always considered the most high-minded of activities—to describe relationships between men and women?

⊞

AMY TAN

"Two Kinds" is a small part of Amy Tan's (1952–) first novel, *The Joy Luck Club* (1989). Tan wrote the book at the urging of a literary agent who suggested that she explore the intergenerational conflicts and relationships among generations of Chinese mothers and daughters in the United States. Tan has also written a second novel, *The Kitchen God's Wife* (1992), and a children's book.

⊞

Two Kinds

My mother believed you could be anything you wanted to be in America. You could open a restaurant. You could work for the government and get good retirement. You could buy a house with almost no money down. You could become rich. You could become instantly famous. 1

"Of course you can be prodigy, too," my mother told me when I was nine. "You can be best anything. What does Auntie Lindo know? Her daughter, she is only best tricky." 2

America was where all my mother's hopes lay. She had come here in 1949 after losing everything in China: her mother and father, her family home, her first husband, and two daughters, twin baby girls. But she never looked back with regret. There were so many ways for things to get better. 3

We didn't immediately pick the right kind of prodigy. At first my mother thought I could be a Chinese Shirley Temple. We'd watch Shirley's old movies on TV as though they were training films. My mother would poke my arm and say, *"Ni kan"*—You watch. And I would see Shirley tapping her feet, or singing a sailor song, or pursing her lips into a very round O while saying, "Oh my goodness." 4

"Ni kan," said my mother as Shirley's eyes flooded with tears. "You already know how. Don't need talent for crying!" 5

Soon after my mother got this idea about Shirley Temple, she took me to a beauty training school in the Mission district and put me in the hands of a student who could barely hold the scissors without shaking. Instead of getting big fat curls, I emerged with an uneven mass of crinkly black fuzz. My mother dragged me off to the bathroom and tried to wet down my hair. 6

"You look like Negro Chinese," she lamented, as if I had done this on purpose. 7

The instructor of the beauty training school had to lop off these soggy clumps to make my hair even again. "Peter Pan is very popular these days," 8 the instructor assured my mother. I now had hair the length of a boy's, with straight-across bangs that hung at a slant two inches above my eyebrows. I liked the haircut and it made me actually look forward to my future fame.

9 In fact, in the beginning, I was just as excited as my mother, maybe even more so. I pictured this prodigy part of me as many different images, trying each one on for size. I was a dainty ballerina girl standing by the curtains, waiting to hear the right music that would send me floating on my tiptoes. I was like the Christ child lifted out of the straw manager, crying with holy indignity. I was Cinderella stepping from her pumpkin carriage with sparkly cartoon music filling the air.

10 In all of my imaginings, I was filled with a sense that I would soon become *perfect*. My mother and father would adore me. I would be beyond reproach. I would never feel the need to sulk for anything.

11 But sometimes the prodigy in me became impatient. "If you don't hurry up and get me out of here, I'm disappearing for good," it warned. "And then you'll always be nothing."

12 Every night after dinner, my mother and I would sit at the Formica kitchen table. She would present new tests, taking her examples from stories of amazing children she had read in *Ripley's Believe It or Not,* or *Good Housekeeping, Reader's Digest,* and a dozen other magazines she kept in a pile in our bathroom. My mother got these magazines from people whose houses she cleaned. And since she cleaned many houses each week, we had a great assortment. She would look through them all, searching for stories about remarkable children.

13 The first night she brought out a story about a three-year-old boy who knew the capitals of all the states and even most of the European countries. A teacher was quoted as saying the little boy could also pronounce the names of the foreign cities correctly.

14 "What's the capital of Finland?" my mother asked me, looking at the magazine story.

15 All I knew was the capital of California, because Sacramento was the name of the street we lived on in Chinatown. "Nairobi!" I guessed, saying the most foreign word I could think of. She checked to see if that was possibly one way to pronounce "Helsinki" before showing me the answer.

16 The tests got harder—multiplying numbers in my head, finding the queen of hearts in a deck of cards, trying to stand on my head without using my hands, predicting the daily temperatures in Los Angeles, New York, and London.

17 One night I had to look at a page from the Bible for three minutes and then report everything I could remember. "Now Jehoshaphat had riches and honor in abundance and . . . that's all I remember, Ma," I said.

After seeing my mother's disappointed face once again, something in- 18
side of me began to die. I hated the tests, the raised hopes and failed expectations. Before going to bed that night, I looked in the mirror above
the bathroom sink and when I saw only my face staring back—and that it
would always be this ordinary face—I began to cry. Such a sad, ugly girl! I
made high-pitched noises like a crazed animal, trying to scratch out the
face in the mirror.

And then I saw what seemed to be the prodigy side of me—because I 19
had never seen that face before. I looked at my reflection, blinking so I
could see more clearly. The girl staring back at me was angry, powerful.
This girl and I were the same. I had new thoughts, willful thoughts, or
rather thoughts filled with lots of won'ts. I won't let her change me, I
promised myself. I won't be what I'm not.

So now on nights when my mother presented her tests, I performed list- 20
lessly, my head propped on one arm. I pretended to be bored. And I was. I
got so bored I started counting the bellows of the foghorns out on the bay
while my mother drilled me in other areas. The sound was comforting and
reminded me of the cow jumping over the moon. And the next day, I
played a game with myself, seeing if my mother would give up on me before eight bellows. After a while I usually counted only one, maybe two
bellows at most. At last she was beginning to give up hope.

Two or three months had gone by without any mention of my being a 21
prodigy again. And then one day my mother was watching *The Ed Sullivan
Show* on TV. The TV was old and the sound kept shorting out. Every time
my mother got halfway up from the sofa to adjust the set, the sound would
go back on and Ed would be talking. As soon as she sat down, Ed would go
silent again. She got up, the TV broke into loud piano music. She sat
down. Silence. Up and down, back and forth, quiet and loud. It was like a
stiff embraceless dance between her and the TV set. Finally she stood by
the set with her hand on the sound dial.

She seemed entranced by the music, a little frenzied piano piece with 22
this mesmerizing quality, sort of quick passages and then teasing lilting
ones before it returned to the quick playful parts.

"*Ni kan*," my mother said, calling me over with hurried hand gestures. 23
"Look here."

I could see why my mother was fascinated by the music. It was being 24
pounded out by a little Chinese girl, about nine years old, with a Peter
Pan haircut. The girl had the sauciness of a Shirley Temple. She was
proudly modest like a proper Chinese child. And she also did this fancy
sweep of a curtsy, so that the fluffy skirt of her white dress cascaded slowly
to the floor like the petals of a large carnation.

25   In spite of these warning signs, I wasn't worried. Our family had no piano and we couldn't afford to buy one, let alone reams of sheet music and piano lessons. So I could be generous in my comments when my mother bad-mouthed the little girl on TV.

26   "Play note right, but doesn't sound good! No singing sound," complained my mother.

27   "What are you picking on her for?" I said carelessly. "She's pretty good. Maybe she's not the best, but she's trying hard." I knew almost immediately I would be sorry I said that.

28   "Just like you," she said. "Not the best. Because you not trying." She gave a little huff as she let go of the sound dial and sat down on the sofa.

29   The little Chinese girl sat down also to play an encore of "Anitra's Dance" by Grieg. I remember the song, because later on I had to learn how to play it.

30   Three days after watching *The Ed Sullivan Show,* my mother told me what my schedule would be for piano lessons and piano practice. She had talked to Mr. Chong, who lived on the first floor of our apartment building. Mr. Chong was a retired piano teacher and my mother had traded housecleaning services for weekly lessons and a piano for me to practice on every day, two hours a day, from four until six.

31   When my mother told me this, I felt as though I had been sent to hell. I whined and then kicked my foot a little when I couldn't stand it anymore.

32   "Why don't you like me the way I am? I'm *not* a genius! I can't play the piano. And even if I could, I wouldn't go on TV if you paid me a million dollars!" I cried.

33   My mother slapped me. "Who ask you be genius?" she shouted. "Only ask you be your best. For you sake. You think I want you be genius? Hnnh! What for! Who ask you!"

34   "So ungrateful," I heard her mutter in Chinese. "If she had as much talent as she has temper, she would be famous now."

35   Mr. Chong, whom I secretly nicknamed Old Chong, was very strange, always tapping his fingers to the silent music of an invisible orchestra. He looked ancient in my eyes. He had lost most of the hair on top of his head and he wore thick glasses and had eyes that always looked tired and sleepy. But he must have been younger than I thought, since he lived with his mother and was not yet married.

36   I met Old Lady Chong once and that was enough. She had this peculiar smell like a baby that had done something in its pants. And her fingers felt like a dead person's, like an old peach I once found in the back of the refrigerator; the skin just slid off the meat when I picked it up.

I soon found out why Old Chong had retired from teaching piano. He   37
was deaf. "Like Beethoven!" he shouted to me. "We're both listening only
in our head!" And he would start to conduct his frantic silent sonatas.

Our lessons went like this. He would open the book and point to differ-   38
ent things, explaining their purpose: "Key! Treble! Bass! No sharps or
flats! So this is C major! Listen now and play after me!"

And then he would play the C scale a few times, a simple chord, and   39
then, as if inspired by an old, unreachable itch, he gradually added more
notes and running trills and a pounding bass until the music was really
something quite grand.

I would play after him, the simple scale, the simple chord, and then I   40
just played some nonsense that sounded like a cat running up and down
on top of garbage cans. Old Chong smiled and applauded and then said,
"Very good! But now you must learn to keep time!"

So that's how I discovered that Old Chong's eyes were too slow to keep   41
up with the wrong notes I was playing. He went through the motions in
half-time. To help me keep rhythm, he stood behind me, pushing down
on my right shoulder for every beat. He balanced pennies on top of my
wrists so I would keep them still as I slowly played scales and arpeggios. He
had me curve my hand around an apple and keep that shape when playing chords. He marched stiffly to show me how to make each finger dance
up and down, staccato like an obedient little soldier.

He taught me all these things, and that was how I also learned I could   42
be lazy and get away with mistakes, lots of mistakes. If I hit the wrong
notes because I hadn't practiced enough, I never corrected myself. I just
kept playing in rhythm. And Old Chong kept conducting his own private reverie.

So maybe I never really gave myself a fair chance. I did pick up the   43
basics pretty quickly, and I might have become a good pianist at that
young age. But I was so determined not to try, not to be anybody different
that I learned to play only the most ear-splitting preludes, the most discordant hymns.

Over the next year, I practiced like this, dutifully in my own way. And   44
then one day I heard my mother and her friend Lindo Jong both talking
in a loud bragging tone of voice so others could hear. It was after church,
and I was leaning against the brick wall wearing a dress with stiff white
petticoats. Auntie Lindo's daughter, Waverly, who was about my age, was
standing farther down the wall about five feet away. We had grown up together and shared all the closeness of two sisters squabbling over crayons
and dolls. In other words, for the most part, we hated each other. I
thought she was snotty. Waverly Jong had gained a certain amount of
fame as "Chinatown's Littlest Chinese Chess Champion."

45　"She bring home too many trophy," lamented Auntie Lindo that Sunday. "All day she play chess. All day I have no time do nothing but dust off her winnings." She threw a scolding look at Waverly, who pretended not to see her.

46　"You lucky you don't have this problem," said Auntie Lindo with a sigh to my mother.

47　And my mother squared her shoulders and bragged: "Our problem worser than yours. If we ask Jing-mei wash dish, she hear nothing but music. It's like you can't stop this natural talent."

48　And right then, I was determined to put a stop to her foolish pride.

49　A few weeks later, Old Chong and my mother conspired to have me play in a talent show which would be held in the church hall. By then, my parents had saved up enough to buy me a secondhand piano, a black Wurlitzer spinet with a scarred bench. It was the showpiece of our living room.

50　For the talent show, I was to play a piece called "Pleading Child" from Schumann's *Scenes from Childhood*. It was a simple, moody piece that sounded more difficult than it was. I was supposed to memorize the whole thing, playing the repeat parts twice to make the piece sound longer. But I dawdled over it, playing a few bars and then cheating, looking up to see what notes followed. I never really listened to what I was playing. I daydreamed about being somewhere else, about being someone else.

51　The part I liked to practice best was the fancy curtsy: right foot out, touch the rose on the carpet with a pointed foot, sweep to the side, left leg bends, look up and smile.

52　My parents invited all the couples from the Joy Luck Club to witness my debut. Auntie Lindo and Uncle Tin were there. Waverly and her two older brothers had also come. The first two rows were filled with children both younger and older than I was. The littlest ones got to go first. They recited simple nursery rhymes, squawked out tunes on miniature violins, twirled Hula Hoops, pranced in pink ballet tutus, and when they bowed or curtsied, the audience would sign in unison, "Awww," and then clap enthusiastically.

53　When my turn came, I was very confident. I remember my childish excitement. It was as if I knew, without a doubt, that the prodigy side of me really did exist. I had no fear whatsoever, no nervousness. I remember thinking to myself, This is it! This is it! I looked out over the audience, at my mother's blank face, my father's yawn, Auntie Lindo's still-lipped smile, Waverly's sulky expression. I had on a white dress layered with sheets of lace, and a pink bow in my Peter Pan haircut. As I sat down I envisioned people jumping to their feet and Ed Sullivan rushing up to introduce me to everyone on TV.

And I started to play. It was so beautiful. I was so caught up in how 54
lovely I looked that at first I didn't worry how I would sound. So it was a
surprise to me when I hit the first wrong note and I realized something
didn't sound quite right. And then I hit another and another followed
that. A chill started at the top of my head and began to trickle down. Yet
I couldn't stop playing, as though my hands were bewitched. I kept thinking my fingers would adjust themselves back, like a train switching to the
right track. I played this strange jumble through two repeats, the sour
notes staying with me all the way to the end.

When I stood up, I discovered my legs were shaking. Maybe I had just 55
been nervous and the audience, like Old Chong, had seen me go through
the right motions and had not heard anything wrong at all. I swept my
right foot out, went down on my knee, looked up and smiled. The room
was quiet, except for Old Chong, who was beaming and shouting, "Bravo!
Bravo! Well done!" But then I saw my mother's face, her stricken face.
The audience clapped weakly, and as I walked back to my chair, with my
whole face quivering as I tried not to cry, I heard a little boy whisper
loudly to his mother, "That was awful," and the mother whispered back,
"Well, she certainly tried."

And now I realized how many people were in the audience, the whole 56
world it seemed. I was aware of eyes burning into my back. I felt the shame
of my mother and father as they sat stiffly throughout the rest of the show.

We could have escaped during intermission. Pride and some strange 57
sense of honor must have anchored my parents to their chairs. And so we
watched it all: the eighteen-year-old boy with a fake mustache who did a
magic show and juggled flaming hoops while riding a unicycle. The
breasted girl with white makeup who sang from *Madame Butterfly* and got
honorable mention. And the eleven-year-old boy who won first prize
playing a tricky violin song that sounded like a busy bee.

After the show, the Hsus, the Jongs, and the St. Clairs from the Joy 58
Luck Club came up to my mother and father.

"Lots of talented kids," Auntie Lindo said vaguely, smiling broadly. 59

"That was somethin' else," said my father, and I wondered if he was re- 60
ferring to me in a humorous way, or whether he even remembered what I
had done.

Waverly looked at me and shrugged her shoulders. "You aren't a genius 61
like me," she said matter-of-factly. And if I hadn't felt so bad, I would have
pulled her braids and punched her stomach.

But my mother's expression was what devastated me: a quiet, blank look 62
that said she had lost everything. I felt the same way, and it seemed as if
everybody were now coming up, like gawkers at the scene of an accident, to
see what parts were actually missing. When we got on the bus to go home,

my father was humming the busy-bee tune and my mother was silent. I kept thinking she wanted to wait until we got home before shouting at me. But when my father unlocked the door to our apartment, my mother walked in and then went to the back, into the bedroom. No accusations. No blame. And in a way, I felt disappointed. I had been waiting for her to start shouting, so I could shout back and cry and blame her for all my misery.

63   I assumed my talent-show fiasco meant I never had to play the piano again. But two days later, after school, my mother came out of the kitchen and saw me watching TV.

64   "Four clock," she reminded me as if it were any other day. I was stunned, as though she were asking me to go through the talent-show torture again. I wedged myself more tightly in front of the TV.

65   "Turn off TV," she called from the kitchen five minutes later.

66   I didn't budge. And then I decided. I didn't have to do what my mother said anymore. I wasn't her slave. This wasn't China. I had listened to her before and look what happened. She was the stupid one.

67   She came out from the kitchen and stood in the arched entryway of the living room. "Four clock," she said once again, louder.

68   "I'm not going to play anymore," I said nonchalantly. "Why should I? I'm not a genius."

69   She walked over and stood in front of the TV. I saw her chest was heaving up and down in an angry way.

70   "No!" I said, and I now felt stronger, as if my true self had finally emerged. So this was what had been inside me all along.

71   "No! I won't!" I screamed.

72   She yanked me by the arm, pulled me off the floor, snapped off the TV. She was frighteningly strong, half pulling, half carrying me toward the piano as I kicked the throw rugs under my feet. She lifted me up and onto the hard bench. I was sobbing by now, looking at her bitterly. Her chest was heaving even more and her mouth was open, smiling crazily as if she were pleased I was crying.

73   "You want me to be someone that I'm not!" I sobbed. "I'll never be the kind of daughter you want me to be!"

74   "Only two kinds of daughters," she shouted in Chinese. "Those who are obedient and those who follow their own mind! Only one kind of daughter can live in this house. Obedient daughter!"

75   "Then I wish I wasn't your daughter. I wish you weren't my mother," I shouted. As I said these things I got scared. I felt like worms and toads and slimy things were crawling out of my chest, but it also felt good, as if this awful side of me had surfaced at last.

"Too late change this," said my mother shrilly.   76

And I could sense her anger rising to its breaking point. I wanted to see   77
it spill over. And that's when I remembered the babies she had lost in
China, the ones we never talked about. "Then I wish I'd never been
born!" I shouted. "I wish I were dead! Like them."

It was as if I had said the magic words, Alakazam!—and her face went   78
blank, her mouth closed, her arms went slack, and she backed out of the
room, stunned, as if she were blowing away like a small brown leaf, thin,
brittle, lifeless.

It was not the only disappointment my mother felt in me. In the years   79
that followed, I failed her so many times, each time asserting my own will,
my right to fall short of expectations. I didn't get straight As. I didn't become class president. I didn't get into Stanford. I dropped out of college.

For unlike my mother, I did not believe I could be anything I wanted to   80
be. I could only be me.

And for all those years, we never talked about the disaster at the recital   81
or my terrible accusations afterward at the piano bench. All that remained unchecked, like a betrayal that was now unspeakable. So I never
found a way to ask her why she had hoped for something so large that failure was inevitable.

And even worse, I never asked her what frightened me the most: Why   82
had she given up hope?

For after our struggle at the piano, she never mentioned my playing   83
again. The lessons stopped, the lid to the piano was closed, shutting out
the dust, my misery, and her dreams.

So she surprised me. A few years ago, she offered to give me the piano,   84
for my thirtieth birthday. I had not played in all those years. I saw the offer as a sign of forgiveness, a tremendous burden removed.

"Are you sure?" I asked shyly. "I mean, won't you and Dad miss it?"   85

"No, this your piano," she said firmly. "Always your piano. You only one   86
can play."

"Well, I probably can't play anymore," I said. "It's been years."   87

"You pick up fast," said my mother, as if she knew this was certain. "You   88
have natural talent. You could been genius if you want to."

"No I couldn't."   89

"You just not trying," said my mother. And she was neither angry nor   90
sad. She said it as if to announce a fact that could never be disproved.
"Take it," she said.

But I didn't at first. It was enough that she had offered it to me. And af-   91
ter that, every time I saw it in my parents' living room, standing in front

of the bay windows, it made me feel proud, as if it were a shiny trophy I had won back.

92   Last week I sent a tuner over to my parents' apartment and had the piano reconditioned, for purely sentimental reasons. My mother had died a few months before and I had been getting things in order for my father, a little bit at a time. I put the jewelry in special silk pouches. The sweaters she had knitted in yellow, pink, bright orange—all the colors I hated—I put those in moth-proof boxes. I found some old Chinese silk dresses, the kind with little slits up the sides. I rubbed the old silk against my skin, then wrapped them in tissue and decided to take them home with me.

93   After I had the piano tuned, I opened the lid and touched the keys. It sounded even richer than I remembered. Really, it was a very good piano. Inside the bench were the same exercise notes with handwritten scales, the same secondhand music books with their covers held together with yellow tape.

94   I opened up the Schumann book to the dark little piece I had played at the recital. It was on the left-hand side of the page, "Pleading Child." It looked more difficult than I remembered. I played a few bars, surprised at how easily the notes came back to me.

95   And for the first time, or so it seemed, I noticed the piece on the right-hand side. It was called "Perfectly Contented." I tried to play this one as well. It had a lighter melody but the same flowing rhythm and turned out to be quite easy. "Pleading Child" was shorter but slower; "Perfectly Contented" was longer but faster. And after I played them both a few times, I realized they were two halves of the same song.

QUESTIONING AND DISCUSSING

Tan, "Two Kinds"

---

1. In *The Joy Luck Club*, the daughter says, "I'm my own person." The mother replies, "How can she be her own person? When did I give her up?" How does this excerpt typify the expectations of parents versus those of their children?

2. How does Amy Tan relate the pressures of being a prodigy? Is it appropriate for parents to have these expectations? How so? How not? Are these pressures culturally specific—unique to the children of immigrant parents, perhaps—or do they transcend culture, ethnicity, and citizenship? Why?

⌗

SHELBY STEELE

A professor of English at San Jose State University, Shelby Steele (1946–) has written essays that have appeared in a wide variety of periodicals, including *The American Scholar, Commentary,* and the *New York Times Magazine.* "On Being Black and Middle Class" is considered among the most controversial of the selections in the series entitled *Best American Essays,* with some of his critics suggesting that Steele has rejected his own people. This essay originally appeared in *Commentary,* a magazine noted for its primarily conservative politics.

⊞

On Being Black and Middle Class

Not long ago, a friend of mine, black like myself, said to me that the term "black middle class" was actually a contradiction in terms. Race, he insisted, blurred class distinctions among blacks. If you were black, you were just black and that was that. When I argued, he let his eyes roll at my naiveté. Then he went on. For us, as black professionals, it was an exercise in self-flattery, a pathetic pretension, to give meaning to such a distinction. Worse, the very idea of class threatened the unity that was vital to the black community as a whole. After all, since when had white America taken note of anything but color when it came to blacks? He then reminded me of an old Malcolm X line that had been popular in the sixties. Question: What is a black man with a PhD? Answer: A nigger.

For many years I had been on my friend's side of this argument. Much of my conscious thinking on the old conundrum of race and class was shaped during my high school and college years in the race-charged sixties, when the fact of my race took on an almost religious significance. Progressively, from the mid-sixties on, more and more aspects of my life found their explanation, their justification, and their motivation in race. My youthful concerns about career, romance, money, values, and even styles of dress became a subject to consultation with various oracular sources of racial wisdom. And these ranged from a figure as ennobling as Martin Luther King, Jr., to the underworld elegance of dress I found in jazz clubs on the South Side of Chicago. Everywhere there were signals, and in those days I considered myself so blessed with clarity and direction that I pitied my white classmates who found more embarrassment than guidance in the fact of *their* race. In 1968, inflated by my new power, I took a mischievous delight in calling them culturally disadvantaged.

3   But now, hearing my friend's comment was like hearing a priest from a church I'd grown disenchanted with. I understood him, but my faith was weak. What had sustained me in the sixties sounded monotonous and off the mark in the eighties. For me, race had lost much of its juju, its singular capacity to conjure meaning. And today, when I honestly look at my life and the lives of many other middle-class blacks I know, I can see that race never fully explained our situation in America society. Black though I may be, it is impossible for me to sit in my single-family house with two cars in the driveway and a swing set in the back yard and *not* see the role class has played in my life. And how can my friend, similarly raised and similarly situated, not see it?

4   Yet despite my certainty I felt a sharp tug of guilt as I tried to explain myself over my friend's skepticism. He is a man of many comedic facial expressions and, as I spoke, his brow lifted in extreme moral alarm as if I were uttering the unspeakable. His clear implication was that I was being elitist and possibly (dare he suggest?) anti-black—crimes for which there might well be no redemption. He pretended to fear for me. I chuckled along with him, but inwardly I did wonder at myself. Though I never doubted the validity of what I was saying, I felt guilty saying it. Why?

5   After he left (to retrieve his daughter from a dance lesson) I realized that the trap I felt myself in had a tiresome familiarity and, in a sort of slow-motion epiphany, I began to see its outline. It was like the suddenly sharp vision one has at the end of a burdensome marriage when all the long-repressed incompatibilities come undeniably to light.

6   What became clear to me is that people like myself, my friend, and middle-class blacks generally are caught in a very specific double bind that keeps two equally powerful elements of our identity at odds with each other. The middle-class values by which we were raised—the work ethic, the importance of education, the value of property ownership, of respectability, of "getting ahead," of stable family life, of initiative, of self-reliance, etc.—are, in themselves, raceless and even assimilationist. They urge us toward participation in the American mainstream, toward integration, toward a strong identification with the society—and toward the entire constellation of qualities that are implied in the word "individualism." These values are almost rules for how to prosper in a democratic, free-enterprise society that admires and rewards individual effort. They tell us to work hard for ourselves and our families and to seek our opportunities whenever they appear, inside or outside the confines of whatever ethnic group we may belong to.

7   But the particular pattern of racial identification that emerged in the sixties and that still prevails today urges middle-class blacks (and all

blacks) in the opposite direction. This pattern asks us to see ourselves as an embattled minority, and it urges an adversarial stance toward the mainstream, an emphasis on ethnic consciousness over individualism. It is organized around an implied separatism.

The opposing thrust of these two parts of our identity results in the double bind of middle-class blacks. There is no forward movement on either plane that does not constitute backward movement on the other. This was the familiar trap I felt myself in while talking with my friend. As I spoke about class, his eyes reminded me that I was betraying race. Clearly, the two indispensable parts of my identity were a threat to each other.

Of course when you think about it, class and race are both similar in some ways and also naturally opposed. They are two forms of collective identity with boundaries that intersect. But whether they clash or peacefully coexist has much to do with how they are defined. Being both black and middle class becomes a double bind when class and race are defined in sharply antagonistic terms, so that one must be repressed to appease the other.

But what is the "substance" of these two identities, and how does each establish itself in an individual's overall identity? It seems to me that when we identify with any collective we are basically identifying with images that tell us what it means to be a member of that collective. Identity is not the same thing as the fact of membership in a collective; it is, rather, a form of self-definition, facilitated by images of what we wish our membership in the collective to mean. In this sense, the images we identify with may reflect the aspirations of the collective more than they reflect reality, and their content can vary with shifts in those aspirations.

But the process of identification is usually dialectical. It is just as necessary to say what we are *not* as it is to say what we are—so that finally identification comes about by embracing a polarity of positive and negative images. To identify as middle class, for example, I must have both positive and negative images of what being middle class entails; then I will know what I should and should not be doing in order to be middle class. The same goes for racial identity.

In the racially turbulent sixties the polarity of images that came to define racial identification was very antagonistic to the polarity that defined middle-class identification. One might say that the positive images of one lined up with the negative images of the other, so that to identify with both required either a contortionist's flexibility or a dangerous splitting of the self. The double bind of the black middle class was in place. . . .

The black middle class has always defined its class identity by means of positive images gleaned from middle- and upper-class white society, and by means of negative images of lower-class blacks. This habit goes back to the institution of slavery itself, when "house" slaves both mimicked the whites they served and held themselves above the "field" slaves. But in the sixties the old bourgeois impulse to dissociate from the lower classes (the "we-they" distinction) backfired when racial identity suddenly called for the celebration of this same black lower class. One of the qualities of a double bind is that one feels it more than sees it, and I distinctly remember the tension and strange sense of dishonesty I felt in those days as I moved back and forth like a bigamist between the demands of class and race.

14   Though my father was born poor, he achieved middle-class standing through much hard work and sacrifice (one of his favorite words) and by identifying fully with solid middle-class values—mainly hard work, family life, property ownership, and education for his children (all four of whom have advanced degrees). In his mind these were not so much values as laws of nature. People who embodied them made up the positive images in his class polarity. The negative images came largely from the blacks he had left behind because they were "going nowhere."

15   No one in my family remembers how it happened, but as time went on, the negative images congealed into an imaginary character named Sam, who, from the extensive service we put him to, quickly grew to mythic proportions. In our family lore he was sometimes a trickster, sometimes a boob, but always possessed of a catalogue of sly faults that gave up graphic images of everything we should not be. On sacrifice: "Sam never thinks about tomorrow. He wants it now or he doesn't care about it." On work: "Sam doesn't favor it too much." On children: "Sam likes to have them but not to raise them." On money: "Sam drinks it up and pisses it out." On fidelity: "Sam has to have two or three women." On clothes: "Sam features loud clothes. He likes to see and be seen." And so on. Sam's persona amounted to a negative instruction manual in class identity.

16   I don't think that any of us believed Sam's faults were accurate representations of lower-class black life. He was an instrument of self-definition, not of sociological accuracy. It never occurred to us that he looked very much like the white racist stereotype of blacks, or that he might have been a manifestation of our own racial self-hatred. He simply gave us a counterpoint against which to express our aspirations. If self-hatred was a factor, it was not, for us, a matter of hating lower-class blacks but of hating what we did not want to be.

17   Still, hate or love aside, it is fundamentally true that my middle-class identity involved a dissociation from images of lower-class black life and a corresponding identification with values and patterns of responsibility that are common to the middle class everywhere. These values sent me a clear message: be both an individual and a responsible citizen; understand

that the quality of your life will approximately reflect the quality of effort you put into it; know that individual responsibility is the basis of freedom and that the limitations imposed by fate (whether fair or unfair) are no excuse for passivity.

Whether I live up to these values or not, I know that my acceptance of them is the result of lifelong conditioning. I know also that I share this conditioning with middle-class people of all races and that I can no more easily be free of it than I can be free of my race. Whether all this got started because the black middle class modeled itself on the white middle class is no longer relevant. For the middle-class black, conditioned by these values from birth, the sense of meaning they provide is as immutable as the color of his skin.   18

I started the sixties in high school feeling that my class-conditioning was the surest way to overcome racial barriers. My racial identity was pretty much taken for granted. After all, it was obvious to the world that I was black. Yet I ended the sixties in graduate school a little embarrassed by my class background and with an almost desperate need to be "black." The tables had turned. I knew very clearly (though I struggled to repress it) that my aspirations and my sense of how to operate in the world came from my class background, yet "being black" required certain attitudes and stances that made me feel secretly a little duplicitous. The inner compatibility of class and race I had known in 1960 was gone.   19

For blacks, the decade between 1960 and 1969 saw racial identification undergo the same sort of transformation that national identity undergoes in times of war. It became more self-conscious, more narrowly focused, more prescribed, less tolerant of opposition. It spawned an implicit party line, which tended to disallow competing forms of identity. Race-as-identity was lifted from the relative slumber it knew in the fifties and pressed into service in a social and political war against oppression. It was redefined along sharp adversarial lines and directed toward the goal of mobilizing the great mass of black Americans in this warlike effort. It was imbued with a strong moral authority, useful for denouncing those who opposed it and for celebrating those who honored it as a positive achievement rather than as a mere birthright.   20

The form of racial identification that quickly evolved to meet this challenge presented blacks as a racial monolith, a singular people with a common experience of oppression. Differences within the race, no matter how ineradicable, had to be minimized. Class distinctions were one of the first such differences to be sacrificed, since they not only threatened racial unity but also seemed to stand in contradiction to the principle of equality which was the announced goal of the movement for racial progress.   21

The discomfort I felt in 1969, the vague but relentless sense of duplicity, was the result of a historical necessity that put my race and class at odds, that was asking me to cast aside the distinction of my class and identity with a monolithic view of my race.

22   If the form of this racial identity was the monolith, its substance was victimization. The civil rights movement and the more radical splinter groups of the late sixties were all dedicated to ending racial victimization, and the form of black identity that emerged to facilitate this goal made blackness and victimization virtually synonymous. Since it was our victimization more than any other variable that identified and unified us, moreover, it followed logically that the purest black was the poor black. It was images of him that clustered around the positive pole of the race polarity; all other blacks were, in effect, required to identify with him in order to confirm their own blackness.

23   Certainly there were more dimensions to the black experience than victimization, but no other had the same capacity to fire the indignation needed for war. So, again out of historical necessity, victimization became the overriding focus of racial identity. But this only deepened the double bind for middle-class blacks like me. When it came to class we were accustomed to defining ourselves against lower-class blacks and identifying with at least the values of middle-class whites; when it came to race were we now being asked to identify with images of lower-class blacks and to see whites, middle class or otherwise, as victimizers. Negative lining up with positive, we were called upon to reject what we had previously embraced and to embrace what we had previously rejected. To put it still more personally, the Sam figure I had been raised to define myself against had now become the "real" black I was expected to identify with.

24   The fact that the poor black's new status was only passively earned by the condition of his victimization, not by assertive, positive action, made little difference. Status was status apart from the means by which it was achieved, and along with it came a certain power—the power to define the terms of access to that status, to say who was black and who was not. If a lower-class black said you were not really "black"—a sellout, an Uncle Tom—the judgment was all the more devastating because it carried the authority of his status. And this judgment soon enough came to be accepted by many whites as well.

25   In graduate school I was once told by a white professor, "Well, but . . . you're not really black. I mean, you're not disadvantaged." In his mind my lack of victim status disqualified me from the race itself. More recently I was complimented by a black student for speaking reasonably correct English, "proper" English as he put it. "But I don't know if I really want to

talk like that," he went on. "Why not?" I asked. "Because then I wouldn't be black no more," he replied without a pause.

To overcome his marginal status, the middle-class black had to identify   26
with a degree of victimization that was beyond his actual experience. In college (and well beyond) we used to play a game called "nap matching." It was a game of one-upmanship, in which we sat around outdoing each other with stories of racial victimization, symbolically measured by the naps of our hair. Most of us were middle class and so had few personal stories to relate, but if we could not match naps with our own biographies, we would move on to those legendary tales of victimization that came to us from the public domain.

The single story that sat atop the pinnacle of racial victimization for us   27
was that of Emmett Till, the Northern black teenager who, on a visit to the South in 1955, was killed and grotesquely mutilated for supposedly looking at or whistling at (we were never sure which, though we argued the point endlessly) a white woman. Oh, how we probed his story, finding in his youth and Northern upbringing the quintessential embodiment of black innocence, brought down by a white evil so portentous and apocalyptic, so gnarled and hideous, that it left us with a feeling not far from awe. By telling his story and others like it, we came to *feel* the immutability of our victimization, its utter indigenousness, as a thing on this earth like dirt or sand or water.

Of course, these sessions were a ritual of group identification, a means   28
by which we, as middle-class blacks, could be at one with our race. But why were we, who had only a moderate experience of victimization (and that offset by opportunities our parents never had), so intent on assimilating or appropriating an identity that in so many ways contradicted our own? Because, I think, the sense of innocence that is always entailed in feeling victimized filled us with a corresponding feeling of entitlement, or even license, that helped us endure our vulnerability on a largely white college campus.

In my junior year in college I rode to a debate tournament with three   29
white students and our faculty coach, an elderly English professor. The experience of being the lone black in a group of whites was so familiar to me that I thought nothing of it as our trip began. But then halfway through the trip the professor casually turned to me and, in an isn't-the-world-funny sort of tone, said that he had just refused to rent an apartment in a house he owned to a "very nice" black couple because their color would "offend" the white couple who lived downstairs. His eyebrows lifted helplessly over his hawkish nose, suggesting that he too, like me, was a victim

of America's racial farce. His look assumed a kind of comradeship: he and I were above this grimy business of race, though for expediency we had occasionally to concede the world its madness.

30   My vulnerability in this situation came not so much from the professor's blindness to his own racism as from his assumption that I would participate in it, that I would conspire with him against my own race so that he might remain comfortably blind. Why did he think I would be amenable to this? I can only guess that he assumed my middle-class identity was so complete and all-encompassing that I would see his action as nothing more than a trifling concession to the folkways of our land, that I would in fact applaud his decision not to disturb propriety. Blind to both his own racism and to me—one blindness serving the other—he could not recognize that he was asking me to betray my race in the name of my class.

31   His blindness made me feel vulnerable because it threatened to expose my own repressed ambivalence. His comment pressured me to choose between my class identification, which had contributed to my being a college student and a member of the debating team, and my desperate desire to be "black." I could have one but not both; I was double-bound.

32   Because double binds are repressed there is always an element of terror in them: the terror of bringing to the conscious mind the buried duplicity, self-deception, and pretense involved in serving two masters. This terror is the stuff of vulnerability, and since vulnerability is one of the least tolerable of all human feelings, we usually transform it into an emotion that seems to restore the control of which it has robbed us; most often, that emotion is anger. And so, before the professor had even finished his little story, I had become a furnace of rage. The year was 1967, and I had been primed by endless hours of nap-matching to feel, at least consciously, completely at one with the victim-focused black identity. This identity gave me the license, and the impunity, to unleash upon this professor one of those volcanic eruptions of racial indignation familiar to us from the novels of Richard Wright. Like Cross Damon in *Outsider,* who kills in perfectly righteous anger, I tried to annihilate the man. I punished him not according to the measure of his crime but according to the measure of my vulnerability, a measure set by the cumulative tension of years of repressed terror. Soon I saw that terror in *his* face, as he stared hollow-eyed at the road ahead. My white friends in the back seat, knowing no conflict between their own class and race, were astonished that someone they had taken to be so much like themselves could harbor a rage that for all the world looked murderous.

33   Though my rage was triggered by the professor's comment, it was deepened and sustained by a complex of need, conflict, and repression in my-

self of which I had been wholly unaware. Out of my racial vulnerability I had developed the strong need of an identity with which to defend myself. The only such identity available was that of me as victim, him as victimizer. Once in the grip of this paradigm, I began to do far more damage to myself than he had done.

Seeing myself as a victim meant that I clung all the harder to my racial 34 identity, which, in turn, meant that I suppressed my class identity. This cut me off from all the resources my class values might have offered me. In those values, for instance, I might have found the means to a more dispassionate response, the response less of a victim attacked by a victimizer than of an individual offended by a foolish old man. As an individual I might have reported this professor to the college dean. Or I might have calmly tried to reveal his blindness to him, and possibly won a convert. (The flagrancy of his remark suggested a hidden guilt and even self-recognition on which I might have capitalized. Doesn't confession usually signal a willingness to face oneself?) Or I might have simply chuckled and then let my silence serve as an answer to his provocation. Would not my composure, in any form it might take, deflect into his own heart the arrow he'd shot at me?

Instead, my anger, itself the hair-trigger expression of a long-repressed 35 double bind, not only cut me off from the best of my own resources, it also distorted the nature of my true racial problem. The righteousness of this anger and the easy catharsis it brought buoyed the delusion of my victimization and left me as blind as the professor himself.

As a middle-class black I have often felt myself *contriving* to be "black." And 36 I have noticed this same contrivance in others—a certain stretching away from the natural flow of one's life to align oneself with a victim-focused black identity. Our particular needs are out of sync with the form of identity available to meet those needs. Middle-class blacks need to identify racially; it is better to think of ourselves as black and victimized than not black at all; so we contrive (more unconsciously than consciously) to fit ourselves into an identity that denies our class and fails to address the true source of our vulnerability.

For me this once meant spending inordinate amounts of time at black 37 faculty meetings, though these meetings had little to do with my real racial anxieties or my professional life. I was new to the university, one of two blacks in an English department of over seventy, and I felt a little isolated and vulnerable, though I did not admit it to myself. But at these meetings we discussed the problems of black faculty and students within a framework of victimization. The real vulnerability we felt was covered over by all the adversarial drama the victim/victimized polarity inspired, and hence went unseen and unassuaged. And this, I think, explains our rather chronic ineffectiveness as a group. Since victimization was not our primary problem—the university had long ago opened its doors to us—we had to contrive to make it so, and there is not much energy in contrivance. What I got at these meetings was ultimately an object lesson in how fruitless struggle can be when it is not grounded in actual need.

38   At our black faculty meetings, the old equation of blackness with victimization was ever present—to be black was to be a victim; therefore, not to be a victim was not to be black. As we contrived to meet the terms of this formula there was an inevitable distortion of both ourselves and the larger university. Through the prism of victimization the university seemed more impenetrable than it actually was, and we more limited in our powers. We fell prey to the victim's myopia, making the university an institution from which we could seek redress but which we could never fully join. And this mind-set often led us to look more for compensations for our supposed victimization than for opportunities we could pursue as individuals.

39   The discomfort and vulnerability felt by middle-class blacks in the sixties, it could be argued, was a worthwhile price to pay considering the progress achieved during that time of racial confrontation. But what may have been tolerable then is intolerable now. Though changes in American society have made it an anachronism, the monolithic form of racial identification that came out of the sixties is still very much with us. It may be more loosely held, and its power to punish heretics has probably diminished, but it continues to catch middle-class blacks in a double bind, thus impeding not only their own advancement but even, I would contend, that of blacks as a group.

40   The victim-focused black identity encourages the individual to feel that his advancement depends almost entirely on that of the group. Thus he loses sight not only of his own possibilities but of the inextricable connection between individual effort and individual advancement. This is a profound encumbrance today, when there is more opportunity for blacks than ever before, for it reimposes limitations that can have the same oppressive effect as those the society has only recently begun to remove.

41   It was the emphasis on mass action in the sixties that made the victim-focused black identity a necessity. But in the eighties and beyond, when racial advancement will come only through a multitude of individual advancements, this form of identity inadvertently adds itself to the forces that hold us back. Hard work, education, individual initiative, stable family life, property ownership—these have always been the means by which ethnic groups have moved ahead in America. Regardless of past or present victimization, these "laws" of advancement apply absolutely to black

Americans also. There is no getting around this. What we need is a form of racial identity that energizes the individual by putting him in touch with both his possibilities and his responsibilities.

It has always annoyed me to hear from the mouths of certain arbiters of   42
blackness that middle-class blacks should "reach back" and pull up those blacks less fortunate than they—as though middle-class status were an un-earned and essentially passive condition in which one needed a large measure of noblesse oblige to occupy one's time. My own image is of reaching back from a moving train to lift on board those who have no tickets. A noble enough sentiment—but might it not be wiser to show them the entire structure of principles, efforts, and sacrifice that puts one in a position to buy a ticket any time one likes? This, I think, is something members of the black middle class can realistically offer to other blacks. Their example is not only a testament to possibility but also a lesson in method. But they cannot lead by example until they are released from a black identity that regards that example as suspect, that sees them as "marginally" black, indeed that holds *them* back by catching them in a double bind.

To move beyond the victim-focused black identity we must learn to make   43
a difficult but crucial distinction: between actual victimization, which we must resist with every resource, and identification with the victim's status. Until we do this we will continue to wrestle more with ourselves than with the new opportunities which so many paid so dearly to win.

QUESTIONING AND DISCUSSING
Steele, "On Being Black and Middle Class"

1. Comment on Shelby Steele's narrative regarding the "double-bound" nature, to him, of being black. How would you argue that society fosters a culture that asks Steele and others to "betray [their] race in the name of [their] class"?

2. How does Steele's contention about "victim-focused black identity" take on ethical considerations? For whom? With what varying implications?

3. Analyze Steele's metaphor in which he is "reaching back from a moving train to lift on board those who have no tickets" and its result. That is, Steele notes that such an effort expresses a "noble enough sentiment," but he concludes that it might be wiser to "show them the entire structure of principles, efforts, and sacrifice that puts one in a position to buy a ticket any time one likes." To what principles might Steele be alluding?

⊞

Robert D. Kaplan

A correspondent for *The Atlantic Monthly* and the author of eight books on travel and foreign affairs, Robert D. Kaplan is also senior fellow at the New America Foundation in Washington. His other books include *Eastward to Tartary: Travels in the Balkans, the Middle East, and the Caucasus* (2000) and *An Empire Wilderness: Travels into America's Future* (1998). The editors of *The Atlantic Monthly* have called his work a combination of "on-the-ground reporting, rich academic context, a deep regard for the past, and an abiding concern for the future." The following is an excerpt from *Warrior Politics: Why Leadership Demands a Pagan Ethos* (2002).

⊞

Machiavellian Virtue

1   Machiavelli was a popularizer of ancient thinking, though he often disagreed with its particulars and gave it his own original and radical twist. Machiavelli believed that because Christianity glorified the meek, it allowed the world to be dominated by the wicked: he preferred a pagan ethic that elevated self-preservation over the Christian ethic of sacrifice, which he considered hypocritical. Nevertheless, one must be careful with Machiavelli. Because he often reduces politics to mere technique and cunning, it is easy to find justification in his writing for almost any policy.

2   The late-twentieth-century Middle East shows Machiavelli's piercing insight into human behavior:

3   In 1988, during the Palestinian Intifada, Israel's defense minister, Yitzhak Rabin, reportedly told Israeli solders to "go in and break their bones," referring to Palestinian protesters. Less violent means had failed to quell the demonstrators, while the use of live bullets resulted in Palestinian casualties that ignited further riots. The outside world was pressuring Israel to compromise with the Palestinians. Instead, Rabin chose to "break their bones." He knew that only enfeebled, poorly led regimes, like that of the late Shah of Iran, compromise with street anarchy. Rabin's actions were condemned by American liberals. But Rabin's standing in Israeli opinion polls began suddenly to rise. In 1992, hard-line Israeli voters switched to the dovish Labor party only because Rabin headed the ticket. Once elected prime minister, Rabin used his new power to make peace with the Palestinians and Jordanians. Rabin, assassinated by a right-wing extremist in 1995, is now a hero for liberal humanists the world over.

4   Rabin's Western admirers prefer to forget his ruthlessness against the Palestinians, but Machiavelli would have understood that such tactics

were central to Rabin's "virtue." In an imperfect world, Machiavelli says, good men bent on doing good must know how to be bad. And because we all share the social world, he adds, virtue has little to do with individual perfection and everything to do with political result. Thus, for Machiavelli, a policy is defined not by its excellence but by its outcome: if it isn't effective, it can't be virtuous.

Like Machiavelli, Churchill, Sun-Tzu, and Thucydides all believed in a   5
morality of results rather than of good intentions. So did Raymond Aron. After Hitler came to power, seeing that France's policy of disarmament and negotiation with Germany were no substitute for military preparedness, Aron wrote, "A good policy is measured by its effectiveness," not by its purity—testimony to the fact that Machiavelli's self-evident truths are independently rediscovered in every age.

Rabin's tough tactics gave him the credibility to make peace; thus, his   6
tactics displayed Machiavellian virtue. Rabin was only as brutal as the circumstances required, and no more. Then he turned his reputation for brutality to the benefit of his fellow citizens—something also recommended by Machiavelli. Rabin did not relent simply to avoid a reputation for violence while allowing disorder to continue. Here, too, he acted like a true *prince*.

By contrast, the decision of the Clinton administration in its first term   7
to make the renewal of China's most-favored-nations trade status dependent solely on an improvement in China's human rights record was not virtuous—not because the policy failed to achieve an improvement in human rights in China, but because it was clear from the start that it would fail. The policy was sanctimonious, undertaken with little hope of practical results, merely to demonstrate what the administration assumed was its superior morality.

In 1999, the United Nations sanctioned a referendum on independence   8
in the Indonesian-held island of East Timor that sparked well-organized attacks by anti-independence militias, in which the capital, Dili, was burned and thousands murdered—in many cases tortured and decapitated. This terror rampage was easily foreseen. For months beforehand, the United Nations had been repeatedly told what would happen if it held elections without security guarantees. Thus, in its startling lack of foresight, weak planning, and chaotic implementation, the U.N.'s exercise in democracy lacked Machiavellian virtue.

In 1957, King Hussein of Jordan dissolved a democratically elected government that was becoming increasingly radical and pro-Soviet, and imposed martial law. Then, in 1970, and again in the 1980s, he cracked down brutally on the Palestinians, who had tried violently to topple his regime. Yet King Hussein's antidemocratic acts saved his kingdom from forces that would have been crueler than himself. Like his "brother in   9 peace," Rabin, the Jordanian monarch employed only so much violence and no more. His violence, therefore, was central to his "virtue."

10   The Chilean dictator Augusto Pinochet, on the other hand, employed excessive violence and thus lacks Machiavellian virtue. Machiavelli would have frowned upon Pinochet, the United Nations in East Timor, and Clinton's initial policy toward China; but he might have lifted a glass in honor of Rabin and King Hussein in the quiet of his Tuscan farmhouse, and smiled.

11   By substituting pagan for Christian virtue, Machiavelli has explained better than any contemporary expert how Rabin and Hussein became what they were. Nor is there anything amoral about Machiavelli's pagan virtue. Isaiah Berlin writes: "Machiavelli's values are not Christian, but they are moral values"—the Periclean and Aristotelian values of the ancient *polis*; the values that secure a stable political community.

12   Thucydides writes about virtue and so do many Roman writers, particularly Sallust. But Machiavelli elaborates on it. "Virtue," or *virtù*, in Machiavelli's Italian, derives ultimately from *vir*, Latin for "man." For Machiavelli, virtue variously means "valor," "ability," "ingenuity," "determination," "energy," and "prowess": manly vigor, that is, but usually in the pursuit of the general good. Virtue presupposes ambition, but not only for the sake of personal advancement.

13   In Chapter 8 of *The Prince*, Machiavelli cites Agathocles the Sicilian, who became ruler of Syracuse in the late fourth century BC, noting that "luck or favour played little or no part" in Agathocles' success. Rather, it was "through overcoming countless difficulties and dangers" that he "rose up through the ranks of the militia, and gained power." Nonetheless, Machiavelli says, "it cannot be called virtue to kill one's fellow-citizens, to betray one's friends, to be treacherous, merciless and irreligious" for no higher purpose, as was the case with Agathocles.

14   Machiavelli's pagan virtue is public virtue, whereas Judeo-Christian virtue is more often private virtue. A famous example of good public virtue and bad private virtue might be President Franklin Delano Roosevelt's somewhat mischievous evasions of truth in getting an isolationist Congress to approve the Lend-Lease Act in 1941, which allowed for the transfer of war supplies to England. "In effect," writes the playwright Arthur Miller about Roosevelt, "mankind is in debt to his lies." In his *Discourses on Livy*, Machiavelli sanctions fraud when it is necessary for the well-being of the *polis*. This is not a new or cynical idea: San-Tzu writes that politics and war constitute "the art of deceit," which, if practiced wisely, may lead to victory and the reduction of casualties. That this is a dangerous precept and easily misused does not strip it of positive applications.

Of course, the military virtue of Machiavelli and Sun-Tzu is not always   15
appropriate to civil leadership. Generals should use deceit; judges should
not. I am talking only about foreign policy, in which violence and the
threat of it are employed without recourse to any court. Though international institutions are strengthening, they are not nearly developed enough
to change this brutal fact.

Niccolò Machiavelli was born in 1469 in Florence to an impoverished   16
member of a noble family. His father could not afford to give him a good
education, and Machiavelli labored under obscure teachers. To some extent, he was self-taught, which saved him from the scholastic abstractions
that tainted the culture of his age. Machiavelli's opportunity came in
1498, with the execution of Girolamo Savonarola, an austere monk
whose extreme politics led to a popular backlash and the election of a
more moderate republican government in the city-state of Florence.
Machiavelli, then twenty-nine, became secretary to the republic's military and diplomatic council. For the next fourteen years he was one of Florence's leading diplomats, traveling in the France of Louis XII and gaining
exposure to civilizations different from his own. When the collapse of the
Borgia dynasty threw central Italy into confusion, Machiavelli, in 1505,
visited the leading oligarchs of Perugia and Siena in an attempt to make
them allies of Florence. The next year, he observed firsthand the fiery subjugation of Perugia and Emilia by the warrior pope Julius II. While sending dispatches to Florence on the progress of Julius's campaign, Machiavelli
had to visit the camps of Florentine soldiers, paying their levies in the
struggle to retake Pisa. Yet as soon as Pisa was recovered in 1509, Florence
found itself threatened by both France and Spain.

Machiavelli's political career ended abruptly in 1512 with the invasion   17
of Italy by Spanish forces loyal to Pope Julius. Faced with the sacking of
their city, the Florentines surrendered, and their republic—with its civic
institutions—was dissolved. A progressive by nature, Machiavelli had replaced the republic's mercenary forces with citizens' militias. But the new
militias failed to save Florence, and the Medici family returned from exile
as the ruling oligarchs. Machiavelli immediately made overtures to them,
but in vain: the Medicis dismissed him from his post, then accused him of
taking part in a conspiracy against the new regime.

After being imprisoned and tortured on the rack, Machiavelli was al-   18
lowed to retire to his farm. It was there, in 1513, that he retreated every
evening to his study and reflected on the history of ancient Greece and
Rome, comparing it with his own considerable government experience,
which, like Thucydides', included military responsibilities, failure, and

public humiliation. The wisdom of both men was a consequence of their mistakes, bad fortune, and suffering. For Machiavelli, the result was *The Prince*, his most famous work on politics, published in 1532, after his death. It was a guide to help both Italy and his beloved Florence survive against intolerant foreign antagonists. In showing the reinstated Medici family how to bring honor upon themselves and Florence, Machiavelli wrote out of deep sadness for the human condition that he knew firsthand:

> I laugh, and my laughter is not within me;
> I burn, and the burning is not seen outside.

19   The Italy that Machiavelli confronted was one divided into towns and city-states, "subject to death-dealing factions, *coups d'état*, assassinations, aggression, and defeat in war." Machiavelli believed that "since one must start from the present state of things, one can only work with the material at hand." Nevertheless, early-Renaissance Italy, as the artistic, literary, and economic record shows, had a deeply rooted civic culture helped by broad cultural commonalities. The anarchic situation common to Côte d'Ivoire, Nigeria, Pakistan, Indonesia, and other places today may actually be worse, so American policymakers, rather than stand on ceremony and condemn outright autocratic elements, will truly have no choice but to work with *the material at hand*. In Indonesia, for example, forcing the new democratic rulers to further alienate the military—before even consolidating their own power and institutions—would more likely lead to the bloody collapse of the country than to speedier democratization.

20   Machiavelli came up in the conversations I had with political and military leaders in Uganda and Sudan in the mid-1980s, in Sierra Leone in the early 1990s, and in Pakistan in the mid-1990s. In all of these places— threatened by corruption, anarchy, and ethnic violence—the challenge was to maintain civil order and the integrity of the state by whatever means available, with whatever allies were available. While the ultimate goal was moral, the means were sometimes offensive. In the cases of Uganda and Pakistan, it meant coups d'état. After General Pervez Musharraf overthrew the elected leader of Pakistan, Nawaz Sharif, in October 1999, Musharraf telephoned the commander in chief for U.S. forces in the Near East, General Anthony C. Zinni, and explained his actions in words that Machiavelli might well have used.

21   Defending Machiavelli, the scholar Jacques Barzun says that if he was indeed a "moral monster," then "a long list of thinkers"—including Aristotle, Saint Augustine, Saint Thomas, John Adams, Montesquieu, Francis Bacon, Spinoza, Coleridge, and Shelley—all of whom "have advised,

approved, or borrowed Machiavellian maxims"—would "form a legion of fellow immoralists." Yet suspicion of Machiavelli has turned his name into a synonym for cynicism and unscrupulousness. It is a hatred fanned originally by the Catholic Counter-Reformation, whose pieties Machiavelli exposed as masks for self-interest. Machiavelli, pre-eminent among Renaissance humanists, put his emphasis on men rather than on God. Machiavelli's stress on political necessity rather than on moral perfection framed his philosophical attack on the Church. Thus, he left the Middle Ages and helped, along with others, inspire the Renaissance by renewing the link with Thucydides, Livy, Cicero, Seneca, and other classical thinkers of the West.

Machiavelli also takes up the same themes as the writers of ancient   22
China. Both Sun-Tzu and the writers of the *Chan-kuo Ts'e*—the discourses of the Warring States period in China—believed, like Machiavelli, that men are naturally wicked and require moral training to be good. Also like Machiavelli, they emphasize the power of individual self-interest to shape and improve the world.

The Prince, as well as Machiavelli's *Discourses on Livy*, are full of bracing   23
insight. Machiavelli writes that foreign invaders will support local minorities over the majority in order "to weaken those who are powerful within the country itself"—which is how European governments behaved in the Middle East in the nineteenth and early-twentieth centuries, when they armed ethnic minorities against the Ottoman rulers. He writes about the difficulty in toppling existing regimes because rulers, no matter how cruel, are surrounded by loyalists, who will suffer if the ruler is deposed; in this, he anticipated the difficulty of replacing dictators such as Saddam Hussein. "All armed prophets succeed whereas unarmed ones fail," he writes, anticipating the danger of a bin Laden. Savonarola was an unarmed prophet who failed, while the medieval popes, along with Moses and Mohammed, were armed prophets who triumphed. Hitler was an armed prophet, and it required an extraordinary effort to vanquish him. Only when Mikhail Gorbachev made it clear that he would not defend Communist regimes in Eastern Europe with force was it possible for the unarmed prophet Václav Havel to succeed.

Nevertheless, Machiavelli may go too far. Wasn't he himself an un-   24
armed prophet who succeeded in influencing statesmen for centuries with only a book? Wasn't Jesus an unarmed prophet whose followers helped bring down the Roman empire? One must always keep in mind that ideas do matter, for better and worse, and to reduce the world merely to power struggles is to make cynical use of Machiavelli. But some academics and

intellectuals go too far in the other direction: they try to reduce the world only to ideas, and to neglect power.

25   Values—good or bad—Machiavelli says, are useless without arms to back them up: even a civil society requires police and a credible judiciary to enforce its laws. Therefore, for policymakers, projecting power comes first; values come second. "The power to hurt is bargaining power. To exploit it is diplomacy," writes the political scientist Thomas Schelling. Abraham Lincoln, the ultimate prince, understood this when he said that American geography was suited for one nation, not two, and that his side would prevail, provided it was willing to pay the cost in blood. Machiavelli's prince, Cesare Borgia, failed to unite Italy against Pope Julius, but Lincoln was sufficiently ruthless to target the farms, homes, and factories of Southern civilians in the latter phase of the Civil War. Thus Lincoln reunited the temperate zone of North America, preventing it from falling prey to European powers and creating a mass society under uniform laws.

26   Virtue is more complex than it seems. Because human rights are a self-evident good, we believe that by promoting them we are being virtuous. But that is not always the case. If the United States had pressed too hard for human rights in Jordan, King Hussein might have been weakened during his struggles for survival in the 1970s and 1980s. The same is true in Egypt, where a U.S. policy dominated completely by human rights concerns would weaken President Hosni Mubarak, whose successor would likely have even less regard for human rights. The same is true for Tunisia, Morocco, Turkey, Pakistan, the Republic of Georgia, and many other countries. Though regimes such as Azerbaijan, Uzbekistan, and China are oppressive, the power vacuum that would likely replace them would cause even more suffering.

27   For Machiavelli, virtue is the opposite of righteousness. With their incessant harping on values, today's Republicans and Democrats alike often sound less like Renaissance pragmatists than like medieval churchmen, dividing the world sanctimoniously between good and evil.

28   Isaiah Berlin's observation that Machiavelli's values are moral but not Christian raises the possibility of several just but incompatible value systems existing side by side. For example, had Lee Kuan Yew of Singapore subscribed to America's doctrine of individual liberties, the meritocracy, public honesty, and economic success fostered by his mild authoritarianism might have been impossible. While Singapore ranks near the top of key indexes on economic freedom—freedom from property confiscation, from capricious tax codes, from burdensome regulations, and so on—the

West African state of Benin, a parliamentary democracy, stands in the bottom quarter of such indexes.

Machiavelli's ideal is the "well-governed *patria*," not individual freedom. The "well-groomed *patria*" may at times be incompatible with an aggressive media, whose search for the "truth" can yield little more than
embarrassing facts untempered by context, so the risk of exposure may
convince leaders to devise new methods of secrecy. The more the barons
of punditry demand "morality" in complex situations overseas, where all
the options are either bad or involve great risk, the more *virtù* our leaders
may need in order to deceive them. Just as the priests of ancient Egypt, the
rhetoricians of Greece and Rome, and the theologians of medieval Europe
undermined political authority, so too do the media. While suspicion of
power has been central to the American Creed, presidents and military
commanders will have to regain breathing space from media assaults to
deal with the challenges of split-second decision making in future warfare. 29

Machiavelli's ideals influenced the Founding Fathers of the United
States. The Founders certainly had more faith in ordinary people than
Machiavelli did. Nevertheless, their recollection of the debacle of Oliver
Cromwell's parliamentary rule in mid-seventeenth-century England made
them healthily suspicious of the masses. "Men are ambitious, vindictive,
and rapacious," writes Alexander Hamilton, echoing Machiavelli (and,
unwittingly, the ancient Chinese). That is why James Madison preferred
a "republic" (in which the whims of the masses are filtered through "their
representatives and agents") over direct "democracy," in which the people
"exercise the government in person. . . ." 30

The core of Machiavelli's wisdom is that primitive necessity and self-
interest drive politics, and that this can be good in itself, because competing self-interests are the basis for compromise, while stiff moral arguments
lead to war and civil conflict, rarely the better options. 31

Machiavelli emphasizes that "all the things of men are in motion and
cannot remain fixed." Thus, primitive necessity is irresistible, because, as
Harvard professor Harvey C. Mansfield explains, "A man or a country
may be able to afford generosity today but what of tomorrow?" The
United States may have the power to intervene in East Timor today, but
then can we afford to fight in the Taiwan Strait and the Korean Peninsula
tomorrow? The answer may well be yes. If we have the means to stop a
large-scale human rights tragedy, it is a good in and of itself to do so—provided that we confront our capabilities not only for this day, but for the
next. In an age of constant crises, "anxious foresight" must be the centerpiece of any prudent policy. 32

Kaplan, "Machiavellian Virtue"

1. What does Robert D. Kaplan seem to argue in this excerpt from his book *Warrior Politics?* What resources does he use to make this argument? Why might this argument be controversial? How might the title of this excerpt seem to be an oxymoron—a contradiction in terms? Does Kaplan seem to take a stand regarding his complex analysis in this chapter?

2. How do you respond to the Machiavellian contention, quoted by Kaplan, that "In an imperfect world [. . .] good men bent on doing good must know how to be bad"? What types of evidence might best support your view?

3. Research Machiavelli and *The Prince.* How do Machiavelli's tenets influence Kaplan's argument? In your view, does Kaplan represent Machiavelli accurately? Is it possible to be "unethically ethical" or "ethically unethical"? Why or why not?

⌗

MARY MCCARTHY

Mary McCarthy's (1912–1989) parents died in the influenza epidemic of 1918; consequently, she was raised by various relatives in Seattle and Minneapolis. Her memoir, *Memories of a Catholic Girlhood,* examines her childhood and her "lapsed" Catholicism. She attended Vassar College, which became the subject of her novel *The Group* (1963). Among her many other distinguished accomplishments were her editorship of the *Partisan Review,* receipt of two Guggenheim Fellowships (1949 and 1959), receipt of the National Medal for Literature (1984), and membership in the National Institute of Arts and Letters. McCarthy wrote more than twenty volumes of fiction, essays, and social commentary. "Cruel and Barbarous Treatment" is part of *The Company She Keeps* (1942).

⌗

Cruel and Barbarous Treatment

1   She could not bear to hurt her husband. She impressed this on the Young Man, on her confidantes, and finally on her husband himself. The thought of Telling Him actually made her heart turn over in a sudden and sicken-

ing way, she said. This was true, and yet she knew that being a potential divorcee was deeply pleasurable in somewhat the same way that being an engaged girl had been. In both cases, there was at first a subterranean courtship, whose significance it was necessary to conceal from outside observers. The concealment of the original, premarital courtship had, however, been a mere superstitious gesture, briefly sustained. It had also been, on the whole, a private secretiveness, not a partnership of silence. One put one's family and one's friends off the track because one was still afraid that the affair might not come out right, might not lead in a clean, direct line to the altar. To confess one's aspirations might be, in the end, to publicize one's failure. Once a solid understanding had been reached, there followed a short intermission of ritual bashfulness, in which both parties awkwardly participated, and then came the Announcement.

But with the extramarital courtship, the deception was prolonged where it had been ephemeral, necessary where it had been frivolous, conspiratorial where it had been lonely. It was, in short, serious where it had been dilettantish. That it was accompanied by feelings of guilt, by sharp and genuine revulsions, only complicated and deepened its delights, by abrading the sensibilities, and by imposing a sense of outlawry and consequent mutual dependence upon the lovers. But what this interlude of deception gave her, above all, she recognized, was the opportunity, unparalleled in her experience, for exercising feelings of superiority over others. For her husband she had, she believed, only sympathy and compunction. She got no fun, she told the Young Man, out of putting horns on her darling's head, and never for a moment, she said, did he appear to her as the comic figure of the cuckolded husband that one saw on the stage. (The Young Man assured her that his own sentiments were equally delicate, that for the wronged man he felt the most profound respect, tinged with consideration.) It was as if by the mere act of betraying her husband, she had adequately bested him; it was supererogatory for her to gloat, and, if she gloated at all, it was over her fine restraint in not-gloating, over the integrity of her moral sense, which allowed her to preserve even while engaged in sinfulness the acute realization of sin and shame. Her overt superiority feelings she reserved for her friends. Lunches and teas, which had been time-killers, matters of routine, now became perilous and dramatic adventures. The Young Man's name was a bright, highly explosive ball which she bounced casually back and forth in these feminine tête-à-têtes. She would discuss him in his status of friend of the family, speculate on what girls he might have, attack him or defend him, anatomize him, keeping her eyes clear and impersonal, her voice empty of special emphasis, her manner humorously detached. *While all the time . . . !*

3   Three times a week or oftener, at lunch or tea, she would let herself tremble thus on the exquisite edge of self-betrayal, involving her companions in a momentous game whose rules and whose risks only she herself knew. The Public Appearances were even more satisfactory. To meet at a friend's house by design and to register surprise, to strike just the right note of young-matronly affection at cocktail parties, to treat him formally as "my escort" at the theater during intermissions—these were triumphs of stage management, more difficult of execution, more nerve-racking than the lunches and teas, because *two* actors were involved. His overardent glance must be hastily deflected; his too-self-conscious readings of his lines must be entered in the debit side of her ledger of love, in anticipation of an indulgent accounting in private.

4   The imperfections of his performance were, indeed, pleasing to her. Not, she thought, because his impetuosities, his gaucheries, demonstrated the sincerity of his passion for her, nor because they proved him a new hand at this game of intrigue, but rather because the high finish of her own acting showed off well in comparison. "I should have gone on the stage," she could tell him gaily, "or been a diplomat's wife or an international spy," while he would admiringly agree. Actually, she doubted whether she could ever have been an actress, acknowledging that she found it more amusing and more gratifying to play herself than to interpret any character conceived by a dramatist. In these private theatricals it was her own many-faceted nature that she put on exhibit, and the audience, in this case unfortunately limited to two, could applaud both her skill of projection and her intrinsic variety. Furthermore, this was a play in which the donnée was real, and the penalty for a missed cue or an inopportune entrance was, at first anyway, unthinkable.

5   She loved him, she knew, for being a bad actor, for his docility in accepting her tender, mock-impatient instruction. Those superiority feelings were fattening not only on the gullibility of her friends, but also on the comic flaws of her lover's character, and on the vulnerability of her lover's position. In this particular hive she was undoubtedly queen bee.

6   The Public Appearances were not exclusively duets. They sometimes took the form of a trio. On these occasions the studied and benevolent carefulness which she always showed for her husband's feelings served a double purpose. She would affect a conspicuous domesticity, an affectionate conjugal demonstrativeness, would sprinkle her conversation with "Darlings," and punctuate it with pats and squeezes till her husband would visibly expand and her lover plainly and painfully shrink. For the Young Man no retaliation was possible. These endearments of hers were sanctioned by law, usage, and habit; they belonged to her rôle of wife and

could not be condemned or paralleled by a young man who was himself unmarried. They were clear provocations, but they could not be called so, and the Young Man preferred not to speak of them. *But she knew. . . .* Though she was aware of the sadistic intention of these displays, she was not ashamed of them, as she was sometimes twistingly ashamed of the hurt she was preparing to inflict on her husband. Partly she felt that they were punishments which the Young Man richly deserved for the wrong he was doing her husband, and that she herself in contriving them was acting, quite fittingly, both as judge and accused. Partly, too, she believed herself justified in playing the fond wife, whatever the damage to her lover's ego, because, in a sense, she actually was a fond wife. She *did* have these feelings, she insisted, whether she was exploiting them or not.

Eventually, however, her reluctance to wound her husband and her solicitude for his pride were overcome by an inner conviction that her love affair must move on to its next preordained stage. The possibilities of the subterranean courtship had been exhausted; it was time for the Announcement. She and the Young Man began to tell each other in a rather breathless and literary style that the Situation Was Impossible, and Things Couldn't Go On This Way Any Longer. The ostensible meaning of these flurried laments was that, under present conditions, they were not seeing enough of each other, that their hours together were too short and their periods of separation too dismal, that the whole business of deception had become morally distasteful to them. Perhaps the Young Man really believed these things; she did not. For the first time, she saw that the virtue of marriage as an institution lay in its public character. Private cohabitation, long continued, was, she concluded, a bore. Whatever the coziness of isolation, the warm delights of having a secret, a love affair finally reached the point where it needed the glare of publicity to revive the interest of its protagonists. Hence, she thought, the engagement parties, the showers, the big church weddings, the presents, the receptions. These were simply socially approved devices by which the lovers got themselves talked about. The gossip-value of a divorce and remarriage was obviously far greater than the gossip-value of a mere engagement, and she was now ready, indeed hungry, to hear What People Would Say. 7

The lunches, the teas, the Public Appearances were getting a little flat. It was not, in the end, enough to be a Woman With A Secret, if to one's friends one appeared to be a woman without a secret. The bliss of having a secret required, in short, the consummation of telling it, and she looked forward to the My-dear-I-had-no-idea's, the I-thought-you-and-Bill-were-so-happy-together's, the How-did-you-keep-it-so-dark's with which her intimates would greet her announcement. The audience of two no longer 8 sufficed her; she required a larger stage. She tried it first, a little nervously, on two or three of her closest friends, swearing them to secrecy. "Bill must hear it first from me," she declared. "It would be too terrible for his pride if he found out afterwards that the whole town knew it before he did. So you mustn't tell, even later on, that I told you about this today. I felt I had to talk to someone." After these lunches she would hurry to a phone booth to give the Young Man the gist of the conversation, just as a reporter, sent to cover a fire, telephones in to the city desk. "She certainly was surprised," she could always say with a little gush of triumph. "But she thinks it's fine." *But did they actually?* She could not be sure. Was it possible that she sensed in these luncheon companions, her dearest friends, a certain reserve, a certain unexpressed judgment?

9   It was a pity, she reflected, that she was so sensitive to public opinion. "I couldn't really love a man," she murmured to herself once, "if everybody didn't think he was wonderful." Everyone seemed to like the Young Man, of course. *But still.* . . . She was getting panicky, she thought. Surely it was only common sense that nobody is admired by everybody. And even if a man were universally despised, would there not be a kind of defiant nobility in loving him in the teeth of the whole world? There would, certainly, but it was a type of heroism that she would scarcely be called upon to practice, for the Young Man was popular, he was invited everywhere, he danced well, his manners were ingratiating, he kept up intellectually. But was he not perhaps *too* amiable, *too* accommodating? Was it for this that her friends seemed silently to criticize him?

10   At this time a touch of acridity entered into her relations with the Young Man. Her indulgent scoldings had an edge to them now, and it grew increasingly difficult for her to keep her make-believe impatience from becoming real. She would look for dark spots in his character and drill away at them as relentlessly as a dentist at a cavity. A compulsive didacticism possessed her: no truism of his, no cliché, no ineffectual joke could pass the rigidity of her censorship. And, hard as she tried to maintain the character of charming schoolmistress, the Young Man, she saw, was taking alarm. She suspected that, frightened and puzzled, he contemplated flight. She found herself watching him with scientific interest, speculating as to what course he would take, and she was relieved but faintly disappointed when it became clear that he ascribed her sharpness to the tension of the situation and had decided to stick it out.

11   The moment had come for her to tell her husband. By this single, cathartic act, she would, she believed, rid herself of the doubts and anxieties that beset her. If her husband were to impugn the Young Man's char-

acter, she could answer his accusations and at the same time discount them as arising from jealousy. From her husband, at least, she might expect the favor of an open attack to which she could respond with the prepared defense that she carried, unspoken, about with her. Further, she had an intense, childlike curiosity as to How Her Husband Would Take It, a curiosity which she disguised for decency's sake as justifiable apprehension. The confidences already imparted to her friends seemed like pale dress rehearsals of the supreme confidence she was about to make. Perhaps it was toward this moment that the whole affair had been tending, for this moment that the whole affair had been designed. This would be the ultimate testing of her husband's love, its final, rounded, quintessential expression. Never, she thought, when you live with a man do you feel the full force of his love. It is gradually rationed out to you in an impure state, compounded with all the other elements of daily existence, so that you are hardly sensible of receiving it. There is no single point at which it is concentrated; it spreads out into the past and the future until it appears as a nearly imperceptible film over the surface of your life. Only face to face with its own annihilation could it show itself wholly, and, once shown, drop into the category of completed experiences.

She was not disappointed. She told him at breakfast in a fashionable 12 restaurant, because, she said, he would be better able to control his feelings in public. When he called at once for the check, she had a spasm of alarm lest in an access of brutality or grief he leave her there alone, conspicuous, and, as it were, unfulfilled. But they walked out of the restaurant together and through the streets, hand in hand, tears streaming "unchecked," she whispered to herself, down their faces. Later they were in the Park, by an artificial lake, watching the ducks swim. The sun was very bright, and she felt a kind of superb pathos in the careful and irrelevant attention they gave to the pastoral scene. This was, she knew, the most profound, the most subtle, the most idyllic experience of her life. All the strings of her nature were, at last, vibrant. She was both doer and sufferer: she inflicted pain and participated in it. And she was, at the same time, physician, for, as she was the weapon that dealt the wound, she was also the balm that could assuage it. Only she could know the hurt that engrossed him, and it was to her that he turned for the sympathy she had ready for him. Finally, though she offered him his discharge slip with one hand, with the other she beckoned him to approach. She was wooing him all over again, but wooing him to a deeper attachment than he had previously experienced, to an unconditional surrender. She was demanding his total understanding of her, his compassion, and his forgiveness. When at last he answered her repeated and agonized I-love-you's by grasping her hand more tightly and saying gently, "I know," she saw that she had won him over. She had drawn him into a truly mystical union. Their marriage was complete.

13   Afterwards everything was more prosaic. The Young Man had to be telephoned and summoned to a conference a trois, a conference, she said, of civilized, intelligent people. The Young Man was a little awkward, even dropped a tear or two, which embarrassed everyone else, but what after all, she thought, could you expect? He was in a difficult position; his was a thankless part. With her husband behaving so well, indeed, so gallantly, the Young Man could not fail to look a trifle inadequate. The Young Man would have preferred it, of course, if her husband had made a scene, had bullied or threatened her, so that he himself might have acted the chivalrous protector. She, however, did not hold her husband's heroic courtesy against him: in some way, it reflected credit on herself. The Young Man, apparently, was expecting to Carry Her Off, but this she would not allow. "It would be too heartless," she whispered when they were alone for a moment. "We must all go somewhere together."

14   So the three went out for a drink, and she watched with a sort of desperation her husband's growing abstraction, the more and more perfunctory attention he accorded the conversation she was so bravely sustaining. "He is bored," she thought. "He is going to leave." The prospect of being left alone with the Young Man seemed suddenly unendurable. If her husband were to go now, he would take with him the third dimension that had given the affair depth, and abandon her to a flat and vulgar love scene. Terrified, she wondered whether she had not already prolonged the drama beyond its natural limits, whether the confession in the restaurant and the absolution in the Park had not rounded off the artistic whole, whether the sequel of divorce and remarriage would not, in fact, constitute an anticlimax. Already she sensed that behind her husband's good manners an ironical attitude toward herself had sprung up. Was it possible that he had believed that they would return from the Park and all would continue as before? It was conceivable that her protestations of love had been misleading, and that his enormous tenderness toward her had been based, not on the idea that he was giving her up, but rather on the idea that he was taking her back—with no questions asked. If that were the case, the telephone call, the conference, and the excursion had in his eyes been a monstrous gaffe, a breach of sensibility and good taste, for which he would never forgive her. She blushed violently. Looking at him again, she thought he was watching her with an expression which declared: I have found you out: now I know what you are like. For the first time, she felt him utterly alienated.

When he left them she experienced the let-down she had feared but also 15 a kind of relief. She told herself that it was as well that he had cut himself off from her: it made her decision simpler. There was now nothing for her to do but to push the love affair to its conclusion, whatever that might be, and this was probably what she most deeply desired. Had the poignant intimacy of the Park persisted, she might have been tempted to drop the adventure she had begun and return to her routine. But that was, looked at coldly, unthinkable. For if the adventure would seem a little flat after the scene in the Park, the resumption of her marriage would seem even flatter. If the drama of the triangle had been amputated by her confession, the curtain had been brought down with a smack on the drama of wedlock.

And, as it turned out, the drama of the triangle was not quite ended by 16 the superficial rupture of their marriage. Though she had left her husband's apartment and been offered shelter by a confidante, it was still necessary for her to see him every day. There were clothes to be packed, and possessions to be divided, love letters to be reread and mementos to be wept over in common. There were occasional passionate, unconsummated embraces; there were endearments and promises. And though her husband's irony remained, it was frequently vulnerable. It was not, as she had at first thought, an armor against her, but merely a sword, out of *Tristan and Isolde*, which lay permanently between them and enforced discretion.

They met often, also, at the houses of friends, for, as she said, "What can 17 I do? I know it's not tactful, but we all know the same people. You can't expect me to give up my friends." These Public Appearances were heightened in interest by the fact that these audiences, unlike the earlier ones, had, as it were, purchased librettos, and were in full possession of the intricacies of the plot. She preferred, she decided, the evening parties to the cocktail parties, for there she could dance alternately with her lover and her husband to the accompaniment of subdued gasps on the part of the bystanders.

This interlude was at the same time festive and heart-rending: her only 18 dull moments were the evenings she spent alone with the Young Man. Unfortunately, the Post-Announcement period was only too plainly an interlude and its very nature demanded that it be followed by something else. She could not preserve her anomalous status indefinitely. It was not decent, and, besides, people would be bored. From the point of view of one's friends, it was all very well to entertain a Triangle as a novelty; to cope with it as a permanent problem was a different matter. Once they had all three gotten drunk, and there was a scene, and, though everyone talked about it afterwards, her friends were, she thought, a little colder, a little more critical. People began to ask her when she was going to Reno.

Furthermore, she noticed that her husband was getting a slight edge in popularity over the Young Man. It was natural, of course, that everyone should feel sorry for him, and be especially nice. *But yet. . . .*

19   When she learned from her husband that he was receiving invitations from members of her own circle, invitations in which she and the Young Man unaccountably were not included, she went at once to the station and bought her ticket. Her good-bye to her husband, which she had privately allocated to her last hours in town, took place prematurely, two days before she was to leave. He was rushing off to what she inwardly feared was a Gay Weekend in the country; he had only a few minutes; he wished her a pleasant trip; and he would write, of course. His highball was drained while her glass still stood half full; he sat forward nervously on his chair; and she knew herself to be acting the Ancient Mariner, but her dignity would not allow her to hurry. She hoped that he would miss his train for her, but he did not. He left her sitting in the bar, and that night the Young Man could not, as he put it, do a thing with her. There was nowhere, absolutely nowhere, she said passionately, that she wanted to go, nobody she wanted to see, nothing she wanted to do. "You need a drink," he said with the air of a diagnostician. "A drink," she answered bitterly. "I'm sick of the drinks we've been having. Gin, whiskey, rum, and what else is there?" He took her into a bar, and she cried, but he bought her a fancy mixed drink, something called a Ramos gin fizz, and she was a little appeased because she had never had one before. Then some friends came in, and they all had another drink together, and she felt better. "There," said the Young Man, on the way home, "don't I know what's good for you? Don't I know how to handle you?" "Yes," she answered in her most humble and feminine tones, but she knew that they had suddenly dropped into a new pattern, that they were no longer the cynosure of a social group, but merely another young couple with an evening to pass, another young couple looking desperately for entertainment, wondering whether to call on a married couple or to drop in somewhere for a drink. This time the Young Man's prescription had worked, but it was pure luck that they had chanced to meet someone they knew. A second or a third time they would scan the faces of the other drinkers in vain, would order a second drink and surreptitiously watch the door, and finally go out alone, with a quite detectable air of being unwanted.

20   When, a day and a half later, the Young Man came late to take her to the train, and they had to run down the platform to catch it, she found him all at once detestable. He would ride to 125th Street with her, he declared in a burst of gallantry, but she was angry all the way because she was afraid there would be trouble with the conductor. At 125th Street, he stood on the platform blowing kisses to her and shouting something that

she could not hear through the glass. She made a gesture of repugnance, but, seeing him flinch, seeing him weak and charming and incompetent, she brought her hand reluctantly to her lips and blew a kiss back. The other passengers were watching, she was aware, and though their looks were doting and not derisive, she felt herself to be humiliated and somehow vulgarized. When the train began to move, and the Young Man began to run down the platform after it, still blowing kisses and shouting alternately, she got up, turned sharply away from the window and walked back to the club car. There she sat down and ordered a whiskey and soda.

There were a number of men in the car, who looked up in unison as she   21
gave her order; observing that they were all the middle-aged, small-businessmen who "belonged" as inevitably to the club car as the white-coated porter and the leather-bound *Saturday Evening Post*, she paid them no heed. She was now suddenly overcome by a sense of depression and loss that was unprecedented for being in no way dramatic or pleasurable. In the last half hour she had seen clearly that she would never marry the Young Man, and she found herself looking into an insubstantial future with no signpost to guide her. Almost all women, she thought, when they are girls never believe that they will get married. The terror of spinsterhood hangs over them from adolescence on. Even if they are popular they think that no one really interesting will want them enough to marry them. Even if they get engaged they are afraid that something will go wrong, something will intervene. When they do get married it seems to them a sort of miracle, and, after they have been married for a time, though in retrospect the whole process looks perfectly natural and inevitable, they retain a certain unarticulated pride in the wonder they have performed. Finally, however, the terror of spinsterhood has been so thoroughly exorcised that they forget ever having been haunted by it, and it is at this stage that they contemplate divorce. "How could I have forgotten?" she said to herself and began to wonder what she would do.

She could take an apartment by herself in the Village. She would meet   22
new people. She would entertain. But, she thought, if I have people in for cocktails, there will always come the moment when they have to leave, and I will be alone and have to pretend to have another engagement in order to save embarrassment. If I have them to dinner, it will be the same thing, but at least I will not have to pretend to have an engagement. I shall give dinners. Then, she thought, there will be the cocktail parties, and, if I go alone, I shall always stay a little too late, hoping that a young man or even a party of people will ask me to dinner. And if I fail, if no one asks me, I shall have the ignominy of walking out alone, trying to look as if I had somewhere to go. Then there will be the evenings at home with a good book when there will be no reason at all for going to bed, and I shall

perhaps sit up all night. And the mornings when there will be no point in getting up, and I shall perhaps stay in bed till dinnertime. There will be the dinners in tea rooms with other unmarried women, tea rooms because women alone look conspicuous and forlorn in good restaurants. And then, she thought, I shall get older.

23   She would never, she reflected angrily, have taken this step, had she felt that she was burning her bridges behind her. She would never have left one man unless she had had another to take his place. But the Young Man, she now saw, was merely a sort of mirage which she had allowed herself to mistake for an oasis. "If the Man," she muttered, "did not exist, the Moment would create him." This was what had happened to her. She had made herself the victim of an imposture. But, she argued, with an accent of cheerfulness, if this were true, if out of the need of a second, a new, husband she had conjured up the figure of one, she had possibly been impelled by unconscious forces to behave more intelligently than appearances would indicate. She was perhaps acting out in a sort of hypnotic trance a ritual whose meaning had not yet been revealed to her, a ritual which required that, first of all, the Husband be eliminated from the cast of characters. Conceivably, she was designed for the rôle of *femme fatale*, and for such a personage considerations of safety, provisions against loneliness and old age, were not only Philistine but irrelevant. She might marry a second, a third, a fourth time, or she might never marry again. But, in any case for the thrifty bourgeois love-insurance, with its daily payments of patience, forbearance, and resignation, she was no longer eligible. She would be, she told herself delightedly, a bad risk.

24   She was, or soon would be, a Young Divorcee, and the term still carried glamor. Her divorce decree would be a passport conferring on her the status of citizeness of the world. She felt gratitude toward the Young Man for having unwittingly effected her transit into a new life. She looked about her at the other passengers. Later she would talk to them. They would ask, of course, where she was bound for; that was the regulation opening move of train conversations. But it was a delicate question what her reply should be. To say "Reno" straight out would be vulgar; it would smack of confidences too cheaply given. Yet to lie, to say "San Francisco" for instance, would be to cheat herself, to minimize her importance, to mislead her interlocutor into believing her an ordinary traveler with a commonplace destination. There must be some middle course which would give information without appearing to do so, which would hint at a *vie galante* yet indicate a barrier of impeccable reserve. It would probably be best, she decided, to say "West" at first, with an air of vagueness and hesitation. Then, when pressed, she might go so far as to say "Nevada." But no farther.

McCarthy, "Cruel and Barbarous Treatment"

1. What about this fictional account might make it appropriate for a discussion of ethics and ethical concerns? How might you frame an argument regarding "what this story is about" in ethical terms, considering the situation, characters, and other factors?

2. Comment on the ethics and self-image of the main female character, the narrator. Is she unusually free-spirited and liberated, or merely selfish? Why? What about McCarthy's tone and descriptive language supports your perspective? What might be the purpose—and effect—of McCarthy's choosing to capitalize certain words, for instance?

3. What are the implications of the title? What about the story suggests these implications?

4. Analyze carefully and comment on the final paragraph of the story and its final lines. What are the various levels at which the notion of "cheating" operates? Why might she say, "'Nevada.' But no farther" if "pressed"?

⊞

JAY BOERSMA

Born and raised in Chicago, Jay Boersma (1947–) is a photographer and digital artist. A graduate of the Rhode Island School of Design, Boersma has created images—digital and traditional—that have appeared in numerous galleries in Chicago and New York. Like "The Recliner of Turin" (1989; below), his images are often revealing of both the surreal and the absurd. Boersma's work is also part of the permanent collection of photography at the Art Institute of Chicago. Boersma was a professor of art for the better part of two decades until 1996, when he became senior creative director for Playboy.com.

⊞

QUESTIONING AND DISCUSSING

Boersma, "The Recliner of Turin"

1. This photograph was made in 1989, before digital imaging became a photographic norm. Jay Boersma superimposed these images in the traditional photographic darkroom. How does the manipulation of any image call into question notions of "truth" and "believing what we see"? Has the advent of computer technology exacerbated an existing problem? Why? Research the various responses that accompanied the advent of photography in the nineteenth century and its reception onward. How does this context illuminate your point of view?

2. To what religious artifact does this photograph allude? (You might want to conduct a bit of research here.) Based on the title and the image, what

might be the artist's attitude toward this artifact—or toward religion generally? What details support your response?

3. What is satire? How is this an example of satire? In your view, are there limits to what you would consider "allowable" if the satire involves the religious beliefs of others—or, for that matter, any beliefs that others hold dear? Why or why not? Defend your point of view carefully.

⊞

QUESTIONS FOR READING AND RESPONDING

Chapter 6 Conversing and Confiding: How Do I Respond?

1. Each of the selections in this section is written by an author who often directly or by implication takes a position of some sort on the ethical dilemmas suggested by the piece, thus inviting the reader to analyze and take a position in response. Choose two of the works you have read in this section—possibly ones that seem the most different from each other—and compare and contrast the ways in which your analysis of one might enhance your analysis of the other. For instance, how might Shelby Steele's discussion of class inform Mary McCarthy's story of divorce? How does Jay Boersma's "Recliner of Turin" similarly enhance your analysis of another selection? Be sure to argue your point of view, using examples from the texts themselves to support your contentions.

2. George Steiner and Amy Tan have each written narratives of immigrant parents and their expectations of their children. How do these narratives differ in the contexts that shaped these writers? How are they similar? Research more about the cultural contexts that influenced these writers, using the evidence you find to support your arguments. How do you respond, given your own experience as someone's parent or child, to these writers?

3. There are those who would argue that criminal defense attorneys need to reread Monroe H. Freedman's essay regarding professional responsibility. Research recent legal decisions as discussed in the media. Does Robert D. Kaplan's "Machiavellian Virtue" seem to override Freedman's delineation of professional responsibility? How so? How not?

4. To what extent might several of these selections depict the destructive aspects of "Machiavellian virtue" in terms of the central character of a story, say, or the people described by a writer like Gail Collins when discussing the victims of gossip? Consider McCarthy's upper-crust divorcée, for instance, or Collins's treatise on political gossip. How, in these instances, is Machiavellian strategy anything but virtuous?

⊞

7

Speaking My Mind

How Can I Persuade?

"If the elders have no values,
their children and grandchildren will turn out badly."
CHINESE PROVERB

CHICAGO TRIBUNE

Real Beauts
Halle Berry? We Don't Think So

1   Last week, *People* magazine trumpeted its 50 Most Beautiful People: Halle Berry, Ashton Kutcher, Eve, Mary-Kate and Ashley, Usher and on and on and on. Sure, these folks are nice to look at (especially that Ashton Kutcher), but is this the kind of beauty that deserves celebration? Didn't think so.

2   The Tempo Subcommittee on Loveliness You Can't Buy From a Surgeon announces its own 10 Most Beautiful People.

- Maurice Cheeks. Was it not lovely when the Portland Trail Blazers coach and Chicago native left his team's bench to put his arm around and to help a 13-year-old girl struggling through the national anthem at an NBA playoff game?
- Mohammed, the Iraqi lawyer, who helped rescue Pfc. Jessica Lynch. After visiting Saddam Hospital in Nasiriyah to visit his wife, a nurse, he discovered a young woman in a bed, bandaged and covered in a white blanket. As he watched, an Iraqi man clad in black slapped the woman twice. In that instant, Mohammed said, he resolved to act because "my heart is cut." He then walked 6 miles until he found some Marines, approached with raised hands, offered his information, and sketched maps to help.
- Dr. Susan Hou. The Loyola University Medical Center physician donated her kidney to one of her patients. "I can't bring about world peace, I can't eliminate world hunger, but I can get one person off dialysis," said Hou, 56.
- Drew Barrymore, who by resisting the overwhelming pressure to starve herself into stick-figure status, is an admirable role model for young women struggling to accept their body images.
- Haki Madhubuti. A rising star of the Black Arts Movement, known for his sharp-edged poetry and courted by major publishers in the 1960s, Madhubuti turned his back on wide fame. He founded Third World Press, the preeminent black publishing house in the U.S.; helped establish two South Side schools emphasizing an African-American curriculum; and in his own non-fiction works, has been a staunch critic of racism and proponent of black pride.

- Dr. Jiang Yanyong, who told the news media that Chinese officials were lying about the number of SARS cases in that country. He was right, but telling the truth is a dangerous business in China. Good for Yanyong for putting public health above his personal safety.
- Ralph Campagna, executive director of the Off The Street Club. He has dedicated his life to giving kids on the West Side a place to go to escape the elements on the street.
- Queen Noor. (Not to be confused with Queen Latifah, who is on *People*'s list). The American-born widow of Jordan's King Hussein. Now queen of an Arab nation, she has become a messenger of conciliation in a world of conflict.
- Laura Hillenbrand. Much like the subject of her non-fiction story, "Seabiscuit," she overcame remarkable odds and Chronic Fatigue Syndrome, to write one of the most inspiring books of the decade.
- Boulder, Colo., cabdriver Mike Brundage last week found 63 $100 bills that a passenger left inside his taxi. When his shift was over, the father of three turned the money in. "I honestly struggled," Brundage, 52, said. "I have a kid in college, and I could have made people happy by keeping it. I have lots of bills, but I know that turning it in was the right thing to do."

QUESTIONING AND DISCUSSING

Chicago Tribune, "Real Beauts"

1. What is the tone of this editorial? What might be the origins of the phrase "real beauts," and why would it be an appropriate choice for part of the title? What else about the title tells you something about the tone? What aspects of the introductory section of the editorial evoke a particular attitude on the part of the editors toward the subject? What is that attitude? How can you tell?

2. When and why does the tone change? Why do you think that the editors chose to revert to the tone of the title and opening paragraph? To what effect?

3. The editorial seems to take a certain position regarding beautiful actors and actresses. What is it? How might this viewpoint seem unfair? (And is it?)

4. What, overall, does the editorial seem to say about values? What does it appear to say about the values we in the United States treasure most?

⊞

DIANE RAVITCH

Diane Ravitch (1939–) served as assistant secretary for educational research and improvement in the U.S. Department of Education under the administration of the first President George Bush. During the administration of President Bill Clinton, Ravitch served on the National Assessment Governing Board. Considered a leader in her field, Ravitch is known for her most influential book, *Left Back: A Century of Battles Over School Reform,* one of several she has published on education and the history of education. The article excerpted here is from a larger work, *The Language Police: How Pressure Groups Restrict What Students Learn* (2003). A former Guggenheim Fellow and recipient of many honors and awards, Ravitch is currently research professor of education at New York University and a senior fellow at the Brookings Institution.

⊞

Thin Gruel

How the Language Police Drain the Life and Content from Our Texts

1   The word *censorship* refers to the deliberate removal of language, ideas, and books from the classroom or library because they are deemed offensive or controversial. The definition gets fuzzier, however, when making a distinction between censorship and selection. Selection is not censorship. Teachers have a responsibility to choose readings for their students based on their professional judgment of what students are likely to understand and what they need to learn. (It is also important to remember that people have a First Amendment right to complain about textbooks and library books they don't like.)

2   Censorship occurs when school officials or publishers (acting in anticipation of the legal requirements of certain states) delete words, ideas, and topics from textbooks and tests for no reason other than their fear of controversy. Censorship may take place before publication, as it does when publishers utilize guidelines that mandate the exclusion of certain language and topics, and it may happen after publication, as when parents and community members pressure school officials to remove certain books from school libraries or classrooms. Some people believe that censorship occurs only when government officials impose it, but publishers censor their products in order to secure government contracts. So the result is the same.

Censors on the political right aim to restore an idealized vision of the   3
past, an Arcadia of happy family life, in which the family was intact, comprising a father, a mother, two or more children, and went to church every
Sunday. Father was in charge, and Mother took care of the children. Father worked; Mother shopped and prepared the meals. Everyone sat
around the dinner table at night. It was a happy, untroubled setting into
which social problems seldom intruded. Pressure groups on the right believe that what children read in school should present this vision of the
past to children and that showing it might make it so. They believe
strongly in the power of the word, and they believe that children will
model their behavior on whatever they read. If they read stories about disobedient children, they will be disobedient; if they read stories that conflict with their parents' religious values, they might abandon their
religion. Critics on the right urge that whatever children read should
model appropriate moral behavior.

Censors from the political left believe in an idealized vision of the fu-   4
ture, a utopia in which egalitarianism prevails in all social relations. In
this vision, there is no dominant group, no dominant father, no dominant
race, and no dominant gender. In this world, youth is not an advantage,
and disability is not a disadvantage. There is no hierarchy of better or
worse; all nations and all cultures are of equal accomplishment and value.
All individuals and groups share equally in the roles, rewards, and activities of society. In this world to be, everyone has high self-esteem, eats
healthy foods, exercises, and enjoys being different. Pressure groups on
the left feel as strongly about the power of the word as those on the right.
They expect that children will be shaped by what they read and will
model their behavior on what they read. They want children to read only
descriptions of the world as they think it should be in order to help bring
this new world into being.

For censors on both the right and left, reading is a means of role model-   5
ing and behavior modification. Neither wants children and adolescents to
encounter books, textbooks, or videos that challenge their vision of what
was or what might be, or that depict a reality contrary to that vision.

I. Censorship from the Right

In the 1980s, after a century of attacks on textbooks—animated by a   6
search for anti-confederate or pro-communist sentiment, or any acknowledgment of evolution—right-wing censors launched an impassioned crusade against immoral books and textbooks and shifted their focus to
religious and moral issues. Groups such as the Reverend Jerry Falwell's

Moral Majority, Phyllis Schlafly's Eagle Forum, the Reverend Donald Wildmon's American Family Association, Dr. James Dobson's Focus on the Family, the Reverend Pat Robertson's National Legal Foundation, and Beverly LaHaye's Concerned Women for America, along with Mel and Norma Gabler's Educational Research Analysts in Texas, pressured local school districts and state boards of education to remove books that they considered objectionable.

7   The New Right attacked textbooks for teaching secular humanism, which they defined as a New Age religion that ignored biblical teachings and shunned moral absolutes. If it was right to exclude the Christian religion from the public schools, they argued, then secular humanism should be excluded too. If it was acceptable to teach secular humanism, they said, then Christian teaching should have equal time. The textbooks, said the critics, failed to distinguish between right and wrong, and thus taught the "situation ethics" of "secular humanism." They disapproved of portrayals of abortion, out-of-wedlock pregnancy, homosexuality, suicide, drug use, foul language, or other behavior that conflicted with their religious values. The right-wing critics also opposed stories that showed dissension within the family; such stories, they believed, would teach children to be disobedient and would damage families. They also insisted that textbooks must be patriotic and teach a positive view of the nation and its history.

8   The teaching of evolution was extensively litigated in the 1980s. The scientific community weighed in strongly on the side of evolution as the only scientifically grounded theory for teaching about biological origins. Fundamentalist Christians, however, insisted the public schools should give equal time to teaching the biblical version of creation. Several southern legislatures passed laws requiring "balanced treatment" of evolution and creationism, but such laws were consistently found to be unconstitutional by federal courts that held that evolution is science, and creationism is religion. In 1987, the United States Supreme Court ruled 7–2 against Louisiana's "balanced treatment" law. Yet fundamentalist insistence on "creation science" or "intelligent design" continued unabated. When states debated the adoption of science textbooks or science standards, critics demanded that competing theories should get equal time. In 2000, Republican primary voters in Kansas defeated two state school board members who had voted to remove evolution from the state's science standards.

9   The religious right mounted numerous challenges to textbooks in the 1980s. The most important was the case of *Mozert v. Hawkins County Board of Education* in Tennessee. In 1983, fundamentalist Christian parents in Hawkins County objected to the elementary school textbooks that were required reading in their schools. The readers were published by

Holt, Rinehart, and Winston (now owned by Harcourt). The parents complained that the textbooks promoted secular humanism, satanism, witchcraft, fantasy, magic, the occult, disobedience, dishonesty, feminism, evolution, telepathy, one-world government, and New Age religion. They also asserted that some of the stories in the readers belittled the government, the military, free enterprise, and Christianity. At first, the parents wanted the textbooks removed from the public schools. Eventually, however, they sought only that their own children be allowed to read alternate books that did not demean their religious views.

The parents received legal support from the Concerned Women for 10 America. The school board was backed by the liberal People for the American Way. The battle turned into an epic left-right political showdown: One side claimed that the case was about censorship, and the other side argued that it was about freedom of religion.

For five years the case garnered national headlines as it wound its way 11 up and down the federal court system. In 1987, the parents lost in federal appeals court, and in 1988, the U.S. Supreme Court decided not to review the appellate court decision. The judges decided that "mere exposure" to ideas different from those of the parents' religious faith did not violate the First Amendment's guarantee of free exercise of religion.

Defenders of the Holt Basic Readers celebrated their legal victory, but 12 it was a hollow one. In *Battleground,* a comprehensive account of the case, author Stephen Bates noted that the Holt readers were "once the most popular reading series in the nation," but were brought to "the verge of extinction" by the controversy associated with the court case.[1] If publishers learned a lesson from the saga of the Holt reading series, it was the importance of avoiding controversy by censoring themselves in advance and including nothing that might attract bad publicity or litigation. The 1986 revision of the series, designed to replace the 1983 edition that was on trial in Tennessee, omitted some of the passages that fundamentalist parents objected to. The Holt readers won the legal battle but were commercially ruined. This was not a price that any textbook publisher would willingly pay.

A third major area for litigation in the 1980s involved efforts to ban 13 books, both those that were assigned in class and those that were available in the school library. The first major test came not in the South, but in the Island Trees Union Free School District in New York. There, the local board directed school officials to remove 10 books from their libraries because of their profanity and explicit sexual content, including Bernard Malamud's *The Fixer,* Richard Wright's *Black Boy,* Kurt Vonnegut's *Slaughterhouse Five,* and Eldridge Cleaver's *Soul on Ice.* The courts traditionally deferred to school officials when it came to curriculum and other policy-making, but in this instance the students who objected to the school officials' decision won by a narrow one-vote margin. In 1982, the U.S. Supreme Court ruled that the students had a "right to receive information." The decision was far from conclusive, however, as the justices wrote seven opinions, none of which had majority support.

14 Many book-banning incidents were never challenged in the courts. In the 1970s and 1980s, school officials in different sections of the country removed certain books from school libraries or from classroom use, including J. D. Salinger's *The Catcher in the Rye*, John Steinbeck's *Grapes of Wrath*, Aldous Huxley's *Brave New World*, George Orwell's *1984*, MacKinley Kantor's *Andersonville*, and Gordon Parks's *Learning Tree*. In most cases, parents criticized the books' treatment of profanity, sex, religion, race, or violence.

15 The battle of the books shifted to Florida in the late 1980s. In Columbia County, a parent (who was a fundamentalist minister) complained to the local school board about a state-approved textbook used in an elective course for high school students. The parent objected to the book because it included Chaucer's "The Miller's Tale" and Aristophanes's *Lysistrata*. The school board banned the book and its decision was upheld in federal district court and in an appellate court. In Bay County, a parent complained about Robert Cormier's *I Am the Cheese*, a work of adolescent fiction that contains some mild profanity and not especially explicit sexual scenes. The school superintendent suppressed not only that book, but required teachers to write a rationale for every book they intended to assign unless it was on the state-approved list. The superintendent then proscribed a long list of literary classics that he deemed controversial, including several of Shakespeare's plays, Charles Dickens's *Great Expectations*, F. Scott Fitzgerald's *Great Gatsby*, and Ernest Hemingway's *A Farewell to Arms*. Parents, teachers, and students sued the local school board and the superintendent to prevent the book-banning, and a federal district judge ruled that it was acceptable to remove books because of vulgar language but not because of disagreement with the ideas in them. The litigation soon became moot, however, when the superintendent retired, and all of the books were restored in that particular district.

16 During the 1980s and 1990s, and after, there were numerous challenges to books by parents and organized groups. Many were directed against adolescent fiction, as authors of this genre became increasingly explicit about sexuality and more likely to utilize language and imagery that some adults considered inappropriate for children. The 30 "most frequently attacked" books from 1965 to the early 1980s included some that offended adults from different ends of the political spectrum. Some were assigned in

class; others were in the school library. The list included such books as *The Adventures of Huckleberry Finn* by Mark Twain, *The Diary of a Young Girl* by Anne Frank, *Black Like Me* by John Howard Griffin, *The Scarlet Letter* by Nathaniel Hawthorne, *The Catcher in the Rye* by J. D. Salinger, and *Go Ask Alice* by anonymous.

By 2000, the American Library Association's list of the "most attacked" books had changed considerably. Most of the classics had fallen away. At the beginning of the new millennium, the most challenged books were of the Harry Potter series, assailed because of their references to the occult, satanism, violence, and religion, as well as Potter's dysfunctional family. Most of the other works that drew fire were written specifically for adolescents. Some of these books were taught in classes; others were available in libraries.[2] 17

The most heated controversy over textbooks in the early 1990s involved a K-6 reading series called Impressions, which was published by Holt, Rinehart, and Winston. The Impressions series consisted of grade-by-grade anthologies with a cumulative total of more than 800 reading selections from authors such as C. S. Lewis, Lewis Carroll, the Brothers Grimm, Rudyard Kipling, Martin Luther King, Jr., and Laura Ingalls Wilder. Its purpose was to replace the old-fashioned "Dick and Jane"-style reader with literary anthologies of high interest for children. 18

The texts may have been altogether too interesting because they captured the avid attention of conservative family groups across the country. Before they became infamous among right-wing groups, the books were purchased by more than 1,500 elementary schools in 34 states. A small proportion of the series' literary selections, some of them drawn from classic fairy tales, described magic, fantasy, goblins, monsters, and witches. 19

Right-wing Christian groups, including Focus on the Family, Citizens for Excellence in Education, and the Traditional Values Coalition, organized against the Impressions series. The controversy became especially fierce in the early 1990s in California. The state-approved textbooks came under fire in half of California's school districts. Large numbers of parents turned out for school board meetings to demand the removal of the readers they claimed were terrifying their children. One district glued together some pages in the books to satisfy critics. Some districts dropped the series. Critics objected to stories about death, violence, and the supernatural. They charged that the series was promoting a New Age religion of paganism, the occult, and witchcraft. In one district, angry parents initiated a recall campaign against two local school board members who supported the books (the board members narrowly survived the recall vote). In another district, an evangelical Christian family filed a lawsuit 20 charging that the district—by using the Impressions textbooks—violated the Constitution by promoting a religion of "neo-paganism" that relied on magic, trances, a veneration for nature and animal life, and a belief in the supernatural. In 1994, a federal appeals court ruled that the textbook series did not violate the Constitution.

21   Public ridicule helped to squelch some of the ardor of those who wanted to censor books. Editorial writers across California uniformly opposed efforts to remove the Impressions series from the public schools, providing important encouragement for public officials who were defending the books. The editorial writers read the books and saw that they contained good literature. Most reckoned that children do not live in a hermetically sealed environment. Children, they recognized, see plenty of conflict and violence on television and in real life as well. They confront, sooner or later, the reality of death and loss. Most know the experience of losing a family member, a pet, a friend. Over the generations, fairy tales have served as a vehicle for children to deal with difficult situations and emotions. Even the Bible, the most revered of sacred documents in Western culture, is replete with stories of violence, betrayal, family dissension, and despicable behavior.

22   One cannot blame parents for wanting to protect their children's innocence from the excesses of popular culture. However, book censorship far exceeds reasonableness; usually, censors seek not just freedom from someone else's views, but the power to impose their views on others. Parents whose religious beliefs cause them to shun fantasy, magic, fairy tales, and ghost stories will have obvious difficulties adjusting to parts of the literature curriculum in public schools today. They would have had equal difficulty adjusting to the literary anthologies in American public schools 100 years ago, which customarily included myths and legends, stories about disobedient children, even tales of magical transformation. It may be impossible for a fundamentalist Christian (or Orthodox Jew or fundamentalist Muslim) to feel comfortable in a public institution that is committed to tolerance and respect among all creeds and promotion of none. This conflict cannot be avoided. Much of what is most imaginative in our culture draws upon themes that will prove objectionable to fundamentalist parents of every religion. Schools may offer alternative readings to children of fundamentalist parents, but they cannot provide readings of a sectarian nature, nor should the schools censor or ban books at the insistence of any religion or political group.

23   Even though the religious right has consistently lost court battles, its criticisms have not been wasted on educational publishers. The Impressions series, for all its literary excellence, was not republished and quietly vanished.

Fear of the pressures that sank the Impressions series has made publish-   24
ers gun-shy about any stories that might anger fundamentalists. Textbook
publishers are understandably wary about doing anything that would unleash hostile charges and countercharges and cause a public blow-up over
their product.

Publishers of educational materials do not want controversy (general   25
publishers, of course, love controversy because it sells books in a competitive marketplace). Even if a publisher wins in court, its books are stigmatized as "controversial." Even if a textbook is adopted by a district or state
over protests, it will lose in other districts that want to avoid similar battles. It is a far, far better thing to have no protests at all. Publishers know
that a full-fledged attack, like the one waged against Impressions, means
death to their product. And the best recipe for survival in a marketplace
dominated by the political decisions of a handful of state boards is to
delete whatever might offend anyone.

II. Censorship from the Left

The left-wing groups that have been most active in campaigns to change   26
textbooks are militantly feminist and militantly liberal. These groups
hope to bring about an equitable society by purging certain language and
images from textbooks.

Lee Burress, a leader of anticensorship activities for many years in the   27
National Council of Teachers of English, describes in *The Battle of the
Books* how feminists and liberals became censors as they sought to "raise
consciousness" and to eliminate "offensive" stories and books. Joan
DelFattore, in *What Johnny Shouldn't Read*, writes that political correctness, taken to its extreme, "denotes a form of intellectual terrorism in
which people who express ideas that are offensive to any group other than
white males of European heritage may be punished, *regardless of the accuracy or relevance of what they say*" (italics in the original). The censors from
the left and right, she says, compel writers, editors, and public officials to
suppress honest questions and to alter facts "solely to shape opinion."
Once a society begins limiting freedom of expression to some points of
view, then "all that remains is a trial of strength" to see whose sensibilities
will prevail.[3]

While the censors on the right have concentrated most of their ire on   28
general books, the censors on the left have been most successful in criticizing textbooks. Although left-wing censors have occasionally targeted
books too, they have achieved their greatest influence by shaping the bias
guidelines of the educational publishing industry. Educational publishers have willingly acquiesced even to the most far-fetched demands for

language censorship, so long as the campaign's stated goal is "fairness." Only a George Orwell could fully appreciate how honorable words like *fairness* and *diversity* have been deployed to impose censorship and uniformity on everyday language.

29   The organization that led the left-wing censorship campaign was the Council on Interracial Books for Children (CIBC). Founded in 1966 in New York City, CIBC was active over the next quarter-century as the best-known critic of racism and sexism in children's books and textbooks. Directing its critiques not as much to the general public as to the publishing industry and educators, CIBC issued publications and conducted seminars for librarians and teachers to raise their consciousness about racism and sexism.

30   CIBC ceased its organizational life in 1990; its most enduring legacy proved to be its guidelines, which explained how to identify racism, sexism, and ageism, as well as a variety of other -isms. They were the original template for the detailed bias guidelines that are now pervasive in the education publishing industry and that ban specific words, phrases, roles, activities, and images in textbooks and on tests. The CIBC guidelines are still cited; they circulate on many Web sites, and they continue to serve as training materials for bias and sensitivity reviewers.[4]

31   CIBC's initial goal was to encourage publishers to include more realistic stories and more accurate historical treatments about blacks, Hispanics, Native Americans, and women. It awarded annual prizes for the best new children's books by minority writers. However, soon after it was founded in the mid-1960s, the nation's political and cultural climate changed dramatically. In the wake of riots and civil disorders in major American cities, including New York, the racial integration movement was swept away by movements for racial separatism and black power. CIBC was caught up in the radicalism of the times. Its goals shifted from inclusion to racial assertiveness, from the pursuit of racial harmony to angry rhetoric about colonialism and the "educational slaughter" of minority children. As its militancy grew, CIBC insisted that only those who were themselves members of a minority group were qualified to write about their own group's experience. It demanded that publishers subsidize minority-owned bookstores, printers, and publishers. It urged teachers and librarians to watch for and exclude those books that violated its bias guidelines.

32   CIBC's critiques of racial and gender stereotyping undoubtedly raised the consciousness of textbook publishers about the white-only world of their products and prompted necessary revisions. However, in the early 1970s, CIBC demanded elimination of books that it deemed "anti-human," racist, and sexist.

CIBC attacked numerous literary classics as racist, including Hugh   33
Lofting's Dr. Dolittle books, Pamela Travers's *Mary Poppins*, Harriet
Beecher Stowe's *Uncle Tom's Cabin*, Theodore Taylor's *The Cay*, Ezra Jack
Keats's books (*Snowy Day* and *Whistle for Willie*), Roald Dahl's *Charlie and
the Chocolate Factory*, and William H. Armstrong's *Sounder*.[5] The American publisher of Dr. Dolittle, agreeing that the series contained stereotypical images of Africans, expurgated the books to remove offensive
illustrations and text. The original version of the books has now disappeared from library shelves and bookstores.

CIBC attacked fairy tales as sexist, asserting that they promote "stereo-   34
types, distortions, and anti-humanism." It charged that such traditional
tales as "Little Red Riding Hood," "Cinderella," "Jack and the Beanstalk,"
"Snow-White," "Beauty and the Beast," "The Princess and the Pea,"
"Rumpelstiltskin," and "Hansel and Gretel" were irredeemably sexist because they portrayed females as "princesses or poor girls on their way to becoming princesses, fairy godmothers or good fairies, wicked and evil
witches, jealous and spiteful sisters, proud, vain, and hateful stepmothers, or
shrewish wives." The "good" females were depicted as beautiful, the "bad"
ones as evil witches. The males were powerful and courageous, while the females were assigned to "traditional" roles as helpers. Typically, the characters in fairy tales rose from poverty to great wealth, CIBC complained, but
no one ever asked about the "socioeconomic causes of their condition"; no
one ever talked about the need for "collective action" to overcome injustice. In the eyes of CIBC, fairy tales were not only rife with sexist stereotypes, but with materialism, elitism, ethnocentrism, and racism too.[6]

CIBC's *Human (and Anti-Human) Values in Children's Books* listed 235   35
children's books published in 1975. Each was evaluated against a checklist that measured whether it was racist, sexist, elitist, materialist, ageist,
conformist, escapist, or individualist; or whether it was opposed to those
values or indifferent to them; whether it "builds a positive image of females/
minorities" or "builds a negative image of females/minorities"; whether it
"inspires action versus oppression"; and whether it is "culturally authentic." Only members of a specific group reviewed books about their own
group: Blacks reviewed books about blacks, Chicanos reviewed books about
Chicanos, and so on. Few of the books reviewed had any lasting significance, and few of them are still in print a quarter-century later. One that
is still read is John D. Fitzgerald's *The Great Brain Does It Again*, which CIBC
rated as racist, sexist, materialist, individualist, conformist, and escapist.

The author Nat Hentoff reacted angrily to what he called CIBC's "righ-   36
teous vigilanteism" Although he agreed with the council's egalitarian goals,

he warned that its bias checklists and its demands for political correctness would stifle free expression. He interviewed other writers who complained about the CIBC checklist but were fearful of being identified. CIBC's efforts to eliminate offensive books and to rate books for their political content, he argued, were creating a climate in which "creative imagination, the writer's and the child's, must hide to survive." Its drive against "individualism," he said, was antithetical to literature and the literary imagination: "Collectivism is for politics," he said, not for writers.[7]

37   In retrospect, CIBC appears to have had minimal impact on general books. Despite having been denounced as racist, *The Cay* and *Sounder* remain commercially successful. Fairy tales continue to enchant children (although they are seldom found in textbooks and are usually bowdlerized). The public was only dimly aware, if at all, of CIBC's lists of stereotypes, its reviews, and its ratings. Publishers kept printing and selling children's books that defied CIBC's strictures.

38   Where CIBC did make a difference, however, was with publishers of K-12 textbooks. Textbook houses could not risk ignoring CIBC or its labeling system. No publisher could afford to enter a statewide adoption process with a textbook whose contents had been branded racist or sexist or ageist or handicapist or biased against any other group. The publishers' fear of stigma gave CIBC enormous leverage. When publishers began writing their own bias guidelines in the late 1960s and early 1970s, they consulted with CIBC or hired members of its editorial advisory board to counsel them about identifying bias. James Banks, a member of the CIBC advisory board, wrote the bias guidelines for McGraw-Hill; his wife, Cherry A. McGee Banks, was one of the main writers of the Scott Foresman–Addison Wesley guidelines.

39   CIBC multiplied its effectiveness when it worked in tandem with the National Organization for Women (NOW), which was also founded in 1966. Unlike CIBC, which operated from New York City, NOW had chapters in every state. CIBC and NOW frequently collaborated to fight sexism and to promote language censorship in the publishing industry and in textbooks. Feminist groups, some associated with NOW, others operating independently, testified at state hearings against unacceptable textbooks, pressured state and local school boards to exclude such books, and lobbied publishers to expunge sexist language from their books. Feminists demanded a 50–50 ratio of girls and boys, women and men, in every book. They counted illustrations to see how many female characters were represented. They noted whether girls and women were in passive or active roles as compared to boys and men. They made lists of the occupations rep-

resented, insisted that women have equal representation in professional roles, and objected if illustrations showed women as housewives, baking cookies, or sewing. They hectored publishers, textbook committees, and school boards with their complaints. And they made a difference.

In 1972, a group called Women on Words and Images published a pamphlet titled *Dick and Jane as Victims: Sex Stereotyping in Children's Readers* that documented the imbalanced representation of boys and girls in reading textbooks. In the most widely used readers of the mid-1960s, boys were more likely to be lead characters and to play an active role as compared to girls, who were portrayed as dependent, passive, and interested only in shopping and dressing up. At textbook hearings around the country, feminist groups brandished the book and demanded changes. Within a year of this pamphlet's appearance, the authors reported that they had drawn national attention to the problem. Publishers consulted with them for advice about how to revise their materials.[8] By the mid-1970s, every major publishing company had adopted guidelines that banned sexist language and stereotypes from their textbooks.

By adopting bias guidelines, the publishers agreed to police their products and perform the censorship demanded by the politically correct left and the religious right. Publishers found it easier to exclude anything that offended anybody, be they feminists, religious groups, racial and ethnic groups, the disabled, or the elderly, rather than to get into a public controversy and see their product stigmatized. It was not all that difficult to delete a story or a paragraph or a test item, and most of the time no one noticed anyway.

The publishers reacted differently to pressure groups from the left and right. Companies did not share the Christian fundamentalist values of right-wing groups; they sometimes fought them in court, as Holt did in the *Mozert v. Hawkins* case described earlier. By contrast, editors at the big publishing companies often agreed quietly with the feminists and civil rights groups that attacked their textbooks; by and large, the editors and the left-wing critics came from the same cosmopolitan worlds and held similar political views. The publishers and editors did not mind if anyone thought them unsympathetic to the religious right, but they did not want to be considered racist by their friends, family, and professional peers. Nor did they oppose feminist demands for textbook changes, which had the tacit or open support of their own female editors. In retrospect, this dynamic helps to explain why the major publishing companies swiftly accepted the sweeping linguistic claims of feminist critics and willingly yielded to a code of censorship.

III. Battered by Left and Right:
The Inside Account of One Textbook Battle

43   Publishing companies zealously protect the confidentiality of their internal discussions. However, in the mid-1980s, when the fundamentalist parents in Hawkins County, Tennessee, sued Holt, Rinehart, and Winston in *Mozert v. Hawkins County Board of Education*, 2,261 pages of correspondence among editors and executives at the company were subpoenaed and entered into the court records. Stephen Bates, in *Battleground*, first reported on the content of these documents, and he made them available to me for this book. These files reveal in clear detail the political warfare waged against Holt's reading series by partisans of both right and left, as well as the private exchanges among editors about how to react to the latest salvo from a left-wing or right-wing group.

44   The Holt reading series reached the market in 1973, just as the great wave of feminist criticism broke over the publishing industry, and it was in trouble with feminists from the beginning. The Holt Basic Readers (not to be confused with Holt's Impressions series discussed earlier) contained a good deal of excellent literature, but by today's standards, the 1973 edition was undeniably sexist: Women and girls played subordinate roles, while men and boys were frequently shown in active and dominant occupations. The first-grade book declared that dolls and dresses were for girls and that trains and planes were for boys. Stories and illustrations contained more male characters than female characters. All of this material had passed through the hands of female authors, female editors, and female text designers, with no one noticing the disparate treatment of boys and girls. But as feminist criticism intensified, Holt, Rinehart, and Winston issued its guidelines on "the treatment of sex roles and minorities" in 1975, and revised its popular readers in 1977 to expand the representation of females and minorities in the text and art and to eliminate any sexist language.

45   As soon as the Holt series was published, the complaints began to pour in from conservative parents as well. The Indianapolis school board said that it would not adopt the series unless certain words, phrases, paragraphs, and stories that offended conservative parents were deleted. These parents objected to stories that included the word *hate* or that seemed to condone lying or bad behavior or anger or family disunity; they positively despised a story called "How to Keep the Cousin You Hate from Spending the Whole Weekend at Your House and Maybe Even Longer" because it used the word *hate* and showed two boys sharing the same bed, which might foster "homosexualism."[9]

No sooner had the editors begun changing offensive words, cutting 46
paragraphs, eliminating problematic stories, and pasting in new material
in response to conservative complaints than the feminist tide rose up and
crashed over them. In 1973, feminists in California attacked every reading textbook considered for statewide adoption, including the Holt Basic
Reading series. NOW lodged a formal complaint with the state's curriculum commission, and a group called the Task Force on Sexism urged the
California State Board of Education to reject dozens of reading and literature textbooks because of their sexism. Feminists lined up to testify
against the textbooks at public hearings and gathered signatures and testimony from large numbers of sympathetic academics. Letters started arriving at the Holt offices with precise counts of the number of females and
males represented in the text and artwork. Holt's California representative cautioned the home office that "the movement is gaining momentum
like you have never seen in this state and I am sure that it is going to
spread to every other state in the same manner."

Even in Texas, known for its conservatism, the state board of education 47
reacted to complaints from feminists. It ruled in 1973 that textbooks
henceforth would have to present both men and women in a variety of
roles and activities, including "women in leadership and other positive
roles with which they are not traditionally identified." This directive co-
existed with the Texas board's existing mandate that textbooks promote
citizenship, patriotism, and "respect for recognized authority," while excluding any selections "which contribute to civil disorder, social strife, or
flagrant disregard of the law." In the fall of 1974, feminists in Oregon and
Arizona joined the protests against reading textbooks, and Holt internally
decided to issue a special revised "California edition" for California, Oregon, and Arizona.

As feminists raised the heat on textbook publishers, other critics objected 48
to the depiction of race and ethnicity in literature books. In 1974, a group
in California called the Standing Committee to Review Textbooks from a
Multicultural Perspective identified racism in such phrases as "the
deputy's face darkened," "the afternoon turned black," and "it's going to
be a black winter." This committee also complained that the reading textbooks were unacceptably biased toward Judeo-Christian teaching, ignoring other religious traditions.

As they began revising the reading books to meet feminist and multi- 49
cultural demands, the Holt editors quickly concluded that the next edition would have to contain a precise ratio of at least 50 percent females
and a representation of minority groups based on their percentage of the

population. The editors began fumbling their way toward a consensus about portraying women and ethnic minorities. They agreed they would show American Indians in business suits, not in traditional "hides and headdress." Girls would be pictured fixing a bicycle tire, not looking for a boy to do it, and a "Caucasian boy or man would be shown unashamedly crying if the situation were appropriate." Girls would be seen working with electricity, studying insects, and solving math problems, while boys would read poetry, chase butterflies, and pay attention to their personal appearance. Older people would not be depicted as living in nursing homes, wearing glasses, or using canes or wheelchairs. Almost overnight, the editors became absorbed in images, stereotypes, males cooking, and females driving tractor trailers.

Literary Quality Takes a Back Seat

50 Even the editors of Holt's high school literature series (Concepts in Literature) joined the effort to expunge older literary works that reflected outmoded views about women and minorities and to increase the representation of authors from these groups. Literary quality became secondary to representational issues. The female editor in charge of the high school series lamented that many of "the best modern works by and about members of these groups" were unacceptable for textbooks because of their language and "candid subject matter." Worse, from Holt's point of view, "attempts to have authors modify such works have rarely met with success." Recognized authors of "the best modern works" by and about women and minorities refused to permit the bowdlerization (or "adaptation," as the editors put it) of their writings to meet the publisher's need for stories that had no offensive language and the right head-count of females and minorities.

51 During 1975, as the textbooks were being revised, the Holt editors worked with a numerical quota system, imposed by their own internal guidelines. These guidelines directed them to "familiarize yourself with the latest U.S. population figures so that our materials reflect current statistics. . . . Counting and chart-keeping should not be regarded as a useless editorial exercise. Careful tallies and analysis of how people are represented will reduce the need for costly reprint corrections and may prevent the loss of an adoption."

52 Trying to comply with these directives, the editors began searching, almost frantically, for new stories to increase the representation of females and minorities. In the internal exchange of memos, Bernard J. Weiss, the editor of the elementary reading series, frequently admitted that a pro-

posed story lacked literary quality but at least it had the right gender and ethnic representation. He said about one story: "I like the ethnic aspect. I like the use of a girl as the lead. I don't like the story. The urban setting is a plus." Another story was added that the editors agreed was "not great literature," but "We gain two points—a female leading character and characters with Spanish-American names." Weiss observed of another selection: "I agree that this story has very little literary merit. . . . However, it does help us to achieve some ethnic balance in a very *unbalanced* book." Stories were freely rewritten to change a character's job or role or ethnicity, even gender. The editors changed the gender of the main character in Judy Blume's story "Freddie in the Middle," which became "Maggie in the Middle," with the author's consent (in the same story, Mrs. Jay became Mrs. Chang, to increase ethnic representation). In another story, a grandmother was added to increase the count of elderly persons in the book. Some stories were added to the revised edition even though Weiss thought they were of poor quality, in order to boost the number of female characters. After extensive revisions, an editor reported numerical success for one volume in the series: "The in-house count shows 146 female and 146 male characters, or a ratio of 1:1. Animal characters were not included in this count."

Despite Holt's valiant efforts to balance its characters by gender and ethnicity, the 1977 revised edition came under fire from feminists and multiculturalists anyway. Seattle's Ethnic Bias Review Committee found the new edition "unacceptable" because "while blacks are emphasized, it is a narrow representation of those in athletics and music," and besides, one of the books contained intolerable ethnic stereotypes: a black waiter and an Asian cook. A textbook adoption committee in New Mexico was not satisfied with Holt's statistics showing the proportion of characters by gender and minority status; it demanded to know the ethnic balance of both characters and authors. (Holt promptly responded with a list identifying their authors as Black, Puerto Rican, Oriental, American Indian, Hispanic, Jewish, Dutch, Polish, Greek, German, Italian, Scandinavian, Japanese, French, or Indian, as well as a breakdown of all main characters by gender and race.)

In 1980, the education task force of Texas NOW battered the Holt readers yet again at state textbook hearings. Holt's editors thought they had achieved a perfect 1:1 balance of male and female characters, but the Texas feminists said that when they added in animals, males actually outnumbered females by 2:1. A feminist critic pointed out, "Children of this age are influenced by a story about Mr. Rabbit just as much as they are by a story about Mr. Jones." Reeling from the latest criticism, the Holt editors invited a feminist critic from Texas, members of the California committee that evaluated textbooks for sexism and racism, and the director of CIBC to review the company's bias guidelines.

55   Editors at Holt learned to look at every potential story through a political lens: What might anger the religious right? What might anger feminists and representatives of racial minorities? Does the story have a strong female character or a positive portrayal of an ethnic minority? Every entry, every chapter, every volume was measured against a detailed checklist to ensure that there was the right proportion of males, females, and minorities; even workbooks, drill sheets, and spelling exercises were carefully scrutinized because California officials would reject the entire series if there was a gender imbalance in any part of it. At the same time that Holt editors were balancing these political demands, they were also simplifying the vocabulary of their readers, in response to complaints that they were too hard.

56   Occasionally Holt editors reminded themselves that the purpose of the reading series was to teach children to read, but their internal notes show that discussion of literary quality, pedagogical effectiveness, and interest level steadily diminished.

57   Ultimately, however, it proved impossible to please everyone. Holt did a better job of reaching out to left-wing pressure groups than to those on the right. The supervising editor of reading books at Holt described right-wingers as the kind of "censors" that one finds in "totalitarian societies," but characterized left-wing critics as "positive pressure groups" with whom the editors were prepared to collaborate. The more that Holt pleased "positive pressure groups" by increasing their feminist and multicultural content, the more the books offended conservatives. As noted earlier, in the mid-1980s, Christians in Tennessee sued their children's school district to stop them from mandating the Holt readers. Eventually the school district won, but afterward the publishing company let the Holt Basic Reading series go out of print. There were no more revisions. The Holt textbooks were destroyed by the censors of left and right. The textbooks became victims in a political ping-pong game that doomed them.

58   By the end of the 1980s, every publisher had complied with the demands of the critics, both from left and right. Publishers had established bias guidelines with which they could impose self-censorship and head off the outside censors, as well as satisfy state adoption reviews. Achieving demographic balance and excluding sensitive topics had become more important to their success than teaching children to read or to appreciate good literature. Stories written before 1970 had to be carefully screened for compliance with the bias guidelines; those written after 1970 were unlikely to be in compliance unless written for a textbook publisher. So long

as books and stories continue to be strained through a sieve of political correctness, fashioned by partisans of both left and right, all that is left for students to read will be thin gruel.

⌗

Banned Words, Images, and Topics
A Glossary That Runs from the Offensive to the Trivial

Diane Ravitch collected more than 20 sets of guidelines produced by state departments of education, textbook publishers, test developers, educational research organizations, and other interest groups. The guidelines ban words, usages, and written and pictorial images from various educational materials. Much of the glossary aims to purify the past and present to the point that both are almost unrecognizable. The forbidden material includes the truly offensive— such as using the term "dummy" to describe a person who is mute or depicting people of color as universally athletic—some legitimate cautions, such as using "hordes" to describe immigrants, and the thoroughly trivial and even the baffling. What follows is a small sample of Ravitch's "Glossary of Banned Words" and "Stereotyped Images To Avoid."

—EDITORS [of original]

A Glossary of Banned Words

Dialect (banned as ethnocentric, use sparingly, replace with *language*) [SF-AW]

Differently abled (banned as offensive, replace with *person who has a disability*) [SF-AW]

Dirty old man (banned as sexist and ageist) [NYC]

Disabled, the (banned as offensive, replace with *people with a disability*) [SF-AW, HAR_1]

Dissenter (ethnocentric, use with caution) [ETS_2]

Distaff side, the (banned as sexist) [ETS_2]

Dogma (banned as ethnocentric, replace with *doctrine, belief*) [SF-AW]

Doorman (banned as sexist, replace with *door attendant*) [HRW_1]

Down's syndrome (banned as offensive, replace with *Down syndrome*) [ETS_2]

Draftsman (banned as sexist, replace with *drafter*) [NES]

Drunk, drunken, drunkenness (banned as offensive when referring to Native Americans) [SF-AW, HM_2]

Duffer (banned as demeaning to older men) [SF-AW]

Dummy (banned as offensive, replace with *people who are speech impaired*) [SF-AW]

Dwarf (banned as offensive, replace with *person of short stature*) [SF-AW, HAR$_1$]

Heretic (use with caution when comparing religions) [ETS$_2$]

Heroine (banned as sexist, replace with *hero*) [SF-AW, HAR$_2$, NES]

Hispanic American (use with caution as some groups object to the term's suggestion of a shared European cultural heritage, replace with specific nationality) [NES]

Homosexual (banned, replace with *person, child*) [AEP]

Hordes (banned as reference to immigrant groups) [CT]

Horseman, horsewoman (banned as sexist, replace with *equestrian*) [HRW$_1$]

Horsemanship (banned as sexist, replace with *riding skill*) [NES]

Hottentot (banned as a relic of colonialism, replace with *Khoi-khoi*) [NYC]

Houseman, housemaid (banned as sexist, replace with *servant, housekeeper*) [HRW$_1$]

Housewife (banned as sexist, replace with *homemaker, head of the household*) [SF-AW, HAR$_1$, HAR$_2$, NES, ETS$_2$]

Hussy (banned as sexist) [SF-AW]

Huts (banned as ethnocentric, replace with *small houses*) [SF-AW]

Pollyanna (banned as sexist, replace with *optimist*) [AIR]

Polo (banned as elitist) [ETS$_1$, ETS$_2$]

Pop (banned as regional bias when referring to soft drink, replace with *Coke, Pepsi* [however, note that brand names are banned by California social content review guidelines]) [AIR]

Postman (banned as sexist, replace with *mail carrier*) [MMH, HRW$_1$]

Postmaster, postmistress (banned as sexist, replace with *post office director*) [HRW$_1$]

Pressman (banned as sexist, replace with *press operator*) [NES]

Primitive (banned as ethnocentric when referring to racial, ethnic, religious, or cultural groups) [SF-AW, HM$_1$, NES, NYC, AIR, ACT, ETS$_2$]

Primitive man (banned as sexist, replace with *primitive peoples*) [HAR$_1$, HAR$_2$, NES]

Profoundly deaf (banned as offensive, replace with *person with loss of hearing*) [HAR₁]

Provider, the (banned as synonym for husband) [HM₁]

Sect (banned as ethnocentric when referring to a religious group, unless it separated from an established religion) [SF-AW, ETS₂]

Senile (banned as demeaning to older persons) [SF-AW, HM₁]

Senility (banned as demeaning, replace with *dementia*) [APA]

Senior citizen (banned as demeaning to older persons) [SF-AW]

Serviceman (banned as sexist, replace with *member of the armed services, gas station attendant*) HRW₁]

Showman (banned as sexist, replace with *showperson, entertainer, producer*) [MMH, HRW₁]

Sickly (banned as demeaning reference to person with disabilities) [ETS₂]

Sightless (banned as offensive, replace with *people who are blind*) [SF-AW]

Sioux (banned as inauthentic, replace with *Lakota, Dakota, or Nakota*) [SF-AW]

Sissy (banned as demeaning) [MMH, SF-AW, NES, CT]

Sissified (banned as demeaning) [HRW₃]

Slave (replace whenever possible with *enslaved person, worker, or laborer*) [AEP]

Sneaky (banned when referring to Asian Americans) [SF-AW]

Snow ball (banned for regional bias, replace with *flavored ice*) [AIR]

Snow cone (banned for regional bias, replace with *flavored ice*) [AIR]

Snowman (banned, replace with *snowperson*) [AEP]

Sob sister (banned as sexist, replace with *exploitive journalist*) NES, AIR]

Soda (banned for regional bias, replace with *Coke, Pepsi* [however, note that brand names are banned by California social content review guidelines]) [AIR]

Songstress (banned as sexist, replace with *singer*) [HM₁]

Sophisticated (banned when it refers to religious practices or beliefs) [SF-AW]

Soul food (banned as regional or ethnic bias) [ETS₁]

Foods to Avoid in Textbooks [HRW₂, for all of the foods below]
Gravies
Gum

Honey
Jam, jelly, preserves
Ketchup
Juice drinks
Pickles
Pies
Potato chips
Pretzels
Salad dressings, mayonnaise
Salad oil, shortening
Salt

Stereotyped Images to Avoid in Texts, Illustrations, and Reading Passages in Tests

Girls and Women/Boys and Men: Images to Avoid
Girls as peaceful, emotional, warm [SF-AW]
Girls as poor at math, science [SF-AW]
Girls as neat [SF-AW, HRW$_3$, MMH]
Girls as shorter, smaller than boys [SF-AW]
Men and boys as strong, brave, silent [AIR, RIV]
Boys as strong, rough, competitive [SF-AW]
Boys as curious, ingenious, able to overcome obstacles [NYC]
Boys as intelligent, logical, mechanical [SF-AW, NYC]
Boys as quiet, easygoing [SF-AW]

People of Color: Images to Avoid
People of color as universally athletic [AIR]
Minority children or adults as passive recipients, observers of action, or victims in need of rescue by others [MA]
People of color who become success by accepting discrimination and working hard [NYC]
People of color who abandon their own culture and language to achieve success [NYC]
People of color as exotic, childlike, folkloric [NYC]
People of color as gangsters and criminals [NYC]
People of color living in poor urban areas [AIR, ETS$_1$]
People of color being angry [AIR]
People of color as politically liberal [AIR]
People of color belonging to any one religion [AIR]
People of color valued as tokens or valued by whites as professional peers [AIR]

People of color sharing a common culture or preferences [AIR]
People of color sharing common dress [AIR]

Persons Who Are Older: Images to Avoid
Older people as meddlesome, demanding, childish, unattractive,
   inactive, victims of ridicule and violence [MMH, NYC]
Older people in nursing homes or with canes, walkers, wheelchairs,
   orthopedic shoes, or eyeglasses [HRW$_1$]
Older people as helpless and dependent on others to take care of
   them [AIR, NYC, ETS$_2$, RIV]
Older people as ill, physically weak, feeble, or dependent [AIR,
   NYC, ETS$_1$]
Older people as funny, absent-minded, fussy, or charming [NES]
Older people who have twinkles in their eyes, need afternoon naps,
   lose their hearing or sight, suffer aches and pains [NES]
Older people who are retired, are at the end of their careers, have
   lived the most fruitful years of their lives, or are engaged in a life
   of leisure activities [NES, NYC]
Older persons who are either sweet and gentle or irritable and
   pompous [HM$_1$]

Sources

[ACT] *Fairness Report for the ACT Assessment Tests*, 1999–2000 (ACT, 2000).

[AEP] Association of Education Publishers online newsletter, speech by Jonathan
   Rosenbloom of TIME Learning Ventures, September 3, 2002.

[AIR] American Institutes for Research, *AIR Principles for Bias, Sensitivity, and
   Language Simplification*, Fall 2000.

[APA] American Psychological Association, *Publication Manual*, 4th ed. (APA,
   1994), pp. 46–60.

[AphilA] American Philosophical Association, *Guidelines for Non-Sexist Use of
   Language*, www.apa.udel.edu/apa/publications/texts/nonsexist.html, 2001.

[CA] California Department of Education, *Standards for Evaluating Instructional Materials for Social Content: 2000 Edition* (California Department of Education, 2001).

[CT] Connecticut Department of Education, *Fairness/Bias review guidelines for the
   Connecticut Mastery Test*, 2002.

[ETS$_1$] Educational Testing Service, *Overview: ETS Fairness Review* (ETS, 1998).

[ETS$_2$] Educational Testing Service, *Sensitivity Review Process: Guidelines & Procedures* (ETS, 1992).

[HAR$_1$] Harcourt, *Striving for Fairness* (unpublished document, for internal use by
   publishing company, 2001).

[HAR₂] Harcourt Horizons, *Editorial Guidelines* (unpublished document, for internal use by publishing company and reviewers of its textbooks, 2001).

[HM₁] Houghton Mifflin, *Eliminating Stereotypes* (Houghton Mifflin, 1981).

[HM₂] Houghton Mifflin, *HMR 2001: Guidelines for Literature Search* (unpublished, for internal use by publishing company, 2001).

[HRW₁] Holt, Rinehart, and Winston School Department, *Guidelines for the Treatment of People and Related Issues*, 1981.

[HRW₂] Holt, Rinehart, and Winston School Department, *Guidelines for Literature Selection*, 1984.

[HRW₃] Holt, Rinehart, and Winston School Department, *The Treatment of Sex Roles*, 1975.

[MA] Massachusetts Department of Education, *Guidelines for Bias Review of the Massachusetts Comprehensive Assessment System*, March 3, 1998.

[MMH] Macmillan McGraw-Hill, *Reflecting Diversity* (1993).

[NES] National Evaluation Systems, *Bias Issues in Test Development*, 1991.

[NYC] New York City Board of Education, *Promoting Bias-Free Curriculum Materials: A Resource Guide for Staff Development*, 1988.

[RIV] *Bias and Sensitivity Concerns in Testing* (Riverside Publishing, 1998).

[SF-AW] Scott Foresman–Addison Wesley, *Multicultural Guidelines*, 1996.

⊞

Excised by the Language Police!
Items Deleted from a Doomed Fourth-Grade Reading Test

Most of the work of the language police goes on behind securely closed doors. In her book, Ravitch relies largely on caches of private documents that became public thanks to court cases.

But as a member of the National Assessment Governing Board (NAGB), charged by President Clinton with developing national tests in reading and math, she was treated to a unique, insider's look at the tests' vetting process. Though Congress never agreed to support the national tests and they were never given, the tests went through a thorough, rather typical, development process, including the review of each potential test item by a "bias and sensitivity review" panel. Though the reviewed questions had previously been approved by numerous education experts, including members of the NAGB, the panel eliminated many of them on the grounds that they were biased or insensitive. Ravitch was baffled by many of their decisions—and even more by the logic of their thinking. We think you will be too.

—EDITORS [of original]

So what did the bias and sensitivity reviewers recommend? The only way to explain their strained interpretations is to give actual examples. I cannot reproduce the actual examples. I cannot reproduce the stories because some of them may yet appear one day as test passages, but I will paraphrase the story sufficiently so that the reader may judge whether the charge of bias is persuasive. The examples, I believe, will demonstrate that the concept of bias has become detached from its original meaning and has been redefined into assumptions that defy common sense.

Women and Patchwork Quilting

The bias and sensitivity reviewers rejected a passage about patchwork quilting by women on the western frontier in the mid-19th century. The passage explained that mothers in that time taught their daughters to sew, and together they made quilts for the girl's dowry when she married. Quilting was an economic necessity because it saved money, and there were no factory-made quilts available until the end of the 19th century. The passage briefly explained how quilts were assembled and described them as works of art. The information in the passage was historically accurate, but the bias and sensitivity panel (as well as the "content expert panel") objected to the passage because it contained stereotypes of females as "soft" and "submissive." Actually, the passage did nothing of the sort. It was a description of why quilting was important to women on the frontier and how it was done. Nothing in the passage excluded the possibility that mothers and daughters were riding the range, plowing the fields, and herding cattle during the day. The reviewers objected to the portrayal of women as people who stitch and sew and who were concerned about preparing for marriage. Historical accuracy was no defense for this representation of women and girls, which they deemed stereotypical.

Class Distinction in the Ancient World

The bias panel did not like a story about growing up in ancient Egypt. The story contrasted how people's ways of living varied in accordance with their wealth and status. Some lived in palaces, others were noblemen, others were farmers or city workers. The size and grandeur of one's house, said the story, depended on family wealth. To the naked eye, the story was descriptive, not judgmental. But the bias and sensitivity reviewers preferred to eliminate it, claiming that references to wealth and class distinctions had an "elitist" tone. The fact that these class distinctions were historically accurate was irrelevant to the reviewers. In the world that they wanted children to read about, class distinctions did not exist—not now nor in the past. The desire to rewrite history is one that continually plagues bias reviewers.

The Even Exchange

This story came from a children's book by an African-American author. It was about an African-American girl who wanted to learn how to jump rope like the other girls in her neighborhood. She meets a neighbor who is an expert at jumping rope, but who is attending summer school because she is not very good at math. The new girl is good at math so the two agree to teach each other what they do best. The bias reviewers did not like this story at all. They found that it had serious bias problems because it showed an African-American girl who was weak in math and was attending summer school. The fact that this character thought of herself as not very good at math was also deeply offensive and stereotypical, the bias reviewers believed. Even though the author was African-American and her book was intended to bolster the self-esteem of black girls, it did not carry any weight with the bias panel. African-American children could be portrayed only in a positive light. Anything that showed weakness suggested negative stereotyping. In this case, one African-American girl was good at math, and the other was not. So far as I could tell, the story showed human variability, not negative racial stereotyping, with each girl displaying different weaknesses and different strengths.

The Silly Old Lady

The bias panel rejected a passage about a silly old woman who keeps piling more and more gadgets on her bicycle until it is so overloaded that it tumbles over. The language was clever, the illustrations were amusing, and the story was higher in literary quality than the other fourth-grade reading passages proposed for the test. But the bias panel rejected it. They felt that it contained a negative stereotype of an eccentric old woman who constantly changed her mind; apparently women, and especially women of a certain age, must be depicted only in a positive light. Why would it upset or distract fourth-grade children to see an older woman acting eccentrically or changing her mind? The bias panel thought that children would get the wrong idea about older women if they read such a story. They might conclude that all women of a certain age behaved in this way.

The Blind Mountain Climber

One of the stranger recommendations of the bias and sensitivity panel involved a true story about a heroic young blind man who hiked to the top of Mount McKinley, the highest peak in North America. The story described the dangers of hiking up an icy mountain trail, especially for a blind person. The panel voted 12–11 to eliminate this inspiring story. First, the majority maintained that the story contained "regional bias" because it was about hiking and mountain climbing, which favors students who live in regions where those activities are common. Second, they rejected the passage because it suggested that people who are blind are somehow at a disadvantage compared to people who have normal sight—that they are "worse off" and have a more difficult time facing dangers than those who are not blind.

"Regional bias," in this instance, means that children should not be expected to read or comprehend stories set in unfamiliar terrain. A story that happened in a desert would be "biased" against children who have never lived in a desert, and a story set in a tropical climate would be biased against those who have never lived in a tropical climate. Consider the impoverishment of imagination that flows from such assumptions: No reading passage on a test may have a specific geographical setting; every event must occur in a generic locale. Under these assumptions, no child should be expected to understand a story set in a locale other than the one that he or she currently lives in or in a locale that has no distinguishing characteristics.

Even more peculiar is the assumption by the panel's majority that it is demeaning to applaud a blind person for overcoming daunting obstacles, like climbing a steep, icy mountain trail. It is not unreasonable, I believe, to consider blindness to be a handicap for a person facing physical danger. By definition, people who are blind cannot see as much or as well as people who have sight. Is it not more difficult to cope with dangerous situations when one cannot see? Yet, perversely, the bias and sensitivity panel concluded that this story celebrating a blind athlete's achievements and his heroism was biased *against* people who are blind. Blindness, apparently, should be treated as just another personal attribute, like the color of one's hair or one's height. In the new meaning of bias, it is considered biased to acknowledge that lack of sight is a disability.

No More Owls

The passage about owls was like a children's encyclopedia entry. It described how their keen eyesight and hearing enabled them to hunt at night for rodents. When I saw that this passage was rejected, I imagined that it was because of the violence associated with hunting (although that's how the owl survives). I was wrong. The passage was rejected because a Native-American member of the bias committee said that owls are taboo for the Navajos. Consequently, the entire committee agreed that the passage should be dropped. The test publisher added a notation that the owl is associated with death in some other cultures and should not be mentioned anymore, neither in texts nor in illustrations.

Here is a classic problem presented by today's bias and sensitivity review process. If any cultural group attributes negative connotations to anything, or considers it taboo or offensive, then that topic will not be referred to, represented, described, or illustrated on tests. But owls exist. They are real birds. They are not creatures of the imagination. Nevertheless, to avoid giving offense, the tests will pretend that owls don't exist. Owls are to be deleted and never again mentioned to the highly vulnerable and sensitive American schoolchild.

Article Endnotes

1. Stephen Bates, *Battleground: One Mother's Crusade, the Religious Right, and the Struggle for Control of Our Classrooms* (Poseidon Press, 1993), p. 319. Another excellent source for these issues is Joan DelFattore, *What Johnny Shouldn't Read: Textbook Censorship in America* (Yale University Press, 1992).
2. The "Ten Most Challenged Books of 2000," according to the American Library Association.
3. Burress, *Battle of the Books*, pp. 116–134; DelFattore, *What Johnny Shouldn't Read*, p. 9.
4. Council on Interracial Books for Children, "Ten Quick Ways to Analyze Children's Books for Sexism and Racism," *Guidelines for Selecting Bias-Free Textbooks and Storybooks* (CIBC, 1980); originally published in the Council on Interracial Books for Children, *Bulletin*, vol. 5, no. 3, 1974, pp. 1–6.
5. CIBC *Bulletin*, Vol. 3, no. 4, 1971.

6. Robert Moore, "From Rags to Witches: Stereotypes, Distortions, and Anti-Humanism in Fairy Tales," CIBC *Bulletin*, vol. 6, no. 7, 1975.

7. Nat Hentoff, "Any Writer Who Follows Anyone Else's Guidelines Ought to Be in Advertising," *School Library Journal* (November 1977), reprinted in *Young Adult Literature: Background and Criticism* (American Library Association, 1980), pp. 454–460. See also Council on Interracial Books for Children, *Human and Anti-Human Values in Children's Books: A Content Rating Instrument for Educators and Concerned Parents: Guidelines for the Future* (CIBC, 1976).

8. Women on Words and Images, *Dick and Jane as Victims: Sex Stereotyping in Children's Readers: An Analysis* (Women on Words and Images, 1972).

9. The quotations that follow are from letters and documents in the Holt files. A copy of these files has been permanently stored in the Hoover Institution Library and Archives as part of my papers. For another discussion of the Holt files, see Bates, *Battleground*.

QUESTIONING AND DISCUSSING

Ravitch, "Thin Gruel"

1. Diane Ravitch begins her essay with an immediate reference to *censorship*. Analyze her definition of the term and the examples she uses to make distinctions, for instance, between *censorship* and *selection*. How does Ravitch articulate her distinctions between these forms of censorship? What values do these positions represent? How does she challenge them?

2. Review the sidebar discussion, "Excised by the Language Police!" The editors write that Ravitch was "baffled" by many of the decisions of the National Assessment Governing Board. In addition to analyzing the examples she presents, analyze Ravitch's language and tone regarding these decisions. What is the "classic problem presented in today's bias and sensitivity review process"? What is your view concerning these issues?

3. There are those who would argue that the efforts on the part of the "language police" have led to teachers being afraid to assign students anything that might be in the least bit controversial—and avoiding argument and challenge altogether, leading, some believe, to a watering down of curricula. How might this development be related to Ravitch's argument in the subsection of the article following the heading "Literary Quality Takes a Back Seat"? Based on Ravitch's article, what is your point of view?

⊞

Jonathan Edwards (1703–1758) was born in East Windsor, Connecticut, where his father was a pastor. When he was not yet thirteen, Edwards entered Yale University and graduated four years later at the top of his class. Upon graduation, he continued his studies in theology and preached in a Presbyterian pulpit in New York. In 1728, Edwards traveled to Northampton, Massachusetts, where his fiery style of preaching brought remarkable religious revivals to the community. However, by 1748, Edwards had alienated much of his congregation as a result of his proposal to admit only those who gave "satisfactory evidence" of being truly converted before they could participate in the act of Communion instead of allowing in anyone who had been baptized. After ministering to a tiny congregation in Stockbridge, Massachusetts, and serving as a missionary to the Housatonic Indians, Edwards was elected president of Princeton in 1757. He was a popular choice, being the most eminent American philosopher-theologian of his time. On March 22, 1758, Edwards died of fever following a vaccination for smallpox, and he was buried in the President's Lot in the Princeton cemetery.

⊞

Sinners in the Hands of an Angry God
Deuteronomy 32.35

Their foot shall slide in due time.

In this verse is threatened the vengeance of God on the wicked unbelieving Israelites, who were God's visible people, and who lived under the means of grace, but who, notwithstanding all God's wonderful works towards them, remained (as in verse 28) void of counsel, having no understanding in them. Under all the cultivations of heaven, they brought forth bitter and poisonous fruit, as in the two verses next preceding the text. The expression I have chosen for my text, "Their foot shall slide in due time," seems to imply the following things, relating to the punishment and destruction to which these wicked Israelites were exposed.

1. That they were always exposed to destruction; as one that stands or walks in slippery places is always exposed to fall. This is implied in the manner of their destruction coming upon them, being represented by their foot sliding. The same is expressed, Psalm 73.18: "Surely thou didst set them in slippery places; thou castedst them down into destruction."

2. It implies that they were always exposed to sudden unexpected destruction. As he that walks in slippery places is every moment liable to fall, he cannot foresee one moment whether he shall stand or fall the next; and when he does fall, he falls at once without warning: which is also expressed in Psalm 73.18–19: "Surely thou didst set them in slippery places; thou castedst them down into destruction: How are they brought into desolation as in a moment!"

3. Another thing implied is, that they are liable to fall of themselves, without being thrown down by the hand of another; as he that stands or walks on slippery ground needs nothing but his own weight to throw him down.

4. That the reason why they are not fallen already, and do not fall now, is only that God's appointed time is not come. For it is said that when that due time, or appointed time comes, their foot shall slide. Then they shall be left to fall, as they are inclined by their own weight. God will not hold them up in these slippery places any longer, but will let them go; and then, at that very instant, they shall fall into destruction; as he that stands on such slippery declining ground, on the edge of a pit, he cannot stand alone, when he is let go he immediately falls and is lost.

The observation from the words that I would now insist upon is this. "There is nothing that keeps wicked men at any one moment out of hell, but the mere pleasure of God." By the mere pleasure of God, I mean His sovereign pleasure, His arbitrary will, restrained by no obligation, hindered by no manner of difficulty, any more than if nothing else but God's mere will had in the least degree, or in any respect whatsoever, any hand in the preservation of wicked men one moment. The truth of this observation may appear by the following considerations.

1. There is no want of power in God to cast wicked men into hell at any moment. Men's hands cannot be strong when God rises up. The strongest have no power to resist Him, not can any deliver out of His hands. He is not only able to cast wicked men into hell, but He can most easily do it. Sometimes an earthly prince meets with a great deal of difficulty to subdue a rebel, who has found means to fortify himself, and has made himself strong by the numbers of his followers. But it is not so with God. There is no fortress that is any defense from the power of God. Though hand join in hand, and vast multitudes of God's enemies combine and associate themselves, they are easily broken in pieces. They are as great heaps of light chaff before the

whirlwind; or large quantities of dry stubble before devouring flames. We find it easy to tread on and crush a worm that we see crawling on the earth; so it is easy for us to cut or singe a slender thread that any thing hangs by: thus easy is it for God, when he pleases, to cast His enemies down to hell. What are we, that we should think to stand before Him, at whose rebuke the earth trembles, and before whom the rocks are thrown down?

2. They deserve to be cast into hell; so that divine justice never stands in the way, it makes no objection against God's using His power at any moment to destroy them. Yea, on the contrary, justice calls aloud for an infinite punishment of their sins. Divine justice says of the tree that brings forth such grapes of Sodom, "Cut it down, why cumbereth it the ground?" Luke 13.7. The sword of divine justice is every moment brandished over their heads, and it is nothing but the hand of arbitrary mercy, and God's will, that holds it back.

3. They are already under a sentence of condemnation to hell. They do not only justly deserve to be cast down thither, but the sentence of the law of God, that eternal and immutable rule of righteousness that God has fixed between Him and mankind, is gone out against them, and stands against them; so that they are bound over already to hell. John 3.18: "He that believeth not is condemned already." So that every unconverted man properly belongs to hell; that is his place; from thence he is, John 8.23: "Ye are from beneath." And thither he is bound; it is the place that justice, and God's word, and the sentence of his unchangeable law assign to him.

4. They are now the objects of that very same anger and wrath of God that is expressed in the torments of hell. And the reason why they do not go down to hell at each moment is not because God, in whose power they are, is not then very angry with them as He is with many miserable creatures now tormented in hell, who there feel and bear the fierceness of His wrath. Yea, God is a great deal more angry with great numbers that are now on earth: yea, doubtless, with many that are now in this congregation, who it may be are at ease, than He is with many of those who are now in the flames of hell.

So that it is not because God is unmindful of their wickedness, and does not resent it, that He does not let loose His hand and cut them off. God is not altogether such an one as themselves, though they may imagine Him to be so. The wrath of God burns against them, their damnation does not slumber; the pit is prepared, the fire is made ready, the furnace is now hot, ready to receive them; the flames do now rage and glow. The glittering sword is whet, and held over them, and the pit hath opened its mouth under them.

5. The devil stands ready to fall upon them, and seize them as his own, at what moment God shall permit him. They belong to him; he has their souls in his possession, and under his dominion. The Scripture represents them as his goods, Luke 11.12. The devils watch them; they are ever by them at their right hand; they stand waiting for them, like greedy hungry lions that see their prey, and expect to have it, but are for the present kept back. If God should withdraw His hand, by which they are restrained, they would in one moment fly upon their poor souls. The old serpent is gaping for them; hell opens its mouth wide to receive them; and if God should permit it, they would be hastily swallowed up and lost.

6. There are in the souls of wicked men those hellish principles reigning that would presently kindle and flame out into hell fire, if it were not for God's restraints. There is laid in the very nature of carnal men a foundation for the torments of hell. There are those corrupt principles, in reigning power in them, and in full possession of them, that are seeds of hell fire. These principles are active and powerful, exceeding violent in their nature, and if it were not for the restraining hand of God upon them, they would soon break out, they would flame out after the same manner as the same corruptions, the same enmity does in the hearts of damned souls, and would beget the same torments as they do in them. The souls of the wicked are in Scripture compared to the troubled sea, Isaiah 57.20. For the present, God restrains their wickedness by His mighty power, as He does the raging waves of the troubled sea, saying, "Hitherto shalt thou come, but no further;" but if God should withdraw that restraining power, it would soon carry all before it. Sin is the ruin and misery of the soul; it is destructive in its nature; and if God should leave it without restraint, there would need nothing else to make the soul perfectly miserable. The corruption of the heart of men is immoderate and boundless in its fury; and while wicked men live here, it is like fire pent up by God's restraints, whereas if it were let loose, it would set on fire the course of nature; and as the heart is now a sink of sin, so if sin was not restrained, it would immediately turn the soul into a fiery oven, or a furnace of fire and brimstone.

7. It is no security to wicked men for one moment that there are no visible means of death at hand. It is no security to a natural man that he is now in health and that he does not see which way he should now immediately go out of the world by any accident, and that there is no visible danger in any respect in his circumstances. The manifold and continued experience of the world in all ages, shows this is no evidence that a man is not on the very brink of eternity, and that the

next step will not be into another world. The unseen, unthought-of ways and means of persons going suddenly out of the world are innumerable and inconceivable. Unconverted men walk over the pit of hell on a rotten covering, and there are innumerable places in this covering so weak that they will not bear their weight, and these places are not seen. The arrows of death fly unseen at noonday; the sharpest sight cannot discern them. God has so many different unsearchable ways of taking wicked men out of the world and sending them to hell, that there is nothing to make it appear that God had need to be at the expense of a miracle, or go out of the ordinary course of His providence, to destroy any wicked man at any moment. All the means that there are of sinners going out of the world are so in God's hands, and so universally and absolutely subject to His power and determination, that it does not depend at all the less on the mere will of God whether sinners shall at any moment go to hell than if means were never made use of or at all concerned in the case.

8. Natural men's prudence and care to preserve their own lives, or the care of others to preserve them, do not secure them a moment. To this, divine providence and universal experience do also bear testimony. There is this clear evidence that men's own wisdom is no security to them from death; that if it were otherwise we should see some difference between the wise and politic men of the world, and others, with regard to their liableness to early and unexpected death: but how is it in fact? Ecclesiastes 2.16: "How dieth the wise man? even as the fool."

9. All wicked men's pains and contrivance which they use to escape hell, while they continue to reject Christ, and so remain wicked men, do not secure them from hell one moment. Almost every natural man that hears of hell, flatters himself that he shall escape it; he depends upon himself for his own security; he flatters himself in what he has done, in what he is now doing, or what he intends to do. Every one lays out matters in his own mind how he shall avoid damnation, and flatters himself that he contrives well for himself, and that his schemes will not fail. They hear indeed that there are but few saved, and that the greater part of men that have died heretofore are gone to hell; but each one imagines that he lays out matters better for his own escape than others have done. He does not intend to come to that place of torment; he says within himself that he intends to take effectual care, and to order matters so for himself as not to fail.

But the foolish children of men miserably delude themselves in their own schemes, and in confidence in their own strength and wisdom; they trust to nothing but a shadow. The greater part of those who heretofore have lived under the same means of grace, and are now dead, are undoubtedly gone to hell; and it was not because they were not as wise as those who are now alive: it was not because they did not lay out matters as well for themselves to secure their own escape. If we could speak with them, and inquire of them, one by one, whether they expected when alive, and when they used to hear about hell, ever to be the subjects of that misery, we doubtless, should hear one and another reply, "No, I never intended to come here: I had laid out matters otherwise in my mind; I thought I should contrive well for myself: I thought my scheme good. I intended to take effectual care; but it came upon me unexpected; I did not look for it at that time, and in that manner; it came as a thief: Death outwitted me: God's wrath was too quick for me. Oh, my cursed foolishness! I was flattering myself, and pleasing myself with vain dreams of what I would do hereafter; and when I was saying, peace and safety, then suddenly destruction came upon me."

10. God has laid Himself under no obligation by any promise to keep any natural man out of hell one moment. God certainly has made no promises either of eternal life or of any deliverance or preservation from eternal death but what are contained in the covenant of grace, the promises that are given in Christ, in whom all the promises are yea and amen. But surely they have no interest in the promises of the covenant of grace who are not the children of the covenant, who do not believe in any of the promises, and have no interest in the Mediator of the covenant.

So that, whatever some have imagined and pretended about promises made to natural men's earnest seeking and knocking, it is plain and manifest that whatever pains a natural man takes in religion, whatever prayers he makes, till he believes in Christ, God is under no manner of obligation to keep him a moment from eternal destruction.

So that, thus it is that natural men are held in the hand of God, over the pit of hell; they have deserved the fiery pit, and are already sentenced to it; and God is dreadfully provoked. His anger is as great towards them as to those that are actually suffering the executions of the fierceness of His wrath in hell, and they have done nothing in the least to appease or abate that anger, neither is God in the least bound by any promise to hold them up one moment; the devil is waiting for them, hell is gaping for them, the flames gather and flash about them, and would fain lay hold on them, and swallow them up; the fire pent up in their own hearts is struggling to break out: and they have no interest in any Mediator, there are no means within reach that can be any security to them. In short, they have no refuge, nothing to take hold of; all that preserves them every moment is the mere arbitrary will, and uncovenanted, unobliged forbearance of an incensed God.

Application

3   The use of this awful subject may be for awakening uncoverted persons in this congregation. This that you have heard is the case of every one of you that are out of Christ. That world of misery, that lake of burning brimstone, is extended abroad under you. There is the dreadful pit of the glowing flames of the wrath of God; there is hell's wide gaping mouth open; and you have nothing to stand upon, nor any thing to take hold of; there is nothing between you and hell but the air; it is only the power and mere pleasure of God that holds you up.

4   You probably are not sensible of this; you find you are kept out of hell, but do not see the hand of God in it; but look at other things, as the good state of your bodily constitution, your care of your own life, and the means you use for your own preservation. But indeed these things are nothing; if God should withdraw His hand, they would avail no more to keep you from falling, than the thin air to hold up a person that is suspended in it.

5   Your wickedness makes you as it were heavy as lead, and to tend downwards with great weight and pressure towards hell; and if God should let you go, you would immediately sink and swiftly descend and plunge into the bottomless gulf, and your healthy constitution, and your own care and prudence, and best contrivance, and all your righteousness, would have no more influence to uphold you and keep you out of hell, than a spider's web would have to stop a fallen rock. Were it not for the sovereign pleasure of God, the earth would not bear you one moment; for you are a burden to it: the creation groans with you; the creature is made subject to the bondage of your corruption, not willingly; the sun does not willingly shine upon you to give you light to serve sin and Satan; the earth does not willingly yield her increase to satisfy your lusts; nor is it willingly a stage for your wickedness to be acted upon; the air does not willingly serve you for breath to maintain the flame of life in your vitals, while you spend your life in the service of God's enemies. God's creatures are good, and were made for men to serve God with, and do not willingly subserve to any other purpose, and groan when they are abused to purposes so directly contrary to their nature and end. And the world would spew you out, were it not for the sovereign hand of Him who hath subjected it in hope. There are black clouds of God's wrath now hanging directly over your heads, full of the dreadful storm, and big with thunder; and were it not for the restraining hand of God, it would immediately burst forth upon you. The sovereign pleasure of God, for the present, stays His rough wind; otherwise it would come with fury, and your destruction would come like a whirlwind, and you would be like the chaff of the summer threshing floor.

The wrath of God is like great waters that are dammed for the present; 6
they increase more and more, and rise higher and higher, till an outlet is
given; and the longer the stream is stopped, the more rapid and mighty is
its course when once it is let loose. It is true that judgment against your
evil works has not been executed hitherto; the floods of God's vengeance
have been withheld; but your guilt in the meantime is constantly increasing, and you are every day treasuring up more wrath; the waters are constantly rising, and waxing more and more mighty; and there is nothing but
the mere pleasure of God that holds the waters back, that are unwilling to
be stopped, and press hard to go forward. If God should only withdraw His
hand from the floodgate, it would immediately fly open, and the fiery
floods of the fierceness and wrath of God, would rush forth with inconceivable fury, and would come upon you with omnipotent power; and if
your strength were ten thousand times greater than it is, yea, ten thousand
times greater than the strength of the stoutest, sturdiest devil in hell, it
would be nothing to withstand or endure it.

The bow of God's wrath is bent, and the arrow made ready on the 7
string, and justice bends the arrow at your heart, and strains the bow, and
it is nothing but the mere pleasure of God, and that of an angry God,
without any promise or obligation at all, that keeps the arrow one moment from being made drunk with your blood. Thus all you that never
passed under a great change of heart, by the mighty power of the Spirit of
God upon your souls, all you that were never born again, and made new
creatures, and raised from being dead in sin, to a state of new, and before
altogether unexperienced light and life, are in the hands of an angry God.
However you may have reformed your life in many things, and may have
had religious affections, and may keep up a form of religion in your families and closets, and in the house of God, it is nothing but His mere pleasure that keeps you from being this moment swallowed up in everlasting
destruction. However unconvinced you may now be of the truth of what
you hear, by and by you will be fully convinced of it. Those that are gone
from being in the like circumstances with you see that it was so with
them; for destruction came suddenly upon most of them, when they expected nothing of it and while they were saying, peace and safety: now
they see that those things on which they depended for peace and safety,
were nothing but thin air and empty shadows.

The God that holds you over the pit of hell, much as one holds a spider 8
or some loathsome insect over the fire, abhors you, and is dreadfully provoked: His wrath towards you burns like fire; He looks upon you as worthy
of nothing else but to be cast into the fire; He is of purer eyes than to bear
to have you in His sight; you are ten thousand times more abominable in

His eyes than the most hateful venomous serpent is in ours. You have offended Him infinitely more than ever a stubborn rebel did his prince; and yet it is nothing but His hand that holds you from falling into the fire every moment. It is to be ascribed to nothing else, that you did not go to hell the last night; that you was suffered to awake again in this world, after you closed your eyes to sleep. And there is no other reason to be given, why you have not dropped into hell since you arose in the morning, but that God's hand has held you up. There is no other reason to be given why you have not gone to hell, since you have sat here in the house of God, provoking His pure eyes by your sinful wicked manner of attending His solemn worship. Yea, there is nothing else that is to be given as a reason why you do not this very moment drop down into hell.

9   O sinner! Consider the fearful danger you are in: it is a great furnace of wrath, a wide and bottomless pit, full of the fire of wrath, that you are held over in the hand of that God, whose wrath is provoked and incensed as much against you, as against many of the damned in hell. You hang by a slender thread, with the flames of divine wrath flashing about it, and ready every moment to singe it, and burn it asunder; and you have no interest in any Mediator, and nothing to lay hold of to save yourself, nothing to keep off the flames of wrath, nothing of your own, nothing that you ever have done, nothing that you can do, to induce God to spare you one moment. And consider here more particularly.

1. Whose wrath it is: it is the wrath of the infinite God. If it were only the wrath of man, though it were of the most potent prince, it would be comparatively little to be regarded. The wrath of kings is very much dreaded, especially of absolute monarchs, who have the possessions and lives of their subjects wholly in their power, to be disposed of at their mere will. Proverbs 20.2: "The fear of a king is as the roaring of a lion: Whoso provoketh him to anger, sinneth against his own soul." The subject that very much enrages an arbitrary prince is liable to suffer the most extreme torments that human art can invent, or human power can inflict. But the greatest earthly potentates in their greatest majesty, and strength, and when clothed in their greatest terrors, are but feeble, despicable worms of the dust, in comparison of the great and almighty Creator and King of heaven and earth. It is but little that they can do when most enraged, and when they have exerted the utmost of their fury. All the kings of the earth, before God, are as grasshoppers; they are nothing, and less than nothing: both their love and their hatred is to be despised. The wrath of the great King of kings,

is as much more terrible than theirs, as His majesty is greater. Luke 12.4–5: "And I say unto you, my friends, Be not afraid of them that kill the body, and after that, have no more that they can do. But I will forewarn you whom you shall fear: fear him, which after he hath killed, hath power to cast into hell: yea, I say unto you, Fear him."

2. It is the fierceness of His wrath that you are exposed to. We often read of the fury of God: as in Isaiah 59.18: "According to their deeds, accordingly he will repay fury to his adversaries." So Isaiah 66.15: "For behold, the Lord will come with fire, and with his chariots like a whirlwind, to render his anger with fury, and his rebuke with flames of fire." And in many other places. So, Revelation 19.15: we read of "the wine press of the fierceness and wrath of Almighty God." The words are exceedingly terrible. If it had only been said, "the wrath of God," the words would have implied that which is infinitely dreadful: but it is "the fierceness and wrath of God." The fury of God! the fierceness of Jehovah! Oh, how dreadful must that be! Who can utter or conceive what such expressions carry in them! But it is also "the fierceness and wrath of Almighty God." As though there would be a very great manifestation of His almighty power in what the fierceness of His wrath should inflict, as though omnipotence should be as it were enraged, and exerted, as men are wont to exert their strength in the fierceness of their wrath. Oh! then, what will be the consequence! What will become of the poor worms that shall suffer it! Whose hands can be strong? And whose heart can endure? To what a dreadful, inexpressible, inconceivable depth of misery must the poor creature be sunk who shall be the subject of this!

Consider this, you that are here present that yet remain in an unregenerate state. That God will execute the fierceness of His anger implies that He will inflict wrath without any pity. When God beholds the ineffable extremity of your case, and sees your torment to be so vastly disproportioned to your strength, and sees how your poor soul is crushed, and sinks down, as it were, into an infinite gloom; He will have no compassion upon you, He will not forbear the executions of His wrath, or in the least lighten His hand; there shall be no moderation or mercy, nor will God then at all stay His rough wind; He will have no regard to your welfare, nor be at all careful lest you should suffer too much in any other sense, than only that you shall not suffer beyond what strict justice requires. Nothing shall be withheld because it is so hard for you to bear. Ezekiel 8.18: "Therefore will I also deal in fury: mine eye shall not spare, neither will I have pity; and though they cry in mine ears with a loud voice, yet I will not hear them." Now God stands ready to pity you; this is a day of mercy; you may cry now with some encouragement of obtaining mercy. But when once the day of mercy is past, your most lamentable and dolorous cries and shrieks will be in vain; you will be wholly lost and thrown away of God as to any regard to your welfare. God will have no other use to put you to, but to suffer misery; you shall be continued in being to no other end; for you will be a vessel of wrath fitted to destruction; and there will be no other use of this vessel, but to be filled full of wrath. God will be so far from pitying you when you cry to Him, that it is said He will only "laugh and mock." Proverbs 1.25–26, etc.

How awful are those words, Isaiah 63.3, which are the words of the great God: "I will tread them in mine anger, and will trample them in my fury, and their blood shall be sprinkled upon my garments, and I will stain all my raiment." It is perhaps impossible to conceive of words that carry in them greater manifestations of these three things, viz., contempt, and hatred, and fierceness of indignation. If you cry to God to pity you, He will be so far from pitying you in your doleful case, or showing you the least regard or favor, that instead of that, He will only tread you under foot. And though He will know that you cannot bear the weight of omnipotence treading upon you, yet He will not regard that, but He will crush you under His feet without mercy; He will crush out your blood, and make it fly and it shall be sprinkled on His garments, so as to stain all His raiment. He will not only hate you, but He will have you in the utmost contempt: no place shall be thought fit for you, but under His feet to be trodden down as the mire of the streets.

3. The misery you are exposed to is that which God will inflict to that end, that He might show what that wrath of Jehovah is. God hath had it on His heart to show to angels and men both how excellent His love is, and also how terrible His wrath is. Sometimes earthly kings have a mind to show how terrible their wrath is, by the extreme punishments they would execute on those that would provoke them. Nebuchadnezzar, that mighty and haughty monarch of the Chaldean empire, was willing to show his wrath when enraged with Shadrach, Meshech, and Abednego; and accordingly gave orders that the burning fiery furnace should be heated seven times hotter than it was before; doubtless, it was raised to the utmost degree of fierceness that human art could raise it. But the great God is also willing to show His wrath, and magnify His awful majesty and mighty power in the ex-

treme sufferings of His enemies. Romans 9.22: "What if God, willing to show his wrath, and to make his power known, endure with much long-suffering the vessels of wrath fitted to destruction?" And seeing this is His design, and what He has determined, even to show how terrible the restrained wrath, the fury and fierceness of Jehovah is, He will do it to effect. There will be something accomplished and brought to pass that will be dreadful with a witness. When the great and angry God hath risen up and executed His awful vengeance on the poor sinner, and the wretch is actually suffering the infinite weight and power of His indignation, then will God call upon the whole universe to behold that awful majesty and mighty power that is to be seen in it. Isaiah 33:12–14: "And the people shall be as the burnings of lime, as thorns cut up shall they be burnt in the fire. Hear ye that are far off, what I have done; and ye that are near, acknowledge my might. The sinners in Zion are afraid; fearfulness hath surprised the hypocrites," etc.

Thus it will be with you that are in an unconverted state, if you continue in it; the infinite might, and majesty, and terribleness of the omnipotent God shall be magnified upon you, in the ineffable strength of your torments. You shall be tormented in the presence of the holy angels, and in the presence of the Lamb; and when you shall be in this state of suffering, the glorious inhabitants of heaven shall go forth and look on the awful spectacle, that they may see what the wrath and fierceness of the Almighty is; and when they have seen it, they will fall down and adore that great power and majesty. Isaiah 66.23–24: "And it shall come to pass, that from one new moon to another, and from one sabbath to another, shall all flesh come to worship before me, saith the Lord. And they shall go forth and look upon the carcasses of the men that have transgressed against me; for their worm shall not die, neither shall their fire be quenched, and they shall be an abhorring unto all flesh."

4. It is everlasting wrath. It would be dreadful to suffer this fierceness and wrath of Almighty God one moment; but you must suffer it to all eternity. There will be no end to this exquisite horrible misery. When you look forward, you shall see a long forever, a boundless duration before you, which will swallow up your thoughts, and amaze your soul; and you will absolutely despair of ever having any deliverance, any end, any mitigation, any rest at all. You will know certainly that you must wear out long ages, millions of millions of ages, in wrestling and conflicting with this almighty merciless vengeance; and then when you have so

done, when so many ages have actually been spent by you in this manner, you will know that all is but a point to what remains. So that your punishment will indeed be infinite. Oh, who can express what the state of a soul in such circumstances is! All that we can possibly say about it gives but a very feeble, faint representation of it; it is inexpressible and inconceivable: For "who knows the power of God's anger?"

10   How dreadful is the state of those that are daily and hourly in the danger of this great wrath and infinite misery! But this is the dismal case of every soul in this congregation that has not been born again, however moral and strict, sober and religious, they may otherwise be. Oh that you would consider it, whether you be young or old! There is reason to think that there are many in this congregation now hearing this discourse that will actually be the subjects of this very misery to all eternity. We know not who they are, or in what seats they sit, or what thoughts they now have. It may be they are now at ease, and hear all these things without much disturbance, and are now flattering themselves that they are not the persons, promising themselves that they shall escape. If they knew that there was one person, and but one, in the whole congregation, that was to be the subject of this misery, what an awful thing would it be to think of! If we knew who it was, what an awful sight would it be to see such a person! How might all the rest of the congregation lift up a lamentable and bitter cry over him! But, alas! instead of one, how many is it likely will remember this discourse in hell? And it would be a wonder, if some that are now present should not be in hell in a very short time, even before this year is out. And it would be no wonder if some persons, that now sit here, in some seats of this meetinghouse, in health, quiet and secure, should be there before tomorrow morning. Those of you that finally continue in a natural condition, that shall keep out of hell longest will be there in a little time! your damnation does not slumber; it will come swiftly, and, in all probability, very suddenly upon many of you. You have reason to wonder that you are not already in hell. It is doubtless the case of some whom you have seen and known, that never deserved hell more than you, and that heretofore appeared as likely to have been now alive as you. Their case is past all hope; they are crying in extreme misery and perfect despair; but here you are in the land of the living and in the house of God, and have an opportunity to obtain salvation. What would not those poor damned hopeless souls give for one day's opportunity such as you now enjoy!

11   And now you have an extraordinary opportunity, a day wherein Christ has thrown the door of mercy wide open, and stands in calling and crying

with a loud voice to poor sinners; a day wherein many are flocking to Him, and pressing into the kingdom of God. Many are daily coming from the east, west, north and south; many that were very lately in the same miserable condition that you are in are now in a happy state, with their hearts filled with love to Him who has loved them, and washed them from their sins in His own blood, and rejoicing in hope of the glory of God. How awful is it to be left behind at such a day! To see so many others feasting, while you are pining and perishing! To see so many rejoicing and singing for joy of heart, while you have cause to mourn for sorrow of heart, and howl for vexation of spirit! How can you rest one moment in such a condition? Are not your souls as precious as the souls of the people at Suffield, where they are flocking from day to day to Christ?

Are there not many here who have lived long in the world, and are not   12
to this day born again? and so are aliens from the commonwealth of Israel, and have done nothing ever since they have lived, but treasure up wrath against the day of wrath? Oh, sirs, your case, in an especial manner, is extremely dangerous. Your guilt and hardness of heart is extremely great. Do you not see how generally persons of your years are passed over and left, in the present remarkable and wonderful dispensation of God's mercy? You had need to consider yourselves, and awake thoroughly out of sleep. You cannot bear the fierceness and wrath of the infinite God. And you, young men, and young women, will you neglect this precious season which you now enjoy, when so many others of your age are renouncing all youthful vanities, and flocking to Christ? You especially have now an extraordinary opportunity; but if you neglect it, it will soon be with you as with those persons who spent all the precious days of youth in sin, and are now come to such a dreadful pass in blindness and hardness. And you, children, who are unconverted, do not you know that you are going down to hell, to bear the dreadful wrath of that God, who is now angry with you every day and every night? Will you be content to be the children of the devil, when so many other children in the land are converted, and are become the holy and happy children of the King of kings?

And let every one that is yet of Christ, and hanging over the pit of hell,   13
whether they be old men and women, or middle-aged, or young people, or little children, now hearken to the loud calls of God's word and providence. This acceptable year of the Lord, a day of such great favors to some, will doubtless be a day of as remarkable vengeance to others. Men's hearts harden, and their guilt increases apace at such a day as this, if they neglect their souls; and never was there so great danger of such person being given up to hardness of heart and blindness of mind. God seems now to be hastily

gathering in His elect in all parts of the land; and probably the greater part of adult persons that ever shall be saved, will be brought in now in a little time, and that it will be as it was on the great outpouring of the Spirit upon the Jews in the apostles' days;[1] The election will obtain, and the rest will be blinded. If this should be the case with you, you will eternally curse this day, and will curse the day that ever you was born, to see such a season of the pouring out of God's Spirit, and will wish that you had died and gone to hell before you had seen it. Now undoubtedly it is, as it was in the days of John the Baptist, the ax is in an extraordinary manner laid at the root of the trees,[2] that every tree which brings not forth good fruit, may be hewn down and cast into the fire.

14   Therefore, let everyone that is out of Christ, now awake and fly from the wrath to come. The wrath of Almighty God is now undoubtedly hanging over a great part of this congregation: Let everyone fly out of Sodom: "Haste and escape for your lives, look not behind you, escape to the mountain, lest you be consumed."[3]

QUESTIONING AND DISCUSSING

Edwards, "Sinners in the Hands of an Angry God"

1. Although Jonathan Edwards is reported to have read the sermon with a "level voice," most members of the congregation were said to be crying audibly during its delivery. What techniques does Edwards use to persuade and influence his audience—originally, his congregation? Why might they be effective? Under what conditions? What values might they demonstrate, and how do you respond to Edwards's rhetorical techniques? Is Edwards unethical in his methods? Why or why not?

2. A central and very famous simile in this sermon involves the following lines: "The God that holds you over the pit of hell, much as one holds a spider or some loathsome insect over the fire, abhors you, and is dreadfully provoked: His wrath towards you burns like fire; He looks upon you as worthy of nothing else but to be cast into the fire; He is of purer eyes than to bear to have you in His sight; you are ten thousand times more abominable in His eyes than the most hateful venomous serpent is in ours." Analyze this simile,

1 In Acts 2 the apostle Peter admonishes a crowd to repent and be converted, saying, "Save yourselves from this untoward generation. Then they that gladly received his word were baptized: and the same day there were added unto them about three thousand souls" (Acts 2.40–41).
2 "And now also the ax is laid unto the root of the trees: therefore every tree which bringeth not forth good fruit is hewn down, and cast into the fire" (Matthew 3.10).
3 Genesis 19.17.

examining, if you wish, its congruence with or difference from your own values (or, if you wish, beliefs).

3. This sermon is a staple of literary anthologies. Why do you think that might be the case?

⊞

SHIRLEY JACKSON

A California native and Syracuse University graduate, Shirley Jackson (1919–1965) is known for her novel *The Haunting of Hill House* (1959), which has been called "one of the greatest horror stories of all time" by no less a horror expert than Stephen King. Celebrated for her stories of suspense, Jackson also wrote about her life as the mother of four children. Many of her stories and other literary works were collected after she died. "The Lottery," which was published in *The New Yorker* in 1948, is one of the most widely anthologized stories of the last century. Although some readers reacted strongly and negatively to the story at the time of its publication, it reflects not only Jackson's own experience living in a small college town in New England but also her experiences with anti-Semitism (her husband was Jewish) and post–World War II discussions of the evils of war and the Holocaust.

⊞

The Lottery

The morning of June 27th was clear and sunny, with the fresh warmth of a full-summer day; the flowers were blossoming profusely and the grass was richly green. The people of the village began to gather in the square, between the post office and the bank, around ten o'clock; in some towns there were so many people that the lottery took two days and had to be started on June 26th, but in this village, where there were only about three hundred people, the whole lottery took less than two hours, so it could begin at ten o'clock in the morning and still be through in time to allow the villagers to get home for noon dinner.

The children assembled first, of course. School was recently over for the summer, and the feeling of liberty sat uneasily on most of them; they tended to gather together quietly for a while before they broke into boisterous play, and their talk was still of the classroom and the teacher, of books and reprimands. Bobby Martin had already stuffed his pockets full of stones, and the other boys soon followed his example, selecting the smoothest and roundest stones; Bobby and Harry Jones and Dickie Delacroix—the villagers pronounced his name "Dellacroy"—eventually made a great pile of stones in one corner of the square and guarded it against the raids of the other boys. The girls stood aside, talking among themselves, looking over their shoulders at the boys, and the very small children rolled in the dust or clung to the hands of their older brothers or sisters.

3   Soon the men began to gather, surveying their own children, speaking of planting and rain, tractors and taxes. They stood together, away from the pile of stones in the corner, and their jokes were quiet and they smiled rather than laughed. The women, wearing faded house dresses and sweaters, came shortly after their menfolk. They greeted one another and exchanged bits of gossip as they went to join their husbands. Soon the women, standing by their husbands, began to call to their children, and the children came reluctantly, having to be called four or five times. Bobby Martin ducked under his mother's grasping hand and ran, laughing, back to the pile of stones. His father spoke up sharply, and Bobby came quickly and took his place between his father and his oldest brother.

4   The lottery was conducted—as were the square dances, the teenage club, the Halloween program—by Mr. Summers, who had time and energy to devote to civic activities. He was a round-faced, jovial man and he ran the coal business, and people were sorry for him, because he had no children and his wife was a scold. When he arrived in the square, carrying the black wooden box, there was a murmur of conversation among the villagers, and he waved and called "Little late today, folks." The postmaster, Mr. Graves, followed him, carrying a three-legged stool, and the stool was put in the center of the square and Mr. Summers set the black box down on it. The villagers kept their distance, leaving a space between themselves and the stool, and when Mr. Summers said, "Some of you fellows want to give me a hand?" there was a hesitation before two men, Mr. Martin and his oldest son, Baxter, came forward to hold the box steady on the stool while Mr. Summers stirred up the papers inside it.

5   The original paraphernalia for the lottery had been lost long ago, and the black box now resting on the stool had been put into use even before Old Man Warner, the oldest man in town, was born. Mr. Summers spoke frequently to the villagers about making a new box, but no one liked to upset even as much tradition as was represented by the black box. There was a story that the present box had been made with some pieces of the box that had preceded it, the one that had been constructed when the first people settled down to make a village here. Every year, after the lottery, Mr. Summers began talking about a new box, but every year the subject was allowed to fade off without anything's being done. The black box

grew shabbier each year; by now it was no longer completely black but splintered badly along one side to show the original wood color, and in some places faded and stained.

Mr. Martin and his oldest son, Baxter, held the black box securely on the stool until Mr. Summers had stirred the papers thoroughly with his hand. Because so much of the ritual had been forgotten or discarded, Mr. Summers had been successful in having slips of paper substituted for the chips of wood that had been used for generations. Chips of wood, Mr. Summers had argued, had been all very well when the village was tiny, but now that the population was more than three hundred and likely to keep on growing, it was necessary to use something that would fit more easily into the black box. The night before the lottery, Mr. Summers and Mr. Graves made up the slips of paper and put them in the box, and it was then taken to the safe of Mr. Summers' coal company and locked up until Mr. Summers was ready to take it to the square the next morning. The rest of the year, the box was put away, sometimes one place, sometimes another; it had spent one year in Mr. Graves' barn and another year underfoot in the post office, and sometimes it was set on a shelf in the Martin grocery and left there.

There was a great deal of fussing to be done before Mr. Summers declared the lottery open. There were the lists to make up—of heads of families, heads of households in each family, members of each household in each family. There was the proper swearing-in of Mr. Summers by the postmaster, as the official of the lottery; at one time, some people remembered, there had been a recital of some sort, performed by the official of the lottery, a perfunctory, tuneless chant that had been rattled off duly each year; some people believed that the official of the lottery used to stand just so when he said or sang it, others believed that he was supposed to walk among the people, but years and years ago this part of the ritual had been allowed to lapse. There had been, also, a ritual salute, which the official of the lottery had had to use in addressing each person who came up to draw from the box, but this also had changed with time, until now it was felt necessary only for the official to speak to each person approaching. Mr. Summers was very good at all this; in his clean white shirt and blue jeans, with one hand resting carelessly on the black box, he seemed very proper and important as he talked interminably to Mr. Graves and the Martins.

Just as Mr. Summers finally left off talking and turned to the assembled villagers, Mrs. Hutchinson came hurriedly along the path to the square, her sweater thrown over her shoulders, and slid into place in the back of the crowd. "Clean forgot what day it was," she said to Mrs. Delacroix, who stood next to her, and they both laughed softly. "Thought my old man was out back stacking wood," Mrs. Hutchinson went on, "and then I looked out the window and the kids were gone, and then I remembered it was the twenty-seventh and came a-running." She dried her hands on her apron, and Mrs. Delacroix said, "You're in time, though. They're still talking away up there."

9   Mrs. Hutchinson craned her neck to see through the crowd and found her husband and children standing near the front. She tapped Mrs. Delacroix on the arm as a farewell and began to make her way through the crowd. The people separated good-humoredly to let her through; two or three people said, in voices just loud enough to be heard across the crowd, "Here comes your Missus, Hutchinson," and "Bill, she made it after all." Mrs. Hutchinson reached her husband, and Mr. Summers, who had been waiting, said cheerfully, "Thought we were going to have to get on without you, Tessie." Mrs. Hutchinson said, grinning, "Wouldn't have me leave m'dishes in the sink, now, would you, Joe?" and soft laughter ran through the crowd as the people stirred back into position after Mrs. Hutchinson's arrival.

10   "Well, now," Mr. Summers said soberly, "guess we better get started, get this over with, so's we can go back to work. Anybody ain't here?"

11   "Dunbar," several people said. "Dunbar, Dunbar."

12   Mr. Summers consulted his list. "Clyde Dunbar," he said. "That's right. He's broke his leg, hasn't he? Who's drawing for him?"

13   "Me, I guess," a woman said, and Mr. Summers turned to look at her. "Wife draws for her husband," Mr. Summers said. "Don't you have a grown boy to do it for you, Janey?" Although Mr. Summers and everyone else in the village knew the answer perfectly well, it was the business of the official of the lottery to ask such questions formally. Mr. Summers waited with an expression of polite interest while Mrs. Dunbar answered.

14   "Horace's not but sixteen yet," Mrs. Dunbar said regretfully. "Guess I gotta fill in for the old man this year."

15   "Right," Mr. Summers said. He made a note on the list he was holding. Then he asked, "Watson boy drawing this year?"

16   A tall boy in the crowd raised his hand. "Here," he said. "I'm drawing for m'mother and me." He blinked his eyes nervously and ducked his head as several voices in the crowd said things like "Good fellow, Jack," and "Glad to see your mother's got a man to do it."

17   "Well," Mr. Summers said, "guess that's everyone. Old Man Warner make it?"

18   "Here," a voice said, and Mr. Summers nodded.

19   A sudden hush fell on the crowd as Mr. Summers cleared his throat and looked at the list. "All ready?" he called. "Now, I'll read the names—heads

of families first—and the men come up and take a paper out of the box. Keep the paper folded in your hand without looking at it until everyone has had a turn. Everything clear?"

The people had done it so many times that they only half listened to   20
the directions; most of them were quiet, wetting their lips, not looking around. Then Mr. Summers raised one hand high and said, "Adams." A man disengaged himself from the crowd and came forward. "Hi, Steve," Mr. Summers said, and Mr. Adams said, "Hi, Joe." They grinned at one another humorlessly and nervously. Then Mr. Adams reached into the black box and took out a folded paper. He held it firmly by one corner as he turned and went hastily back to his place in the crowd, where he stood a little apart from his family, not looking down at his hand.

"Allen," Mr. Summers said. "Anderson. . . . Betham."   21

"Seems like there's no time at all between lotteries any more," Mrs.   22
Delacroix said to Mrs. Graves in the back row. "Seems like we got through the last one only last week."

"Time sure goes fast," Mrs. Graves said.   23

"Clark. . . . Delacroix."   24

"There goes my old man," Mrs. Delacroix said. She held her breath   25
while her husband went forward.

"Dunbar," Mr. Summers said, and Mrs. Dunbar went steadily to the box   26
while one of the women said, "Go on, Janey," and another said, "There she goes."

"We're next," Mrs. Graves said. She watched while Mr. Graves came   27
around from the side of the box, greeted Mr. Summers gravely, and se-lected a slip of paper from the box. By now, all through the crowd there were men holding the small folded papers in their large hands, turning them over and over nervously. Mrs. Dunbar and her two sons stood to-gether, Mrs. Dunbar holding the slip of paper.

"Harburt. . . . Hutchinson."   28

"Get up there, Bill," Mrs. Hutchinson said, and the people near her   29
laughed.

"Jones."   30

"They do say," Mr. Adams said to Old Man Warner, who stood next to   31
him, "that over in the north village they're talking of giving up the lottery."

Old Man Warner snorted. "Pack of crazy fools," he said. "Listening to   32
the young folks, nothing's good enough for *them*. Next thing you know, they'll be wanting to go back to living in caves, nobody work any more, live *that* way for a while. Used to be a saying about 'Lottery in June, corn be heavy soon.' First thing you know, we'd all be eating stewed chickweed and acorns. There's *always* been a lottery," he added petulantly. "Bad enough to see young Joe Summers up there joking with everybody."

33   "Some places have already quit lotteries," Mrs. Adams said.

34   "Nothing but trouble in *that*," Old Man Warner said stoutly. "Pack of young fools."

35   "Martin." And Bobby Martin watched his father go forward. "Overdyke. . . . Percy."

36   "I wish they'd hurry," Mrs. Dunbar said to her older son. "I wish they'd hurry."

37   "They're almost through," her son said.

38   "You get ready to run tell Dad," Mrs. Dunbar said.

39   Mr. Summers called his own name and then stepped forward precisely and selected a slip from the box. Then he called, "Warner."

40   "Seventy-seventh year I been in the lottery," Old Man Warner said as he went through the crowd. "Seventy-seventh time."

41   "Watson." The tall boy came awkwardly through the crowd. Someone said, "Don't be nervous, Jack," and Mr. Summers said, "Take your time, son."

42   "Zanini."

43   After that, there was a long pause, a breathless pause, until Mr. Summers, holding his slip of paper in the air, said, "All right fellows." For a minute, no one moved, and then all the slips of paper were opened. Suddenly, all the women began to speak at once, saying, "Who is it," "Who's got it?," "Is it the Dunbars?," "Is it the Watsons?" Then the voices began to say, "It's Hutchinson. It's Bill," "Bill Hutchinson's got it."

44   "Go tell your father," Mrs. Dunbar said to her older son.

45   People began to look around to see the Hutchinsons. Bill Hutchinson was standing quiet, staring down at the paper in his hand. Suddenly, Tessie Hutchinson shouted to Mr. Summers, "You didn't give him time enough to take any paper he wanted. I saw you. It wasn't fair!"

46   "Be a good sport, Tessie," Mrs. Delacroix called, and Mrs. Graves said, "All of us took the same chance."

47   "Shut up, Tessie," Bill Hutchinson said.

48   "Well, everyone," Mr. Summers said, "That was done pretty fast, and now we've got to be hurrying a little more to get it done in time." He consulted his next list. "Bill," he said, "you draw for the Hutchinson family. You got any other households in the Hutchinsons?"

49   "There's Don and Eva," Mrs. Hutchinson yelled. "Make *them* take their chance!"

50   "Daughters draw with their husbands' families, Tessie," Mr. Summers said gently. "You know that as well as anyone else."

51   "It wasn't *fair*," Tessie said.

"I guess not, Joe," Bill Hutchinson said regretfully. "My daughter draws   52
with her husband's family, that's only fair. And I've got no other family except the kids."

"Then, as far as drawing for families is concerned, it's you," Mr. Sum-   53
mers said in explanation, "and as far as drawing for households is concerned, that's you, too. Right?"

"Right," Bill Hutchinson said.   54

"How many kids, Bill?" Mr. Summers asked formally.   55

"Three," Bill Hutchinson said. "There's Bill, Jr., and Nancy, and little   56
Dave. And Tessie and me."

"All right, then," Mr. Summers said. "Harry, you got their tickets back?"   57

Mr. Graves nodded and held up the slips of paper. "Put them in the box,   58
then," Mr. Summers directed. "Take Bill's and put it in."

"I think we ought to start over," Mrs. Hutchinson said, as quietly as she   59
could. "I tell you it wasn't *fair*. You didn't give him time enough to choose.
*Every*body saw that."

Mr. Graves had selected the five slips and put them in the box, and he   60
dropped all the papers but those onto the ground, where the breeze caught
them and lifted them off.

"Listen, everybody," Mrs. Hutchinson was saying to the people around her.   61

"Ready, Bill?" Mr. Summers asked, and Bill Hutchinson, with one quick   62
glance around at his wife and children, nodded.

"Remember," Mr. Summers said, "take the slips and keep them folded   63
until each person has taken one. Harry, you help little Dave." Mr. Graves
took the hand of the little boy, who came willingly with him up to the
box. "Take a paper out of the box, Davy," Mr. Summers said. Davy put his
hand into the box and laughed. "Take just *one* paper," Mr. Summers said.
"Harry, you hold it for him." Mr. Graves took the child's hand and removed the folded paper from the tight fist and held it while little Dave
stood next to him and looked up at him wonderingly.

"Nancy next," Mr. Summers said. Nancy was twelve, and her school   64
friends breathed heavily as she went forward, switching her skirt, and took
a slip daintily from the box. "Bill, Jr.," Mr. Summers said, and Billy, his
face red and his feet over-large, nearly knocked the box over as he got a
paper out. "Tessie," Mr. Summers said. She hesitated for a minute, looking
around defiantly, and then set her lips and went up to the box. She
snatched a paper out and held it behind her.

"Bill," Mr. Summers said, and Bill Hutchinson reached into the box   65
and felt around, bringing his hand out at last with the slip of paper in it.

The crowd was quiet. A girl whispered, "I hope it's not Nancy," and the   66
sound of the whisper reached the edges of the crowd.

67   "It's not the way it used to be," Old Man Warner said clearly. "People ain't the way they used to be."

68   "All right," Mr. Summers said. "Open the papers. Harry, you open little Dave's."

69   Mr. Graves opened the slip of paper and there was a general sigh through the crowd as he held it up and everyone could see that it was blank. Nancy and Bill, Jr., opened theirs at the same time, and both beamed and laughed, turning around to the crowd and holding their slips of paper above their heads.

70   "Tessie," Mr. Summers said. There was a pause, and then Mr. Summers looked at Bill Hutchinson, and Bill unfolded his paper and showed it. It was blank.

71   "It's Tessie," Mr. Summers said, and his voice was hushed. "Show us her paper, Bill."

72   Bill Hutchinson went over to his wife and forced the slip of paper out of her hand. It had a black spot on it, the black spot Mr. Summers had made the night before with the heavy pencil in the coal-company office. Bill Hutchinson held it up, and there was a stir in the crowd.

73   "All right, folks," Mr. Summers said. "Let's finish quickly."

74   Although the villagers had forgotten the ritual and lost the original black box, they still remembered to use stones. The pile of stones the boys had made earlier was ready; there were stones on the ground with the blowing scraps of paper that had come out of the box. Mrs. Delacroix selected a stone so large she had to pick it up with both hands and turned to Mrs. Dunbar. "Come on," she said. "Hurry up."

75   Mrs. Dunbar had small stones in both hands, and she said, gasping for breath, "I can't run at all. You'll have to go ahead and I'll catch up with you."

76   The children had stones already, and someone gave little Davy Hutchinson a few pebbles.

77   Tessie Hutchinson was in the center of a cleared space by now, and she held her hands out desperately as the villagers moved in on her. "It isn't fair," she said. A stone hit her on the side of the head.

78   Old Man Warner was saying, "Come on, come on, everyone." Steve Adams was in the front of the crowd of villagers, with Mrs. Graves beside him.

    "It isn't fair, it isn't right," Mrs. Hutchinson screamed, and then they were upon her.

QUESTIONING AND DISCUSSING

Jackson, "The Lottery"

1. "The Lottery" clearly raises a variety of ethical questions. How do the villagers seem to justify the process of the lottery and its outcomes?
2. Looking closely at the text, examine how the lottery has continued, why "there has *always* been a lottery." Explore the logic—or lack of it—behind the lottery and the villagers' attitude toward it.
3. Consider the various lessons of the story, looking again at the text for your examples. How might the story represent more than the brutal traditions of one small town?

LANGSTON HUGHES

A mainstay among those associated with the literary and cultural movement known as the Harlem Renaissance, Langston Hughes (1902–1967) was born in Joplin, Missouri. He moved from place to place in his youth, living primarily with his grandmother in Lawrence, Kansas. At times, he also lived with his mother in Detroit and Cleveland, where he published poems and stories in the school newspaper, *The Central High Monthly*. While his mother supported his ambitions to be a poet, Hughes's aspirations conflicted with the wishes of his father, a businessman who had gone to Mexico in response to the racism he had encountered in the United States. Unlike other, more traditional black poets such as Countee Cullen, Hughes preferred to focus on the oral, improvisational, and musical traditions of black culture, transferring them to fiction and poetry. Hughes was a world traveler and a man with extensive political commitments who eventually became militant on the subject of race but who nonetheless gave voice to an ironic humor in his work.

Salvation

I was saved from sin when I was going on thirteen. But not really saved. It happened like this. There was a big revival at my Auntie Reed's church. Every night for weeks there had been much preaching, singing, praying, and shouting, and some very hardened sinners had been brought to Christ, and the membership of the church had grown by leaps and bounds. Then just before the revival ended, they held a special meeting for children, "to bring the young lambs to the fold." My aunt spoke of it for days ahead. That night I was escorted to the front row and placed on the mourners' bench with all the other young sinners, who had not yet been brought to Jesus.

2   My aunt told me that when you were saved you saw a light, and something happened to you inside! And Jesus came into your life! And God was with you from then on! She said you could see and hear and feel Jesus in your soul. I believed her. I had heard a great many old people say the same thing and it seemed to me they ought to know. So I sat there calmly in the hot, crowded church, waiting for Jesus to come to me.

3   The preacher preached a wonderful rhythmical sermon, all moans and shouts and lonely cries and dire pictures of hell, and then he sang a song about the ninety and nine safe in the fold, but one little lamb was left out in the cold. Then he said: "Won't you come? Won't you come to Jesus? Young lambs, won't you come?" And he held out his arms to all us young sinners there on the mourners' bench. And the little girls cried. And some of them jumped up and went to Jesus right away. But most of us just sat there.

4   A great many older people came and knelt around us and prayed, old women with jet-black faces and braided hair, old men with work-gnarled hands. And the church sang a song about the lower lights are burning, some poor sinners to be saved. And the whole building rocked with prayer and song.

5   Still I kept waiting to *see* Jesus.

6   Finally all the young people had gone to the altar and were saved, but one boy and me. He was a rounder's son named Westley. Westley and I were surrounded by sisters and deacons praying. It was very hot in the church, and getting late now. Finally Westley said to me in a whisper: "God damn! I'm tired o' sitting here. Let's get up and be saved." So he got up and was saved.

7   Then I was left all alone on the mourners' bench. My aunt came and knelt at my knees and cried, while prayers and songs swirled all around me in the little church. The whole congregation prayed for me alone, in a mighty wail of moans and voices. And I kept waiting serenely for Jesus, waiting, waiting—but he didn't come. I wanted to see him, but nothing happened to me. Nothing! I wanted something to happen to me, but nothing happened.

8   I heard the songs and the minister saying: "Why don't you come? My dear child, why don't you come to Jesus? Jesus is waiting for you. He wants you. Why don't you come? Sister Reed, what is this child's name?"

"Langston," my aunt sobbed.   9

"Langston, why don't you come? Why don't you come and be saved?   10
Oh, Lamb of God! Why don't you come?"

Now it was really getting late. I began to be ashamed of myself, holding   11
everything up so long. I began to wonder what God thought about Westley, who certainly hadn't seen Jesus either, but who was now sitting
proudly on the platform, swinging his knickerbockered legs and grinning
down at me, surrounded by deacons and old women on their knees praying. God had not struck Westley dead for taking his name in vain or for
lying in the temple. So I decided that maybe to save further trouble, I'd
better lie, too, and say that Jesus had come, and get up and be saved.

So I got up.   12

Suddenly the whole room broke into a sea of shouting, as they saw me   13
rise. Waves of rejoicing swept the place. Women leaped in the air. My
aunt threw her arms around me. The minister took me by the hand and
led me to the platform.

When things quieted down, in a hushed silence, punctuated by a few   14
ecstatic "Amens," all the new young lambs were blessed in the name of
God. The joyous singing filled the room.

The night, for the last time in my life but one—for I was a big boy   15
twelve years old—I cried. I cried, in bed alone, and couldn't stop. I buried
my head under the quilts, but my aunt heard me. She woke up and told my
uncle I was crying because the Holy Ghost had come into my life, and because I had seen Jesus. But I was really crying because I couldn't bear to
tell her that I had lied, that I had deceived everybody in the church, and
I hadn't seen Jesus, and that now I didn't believe there was a Jesus any
more, since he didn't come to help me.

Questioning and Discussing

Hughes, "Salvation"

1. "I was saved from sin when I was going on thirteen. But not really saved."
   How do these opening lines prepare the reader for the conflict that follows?
   What does Hughes seem to be saying about faith?

2. What are the various ethical dilemmas that the young Hughes faces in this
   selection? How does the narrative's development prepare you for these
   dilemmas?

3. "So I sat there calmly in the hot, crowded church, waiting for Jesus to come
   to me." Comment on the effect of this sentence and Hughes's saying, "I

began to wonder what God thought about Westley, who certainly hadn't
seen Jesus either, but who was now sitting proudly on the platform [. . .]

⌗

LISA SCHMEISER

In the early 1990s, Lisa Schmeiser (1972–) spent five and a half consecutive years, in
her words, "at schools with 'Polytechnic' in the name," earning a BS in biology from
the Virginia Polytechnic Institute and an MS in technical communications from Rensse-
laer Polytechnic Institute. Recently, Schmeiser has written or coauthored three books on
Web design and site maintenance. By day, she is a senior associate editor at *Macworld*
magazine. By night, as Schmeiser puts it, she is a "bilious television critic for the Minneapolis *City Paper, Television without Pity,* and *Tevee.*" "Do Geeks Need to Go to
College?"—one among Schmeiser's many freelance articles—originally appeared in the
technology section of *Salon,* the well-established and award-winning online magazine.

⌗

Do Geeks Need to Go to College?

1   When Brad Scott of *Clear Ink* has to devise the information architecture
for a new Web site, he just asks himself where the site's bathrooms will be.

2   Scott, a one-time interior design major turned information architect, is
speaking only metaphorically, of course. But he says learning about "critical adjacencies of space"—such as putting restrooms near conference
rooms so that meeting attendees can quickly duck in and out—carries
over to Web design, where the "critical adjacencies" are of information.

3   Scott's migration from architecture into the technology industry isn't
atypical: Talk to a group of tech workers, and you may find that the majority of them drifted into the industry from a completely different discipline.

4   The Web industry is creating jobs at a clip, and many of those jobs are
going to college graduates without academic computing experience—and
people who skipped college altogether. No one has taken a formal count of
these two groups, but they haven't gone unnoticed. And their success raises
the question of whether a computer science education, or even any higher
education, is a prerequisite to competing in the high-tech job market.

5   The relevance of higher education to high-tech jobs is under scrutiny,
thanks to the rising number of success stories featuring someone who ma-
jored in a right-brained specialty, bypassed college or dropped out—the

most famous example being Harvard dropout Bill Gates. In December, *Forbes* asked if investing in a college education was a smart way to spend time investing in a career. Among the numbers the article cited: Close to fifteen percent of the Forbes 400 either dropped out of college or avoided it altogether, and those executives boast an average net worth of $4.8 billion. A few weeks later, *U.S. News and World Report* ran a related article: More boys are opting out of college to pursue jobs in a booming economy.

There is ample incentive to trade higher education for high-salaried, high-tech jobs. *Forbes* noted that a college degree costing $120,000 might actually be worth more as a mutual fund with a five percent interest rate; if a teenager's parents sink the $30,000 they would have spent on the first year's tuition into a mutual fund for their child, he'll have $500,000 by the time he turns fifty. Many college graduates, especially those who spend their early postgraduate years paying off student loans, will never see that much in the bank. The article also contents that colleges are unable to keep up with the proliferation of programming languages and technologies driving today's job market, and thus do not outfit their students with the necessary job skills. Is it any wonder would-be tech tyros rethink college?   6

The übergeek news portal *Slashdot* posted a link to the *Forbes* article and found itself hosting a three hundred-plus-message argument on the merits of education in relation to high-tech jobs. The respondents were evenly split: Some younger programmers argued that their practical experience and high salaries offset the disadvantages of lacking a degree, while others argued that a formal education leads to a higher caliber of technical work later in life.   7

But does that formal education even have to be in engineering, or will any old degree do? Scott is joined by Web producer Satya Kuner and Jason Monberg, the CTO of Sparks, in believing that their nontechnical degrees have enhanced their work in the tech industry.   8

Kuner contends that her background as a dance major improved her job performance when she was charged with doing technical support for Unix, C, and Perl programming. As part of her job, she had to walk users through solutions to thorny code errors, then log the events in a database for other workers. She credits the improvements she made to the company's database to the communication skills she learned in college, saying, "Lots of geeks I know can't provide clear instructions because they can't fathom that someone couldn't know something."   9

Humanities-based skills can also improve the traditional code-writing process. According to Kuner, artists bring a novel perspective to code composition, allowing them to extend the uses to which a programming language is put. Monberg, who holds a degree in sociology, has noticed that coding and engineering groups that include people trained outside the   10 discipline are more open to innovation. "It opens the door to a more en-gaging cross-pollinating environment," he says. "Individual contributors are not completely locked into thinking only about their specific task."

11 Nor are individuals locked into one set of job skills: Scott, Kuner, and Monberg all acquired specific technical skills on a compressed schedule in response to job demands, and they believe that their college education helped flatten the learning curve—even if the connections between Unix and dancing, interior design or sociology aren't readily apparent.

12 College provided a mental model for learning subsequent skills, which complements the one constant in high tech: the need to keep learning. Any high-tech worker, regardless of academic background, must stay abreast of new skills to keep up in the field.

13 Perhaps, as those *Slashdot* posters argued, the learning can take place on site at a sixty thousand dollar programming job. But judging by the posts complaining, "if only Bill Gates took an OS class," there are also unar-guable merits to a technical university education for engineers. Monberg himself admits that there are times when a computer science education would have come in handy: "When you get down to it, earning a CS de-gree provides one with some very basic practical experience."

14 At the heart of the higher-education debate lies the question: Do high-tech workers miss out on some crucial educational event if they skip col-lege? There's no denying that high tech offers something few other disciplines do—the ability to enter and move up in an industry based on applicable skills and experience, instead of requiring a degree to even en-ter the arena. But having a degree doesn't prevent high-tech workers from picking up experience elsewhere. The learning skills one uses to pick up programming languages and systems operations are highly individual and can be acquired from disciplines as diverse as music or biology. They can also be picked up through a combination of time spent on a computer and a curiosity to learn more: Kuner, Monberg, and Scott all honed their tech-nical chops through self-teaching.

15 What can't be picked up through hard programming experience is the discipline-specific experience that any college graduate possesses. To a bi-ology major like me, object-oriented programming didn't make much sense when it was explained in terms of classes and constructors. But when I could map the general ideas to familiar ground—the immune system's dif-ferent types of cells and the chemical signals they send to each other are similar to classes of code objects and the embedded functional signals they each have—I picked up the programming concept and expanded on it in ways my computer-engineering coworkers hadn't pondered yet.

16 As more graduates combine their intellectual experience with practical technical skills, observers may recast the higher-education question. In-

stead of wondering whether college is relevant, we may ask what kind of degrees will allow high-tech workers and companies to stay fresh and keep innovating.

QUESTIONING AND DISCUSSING

Schmeiser, "Do Geeks Need to Go to College?"

1. Lisa Schmeiser argues several important points in this essay. What are they? Are any of her arguments tempered by the knowledge that this essay was written just *before* the dot-com "bust"? Does this information alter—or enhance—her major points? Explain your perspective, looking to the text to support your point of view.

2. "More boys are opting out of college to pursue jobs in a booming economy," *Forbes* magazine proclaimed at the time this article was published. What are the potential long-term implications of that type of decision? How does Schmeiser argue against it?

3. Looking at the essay for your support, discuss the ways in which Schmeiser articulates the value of—and what appear to be *her values* regarding—a liberal education. Is Schmeiser persuasive? Explain.

⊞

ALFRED, LORD TENNYSON

Likely the most influential and popular English poet of the nineteenth century, Alfred, Lord Tennyson (1809–1892), was born in Somersby, Lincolnshire. Tennyson was encouraged to devote his life to writing poetry by his friends at Cambridge University, who together were called "the Apostles." Tennyson became close to Arthur Hallam, a member of that group; Hallam's sudden death in 1833 prompted Tennyson to write one of his most celebrated poems, the long elegy *In Memoriam*. Despite the fact that his sixty-year span of writing manifests a range of verse styles, Tennyson is particularly known for a type of poem created by the ancient Greeks called the *idyl*, a poem about country life. Idyls typically feature a monologue spoken by a mythological figure; the character tells a story in a rich setting that helps to evoke a particular context and mood. Although some of these characters are maidens (as in Tennyson's "Lady of Shalott"), others, such as the speaker in the poem that follows, are heroes or prophets, all advanced in age. As is the case with "Ulysses," many of these characters, by implication, urge their Victorian-era readers to act heroically.

⊞

Ulysses

    It little profits that an idle king,
By this still hearth, among these barren crags,
Matched with an agéd wife, I mete and dole
Unequal laws unto a savage race,
That hoard, and sleep, and feed, and know not me.   5

    I cannot rest from travel; I will drink
Life to the lees. All times I have enjoyed
Greatly, have suffered greatly, both with those
That loved me, and alone; on shore and when
Through scudding drifts the rainy Hyades   10
Vexed the dim sea. I am become a name;
For always roaming with a hungry heart
Much have I seen and known—cities of men
And manners, climates, councils, governments,
Myself not least, but honored of them all—   15
And drunk delight of battle with my peers,
Far on the ringing plains of windy Troy.
I am a part of all that I have met;
Yet all experience is an arch wherethrough

Gleams that untraveled world, whose margin fades   20
For ever and for ever when I move.
How dull it is to pause, to make an end,
To rust unburnished, not to shine in use!
As though to breathe were life. Life piled on life
Were all too little, and of one to me   25
Little remains; but every hour is saved
From that eternal silence, something more,
A bringer of new things; and vile it were
For some three suns to store and hoard myself,
And this gray spirit yearning in desire   30
To follow knowledge like a sinking star,
Beyond the utmost bound of human thought.

   This is my son, mine own Telemachus,
To whom I leave the scepter and the isle—
Well-loved of me, discerning to fulfill   35
This labor by slow prudence to make mild
A rugged people, and through soft degrees
Subdue them to the useful and the good.
Most blameless is he, centered in the sphere
Of common duties, decent not to fail   40
In offices of tenderness, and pay
Meet adoration to my household gods,
When I am gone. He works his work, I mine.

   There lies the port; the vessel puffs her sail:
There gloom the dark, broad seas. My mariners,   45
Souls that have toiled, and wrought, and thought with me—
That ever with a frolic welcome took
The thunder and the sunshine, and opposed
Free hearts, free foreheads—you and I are old;
Old age hath yet his honor and his toil.   50
Death closes all; but something ere the end,
Some work of noble note, may yet be done,
Not unbecoming men that strove with Gods.
The lights begin to twinkle from the rocks;
The long day wanes; the slow moon climbs; the deep   55
Moans round with many voices. Come, my friends.
'Tis not too late to seek a newer world.
Push off, and sitting well in order smite

The sounding furrows; for my purpose holds
To sail beyond the sunset, and the baths   60
Of all the western stars, until I die.
It may be that the gulfs will wash us down;
It may be we shall touch the Happy Isles,
And see the great Achilles, whom we knew.
Though much is taken, much abides; and though   65
We are not now that strength which in old days
Moved earth and heaven, that which we are, we are:
One equal temper of heroic hearts,
Made weak by time and fate, but strong in will
To strive, to seek, to find, and not to yield.   70

QUESTIONING AND DISCUSSING

Tennyson, "Ulysses"

1. Why might a nineteenth-century poet look to a hero of ancient Greek
   mythology for the subject of his poem? For what purpose?

2. Based on evidence from the poem, what are the aged Ulysses' aspirations?
   What does he seem to value most? Consider "Old age hath yet his honor
   and his toil. /Death closes all; but something ere the end,/Some work of
   noble note, may yet be done," and "'Tis not too late to seek a newer world."

3. How does Tennyson make this a poem about something more than an elderly explorer-king? What are the lessons to be learned from the poem that
   might—even now—inform our attitudes and understanding of older persons
   in the world? What evidence from the poem supports your perspective?

⊞

Robert Grudin

Robert Grudin (1938–) specializes in Renaissance and comparative literature at the University of Oregon, where he is professor in the Department of English. He was educated at Harvard University; Trinity College, Dublin; and the University of California at Berkeley, where in 1969 he earned a PhD in comparative literature. Grudin has written on a wide range of subjects and is known not only for his literary studies but also as a social and moral philosopher. His books include *Mighty Opposites: Shakespeare and Renaissance Contrariety* (1979), *Time and the Art of Living* (1982), and *The Grace of Great Things: Creativity and Innovation* (1990). *Time and the Art of Living* develops a "personal philosophy of life," in Grudin's words, using science, literature, art, philosophy, history, and personal reflection as its contexts. The essay that follows is part of *The Grace of Great Things*, which studies the ways in which new ideas and new forms are transmuted in the contemporary world.

⌗

Ideology and Moral Philology

But the Idols of the Market Place are the most troublesome of all—idols which have crept into the understanding through the alliances of words and names. For men believe that their reason governs words, but it is also true that words react on the understanding, and this it is that has rendered philosophy and the sciences sophistical and inactive.

—Francis Bacon, *Novum Organum*

Nothing so needs reforming as other people's habits.

—Mark Twain, *Pudd'nhead Wilson*

What do I mean by "ideology"? Let me begin by looking at two ways of comparing human beings with apes.

Traditional satire (for example, *Gulliver's Travels*) dwelt on similarities between human beings and apes as means of illustrating the chronic limitations of human nature. The ape's behavioral patterns, its grooming, its play, its mating, its social interactions, were exploited by satirists as a destructive mimicry of similar mechanisms in humanity. This satire is based on a world view deeply skeptical of human virtue and highly critical of human pretensions to progress and excellence.

Modern science, on the other hand, characteristically sees the same ape/human similarities as proof of the remarkable intelligence of apes. (After all, if they're so like us, they've got to be bright!) This opinion is based on a world view deeply rooted in the idea of progress and the sense of human excellence.

4   To understand the difference between the classical view and our own is to begin to appreciate the power of ideology. It is also to exercise one of the important talents that human beings have and apes do not: the faculty of self-examination.

5   Ideology is at once the matrix from which creativity is born and the barrier against which it strains. As a pattern of ideas absorbed by us as children from our society, ideology gives each of us intellectual viability among our fellows and introduces us to a variety of important issues. But as an essentially unphilosophical system, born of social necessity, governed by historical circumstance, incomplete, arbitrary, and insidiously tyrannical, ideology is unfriendly to independent thought. Creativity has no choice but to grow in ideology, no goal except to move beyond it.

6   The conflict between ideology and creativity may be illustrated by comparing ideology with philosophy. Let us say that both philosophy and ideology are systems of ideas on which people base their judgments and actions. Philosophy is an open system. Its premises are clear, and it retains, in addition to these premises, a method by which they may be reexamined.

7   Ideology, on the other hand, is a closed system whose premises, whether explicit or implicit, are unavailable to scrutiny. Ideology causes us to judge and to act automatically, uninquisitively. We do not question our own judgments or actions and have not the means of questioning them if we wanted to. When others question them, we fall back to generalizations which, though we have not examined them, we accept as unimpeachable; we use these generalizations to displace responsibility for error from ourselves to our questioners. While philosophy evolves, more often than not, by recognizing its own excesses or failings, ideology can never see itself as "wrong." When it evolves at all, ideology evolves unconsciously, not through distinct reforms of self-awareness but through slow, unconscious cultural realignments.

8   These factors can make ideology a vehicle for laziness and self-deceit. Ideology enables us to pass judgments on a variety of issues while lacking adequate information or analytic skill or commitment to discovering the truth. And ideology not only substitutes for information, analysis, and commitment, but also for conscience. The fact that a given action or lack of action conforms to our ideology absolves us from having to worry about it or take responsibility for it. With ideology we may appear to be well informed, analytically skillful, inquisitive, conscientious, and morally responsible without really being so.

9   This does not mean, of course, that ideologies are universally debilitating, or that they are all equally so. Some ideologies (for example, liberal-

ism) actually have values such as inquiry and enlightenment built into them, while in others such values are prohibited. What it does mean is that a system is ideological to the extent that its values are assumed and unexamined, and that even edifying words like "enlightenment," if thus assumed and unexamined, can lose much of their positive force and function instead as false counters, near-empty clichés, or instruments of reaction. In this respect ideology is a kind of moral computer program, which is excellent at arranging information, providing precedents, expediting connections, and suggesting conclusions, but which cannot analyze its own structure or consciously evolve from it.

Recognizing the operation of ideology in others is a minor matter compared to locating it in ourselves and our peers. Ideology lies deep and is well protected. The mechanisms with which people defend ideology are precisely those with which they defend their personal integrity. For this very reason, the identification and analysis of one's own ideology are critical steps in the progress toward self-knowledge. Later in this chapter I will suggest a method by which these steps may be taken. A more suitable beginning, however, may be found in an examination of what may be called microideologies—modal or periodic value systems that we adopt or put aside as occasion warrants. 10

Microideology describes our behavior and sense of identity as they change in response to typical personal interactions: with our parents or our children, with friends, colleagues, or strangers, with our own or the opposite sex. These changes occur painlessly, often unconsciously, but they can be so profound as to activate, within the same individual, strikingly different presentations of character. To understand these expressions and their roots in circumstance is to understand, in little, a key factor of ideology. A homely enough set of such systems operates the way people generally behave in street traffic. 11

As pedestrians we are midgets in a giant world. We are deeply aware of our own physical weakness, in terms of limited speed and energy; we sense that we would not fare well in collisions with cars or bicycles. We view these potential antagonists with distaste and fear. Car drivers, faceless in their instruments of power and pollution, are potential homicides, sinister agents of a callous system. Bicyclists are mere outlaws, debased cowboys who combine the unbridled ambitions of the tyrant with the furtive quickness of the sneak. Conscious of the superior power of car drivers and bicyclists, we are ardent democrats and great believers in the law. Our Constitution, a great text written in stop signs, traffic lights, and speed limits, is defended with zeal and indignation, and nothing is quite so righteously satisfying as the knowledge that, by stepping into a pedestrian crossing at the right time, we have caused a car to stop. 12

13   As bicyclists we are strong advocates of the conservation of energy. Stop signs—the restrictive machinery of a callous system—pedestrians, and cars have importance to us less as independent moral entities than as obstacles that threaten us with the unthinkable toil of having to stop our bikes and pedal them back up to speed. As such, stodgy pedestrians and obscene cars are figures of reaction and oppression. They lack our spirit of adventure; they breed in the staleness of closed systems. Aware of our own maverick status, we feel entitled to use our wits. The bicyclian politics, which springs from a profoundly liberal commitment to the sharing of other people's rights, is seen to apply without discrimination on road, sidewalk, and lawn.

14   As car drivers we are important people in a hurry. Because we need not worry about our own vulnerability or energy, our main concern is time. We deplore the unreasonable regulations—born of a callous system—that delay our swift procedure from place to place, but more bitterly we resent the assorted rabble, some on foot and some on two-wheeled toys, who flaunt ill-bestowed liberty by milling around in the street. These loiterers and guerrillas are small, weak, and probably poor; they have no strength except in number; in spite of this they get ridiculously upset when someone fails to notice them. Doubtless sprung from the god of war, we are so imbued with epic high spirits that often we cannot tolerate even our own kind.

15   Though they may be somewhat exaggerated, the preceding examples suggest that generic value shifts characterize our normal daily journeys from task to task. I am concerned here less with the marvelous swiftness of these transformations than with the nature of the value systems involved. These value systems share a number of characteristics.

- First, each system is shared by all or almost all members of the class or set.
- Second, each is based on a subjective and limited understanding of the total situation (in this case, traffic).
- Third, each system has little regard for its own internal consistency or significance in context.
- Fourth, in each system ethical standards develop not out of inquiry but directly out of the necessities of the particular situation.
- Fifth, these standards are not merely accepted but asserted sanctimoniously and defensively against members of other sets.

16   A sixth characteristic, implicit in all three examples, is perhaps most illuminating of all: the value systems of walker, biker, and driver, confusing and contradictory as they are, seem actually to assist them in carrying out

the specific tasks they address. They allay doubt; they tranquilize anxiety; they rationalize aggressiveness; they dispel responsibility. As support systems and protective shells, they aid us in navigating through the complex challenges of modern life. Much more comfortably than philosophy, ideology makes practical sense of the world. It assures us that experience has coherence and can be explained. It gives us confidence in ourselves as participants in a meaningful project.

To discuss the "limitations" of ideology is to discuss only half the problem. As important as the things we cannot do with ideology is the fact that we cannot do without it.   17

Such, in microcosm, is the nature of ideology. With one major exception, the same principles that apply to walkers, bicyclists, and drivers apply to liberals and conservatives, to Marxists, Freudians, feminists, and fundamentalists. The exception is that these latter ideologies, these supersystems, do not change when we get on or off a bicycle or in or out of a car. They are wedged firmly into our identity because they spring, rather than from temporary requirements, from the historical necessities of a whole nation, social class, or intellectual movement, and because they address, rather than some temporary role, our general condition as individuals in society.   18

A particular understanding of ideology is characteristic of the young. Younger generations who reject established values generally have no idea that their own revolutionary program will harden into protective ideologies. Moreover, they reject elements of systems without inquiring into the bases of systems. The hippies, for example, rebelled against the capitalism and conservatism of their parents while unconsciously retaining the materialism and anti-intellectualism on which those elements were based. This mistake left the hippies not only with empty heads but with hungry bellies; the upshot was a counterrevolution (the yuppies) which, with all the joy of new discovery, reinstated the old order. Thus revolution, by surprise, becomes a force of continuity, and generations, like tourists lost in a strange city, find themselves returning by various alleyways to the same square.   19

It is not enough simply to isolate and denounce ideology. To gain at least partial freedom from it, we must first make peace with it; we must understand its inevitable prevalence in others and our own vulnerability to it. The liberal arts afford various ways of meeting this challenge. Cultural history, as applied by many scholars, offers insights into the phenomenon of ideology by examining various ideologies of the past. Such insights are particularly informative when they apply to our own political and cultural background. Philosophy, anthropology, sociology, psychology, economics, and political science have all sponsored examinations of the substrata that lie beneath generally accepted ideas.   20

21   Perhaps more helpful than any of these, curiously enough, is the study of literature. Though they never bothered to invent the word, great satirists like Chaucer and Swift were profound students of ideology, as were major novelists like Hawthorne, Flaubert, Tolstoy, James, and Conrad. One of the primary functions of good fiction and drama is to establish a limited point of view—quite often one which is unquestioningly accepted by large elements of the author's own society—and play off against it ironically. Understanding literature properly, we may learn to recognize as such the oversights and contradictions that attend our own points of view.

22   But none of these studies addresses the whole. None persistently explores those areas which might be called the heart of ideology; the premises of our view so profound as to be unspoken, the topics so long neglected as to be forgotten. For people to explore these idiosyncrasies in their own ideology is almost as unlikely as it is for them to see through the backs of their own heads. One method, however, offers some hope of progress. To address it, we must return again to the distinction between philosophy and ideology.

23   I called philosophy an "open" system and spoke of it as combining a structure of ideas with an instrument of self-scrutiny. Philosophy, as defined above, is not purely conceptual: it is rather an interplay of concept and method. In this relation, method does not merely "apply" concepts: it studies and tests and reforms them, overseeing them the way a cat oversees her kittens. Because of this interplay, concepts (words or groups of words) are continuously reviewed, reassessed, and subjected to hypothetical variations.

24   Ideology, on the other hand, seems to be preeminently conceptual. Though given ideologies (for example, Marxism, feminism) may have built-in methods, the methods are not employed in self-analysis but exist as a way of criticizing other ideologies and globally asserting their own root concepts. How are these concepts structured? We may see them as radiating out from a series of key words, comprising the ideas and feelings that these words evoke and the relations between one set of words, ideas, and feelings and another.

25   Take, for example, the final words of the American Pledge of Allegiance: "with liberty and justice for all." The ideologue in me still feels a glow of pleasure at hearing these words. Yet history can point to no relationship as dynamically insecure as that between liberty and justice. Full-blooded ideologues do not analyze such interactions. By definition, ideologues analyze nothing that relates to their ideology. Instead they rely on the power commanded by the key word, either as support for a position of their own or as a bludgeon against a position held by someone else.

It follows, then, that ideology may be approached through a study of   26
words, which might be called moral philology. It would analyze key words
in an effort to establish the parent concepts they evoke. It would assemble and correlate, appreciate and criticize, the set of parent concepts suggested by groups of key words. Specifically, this study would ask the
following questions about key words:

Does a given word suggest a single concept, or more than one?
If more than one, what do the concepts suggested have in common?
If more than one, do the concepts suggested contradict one another, and
    if so, how?
What do we intend when we use the key word?
Is our intention satisfied by the parent concept or concepts?
If not, how?
Are the constructs suggested by groups of key words harmonious or self-
    contradictory?

Such a study is far from new. It was an important part of the Socratic   27
method of inquiry (dialectic) as evidenced in Platonic dialogues like the
Euthyphro, the Symposium, and the Republic. In these dialogues Socrates
takes three key words ("piety," "love," and "justice," respectively), pins down
the concepts that they evoke, and subjects them to scrutiny. Socrates took
a good deal of heat for his dogged adherence to this method, and more
than anything else it may have been the cause of his condemnation and
death. But society's violent response to moral philology is a testament to
the potentially revolutionary power of this method.

Because of its perennial relevance, moral philology has never wholly   28
disappeared from the rolls, but neither has it ever achieved much currency
as a teaching method and a means of self-examination. It is a difficult
study and (on the surface) a rather dry one. But it is perhaps unchallenged
in exploring the ways of ideology and in devising means of escape from
fixed channels. Whatever its limitations, moral philology has the unique
advantage of beginning with an analysis of those very constructs which
are to be the basis of its later judgments. To do this is to avoid the self-
defeating habit (typical of many other analytic approaches) of using these
very key words, without examination, as the bases for further exploration
and analysis.

The reassessment of key words is perhaps the most accessible and effec-   29
tive method of self-scrutiny available to us. And self-scrutiny, whether
individual or cultural, is an important medium for innovation and a prerequisite for renewal.

QUESTIONING AND DISCUSSING

Grudin, "Ideology and Moral Philology"

1. Explore the ways in which Robert Grudin defines *ideology*. What is its relationship to value systems? How does Grudin demonstrate this? Are his arguments persuasive? Why or why not?

2. What does Grudin mean when he says that in each of the value systems that he discusses, "ethical standards develop not out of inquiry but directly out of the necessities of the particular situation"?

3. What is the relationship among ideology, ethics, and "moral philology"?

4. Respond to Grudin's contention that "self-scrutiny, whether individual or cultural, is an important medium for innovation and a prerequisite for renewal." Why might this be important—or an ethical necessity?

⊞

ALAN M. DERSHOWITZ

Well-known law professor, author, and attorney Alan M. Dershowitz (1938–) received his BA from Brooklyn College in 1959 and his JD from Yale Law School in 1962. He has been described by *Business Week* as "a feisty civil libertarian and one of the nation's most prominent legal educators," by the New York Criminal Bar Association as a man who has made an "outstanding contribution as a scholar and dedicated defender of human rights," and by the Anti-Defamation League of the B'nai B'rith (which gave Dershowitz the William O. Douglas First Amendment Award) as a man demonstrating "compassionate, eloquent leadership and persistent advocacy in the struggle for civil and human rights." At Yale Law School, Dershowitz was editor of the *Yale Law Journal* and graduated first in his class. He became a member of the Harvard Law faculty at twenty-five; he became a full professor at twenty-eight, the youngest person in the school's history to have done so. The consummate defense attorney, his famous and infamous clients have included Anatoly Shcharansky, O. J. Simpson, David Crosby, Mike Tyson, Senator Alan Cranston, various death row inmates, Jim Bakker, and *Penthouse*.

Assimilation Is a Greater Problem Than Anti-Semitism for American Jews

Contrary to the beliefs of many Jews, anti-Semitism is no longer a problem in America; the greater danger for American Jews is assimilation. Many Jews are too willing to emphasize their history of persecution as a way to retain their Jewish identity. Since anti-Semitism and its attendant oppression have vanished from most segments of society, this focus is no longer relevant. However, Jewish life is at risk of disappearing because of high intermarriage rates and low birth rates. American Jews need to move toward a more positive Jewish state of mind in order to counter the effects of assimilation.

The good news is that American Jews—as *individuals*—have never been more secure, more accepted, more affluent, and less victimized by discrimination or anti-Semitism. The bad news is that American Jews—as a *people*—have never been in greater danger of disappearing through assimilation, intermarriage, and low birthrates. The even worse news is that our very success as individuals contributes to our vulnerability as a people. The even better news is that we can overcome this new threat to the continuity of American Jewish life and emerge with a more positive Judaism for the twenty-first century—a Judaism that is less dependent on our enemies for its continuity, and that rests more securely on the considerable, but largely untapped, strengths of our own heritage.

American Jewish life is in danger of disappearing, just as most American Jews have achieved everything we ever wanted: acceptance, influence, affluence, equality. As the result of skyrocketing rates of intermarriage and assimilation, as well as "the lowest birth rate of any religious or ethnic community in the United States," the era of enormous Jewish influence on American life may soon be coming to an end.[1] Although Jews make up just over 2 percent of the population of the United States—approximately 5.5 million[2] out of 262 million—many Americans mistakenly believe that we constitute a full 20 percent of the American people, because of our disproportionate visibility, influence, and accomplishments.[3] But our numbers may soon be reduced to the point where our impact on American life will necessarily become marginalized. One Harvard study predicts that if current demographic trends continue, the American Jewish community is likely to number less than 1 million and conceivably as few as 10,000 by the time the United States celebrates its tricentennial in 2076.[4] Other projections suggest that early in the next century, American Jewish life as we know it will be a shadow of its current, vibrant self—consisting primarily of isolated pockets of ultra-Orthodox Hasidim.[5]

3   Jews have faced dangers in the past, but this time we may be unprepared to confront the newest threat to our survival *as a people,* because its principal cause is our own success as *individuals.* Our long history of victimization has prepared us to defend against those who would destroy us out of hatred; indeed, our history has forged a Jewish identity far too dependent on persecution and victimization by our enemies. But today's most serious threats come not from those who would persecute us, but from those who would, without any malice, kill us with kindness—by assimilating us, marrying us, and merging with us out of respect, admiration, and even love. The continuity of the most influential Jewish community in history is at imminent risk, unless we do something dramatic *now* to confront the quickly changing dangers.

Thoughts on Jewish Survival

4   This viewpoint is a call to action for all who refuse to accept our demographic demise as inevitable. It is a demand for a new Jewish state of mind capable of challenging the conventional wisdom that Judaism is more adaptive to persecution and discrimination than it is to an open, free, and welcoming society—that Jews paradoxically need enemies in order to survive, that anti-Semitism is what has kept Judaism alive. This age-old perspective on Jewish survival is illustrated by two tragic stories involving respected rabbinical leaders.

5   The first story takes place in 1812, when Napoleon was battling the czar for control of the Pale of Settlement (the western part of czarist Russia), where millions of Jews were forced to live in crowded poverty and under persecution and discrimination as second-class subjects. A victory for Napoleon held the promise of prosperity, first-class citizenship, freedom of movement, and an end to discrimination and persecution. A victory for the czar would keep the Jews impoverished and miserable. The great Hasidic rabbi Shneur Zalman—the founder of the Lubavitch dynasty—stood up in his synagogue on the first day of Rosh Hashanah to offer a prayer to God asking help for the leader whose victory would be good for the Jews. Everyone expected him to pray for Napoleon. But he prayed for the czar to defeat Napoleon. In explaining his counterintuitive choice, he said: "Should Bonaparte win, the wealth of the Jews will be increased and their [civic] position will be raised. At the same time their hearts will be estranged from our Heavenly Father. Should however our Czar Alexander win, the Jewish hearts will draw nearer to our Heavenly Father, though the poverty of Israel may become greater and his position lower."[6]

6   This remarkable story is all too typical of how so many Jewish leaders throughout our history have reasoned about Jewish survival. Without

tsuris—troubles—we will cease to be Jewish. We *need* to be persecuted, impoverished, discriminated against, hated, and victimized in order for us to retain our Jewishness. The "chosen people" must be denied choices if Judaism is to survive. If Jews are given freedom, opportunity, and choice, they will choose to assimilate and disappear.

The story recurs, with even more tragic consequences, on the eve of the Holocaust. Another great Eastern European rabbi, Elchanan Wasserman—the dean of the Rabbinical College in Baranowitz, Poland—was invited to bring his entire student body and faculty to Yeshiva College in New York or to the Beis Medrish Letorah in Chicago, both distinguished Orthodox rabbinical colleges. He declined the invitations because "they are both places of spiritual danger, for they are run in a spirit of freethinking." The great rabbi reasoned, "What would one gain to escape physical danger in order to then confront spiritual danger?" Rabbi Wasserman, his family, his students, and their teachers remained in Poland, where they were murdered by the Nazis.*   [7]

I call the approach taken by these rabbis the Tsuris Theory of Jewish Survival. Under this theory, the Jews need external troubles to stay Jewish. Nor has this fearful, negative perspective on Jewish survival been limited to ultra-Orthodox rabbis. Many Jewish leaders, both religious and secular, have argued that Jews *need* enemies—that without anti-Semitism, Judaism cannot survive. Theodor Herzl, the founder of political Zionism and a secular Jew, believed that "our enemies have made us one. . . . It is only pressure that forces us back to the parent stem."[7] In a prediction that reflects an approach to the survival of Judaism strikingly similar to that of the founder of the Lubavitch Hasidim, Herzl warned that if our "Christian hosts were to leave us in peace . . . for two generations," the Jewish people would "merge entirely into surrounding races."[8] Albert Einstein agreed: "It may be thanks to anti-Semitism that we are able to preserve our existence as a race; that at any rate is my belief."[9] Jean-Paul Sartre, a non-Jew, went even further, arguing that the "sole tie that binds [the Jewish people together] is the hostility and disdain of the societies which surround them." He believed that "it is the anti-Semite who makes the Jew."[10]**   [8]

---

*As he was being taken to his death with his "head erect," Rabbi Wasserman reportedly said: "The fire which will consume our bodies will be the fire through which the people of Israel will arise to a new life." *Encyclopedia Judaica*, vol. 16 (Jerusalem: Ketet, 1972), p. 362.

**The famed Russian writer Ilya Ehrenberg, an assimilated Jew who considered converting to Catholicism, insisted that he would remain a Jew "as long as there was a single anti-Semite left on earth." Joshua Rubenstein, *Tangled Loyalties* (New York: Basic Books, 1996), p. 13.

The Jewish Pendulum

9   If the Tsuris Theory of Jewish identity, survival, and unity is true, then Jews are doomed to live precariously on a pendulum perennially swinging in a wide arc between the extremes of persecution and assimilation. As the pendulum swings away from the Scylla of persecution, it inevitably moves toward the Charybdis of assimilation. In this reactive view, Jews have little power over their ultimate destiny. Our enemies always call the shots, either by persecuting us, in which case we fight back and remain Jewish, or by leaving us alone, in which case we assimilate. The only other alternative—the one proposed by Herzl—is for all Jews to move to Israel, where they control their own destiny. But most Jews will continue to ignore that option, certainly if our "hosts" continue to leave us in peace in our adopted homelands. In this respect, aliyah (emigration) to Israel has also been largely determined by our external enemies, since most Jews who have moved to the Jewish homeland have done so in reaction to anti-Semitism and persecution in their native countries.[11]

10   Historically, therefore, there has been some descriptive truth to this pendulum view of persecution alternating with assimilation. Jews have retained their Jewish identity, at least in part, because of tsuris. Our enemies herded us into ghettos, created pales of settlement, discriminated against us, excluded us from certain livelihoods while pressing us into others.[12] We stuck together and remained Jews, resisting as best we could the persecution by our enemies.

11   But there is more—much more—to Jewish identity than collective self-defense. There is something important that is worth defending. After all, until anti-Semitism changed from religious bigotry to "racial" bigotry—roughly near the end of the nineteenth century—persecuted Jews generally had the option of conversion. Unlike Hitler, our religiously inspired persecutors—the Crusaders, the Inquisitors, Martin Luther, and the pogromists—did distinguish between Jews who converted to Christianity and Jews who did not.[13] Indeed, it was precisely their religious mission to convert the Jews, by whatever methods it took.

12   Many Jews did convert—some at knifepoint, others to advance themselves. The story about Professor Daniel Chwolson illustrates the latter phenomenon. Chwolson, a Russian intellectual of the nineteenth century, had converted from Judaism to Russian Orthodoxy as a young man, but he continued to fight against anti-Semitism. This led a Jewish friend to ask him why he had converted: "Out of conviction," the great man said. "What conviction?" his Jewish friend inquired. Chwolson responded: "Out of a firm conviction that it would be far better to be a professor in St. Petersburg than a Hebrew school teacher in Shklop." Yet despite the material

advantages of conversion, most Jews resisted it. Clearly, those Jews—who sacrificed so much—remained Jewish not only in reaction to their enemies. More than our fabled "stiff-neckedness" was involved. There are substantive principles that Jews have been so stubborn about—that we have been willing to fight and even die for. For Jews who define their Jewishness in theological terms, it is easy to find that principle: It is God's will. For the large number of Jews who are skeptical about being God's "chosen people," the principle is more elusive, but it is palpable to most of us, though difficult to articulate. It is a disturbing reality, however, that for a great many Jews, their Jewish identity has been forged and nurtured by our external enemies who have defined *us* as victims of *their* persecution.

Becoming Positively Jewish

Now, after two millennia of persecution and victimization, we may well be moving into a new era of Jewish life during which we will not be persecuted or victimized. If this comes to pass, we will need to refocus our attention on defining the positive qualities of Jewish life that ought to make us want to remain Jews without "help" from our enemies. We must become positively Jewish instead of merely reacting to our enemies. 13

If Herzl's and Sartre's entirely negative view of the reason for Jewish survival were to persist even as we enter this new era of equality and acceptance, then Judaism would not deserve to endure. If Jewish life cannot thrive in an open environment of opportunity, choice, freethinking, affluence, success, and first-class status—if we really do need tsuris, czars, pogroms, poverty, insularity, closed minds, and anti-Semitism to keep us Jewish—then Jewish life as we know it will not, and should not, survive the first half of the twenty-first century. We have been persecuted long enough. The time has come to welcome the end of our victimization without fear that it will mean the end of our existence as a people. We must no longer pray for the czar's victory out of fear that the end of our collective tsuris and the success of individual Jews will mean the failure of Judaism. 14

I believe that Jewish life can thrive in the next century, not *despite* the end of institutional anti-Semitism, the end of Jewish persecution, and the end of Jewish victimization, but *because* of these positive developments. The ultimate good news may be that the denouement of negative Judaism— Jewish identification based largely on circling the wagons to fend off our enemies—compels us to refocus on a more positive and enduring Jewish identification, which will be more suitable to our current situation and the one we will likely be facing in the twenty-first century, when Jews will have the unconstrained choice whether to remain Jewish or to assimilate. 15

We may be entering a true Jewish golden age, during which we will prove, once and for all, that Jews do not need enemies to survive. To the contrary: We can thrive best in an open society where we freely choose to be Jews because of the positive virtues of our 3,500-year-old civilization.

16   I say we *may* be entering this golden age; there are no guarantees. Many Jews believe that the end is near, because increasing rates of assimilation and intermarriage are propelling us toward a demographic Armageddon. A recent apocalyptic article in a Jewish journal concluded that "Kaddish time" is fast approaching for the American Jewish community. (Kaddish is the prayer for the dead.) But reports of the death of Judaism may be premature—*if* we can change the way we think, and act, about Jewish survival. If we refuse to change, if we accept the current demographic trends as intractable, then Jewish life in America may indeed be doomed.

17   The challenge is to move the Jewish state of mind beyond its past obsession with victimization, pain, and problems and point it in a new, more positive direction, capable of thriving in an open society. For unless we do, we may become the generation that witnesses the beginning of the end of one of the most influential civilizations in the history of our planet—a unique source of so much goodness, compassion, morality, creativity, and intelligence over the past several millennia. The demise of Jewish life as we have come to know it would be a tragedy not only for the Jewish people collectively, but also for most of us individually—and for the world at large.

Internal Dangers to Judaism

18   The thesis of this viewpoint is that the long epoch of Jewish persecution is finally coming to an end and that a new age of internal dangers to the Jewish people is on the horizon. Institutional anti-Semitism is on its last legs as governments, churches, universities, and businesses embrace Jews. No Jew today needs to convert in order to become a professor, a banker, or a corporate CEO. Although anti-Semitism persists in many quarters, today's overt anti-Semites—the skinheads, militias, Holocaust deniers, and Farrakhan followers—have become marginalized. They continue to constitute a nuisance and pose a potential threat, but they do not have a significant day-to-day impact on the lives of most Jews, as anti-Semites in previous generations did. Today's marginalized anti-Semites do not decide which jobs we can hold, which universities we can attend, which neighborhoods we can live in, which clubs we can join, or even whom we can date and marry. We no longer look *up* to anti-Semites as the elites in our

society who determine our fate. We look *down* on anti-Semites as the dregs of our society who make lots of noise but little difference.

As Jews and Israel become more secure against external threats, the internal threats are beginning to grow, as graphically illustrated by the assassination of an Israeli prime minister [Yitzhak Rabin] by a Jew, the growing conflict between fundamentalist Jews and more acculturated Jews, the increasing trends toward intermarriage and assimilation, and the decline of Jewish literacy. 19

For thousands of years, Jews have been embattled. Surrounded by enemies seeking to convert us, remove us, even exterminate us, we have developed collective defense mechanisms highly adaptive to combating persecution by anti-Semites. But we have not developed effective means of defending the Jewish future against our own actions and inactions. This is our urgent new challenge—to defend the Jewish future against voluntary self-destruction—and we must face it squarely, if we are to prevent the fulfillment of Isaiah's dire prophecy "Your destroyers will come from your own ranks." 20

We must take control of our own destiny by changing the nature of Jewish life in fundamental ways. The survival of the Jewish people is too important—to us and to the world at large—to be left in the hands of those ultra-Orthodox rabbis who would rather face Armageddon than change the religious status quo. Just as Jews of the past changed the nature of Jewish life in order to adapt to external necessities and to survive the ravages of their external enemies, so, too, must today's Jews change the nature of Jewish life to adapt to new internal necessities and to survive the demographic challenges of intermarriage, assimilation, low birthrates, and the breakdown of neighborhoods and communities. 21

A hundred years ago, Theodor Herzl identified the "Jewish question" of the twentieth century as the literal survival of Jews in the face of external enemies committed to our physical annihilation—Jew-haters in every nation where Jews lived as a minority. His solution—the creation of a secular Jewish state—was to change the nature of Jewish life in dramatic and unanticipated ways. A hundred years later, the "Jewish question" of the twenty-first century is survival in the face of our internal challenges. Herzl also anticipated that this new "Jewish question" might arise if and when our Christian hosts were to leave us in peace. This is now coming to pass. The solution to *this* Jewish question also requires the creation of yet another Jewish state: a new Jewish state of *mind!* 22

This viewpoint continues where *Chutzpah* (1991) left off, in exploring the larger issue of being Jewish today. In the concluding paragraphs of that book I issued the following challenge: 23

We have learned—painfully and with difficulty—how to fight others. Can we develop Jewish techniques for defending against our own success?

Pogo once said: "We have [met] the enemy and he is us!" As Jews, we have not yet been given the luxury of seeing ourselves as the enemy. There are still too many external enemies who challenge the very physical survival of the Jewish people in Israel and throughout the world. But as we become stronger in the face of our external enemies, we must prepare to confront ourselves.

24   In confronting ourselves, we must face the reality that the generation of Jews I wrote about in *Chutzpah*—those of us who remember the Holocaust, the creation of Israel and the moral threats to its survival, the movements to save Soviet, Syrian, and Ethiopian Jewry, the struggle against institutional anti-Semitism—is aging. Our children, who have no actual memory of embattled Judaism fighting for the life, liberty, and equality of endangered Jews, are now the crossroads generation that will determine what Jewish life in America and around the world will be in the coming century. It is to that younger generation of Jews, as well as to their parents, that I address this volume.

Anti-Semitism Has Declined

25   The last decade of the twentieth century has witnessed the end of state-sponsored and church-supported anti-Semitism. The fall of the Soviet Union, a nation that, since the time of Stalin, had been a major source of international anti-Semitism, had a domino effect on ending the state sponsorship of this oldest of bigotries. Other nations within the Soviet sphere of influence stopped espousing anti-Semitism as a matter of government policy. Even most Arab and Islamic countries dropped their overtly anti-Semitic policies. As a result, the United Nations has changed its tone, condemning anti-Semitism and reducing somewhat its pro-Arab and anti-Israel bias. Equally important, the Catholic church—the single institution most responsible for the persecution of Jews over the past two millennia—approved diplomatic relations with Israel, thus annulling its entrenched view that Jewish "homelessness, was the Divine judgment against Jews" for rejecting Jesus. The American Lutheran Church explicitly rejected Martin Luther's anti-Semitic teachings.

26   Bill Clinton's presidency marked the end of discrimination against Jews in the upper echelons of government. For the first time in American history, the fact that an aspirant for high appointive office was a Jew became irrelevant in his or her selection. President Clinton—our first president who grew up in an age when anti-Semitism was unacceptable—selected several Jewish cabinet members, two Jewish Supreme Court justices, nu-

merous Jewish ambassadors and other high-level executive and judicial officials. Nor, apparently, was Jewishness a bar to election to the United States Congress, which has ten Jewish senators and more than two dozen Jewish representatives, several from states with tiny Jewish populations.* Though we have still not had a Jew at the top of either party's ticket, it is fair to say that in today's America, a Jew can aspire to any office, any job, and any social status.

The wealth of individual Jews grew perceptibly during this decade, with   27
25 percent of America's richest people being of Jewish background. (If only earned, as distinguished from inherited, wealth is counted, the percentage would be even higher.)[14] An American Leadership study in 1971–72 found that Jews represented more than 10 percent of America's top "movers and shakers in business," a higher percentage than any other ethnic group.[15] Jews' per capita income is nearly double that of non-Jews. Twice the percentage of Jews as non-Jews earn more than $50,000 a year. And twice the percentage of non-Jews earn less than $20,000.[16] Jewish charitable giving has increased along with Jewish wealth. Jews are now among the largest contributors to universities, museums, hospitals, symphonies, opera, and other charities. "In 1991, the United Jewish Appeal raised more money than any other charity in America, including the Salvation Army, American Red Cross, Catholic Charities and the American Cancer Society."[17] Yet only one-tenth of Jewish philanthropists limit their giving to Jewish charities alone, while one-fourth give only to non-Jewish causes.[18]

A Jew today can live in any neighborhood, even those that were for-   28
merly "restricted." Jews live alongside white Anglo-Saxon Protestants in the most "exclusive" neighborhoods throughout the country—Grosse Pointe, Greenwich, Fifth Avenue, Beacon Hill. And they have been welcomed into the "best" families, including the Roosevelts, Kennedys, Cuomos, and Rockefellers. Economically, socially, and politically, we have become the new WASPs, as a perusal of the sponsor list of any major charitable or cultural event will show. Indeed, terms such as "J.A.S.P." (Jewish Anglo-Saxon Protestant) and "W.A.S.H." (White Anglo-Saxon Hebrew) have become current in some circles to denote the full social acceptance that Jews increasingly enjoy.[19]

Of America's Nobel Prize winners in science and economics, nearly 40   29
percent have been Jews.[20] Of America's 200 most influential intellectuals, half are full Jews, and 76 percent have at least one Jewish parent.[21] Jews attend Ivy League colleges at ten times their presence in the general population.[22] It is no wonder that so many non-Jews believe that we constitute so

---

*The Daily Telegraph, December 31, 1993. Jewish Week, Nov. 8, 1996, p. 11, puts the number of Jewish representatives at thirty-one, while the Los Angeles Jewish Times puts the number at twenty-five.

much higher a percentage of the American population than we actually do. Jews today are equal in virtually every way that matters. What could not have been said even at the end of the 1980s can be said today: American Jews are part of the American mainstream; we are truly victims no more.

A Misperception

30   Yet despite these enormous gains, many older Jews do not seem to be able to give up their anachronistic status as victims. A recent book on the American Jewish community notes: "[A]bout a third [of affiliated Jews in San Francisco said] that Jewish candidates could not be elected to Congress from San Francisco. Yet three out of four Congressional representatives . . . *were*, in fact, well identified Jews at the time the poll was conducted. And they had been elected by a population that was about 95 percent non-Jewish."[23]

31   Nor is this misperception limited to California. According to journalist J. J. Goldberg, "[T]he percentage of Jews who tell pollsters that anti-Semitism is a 'serious problem' in America nearly doubled during the course of the 1980s, from 45 percent in 1983 to almost 85 percent in 1990."[24] Yet by every objective assessment, the problem was less serious in 1990 than it was in 1983, and the trend has clearly been in the direction of improvement.

32   When I speak to older Jewish audiences, I am often accused, sometimes stridently, of minimizing anti-Semitism and am told that it is worse than ever. Social scientists call this dramatic disparity between the reality of declining anti-Semitism and the widespread belief that it is increasing a "perception gap" between what is actually happening and Jewish "sensibilities."[25] Some of the Jews who believe this are similar in this respect to some feminists and black activists I know, who insist that the plight of women and blacks is worse than it ever was.* These good and decent people, whose identities are so tied up with their victimization, are incapable of accepting the good news that their situation is improving. It is not even a matter of perceiving the glass as half full or half empty. They see the glass as broken, even though it is intact and quickly filling up. As the sociologist Marshall Sklare puts it: "American Jews respond more readily to bad news than to good news."[26]

33   I am reminded of the story of the two Jews reading their newspapers over a cup of coffee in a late-nineteenth-century Viennese café. Kurt is reading the liberal Yiddish-language newspaper and shaking his head from

---

*Among blacks and women, it tends to be members of the younger generation who believe that matters are worse than ever.

side to side, uttering soft moans of "Oy vey" and "Vey is meir." Shmulie is reading the right-wing, anti-Semitic German-language tabloid and smiling. Kurt, noticing what Shmulie is reading, shouts at his friend, "Why are you reading that garbage?" Shmulie responds, "When I used to take your newspaper, all I would read about was Dreyfus being falsely accused, the Jews of Russia being subjected to pogroms, anti-Semitic laws being enacted all over Europe, and the grinding poverty of the Jews in the Holy Land. Now, ever since I take this paper, I read about how the Jews control the banks, the press, the arts; how Jews hold all political power behind the scenes; and how we will soon take over the world. Wouldn't you rather read such good news than such bad news?"

With some of today's older Jews, it is exactly the opposite: they refuse to read the good news, even when it is demonstrably true. The insist on focusing on the "oys" rather than the joys of Judaism, as Rabbi Moshe Waldoks put it.[27] This is understandable, in light of the long history of persecution. Like an individual victim of a violent crime who sees his assailant around every corner, the Jewish people have been traumatized by our unrelenting victimization at the hands of Jew-haters. It is impossible for anyone who did not personally experience the Holocaust, or the other repeated assaults on Jewish life throughout our history, to comprehend what it must have been like to be victimized by unrelenting persecution based on primitive Jew-hating. We continue to see anti-Semitism even where it has ceased to exist, or we exaggerate it where it continues to exist in marginalized form. Indeed, some Jewish newspapers refuse to print, and some Jewish organizations refuse to acknowledge, the good news, lest they risk alienating their readerships or losing their membership. For example, in November of 1996 I saw a fundraising letter from a Jewish organization which claimed that "anti-Semitism . . . appears to be growing more robust, more strident, more vicious—*and* more 'respectable.'" Well-intentioned as this organization is, it seeks support by exaggerating the threats we currently face and by comparing them to those we faced during the Holocaust.

The Causes of Contemporary Assimilation

My students, my children, my friends' children—our next generation— understand our new status: they do not want to be regarded as victims. They do not feel persecuted, discriminated against, or powerless. They want to read the new good news, not the old bad news. A 1988 poll of Jewish students at Dartmouth College made the point compellingly: When asked whether they believed that their Jewishness would in any way hamper their future success, not a single student answered in the affirmative.

That is the current reality, and it is different from the reality my parents faced—and even from the reality many of my generation perceived when we were in college or beginning our careers. The coming generation of Jewish adults will not remain Jews *because* of our enemies or because of our perceived status as victims.* They crave a more positive, affirmative, contemporary, and relevant Jewish identity. Unless we move beyond victimization and toward a new Jewish state of mind, many of them will abandon Judaism as not relevant to their current concerns.

36   If we are to counteract this trend, we must understand the dynamics of contemporary assimilation and not confuse them with past episodes of assimilation, which were based largely on the perceived need to escape from the "burdens" of Jewish identification. Today, there are no burdens from which to escape. Being Jewish is easy, at least in relation to external burdens. Jews today assimilate not because Christianity or Islam is "better" or "easier," but because Jewish life does not have a strong enough positive appeal to offset the inertial drift toward the common denominator. Jews do not convert to Christianity; they "convert" to mainstream Americanism, which is the American "religion" closest to Judaism. They see no reason not to follow their heart in marriage, their convenience in neighborhoods, their economic opportunities in jobs, their educational advantages in schools, their conscience in philosophy, and their preferences in lifestyle. Most Jews who assimilate do not feel that they are giving up anything by abandoning a Jewishness they know little about. They associate the Judaism they are abandoning with inconvenient rituals and rules that have no meaning to them. As one young woman remembers her Jewishness: "An old man saying no."[28]

37   We must recognize that many of the factors which have fueled current assimilation and intermarriage are *positive* developments for *individual* Jews: acceptance, wealth, opportunity. Most Jews do not want to impede these developments. Indeed, they want to encourage them. For that reason, we must accept the reality that many Jews will continue to marry non-Jews, but we should not regard it as inevitable that these marriages will necessarily lead to total assimilation. We can take positive steps to stem that tide—but it will take a change in attitude toward mixed marriages, and indeed toward the tribalism that has understandably characterized Jewish attitudes toward outsiders for so much of our history.

Notes

1. Yehuda Rosenman, "Research on the Jewish Family and Jewish Education," in *Facing the Future: Essays on Contemporary Jewish Life*, ed. Steven Bayme (New York: Ktav, 1989), p. 156. Accord-

*In response to this generational perception gap, one of my students suggested that I title this book *Ghetto-ver It!*

ing to Seymour Martin Lipset, in *American Exceptionalism: A Double-Edged Sword* (New York: W. W. Norton, 1996), the average American Jewish woman bears 1.1 children (p. 175).

2. There is significant dispute over this figure because it depends on the definition of who is counted as a Jew. If one included only Jews as defined by Orthodox and Conservative religious laws, the number would be lower. J. J. Goldberg, in *Jewish Power* (Reading, Mass.: Addison-Wesley, 1996), puts the percentage at 2.5. He also cites one expert who says that there are 8 million members of the "Jewish political community," in which he includes non-Jewish spouses and children of Jews (p. 57).

3. A 1992 survey by Martilla & Kiley for the Anti-Defamation League found the median estimate by gentiles of the size of the U.S. Jewish population to be slightly lower, but still whopping, at 18 percent. The study also found that only 10 percent of gentile Americans believe that Jews constitute less than 5 percent of the U.S. population. See Lipset, p. 151; see also Goldberg. Mark Twain noticed the disparity between the tiny number of actual Jews and their enormous perceived influence in a remarkable essay in *Harper's Monthly*, September 1899.

4. Elihu Bergman, "The American Jewish Population Erosion," *Midstream*, October 1977, pp. 9–19.

5. As a deliberate survival strategy, America's ultra-Orthodox Jews attempt "to recreate the world that had existed in pre-war Europe" (Jerome R. Mintz, *Hasidic People: A Place in the New World* [Cambridge, Mass: Harvard University Press, 1992], p. 29). To this end, they take pains to keep secular American influences at bay. Rabbi Elliot Kohn of Kiryas Joel, a Hasidic village in the foothills of upstate New York, explains, "We want isolation. That's why we have no TV's or radios," and that is why such communities use the Yiddish tongue rather than English, dress distinctively, and eschew secular studies (quoted in Don Lattin, "Church-State Conflict in a Jewish Town," *San Francisco Chronicle*, March 25, 1994, p. A1). See also Marc D. Stern, "Orthodoxy in America: The Trend Toward Separatism," *Congress Monthly* (New York: American Jewish Congress), January 1992, pp. 10–12; Egon Mayer, *From Suburb to Shtetl: The Jews of Boro Park* (Philadelphia: Temple University Press, 1979).

6. Simon Dubnow, *History of the Jews in Russia and Poland*, trans. I. Friedlander (1916; reprint, New York: Ktav, 1975) pp. 356–57.

7. Theodor Herzl, *The Jewish State*, trans. Jacob M. Alkow (1896; reprint, New York: Dover, 1988), p. 92.

8. Ibid., p. 91.

9. Albert Einstein, *About Zionism: Speeches and Letters*, trans. Leo Simon (New York: Macmillan, 1931), p. 33.

10. Jean-Paul Sartre, *Anti-Semite and Jew: An Exploration of the Etiology of Hate*, trans. George J. Becker (1948; reprint, New York: Schocken Books, 1995), pp. 69, 91. It should be noted that Christian theological anti-Semites had long espoused a version of this argument. The Apostle Paul was the first to enunciate a doctrine that Jews survive not because of the strength of their faith, their culture, or their ethnic cohesiveness, but rather because God preserves them in a wretched state, by reason of what one might term divine anti-Semitism. Saint Augustine elaborated that God maintains the Jews as wretches and *as* Jews in order to bear out scriptural prophecies about punishing the Jews for rejecting Jesus (see Augustine, *The City of God*, trans. Marcus Dods [New York: Random House, 1950], pp. 656–58). Similarly, the very devout Pascal wrote in *Pensées* that Jesus preserves Jews in such impossibly abject conditions in order to prove his omnipotence generation after generation.

11. Today, 4.6 million Jews live in Israel, a number that is growing thanks to immigration by former Soviet Jews and the positive Jewish birthrate in Israel, which contrasts with the negative birthrate of every Diaspora Jewish community in the world. Israel is thus well on its way to surpassing America in its Jewish population. (To get a sense of Israel's dynamic growth rate, consider that only 600,000 Jews lived there in 1948.) Demographers predict that in the near future, the majority of the world's Jews will reside in Israel, for the first time since the destruction of the Second Temple nearly two thousand years ago (see Herb Keinon, "In 10 Years Most Jews Will Be Living in Israel," *Jerusalem Post*, Jan. 7. 1991).

12. Dubnow, passim.

13. Spain distinguished in practice, though perhaps not in theory. The forced conversions attendant upon the Christian "reconquest" of Iberia involved massive Jewish populations, and many converts practiced Judaism in secret—the Spanish called them Marranos, meaning "swine." As a result, Spanish clergy came to view *all* Jewish converts with suspicion. In 1449, the *estatuto de limpieza de sangre* ("the statute of purity of blood") was enacted, which barred converts and their progeny from holding positions in the church hierarchy. This was Europe's first "racial" anti-Semitic legislation: even Christians in good faith, generations removed from ancestors who converted from Judaism, were denied certain rights on the basis of their "blood." A Spanish pope, Alexander VI, decreed the *limpieza* law to be in force in all Christendom in 1495. His successor, the Italian pope Julius II, quickly abolished the "purity of blood" sanctions against Christians of Jewish descent, decrying distinctions based on race rather than religion as "detestable customs and real corruption." Nevertheless, the "purity of blood" policy became even more widespread in Spain, "until it dominated all Spanish ecclesiastical organizations—and, through them, also a major part of Spain's public opinion" (Benzion Netanyahu, *The Origins of the Inquisition in Fifteenth Century Spain* [New York: Random House, 1995], p. 1063. See also Bernard Lewis, *Semites and Anti-Semites: An Inquiry into Conflict and Prejudice* [New York: W. W. Norton, 1986], pp. 82–84).

14. *Forbes*, Oct. 14, 1996, pp. 100–295. A perusal of the 1996 *Forbes* list of the four hundred richest people in America makes clear how difficult it will soon be to identify people by their Jewish background. But by any standard, the number of Jews on the list is highly disproportionate to their percentage in the population. Even if one were to count only Jews who strongly identify with their heritage—such as Wexner, Soros, Spielberg, Milken, Fisher, Taubman, Pritzker, Bronfman, Lauder, Perlman, Tisch, Le Frak, Lee, Geffen, Lauren, Stern, Rich, Green, Heyman, Peltz, Wasserman, Redstone, and others too numerous to list here—the percentage is amazing.

15. Seymour Martin Lipset and Earl Raab, *Jews and the New American Scene* (Cambridge, Mass.: Harvard University Press, 1995), p. 26. The study was conducted in 1971–72. The percentage is higher now.

16. Steven Cohen, *The Dimensions of American Jewish Liberalism* (New York: American Jewish Congress, 1989), pp. 28–29.

17. Barry A. Kosmin, *The Dimensions of Contemporary Jewish Philanthropy* (New York: Council of Jewish Federations), p. 28. See also *Los Angeles Times*, Nov. 2, 1992. The UJA replaced the Salvation Army at the top of the Philanthropy 400, an annual ranking of nonprofit groups by the *Chronicle of Philanthropy*. The UJA raised $668.1 million in 1991, up 57 percent from the preceding year. Most of the money helped resettle Soviet Jews.

18. This finding by the National Jewish Population Survey of 1990 reflects the widespread Jewish distaste for nonuniversalist Jewish charities. A 1989 survey of American Jewish attitudes toward Jewish identity revealed that 31 percent of American Jews believe that "Jewish charities and organizations place too much emphasis on helping only Jews and not enough on helping all people in need whether they're Jewish or not" (Stephen M. Cohen, *Content or Continuity? The 1989 National Survey of American Jews* [New York: American Jewish Committee, 1991], p.59).

19. Richard L. Zweigenhaft and G. William Domhoff, in *Jews in the Protestant Establishment* (New York: Praeger, 1982), credit the term "J.A.S.P." to Peter I. Rose (p. 107). See also Robert C. Christopher, *Crashing the Gates: The De-WASPing of America's Power Elite* (New York: Simon & Schuster, 1989), pp. 43–44.

20. See Charles Silberman, *A Certain People: American Jews and Their Lives Today* (New York: Summit Books, 1985), p. 145. Silberman has updated the statistics originally presented in Harriet Zuckerman, *Scientific Elite: Nobel Laureates in the United States* (New York: Columbia University Press, 1977), p. 68.

21. David Brion Davis, review of Edward S. Shapiro, *The Jewish People in America*, vol. 5: *A Time for Healing: American Jewry Since World War II*, in *New Republic*, April 12, 1993. (Shapiro summarized several sociological surveys.) Moreover, the 1986 edition of the *World Almanac and Book of Facts* ranked eight Jewish women, whose occupations range from historian to syndicated columnist to women's rights leader to novelist, as among "America's 25 Most Influential Women"—

fully 32 percent of the total. Cited in Jacob Rader Marcus, ed., *The Jew in the American World: A Source Book* (Detroit: Wayne State University Press, 1996), p. 519.

22. Depending on the year, somewhere between 25 and 40 percent of the students at Ivy League schools are Jewish (Norman F. Cantor, *The Sacred Chain: The History of the Jews* [New York: HarperCollins, 1994], p. 400). If we use a low figure of 30 percent, and then take a high estimate of Jews as 2.5 percent of the general U.S. population, we can calculate the rate of disproportional Jewish representation in the Ivies as twelve times greater than Jewish presence in the overall population.

23. Lipset and Raab, p. 75. The poll was conducted in 1985. As of 1996, both of California's U.S. senators are Jewish, as are eight other members of Congress from the state.

24. Goldberg, p. 6.

25. Ibid.

26. Quoted in Goldberg, p. 147.

27. Quoted in Rodger Kamenetz, *The Jew in the Lotus* (San Francisco: Harper-San Francisco, 1994), p. 48.

28. Ibid.

QUESTIONING AND DISCUSSING

Dershowitz, "Assimilation Is a Greater Problem Than Anti-Semitism for American Jews"

1. Although Alan M. Dershowitz talks specifically about American Jews, one can argue that the unique ways of life of any minority group risk disappearance in the United States just as these groups "have achieved everything [they] have ever wanted." Research the idea of *assimilation* and the pressures in the United States for us to "be like everyone else." In what ways might our alleged valuing of diversity actually be restrictive?

2. Is it true that without *tsuris*—troubles—Jews or members of other minorities cannot define themselves?

3. Analyze Dershowitz's arguments when he claims, "Today's most serious threats come not from those who would persecute [. . .] but from those who would, without any malice, kill [. . .] with kindness." Why does he believe this?

4. Many argue that there has been a resurgence of anti-Semitic activity, particularly on some college campuses. Review recent articles about anti-Semitism and other forms of discrimination. Do you agree with Dershowitz that anti-Semitism—and other forms of discrimination and racism—is on the decline? How do these forms of discrimination reflect on our professed valuing of diversity and ethical conduct in the United States?

⊞

PATRICIA HILL COLLINS

Dr. Patricia Hill Collins (1948–) has written extensively on issues of race, gender, social class, and nationality as they specifically relate to African American women. Collins is the chair of the Department of African American Studies at the University of Cincinnati, where she is a professor of sociology. She received her BA and PhD in sociology from Brandeis University and an MAT from Harvard University. This excerpt comes from her first book, *Black Feminist Thought: Knowledge, Consciousness, and the Politics of Empowerment,* published in 1990, which won the Jessie Bernard Award of the American Sociological Association for significant scholarship in gender studies and the C. Wright Mills Award of the Society for the Study of Social Problems. Collins has taught at several institutions, has held editorial positions with professional journals, and has lectured widely in the United States and abroad.

⊞

The Politics of Black Feminist Thought

1 In 1831 Maria W. Stewart asked, "How long shall the fair daughters of Africa be compelled to bury their minds and talents beneath a load of iron pots and kettles?" Orphaned at age five, bound out to a clergyman's family as a domestic servant, Stewart struggled to gather isolated fragments of an education when and where she could. As the first American woman to lecture in public on political issues and to leave copies of her texts, this early U.S. Black woman intellectual foreshadowed a variety of themes taken up by her Black feminist successors (Richardson 1987).

2 Maria Stewart challenged African-American women to reject the negative images of Black womanhood so prominent in her times, pointing out that race, gender, and class oppression were the fundamental causes of Black women's poverty. In an 1833 speech she proclaimed, "Like King Solomon, who put neither nail nor hammer to the temple, yet received the praise; so also have the white Americans gained themselves a name . . . while in reality we have been their principal foundation and support." Stewart objected to the injustice of this situation: "We have pursued the shadow, they have obtained the substance; we have performed the labor, they have received the profits; we have planted the vines, they have eaten the fruits of them" (Richardson 1987, 59).

3 Maria Stewart was not content to point out the source of Black women's oppression. She urged Black women to forge self-definitions of self-reliance and independence. "It is useless for us any longer to sit with

our hands folded, reproaching the whites; for that will never elevate us," she exhorted. "Possess the spirit of independence. . . . Possess the spirit of men, bold and enterprising, fearless and undaunted" (p. 53). To Stewart, the power of self-definition was essential, for Black women's survival was at stake. "Sue for your rights and privileges. Know the reason you cannot attain them. Weary them with your importunities. You can but die if you make the attempt; and we shall certainly die if you do not" (p. 38).

Stewart also challenged Black women to use their special roles as mothers to forge powerful mechanisms of political action. "O, ye mothers, what a responsibility rests on you!" Stewart preached. "You have souls committed to your charge. . . . It is you that must create in the minds of your little girls and boys a thirst for knowledge, the love of virtue, . . . and the cultivation of a pure heart." Stewart recognized the magnitude of the task at hand. "Do not say you cannot make any thing of your children; but say . . . we will try" (p. 35).

Maria Stewart was one of the first U.S. Black feminists to champion the utility of Black women's relationships with one another in providing a community of Black women's activism and self-determination. "Shall it any longer be said of the daughters of Africa, they have no ambition, they have no force?" she questioned. "By no means. Let every female heart become united, and let us raise a fund ourselves; and at the end of one year and a half, we might be able to lay the corner stone for the building of a High School, that the higher branches of knowledge might be enjoyed by us" (p. 37). Stewart saw the potential for Black women's activism as educators. She advised, "Turn your attention to knowledge and improvement; for knowledge is power" (p. 41).

Though she said little in her speeches about the sexual politics of her time, her advice to African-American women suggests that she was painfully aware of the sexual abuse visited upon Black women. She continued to "plead the cause of virtue and the pure principles of morality" (p. 31) for Black women. And to those Whites who thought that Black women were inherently inferior, Stewart offered a biting response: "Our souls are fired with the same love of liberty and independence with which your souls are fired. . . . [T]oo much of your blood flows in our veins, too much of your color in our skins, for us not to possess your spirits" (p. 40).

Despite Maria Stewart's intellectual prowess, the ideas of this extraordinary woman come to us only in scattered fragments that not only suggest her brilliance but speak tellingly of the fate of countless Black women intellectuals. Many Maria Stewarts exist, African-American women whose minds and talents have been suppressed by the pots and kettles symbolic of Black women's subordination (Guy-Sheftall 1986). Far too many

African-American women intellectuals have labored in isolation and obscurity and, like Zora Neale Hurston, lie buried in unmarked graves.

8   Some have been more fortunate, for they have become known to us, largely through the efforts of contemporary Black women scholars (Hine et al. 1993; Guy-Sheftall 1995b). Like Alice Walker, these scholars sense that "a people do not throw their geniuses away" and that "if they are thrown away, it is our duty as artists, scholars, and witnesses for the future to collect them again for the sake of our children, . . . if necessary, bone by bone" (Walker 1983, 92).

9   This painstaking process of collecting the ideas and actions of "thrown away" Black women like Maria Stewart has revealed one important discovery. Black women intellectuals have laid a vital analytical foundation for a distinctive standpoint on self, community, and society and, in doing so, created a multifaceted, African-American women's intellectual tradition. While clear discontinuities in this tradition exist—times when Black women's voices were strong, and others when assuming a more muted tone was essential—one striking dimension of the ideas of Maria W. Stewart and her successors is the thematic consistency of their work.

10   If such a rich intellectual tradition exists, why has it remained virtually invisible until now? In 1905 Fannie Barrier Williams lamented, "The colored girl . . . is not known and hence not believed in; she belongs to a race that is best designated by the term 'problem,' and she lives beneath the shadow of that problem which envelops and obscures her" (Williams 1987, 150). Why are African-American women and our ideas not known and not believed in?

11   The shadow obscuring this complex Black women's intellectual tradition is neither accidental nor benign. Suppressing the knowledge produced by any oppressed group makes it easier for dominant groups to rule because the seeming absence of dissent suggests that subordinate groups willingly collaborate in their own victimization (Scott 1985). Maintaining the invisibility of Black women and our ideas not only in the United States, but in Africa, the Caribbean, South America, Europe, and other places where Black women now live, has been critical in maintaining social inequalities. Black women engaged in reclaiming and constructing Black women's knowledges often point to the politics of suppression that affect their projects. For example, several authors in Heidi Mirza's (1997) edited volume on Black British feminism identify their invisibility and silencing in the contemporary United Kingdom. Similarly, South Africa businesswoman Danisa Baloyi describes her astonishment at the invisibility of African women in U.S. scholarship: "As a student doing research in the United States, I was amazed by the [small] amount of information on

Black South African women, and shocked that only a minuscule amount was actually written by Black women themselves" (Baloyi 1995, 41).

Despite this suppression, U.S. Black women have managed to do intel- 12 lectual work, and to have our ideas matter. Sojourner Truth, Anna Julia Cooper, Ida B. Wells-Barnett, Mary McLeod Bethune, Toni Morrison, Barbara Smith, and countless others have consistently struggled to make themselves heard. African women writers such as Ama Ata Aidoo, Buchi Emecheta, and Ellen Kuzwayo have used their voices to raise important issues that affect Black African women (James 1990). Like the work of Maria W. Stewart and that of Black women transnationally, African-American women's intellectual work has aimed to foster Black women's activism.

This dialectic of oppression and activism, the tension between the sup- 13 pression of African-American women's ideas and our intellectual activism in the face of that suppression, constitutes the politics of U.S. Black feminist thought. More important, understanding this dialectical relationship is critical in assessing how U.S. Black feminist thought—its core themes, epistemological significance, and connections to domestic and transnational Black feminist practice—is fundamentally embedded in a political context that has challenged its very right to exist.

The Suppression of Black Feminist Thought

The vast majority of African-American women were brought to the 14 United States to work as slaves in a situation of oppression. Oppression describes any unjust situation where, systematically and over a long period of time, one group denies another group access to the resources of society. Race, class, gender, sexuality, nation, age, and ethnicity among others constitute major forms of oppression in the United States. However, the convergence of race, class, and gender oppression characteristic of U.S. slavery shaped all subsequent relationships that women of African descent had within Black American families and communities, with employers, and among one another. It also created the political context for Black women's intellectual work.

African-American women's oppression has encompassed three interde- 15 pendent dimensions. First, the exploitation of Black women's labor essential to U.S. capitalism—the "iron pots and kettles" symbolizing Black women's long-standing ghettoization in service occupations—represents the economic dimension of oppression (Davis 1981; Marable 1983; Jones 1985; Amott and Matthaei 1991). Survival for most African-American women has been such an all-consuming activity that most have had few opportunities to do intellectual work as it has been traditionally defined.

The drudgery of enslaved African-American women's work and the grinding poverty of "free" wage labor in the rural South tellingly illustrate the high costs Black women have paid for survival. The millions of impoverished African-American women ghettoized in Philadelphia, Birmingham, Oakland, Detroit, and other U.S. inner cities demonstrate the continuation of these earlier forms of Black women's economic exploitation (Brewer 1993; Omolade 1994).

16   Second, the political dimension of oppression has denied African-American women the rights and privileges routinely extended to White male citizens (Burnham, 1987; Scales-Trent 1989; Berry 1994). Forbidding Black women to vote, excluding African-Americans and women from public office, and withholding equitable treatment in the criminal justice system all substantiate the political subordination of Black women. Educational institutions have also fostered this pattern of disenfranchisement. Past practices such as denying literacy to slaves and relegating Black women to underfunded, segregated Southern schools worked to ensure that a quality education for Black women remained the exception rather than the rule (Mullings 1997). The large numbers of young Black women in inner cities and impoverished rural areas who continue to leave school before attaining full literacy represent the continued efficacy of the political dimension of Black women's oppression.

17   Finally, controlling images applied to Black women that originated during the slave era attest to the ideological dimension of U.S. Black women's oppression (King 1973; D. White 1985; Carby 1987; Morton 1991). Ideology refers to the body of ideas reflecting the interests of a group of people. Within U.S. culture, racist and sexist ideologies permeate the social structure to such a degree that they become hegemonic, namely, seen as natural, normal, and inevitable. In this context, certain assumed qualities that are attached to Black women are used to justify oppression. From the mammies, jezebels, and breeder women of slavery to the smiling Aunt Jemimas on pancake mix boxes, ubiquitous Black prostitutes, and ever-present welfare mothers of contemporary popular culture, negative stereotypes applied to African-American women have been fundamental to Black women's oppression.

18   Taken together, the supposedly seamless web of economy, polity, and ideology function as a highly effective system of social control designed to keep African-American women in an assigned, subordinate place. This larger system of oppression works to suppress the ideas of Black women intellectuals and to protect elite White male interests and worldviews. Denying African-American women the credentials to become literate certainly excluded most African-American women from positions as scholars, teach-

ers, authors, poets, and critics. Moreover, while Black women historians, writers, and social scientists have long existed, until recently these women have not held leadership positions in universities, professional associations, publishing concerns, broadcast media, and other social institutions of knowledge validation. Black women's exclusion from positions of power within mainstream institutions has led to the elevation of elite White male ideas and interests and the corresponding suppression of Black women's ideas and interests in traditional scholarship (Higginbotham 1989; Morton 1991; Collins 1998a, 95–123). Moreover, this historical exclusion means that stereotypical images of Black women permeate popular culture and public policy (Wallace 1990; Lubiano 1992; Jewell 1993).

U.S. and European women's studies have challenged the seemingly hegemonic ideas of elite White men. Ironically, Western feminisms have also suppressed Black women's ideas (duCille 1996, 81–119). Even though Black women intellectuals have long expressed a distinctive African-influenced and feminist sensibility about how race and class intersect in structuring gender, historically we have not been full participants in White feminist organizations (Giddings 1984; Zinn et al. 1986; Caraway 1991). As a result, African-American, Latino, Native American, and Asian-American women have criticized Western feminisms for being racist and overly concerned with White, middle-class women's issues (Moraga and Anzaldua 1981; Smith 1982a; Dill 1983; Davis 1989). [19]

Traditionally, many U.S. White feminist scholars have resisted having Black women as full colleagues. Moreover, this historical suppression of Black women's ideas has had a pronounced influence on feminist theory. One pattern of suppression is that of omission. Theories advanced as being universally applicable to women as a group upon closer examination appear greatly limited by the White, middle-class, and Western origins of their proponents. For example, Nancy Chodorow's (1978) work on sex role socialization and Carol Gilligan's (1982) study of the moral development of women both rely heavily on White, middle-class samples. While these two classics made key contributions to feminist theory, they simultaneously promoted the notion of a generic woman who is White and middle class. The absence of Black feminist ideas from these and other studies placed them in a much more tenuous position to challenge the hegemony of mainstream scholarship on behalf of all women. [20]

Another pattern of suppression lies in paying lip service to the need for diversity, but changing little about one's own practice. Currently, some U.S. White women who possess great competence in researching a range of issues acknowledge the need for diversity, yet omit women of color from their work. These women claim that they are unqualified to understand or [21] even speak of "Black women's experiences" because they themselves are not Black. Others include a few safe, "hand-picked" Black women's voices to avoid criticisms that they are racist. Both examples reflect a basic unwillingness by many U.S. White feminists to alter the paradigms that guide their work.

22   A more recent pattern of suppression involves incorporating, changing, and thereby depoliticizing Black feminist ideas. The growing popularity of post-modernism in U.S. higher education in the 1990s, especially within literary criticism and cultural studies, fosters a climate where symbolic inclusion often substitutes for bona fide substantive changes. Because interest in Black women's work has reached occult status, suggests Ann duCille (1996), it "increasingly marginalizes both the black women critics and scholars who excavated the fields in question and their black feminist 'daughters' who would further develop those fields" (p. 87). Black feminist critic Barbara Christian (1994), a pioneer in creating Black women's studies in the U.S. academy, queries whether Black feminism can survive the pernicious politics of resegregation. In discussing the politics of a new multiculturalism, Black feminist critic Hazel Carby (1992) expresses dismay at the growing situation of symbolic inclusion, in which the texts of Black women writers are welcome in the multicultural classroom while actual Black women are not.

23   Not all White Western feminists participate in these diverse patterns of suppression. Some try to build coalitions across racial and other markers of difference, often with noteworthy results. Works by Elizabeth Spelman (1988), Sandra Harding (1986, 1998), Margaret Andersen (1991), Peggy McIntosh (1988), Mab Segrest (1994), Annie Fausto-Sterling (1995), and other individual U.S. White feminist thinkers reflect sincere efforts to develop a multiracial, diverse feminism. However, despite their efforts, these concerns linger on.

24   Like feminist scholarship, the diverse strands of African-American social and political thought have also challenged mainstream scholarship. However, Black social and political thought has been limited by both the reformist postures toward change assumed by many U.S. Black intellectuals (Cruse 1967; West 1977–78) and the secondary status afforded the ideas and experiences of African-American women. Adhering to a male-defined ethos that far too often equates racial progress with the acquisition of an ill-defined manhood has left much U.S. Black thought with a prominent masculinist bias.

25   In this case the patterns of suppressing Black women's ideas have been similar yet different. Though Black women have played little or no part in dominant academic discourse and White feminist arenas, we have long

been included in the organizational structures of Black civil society. U.S. Black women's acceptance of subordinate roles in Black organizations does not mean that we wield little authority or that we experience patriarchy in the same way as do White women in White organizations (Evans 1979; Gilkes 1985). But with the exception of Black women's organizations, male-run organizations have historically either not stressed Black women's issues (Beale 1970; Marable 1983), or have done so under duress. For example, Black feminist activist Pauli Murray (1970) found that from its founding in 1916 to 1970, the *Journal of Negro History* published only five articles devoted exclusively to Black women. Evelyn Brooks Higginbotham's (1993) historical monograph on Black women in Black Baptist churches records African-American women's struggles to raise issues that concerned women. Even progressive Black organizations have not been immune from gender discrimination. Civil rights activist Ella Baker's experiences in the Southern Christian Leadership Conference illustrate one form that suppressing Black women's ideas and talents can take. Ms. Baker virtually ran the entire organization, yet had to defer to the decision-making authority of the exclusively male leadership group (Cantarow 1980). Civil rights activist Septima Clark describes similar experiences: "I found all over the South that whatever the man said had to be right. They had the whole say. The woman couldn't say a thing" (C. Brown 1986, 79). Radical African-American women also can find themselves deferring to male authority. In her autobiography, Elaine Brown (1992), a participant and subsequent leader of the 1960s radical organization the Black Panther Party for Self-Defense, discusses the sexism expressed by Panther men. Overall, even though Black women intellectuals have asserted their right to speak both as African-Americans and as women, historically these women have not held top leadership positions in Black organizations and have frequently struggled within them to express Black feminist ideas (Giddings 1984).

Much contemporary U.S. Black feminist thought reflects Black women's 26 increasing willingness to oppose gender inequality within Black civil society. Septima Clark describes this transformation:

> I used to feel that women couldn't speak up, because when district meetings were being held at my home . . . I didn't feel as if I could tell them what I had in mind . . . But later on, I found out that women had a lot to say, and what they had to say was really worthwhile. . . . So we started talking, and have been talking quite a bit since that time. (C. Brown 1986, 82)

African-American women intellectuals have been "talking quite a bit" 27 since 1970 and have insisted that the masculinist bias in Black social and political thought, the racist bias in feminist theory, and the heterosexist bias in both be corrected (see, e.g., Bambara 1970; Dill 1979; Jordan 1981; Combahee River Collective 1982; Lorde 1984).

28 Within Black civil society, the increasing visibility of Black women's ideas did not go unopposed. The virulent reaction to earlier Black women's writings by some Black men, such as Robert Staples's (1979) analysis of Ntozake Shange's (1975) choreopoem, *For Colored Girls Who Have Considered Suicide*, and Michele Wallace's (1978) controversial volume, *Black Macho and the Myth of the Superwoman*, illustrates the difficulty of challenging the masculinist bias in Black social and political thought. Alice Walker encountered similarly hostile reactions to her publication of *The Color Purple*. In describing the response of African-American men to the outpouring of publications by Black women writers in the 1970s and 1980s, Calvin Hernton offers an incisive criticism of the seeming tenacity of a masculinist bias:

> The telling thing about the hostile attitude of black men toward black women writers is that they interpret the new thrust of the women as being "counter-productive" to the historical goal of the Black struggle. Revealingly, while black men have achieved outstanding recognition throughout the history of black writing, black women have not accused the men of collaborating with the enemy and setting back the progress of the race. (1985, 5)

29 Not all Black male reaction during this period was hostile. For example, Manning Marable (1983) devotes an entire chapter in *How Capitalism Underdeveloped Black America* to how sexism has been a primary deterrent to Black community development. Following Marable's lead, work by Haki Madhubuti (1990), Cornel West (1993), Michael Awkward (1996), Michael Dyson (1996), and others suggests that some U.S. Black male thinkers have taken Black feminist thought seriously. Despite the diverse ideological perspectives expressed by these writers, each seemingly recognizes the importance of Black women's ideas.

Black Feminist Thought as Critical Social Theory

30 Even if they appear to be otherwise, situations such as the suppression of Black women's ideas within traditional scholarship and the struggles within the critiques of that established knowledge are inherently unstable. Conditions in the wider political economy simultaneously shape Black women's subordination and foster activism. On some level, people who are oppressed usually know it. For African-American women, the knowledge gained at intersecting oppressions of race, class, and gender

provides the stimulus for crafting and passing on the subjugated knowledge of Black women's critical social theory (Collins 1998a, 3–10).

As an historically oppressed group, U.S. Black women have produced 31 social thought designed to oppose oppression. Not only does the form assumed by this thought diverge from standard academic theory—it can take the form of poetry, music, essays, and the like—but the *purpose* of Black women's collective thought is distinctly different. Social theories emerging from and/or on behalf of U.S. Black women and other historically oppressed groups aim to find ways to escape from, survive in, and/or oppose prevailing social and economic injustice. In the United States, for example, African-American social and political thought analyzes institutionalized racism, not to help it work more efficiently, but to resist it. Feminism advocates women's emancipation and empowerment, Marxist social thought aims for a more equitable society, while queer theory opposes heterosexism. Beyond U.S. borders, many women from oppressed groups also struggle to understand new forms of injustice. In a transnational, postcolonial context, women within new and often Black-run nation-states in the Caribbean, Africa, and Asia struggle with new meanings attached to ethnicity, citizenship status, and religion. In increasingly multicultural European nation-states, women migrants from former colonies encounter new forms of subjugation (Yuval-Davis 1997). Social theories expressed by women emerging from these diverse groups typically do not arise from the rarefied atmosphere of their imaginations. Instead, social theories reflect women's efforts to come to terms with lived experiences within intersecting oppressions of race, class, gender, sexuality, ethnicity, nation, and religion (see, e.g., Alexander and Mohanty 1997; Mirza 1997).

Black feminist thought, U.S. Black women's critical social theory, re- 32 flects similar power relationships. For African-American women, critical social theory encompasses bodies of knowledge and sets of institutional practices that actively grapple with the central questions facing U.S. Black women as a collectivity. The need for such thought arises because African-American women as a *group* remain oppressed within a U.S. context characterized by injustice. This neither means that all African-American women within that group are oppressed in the same way, nor that some U.S. Black women do not suppress others. Black feminist thought's identity as a "critical" social theory lies in its commitment to justice, both for U.S. Black women as a collectivity and for that of other similarly oppressed groups.

Historically, two factors stimulated U.S. Black women's critical social 33 theory. For one, prior to World War II, racial segregation in urban housing became so entrenched that the majority of African-American women lived in self-contained Black neighborhoods where their children attended overwhelmingly Black schools, and where they themselves belonged to all-Black churches and similar community organizations. Despite the fact that ghettoization was designed to foster the political control and economic exploitation of Black Americans (Squires 1994), these all-Black neighborhoods simultaneously provided a separate space where African-American women and men could use African-derived ideas to craft distinctive oppositional knowledges designed to resist racial oppression.

34   Every social group has a constantly evolving worldview that it uses to order and evaluate its own experiences (Sobel 1979). For African-Americans this worldview originated in the cosmologies of diverse West African ethnic groups (Diop 1974). By retaining and reworking significant elements of these West African cultures, communities of enslaved Africans offered their members explanations for slavery alternative to those advanced by slave owners (Gutman 1976; Webber 1978; Sobel 1979). These African-derived ideas also laid the foundation for the rules of a distinctive Black American civil society. Later on, confining African-Americans to all-Black areas in the rural South and Northern urban ghettos fostered the solidification of a distinctive ethos in Black civil society regarding language (Smitherman 1977), religion (Sobel 1979; Paris 1995), family structure (Sudarkasa 1981b), and community politics (Brown 1994). While essential to the survival of U.S. Blacks as a group and expressed differently by individual African-Americans, these knowledges remained simultaneously hidden from and suppressed by Whites. Black oppositional knowledges existed to resist injustice, but they also remained subjugated.

35   As mothers, othermothers, teachers, and churchwomen in essentially all-Black rural communities and urban neighborhoods, U.S. Black women participated in constructing and reconstructing these oppositional knowledges. Through the lived experiences gained within their extended families and communities, individual African-American women fashioned their own ideas about the meaning of Black womanhood. When these ideas found collective expression, Black women's self-definitions enabled them to refashion African-influenced conceptions of self and community. These self-definitions of Black womanhood were designed to resist the negative controlling images of Black womanhood advanced by Whites as well as the discriminatory social practices that these controlling images supported. In all, Black women's participation in crafting a constantly changing African-American culture fostered distinctively Black and women-centered worldviews.

36   Another factor that stimulated U.S. Black women's critical social theory lay in the common experiences they gained from their jobs. Prior to

World War II, U.S. Black women worked primarily in two occupations—agriculture and domestic work. Their ghettoization in domestic work sparked an important contradiction. Domestic work fostered U.S. Black women's economic exploitation, yet it simultaneously created the conditions for distinctively Black and female forms of resistance. Domestic work allowed African-American women to see White elites, both actual and aspiring, from perspectives largely obscured from Black men and from these groups themselves. In their White "families," Black women not only performed domestic duties but frequently formed strong ties with the children they nurtured, and with the employers themselves. On one level this insider relationship was satisfying to all concerned. Accounts of Black domestic workers stress the sense of self-affirmation the women experienced at seeing racist ideology demystified. But on another level these Black women knew that they could never belong to their White "families." They were economically exploited workers and thus would remain outsiders. The result was being placed in a curious *outsider-within* social location (Collins 1986b), a peculiar marginality that stimulated a distinctive Black women's perspective on a variety of themes (see, e.g., Childress 1986).

Taken together, Black women's participation in constructing African-American culture in all-Black settings and the distinctive perspectives gained from their outsider-within placement in domestic work provide the material backdrop for a unique Black women's standpoint. When armed with cultural beliefs honed in Black civil society, many Black women who found themselves doing domestic work often developed distinct views of the contradictions between the dominant group's actions and ideologies. Moreover, they often shared their ideas with other African-American women. Nancy White, a Black inner-city resident, explores the connection between experience and beliefs:

> Now, I understand all these things from living. But you can't lay up on these flowery beds of ease and think that you are running your life, too. Some women, white women, can run their husband's lives for a while, but most of them have to . . . see what he tells them there is to see. If he tells them that they ain't seeing what they know they *are* seeing, then they have to just go on like it wasn't there! (in Gwaltney 1980, 148)

Not only does this passage speak to the power of the dominant group to suppress the knowledge produced by subordinate groups, but it illustrates how being in outsider-within locations can foster new angles of vision on oppression. Ms. White's Blackness makes her a perpetual outsider. She could never be a White middle-class woman lying on a "flowery bed of ease." But her work of caring for White women allowed her an insider's view of some of the contradictions between White women thinking that they are running their lives and the patriarchal power and authority in their households.

38   Practices such as these, whether experienced oneself or learned by listening to African-American women who have had them, have encouraged many U.S. Black women to question the contradictions between dominant ideologies of American womanhood and U.S. Black women's devalued status. If women are allegedly passive and fragile, then why are Black women treated as "mules" and assigned heavy cleaning chores? If good mothers are supposed to stay at home with their children, then why are U.S. Black women on public assistance forced to find jobs and leave their children in day care? If women's highest calling is to become mothers, then why are Black teen mothers pressured to use Norplant and Depo Provera? In the absence of a viable Black feminism that investigates how intersecting oppressions of race, gender, and class foster these contradictions, the angle of vision created by being deemed devalued workers and failed mothers could easily be turned inward, leading to internalized oppression. But the legacy of struggle among U.S. Black women suggests that a collectively shared, Black women's oppositional knowledge has long existed. This collective wisdom in turn has spurred U.S. Black women to generate a more specialized knowledge, namely, Black feminist thought as critical social theory. Just as fighting injustice lay at the heart of U.S. Black women's experiences, so did analyzing and creating imaginative responses to injustice characterize the core of Black feminist thought.

39   Historically, while they often disagreed on its expression—some U.S. Black women were profoundly reformist while more radical thinkers bordered on the revolutionary—African-American women intellectuals who were nurtured in social conditions of racial segregation strove to develop Black feminist thought as critical social theory. Regardless of social class and other differences among U.S. Black women, all were in some way affected by intersecting oppression of race, gender, and class. The economic, political, and ideological dimensions of U.S. Black women's oppression suppressed the intellectual production of individual Black feminist thinkers. At the same time, these same social conditions simultaneously stimulated distinctive patterns of U.S. Black women's activism that also influenced and was influenced by individual Black women thinkers. Thus, the dialectic of oppression and activism characterizing U.S. Black women's experiences with intersecting oppressions also influenced the ideas and actions of Black women intellectuals.

40   The exclusion of Black women's ideas from mainstream academic discourse and the curious placement of African-American women intellec-

tuals in feminist thinking, Black social and political theories, and in other important thought such as U.S. labor studies has meant that U.S. Black women intellectuals have found themselves in outsider-within positions in many academic endeavors (Hull et al. 1982; Christian 1989). The assumptions on which full group membership are based—Whiteness for feminist thought, maleness for Black social and political thought, and the combination for mainstream scholarship—all negate Black women's realities. Prevented from becoming full insiders in any of these areas of inquiry, Black women remained in outsider-within locations, individuals whose marginality provided a distinctive angle of vision on these intellectual and political entities.

Alice Walker's work exemplifies these fundamental influences within   41
Black women's intellectual traditions. Walker describes how her outsider-within location influenced her thinking: "I believe . . . that it was from this period—from my solitary, lonely position, the position of an outcast—that I began really to see people and things, really to notice relationships" (Walker 1983, 244). Walker realizes that "the gift of loneliness is sometimes a radical vision of society or one's people that has not previously been taken into account" (p. 264). And yet marginality is not the only influence on her work. By reclaiming the works of Zora Neale Hurston and in other ways placing Black women's experiences and culture at the center of her work, she draws on alternative Black feminist worldviews.

Developing Black Feminist Thought

Starting from the assumption that African-American women have cre-   42
ated independent, oppositional yet subjugated knowledges concerning our own subordination, contemporary U.S. Black women intellectuals are engaged in the struggle to reconceptualize all dimensions of the dialectic of oppression and activism as it applies to African-American women. Central to this enterprise is reclaiming Black feminist intellectual traditions (see, e.g., Harley and Terborg-Penn 1978; Hull et al. 1982; James and Busia 1993; and Guy-Sheftall 1995a, 1995b).

For many U.S. Black women intellectuals, this task of reclaiming Black   43
women's subjugated knowledge takes on special meaning. Knowing that the minds and talents of our grandmothers, mothers, and sisters have been suppressed stimulates many contributions to the growing field of Black women's studies (Hull et al. 1982). Alice Walker describes how this sense of purpose affects her work: "In my own work I write not only what I want to read—understanding fully and indelibly that if I don't do it no one else is so vitally interested, or capable of doing it to my satisfaction—I write all the things I *should have been able to read*" (Walker 1983, 13).

44   Reclaiming Black women's ideas involves discovering, reinterpreting, and, in many cases, analyzing for the first time the works of individual U.S. Black women thinkers who were so extraordinary that they did manage to have their ideas preserved. In some cases this process involves locating unrecognized and unheralded works, scattered and long out of print. Marilyn Richardson's (1978) painstaking editing of the writings and speeches of Maria Stewart, and Mary Helen Washington's (1975, 1980, 1987) collections of Black women's writings typify this process. Similarly, Alice Walker's (1979a) efforts to have Zora Neale Hurston's unmarked grave recognized parallel her intellectual quest to honor Hurston's important contributions to Black feminist literary traditions.

45   Reclaiming Black women's ideas also involves discovering, reinterpreting, and analyzing the ideas of subgroups within the larger collectivity of U.S. Black women who have been silenced. For example, burgeoning scholarship by and about Black lesbians reveals a diverse and complex history. Gloria Hull's (1984) careful compilation of the journals of Black feminist intellectual Alice Dunbar-Nelson illustrates the difficulties of being closeted yet still making major contributions to African-American social and political thought. Audre Lorde's (1982) autobiography, *Zami*, provides a book-length treatment of Black lesbian communities in New York. Similarly, Kennedy and Davis's (1994) history of the formation of lesbian communities in 1940s and 1950s Buffalo, New York, strives to understand how racial segregation influenced constructions of lesbian identities.

46   Reinterpreting existing works through new theoretical frameworks is another dimension of developing Black feminist thought. In Black feminist literary criticism, this process is exemplified by Barbara Christian's (1985) landmark volume on Black women writers, Mary Helen Washington's (1987) reassessment of anger and voice in *Maud Martha*, a much-neglected work by novelist and poet Gwendolyn Brooks, and Hazel Carby's (1987) use of the lens of race, class, and gender to reinterpret the works of nineteenth-century Black women novelists. Within Black feminist historiography the tremendous strides that have been made in U.S. Black women's history are evident in Evelyn Brooks Higginbotham's (1989) analysis of the emerging concepts and paradigms in Black women's history, her study of women in the Black Baptist Church (1993), Stephanie Shaw's (1996) study of Black professional women workers during the Jim Crow era, and the landmark volume *Black Women in the United States: An Historical Encyclopedia* (Hine et al. 1993).

47   Developing Black feminist thought also involves searching for its expression in alternative institutional locations and among women who are not commonly perceived as intellectuals. As defined in this volume, Black women intellectuals are neither all academics nor found primarily in the

Black middle class. Instead, all U.S. Black women who somehow contribute to Black feminist thought as critical social theory are deemed to be "intellectuals." They may be highly educated. Many are not. For example, nineteenth-century Black feminist activist Sojourner Truth is not typically seen as an intellectual. Because she could neither read nor write, much of what we know about her has been recorded by other people. One of her most famous speeches, that delivered at the 1851 women's rights convention in Akron, Ohio, comes to us in a report written by a feminist abolitionist some time after the event itself (Painter 1993). We do not know what Truth actually said, only what the recorder claims that she said. Despite this limitation, in that speech Truth reportedly provides an incisive analysis of the definition of the term *woman* forwarded in the mid-1800s:

> That man over there says women need to be helped into carriages, and lifted over ditches, and to have the best place everywhere. Nobody ever helps me into carriages, or over mud puddles, or gives me any best place! And ain't I a woman? Look at me! Look at my arm! I have ploughed, and planted, and gathered into barns, and no man could head me! And ain't I a woman? I could work as much and eat as much as a man—when I could get it—and bear the lash as well! And ain't I a woman? I have borne thirteen children, and seen them most all sold off to slavery, and when I cried out with my mother's grief, none but Jesus heard me! And ain't I a woman? (Loewenberg and Bogin 1976, 235)

By using the contradictions between her life as an African-American 48 woman and the qualities ascribed to women, Sojourner Truth exposes the concept of woman as being culturally constructed. Her life as a second-class citizen has been filled with hard physical labor, with no assistance from men. Her question, "and ain't I a woman?" points to the contradictions inherent in blanket use of the term *woman*. For those who question Truth's femininity, she invokes her status as a mother of thirteen children, all sold off into slavery, and asks again, "and ain't I a woman?" Rather than accepting the existing assumptions about what a woman is and then trying to prove that she fit the standards, Truth challenged the very standards themselves. Her actions demonstrate the process of deconstruction—namely, exposing a concept as ideological or culturally constructed rather than as natural or a simple reflection of reality (Collins 1998a, 137–45). By deconstructing the concept *woman*, Truth proved herself to be a formidable intellectual. And yet Truth was a former slave who never learned to read or write.

Examining the contributions of women like Sojourner Truth suggests 49 that the concept of *intellectual* must itself be deconstructed. Not all Black women intellectuals are educated. Not all Black women intellectuals work in academia. Furthermore, not all highly educated Black women, especially those who are employed in U.S. colleges and universities, are *automatically* intellectuals. U.S. Black women intellectuals are not a female segment of William E. B. DuBois's notion of the "talented tenth." One is neither born an intellectual nor does one become one by earning a degree. Rather, doing intellectual work of the sort envisioned within Black feminism requires a process of self-conscious struggle on behalf of Black women, regardless of the actual social location where that work occurs.

50   These are not idle concerns within new power relations that have greatly altered the fabric of U.S. and Black civil society. Race, class, and gender still constitute intersecting oppressions, but the ways in which they are now organized to produce social injustice differ from prior eras. Just as theories, epistemologies, and facts produced by any group of individuals represent the standpoints and interests of their creators, the very definition of who is legitimated to do intellectual work is not only politically contested, but is changing (Mannheim 1936; Gramsci 1971). Reclaiming Black feminist intellectual traditions involves much more than developing Black feminist analyses using standard epistemological criteria. It also involves challenging the very terms of intellectual discourse itself.

51   Assuming new angles of vision on which U.S. Black women are, in fact, intellectuals, and on their seeming dedication to contributing to Black feminist thought raises new questions about the production of this oppositional knowledge. Historically, much of the Black women's intellectual tradition occurred in institutional locations other than the academy. For example, the music of working-class Black women blues singers of the 1920s and 1930s is often seen as one important site outside academia for this intellectual tradition (Davis 1998). Whereas Ann duCille (1993) quite rightly warns us about viewing Black women's blues through rose-colored glasses, the fact remains that far more Black women listened to Bessie Smith and Ma Rainey than were able to read Nella Larsen or Jessie Fauset. Despite impressive educational achievements that have allowed many U.S. Black women to procure jobs in higher education and the media, this may continue to be the case. For example, Imani Perry (1995) suggests that the music of Black women hip-hop artists serves as a new site of Black women's intellectual production. Again, despite the fact that hip-hop contains diverse and contradictory components (Rose 1994) and that popularity alone is insufficient to confer the title "intellectual," many more Black women listen to Queen Latifah and Salt 'N' Pepa than read literature by Alice Walker and Toni Morrison.

52   Because clarifying Black women's experiences and ideas lies at the core of Black feminist thought, interpreting them requires collaborative leadership among those who participate in the diverse forms that Black women's

communities now take. This requires acknowledging not only how African-American women outside of academia have long functioned as intellectuals by representing the interests of Black women as a group, but how this continues to be the case. For example, rap singer Sister Souljah's music as well as her autobiography *No Disrespect* (1994) certainly can be seen as contributing to Black feminist thought as critical social theory. Despite her uncritical acceptance of a masculinist Black nationalist ideology, Souljah is deeply concerned with issues of Black women's oppression, and offers an important perspective on contemporary urban culture. Yet while young Black women listened to Souljah's music and thought about her ideas, Souljah's work has been dismissed within feminist classrooms in academia as being "nonfeminist." Without tapping these nontraditional sources, much of the Black women's intellectual tradition would remain "not known and hence not believed in" (Williams 1987, 150).

At the same time, many Black women academics struggle to find ways 53 to do intellectual work that challenges injustice. They know that being an academic and an intellectual are not necessarily the same thing. Since the 1960s, U.S. Black women have entered faculty positions in higher education in small but unprecedented numbers. These women confront a peculiar dilemma. On the one hand, acquiring the prestige enjoyed by their colleagues often required unquestioned acceptance of academic norms. On the other hand, many of these same norms remain wedded to notions of Black and female inferiority. Finding ways to temper critical responses to academia without unduly jeopardizing their careers constitutes a new challenge for Black women who aim to be intellectuals within academia, especially intellectuals engaged in developing Black feminist thought (Collins 1998a, 95–123).

Surviving these challenges requires new ways of doing Black feminist 54 intellectual work. Developing Black feminist thought as critical social theory involves including the ideas of Black women not previously considered intellectuals—many of whom may be working-class women with jobs outside academia—as well as those ideas emanating from more formal, legitimated scholarship. The ideas we share with one another as mothers in extended families, as othermothers in Black communities, as members of Black churches, and as teachers to the Black community's children have formed one pivotal area where African-American women have hammered out a multifaceted Black women's standpoint. Musicians, vocalists, poets, writers, and other artists constitute another group from which Black women intellectuals have emerged. Building on African-influenced oral traditions, musicians in particular have enjoyed close associations with the larger community of African-American women constituting their audience. Through their words and actions, grassroots political activists also contribute to Black women's intellectual traditions. Producing intellectual work is generally not attributed to Black women artists and political activists. Especially in elite institutions of higher education, such women are typically viewed as objects of study, a classification that creates a false dichotomy between scholarship and activism, between thinking and doing. In contrast, examining the ideas and actions of these excluded groups in a way that views them as subjects reveals a world in which behavior is a statement of philosophy and in which a vibrant, both/and, scholar/activist tradition remains intact.

Objectives of the Volume

55 African-American women's social location as a collectivity has fostered distinctive albeit heterogeneous Black feminist intellectual traditions that, for convenience in this volume, I call *Black feminist thought*. Investigations of four basic components of Black feminist thought—its thematic content, its interpretive frameworks, its epistemological approaches, and its significance for empowerment—constitute the core of this volume. All four components have been shaped by U.S. Black women's placement in a political context that is undergoing considerable change. Thus, Black feminist thought's core themes, interpretive frameworks, epistemological stances, and insights concerning empowerment will reflect and aim to shape specific political contexts confronting African-American women as a group.

56 In this volume, I aim to describe, analyze, explain the significance of, and contribute to the development of Black feminist thought as critical social theory. In addressing this general goal, I have several specific objectives. First, I summarize selected core themes in Black feminist thought by surveying their historical and contemporary expression. Drawing primarily on the works of African-American women scholars and on the thought produced by a wide range of Black women intellectuals, I explore several core themes that preoccupy Black women thinkers. The vast majority of thinkers discussed in the text are, to the best of my knowledge, U.S. Black women. I cite a range of Black women thinkers not because I think U.S. Black women have a monopoly on the ideas presented but because I aim to demonstrate the range and depth of thinkers who exist in U.S. Black civil society. Placing the ideas of ordinary African-American women as well as those of better-known Black women intellectuals at the center of analysis produces a new angle of vision on Black women's concerns. At the same time, Black feminist thought cannot be developed in isolation from the thoughts and actions of other groups. Thus, I also include the ideas of diverse thinkers who make important contributions to developing Black

feminist thought. Black women must be in charge of Black feminist thought, but being in charge does not mean that others are excluded.

Using and furthering an interpretive framework or paradigm that has 57 come to be known as race, class, and gender studies constitute a second objective of *Black Feminist Thought*. Rejecting additive models of oppression, race, class, and gender studies have progressed considerably since the 1980s. During that decade, African-American women scholar-activists, among others, called for a new approach to analyzing Black women's experiences. Claiming that such experiences were shaped not just by race, but by gender, social class, and sexuality, works such as *Women, Race and Class* by Angela Davis (1981), "A Black Feminist Statement" drafted by the Combahee River Collective (1982), and Audre Lorde's (1984) classic volume *Sister Outsider* stand as groundbreaking works that explored interconnections among systems of oppression. Subsequent work aimed to describe different dimensions of this interconnected relationship with terms such as *intersectionality* (Crenshaw 1991) and *matrix of domination*. In this volume, I use and distinguish between both terms in examining how oppression affects Black women. Intersectionality refers to particular forms of intersecting oppressions, for example, intersections of race and gender, or of sexuality and nation. Intersectional paradigms remind us that oppression cannot be reduced to one fundamental type, and that oppressions work together in producing injustice. In contrast, the matrix of domination refers to how these intersecting oppressions are actually organized. Regardless of the particular intersections involved, structural, disciplinary, hegemonic, and interpersonal domains of power reappear across quite different forms of oppression.

My third objective is to develop an epistemological framework that can 58 be used both to assess existing Black feminist thought and to clarify some of the underlying assumptions that impede its development. This issue of epistemology raises some difficult questions. I see the need to define the boundaries that delineate Black feminist thought from other arenas of intellectual inquiry. What criteria, if any, can be applied to ideas to determine whether they are in fact Black and feminist? What essential features does Black feminist thought share with other critical social theories, particularly Western feminist theory, Afrocentric theory, Marxist analyses, and postmodernism? Do African-American women implicitly rely on alternative standards for determining whether ideas are true? Traditional epistemological assumptions concerning how we arrive at "truth" simply are not sufficient to the task of furthering Black feminist thought. In the same way that concepts such as woman and intellectual must be challenged, the process by which we arrive at truth merits comparable scrutiny. While

I provide a book-length treatment of these theoretical concerns in *Fighting Words: Black Women and the Search for Justice*, here I focus on the distinguishing features of a Black feminist epistemology.

59   I aim to use this same epistemological framework throughout the volume. Alice Walker describes this process as one whereby "to write the books one wants to read is both to point the direction of vision and, at the same time, to follow it" (1983, 8). This was a very difficult process for me, one requiring that I not only develop standards and guidelines for assessing U.S. Black feminist thought but that I then apply those same standards and guidelines to my own work while I was creating it. For example, in Chapters 2 and 10 I argue that Black women intellectuals best contribute to a Black women's group standpoint by using their experiences as situated knowers. To adhere to this epistemological tenet required that, when appropriate, I reject the pronouns, "they" and "their" when describing U.S. Black women and our ideas and replace these terms with the terms "we," "us," and "our." Using the distancing terms "they" and "their" when describing my own group and our experiences might enhance both my credentials as a scholar and the credibility of my arguments in some academic settings. But by taking this epistemological stance that reflects my disciplinary training as a sociologist, I invoke standards of certifying truth about which I remain ambivalent.

60   In contrast, by identifying my position as a participant in and observer of Black women's communities, I run the risk of being discredited as being too subjective and hence less scholarly. But by being an advocate for my material, I validate epistemological tenets that I claim are fundamental for Black feminist thought, namely, to equip people to resist oppression and to inspire them to do it (Collins 1998a, 196–200). To me, the suppression of Black women's intellectual traditions has made this process of feeling one's way an unavoidable epistemological stance for Black women intellectuals. As Walker points out, "she must be her own model as well as the artist attending, creating, learning from, realizing the model, which is to say, herself" (1983, 8)

61   Finally, I aim to further Black feminist thought's contributions to empowering African-American women. Empowerment remains an illusive construct and developing a Black feminist politics of empowerment requires specifying the domains of power that constrain Black women, as well as how such domination can be resisted. Ideally, Black feminist thought contributes ideas and analytical frameworks toward this end. Moreover, it is important to remember that Black women's empowerment can occur only within a transnational context of social justice. While focused on U.S. Black women, U.S. Black feminism constitutes one of many histori-

cally specific social justice projects dedicated to fostering the empowerment of groups within an overarching context of justice. In this sense, Black feminist thought constitutes one part of a much larger social justice project that goes far beyond the experiences of African-American women.

QUESTIONING AND DISCUSSING

Collins, "The Politics of Black Feminist Thought"

1. In Patricia Hill Collins's complex essay, she enumerates the "far too many African-American women intellectuals" who have "labored in isolation and obscurity." Who are some of these women? Why is their work and thinking so important?

2. Collins argues that there is a "dialectic of oppression and activism," a "tension between the suppression of African-American women's ideas and our intellectual activism in the face of that suppression." What does Collins mean by this? What is the political context that challenges the "right to exist" of black feminist thought? How has the suppression of black feminist ideas been "similar" to bias against other women yet "different"?

3. What are the historical factors that "stimulated U.S. Black women's critical social theory"?

4. How does Collins attempt to redefine standard terms such as *intellectual*?

5. Does Collins convince you of the uniqueness of the suppression of African-American women's intellectual thought? Why or why not?

⌗

BRUCE DAVIDSON

Film director and photographer Bruce Davidson (1933–) grew up in Oak Park, Illinois, and studied at the Rochester Institute of Technology and the Yale University School of Design. A Guggenheim Fellow, Davidson in 1967 received the first photography grant awarded by the National Endowment for the Arts. His work is in the permanent collections of the Smithsonian Institution, the Metropolitan Museum of Art, the Museum of Modern Art, and the Art Institute of Chicago.

⊞

QUESTIONING AND DISCUSSING

Davidson, *Subway*

1. This is one of a number of images from Bruce Davidson's book of photographs entitled *Subway*. About them, Davidson has written, "I wanted to transform the subway from its dark, degrading, and impersonal reality into images that open up our experience again to the color, sensuality, and vitality of the individual souls that ride it each day." To what extent does this image accomplish this? Why or why not?

2. Comment on the arrangement of each visual component of this image. What are the effects of the ways in which Davidson has chosen to compose this photograph? Why might he have made these choices, and for what effect?

3. How might you explain the "theme" of this image? What is the evidence that supports this theme? Might Davidson be suggesting something that goes beyond the subway—and this one man? Why or why not?

⊞

QUESTIONS FOR READING AND RESPONDING

Chapter 7 Speaking My Mind: How Can I Persuade?

1. Although this could be said for most—if not all—of the selections in this volume, this chapter presents a number of works in which the authors attempt to influence the belief systems of their audiences. Compare and contrast the methods used by Jonathan Edwards in "Sinners in the Hands of an Angry God," for instance, with those of Robert Grudin in "Ideology and Moral Philology," Langston Hughes in "Salvation," and Diane Ravitch in "The Language Police." In what ways are these methods vastly different— and yet similar?

2. Alan M. Dershowitz's essay on assimilation, the *Chicago Tribune* editorial about beautiful people, Tennyson's "Ulysses," Shirley Jackson's "The Lottery," Patricia Hill Collins's "The Politics of Black Feminist Thought," and Lisa Schmeiser's "Do Geeks Need to Go to College?" each deals with questions of what we as individuals and as a society do or do not value. Select three of these pieces and discuss the ways in which values—good or otherwise— influence us, using evidence from the texts to support your points of view.

3. Several of the selections in this chapter speak to a conflict between isolation and membership in particular groups of society. Consider, for instance, the image of the man at the subway door photographed by Bruce Davidson; the story of the aged conqueror in Tennyson's "Ulysses"; the tensions of membership versus assimilation as described by Alan Dershowitz; the "geeks" described by Lisa Schmeiser; the status of those who are "saved" as explained by Langston Hughes; and other examples from this chapter. Selecting at least three for your discussion, explain how these selections might illustrate that belonging to one group might erase one's membership in another. What is the value of the ways in which we as human beings identify with one group or another? To what effect? Be sure to argue a point of view, selecting specific examples from these visual or written texts to prove your points.

⊞

8

Taking a Stand

What Are My Politics?

"Puritanism: the haunting fear
that someone, somewhere,
may be happy."
H. L. MENCKEN

In a recent book documenting the history of the magazine entitled *About Town: The New Yorker and The World It Made* (Scribner's), author Ben Yagoda says, "Writing a book about *The New Yorker* is like entering its world with its colorful, talented and influential parade of editors, writers and artists." For seventy-five years, the magazine is said to have set the tone regarding literature, society, and the arts. *The New Yorker* "resonates throughout the culture" as a repository for "increasingly high standards of English prose, taste, and civility," standards often marked with a wry, sophisticated sense of humor. The following cartoon, drawn by Frank Cotham and published in a recent edition, in many ways demonstrates this sophistication.

⊞

"This Is What Happens When Ethical Standards Are Set Artificially High"

"This is what happens when ethical standards are set artificially high."

QUESTIONING AND DISCUSSING

The New Yorker, "This Is What Happens When Ethical Standards Are Set Artificially High"

1. This cartoon depicts a rather absurd situation. What is the source of this absurdity?

2. Is it ever possible for "ethical standards to be set artificially high"? Why or why not? What does the cartoon suggest about the reasons that these men might be in jail? What kind of crime—homicide, robbery, white collar— does the dialogue line suggest?

3. Does this cartoon imply that ethical standards are somehow relative—that is, that they depend on the situation? Are such standards malleable? How so? How not? Is there an example of a situation for which ethical standards might "depend"? What might that be, if such a situation is possible?

⊞

HANNA ROSIN

A graduate of Stuyvesant High School in New York City and Stanford University, Hanna Rosin was an assistant editor of *The New Republic* and now writes for the editorial page of the *Washington Post*. Her work frequently concerns religious and social issues.

✤

Separation Anxiety
The Movement to Save Marriage

1   For the past three years, family values crusaders have been like wandering tribes, fervent and armed but with no place to go. In a euphoric moment after Clinton's election, the tribes united when left-wing communitarians joined their erstwhile conservative foes: a Democratic president declared the answer to poverty was "stable, intact families," and Donna Shalala, parroting the famous *Atlantic Monthly* article, professed that Dan Quayle was right. But the bipartisan convergence deprived both sides of an enemy. "We were lost," sighs David Blankenhorn, from the liberal Institute for American Values. "We had no momentum."

2   Then this year came a revelation, "like a bolt of lightning," recalls Blankenhorn. The enemy, he and his colleagues realized, was divorce law and, more specifically, "no-fault" divorce reform of the '70s, which allows couples to end their marriage without blame. Instead of having to choose from a menu of sins—adultery, mental cruelty, desertion, imprisonment— no-fault freed a new generation to break up simply because of "irreconcilable differences." "When you change the laws to make divorce quick and easy, you don't need a PhD to know what will happen," he adds. "You'll erode the American family."

3   Blankenhorn's epiphany sparked a string of conversions. In January, Iowa's Republican governor, Terry Branstad, launched the "Campaign for the Family" and drafted a bill requiring stronger grounds for divorce. Then, on Valentine's Day, a Michigan state representative, Republican Jessie Dalman, introduced a bill overturning the state's no-fault law, arguing that it "cheapens commitment and degrades lifelong love." By April, eighteen states had followed, introducing laws forcing marriage deserters to confess their sin or stick it out. In the meantime, Democrats in Washington turned up the rhetorical heat: in *It Takes a Village*, Hillary Clinton writes that she is "ambivalent about no-fault divorce when children are

involved." And her husband agrees, telling congressmen at his national prayer breakfast in February, "It may be that it ought to be a little harder to get a divorce. . . ."

The new divorcephobes accept as an axiom that the no-fault reform 4
wrecked a generation of marriages. "To me, this is like debating whether the earth is round," says Blankenhorn. But the truth is more complicated. The reform may have contributed to a rise in divorce rates—but only compared to the pent-up, atypical '50s. Outside this historical blip, the rate has been steadily climbing since the Civil War, worldwide. The end of marriage begins not with Dr. Spock, but with John Milton, who in his "Doctrine and Discipline of Divorce" declared that without it marriage sours into "drooping and disconsolate household captivity." The more worrisome phenomenon these days is that fewer families form in the first place—a trend that nixing no-fault is likely to encourage by scaring off the already marriage-shy.

How did divorce, once seen as the path to personal happiness, start look- 5
ing like the seed of America's destruction? The turn begins in the '80s with a defector from the feminist line. When Harvard professor Lenore Weitzman polled 228 women divorced under California's 1969 no-fault statute, she expected to find reduced levels of bitterness and acrimony. Instead, she stumbled on what she called the "new poor," a class of disillusioned women whose incomes had dropped 70 percent after their marriages ended.

Weitzman's portrait of female suffering permanently complicated the 6
easy equation between divorce and women's autonomy, although it's now thought to be exaggerated; the standard figure for income loss has been revised down to 30 percent. It took research on another set of victims— children—to really jump[-]start the anti-divorce movement. The study on children most often quoted by divorcephobes is "Growing Up With a Single Parent," published last year by professors Sara McLanahan of Princeton and Gary Sandefur of the University of Wisconsin. The two researchers concluded that, regardless of the race or education of the parents, children who grow up in single-parent homes fare worse at every stage of life: they get lower grades from middle school on and are more likely to drop out of high school; they get worse-paying jobs and are more likely to be unemployed and even to end up in jail. "The evidence is clear," they concluded. "Children who grow up with one parent are definitely worse off."

This research did for the anti-divorce movement what secondhand 7
smoke did for tobaccophobes: it created innocent bystanders. "Children are the quintessential vulnerable citizens. They need and deserve our help," wrote William Galston, Clinton's former domestic policy adviser

and an early disciple of the anti-divorce movement. He could now frame the issue in terms only a brute could argue with. "In the end it comes down to a moral question: Is our society willing to put the well-being of children first, even when it may restrain our passion for unfettered autonomy?" What politician could resist? Jessie Dalman's press packet includes a copy of a hand-scrawled letter from a grateful tyke: "Dear Honorable Jessie Dalman, I wanted to write to you and let you know I am supporting you and your stand of divorce reform and I am praying for you. Love, Drew."

8   Drew may be convinced, but the researchers who interviewed his cohorts are baffled. "That sounds like a bad idea," says Sandefur, when asked about the anti-no-fault movement. "People who get divorced probably should get divorced. The worst thing for kids is to be around a constant state of warfare." McLanahan is equally bewildered. "It's a bit of a sham," she says. "Just an easy fix that will appeal to voters."

9   To prove no-fault's pernicious influence, the Galstonites rely on a study published last year in the *Journal of Marriage and the Family,* which showed that the divorce rate increased by 15 to 25 percent in the three years following the switch to no-fault in forty-four of the fifty states. But, as Andrew Cherlin, another researcher often cited by Galston, points out, they're missing the first rule of statistics: correlation does not prove causation. The divorce rate has been rising steadily since the 1800s, and it surged in the early '60s—fifteen years before no-fault laws were widespread. The sudden spike in the three years following the reform came from a backlog of cases.

10   Like it or not, the country is accustomed to divorce; the only thing squelching no-fault will do is to recreate the sham of another era, when couples who wanted to divorce were obliged to invent affairs and abuse. "In New York, where adultery was the only grounds for divorce, people set up an appointment in a hotel room with a model and a photographer," recalls Herbert Jacob, a professor at Northwestern University who studies divorce. "If the judge wanted mental cruelty, your lawyer would tell you to say he called you names. If the judge wanted physical cruelty, the lawyer would recess, and you'd come back in a few minutes and say he slapped you."

11   Family boosters balk when they are called retrograde, and even the most conservative among them have learned to defend the reform in feminist terms. "We only want to return justice to marital dissolution," says Kristi Hamrick of the right-wing Family Research Council. "Returning fault gives women a powerful weapon." If the abandoned wife can pin blame on her husband, goes the argument, she can wangle a better settlement. But even this new twist is grounded in Victorian wisdom. "There's a lot of truth in the stereotype," Hamrick continues. "A gentleman decides to change his old wife for a new trophy model, so he writes one check and

leaves. Our way gives the woman back some power." In fact, in up to 65 percent of cases, it's the woman who asks to get out of the marriage. And the image of the vulnerable wife rendered helpless by divorce is out of date: in the age group most likely to divorce, 30 percent of women had jobs in 1960; now, three-quarters do.

A truly feminist, pro-child divorce reform would look something like this: dock alimony and child support automatically from the sole or primary wage-earner's paycheck, and let whoever has primary custody of the children keep the house. To punish trophy hunters, force them to support the first set of children at the same living standard as the second. This was the radical track Weitzman, who opposed returning to a fault system, suggested in her book and still supports: "Society's views of marriage are reflected in its post-divorce laws," she says. "If we don't reward a mother with alimony, what we are really saying is we don't care about someone dedicating her life to supporting a family." 12

Since the days of Weitzman's research, state laws have advanced—by splitting pensions, for example, or shaming deadbeat dads. Wisconsin even ensures mothers tax-supported child support. But most states are far behind for what some researchers suspect is a sinister reason: many legislators are divorced men. As Galston points out, the first no-fault statute was drafted by California Assemblyman James Hayes, who divorced his wife of twenty-five years to marry a younger woman. Fourteen of the fifteen people who testified for the law were men; ten were divorced. 13

For Galston, drawing attention to the sins of the overclass is a matter of playing fair, making sure "family values" does not become another way to demonize the poor: "This change is about us, not them," says Galston. But the movement's greatest fault is confounding "us" and "them." In Maggie Gallagher's The Abolition of Marriage, there is a chapter describing the author's apocalyptic visions of a "post-marriage" society. It opens with Raphael Rympel, a Haitian schoolboy shot dead in the playground. This happened in Crown Heights, but "there is no escape from Crown Heights," Gallagher writes, "because every neighborhood in America is just like it," by which she means that every neighborhood in America is an open sore left by divorce culture. The poor children there are no worse off than Melissa, a smart and pretty pre-law student who, as a child of divorce, is haunted by fears of abandonment. "Even most concentration camp survivors grow up to be law-abiding citizens," Gallagher memorably puts it, explaining why outward success is deceptive. 14

To show that divorce doesn't discriminate, Gallagher cites a well-known study by Judith Wallerstein, in which sixty mostly affluent California families were tracked for ten years. Only one-third of the divorced dads chose to pay for their children's college; 60 percent of the children 15 did worse in school than their fathers. If these white, educated, upper-middle-class children can't hack it, Gallagher suggests, just imagine what happens to the black and poor. She seems to forget that it's only in white, middle-class America that too much anxiety seems as bad as too little money. Comparing the two is like saying if Woody Allen can't keep his family together, imagine what will happen to the rest of us.

16   It's hard to imagine the family faithfuls really believe that changing divorce law is the best they can do for the Raphael Rympels of this world. At least for the politicians of the movement, dragging the Rympels into the debate is useful for other reasons. Governor Branstad of Iowa began our conversation by citing the usual litany of doomsday statistics: "Poverty, drug abuse, juvenile delinquency, the crime rate, are all associated with the breakup of the traditional family." But in his "Campaign for the Family" it's not the juveniles he is concerned about. "If a child grows up angry in a broken home and feels like nobody loves them, it's likely they'll become a drug addict and rob you."

17   And if it's not the underclass he's worried about, Branstad can rest easy. In the last few years, there's been a yuppie stampede to America's altars: a 1993 University of Pennsylvania study found female college graduates were marrying younger than they did in the '70s. We've always been the most marriage-happy Western country, and lately we've started to celebrate it with a vengeance. In movies, books and syrupy newspaper features, America is suddenly awash in nuptial splendor. Screen hits of the '70s celebrating wives unshackled by divorce—*An Unmarried Woman, Kramer vs. Kramer*—have been replaced by parables of couples who stick together through affairs, alcoholism and streams of verbal abuse: *Flirting with Disaster, Something to Talk About, When a Man Loves a Woman, Leaving Las Vegas,* [and the television series] *Married with Children.* In bookstores, *The Creative Divorce,* a best-seller of the divorce decade, has been superseded by *The Good Marriage,* Judith Wallerstein's book of secrets to making love last.

18   It's a shift the Galstonites, in their self-styled Jeremiad prose, recognize. "The people of your generation, the children of divorce, are displaying a yearning for restabilization," Galston explains. "Faced with the reality of divorce, Generation X is expressing the ardent hope that 'This won't happen to me.'" Then, pausing for a sip of coffee, he lets me in on the cosmic secret: "Sociologists think this might be the Great Awakening."

19   Heralding it in is a burgeoning cottage industry of marriage supporters, the cheerleaders for the anti-no-fault movement. Across the country, groups dedicated to ending the plague of divorce are spreading the gospel of a new kind of sustainable union—the "good-enough marriage." Christian columnist Michael McManus is the Johnny Appleseed of this pro-marriage movement. The concept of no-fault offends him, he says,

because it promotes the kind of starry-eyed romantic expectations no marriage can fulfill and prompts couples to give up too quickly. "Abraham did not get along with Sarah," he says. "No marriage is perfect."

McManus and his acolytes are convincing churches across the country to   20 implement what they call "community marriage policies"—an elaborate network of marriage support where those considering divorce are barraged by caring peer couples who have come back from the brink. In the last year, the number of pledging communities has jumped from fourteen to forty-two, McManus says. First to implement the scheme was Modesto, California, well-known as a laboratory of experimental spirituality. The policy seems to have worked there: since it began a decade ago, divorce is down 7 percent, although the population increased by 40 percent. Couples who apply to marry in one of the Modesto churches must go through as many as ten two-hour counseling sessions and take a personality test designed to detect fault lines. About 10 percent of these couples break their engagements.

McManus's miracle program is Retrouvaille, an intense peer counseling   21 system founded in Quebec in the '60s, which claims to save 90 percent of the 5,000 floundering couples who participate each year. The program operates on a kind of reverse Tolstoy principle—all unhappy families are unhappy in the same way. They all fail because of "poor communication," because husband and wife "mistake feeling for thought." Couples trained in the Retrouvaille method repeat their intimate tragedies in rehearsed monotone: McManus, for example, tells me with no hesitation that, though both his parents were alcoholics, he "grew up a whole person" because they stayed together. In the Retrouvaille world, no marriage is too broken; McManus has patched together alcoholics, abusers, even one wife and her bisexual husband who'd been having affairs for eight years.

McManus is lit by a kind of cultish fervor that pities all who do not pos-   22 sess it. One Friday afternoon, the 6'7" preacher is crammed into a chair at a Washington studio, the pro-marriage guest on a trashy low-budget show called *NewsTalk* being filmed in New York. The subject is "Should couples stay together for the sake of the children?" and the other guests are divorced women and couples who have saved their marriage. When a divorced mother describes why her marriage was irretrievable, McManus leans over to me and whispers, "She hadn't heard of Retrouvaille." When the talk-show host doesn't mention Retrouvaille, McManus throws a fit: "What are you doing? Talk about Retrouvaille. R-E-T-R-O-UV-A-I-L-L-E. That's why I came. They told me I could. . . ." He is cut off, and a production assistant is called in. "But they told me they would talk about it," he says petulantly. "All you want to do is focus on the negative."

This patient patronizing, waiting to erupt into angry judgment, is not   23 unique to the religious preachers of the pro-marriage movement. In what communitarian guru Michael Lerner calls his "Progressive, Ethical Covenant with American Families," the manifesto for a two-day worryfest held in April, he confuses political platforms ("Reduce the work week") with moral ones such as "Support people to work through difficulties in relationships" and "Support single people and those leaving oppressive relationships." These seem innocuous and obvious enough, until you get to the dogmatic details: divorce is a result of the "supermarket mentality" and "market consciousness" of America. Yet, at the same time, "we want to reject attempts to stigmatize the decision to leave an oppressive relationship," given "the distortions in human relationships fostered by the legacy of patriarchy and the dynamics of a society dominated by materialism and selfishness." The actual advice must be irrelevant, since the two platforms are exactly contradictory; what's important is achieving that perfect pedagogic pitch.

24   Across the states, it's this tone that is winning out over substance. Most of the no-fault bills are in embryonic stages, and, at best, a few will squeak through this year. In Iowa, Governor Branstad has given up on repealing no-fault this session but is fighting for a series of community forums discussing "the importance of strong families" and a requirement that divorcing parents attend re-education classes to learn about the impact of divorce on their children. It's like McManus becoming incensed that the schools teach "math and science but not marriage." But at least McManus has been to the brink and back and understands that marriage is a messy business. For the rest, it's just a matter of night school.

QUESTIONING AND DISCUSSING

Rosin, "Separation Anxiety"

---

1. Hanna Rosin begins her article as follows: "For the past three years, family values crusaders have been like wandering tribes, fervent and armed but with no place to go." How does this opening line indicate the author's attitude and tone toward her subject? What is the effect of this sentence? Comment on her use of simile.

2. From what contexts does Rosin speak? That is, what is the political climate of the time—1996, when this article was written—that apparently shapes Rosin's perspective? What did Secretary of Human Services Donna Shalala mean when she said that "Dan Quayle [vice president under the first President Bush] was right"?

3. Why does Rosin put "family values" in quotation marks within the article? What is her critique of those who would advocate "family values"?

4. Do you agree with Rosin that, based on evidence presented in the article, "tone is winning out over substance"? Why or why not? How effectively does Rosin argue her point of view? Use examples from the text to prove your points.

⊞

JONATHAN RAUCH

Jonathan Rauch (1960–) attended Yale University and wrote for the *Winston-Salem Journal* in North Carolina for two years. Currently a freelance writer, he writes a bi-weekly column for *National Journal* in Washington, DC, on issues related to public policy and government. Rauch has written four books, including *Kindly Inquisitors* (1993), which deals with attacks on freedom of thought; and *Government's End: Why Washington Stopped Working* (1999). He also serves as writer-in-residence for the Brookings Institution in Washington. He became openly gay in 1991 when, while writing in *The New Republic,* he critiqued hate crimes laws from the perspective of a gay person.

⊞

The Case for Gay (and Straight) Marriage
For Better or Worse?

Whatever else marriage may or may not be, it is certainly falling apart.   1
Half of today's marriages end in divorce, and, far more costly, many never begin—leaving mothers poor, children fatherless and neighborhoods chaotic. With timing worthy of Neville Chamberlain, homosexuals have chosen this moment to press for the right to marry. What's more, Hawaii's courts are moving toward letting them do so. I'll believe in gay marriage in America when I see it, but if Hawaii legalizes it, even temporarily, the uproar over this final insult to a besieged institution will be deafening.

Whether gay marriage makes sense—and whether straight marriage   2
makes sense—depends on what marriage is actually for. Current secular thinking on this question is shockingly sketchy. Gay activists say: marriage is for love, and we love each other, therefore we should be able to marry. Traditionalists say: marriage is for children, and homosexuals do not (or should not) have children, therefore you should not be able to marry. That, unfortunately, pretty well covers the spectrum. I say "unfortunately"

because both views are wrong. They misunderstand and impoverish the social meaning of marriage.

3   So what is marriage for? Modern marriage is, of course, based upon traditions that religion helped to codify and enforce. But religious doctrine has no special standing in the world of secular law and policy (the "Christian nation" crowd notwithstanding). If we want to know what and whom marriage is for in modern America, we need a sensible secular doctrine.

4   At one point, marriage in secular society was largely a matter of business: cementing family ties, providing social status for men and economic support for women, conferring dowries, and so on. Marriages were typically arranged, and "love" in the modern sense was no prerequisite. In Japan, remnants of this system remain, and it works surprisingly well. Couples stay together because they view their marriage as a partnership: an investment in social stability for themselves and their children. Because Japanese couples don't expect as much emotional fulfillment as we do, they are less inclined to break up. They also take a somewhat more relaxed attitude toward adultery. What's a little extracurricular love provided that each partner is fulfilling his or her many other marital duties?

5   In the West, of course, love is a defining element. The notion of lifelong love is charming, if ambitious, and certainly love is a desirable element of marriage. In society's eyes, however, it cannot be the defining element. You may or may not love your husband, but the two of you are just as married either way. You may love your mistress, but that certainly doesn't make her your spouse. Love helps make sense of marriage emotionally, but it is not terribly important in making sense of marriage from the point of view of social policy.

6   If love does not define the purpose of secular marriage, what does? Neither the law nor secular thinking provides a clear answer. Today marriage is almost entirely a voluntary arrangement whose contents are up to the people making the deal. There are few if any behaviors that automatically end a marriage. If a man beats his wife, which is about the worst thing he can do to her, he may be convicted of assault, but his marriage is not automatically dissolved. Couples can be adulterous ("open") yet remain married. They can be celibate, too; consummation is not required. All in all, it is an impressive and also rather astonishing victory for modern individualism that so important an institution should be so bereft of formal social instruction as to what should go on inside of it.

7   Secular society tells us only a few things about marriage. First, marriage depends on the consent of the parties. Second, the parties are not children. Third, the number of parties is two. Fourth, one is a man and the other a woman. Within those rules a marriage is whatever anyone says it is.

Perhaps it is enough simply to say that marriage is as it is and should not   8
be tampered with. This sounds like a crudely reactionary position. In fact,
however, of all the arguments against reforming marriage, it is probably
the most powerful.

Call it a Hayekian argument, after the great libertarian economist F. A.   9
Hayek, who developed this line of thinking in his book *The Fatal Conceit.*
In a market system, the prices generated by impersonal forces may not
make sense from any one person's point of view, but they encode far more
information than even the cleverest person could ever gather. In a similar
fashion, human societies evolve rich and complicated webs of nonlegal
rules in the form of customs, traditions and institutions. Like prices, they
may seem irrational or arbitrary. But the very fact that they are the customs that have evolved implies that they embody a practical logic that
may not be apparent to even a sophisticated analyst. And the web of custom cannot be torn apart and reordered at will because once its internal
logic is violated it falls apart. Intellectuals, such as Marxists or feminists,
who seek to deconstruct and rationally rebuild social traditions, will produce not better order but chaos.

So the Hayekian view argues strongly against gay marriage. It says that   10
the current rules may not be best and may even be unfair. But they are all
we have, and, once you say that marriage need not be male-female, soon
marriage will stop being anything at all. You can't mess with the formula
without causing unforeseen consequences, possibly including the implo-
sion of the institution of marriage itself.

However, there are problems with the Hayekian position. It is unten-   11
able in its extreme form and unhelpful in its milder version. In its extreme
form, it implies that no social reform should ever be undertaken. Indeed,
no laws should be passed, because they interfere with the natural evolution of social mores. How could Hayekians abolish slavery? They would
probably note that slavery violates fundamental moral principles. But in
so doing they would establish a moral platform from which to judge social
rules, and thus acknowledge that abstracting social debate from moral
concerns is not possible.

If the ban on gay marriage were only mildly unfair, and if the costs of   12
changing it were certain to be enormous, then the ban could stand on
Hayekian grounds. But, if there is any social policy today that has a fair claim
to be scaldingly inhumane, it is the ban on gay marriage. As conservatives
tirelessly and rightly point out, marriage is society's most fundamental institution. To bar any class of people from marrying as they choose is an extraordinary deprivation. When not so long ago it was illegal in parts of America
for blacks to marry whites, no one could claim that this was a trivial

disenfranchisement. Granted, gay marriage raises issues that interracial marriage does not; but no one can argue that the deprivation is a minor one.

13 To outweigh such a serious claim it is not enough to say that gay marriage might lead to bad things. Bad things happened as a result of legalizing contraception, but that did not make it the wrong thing to do. Besides, it seems doubtful that extending marriage to, say, another 3 or 5 percent of the population would have anything like the effects that no-fault divorce has had, to say nothing of contraception. By now, the "traditional" understanding of marriage has been sullied in all kinds of ways. It is hard to think of a bigger affront to tradition, for instance, than allowing married women to own property independently of their husbands or allowing them to charge their husbands with rape. Surely it is unfair to say that marriage may be reformed for the sake of anyone and everyone except homosexuals, who must respect the dictates of tradition.

14 Faced with these problems, the milder version of the Hayekian argument says not that social tradition shouldn't be tampered with at all, but that they shouldn't be tampered with lightly. Fine. In this case, no one is talking about casual messing around; both sides have marshaled their arguments with deadly seriousness. Hayekians surely have to recognize that appeals to blind tradition and to the risks inherent in social change do not, a priori, settle anything in this instance. They merely warn against frivolous change.

15 So we turn to what has become the standard view of marriage's purpose. Its proponents would probably like to call it a child-centered view, but it is actually an anti-gay view, as will become clear. Whatever you call it, it is the view of marriage that is heard most often, and in the context of the debate over gay marriage it is heard almost exclusively. In its most straightforward form it goes as follows (I quote from James Q. Wilson's fine book *The Moral Sense*):

> A family is not an association of independent people; it is a human commitment designed to make possible the rearing of moral and healthy children. Governments care—or ought to care—about families for this reason, and scarcely for any other.

16 Wilson speaks about "family" rather than "marriage" as such, but one may, I think, read him as speaking of marriage without doing any injustice to his meaning. The resulting proposition—government ought to care about marriage almost entirely because of children—seems reasonable. But there are problems. The first, obviously, is that gay couples may have children, whether through adoption, prior marriage or (for lesbians) artificial insemination. Leaving aside the thorny issue of gay adoption, the point is that if the mere presence of children is the test, then homosexual relationships can certainly pass it.

You might note, correctly, that heterosexual marriages are more likely to produce children than homosexual ones. When granting marriage licenses to heterosexuals, however, we do not ask how likely the couple is to have children. We assume that they are entitled to get married whether or not they end up with children. Understanding this, conservatives often make an interesting move. In seeking to justify the state's interest in marriage, they shift from the actual presence of children to the anatomical possibility of making them. Hadley Arkes, a political science professor and prominent opponent of homosexual marriage, makes the case this way:

> The traditional understanding of marriage is grounded in the "natural teleology of the body"—in the inescapable fact that only a man and a woman, and only two people, not three, can generate a child. Once marriage is detached from that natural teleology of the body, what ground of principle would thereafter confine marriage to two people rather than some larger grouping? That is, on what ground of principle would the law reject the claim of a gay couple that their love is not confined to a coupling of two, but that they are woven into a larger ensemble with yet another person or two? What he seems to be saying is that, where the possibility of natural children is nil, the meaning of marriage is nil. If marriage is allowed between members of the same sex, then the concept of marriage has been emptied of content except to ask whether the parties love each other. Then anything goes, including polygamy. This reasoning presumably is what those opposed to gay marriage have in mind when they claim that, once gay marriage is legal, marriage to pets will follow close behind.

But Arkes and his sympathizers make two mistakes. To see them, break down the claim into two components: (1) Two-person marriage derives its special status from the anatomical possibility that the partners can create natural children; and (2) Apart from (1), two-person marriage has no purpose sufficiently strong to justify its special status. That is, absent justification (1), anything goes.

The first proposition is wholly at odds with the way society actually views marriage. Leave aside the insistence that natural, as opposed to adopted, children define the importance of marriage. The deeper problem, apparent right away, is the issue of sterile heterosexual couples. Here the "anatomical possibility" crowd has a problem, for a homosexual union is, anatomically speaking, nothing but one variety of sterile union and no different even in principle: a woman without a uterus has no more potential for giving birth than a man without a vagina.

It may sound like carping to stress the case of barren heterosexual marriage: the vast majority of newlywed heterosexual couples, after all, can have children and probably will. But the point here is fundamental. There are far more sterile heterosexual unions in America than homosexual ones. The "anatomical possibility" crowd cannot have it both ways. If the possibility of children is what gives meaning to marriage, then a post-menopausal woman who applies for a marriage license should be turned away at the courthouse door. What's more, she should be hooted at and condemned for stretching the meaning of marriage beyond its natural basis and so reducing the institution to frivolity. People at the Family Research Council or Concerned Women for America should point at her and say, "If she can marry, why not polygamy?"

21   Obviously, the "anatomical" conservatives do not say this, because they are sane. They instead flail around, saying that sterile men and women were at least born with the right-shaped parts for making children, and so on. Their position is really a nonposition. It says that the "natural children" rationale defines marriage when homosexuals are involved but not when heterosexuals are involved. When the parties to union are sterile heterosexuals, the justification for marriage must be something else. But what?

22   Now arises the oddest part of the "anatomical" argument. Look at proposition (2) above. It says that, absent the anatomical justification for marriage, anything goes. In other words, it dismisses the idea that there might be other good reasons for society to sanctify marriage above other kinds of relationships. Why would anybody make this move? I'll hazard a guess: to exclude homosexuals. Any rationale that justifies sterile heterosexual marriages can also apply to homosexual ones. For instance, marriage makes women more financially secure. Very nice, say the conservatives. But that rationale could be applied to lesbians, so it's definitely out.

23   The end result of this stratagem is perverse to the point of being funny. The attempt to ground marriage in children (or the anatomical possibility thereof) falls flat. But, having lost that reason for marriage, the anti-gay people can offer no other. In their fixation on excluding homosexuals, they leave themselves no consistent justification for the privileged status of heterosexual marriage. They thus tear away any coherent foundation that secular marriage might have, which is precisely the opposite of what they claim they want to do. If they have to undercut marriage to save it from homosexuals, so be it!

24   For the record, I would be the last to deny that children are one central reason for the privileged status of marriage. When men and women get together, children are a likely outcome; and, as we are learning in ever more unpleasant ways, when children grow up without two parents, trouble ensues. Children are not a trivial reason for marriage; they just cannot be the only reason.

25   What are the others? It seems to me that the two strongest candidates are these: domesticating men and providing reliable caregivers. Both pur-

poses are critical to the functioning of a humane and stable society, and both are much better served by marriage—that is, by one-to-one lifelong commitment—than by any other institution.

Civilizing young males is one of any society's biggest problems. Wherever unattached males gather in parks, you see no end of trouble: wildings in Central Park, gangs in Los Angeles, soccer hooligans in Britain, skinheads in Germany, fraternity hazings in universities, grope-lines in the military and, in a different but ultimately no less tragic way, the bathhouses and wanton sex of gay San Francisco or New York in the 1970s.

For taming men, marriage is unmatched. "Of all the institutions through which men may pass—schools, factories, the military—marriage has the largest effect," Wilson writes in *The Moral Sense*. (A token of the casualness of current thinking about marriage is that the man who wrote those words could, later in the very same book, say that government should care about fostering families for "scarcely any other" reason than children.) If marriage—that is, the binding of men into couples—did nothing else, its power to settle men, to keep them at home and out of trouble, would be ample justification for its special status.

Of course, women and older men don't generally travel in marauding or orgiastic packs. But in their case the second rationale comes into play. A second enormous problem for society is what to do when someone is beset by some sort of burdensome contingency. It could be cancer, a broken back, unemployment or depression; it could be exhaustion from work or stress under pressure. If marriage has any meaning at all, it is that, when you collapse from a stroke, there will be at least one other person whose "job" is to drop everything and come to your aid; or that when you come home after being fired by the postal service there will be someone to persuade you not to kill the supervisor.

Obviously, both rationales—the need to settle males and the need to have people looked after—apply to sterile people as well as fertile ones, and apply to childless couples as well as to ones with children. The first explains why everybody feels relieved when the town delinquent gets married, and the second explains why everybody feels happy when an aging widow takes a second husband. From a social point of view, it seems to me, both rationales are far more compelling as justifications of marriage's special status than, say, love. And both of them apply to homosexuals as well as to heterosexuals.

Take the matter of settling men. It is probably true that women and children, more than just the fact of marriage, help civilize men. But that hardly means that the settling effect of marriage on homosexual men is negligible. To the contrary, being tied to a committed relationship plainly helps stabilize gay men. Even without marriage, coupled gay men have steady sex partners and relationships that they value and therefore tend to be less wanton. Add marriage, and you bring a further array of stabilizing influences. One of the main benefits of publicly recognized marriage is that it binds couples together not only in their own eyes but also in the eyes of society at large. Around the partners is woven a web of expectations that they will spend nights together, go to parties together, take out mortgages together, buy furniture at Ikea together, and so on—all of which helps tie them together and keep them off the streets and at home. Surely that is a very good thing, especially as compared to the closet-gay culture of furtive sex with innumerable partners in parks and bathhouses.

31   The other benefit of marriage—caretaking—clearly applies to homosexuals. One of the first things many people worry about when coming to terms with their homosexuality is: Who will take care of me when I'm ailing or old? Society needs to care about this, too, as the AIDS crisis has made horribly clear. If that crisis has shown anything, it is that homosexuals can and will take care of each other, sometimes with breathtaking devotion—and that no institution can begin to match the care of a devoted partner. Legally speaking, marriage creates kin. Surely society's interest in kin-creation is strongest of all for people who are unlikely to be supported by children in old age and who may well be rejected by their own parents in youth.

32   Gay marriage, then, is far from being a mere exercise in political point-making or rights-mongering. On the contrary, it serves two of the three social purposes that make marriage so indispensable and irreplaceable for heterosexuals. Two out of three may not be the whole ball of wax, but it is more than enough to give society a compelling interest in marrying off homosexuals.

33   There is no substitute. Marriage is the only institution that adequately serves these purposes. The power of marriage is not just legal but social. It seals its promise with the smiles and tears of family, friends and neighbors. It shrewdly exploits ceremony (big, public weddings) and money (expensive gifts, dowries) to deter casual commitment and to make bailing out embarrassing. Stag parties and bridal showers signal that what is beginning is not just a legal arrangement but a whole new stage of life. "Domestic partner" laws do none of these things. I'll go further: far from being a substitute for the real thing, marriage-lite may undermine it. Marriage is a deal between a couple and society, not just between two people: society recognizes the sanctity and autonomy of the pair-bond, and in exchange each spouse commits to being the other's nurse, social worker and policeman of first resort. Each marriage is its own little society within society. Any step that weakens the deal by granting the legal benefits of marriage without also requiring the public commitment is begging for trouble.

34   So gay marriage makes sense for several of the same reasons that straight

marriage makes sense. That would seem a natural place to stop. But the logic of the argument compels one to go a twist further. If it is good for society to have people attached, then it is not enough just to make marriage available. Marriage should also be expected. This, too, is just as true for homosexuals as for heterosexuals. So, if homosexuals are justified in expecting access to marriage, society is equally justified in expecting them to use it. I'm not saying that out-of-wedlock sex should be scandalous or that people should be coerced into marrying. The mechanisms of expectation are more subtle. When grandma cluck-clucks over a still-unmarried young man, or when mom says she wishes her little girl would settle down, she is expressing a strong and well-justified preference: one that is quietly echoed in a thousand ways throughout society and that produces subtle but important pressure to form and sustain unions. This is a good and necessary thing, and it will be as necessary for homosexuals as heterosexuals. If gay marriage is recognized, single gay people over a certain age should not be surprised when they are disapproved of or pitied. That is a vital part of what makes marriage work. It's stigma as social policy.

If marriage is to work it cannot be merely a "lifestyle option." It must be   35
privileged. That is, it must be understood to be better, on average, than other ways of living. Not mandatory, not good where everything else is bad, but better: a general norm, rather than a personal taste. The biggest worry about gay marriage, I think, is that homosexuals might get it but then mostly not use it. Gay neglect of marriage wouldn't greatly erode the bonding power of heterosexual marriage (remember, homosexuals are only a tiny fraction of the population)—but it would certainly not help. And heterosexual society would rightly feel betrayed if, after legalization, homosexuals treated marriage as a minority taste rather than as a core institution of life. It is not enough, I think, for gay people to say we want the right to marry. If we do not use it, shame on us.

QUESTIONING AND DISCUSSING

Rauch, "The Case for Gay (and Straight) Marriage"

1. Jonathan Rauch's argument, certainly the first part of it, is fairly direct: "Whatever else marriage may or may not be, it is certainly falling apart." How does Rauch argue his thesis? What are his most and least effective examples? Is his an argument that has to do with ethics? Why or why not?

2. What are the various historical contexts that Rauch discusses? How do these contribute to his arguments about gay marriage? Why does Rauch introduce the "Hayekian" argument? What might be his rhetorical purpose in doing so?

3. What is the "anatomical" argument? How does Rauch use this to bolster his own point of view? To what end?

4. Why is it important that marriage be "privileged"? What is the effect of Rauch's using this point as part of his argument in support of gay marriage? How does it potentially undercut his critics to argue that marriage should be privileged as he argues that it is desirable and appropriate for gays? Overall, what does Rauch seem to value about marriage?

⊞

WILFRED OWEN

Wilfred Owen (1893–1918), a celebrated "World War I poet," was born in Oswestry, England. Owen's collection of poetry reflects in its entirety and with painful clarity the agony and horrors of war and the ironies separating those fighting the war and the often well-meaning patriots at home. Educated at the Birkenhead Institute and London University, Owen lived as a teacher in France during World War I until he visited a hospital for the wounded and decided to return to England and enlist in January of 1917. While spending time in a hospital due to war injuries, Owen met poet Siegfried Sassoon, who advised and encouraged Owen regarding his poetry. Sassoon introduced Owen to H. G. Wells and helped to get some of Owen's work published in *The Nation*. After being deemed fit for battle, Owen returned to the front. On November 4, 1918, he was caught in German machine-gun fire and was killed only a week before the end of the war. After his death, Sassoon helped to arrange for a complete edition of Owen's work to be published in 1931. In 1962, the composer Benjamin Britten incorporated some of Owen's powerful verses into his *War Requiem*.

⊞

Dulce et Decorum Est

Bent double, like old beggars under sacks,
Knock-kneed, coughing like hags, we cursed through sludge,
Till on the haunting flares we turned our backs,
And towards our distant rest began to trudge.
Men marched asleep. Many had lost their boots,   5
But limped on, blood-shod. All went lame, all blind;
Drunk with fatigue; deaf even to the hoots
Of gas-shells dropping softly behind.

Gas! GAS! Quick, boys!—An ecstasy of fumbling,
Fitting the clumsy helmets just in time,　　　　　　　　　　10
But someone still was yelling out and stumbling
And flound'ring like a man in fire or lime.—
Dim through the misty panes and thick green light,
As under a green sea, I saw him drowning.

In all my dreams before my helpless sight　　　　　　　　15
He plunges at me, guttering, choking, drowning.

If in some smothering dreams, you too could pace
Behind the wagon that we flung him in,
And watch the white eyes writhing in his face,
His hanging face, like a devil's sick of sin,　　　　　　　20
If you could hear, at every jolt, the blood
Come gargling from the froth-corrupted lungs
Bitter as the cud
Of vile, incurable sores on innocent tongues,—
My friend, you would not tell with such high zest　　　25
To children ardent for some desperate glory,
The old lie: *Dulce et decorum est*
Pro patria mori.

QUESTIONING AND DISCUSSING

Owen, "Dulce et Decorum Est"

---

1. The title and its extension in the last line of the poem come from the Roman poet Horace and translate as follows: "It is sweet and becoming to die for one's country." How do you read this title? How does it contrast with and comment on the events described in the poem? What appears to be Owen's attitude toward war?

2. Comment on the effectiveness of Owen's use of figurative language and his other descriptions: "an ecstasy of fumbling" (9), "Dim through the misty panes and thick green light / As under a green sea [. . .]" (13,14), "the blood / Come gargling from the froth-corrupted lungs / Bitter as the cud [. . .]" (21–23). How do these—and other examples you find—contribute to the meaning of the poem and shape your reaction to it?

3. Who is the person being addressed in the poem? ("My friend, you would not tell with such high zest / To children ardent for some desperate glory, / The old lie [. . .]" [25–27]). What perceptions might that "friend" have about war

that Owen seeks to correct? How does this poem transcend, if it does, the war—World War I—about which it was written?

⊞

Studs Terkel

Studs Terkel (1912–), broadcaster and author, grew up in Chicago. He graduated from the University of Chicago in 1932 and earned a JD at the Chicago Law School in 1934. He has acted in radio soap operas; has been a disk jockey, a sports commentator, and a TV host; and for the past two decades has traveled all over the world conducting on-the-spot interviews. He has questioned the American people on topics such as the Great Depression, World War II, and their jobs, and he has written and published best-selling books that share portraits of those he has interviewed. All of his books have received international acclaim, and they have been translated into every major Western language as well as into Hungarian and Japanese. In addition to a host of other honors, Terkel won the Pulitzer Prize for nonfiction for his 1984 book, *The Good War*, from which this selection is taken. Until recently a long-time radio host on Chicago's WFMT, Terkel welcomed to his program a variety of writers, political figures, musicians, and other intriguing personalities.

⊞

From *The Good War*

Introduction

"I was in combat for six weeks, forty-two days. I remember every hour, every minute, every incident of the whole forty-two days. What was it—forty years ago?" As he remembers aloud, the graying businessman is transformed into a nineteen-year-old rifleman. Much too tall for a rifleman, his mother cried.

This is a memory book, rather than one of hard fact and precise statistic. In re-calling an epoch, some forty years ago, my colleagues experienced pain, in some instances; exhilaration, in others. Often it was a fusing of both. A hesitancy, at first, was followed by a flow of memories: long-ago hurts and small triumphs. Honors and humiliations. There was laughter, too.*

---

*Hard Times: An Oral History of the Great Depression (New York: Pantheon Books, 1970), p. 3.

In 1982, a woman of thirty, doing just fine in Washington, D.C., let me 1
know how things are in her precincts: "I can't relate to World War Two.
It's in schoolbook texts, that's all. Battles that were won, battles that were
lost. Or costume dramas you see on TV. It's just a story in the past. It's so
distant, so abstract. I don't get myself up in a bunch about it."

It appears that the disremembrance of World War Two is as disturbingly 2
profound as the forgettery of the Great Depression: World War Two, an
event that changed the psyche as well as the face of the United States and
of the world.

The memory of the rifleman is what this book is about; and of his sud- 3
den comrades, thrown, hugger-mugger, together; and of those men,
women, and children on the home front who knew or did not know what
the shouting was all about; and of occasional actors from other worlds, accidentally encountered; and of lives lost and bucks found. And of a moment in history, as recalled by an ex-corporal, "when buddies felt they
were more important, were better men who amounted to more than they
do now. It's a precious memory."

On a September day in 1982, Hans Göbeler and James Sanders are toast- 4
ing one another in Chicago. Mr. Göbeler had been the mate on a German
submarine, U-505. Mr. Sanders had been the junior flight officer on the
U.S.S. *Guadalcanal*. Thirty-eight years before, one tried his damnedest, as
a loyal member of his crew, to sink the other's craft about two hundred
miles off the coast of West Africa. Now they reminisce, wistfully.

"Every man, especially the youth, can be manipulated," says Mr. Gö- 5
beler. "The more you say to him that's the American way of life, the German way of life, they believe it. Without being more bad than the other
is. There's a great danger all the time." Mr. Sanders nods. "It could happen. People could be fooled. Memory is short."

*For me, it was forty-odd years ago. I was in the air force, 1942–1943. I never
saw a plane; if I did, I wouldn't have had the foggiest idea what to do with it.
Mine was limited service. Perforated eardrum. It was stateside all the way, safe
and uneventful. Yet I remember, in surprising detail, the uneventful events; and
all those boy-faces, pimply, acned, baby-smooth. And bewildered.*

*From Jefferson Barracks, Missouri, to Fort Logan, Colorado, to Basic Train-
ing Center 10, North Carolina, my peregrinations were noncombative in nature. How I became a sergeant may have had something to do with my age. I
was ten years older than the normal GI and, willy-nilly, became the avuncular
one to the manchildren. Special Services, they called it.*

*The other barracks elder was a crooked ex-bailiff from New Orleans. He was
forty. Propinquity, the uniform, and the adventure made us buddies. Even now,*

I remember those wide-eyed wonders, our nightly audience, as Mike and I held forth. Who knows? Perhaps we were doing the state some service in giving these homesick kids a laugh or two. In any event, they were learning something about civics hardly taught in school, especially from Mike.

When he and I, on occasion, goofed off and, puffing five-cent Red Dot cigars, observed from the warm quarters of the PX toilet our young comrades doing morning calisthenics in the biting Rocky Mountain air, it was without any sense of shame. On the contrary. Mike, blowing smoke rings, indicated the scene outside and, in the manner of General MacArthur, proclaimed, "Aintchu proud of our boys?" I solemnly nodded. The fact is we were proud of them; and they, perversely, of us. Memento mores.

6   Seated across the celebratory table from Hans Göbeler and Jim Sanders, I think of the nineteen-year-old rifleman. "It was sunshine and quiet. We were passing the Germans we killed. Looking at the individual German dead, each took on a personality. These were no longer an abstraction. They were no longer the Germans of the brutish faces and the helmets we saw in the newsreels. They were exactly our age. These were boys like us."

7   "Boys" was the word invariably used by the combat-protagonists of this book. The references were to enemy soldiers as well as our own. The SS were, of course, another matter. Even the most gentle and forgiving of our GIs found few redeeming attributes there. So, too, with the professional warrior of Imperial Japan. As for the Japanese citizen-soldier, let a near-sighted, bespectacled American corporal (now a distinguished near-sighted, bespectacled economist) tell it: "In Guam, I saw my first dead Japanese. He looked pitiful, with his thick glasses. He had a sheaf of letters in his pocket. He looked like an awkward kid who'd been taken right out of his home to this miserable place."

8   Paul Douglas, the liberal Illinoisan, volunteered for the marines at fifty "to get myself a Jap." True, it did no harm to his subsequent campaign for the United States Senate. There was nothing unusual in Mr. Douglas's pronouncement. "Jap" was a common word in our daily vocabulary. He was a decent, highly enlightened man caught up in war fever as much as fervor. It was the doyen of American journalists, Walter Lippmann, who strongly urged internment for Niseis and their fathers and mothers.

9   For the typical American soldier, despite the perverted film sermons, it wasn't "getting another Jap" or "getting another Nazi" that impelled him up front. "The reason you storm the beaches is not patriotism or bravery," reflects the tall rifleman. "It's that sense of not wanting to fail your buddies. There's sort of a special sense of kinship."

10   An explanation is offered by an old-time folk singer who'd been with an

anti-aircraft battery of the Sixty-second Artillery: "You had fifteen guys who for the first time in their lives were not living in a competitive society. We were in a tribal sort of situation, where we could help each other without fear. I realized it was the absence of phony standards that created the thing I loved about the army."

There was another first in the lives of the GIs. Young kids, who had never wandered beyond the precinct of their native city or their small hometown or their father's farm, ran into exotic places and exotic people, as well as into one another, whom they found equally exotic.

"The first time I ever heard a New England accent," recalls the midwesterner, "was at Fort Benning. The southerner was an exotic creature to me. People from the farms. The New York street-smarts." (Author's note: The native New Yorker was probably the most parochial, most set in his ways, and most gullible.)

One of the most satisfying moments during my brief turn as a "military man" came at a crap game. It was in Jefferson Barracks. A couple of hotshots from New York and Philadelphia had things seemingly going their way. I and several others lost our pokes in short order. Along came this freckled, skinny kid off an Arkansas farm, his Adam's apple bobbing wildly. It appeared that the easterners had another pigeon. An hour or so later, the street-smart boys were thoroughly cleaned out by the rube. It was lovely. City boys and country boys were, for the first time in their lives, getting acquainted.

"When I woke up the first morning on the troop train in Fulton, Kentucky, I thought I was in Timbuktu. Of course, I was absolutely bowled over by Europe, the castles, the cathedrals, the Alps. It was wonderment for a nineteen-year-old."

Of course, there were songs learned that their mothers never taught them. And swearing. And smoking. "We were told that the next morning we would be on the attack. By this time, I had taken up cigarette smoking, wondering what my mother would think when I came back. I felt sickish, I was cold, I was scared. And I couldn't even get one last cigarette."

In tough circumstances, as a war prisoner or under siege or waiting for Godot, what was most on the soldier's mind was not women nor politics nor family nor, for that matter, God. It was food. "In camp," a prisoner of the Japanese recalls, "first thing you talked about is what you wanted in your stomach. Guys would tell about how their mother made this. Men would sit and listen very attentively. This was the big topic all the time. I remember vividly this old Polack. One guy always wanted him to talk about how his mother made the cabbage rolls, the *golabki*. He had a knack of telling so you could almost smell 'em. You'd see some of the fellas just lickin' their lips. Tasting it. You know?"

16 Food. Fear. Comradeship. And confusion. In battle, the order of the day was often disorder. Again and again survivors, gray, bald, potbellied, or cadaverous, remember chaos.

17 The big redhead of the 106th Infantry Division can't forget his trauma. "So there I am wandering around with the whole German army shooting at me, and all I've got is a .45 automatic. There were ample opportunities, however, because every place you went there were bodies and soldiers laying around. Mostly Americans. At one time or another, I think I had in my hands every weapon the United States Army manufactured. You'd run out of ammunition with that one, you'd throw it away and try to find something else."

18 The lieutenant had an identical experience some five days after D-Day. "We were in dug-in foxholes, in a very checkered position. There were Germans ahead of us and Germans in the back of us. Americans over there ahead of these Germans. There was no straight front line. It was a mess."

19 A mess among the living, perhaps. There was order, of a sort, among the dead. At least for the Germans. A Stalingrad veteran is haunted by the memory of the moment. "I was sleeping on the bodies of killed German soldiers. The Germans were very orderly people. When they found they didn't have time to bury these bodies, they laid them next to each other in a very neat and orderly way. I saw straight rows, like pieces of cordwood. Exact."

20 A woman, born in 1943, cannot forget the camp photographs in *Life*. She had been casually leafing through some old issues in a Pennsylvania school library. She was twelve at the time. "In those grainy photos, you first think it's cords of wood piled up. You look again, it shows you human beings. You never get the picture out of your eye: the interchangeability of the stacks of human bodies and the stacks of cords of wood. There is something curious about the fascination with horror that isn't exhausted anywhere. Prior to finding these pictures, there were merely hints of something to a sheltered girl, nothing she could put together."

21 Between the winter of 1941 and the summer of 1945, Willie and Joe, dogfaces, and their assorted buddies grew up in a hurry. It wasn't only the bullet they bit. It was the apple. Some lost innocence, abroad. "I went there a skinny, gaunt mama's boy, full of wonderment," says the rifleman. "I came back much more circumspect in my judgment of people. And of governments."

22 Others were not quite so touched. "I got one eye. My feet hangs down. I got a joint mashed in my back. I got a shoulder been broke. Feel that knot right there." The Kentucky guardsman offers a litany of war wounds,

but is undaunted. "I'd go fight for my country right today. You're darn   23
right. I'd go right now, boy."
   They all came back home. All but 400,000.

*At home, the fourteen-year-old Victory girl grew up in a hurry, too. "What I
feel most about the war, it disrupted my family. That really chokes me up,
makes me feel very sad that I lost that. On December 6, 1941, I was playing
with paper dolls: Deanna Durbin, Sonja Henie. I had a Shirley Temple doll that
I cherished. After Pearl Harbor, I never played with dolls again."*   24

After the epochal victory over fascism, the boys came back to resume their
normal lives. Yet it was a different country from the one they had left.

> In 1945, the United States inherited the earth. . . . at the end of World War
> II, what was left of Western civilization passed into the American account.
> The war had also prompted the country to invent a miraculous economic
> machine that seemed to grant as many wishes as were asked of it. The con-
> tinental United States had escaped the plague of war, and so it was easy
> enough for the heirs to believe that they had been anointed by God.*   25

We had hardly considered ourselves God's anointed in the thirties. The
Great Depression was our most devastating experience since the Civil   26
War. Somewhere along the line, our money machine had stripped its gears.
   A Wall Street wise man, adviser to four presidents, non-explained:
"The Crash was like a thunderclap. Everybody was stunned. Nobody
knew what it was about. The Street was general confusion. They didn't
understand any more than anybody else. They thought something would   27
be announced." He neglected to tell me by whom.
   The sixteen million Americans out in the cold reached for abandoned
newspapers on park benches and—would you believe?—skipped over the
sports section and flipped feverishly to Help Wanted. A hard-traveling
survivor recalls an ad being answered at the Spreckels sugar refinery in
San Francisco: "A thousand men would fight like a pack of Alaskan dogs   28
to get through. You know dang well, there's only three or four jobs."
   With the German invasion of Poland in 1939, it all changed. The
farewell to a dismal decade was more than ceremonial: 1939 was the end
and the beginning. Hard Times, as though by some twentieth-century   29
alchemy, were transmuted into Good Times. War was our Paracelsus.
   True, the New Deal had created jobs and restored self-esteem for millions of Americans. Still, there were ten, eleven million walking the

---

*Lewis H. Lapham, "America's Foreign Policy: A Rake's Progress," *Harper's*, March 1979.

streets, riding the rods, up against it, despairing. All this changed under the lowering sky of World War Two. What had been a country psychically as well as geographically isolated had become, with the suddenness of a blitzkrieg, engaged with distant troubles. And close-at-hand triumphs.

30   Our huge industrial machine shifted gears. In a case of Scripture turned upside down, plowshares were beaten into swords (or their twentieth-century equivalents: tanks, mortars, planes, bombs). In the words of President Franklin D. Roosevelt, Dr. New Deal was replaced by Dr. Win The War.

31   Thomas (Tommy the Cork) Corcoran, one of FDR's wonder boys, remembers being called into the Oval Office: "'Tommy, cut out this New Deal stuff. It's tough to win a war.' He'd heard from the people who could produce the tanks and other war stuff. As a payoff, they required an end to what they called New Deal nonsense."

32   James Rowe, who had been a young White House adviser, recalls: "It upset the New Dealers. We had a big PWA building program. Roosevelt took a big chunk of that money and gave it to the navy to build ships. I was shocked. A large number of businessmen came down as dollar-a-year men. Roosevelt was taking help anyplace he could get it. There was a quick change into a war economy."

33   And prosperity came. Boom had a double meaning.

34   For the old Iowa farmer, it was something else. Oh yes, he remembered the Depression and what it did to the farmers: foreclosures the norm; grain burned; corn at *minus* three cents a bushel; rural despair. Oh yes, it changed with the war. "That's when the real boost came. The war—" There is a catch in his voice. He slumps in his rocker. His wife stares at the wallpaper. It is a long silence, save for the *tick-tock* of the grandfather's clock. "—it does something to your country. It does something to the individual. I had a neighbor just as the war was beginning. We had a boy ready to go to service. This neighbor told me what we needed was a damn good war, and we'd solve our agricultural problems. And I said, 'Yes, but I'd hate to pay with the price of my son.' Which we did." He weeps. "It's too much of a price to pay."

35   The retired Red Cross worker wastes no words: "The war was fun for America. I'm not talking about the poor souls who lost sons and daughters. But for the rest of us, the war was a hell of a good time. Farmers in South Dakota that I administered relief to and gave 'em bully beef and four dollars a week to feed their families, when I came home were worth a quarter-million dollars, right? It's forgotten now."

36   It had, indeed, become another country. "World War Two changed everything," says the retired admiral. "Our military runs our foreign policy. The State Department has become the lackey of the Pentagon. Before World War Two, this never happened. Only if there was a war did they

step up front. The ultimate control was civilian. World War Two changed all this."

It is exquisite irony that military work liberated women from the private world of *Küche, Kinde, Kirche*. "I remember going to Sunday dinner one of the older women invited me to," the ex-schoolteacher remembers. "She and her sister at the dinner table were talking about the best way to keep their drill sharp in the factory. I never heard anything like this in my life. It was just marvelous. But even here we were sold a bill of goods. They were hammering away that the woman who went to work did it to help her man, and when he came back, she cheerfully leaped back to the home."

Though at war's end these newborn working women were urged, as their patriotic duty Over Here, to go back home where they "naturally belonged" and give their jobs back to the boys who did their patriotic duty Over There, the taste for independence was never really lost. Like that of Wrigley's chewing gum, found in the pack of every GI, its flavor was longer-lasting. No matter what the official edict, for millions of American women home would never again be a Doll's House.

War's harsh necessity affected another people as well: the blacks. Not much happened to change things in the years between the two world wars. Big Bill Broonzy, the blues singer, commemorated his doughboy life in World War One:

When Uncle Sam called me, I knew I would be called the real McCoy.
But when I got in the army, they called me soldier boy.
I wonder when will I be called a man?

As in 1917, black servicemen were almost exclusively in labor battalions: loading ships, cleaning up, kitchen work, digging one thing or another. They were domestics abroad as well as at home. Mythology had long been standard operating procedure: blacks were not to be trusted in combat. To this, Coleman Young offered a wry touch of history: "The black Tenth Calvary was with Teddy Roosevelt at San Juan Hill. They saved his ass." As the war dragged on, and casualties mounted alarmingly, black soldiers were sent up front. Grudgingly, they were allowed to risk their lives in combat. Lieutenant Charles A. Gates tells of the 761st Tank Battalion. All black. "We were very well disciplined and trained. The German army was confused. They couldn't see how we could be in so many places at the same time." There was astonishment on the part of our generals as well as theirs. It took thirty-five years for the 761st to get a Presidential Unit Citation.

These were rare adventures for black GIs in World War Two. A schoolteacher recalls his days as a sergeant with the Quartermaster Corps: "That's where most of us were put. We serviced the service. We handled food, clothing, equipage. We loaded ammunition, too. We were really stevedores and servants."

42 At home, things were somewhat different. Like women, blacks were called upon. Their muscles and skills, usually bypassed, were needed in defense plants. The perverse imperatives of war brought about relatively well-paying jobs for black men and women who would otherwise have been regarded with less than benign neglect. Even this might not have come about had it not been for the constant pressure from the black community.

43 "I got a call from my boss. 'Get your ass over here, we got a problem.'" Joseph Rauh, working in Washington, remembers June of 1941. "'Some guy named Randolph is going to march on Washington unless we put out a fair employment practices order.* The President says you gotta stop Randolph from marching. We got defense plants goin' all over this goddamn country, but no blacks are bein' hired. Go down to the Budget Bureau and work something out.'"

44 It was not noblesse oblige that brought forth Executive Order 8802, establishing the Fair Employment Practice Committee.

45 Wartime prosperity had extended into an exhilarating period of postwar prosperity. The United States had become the most powerful industrial as well as military power in the world. Its exports were now as truly worldwide as its politics. For the returning GI, it was a wholly new society. And a new beginning.

46 "I had matured in those three years away," says the middle manager of a large corporation. He had come from a family of blue-collar workers in a blue-collar town. "I wanted to better myself more than, say, hitting the local factory. Fortunately, I was educated on the GI Bill. It was a blessing. The war changed our whole idea of how we wanted to live when we came back. We set our sights pretty high. All of us wanted better levels of living. I am now what you'd call middle class."

47 The suburb, until now, had been the exclusive domain of the "upper class." It was where the rich lived. The rest of us were neighborhood folk. At war's end, a new kind of suburb came into being. GI Joe, with his persevering wife/sweetheart and baby, moved into the little home so often celebrated in popular song. Molly and me and baby makes three. It was not My Blue Heaven, perhaps, but it was something only dreamed of before. Thanks to the GI Bill, two new names were added to American folksay: Levittown and Park Forest.

48 A new middle class had emerged. Until now, the great many, even before

---

*A. Philip Randolph, president of the Brotherhood of Sleeping Car Porters. He and other black leaders were planning a march urging the administration to pass a fair employment practices act.

the Depression, had had to scuffle from one payday to the next. "When you went to the doctor's," remembers the California woman, "it may have been ten dollars, but that was maybe a third of my father's salary as a milkman."

"The American myth was alive," reminisces a Sioux Falls native. "Re- 49 member the '49 cars in the *National Geographic?* Postwar cars. New design, new body style. In the colored Sunday funnies there'd be ads for the new cars. We'd been driving Grandpa Herman's old prewar Chrysler. It was the only car on the block. Now everybody was getting a car. Oh, it was exciting."

It was, indeed, a different world to which Telford Taylor returned from 50 Germany. He had been the chief American prosecutor during twelve of the thirteen Nuremberg trials. "When I came back home in 1949, I was already in my early forties. I'd been away from home seven years and was out of touch with things politically. I thought that Washington was still the way I'd left it in 1942. By 1949, it was a very different place. I had left Washington at a time when it was still Roosevelt, liberalism, social action, all these things. When I came back in the late forties, the Dies Committee . . . the cold war. I was a babe in the woods. I didn't know what hit me."

The cold war. Another legacy of World War Two. 51

The year Telford Taylor returned to the States, Archibald MacLeish 52 wrote a singularly prescient essay:

> Never in the history of the world was one people as completely dominated, intellectually and morally, by another as the people of the United States by the people of Russia in the four years from 1946 through 1949. American foreign policy was a mirror image of Russian foreign policy: whatever the Russians did, we did in reverse. American domestic politics were conducted under a kind of upside-down Russian veto: no man would be elected to public office unless he was on record as detesting the Russians, and no proposal could be enacted, from a peace plan at one end to a military budget at the other, unless it could be demonstrated that the Russians wouldn't like it. American political controversy was controversy sung to the Russian tune; left-wing movements attacked right-wing movements not on American issues but on Russian issues, and right-wing movements replied with the same arguments turned round about. . . .
>
> All this . . . took place not in a time of national weakness or decay but precisely at the moment when the United States, having engineered a tremendous triumph and fought its way to a brilliant victory in the greatest of all wars, had reached the highest point of world power ever achieved by a single state.*

---

*MacLeish's piece of 1949, "The Conquest of America," was reprinted in the *Atlantic Monthly,* March 1980.

53 The ex-admiral says it his way: "World War Two has warped our view of how we look at things today. We see things in terms of that war, which in a sense was a good war. But the twisted memory of it encourages the men of my generation to be willing, almost eager, to use military forces anywhere in the world."

54 In a small midwestern rural town, a grandmother, soft and gentle, is certain she speaks for most of the townsfolk. "People here feel that we should have gone into Vietnam and finished it instead of backing off as we did. I suppose it's a feeling that carried over from World War Two when we finished Hitler. I know the older men who fought in that war feel that way."

55 Big Bill Broonzy put it another way. It happened quite inadvertently one night in a Chicago nightclub. He had been singing a country blues about a sharecropper whose mule had died. It was his own story. During the performance, four young hipsters made a scene of walking out on him. I, working as MC that night, was furious. Big Bill laughed. He always laughed at such moments. Laughin' to keep from cryin', perhaps. "What do these kids know 'bout a mule? They never seen a mule. How do you expect somebody to feel 'bout somethin' he don't know? When I was in Europe, all those places, Milano, Hamburg, London, I seen cities bombed out. People tellin' me 'bout bombin's. What do I know 'bout a bomb? The only bomb I ever did see was in the pictures. People scared, cryin'. Losin' their homes. What do I know 'bout that? I never had no bomb fall on me. Same thing with these kids. They never had no mule die on 'em. They don't even know what the hell I'm talkin' 'bout."

56 Big Bill, at that moment, set off the most pertinent and impertinent of challenges: Must a society experience horror in order to understand horror? Ours was the only country among the combatants in World War Two that was neither invaded nor bombed. Ours were the only cities not blasted into rubble. Our Willie and Joe were up front; the rest of us were safe, surrounded by two big oceans. As for our allies and enemies, civilian as well as military were, at one time or another, up front: the British, the French, the Russians (twenty million dead; perhaps thirty million, says Harrison Salisbury), as well as the Germans, the Italians, the Japanese. Let alone the Slavs of smaller spheres. And, of course, the European Jews. And the Gypsies. And all kinds of *Untermenschen*.

57 True, an inconsolable grief possessed the families of those Americans lost and maimed in the Allied triumph. Parks, squares, streets, and bridges have been named after these young heroes, sung and unsung. Yet it is the casual walkout of the four young hipsters in that Chicago nightclub that may be the rude, fearsome metaphor we must decipher.

58 The elderly Japanese *hibakisha* (survivor of the atom bomb), contemplates the day it fell on Hiroshima. He had been a nineteen-year-old sol-

dier passing through town. "The children were screaming, 'Please take these maggots off our bodies.' It was impossible for me, one soldier, to try to help so many people. The doctor said, 'We can't do anything. Sterilize their wounds with salt water.' We took a broom, dipped it into the salt water, and painted over the bodies. The children leaped up: 'I'm gonna run, I must run.'" The interpreter corrects him: "In the local dialect, it means 'thank you.'"

The tall young rifleman understands the horror. He was being retrained, 59 after his European near-misses, for the invasion of Japan when the first atom bomb was dropped. "We ended halfway across the Pacific. How many of us would have been killed on the mainland if there were no bomb? Someone like me has this specter." So does his quondam buddy: "We're sitting on the pier in Seattle, sharpening our bayonets, when Harry dropped that beautiful bomb. The greatest thing ever happened. Anybody sitting at the pier at that time would have to agree." The black combat correspondent sees it somewhat differently: "Do you realize that most blacks don't believe the atom bomb would have been dropped on Hiroshima had it been a white city?" Witnesses to the fire bombings of Dresden may dispute the point.

The crowning irony lay in World War Two itself. It had been a different 60 kind of war. "It was not like your other wars," a radio disk jockey reflected aloud. In his banality lay a wild kind of crazy truth. It was not fratricidal. It was not, most of us profoundly believed, "imperialistic." Our enemy was, patently, obscene: the Holocaust maker. It was one war that many who would have resisted "your other wars" supported enthusiastically. It was a "just war," if there is any such animal. In a time of nuclear weaponry, it is the language of a lunatic. But World War Two . . .

It ended on a note of hope without historic precedent. *On a Note of Tri-* 61 *umph* is what Norman Corwin called his eloquent radio program heard coast-to-coast on V-E Day, May 8, 1945.

Lord God of test-tube and blueprint
Who jointed molecules of dust and shook them till their name was Adam,
Who taught worms and stars how they could live together,
Appear now among the parliaments of conquerors and give instruction to
*   their schemes:*
Measure out new liberties so none shall suffer for his father's color or the
*   credo of his choice. . . .*

The day of that broadcast is remembered for a number of reasons by a 62 West Coast woman. "V-E Day. Oh, such a joyous thing! And San Francisco was chosen for the first session of the UN. I was ecstatic. Stalin,

Churchill, and Roosevelt met, and somehow war never again would happen." She was an usher at the War Memorial Opera House, where the UN
first met in June of '45. "I was still in my little Miss Burke School uniform.
Little middy and skirt. I was part of it. And so deeply proud. When the
Holocaust survivors came out, I felt we were liberating them. When the
GIs and Russian soldiers met, they were all knights in shining armor, saving humanity." She laughs softly. "It's not that simple. World War Two
was just an innocent time in America. I was innocent. My parents were
innocent. The country was innocent. Since World War Two, I think I
have a more objective view of what this country really is."

63   The Red Cross worker thinks of then and now. "To many people, it
brought about a realization that there ain't no hidin' place down here.
That the world is unified in pain as well as opportunity. We had twenty,
twenty-five years of greatness in our country, when we reached out to the
rest of the world with help. Some of it was foolish, some of it was mis-
spent, some was in error. Many follies. But we had a great reaching out. It
was an act of such faith." He tries to stifle an angry sob. "Now, we're being
pinched back into the meanness of the soul. World War Two? It's a war I
still would go to."

64   The ex-captain, watching a Dow-Jones ticker, shakes his head. "I don't
have as much trust in my fellow man as I once did. I have no trust in my
peers. They're burnt-out cases. In the war, I was trying to do something
useful with my life . . . "

65   A thousand miles away, the once and forever tall young rifleman,
though gray and patriarchal, stares out the window at the Chicago sky-
line, the Lake, and beyond. "World War Two has affected me in many
ways ever since. In a short period of time, I had the most tremendous experiences of all of life: of fear, of jubilance, of misery, of hope, of comradeship, and of endless excitement. I honestly feel grateful for having been a
witness to an event as monumental as anything in history and, in a very
small way, a participant."

A Sunday Morning

John Garcia

*A huge man, built along the lines of a sumo wrestler. He manages a complex of
apartment buildings in Los Angeles. He could quite easily be the bouncer, too.
He is resigned to the assortment of illnesses that plague him; his manner is easygoing. "With my age, my love for food, that's caused diabetes, the whole bit."
He is a Hawaiian.*

I was sixteen years old, employed as a pipe fitter apprentice at Pearl Har- 66
bor Navy Yard. On December 7, 1941, oh, around 8:00 AM, my grandmother woke me. She informed me that the Japanese were bombing Pearl
Harbor. I said, "They're just practicing." She said, no, it was real and the
announcer is requesting that all Pearl Harbor workers report to work. I
went out on the porch and I could see the anti-aircraft fire up in the sky. I
just said, "Oh, boy."

I was four miles away. I got on my motorcycle and it took me five, ten 67
minutes to get there. It was a mess.

I was working on the U.S.S. *Shaw.* It was on a floating dry dock. It was in 68
flames. I started to go down into the pipe fitter's shop to get my toolbox
when another wave of Japanese came in. I got under a set of concrete steps
at the dry dock where the battleship *Pennsylvania* was. An officer came by
and asked me to go into the *Pennsylvania* and try to get the fires out. A
bomb had penetrated the marine deck, and that was three decks below. Under that was the magazines: ammunition, powder, shells. I said, "There ain't
no way I'm gonna go down there." It could blow up at any minute. I was
young and sixteen, not stupid, not at sixty-two cents an hour. (Laughs.)

A week later, they brought me before a navy court. It was determined 69
that I was not service personnel and could not be ordered. There was no
martial law at the time. Because I was sixteen and had gone into the water, the whole thing was dropped.

I was asked by some other officer to go into the water and get sailors out 70
that had been blown off the ships. Some were unconscious, some were
dead. So I spent the rest of the day swimming inside the harbor, along
with some other Hawaiians. I brought out I don't know how many bodies
and how many were alive and how many dead. Another man would put
them into ambulances and they'd be gone. We worked all day at that.

That evening, I drove a truckload of marines into Palolo Valley because 71
someone reported that the Japanese had parachuted down there. Because
of the total blackout, none of the marine drivers knew how to get there.
It was two miles away. There were no parachuters. Someone in the valley
had turned their lights on and the marines started shootin' at that house.
The lights went out. (Laughs.)

I went back to my concrete steps to spend the night there. Someone on 72
the *Pennsylvania* was walking along the edge of armored plate. He lit a cigarette. All of a sudden, a lot of guns opened up on him. I don't know if he
was hit.

The following morning, I went with my tools to the *West Virginia.* It 73
had turned turtle, totally upside down. We found a number of men inside.
The *Arizona* was a total washout. Also the *Utah.* There were men in there,

too. We spent about a month cutting the superstructure of the *West Virginia*, tilting it back on its hull. About three hundred men we cut out of there were still alive by the eighteenth day.

How did they survive?

74 I don't know. We were too busy to ask. (Laughs.) It took two weeks to get all the fires out. We worked around the clock for three days. There was so much excitement and confusion. Some of our sailors were shooting five-inch guns at the Japanese planes. You just cannot down a plane with a five-inch shell. They were landing in Honolulu, the unexploding naval shells. They have a ten-mile range. They hurt and killed a lot of people in the city.

75 When I came back after the third day, they told me that a shell had hit the house of my girl. We had been going together for, oh, about three years. Her house was a few blocks from my place. At the time, they said it was a Japanese bomb. Later we learned it was an American shell. She was killed. She was preparing for church at the time.

76 My neighbors met me. They were mostly Japanese. We all started to cry. We had no idea what was happening, what was going to happen.

77 Martial law had been set in. Everyone had to work twelve hours, six to six. No one on the streets after 6:00 PM. No one on the streets before 6:00 AM. The military took over the islands completely. If you failed to go to work, the police would be at your door and you were arrested. You had to do something, filling sandbags, anything. No one was excused. If you called in sick, a nurse would come to your house to check on you. If you failed to be there or were goofing off, you went to jail. All civil liberties were suspended.

78 There was no act of treason by anyone that I know of. There were spies, but they were all employed by the Japanese embassy. If they had arrested the ordinary Japanese, there would be no work force at Pearl Harbor. There were 130,000 Japanese on the islands. There'd be no stores, no hotels, nothing. You'd have to shut the city down. They suffered a lot of insults, especially by the servicemen. They took it without coming back.

79 I tried to get in the military, but they refused. They considered my work essential for the war effort. I was promoted to shop fitter and went from $32 a week to $125. But I kept trying for a year to get in the fight. Finally, I wrote a letter to President Roosevelt. I told him I was angry at the Japanese bombing and had lost some friends. He okayed that I be accepted. I went into the service and went down to $21 a month. (Laughs.)

My grandmother signed for me because I was only seventeen. She said she would never see me alive again. It turned out prophetic because she died one day before I got home. January 1946.

They wanted to send me to Texas for training. I got on the stick and wrote to the President again. I wasn't interested in Texas, I wanted to go into combat. I got an answer from the White House requesting that I be put into a combat outfit. I got thirty days washing dishes for not following the chain of command. (Laughs.)

"When I went into the military, they asked, 'What race are you?' I had no idea what they were talking about because in Hawaii we don't question a man's race. They said, 'Where are your parents from?' I said they were born in Hawaii. 'Your grandparents?' They were born in Hawaii. 'How about your great-grandparents?' I said they're from Europe, some from Spain, some from Wales. They said, 'You're Caucasian.' I said, 'What's that?' They said, 'You're white.' I looked at my skin. I was pretty dark, tanned by the sun. I said, 'You're kidding.' (Laughs.) They put me down as Caucasian and separated me from the rest of the Hawaiians.

Some of my new buddies asked me not to talk to three of the men. I asked why. They said, 'They're Jews.' I said, 'What's a Jew?' They said, 'Don't you know? They killed Jesus Christ.' I says, 'You mean them guys? They don't look old enough.' They said, 'You're tryin' to get smart?' I said, 'No. It's my understanding he was killed about nineteen hundred years ago.'"

I joined the Seventh Infantry Division in time for the run to Kwajalein in the Marshall Islands. It took six days to take it. We went back to Hawaii. I don't know what we were preparing for, but we practiced and practiced and practiced swimming, some other Hawaiians and me. I said, "Eleanor must be coming here." I was taken to the FBI in Honolulu and asked how did I know the President was coming. I said I don't know. They said, "You said Eleanor was coming." I said, "Yeah, I just figured somebody important was coming because we've been practicing this show for two months." They said, "Okay, keep your mouth shut."

All of a sudden one day they told us there'd be a swimming show. We threw oil in the water, set the water on fire, and dove into it. Then they told us to get dressed and get ready for the parade. We were all searched for ammunition. No one could have ammunition in his rifle, no pocket knives. But we had bayonets. (Laughs.) As we went past the parade stand, we saw General MacArthur and President Roosevelt.

84   We knew something was up but we didn't know where we were gonna go. A rumor came down that we were going into Africa after Rommel. The main body of the Seventh had trained in the Mojave Desert, but was sent to the Aleutians. They had figured on Africa. So we thought for sure it was Africa for us. We got orders for the Pacific. They said Yap.

"I had been made a sergeant by this time because we were given jungle training and I knew the tropics. So they sent me to Alaska. (Laughs.) After three weeks, they had to send me back because I was shaking. It was too damn cold. (Laughs.)"

85   Several nights later, a broadcast came from Tokyo Rose: "Good evening, men of the Seventh Infantry. I know you're on your way to the Philippines." She was right. (Laughs.) We were there from October of '44 until March of '45. Totally combat.

86   I fought very carefully, I fought low. There were a couple of Japanese boys, our interpreters, who were a little bit heroic. They would climb on board a Japanese tank going by, knock on the things, converse in Japanese, and as soon as the door popped open, they'd drop a hand grenade—boom!

87   Our next stop was Okinawa. We landed there on April 1, '45. No opposition. Several days later, we got word that President Roosevelt had died. We were all sort of down—boom! They said a man called Truman replaced him. I said, "Who is Truman?" We were there eighty-two days. I did what I had to do. When I saw a Japanese, I shot at him and ducked. Shot and ducked, that's all I did. I was always scared until we took Hill 87.

88   We buried General Ushijima and his men inside a cave. This was the worst part of the war, which I didn't like about Okinawa. They were hiding in caves all the time, women, children, soldiers. We'd get up on the cliff and lower down barrels of gasoline and then shoot at it. It would explode and just bury them to death.

89   I personally shot one Japanese woman because she was coming across a field at night. We kept dropping leaflets not to cross the field at night because we couldn't tell if they were soldiers. We set up a perimeter. Anything in front, we'd shoot at. This one night I shot and when it came daylight, it was a woman there and a baby tied to her back. The bullet had all gone through her and out the baby's back.

90   That still bothers me, that hounds me. I still feel I committed murder. You see a figure in the dark, it's stooped over. You don't know if it's a soldier or a civilian.

91   I was drinking about a fifth and a half of whiskey every day. Sometimes homemade, sometimes what I could buy. It was the only way I could kill. I had friends who were Japanese and I kept thinking every time I pulled a

trigger on a man or pushed a flamethrower down into a hole: What is this person's family gonna say when he doesn't come back? He's got a wife, he's got children, somebody.

They would show us movies. Japanese women didn't cry. They would accept the ashes stoically. I knew different. They went home and cried.   92

I'd get up each day and start drinking. How else could I fight the war? Sometimes we made the booze, sometimes we bought it from the navy. The sailors stole it from their officers. (Laughs.) Sometimes it cost us seventy-five dollars a bottle, sometimes it cost us a Japanese flag. You'd take a piece of parachute silk, make a circle on it, put a few bullet holes in it, give it to the navy, and they'd give you a bottle of whiskey.   93

I drank my last drink on the night of August 14, 1945, I think it was. When we heard from Swedish radio that the Japanese wanted to contact the Americans in order to end the war, we just went wild. Every soldier just took a gun and started shooting. I got into my trench and stayed there because the bullets were all over. Thirty-two men out of our outfit were killed that night by stray celebrating bullets.   94

I haven't touched a drop since. I wasn't a drinking man before. I started in the Philippines when I saw the bodies of men, women, and children, especially babies, that were hit by bombs. They were by the side of the road, and we would run over them with our tanks.   95

Oh, I still lose nights of sleep because of that woman I shot. I still lose a lot of sleep. I still dream about her. I dreamed about it perhaps two weeks ago . . . (He lets out a deep breath; it's something more turbulent than a sigh.)   96

Aaaahh, I feel that if countries are gonna fight a war, find yourself an island with nobody and then just put all your men in there and let them kill each other. Or better, send the politicians, let them fight it out. Yeah, like this stupid race that we're having of atomic wars. So much money is being devoted to killing people and so little to saving. It's a crazy world.   97

I was a policeman for fifteen years in Washington, D.C. When I was involved in a hostage situation, I just waited. Eventually, the person gave up. There's no need to be playing gung ho and going in there with guns blazing. I worked always in black neighborhoods. I would not shoot. I would talk and talk and talk. In one instance, there were three men holed up. I took off my gun and I went in. I said, "You guys can kill me, but you're not gonna walk out of here because there's a lot of men waiting for you. You can give me your gun and walk out and do some time, but you're not gonna do it inside of a box." They said, "Man, you're crazy." I said, "I don't think you are." All three of them gave me the gun, and we walked out. It's just that I'm not a killer.   98

Dennis Keegan

Santa Rosa, California. He came in during the conversation with his younger brother, Frank. He is a lawyer, successful, solid, and though easy with talk, is matter-of-fact in style.

99   I'd been to mass at Saint Rose and was on the floor reading the funny paper when we got the news of Pearl Harbor. We had the radio on, probably listening to Glenn Miller or Benny Goodman. It didn't really mean a thing for a while. Of course, we already had a brother, Bill, who was already in Canada, training to fly Spitfires. But these places were so far away from us. It just didn't seem possible that we were at war.

100   A friend and I were in San Francisco that Sunday night. We were stopped on the Golden Gate Bridge by a national guardsman. He looked in the car. It was a battered Chevvy. We heard later that a woman was killed on the bridge that night because she didn't respond to a guardsman's order to halt.

101   We decided to drive downtown. That was an eye-opener. Market Street was bedlam. The United Artists Theatre had a huge marquee with those dancing lights, going on and off. People were throwing everything they could to put those lights out, screaming Blackout! Blackout! They theater people had not been told to turn them off. Once in a while, they'd hit a light.

102   No cars could move. The streets were full of people, blocking the tracks, the trolley line. People were throwing rocks, anything they could find. A streetcar came along, one of those old-fashioned, funny San Francisco streetcars. It had a big round light. A man ran up with a baseball bat and smashed the light. But the city was lustrous, all the office building lights were on. I said to my friend, "Let's get the hell out of here before they smash our headlights."

103   I was a senior at the University of San Francisco. I had room and board with a lady and her daughter. I flipped on the lights because it was pitch dark. Mrs. Kelleher screamed, "Dennis, turn the lights out! The Japs are comin'! The Japs are comin'!" She and her daughter were sitting on the couch, clutching one another in absolute abject terror. "The Golden Gate Bridge has been bombed!" I said, "Mrs. Kelleher, I just drove over there a few minutes ago. There's nothing wrong with the bridge." But they were so terror-stricken, I turned out the lights.

104   Their son Frank was in the ROTC at USF. He got a call: For God's sake, get over here. We're gonna make a stand at the university! They'd been listening to the radio all day and were convinced the Japanese were here. They had landed all over the coast and had taken the Presidio. They would repeat it on the radio, again and again. Total hysteria.

The next morning, when we discovered that there weren't any Japs on   105
the corner of Twelfth and Balboa, the fear subsided. We made it through
the black night and we weren't bombed. We had our breakfast and everything was pretty routine. We were simmering but we weren't boiling.

Bill, who was in Canada, called our mother to find out if we were okay.   106
He'd heard in Canada that San Francisco had been bombed and most of
the West Coast. Mrs. Thurston, our doctor's wife, packed up and left. Back
to Alabama, where she came from. The doctor said, "You go, I'm not
leavin'." She took the jewelry, all the money, everything, and left him
alone in the big beautiful house.

Within a week we had a company of Texas National Guard boys. Six or   107
seven hundred of them, camped in the old Fairgrounds building. They
had been sent here to protect us. Everybody came out here to protect us
from the anticipated invasion. The papers didn't help any. The *Examiner*
had a headline: Japanese Invade West Coast. All we had out here were
Hearst papers. We reacted like a bunch of nuts.

I went down to San Francisco to enlist. I couldn't pass the eye test for   108
the navy. I thought, The army will get me if I don't get my butt out of
here. So I hopped down and got my seaman's papers and climbed aboard
a Standard Oil tanker and got the hell out of there as fast as I could.

Ron Veenker

He is a teacher at a small college in Kentucky. He is forty-four.

*He was raised in a Frisian community in Sioux Falls, South Dakota. "Frisian
is a kind of Middle German language. They who knew High German in this
community kept a very low profile. Every once in a while they'd break out in
German, someone would say shoo, shoo, shoo, shoo, shoo. There was one fellow who would not shut up with the German. Everybody was afraid the whole
community would suffer because of him. Anybody who had a German background was almost a pariah.*

*"But if we wanted to be in big trouble, we'd get angry and call the other kid a
dirty Jap rat. That was the filthiest thing you could say."*

I was four years old when the silence on December 7 terrified me. There   109
had always been a lot of hilarity on Sundays. Not this time.

I was five when I visited California to stay with my other grandmother.   110
We were standing at a trolley stop. A Japanese man about thirty-five, all
bent over, smiling, came up. He had a pack of gum with a stick extended,
which he handed to me. He had nothing but kindness on his face. I intu-
ited it. Kids and dogs, you know. (Laughs.) My grandmother picked me up
and ran two blocks, lickety-kite. And waited for the trolley at another stop.

111 Very soon after that, I noticed that all our neighbors were not there any more. Nobody talked about it. These were Japanese truck-garden people, who had been there a long time. Their homes had pagoda architecture. I walked down this lane past all their homes on my way to school in the morning. It was so quiet, it was eerie. I had been used to hearing people. They'd been taken away.

112 I'd been told the Japanese were something to fear. Even their empty homes I feared. I would start to whistle. I'll never forget the song "Pistol-Packin' Mama." I'd start to sing at the top of my lungs and I'd run. Every morning I'd come to school so tired. I would have been about seven then.

113 My great-grandmother was still alive. She was an alcoholic. My grandmother would give the old woman a jug of wine and go off to work. Great-Grandma would sit there, get bombed all day. I awakened one night, hearing a great commotion. Like airplanes going over. I swear I could hear flak from the anti-aircraft. I looked out the window and saw searchlights. There were explosions in the sky. Down below, I saw my great-grandmother wandering around the back yard in a nightgown, dazed. I've always associated that with the rumor that the Japanese once attacked Los Angeles.

Peter Ota

114 I think back to what happened—and sometimes I wonder: Where do I come from?

He is a fifty-seven-year-old Nisei. His father had come from Okinawa in 1904, his mother from Japan. He's an accountant. His father had worked on farms and in the coal mines of Mexico. After thirty-seven years building a fruit and vegetable business, he had become a successful and respected merchant in the community. He was a leader in the Japanese Chamber of Commerce of Los Angeles.

115 On the evening of December 7, 1941, my father was at a wedding. He was dressed in a tuxedo. When the reception was over, the FBI agents were waiting. They rounded up at least a dozen wedding guests and took 'em to county jail.

116 For a few days we didn't know what happened. We heard nothing. When we found out, my mother, my sister, and myself went to jail. I can still remember waiting in the lobby. When my father walked through the door, my mother was so humiliated. She didn't say anything. She cried. He was in prisoner's clothing, with a denim jacket and a number on the back.

117 The shame and humiliation just broke her down. She was into Japanese culture. She was a flower arranger and used to play the *biwa*, a Japanese stringed instrument. Shame in her culture is worse than death. Right af-

ter that day she got very ill and contracted tuberculosis. She had to be sent to a sanitarium. She stayed behind when we were evacuated. She was too ill to be moved. She was there till she passed away.

My father was transferred to Missoula, Montana. We got letters from 118 him—censored, of course—telling us he was all right. It was just my sister and myself. I was fifteen, she was twelve. In April 1942, we were evacuated to Santa Anita. At the time we didn't know where we were going, how long we'd be gone. We didn't know what to take. A toothbrush, toilet supplies, some clothes. Only what you could carry. We left with a caravan.

Santa Anita is a race track. The horse stables were converted into liv- 119 ing quarters. My sister and I were fortunate enough to stay in a barracks. The people in the stables had to live with the stench. Everything was communal. We had absolutely no privacy. When you went to the toilet, it was communal. It was very embarrassing for women especially. The parent actually lost control of the child. I had no parents, so I did as I pleased. When I think back what happened to the Japanese family . . .

We had orders to leave Santa Anita in September of 1942. We had no 120 idea where we were going. Just before we left, my father joined us. He was brought into camp on the back of an army state truck, he and several others who were released from Missoula. I can still picture it to this day: to come in like cattle or sheep being herded in the back of a pickup truck bed. We were near the gate and saw him come in. He saw us. It was a sad, happy moment, because we'd been separated for a year.

He never really expressed what his true inner feelings were. It just 121 amazes me. He was never vindictive about it, never showed any anger. I can't understand that. A man who had worked so hard for what he had and lost it overnight. There is a very strong word in Japanese, *gaman*. It means to persevere. Old people instilled this into the second generation: You persevere. Take what's coming, don't react.

He had been a very outgoing person. Enthusiastic. I was very, very im- 122 pressed with how he ran things and worked with people. When I saw him at Santa Anita, he was a different person.

We were put on a train, three of us and many trains of others. It was 123 crowded. The shades were drawn. During the ride we were wondering, what are they going to do to us? We Niseis had enough confidence in our government that it wouldn't do anything drastic. My father had put all his faith in this country. This was his land.

Oh, it took days. We arrived in Amache, Colorado. That was an expe- 124 rience in itself. We were right near the Kansas border. It's a desolate, flat, barren area. The barracks was all there was. There were no trees, no kind of landscaping. It was like a prison camp. Coming from our environment, it was just devastating.

125　School in camp was a joke. Let's say it was loose. If you wanted to study, fine. If you didn't, who cared? There were some teachers who were conscientious and a lot who were not. One of our basic subjects was American history. They talked about freedom all the time. (Laughs.)

126　After a year, I was sent out to Utah on jobs. I worked on sugar beet farms. You had to have a contract or a job in order to leave camp. The pay was nominal. We would have a labor boss, the farmer would pay us through him. It was piecework. Maybe fifteen of us would work during the harvest season. When it was over, we went back to camp.

127　If you had a job waiting, you could relocate to a city that was not in the Western Defense Command. I had one in Chicago, as a stock boy in a candy factory. It paid seventy-five cents an hour. I was only in camp for a year. My sister was in until they were dismantled, about three and a half years. My father was in various camps for four years.

128　I went from job to job for a year. I had turned draft age, so I had to register. It's ironic. Here I am being drafted into the army, and my father and sister are in a concentration camp waiting for the war to end.

129　I was in the reserve, not yet inducted, in the middle of 1944, when I received a wire from my father saying that my mother was very ill. I immediately left Chicago for Amache, Colorado, to get my clearance from the Western Defense Command. It took several days. While I was waiting, my mother passed away.

130　Since we wanted her funeral to be at the camp where my father and sister were, I decided to go on to California and pick up her remains. At Needles, California, I was met at the train by an FBI agent. He was assigned to me. He was with me at all times during my stay there. Whether I went to sleep at night or whether I went to the bathroom, he was by my side.

131　As soon as we stepped off the train at the Union Station in Los Angeles, there was a shore patrol and a military police who met me. They escorted me through the station. It was one of the most . . . (He finds it difficult to talk.) I don't even know how to describe it. Any day now, I'd be serving in the same uniform as these people who were guarding me. The train stations at that time were always filled. When they marched me through, the people recognized me as being Oriental. They knew I was either an escaped prisoner or a spy. Oh, they called out names. I heard "dirty Jap" very distinctly.

132　After we got to the hotel, the FBI agent convinced the military that it wasn't necessary for them to stay with me. But he had to. He was disgusted with the whole situation. He knew I was in the reserve, that I was an American citizen. He could see no reason for him to be with me. But he was on assignment. We spoke personal things. His wife was having a baby, he couldn't be with her. He thought it was ridiculous.

I was in the armored division at Fort Knox. We were sent to Fort Mead   133
for embarkation when the European war ended. They didn't know what
to do with us Japanese Americans. We were in our own units. Should they
send us to the Pacific side? They might not be able to tell who was the enemy and who was not. (Laughs.)

The war ended while I was at Fort McDowell on San Francisco Bay.   134
That was the receiving point for Japanese prisoners captured in the war. I
went back with a boatload of them. I didn't know how they'd react to me.
I was very surprised. The professional soldiers who were captured during
the early days of the war in Guadalcanal, Saipan, never believed the war
ended. They would always say, when the subject came up, it was propaganda. The civilian soldiers were very different. We could get along with
them. They were very young —boheitai, boy soldiers. We could relate to
them as to children. They were scared. They had nothing to go back to.
Okinawa was devastated. A lot of them lost their families.

My furloughs were spent in camp, visiting my father and sister. Going to   135
camp was like going home for me, to see my family. We made the best of
what we had. We celebrated Christmas in the American fashion. We tried
to make our lives go easy.

We came back to Los Angeles at the end of the war, believing that there   136
was no other way but to be American. We were discouraged with our Japanese culture. My feeling at the time was, I had to prove myself. I don't
know why I had to prove myself. Here I am, ex-GI, born and raised here.
Why do I have to prove myself? We all had this feeling. We had to prove
that we were Americans, okay?

My mother and father sent me to a Japanese school teaching the culture.   137
My wife and I did nothing with our children in that respect. We moved to
a white community near Los Angeles. It was typical American suburb living. We became more American than Americans, very conservative. My
wife and I, we talk about this. We thought this was the thing we had to do:
to blend into the community and become part of white America.

My children were denied a lot of the history of what happened. If you   138
think of all those forty years of silence, I think this stems from another
Japanese characteristic: when shame is put on you, you try to hide it. We
were put into camp, we became victims, it was our fault. We hide it.

My oldest daughter, Cathy, in her senior year at college, wanted to write   139
a thesis about the camp experience. She asked if we knew people she
might interview. Strange thing is, many people, even now, didn't want to
talk about it. Some of the people she did talk to broke down. Because
this was the first time they had told this story. This is the same thing I
did. When I first went into detail, it just broke me up. When it came out,

I personally felt good about it. It was somethin' that was inside of me that I've wanted to say for a long time.

How do the Sansei feel about it—your daughter's generation?

140 Very angry. They keep saying, "Why did you go? Why didn't you fight back?" They couldn't understand it. They weren't raised in our culture. Today, I would definitely resist. It was a different situation at that time. This is what we tried to explain to our daughter. Today if this happened, I think a majority of the Japanese would resist.*

141 When I think back to my mother and my father, what they went through quietly, it's hard to explain. (Cries.) I think of my father without ever coming up with an angry word. After all those years, having worked his whole life to build a dream—an American dream, mind you—having it all taken away, and not one vindictive word. His business was worth more than a hundred thousand. He sold it for five. When he came out of camp, with what little money he had he put a down payment on an apartment building. It was right in the middle of skid row, an old rooming house. He felt he could survive by taking in a little rent and living there. My sister worked for a family as a domestic. He was afraid for her in this area. He died a very broken man.

142 My wife and I, we're up on cloud nine right now. Our daughter just passed the California bar. Guess what she's doing? She works for the redress and reparations group in San Diego.** How's that?

Yuriko Hohri

She lives with her husband in Chicago. He is national chair of the Council for Japanese American Redress. She is active, too.

143 The war became real for me when the two FBI agents came to our home in Long Beach. It was a few months after December 7. It was a rainy Saturday morning. My three sisters, my mother, and myself were at home doing chores. I was twelve.

---

*Jun Kurose, a Nisei internee from Seattle: "When we were told to evacuate, the American Friends Service Committee said: 'Don't go, we will help you.' . . . Some of the Japanese were saying, 'Stay out of this, you're making it rougher for us.' If we'd listened to the Friends, we might have been able to avert much suffering. We went willingly, we really did." (From *American Dreams: Lost and Found* [New York: Pantheon Books, 1980], p. 168.)

**A movement for redress of grievances has come into being on behalf of Japanese Americans who were interned during the war years.

A black car came right into the driveway. One man went into the 144
kitchen. As I watched, he looked under the sink and he looked into the
oven. Then he went into the parlor and opened the glass cases where our
most treasured things were. There were several stacks of *shakuhachi* sheet
music. It's a bamboo flute. My father played the *shakuhachi* and my mother
played the *koto*. At least once a month on a Sunday afternoon, their
friends would come over and just enjoy themselves playing music. The
man took the music.

I followed the man into my mother and father's bedroom. Strangers do 145
not usually go into our bedrooms when they first come. As I watched, he
went into the closet and brought out my father's golf clubs. He turned the
bag upside down. I was only concerned about the golf balls, because I
played jacks with them. He opened the *tansu*, a chest of drawers. My
mother and sisters were weeping.

My father was at work. He took care of the vegetable and fruit sections 146
for two grocery stores. He was brought home by the agents. He was taken
to a camp in Tujunga Canyon. My grandmother and I went to visit him.
It was a different kind of visit. There was a tall barbed-wire fence, so we
were unable to touch each other. The only thing we could do was see each
other. My father was weeping.

Our family moved to my grandmother's house—my mother's mother. 147
At least six of my uncles were at home, so it was very crowded. My next
recollection is that my mother, my three little sisters, and I were on this
streetcar. My mother had made a little knapsack for each of us, with our
names embroidered. We had a washcloth, a towel, soap, a comb. Just
enough for us to carry. It was the first time we took a streetcar. Because we
always went by my father's car.

We went to Santa Anita. We lived in a horse stable. We filled a cheese- 148
cloth bag with straw—our mattress. The sides of the room did not go up
to the ceiling, so there was no privacy at all. They were horse stalls. We'd
have fun climbing up. The floors were asphalt. I do remember what we
called stinky bugs. They were crunchy, like cockroaches, large, black. Oh,
it's really—(Laughs, as she shakes her head.) We had apple butter. To this
day, I cannot taste apple butter.

*She shows her internee's record, which she had saved all these years: her name,
birthdate, internment date, places of internment. At the bottom of the sheet, in
large print:* KEEP FREEDOM IN YOUR FUTURE WITH U.S. SAVINGS BONDS.

Our teachers were young Nisei internees. There was a lot of rotation among 149
them. The schooling was informal. Oh, I learned how to play cards there.

150   In the mornings, a man would knock on the door. There was a sort of bed check at night. There were searchlights always going.

151   All during this time, I was writing letters to Attorney General Biddle. I was asking him to release my father. I said we are four growing girls. We need our father here. Period.

152   We left Santa Anita in October 1942. It was a very long train with many, many cars. The stops were made at night with all the shades drawn. We wound up in Jerome, Arkansas. It was in the swamps. The toilet facilities had not yet been finished. The minute we got off, we had to go to the bathroom. I was standing in line, next thing I know people were looking down at me. I had fainted.

153   We could hardly walk because the clay would grab hold of your shoe or boot. It was very cold. They issued us all navy peacoats. You could see the soldier with his gun in the tower. It was trained in our direction.

154   My father was released shortly before we left Jerome. He appeared one day in April 1944. He said this was no place for a family to be reared. We left before other families because my father had a sponsor. This is where the American Friends Service Committee came into our lives. Our sponsor was a Quaker who lived in Des Moines, Iowa.

155   All I remember of Des Moines is that I was much ahead of my class in algebra. I think it had something to do with my Nisei algebra teacher in camp. His name is Paul Shimokobo. He later became my neighbor in Chicago. He died a few years ago. He must have been a very good teacher.

156   My classmates were sort of standoffish. But there was a black girl, Marguerite Desleigh. She treated me like an ordinary person. She invited me to her home. It was very beautiful. We became friends.

157   What else can I say? I'm just pleased to be alive.

QUESTIONING AND DISCUSSING

Terkel, *The Good War*

1. Discuss the various meanings of the title. In what ways could World War II have been described as a "good" war? In what ways might the title also be ironic?

2. Terkel writes, "This is a memory book, rather than one of hard facts and precise statistic." What are the values that are implied, then, by a book that is about "memory" rather than "precise statistic"? How are the narratives and memories inscribed by this book suggested to be as valuable as "hard fact"—or, perhaps, more valuable? Why?

3. What seems to be Terkel's strategy in selecting the people and stories that populate this excerpt? For what purpose? Which of these stories do you find the most compelling? Why?

4. Terkel relates the attitude of a woman who was thirty in 1982, when this book was published. She says, "I can't relate to World War Two. It's in schoolbook texts, that's all." Part of Terkel's project seems to be to make readers value important historical, political, and social events that weren't necessarily part of their life experiences. Why?

5. Are there similar, world-changing events that occurred in or just before your lifetime about which you feel equally removed or indifferent? Research one of these events, perhaps interviewing a veteran of the Korean or Vietnam conflicts or someone who recalls the day President Kennedy was assassinated. How does learning more about these events through others' experiences make the events more real and vivid?

⊞

ALLEEN PACE NILSEN

Alleen Pace Nilsen (1936–) has been a professor of English at Arizona State University and at other institutions. In 1967, Nilsen lived in Afghanistan, where she studied the cultural and behavioral attitudes toward women in that society. The cultural and societal upheavals of that time were fertile soil for Nilsen's work; when she returned to the United States, she began to study the dictionary to find cultural bias toward men and women in American English. She is also interested in what teenagers read, and she has coauthored the volume *Literature for Today's Young Adults*. The following essay—which takes on additional interest in light of the United States' renewed involvement in Afghanistan in the early twenty-first century—is from her study of American language.

⊞

Sexism in English: A 1990s Update

Twenty years ago I embarked on a study of the sexism inherent in American English. I had just returned to Ann Arbor, Michigan, after living for two years (1967–69) in Kabul, Afghanistan, where I had begun to look critically at the role society assigned to women. The Afghan version of the *chaderi* prescribed for Moslem women was particularly confining. Afghan jokes and folklore were blatantly sexist, such as this proverb: "If you see an old man, sit down and take a lesson; if you see an old woman, throw a stone."

2   But it wasn't only the native culture that made me question women's roles, it was also the American community.

3   Most of the American women were like myself—wives and mothers whose husbands were either career diplomats, employees of USAID, or college professors who had been recruited to work on various contract teams. We were suddenly bereft of our traditional roles: some of us became alcoholics, others got very good at bridge, while still others searched desperately for ways to contribute either to our families or to the Afghans. The local economy provided few jobs for women and certainly none for foreigners; we were isolated from former friends and the social goals we had grown up with.

4   When I returned in the fall of 1969 to the University of Michigan in Ann Arbor, I was surprised to find that many other women were also questioning the expectations they had grown up with. In the spring of 1970, a women's conference was announced. I hired a baby-sitter and attended, but I returned home more troubled than ever. The militancy of these women frightened me. Since I wasn't ready for a revolution, I decided I would have my own feminist movement. I would study the English language and see what it could tell me about sexism. I started reading a desk dictionary and making notecards on every entry that seemed to tell something about male and female. I soon had a dog-eared dictionary, along with a collection of notecards filling two shoe boxes.

5   Ironically, I started reading the dictionary because I wanted to avoid getting involved in social issues, but what happened was that my notecards brought me right back to looking at society. Language and society are as intertwined as a chicken and an egg. The language a culture uses is telltale evidence of the values and beliefs of that culture. And because there is a lag in how fast a language changes—new words can easily be introduced, but it takes a long time for old words and usages to disappear—a careful look at English will reveal the attitudes that our ancestors held and that we as a culture are therefore predisposed to hold. My notecards revealed three main points. Friends have offered the opinion that I didn't need to read the dictionary to learn such obvious facts. Nevertheless, it was interesting to have linguistic evidence of sociological observations.

Women Are Sexy; Men Are Successful

6   First, in American culture a woman is valued for the attractiveness and sexiness of her body, while a man is valued for his physical strength and accomplishments. A woman is sexy. A man is successful.

A persuasive piece of evidence supporting this view are the eponyms— 7
words that have come from someone's name—found in English. I had a
two-and-a-half-inch stack of cards taken from men's names but less than
a half-inch stack from women's names, and most of those came from
Greek mythology. In the words that came into American English since we
separated from Britain, there are many eponyms based on the names of famous American men: *Bartlett pear, boysenberry, diesel engine, Franklin stove,
Ferris wheel, Gatling gun, mason jar, sideburns, sousaphone, Schick test,* and
Winchester rifle. The only common eponyms taken from American women's
names are *Alice blue* (after Alice Roosevelt Longworth), *bloomers* (after
Amelia Jenks Bloomer), and *Mae West jacket* (after the buxom actress).
Two out of the three feminine eponyms relate closely to a woman's physical
anatomy, while the masculine eponyms (except for *sideburns* after General
Burnsides) have nothing to do with the namesake's body but, instead,
honor the man for an accomplishment of some kind.

Although in Greek mythology women played a bigger role than they 8
did in the biblical stories of the Judeo-Christian culture and so the names
of goddesses are accepted parts of the language in such place names as
Pomona from the goddess of fruit and *Athens* from Athena and in such
common words as *cereal* from Ceres, *psychology* from Psyche, and *arachnoid*
from Arachne, the same tendency to think of women in relation to sexuality is seen in the eponyms *aphrodisiac* from Aphrodite, the Greek name
for the goddess of love and beauty, and *venereal disease* from Venue, the
Roman name for Aphrodite.

Another interesting word from Greek mythology is *Amazon.* According 9
to Greek folk etymology, the *a* means "without" as in *atypical* or *amoral,*
while *mazon* comes from *mazos* meaning "breast" as still seen in *mastec-
tomy.* In the Greek legend, Amazon women cut off their right breasts so
that they could better shoot their bows. Apparently, the storytellers had a
feeling that for women to play the active, "masculine" role the Amazons
adopted for themselves, they had to trade in part of their femininity.

This preoccupation with women's breasts is not limited to ancient sto- 10
ries. As a volunteer for the University of Wisconsin's *Dictionary of American Regional English (DARE),* I read a western trapper's diary from the
1930s. I was to make notes of any unusual usages or language patterns. My
most interesting finding was that the trapper referred to a range of mountains as *The Teats,* a metaphor based on the similarity between the shapes
of mountains and women's breasts. Because today we use the French
wording, *The Grand Tetons,* the metaphor isn't as obvious, but I wrote to
mapmakers and found the following listings: *Nippletop* and *Little Nipple
Top* near Mount Marcy in the Adirondacks; *Nipple Mountain* in Archuleta
County, Colorado; *Nipple Peak* in Coke County, Texas; *Nipple Butte* in

Pennington, South Dakota; *Squaw Peak* in Placer County, California (and many other locations); *Maiden's Peak* and *Squaw Tit* (they're the same mountain) in the Cascade Range in Oregon; *Mary's Nipple* near Salt Lake City, Utah; and *Jane Russell Peaks* near Stark, New Hampshire.

11　　Except for the movie star Jane Russell, the women being referred to are anonymous—it's only a sexual part of their body that is mentioned. When topographical features are named after men, it's probably not going to be to draw attention to a sexual part of their bodies but instead to honor individuals for an accomplishment. For example, no one thinks of a part of the male body when hearing a reference to Pike's Peak, Colorado, or Jackson Hole, Wyoming.

12　　Going back to what I learned from my dictionary cards, I was surprised to realize how many parts of words we have in which the feminine word has acquired sexual connotations while the masculine word retains a serious businesslike aura. For example, a *callboy* is the person who calls actors when it is time for them to go on stage, but a *callgirl* is a prostitute. Compare *sir* and *madam*. *Sir* is a term of respect, while *madam* has acquired the specialized meaning of a brothel manager. Something similar has happened to *master* and *mistress*. Would you rather have a painting by an *old master* or an *old mistress*?

13　　It's because the word *woman* had sexual connotations, as in "She's his woman," that people began avoiding its use, hence such terminology as *ladies' room*, *lady of the house*, and *girls' school* or *school for young ladies*. Feminists, who ask that people use the term *woman* rather than *girl* or *lady*, are rejecting the idea that *woman* is primarily a sexual term. They have been at least partially successful in that today *woman* is commonly used to communicate gender without intending implications about sexuality.

14　　I found two hundred pairs of words with masculine and feminine forms, e.g., *heir-heiress*, *hero-heroine*, *steward-stewardess*, *usher-usherette*. In nearly all such pairs, the masculine word is considered the base, with some kind of a feminine suffix being added. The masculine form is the one from which compounds are made, e.g., from *king-queen* comes *kingdom* but not *queendom*, from *sportsman-sportslady* comes *sportsmanship* but not *sportsladyship*. There is one—and only one—semantic area in which the masculine word is not the base or more powerful word. This is in the area dealing with sex and marriage. When someone refers to a *virgin*, a listener will probably think of a female, unless the speaker specifies *male* or uses a masculine pronoun. The same is true for *prostitute*.

15　　In relation to marriage, there is much linguistic evidence showing that weddings are more important to women than to men. A woman cherishes the wedding and is considered a bride for a whole year, but a man is referred to as a groom only on the day of the wedding. The word *bride* appears in *bridal attendant, bridal gown, bridesmaid, bridal shower,* and even *bridegroom. Groom* comes from the Middle English *grom,* meaning "man," and in the sense is seldom used outside of the wedding. With most pairs of male/female words, people habitually put the masculine word first, *Mr. and Mrs, his and hers, boys and girls, men and women, kings and queens, brothers and sisters, guys and dolls,* and *host and hostess,* but it is the *bride and groom* who are talked about, not the *groom and bride.*

The importance of marriage to a woman is also shown by the fact that   16
when a marriage ends in death, the woman gets the title of *widow.* A man gets the derived title of *widower.* This term is not used in other phrases or contexts, but *widow* is seen in *widowhood, widow's peak,* and *widow's walk.* A *widow* in a card game is an extra hand of cards, while in typesetting it is an extra line of type.

How changing cultural ideas bring changes to language is clearly visible   17
in this semantic area. The feminist movement has caused the differences between the sexes to be downplayed, and since I did my dictionary study two decades ago, the word *singles* has largely replaced such sex specific and value-laden terms as *bachelor, old maid, spinster, divorcee, widow,* and *widower.* And in 1970 I wrote that when a man is called *a professional* he is thought to be a doctor or a lawyer, but when people hear a woman referred to as *a professional* they are likely to think of a prostitute. That's not as true today because so many women have become doctors and lawyers that it's no longer incongruous to think of women in those professional roles.

Another change that has taken place is in wedding announcements.   18
They used to be sent out from the bride's parents and did not even give the name of the groom's parents. Today, most couples choose to list either all or none of the parents' names. Also it is not much more likely that both the bride and groom's picture will be in the newspaper, while a decade ago only the bride's picture was published on the "Women's" or the "Society" page. Even the traditional wording of the wedding ceremony is being changed. Many officials now pronounce the couple "husband and wife" instead of the old "man and wife," and they ask the bride if she promises "to love, honor, and cherish," instead of "to love, honor, and obey."

Women Are Passive; Men Are Active

The wording of the wedding ceremony also relates to the second point   19
that my cards showed, which is that women are expected to play a passive or weak role while men play an active or strong role. In the traditional ceremony, the official asks, "Who gives the bride away?" and the father answers, "I do." Some fathers answer, "Her mother and I do," but that doesn't solve the problem inherent in the question. The idea that a bride

is something to be handed over from one man to another bothers people because it goes back to the days when a man's servants, his children, and his wife were all considered to be his property. They were known by his name because they belonged to him, and he was responsible for their actions and their debts.

20　　The grammar used in talking or writing about weddings as well as other sexual relationships shows the expectation of men playing the active role. Men *wed* women while women *become* brides of men. A man *possesses* a woman; he *deflowers* her; he *performs*; he *scores*; he *takes away* her virginity. Although a woman can *seduce* a man, she cannot offer him her virginity. When talking about virginity, the only way to make the woman the actor in the sentence is to say that "She lost her virginity," but people lose things by accident rather than by purposeful actions, and so she's only the grammatical, not the real-life, actor.

21　　The reason that women tried to bring the term *Ms.* into the language to replace *Miss* and *Mrs.* relates to this point. Married women resent being identified only under their husband's names. For example, when Susan Glascoe did something newsworthy, she would be identified in the newspaper only as Mrs. John Glascoe. The dictionary card showed what appeared to be an attitude on the part of the editors that it was almost indecent to let a respectable woman's name march unaccompanied across the pages of a dictionary. Women were listed with male names whether or not the male contributed to the woman's reason for being in the dictionary or in his own right was as famous as the woman. For example, Charlotte Brontë was identified as Mrs. Arthur B. Nicholls, Amelia Earhart as Mrs. George Palmer Putnam, Helen Hayes as Mrs. Charles MacArthur, Jenny Lind as Mme. Otto Goldschmit, Cornelia Otis Skinner as the daughter of Otis, Harriet Beecher Stowe as the sister of Henry Ward Beecher, and Edith Sitwell as the sister of Osbert and Sacheverell. A very small number of women got into the dictionary without the benefit of a masculine escort. They were rebels and crusaders: temperance leaders Frances Elizabeth Caroline Willard and Carry Nation, women's rights leaders Carrie Chapman Catt and Elizabeth Cady Stanton, birth control educator Margaret Sanger, religious leader Mary Baker Eddy, and slaves Harriet Tubman and Phillis Wheatley.

22　　Etiquette books used to teach that if a woman had *Mrs.* in front of her name, then the husband's name should follow because *Mrs.* is an abbreviated form of *Mistress* and a woman couldn't be a mistress of herself. As with many arguments about "correct" language usage, this isn't very logical because *Miss* is also an abbreviation of *Mistress*. Feminists hoped to simplify matters by introducing *Ms.* as an alternative to both *Mrs.* and *Miss*, but what happened is that *Ms.* largely replaced *Miss*, to become a catch-all business title for women. Many married women still prefer the title *Mrs.*, and some resent being addressed with the term *Ms.* As one frustrated newspaper reporter complained, "Before I can write about a woman, I have to know not only her marital status but also her political philosophy." The result of such complications may contribute to the demise of titles, which are already being ignored by many computer programmers who find it more efficient to simply use names, for example in a business letter: "Dear Joan Garcia," instead of "Dear Mrs. Joan Garcia," "Dear Ms. Garcia," or "Dear Mrs. Louis Garcia."

The titles given to royalty provide an example of how males can be disadvantaged by the assumption that they are always to play the more powerful role. In British royalty, when a male holds a title, his wife is automatically given the feminine equivalent. But the reverse is not true. For example, a *count* is a high political officer with a *countess* being his wife. The same is true for a *duke* and a *duchess* and a *king* and a *queen*. But when a female holds the royal title, the man she marries does not automatically acquire the matching title. For example, Queen Elizabeth's husband has the title of *prince* rather than *king*, but if Prince Charles should become king while he is still married to Lady or Princess Diana, she will be known as the queen. The reasoning appears to be that since masculine words are stronger, they are reserved for true heirs and withheld from males coming into the royal family by marriage. If Prince Phillip were called *King Phillip*, it would be much easier for British subjects to forget where the true power lies. 23

The names that people give their children show the hopes and dreams they have for them, and when we look at the differences between male and female names in a culture, we can see the cumulative expectations of that culture. In our culture girls often have names taken from small, aesthetically pleasing items, e.g., *Ruby*, *Jewel*, and *Pearl*. *Esther* and *Stella* mean "star," *Ada* means "ornament," and *Vanessa* means "butterfly." Boys are more likely to be given names with meanings of power and strength, e.g., *Neil* means "champion," *Martin* is from Mars, the God of War, *Raymond* means "wise protection," *Harold* means "chief of the army," *Ira* means "vigilant," *Rex* means "king," and *Richard* means "strong king." 24

We see similar differences in food metaphors. Food is a passive substance just sitting there waiting to be eaten. Many people have recognized this and so no longer feel comfortable describing women as "delectable morsels." However, when I was a teenager, it was considered a compliment to refer to a girl (we didn't call anyone a *woman* until she was middle-aged) as a *cute tomato*, *a peach*, *a dish*, a *cookie*, *honey*, *sugar*, or *sweetie-pie*. When being affectionate, women will occasionally call a man *honey* or *sweetie*, but in general, food metaphors are used much less often with men 25 than with women. If a man is called *a fruit*, his masculinity is being questioned. But it's perfectly acceptable to use a food metaphor if the food is heavier and more substantive than that used for women. For example pin-up pictures of women have long been known as *cheesecake*, but when Burt Reynolds posed for a nude centerfold the picture was immediately dubbed *beefcake*, c.f., *a hunk of meat*. That sexual references to men have come into the language is another reflection of how society is beginning to lessen the differences between their attitudes toward men and women.

26 Something similar to the *fruit* metaphor happens with references to plants. We insult a man by calling him a *pansy*, but it wasn't considered particularly insulting to talk about a girl being a *wallflower*, a *clinging vine*, or a *shrinking violet*, or to give girls such names as *Ivy, Rose, Lily, Iris, Daisy, Camellia, Heather*, and *Flora*. A plant metaphor can be used with a man if the plant is big and strong, for example, Andrew Jackson's nickname of *Old Hickory*. Also, the phrases *blooming idiots* and *budding geniuses* can be used with either sex, but notice how they are based on the most active thing a plant can do, which is to bloom or bud.

27 Animal metaphors also illustrate the different expectations for males and females. Men are referred to as *studs, bucks*, and *wolves* while women are referred to with such metaphors as *kitten, bunny, beaver, bird, chick*, and *lamb*. In the 1950s we said that boys went *tomcatting*, but today it's just *catting around* and both boys and girls do it. When the term *foxy*, meaning that someone was sexy, first became popular it was used only for girls, but now someone of either sex can be described as *a fox*. Some animal metaphors that are used predominantly with men have negative connotations based on the size and/or strength of the animals, e.g., *beast, bullheaded, jackass, rat, loanshark*, and *vulture*. Negative metaphors used with women are based on smaller animals, e.g., *social butterfly, mousy, catty*, and *vixen*. The feminine terms connote action, but not the same kind of large scale action as with the masculine terms.

Women Are Connected with Negative Connotations; Men with Positive Connotations

28 The final point that my notecards illustrated was how many positive connotations are associated with the concept of masculine, while there are either trivial or negative connotations connected with the corresponding feminine concept. An example from the animal metaphors makes a good illustration. The word *shrew* taken from the name of a small but especially vicious animal was defined in my dictionary as "an ill-tempered scolding woman," but the word *shrewd* taken from the same root was defined as

"marked by clever, discerning awareness" and was illustrated with the phrase "a shrewd businessman."

Early in life, children are conditioned to the superiority of the masculine role. As child psychologists point out, little girls have much more freedom to experiment with sex roles than do little boys. If a little girl acts like a *tomboy*, most parents have mixed feelings, being at least partially proud. But if their little boy acts like a *sissy* (derived from *sister*), they call a psychologist. It's perfectly acceptable for a little girl to sleep in the crib that was purchased for her brother, to wear his hand-me-down jeans and shirts, and to ride the bicycle that he has outgrown. But few parents would put a boy baby in a white and gold crib decorated with frills and lace, and virtually no parents would have their little boys wear his sister's hand-me-down dresses, nor would they have their son ride a girl's pink bicycle with a flower-bedecked basket. The proper names given to girls and boys show this same attitude. Girls can have "boy" names—*Cris, Craig, Jo, Kelly, Shawn, Teri, Toni,* and *Sam*—but it doesn't work the other way around. A couple of generations ago, *Beverley, Frances, Hazel, Marion,* and *Shirley* were common boys' names. As parents gave these names to more and more girls, they fell into disuse for males, and some older men who have these names prefer to go by their initials or by such abbreviated forms as *Haze* or *Shirl*.

When a little girl is told to *be a lady*, she is being told to sit with her knees together and to be quiet and dainty. But when a little boy is told to *be a man* he is being told to be noble, strong, and virtuous—to have all the qualities that the speaker looks on as desirable. The concept of manliness has such positive connotations that it used to be a compliment to call someone a *he-man*, to say that he was doubly a man. Today many people are more ambivalent about this term and respond to it much as they do to the word *macho*. But calling someone a *manly man* or a *virile man* is nearly always meant as a compliment. *Virile* comes from the Indo-European *vir* meaning "man," which is also the basis for *virtuous*. Contrast the positive connotations of both *virile* and *virtuous* with the negative connotations of *hysterical*. The Greeks took this latter word from their name for *uterus* (as still seen in *hysterectomy*). They thought that women were the only ones who experienced uncontrolled emotional outbursts, and so the condition must have something to do with a part of the body that only women have.

Differences in the connotations between positive male and negative female connotations can be seen in several pairs of words that differ denotatively only in the matter of sex. *Bachelor* as compared to *spinster* or *old maid* has such positive connotations that women try to adopt them by using the term *bachelor-girl* or *bachelorette*. *Old Maid* is so negative that it's

29

30

31

the basis for metaphors: pretentious and fussy old men are called *old maids*, as are the leftover kernels of unpopped popcorn, and the last card in a popular children's game.

32   *Patron* and *matron* (Middle English for *father* and *mother* have such different levels of prestige that women try to borrow the more positive masculine connotations with the word *patroness*, literally "female father." Such a peculiar term came about because of the high prestige attached to *patron* in such phrases as *a patron of the arts* or *a patron saint*. *Matron* is more apt to be used in talking about a woman in charge of a jail or a public restroom.

33   When men are doing jobs that women often do, we apparently try to pay the men extra by giving them fancy titles, for example, a male cook is more likely to be called a *chef* while a male seamstress will get the title of *tailor*. The armed forces have a special problem in that they recruit under such slogans as "The Marine Corps builds men!" and "Join the Army! Become a man!" Once the recruits are enlisted, they find themselves doing much of the work that has been traditionally thought of as "women's work." The solution to getting the work done and not insulting anyone's masculinity was to change the titles as shown below:

waitress	orderly
nurse	medic or corpsman
secretary	clerk-typist
assistant	adjutant
dishwasher or kitchen helper	KP (kitchen police)

34   Compare *brave* and *squaw*. Early settlers in America truly admired Indian men and hence named them with a word that carried connotations of youth, vigor, and courage. But they used the Algonquin's name for "woman" and over the years it developed almost opposite connotations to those of *brave*. *Wizard* and *witch* contrast almost as much. The masculine *wizard* implies skill and wisdom combined with magic, while the feminine *witch* implies evil intentions combined with magic. Part of the unattractiveness of both *witch* and *squaw* is that they have been used so often to refer to old women, something with which our culture is particularly uncomfortable, just as the Afghans were. Imagine my surprise when I ran across the phrases *grandfatherly advice* and *old wives' tales* and realized that the underlying implication is the same as the Afghan proverb about old men being worth listening to while old women talk only foolishness.

35   Other terms that show how negative we view old women as compared to young women are *old nag* as compared to *filly*, *old crow* or *old bat* as compared to *bird*, and of being *catty* as compared to being *kittenish*. There is no

matching set of metaphors for men. The chicken metaphor tells the whole story of a woman's life. In her youth she is a *chick*. Then she marries and begins *feathering her nest*. Soon she begins feeling *cooped up*, so she goes to *hen parties* where she *cackles* with her friends. Then she has her *brood*, begins to *henpeck* her husband, and finally turns into an *old biddy*.

I embarked on my study of the dictionary not with the intention of prescribing language change but simply to see what the language would tell me about sexism. Nevertheless I have been both surprised and pleased as I've watched the changes that have occurred over the past two decades. I'm one of those linguists who believes that new language customs will cause a new generation of speakers to grow up with different expectations. This is why I'm happy about people's efforts to use inclusive language, to say *he or she* or *they* when speaking about individuals whose names they do not know. I'm glad that leading publishers have developed guidelines to help writers use language that is fair to both sexes, and I'm glad that most newspapers and magazines list women by their own names instead of only by their husbands' names and that educated and thoughtful people no longer begin their business letters with "Dear Sir" or "Gentlemen," but instead use a memo form or begin with such salutations as "Dear Colleagues," "Dear Reader," or "Dear Committee Members." I'm also glad that such words as *poetess*, *authoress*, *conductress*, and *aviatrix* now sound quaint and old-fashioned and that *chairman* is giving way to *chair* or *head*, *mailman* to *mail carrier*, *clergyman* to *clergy*, and *stewardess* to *flight attendant*. I was also pleased when the National Oceanic and Atmospheric Administration bowed to feminist complaints and in the late 1970s began to alternate men's and women's names for hurricanes. However, I wasn't so pleased to discover that the change did not immediately erase sexist thoughts from everyone's mind, as shown by a headline about Hurricane David in a 1979 New York tabloid, "David Rapes Virgin Islands." More recently a similar metaphor appeared in a headline in the *Arizona Republic* about Hurricane Charlie, "Charlie Quits Carolinas, Flirts with Virginia."

36

What these incidents show is that sexism is not something existing independently in American English or in the particular dictionary that I happened to read. Rather, it exists in people's minds. Language is like an X-ray in providing visible evidence of invisible thoughts. The best thing about people being interested in and discussing sexist language is that as they make conscious decisions about what pronouns they will use, what jokes they will tell or laugh at, how they will write their names, or how they will begin their letters, they are forced to think about the underlying issue of sexism. This is good because as a problem that begins in people's assumptions and expectations, it's a problem that will be solved only when a great many people have given it a great deal of thought.

37

Nilsen, "Sexism in English"

1. How did Alleen Pace Nilsen's having lived in a culture overseas teach her particular lessons about her own culture? What are these lessons? What is Nilsen's overall argument?

2. What types of examples does Nilsen use to support her larger point? Are they effective? How so? What other examples from various culture(s) within the United States might you use to update this article further from its 1990s perspective?

3. There was a time when the title *Ms.* was new, an attempt to change the meanings of and judgments implied by the titles *Miss* and *Mrs.* The word *stewardess* has been replaced by *flight attendant.* Most *waitresses* are also called *waiters* and often everyone waiting tables in restaurants is now called a member of the *waitstaff.* The media have outraged grammarians and others concerned about correct usage by using *they*—a plural—to substitute for a singular *she* or *he* (the traditional default pronoun) when referring generally to a single individual. Have changes such as these to make language less "loaded" been effective? Why or why not?

⊞

AUDRE LORDE

Audre Lorde (1934–1992) names herself "a Black feminist lesbian mother poet" because her identity and her work are based on many divergent perspectives once perceived as incompatible: pride, love, anger, fear, racial and sexual oppression, urban neglect, and personal survival. Lorde was born in New York City to Frederic and Linda Lorde, immigrants from the West Indies. She received her bachelor's degree from Hunter College and her master's degree in library science from Columbia University. In 1968, she received a National Endowment for the Arts grant and became a poet-in-residence at Tougaloo College, a small, historically black institution in Mississippi. Drawing upon her experiences as a teacher and a writer, Lorde published her first volume of poetry in 1968. She went on to write six more volumes, and by 1982, she had expanded her prose writing as well. An influential writer, Lorde believed that her writing was more than a choice or vocation. It was a responsibility—one that blends rage with love, anger with hope and renewal—that was necessary for her survival and the survival of others.

⊞

The Transformation of Silence into Language and Action

I have come to believe over and over again that what is most important to me must be spoken, made verbal and shared, even at the risk of having it bruised or misunderstood. That the speaking profits me, beyond any other effect. I am standing here as a Black lesbian poet, and the meaning of all that waits upon the fact that I am still alive, and might not have been. Less than two months ago I was told by two doctors, one female and one male, that I would have to have breast surgery, and that there was a 60 to 80 percent chance that the tumor was malignant. Between that telling and the actual surgery, there was a three-week period of the agony of an involuntary reorganization of my entire life. The surgery was completed, and the growth was benign.

But within those three weeks, I was forced to look upon myself and my living with a harsh and urgent clarity that has left me still shaken but much stronger. This is a situation faced by many women, by some of you here today. Some of what I experienced during that time has helped elucidate for me much of what I feel concerning the transformation of silence into language and action.

3   In becoming forcibly and essentially aware of my mortality, and of what I wished and wanted for my life, however short it might be, priorities and omissions became strongly etched in a merciless light, and what I most regretted were my silences. Of what had I *ever* been afraid? To question or to speak as I believed could have meant pain, or death. But we all hurt in so many different ways, all the time, and pain will either change or end. Death, on the other hand, is the final silence. And that might be coming quickly, now, without regard for whether I had ever spoken what needed to be said, or had only betrayed myself into small silences, while I planned someday to speak, or waited for someone else's words. And I began to recognize a source of power within myself that comes from the knowledge that while it is most desirable not to be afraid, learning to put fear into a perspective gave me great strength.

4   I was going to die, if not sooner then later, whether or not I had ever spoken myself. My silences had not protected me. Your silence will not protect you. But for every real word spoken, for every attempt I had ever made to speak those truths for which I am still seeking, I had made contact with other women while we examined the words to fit a world in which we all believed, bridging our differences. And it was the concern and caring of all those women which gave me strength and enabled me to scrutinize the essentials of my living.

5   The women who sustained me through that period were Black and white, old and young, lesbian, bisexual, and heterosexual, and we all shared a war against the tyrannies of silence. They all gave me a strength and concern without which I could not have survived intact. Within those weeks of acute fear came the knowledge—within the war we are all waging with the forces of death, subtle and otherwise, conscious or not— I am not only a casualty, I am also a warrior.

6   What are the words you do not yet have? What do you need to say? What are the tyrannies you swallow day by day and attempt to make your own, until you will sicken and die of them, still in silence? Perhaps for some of you here today, I am the face of one of your fears. Because I am woman, because I am Black, because I am lesbian, because I am myself— a Black woman warrior poet doing my work—come to ask you, are you doing yours?

7   And of course I am afraid, because the transformation of silence into language and action is an act of self-revelation, and that always seems fraught with danger. But my daughter, when I told her of our topic and my difficulty with it, said, "Tell them about how you're never really a whole person if you remain silent, because there's always that one little piece inside you that wants to be spoken out, and if you keep ignoring it, it gets mad-

der and madder and hotter and hotter, and if you don't speak it out one day it will just up and punch you in the mouth from the inside."

In the cause of silence, each of us draws the face of her own fear—fear of contempt, of censure, or some judgment, or recognition, of challenge, of annihilation. But most of all, I think, we fear the visibility without which we cannot truly live. Within this country where racial difference creates a constant, if unspoken, distortion of vision, Black women have on one hand always been highly visible, and so, on the other hand, have been rendered invisible through the depersonalization of racism. Even within the women's movement, we have had to fight, and still do, for that very visibility which also renders us most vulnerable, our Blackness. For to survive in the mouth of this dragon we call america, we have had to learn this first and most vital lesson—that we were never meant to survive. Not as human beings. And neither were most of you here today, Black or not. And that visibility which makes us most vulnerable is that which also is the source of our greatest strength. Because the machine will try to grind you into dust anyway, whether or not we speak. We can sit in our corners mute forever while our sisters and our selves are wasted, while our children are distorted and destroyed, while our earth is poisoned; we can sit in our safe corners mute as bottles, and we will still be no less afraid.

In my house this year we are celebrating the feast of Kwanza, the African-american festival of harvest which begins the day after Christmas and lasts for seven days. There are seven principles of Kwanza, one for each day. The first principle is Umoja, which means unity, the decision to strive for and maintain unity in self and community. The principle for yesterday, the second day, was Kujichagulia—self-determination—the decision to define ourselves, name ourselves, and speak for ourselves, instead of being defined and spoken for by others. Today is the third day of Kwanza, and the principle for today is Ujima—collective work and responsibility—the decision to build and maintain ourselves and our communities together and to recognize and solve our problems together.

Each of us is here now because in one way or another we share a commitment to language and to the power of language, and to the reclaiming of that language which has been made to work against us. In the transformation of silence into language and action, it is vitally necessary for each one of us to establish or examine her function in that transformation and to recognize her role as vital within that transformation.

For those of us who write, it is necessary to scrutinize not only the truth of what we speak, but the truth of that language by which we speak it. For others, it is to share and spread also those words that are meaningful to us. But primarily for us all, it is necessary to teach by living and speaking those truths which we believe and know beyond understanding. Because in this way alone we can survive, by taking part in a process of life that is creative and continuing, that is growth.

12   And it is never without fear—of visibility, of the harsh light of scrutiny and perhaps judgment, of pain, of death. But we have lived through all of those already, in silence, except death. And I remind myself all the time now that if I were to have been born mute, or had maintained an oath of silence my whole life long for safety, I would still have suffered, and I would still die. It is very good for establishing perspective.

13   And where the words of women are crying to be heard, we must each of us recognize our responsibility to seek those words out, to read them and share them and examine them in their pertinence to our lives. That we not hide behind the mockeries of separations that have been imposed upon us and which so often we accept as our own. For instance, "I can't possibly teach Black women's writing—their experience is so different from mine." Yet how many years have you spent teaching Plato and Shakespeare and Proust? Or another, "She's a white woman and what could she possibly have to say to me?" Or, "She's a lesbian, what would my husband say, or my chairman?" Or again, "This woman writes of her sons and I have no children." And all the other endless ways in which we rob ourselves of ourselves and each other.

14   We can learn to work and speak when we are afraid in the same way we have learned to work and speak when we are tired. For we have been socialized to respect fear more than our own needs for language and definition, and while we wait in silence for that final luxury of fearlessness, the weight of that silence will choke us.

15   The fact that we are here and that I speak these words is an attempt to break that silence and bridge some of those differences between us, for it is not difference which immobilizes us, but silence. And there are so many silences to be broken.

QUESTIONING AND DISCUSSING

Lorde, "The Transformation of Silence into Language and Action"

1. How does Audre Lorde explain "the transformation of silence into language and action"? How is this transformation of silence political? What in the essay proves your points?

2. How is self-revelation "fraught with danger"? Why?

3. What does Lorde mean when she writes about "the mockeries of separation"? Do you agree with her? Why or why not?

4. What appear to be Lorde's values—and the ethical appeal that she makes? Consider, particularly, lines such as "Because the machine will try to grind you into dust anyway, whether or not we speak."

⊞

GEORGE ORWELL

George Orwell, (1903–1950), best known for his political satires such as *Animal Farm* and *1984*, was born Eric Arthur Blair in Bengal, India. In 1907, his family returned to England, where Orwell attended preparatory school until 1921, when he continued the family tradition of living east of Suez by joining the Indian Imperial Police. He resigned his post at the beginning of 1928, returning to Europe with a desire to explore writing while investigating the lives of the urban poor. By 1932, poverty forced Orwell to abandon his wandering adventures, and he became a schoolteacher. The alias *George Orwell* was born at this time, mainly because the budding author feared that a poor reception of his second book would damage any further literary ambitions. During the next decade, Orwell became a fierce socialist, his politics reflected in his works written at the time. At the outbreak of World War II, Orwell attempted to enlist to fight Nazi aggression, but he was turned down because of health reasons. It was toward the end of the war and in its aftermath that Orwell completed several of his most famous works, *Animal Farm* and *1984*. Another essay by Orwell, *Shooting an Elephant*, appears in Chapter 1.

⊞

Politics and the English Language

Most people who bother with the matter at all would admit that the English language is in a bad way, but it is generally assumed that we cannot by conscious action do anything about it. Our civilization is decadent and our language—so the argument runs—must inevitably share in the general collapse. It follows that any struggle against the abuse of language is a sentimental archaism, like preferring candles to electric light or hansom cabs to airplanes. Underneath this lies the half-conscious belief that language is a natural growth and not an instrument which we shape for our own purposes.

Now, it is clear that the decline of a language must ultimately have political and economic causes: it is not due simply to the bad influence of this or that individual writer. But an effect can become a cause, reinforcing the original cause and producing the same effect in an intensified form, and so on indefinitely. A man may take to drink because he feels himself to be a failure, and then fail all the more completely because he drinks. It is rather the same thing that is happening to the English language. It becomes ugly and inaccurate because our thoughts are foolish, but the slovenliness of our language makes it easier for us to have foolish thoughts. The point is that the process is reversible. Modern English, especially written English, is full of bad habits which spread by imitation and which can be avoided if one is willing to take the necessary trouble. If one gets rid of these habits one can think more clearly, and to think more clearly is a necessary first step towards political regeneration: so that the fight against bad English is not frivolous and is not the exclusive concern of professional writers. I will come back to this presently, and I hope that by that time the meaning of what I have said here will have become clearer. Meanwhile, here are five specimens of the English language as it is now habitually written.

3   These five passages have not been picked out because they are especially bad—I could have quoted far worse if I had chosen—but because they illustrate various of the mental vices from which we now suffer. They are a little below the average, but are fairly representative samples. I number them so that I can refer back to them when necessary:

> "(1) I am not, indeed, sure whether it is not true to say that the Milton who once seemed not unlike a seventeenth-century Shelley had not become, out of an experience ever more bitter in each year, more alien (*sic*) to the founder of that Jesuit sect which nothing could induce him to tolerate."
> Professor Harold Laski (Essay in *Freedom of Expression*).

> "(2) Above all, we cannot play ducks and drakes with a native battery of idioms which prescribes such egregious collocations of vocables as the Basic *put up with* for *tolerate* or *put at a loss* for *bewilder*."
> Professor Lancelot Hogben (*Interglossa*).

> "(3) On the one side we have the free personality: by definition it is not neurotic, for it has neither conflict nor dream. Its desires, such as they are, are transparent, for they are just what institutional approval keeps in the forefront of consciousness; another institutional patter would alter their number and intensity; there is little in them that is natural, irreducible, or culturally dangerous. But *on the other side,* the social bond itself is nothing but the mutual reflection of these self-secure integrities. Recall the definition of love. Is not this the very picture of a small academic? Where is there a place in this hall of mirrors for either personality or fraternity?"
> Essay on psychology in *Politics* (New York).

"(4) All the 'best people' from the gentlemen's clubs, and all the frantic fascist captains, united in common hatred of Socialism and bestial horror of the rising tide of the mass revolutionary movement, have turned to acts of provocation, to foul incendiarism, to medieval legends of poisoned wells, to legalize their own destruction of proletarian organizations, and rouse the agitated petty-bourgeoisie to chauvinistic fervor on behalf of the fight against the revolutionary way out of the crisis."

Communist pamphlet.

"(5) If a new spirit *is* to be infused into this old country, there is one thorny and contentious reform which must be tackled, and that is the humanization and galvanization of the B.B.C. Timidity here will bespeak cancer and atrophy of the soul. The heart of Britain may be sound and of strong beat, for instance, but the British lion's roar at present is like that of Bottom in Shakespeare's *Midsummer Night's Dream*—as gentle as any sucking dove. A virile new Britain cannot continue indefinitely to be traduced in the eyes or rather ears, of the world by the effete languors of Langham Place, brazenly masquerading as 'standard English.' When the Voice of Britain is heard at nine o'clock, better far and infinitely less ludicrous to hear aitches honestly dropped than the present priggish, inflated, inhibited, school-ma'amish arch braying of blameless bashful mewing maidens!"

Letter in *Tribune*.

Each of these passages has faults of its own, but, quite apart from avoid-   4
able ugliness, two qualities are common to all of them. The first is staleness
of imagery: the other is lack of precision. The writer either has a meaning
and cannot express it, or he inadvertently says something else, or he is almost indifferent as to whether his words mean anything or not. This mixture of vagueness and sheer incompetence is the most marked characteristic
of modern English prose, and especially of any kind of political writing. As
soon as certain topics are raised, the concrete melts into the abstract and no
one seems able to think of turns of speech that are not hackneyed: prose
consists less and less of *words* chosen for the sake of their meaning, and
more and more of *phrases* tacked together like the sections of a prefabricated
hen-house. I list below, with notes and examples, various of the tricks by
means of which the work of prose-construction is habitually dodged:

Dying Metaphors

A newly invented metaphor assists thought by evoking a visual image,   5
while on the other hand a metaphor which is technically "dead" (e.g.
iron resolution) has in effect reverted to being an ordinary word and can
generally be used without loss of vividness. But in between these two

classes there is a huge dump of worn-out metaphors which have lost all evocative power and are merely used because they save people the trouble of inventing phrases for themselves. Examples are: *Ring the changes on, take up the cudgels for, toe the line, ride roughshod over, stand shoulder to shoulder with, play into the hands of, no axe to grind, grist to the mill, fishing in troubled waters, on the order of the day, Achilles' heel, swan song, hotbed.* Many of these are used without knowledge of their meaning (what is a "rift," for instance), and incompatible metaphors are frequently mixed, a sure sign that the writer is not interested in what he is saying. Some metaphors now current have been twisted out of their original meaning without those who use them even being aware of the fact. For example, *toe the line* is sometimes written *tow the line*. Another example is *the hammer and the anvil*, now always used with the implication that the anvil gets the worst of it. In real life it is always the anvil that breaks the hammer, never the other way about: a writer who stopped to think what he was saying would be aware of this, and would avoid perverting the original phrase.

Operators or Verbal False Limbs

6   These save the trouble of picking out appropriate verbs and nouns, and at the same time pad each sentence with extra syllables which give it an appearance of symmetry. Characteristics phrases are: *render inoperative, militate against, make contact with, be subjected to, give rise to, give grounds for, have the effect of, play a leading part (role) in, make itself felt, take effect, exhibit a tendency to, serve the purpose of, etc., etc.* The keynote is the elimination of simple verbs. Instead of being a single word, such as *break, stop, spoil, mend, kill,* a verb becomes a *phrase*, made up of a noun or adjective tacked on to some general-purpose verb such as *prove, serve, form, play, render*. In addition, the passive voice is wherever possible used in preference to the active, and noun constructions are used instead of gerunds (*by examination of* instead of *by examining*). The range of verbs is further cut down by means of the *-ize* and *de-* formation, and the banal statements are given an appearance of profundity by means of the *not un-* formation. Simple conjunctions and prepositions are replaced by such phrases as *with respect to, having regard to, the fact that, by dint of, in view of, in the interests of, on the hypothesis that*; and the ends of sentences are saved from anticlimax by such resounding commonplaces as *greatly to be desired, cannot be left out of account, a development to be expected in the near future, deserving of serious consideration, brought to a satisfactory conclusion,* and so on and so forth.

Pretentious Diction

Words like *phenomenon, element, individual* (as a noun), *objective, categori-* 7
cal, effective, virtual, basic, primary, promote, constitute, exhibit, exploit, uti-
lize, eliminate, liquidate, are used to dress up simple statements and give an
air of scientific impartiality to biased judgments. Adjectives like *epoch-*
making, epic, historic, unforgettable, triumphant, age-old, inevitable, inex-
orable, veritable, are used to dignify the sordid processes of international
politics, while writing that aims at glorifying war usually takes on an archaic color, its characteristic words being: *realm, throne, chariot, mailed*
fist, trident, sword, shield, buckler, banner, jackboot, clarion. Foreign words
and expressions such as *cul de sac, ancien régime, deus ex machina, mutatis*
mutandis, status quo, gleichschaltung, weltanschauung, are used to give an air
of culture and elegance. Except for the useful abbreviations *i.e., e.g.,* and
etc., there is no real need for any of the hundreds of foreign phrases now
current in English. Bad writers, and especially scientific, political and sociological writers, are nearly always haunted by the notion that Latin or
Greek words are grander than Saxon ones, and unnecessary words like
expedite, ameliorate, predict, extraneous, deracinated, clandestine, subaqueous
and hundreds of others constantly gain ground from their Anglo-Saxon
opposite numbers. The jargon peculiar to Marxist writing (*hyena, hang-*
man, cannibal, petty bourgeois, these gentry, lacquey, flunkey, mad dog, White
Guard, etc.) consists largely of words and phrases translated from Russian,
German or French; but the normal way of coining a new word is to use a
Latin or Greek root with the appropriate affix and, where necessary, the
-ize formation. It is often easier to make up words of this kind (*deregional-*
ize, impermissible, extramarital, nonfragmentatory and so forth) than to think
up the English words that will cover one's meaning. The result, in general,
is an increase in slovenliness and vagueness.

Meaningless Words

In certain kinds of writing, particularly in art criticism and literary criti- 8
cism, it is normal to come across long passages which are almost completely
lacking in meaning. Words like *romantic, plastic, values, human, dead, sen-*
timental, natural, vitality, as used in art criticism, are strictly meaningless in
the sense that they not only do not point to any discoverable object, but
are hardly ever expected to do so by the reader. When one critic writes,
"The outstanding feature of Mr. X's work is its living quality," while another writes, "The immediately striking thing about Mr. X's work is its peculiar deadness," the reader accepts this as a simple difference of opinion.
If words like *black* and *white* were involved, instead of the jargon words

dead and *living*, he would see at once that language was being used in an improper way. Many political words are similarly abused. The word *Fascism* has now no meaning except in so far as it signifies "something not desirable." The words *democracy, socialism, freedom, patriotic, realistic, justice,* have each of them several different meanings which cannot be reconciled with one another. In the case of a word like *democracy,* not only is there no agreed definition, but the attempt to make one is resisted from all sides. It is almost universally felt that when we call a country democratic we are praising it: consequently the defenders of every kind of régime claim that it is a democracy, and fear that they might have to stop using the word if it were tied down to any one meaning. Words of this kind are often used in a consciously dishonest way. That is, the person who uses them has his own private definition, but allows his hearer to think he means something quite different. Statements like *Marshal Pétain was a true patriot, The Soviet Press is the freest in the world, The Catholic Church is opposed to persecution,* are almost always made with intent to deceive. Other words used in variable meanings, in most cases more or less dishonestly, are: *class, totalitarian, science, progressive, reactionary, bourgeois, equality.*

9   Now that I have made this catalogue of swindles and perversions, let me give another example of the kind of writing that they lead to. This time it must of its nature be an imaginary one. I am going to translate a passage of good English into modern English of the worst sort. Here is a well-known verse from *Ecclesiastes:*

> "I returned and saw under the sun, that the race is not to the swift, nor the battle to the strong, neither yet bread to the wise, nor yet riches to men of understanding, nor yet favor to men of skill; but time and chance happeneth to them all."

10   Here it is in modern English:

> "Objective consideration of contemporary phenomena compels the conclusion that success or failure in competitive activities exhibits no tendency to be commensurate with innate capacity, but that a considerable element of the unpredictable must invariably be taken into account."

11   This is a parody, but not a very gross one. Exhibit (3), above, for instance, contains several patches of the same kind of English. It will be seen that I have not made a full translation. The beginning and ending of the sentence follow the original meaning fairly closely, but in the middle the concrete illustrations—race, battle, bread—dissolve into the vague phrase "success or failure in competitive activities." This had to be so, because no modern writer of the kind I am discussing—no one capable of using

phrases like "objective consideration of contemporary phenomena"—
would ever tabulate his thoughts in that precise and detailed way. The
whole tendency of modern prose is away from concreteness. Now analyze
these two sentences a little more closely. The first contains forty-nine
words but only sixty syllables, and all its words are those of everyday life.
The second contains thirty-eight words of ninety syllables: eighteen of its
words are from Latin roots, and one from Greek. The first sentence contains six vivid images, and only one phrase ("time and chance") that
could be called vague. The second contains not a single fresh, arresting
phrase, and in spite of its ninety syllables it gives only a shortened version
of the meaning contained in the first. Yet without a doubt it is the second
kind of sentence that is gaining ground in modern English. I do not want
to exaggerate. This kind of writing is not yet universal, and outcrops of
simplicity will occur here and there in the worst-written page. Still, if you
or I were told to write a few lines on the uncertainty of human fortunes,
we should probably come much nearer to my imaginary sentence than to
the one from *Ecclesiastes*.

    As I have tried to show, modern writing at its worst does not consist in   12
picking out words for the sake of their meaning and inventing images in
order to make the meaning clearer. It consists in gumming together long
strips of words which have already been set in order by someone else, and
making the results presentable by sheer humbug. The attraction of this
way of writing is that it is easy. It is easier—even quicker, once you have
the habit—to say *In my opinion it is a not unjustifiable assumption that* than
to say *I think*. If you use ready-made phrases, you not only don't have to
hunt about for words; you also don't have to bother with the rhythms of
your sentences, since these phrases are generally so arranged as to be more
or less euphonious. When you are composing in a hurry—when you are
dictating to a stenographer, for instance, or making a public speech—it is
natural to fall into a pretentious, Latinized style. Tags like *a consideration
which we should do well to bear in mind* or *a conclusion to which all of us would
readily assent* will save many a sentence from coming down with a bump.
By using stale metaphors, similes and idioms, you save much mental effort, at the cost of leaving your meaning vague, not only for your reader
but for yourself. This is the significance of mixed metaphors. The sole aim
of a metaphor is to call up a visual image. When these images clash—as in
*The Fascist octopus has sung its swan song, the jackboot is thrown into the melt-
ing pot*—it can't be taken as certain that the writer is not seeing a mental
image of the objects he is naming; in other words he is not really thinking.
Look again at the examples I gave at the beginning of this essay. Professor
Laski (1) uses five negatives in fifty-three words. One of these is superfluous,

making nonsense of the whole passage, and in addition there is the slip *alien* for *akin,* making further nonsense, and several avoidable pieces of clumsiness which increase the general vagueness. Professor Hogben (2) plays ducks and drakes with a battery which is able to write prescriptions, and, while disapproving of the everyday phrase *put up with,* is unwilling to look *egregious* up in the dictionary and see what it means. (3), if one takes an uncharitable attitude towards it, is simply meaningless: probably one could work out its intended meaning by reading the whole of the article in which it occurs. In (4), the writer knows more or less what he wants to say, but an accumulation of stale phrases chokes him like tea leaves blocking a sink. In (5), words and meaning have almost parted company. People who write in this manner usually have a general emotional meaning—they dislike one thing and want to express solidarity with another—but they are not interested in the detail of what they are saying. A scrupulous writer, in every sentence that he writes, will ask himself at least four questions, thus: What am I trying to say? What words will express it? What image or idiom will make it clearer? Is this image fresh enough to have an effect? And he will probably ask himself two more: Could I put it more shortly? Have I said anything that is avoidably ugly? But you are not obliged to go to all this trouble. You can shirk it by simply throwing your mind open and letting the ready-made phrases come crowding in. They will construct your sentences for you—even think your thoughts for you, to a certain extent—and at need they will perform the important service of partially concealing your meaning even from yourself. It is at this point that the special connection between politics and the debasement of language becomes clear.

13   In our time it is broadly true that political writing is bad writing. Where it is not true, it will generally be found that the writer is some kind of rebel, expressing his private opinions and not a "party line." Orthodoxy, of whatever color, seems to demand a lifeless, imitative style. The political dialects to be found in pamphlets, leading articles, manifestos, White Papers and the speeches of under-secretaries do, of course, vary from party to party, but they are all alike in that one almost never finds in them a fresh, vivid, home-made turn of speech. When one watches some tired hack on the platform mechanically repeating the familiar phrases—*bestial atrocities, iron heel, bloodstained tyranny, free peoples of the world, stand shoulder to shoulder*—one often has a curious feeling that one is not watching a live human being but some kind of dummy: a feeling which suddenly becomes stronger at moments when the light catches the speaker's spectacles and turns them into blank discs which seem to have no eyes behind them. And this is not altogether fanciful. A speaker who uses that kind of phraseology has gone

some distance towards turning himself into a machine. The appropriate noises are coming out of the larynx, but his brain is not involved as it would be if he were choosing his words for himself. If the speech he is making is one that he is accustomed to make over and over again, he may be almost unconscious of what he is saying, as one is when one utters the responses in church. And this reduced state of consciousness, if not indispensable, is at any rate favorable to political conformity.

In our time, political speech and writing are largely the defence of the indefensible. Things like the continuance of British rule in India, the Russian purges and deportations, the dropping of the atom bombs on Japan, can indeed be defended, but only by arguments which are too brutal for most people to face, and which do not square with the professed aims of political parties. Thus political language has to consist largely of euphemism, question-begging and sheer cloudy vagueness. Defenceless villages are bombarded from the air, the inhabitants driven out into the countryside, the cattle machine-gunned, the huts set on fire with incendiary bullets: this is called *pacification*. Millions of peasants are robbed of their farms and sent trudging along the roads with no more than they can carry: this is called *transfer of population* or *rectification of frontiers*. People are imprisoned for years without trial, or shot in the back of the neck or sent to die of scurvy in Arctic lumber camps: this is called *elimination of unreliable elements*. Such phraseology is needed if one wants to name things without calling up mental pictures of them. Consider for instance some comfortable English professor defending Russian totalitarianism. He cannot say outright, "I believe in killing off your opponents when you can get good results by doing so." Probably, therefore, he will say something like this: 14

"While freely conceding that the Soviet régime exhibits certain features which the humanitarian may be inclined to deplore, we must, I think, agree that a certain curtailment of the right to political opposition is an unavoidable concomitant of transitional periods, and that the rigors which the Russian people have been called upon to undergo have been amply justified in the sphere of concrete achievement." 15

The inflated style is itself a kind of euphemism. A mass of Latin words falls upon the facts like soft snow, blurring the outlines and covering up all the details. The great enemy of clear language is insincerity. When there is a gap between one's real and one's declared aims, one turns as it were instinctively to long words and exhausted idioms, like a cuttlefish squirting out ink. In our age there is no such thing as "keeping out of politics." All issues are political issues, and politics itself is a mass of lies, evasions, folly, hatred and schizophrenia. When the general atmosphere is bad, language must suffer. I should expect to find—this is a guess which I have not 16 sufficient knowledge to verify—that the German, Russian and Italian languages have all deteriorated in the last ten to fifteen years, as a result of dictatorship.

17   But if thought corrupts language, language can also corrupt thought. A bad usage can spread by tradition and imitation, even among people who should and do know better. The debased language that I have been discussing is in some ways very convenient. Phrases like *a not unjustifiable assumption, leaves much to be desired, would serve no good purpose, a consideration which we should do well to bear in mind*, are a continuous temptation, a packet of aspirins always at one's elbow. Look back through this essay, and for certain you will find that I have again and again committed the very faults I am protesting against. By this morning's post I have received a pamphlet dealing with conditions in Germany. The author tells me that he "felt impelled" to write it. I open it at random, and here is almost the first sentence that I see: "(The Allies) have an opportunity not only of achieving a radical transformation of Germany's social and political structure in such a way as to avoid a nationalistic reaction in Germany itself, but at the same time of laying the foundations of a cooperative and unified Europe." You see, he "feels impelled" to write—feels, presumably, that he has something new to say—and yet his words, like cavalry horses answering the bugle, group themselves automatically into the familiar dreary pattern. This invasion of one's mind by ready-made phrases (*lay the foundations, achieve a radical transformation*) can only be prevented if one is constantly on guard against them, and every such phrase anaesthetizes a portion of one's brain.

18   I said earlier that the decadence of our language is probably curable. Those who deny this would argue, if they produced an argument at all, that language merely reflects existing social conditions, and that we cannot influence its development by any direct tinkering with words and constructions. So far as the general tone or spirit of a language goes, this may be true, but it is not true in detail. Silly words and expressions have often disappeared, not through any evolutionary process but owning to the conscious action of a minority. Two recent examples were *explore every avenue* and *leave no stone unturned*, which were killed by the jeers of a few journalists. There is a long list of flyblown metaphors which could similarly be got rid of if enough people would interest themselves in the job; and it should also be possible to laugh the *not un-* formation out of existence, reduce the amount of Latin and Greek in the average sentence, to drive out foreign phrases and strayed scientific words, and, in general, to make pretentiousness unfashionable. But all these are minor points. The defence of the English language implies more than this, and perhaps it is best to start by saying what it does *not* imply.

To begin with it has nothing to do with archaism, with the salvaging of obsolete words and turns of speech, or with the setting up of a "standard English" which must never be departed from. On the contrary, it is especially concerned with the scrapping of every word or idiom which has outworn its usefulness. It has nothing to do with correct grammar and syntax, which are of no importance so long as one makes one's meaning clear, or with the avoidance of Americanisms, or with having what is called a "good prose style." On the other hand it is not concerned with fake simplicity and the attempt to make written English colloquial. Nor does it even imply in every case preferring the Saxon word to the Latin one, though it does imply using the fewest and shortest words that will cover one's meaning. What is above all needed is to let the meaning choose the word, and not the other way about. In prose, the worst thing one can do with words is to surrender to them. When you think of a concrete object, you think wordlessly, and then, if you want to describe the thing you have been visualizing you probably hunt about till you find the exact words that seem to fit. When you think of something abstract you are more inclined to use words from the start, and unless you make a conscious effort to prevent it, the existing dialect will come rushing in and do the job for you, at the expense of blurring or even changing your meaning. Probably it is better to put off using words as long as possible and get one's meaning as clear as one can through pictures or sensations. Afterwards one can choose— not simply accept—the phrases that will best cover the meaning, and then switch round and decide what impression one's words are likely to make on another person. This last effort of the mind cuts out all stale or mixed images, all prefabricated phrases, needless repetitions, and humbug and vagueness generally. But one can often be in doubt about the effect of a word or phrase, and one needs rules that one can rely on when instinct fails. I think the following rules will cover most cases:

(I)   Never use a metaphor, simile or other figure of speech which you are used to seeing in print.
(II) Never use a long word where a short one will do.
(III) If it is possible to cut a word out, always cut it out.
(IV) Never use the passive when you can use the active.
(V)   Never use a foreign phrase, a scientific word or a jargon word if you can think of an everyday English equivalent.
(VI) Break any of these rules sooner than say anything outright barbarous.

These rules sound elementary, and so they are, but they demand a deep change of attitude in anyone who has grown used to writing in the style now fashionable. One could keep all of them and still write bad English, but one could not write the kind of stuff that I quoted in those five specimens at the beginning of this article.

21   I have not here been considering the literary use of language, but merely language as an instrument for expressing and not for concealing or preventing thought. Stuart Chase and others have come near to claiming that all abstract words are meaningless, and have used this as a pretext for advocating a kind of political quietism. Since you don't know what Fascism is, how can you struggle against Fascism? One need not swallow such absurdities as this, but one ought to recognize that the present political chaos is connected with the decay of language, and that one can probably bring about some improvement by starting at the verbal end. If you simplify your English, you are freed from the worst follies of orthodoxy. You cannot speak any of the necessary dialects, and when you make a stupid remark its stupidity will be obvious, even to yourself. Political language— and with variations this is true of all political parties, from Conservatives to Anarchists—is designed to make lies sound truthful and murder respectable, and to give an appearance of solidity to pure wind. One cannot change this all in a moment, but one can at least change one's own habits, and from time to time one can even, if one jeers loudly enough, send some worn-out and useless phrase—some *jackboot, Achilles' heel, hotbed, melting pot, acid test, veritable inferno* or other lump of verbal refuse—into the dustbin where it belongs.

QUESTIONING AND DISCUSSING

Orwell, "Politics and the English Language"

1. George Orwell notes that "the decline of a language must ultimately have political and economic causes [. . .]." How does Orwell support his point of view? With what types of examples? For what purpose?

2. In perhaps one of the most quoted lines from this essay, Orwell writes, "In our time, political speech and writing are largely a defence of the indefensible." Discuss this line, not only analyzing Orwell's examples but also examples from our own political time and contexts.

3. Research various types of writing that might be called "political." Is political writing always "bad" writing, as Orwell writes? Why or why not? Does Orwell's writing here reveal his own biases? (This could lead you to discuss the issue of whether or not anything is ever truly objective.)

4. If Orwell believed in 1946 that "the English language is in a bad way," what, given your observations of contemporary political speeches, writing, and the

like, might he say today? What light does Orwell's essay shed on your own view of politics and the English language as they relate to the United States?

⊞

ADAM BELLOW

Adam Bellow (1957–   ) is the former editorial director of the Free Press and is currently an editor-at-large for Doubleday. His articles and reviews have appeared in *Talk, The National Review,* and *The Atlantic Monthly,* publications that represent different points on the political spectrum. *In Praise of Nepotism: A Natural History* was published in 2003. In this controversial book, of which the following is an excerpt, Bellow draws on modern evolutionary theory to refute the notion that nepotism is unfair and attempts to prove, instead, that it is rooted in human biological nature.

⊞

In Praise of Nepotism

For almost two years leading up to the November 2000 elections, expectations focused on Vice President Albert Gore Jr. and Texas Governor George W. Bush. Both were the sons of important political families. Their rivalry sparked an immediate interest in the "return" of political dynasties.

Gore, an able and hardworking politician, was described as a child of privilege whose public career had begun literally at birth, when his father persuaded the local paper to carry the news on the front page. After twenty-four years of government service Gore had compiled an impressive record. Bush, too, was a talented politician, a two-term governor who had smoothly assumed control of his father's political network. Yet he suffered even more from the "silver-spoon" label. Following closely in his father's footsteps without equaling his accomplishments, Bush seemed derivative, uncertain: a bad copy of his father. For many, he was aptly described by a comment aimed at the senior Bush in 1988 by the Texas commissioner of agriculture, Jim Hightower, now a radio personality: "He is a man who was born on third base and thinks he hit a triple."

Many people were offended by the idea that the presidency could be claimed as a birthright, as though it were family property. But others saw in Bush the authenticity Gore lacked, suggesting that the rebellious youth who eventually accepts mature responsibilities is better liked and trusted than the dutiful son who suppresses his true inclinations in order to please a demanding father. In effect, then, the 2000 election was a referendum not on the validity of dynastic succession in a democracy but on which kind of successor we prefer. The Prodigal Son won out over the Dutiful Son. The glad-handing frat boy defeated the humorless wonk.

4   No sooner had Bush taken office (thanks partly to the decision of a Supreme Court dominated by Reagan-Bush appointees) than he began doling out appointments to relatives of other leading Republicans. Michael Powell, the son of Secretary of State Colin Powell, became chairman of the Federal Communications Commission. Elaine Chao, the wife of Senator Mitch McConnell, became Secretary of Labor. Chao's chief labor attorney, Eugene Scalia, is the son of Supreme Court Justice Antonin Scalia, and Justice William Rehnquist's daughter went to Health and Human Services. Elizabeth Cheney, the Vice President's daughter, became a deputy assistant secretary of state, and her husband became chief counsel for the Office of Management and Budget. In a crowning act of nepotistic chutzpah, Bush acceded to Senator Strom Thurmond's request that he appoint the twenty-eight-year-old Strom Thurmond Jr. U.S. attorney for South Carolina.

5   Helen Thomas, the former UPI Washington correspondent, declared in a column that the Bush Administration had become "a family affair, reeking of nepotism." (Nepotism is often said to reek, as though it were a pile of dirty laundry.) "You'd think an administration headed by the son of a former president might be a teensy bit leery of appearing to foster a culture of nepotism," Andrew Sullivan wrote in *The New Republic*. Sullivan produced a long list of people who had gotten jobs in Washington through such connections, and concluded, "All this nepotism is a worrisome sign that America's political class is becoming increasingly insular."

6   The 2002 midterm elections greatly strengthened this impression. All over the country sons and daughters, brothers and sisters, wives and widows of elected officials were strongly in evidence. Most prominent was Florida's governor, Jeb Bush, re-elected by a healthy margin. In Massachusetts, Mitt Romney, son of the former Michigan governor George Romney, became governor. In New Hampshire, John E. Sununu, son of a former governor and presidential chief of staff, beat the sitting governor, Jeanne Shaheen, for a U.S. Senate seat. In Arkansas, Tim Hutchinson, whose brother Asa was a congressman and is now an undersecretary in the Department of Homeland Security, lost his Senate seat to the state attorney general, Mark Pryor, son of the former Arkansas governor and senator David Pryor. Lucille Roybal-Allard, who occupies the California congressional seat once held by her father, was also re-elected. And in North Carolina, Elizabeth Dole, the wife of Bob Dole, won a Senate race against

Erskine Bowles, a former Clinton chief of staff (and the son of a state politician). Meanwhile, the position of House minority leader was claimed by Representative Nancy Pelosi, the daughter of a five-term Maryland congressman and Baltimore mayor, who had risen swiftly in California politics in part through her skillful use of dynastic connections. Pelosi was opposed by Harold Ford Jr., a young black congressman who had succeeded to his father's seat in Tennessee.

The widespread perception of a tilt toward nepotism is correct: the 7 American political class, along with other sectors of our society, is increasingly filled with the offspring of established parents. This phenomenon has gone largely unnoticed or has been apprehended in a piecemeal fashion. The few who have commented on it have voiced alarm that we are returning to a society based on heredity status, complete with a corporate aristocracy and a political House of Lords. Where I differ from these critics is in not seeing the trend as an ominous departure from American principles. Occupational traditions within families are very much a part of our national fabric—much more so than most people realize. Their eclipse since World War II has been the exception in American history, not the rule, and their return is an encouraging sign, not a cause for alarm. Indeed, this is the kind of nepotism of which this country needs not less but more.

The proliferation of family ties has been broadly described as a "new nepo- 8 tism" or a "new dynasticism" in American politics. There is an undeniable advantage to bearing a recognizable name in a media-driven electoral system, and to having easy access to parents' fundraising and political networks. Whatever the cause, the dramatic surge in family succession signals a quiet revolution as a new generation comes forward to claim its inheritance. Some Americans have viewed the new successors as opportunists trading on their famous names and family connections. But many others embrace the notion that continuing a family tradition has a dignity and value of its own.

Take business, for example. Every year the business press devotes con- 9 siderable ink to the ups and downs of business heirs such as H. Fisk Johnson, of Johnson Wax, and Lachlan Murdoch, the thirty-one-year-old heir apparent to the multi-billion-dollar media conglomerate run by his father, Rupert Murdoch. At other large firms family leadership is making a comeback: Harold McGraw III is the first family member to head the McGraw-Hill publishing company since 1983, and Ford Motor's CEO, William Ford, is the first family member to run the business in a generation. These and other family appointments (such as those of Motorola's Christopher

Galvin and the chewing-gum magnate William Wrigley Jr.) were called signs of a new nepotism in American business, with new expectations: observers and stockholders called on these scions to take their firms in bold new directions, rather than simply continuing their fathers' work.

10 Craft and service professions are often family dominated. The Lairds of New Jersey have been making liquor since 1780; the Coors family of Colorado has been making beer since 1873. Brown-Forman, maker of Jack Daniel's and Southern Comfort, has been a family business for more than 130 years and ascribes its success to a policy of "planned nepotism." Many other specialties, such as glass-blowing, candy making, circus performing, and fireworks, are passed down through families. Funeral homes are also frequently family owned.

11 In fact, the great majority of American businesses are family owned or controlled, including many Fortune 500 companies. Thus nepotism in business is perhaps to be expected. More surprising is the rapid growth of family succession in areas such as entertainment, the arts, and sports.

12 The men who built the movie industry in the 1920s and 1930s were nepotists on a grand scale, and some of Hollywood's greatest figures owed their breaks to family ties—though many of them denied it. In the 1960s and 1970s there were dozens of second-generation actors, including Jane and Peter Fonda, Tatum O'Neal, Michael Douglas, Sally Field, and Sissy Spacek (the cousin of Rip Torn). Today there are hundreds—far too many to list. Kate Hudson is the daughter of Goldie Hawn. Gwyneth Paltrow, the daughter of Blythe Danner and the late Bruce Paltrow, got her break when "uncle" Steven Spielberg cast her in *Hook*. Family ties also prevail among producers, directors, and writers, and also film and sound editors, cinematographers, makeup artists, costume and set designers, stunt men, and musicians—among them the Newman family, which has included eight composers.

13 Television is another industry in which who you know can mean as much as what you know. The actor, writer, and director Rob Reiner, son of the writer and comedian Carl Reiner, got his break when his father's friend Norman Lear cast him in *All in the Family*. Aaron Spelling cast his daughter, Tori, in *Beverly Hills 90210*; his son Randy is also an actor. The producer Steven Bochco has cast several family members in his shows, and his son Jesse co-produces *NYPD Blue*. "Bochco," he says good-naturedly, "is Polish for nepotism."

14 Today the music industry is bursting with successors: in 1998, Sean Lennon and Jakob Dylan both released CDs (Sean's half-brother Julian had a brief musical career in the 1980s). Both the sons of Ringo Starr are drummers (Zak Starkey now plays for The Who). By the time he was

twenty-four Enrique Iglesias, the son of Julio, had put out four CDs and had sold more than 14 million records; his older brother is also pursuing a career as a singer. Whitney Houston got her start singing backup with her mother, Cissy Houston, and is a cousin of Dionne Warwick's. Norah Jones, the daughter of Ravi Shankar, was showered with Grammys at this year's award ceremony. This is not to mention the well-known and extensive family ties in Motown, jazz, and country and western.

Family traditions have also been known among writers, but never before in such numbers. Martin Amis started publishing novels at an early age and has now upstaged his father, Kingsley Amis. Margaret Drabble and A. S. Byatt are sisters, and the three Barthelme brothers have all published multiple books. Susan Minot's sister Eliza has published a book based on the same family events depicted in Minot's own debut novel. The daughters and niece of John McPhee have written several books. I myself am the son of the novelist Saul Bellow, and I got my job in publishing through what might be called the neocon family network—the same network that aided John Podhoretz, William Kristol, Daniel Wattenberg, Jonah Goldberg, and Joshua Gilder, all children of well-known conservatives.

Many children of doctors and lawyers become doctors and lawyers themselves, and with the entrance of large numbers of women into these professions, the proportion of professional families has sharply increased. (One study has found that the children of doctors are 14 percent more likely to be admitted to medical school than non-successors.) Military families have also been known in every era of American history, bearing such distinguished names as Perry, Lee, MacArthur, and Patton; Custer got several of his relatives killed at Little Big Horn. Religious pulpits, too, are often handed down from father to son. Martin Luther King Jr. was the son of a prominent Baptist preacher who was also a civil-rights leader. In 2000 the Reverend Billy Graham handed the reins of his religious organization to his son Franklin; Graham's daughter also has her own ministry. The sons of the architect I. M. Pei work for their father and continue his tradition.

Nor are such tendencies confined to elite professions. The father-son tradition in labor unions continues, especially in the building trades. The prevalence of family ties in police and fire departments is also well established; the strength of these traditions was brought home viscerally in the lists of dead firemen after the World Trade Center disaster.

We think of sport as a Darwinian arena in which only the fittest survive—and so it is. Yet family ties increasingly permeate sports and sports-related professions. Take baseball: the left fielder Barry Bonds is the son of the coach and former outfielder Bobby Bonds and the godson of Willie

Mays. There are also assorted Alomars, Alous, Bells, Boones, Berras, Macks, Motas, Roses, Sislers, and Stottlemyres. Much the same holds true for football, basketball, hockey, stockcar racing, and boxing: Laila Ali, the daughter of Muhammad Ali, and Jacqui Frazier-Lyde, the daughter of Ali's old rival Joe Frazier, have entered the world of women's professional boxing and seem slated to carry that rivalry into a new generation.

19   No social scientist has studied modern American nepotism. But you don't need a degree in sociology to realize that there is a new boom in generational succession. The question is, what does it mean? Why is it happening now in the most democratic and individualistic society on earth? Doesn't it fly in the face of our commitment to merit and equal opportunity? Are we creating a new caste hierarchy based on occupation, similar to that of the medieval guilds? More to the point, how will we square our embrace of the new nepotism with our traditional aversion to the old?

20   Think back to the days before the widespread class mixing and upward mobility brought about by World War II, not to mention the civil-rights and feminist movements. In the 1920s and 1930s a certain kind of nepotism was everywhere for a certain class of people. A young man of good family who went to Groton or Choate was admitted as a matter of course to Harvard, Princeton, or Yale, after which he joined his father's Wall Street firm and one or more exclusive clubs, where he mingled with men of his set. If he didn't go to work for his father, he worked for a friend of his father's or the father of a friend, and if he married the boss's daughter, he could expect to be put on the fast track to the executive suite. Whether or not he rose all the way to the top, he would always be provided for.

21   No one (or almost no one, at any rate) can simply pick up the phone these days and get his kid a high-paying job, a record deal, or a spot on the national ticket. Few of today's successors got their jobs through what we would consider to be egregious nepotism. But more and more that kind of outright intervention isn't necessary. The whole thing works by a kind of natural osmosis. Growing up around a business or a vocation creates an early interest in the field, and a desire to please or imitate one's parents can exert a potent influence. But successors have a powerful advantage other people do not enjoy. Doors open, and people often prove happy to do favors for the children of colleagues who they hope may one day return the favor. All that is required to profit from this kind of opportunity is a willingness to take advantage of it.

22   It is worth dwelling for a moment on the differences between the old nepotism and the new. The old nepotism involved parents' hiring their

children outright or pulling strings in their behalf. It was also highly coercive: obedient daughters married according to their parents' wishes, and dutiful sons allowed their fathers to chart their careers and often to select brides for them as well. The new nepotism operates not from the top down but from the bottom up: it is voluntary, not coercive; it springs from the initiative of children, not the interest of parents; it tends to seem "natural" rather than planned. Although not nepotism in the classic sense, it is rightly called nepotism because it involves exploiting the family name, connections, or wealth. The method may be different, but the result is much the same.

Mainly, however, the new nepotism differs in combining the privileges 23 of birth with the iron rule of merit in a way that is much less offensive to democratic sensibilities. This is what explains the astonishing latitude— in effect, the room to fail—that we seem perfectly willing to grant the new successor generation. Americans increasingly feel that there is nothing wrong with hiring a relative or giving someone else's relative a break, so long as he or she is qualified. We even say that pulling strings to help relatives who are qualified is not really nepotism. But this leaves us in the inconsistent position of arguing that hiring a relative is or is not nepotism depending on the relative's performance.

We have tied ourselves in knots around this question for a simple rea- 24 son: we have long viewed nepotism as something bad by definition. That negative view of nepotism, however, is not a natural or a God-given law but an artifact of social and cultural history.

Dictionaries trace the word "nepotism" to the Latin root *nepos*, meaning 25 "nephew" or "grandson." But this etymology is misleadingly narrow. The word derives more directly from the Italian *nipote*, which can refer to almost any family member, of any generation, male or female. *Nipotismo* came into wide use in the fifteenth and sixteenth centuries to describe the corrupt practice of appointing papal relatives to office, usually illegitimate sons described as nephews, and for a long time this ecclesiastical connection continued to be reflected in dictionaries. (Even today some dictionaries give "illegitimate son of an ecclesiastic" as one definition of "nephew.") The modern definition of "nepotism" is simply favoritism based on kinship, but most people today use the term very narrowly, to mean hiring not just a relative but one who is grossly incompetent. The word is also used very broadly, to describe a range of affinities that go well beyond the family.

From the working man's perspective, nepotism means hiring or promot- 26 ing the boss's son-in-law, nephew, or girlfriend over the heads of more qualified candidates. This violates our basic sense of fairness and elicits revulsion and anger toward those who practice nepotism and—even more, perhaps—those who profit from it. Yet in family businesses nepotism is often the rule, and it is usually accepted as the way things are by everyone involved. In such cases nepotism appears to be a problem only when the beneficiary is manifestly unqualified.

27   Economists view nepotism as an obstacle to healthy change in business firms, one that results in waste and inefficiency. Yet some acknowledge that nepotism may be a rational practice, because it can reduce the cost of extensive talent searches. Still others argue that hiring family members is the best way to promote important values of trust and solidarity. And despite official anti-nepotism policies, many executives admit that they prefer to hire the relatives of current employees, because their experience suggests that the proven conduct of a relative best predicts the behavior of a prospective worker.

28   From a feminist perspective, the word "nepotism" evokes a long history of slights against women, given that in historical practice it has favored sons over daughters. Even after the feminist revolution nepotism continues to play a role in rearguard efforts to preserve the male monopoly on power. This is evident from the intensity of the feminist campaign against exclusive men's clubs, old-boy networks, and the "glass ceiling" that blocks the advancement of female executives. From the perspective of black Americans, nepotism may be perceived as tantamount to racism, since favoritism toward whites, whether relatives or not, is objectively no different from discrimination against blacks.

29   For most Americans, nepotism is first and last a class issue—a way for the rich to warehouse their unemployable offspring while keeping the lower classes in their place. In fact, however, systematic nepotism has been practiced more or less continuously by both the upper and lower classes, without ambivalence or apology. It was the middle class that pushed the merit principle, rising as it did through the institutions of the market and the state, in which promotion depends on bureaucratic efficiency. This is one of the things that make the new nepotism such a surprising development—it is essentially a middle-class phenomenon.

30   The old nepotism can be seen now as illegitimate and undesirable, a form of social cheating. But it was based on positive impulses. Parents have a natural impulse to pass something on to their children, just as children wish to accept whatever their parents have to give. The sum of these transactions is the way we pass on our cultural traditions and values.

When we talk about nepotism, what we are really talking about is the transmission of property, knowledge, and authority from one generation to the next.

All societies are organized at the most basic level around the processes   31
of marriage, reproduction, and succession. Every society therefore evolves a "nepotistic formula" geared to its needs and conditions. These formulas arise as adaptations to a given set of social and ecological conditions. The unique features of the American nepotistic formula are the result of a long historical process whose dominant trend has been the breakup of the large extended families typical of agrarian societies and the emergence of the nuclear family as the fundamental unit of industrial civilization. Concurrent with this trend has been the American project of creating a truly egalitarian society—our attempt to fulfill the promise that has been at the heart of American democracy for more than two hundred years. This project has involved a long war between the hereditary principle and the principle of merit.

The American war against nepotism began in the eighteenth century,   32
with the abolition of English inheritance practices such as primogeniture and entail, in which the family estate was passed intact to the oldest son. The replacement of these practices with a more egalitarian pattern of partible inheritance swept the country after the American Revolution. This democratic change was thanks largely to Thomas Jefferson, who hoped to break up the great landed estates of the Colonial period. The trend continued in the nineteenth century, with laws against polygamy and the marriage of cousins, and with the creation of a federal civil service based on merit and efficiency rather than on family connections. Nevertheless, family interests continued to be important in the construction of ethnic institutions, including the American Catholic Church, the urban political machine, and the early labor movement.

In the twentieth century the war on nepotism entered a progressive   33
phase, with strictures on the use of political patronage to benefit kin. This phase culminated in the historic New Deal and civil-rights legislation, which uprooted the last legal barriers to equal opportunity. It was at this time that anti-nepotism policies began to be widely adopted in most large-scale institutions, both public and private. Just as the merit system seemed to have triumphed, however, the same civil-rights provisions were used to challenge anti-nepotism rules as themselves discriminatory— especially against women, who were often barred from employment at schools and companies where their husbands also worked. The rapid rollback of no-spouse rules at universities, law firms, and newspapers and in

many other environments has led to a proliferation of professional marriages and sparked the current boom in generational succession.

34 The new nepotism is a serious matter, because it bears on the formation of elites in a democracy. Elites and upper classes have always been controversial for Americans, and since the Revolution we have viewed them with particular suspicion. Yet a century of sociology has concluded that an elite is a practical necessity for any society. The real question is, what kind of elite will you have—an open, meritocratic elite that is continually refreshed from other strata of society, or a closed and exclusive elite that withdraws into castelike isolation and merely seeks to perpetuate its privileges?

35 The tendency in American life since World War II has been toward individualism, mobility, and the dissipation of family bonds. The "return" of nepotism therefore seems especially disturbing. Critics from both left and right have pointed out the worrisome consequences of reviving the hereditary principle. Several writers have recently argued that after a long period of extreme social mobility and mixing, the United States is undergoing a new process of stratification. Call it what you like, the overclass, the cognitive elite, the meritocracy, today's American elite increasingly lives in its own segregated communities, sends its children to the same exclusive schools, marries within its own class, and acts in other ways to pass on its accumulated wealth, position, and privileges. In other words, the American meritocracy appears to be turning into an exclusive, inbred caste.

36 Such, at any rate, might be the argument for those who deny the legitimacy of the hereditary principle. But this is not my view. Rather, I would suggest that the new nepotism represents a valuable corrective to the excesses of meritocracy. The late historian and cultural critic Christopher Lasch argued that an elite that regards itself as fit to rule by virtue of its merit owes no gratitude or deference to anyone. It has no ethical tie to the mass of ordinary people, and is therefore unresponsive to their needs. We spent two centuries trying to get nepotism out of government, but Lasch suggests that meritocracy unleavened by nepotism lacks a necessary humanizing element.

37 The idea would be a balance between these two principles—a balance we appear to have struck with our new and distinctly American form of meritocratic nepotism. The new nepotism is therefore not the return of something tribal and archaic but the transformation of an ancient practice into a new and more acceptable form—one that can satisfy the per-

manent human impulses behind nepotism without violating the American
social compact.

Since we are clearly not going to get rid of the new nepotism anytime   38
soon, Americans must come to terms with it. That means learning to
practice it in accordance with the unwritten rules that have made it, on
balance, a wholesome and positive force. If history shows anything, it is
that nepotism in itself is neither good nor bad. It's the way you practice it
that matters. Those who observe the hidden rules of nepotism are rewarded and praised; those who do not are punished, often savagely. These
rules—derived from my own study of a number of dynastic families, from
the biblical House of David to the Kennedys and the Bushes—can be reduced to the following simple injunctions:

1. *Don't embarrass me.* The first rule of patronage has always been that
   the protégé's actions and manner reflect on the patron. By holding a
   patron responsible for his protégé's performance, the Mandarins of
   the Chinese imperial bureaucracy introduced a powerful corrective to
   the potential for nepotistic abuses. This is also the corrective built
   into the modern nepotistic equation.
2. *Don't embarrass yourself,* or *You have to work harder than anyone else.* If
   the protégé is obliged to respect the patron, he is equally obliged to
   respect himself and his colleagues. A democratic society is founded
   on a moral commitment to equal opportunity, and those who enjoy
   advantages of birth must make an effort to counteract the natural resentment of those who do not. That is why "good" business heirs display outstanding dedication—arriving early, leaving late, and in
   other respects going out of their way to win the approval of their colleagues. This is what distinguishes the new nepotism from the old:
   other people must prove their merit before the fact, but nepotees
   must prove it after.
3. *Pass it on.* Although nepotism is considered selfish, it proceeds from a
   generous impulse to pass something on to one's children, and this we
   think of as entirely praiseworthy. But if nepotism is in some respects a
   two-way street, it is also a one-way transaction. We therefore express
   our gratitude to our parents in the form of generosity to our children.
   This wholesome consciousness implies a certain humility and an acceptance of mortality.

Above all, it is high time for us to get over our ambivalence about the "re-   39
turn" of dynastic families. This country is now old enough to have accumu-

lated a large number of great families, and we can no longer deny their many obvious and constructive contributions. Americans admire the Adamses, the Roosevelts, and the Kennedys not just for their unity—a value that is becoming increasingly difficult to preserve in our mobile society—but for their sense of common purpose and the spirit of public service that they foster. There is much to be said for these "aristocratic" features of dynastic families, and as long as those families observe the meritocratic rules of the new nepotism, we really have no basis for complaint. Indeed, we should not only respect great families but try to be more like them. Rather than simply seeking to punish or stamp out the bad kind of nepotism, we should reward and encourage the good.

40   The risks inherent in the return of dynastic nepotism have been exaggerated and fail to take into account both the progress of meritocracy and the power of social envy in a democracy. Dynastic heirs walk on very thin ice in our society: we readily grant them the benefit of the doubt, but we hold them to extremely high standards, and at the first sign of their failing to meet those standards, the hammer comes down hard.

41   Nepotism may be objectively discriminatory, but given that people are going to practice it anyway, we may as well infuse it with meritocratic principles so that all can benefit. Let families compete for public honors; this has always been the soul of republican virtue, and it is up to us to recover this tradition in every generation. The spirit of family enterprise gives dignity and meaning to our lives, and is not only a spur to achievement but also a check on excessive ambition. It links the generations in a chain of generosity and gratitude. We would all be better off if we reflected more consistently and deeply not only on our debt to our ancestors but also on what we owe our descendants.

Questioning and Discussing

Bellow, "In Praise of Nepotism"

1. This controversial article was written by a man whose father is a prize-winning novelist. Analyze the article to determine if Adam Bellow's own, possibly privileged, position influences the position he takes. What evidence is there—either way? What, exactly, is Bellow's view of nepotism? How effective are his examples? Why?

2. As Bellow notes, "You don't need a degree in sociology to realize that there is a new boom in generational succession. The question is, what does it mean?" Looking at the article carefully, determine how Bellow replies to his own question.

3. Analyze the validity of the following statement: "Dynastic heirs walk on very thin ice in our society: we readily grant them the benefit of the doubt, but we hold them to extremely high standards, and at the first sign of their failing to meet those standards, the hammer come down hard." Looking elsewhere in Bellow's article and based on your own reading or experience, is this statement true, in your view? Do the advantages of being "dynastic heirs" outweigh any negative aspects? Why? Does this pronouncement reflect Bellow's own interest? Why or why not?

4. Comment on Bellow's conclusion: "We would all be better off if we reflected more consistently and deeply not only on our debt to our ancestors but also on what we owe our descendants." Is this conclusion beside the point? Why or why not?

Ansel Adams

One of the world's most famous photographers, Ansel Adams (1902–1984) was born in San Francisco. His early interests focused on music, specifically the piano, rather than photography. But his 1916 photographs of Yosemite Valley inspired his study, and he returned to Yosemite every summer, eventually associating himself with a conservation society, the Sierra Club. In 1931, his work was exhibited at the Smithsonian, and in 1932, Adams, along with other noted photographers, including Edward Weston and Imogen Cunningham, formed Group f/64, philosophically espousing the perfection of the image through technically exacting photographs. In addition to creating a wide and justifiably celebrated body of work that captures natural outdoor beauty, particularly that of the Southwest and West, Adams also worked as a photomuralist during World War II for the Department of the Interior. At this time he also began his famous "zone system" to help visualize the image before the final print. The image of Roy Takeno that follows is from that series of photographs taken for the government documenting the Manzanar camp at which Japanese-Americans were held during World War II.

QUESTIONING AND DISCUSSING

Adams, "Free Press"

1. This image was made by celebrated photographer Ansel Adams in 1943, during the period when the United States confined American citizens of Japanese descent in internment camps. The precise title is "Roy Takeno

reading paper in front of office." Research these Japanese interment camps to understand the context of this image. Consider also the federal programs that supported often well-known photographers to document life in the United States during that era.

2. Contemplating the photograph and the political and historical contexts in which it was taken, carefully analyze the content of this image. What are the ironies inherent in this photograph? How is it on its surface a document of a moment in someone's life in the interment camp—and also an editorial comment on that life?

3. Analyze and comment on the historical, political, and racial contexts that might have made the U.S. government decide to make Americans of Japanese descent leave their homes and relocate to internment camps. How does this event in our history illuminate current events and the values we reveal in our responses to them?

⌗

QUESTIONS FOR READING AND RESPONDING

Chapter 8 Taking a Stand: What Are My Politics?

1. Each of the authors or artists in this chapter takes a type of political stand, whether implicitly or explicitly. Using three of the selections and analyzing each one carefully, create categories based on the values demonstrated by each author/artist and discuss how specific examples from and qualities of each selection support those categories.

2. Several of the authors have particular perspectives on war. Using examples from Wilfred Owen and Studs Terkel, analyze each writer's views and purposes for writing about war.

3. Investigate current research involving the issues (divorce, gay marriage) featured in Hanna Rosin's and Jonathan Rauch's essays. What information do you find that either supports or refutes their various positions? As a result of your research, do you find Rosin's and Rauch's arguments more or less effective? Why? What were your views before you read these essays and conducted your research? Have you changed or modified your point of view? Why or why not?

4. Compare and contrast the work of Audre Lorde, George Orwell, and Alleen Pace Nilsen regarding issues related to language and the values conveyed through language. How are their positions political? Use examples from their texts to support your point of view.

5. Compare the Ansel Adams photograph with *The New Yorker* cartoon. How does each raise issues of ethics and values? Through what means? With what effect?

6. Adam Bellow and Studs Terkel deal to some extent with the issue of "generations." How do their views differ? What are their purposes, and how would you describe the types of values their works imply?

⌗

Index of Authors and Titles

⊞

Credits

⊞

The authors and editors wish to thank the following persons and publishers for permission to include the works or excerpts mentioned.

Text

Chapter 1: P. 4, "Ethics," from *Waiting for My Life* by Linda Pastan. Copyright © 1981 by Linda Pastan. Used by permission of W. W. Norton & Company, Inc. P. 5, "The Blue Hotel" by Stephen Crane from *The Works of Stephen Crane*, ed. by Fredson Bowers, pp. 376–396. Copyright © 1973. Reprinted with permission of the University of Virginia Press. P. 30, "When We Dead Awaken": Writing as Re-Vision, from *Arts of the Possible: Essays and Conversations* by Adrienne Rich. Copyright © 2001 by Adrienne Rich. Used by permission of the author and W.W. Norton & Company, Inc. "The Loser," copyright © 1993, 1967, 1963 by Adrienne Rich; The lines from "Snapshots of a Daughter-in-Law." Copyright ©1993, 1967, 1963 by Adrienne Rich; "Orion." Copyright © 1993 by Adrienne Rich. Copyright © 1969 by W.W. Norton & Company, Inc.; "Planetarium." Copyright © 1993 by Adrienne Rich. Copyright © 1971 by W.W. Norton & Company, Inc, from *Collected Early Poems: 1950–1970* by Adrienne Rich. Used by permission of the author and W.W. Norton & Company, Inc. P. 44, reprinted with permission from *Psychology Today* magazine, Copyright © (1974) Sussex Publishers, Inc. P. 65, Excerpt from *Shooting an Elephant and Other Essays*, by George Orwell, copyright 1950 by Harcourt, Inc., and renewed 1979 by Sonia Brownell Orwell, reprinted by permission of Harcourt, Inc. P. 72, "Everyday Use" from *In Love & Trouble: Stories of Black Women*, copyright 1973 by Alice Walker, reprinted by permission of Harcourt, Inc. P. 81, "What Do Children Owe Elderly Parents?" by Daniel Callahan from *The Hastings Center Report*, V. 5, No. 2, April 1985, pp. 31–37. Reproduced by permission. © The Hastings Center. P. 92, "The Thin Envelope: Why College Admissions Has Become Unpredictable" by Louis Menand, *The New Yorker*, April 7, 2003, pp. 88–92. © 2003 by Louis Menand reprinted with the permission of the Wylie Agency Inc.

Chapter 2: P. 106, "U.S. Government to Discontinue Long-term, Low-Yield Investment in Nation's Youth," *The Onion*, September 2, 2003. Reprinted with permission of *The Onion*. Copyright 2003, by Onion, Inc. www.theonion.com. P. 110, "Pornography" by Margaret Atwood, copyright © 1983 by O.W. Toad, Ltd. first appeared in *Chatelaine* Magazine. Reprinted by permission of the author. P. 116, "Understanding Afrocentrism: Why Blacks Dream of a World Without Whites" by Gerald Early. Copyright © 1995. Reprinted by permission of the author. P. 141, from *Thirteen Ways of Looking at a Black Man* by Henry Louis Gates, Jr., copyright © 1997 by Henry Louise Gates, Jr. Used by permission of Random House, Inc. P. 153, "Old Horse," anonymous from *Lutheran Life*, Vol. 71, November 1959. P. 156, pp. 118–32 from *Jewish Literacy* by Rabbi Joseph Telushkin. Copyright © 1991 by Rabbi Joseph Telushkin. Reprinted by permission of HarperCollins Publishers Inc. P. 166, From *Exile and The Kingdom* by Albert Camus, translated by Justin O'Brien, copyright © 1957, 1958 by Alfred A. Knopf, a division of Random House, Inc. Used by permission of Alfred A. Knopf, a division of Random House, Inc. P. 177, from "The Shawl" by Cynthia Ozick, copyright © 1980, 1983 by Cynthia Ozick. Used by permission of Alfred A. Knopf, a division of Random House, Inc. P. 182, from *The Virtual Community* by Howard Rheingold. Copyright © 1993 by Howard Rheingold. Reprinted by permission of Perseus Books PLC, a member of Perseus Books, L.L.C.

Chapter 3: P. 199, "Good Country People" from *A Good Man Is Hard to Find and Other Stories*, copyright 1955 by Flannery O'Connor and renewed 1981 by Regina O'Connor, reprinted by permission of Harcourt, Inc. P. 217, Reynolds Price, "Dear Harper: A Letter to a Godchild About God." © 2000 Reynolds Price, originally appeared in Forbes ASAP, 2000. Reprinted by permission of Author. P. 229, "American Electric: Did Franklin Fly That Kite?" by Adam Gopnik, *The New Yorker*, June 30, 2003, pp. 96–100. Reprinted by permission of the author. P. 239, All pages from "A Very Old Man with Enormous Wings" from *Leaf Storm and Other Stories* by Gabriel García Márquez. Translated by Gregory Rabassa. Copyright © 1971 by Gabriel García Márquez. Reprinted by permission of HarperCollinsPublishers Inc. P. 245, "Ethical Issues Concerning Human Cloning," by Herbert Wray, Jeffery L. Sheler, and Traci Watson, *U.S. News & World Report*, March 10, 1997. Copyright 1997 *U.S. News & World Report*, L.P. Reprinted with permission. P. 270, Svi Shapiro, "A Parent's Dilemma: Public vs. Jewish Education," from *Tikkun*, 11(6), November/December 1996, pp. 59–64. Reprinted from *Tikkun: A Bimonthly Jewish Critique of Politics, Culture & Society*. www.tikkun.org. P. 281, "Moral and Ethical Dilemmas in the Special-Care Nursery," by Raymond Duff and A.G.M. Campbell, *New England Journal of Medicine* 289, 1973, pp. 890–894. Copyright © 1973 Massachusetts Medical Society. All rights reserved. P. 292, copyright ©1994 by Michael Dorris, reprinted with the permission of The Wylie Agency, Inc. P. 297, "Three Generations of Native American Women's Birth Experience," by Joy Harjo, *Ms. Magazine*, July/August 1991, pp. 28–30. Reprinted by permission of *Ms. Magazine*, © 1991.

Chapter 4: P. 308, "NBC has its eye on reality series coming to Bravo" by Gail Shister, *Philadelphia Inquirer*, February 12, 2003. Reprinted by permission of the *Philadelphia Inquirer*. P. 310, reprinted by arrangement with the Estate of Martin Luther King Jr., c/o Writers House as agent for the proprietor New York, NY. Copyright 1963 Martin Luther King Jr., copyright renewed 1991 Coretta Scott King. P. 327, reprinted with the permission of Simon & Schuster Adult Publishing Group from "Why I Am Not a Christian" by Bertrand Russell. Copyright © 1957, 1985 by George Allen & Unwin Ltd. P. 341, Reprinted with the permission of Scribner, an imprint of Simon & Schuster Adult Publishing Group, from *The Other America: Poverty in The United States* by Michael Harrington. Copyright © 1962, 1969, 1981 by Michael Harrington; copyright renewed © 1990 by Stephanie Harrington. P. 357, from *The Sacred Hoop* by Paula Gunn Allen. Copyright © 1986, 1992 by Paula Gunn Allen. Reprinted by permission of Beacon Press, Boston. P. 365, "The Man Who Went to Chicago," from *Eight Men* by Richard Wright. Copyright 1940, © 1961 by Richard Wright. Copyright renewed 1989 by Ellen Wright. Introduction by Paul Gilmore. Reprinted by permission of HarperCollins Publishers Inc. P. 393, "The Media's Image of Arabs" by Jack Shaheen, *Newsweek*, February 29, 1988. Reprinted by permission of the author. P. 396, from *Rooted Against the Wind* by Gloria Wade-Gayles. Copyright © 1996 by Gloria Wade-Gayles. Reprinted by permission of Beacon Press, Boston. P. 404, "My Own People" by Anzia Yezierska from *Hungry Hearts*, 1997. Reprinted by permission of Ayer Company Publishers.

Chapter 5: P. 421, Reprinted courtesy of www.cheathouse.com. P. 422, ©SLATE/Distributed by United Feature Syndicate, Inc. P. 436, "Doin' Time with a New Ticker" by Steve Lopez, *The Los Angeles Times*, January 28, 2002, p. B1. Copyright 2002, *Los Angeles Times*. Reprinted with permission. P. 438, "Change of Heart" from *60 Minutes*, CBS News, September 14, 2003. Reprinted by permission of CBS News/60 Minutes. P. 475, "Aria: Memoir of a Bilingual Childhood" by Richard Rodriguez. Copyright © 1980 by Richard Rodriguez. Originally appeared in *The American Scholar*. Reprinted by permission of Georges Borchardt, Inc. for the author. P. 486, Reprinted with the permission of Simon & Schuster Adult Publishing Group, from *Wealth against Commonwealth* by Henry Demarest Lloyd, edited by Thomas C. Cochran. Copyright © 1963 by Prentice-Hall, Inc. P. 496, "The War Against Boys" by Christina Hoff Sommers, *The Atlantic Monthly*, May 2000. Reprinted by permission of the author.

Chapter 6: P. 506, "Get a Leash" by Randy Cohen, *The New York Times* Magazine, November 4, 2001. Reprinted by permission of the author. Randy Cohen writes "The Ethicist" for *The New York Times* Magazine, where this originally appeared. P. 508, Reprinted from *Michigan Law Review*, June 1966, Vol. 64, No. 8. Copyright 1966 by The Michigan Law Review Association. Professor Freedman has expanded and updated his analysis in Freedman & Smith, Understanding Lawyers' Ethics (Matthew Bender, 2004, 3rd edition). P. 521, "Heraldry" by George Steiner from *Errata*. Reprinted by permission of the Publisher, Weidenfeld & Nicolson, a division of The Orion Publishing Group. P. 529, text as submitted from *Scorpion Tongues* by Gail Collins. Copyright © 1998 by Gail Collins. Reprinted by permission of HarperCollins Publishers Inc. P. 544, Reprinted with permission of the author and publisher from the Summer 2002 issue of *Reform Judaism* magazine, published by the Union for Reform Judaism. P. 554, "Etta Mae Johnson," from *The Women of Brewster Place* by Gloria Naylor, copyright © 1980, 1982 by Gloria Naylor. Used by permission of Viking Penguin, a division of Penguin Group (USA) Inc. P. 569, "Two Kinds," from *The Joy Luck Club* by Amy Tan, copyright © 1989 by Amy Tan. Used by permission of G.P. Putnam's Sons, a division of Penguin Group (USA) Inc. P. 579, "On Being Black and Middle Class" by Shelby Steele, *Commentary Magazine*, 1988. Reprinted by permission of Dr. Shelby Steele, Senior Fellow, The Hoover Institution, Stanford University. P. 590, from *Warrior Politics* by Robert D. Kaplan, copyright © 2002 by Robert D. Kaplan. Used by permission of Random House, Inc. P. 598, from Mary McCarthy, *The Company She Keeps*. Copyright © 1991. Reprinted by permission of The Mary McCarthy Literary Trust.

Chapter 7: P. 614, "Halle Berry? We Don't Think So," *Chicago Tribune*, May 5, 2003, Section 5. Reprinted by permission. P. 616, "Thin Gruel: How the Language Police Drain the Life and Content from Our Texts" by Diane Ravitch, *American Educator*, Summer 2003. Reprinted with permission from the Summer 2003 issue of the *American Educator*, the quarterly journal of the American Federation of Teachers. From *The Language Police* by Diane Ravitch, copyright © 2003 by Diane Ravitch. Used by permission of Alfred A. Knopf, a division of Random House, Inc. P. 644, "Sinners in the Hands of an Angry God" by Jonathan Edwards from *The Works of Jonathan Edwards*, Volume 7, edited by Sereno E. Dwight. Reprinted by permission of the publisher, Yale University Press. P. 659, "The Lottery" from *The Lottery and Other Stories* by Shirley Jackson. Copyright © 1948, 1949 by Shirley Jackson. Copyright renewed 1976, 1977 by Laurence Hyman, Barry Hyman, Mrs. Sarah Webster and Mrs. Joanne Schnurer. Reprinted by permission of Farrar, Straus and Giroux, LLC. P. 667, "Salvation" from *The Big Sea* by Langston Hughes. Copyright © 1940 by Langston Hughes. Copyright renewed 1968 by Arna Bontemps and George Houston Bass. Reprinted by permission of Hill & Wang, a division of Farrar, Straus and Giroux, LLC. P. 670, "Do Geeks Need to Go to College?" by Lisa Schmeiser, *Salon Magazine*, April 12, 1999. This article first appeared in Salon.com, at http:www.Salon.com. An online version remains in the *Salon* archives. Reprinted with permission. P. 674, "Ulysses" by Alfred Lord Tennyson from *The Norton Introduction to Literature*, 7/e, 1998, pp. 1139–1141. Reprinted by permission of W.W. Norton & Company, Inc. P. 677, "Ideology and Moral Philology," from *The Grace of Great Things* by Robert Grudin. Copyright © 1990 by Robert Grudin. Reprinted by permission of Houghton Mifflin Company. All rights reserved. P. 684, from *The Vanishing American Jew* by Alan Dershowitz. Copyright © 1997 by Alan M. Dershowitz. By permission of Little, Brown and Company, (Inc.). P. 700, Copyright © 2000 from *Black Feminist Thought: Knowledge, Consciousness, and the Politics of Empowerment*, 2/e by Patricia Hill Collins. Reproduced by permission of Routledge/Taylor & Francis Books, Inc., and the author.

Chapter 8: P. 728, "Separation Anxiety: The Movement to Save Marriage" by Hanna Rosin, *The New Republic*, May 6, 1996. Reprinted by permission of *The New Republic*, © 1996 The New Republic LLC. P. 735, "For Better or Worse? The Case for Gay (or Straight) Marriage" by Jonathan Rauch. © Jonathan Rauch. First published in *The New Republic*, May 6, 1996. Reprinted by permission of the author. P. 744, By Wilfred Owen from *The Collected Poems of Wilfred Owen*, copyright © 1963 by Chatto & Windus, Ltd. Reprinted by permission of New Directions Publishing Corp. P. 746, reprinted by permission of Donadio & Olson, Inc. Copyright 1984 by Studs Terkel. P. 773, "Sexism in English: A 1990s Update" by Alleen Pace Nilsen. Copyright © 1990. Reprinted by permission of the author. P. 785, "Transformation of Silence into Language and Action," by Audre Lorde, paper delivered at the Modern Language Association's "Lesbianism and Literature Panel," Chicago, IL, December 28, 1977. © Estate of Audre Lorde, Reprinted by permission of The Charlotte Sheedy Literary Agency. P. 789, excerpt from *Shooting an Elephant and Other Essays*, by George Orwell, copyright 1950 by Harcourt, Inc., and renewed 1979 by Sonia Brownell Orwell, reprinted by permission of Harcourt, Inc. P. 798, from *In Praise of Nepotism: A Natural History* by Adam Bellow, copyright © 2003 by Adam Bellow. Used by permission of Doubleday, a division of Random House, Inc.

Photos and cartoons

Chapter 1:
P. 2, © David Butow/Corbis Saba. P. 102, © Ruth Orkin.

Chapter 2:
P. 104, © Paul Almasy/Corbis. P. 106, reprinted with permission of *The Onion*. Copyright © 2003 by Onion, Inc. www.theonion.com. P. 108, reprinted with permission of *The Onion*. Copyright © 2003 by Onion, Inc. www.theonion.com. P. 194, Special Collections, University of Arizona Library, University of Arizona. Arizona Photograph Collection, Students 1891–1900, File 4, Folder 1, UA Class of 1898–1899.

Chapter 3:
P. 196, © Getty Images. P. 198, MAD #362 © 1997 E.C. Publications, Inc. All Rights Reserved. Used with permission. P. 304, Library of Congress.

Chapter 4:
P. 306, © AP/Wide World Photos/Katsumi Kasahara. P. 415, Library of Congress.

Chapter 5:
P. 418, © TimeLife Pictures. P. 502, Library of Congress.

Chapter 6:
P. 504, © Hulton-Deutsch Collection/Corbis. P. 610, © Jay Boersma.

Chapter 7:
P. 612, © Corbis. P. 722, © Bruce Davidson/Magnun Photos.

Chapter 8:
P. 724, © Bettman/Corbis. P. 726, © The New Yorker Collection, 2003, Frank Cotham, from cartoonbank.com. All rights reserved. P. 814, Library of Congress.